Creating Meaning Through Literature and the Arts

An Integration Resource for Classroom Teachers

Third Edition

Claudia E. Cornett
Professor Emerita, Wittenberg University

PEARSON

Merrill
Prentice Hall

Upper Saddle River, New Jersey
Columbus, Ohio

Library of Congress Cataloging-in-Publication Data

Cornett, Claudia E.

    Creating meaning through literature and the arts: An integration resource for classroom teachers / Claudia E. Cornett.—3rd ed.

      p. cm

    Includes bibliographical references and index.

    ISBN 0-13-171878-9 (alk. paper)

  1. Arts—Study and teaching. 2. Literature—Study and teaching. 3. Interdisciplinary approach in education. I. Title.

LB1591.C67 2007

372.64—dc22   2006046209

Vice President and Executive Publisher: Jeffery W. Johnston
Senior Editor: Linda Ashe Bishop
Development Editor: Ben Prout
Senior Production Editor: Mary M. Irvin
Design Coordinator: Diane C. Lorenzo
Senior Editorial Assistant: Laura Weaver
Production Coordination: Carlisle Publishing Services
Cover Designer: Candace Rowley
Production Manager: Pamela D. Bennett
Director of Marketing: David Gesell
Marketing Manager: Darcy Betts Prybella
Marketing Coordinator: Brian Mounts

This book was set in Bembo by Carlisle Publishing Services. It was printed and bound by Von Hoffman Press. The cover was printed by Phoenix Color Corp.

Cover Image: The "Starry Night" mural was painted by first graders in the classrooms of Bebe Cifaldi, Laurie Keniry, Cora Lugo, Beverly Ohemeng, and Gena Weber at the Hilton Head School for the Creative Arts.
Photo Credits: p. 186, Hollie Steele; p. 278, Wrenn Cook; all other photos, Susan Rudeen Jarrett.

Pearson Prentice Hall™ is a trademark of Pearson Education, Inc.
Pearson® is a registered trademark of Pearson plc
Prentice Hall® is a registered trademark of Pearson Education, Inc.
Merrill® is a registered trademark of Pearson Education, Inc.

Pearson Education Ltd.   Pearson Education Australia Pty. Limited
Pearson Education Singapore Pte. Ltd.   Pearson Education North Asia Ltd.
Pearson Education Canada, Ltd.   Pearson Educación de Mexico, S.A. de C.V.
Pearson Education—Japan   Pearson Education Malaysia Pte. Ltd.

10 9 8 7 6 5 4 3 2 1
ISBN: 0-13-171878-9

With love to Charles, because you give me roots and wings,
and you did as much work on this book as I did.

And to Sarah and all those like her
who are just beginning their teaching journey.

About the Author

Claudia Cornett is a Professor Emerita at Wittenberg University, where she was a recipient of the Distinguished Teaching Award. During her tenure at Wittenberg, she directed the Reading Center and taught graduate and undergraduate courses in all aspects of literacy, literature, and arts integration. Before moving to the college level, she taught grades 1–8, was a reading specialist, and earned a Ph.D. in Curriculum and Instruction from Miami University.

Claudia is the author of numerous books and articles about literacy, bibliotherapy, the strategic use of humor, and the arts as teaching tools. She also wrote and is featured in *Sounds Abound*, an instructional television series on early literacy broadcast on PBS stations during school programming. Currently she hosts a weekly segment on educational television called *Art Chat,* which features interviews with artists in their studios.

Claudia regularly presents keynote speeches and conducts professional development for educators throughout the United States, Europe, and Canada. Her current research focuses on addressing literacy issues using an arts-based teaching model.

Claudia lives with her husband, a retired school superintendent, in historic Lebanon, Ohio. She can be reached at ccornett@wittenberg.edu.

Foreword

There is a quiet but determined movement throughout K–12 education in this country led by teachers who have discovered the power of integrating the arts into their teaching. Each year more teachers are incorporating the arts into their classrooms, often in partnership with arts specialists. These educators are using a variety of teaching strategies that lead to active student participation. This, in turn, leads to livelier classrooms.

Because our lives do not naturally fall into 50-minute segments during which we focus on one subject at a time, many educators are also taking a second look at integrating multiple disciplines in their instruction, with an eye on making learning more meaningful for students. These ideas—teaching by integrating subjects and using the arts to teach other curriculum areas—are not new to education; indeed, they have been advocated by arts groups and many educational institutions for years.

In the 1960s, arts education began to enjoy the spotlight through the work of such organizations as the National Endowment for the Arts and the John D. Rockefeller III Fund. Since then, educators and arts organizations have worked together more closely to provide arts education experiences for students. Over the intervening years, hundreds of arts organizations have made it part of their mission to support the classroom teacher in efforts to teach in, through, and about the arts.

Practitioners in the arts education field have begun to realize that professional development in the arts is valued not only by experienced teachers, but by university students learning to become teachers as well. Indeed, professional development in the arts for practicing teachers is such a growing field precisely because course work in the arts is limited or nonexistent for preservice teachers. It is time to provide more resources and information about the arts and integration at the undergraduate level. With this book, Claudia Cornett has provided such a resource.

Creating Meaning Through Literature and the Arts will be a valuable resource to preservice teachers and veteran teachers who are new to the concept of arts integration. Educators will find basic information about the four arts disciplines of dance, drama, visual art, and music; diverse applications of literature; strategies and lesson plans for interdisciplinary teaching; resource lists; and an extensive bibliography. Readers will enjoy Dr. Cornett's incorporation of many practical examples and appreciate the Research Updates, which highlight arts and education research and facts. Additionally, readers can witness integration through classroom vignettes placed throughout the chapters. In these "snapshots" and "spotlights," actual lessons are described in which the arts are integrated into teaching and learning. As teachers continue to hear the cry for education reform, school change, and school improvement with ever-increasing frequency, many have turned to the arts. With her book, Dr. Cornett has provided a tool to guide teachers on the path toward making the arts a meaningful part of the classroom experience.

Barbara Shepherd
Director, National Partnerships
The Kennedy Center
Washington, DC

Preface

Come to the edge, he said.
They said, we are afraid.
Come to the edge, he said.
They came.
He pushed them and they flew.

French poet and art critic
Guillaume Apollinaire, 1880–1918

Since the first edition of this book, arts integration has blossomed. Across the United States, and now in Canada, the United Kingdom, and Australia, thousands of teachers have felt compelled to "come to the edge." Their courage to make the arts the "fourth R" has been rewarded. Mounting research now links the arts with academic achievement. More importantly, teachers report how the arts engage students in phenomenal ways. Students become intrinsically motivated and develop important social and emotional skills. Arts-based learning restructures how students think and feel by changing them into active meaning makers. This deep change goes beyond measures used in standardized testing. What's more, students, teachers, and parents are just plain happier.

Fueling the Flame

The engine of arts integration is being fueled by many sources. Most prominent are:

- Research that confirms the arts "level the playing field" for disadvantaged students
- No Child Left Behind and other legislation that designate the arts as core disciplines
- New standards for teacher preparation that specify what classroom teachers need to know and be able to do in the arts
- Annenberg, Ford, and other foundations that have given millions of dollars to support arts-based education
- National organizations like the Kennedy Center's Partners in Education and Arts Education Partnership that support school efforts to put arts-based research into practice

Unlike other educational reforms, the foundation for arts integration has been built by a broad-based coalition. Educators, arts and cultural organizations, government agencies, and hundreds of businesses and corporations have joined forces. They are united by one goal: to improve education and thereby improve everyone's lives. Collaboration among such diverse groups has caused integration to be honed into a powerful tool. *Meaningful* arts integration creates the conditions for two-way transfer of learning from the arts to traditional academic areas and vice versa.

Features New to This Edition

This book tells the story of how arts integration has grown so much so fast. It is the story of hundreds of arts-based schools. Some are brand new, such as Hilton Head School for the Creative Arts. The featured school for this edition is Ashley River Creative Arts, about to celebrate 25 years of arts integration. Old and new, public, magnet, and charter, these schools are combining research, standards, and constructivist beliefs to transform education. In particular, they view literacy as greater than the language arts. All communication forms used to understand and express thoughts and feelings are embraced, with the arts in both leading and supporting roles. From an arts-based perspective, literacy *is* the arts.

This third edition describes why arts integration is an important school reform and how it is implemented. While there is no one right way, common building blocks make the arts integral, not add-ons. At center stage is the classroom teacher. In the pages that follow I have synthesized *what* teachers new to arts integration need to know and be able to do. New to this edition is an *Arts Integration Blueprint* that shows how using the arts as learning tools need not be at odds with "arts for art's sake." Indeed, the stars of the curriculum, reading and math, are primarily valued as means to understand and express meaning. The arts are equally and uniquely needed to do the same.

Integration is the opposite of isolation. Arts integration unites, combines, and orchestrates learning, raising the act of teaching to an art. The arts were our first communication tools. They have long been valued for their power to uplift and elevate. They are now part of the inner circle of learning, an essential piece of the educational puzzle.

Book Organization

This edition has two parts. Part 1 is an overview of arts integration in three chapters. Chapter 1 introduces arts integration. Chapter 2 describes the beliefs, research, and theories at the heart of arts integration. Chapter 3 is an overview of the *Arts Integration Blueprint,* a set of 10 building blocks common in most schools.

Part 2 begins an in-depth look at the integration of each of the five arts with two chapters each for literature, visual art, drama, dance, and music. Even-numbered chapters explain practical ideas for using the *Blueprint* (e.g., planning units and lesson plans, arts literacy, best practices, differentiating instruction, assessment *for* learning). Odd-numbered chapters with blue tabs are compendia of Seed Strategies—brief idea starters in the categories of energizers, teaching arts elements and concepts, and curricular areas.

Text Features

- **Chapter questions** introduce each chapter.
- **Research Updates** summarize arts-based studies related to the subject of each chapter.
- **Ready References** outline sources and information teachers often need. Included is the basic arts knowledge base recommended for classroom teachers by the new standards of the Interstate New Teachers Assessment and Support Consortium (INTASC).
- **Planning Pages** show examples of actual arts-integrated lesson and unit plans in each chapter.
- **Snapshots and Spotlights** of actual teachers, classrooms, students, and artists help paint the big picture of how arts strategies are orchestrated in lessons. Strategies are cited in bold print to help focus on how teachers make meaningful integration happen. *Note:* Most of the teachers in this book have given me permission to use their real names. A few names are pseudonyms.
- The **appendices** identify important tools that support arts integration and include key websites, a dozen assessment tools, a School Registry to locate arts-based schools, an extensive arts-based bibliography of children's books, strategies for differentiating for students with special needs, and guidelines for arts-based field trips.

Acknowledgments

This book reflects the dedication of many educators to arts integration. In particular, I want to thank Jayne Ellicott, Principal, Ashley River Creative Arts, and Cathie Middleton, Assistant Principal, for being true collaborators. The teachers of Ashley River were a delight to work with and give this book life. I want to acknowledge every one of them:

Elizabeth Allen, Susan Brandon, Ann Cheek, Bernadette Chilcote, Chris Crawford, Natascha Ferguson, Robin Fountain, Janelle Fredrich, Alison Graham, Jennifer Hanson, Cindy Hines, Sylvia Horres, Ismaker Kadrie, Marty Kearney, Michelle Lowe, Barbara Lunsford, Mary Mac Jennings, Jeff Jordan, Bill Langston, Cheryl Leonard, Deborah Menick, Dianne O'Neill, Susan Peebles, Fannie Petros, Carole Rathbun, Jill Roberts, Linda Roberts, CJ Rozzi, Ashley Sires, Cherrie Sneed, Jill Sneed, Kathryn Stonaker, Stacey Sturgell, Lisa Trott, Judy Trotter, Amy Walker, Joyce Wiggins

Over the years I have been fortunate to work with so many others who have contributed to this book in some measure, including Hollie Steele and Carolyn Attaway at Battle Academy in Chattanooga, Tennessee; Rodney Van Valkenburg, Allied Arts of Greater Chattanooga; Kristy Smith, Beaufort County Schools; Wrenn Cook, Columbia College; Ava Hughes, Arts Partnership of Greater Spartanburg; Mary Lou Hightower, University of South Carolina; Christine Fisher and Ray Doughty, South Carolina ABC Schools; Gretch Keefner, Principal, and teachers at Hilton Head School for the Creative Arts (Colleen Skibo, Tara Caron, Erin Duffy, Tennille Kasper, Karen Cauller, and Marcia Underwood); Terry Bennett, Principal, and teachers at Lady's Island Elementary; Amy Goldin, New York University Steinhardt School and Progressive School of Long Island; Debbie Fahmie, Tallahassee, Florida; the Executive Board of the South Carolina Alliance for Arts Education; and the Beaufort Art Association.

On a more personal level I want to thank Bob and Robyn Cornett for their love and understanding and the many good friends who have been so supportive during the writing process, especially Virginia and Rudy Lucas, Susan and Pete Palmer, Chuck and Gloria Dalvini, and Marion and Frank Mayes. And to Collette Kelly, I want to say I'm still amazed at what you set in motion.

I also wish to thank the reviewers of my manuscript for their comments and insights; this is a better book for their efforts: Laura Dougherty, Illinois State University; Darlene Gaskill, Oral Roberts University; Janette Knowles, Ohio Dominican University; and Steve Thunder-McGuire, University of Iowa.

Thanks to all the folks at Merrill/Prentice Hall who work so artfully to turn typed pages into beautiful books. In particular, I want to acknowledge Senior Editor Linda Bishop, her assistant Laura Weaver, Senior Production Editor Mary Irvin, and Carol Sykes for her work on the photographs. Thanks also to Norine Strang at Carlisle Publishing Services who was a good shepherd.

Of course, first and last, time present and time past, there is my husband, Charles, to whom this book is dedicated. Without his superb research skills and insightful suggestions I would not have made it. He made me laugh every day and once again made sure I ate supper.

Claudia Cornett

Teacher Preparation Classroom

MERRILL PRENTICE HALL

Your Class. Their Careers. Our Future. Will your students be prepared?

We invite you to explore our new, innovative and engaging website and all that it has to offer you, your course, and tomorrow's educators! Organized around the major courses pre-service teachers take, the Teacher Preparation site provides media, student/teacher artifacts, strategies, research articles, and other resources to equip your students with the quality tools needed to excel in their courses and prepare them for their first classroom.

This ultimate on-line education resource is available at no cost, when packaged with a Merrill text, and will provide you and your students access to:

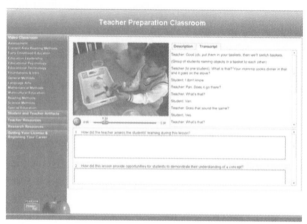

Online Video Library. More than 150 video clips—each tied to a course topic and framed by learning goals and Praxis-type questions—capture real teachers and students working in real classrooms, as well as in-depth interviews with both students and educators.

Student and Teacher Artifacts. More than 200 student and teacher classroom artifacts—each tied to a course topic and framed by learning goals and application questions—provide a wealth of materials and experiences to help make your study to become a professional teacher more concrete and hands-on.

Research Articles. Over 500 articles from ASCD's renowned journal *Educational Leadership*. The site also includes Research Navigator, a searchable database of additional educational journals.

Teaching Strategies. Over 500 strategies and lesson plans for you to use when you become a practicing professional.

Licensure and Career Tools. Resources devoted to helping you pass your licensure exam; learn standards, law, and public policies; plan a teaching portfolio; and succeed in your first year of teaching.

How to ORDER *Teacher Prep* for you and your students:
For students to receive a *Teacher Prep* Access Code with this text, instructors **must** provide a special value pack ISBN number on their textbook order form. To receive this special ISBN, please email
Merrill.marketing@pearsoned.com and provide the following information:
- Name and Affiliation
- Author/Title/Edition of Merrill text

Upon ordering *Teacher Prep* for their students, instructors will be given a lifetime *Teacher Prep* Access Code.

Contents

Part 1
Arts Integration

Chapter 1
An Introduction to Arts Integration 1

Stop the Beatings 1
Remarkable Meaning Makers 2
The Arts and Integration 6
  History and Nature of the Arts 6
  What Is Art? 7
  Arts–Added Education 7
What Is Integration? 8
What Is Meaningful Arts Integration? 10
  In the News 10
  Arts for Learning Sake 10
  Definition and Principles 11
  Meaningful Arts Integration 12
Levels and Models of Arts Integration 12
  Five Minutes a Day? 12
  With, About, In, and Through the Arts 13
  Arts-Based Reform: National and Regional
    Models 14
Why Integrate the Arts? 15
  Arts and Academics 15
  Unique Contributions of the Arts: Process and
    Content 16
  National Initiatives and Legislation 20
The Arts and the 21st-Century Workforce 23
Conclusion 25
Resources 25
Children's Literature References 25

Chapter 2
Philosophy, Research, and Theories That Support Arts Integration 26

Arts Integration Philosophy 28
  Philosophical Overview 28
  People 29
  Principles of Learning 30
  Places 31
  Programs 32
  Pedagogy 32
  Mission Statement 33
Research on Arts Integration 34
**Academic Achievement (as Measured by Test
  Scores) 35**
Cognitive Effects 35
Literacy and Math 36
Motivational/Affective Effects 36
Social Effects 36
Learning Environment 37
Diverse Learners 37
Brain Research 37
  Misconceptions 37
  Brain Facts and Educational Implications 38
  New Brain Research 40
Arts Integration and Learning Theories 40
  Multiple Intelligences (MI) Theory 40
  Erikson's Stage Theory 43
  Piaget's Stages of Cognitive Development 43
  Maslow's Hierarchy of Needs 45
  Vygotsky's Social Development 46
  Child Development and the Arts 47

Creativity and Creative Problem Solving (CPS) 47
Predispositions 47
Problem Based 48
What Is Creativity? 48
Creativity in Action 49
The Creative Problem Solving (CPS) Process 50
Creative Planning and Teaching 52
Conclusion 55
Resources 55
Children's Literature References 55

Chapter 3
Arts Integration Blueprint 56

How to Plan and Implement Arts Integration 57
Teaching With, About, In, and Through the Arts 57
More than Entertainment 58
Blueprint I: Philosophy of Arts Integration 60
Blueprint II: Arts Literacy 61
Teacher Standards 61
Purposes of the Arts 62
Processes/Skills 63
People 65
Products 65
Arts Elements and Concepts 66
Blueprint III: Collaborative Integrated Arts Planning 66
Planning Overview 66
Blueprint IV: Aesthetic Learning Environment 72
Blueprint V: Literature as a Core Art Form 73
Blueprint VI: Best Teaching Practices 74
What You Teach Is Who You Are 75
Inside-Out Motivation 75
Engagement and Active Learning 76
Creative Problem Solving (CPS) 76
Explicit Teaching 78
Apply, Practice, Rehearse 79
Aesthetic Orienting 79
Process and Product 80
Management: Behavior, Time, and Materials 81
Independence and Self-Discipline 82
Blueprint VII: Instruction Design 82
Instructional Design 82
Blueprint VIII: Adaptations for Diverse Needs 85
Student Needs: 10 Ways to Diversify Instruction 86
Interventions for Special Needs Populations 87
Blueprint IX: Assessment for Learning 87
Definition and Purposes 88
Evidence Driven 88
Issues 88
For/Of 88
Assessing Assessment 89
Assessment Tools 89
Blueprint X: Arts Partnerships 91
Direct Service 91
Arts Specialists 91
Arts Agencies/Organizations 93
Arts Directory 93
Conclusion 93
Resources 93
Children's Literature References 93

Part 2
Integrating Literature and the Arts Throughout the Curriculum

Chapter 4
Integrating the Literary Arts 94

Literature at the Core 94
What Are the Literary Arts? 96
Blueprint I: Philosophy of Arts Integration 97
Why Integrate Literature? 97
Blueprint II: Arts Literacy: Literary Content and Skills 102
What Teachers Need to Know 102
Blueprint III: Collaborative Planning 112
National Standards: Literary Arts 112
Integrated Units 113
Unit Structures 113
Field Trip or Literary Event 114
Special Connections 115
Two-Pronged Lesson Plan 115
Blueprint IV: Aesthetic Literary Environment 117
Literature Collections 117
Blueprint V: Literature as a Core Art Form 117
Creativity 117
Unity and Balance 117
Taste 117
Selection Sources 118
Blueprint VI: Best Teaching Practices 121
What You Teach Is Who You Are 121
Explicit Teaching 124
Aesthetic Orienting 125

Stretching Time   126
Independence and Self-Discipline   126

Blueprint VII: Instructional Design: Routines and Structures   126

Blueprint VIII: Adaptations for Diverse Needs   130
Developmental Stages   130
Matching Books and Students   130

Blueprint IX: Assessment for Learning   131

Blueprint X: Arts Partnerships   131
Author/Artist Visits   131

Conclusion   132
Resources   132
Children's Literature References   133

Chapter 5
Seed Strategies for Literature and Poetry   135

Chapter Organization   136

I. Energizers and Warm-Ups   136

II. Teaching About Literature: Elements and Genre Traits   138

III. Connecting Literature to Curricular Areas   139
Science Focus   139
Social Studies Focus   140
Literacy: Reading and Language Arts Focus   143
Math Focus   145
Special Focus: Poetry Sharing and Writing   146
General Principles for Poetry Integration   147
Ongoing Poetry Routines   147
Poetry Sharing and Performance   148
Memorizing Poetry   148
Composing Poetry: Written and Oral   148

Conclusion   150
Resources   150

Chapter 6
Integrating Visual Art Throughout the Curriculum   152

Visual Imagery and Literacy   152

Blueprint I: Arts Integration Philosophy   155
Why Should Teachers Integrate Art?   155

Blueprint II: Arts Literacy: Content and Skills   159
What Do Teachers Need to Know to Integrate Art?   159

Blueprint III: Collaborative Integrated Art Planning   167

Unit Planning   167

Blueprint IV: Aesthetic Learning Environment   172
Immersion   174
Art Sources   174

Blueprint V: Literature as a Core Art Form   175
Visual Art-Based Literature   175

Blueprint VI: Best Teaching Practices   176
Teacher Roles: Guide and Director   176
Creative Problem Solving and Authentic Art   177
Explicit Teaching   177
Aesthetic Orienting   178
Process and Product   179

Blueprint VII: Instructional Design: Routines and Structures   179
Energizers and Warm-Ups   179
Daily Routines and Rituals   179
Art Discussions   180
Stations and Centers   180

Blueprint VIII: Adaptations for Diverse Needs   181
Visual Art and Child Development   181
Differentiating Instruction   184
Websites   185

Blueprint IX: Assessment for Learning   185

Blueprint X: Arts Partnerships   186
Conclusion   188
Resources   188
Children's Literature References   189

Chapter 7
Visual Art Seed Strategies   190

Chapter Organization   191

I. Energizers and Warm-Ups   192

II. Teaching Art Concepts and Elements   193

III. Using Different Media   196
General Tips   196
Mixing Colors: Color Triangles   196
Drawing and Rubbing   198
Painting and Painting Tools   199
Printmaking   199
Collage   200
Artistic Techniques: Enlarge, Simplify, Crop   200
Displays and Bulletin Boards   201
Murals   201
Mixed Media   201
Photography   202
Three-Dimensional Art   202
Bookmaking   205

IV. Connecting Visual Art to Curricular Areas 205
Science Focus 205
Social Studies Focus 207
Literacy: Reading and Language Arts Focus 208
Math Focus 213
Conclusion   214
Resources   214
Children's Literature References   215

Chapter 8
Integrating Drama Throughout the
Curriculum 216

Drama in Education 216

Blueprint I: Philosophy of Arts Integration 218
Why Should Teachers Integrate Drama? 219

Blueprint II: Arts Literacy: Content and Skills 223
What Do Teachers Need to Know to Integrate Drama? 223

Blueprint III: Collaborative Planning 227
Meaningful Connections 227
The National Standards for the Arts: American Goals 227
Unit Planning 228

Blueprint IV: Aesthetic Learning Environment 229

Blueprint V: Literature as a Core Art Form 231

Blueprint VI: Best Teaching Practices 231
What You Teach Is Who You Are 231
Creative Problem Solving 234
Explicit Teaching 235
Management: Time, Space, Students 235
Discipline for Independence 237

Blueprint VII: Instructional Design: Routines and Structures 238
Structuring Lessons 238
Clubs 239

Blueprint VIII: Adaptations for Diverse Needs 239

Blueprint IX: Assessment for Learning 240
Coaching: Formative Feedback 240
Observation Records 241
Rubrics and Checklists 241
Peer Feedback 241
Program Evaluation 242

Blueprint X: Arts Partnerships 242
Arts Agency Collaborations 242
Arts Education Partnership *(http://aep-arts.org)* 242
Teaching Artists and Artist Residencies 242
When There Is No Drama Specialist 245

Conclusion 246
Resources 246
Children's Literature References 246

Chapter 9
Drama and Storytelling Seed Strategies 247

Chapter Organization 249
Drama Reminders 249

I. Energizers and Warm-Ups 249

II. Pantomime Strategies 251

III. Verbal Improvisation Strategies 257

IV. Connecting Drama to Curricular Areas 262
Science Focus 262
Social Studies Focus 263
Literacy: Reading and Language Arts Focus 263
Math Focus 266

Special Section: Storytelling, an Integrated Art Form 267
Why Storytelling? 267
Storytelling Strategies and Resources 268
Storytelling Sources and Resources 273
Conclusion 274
Resources 274
Children's Literature References 274

Chapter 10
Integrating Dance and Movement 276

Two Ways 276

Teaching With, About, In, and Through 278
Relax! You Need Not Be a Dancer Yourself 278

Blueprint I: Philosophy of Arts Integration 279
Why Should Teachers Integrate Dance and Movement? 279

Blueprint II: Arts Literacy: Content and Skills 283
What Do Teachers Need to Know to Integrate Dance? 284
Sources for Materials 287
Teaching Approach 288

Blueprint III: Collaborative Planning 289
National Standards for Dance 289
Arts with Arts Integration 290

Blueprint IV: Aesthetic Learning Environment 294

Blueprint V: Literature as a Core Art Form 295

Blueprint VI: Best Teaching Practices 296

What You Teach Is Who You Are   296
Engagement and Active Learning   296
Creative Problem Solving   297
Explicit Teaching   298
Aesthetic Orienting   298
Apply–Practice–Rehearse   298
Process or Product   299
Management: Behavior, Time, and Materials   299

Blueprint VII: Instructional Design: Routines and Structures   300
IDC Lesson Framework   300
Routines and Rituals   301
Lessons That Flop   301
Four Corners Stations   302
Clubs   302

Blueprint VIII: Adaptations for Diverse Needs   302
Adaptations for Special Needs   303

Blueprint IX: Assessment for Learning   303
General Criteria: Observing Dance and Dance Making   303
Feedback   303
Anecdotal Records   303
Group Debriefing   303
Self-Assessment   304
Portfolio Entries   304

Blueprint X: Arts Partnerships   304
Initiating Collaboration   304
Residencies   305
Conclusion   305
Resources   305
Children's Literature References   306

Chapter 11
Dance Seed Strategies 307

Chapter Organization   309

I. Energizers and Warm-Ups   309

II. Dance BEST Elements and Concepts   311

III. Connecting Dance to Curricular Areas   314
Science Focus   314
Social Studies Focus   316
Literacy: Reading and Language Arts Focus   318
Math Focus   320

IV. Multiarts Focus: Dance Integrated with Other Arts   321
Conclusion   322
Resources   322
Children's Literature References   322

Chapter 12
Integrating Music Throughout the Curriculum 323

In the News   323
Music Research: It's Only Natural   325

Blueprint I: Philosophy of Arts Integration   326
Why Integrate Music?   326

Blueprint II: Arts Literacy: Content and Skills   330
What Do Teachers Need to Know to Integrate Music?   330

Blueprint III: Collaborative Planning   338
Nine National Standards for Music K–8   338
Respected, Not Trivialized   338
Complementary Connections   338
Unit Centers   340
Two-Pronged Integrated Plans   342

Blueprint IV: Aesthetic Learning Environment   342
Background Music: Research   342
Besides Background Music   344

Blueprint V: Literature as a Core Art Form   344

Blueprint VI: Best Teaching Practices   347
What You Teach Is Who You Are   347
Engagement and Active Learning   348
Creative Problem Solving   350
Explicit Teaching   351
Aesthetic Orienting   351
Management   352
Practice and Independence   352

Blueprint VII: Instructional Design: Routines and Structures   353
Lesson Introductions   353
Daily and Weekly Routines   353
Energizers and Warm-Ups   354
Centers, Stations, Displays   354
Schoolwide Structures   354

Blueprint VIII: Adaptations for Diverse Needs   355
Nature and Nurture   355
Musical Development   355

Blueprint IX: Assessment for Learning   356
Two-Pronged Planning   356
Feedback   356
Interest Inventories   356
Program Evaluation   356

Blueprint X: Arts Partnerships   356
Music Teachers   357
Technology   357
Conclusion   358

Resources   358
Children's Literature References   358

Chapter 13
Music Seed Strategies   359

Chapter Organization   359
I. Energizers and Warm-Ups   360
II. Music Elements and Concepts and Elements
362
III. Connecting Music to Curricular Areas   365
   Science Focus   366
   Social Studies Focus   368
   Literacy: Reading and Language Arts Focus   369
   Math Focus   375
Conclusion   377
Resources   377
Children's Literature References   378

Epilogue   379

Bibliography   380

Appendix A
Developmental Stages and the Arts   389

Appendix B
Adapting Arts-Based Lessons for Students with
Diverse Needs   392

Appendix C
Assessment Tools and Resources   394

Appendix D
Discipline Prevention and Intervention   399

Appendix E
Book Report Alternatives   401

Appendix F
Artistic Birthday Buddies Project   403

Appendix G
Arts-Based Field Trips   404

Appendix H
Websites   406

Appendix I
School Registry of Arts-Based Schools   407

Appendix J
Arts-Based Children's Literature   409

Seed Strategies Index   420

Subject Index   423

An Introduction to Arts Integration

Questions to Guide Reading

1. Why has arts integration become a focus of school reform?

2. How do arts-based schools change curricula and teaching?

3. What is *meaningful* arts integration?

4. How is arts integration implemented in different ways?

5. What unique contributions to learning do the arts make? Why do these often go unnoticed with traditional tests?

6. What national initiatives support arts integration?

7. How are the arts connected to the economy and workplace?

We have an achievement gap partly because we have an arts gap among the haves and the have not children. (Annenberg Institute for School Reform. 2003)

You may have seen the American Express ads that feature Sting and Sheryl Crow promoting music lessons to increase math and science learning. The idea of using the arts to boost academic performance is now barbershop conversation. For those fixated on test scores, mixing the arts and education may seem like another quick fix. The relationship between education and the arts, however, is complex, and there is a long history of efforts to put the two together. In the 16th century Johann Comenius was arguing that "things, not words . . . change school from prison to a scholae ludus (play site), where curiosity is aroused and satisfied." He urged teachers to "Stop beatings. Reduce rote learning and engage the child's interest through music and games and through handling objects, through posing problems (project learning) and stirring imagination by dramatic accounts of the big world."

Stop the Beatings

Four hundred years later we thankfully have stopped the beatings. What about the rest of Comenius's proposal? The most recent National Assessment of Educational Progress, a congressionally mandated standardized test, released new findings that show the reading skills of high school students aren't improving. Scores are flat. Two thirds of American adolescents read at or below basic level. They can do literal thinking, but not inference, analysis, or critique. The same goes for writing. Students can create simple narratives and informational paragraphs but not extended text or persuasive arguments. Students achieving in some bit of reading at grade 3 may not be reading at all by grade 8. More troubling, achievement gaps between rich and poor, miniority and majority populations seem to be widening (Shanahan, 2004, p. 255).

We have to do more than stop the beatings. Some schools are. An increasing number are becoming Comenius schools—without even knowing it. Now numbering in the hundreds, these "arts-based" schools are popping up in every state and in Canada, Australia, and the United Kingdom. Comenius's great ideas have been rediscovered and reworked and now boast a research base that goes much

Pantomiming escaping slaves.

perspectives and cultures; to be motivated to do excellent work; to take risks and persevere against the odds; to value democratic ideas; and to continue learning throughout life. The arts provide important means to achieve these goals that include distinct problem-solving processes and a world arts treasury that can reignite students with the imagination and passion inherent in its creators. Indeed the arts are often regarded as "the sense and soul of the curriculum" powerful instructional tools—essential in meeting the goals of standards-based educational reform.

What actually happens in these newly fashioned 21st-century arts-based schools that are implementing seeds of ideas developed 400 years ago? Here is a look into a first grade at one of the American's oldest arts-based schools.

beyond the narrow gauge of standardized tests. Arts integration is part of a broad-based revival of interest in whole child learning translating into long-term differences in children's personal, emotional, and cognitive growth (Ruppert, 2006).

Remarkable Meaning Makers

The concept of arts integration goes beyond using art, singing, and drama for self-expression. The arts are viewed as indispensable sources of cultural and historical information, givers of diverse perspectives and values, and remarkable tools to make meaning. The arts contribute to an overall culture of excellence in schools. They are treated as vital communication vehicles that connect students to one another and give them an understanding of their creative ancestry. The arts provide a ready way to perceive new relationships, to notice patterns and connect ideas across school subjects. Works of art and artistic thinking link social studies, mathematics, science, and geography "opening lines of inquiry, revealing that art, like life, is lived in a complex world not easily defined in discrete subjects" (J. Paul Getty Trust, 1993).

"The challenge to American education has never been simply to raise test scores" (Deasy & Stevenson, p. xiv). The goals are much greater. American education is expected to cause students to think at higher levels; to respect diverse

Classroom Snapshot:
Music/Literacy/Social Studies

The background music is barely audible. The lights are off. Judy Trotter sits on the arm of a wingback chair. There is complete silence as she closes the picture book she has just finished reading to her first graders. The book is *Barefoot* (Edwards, 1997). It is about slaves running from their captors.

"Find your personal space," Judy tells them, almost in a whisper. Students slowly stand up. They begin to spread out and adjust so no one is within reach of another.

Judy waits for students to look at her and then says, "OK, show me walking in place—barefoot. Begin."

In their personal "space bubbles," 17 children begin to drag, shuffle, slide, and tiptoe to a slow steady beat. Background percussion sets the tempo. Judy "side coaches" to increase engagement.

"I see faces full of effort. Good job of concentrating. I see everyone thinking about walking with bare feet in mud, on rocks, through water. Careful, don't let them hear you," she warns.

"Stop!" Judy calls. Students relax and become first graders again. Judy stops the CD.

"Who were the other people in the story?" she asks. Students talk about the slave hunters, what they were like, what they wanted, and how they felt.

"Now let's pantomime their feelings," Judy tell them. "Places!"

Once again in their personal spaces the children are at the ready.

"Action!" Judy calls and a contrasting mime of "boots" begins. This time, students slash, stomp, squat, peer, and glare.

"Freeze," Judy directs. This follow-up to the read-aloud continues with a *narrative pantomime* (Heinig, 1993). Judy retells the plot as students mime the major events in this story set during the Civil War. No props are used, except a flashlight to suggest stars that mapped the path for escaping slaves. ☀

Teacher Spotlight:
Meaningful Integration

The mind should "act as a waffle iron on batter." (I. Kant)

Judy Trotter has been teaching fourth and first grade off and on at Ashley River Creative Arts Elementary for more than 15 years. She is uncompromising when she declares, "Teaching through the arts is the best way to teach."

"Teachers get in a testing panic and think they don't have time for the arts. They get worried about our state PACT test. But if students truly learn, they will do well on the tests," Judy states confidently. "Teaching should not be about teaching to the test. Teaching should be structured so students learn for the pure joy of it."

After teaching at this renowned school for so long, Judy says she is "always thinking about arts connections." Currently she is also doing another arts-based read-aloud (Cornett, 2006) of the chapter book *Because of Winn Dixie* (DiCamillo, 2000). She is animated as she describes how you can take any story and "go off in any arts direction."

"It just flows," she says. "The arts are a natural connection." That *natural* connection has to do with her concern about *meaningful* arts integration. She talks passionately about her deep commitment to "social justice, big ideas, and compassion." A main focus of her teaching is passing on particular values and the capacity to take new perspectives, including "a respect for the unknown."

It is clear Judy believes that balanced and meaningful teaching means school life should mirror outside life. "I believe in teaching the whole child," Judy explains. "Art is everywhere. It is totally integrated into our daily lives. We live in the arts and should be able to learn through arts. They enrich life and learning."

Assessment

Judy talks just as passionately about assessment. "We must work with the standards," she insists, "but I use many ways to gauge student progress—journals, for example, for poetry, math, writing, science, and social studies." She laughs, "They know they have to prove they have learned it!" The journals, she explains, are black and white composition books.

Like all the Ashley River teachers, Judy plans standards-based units that use the arts as central teaching tools. "We were immersed in Asian culture at the time of the tsunami," she notes. Students learned to use paintbrushes to write in black paint. They studied the picture book art of Soerpiet, a Korean illustrator known for watercolors. Students listened to Chinese CDs and made costumes to celebrate Chinese New Year. She describes how she read poems to Chinese music and asked the children to take an imaginary trip to China. Previously the students had watched a CD-Rom of China. "Of course, there was a Chinese celebration," Judy says excitedly.

It is a routine to end each unit with exhibits and performances that show what the students have learned. While teaching fourth grade, Judy recalls a favorite unit on Western Expansion during which they studied composers of the period. They listened to Aaron Copland's pieces, pretended they were on a wagon train, and wrote journal entries in a diary (Pretend and Write drama strategy).

Music, Movement, and Management

Judy is equally committed to preparing new teachers to integrate the arts meaningfully and is on the faculty at the College of Charleston. She also does workshops for practicing teachers on using music and movement strategies. How does she respond to concerns about students dancing?

Arts-based read aloud to prepare for pantomime.

"I do it with them!" she explains. "I teach my students how to control their voices and bodies. We take movement breaks daily." To help students put forth their best concentration efforts, her favorite strategy is to use "fast pass." Students earn a yarn necklace "that is a fast pass so you don't have to wait in line." (She thought of this while on vacation at Disney World.) She also uses a "compliment chain" in which a hook is added anytime someone compliments a classmate. "We celebrate when it gets to a goal point."

What's next? Judy is excited about the current African culture unit using *Follow the Drinking Gourd* (Winter, 1997) and folk tales. "We will compare the art of the Chinese with African art. "I want students to value how other people sound and look—deep down all people are so much the same. This is one of the big ideas behind the arts."

Meaningful Aspects

Judy Trotter's lessons are examples of meaningful arts integration. She uses drama, visual art, dance, and music as teaching tools *and* as content to reach unit objectives. Visual art stirs children's emotions. Drawing is prominent in the writing process. Songs and poetry are used to summarize content and make facts memorable. Background music engages the senses. Drama brings history to life making it vivid and real. Dance activates kinesthetic thinking and brings the joy of movement into the learning process. At Ashley River these aspects of arts integration are made a reality through collaborative planning by grade-level teams who plan using science, social studies, literacy, math, and arts standards. Arts specialists consult with teams to ensure arts standards are given equity with core academic areas.

Curriculum, Instruction, and Assessment

Teachers at Ashley River use multiple forms of assessment, including observation checklists and rubrics, both for academic areas and arts products and processes. Arts-based lessons taught during the literacy block are frequently connected to science and social studies units. Students are engaged throughout lessons, cognitively, physically, emotionally, and socially using best practices for teaching reading and writing *and* for teaching the arts. Teachers explicitly teach how to transform ideas using the arts to construct individual interpretations of content. Teachers not only pose problems but teach how to problem solve; they ask many open-ended questions, expecting a range of "right" answers. Ashley River teachers present the arts as communication vehicles all people routinely use to understand, respond to, and express thoughts and feelings. In this way the arts are shown respect as powerful forms of literacy used to create personal meaning. Ashley River teachers act on the maxim "A mind should be well made rather than well filled" (Immanuel Kant).

School Spotlight:

Happy 25th Anniversary!

The arts are not an educational option; they are basic. (John Goodlad)

Ashley River Creative Arts Elementary is about to celebrate its 25th year as a K–5 integrated arts school. In 2½ decades this small school in Charleston, South Carolina, has become one of the most famous arts-based schools in the United States. It is a National Blue Ribbon School and was honored as a Kennedy Center "Creative Ticket School of Excellence." It's fitting that the mascot is a unicorn, a fanciful creature associated with hope and creativity.

Beginnings

"This is a school born of the imagination of the first principal," explains Jayne Ellicott, principal since 1994. She should know. Ellicott was Rose Maree Myers' assistant when the school opened in 1984. "Rose Maree was a visual art teacher with a theatre background. She had a very musical son who was not academically inclined. Her vision was to use the power of the arts to give all children a love of learning."

Ms. Ellicott witnessed the transformation of a condemned building with broken windows and weeds above the roof into what began as a magnet school. At first, half the students were "zoned in," and the other half were chosen by lottery. By the third year all students were chosen from a waiting list. Now, all students are chosen by lottery each January.

Ms. Ellicott is convinced Ashley River started with an advantage because they didn't try to force an arts-based program on an existing school. The first faculty was hand-picked for their commitment to using the arts as core instructional methods. From the get-go, teachers knew they were being hired to *create* an integrated arts school. Ms. Ellicott remembers, "It was hard to gel that personality force, but Rose Maree inspired the faculty to trust her and she was very goal centered."

Excitement and Focus

Twenty-five years ago it was this combination of excitement and focus that motivated the administration and teachers to do evening and Saturday professional development. Jayne Ellicott smiles as she reminisces about weekly meetings during which Rose Maree would demonstrate integrated arts lessons. As with most teachers new to arts integration, some were intimidated by dance and movement, others by the prospect of visual art. For some, music was the challenge. "We didn't have any special supplies. We didn't even have ceiling tiles and very few electric plugs that first year," she laughs. But she suggests that those limitations were the catalyst for the teachers to bond.

According to Ms. Ellicott, arts integration requires hard work that includes collaboration among teachers within grade levels and with arts specialists. This is achieved in many ways, including monthly meetings with specialists at each grade level. The focus is on the basics, but the arts are the "delivery path." Ongoing informal interactions among specialists and teachers also happen at lunch, in the halls, and after school. She insists that "doors to classrooms need to be open so anyone can walk by, enjoy, and even come in and participate."

Beyond Test Scores

All of Ashley River's students now do well on PACT (South Carolina's state academic test), but Ms. Ellicott points to what she considers more important indicators of the school's success. "Our students show they know and understand in many ways. They know what to do with free time and they all think they can become 'expert' at something—painting, dancing, playing an instrument."

Ms. Ellicott cites other results she attributes to their arts-based approach by contrasting students who enter as kindergarteners and remain versus latecomers. "Late arrivals have trouble because our students all learn early on to cooperate, communicate, and process information on a higher scale. They quickly learn to plan and work together when they are engaged in the arts. They learn to achieve consensus and are more confident. For example, in drama class I've seen even the most shy student just bellow out!"

Two Things

Ms. Ellicott credits most of the school's success to the arts-based curriculum, but points out that parents decide their children will be at Ashley River and that choice makes a difference. Ms. Ellicott emphasizes that the school does not select academically gifted kids over other children, nor do they have more money than other schools. AR does have a strings teacher, a drama specialist, and an extra music teacher, which is three more teachers than "normal." Parents furnish the instruments for the strings program. The extra teachers, along with special equipment like musical Orff instruments and a photography lab, are funded by aggressive pursuit of grants like those from ABC (Arts in the Basic Curriculum) provided by the State Arts Commission. "We have used start-up grant monies, Wachovia Bank matching grants, Sam's Club's, Project Artistic (U.S. Department of Educa-

tion), and individual donors. We continue to invite private benefactors to be a part of Ashley River's mission," Ms. Ellicott explains.

Problems and Opportunities

Is Ashley River without problems? "No," admits Ms. Ellicott. "We have all the same issues as any school." Nineteen percent of the students are on free/reduced lunch. Forty percent of the students have learning disabilities. Thirty-eight percent are from a minority group. Parents think that kids who couldn't make it somewhere else can make it at AR, she says. "We are able to work through our problems using arts tools that focus on cooperation, persistence, more risk taking and experimentation, and respect for diverse ideas."

Over the years Ashley River has added many choice arts opportunities for students, like the Drama Troupe (fourth and fifth grade), a chorus, a strings/violin club, a ballet club, and a clay club. These have proven to be important curricular adjuncts and powerful public relations tools. Ms. Ellicott recalls the reaction when she took the strings group to a local Rotary meeting. "Community leaders were shocked to see kindergartners play the violin. I saw tears in the audience."

Passion

Jayne Ellicott sits in her office papered with children's art and writing. She reflects on the years past and yet to come. "There is so much about the adult world that has nothing to do with standards and measurement, so much that is more important that we don't and can't measure. I watch the

Assistant Cathie Middleton and Principal Jayne Ellicott, Ashley River Creative Arts Elementary.

Research Update 1.1 **Arts and Learning**

- **Minneapolis, MN.** Arts-integrated schools reported substantial effects for all students. The greatest impact was for disadvantaged students. "Students become better thinkers, develop higher-order skills, and deepened their inclination to learn" (Rabkin & Redmond, 2005).
- **Escondido, CA.** K–5 multilingual students made significant gains in English and comprehension with arts integration. The SUAVE program received a development and dissemination grant in 2003 (list at *http://web99.ed.gov*).
- **Tucson, AZ.** Students at Opening Minds through the Arts (OMA) schools have significantly higher scores in math, reading, and writing than non-OMA students. The arts have closed the gap between minority and white students (*Arts Education: Improving Students' Academic Performance,* March 2005 broadcast: *www.ed.gov*).
- **South Carolina.** Arts in Basic Curriculum (ABC) evaluators analyzed 3 years of state tests in English/language arts and math. They found a steady increase in the percent of students identified as proficient or advanced in ABC schools, as compared to the comparison group (Horowitz, 2004, p. 27).

- **New York City; Hartford, CT; Philadelphia, PA; Baltimore, MD.** A 3-year study of 2,000 students found a significant relationship between rich school arts programs and creative, cognitive, and personal competencies needed for academic success. The study suggests that transfer of learning involves "certain habits of mind which have salience across subject areas." A key factor was to "invite thinking to travel back-and-forth across subject boundaries" (Burton et al., 2000).
- **Chicago.** Twenty-three arts-integrated CAPE schools showed test scores rising up to two times faster than in demographically comparable schools (Deasy, 2002).
- **Hamilton, OH.** Students involved in the SPECTRA arts program made more gains in reading vocabulary, comprehension, and math than a control. Creativity measures were four times higher and gains held during a second-year evaluation (Luftig, 1994).
- **Test scores of arts-involved students are generally higher than those who aren't.** The arts help students "exercise your mind in unique ways." See SAT Results at *www.collegeboard.com* (Deasy, 2002; National Center for Education Statistics: *http://nces.ed.gov*).

---

kindergartners bowing away on the violin or the little ballet dancers (boys and girls) with their underpants hanging out. I wish that every teacher would be a believer. Not all do. You have to have the passion that the arts are making this difference. Of course, I think all it takes is walking through a classroom to see how the arts transform learning. I just happen to work with teachers who are believers." ✺

The Arts and Integration

Research Updates appear throughout this book. In the first one (1.1) there is a sampling of what is happening at schools across the nation. These research results explain why hundreds of American schools, like Ashley River, have chosen arts-based reform. However, there is more to arts integration than test scores can show. What is it about the arts that educators find so compelling?

History and Nature of the Arts

Ars Longa, Vita Brevis (Life is short. Art is long.)

The arts are time-honored ways of communicating that predate both literacy and numeracy. From their earliest be-

ginnings our human ancestors seemed to feel a need to make art. Theologian Karen Armstrong (2004, p. xix) traces the source of art and religion to identical human needs. She makes the case that both appeared at the same time as people tried to make sense of their existence. Stunning cave paintings in southern France date back more than 30,000 years (Chauvet, Deschamps, & Hilliare, 1996) as do flutes carved from bone. (Compare these to the first written system, cuneiform, which is 5,000 years old.) These paintings, flutes, and ancient drums were not decorations in the lives of early people. These tools were used to think about life's mysteries and express possible meanings.

Words used by our ancestors had practical roots as well, and like painting and drumming, this verbal language evolved into art forms. Storytelling emerged and timeless folktales survive to proclaim the power of early word art. Every culture still uses stories to pass on core beliefs and values about persistent human concerns. Stories show commonalities among people too, regardless of ethnicity. For example, themes about hopes for "fairy tale endings" transcend cultural differences and time periods, as demonstrated by more than 300 versions of the Cinderella story. Interest in this particular story form persists into the 21st century with new versions every year, including *Adelita* (2002), a Mexican version called *Chickerella (*2005), and even a jazz age version,

Ella's Big Chance (2004). Early verbal arts also record curious customs and troublesome rituals. For example, the Mother Goose rhyme "Eeny meeny miny mo" has been traced to an epoch when human sacrifices were "counted out."

Ken Robinson, professor at University of Warwick, points out "If the human mind was restricted to academic intelligence, most of human culture would not have happened" (2000, p. 5). Imagine a world without stories, music, theatre, paintings, architecture, or dance. Robinsion suggests these fruits of our creative nature "are rather large factors to leave out of a model of human intelligence" (p. 5). Arts-based schools place these "large factors" at the core of learning.

What Is Art?

Someone once said, "One moment's pain is another moment's privilege." That explains how art emerges from traumatized hurricane victims. Jazz pieces, plays, paintings, sculpture, and dances release psychological pain and allow the rest of us to empathize. This is a universal message of art: pain is universal. Mozart's symphony, written at age 16, is now understood to reflect his struggle to come of age (Lockwood, 2005). Picasso's "Guernica" depicts the deep desperation and horrors of war. Art brings us together in a "third space" of new understanding (Deasy & Stevenson, 2005).

We seem driven to use the arts to explain ourselves, answer questions, and console one another. But why? Any answer would have to tackle the impossible task of finally defining art. To use words to explain communication that exists because words are inadequate is a conundrum. It is possible, however, to consider unique aspects of the arts and their special contributions that give spark and substance to life. Literature, music, art, drama, and dance are unique meaning makers that open vital communication channels in unmatchable ways.

Consider, for example, how meaning is altered when the art form of poetry is used instead of ordinary prose to convey a message. On a Hilton Head Island restaurant menu, I recently read, "Our feature is blackened swordfish with grilled vegetables." This simple informational prose offers customers important facts. The writer probably spent very little time selecting each word for its emotional impact, although I have to admit it made me salivate. For contrast, read aloud this short poem with an aabb rhyme scheme.

Mahi mahi, swordfish steak
Shrimp scampi, crab cakes
Blackened broiled, potato-breaded
I love fish, except with heads-on.

This poem gives information, but now poetic devices like rhyme, rhythm, and assonance (repetition of vowel sounds) direct attention to the sound as well as the message. The poem is meant to be heard, not just read silently. A first reading might bring the urge to read it again—just for the sound of it. The poet wrote with an ear to musical elements of language as well as to the sense she wanted to share. Language choices are creative, and a new perspective is offered on the topic of seafood. We feel something about the words—delight, perhaps, at the poet's inventiveness. In sum, poetry uses words, as does prose, but it is different in the kind and degree of intended emotional and sensory impact. This is one significant piece of the "what is art" puzzle.

Beyond Words. Like poetry, visual art is made to communicate ideas and feelings, but the communication is beyond words. Visual images, left open to interpretation, cause fine art, and even decorative art, to engage us cognitively and emotionally and may even stimulate a physical response. Visualize Leonardo da Vinci's *Mona Lisa* and, for contrast, the red and white label of a Campbell's soup can. Both pieces were made using the art elements of color, shape, size, and texture and composition principles such as unity and balance. An artist for Campbell's Soup Company undoubtedly worked hard to create a design that would catch attention and raise associations with "m-m-m good" feelings. Red is a warm color, set off with white, and is faintly patriotic. The touch of gold adds a classy feel.

Now imagine Andy Warhol's *paintings* of soup cans. Warhol's art and da Vinci's paintings are both classified as fine art. They provoke a different kind and degree of cognitive and affective involvement than advertisement or decorative art. The intensity of engagement derives from art's power to cause us to question and wonder.

Don't Be Dull. Some complain that fine art is hard to understand, but that is often art's purpose. Artists work to intentionally disconcert. The goal is to create cognitive dissonance and emotional reactions that jar the viewer out of complacency. The goal is not to merely please but to provoke a somatic (bodily) response. Art can awe us with its beauty, but it can also gag us with disgust. I'm thinking here about an art exhibit in Cincinnati, in which a cross was suspended in a jar of urine or the "dung" art made during the late 1990s.

It is likely that da Vinci intended to leave us with more questions than answers about Mona Lisa. "Why is she smiling?" "Who is she?" "Why did he use those colors?" "How did he get that expression on her face?" "How did he do that?" Now Dan Brown's *The Da Vinci Code* has even further heightened interest in possible meanings of da Vinci's art. The Louvre finally had to cover Mona Lisa with a glass box.

Arts-Added Education

The arts, by nature, address core concerns of education—getting attention, keeping attention, motivating, provoking deep thought, and expanding perspective. The arts engage us intellectually and emotionally. That capacity to engage is a major reason educators are drawn to arts-based education. Learning never gets off the starting line without it. It's a simple idea that has been difficult to implement, until now.

Engagement Through the Arts.
Engagement has become a buzz word in education. It is used so commonly that it is worth taking time to consider the meaning: concentrated focus for the purpose of understanding. Getting attention is not enough. Even concentrated focus, devoid of understanding, is not engagement. It may be entertainment, but not engagement.

Didactic teaching approaches that rely on "telling" and "assigning" lack the potential to engage students. Worksheets rarely captivate, and answering questions at the end of chapters is often perceived as busy work. True-false, fill-in, and multiple-choice tests can't show deep understanding that results from independent problem solving. Arts-based teaching rejects such practices and substitutes genuine cognitive, emotional, and physical engagement.

Motivation and Interest.
The arts possess strong and unusual motivational properties. They capture our attention and trigger interest. But when the arts are meaningfully used as teaching and learning tools, their crowd-pleasing attributes are just the beginning. The arts can be intentionally employed to invite multiple interpretations and stimulate natural problem-solving tendencies. Teachers who use the arts as teaching tools take advantage of the engaging power of literature, music, art, drama, and dance. Students think about "why?" and "what if?" and teachers coach them to search for a range of possible solutions. Students change their minds and have changes of heart in response to significant arts experiences. Eisner (2002) reminds us that parents send their children to schools to have their "minds made" (p. 9). Indeed, the arts can be mind-altering devices.

Researcher, Sam Intrator, (2004–2005) shadowed students for 130 days and concluded that engagement is the "grail of teaching." He observed that pupils were "most vibrant when creating" and stressed the importance of encouraging original ideas to engage (p. 4). Teaching for engagement allows teachers to dispense with questionable motivational aids like stickers and stamps. The arts engender deep engagement, which produces intrinsic motivation to work at difficult tasks—long-term projects, exhibits, and performances. Students persist even when there are bumps in the road. The arts charge learning with energy and intensity. Arts advocate Eric Booth (2003) explains that "bringing artistic experiences into the learning equation does something exciting to learning" (p. 15). The "something" he refers to is a "kind of alertness" or "awakeness" that changes any

learning connected to the arts. He could have used the word *engagement*. As an example, Vincent Marron from North Carolina A+ Schools tells the story of a reporter who went to interview the great cellist, Pablo Casals. When he arrived, the 95-year-old Casals was practicing. The reporter asked why, after all his successes, he needed to practice. Casals replied, "I think I'm getting better" (2003, p. 15). That's engagement.

Head, Heart, Hands.
Arts integration is an approach that unites head, heart, and hands. The arts are learning and teaching tools without equal in their potential to cause mental, physical, emotional, and even spiritual response. The artistic properties of any work, topic, or theme can be explored and expressed through paintings, songs, poems, and dances. For example, in one arts-based science unit on plants, students learned about photosynthesis and plant characteristics through singing songs, creating process dances, and assuming roles in drama. They figured out how to give monologues in the role of a bean sprout and how to use movement to show the "rootedness" of plants. This kind of mental and physical problem solving transforms how kids think. The experiences are memorable because they integrate mind, body, and emotions. Imagine fourth graders showing what they know about converting sunshine and water into energy through pantomime and dance. Imagine students eager to come to school and begging to stay in from recess to prepare for learning performances. Imagine a teacher who knows how to assess science standards using rubric criteria to observe these kinds of artistic student presentations. Imagine this and you've glimpsed engaged learning through arts integration.

What Is Integration?

> *Interdisciplinary learning is "learning to know something by its relation to something else."* (Leonard Bernstein)

Integration is not a 21st-century notion. At the start of this chapter I mentioned that Comenius was making integrated proposals in the 1500s. Hundreds of years later in the United States, the "Committee of Ten" (1892) recommended "one hour per week be given over to nature study . . . and that all work be conducted without the aid of a textbook. In addition, every attempt should be made to correlate the science observations with work in language, drawing, and literature." In 1935 the National Council of Teachers of English defined *integration* as the unification of all subjects and experiences.

Definition.
Throughout its history the concept of integration has operated under many labels: interdisciplinary instruction, unit teaching, the project approach, inquiry method, and whole language. By any name it is combining

diverse elements into harmonious wholes with a synergistic result. Synergisms are valued because, while individual elements maintain their integrity, the "sum is more than all the parts." What is a buckle without its belt or a sleeve without a shirt? The part is not usable, nor understandable, without the whole. In art terms it is putting figures against a background or giving particulars a context. In life terms integration is how we live.

Efficiency and Relevance.

A practical argument for integration is that there is just too much to know. It is impossible to teach it all. The Harvard University's library acquired more volumes in the last 5 years than in the previous 100 years, and the Internet testifies to the immense store of information on millions of websites. Instead of continuing to cram in and cover more, arts integration connects big ideas through creative inquiry about important questions. Isolated facts and outdated information are dropped from the curriculum by setting priorities and allocating time to what is most important in our integrated world. Integration creates an economy of time and materials. More is achieved with what is at hand. Instructional time is blocked for science and social studies units. Literacy instruction is linked. Informational science materials are used for reading instruction. Stories and poems from literature anthologies are used in social studies. Teachers do grade-level planning for these integrated units and join with arts specialists to teach to standards for both academics and the arts. Integration connects traditionally segmented areas of the curriculum. The result is an educational approach that is more consistent with 21st-century living and working conditions that demand multitasking and group problem solving to create innovative solutions. It's not surprising that a meta-analysis of 30 studies showed students in integrated programs consistently outperformed those in traditional classrooms on national and state tests (Hartzler, 2000).

A school day organized around isolated skill teaching and fragmented into subjects is poorly matched with life. Making school more lifelike is key to motivating students to learn. Integration is about using information and meaning-making skills to solve important and interesting problems, which adds purpose and relevancy to learning. Arts integration brings a creative problem-solving orientation to bear on the entire curriculum by causing students to seek diverse connections and build new relationships among ideas.

Holistic Learning.

Gestalt psychologists explain that humans are predisposed to bring pieces and parts together into comprehensible wholes. The integration process results in a sense of completeness because meaning is constructed from disconnected ideas. Units are developed around significant life questions and major themes—important "truths" that pull together disparate facts. Meaningful and natural connections are sought, not superficial ones like counting beans in *Jack and the Beanstalk* and calling that integration of math and literature.

Of course, students of any age and stage need to attend to parts, details, and facts as they study subjects and learn skills. In reading students need to notice the differences among similar letters like *b* and *d*. A key to student motivation, however, is for them to see purpose. Isolated concepts and skills are hard to perceive as worthy. Letters are pretty meaningless until they are ordered in patterns to make whole words. Words have minimal meaning until they are placed or integrated into the context of a phrase, sentence, paragraph, or story. What does *run* mean? Is it a verb, as in "to run away," or is it a noun, as in "a run in my hose"? I could have a "run of bad luck" or "run into" another car or have a "dog run" in my backyard. Meaning changes based on context.

Whole to Part.

Even adults who are novices at a task tend to proceed from whole to part, from the gross to the particular, dwelling first on the most obvious, such as large shapes and intuited feelings. Anyone who has first used computer-drawing tools has experienced the compulsion to play around with the mouse. Psychologist Daniel Goleman (1995) explains the evolutionary significance of reacting first to the holistic experience and then to details by describing a jogger who spies a long slender dark curved something coming along his path. "Snake!" screams the ancient emotional impulse and the jogger stops dead in his tracks. Saved from a poisonous bite by primitive instincts, she now uses newer (in evolutionary time) powers of logic to see the details of the something. This time it's just a stick. Think of the consequences if we routinely stopped to analyze the pieces before responding to the whole.

The arts play an important role in integrating wholes and parts. Literature, visual art, drama, dance, and music can interact with science, social studies, math, and literacy to multiply learning about life skills, key concepts, and themes. Traditional lines between curricular areas become muddied. "Is it art or science as a child mixes colors and discovers that blue and yellow make green? The child notices curves and angles in letters and then makes them with his or her own body or draws them in the air; is this language arts or dance?" (Stinson, 1988, p. 95). The answer is, this is authentic learning divorced from outdated artificial boundaries that impede learning. The public, parents, and certainly professional educators are tired of temporary, piecemeal, and simplistic school fixes. Children are whole, integrated persons when they arrive at school. We know how to fully engage students in experiences planned with transfer and connectedness in mind. We know how to teach students communication and problem solving that support personal success and give children the skill and will to give back to their communities. That know-how is bound up in arts integration. Example results appear in Research Update 1.2.

Research Update 1.2   Arts and Achievement

- **Arts integration** is significantly related to gains in reading scores for students in grades 3–5 and is more effective for English language learners and students from low socioeconomic homes (Ingram & Riedel, 2003).
- **Students** in the 130 arts-based Waldorf schools outperformed national averages on the SAT (Oppenheimer, 1999).
- **Los Angeles.** All 3,500 students in a program that integrated the arts into literature and social studies wrote higher-quality essays, showed deeper understanding of history, and made more interdisciplinary references than nonarts students (Aschbacher & Herman, 1991).
- **Los Angeles, Boston, & Cambridge, MA.** In the arts-based Different Ways of Knowing programs, 920 elementary students in 52 classrooms had significant gains in achievement and motivation. High-risk students with 2 years gained 16 points on standardized tests. Arts students had significantly higher grades across the board. Nonarts students showed no gains (Catterall, 1995). See more research at http://differentways.org.
- **Wilmington, NC.** Student disciplinary actions dropped from 130 to 50 and suspensions from 32 to 3 during the first year of involvement in the A+ School Program of arts integration. In addition, state writing test scores for fourth graders improved 30 percentile points (from 35th to 65th percentile).
- **Canada.** A 3-year study of more than 6,000 elementary students in Learning to Read Through the Arts showed an 11-point increase in math in the 170 schools. Literacy scores remained the same, but students reported being happier about school and researchers saw them as more engaged (Upitis & Smithirin, 2003). Website: www.ltta.ca.
- **Coast to coast.** A study of 10 "high-poverty" schools in the continental United States found that arts integration and arts education contributed significantly to closing the achievement gap (Deasy & Stevenson, 2005).
- **SAT** scores for students who studied visual art are 47 points higher in math and 31 points for the verbal portion over nonarts students. Students with music backgrounds averaged 49 points higher on combined scores. Students with drama and dance backgrounds scored 44 points and 27 points higher, respectively. See SAT Results at www.collegeboard.com.

What Is Meaningful Arts Integration?

In the News

Dallas, Texas (2005). Four thousand five hundred teachers now integrate field trips and arts residencies into literacy, science, and social studies. More than 150 public schools work with museums, theatres, and other arts groups to boost academic achievement. ArtsPartners teachers replace "drive-by art" field trips with learning tied to the state-mandated curriculum. Standardized tests show bigger strides in literacy, especially writing. Scores of students with the most arts involvement rose 10 points—as compared to 3 points for the control group. Hogg Elementary students—mostly ELLs (English language learners) from poor neighborhoods—are turning out writing like advantaged students. By fourth grade they write like sixth graders (Ford Foundation, 2005).

Arts for Learning Sake

Booth (2003) traces the role of arts in American schools beginning with "arts for art's sake," moving to "arts for the sake of the workplace," and now a current emphasis on "arts for learning sake." He believes the third focus will dominate the 21st century. Arts for learning is embodied in the arts integration visitors see at Ashley River Creative Arts and hundreds of other schools nationwide (Richmond-Cullen, 2005; School Registry in the Appendix). Large-scale arts-based reform projects have now been implemented in inner cities like New York, Minneapolis, Washington, D.C., and Chicago. Like Ashley River, these schools have chosen arts integration because of theoretical, philosophical, and research support for the kinds of learning engagement that the arts make possible. In particular, arts integration has earned a special reputation for success with disadvantaged, minority, and at-risk students (Deasy & Stevenson, 2005).

Arts integration is not one model, nor is it a prescribed program. The concept of arts integration is primarily a research-based set of beliefs implemented using a variety of curriculum and instructional designs. It also goes by many aliases: arts infusion, arts immersion, arts-based, arts at the core, Arts PROPEL, arts plus, A1, and A+. Mello (2004) and others draw distinctions among some of these terms, suggesting that arts-based involves teaching arts content while arts infusion does not. In this book, however, the labels *arts-*

based and *arts-infused* are synonymous with arts integration; both arts content and arts processes are taught in connection with other academic areas resulting in mutual benefits.

Different Ways of Knowing (DWoK), implemented in 3,000 classrooms in Kentucky and other states, is another example of a model with an arts integration focus (www. differentways.org). More than 500 arts-based magnet schools and scores of charter schools are now affiliated with arts organizations (Fineberg, 2002). Arts integration may also be subsumed under interdisciplinary and inquiry learning (*Authentic Connections,* 2002). Schools implementing multiple intelligences research quickly find themselves involved in arts integration, as well, since three of the intelligences are arts: music, visual/spatial, and kinesthetic (dance and drama). Gardner's other five are also arts linked. For example, verbal intelligence is used with the literary arts in poetry and songs.

Definition and Principles

The National Endowment for the Arts (Weich, 1995) has taken the position that it is impossible to make schools more effective centers of learning without the arts. From Charleston, South Carolina, to Maui, Hawaii, schools have gotten the message and are using the arts as essential teaching tools—not just in the occasional art class or interdisciplinary unit but as pedagogical pillars. These schools share a common belief: Literature, visual art, drama, dance, and music have the power to energize and humanize the curriculum. Integrated arts schools are acting on research that confirms how arts experiences help "level the educational playing field" for disadvantaged students and "close the achievement gap" (Deasy & Stevenson, 2005; Fiske, 1999; Rabkin & Redmond, 2005). The arts are no longer on the curricular fringe of public education. They are an acknowledged part of national strategies to transform schools (Barton, 2005; Boston, 1996; Huckabee, 2005).

Characteristics. Based on a study of a large-scale project in Minneapolis, researchers concluded "the amount of arts integration matters." More than mere exposure to the arts is necessary to affect substantial gains in learning. When teachers integrated the arts into their mathematics lessons "a lot," for example, students showed greater gains than those who integrated "very little" (Ingram & Seashore, 2003, pp. 4–5). The potential for the arts to invigorate learning is demonstrated in the academic superiority of students in schools that devote 25 percent or more of the curriculum to arts courses (Horowitz, 2004; Perrin, 1994).

In addition to "more arts," what makes for quality arts integration? Although instruction varies within arts-based schools, some common overall practices promote change. Here is a synthesis of findings from diverse arts integration projects (Deasy & Stevenson, 2005; Freeman, Seashore, & Werner, 2003; Horowitz, 2004; Ingram & Seashore, 2003).

Changed beliefs and perceptions. Teachers change their views of students. They see struggling readers and writers blossom when given arts options. Teachers become learning coaches and facilitators rather than knowledge dispensers. Students explore, experiment, and make personally meaningful connections. Teachers find unknown strengths and see themselves as leaders; A+ teachers in North Carolina became more resilient to problems like funding cuts or loss of their principal (Horowitz, 2004).

Application of research and theory. Teachers design hands-on/brains-on multisensory instruction using theories like multiple intelligences and brain research. They engage students more directly in problem solving. Students learn to give original interpretations and solutions.

Reaching diverse learners. Arts experiences reveal different aspects of students so teachers deepen their understanding of abilities and potential. Overlooked students become significant players in the learning game as teachers learn alternative strategies and assessments.

Increased culture of excellence. Schools and classrooms become aesthetic places. Physical and psychological changes create stimulating environments with high expectations.

Increased repertoire. Teachers expand their toolkits through collaborative planning and coteaching with arts specialists. They acquire arts strategies that are new ways to engage students and parallel best practices for teaching reading and writing. Students are motivated to revise and rework through arts-based processes like expert use of critique.

More arts instruction and two-way transfer. The arts are placed on an equal footing with other subjects. The arts are used as teaching tools in core subjects, but it doesn't stop there. The arts are also seen as forms of literacy central to teaching and learning. Core academic content and skills are just as likely to be used to teach arts content. For example, units may focus on an artist or art form like picture book artist Eric Carle or a study of historical ballads.

Units centered on Big Ideas and Important Questions. Grade-level integrated units and schoolwide curricular themes are organizing features. Students learn to synthesize and apply arts-based problem solving beyond school walls.

Networking. Partnerships with artists, arts agencies, and the community make arts integration work. For example, at Normal Park Museum Magnet in Chattanooga, Tennessee, family nights involve parents in the arts and "openings" of student exhibits draw others into the excitement of arts integration.

Meaningful Arts Integration

From a broad research and experience base, a general definition of meaningful arts integration has emerged. *Arts integration is the meaningful use of arts processes and content to introduce, develop, or bring closure to lessons in any academic area.* The goal is to transform learning by using the arts to actively engage learners in problem solving that creates understanding and expands expressive communication abilities.

Ten Building Blocks.   Important to this definition is the provision that the arts can be powerful teaching and learning tools if used *meaningfully.* Just as literacy educators have fought to maintain the integrity of literature as an art form in literature-based programs, so the arts community has rightly insisted that music, visual art, drama/theatre, and dance/movement be *used*, not abused. Meaningful arts integration entails more than cosmetic changes to schools and classrooms.

While there is no one right way to integrate the arts, there are common characteristics among the many programs used nationwide. Here are 10 building blocks shared in successful arts integration designs. Most are supported by the Consortium of National Arts Education Associations (*Authentic Connections*, 2002). These are presented here as "general operating principles."

Meaningful Use of the Arts Is Facilitated by . . .

1. *Philosophy of education.*   Arts-based learning is built on strong beliefs about and value for diversity, creative inquiry, active learning (hands-on/brains-on), and student independence. Of particular importance is a belief in the capacity of individuals to construct personal meaning using a variety of communication tools (language arts and arts) and materials.

2. *Arts literacy: content and skills.*   Basic arts concepts and processes are explicitly taught by classroom teachers and arts specialists to increase students' capacities to communicate and problem solve. The arts are integral to the literacy curriculum.

3. *Collaborative planning.*   Classroom teachers and arts specialists co-plan standards-based lessons and units that focus on relationships among big ideas, key concepts, and skills—especially those that transcend individual disciplines. Shared connections take advantage of the natural fit between areas of study and arts content and processes.

4. *Aesthetic learning environments.*   Physical and psychological changes create classroom ecologies that facilitate attitudes toward learning, celebrate differences (including cultural and ethnic), and promote respect and risk taking.

5. *Literature as a core art form.*   Over the past 3 decades high-quality literature has become the primary material to deliver literacy instruction. Every literary genre, from poetry to science fiction, is now used throughout academic areas. Literature is the most readily available arts material and has become the most frequently integrated art form.

6. *Best practices.*   Research- and wisdom-based methods are used for all instructional areas, including the arts. This includes explicit teaching (what-why-how) of authentic arts concepts and processes (e.g., Create, Perform, Respond) and use of high-quality materials and arts examples. Transfer of learning is sought through explicit connections. Coteaching with artists and arts specialists is an important vehicle for building an arts knowledge and skill base among classroom teachers.

7. *Instructional design: routines and structures.*   A thorough and predictable focus on arts-based learning is assured through pronged lessons and by specific routines in the classroom and school schedule. Lessons have a clear introduction, development, and conclusion. Routines range from using energizers to start lessons to morning rituals like arts-based literacy openers and school arts clubs. Time for long-term projects and pursuit of interests is built into the schedule.

8. *Adaptations for diversity.*   Arts communication processes and materials, including multiple intelligences interventions and multisensory methods, expand options for learners to comprehend and express.

9. *Assessment for learning.*   Assessment is primarily used as a motivational tool. Learning criteria are made clear at the outset and continuous feedback on progress increases the likelihood that students will meet criteria. Multiple assessments are used with focus on students "showing they know" through long-term projects, arts-based performances, and exhibits.

10. *Arts partnerships.*   Co-planning and coteaching with arts specialists from within and outside the school are necessary. Teaching artists may be brought in to plan, coach teachers, and/or do residencies with students. Partnerships with community arts agencies are sought.

A more comprehensive discussion of principles 2–10 forms the bulk of Chapter 3. Use of the building blocks and principles related to each art form is explained in the individual arts chapters of this book. A section in Chapter 2 addresses the first principle about the philosophy on which arts integration is founded.

Levels and Models of Arts Integration

Five Minutes a Day?

We had a few minutes left in class today, just enough time where it's too late to start something but we needed to fill the gap. I dug out my Claude Monet book and had students guess the focus of the painting "Winterscapes" (without looking at the ti-

tle). I couldn't believe it—middle schoolers who were joking with me one minute turned serious, intently looking at the painting. Some even commented, "I like the way he did that in the back." I responded by saying, "You mean the horizon in the background?" and a boy said, "Yeah, that!"

*They were different people. When I first asked if they had heard of Claude Monet, they said they knew of "Jean Claude van Damme." Anyway, it was such a fleeting but intense experience. Also, they now beg me every day to do drama from the novel we are reading. I feel I'm depriving them if I don't do it. Anyway, integrating the arts, I believe, even if it's just 5 minutes a day, is so incredible—especially to see it at the middle school. (*Bethany Gray, education major, Wittenberg University)

With, About, In, and Through the Arts

In 1997, Jane Remer, from Americans for the Arts, spoke at the Kennedy Center Partners in Education conference on arts integration. She presented the concept of teaching *with* and *about* the arts. In this book that idea is expanded to teaching *with*, *about*, *in*, and *through* the arts to conceptualize levels of integration.

Bethany Gray is an example of a teacher who is just starting out. Like other arts integration novices, she is gradually increasing amounts and intensity as an arts knowledge and skill base is built. Teachers in schools going through a whole school reform may be involved in a year of professional development and collaborative planning with arts specialists before beginning. Individual teachers who begin on their own may be like Bethany; they have taken undergraduate integrated arts courses or enroll in graduate classes. Lesley College in Boston is one of a growing number of institutions offering degree programs related to arts integration; certification programs are under consideration in several states like Maryland *(www.aems-educ.org)*. Other teachers strike out on their own with self-study using books, articles, websites, and professional development videos (see Bibliography and Appendices). The Annenberg Foundation's video series for teachers can be viewed online *(www.learner.org)*. To locate an arts-based school near you, consult the School Registry in the Appendix.

Level One: With. Teachers usually begin at a modest level and teach *with* the arts. They experiment with a few arts strategies in an arts area of most interest. Bethany was using the Close Looking strategy along with open questions to promote student inquiry. She also is experimenting with drama, which has a strong research connection to comprehension (Deasy, 2002). Daily arts routines like Art

Print Discussions or Poem a Day (see Chapter 3 Classroom Snapshot) are easy to begin and have natural connections to the literacy curriculum. Another starting place is to set up arts-based centers and stations for independent follow-up work by students (see Chapter 3, Blueprint VII).

Level Two: About and In. More meaningful integration happens when teachers have opportunities to observe artists and co-plan with arts specialists. The goal is to plan lessons that include teaching *about* arts content that naturally connects to established units, most often in science and social studies. Songs, dances, music, and art from historical periods and different cultures are frequently the first kinds of arts content classroom teachers use. At first, arts works may be used to introduce lessons. Eventually, as in Judy Trotter's room, the art form becomes the material for literacy and social studies, science, and math. At the same time teachers begin to involve students *in* using the ways of thinking, creating, and responding that are the province of the arts.

Once again, teachers normally start with an arts area that is personally comfortable. Each of us has natural inclinations and competencies in arts areas. Teachers should begin with a strength—an arts area they feel they know something about and feel comfortable doing. Modest creative challenges provide a success orientation for students and for teachers. For example, a teacher who plays a musical instrument may accompany students on the guitar or flute as they sing curriculum-related songs. Students see a whole new dimension of a teacher who takes this risk, and the class is bonded through the unique power of music to bring groups together. Depth of teaching *about* and *in* depends on the arts knowledge base of teachers.

Level Three: Through. The fullest arts integration is teaching *through* the arts. This involves creating an aesthetic school and classroom environment in which substantial content units are taught using the arts as both learning tools and unit centers. Both academic and arts standards are used to co-plan these units with arts specialists. Lessons are taught using best practices connected to arts-based learning. All of the 10 building blocks for arts integration are in place, including assessment *of* and *through* the arts.

At any level, arts-based instructional implications should derive from a knowledge base about best teaching practices and learning theories. Chapter 2 provides an overview of trail-blazing brain research, Gardner's multiple intelligences, Erikson's life stages, Piaget's developmental stages, Maslow's hierarchy of needs, Vygotsky's social development, and the creative problem-solving process integral to all meaning making. Scripp (2003) advises that "Only if schools become communities of problem-solvers and collaborators will what is today's innovation become tomorrow's new standard of practice" (p. 139). These theoretical sources, accompanied by knowledge of arts-based research, create conditions for educators to devise unique and appropriate variations on the innovative practice of arts integration.

Arts-Based Reform: National and Regional Models

In a recent study, three fourths of schools undergoing restructuring were using interdisciplinary designs like arts integration as reform options (Grossman, Wineburg, & Beers, 2000). A variety of national and regional models has emerged, such as the Annenberg Foundation arts education initiatives, the Kenen Institute's A+ programs in North Carolina, and the Galef Institute's DWOK (Different Ways of Knowing) program. The U.S. Department of Education has made grants to multiple sites to develop arts-integrated curricula. One highly successful example is Tucson's "Opening Minds Through the Arts," a consortium of the Tucson Symphony Opera, the University of Arizona, and the Tucson Arts Connection (Deasy & Stevenson, 2005). The focus is music integration. Other recipients of grants, from $500,000 to $1 million, include Rockford, Illinois, schools, the Mississippi Arts Commission (state arts agency), and ArtsConnection in New York City for an arts/literacy project (Fineberg, 2002).

Schools at all grade levels in all 50 states and in Canada, Australia, and the United Kingdom are now undergoing arts-based school reform (see School Registry in Appendix). Comprehensive research reports such as *Champions of Change* (Fiske, 1999), *Gaining the Arts Advantage: Lessons from School Districts That Value Arts Education* (Longley, 1999), *Critical Links* (Deasy, 2002), and *Third Space* (Deasy & Stevenson, 2005) document reforms that show how learning can be transformed with arts integration.

Whole School Reform.   Increasingly the arts are becoming leading contenders in school reform (Deasy & Stevenson, 2005; Ruppert, 2006). Why? Arts interventions that create arts-rich school environments and integrate the arts into academic areas are supported by a "sufficient number of studies to matter" (Catterall, 2003, p. 105). Schools enjoy the benefits of increased student motivation and engagement, higher test scores, growth in use of higher-order thinking and problem-solving skills, increased creative capacities, broader multicultural understanding, increased graduation rates, and higher attendance for students and teachers. School faculties are revitalized with more teacher collaboration and transformation of instructional practice. Communities become more involved and supportive (Deasy, 2002; Deasy & Stevenson, 2005; Fiske, 1999; Jack,

2005; Larson, 1997). For example, daily attendance increased up to 94 percent, and 83 percent of students achieved at or above national norms in reading and math after the arts were integrated into the curriculum at Guggenheim Elementary School in inner-city Chicago. Of course, making sure kids are in school is of significant educational, social, and economic value. The annual cost of truancy to the nation is $228 billion, and 85 percent of all daytime crime is committed by truant youth. Then there is the cost to train unskilled youth who drop out—about $30 billion annually (Boston, 1996).

A single model for arts integration does not—and should not—exist. As Marron (2003) points out "it is the process of developing and implementing these methods that evokes a change of school culture" (p. 95). Described next are examples of arts-based whole school reforms implemented across the country (Horowitz, 2004). Information about their programs is available at their websites.

A+ Schools. This North Carolina effort involves more than 35 participating schools. Douglas A+ Creative Elementary Arts and Science Magnet School in Raleigh is considered a model school. The A+ label is now viewed as a symbol of excellence. The North Carolina network is nationally recognized as a top education reform effort and has spread to Oklahoma, South Dakota, and Arkansas. Website: *http://aplus-schools.uncg.edu.*

Arts for Academic Achievement. The Minneapolis Annenberg Challenge for Arts Education is a partnership between the Minneapolis Public Schools and the Minnesota Center for Arts Education (website: *www.annenberginstitute. org/challenge.index.html).* Schools are categorized at three levels of integration: (1) minimal arts with one arts specialist, (2) actively working toward arts integration with two or more arts specialists, and (3) more than two arts specialists and long-term partnerships with local arts organizations. Research findings are available at *www.mpls. k12.mn.us/Arts_for_Academic_Achievement.html.*

Arts in the Basic Curriculum Project (ABC). This is a statewide initiative by the South Carolina Department of Education, the South Carolina Arts Commission, and Winthrop University. The project has a grants program to support implementation of arts-based education. ABC schools have strong school ecologies and high levels of support for arts immersion. Arts classes are provided weekly in all four arts disciplines. Arts teachers participate in team planning with classroom teachers. ABC schools were found to more likely follow the state's curriculum and focus on arts education standards. More than 40 schools statewide have been coached through the planning and implementation of ABC. Website: *www.winthrop.edu/abc.*

The Annenberg Challenge for Arts Education. This New York City reform is administered by the Center for Arts Education. The grants program partners schools with colleges, community organizations, and cultural institutions such as museums, musical groups, and dance companies. In 2005, the center published *Promising Practices: The Arts and School Improvement,* profiling 9 of the 81 public schools. Collaborations include frequent visits to arts partner organizations, working with artists at the schools, family days and workshops conducted by arts organizations, and co-planning among teachers and community arts organizations. The book and other information is available online at *www.cae-ncy.org.*

Transforming Education Through the Arts Challenge (TETAC). Thirty-five schools in eight states are supported by the J. Paul Getty Trust and the Annenberg Challenge for Arts Education. TETAC is managed by the National Arts Education Consortium, a coalition of universities and schools. Research findings are available at *www.arts.ohio-state.edu/NAEC/* or *www.aep-arts.org.*

Chicago Arts Partnerships in Education (CAPE). Arts partnerships are created to integrate the arts into Chicago public schools. Teachers and schools are matched with artists and artistic resources. Curricula are developed and delivered through collaborative planning and arts-integrated instruction. The initiative comprises 19 partnerships in 30 Chicago schools and involves 45 professional arts organizations and 11 community organizations. Find research on CAPE in *Champions of Change: The Impact of Arts on Learning* (Fiske, 1999). Two more recent studies of CAPE and (1) the effect of arts integration on learning and (2) using professional artists can be found at the CAPE website: *www.capeweb.org.*

Changing Education Through the Arts (CETA). Since 1999, the Kennedy Center has now partnered with 18 schools in 14 districts in the Washington, D.C., metropolitan area (including Virginia and Maryland) to effect arts-based school reform through professional development. Schools have high populations of ELLs so kids can work together in the arts when they can't in other areas; for example, making a tableau is not dependent on English fluency. There has been an upward trend in test scores in CETA schools, and 25 more are on a waiting list. In 2001 an arts coaches program was added in which artists plan, conduct class demonstrations, and coteach. An emphasis is placed on reflection after teaching. CETA demands a multiple year commitment from teachers and principals (Duma, 2005). Website: *www.kennedycenter.org.*

Dallas ArtsPartners. This is a collaborative partnership between the Dallas Independent School District and 62 arts organizations. Website: *www.dallasartspartners.org.*

Why Integrate the Arts?

Arts and Academics

Rodney Van Valkenburg, Director of Arts Education, Allied Arts of Greater Chattanooga, believes that the reason the arts work is that "the skills necessary to be a good artist are the same skills that are needed to be a good student: self-control of your body, voice, and mind" (interview, August 2005). Chapter 3 focuses on research that shows strong positive relationships between the arts and academic achievement. This conclusion is derived from several important research reports, most notably *Third Space* (Deasy & Stevenson, 2005), *Critical Links* (Deasy, 2002), and *Champions of Change* (Fiske, 1999), which summarize positive findings from dozens of studies. The case for arts-based learning is convincing enough that in 2004 Secretary of Education Rod Paige wrote a personal letter to all school superintendents emphasizing the significance of the arts in achievement. He reminded the nation's educational leaders "the arts are a core academic subject under the *No Child Left Behind Act*" and lamented the "disturbing and just plain wrong" notion that NCLB should be used to shrink the role of the arts in schools. He refers to the National Longitudinal Study of 25,000 students, which showed a strong correlation between the arts and better test scores. What's more, high arts students "performed more community service, watched fewer hours of television, reported less boredom in school, and were less likely to drop out of school." Paige points out that the findings held for students from the lowest socioeconomic quartile "belying the assumption that socioeconomic status, rather than arts engagement, contributes to such gains in academic achievement and social involvement." Read Paige's letter at *www.ed.gov/policy/elsec/guid/secletter/040701.html.*

Achievement Gap. Compelling support for arts-based education, especially for disadvantaged populations, comes from striking successes with at-risk youth. As Richard Riley, former Secretary of Education, put it, "The arts teach young people how to learn by giving them the first step: the desire to learn." Student testimonials also point to how the arts can be a feel-good alternative to drugs and other destructive means to "get high." In addition, the arts contribute to increased self-esteem and the development of creative problem-solving skills that build independence and lower recidivism rates (Deasy, 2002; Fiske, 1999).

What Matters Most? To paraphrase Albert Einstein, everything that counts isn't countable and what we can count may not count. Many well-rounded successful people were not straight A students. High scores do not guarantee desirable social and moral behavior. What matters most in a broader view of success? Ferrero (2005) reminds us "schooling is always and inevitably about cultivating persons" (p. 26).

At a recent professional development workshop on arts integration, teachers brainstormed characteristics of an "ideal student." While not a scientific study, this was an informative exercise. Teachers readily listed: alert, engaged, open, cooperative, thinking, respectful, polite, responsible, disciplined, skillful, self-motivated, positive, hardworking, curious, confident, secure, loving, energetic, independent, problem solver, and persistent. It took about 5 minutes for groups to completely fill a piece of chart paper. Surprisingly, not one list included high test scores or grades. Not one even listed good reader. The ensuing discussion showed that teachers expect good grades to result from "ideal" cognitive, social, and personal behaviors and demeanors. According to Dick Allington (2005), president of International Reading Association, our fund of professional wisdom, built from thousands of years of teaching experience, is a valid source in designing curricula and instruction that yield both high scores and other important results. In the Chattanooga workshop we figured we had 800 years of teaching experience. The next step was to examine if and how arts integration might contribute to developing these ideal people attributes.

Unique Contributions of the Arts: Process and Content

> *The kids love to be here. They can't wait to start each day.* (Jayne Ellicott, Principal)

Education reformer John Goodlad thinks contemporary Americans are overly pressured by macho societal images that exult athleticism over aesthetics and see the arts as a luxury, not a necessity. This was readily apparent at a recent Senate Education Committee meeting in Columbus, Ohio. The state capitol had just been refurbished to preserve its stunning architectural features. Ironically, the hearing room, boasting regilded Corinthian columns and magnificent wall paintings, was the site for testimony on an amendment that would deter students from taking arts courses. Goodlad calls for a change led by a "large and sympathetic army of educators ready and willing to march for the arts" (Remer, 1996, p. 67). The nation appears ready to follow. A May 2005 Harris poll shows the American public overwhelmingly believes the arts are vital to a well-rounded education (Ruppert, 2006).

Chapter 3 goes into more detail about research that connects the arts and achievement. In this section the focus is on contributions the arts make that go beyond the capabilities of standardized test scores. Ready Reference 1.1 summarizes these special contributions to learning. The following discus-

sion elaborates on them. Are the arts the "fourth R"? Is there more than readin', ritin', and rithmetic'? Judge for yourself as you consider the contributions the arts make to learning.

1. Communication through the Arts.   The arts are widely acknowledged as unmatched communication vehicles. This is an overarching justification for arts integration. As Eisner (2000) reminds us, the limits of language do not determine the limits of our thinking. Thoughts cannot be reduced to words. Without the vital communication channels the arts provide, many ideas and feelings remain trapped. Through the arts we are given special tools to look inward to understand ourselves and outward to understand others.

Arts integration balances the current literacy curriculum that gives inordinate weight to reading and writing. School curricula needs to be realigned with an accurate model of communication. Literacy needs to be redefined to include *all* means people use to understand, respond to, and express thoughts and feelings. This definition more clearly explains the role of the arts and other necessary forms of literacy in the 21st century (e.g., computer literacy, media literacy).

Communication through the arts is interrelated with the cognitive, social, and personal/emotional effects of the arts. Arts contributions in these areas further justify the integration of the arts into daily learning.

2. Content of the Arts.   The arts are not just process. A vast worldwide treasury of art products is readily available for the classroom. The Internet provides virtual tours of museums like the Louvre, and there is a website on nearly every artist, art form, art style, and art period (e.g., www.songs-of-the-century.com). Every genre of music from any conceivable culture can be downloaded or found on CDs. The work of local poets, playwrights, composers, and artists are important "texts" as well.

Specific artworks can be used to introduce and/or develop lessons and units. These art forms are sources from which students can derive new perspectives about the myriad topics about which art is made. In addition, arts texts can be studied as models of skill and technique. Students can be taught how to work backwards from a finished product to understand the kinds of thinking and values it represents.

3. Cognitive/Intellectual Capacities.   The arts are deeply cognitive. No art is understood or created without higher-level thinking. Artistic thinking is characterized by careful observation, pattern finding, new perspectives, qualitative judgment, and use of metaphors and symbols. The arts are used to transform and represent what is noticed and imagined. These kinds of thinking are equally important in science, math, and history (Eisner, 2005).

The arts draw us into shared views with artists, actors, musicians, and poets. Their provocative nature charges us to respond. It can happen with a song like John Lennon's "Imag-

Ready Reference 1.1 Fourteen Unique Gifts of the Arts

1. *Communication.* Literacy includes *all* communication processes used to understand, respond to, and express thoughts and feelings. The arts are unparalleled communication vehicles. They are symbolic languages that exist because all thoughts cannot be captured with words. Arts communication is interrelated with the cognitive, social, and personal effects of the arts.

2. *Content of the arts.* The arts are not just process. A vast worldwide arts treasury stands ready to change hearts and minds.

Intellectual. It takes high-level thinking to understand and create through the arts.

3. *Creative problem solving (CPS)* is the process used to construct meaning and is at the core of the arts. It is grounded in seeking connections and synthesizing diverse solutions.

4. *Critical thinking* is a part of CPS. It is a focus of the arts where quality is highly valued. In particular, arts criticism involves analysis of details and patterns, compiling evidence, and using criteria to make judgments.

5. *Comprehension* is understanding. Across disciplines understanding is actively created when we problem solve to make sense. The arts stress personal meaning making using thinking such as visualizing, taking divergent perspectives, and making original connections among ideas.

6. *Composition* is the process of expressing meaning. The arts contribute special principles, techniques, and materials to the composition process and add a range of composition forms.

Social Capacities. Meaning may ... cumstances.

7. *Culture.* The arts uniquely reco... lived throughout history. They als... texts for growth, including positive c... ...mates.

8. *Cooperation/collaboration.* The a... involve students in group problem solving (e.g., ensembles, choirs, troupes, skits).

9. *Community.* The arts create a sense of belonging based on respect for the distinctive contributions of each person.

10. *Compassion.* The arts build empathy by providing experiences that cause new perspective.

Personal/Emotional Capacities. The arts engage the emotions.

11. *Commitment/interest.* The arts develop intrinsic motivation because they are inherently engaging. Persistence, based on curiosity and choice, gives satisfaction, and people feel the rewards of commitment.

12. *Concentration.* The arts capture attention and develop concentration because they are emotionally compelling.

13. *Confidence.* The arts develop the courage to take risks and take pride in unique contributions to solving problems.

14. *Competence/control.* The arts develop skills with tools and materials and control over mind, voice, and body. They build special strategies to plan, think, work, and produce. Artists feel free to break rules because they've mastered them.

ine" or a dance performance such as "River Dance." We sing along and feel our pulse entrain to the tempo. We do indeed begin to imagine different worlds in which we are Celtic dancers or where worldwide peace is possible. Actors transform our thinking about place, time, events, and people in films like *Hotel Rwanda*; the arts speak to us directly in old languages (e.g., "a picture is worth a thousand words").

Students who can use a keyboard, paint, or slab of marble to communicate and solve problems are, according to Howard Gardner (1993) using intelligences that are central to life. The arts link cognition to emotion, and students begin to see life links. They recognize the changes in their own capacities and feel pride that stimulates them to be more diligent and to want to learn from one another. Center stage in the cognitive contributions of the arts are four processes:

Creative Problem Solving (CPS). This process is at the core of the arts and is how meaning is constructed. It is grounded in seeking and synthesizing diverse problem solutions. CPS purposefully capitalizes on mistakes, makes paradoxical connections, and embraces surprises. The novel, different, and abnormal are valued. Key processes include data gathering (e.g., brainstorming, observation, and research), experimenting, incubating ideas, and connecting and transforming ideas. Synthesis produces new compositions that are critiqued and tweaked before a final solution is accepted.

Business leaders consider CPS to be one of the most important skill sets in the 21st century. It produced plasma TV, hybrid cars, the iPod nano, and humble Velcro. CPS is also a key means to achieve the central goal of literacy—to

meaning. Literacy is qualitative communica-
...ncy in reading, writing, and speaking and depth of
...rstanding. Rather than teach a set of good reader strategies and a separate set of writing process steps, CPS can be
used to streamline. CPS also parallels the scientific method,
which makes sense since the essence of science is solving
problems creatively.

Critical thinking. This part of CPS is a particular focus
of the arts where quality is highly valued. There is a heightened focus on thoughtful and skilled use of ideas, techniques, and materials. For example, arts critique entails
closely analyzing details and patterns, compiling evidence,
and using evaluation criteria to make judgments (Soep,
2005). Students use these processes to reach judgments of
their own work and that of others. Opinions matter but
need to be supported with evidence.

Even young children can be prompted to discover details in paintings, interpret messages in music, and draw conclusions supported by "text" evidence. Children persist at
this hard brainwork because it is self-rewarding. They become enamored of details and patterns in the same ways artists
like Claude Monet got hooked on haystacks. He persisted because he was intrigued by questions about light. According to
Lucy Calkins, writers also dwell on "few seminal issues" and
do the same kind of intellectual tinkering through writing.

Blessed with so many things, students may not have
learned that little things can make large differences. The arts
help refocus on the tremendous potential of a single word
or a slight gesture to speak volumes—as Mr. Spock's raised
eyebrow demonstrates. As Elliot Eisner reminds us, "the
subtle is significant."

Comprehension. An artful view of comprehension
places emphasis on deep understanding, not on the number
of books read or how many words are written. In the arts
and across disciplines, understanding is actively created
when people seek to make sense and have the problem-
solving skills to do so. The arts stress this personal meaning
making with special attention to visualizing, taking perspectives, and making original connections among ideas.

Long before the release of the National Reading Panel's
(NRP) report, which was used to draft the No Child Left
Behind Act, comprehension was viewed as the ultimate
measure of reading. The NRP made comprehension one of
the five support pillars of reading and reiterated the importance of placing priority on deep cognitive understanding.
Unfortunately, the amount of instructional time given to
phonological and phonemic awareness, phonics, and vocabulary often outweighs that given to research-based comprehension strategies. Early positive effects of dwelling on
lower-level pieces of reading eventually fade; by fourth grade

many slip into a decline. Without tools to create meaning,
many students simply don't develop comprehension capabilities (Kamil, 2004; Williams, 2002). Arts "texts" (e.g., pictures,
songs, paintings) hold promise for halting the decline when
they are used to engage young children in higher-order
thinking long before they have print decoding fluency.

Composition. This is the process of expressing meaning.
Problems (self-chosen or imposed) generate the purposes for
both reading and writing. Reading is "creating meaning from
print," and the problem for every reader is to make sense or
comprehend text. Writing is the reverse. Writers construct
meaning through expression rather than reception.

The arts contribute special principles, techniques, and
materials to the composing meaning process. They add
many possibilities to the forms compositions can take and
use the same set of cognitive skills necessary for reading
comprehension and written composition. Students who,
from early childhood, have been involved in creating, responding, and performing in the arts have a history of using
the creating meaning problem-solving process. The arts are
crucial to young children's understanding and often are the
only ways they can express feelings and ideas (Cunningham
& Shagoury, 2005). Teachers can build on this arts-based
foundation by clearly showing how reading comprehension
and written composition use the same problem-solving
process used to view and do art, drama, and dance and listen
to and make music. For example, at a Connecticut elementary school, students are explicitly taught how to combine
the visual art and writing process. Students keep sketch journals and make drawings to plan writing. They are taught to
use the parallel composition processes to complement one
another. These students have an arts advantage because they
have engaged in higher-order cognitive work long before
they have the skills to do this kind of thinking with print.

4. Social Capacities.

*Very little that has come down through the ages has not in some
way filtered through something that we can all identify as the arts.*
(Sherri Geldin, Wexner Art Center, Columbus, Ohio)

People are group animals. Meaning is made and altered by
social circumstances. The measure of a satisfying life rests on
social relationships. The arts make significant contributions
to our social development as individuals and groups.

Culture. Eisner (2002a) explains how the two meanings
of culture relate to the arts. First, culture has to do with
shared ways of living.

The arts are culture vaults that house records of ways humans have lived throughout history. Pots, paintings, and plays

show what we value, what we worry about, and what is important to us. The arts are a kind of museum of collective memories (Paige & Huckabee, 2005). Demographic projections predict that minorities, with distinct cultures, will become the majority in the United States in 40 years. Currently, some 400 languages are now spoken in schools nationwide. To live in harmony in such diversity requires appreciation for contributions every culture makes to a society. One source for such understanding is the arts. They are naturally interdisciplinary and provide a neutral ground to learn varied communication symbols, content disciplines, values, and beliefs. The arts help us better understand the joys and sorrows of others. For example, think of how musical theatre, like *Les Miserables,* has engaged audiences in vicarious suffering caused by poverty and loss.

Second, a culture is a rich medium for growing things. The arts provide stimulating contexts for growth when they are used to alter school and classroom ecologies. The arts are a medium for growing children's brains.

Cooperation/collaboration. The arts build cooperation by involving students in group problem solving through ensembles, choirs, troupes, and skits. Through arts experiences, they learn to work as a team, to respect diverse points of view, and to see that relationships among people and ideas matter. These ways of working are critical to the workplace and family success.

Community. The arts create a sense of belonging based on delight and respect for each person's distinctive contributions. Experiences as audience members and as performers connect students in reciprocal relationships. As concertgoers and museum visitors they are bound together in listening and viewing experiences that create shared background. They experience the dependent relationship of arts consumers and producers that builds a sense of community.

Most close to home is the classroom community on which the arts make an indelible mark. An artful view of learning sets in motion a cascade of physical and psychological changes. In Jayne Ellicott's words, "Arts integration makes school a happier place."

Compassion. Compassion means to be in passion with another. The arts develop concern for, sensitivity to, and "response ability." The arts build empathy through experiences that cause students to grasp another's understanding. The arts intentionally invite empathy by their emphasis on and respect for the unusual, different, and extraordinary. Like respect, empathy comes from acknowledging the circumstances of another person and leads to compassion when one person fully imagines himself in those circumstances. Such deep understanding allows students to see how arts materials and processes can communicate ideas in ways that have eluded them.

5. Personal/Emotional Capacities. No longer do educators divorce emotion from cognition. Brain and psychological research confirms what experience has long told us: Students are whole beings. Active engagement is a key to academic success. Engagement is more than entertainment, however. Engagement is not merely hands on, but brains and hearts on. The arts turn the emotional brain on to uplift spirits and give hope in the form of a good laugh, a beautiful song, or a satisfying painting. Enthusiasm for learning is sparked when students feel the joys of playing with ideas and experience the pride of creative discovery. The arts, unlike schooling, have never tried to compartmentalize people, and they make unique contributions to integrating the personal and emotional into learning.

Commitment/interest. The arts engage people in uncommon ways. Artistic work is characterized by intense involvement, joy, and delight at surprises. Artists report they rarely feel their work is finished and return to the same themes and topics over and over. It isn't unusual to hear an artist say she is "addicted" to making art or music or dance. The arts are inherently interesting. Artists persist because they are curious and have choices. Arts integration gives students opportunities to experience the intrinsic motivation of artists: satisfaction, a commitment to complete what they begin, and the feeling of a job well done.

Students feel ownership of artwork in ways that never happen with textbooks, worksheets, or computer work. A special education teacher recently described a textile art project during a family folklore unit. Her 11 students gathered fabric from family members and eventually created a quilt to honor important events and people. The products were so striking that the teacher offered to buy them. The students were from poor families, and she thought her offer would both help them out and create a permanent school display. The students, however, would not give up their art. One irate grandmother came to school to protest. Tearfully she objected to her granddaughter selling something so beautiful and personal.

Just as sports encourage some students to stay in school, the arts can provide motivation to learn. A sculpture project in social studies or learning to play the recorder in music class can become the main reasons for students to come to school. Great teachers from children's literature come to mind: Jesse's music teacher, Miss Edmunds, in *Bridge to Terabithia* (Paterson, 1979), who helped him find beauty in his dismal life, and Mr. Isobe, in *Crow Boy* (Yashima, 1965), who tacked up an outcast child's art and changed Chibi's life with a stage performance.

Concentration/attention. The arts are compelling. They capture attention and sustain concentration because they are provocative. There is a print literacy connection here. Unlike the details in a work of art or the nuances of sounds in a musical piece, letters can seem unattractive. In the arts, details are not presented out of context, but always within a song, dance, or painting. Details have meaning and can be discovered and enjoyed with minimal background because we are born with the capacity to communicate through the arts. Reading and writing, on the other hand, are accrued skills. Letters are mindless details until they are set within words that are set within phrases and sentences that make up paragraphs and eventually full texts. Unfortunately, many children lack the persistence to wade through years of skill drill, never knowing the intrinsic rewards that await them when they achieve print fluency. The arts can give such children hope. Children who have learned to "read" art have experienced the good feeling that comes from creating your own story about a picture. These children can be helped to concentrate and persist with print, which is just another symbol system. The arts make learning concrete, especially for young and struggling learners. They cause us to want to attend and concentrate which bears fruit when students experience inherent joys of creating meaning.

Confidence/courage. Tom Stang, a teacher in an arts-based program for troubled youth in Phoenix believes "the arts are the soul of the education program" (Larson, 1997, p. 94). Problem students often become the high achievers in arts learning settings. Success in the arts can be a bridge to success in other areas of learning, as is demonstrated in case studies of disadvantaged students in New York City involved in ArtsConnection (Oreck, Baum, & McCartney, 1999). Students used more self-regulatory behaviors and had a sense of identity that made them more confident and resilient. One elementary student explained, "It's like I became addicted to dance" (Oreck, p. 70).

The arts develop the courage to take risks and experiment. Pride in one's unique contributions develops as teachers and peers positively respond to efforts. The arts create confidence in one's ability to do original problem solving. Confidence increases willingness to take more risks and be more flexible.

Competence/control. The arts develop self-control and skill with special tools and materials. They build special strategies to plan, think, work, and produce. Self-chosen practice and rehearsal is motivated by the desire to produce quality work. Anyone who ever learned to play an instrument knows that thousands of hours of practice are necessary to become good. Adults who recall "forced lessons" by parents are often thankful. One college student's journal entry speaks for so many: "At first I just wanted to make my parents proud and I loved the applause at recitals. Eventually I found out I could get so much out of just playing—for myself. I could relax, escape, and really just change from a negative mood to a positive frame of mind by sitting down and playing for an hour or so. Other kids got high or zoned out with drugs or booze. I guess I just got high on music!"

It is simplistic to advise students to "just say no." Students have to be shown healthy ways to feel good—alternatives to sticking a destructive substance up their noses, down their throats, or in their veins. The arts provide these alternatives, giving students control over minds, bodies, and emotions.

National Initiatives and Legislation

Several important national initiatives support arts integration. First is the creation of national standards about what students should know and be able to do in every academic area and the arts. The standards were generated by the major professional organizations for each discipline (e.g., National Council of Teachers of Math) and represent the most current research and professional wisdom. Standards have also been created for new teachers that include what classroom teachers should know and be able to do in the arts (Interstate New Teacher Assessment and Support Consortium, 2002). The standards provide impetus for integrating the arts by clarifying the importance of "whole child" education that acknowledges the interconnectedness among body, mind, and emotions (e.g., see the September 2005 issue of *Educational Leadership*). Academic and arts standards call for students to meet goals that will be impossible to achieve without the concerted efforts of classroom teachers and arts specialists.

Second, *No Child Left Behind* designates the arts as core subjects and makes demands that are unachievable without the arts. In particular, disadvantaged students, under the greatest pressure, have responded in remarkable ways to arts-based learning.

Third, several national government-affiliated organizations now exist for the express purpose of reforming education using arts-based models. These include the Kennedy Center's Partners in Education and the Arts Education Partnership.

The Standards Movement. National and state standards documents now drive curriculum development, instruction, and assessment strategies in American classrooms. Both teachers and artists need to be mindful of publications that articulate content and performance standards in curricular areas, including each of the arts disciplines. Nearly every state department of education includes downloadable standards for each subject area at their websites. Another recommended source is *Standards for Excellence* (1998), available from the Council for Basic Education. The Association for Supervision and Curriculum Development (ASCD) also has a fully developed library of standards for each subject in public school curricula that includes a CD-ROM, charts, and a handbook, available through its website (*www.ascd.org*).

The *National Standards for the Arts* (1994) were developed by the Consortium of National Arts Education Associations. These standards call for arts-based education for all children. The document is the result of an extended process of consensus building and includes a review of state-level arts education frameworks, national forums, and examination of standards from other countries. The standards represent agreement on what U.S. students should know and be able to do in each of the arts by the time they complete high school. While the Standards are voluntary, they are currently being used at state and local levels. For examples go the department of education for most states. South Carolina's can be retrieved at *www.myscschool.com* or *www.winthrop.edu/abc/*. Also recommended is the Ohio Department of Education website *http://ode.state.oh.us*.

Four arts. The standards address four arts disciplines: dance, music, theatre, and the visual arts. Grouped by grade levels K–12, they suggest a basic body of knowledge and skills required to make sense and make use of the arts. The knowledge and skills are organized into: (1) communication in each art form, (2) ability to think critically about art forms, (3) acquaintance with exemplary works of art from a variety of cultures and periods, and (4) ability to relate types of arts knowledge and skills within and across arts disciplines. Standards specify desired results. Teachers design the actual instruction and choose materials to meet the Standards.

The main K–8 standards are in Ready References in the arts chapters of this book. Teaching strategies in the chapters meet one or more of the Standards, if they are developed and implemented appropriately. The literature chapter shows the standards prepared by the National Council of the Teachers of English and the International Reading Association.

A full copy of the *National Standards for the Arts* is available from the Music Educators National Conference (*www.menc.org*).

Interstate New Teacher Assessment and Support Consortium (INTASC). Standards aren't just for K–12 students. Teacher licensure has also come under the purview of the standards movement. Working under the Council of Chief State School Officers, representatives of major pro-

fessional organizations collaborated to create model standards for licensing new teachers that were published in 1992. The standards are consistent with the advanced certification standards of the National Board for Professional Teaching Standards. The 10 INTASC principles are currently used by universities throughout the United States to organize undergraduate and graduate teacher preparation. In 2002, INTASC published the arts education section, which describes what classroom teachers and arts specialists need to know and be able to do in the arts. The standards can be downloaded at *www.ccsso.org/intasc*.

National Assessment. With the setting of goals and standards comes assessment, the process of collecting evidence. That evidence can be used for many purposes, one of which is to make a determination about the extent to which standards are being met. *Champions of Change* writer warns that in a "society that values measurements and uses data-driven analysis to inform decisions about allocation of scarce resources, photographs of smiling faces are not enough to gain or even retain support. Such images alone will not convince skeptics . . ." (Fiske, 1999). Educators can feel threatened by assessment, but a clear destination makes the success of the learning journey more likely. On the other hand, standards don't specify some of our most valued goals for students. There is a firestorm over what constitutes appropriate assessment for skills like cross-disciplinary problem solving. Such higher-order thinking is difficult to assess out of context and with paper-and-pencil tests.

Schools currently use many state and local assessments, and there is one national assessment. For more than 20 years the National Assessment of Educational Progress (NAEP), known as the Nation's Report Card, has been the barometer of achievement for American students for reading, writing, math, and science. Groups of students in grades 4, 8, and 12 across the country are tested to determine how students perform based on standards for essential subjects. In the spring of 1997 the four arts areas were added, and eighth graders were tested. The assumption is that if something is worth assessing, we must or should be teaching it *(www.nces.ed.gov/nationsreportcard/)*. Chapter 3 and each arts chapter includes extended discussions of assessment.

Goals 2000. Setting the stage for NCLB was the Goals 2000: Educate America Act of 1994. The legislation designated the arts as core disciplines and proposed that all American children should be competent in the arts. The Act strove to make children ready for school at the start and targeted a 90% graduation rate. It declared the right of children to be educated in safe, disciplined, and drug-free schools. Three other provisions set goals for employment readiness, professional development for educators, and parent involvement.

All these provisions have arts connections, but designating the arts as "core disciplines" initially drew the most attention. For the first time, many began to seriously examine potential relationships between arts and learning.

Young children.   Research on young children showed arts-involved children seemed to be better prepared to start school (Welch, 1995). Other studies confirmed what early childhood educators had long known. Arts experiences can create what Lewis (2002) calls a "reverential spell" that deeply affect young children and invites them into learning. Children hear and sing nursery rhymes (literature and music) that build a language foundation on which teachers build reading and writing skills. This literary heritage invites children to move and sing "Ring around the rosie" and "London Bridge is falling down." Children dance, sing, laugh, and learn to love language and school. As they explore meaning making through chalk, paint, clay, and collage, they learn to take risks, experiment, and problem solve. They see how they can make an individual mark with materials that respond to the will of children engaged in experimentation. Children delight in manipulating color, line, shape, and texture. This delight can last a lifetime, be the start of an art avocation, or lead to one of hundreds of arts-related careers.

Ninety percent graduation rate?   Children who start school expecting success and continue to enjoy learning are more likely to stay in school. According to Welch (1995), arts programs are related to dropout prevention. Programs such as the Duke Ellington School's in Washington, D.C., are examples using the arts to motivate students: Ninety percent of the participants in the Boys Choir of Harlem go on to college (Gregorian, 1997).

Signs of being at risk develop early. We can't wait until high school to make learning relevant and exciting. As Howard Gardner explained in *Creating Minds* (1993), it is often unconventional "creative spirits" such as Einstein and Freud who make the breakthroughs in science and math. We cannot afford to lose creative thinkers who may dismiss science and math as dismal piles of facts, dates, and graphs. Instead, students need to be involved in integral connections among math, science, visual intelligence, kinesthetic knowing (dance/drama), and musical thinking. Meaningful connections among disciplines and the arts give students more means to enjoy learning and achieve understanding, and reasons to return to the arts in the future.

Safe schools.   Research studies also link arts-based education to a positive school environment (Deasy, 2002; Welch, 1995). The arts transform classrooms, and schools become places of discovery. The culture is changed, conditions for learning improve, and there is more collaboration among teachers and integration of disciplines. The physical appearance of a school building and its classrooms are altered as teachers rearrange desks to make room for movement, walls are painted, and director's chairs, plants, and easels are brought in. The dynamics between teachers and students change as both uncover hidden strengths.

No Child Left Behind.   When the NCLB Act was signed in 2002, it promised to eliminate the achievement gap, improve teacher quality, empower parents, and promote school safety. The law mandated expectations that caused some schools to narrow the curriculum and teach to the test. This happens despite a body of evidence that the best schools focus on teaching for understanding (Allington, 2005). Indeed, overly directing students' attention to test performance, instead of targeting learning, decreases motivation and depth of learning (Guthrie, 2004).

NCLB continued the Goals 2000 designation of the arts as "core academic skills," suggesting the place of the arts in schools should be comparable to that of the language arts, math, and science. In a May 2005 speech, Assistant Secretary, U.S. Department of Education, Susan Scalafani called learning in and through the arts "central" to fulfilling the NCLB's goal of improved student achievement. This broad support of the arts can be confounded, however, by accountability and research policies. Scientific research places almost all the weight on quantitative data, although qualitative studies more clearly reveal the effects of the arts.

NCLB proved to be both an opportunity and a challenge. The law expects students with special needs to meet the same academic standards as other students. This is an opportunity for educators whose work is grounded in the use of the arts; success of at-risk students in arts-based learning circumstances is well documented (Deasy, 2002; Deasy & Stevenson, 2005). Promising examples of narrowing achievement gaps through the arts have emerged in schools from Cleveland to Los Angeles. Bringing the capacity and expertise of the arts community to bear on this problem links an educational partnership that is just beginning to be tapped.

Two documents summarize hundreds of studies of arts-based learning (Deasy, 2002; Fiske, 1999). Such efforts help address the demand for scientifically based practices. Teachers concerned about curriculum constriction and teaching to the test, which creates low morale, can be bolstered by research that connects quality arts integration with academic achievement. Mandatory high-stakes testing puts a premium on instructional time, but narrowing the curriculum leads to decreases rather than increases in test scores (Yen & Ferrara, 1997). It is important to remember that a test is just a sample of what a student can do. Teachers need no longer feel they are pitting the arts against academics (Gunzenhauser & Gerstl-Pepin, 2002).

A recent Gallup Poll shows that the public does not support many of the provisions of NCLB, especially the focus on a single standardized test, expectations for special education, school transfers, and the adequate yearly progress (AYP) formula (Rose & Gallup, 2005). A RAND Corporation study released in December 2004 expressed deep doubts that students could reach the goal of universal proficiency in reading by 2014. The researchers noted that many children were not moving beyond basic decoding skills to fluency and comprehension. Aggressive arts integration builds a strong bridge between low-level thinking and the higher-order skills needed for comprehension. For more information on the arts and NCLB, check out *No Subject Left Behind: A Guide to Arts Education Opportunities in the 2001 NCLB Act* (2004) at *www.symphoy.org/govaff/what/042502education.shtml*.

Arts Education Partnership (AEP).

First created under Goals 2000, AEP is a national coalition of arts, education, business, philanthropic, and government organizations. The primary focus is helping states and local school districts integrate the arts into their educational improvement plans. The partnership was formed through a cooperative agreement among the National Endowment for the Arts, the U.S. Department of Education, the National Assembly of State Arts Agencies, and the Council of Chief State School Officers. AEP sponsors nationwide forums and publishes a quarterly newsletter featuring articles and resources related to promising practices. Its website is a recommended starting place: *www.aep-arts.org*.

The Partners in Education of the John F. Kennedy Center for the Performing Arts.

This nationwide program based in Washington, D.C., fosters partnerships among arts agencies and schools. There are now Kennedy Center teams in 43 states, Washington, D.C., and Mexico, with Ohio and South Carolina boasting the most sites. Schools and arts agencies partner to provide professional development to classroom teachers interested in using the arts as teaching tools. Teams use local artists and Kennedy Center teaching artists for workshops. The program also has a grants program for arts-based research and offers workshops to train artists for classroom teaching. Barbara Shepherd, Director of Kennedy Center National Partnerships, puts high priority on "institutionalizing" arts in education through total education reform, including changing concepts about teaching, beginning at the preservice level. Her greatest wish is for "every student and classroom to have access to a teacher who can integrate the arts plus arts specialists and visiting professional artists" (May 2005 phone interview). The annual conference of Partners in Education brings teams together to plan. ArtsEdge is a premiere arts education website that grew out of the program and is a must visit for all educators. To find out about memberships, visit the Kennedy Center website: *www.kennedy-center.org/education/partners/*.

The Arts and the 21st-Century Workforce

> *You know, I often say that I might not have been president if it hadn't been for school music.* (Bill Clinton, *Good Morning America*, June 16, 2000)

President Clinton translated his school experiences into a theory of education that connects the arts with the motivation and self-discipline necessary for school and career achievement. He is not alone among American civic and business leaders.

The National Governors Association concurs that the arts provide a competitive advantage. Its report, *The Impact of Arts Education on Workforce Preparation*, points out that the arts help build the workforce of tomorrow (2002). It describes how arts-based education increases academic performance and lowers juvenile crime. In school and after-school programs the arts are proving to be "innovative and cost-effective ways to produce successful students and productive employees." The report touts "creative approaches" for their ability to improve classroom performance and build self-esteem. "If you look into the faces of children who are involved in a creative activity, you will see their enthusiasm for learning and their pride in being part of a creative experience," said Alabama Governor Don Siegelman, chair of NGA's Economic Development and Commerce Committee. (Access report online at: *www.nga.org*.)

The NGA report describes the 21st-century workplace as demanding less tangible assets, like flexibility, interpersonal skills, and problem solving. Richard Gurin, CEO of Binney and Smith, thinks "the basic problem gripping the American workplace is . . . the crisis of creativity" (quoted in Boston, 1996, p. 2). In the world of work, questions and problems seldom have just one answer. American business survives and thrives on new ideas. Our economy depends on individuals who can imagine and produce products sought around the globe. The unique language, symbol systems, and technologies that students master to become successful in the arts prepare them for a world guaranteed to change in unimaginable ways.

According to the chairman of Sisco Systems, 80% of the jobs that people will be doing 10 years from now haven't even been conceptualized (speech, Wake Forest University). Involvement in the arts prepares students to solve future problems by encouraging risk taking, experimentation, and freedom to fail. Finding multiple solutions, trying new ideas, and capitalizing on mistakes are artistic orientations. As Aristotle observed, "Art loves chance. He who errs willingly is the artist."

Research confirms the long-term benefits of arts education for working in the new economy (Richmond-Cullen,

2005). The arts deliver precisely the kinds of thinking and working skills needed in the workplace of the new millenium: analysis, synthesis, evaluation, and critical judgment. The arts nourish imagination and creativity while focusing deliberately on content and end products. The workplace demands collaboration and teamwork, technological competencies, flexible thinking, an appreciation for diversity, and self-discipline—all of which are integral to arts learning. Arts-based education also boosts school attendance and communication skills. The arts contribute to lower recidivism rates, increased self-esteem, and the acquisition of job skills, especially for at-risk populations. The arts give students an understanding of the skill, discipline, perseverance, and sacrifice necessary for achievement in the workplace and in personal life (Psilos, 2002).

Rabkin and Redmond (2005) point out that while the new economy may require creative problem solving and teamwork, many schools in low-income areas dwell on basic skills, tests, and discipline. "The student boredom and academic failure that follow prompt calls for more testing and discipline" (p. 46). Concurrent with a preoccupation with "back to basics" is a strong commitment to school restructuring, school-based decision making, and standards. Americans are beginning to realize "the breadth and depth of the contribution arts education can make, both to education reform and to the quality of the workforce" (Boston, 1996, p. 3).

The world of work needs and wants artistic thinkers and creative problem solvers. There is a premium on employees who can use diverse problem-solving approaches—people who readily combine intuition with analysis, synthesis, and evaluation to solve problems and make judgments (Boston, 1996).

Big Business. The arts are an enormous, often unacknowledged, part of daily life, and comprise a $300 billion business. The economic impact is staggering (Florida, 2004). One Cezanne exhibit in Philadelphia generated more than $100 million in revenue. With more than 578,000 arts-centric businesses employing nearly 3 million people, arts education becomes a critical tool in fueling the creative industries of the future with arts-trained workers (Richmond-Cullen, 2005; U.S. Bureau of Labor Statistics *www.bis.gov*). In South Carolina alone, the arts supported $700 million in wages and salaries, 30,000 jobs, and $1.9 billion in economic output (South Carolina Arts Commission, 2002).

Rabkin and Redmond (2005) argue that students will not "learn to think for themselves if their school expects them to stay in line and keep quiet" (p. 46). The arts not only prepare students for collaborative workplaces and the creative problem solving valued in the new millenium, they are themselves important career destinations. Arts-related professions are wide ranging—from architect to dance teacher, set designer to car designer. The nonprofit arts industry alone employs more than 1.5 million people. Constricted education does not allow students to see these as career options, nor are they being prepared for most jobs.

Teacher Spotlight:
First-Year Teacher

This book is for teachers, and the chapter began with a vignette about Judy Trotter, a veteran teacher. It is appropriate to end with another real teacher. This time it is a first-year teacher, also at Ashley River Creative Arts.

Fannie Petros first visited Ashley River during a practicum when she was an undergraduate at the College of Charleston. She recalls a teacher showing students how to draw math story problems. "This wasn't a typical school. The doors were open, there was art everywhere and so much active participation."

Fannie says her fellow teachers became her most valuable resources for arts integration when she was hired. "Their strongest message is to use your imagination to create what you need," she says. She adopted their concept of arts integration that focuses on active hands-on learning. "Kids have to create their own meanings, and they do this through exploration."

Fannie believes arts-based learning causes students and teachers to "think of the whole picture of learning, not just one aspect." She speaks as a teacher and as a student. She graduated from the Chattanooga School for the Arts and Sciences, a K-12 arts-based school.

Fannie notes that it takes time to plan for the core curriculum and be true to the school's arts-based mission statement. "But it is worth it. When you see how much the kids love to be here and they are really getting it, you know. Even with the lowest kids it is clicking. It's why I became a teacher."

Fannie believes the arts give students learning advantages. "I see that ah-ha moment when kids learn through the arts—especially ones who weren't succeeding otherwise. I tell them when they accept their Oscars, they better remember their first grade teacher!"

Fannie especially loves to dovetail the arts with literacy. Every day the kids sing and "act out" words—even high frequency words. She emphasizes spelling patterns using musical elements like rhythm. If they are learning the word *low*, they spell it in a low voice. "As a student I hated vocabulary. My students love it." Like the other AR teachers, Fannie connects literacy to science and social studies. During a recent unit, students studied Chinese culture through reading, writing, and origami. They also learned and performed the Chinese dragon dance. "Students learn to be in an audience and in front of an audience. It builds so much confidence when you are in the spotlight," she explains. "Right now, we're so excited because we are learning about Grandma Moses!"

Conclusion

Arts integration creates a different classroom ethos. Much instruction takes place in a project-centered curriculum that targets creative problem solving. Students learn content using arts strategies that are intellectually challenging and emotionally engaging. Risk taking is encouraged as teachers consistently support thinking about possibilities using arts perspectives. Visual art provokes reflection while satisfying the need to produce and complete quality work. Dance uses the body to communicate feelings and ideas. Drama invites the suspension of disbelief and consideration of "what if." Music "soothes the soul" while giving insight into people and events. Concentrated work is punctuated with gleeful play. Curiosity is aroused, and learning proceeds with a sense of wonder and mystery. Students learn multiple ways to understand and express themselves that boost learning.

To ensure that arts integration is more than a curricular veneer, educators strive to plan *meaningful* use of the arts. Diverse models have developed to meet the needs of individual schools, but shared building blocks exist that were introduced in this chapter. Teachers are eased into an artistic view of education by first teaching *with* the arts and moving more deeply into teaching *about* and *in* the arts. The goal is teaching *through* the arts, using the arts as primary learning and communication vehicles. The success of arts integration depends on increasing the degree or quality of arts-based work by growing the classroom teacher's arts literacy, usually through collaborative work with teaching artists.

All the chapters build on ideas introduced in this chapter, especially the "with, about, in, through" progression and the 10 building blocks. In the next chapter the philosophy (beliefs) that support arts integration are discussed, along with more specific research and educational theories that connect to arts integration. In particular, the Creative Problem Solving (CPS) process is described to help teachers learn how to orchestrate higher-order thinking using problem solving to construct meaning.

Student Spotlight:
Day's End

A boy who had been miming plant parts stopped by where I was taking notes. "Write down that I like learning through the arts," he says. "I like that my teacher wants us to be different and not just be good test takers." He points to a quote above the door. They are

words from Dr. Seuss, "Say what you think and be who you are. Those that mind don't matter and those that matter won't mind" (Ashley River Creative Arts, February 2005).

Resources

See the Appendix for further study, including more websites.

Recommended Videos

Annenberg Videos

Arts for life. (1990). The Getty Center for Education in the Arts (15 min./arts integration rationale and classroom examples).

Teaching in and through the arts. (1995). The Getty Center for Education in the Arts (25 min./classroom examples).

The arts: Tools for teaching. (1994). Washington, DC: John F. Kennedy Center for the Performing Arts.

The arts and children: A success story. Arts Education Partnership (15 min./why integrate the arts).

Recommended Websites

These sites link to hundreds of other useful online resources.

Artsedge: *http://artsedge.kennedy-center.org (comprehensive site)*

Arts Education Partnership: *http://aep-arts.org (comprehensive site)*

A4L: *www.arts4learning.org. (Locate artists and art programs by subject, grade, and cultural. Teaching resources)*

Young Audiences: *www.youngaudiences.org (videos and a booklet of success stories)*

Children's Literature References

Aliki. (2003). *Ah, music!* New York: HarperCollins.

Auch, M., & Auch, H. (2005). *Chickarella.* New York: Holiday House.

dePaola, T. (2002). *Adelita: A Mexican Cinderella story.* New York: G.P. Putnam's Sons.

DiCamillo, K. (2000). *Because of Winn-Dixie.* Cambridge, MA: Candelwick.

Edwards, P. (1997). *Barefoot.* New York: Harper Trophy.

Hughes, S. (2004). *Ella's big chance: A jazz-age Cinderella.* New York: Simon & Schuster.

Krull, K. (1995). *Lives of the musicians: Good times, bad times, and what the neighbors thought.* San Diego, CA: Harcourt Brace.

Lionni, L. (1987). *Frederick.* New York: Knopf.

McCully, E. A. (1992). *Mirette on the high wire.* New York: Putnam.

Paterson, K. (1979). *Bridge to Terabithia.* New York: Harper & Row.

Pinkwater, D. (1993). *The big orange splot.* New York: Scholastic.

Winter, J. (1997). *Follow the drinking gourd.* New York: Knopf.

Wisniewski, D. (1997). *Golem.* New York: Clarion.

Yashima, T. (1965). *Crow boy.* New York: Scholastic.

Philosophy, Research, and Theories That Support Arts Integration

Questions to Guide Reading

1. How do philosophical beliefs shape arts integration?

2. What does research show about the arts and academics?

3. How does arts integration draw on brain research?

4. How are these theories used in arts integration: multiple intelligences, Piaget's stages, Erikson's stages, Maslow's hierarchy of needs, and Vygotsky's ZPD?

5. How do the arts help teachers adapt for diverse student characteristics (cognitive, social, emotional, and physical)?

6. How is the creative problem solving (CPS) process central to arts integration and learning in general?

Art engages the world. Artists make work about things, ideas, questions, relationships, emotions, problems, and solutions. Arts integration is modeled on the methods and purposes of real artists. (Rabkin & Redmond, 2005)

Answers to the question "WHY integrate the arts?" are central to this chapter. To begin with shared beliefs about learning and teaching create a philosophy of arts integration. This philosophy is based on a growing body of research findings and on theoretical models of learning. Of course, teachers need to known *how* to put all this into practice and so teaching implications are included for each area.

In the opening School Spotlight, notice how beliefs, research, and theories play significant roles in arts-based school reform and sustainability of efforts at one elementary school.

School Spotlight:

Schoolwide Reform

A flamboyant mural across the front of Lady's Island Elementary School (LIES) is one sign that this is no ordinary school. LIES is the first of its kind in the district, a site-based, deregulated school of choice in which arts infusion is the guiding philosophy.

Inside the front doors dozens of American flags, painted on ceiling tiles, greet visitors. A primary class sits on a colorful rug next to a piano with a sign that reads "Sing Your Way to Reading." A huge shrimp sculpture comically gazes down the center hall, and children's mobiles dance overhead. The halls are covered with every sort of student art, from cartoons to portraits to abstracts. Much of it is framed. On each classroom door is a teacher's name on a large artist's palette. All this before you even reach the office.

This is Terry Bennett's school. It is obvious how he feels about his job as principal—he smiles all the time. It is a place full of energy created by happy teachers and students. But just a few years ago this little school on an island in South Carolina was in turmoil. Changes in racial makeup, caused by a new elementary school built in a bedroom community, left LIES with just over 200 students, 75 percent of them on free or reduced lunch. A massive faculty exodus left only 50 percent of the teachers. It was a school without a focus. How did Mr. Bennett lead the transition to arts integration? He outlined the step-by-step process.

1. *Identify Strengths.* "When I came here in 1999, I knew we needed a focus. I had many conversations with teachers, parents, and school leaders. I didn't ask about problems. I already knew those. I wanted to identify strengths. I didn't begin with the idea to infuse the arts. The arts just emerged as areas of expertise and interest. Also, I noticed there weren't any discipline problems coming from the art and music classes. That told me something."

2. *Gather Research.* Mr. Bennett went looking for connections between the arts and academics. "I was surprised to find so much. The National Assessment of Educational Progress in Arts Education showed that students who received arts instruction outperformed other students. Another study by the Wolf Trap Institute for Early Learning Through the Arts explained how the arts prepare children for

Entry to Ashley River Creative Arts Elementary.

their first years of school. Brain research is showing that stimuli provided by pictures, songs, movement, and drama are essential for children to develop to full potential. These activities are the languages of the child, the multiple ways in which kids understand and interpret the world. The arts pave the way for the child to use [written] language to read and write."

Because of the nature of the LIES school population, Mr. Bennett was most interested in research on at-risk students. Findings show that active engagement in the arts improves self-esteem, confidence, leadership skills, and overall academic performance (Heath, 1999).

"I shared all this with teachers and parents. I even wrote a letter to the local newspaper outlining Catterall's analysis of 25,000 students as they moved from grade 8 to grade 10. He found significant correlations between the arts and higher grades, higher scores on standardized tests, better attendance rates, and participation in community affairs." Bennett also publicized the finding that students from poorer families improved more rapidly than other students when there were arts involved.

"Of course, everyone is impressed by College Board reports that show students who study the arts more than 4 years score 59 points higher on the verbal and 44 points higher on the math portions of the SAT than nonarts students. That is 103 points higher on the SAT!"

3. *Mission Statement.* The South Carolina Arts in the Basic Curriculum (ABC). ABC Program Director Christine Fisher presented an overview of arts integration to the LIES faculty. Her message was that they could address problems with attendance, achievement, and teacher turnover by using the arts so." Mr. Bennett and the music teacher then attended an ABC workshop to develop a mission statement. "That was our first year together as a school team." Note: The LIES mission statement and beliefs can be viewed on its website: *http://web.beaufort.K12.SC./US/education/school/school. php?sectionid=21.*

4. *Plan of Action.* "I'm not an artist. What I am is a leader. My staff needed someone to suggest and to push them—to support them," Mr. Bennett explains. By 2000 the school staff had developed a schoolwide plan to bring in artists in residence and to integrate the arts throughout the traditional academic curriculum.

5. *Professional Development.* Mr. Bennett believes in "in-house" professional development. "Our arts specialists took on leadership roles from the beginning. They have a regular place on every faculty meeting agenda." They also worked with the district arts coordinator, Kristy Smith, to bring in outside consultants to kick off the school year. "Our focus there was to give classroom teachers arts integration strategies," he says. In addition, teams began to visit other arts-based schools such as nearby Ashley River Creative Arts in Charleston.

6. *Implementation.* "During the first year we jumped in. We're not 'there' yet, but teachers are going toward more and more integrated units, and there is an increasing tie-in between what goes on between arts classrooms and regular classrooms." Like every school, a common planning time for classroom teachers to collaborate with arts specialists is the goal.

"We've got kindergartners studying Warhol and Rodin. Classroom teachers do units on local artists, too, like Jonathan Green. Projects and performances are emphasized because they encourage students to apply complex knowledge and skills from several areas simultaneously," Mr. Bennett adds LIES also partners with local arts agencies and has started after-school arts clubs like one for strings. "One child was in my office whining about something the other day and I said, jokingly, 'Let me play my fiddle.' She said, 'You're not holding it right!'"

In addition to art and music, students now dance once a week in place of PE. The certified dance teacher uses PE standards.

7. Maturation and Evaluation. Enrollment continues to rise with over half choosing to attend because of the arts focus. The gifted and talented program also identifies artistic abilities. "Students are happier. Every child likes some art form, and they touch all four every day. With happiness comes better attendance. I hear kids say things like, 'I don't want to be absent on Monday because my class has art on Monday.'"

Test scores started up right away. "I attribute this to arts infusion. Teachers are teaching a new way, but emphasizing state standards. We're teaching the same things by teaching differently," Mr. Bennett says.

"We believe what Richard Riley, U.S. Secretary of Education said, 'The creativity of the arts and the joy of music should be central to the education of every American child.'"

LIES Update

In 2005 the cafeteria was remodeled into three arts spaces: (1) a music and strings classroom with extra storage for instruments, (2) a dance classroom with dance floor, and (3) a drama classroom. The arts spaces are the center of the building. Teachers completed a yearlong curriculum map project to ensure the arts-integrated curriculum meets state standards. Test scores keep going up. Students exceeded all 17 areas required for NCLB. Last year the third grade state PACT scores were excellent: 97% scored at the basic level or above in mathematics, and 93% scored at basic or above in English/language arts.

"The local phone book features art work from students at LIES. Businesses display framed work throughout the community," Mr. Bennett says proudly. For the fifth year LIES students were in the South Carolina Honors choir. And teacher Deborah Smith was one of the Milken Foundation National Educator Award winners. She believes an integrated arts approach was a key.

Terry Bennett thinks these changes show the arts are "not only the heart of the building but also its soul." He is both reflective and indomitable when he adds, "We con-

tinue to struggle with scheduling, funding, state and national requirements—just like every school. However, our focus on student achievement with arts integration has not diminished. We continue to be Beaufort's Best Kept Secret!"

Arts Integration Philosophy

Knowing how to shift intellectual gears beats rigid thinking every time. (Bruce Boston, 1996)

All of us possess a framework of beliefs that shape our perceptions and determine our behavior, including how we teach. Philosophy matters. Beliefs and values "create our sense of what makes life worth living, and therefore what is worth teaching" (Ferrero, 2005, p. 21). Beliefs should be informed by both research and professional wisdom and be judged by how well they support student growth and happiness (Noddings, 2005, p. 10). Ferrero reminds us, however, that beliefs and values have to do with normative questions "not easily settled by empirical means" (p. 22). In other words, experimental research conclusions may have little effect on the "should and ought to" beliefs held by teachers, parents, and students.

The following are shared beliefs among educators involved in arts integration. They form interlocking conditions for learning and are in no order. They are organized around six Ps: philosophy, people, principles, places, programs, and pedagogy.

Philosophical Overview

Those who choose to implement arts integration generally assume a constructivist view of learning. There is deep belief in making learning purposeful and relevant by tapping interests and engaging students in hands-on/brains-on experiences. A developmental view of learning guides planning and focuses attention on the special strengths, differences, and needs of every learner. A main goal is to expand each student's capacity to problem solve and create new meanings—a process that is believed to promote feelings of ownership and involvement.

Constructivism. Constructivists believe that people learn best when they feel free and able to understand, respond to, and express ideas and feelings using their own life experiences and worldviews (Au, 2002, p. 395). Interest drives the search for meaning by engaging and motivating. This means teachers should (1) teach for meaning and understanding (not for the test or grades), (2) create learning environments that are low in threat and high in challenge, (3) immerse students in experiences that call for creative problem solving, and (4) teach to interests. Bruer (1999) suggests that "no reasonable parent or informed educator would take issue with these ideas"(p. 2).

Constructivism is supported by 30 years of psychological research that shows the mind constructs knowledge by connecting new information to existing understandings (Bruer, 1999; Ferrero, 2005). All knowledge is interconnected and interdependent. The key point is *personal* meaning making that is heavily influenced by social circumstances and context. Active engagement in meaning construction is believed to result in deeper understanding and motivation. Active engagement focuses on transforming ideas (e.g., from written to visual) through thinking, doing, and feeling. Meaning is "imposed," not "just uncovered" (Au, 2002, p. 29). In the arts this translates into a broad array of actions, such as making, molding, moving, creating, doing, acting, and singing. Among other important beliefs:

- Effective communication depends on possessing multiple ways to understand, respond to, and express thoughts and feelings.
- Arts and academic discipline-specific content and skills are important for the distinct contribution each makes.
- Literacy is effective communication of ideas and feelings using all symbol or sign systems: reading, writing, speaking, listening, visual art, music, drama, and dance.
- The Creative Problem Solving (CPS) process is used to make meaning across disciplines. There are many right answers.

Creativity.   Arts integration rests on a strong belief that people are innately creative and can learn to intentionally use inherent creative abilities to solve problems. The arts provide a fertile environment for developing skills necessary to creativity, such as brainstorming, data gathering from diverse sources, experimentation, questioning, critiquing, synthesizing, and evaluation based on evidence and aesthetic criteria.

Creativity blooms in an environment where students feel safe taking risks and asking questions. Students must feel free to experiment without concern that initial ideas will be criticized or ridiculed. Students need flexible time blocks to work on long-term projects, performances, and exhibits that synthesize learning. Humor and play are essential to creative thinking, while time restraints and close surveillance can be inhibitors.

People

Teachers and students have common and diverse physical, emotional, cognitive/communication, social, and moral dimensions.

Teachers.   "Research confirms that teachers are the single most important factor in raising student achievement"

(PEN, 2004). According to Booth (2003 ___ what you teach is who you are" (p. 2 ___ means using the arts as teaching tools an ___ of teaching to an art. The "artistic teach ___ large. Quality arts integration depends on ___ ted teachers who radiate possibilities and in ___ a "magic circle" that "awakens the dormant ___ participate" (Keppel, 2003, p. 29). These teachers talk passionately about their belief in "hands-on/minds-on" learning and readily do "extra work" because they believe the "cause is great." They share high degrees of: *act out/panto-mime*

- *Enthusiasm*   for engaging and stretching all students
- *Desire to learn*   new research, theories, and methods
- *Flexibility*   to change schedules and materials and take advantage of teachable moments
- *Openness*   to experiment with creative variations
- *Collaborative*   planning and coteaching
- *Passion*   about the transformative power of the arts
- *Creative solutions*   for learning problems
- *Optimism*   about teaching and reaching all children
- *Humor*   that is used a source for creative ideas
- *Artistry*   in which one-of-a-kind imprints are made on each child by using an artistic approach
- *Mentorship*   of students by sharing personal abilities and interests (play instruments, read, paint, and dance) (Students choose to apprentice themselves to these "masters.")
- *Relationships*   that form the core of classroom discipline
- *Courage/confidence*   to make mistakes and not be threatened by the ideas of colleagues.

Learners: Development and Differences.   Learners mature through predictable physical, cognitive, emotional, social, and moral stages. These stages are definable, but not rigid. Piaget and others have described broad stages of development; however, every brain has its own genetic blueprint. Rarely, do any two people, even twins, develop in exactly the same way or at the same rate. Learning is a result of experiences, which differ for every person, in either actuality or the perception of the experience. Learning changes the brain.

Genuine efforts to reach educational excellence require that educators consider commonalities of learners while addressing special capacities and needs. Focusing on the strengths, needs, and differences makes full development possible. Arts-based instruction and materials have to be matched to general developmental needs, as well as individual needs, for optimum growth. Arts integration offers increased possibilities for instructional adaptation because it adds options. In integrated arts classrooms, teachers structure learning so students are provided with appropriate challenges that allow them to express themselves in unique ways.

Diversity, not uniformity, is a significant measure of the effectiveness of arts integration. At arts integration schools, considerable attention is paid to teaching in a culturally responsive manner (Cambourne, 2002). A learner's own purposes or goals are central, and knowledge and meaning are socially constructed through negotiation, evaluation, and transformation. As our student bodies grow more diverse, it behooves us to adjust. A growing body of research supports the effectiveness of constructivist approaches in promoting the achievement of diverse students (Au, 2002).

Chapter 3 includes a discussion of developmental and individual differences, as well as ways to adapt for arts integration. There are also suggestions for diversifying lessons in arts chapters. The Appendix has a developmental continuum.

Principles of Learning

Beliefs about how students learn best form learning principles. The following learning principles go hand in hand with pedagogical beliefs.

Humans are predisposed to communicate. We are distinctive among animals in our intense need and ability to understand and express ourselves. The arts existed before words and persist because words are not up to the task of capturing the wide range of human thoughts and feelings. In arts integration students are taught that the arts are basic communication tools. They become an integral part of the literacy curriculum and expand students' options for comprehension and expression of ideas and feelings.

The drive to create personal meaning is powerful. The need to make sense appears in infancy. This "explanatory drive" (Gopnik, Kuhl, & Meltzoff, 1999) persists throughout life.

Arts-based learning is initiated by tapping into individual interests to motivate students and proceeds by capitalizing on the need to create sense. Art making and understanding begin with a problem and, from the outset, there is an expectation that the final product or perspective be distinctive in nature. In particular, the arts emphasize developing knowledge and skills so learners can act independently. The arts culminate in externalizing internal thoughts and feelings by "showing" them through dance, mime, sculpture, or any other art mediums.

Meaningfulness is key to meaning construction. John Dewey believed school should not be seen as preparation for life because it is life. Learners want to be involved in important and purposeful work that contributes to their own happiness and the happiness of others. Arts-based learning focuses on solving problems, using diverse materials and strategies connected to the real world and so

perceived as meaningful. Students are taught how to problem solve and are given authentic contexts to do so.

Cognition, emotions, and the physical body are interconnected. Students need experiences that call for the integration of multiple body and mind systems. This means that teachers need to orchestrate experiences that are thought provoking, aesthetic, concrete, and physical. As Given (2002) notes, students have individual strengths (emotional needs), they need to belong (social needs), they need to know and self-monitor (cognitive needs), and they need to act (physical needs).

Arts-based teaching activates all the perceptual senses. The arts are about making and doing so they change how we think and how we feel. They use alternative channels for perception and expression, including moving and touching. Image-based thinking, rather than word-based, allows thinking without words. Visual, sound, emotional, and physical images move through our minds and bodies and are projected using dance, drama, music, and art. Teachers that embark on arts integration employ the power of emotion to boost learning by acknowledging that every thought, decision, and response are accompanied and often determined by emotion. Teaching strategies like warm-ups, open questions, and feedback invite cognitive, affective, and physical engagement.

People are innately social. Social interactions among peers and with the teacher change the quantity and quality of meaning making (Au, 2002). This is because relationships fill needs to belong and be heard, recognized, and respected (Gopnik et al., 1999; Maslow, 1970). Learning to learn from and work with others is essential to success in the classroom and the workplace, where cooperation is needed to solve problems and create new products. Healthy personal relationships depend on cooperation and respect.

The arts provide multiple opportunities for students to learn important group skills through choirs, ensembles, and clubs. In each of these arenas, students must tackle inevitable problems that arise when two or more people assemble. Audiences are a social force that can cause shy and reluctant students to blossom. Students learn how to take on the role of an audience member, too, which increases their social adeptness and capacity to enjoy, appreciate, and gain aesthetic satisfaction.

Wholes and parts are processed simultaneously. The brain makes sense by sorting and connecting. This requires attention to the big picture and small details. Students must learn how isolated skills and individual concepts add up to big understandings. Listening to a whole song or seeing a whole painting provokes cognitive and emotional responses. The whole experience comes into focus as details are noticed. The details, in turn, have meaning because they are part of the whole, just as letters are meaningless until they are put into words.

Whole with part teaching causes students to stand back and move in close to create meaning. Arts-based teaching combines zoom out and zoom in with a focus on aesthetic knowing through all senses. Students are explicitly taught pieces, parts, and elements of the arts as means to understand, respond to, and express meaning—not as ends in and of themselves.

Understanding results from transformation.

> *One of the reasons the arts are effective is that they put students' knowledge to work. You can't act, paint, or dance unless you know something about your subject.* (Rodney Van Valkenburg, Allied Arts of Greater Chattanooga)

Meaning is constructed by acting on, representing, or changing ideas. This transformation depends on connecting the new to the known.

Arts integration focuses on teaching students to make novel links among disparate ideas. Hooking to previous experience is vital so teachers often begin lessons with brainstorming what is known about a topic. Students are drawn to significant details by prompting them to take time to notice and find patterns. Asking and coaching is valued over telling and pointing out. Specific arts elements and concepts (details) are explicitly taught as thinking anchors to facilitate transformation. Students are taught to use creative problem solving, which includes synthesizing patterns to arrive at new perspectives and products. This transformation yields deep understanding.

Meaningful work with artists and arts content and materials also causes students to *be* transformed. Over time they build a reservoir of knowledge and skills to work in new ways. Many implementations of arts integration are yoked to multiple intelligences theory for this purpose.

People seek independence. From toddlerhood on, it is obvious that children want to do it themselves and in their own way. Learners feel more confident when they gain the competence to solve their own problems. The arts are about expanding ways to understand, respond, and express meaning independently. Arts-based teaching focuses on explicit teaching of arts concepts and skills that provide students expanded communication options. Teachers move students toward independence by explicitly teaching problem-solving strategies, scaffolding practice, and providing time to work independently, with feedback. Students also need to understand that independence is gained through hard work. Artists provide significant role models of hardworking people who persist at overcoming obstacles to independence.

Learning is conscious and unconscious. Attention, concentration, and focus are necessary for learning. Attention is critical to memory, but human beings have both conscious and unconscious attentive capabilities. Children learn language, behavior, values, and beliefs by both direct and indirect attention (Schacter, 1996). Concentration involves sustained attention and is best achieved through deep engagement in creative problem solving ("flow" is the most engaged state). Arts-based learning occurs in contexts set up to maximize attention. Background music and art exhibits are attended to directly, at times, but they are a pervasive part of learning aesthetically. Teachers use specific attention getters to capture students' focus, sustain concentration, and give time for incubation through unconscious processes. Lessons routinely include conscious reflection and self-evaluation.

Depth of learning is increased by instrinsic motivation. The arts develop internal motivation because they purposefully focus on inside-out meaning construction. The motivational character of the arts stems from curiosity, wonder, and yearning. Fun is taken seriously and tapped for its *fundamental* role in engaging through movement, novelty, challenge, surprise, and group work. A focus on time to pursue interests and having choices are particularly key to intrinsic motivation (Guthrie, 2004) and account for large effect sizes in comprehension.

Arts integration minimizes extrinsic reinforcers such as stickers and praise, because they decrease interest in learning for its own sake. These external controls are not needed when students are motivated by arts engagement. However, learners must believe they are capable of creative problem solving. If problems are too difficult or students lack knowledge or skill to participate, they can become overly frustrated or bored.

Arts integration relies on noncompetitive social interaction in which groups work to solve problems and share ideas, which may result in individual products. Competitive practices are minimized because they can threaten and cause students to lose hope or give up. Arts integration motivates individuals by helping them find unique contributions each can make. This also increases the likelihood of more complex understanding.

Places

Learning Climate. Learning can't be separated from its context. The teacher must create an environment that convinces learners they need to engage as deeply as possible (Cambourne, 2002). It is impossible to imagine deep engagement in sterile or unpleasant classrooms. Arts integration emphasizes creating an aesthetic learning ecology in which sights, sounds, and smells are used to stimulate the senses.

The psychological feel of a classroom also affects student success. Students will not take risks if they do not feel that it is physically and psychologically safe to make mistakes. The teacher's personality, beliefs, and teaching approach are the greatest determiners of climate. Caine and Caine (2005) recommend that the classroom be low threat and high challenge, which creates a "relaxed alertness"—an optimal state in which fear and pleasure centers of the brain are moderated.

Freedom.   Albert Einstein once commented that it was "nothing short of a miracle that the modern methods of instruction have not yet entirely strangled the holy curiosity of inquiry." He called curiosity a "delicate little plant" that needs freedom as much as stimulation to thrive. As we consider the reasons behind the growing momentum for arts integration, we should evaluate the importance of freedom in schooling. Worldwide, America is nearly synonymous with freedom. School structure and classroom practices need to align with the principles of our democracy if we want continued freedom for Americans and the spread of freedom to others throughout the world.

How does arts integration contribute to the perpetuation of freedom? The concept of arts integration is rooted in core values that find coercion and conformity repellent. Like Einstein, thoughtful educators and arts advocates worry about the potential for "rank and ruin" if educational practices don't promote "engagement of seeing and searching" possible only in a climate that celebrates risk taking, freedom of expression, and individual differences that give strength to a society. Students learn democratic values by living them as citizens of the school. Children at arts-based schools learn to make thoughtful decisions and manage their own behavior because they are given the reigns to experiment. Mistakes are viewed as opportunities. Self-reflection and critique are emphasized to increase quality of work and depth of learning.

Responsibility.   When Thomas Edison finished an early prototype of his light bulb, he called a boy to take it to the factory. The boy dropped it on the way. Edison had to start all over. When he had another light bulb, many days later, he sent for the same boy. He told him to take it to the factory. Edison would certainly have liked the idea that the arts give second chances to so many.

The root of the word *responsibility* is response. The arts uniquely value risk taking and experimentation with the proviso that learners reflect on the consequences of their actions. Children become responsible when they are taught appropriate ways to respond using myriad arts tools, materials, and techniques. These options balance freedom with responsibility.

Programs

Meaningful arts integration is shaped by local educators and arts specialists based on the needs and resources of each school. There is not one implementation model. Some programs are district- or schoolwide. Some use grants to fund artist residencies and provide collaborative planning time for teachers and specialists. Others involve individual teachers that plan together with in-house arts specialists using limited budgets. All successful programs are the result of intentional design that addresses standards, are grounded in research, and provide ongoing professional development to increase best practices in the arts, collaborative planning, and coteaching skills.

Most programs start small, with emphasis on teacher comfort and arts predispositions. Some schools, such as Hilton Head Creative Arts, spend a year or more studying research and visiting schools (Keefner, 2005). All schools must eventually construct a philosophy that guides the program design. This includes a mission statement and consensus operating principles to make clear how teachers agree to put beliefs into action.

Most arts integration programs share the goal of integrating multiple art forms throughout the curriculum. Overlapping concepts and skills are found among arts and academic areas. At first, just one art may be used and perhaps one or two integrated units per year. Some schools dedicate a specific amount of school time to integration (e.g., arts-based literacy block). The speed and quality of integration is determined by the arts knowledge depth and the pedagogical base of teachers and arts specialists.

Pedagogy

Quality arts integration rests on good teaching. Research confirms that the effects on learning depend on the length and specific nature of arts integration. The pedagogy of quality arts integration draws on three sources: (1) general, research-based, best teaching practices (Allington, 2005; Zemelman, Daniels, & Hyde, 1998), (2) general practices that relate to the arts, and (3) practices peculiar to each art form.

Teacher Roles.   Arts integration envisions teachers in many different roles to meet cognitive, emotional, and physical needs of students (Given, 2002):

- Specialists and generalists
- Mentors and models
- Collaborators in co-planning and coteaching
- Facilitators and coaches
- Managers, directors, and guides
- Talent scouts
- Colearners with students
- Motivators, assessors, and evaluators

Instruction. Best teaching practices closely related to arts integration are discussed in Chapter 3. Specific arts practices are addressed in separate arts chapters. Basic beliefs about pedagogy are summarized here using six Ts of effective teaching (adapted from Allington, 2002):

Talk. Allington (2005) suggests that "even small amounts of conversation produce huge comprehension benefits." Focused conversation among students increases learning. Arts integrated classrooms are not dominated by teacher talk. Instead, teachers use mini-lessons to introduce and demonstrate, and students are quickly set to work to solve problems. They learn to take turns, share ideas, and actively listen to others as they brainstorm solutions. Students learn to question, clarify, and reflect. Through drama students learn to be comfortable improvising and controlling their voices and bodies. They learn to subdue their own volume as background music is played. Most of all, students learn that voicing their own ideas is valued.

Tasks. The major task is to actively engage students in constructing meaning about authentic problems. This communication task has three parts: (1) creating understanding, (2) responding, and (3) expressing ideas and feelings. Meaning construction is accomplished using the creative problem solving process, associated with the arts, and aligned with the reading/writing processes and the scientific method.

Students engage in sustained inquiry and self-monitoring. Specific arts content, skills, and materials are taught for use during problem solving. These expand the communication possibilities and enable students to transform ideas. Transformation creates feelings of ownership.

Texts. Texts are not limited to printed material. Texts include paintings, sculpture, architecture, songs, musical pieces, and dances. Students are taught to read all types of texts that record ideas, values, and emotions. Classroom teachers and arts specialists work in concert to teach students the arts literacy needed to "read" arts texts by decoding each art's symbol system.

Time. Time is used flexibly and adjusted to students and task characteristics. In general, different students need different amounts of time to learn the same thing. Time is a huge variable in learning. Because the creative problem solving process is central to arts integration, teachers plan time differently to accommodate this process. For example, incubation time is given for students to take time away from a piece of writing or art so they can return with a fresh perspective. One prominent feature is long-term projects that deepen understanding through higher-order thinking used in creative problem solving. The result is exhibits and performances that synthesize learning over time.

Transfer. The promise of transfer of learning from arts experiences to academic areas has intensified research efforts and increased hope, especially for disadvantaged students. Significant arts involvement appears to narrow the gap between students from low-income families and those from more affluent backgrounds (Catterall, 2003; Deasy & Stevenson, 2005). The arts hold potential to develop generic higher-order thinking, problem-solving skills, and motivational dispositions common to success in school and life. For example, the arts promote curiosity, inquiry, persistence, experimentation, synthesis, and flexible thinking—all of which are important beyond the school walls and critical to 21st-century job success (*Impact of Arts Education,* 2002).

Pedagogical issues related to transfer depend on how explicit the teacher is about common links between learning in the arts and other subjects. For example, transfer is more likely when teachers demonstrate parallels between CPS and the reading and writing processes. Transfer can go back and forth. Students who understand that the written composition process shares much with the composition process in visual art are likely to use skills from each to enrich both. This is two-way transfer. Three-way transfer is the ultimate goal—arts to academics, academics to arts, and both to life.

Tests. The arts have a long history of using nontraditional ways to show achievement—primarily portfolios, performances, and exhibitions. In arts integration these assessment tools are fully employed. Instead of relying on paper tests, students "show they know." They externalize learning by creating dance, drama, visual art, music, and poetry responses that synthesize ideas. Portfolios of work, rubrics, and self-evaluation are common and combine with performances and exhibits to do more than gauge what was learned. These "tests" motivate students to want to learn. When assessment is used *for* learning and not just *of* learning, it is viewed as less threatening and more valuable (Stiggins, 2002). "How am I doing?" is a question students ask because they earnestly want to improve, not just get a higher grade. Hope is sustained through a belief that there is a strong chance of success.

Mission Statement

Schools embarking on arts integration usually begin by creating a philosophical statement of beliefs that embraces the power of arts to facilitate learning. When individual teachers or groups integrate the arts on their own, they too must begin with clarity about what they believe is right and good for students. More and more the word *arts* is becoming a part of school names, as with Hilton Head Creative Arts (renamed 2006), formerly the Island Academy.

At Hand Middle School in Columbia, South Carolina, the staff developed a five-year plan based on the mounting

ng cognition to the arts. According to their
ـtatement, "all students should be enriched by
ـ ـ to the fine arts through high quality, comprehensive
ـ ـe arts courses and the integration of the fine arts into every
subject." Principal Marissa Vickers calls the arts an "integral
component" and an "anchor" for students' daily learning. Examples of arts integration at Hand include: use of familiar
melodies to learn the order of the planets and the muscular
system, focus on using descriptive adjectives first in art and
then in writing, setting original poetry to music, drawing editorial cartoons in social studies, and dance and drama performances of science content like the laws of motion and rain
forest destruction (*http://hornet.richlandone.org/*).

Research on Arts Integration

> The best arts integration programs demonstrate a strategy that
> can help close the achievement gap and make schools happier
> places. It is a strategy within reach of most schools and districts,
> even those in the poorest communities. (Rabkin & Redmond,
> 2005)

The track record for arts integration as a tool for academic
gain continues to strengthen. As more teachers use the motivation and communication powers of the arts, reports of
increased concentration, more cooperation, better comprehension, and greater self-discipline among students are
on the rise (Deasy, 2002; Deasy & Stevenson, 2005). Studies of successful people show that persistence pays off; the
arts increase persistence. Persistence derives from motivation; in arts-based schools it becomes apparent that it was-
n't that students couldn't learn—it was that they wouldn't.
The arts make students want to learn. What's more, students become more resilient to setbacks when they have
the opportunity to learn through arts-based inquiry lessons that emphasize experimentation and learning from
mistakes.

Controllables.   Teachers can feel helpless when faced
with evidence that the most powerful correlates of academic achievement (IQ, parent's income, and education)
are beyond their control. Fortunately, several controllable
factors correlate with high scores and with important attributes not measured by tests. Arts integration is one of
those "controllables." A solid body of evidence correlates
meaningful teaching through the arts with higher academic
achievement and desirable personal and social behaviors
(Deasy, 2002; Ruppert, 2006).

Researchers will probably never be able to identify all
the particulars of arts integration that cause the strong correlations. Consider how just one factor, the teacher, plays
a major role. A charismatic, highly skilled teacher can

make the most boring worksheet into a significant learning event, while a dull, rigid teacher can corrupt the most
wonderful piece of literature. Arts integration intentionally dwells on "live performers," leaving it highly vulnerable to people influence. Arts integration is also defined in
numerous ways and implemented to different degrees. It is
difficult to create a research design that deals with such
complexities. In whole school reform it is particularly
hard to use the classic experimental design that yields
cause-effect findings with random sampling and control
groups. Who would want their children to be in a control
that uses less than the best of what is known about good
instruction?

Furthermore, the standard for success of educational
programs is often an unrealistic expectation of 100%. Scientific research is held up as model, despite the acceptance
of much lower effectiveness levels in scientific fields. For
example, pharmaceuticals are offered as research models
even though 90% of drugs only work with 30–50% of the
population (Allen Roses, geneticist and vice president of
GlaxoSmithKline quoted in Connor, 2003). Imagine pro-
posing an educational approach that only works with one
third to one half of kids. The consequences of overreliance
on "scientific research" have become apparent as more
and more "proven" treatments, such as silicone implants
and Vioxx, have been shown to have life-threatening side
effects.

Testing Inadequacies.   A compelling argument is
made that measuring complex thinking in the arts is beyond the capabilities of current tests. Hetland and Winner
(2000) call the research on the arts-academics connection
"inconclusive," but make the case that the arts should not
be justified by their ability to increase test scores. The arts
have inherent merits such as an unquestioned ability to
compel interest, induce empathy, and give new perspectives. These and many of the other important influences of
the arts are not easily measured in standardized testing formats (Efland, 2002). Artistic processes resist standardiza-
tion. As Eisner (2002) is quick to point out, that which is
easily measured may not matter and what matters is not
easy to measure.

Scripp (2003) argues further that "one-way cause and
effect" models of research are appropriate when it is only
possible that the treatment affects the outcome. He points
out, for example, that smoking causes cancer, but cancer
does not cause smoking. Arts-based learning is not a one-
way street. Learning in music enhances math, but math undoubtedly enriches music achievement. One-way transfer is
unlikely and is a constricted view of learning. That said,
most available research looks at what the arts might do for
academics, not the other way around.

Meta-analysis. A relatively new methodology, meta-analysis, allows researchers to examine a wide range of research and draw conclusions by averaging effect sizes across studies. One controversial study can no longer be used to "discredit the general trends of a diverse collection of research over time" (Scripp, 2003, p. 127). Meta-analysis has added a degree of stability to interpretation of results. Of special importance is "triangulation" that uses "multiple ways of assessing learning outcomes which may corroborate each other and lend credence to inferences about what leads to what" (Catterall, 2003, p. 114). A growing body of work compares results across multiple studies, and dozens of studies are finding the same thing: Significant arts involvement changes how children think and how they feel about learning. That fact is reflected in test scores and in vast quantities of survey, interview, observation, and anecdotal evidence.

Research Findings. The following findings are organized according to the diverse relationships found between arts engagement and (1) academic achievement, (2) cognitive/ higher-order thinking, (3) literacy/math, (4) affective/ motivational changes, (5) social growth, (6) learning environment, and (7) diverse learners. In general, the literature reports data to support an array of positive influences. The subsequent summary describes important research findings. Many studies were descriptive in nature and yield correlational findings from which potential causal relationships between the arts and other areas are inferred. Most of these conclusions were drawn from syntheses of large numbers of studies. The quantity of studies that continue to produce similar findings is important and alleviates, to some extent, concerns about the ability to conclusively discern cause-effect relationships.

There have been several important digests of research on the effects on students and teachers involved in arts-based teaching and learning. The information that follows comes mostly from: Catterall, 1998; Catterall et al., 1999; Darby & Catterall, 1994; Deasy, 2002; Deasy & Stevenson, 2005; Fiske, 1999; Horowitz, 2004; Keirstead & Graham, 2004; Project Zero, 2000; Rooney, 2004; and a Canadian study reported on by Upitis & Smithrin, 2003. Additional references are included after some conclusions to help locate particular studies.

Academic Achievement

(as Measured by Test Scores)

1. ***Arts-involved students score higher than other students.*** Differences range significantly from 16 to 18 percentage points (test scores). Students whose parents had

lower incomes scored lower, but their scores were still significant. Research includes Darby and Catterall, 1994 (a meta-analysis of 188 reports); Catterall et al., 1999; Fiske, 1999; Harvard's Project Zero, 2000; Catterall, 1998 (analysis of National Educational Longitudinal Survey of more than 25,000 students over 10 years); Deasy, 2002; and Upitis and Smithrin, 2003.

2. ***Greater arts integration yields higher test scores.*** Longer and more intense work in the arts had more impact. This effect was particularly strong for low-income and ESL students (Fiske, 1999; Ingram & Riedel, 2003; Stronge, 2002).

3. ***Academic achievement builds over time.*** "Gain scores" (year-over-year comparisons) were significantly higher for third, fourth, and fifth graders in arts integrated classrooms (Ingram & Riedel, 2003).

4. ***Arts experiences especially benefit "undereducated"*** students (Deasy 2002; Deasy & Stevenson, 2005; Upitis & Smithrin, 2003). See additional findings under "Diverse Learners."

Cognitive Effects

Schools that integrate the arts develop essential thinking such as

> *careful observation of the world; mental representation of what is observed or imagined; abstraction from complexity; pattern recognition and development; qualitative judgment; symbolic, metaphoric, and allegorical representation.* (Rabkin & Redmond, 2005, pp. 46-47)

These are the same kinds of thinking used in science, math, social studies, reading, and writing. Basically this is thought to be why students in arts-based schools reach higher academic standards. Teaching students to use complex thinking beyond literal or memory levels is difficult, and there has been only limited success using traditional methods (Kamil, 2004). No one debates that the arts engage higher-order thinking. The problem is that these effects may not show up in test results or on traditional measures of academic achievement (Efland, 2002). Here are the findings to date.

1. ***Arts experiences engage and strengthen higher-order thinking.*** These include increases in comprehension/ meaning construction, spatial reasoning (the capacity for organizing and sequencing ideas), conditional reasoning (theorizing about outcomes and consequences), problem solving/decision making, and the components of creative thinking (originality, elaboration, and flexibility) (Deasy, 2002; Efland, 2002; Eisner, 2002a; Horowitz, 2004;

Mardiropsian & Fox, 2003; Psilos, 2002; Winner & Hetland, 2000a, 2000b).

2. *Critical thinking is developed through the arts.* For example, students used more "evidentiary reasoning" and broadened their understanding of interpretation itself from discussing paintings (Horowitz, 2004; Project Zero, 2003).

3. *Creativity as a "capacity for learning" is expanded.* High arts students are more fluent, flexible, original, elaborative, and willing to resist closure (A+ Schools, 2001; Burton et al., 1999; New American Schools, 2003).

4. *Spatial reasoning, organization, planning, self-direction and self-assessment improve.* Music, in particular, has been found to enhance spatial thinking (Burton et al., 1999; Darby & Catterall, 1994; Deasy, 2002; Fiske, 1999; Psilos, 2002).

Literacy and Math

1. *Arts instruction enhances and complements basic reading instruction.* This includes learning letter names and sounds, spelling, and phonics (Deasy, 2002).

2. *The arts offer additional ways to understand and represent ideas and feelings.* This includes improved language and literacy skills related to use of drama and music. For example, dramatic enactments of stories and text improve writing, reading comprehension, and ability to read materials not seen before. The effects are even more significant for children from economically disadvantaged circumstances and those with reading difficulties. Planning and organizing skills inherent in music are parallel with planning and producing writing (Deasy, 2002).

3. *Increased communication leads to other effects.* Students are more cooperative, have greater rapport with teachers, show more sustained focus, and are more willing to perform and exhibit learning (Burton et al., 1999; Darby & Catterall, 1994; Deasy, 2002; Rooney, 2004).

4. *Music instruction develops math-related skills.* Spatial reasoning and spatial-temporal reasoning skills used in music are fundamental to understanding and using mathematical ideas and concepts (Deasy, 2002).

Motivational/Affective Effects

Motivation to pursue and sustain learning is essential to achievement. Learning in the arts nurtures motivation through active engagement, boosting self-confidence and self-efficacy. These increase attendance, educational aspirations, and ownership of learning. Arts-based teaching makes learning more equitable by broadening access to understanding and ways to express meaning (Annenberg, 2002;

Darby & Catterall, 1994; Fogg & Smith, 2001; Morrow, 2001; Rooney, 2004).

1. *Self-esteem, flexibility, and willingness to take risks, experiment, and tolerate uncertainty increases.* (A+ Schools, 2001; Catterall et al., 1999; Eisner, 2002a; Jensen, 2001; Ritter, 1999; Rooney, 2004; Stronge, 2002).

2. *Fewer at-risk behaviors were found.* In particular, students involved in music showed this pattern (New American Schools, 2003).

3. *Empathy for others increased.* Drama, in particular, was found to show this effect. Stereotypical views toward minority cultures decreased when arts instruction focused on Native American music and culture (Catterall et al., 1999; Edwards, 1994).

4. *Students stay in school longer and have more positive attitudes.* (Catterall et al., 1999).

Social Effects

Studies of arts-based learning experiences in drama, music, dance, and multiarts activities show student growth in self-control, conflict resolution, collaboration, empathy, and social tolerance.

1. *Quality of classroom participation increased.* Students involved as makers and doers in the arts showed the greatest ability to collaborate, reflect, and make choices (Deasy, 2002; Fiske, 1999).

2. *Self-discipline/regulation increased.* Students were more cooperative, paid attention, persevered, did more problem solving, took initiative, asked questions, took positive risks, used feedback, and prepared. Greater communication skills developed through the arts enhanced ability to achieve consensus (Burton et al., 1999; Deasy, 2002).

3. *The arts make education more equitable.* The arts are "instruments of cognitive growth and agents of motivation," so unfair access to the arts "brings consequences of major importance to our society" (Catterall et al., 1999, p. 17). The National Assessment of Educational Progress [NAEP] data demonstrates how the arts can level the educational playing field. For example, among all areas in which students were tested, music scores reflected the narrowest gap between varying races and minorities.

4. *Arts-based instruction can increase family and community support.* (Annenberg, 1998). Dramatic increases were found in "syntactic complexity, hypothetical reasoning, and questioning approaches" that enable planning and give youth "language with which to collaborate productively and respectfully," allowing them to participate in social enterprises to improve their communities (Heath & Roach, 1999, p. 27).

Learning Environment

It is critical that students learn in a positive context. The arts help create the kind of learning environment that boosts success by "fostering teacher innovation, a positive professional culture, community engagement, increased student attendance and retention, effective instructional practice, and school identity" (Deasy, 2002, pp. iii–iv).

1. *The arts enhance learning by creating "strong school ecologies."* A "complex web of stimulation and influence creates an enhanced learning environment [which is] key to academic achievement" (Rooney, 2004). The arts-infused environment increases opportunities for engaged, active, interdisciplinary teaching and learning (A+ Schools, 2001; Burton et al., 1999; Fiske, 1999; Fogg & Smith, 2001; Seaman, 1999).

2. *The arts promote a greater spirit of cooperation and participation.* Teachers work more collaboratively and are more creative, artistic, and enthusiastic. They think more deeply and are more open and flexible. Teachers involved in arts integration are more likely to participate in professional development and acquire a broader repertoire of teaching strategies (A+ Schools, 2001; Burton et al., 1999; Rooney, 2004).

Diverse Learners

Imagine Leonardo da Vinci in an average American school. "This illegitimate son of a poor woman, a left-handed writer who loved to draw and challenge conventional thought, would be labeled an at-risk special education candidate . . ." (Murfee, 1995, p. 8). The arts engage and offer challenges for all students—at risk, disadvantaged, delayed, and gifted from every cultural background. Arts integration presents a menu of learning opportunities that widen success possibilities by increasing participation by all students. The open-ended problem-solving nature of arts integration encourages individuality. In addition, arts teachers tend to be more diverse so students interact with role models from various backgrounds. Findings from large-scale projects such as South Carolina's ABC schools show that arts integration offers hope for increasing the capacities of all children, especially diverse learners. For more in-depth information about research programs for diverse learners, visit the Very Special Arts website: *www.vsarts.org.*

1. *Arts-based teaching engages a wide range of learners.* By introducing flexibility, teachers can better promote individuality and diversity. All arts-involved students showed higher levels of learning, especially at-risk and underachieving students (Deasy, 2002; Eisner, 2002a, 2000b; Fiske, 1999; Goldberg & Phillips, 2000; Ingram & Riedel, 2003; Mason, Thormann, & Steedly, 2004; New American Schools, 2003; Stronge, 2002; Upitis & Smithrin, 2003). Students who have struggled with traditional modes of instruction find success in inclusive environments that build on commonalities, while respecting differences.

2. *Arts-based teaching and learning "opens avenues."* Students who are not part of the dominant culture benefit from the expanded opportunities for learning the arts provide (Annenberg, 2003; Darby & Catterall, 1994; Mason et al., 2004).

3. *Significant relationships and improvements in reading, writing, and math were found.* This research focused on disadvantaged low-scoring students involved in the arts experiences such as using multimedia from photographs, objects, and videos to advanced computer software (Ingram & Riedel 2003; National Center to Improve Practice, (*www2. edc.org/ NCIP/*).

Brain Research

Since the early Greeks, we have known that the brain is the locus of cognition. Beyond that the brain was a mystery. By the mid 20th century, technology allowed neuroscientists to see the brain in action. Noninvasive tools like PET (positron emission tomography) and MRI (magnetic resonance imaging) yielded images of brain growth and development. Unfortunately, some educators drew from these studies instructional implications that had little basis in scientific fact. Educators are now accused of oversimplifying research to create "neuromyths" based more on psychology than science. According to Hall (2005), there is no "grand scheme of brain-based education" that will instantly transform learning" (pp. 27–28).

Brain science is just beginning to shed light on a few areas of learning, including language, literacy, numeracy, dyslexia, and the links with emotion (Bruer, 1999). We really know relatively little about thinking and learning "at the level of brain areas, neural circuits, or synapses" or "how the brain thinks, remembers, and learns" (p. 648). A cautious approach is recommended that acknowledges incomplete knowledge but the reality of children waiting to be taught every day.

Misconceptions

There are basically three areas of misunderstanding.

1. *Constructivism.* The constructivist view of learning is based on more than three decades of psychological research (Bruer, 1999). It is psychological, not brain, research that yielded findings about memory and the effects of prior knowledge on learning. Bruer says "to claim that these are 'brain-based' findings is misleading" (p. 649).

2. *Left–right brain dichotomy.* There really is no evidence that people do anything but use their whole brains, unless the corpus collosum is severed. Split-brain models are "simply too crude." Such is the conclusion of Christopher Chabris and Stephen Kosslyn, leading researchers in spatial reasoning and visual imagery, who reject "folk theory" that lumps "conglomerations of complex mental abilities, such as spatial reasoning, to one hemisphere or the other" (Bruer, 1999, p. 650). Different brain areas are specialized for different tasks, but that specialization occurs at "a finer level of analysis than 'using visual imagery,'" (p. 651). Visual imagery is a useful strategy, but the belief that mental picturing is a function of the right hemisphere is simply false. Neither are speech, writing, and reading skills simply left hemisphere (Shaywitz, 2004). Subsystems of both hemispheres are used to hear phonemes in words, decode the pronunciation of written words, give meaning to words, construct the gist of a written text, and infer as we read. Simply stated, "both hemispheres are involved in all activities" (Bruer, 1999, p. 648).

3. *Windows of development.* Neuroscience "has not established that there is a sensitive period between the ages of 4 and 10 during which children learn more quickly, easily, and meaningfully" (Bruer, 1999, p. 648). Neuroscientist Harry Chugani believes, however, that there is a biological window of opportunity when learning is easy, efficient, and durable, presenting once-in-a-lifetime opportunities to learn. The debate continues about whether the time of excess brain connectivity gives children greater opportunity to retain and increase efficiency of connections. It is accepted that there are critical periods for "species-wide skills, such as seeing, hearing, and acquiring a first language; but these seem to be the exception rather than the rule in human development" (p. 655). Much, if not most, learning takes place after age 10 when pruning is complete. We may actually be more efficient learners after puberty when our brains are growing less.

Brain Facts and Educational Implications

Good teachers know that lecturing on the American Revolution is far less effective than acting out a battle. (Robert Sylwester, University of Oregon)

Here are educational implications from brain research that have bearing on arts integration.

Brain Development. During gestation the brain adds about 250,000 neurons per minute. Brain neurons at this stage have been likened to "a spaghetti-like mass" (Hall, 2005, p. 28; Lindsey, 1998–99, p. 2). At birth the brain has 100 billion neurons, which in turn make more than 50 trillion synapses (Begley, 1996). In early childhood, neurons begin to hook up according to sensory input. This process is known as "synaptogenesis" (Hall, 2005, p. 28); the growth happens "like a budding and branching tree," depending on which areas are stimulated. By age 3, trillions of connections among neurons will have been created, more than the brain can possibly use.

Over time, unused, seldom used, and redundant connections are eliminated. As early as age 10 a "draconian pruning" occurs and some neurons die (Hall, 2005, p. 28; Nash, 1997, p. 50). The elimination of connections is not genetically predetermined (Simmons & Sheehan, 1997). While synapse pruning is scientific fact, no reliable studies have compared adult synaptic connectivity with differences in experiences of individuals before puberty. It is not known whether adults with greater synaptic density are more intelligent and developed.

Implications. Arts integration creates a highly stimulating learning environment for all children. Since the brain is constantly changing during childhood, it is important to be responsive to individual maturational strengths and needs as well (Hansen & Monk, 2002). Arts integration focuses on the "power of one," in which each child is valued for his/her uniqueness, while there is sensitivity to general developmental patterns. Strengths and needs are assessed and teaching focuses on developing, not suppressing differences.

Environmental Influences. The human brain has infinite potential, but the environment has a great influence on whether a child "grows up intelligent or dull, fearful or self-assured, articulate or tongue-tied" (Begley, 1996, p. 56). The number and complexity of brain synapses is altered by the conditions under which children live; there is no preprogrammed unfolding (Bransford et al., 1999). Studies of animals raised with playmates and toys show they grew 25 percent more synapses than deprived ones. With all this research, however, we don't know if bigger is better. Einstein had a relatively small brain.

Research also confirms the negative impact of early stress on brain function (Lindsey, 1998–99). Stress causes the amygdala to flood the brain with chemicals potentially harmful to development of the cortex, which causes problems with understanding. The result is that "children who don't play much or are rarely touched develop brains 20% to 30% smaller than normal" (Nash, 1997, p. 51). Experiments also show how kittens remain blind in one eye when the eye, sewn shut at birth, is reopened. Other kittens raised in an environment with only horizontal lines grew to be cats that could not see vertical lines. The horizontal cats ran right into vertical bars as if they didn't exist (Hubel, 1988). There seems to be a window for human visual acuity development that lasts until about age 8. When the brain does not receive the right information, results can be devastating. Children born with cataracts became permanently blind in affected eyes if the clouded lens was not removed by age 2. Studies also show brain development is inhibited by restricted physical activity (Begley, 1996). For example, a child in a body cast until age 4 never learns to walk smoothly.

Implications. The hypothesis is that if a child's environment is dull, fewer neural connections are made. Arts integration happens in a "synapse-stimulating" aesthetic environment. Arts integration philosophy is grounded in beliefs about encouraging students to experiment and feeling free to fail. Teachers attempt to create safe conditions of low threat and high challenge so students feel free to take risks and are surrounded by multisensory stimulation. The arts have the power to relax and calm through physical work, background music, and even the use of color on classroom walls. Songs and movement are integrated throughout the curriculum. Drama and dance allow students to move and learn kinesthetically. It is common for them to work in groups and to be out of their seats. Student passivity is replaced with hands-on art and drama problem solving. Project and performance-based learning drives instruction, making assessment of thinking processes (strategies and skills) and products (information and concepts) more like that in the 21st-century workplace.

Experiences. Pioneering brain research implies links between types of brain activity and how the brain comes to be structured (Bransford et al., 1999). "The number of synaptic connections in the brain is influenced by experience" (Hansen & Monk, 2002, p. 352). The manner in which a child is raised affects how the brain chooses to wire itself for life (Simmons & Sheehan, 1997). The environment affects not only the number, but also the way these connections are "wired" (Lindsey, 1998–99). Each child's brain can form quadrillions of connections, but the number and strength depend on the transformative power of repeated experience. As Nash (1997) points out "the potential for greatness may be encoded in the genes, but whether that potential is realized . . . is etched by experience in those critical early years" (p. 56).

Implications. New views of intelligence consider how cultural, social, and environmental factors can raise or lower intellectual capacities. The potential of substantial arts experiences, such as learning to play keyboards, has gotten significant attention in recent years. Music is heard and a link is made, beautiful colors and shapes surround a child and connections are forged, a baby is rocked or cuddled and another circuit is wired. The key is not simple exposure. A pattern of repeated stimuli sculpts the brain. Arts-based experiences

cover a vast range, including daily poetry sharing, reading aloud, singing, storytelling, and dramatic conversations that stimulate growth in the auditory cortex. The lesson for us is that "every musical [arts] experience that we offer our students affects their brains, bodies and feelings. In short, it changes their minds permanently"(Reimer, 2004, p. 25).

We learn the things in which we engage the most. Students seek experiences connected to interests, and the arts are inherently interesting. Engaged students enjoy the arts and repeat and extend these activities by choice. This intensity of effort and concentrated focus changes the brain (Zull, 2005).

It is now clear that children at younger ages than previously thought are capable of complex deductive thinking and empathy (Lindsey, 1998–99; Wingert & Brant, 2005). Babies are being taught to use sign language long before they use words. The arts expand communication in the same way. Arts integration embraces the concept that the limits of language are not the limits of thinking (Eisner, 2002a). Arts integration diversifies and intensifies children's experiences. Music, art, movement, and drama become valued avenues to make meaning, and they give opportunities to use innate capacities to empathize. The hope is if they use it, they won't lose it during synapse pruning.

Emotion. Brain changes are most extensive and powerful when emotion is part of learning. The chemicals of emotion, such as adrenalin, serotonin, and dopamine modify synapses. Modification of synapses is the very root of learning. Connections may not occur at all if the emotion chemicals and structures in the brain are not engaged (Zull, 2005).

Implications.

Emotion drives attention, and attention drives learning. (Robert Sylwester)

The arts are arguably the most important tool a teacher has to engage the emotions. Artists create things to engage others emotionally so art pieces are compelling instructional materials. Creating art is emotionally engaging as well. "The arts, then, change the brain of both the creator, and the consumer" (Zull, 2005). Arts-based lessons employ emotions to release memory proteins. Students are intentionally engaged in experiences that call for feelings to be felt and expressed.

The importance of the arts in school is strongly associated with motivation and interest. Arts-based instruction gives students freedom and ownership that are "part and parcel of the neurochemistry of the arts" (Zull, 2005). Creating meaning through the arts employs diverse media and alternative sign systems to expand ways to express feelings and ideas. Creativity is based on the decisions made by the creator, which causes the brain's reward system to kick in

(Zull, 2005). Chemicals, such as dopamine, are released in the region of cortex used to create ideas, problem solve and make decisions, and plan actions. Students feel satisfaction and pride when they create original ideas and objects.

Play taps into brain chemicals involved in pleasure: Dopamine causes elation and excitement, and endorphin and norepinephrine heighten attention (Brownlee, 1997). Arts integration includes dramatic play, movement exploration, and experimentation with art materials. These all have the potential to alter brain chemistry by creating a feeling of optimism and well-being.

Shared Networks.   According to Posner and Rothbart (2005), "MRI studies have revealed common (neural) networks underlying many important tasks, such as reading and number skills" (p. 99).

Implications.   Accumulated studies in neuroscience in the past decade link music and cognitive development (Rauscher & Shaw, 1997). Significant relationships between math achievement and music performance in elementary students have also been found (Deasy, 2002). Anaylsis of music at a basic level reveals obvious connections to counting and proportions (Catterall, 1999). One theory emerging from these brain image studies is that brain networks are shared by tasks like music and math (Scripp, 2003). To some, close associations between music and math seem almost impossible to understand except with neurological explanations. There seem to be "underlying deep principles and rich learning processes that can be made explicit" through arts integration (Scripp, 2003, p. 130). This suggests two-way transfer potential between the arts and other areas.

Continued Growth.   By adulthood the number of neurons in the brain reaches 100 trillion (Hall, 2005). The brain continues to grow much longer than previously thought—at least into the second decade of life (Bruer, 1999; Hansen & Monk, 2002).

New Brain Research

In 2005 Dana Foundation launched a $2 million study to identify neural relationships between the arts and cognition. The goal is to "identify brain regions that, if activated by arts training, could be used in other tasks" (Gazzaniga, 2005, p. 7). The cognitive skills that will be examined include attention, memory, transfer between hemispheres, language and literacy/reading, social interaction, and math ability. Brain imaging technology makes it possible to discern whether "drama students have acquired a particular skill, what the brain-based mechanism underlying the skill is, and how well it generalizes to different domains" (p. 7).

A second area of inquiry is sensitive periods during which the arts, like language, may be learned most easily.

Researchers will investigate sensitive periods in dance, drama, painting, and music (p. 8). The results will provide the first "vigorous scientific attempt to create a comprehensive picture of the role of education in arts in changing the brain" (p. 9). Follow the progress and get the results in a couple of years at the foundation's website (*www.dana.org*).

Until such findings are available, teachers need to move forward. Children are growing up. The moral imperative is to act on research at hand and accumulated wisdom from educators involved in long-term arts integration.

Arts Integration and Learning Theories

Theories are more than hunches. They are sets of well-founded assumptions that explain phenomena. The "well-founded" part means conclusions are drawn from a wide range of research, and not just experimental designs. Research is an investigative process to make discoveries. The theories in this chapter were mostly constructed from systematic observations of children and adults. They describe patterns observed by now famous researchers like Jean Piaget and Howard Gardner. Each theory is followed by implications for using the theory for arts integration.

Multiple Intelligences (MI) Theory

Harvard researcher Howard Gardner has become an educational celebrity because of his multiple intelligences theory (1983, 1993). Decades of work with normal and gifted children, as well as brain-injured adults, led him to reject a narrow concept of intelligence as a single general capacity (Armstrong, 2000; Blythe & Gardner, 1990). Gardner pluralized intelligence and reconceptualized it to include multiple capacities humans use to solve problems and create products that are valued in cultural settings.

Multiple intelligences theory presents the arts as distinct modes of thinking that fall under the umbrella of intelligence. Originally Gardner described seven "ways of knowing," but an eighth intelligence, naturalistic, was added later, and there is a list of more possibilities (Ready Reference 2.1). Four of the eight intelligences are arts domains: verbal (literary arts), visual/spatial (visual art), musical, and body/kinesthetic (dance/drama). The other four are linked. Logical, interpersonal, and intrapersonal intelligences are used during creative problem solving in the arts, including emphasis on self-reflection and critiquing. The arts also involve high-level cooperative work with others (e.g., choirs, plays).

Gardner explains that intelligences seldom operate "in isolation" (Blythe & Gardner, 1990, p. 33) and believes that

Ready Reference 2.1 Gardner's Eight Intelligences

Verbal: "Word lovers" (T. S. Eliot,* Paul Lawrence Dunbar) GOOD AT and LIKE TO: See and hear words, talk and discuss, tell stories, read and write (poetry, literature), memorize (names, facts), use or appreciate humor, use word play, and do word puzzles.

Visual: "Imagers" (Mary Cassatt, Pablo Picasso*) GOOD AT and LIKE TO: Think in pictures and see spatial relationships, draw, build, design and create, daydream and imagine, look at pictures, watch movies, read maps and charts, and do mazes and puzzles.

Musical: "Music lovers" (Igor Stravinsky,* Louis Armstrong) GOOD AT and LIKE TO: Sing, hum, and listen to music, play instruments, respond to music (tap rhythms), compose, pick up sounds, remember melodies, and notice pitches and rhythms.

Interpersonal: "People–people" (Muhatma Gandhi,* Mother Teresa) GOOD AT and LIKE TO: Have lots of friends, join groups, talk out or mediate and resolve conflicts, empathize and understand, share, compare, relate, cooperate, interview others, and lead and organize.

Intrapersonal: "Loners" (Sigmund Freud,* James Baldwin) GOOD AT and LIKE TO: Reflect on feelings, intentions, dreams, and goals; work alone; have own space; self-pace work; pursue own interests; and do original thinking.

Logical: "Reasoners" (Albert Einstein,* Marie Curie) GOOD AT and LIKE TO: Experiment, ask questions, problem solve, figure out how things work, explore abstract relationships, discover patterns, classify, reason and use logic (inductive and deductive), do math, and play logic games.

Kinesthetic: "Movers" (Martha Graham,* Alvin Ailey) GOOD AT and LIKE TO: Dance and use body to communicate; touch and use hands, face, gestures; do hands-on learning; prefer kinesthetic–tactile activities, sports, and drama.

Naturalistic: "Nature lovers" (Jacques Cousteau, Jane Goodall) GOOD AT and LIKE TO: Have and raise pets, visit zoos and parks, study animals and nature, garden, be out of doors.

*Exemplars in *Creating Minds* (Gardner, 1993) who expressed extreme "intelligence" in at least one area, but used all intelligences. None were very successful in school settings.

---

everyone has capacities in all eight areas. If this is so, education should develop all modes of understanding and expression. He implies that this broadened focus increases student performance. Arts-based intelligences are a large chunk of developing breadth in students' ways of knowing. Gardner argues, further, that everyone has strengths in particular intelligences, and those strengths are instructional guideposts. Unfortunately, American education has historically privileged those with verbal and logical intelligences. Students with proclivities in the other domains have been misunderstood and neglected. Gardner thinks it is educational malpractice to continue to serve education in the same way to all students. He urges teachers to draw on stronger intelligences as vehicles to reach less dominant areas.

For example, musically inclined students learn fractions by using eighth, quarter, and whole notes as examples. By listening and comparing varying note values, they grasp the concept of fractions—sometimes for the first time. Musically smart students are invited to compose melodies or rhythms to express understanding and use the mnemonic power of music to boost memory. For example, a group of students stuck on prepositions wrote "preposition lyrics" set to "Yankee Doodle." (The first line is "Out, from, under, in between, over, of, into, through.") Another class used the tune to "Turkey in the Straw" to summarize bodily processes: "Oh, the bile from the liver it emulsifies the fats (3X), and it does it in the small intestine." Music adds new viewpoint, too. For example, students studying real people or literary characters can do music "imaging" to force deeper understanding (e.g., thinking of melodies the spider Charlotte in *Charlotte's Web* might have hummed or sung as she spun her web).

MI Theory into Practice. Gardner thinks deep understanding only happens when ideas and skills are transformed from one domain to another. The arts offer diverse means of transformation. Thinking and learning is made visible, and the arts become important assessment pieces that both delight and inform classroom audiences and participants. Arts-based schools across America now use MI theory. Here are a dozen example strategies.

1. *Informal intelligences assessment.* Teachers profile students' strengths and preferences to differentiate instruction and guide students in making choices. The information in Ready Reference 2.1 can be used to construct a self-assessment checklist. An informal assessment can also be done using the following MI-based questions. Ask students to step (or dance) forward from a circle or line to respond. Check off students on an MI list. Ask, "How many of you like to…"

- Draw? Make mental pictures? Enjoy TV or movies, look at pictures, make art? (visual)
- Read? Write? Listen to stories? (verbal/word smart)
- Play sports? Dance? Make things with your hands? (body/ kinesthetic)
- Do math or science experiments? (logical/math)
- Listen to music, sing, or play an instrument? (musical)
- Be with groups of people? (interpersonal/people–person)
- Work alone? Think about your own ideas and dreams? (intrapersonal)
- Be outside? Be around animals and nature? (naturalistic)

2. *MI planning.* Teachers can code lesson plans to track intelligences used to provide a balance of learning activities. Use a spreadsheet to graph the days of the week along one axis and the eight intelligences along the other. Map out the music, art, dance or movement, drama, and literature (linguistic intelligence) addressed each day to make sure no area is neglected. Use the ideas in the following arts chapters to present academic content in alternative ways and to give arts response options to students. Teachers also design centers or stations that offer students eight ways to transform ideas and "show they know."

3. *Eight-minute energizer.* (Armstrong, 1994). This is a class routine. Teachers spend a minute on each intelligence:

- Visual: Make pictures in your head (e.g., places you'd like to visit, colors and shapes that are happy). Take students on a fantasy journey by describing an imaginary trip to a place. Relate this to a unit under study (e.g., planets).
- Verbal: Write down all the words you can think of (e.g., that start with a letter or rhyme—pick any category). Make up quick poems or riddles. Write a class motto or chant.
- Musical: Hum or sing together. Play a piece of music and move to it. Choose a song for a Class Anthem and sing it regularly. *Example:* "High Hopes," "When You Wish Upon a Star."
- Intrapersonal: Think about a goal. What would you like to do or be, and how could you do it? How could you be a better person or student? Drop it in the Tomorrow Box.
- Interpersonal: Get a partner and give each other honest compliments or share about an interest.
- Logical: Do quick math. *Example:* add, subtract, or multiply in your head. Do logic puzzles like Plexers or Mindbogglers. Do Quick Categories (e.g., table, chair, sofa are _____.
- Kinesthetic: Do physical warm-ups (see Drama and Dance Seed Strategies in Chapters 8 and 10). *Examples:* toe touches, waist stretches, sky reaches, jumping jacks.

- Naturalistic: Use a magnifying glass to study a plant or animal for 30 seconds and then share all the things you noticed. Look out the window at nature and share observations.

4. *Assessment criteria.* Students need to have clear criteria for quality work before they begin work. This permits students to (1) explore mutiple ways to meet the criteria and (2) self-examine or critique work against the criteria. Optimally, the teacher and students codevelop criteria and apply them to projects, performances, exhibits, portfolios, and written materials. The key is to decide what goals or competencies are to be achieved through a learning event, not just to describe what students will experience. It is unfair to grade work unless students know, in advance, the concepts and skills that the work should show. This emphasis on clear criteria liberates creative thinking. It gives focus to the problem-solving process and prepares students to deal with the limitations of time, materials, money, and the people you work with, all of which are part of any real-life workplace.

5. *Inform parents.* Invite parents to evaluate their intelligences. Do a short MI overview for a PTO meeting and include short MI ideas in class newsletters. Share websites such as *http://newhorizons.org/strategies/front_strategies.html.*

6. *Explicit teaching and goal setting.* Plan a unit or series of lessons on multiple intelligences so students expand their concept of "knowing." Create a goal-setting form as each intelligence is studied. Include a sentence description for each intelligence (Ellison, 1992). Ask students to think of how to achieve their goals in different ways. Encourage the use of all intelligences by taking time each week to discuss what they tried. (Sources for MI posters: Illinois Renewal Institute, 800-348-4474; or Zephyr Press, 3316 N. Chapel Ave., Box 6606-A, Tucson, AZ 85728-6006).

7. *MI people resources.* Match the intelligences with authors, artists, athletes, or fictional characters (e.g., Charlotte in *Charlotte's Web* is verbal and kinesthetic) or use Gardner's eight exemplars from *Creating Minds* (1993) to study different intelligences. Students can also find peer examples using a Bingo game format. Make cards with different intelligence characteristics in each box. Students circulate and find names of peers that fit in each. A "Career Day" can be organized around invited guests from each of the eight intelligences to round out the search for diversity.

8. *Apprenticeships.* Invite local artists, musicians, dancers, and actors to mentor students who have propensities in these intelligences. A combination of shadowing a mentor, discussing, and being coached on projects can profoundly influence learning.

9. *Choice and interest.* Learners are more motivated when they are given choices and work is connected to interests. Students also need to have the choice, at times, to work alone. Invite students to think of alternate ways to express understanding using different intelligences. Offer options other than traditional reports to synthesize content (e.g., write stories, poems, songs; construct games; make charts, drawings, sculptures, tableau; or create dances).

10. *Co-planning.* If teachers share their MI profiles with one another, they can intentionally draw on one another's strengths as they plan. Collaborative planning with arts specialists is an important way to discover alternatives to instructional goals.

11. *Field-based learning.* Class trips to places that focus on a particular intelligence can be powerful (e.g., symphony for music, art museum for art, library for verbal, dance concert for body). Discuss the MI focus of each.

12. *MI schools.* Visits to schools using MI theory are the best way to understand how the arts are integral to implementing this theory. Two schools that call themselves MI schools are the Key School in Indianapolis and Arts PROPEL schools in Pittsburgh. Check the School Registry in the Appendix for other contacts or visit these websites: *www.greatschools.net* or *http://schoolmatch.com.*

Erikson's Stage Theory

Erik Erikson was a brilliant psychologist who spent his early years studying art. At an invitation from Sigmund Freud to study psychoanalysis, he changed his direction and in 1950 published *Childhood and Society*, a classic book about the influence of culture on child development. He concluded that all cultures place common demands on individuals, and each person develops a sense of self and how to relate to others in response to crises. Erikson organized these crises into eight stages.

The initial struggle is for the child to learn to trust and become hopeful. During the toddler period, the child must resolve the conflict between autonomy versus shame and doubt. If autonomy and independence are developed, the child will have a sense of will. During the preschool years, the child struggles with initiative versus guilt and develops a strong sense of purpose—if supported in attempts to take initiative. When a child starts school, she is usually struggling with the conflicts between industry and inferiority. If this crisis is successfully resolved, there is a growing sense of competence. During the adolescent years, the crisis is between self-identify and role confusion, with successful resolution leading to "fidelity"—a kind of being true to yourself. The final crises are beyond the scope of this book but involve intimacy versus isolation (young adults) to gain love relationships, generativity versus rejectivity (adults) to learn caring; and integrity versus despair (mature adults) to gain wisdom (Erikson, 1950).

Erikson's Stages and the Arts. Arts integration can contribute to a sense of industry and competence (the two major crises for primary and intermediate children).

Early childhood (ages 2–6). The crisis of initiative versus guilt is successfully confronted by building on the independence (autonomy) developed in the previous stage. Arts integration encourages risk taking within an encouraging environment. The arts offer opportunities for children to actively pursue intrinsically rewarding activities that involve use of imagination. Making and acting on choices develops as students engage in dramatic play. Drama and dance give children vehicles to explore grown-up roles and body movement without worrying about making mistakes. Arts experiences teach children that not every activity in school has to yield a "correct" answer and that being different shouldn't make you feel ashamed or guilty.

Elementary. The arts enable students to discover pleasure and pride that result from working hard and being productive. These are critical experiences in resolving the crisis of industry versus inferiority. The arts allow students to create unique products through which they can feel they are conquering materials and skills. Teachers promote a sense of industry through the arts by giving students choices about how to show thoughts and feelings with original writing or arts making during social studies and science units. Group work in drama, dance, music, and art gives opportunities to develop competence in peer interactions. Without these kinds of experiences, children can develop feelings of inferiority.

Of particular importance is giving students adequate think time so that more try to answer questions and feel more confident about speaking up. Teachers also need to use techniques that encourage students to persist when initial responses are incomplete or inaccurate. Dignifying incorrect answers shows respect for sincere efforts. For example, if a student says, "Abraham Lincoln freed the slaves" when asked, "What do you know about the first president?" a teacher might say, "Lincoln was an important president, but not the first." This is an honest response and allows the student to save face.

In a 35-year study of 450 males, a correlation was found between willingness to work hard in childhood and later success in personal relationships, life adjustment, and income (Valliant & Valliant, 1981). Arts integration focuses on engendering the desire to do hard work by using the intrinsic motivational properties of the arts. Artistic work is imbued with the promise of personal transformation.

Piaget's Stages of Cognitive Development

Jean Piaget, a Swiss biologist and epistemologist, is famous for a four-stage theory based on observing children. He reasoned that the key stimulus for development was interaction with the environment. Piaget thought that, along with genetically programmed biological changes, touching, seeing,

Ready Reference 2.2   Piaget's Stages of Development

Sensorimotor Thinking: Birth to 2 Years

- Explores using senses. Relies on nonverbal communication. Reaches, puts objects in mouth.
- Realizes objects exist when not seen. Evidence: A toy taken away isn't missed because it isn't seen, but once a child gains "object permanence," she remembers the toy and cries to get it back.
- Gains control of body actions. Evidence: Sees something and tries to get it by crying and crawling.

Preoperational: 2 to 7 Years

- Starts to think with images and symbols. Evidence: Uses symbols for objects and people. Likes fantasy, imaginative play, and pretend.
- Rapid language and concept growth. Evidence: 2,000-word vocabulary by age 4 is common.
- Trouble reversing actions. Can't understand how objects can change shape but still be the same object. Evidence: Doesn't think a tall glass of water poured into a short fat glass is the same amount.
- Difficulty seeing other points of view because of egocentrism (self-centered). Evidence: Happily talks to self. Thinks everyone thinks, feels, and sees as they do.

Concrete Operations (Hands-on Thinking): 7 to 11 Years

- Basic concepts of objects, numbers, time, space, and cause-effect links develop.
- Reversibility (two-way thinking) develops. Can group by different categories. Understands a group can be a subset. Example: Knows animals and plants are both "living things."
- Needs concrete objects to draw conclusions. Basic logic develops but tied to physical reality. Can't do hypothetical problem solving.

Formal Operations (Abstract Reasoning): 11 to 15 Years

- Makes logical predictions, thinks hypothetically, and can do metacognition (self-questions; thinks about own thinking).
- Understands sarcasm, puns, argumentation, and abstract thinking. Generates diverse solutions for problems and can evaluate alternatives based on many criteria (e.g., moral, legal, economic). Can form and test hypotheses and use scientific method.

Sources: Ginsberg & Opper, 1969; Piaget, 1950, 1952, 1954.

---

hearing, tasting, smelling, moving, and interacting with people cause children to make discoveries that alter their worldview. In other words, children develop intellectually by experimenting. What adults see as play is serious work. Piaget believed children mentally organize reality into psychological structures used to understand. He called these cognitive structures *schema.* A person either *assimilates* new information into schema or creates new or modifies old cognitive structures through the process of *accommodation*—thinking is adjusted based on new information. For example, a child might not recognize a beanbag chair as a chair and call it a "ball" because he is trying to understand using old schema. Once the child is shown how to sit in the chair, this new information is assimilated. Accommodation occurs if new information is added about the category of "furniture." Most learning involves both assimilation and accommodation.

Piaget thought these stages were natural and sequential, building on one another in a progression toward more complex thinking (Ready Reference 2.2). Indeed there is a genetic predisposition toward increasingly complex cognitive development that involves continually trying to achieve equilibrium when something is not understandable. We are

innately programmed to want to make sense. Piaget cautioned, however, against trying to hurry development. He believed it took too long to teach something to a child who was not ready. His flexible age guidelines show a developmental progression and suggest learning expectations be appropriate to development (Piaget, 1980).

Piaget believed a child's thinking is consistent with his or her stage across situations, but more recent research shows that children show characteristics of one stage in certain situations and can think at a higher or lower stage in other situations. For example, Gelman (1979) reported incidences of 4-year-olds speaking in simpler sentences when they talked to 2-year-olds, indicating they considered the needs of the younger child. This behavior was thought by Piaget to not develop until around age 7. More recently, studies of baby brains show that young children are much more intellectually sophisticated than their communication capabilities can show. Wingert and Brant (2005) report research that babies have "startling powers of deduction and ability to notice details and patterns." Infants can discern small differences, especially in faces, that adults and older children no longer notice. Until 3 months, babies can recognize a scrambled photograph of mom just as quickly as a normal photo—a kind of "Picasso think" (Wingert & Brant, 2005).

Piaget and Arts Integration.

Piaget's theory supports arts integration on many fronts. The following are teaching implications followed by connections to the arts.

Preoperational and concrete operational learners need...

1. Concrete experiences. Arts integration increases the hands-on options and expands purposes and methods for common teaching adjuncts. Drama and dance are literally hands on. Both use the whole body to transform concepts. For example, a tableau or frozen body picture can be used to depict understanding of critical moments in a plot or in science to show relationships among parts of a cell. Music provides participatory experiences when students listen and respond to, sing, and create songs.

2. Short explanations with application. The arts focus on "doing" and problem solving, so they are natural for this implication. A 5-minute mini-lesson on pantomime can give enough options to use the face, body, and in-place movements to "become" a character. Students can then evoke real-life or fictional characters and, in pairs, become "frozen statues" to convey understanding. Depth of understanding is increased when students are asked to discuss observations about themselves and others, which boosts application of learning.

3. Engagement first. Artists are always seeking strategies to jump-start creative thinking. It is not surprising that there are dozens of arts warm-ups. Each of the Seed Strategy chapters has a section on energizers. The idea is to gradually involve students so they feel successful. Engagement strategies hook students so they willingly participate in longer, more complex work. Strategies include open questions like "What do you think of when I say *dance*?" and activities that involve solving problems using imagination, intellect, voice and body, and diverse art materials. Students should be engaged before assemblies and arts performance, too, using previews to prepare them for what is to be experienced. By giving "listen fors" (a character's line or song), students are more likely to stay actively engaged in the expectation of finding connections.

4. Field trips and guests. Museums, concerts, and plays are all examples of rich experiences that extend learning. Guest artists, storytellers, and musicians give students direct experiences.

5. Coaching. Children need help thinking through problems. The arts have long used the concept of coaching to support problem solving. There is a tradition and a wealth of readily available strategies. Coaching is discussed in all the arts chapters but, for now, suffice it to say that it involves questioning, prompting, and encouraging students before and during work. Descriptive feedback is used more than praise.

6. Life-centered curriculum. A study of 91 showed the arts significantly contribute to developing kind of flexible and adaptable knowledge businesses seek today's workers (Longley, 1999). Real-life success comes from hard work, self-control and discipline, cooperation, problem solving, flexibility, humor, responsibility, motivation, productivity, risk taking, and passion. These are all developed through the arts and arts-based learning focuses on explicitly teaching how to solve problems in a creative manner. Ready Reference 2.5, presented later in the chapter, summarizes this essential process.

7. Exploration and cognitive variety. Literature, art, drama, dance, and music are distinct ways of thinking, with special languages and symbol systems. Each permits different ways of expressing and receiving ideas and feelings. The arts add ways to explore. Just teaching basic arts concepts expands abilities to think in new categories. For example, once students know that dance includes locomotor and nonlocomotor movements, they can brainstorm some of each and experiment with a range of movement. In the area of language arts, verbs and adverbs might then be moved in place and from point to point. The verb *lean* can be shown with different body parts, in place, and in motion across space. Adverbs can be added for interest and to elaborate meaning. So, we can lean quickly, slowly, casually, lazily, rigidly, and hungrily.

8. Higher-order thinking. Piaget believed there is a natural inclination for higher-order thinking to develop, but it depends on experiences. Complex thinking is a major goal of education, but it is difficult to teach. The arts provide a rich context for cognitive development because they thrive on changing points of view and mental experimentation. Mistakes are not seen as failures so children feel safe using paint or clay to think through problems. Elementary children may not have the verbal language to explain perspective, but art materials allow them to edge into this type of thinking.

Maslow's Hierarchy of Needs

In the 1970s, Abraham Maslow proposed a theory of motivation that has become widely used in psychology, business, and education. The theory gives teachers a tool for understanding why children do what they do—or don't do. Maslow's research caused him to conclude that people were motivated by specific needs. He categorized these needs and organized them into a hierarchy, with the basic needs for surviving, like food, clothes, and a place to live, on the bottom (Ready Reference 2.3). He posited that once lower-level survival needs and safety needs were met, people moved up the ladder. He thought the three top levels, including the need for beauty, represented needs that were never filled, so people continued to always seek more in these areas, in contrast to low-level needs.

2.3 Maslow's Hierarchy of Needs

...illment
...or beauty and order
Kno...   ...intellectual needs
Approval and recognition from others
Belonging, love, acceptance by others
Physical and psychological safety

Lowest level: Survival needs, including food, clothes, water, shelter

---

Source: Maslow (1970).

Maslow and Arts Integration. Maslow's theory of needs-based motivation summarized in Ready Reference 2.3 suggests that children who are hungry, thirsty, too hot, afraid, or worried will see little purpose in aesthetically focused arts activities. Arts integration will not feed and clothe children, but the arts are communication vehicles that can give them significant ways to release fears and concerns. In arts integrated schools, the psychological safety of children is an important focus. Risk taking is squelched in threatening environments, and creativity withers without risk taking. Comfort and safety needs (second level) are routinely met using strategies that derive from an arts-based philosophy—teaching how mistakes are normal and instructive, giving second chances after genuine effort, and offering choices of types of art materials and alternative writing forms. Humor and creative thinking are parallel in nature and both are problem based so it isn't surprising that a lot of laughing goes on when the arts are integrated. Humor is a tension reliever and can be used intentionally to relax students. Riddles can activate problem solving and cause children to release stress. Teachers who poke fun at their own mistakes show students how to deal with embarrassing moments and bond learners together in laughter.

American culture places high value on diverse thinking. The popularity of blogging is a recent manifestation of this value. The human need for group approval, however, is very powerful (third level). It is common at the start of arts integration for students to doubt that they have unique and different ideas. They may feel compelled to copy or imitate peers. Some students are actually afraid of being different and worry about being laughed at and ostracized. Teachers need to be sensitive to belonging needs of students. Teachers can share stories about artists who have taken risks by being different (e.g., cubism was thought ridiculous by Picasso's contemporaries) and celebrate novel responses with clear descriptive feedback: "Joe painted his sky with orange and red in it." The need for group approval can also be met by forming learning circles to collaborate on projects, such as writing songs and poems. Dance and drama naturally demand group work and can fulfill belonging needs while en-

couraging experimentation with different ways of thinking in a pretend context.

Children are not easily pigeonholed and may have needs operating simultaneously at several of Maslow's levels. Stories about people who deny themselves survival and safety needs to pursue artistic works, aesthetic needs, and self-fulfillment can help students think about the motivational power of higher-order needs. For example, students might find out why Monet and other Impressionists made paintings others thought looked unfinished (see *Lives of the Musicians,* 1993, by Kathleen Krull).

Maslow helps us understand that while we are motivated to get some things, many activities are self-motivating. Teachers who use arts integration find they can design a classroom around arts experiences that require no extrinsic rewards (food, stickers). Work in the arts is intrinsically motivating. Just being in a beautiful room or listening to music can be emotionally and cognitively satisfying. With the help of students, teachers can fill the classroom with plants, student artwork, background music, and even potpourri. Another powerful intrinsic motivator is interest, which can be developed through regular times to work on interest-based projects. Choice also satisfies the basic need for control over one's circumstances. Achievement needs can be addressed by allowing time and other opportunities to pursue independent projects involving the arts. For example, students might study a person or topic in the arts that connects to a unit. Teachers can encourage being curious and wondering with a "Wonder Box" to drop questions and topics that students would like to learn about or information they would like to share. Facts and idiosyncrasies about artists or artworks can cause otherwise apathetic students to become excited about learning.

Vygotsky's Social Development

Russian psychologist Lev Vygotsky (1978, 1986) is another researcher who has given educators a theory that supports arts integration and from which teaching strategies have been derived. Unlike Piaget, Vygotsky thought teachers should intervene in children's learning. He called this intervention *scaffolding*. The idea is to use techniques to bridge the gap between where a child is functioning and a stage just out of reach, but attainable. He called this developmental position the *zone of proximal development* (ZPD) and demonstrated how students can often solve problems with help (cues, suggestions, steps, encouragement) when they cannot do so independently.

Vygotsky and Arts Integration. Using ZPD theory begins with observing students. Teachers must determine when students can proceed independently, when they can succeed with some assistance, and when the problem or activity is not appropriate at all. Determining this match involves instructional creative problem solving to find appropriate scaffolds. Vygotsky believed social interactions with others was a key scaffold for cognition. Problem solving during drama and dance almost always is done in groups, and learners can both view and do art in pairs, trios, quads, or whole groups, like murals. By listening to each other tell what they see in a piece of art or hear in a piece of music, everyone has the chance to get another perspective and make new connections (peer scaffolding). An example of peer scaffolding using literature is "Junior Great Books" literature discussions that start with an open question. The questioner initiates the discussion with one question for which there are many answers. For example, "Why did Jack go up the beanstalk the third time when he already had all the money he would ever want?" While there are clues in the story, there is not one answer, so students must interpret text clues. This co-construction of meaning leaves everyone, including the teacher, with ideas beyond individual realms of meaning.

Child Development and the Arts

Maslow, Piaget, Vygotsky, and others each give us a piece of the whole picture of child development. Teachers draw on these and other theories to create arts-based lessons. Arnheim (1989) urges teachers not to "foist upon the learner technical tricks that go beyond his or her stage of conception." He strongly advises that art knowledge "naturally emerge from the demands of the task" with an emphasis on learners "discovering" rather than being told or shown what to do (p. 42). Social learning theorists advise educators to keep in mind that students are usually most successful applying or practicing new learning in a group situation, before going it alone. Telling students to "write a song" or "make a play" or "make up a dance" is overwhelming—even many teachers would need scaffolding through the creative problem-solving process for each of these tasks.

Choosing and creating developmentally appropriate experiences for students is like a doctor writing a prescription for a patient. Teachers need information about developmental patterns as guideposts to think about specific children and adapt daily instruction. The Appendix includes a developmental chart to help teachers think about what's appropriate for primary, intermediate, and middle school students. Classroom teachers should also consult with school arts specialists about appropriate materials, tools, and processes for specific students.

Creativity and Creative Problem Solving (CPS)

Vicious terrorist attacks, horrific genocides, brutal land mines, terrible diseases like AIDS and Ebola—the kinds and quantities of 21st-century problems are overwhelming. What's more, most are new, at least in their degree. New problems call for new solutions. It is not possible to Google any one of these plagues and get *the* answer. Solutions have to be created, mostly by the next generation—today's children.

It is common to associate creative thinking with artists. The arts invite us to explore the unusual and create something different, even if it's just a new interpretation of a movie. But creative thinking is also a vital daily survival skill set. Those who strive to stretch a personal budget or create new ways to construct in earthquake regions use innate abilities to think creatively. Memorizing facts and rote skill application, too often the focus of formal education, aren't enough for these tasks.

Predispositions

Fortunately, children come to school predisposed to problem solve creatively, particularly using the arts. Even before birth, fetuses respond to musical rhythms, pitches, and volumes. Young children are compelled to pretend, make up songs, experiment with art tools, and explore ways to move their bodies. When we tap this natural excitement, we build the intrinsic motivation to do difficult higher-order thinking. Arts integration is founded on the premise that the arts set the stage for learning. At the center of thinking through the arts is creative problem solving. In other words, creativity is the source of the arts. It is also the source of discoveries in science, math, and history and has given us magnificent books and poems as well.

The need to encourage and teach creativity has become a pressing societal issue. Diverse theories and research give us information about the sources of creativity, its nature, and its development. It seems that Plato's concept of a muse that can spark creative work can actually be summoned. Educators now have access to the same strategies used in think tanks around the world. We no longer need to wait for the muse's visit, and we know enough to jettison simplistic notions

Learning from a social studies unit synthesized into an exhibit at Hilton Head Creative Arts.

about using low-level rewards to step up active engagement in learning. In this section, creativity and creative problem solving are discussed with regards to their central role in re-structuring schooling using an integrated arts approach.

Problem Based

What is known is that creative thinking has its origins in problems. Using poetry as an example, Robert Frost explained, "A poem . . . begins as a lump in the throat, a sense of wrong, a homesickness, a lovesickness. It finds the thought, and the thought finds the words." The personal struggle to make sense—perhaps the most ancient human problem—has honed human practices like noticing patterns. It is clear creativity emerges from connecting careful observations and details. Summoning visualization capabilities is another key. These mental gifts can be developed and by teaching them we do more than "disturb the universe." We re-create it through our students.

What Is Creativity?

The most important things in life are hard to define: love, happiness, art. Creativity is no exception. I especially like Perkins's (1987–88) definition that implies everyday people have what it takes. He believes creativity is simply "using ordinary resources of the mind in extraordinary ways" (p. 38). To use one's experiences, thinking skills, and knowledge in novel and appropriate ways to produce something somewhat new seems doable. Context is crucial. Societies value original products needed by specific groups. What is deemed creative

in one culture or time period is not in another. For example, re-stickable mini notes probably wouldn't have been hot among 12th-century European peasants. Modern conveniences, like the paper clip, are no longer considered creative, but they must have delighted first users.

Creativity Theories.   Researchers have tried to make sense out of the elusive concept of creativity using four angles.

1. *Observing creative people, especially adults.*   This has been the focus of researchers such as MacKinnon (1978), Torrance (1962, 1973), and Tardif and Sternberg (1988).

2. *Studying the stages or process.*   Study of the development of creativity and the problem-solving process goes back to Plato. He thought creativity was a divinely inspired, mystical process manifested in bursts of insight. Aristotle explained creativity with natural laws used to understand any thinking. His work was later used by many theorists including Perkins, Guilford, and Weisberg. Other notable theorists using the stages and process approach are Wallace (1926), Csikszentmihalyi (1990), Maslow, and Vygotsky.

3. *Identifying influences.*   B. F. Skinner concluded creativity was a function of behavioral influences: It occurs naturally and, if reinforced, is repeated.

4. *Developing an interactive theory.*   Creativity is viewed as an interaction among cognitive processes (e.g., divergent thinking), functioning in particular domains (e.g., math or science), and environment (culture and time period). Sternberg, Gardner, Csikszentmihalyi, and Amabile have all proposed variations on this theory.

Creativity Profile.

Creative children look twice, listen for smells, dig deeper, build dream castles, get from behind locked doors, have a ball, plug in the sun, get into and out of deep water, sing in their own key. (Paul Torrance, 1973)

Creative characteristics often emerge in childhood (Csik-szentmihalyi, 1990; Dacey, 1989; Gardner, 1993; Getzels & Jackson, 1962; Tardif & Sternberg, 1988). Attributes associated with creativity are listed in Ready Reference 2.4. This list helps crystalize the dimensions of creativity students possess. Use it to observe students, to set goals and to plan an environment that encourages creative thinking. No two learners have the same profile and there is no "right" profile, but we all possess degrees of most of the characteristics. Some traits are even undesirable under certain

Ready Reference 2.4 Creativity Profile

Rate yourself on these creative charactertistics. Use 1=not evident to 5=very evident. Follow with goal setting.

Personality Characteristics

1. Curious and questioning
2. Likes to explore; seeks adventure
3. Spontaneous, impulsive, uninhibited
4. Emotionally secure
5. Risk taker, but not reckless; courageous
6. Nonconforming; opinions of others not a priority
7. Confident in own worth and work
8. Loses track of time; dislikes deadlines
9. Strong sense of destiny
10. Independent; unlikely to follow the crowd
11. Likes original ideas
12. Skeptical of authority; resists "right" answers
13. Easily bored with routine
14. Heightened sense of humor
15. Critical of self
16. Not often satisfied, but not easily discouraged
17. Likes to work alone; may appear aloof; may not fit in or seek out groups
18. Motivated, hardworking, and persistent; not easily frustrated; willing to struggle and sustain effort
19. Playful, almost childlike, in sense of wonder and delight
20. Tolerant of ambiguity; doesn't need a right answer
21. Broad interests and hobbies
22. Empathetic; feels others' pain

Cognitive Characteristics

1. Approaches problems playfully; likes to experiment
2. Inclination to explore possibilities versus do critical thinking or say, "It won't work"
3. Likes open-endedness
4. Is a problem finder
5. Uses mistakes to solve problems
6. Fluent; likes to brainstorm and generate ideas
7. Flexible; shifts perspectives and categories quickly
8. Original; creates unique ideas and likes to transform
9. Elaborates; can flesh out ideas with details
10. Observant; notices details; senses are acute
11. Intelligent, but understands that intellect does not guarantee high creativity; threshold level is necessary
12. Logical; uses details and evidence to support ideas
13. Imaginative and resourceful; combines ideas in new ways with vivid detail
14. Uses hunches and guesses; intuitive
15. Seeks possibilities; likes variety, divergence, and novelty
16. Visualizes; uses metaphoric thinking to problem solve
17. Organizer; likes to create order from chaos
18. Prefers complexity and asymmetry
19. Goal and task oriented; focused
20. Sets own standards to judge

Sources: Barron, 1969; Dacey, 1989; Isaksen and Treffinger, 1985; MacKinnon, 1978; Tardif & Sternberg, 1988; Torrance, 1962.

circumstances. Teachers should especially encourage desirable behaviors for which students have tendencies. Teachers can choose to develop any of the traits in themselves as well.

Creativity in Action

An understanding of the process of CPS has emerged from the work of researchers such as Csikszentmihalyi (1990) and Wallace (1926). Here is a glimpse into the process at work.

National Public Radio Interview (August 27, 1995).
"It takes an enlightened stubbornness to produce anything," declared a man with a British accent. Trevor Baylis was talking about the fruits of his own stubbornness. It all started when he was watching a TV program on the AIDS problem in Africa. Baylis became aware of ballooning disease statis-

tics and efforts to educate the African population by radio. The part of the problem that intrigued Baylis was the inability of people to afford or obtain batteries. It cost a month's salary to buy batteries, and some people actually gave up precious rice to buy them. Baylis began to visually imagine being in Africa in a pith helmet with a monocle and glass of gin. This input triggered the image of a wind-up radio.

"It just popped into my head," he laughed.

He said it seemed so simple he was sure someone else must have already thought of it. But he investigated and his inquiries showed no one had.

"Everyone has a good original idea, but most don't come to fruition because we worry about humiliation—people laughing, or that our idea is not new," Baylis said.

He wasn't worried. He experimented with different springs and was able to make a radio that would play for 40 minutes with 20 seconds of winding. Now the Third World

Ready Reference 2.5   Creative Problem Solving (CPS) Process

I. *Before: Get Ready*
1. Set purpose: Problem is presented or found.
2. Motivate: "Can do, will do, want to do" attitude.
3. Propose solutions: Preview, predict, brainstorm.

II. *During/Drafting:* Make sense by connecting.
1. Gather data/find facts: Read, research, interview.
2. Explore and experiment: Visualize, empathize, SCAMPER (substitute, combine, adapt, modify, put to use, eliminate, reverse/rearrange)
3. Question/clarify: Metacomprehension/fix-ups
4. Focus: Zoom in to critique details. Zoom out for patterns.

5. Time out: Incubation
6. Insight: Ah ha!
7. Connect and transform: Insight (Ah-ha) to organize, summarize, and synthesize using FFOE and metaphorical thinking.

III. *After* (Responses and Solutions)
1. Evaluate: What works? (preset criteria)
2. Revise: Edit, reorganize, elaborate.
3. Publish: Make public (performance, exhibits).

Sources: Csikszentmihalyi, 1990; Dewey, 1920; Wallace, 1926.

has a cheap way to use mass communication. By the summer of 2005 wind-up radios were available worldwide.

Baylis's story illustrates the stages people go through when they do creative problem solving. These are not just chance. We can manage the processes by knowing the conditions necessary to "prime the pump" of imaginative (image-based) thinking.

The Creative Problem Solving (CPS) Process

I never do a painting as a work of art. All of them are researches. I search constantly and there is a logical sequence in all this search. Pablo Picasso, quoted in Gardner (1973)

Many great thinkers and researchers have studied how people go about solving problems creatively (Csikszentmihalyi, 1990; Dewey, 1997; Eberle, 1971; Osborne, 1963; Wallace, 1926). The goal has always been to actively construct new meanings that result in understanding and expression of ideas and feelings. The language arts (reading, writing, speaking, and listening) are important tools, but so are the arts (music, art, drama, and dance). For example, visualizing is one of the most frequently used ways people think through problems. It involves imagining visual art elements inside your head. CPS is contrasted with linear problem solving in which one answer is sought and may even be known (e.g., solving multiplication problems). During CPS divergent perspectives are actively pursued, and surprises are embraced. Uncommon tools and materials are tried. For example, visual artist Gay Torrey paints her thoughts about people and places using lace and bubble wrap. She says she

thrives on finding bizarre ways to express her ideas, including printing from a dead fish coated in tempera.

Parallel Processes. It shouldn't be surprising that a common working process is shared among fields in which creative thinking is necessary. Scientists use CPS, but call it the *scientific method.* Readers who expect to construct personal meanings use the CPS process to make sense from print. Writers routinely use prewriting, drafting, and post-writing—thinking and working processes congruent with CPS. Diverse labels are inevitable, but students need to understand the commonalities among the processes for constructing personal meaning. In this book CPS is featured to help streamline the complex way people engage higher-order thinking to solve problems.

Description. The CPS process begins with the supposition that there are many solutions to any problem. It is dysfunctional outside a context where free thinking is valued, time is flexible, and risk taking is supported. There is a general order, but the steps are recursive and flexible. People go back and forth among questioning, data gathering, experimenting, prioritizing, synthesizing, and evaluating. Readers, writers, painters, dancers, and musicians move in and out of these kinds of thinking during CPS, continually referring to the problem under investigation and redefining the problem as they proceed. Viewed simplistically, brain hemispheres collaborate to work the problem: left (conscious), right (unconscious), left–right (insight on problem), and finally left again (evaluation). CPS is a whole brain experience. Think about Mr. Baylis and your own experiences related to this description of the CPS process.

Before (Get Ready).

1. *Set purpose:* A problem is presented or found and described. There is conscious awareness that a problem exists or a desire to do problem finding—a personal decision to look for new uses, products, and the like. Problem seekers capture fleeting idea sparks through sketch journals, idea notebooks, or photographs. Musical artists record bits of sound or patterns and, like the composer in the television ad, can be inspired by the arrangement of birds on a set of telephone wires that seem to depict a musical score. In school problems are often presented to students. For example, "Figure out how to summarize the story's themes through tableau."

2. *Motivate:* A "can do, will do, want to do" attitude is needed. The perception of important goals, choice, interest, and emotion cause motion or movement toward goals.

3. *Propose solutions:* Possibilities or hypotheses are generated by previewing to get an overview (e.g., text walk-through), predicting from background, and brainstorming. (Scientist Linus Pauling said, "The best way to have a good idea is to have lots of ideas.") Judgment of ideas is withheld for later. The classic "brainstorming" rules are: Quantity first! Generate many ideas. Cluster to organize ideas (Osborne, 1963).

4. *Question:* Questions are generated. Basic ones are: "What do I know already? What do I need to know? How can I get to know?" (plan, resources, information).

During/Drafting.
Sense is created and problems solved by finding ideas and making new connections.

1. *Gather data:* As John Dewey explained "we can have facts without thinking, but we cannot have thinking without facts." Cultivation of creative thinking depends on commitment to growing a depth of knowledge in the areas where creative work is to be done (e.g., arts literacy). No one creates in a vacuum or without building on foundations laid by others. Ideas must be gathered for solving the problem by reading, listening, and observing (facts, details, and patterns). This includes any kind of research, including work on the Internet. Much of creativity is attributed to taking an observant mental stance to notice more. This feeds the engine of the brain, as does collaboration with others. Artistic thinkers are known to seek out unusual perspectives from other people and use novel sources.

2. *Explore and experiment:* This stage uses divergent thinking versus convergent thinking. The search is for many diverse possibilities. As with all higher-order cognition, creative problem solving seems messy and disorganized as problem solvers collect data and play with materials and ideas. The following are common ways to explore:

Visualize: The root of imagination is image. Visualization is creating mental images or picturing. Ein-

stein claimed that this was how he did most of his thinking that led to his greatest discoveries.

Empathize: German scholar Theodore Lipps coined the term *empathy* at the turn of the 20th century to explain what audiences had to do to understand art. Empathy is more than sympathy. It is deliberately trying to make meaning from the ideas of others. It is also more than "critical distance," because imagination is used to see and feel as others do.

Scamper: Catterall (2003) suggests that "If you haven't played with the ideas, your product probably isn't finished" (p. 166). SCAMPER (Eberle, 1971) is a set of verbs to cause mental play with ideas. They are: substitute, combine, adapt, modify, put to other use, eliminate, reverse/rearrange. SCAMPER time can be scheduled as a warm-up to use "what-if" thinking to stretch the imagination. For example, if students complain about a short recess, ask, "What if we had only recess at school?" Ask students to generate "what ifs" for 1 minute using SCAMPER.

3. *Question/clarify:* Continual self-questioning using the four Ws and H (who, what, where, why, and how) and the question "Is this making sense?" is at the heart of constructing meaning. If the answer is "no," students need independent fix-ups to redirect meaning making. For example, a student would know to reread, read aloud, read ahead, and visualize.

4. *Focus:* According to Jean Piaget (1950), "The second goal of education is to form minds which can be critical, can verify, and not accept everything they are offered." This step zooms in. Ideas are analyzed and critiqued. Details are important. Evidence is accumulated.

5. *Time out:* Creative solutions need time. The brain has to combine its assets in a way that isn't completely conscious. Incubation is an unconscious or idle period. Sleep, rest, and time away from the work allow the subconscious to take charge.

6. *Connect:* This is the insight or "ah-ha" stage. A light goes on and there is a conscious focus on newfound ways to organize and summarize to make sense. Thinking is nearly impossible without connections, especially visual ones so key to meaning making. Gestalt psychology explains the human tendency to bring together disparate pieces, to connect the dots and create a coherent whole. In essence, we seek to understand by relating the new to known ideas.

Sometimes organizational frames are used to help summarize. Examples are: Learned-Wonder-Like (LWL), Interesting, Questions, Useful (IQU), and Exciting, Puzzling, Connecting (EPC).

Another tool, FFOE, causes more connections and fleshes out ideas: (1) Fluent: Generate many possibilities, (2) Flexible: Change Point of View (POV) and organize differently, (3) *Original:* Make unique connections and don't take the first idea, and (4) *Elaborate:* Add details and examples/nonexamples.

7. *Transform:* At this stage best ideas are synthesized and ranked. This goes beyond summarizing. Questions like "What do I now know/feel? How can I best communicate it?" provoke thinking about altering the ways ideas might be represented. Artists intentionally strive for audiences to experience a cognitive and emotional reaction so they ask questions like "How can I cause them to want them to stop and say 'How did she do that?'" (Gay Torrey, visual artist). Metaphors and analogies are examples of creative connections that transform thinking. For example, a "bridge" is a metaphor for teacher. The image pulls together important relationships like supporting and transporting students.

After (Responses and Solutions).

1. *Evaluate:* Reflection on "what works" is made using preset criteria to judge (e.g., quality, time, money, values). This includes self-evaluation using checklists and rubrics.

2. *Revise:* The solution is edited, reorganized, and reworked as needed. It's like Regis saying, "Is that your FINAL answer?"

3. *Publish:* Publish means to "make public." This happens through any sharing: performances, exhibits, author/artist chair. Efforts are celebrated.

Creative Planning and Teaching

Development of creativity should be a high-placed criterion for sorting out what goes in and should come out of today's jam-packed curricula (Starko, 1995). Teachers who fill children's days with dull worksheets and maintain silence with glares are not part of a success strategy. Time is limited. Children spend about a third of their childhood in school. The future depends on focusing classroom assets on essential skills and critical concepts. If humans are to survive and thrive, one essential skill set is the CPS process. The arts provide fertile ground for growing such indispensable higher-order thinking.

This ability to produce creative solutions is valued in fields from advertising to fashion design. Not to be overlooked is the role CPS plays in lesson designs. This entails focus on known destinations (standards/goals) with the belief that there are infinite means of achieving these targets. Celebrated teachers are known for this kind of creative work. Film depictions dramatize the power of CPS in teaching. In *Dead Poets' Society*, for example, Robin Williams portrays a teacher who uses the power of literature and drama to move students. *Fame* (1980) tells the story of a New York City high school specializing in the performing arts, and *Mr. Holland's Opus* (1996) portrays an inspirational

music teacher. In *Music of the Heart* (1999), an inner-city teacher challenges her students to learn the violin well enough to perform at Carnegie Hall.

Valuing Creativity.

> *To engender creativity, first we must value it.* (Sternberg and Lubar, 1991)

Teachers don't go around saying, "I can't do math" or "I can't read." If they did, we would think they should be fired. Some teachers, however, seem to feel no shame in saying, "I am not creative." In doing so they limit themselves and their students. Emergence of innate creative abilities depends on belief that everyone possesses them and a deep value for the problem solving that creativity makes possible. It is unacceptable for a teacher to claim that she or he cannot do important life-linked creative thinking that students need to be taught.

Practice the CPS Process. Here are facts about CPS, followed by an "if–then" frame. Consider the proposition (if) and think of ways a teacher may put the information into practice (then).

1. When people have blocks of time to become deeply involved in a creative problem, they can enter a mental state called *flow* (Csikszentmihali, 1990). Decades of cross-cultural research on happiness from Tokyo teens to Italian farmers found people who recalled being so engaged they lost track of time. Flow is an optimal active experience that is highly motivating. You feel focused, exhilarated, and satisfied. People freely spend large amounts of time and energy during flow. They report a sense of discovery from connecting ideas that feel like a "new reality." The whole world seems closed out. *If this is true, then teachers should . . .*

2. Creativity involves a leap that transcends logic but is built on a base of knowledge and skills. Expertise is absolutely necessary. You cannot create without a reservoir of ideas or skills. *If this is true, then teachers should . . .*

3. The creative process is facilitated by (a) knowing strategies, like SCAMPER, to manipulate ideas in content areas, (b) finding new problems, and (c) working with content in new ways. *If this is true, then teachers should . . .*

4. Motivation and positive attitude play a prominent role. These mental states keep individuals committed to a task long enough for exploration, problem finding, and creative thinking to happen at all. *If this is true, then teachers should . . .*

5. There is no creation without frustration. Creative problem solving is bringing order to chaos, relating the unrelated, discovering patterns, and raising and answering

questions. These are higher-order thinking processes. The process is a struggle and is messy. Teachers who substitute activities requiring that students follow directions may think they are helping students by making it easy. They really rob students of opportunities to become resilient and independent—the products of overcoming obstacles. Feelings of accomplishment and pride stem from successful struggles. *If this is true, then teachers should . . .*

6. Producing and consuming humor use thinking processes similar to creative thinking. Humor is rooted not in happiness, but in conflict and problems, just like creative thinking. Even a riddle is a problem to be solved creatively. *If this is true, then teachers should . . .*

7. We can accumulate important data to fuel the fire of creativity by looking and listening carefully, observing details, and noticing patterns. *If this is true, then teachers should . . .*

8. We stand on the shoulders of our ancestors in our creative efforts, building bit by bit in a long, constantly evolving effort. We must know the past to envision the future. *If this is true, then teachers should . . .*

9. The CPS process is goal oriented and focused. It demands concentration. *If this is true, then teachers should . . .*

10. There is a difference between problem solving and problem finding. The latter is as much needed as the former. Consider these problem types: (1) ones given to us with known solutions (most school problems), (2) ones given with solutions unknown, and (3) problems sought and found, and without known solutions. Example: Advertisers try to create markets for products we don't even know we need or want. *If this is true, then teachers should . . .*

11. Creative problem solving includes many types of thinking, including metaphoric (comparisons), divergent (open ended), and combining opposites (e.g., jumbo shrimp). *If this is true, then teachers should . . .*

12. The CPS process is parallel to the scientific method, the writing process, and the reading process. *If this is true, then teachers should . . .*

13. Teachers can intentionally boost creativity, and they unintentionally inhibit it. *If this is true, then teachers should . . .*

Creativity Deprivation. Struggling learners may actually be harmed if engagement in CPS is postponed until skills like decoding and spelling are mastered. Young children who are denied opportunities to use problem solving may not develop internal motivation to create meaning. Left to low- level memory or following direction tasks, they can develop distaste for learning. What is to sustain attention to the squirrelly details of our alphabet? Letters like *d, b, p,* and *q* are all just circles with sticks, devoid of meaning. They do not conform to a child's world where a shoe or crayon is still a shoe and a crayon, no matter what direction you turn them. Parents and teachers may not always look favorably on creative behaviors such as wanting to "do their own thing " and resisting conforming to adult expectations. Just like Lionni's main character in *Frederick,* creative behaviors may cause children to be seen as troublemakers. Studies document the decline in children's creative thinking as they move through school. Some conclude that fourth grade is the peak of creativity for many learners. Ready Reference 2.6 lists common creativity inhibitors. More are available at *www.goshen. edu/art/ed/creativitykillers.html.*

Ready Reference 2.6 Creativity Killers

Here are common inhibitors to creative thinking.

1. Tests: too often, too soon, or too long.
2. Positive evaluations and successes: can inhibit risk taking.
3. Hovering: students feel overly monitored as they work.
4. Extrinsic reinforcers: focus on "getting things" rather than learning for its own sake (grades, points, stamps, praise).
5. Worry and fear: not feeling safe enough to take risks.
6. Competition: especially if there is great hope for success.
7. Products: overemphasis on final product versus learning.
8. Choice: little or no choice about assignments.
9. Overemphasis on order, neatness, and following directions.
10. Preponderance of questions that are literal or have "right" answers.
11. Time: lack of incubation or wait time to think.
12. Data: insufficient information, skills, or materials.
13. Rush to judgment: "That won't work" right off the bat.
14. Learned helplessness: doing things *for* children that they could do themselves.
15. Lack of time to pursue interests.
16. Solemnity: taking things too seriously (e.g., teachers that rarely laugh, play, or use humor).
17. "One-way" thinking: stereotyped or dictated art that emphasizes "staying in the lines" and one right answer.
18. Predigested activities: focus on following directions or copying models.

Source: Lowenfeld & Brittain, 1975, pp. 22–25.

Creativity Boosters.

> *I have no special gift. I am only passionately curious.* (Albert Einstein)

Enhancing creativity rests on developing habits that include celebrating differences of mind, spirit, and body. Students are taught to make diverse choices within moral limits and employ personal interest. I think here of the boy, Philo Farnsworth, reading old science magazines in the attic of his family's Iowa farmhouse. Time to pursue a teenage fascination with electrons led him to visualize the rows of his plowed field as a metaphor that created the cathode ray tube. Farnsworth thus gave us television.

Any subject can be the basis for CPS, if we provide opportunities to learn information and teach how to apply it to problems. Playing creative games and puzzles is not enough. Learners must have a knowledge base and be taught to question, change, elaborate, and transform ideas. Such teaching also must forecast the consequences of human creating. As the Jewish folktale about the golem reminds us, creativity, mindless of morality, is a destroyer. (*Golem,* by David Wisniewski, won the Caldecott Medal in 1997.) Ready Reference 2.7 lists creativity boosters. Also, check *http://creativeeducationfoundation.org/*.

Final Suggestions.   This entire book is about how to teach using CPS in the framework of arts integration. Here are a few ideas to keep in mind.

- Use CPS personally when you plan lessons and learning experiences and in your other life pursuits as well.
- Display the process (in simplified form) to use as reference.

Ready Reference 2.7   Creative Thinking Boosters

1. Brainstorming steps: Go for quantity. List all ideas, even way-out. Keep driving, don't brake! Piggyback on ideas. Set a time limit. Group ideas and evaluate (Osborne, 1963). Notes: Individual before group brainstorming can produce more ideas. Giving evaluation criteria before brainstorming reduces the number of ideas, but may increase quality.
2. Reverse brainstorm. Squeeze out nonexamples—opposites instead of examples.
3. Word association (like brainstorming): List or web ideas connected to a word. Use to introduce any lesson. Example: Associate ideas for *foundations* for "The Three Little Pigs."
4. Question frames: Prompt with stems: "How might we _____?" "What if_____?" "What are all the ways_____?" "An idea nobody would think of is_____." Focus on a problem under study: How might we move if it were winter and we were marching from Valley Forge?
5. Stumped or stymied? Take a time out. Listen to music or do something physical: stretch, bend, or dance.
6. Turn mistakes into opportunities. Make lemonade! Be open to surprises. See *The Big Orange Splot* by D. M. Pinkwater (1993) and the Itzhak Perlman story in the music chapter.
7. Gather data. Read, observe, discuss, use the Internet to get ideas and different perspectives. Look at past work, reread, examine others' ideas.
8. Don't take first idea. Sleep on it. Generate lots of possibilities. The best idea may come right after you think you've run out.

9. Mind meld. Open an encyclopedia, dictionary, or magazine and pick an idea (noun, verb). Combine it with the one you are trying to develop. Don't worry about weird ideas. Example: I spotted scissors by my computer. I can force a relationship between the scissors and this chapter: I want to *cut out* drab teaching and can make *points* for why teachers should use arts-based teaching. Scissors and the arts can be *tools or weapons.* There are *different kinds* of scissors (pinking, pruning, etc.), just as there are various ways to integrate the arts.
10. Thinking hats (adapted from deBono, 1991): Get with four people. Each person "wears a hat" or takes a perspective:

    - Hat 1 describes what is known.
    - Hat 2 gives feelings about the problem.
    - Hat 3 tells what is not known.
    - Hat 4 thinks of associations or images.
    - Hat 5 lists ideas not at all related—opposites or nonexamples.

    This is similar to "cubing" (Neeld, 1986) in which a topic is explored in six ways: (1) Describe it. List its parts. (2) Tell how it feels. (3) What do you associate with it? (4) Use or apply it. (5) Compare or tell what it is like. (6) Argue for or against it. This can be timed (e.g., spend 2 minutes on each "side" of the cube, or do one or two sides a day).
11. SCAMPER. See Ready Reference 2.5 on CPS.

- Explictly teach CPS using mini-lessons on each aspect.
- Demonstrate relationships between (1) arts problem solving and CPS and (2) making meaning during reading, writing, science, and math and CPS.
- Look for teachable moments to connect CPS to daily life.
- When kids get stuck, refer them to CPS processes like data gathering, brainstorming, and SCAMPER.
- Plan regular time for students to do choice CPS.

Teacher Spotlight:
Risk, Creativity, and Children

A common justification for arts integration is that the arts encourage students to take more risks. Fifth-grade teacher Carol Rathbun has had the opportunity to judge the importance of "risk" during her 20 years at Ashley River. "Most children were 'at risk' in my first classes," she explains. "I was 'at risk' myself. I had to take risks to help my at-risk students." The arts proved to be an avenue of success.

"I believe every child is creative—especially the one that painted Paul Revere green." Carol says. She includes all the arts, but particularly likes movement and drama. For example, during an immigration unit students recently moved along timelines as they assumed roles of people on Ellis Island. Each had prepared a monologue about the immigration experience. "I think impromptu is the best use of drama." she explains. Carol draws this conclusion from comments of students who return to visit her. "It is drama they recall, especially creating the Plantation House!" She becomes more serious as she points out they "vividly remember how it felt for brother to be against brother on the battlefield."

Conclusion

Research now substantiates what some teachers and parents already knew intuitively—that the arts are critical to learning (Murfee, 1995).

This chapter has concentrated on the philosophical beliefs, research, and theories that suggest arts integration is a moral imperative. It is the right thing to do. The chapter culminated in a description of the theory of creative problem solving (CPS) that is at the heart of artistic thinking. CPS is central to meaning making because it orchestrates higher-order thinking needed to construct sense. The role of philosophy, theory, and research cannot be underestimated in both initiating and sustaining arts integration.

Resources

See the Appendix for further study recommendations.

Recommended Videos

Journey within. (1990). Renascence Films. (Illustrates the uses of art and the importance of play and freedom in the learning.) Website: www.touchstonecenter.net/publications.html.

The beginning. A wiggleman's tale (This is an oldie but a goodie cartoon short to make you think outside the box.) Available from jonasfilms.com.

Children's Literature References

Krull, K. (1995). *Lives of the musicians.* Orlando, FL: Harcourt, Brace, Jovanovich.

Lionni, L. (1987). *Frederick.* New York: Knopf.

Pinkwater, D. (1993). *The big orange splot.* New York: Scholastic.

Wisniewski, D. (1997). *Golem.* New York: Clarion.

3

Arts Integration Blueprint

Questions to Guide Reading

1. How are philosophical beliefs, research, and learning theories put into practice in arts integration?

2. What is teaching *with, about, in,* and *through* the arts?

3. How can the Arts Integration Blueprint be used?

In previous chapters the WHY question was addressed with focus on the philosophy, research, and unique contributions the arts make to learning. This chapter moves ahead to WHAT teachers need to know and HOW to implement arts integration using the Arts Integration Blueprint. The opening School Spotlight features a school that collaboratively plans units—a key component in the Blueprint. This school also shows how reform is driven by research. Notice, however, how many important effects of arts integration would not be assessed by traditional tests.

School Spotlight:

Tanglewood Middle School

At Tanglewood Middle School the motto is, "I can create art. I am an artist. There is art in me," explains Karen Kapp, principal of this school located in an impoverished area of Greenville, South Carolina. Tanglewood recently adopted an arts integration approach using inquiry-based units.

"The arts captured the children internally from the start by awakening their emotions and physical self. We now have kids with fire on the inside," Kapp says proudly (April 28, 2005, interview).

Tanglewood's model is based on the Chicago Teacher's Center model. Teacher comfort with an art form was an important criterion for getting started. The goal was for teachers to learn to use the art form by working with an artist. The first arts-based units were designed around "essential questions" and were approximately 3 weeks in length. Two planning sessions with an artist were followed by eight sessions with students.

Ms. Kapp cites the school's 2005 Arts Project progress report as evidence of the power of arts integration. It shows: (1) Students scoring *below basic* improved 12% in English/language arts on the South Carolina's state test. Similarly, students scoring *basic* improved 16% and students scoring *proficient* and *advanced* increased 9% the first year of arts integration at Tanglewood Middle School. (2) Students scoring *below basic* in math improved 8% in one year; those scoring *basic* increased 4% and *proficient* and *advanced* scores improved 6% in one year. (3) Tanglewood made dramatic adequate yearly progress (AYP). In two years of arts infusion, the school met 20 of 23 AYP targets.

Kapp thinks the effects of arts infusion are especially visible in special education classes. "Students examined the Mona Lisa and discussed da Vinci. Students who were off the charts are completely engaged and making their own pieces."

The school climate has also changed significantly. "There is just more spirit and engagement," she says, using words like "passionate," "energized," and "missionary zeal" to describe the teachers. "Teacher attendance is the highest in the district—a complete reversal."

Tanglewood's implementation plan is unique, but its results are similar to many integrated arts schools: more engaged students, better test scores, and greater teacher enthusiasm.

How to Plan and Implement Arts Integration

If you believe in great things, other people will too. (O. W. Holmes)

Teaching With, About, In, and Through the Arts

In schools across America, arts integration is developing along a continuum from using one or two art forms to a small degree to complete arts infusion. The latter includes a deep respect for the arts as separate disciplines, with a focus on using the arts as investigative tools. For example, in social studies, concepts like *courage* may be examined from the viewpoint of a poet, painter, musician, and dancer. Students may be led to a key moment in French history through Rodin's immense sculpture of "The Burghers of Calais." It would be difficult not to be moved by the courage of these figures who stand frozen about to give their lives. The message comes through mass and shape. This kind of art can give a richness of perspective that changes what students *know*, what they can and will *do*, and most importantly, what they might *be* (Drake & Burns, 2004).

In a fully integrated arts design, teachers present skills and information about and from the arts *and* use the arts as teaching and learning vehicles. Booth (2003) calls this using the arts for art's sake *and* for learning's sake. The levels leading up to teaching *through* the arts are:

Teaching With.   At this beginning level, teachers use the arts casually for enjoyment and to give students chances to work creatively. Usually these are isolated experiences and students explore art materials or ideas with minimal teacher guidance. For example, students may sing songs related to a holiday or have time to draw after reading. These activities are usually not keyed to standards, and arts activities may not relate at all to units in science, social studies, math, or literacy.

Teaching About and In.   Gradually teachers build an arts knowledge base that allows them to plan lessons for

Me, Myself, and I: Self portraits painted by Ashley River students.

students to learn *about* and do work *in* the arts. The goal is to have students do creative problem solving through the arts and develop personal artistry. Teachers begin to co-plan with arts specialists and artists to construct lessons that connect arts content and skills to other curricular areas. Often music and art teachers help teachers locate artwork and music from historical periods or particular cultures to introduce social studies units. Classroom teachers teach rudimentary arts content and skills to give students the means to problem solve using the arts. An investigation of van Gogh's struggles and triumphs may be paired with social studies. The events of van Gogh's life become an historical lens to view the times. Map and globe skills may be used to pinpoint his life journey. Literacy is developed around reading biographies and writing about van Gogh in forms that range from informational reports to poems.

Teachers begin to give substance to casual routines, like opening songs. They do mini-lessons about composers, display musical elements charts, and ask students to do close listening to make meaning. When teaching *about* and *in* the arts, there is a conscious effort to develop aesthetic thinking. Students are engaged in exploration, creation, response, performance, reflection, and evaluation. Lessons are tied to district standards, and there is an effort to assess arts literacy, along with growth in linked curricular areas.

Teaching Through.   At this level the arts are prominent through daily arts routines, an aesthetic classroom environment, and as both content and means of learning in co-planned, standards-based units. Units are often science and social studies based and center on big ideas and key questions. The arts, language arts, and math become problem-solving tools to explore unit questions. The creative problem solving (CPS) process is explicitly taught and applied.

Teaching through the arts seeks high aesthetic standards and involves students in significant arts experiences connected to units. Lessons producing "25 identical Kachina dolls from a pattern or slopping paint thoughtlessly on brown kraft paper to represent ancient cave drawings" are questioned (Remer, 1996, p. 339). Teachers become more selective and choose to not integrate some lessons. For example, "dancing in geometric patterns does not substitute for learning to calculate area and perimeter" (p. 339). Artifacts are studied to uncover cultural history and values from particular times and places. The emphasis in teaching *through* the arts is meaning making *using* the arts.

More than Entertainment

Teachers actually move in and out of phases of teaching *with, about, in,* and *through* the arts. Each level offers entry points to fit student needs, curricular structures, materials, time constraints, and teacher background. Teachers need to feel comfortable gradually developing arts literacy and pedagogy. The type and pace depends on the people involved. Too much, too soon can overwhelm even the best. Teachers choose at various times to integrate multiple arts or just one and when to plan alone or plan collaboratively. The goals are the same for all these models—to make natural and meaningful arts connections that add depth to learning.

Most of the study about and collaborative planning for arts integration comes to fruition in individual classrooms. While an artist residency can be a unit centerpiece and coteaching with arts specialists is desirable, the sustainability of arts integration rests with the classroom teacher. In the following Classroom Snapshot a teacher organizes the day around arts-based literacy routines and science and social studies units.

Classroom Snapshot:
Arts Routines and Inquiry Units

When children create they are making sense of the world.
(Robert Alexander)

A long wall outside the classroom displays a timeline of artists' birthdays. It is at a level so primary students can write and read comments about artists. These appear in "speech bubbles" along the timeline. To the left of the door is a large framed watercolor mural painted by students—the culmination of a study of Monet's water lilies. An invitation to walk through "Monet's Garden" refers to an actual garden outside that children tend.

Inside the room wooden easels display framed prints by Monet, van Gogh, da Vinci, and Rembrandt. A van Gogh learning center is in one corner with baskets of art materials. Above is a display of his portraits and landscapes. A stack of "Arts for Life" journals is on the bookshelf. A yellow crate holds arts-based books, including biographies and informational books like *Painting with Children* and *Crayons.* In one corner a sign says "Book Nook." Pillows and a bean bag chair make it look inviting. A recipe box holds student recommendation cards with comments and a "smiley face" rating for books. A ficus tree fills another corner, and philodendron tentacles crawl along the windowsill.

The bell rings and Ms. Lucas turns up the CD player. The room fills with Vivaldi. Smiling children burst in. One boy shouts "The Four Seasons!" A debate ensues about which season is playing as kids hang up coats and greet Ms. Lucas with "bonjour" and "goedemorgan." Ms. Lucas explains how she teaches a bit of the language of each focus artist. So far they know greetings in German, Italian, Russian, French, and now, Dutch, for van Gogh. Students scurry to get their journals. They settle at their desks or at learning centers. Some use materials at the Art Center, which offers many tools and media. Ms. Lucas hands me a blank wallpaper book with "Arts for Life" on the front. We are the only two not on task, so I find a spot to write, and so does she. Inside the cover there is a note that says, "The arts are what give heart to our lives. Imagine a day without literature, music, art, dance, or drama. Write or do a piece of art about how the arts are a part of your life." I count 27 engaged second graders as Vivaldi plays on.

After about 10 minutes, Ms. Lucas says, "Find a place to pause." Students put away the journals. An agenda on the board lists the order of events. The children seem well rehearsed in the arts-based literacy routines. A few examples are:

Composer of the Day.   Rae Lyn and Jake give a 1-minute report on Vivaldi, telling interesting facts from his life.

Art Docent.   Tony sits in a red chair and talks about a self-portrait made on wet cloth with chalk. He says his inspiration was van Gogh's poses, lines, and colors. The audience comments and asks questions like, "How did you do that?"

Poem a Day (PAD).   Two children put up a transparency of Lillian Moore's poem of questions, "Yellow Weed." Missy points at the poem poster while Douglas reviews the directions for "echoic" reading. Missy and Douglas take turns reading lines, with the class echoing the music of their voices: dynamics, tempo, pitch, pauses, and stress. The class applauds and Ms. Lucas asks what they want to say about the poem. They talk about their feelings and particular words.

Sing In. Ms. Lucas asks for song nominations, and there is agreement on "Oats, Peas, and Beans" and "The Green Grass Grew All Around." Song posters on a clothesline feature lyrics in large letters. Julian chooses a pink pointer and takes charge: "We'll start with the oats song. Everyone stand up and take a deep breath. Now, ready, 1–2–3–begin!" When they sing "The Green Grass Grew All Around," another student hands out word cards (ground, hole, root, tree, branch, etc.) and corresponding pictures. Students put them in a pocket chart as they sing this cumulative song.

Unit Questions

The arts routines take about 15 minutes, and Ms. Lucas uses each to reinforce literacy skills by asking about phonic patterns in poems and songs. The rest of the morning is organized around a science unit that addresses key questions: "How do plants affect people? What causes these effects? What affects plants?" The central concern is an exploration of causes and effects. Students work in centers, student-led learning circles, independent inquiry work, and guided groups with Ms. Lucas. She explains that almost all literacy skills are connected to science and social studies units. For example, in this unit students are reading informational books, like Sylvia Johnson's *Why Flowers Have Colors* and Barbara Cooney's *Miss Rumphius*, and writing observation reports, poetry, and reader's theatre scripts using books they've read. Every unit uses the literary arts, visual art, drama, dance, and music to introduce and offer response options to unit content.

People Focus

Every unit also has a focus on scientists, composers, and poets who have wrestled with the questions the unit addresses. van Gogh is part of the plant unit because of his expressive plant paintings. The goal is to find meaningful connections and go further to explore why he painted the *way* he did and *what* he did (causes). Science is treated as the study of people who discover relationships among living and nonliving things, not as a study of isolated things and processes. Vivaldi's compositions on seasons connect to the effects of the seasons on plants. Students also investigate the effects of his music on people. Vivaldi's messages about the seasons are different from that in informational books on the cycle of seasons and plant life, and yet there is overlap. Ms. Lucas explains students need to both know and feel when learning. Much thought has gone into the role of emotional intelligence in structuring these integrated units.

Assessment.

Each unit culminates in a portfolio of work. Unit questions are followed by a table of contents:

I.   Music and plants: songs and pieces
II. Art and plants: artists and their artwork
III. Drama and plants: scripts and drama workshops
IV. Dance/movement and plants
V.   Literature and plants: fiction and nonfiction
VI. Writing about plants: informational and creative writing

Bulges indicate audio and videotapes. Ms. Lucas explains that boxes are used for portfolios when art projects are three-dimensional. Highlights are presented at the unit culmination when relatives and friends come to "Portfolio Performances."

After lunch Ms. Lucas uses similar strategies with a social studies unit. Sometimes the units are combined, but combinations are not forced. For the same reason, math is integrated only as there is a fit; counting bricks in *The Three Little Pigs* is not an authentic math/literature link. Students get direct instruction in math, reading, and language arts, as needed, and lessons may be taught separate from the units. Ms. Lucas tries to tie skill-based lessons to units so that students see the relevance of skills.

Day's End

Another set of student-led routines wraps up the day. Students sing and tell what they liked learning. There are "book ads" to advertise "must-reads." A grand finale is a pantomime in which students assume roles as seeds and grow into tall irises. The silent drama is interrupted by the bell. Out the door they go with calls of "arrivederci" and "bonsoir!"

"You know so much about the arts. Are you an artist?" I ask.

"I am learning a lot, just like my students. Am I an artist? Of course, aren't you?" Ms. Lucas cocks her head. "Would any teacher say she isn't a reader or can't do math or write?"

"Some say being an artist is different," I suggest.

"Being an artist is a part of being human. To say you aren't an artist—not a creative being with unique ways to understand and express yourself—is to say you're less than human. Teachers must be artists. Anything less than an artist-teacher is just not good enough for my children or anyone's children." Ms. Lucas has the face of a veteran teacher who is confident that the arts have changed the lives of her students. For Ms. Lucas arts integration is a philosophy of teaching and life.

Research Update 3.1   Arts Integration and Achievement

- **Chicago.**   Thirty-seven arts-based CAPE schools outscored nonarts schools on the Illinois Test of Basic Skills and the Illinois State IGAP test (reading and math). By sixth grade, more than 60% of CAPE students were performing at grade level. This gain is sizable and significant. By ninth grade CAPE students were a full grade level higher than non-CAPE students in reading (Fiske, 1999).
- **New York, Connecticut, Virginia, and South Carolina.**   In a study of 2,000 students, grades 4–8, researchers found "significant relationships between rich in-school arts programs and creative, cognitive, and personal competencies needed for academic success" (Burton, Horowitz, & Abeles, 1999, p. 36).
- **Bronx, NY.**   At St. Augustine School, 98% of students were at grade level after participating in an arts-integrated curriculum (Hanna, 1992).
- **Milwaukee, WI.**   Elm Elementary is number 1 in academic performance out of 103 schools. It was in the bottom 10 percent. What changed? The staff introduced a comprehensive arts program.

- **Charleston, SC.**   More than 90% of students in grades 1–3 have met basic skills standards in reading and math at Ashley River Creative Arts Elementary. Ninety-six percent meet basic standards in other subjects as well. These rates are about 10 percent higher than other South Carolina schools.
- **Augusta, GA.**   Students at the Redcliffe Elementary Arts Infusion School showed gains on the Stanford Achievement Test for each year of the project (Greater Augusta Arts Council).
- **Dallas, TX.**   Partnership for Arts, Culture, and Education, Inc. (PACE) reports that integrating the arts into the core curriculum positively affects academic performance. Three urban elementaries were studied. After 4 years, students in the integrated arts school had higher average standardized test scores in language arts than students from the other schools (*Inside OSBA's Briefcase*, July 3, 1997, Vol. 28, no. 27).

Visit Postscript

Ms. Lucas's students face poverty, drugs, violence, and parent apathy every day. The school district struggles financially, and arts specialists are at a premium. Teachers work to align instruction with standards and No Child Left Behind mandates, just like teachers across the country. The district is in a partnership with local arts agencies, and together they provide arts-based professional development through the Kennedy Center's Partners in Education program. Teachers say they need to learn more about arts concepts and skills to do more meaningful integration. They want to find more time to co-plan with arts specialists to plan complementary connections with science, social studies, math, and literacy. ✷

Arts Integration Blueprint

What is now proved was once only imagined. (William Blake)

Research Update 3.1 describes results of arts integration in schools across the United States. Teaching *with, about, in,* and *through* the arts outlines degrees of integration used in these schools. Successful schools also share principles of implementation. The Arts Integration Blueprint is a structure to use these principles to plan, teach, and assess. It is based on the philosophy, research, and theories in Chapter 2, along with professional wisdom honed in the "crucible of the classroom." The Blueprint goes beyond the *why* to answer *what* and *how* questions. It includes 10 building blocks that support the goal of creating meaning by problem solving through the arts. Each building block includes questions that educators address as they work toward quality arts integration. The building blocks appear in Ready References 3.1 and 3.2. Each is discussed in the following section. Implementation, as it applies to five art forms, is presented in subsequent chapters.

Blueprint I: Philosophy of Arts Integration

Beliefs about the goals of education, teaching, and learning direct arts integration implementation. These include strong values for diversity, creative inquiry, active learning ("hands–head–heart"), and student independence. Of particular importance is a belief in the capacity of individuals to construct personal meanings using a variety of communication tools (language arts and arts) and materials.

Ready Reference 3.1 ## Arts Integration Blueprint Questions

These questions are prompts for planning.

1. *Philosophy of arts integration.* What and how do students need to learn to be happy and successful in the 21st century? How does arts integration align with these needs?
2. *Arts literacy: Content and skills.* What arts literacy is necessary to teach students to use each art form to understand, respond to, and express ideas and feelings effectively?
3. *Collaborative planning.* What are the important overarching understandings and processes students need? What concepts and processes are shared among disciplines? What unusual contributions do the arts make to learning/teaching?
4. *Aesthetic learning environments.* How can learning ecologies be created to facilitate aesthetic attitudes toward learning?
5. *Literature as a core art form.* How can literature integration be used as a model for arts integration? How can the vast store of arts-based literature be used throughout the curriculum?
6. *Best teaching practices.* What teaching methods align with the philosophy of arts integration? What pedagogy, both general and arts specific, is supported by research and professional wisdom?
7. *Instructional design: Routines and structures.* What organizational features support systematic implementation of arts integration? What lesson sequence works best? How is time organized? What are common routines and structures?
8. *Adaptations for diversity.* How can the arts be used to motivate students and help meet the wide range of needs? How can arts teaching be adapted for strengths and needs?
9. *Assessment for learning.* How can arts-based assessments enhance learning and teaching?
10. *Arts partnerships.* Who are potential arts specialists that may partner with teachers? How can collaboration for arts integration happen? What special knowledge and skills do artists bring to the planning, teaching, and assessment processes?

Chapter 2 described the six Ps: philosophy, people, principles, places, programs, and pedagogy.

Blueprint II: Arts Literacy

I'm listening to a local radio station in Brevard, North Carolina, home of the well-known summer music series. A girl group is singing a country song about redneck women who live in trailers and keep Christmas lights up all year long. The song is a celebration of the freedom to live as you like. There is a toe-tapping rhythm and a catchy refrain. After two verses, I sing along. Art takes many forms.

Eesteemed arts educators believe it is well within the classroom teacher's capabilities to engage students in the many forms of arts. The meaningfulness depends on the ongoing arts literacy development of teachers. What is the minimum level needed to make meaningful arts connections? Arnheim (1988) explains how a teacher might begin by talking with children about art, maybe looking at Australian aborigine bark paintings to see what they tell about a people. He sees teachers then leading students to art making so they see the "kinship between the simply shaped but impressive and beautiful paintings of a distant race and their own artwork" (p. 48).

Teacher Standards

National educational and arts organizations recently collaborated to produce a document outlining the arts knowledge and skills needed by classroom teachers. The *Model Standards for Licensing Classroom Teachers and Specialists in the Arts* (INTASC, 2002) acknowledge that even in nonintegrated schools, much arts instruction is provided by generalist teachers. The Standards are organized around the 10 principles of good teaching used in the original Interstate New Teacher Assessment and Support Consortium (INTASC) document that teacher preparation programs use. Principle #1 addresses subject matter knowledge; for the arts that includes the information in this next section. The Standards can be retrieved at *www.ccsso.org/intasc*.

The classroom teacher provides the context for the arts to be made integral to the general curriculum, especially literacy, while the arts specialist provides depth. Classroom teachers need to coteach these areas of arts literacy:

- Purposes of the arts (WHY)
- Processes of the arts (HOW)
- People (WHO)
- Arts products as texts (WHAT)
- Arts elements, skills, and concepts (WHAT)

Ready Reference 3.2   Arts Integration Blueprint Chart

	1 Arts Integration Philosophy	2 Arts Literacy	3 Collaborative Planning	4 Aesthetic Learning Environment	5 Literature as a Core Art
W H A T	Stated beliefs about learning and literacy Focus on constructing meaning through "head, hands, heart" creative problem solving. Ps: philosophy, people, principles, places, program, pedagogy	Literature, Art, Drama, Dance, Music (LADDM) Knowledge: Content, Products, Skills, People, Artistic thinking, Techniques, Tools, Materials	Systematic planning –Standards –5 unit types –Schoolwide –Field-based –Materials –Assessment –2-pronged focus	Psychological Climate and Physical Spaces/Places: –Arrangement –Movement –Performances –Displays –Storage –Classroom –School campus	Arts-Based Literature: Every literary genre from biography to picture books that have a connection to the arts including DVDs, CDs, etc.
W H Y	Guide: planning, teaching, assessment, and evaluation	Arts for learning's sake AND arts for art's sake	Ownership, higher-quality results	Social contexts that promote creative problem solving/meaning making	Literature is the most used art form in the elementary curriculum Natural fit
H O W	School mission statement and consensus operating principles	Teachers and specialists explicitly teach as there is a fit -Literacy connection -Visuals	During school day, summer, weekly, monthly, written, casual Professional development, teacher reference library, text studies, websites	Teacher philosophy and personality: alter physical and psychological environment Anesthetic or aesthetic?	Selection Sources: Class library of arts-based books Coding collections

Purposes of the Arts

Literacy is the ability to both understand and express thoughts and feelings effectively. In the 21st century that includes using all means of communication—language arts plus dance, music, drama, poetry, and visual art. Each art form has its own language. The symbol systems are like alphabets and range from musical notation to the visual art elements of color, shape, and line. Language arts (verbal), visual arts, and performing arts all share the same purpose: to communicate ideas, emotions, and values. Messages are created and sent using symbols chosen by artists. How those messages are understood depends on the receiver's ability to "read" art texts ranging from picture book illustrations to body language. Hands-on arts experiences are important

6 Best Teaching Practices	7 Instructional Design	8 AdaptatioStans For Diverse Needs	9 Assessment For Learning	10 Arts Partnerships
1. Teacher as Person 2. Inside-Out Motivation 3. Engagement/ Active Learning 4. Creative Problem Solving (CPS) 5. Explicit Teaching 6. Apply, Practice, Rehearse 7. Aesthetic Orienting 8. Process or Product 9. Managing Behavior, Time, and Materials 10. Independence and Self-Discipline	Scheduling time, events, spaces. Schoolwide and classroom structures, predictable routines: –IDC design –Energizers/ warm-ups –Opening/wrap-up routines –Performances and Exhibits –Centers –Groupings –Clubs/Projects	Adapting: Place Amount Rate Time Instruction Curriculum Utensils Level Assistance Response	Clear expectations motivate Data gathered to gauge progress Focus on performances, displays, long-term projects Program evaluation	Collaboration among general educators, artists, art teachers, teaching artists, arts agencies, universities, community groups, parents
Research and professional wisdom in arts and education, should direct instruction	Make sure the arts are integral Institutionalize routines, rituals, and structures	Individuals have different strengths and needs	Motivate learning and gauge progress Standards and goals-based: Know-Do-Be	It takes a village . . . Funding issues Resources Expertise
Coteach, coached teaching, solo Informed by: research updates, PD, professional journals, Websites: artsedge, aep, ased	Set up ongoing structures and routines—many of which should become student led	Assess, with focus on observation and consultation with students and parents Adjust for success	Tell, show, develop criteria collaboratively Arts portfolios, rubrics, and checklists for teacher, peer and self-evaluation	Joint planning: Lessons, grants, and fund raising Features: parent nights (display openings), School Arts Directory

means of helping students understand how the arts are basic ways people solve problems—specifically, communication problems. Because the arts are so personal, they can uniquely help students grasp the concept that it is not what you "take" from a text, but what you "make" of it (Eisner, 2002a). Ready Reference 3.3 lists topics for discussions and writing about arts themes.

Processes/Skills

While the main purpose of the arts is to communicate, the process that drives artistic decisions about *what* to communicate and *how* is creative problem solving (CPS). In the arts the problem is often self-chosen and has to do with how to develop a new meaning. Not all problem solving is creative and not all cognition is artistic. Artistic

 **Topics for Arts Mini-Lessons**

Use these questions for conversations or journaling to help teach the complex relationships among the arts and life.

Literacy and Communication

- How do people communicate ideas and feelings (understand, respond, express)? How are the arts ways to communicate?
- What is literacy? Compare to communication. How are the arts languages or forms of literacy?
- How are the arts different from and like the language arts?
- What does it mean to read? What "texts" do we read? How is reading art or music different from reading books?
- What are arts words and processes that are common across disciplines (line, play, shape, composition)?

Nature of the Arts

- How are the arts a part of daily life (economics, business, social, clothes, iPods, Internet, concerts)?
- What is art?
- Why does art exist? What is the function or purpose of the arts now? Originally?
- How does something become art?
- What is good art?
- What makes something music, visual art, drama/theatre, dance, literature/poetry?
- When are arts practical or serve a functional role? What arts used to be functional and now exist just for aesthetic purposes (e.g., horse training/dancing)?
- What is beauty? Why is it an important idea?
- What does "arts for art's sake" mean? What disciplines exist for their own sake?
- How would life be different if the arts disappeared? (Lowry's *The Giver* uses this theme.)

Cognition, Emotion, and Motivation

- What makes us want to learn? How do the arts connect?
- What role does problem solving play in the arts? How do we solve daily problems?
- How do people think/feel when they are engaged in the arts (music, visual art, drama, dance, and literature)?
- What is the role of "transforming ideas" in understanding? What do the arts have to do with transformation?

- How is the process of making art like problem-solving processes in reading, writing, and scientific method?
- How are images used during thinking? Can you think without visual images?
- What do the senses have to do with the learning? The arts?

Creativity and Imagination

- What is creativity?
- How are problem solving and creativity related?
- How are all people creative? Why do they have to be?
- How is creativity related to survival?
- What do the arts have to do with creativity?
- Why do artists practice/redo/rework/rehearse so much?
- What is imagination? How is imagination used in problem solving? Daily life? Reading? Writing? Arts?

Artistic Thinking

- What do artists do? How do they think during art making?
- How does making, viewing, or listening to the arts feel?
- How do artists think? What does it mean to think artistically?
- How do materials change how we think?
- What do artists value?

Other

- What do these have to do with life: imagination, images, experimentation, problem solving, thinking, creativity, diversity, culture, performance/exhibition, emotions, and motivation. Relate these to the arts.
- What do these clichés mean, and why have they become cliché (e.g., a picture is worth a thousand words; arts for art's sake)?
- Why do people say they can't sing, dance, or draw when they don't say that so readily about reading, writing, or math? What does this thinking do to the possibility of singing, dancing, making art, etc.?
- Why do we applaud? (chimps and seals do, too)

---

thinking, feeling, being, and doing are born of imaginings. "What if?" and "Why not?" are key questions. Thinking without words is common. Creative writers, for example, often begin with visual images of places and characters. Many argue that nearly all thinking is in images, not in words, and that learning through images is superior. Indeed, visual brain receptors outnumber auditory receptors 30 to 1. Even nonfiction writing, like this text, is done by making mental images of real and imagined teachers, students, and school contexts. Try to think about what happened yesterday using only words. How much of your thinking is in visual images?

Arts skills and techniques include ways artists understand, respond to, and represent ideas. The skills range from learning how to focus so you don't get dizzy while dancing (e.g., find a spot on the wall) to painting techniques like dry brush. Teaching artists are quick to point out that acquiring new ways to view and do the arts is a self-motivating journey.

Artistic processes are not confined to the arts; they are used across academic disciplines. Think about how these verbs, which exemplify artistic work, relate to science and math: *wonder, seek, discover, notice, perceive, visualize, empathize, experiment, connect, capture, transform, compose, create, synthesize, reflect, criticize,* and *judge.* These are embodied in CPS used across subjects. Essential to arts integration is explicitly teaching the processes just described with CPS as a unifying structure. CPS streamlines learning, rather than artificially compartmentalizing and isolating.

People

Artists themselves are rich content for study. CPS is given a face when students learn about artists through residencies, websites, books, and videos. An ongoing chart of "found" artist characteristics is a resource for problem-solving strategies to try out. These attributes often emerge.

- "You can't break the rules until you've mastered them," explains Joan Templar, an accomplished visual artist and art professor. She creates dramatic abstract works from joint compound and collage materials. Most artists, from Picasso to Michelangelo, studied the masters before striking out on original paths. This knowledge and skill base in using materials and tools opens up choices.
- Artists are highly observant. They notice details and patterns—and not just in formal art. Anything can be aesthetically perceived, as in the "not what you take from a 'text' but what you make of it" point suggested earlier. An artist looks at an old tire and sees a unique tread pattern. The wear makes a kind of thumbprint. Artists take delight in the individuality of people, nature, and objects.
- Artists study other artists and adapt ideas to create original works. Each artist has unique ways of working—style, techniques, and materials. Any or all of these can ignite a fire in students. I think here of the popular video of Eric Carle painting his collage papers. He has inspired students from first grade through college to try the technique that gave us *The Very Hungry Caterpillar* and many other vibrant picture books.
- Artists use strategies to start up and get unstuck. For example, they often rework one piece or continue to work with one idea for a long time (e.g., Monet repeatedly painted haystacks). This suggests that students

reread books, write on the same topics, and study a subject for an extended time—ideas that heretofore were considered problematic or even cheating.

Artists routinely start where they last worked, but tweak ideas. They often take the work of others and give it a new twist. In the picture book field this popular idea produced an assortment of new fairy tales versions like *Sleeping Ugly* (Yolen). "Go away and come back" is an idea to get fresh perspective. Time gives distance. Artists say they find new insights after putting the work aside for a day or so. This aligns with research on creativity that shows incubation time is needed both to achieve critical distance and to forge new connections and discover new perspectives. Students who use this strategy feel more satisfied with their products because their work is of higher quality and greater complexity.

- Successful artists are known for their persistence and resilience. Dr. Seuss is an example. Theodore Geisel persisted to publish his first book, *And to Think I Saw It on Mulberry Street,* after getting 43 rejections. Students need models that delight in hard work and show that effort is the key to success—not just talent. Students need to know that the path to success is interesting, long, and rocky. Artist studies are rich sources for students to see that they are not alone in their struggles.

Products

The arts take forms from watercolors to contra dances. These products are "texts" that preserve culture and history. While arts products may look pretty and entertain, the focus of integration is deeper. Students learn to "read" nonprint art as well as literary art forms. They learn to dig for cultural information from historical periods and use the arts as windows to see how people think, feel, and live. The goal is to understand others, at a deep level, so students grow into adults who maintain healthy relationships.

Directed hands-on examination of cultural artifacts is one stepping-stone to understanding the values and lifestyles of any group. Students can be coached to hypothesize about what is expressed in any dance, painting, sculpture, or song. Through questioning they can realize that people use the arts to say what is most important.

Picture book art is readily available as "text" to teach students to "decode" visual art. Of course, reading art depends on learning art elements and how to investigate possible meanings in the composition. For example, picture book artists often direct the reader's eyes to move to the next page.

Each of the arts chapters of this book features examples of the many arts products that can be used as texts to develop literacy aspects from vocabulary to comprehension. Arts products are also suggested to introduce, develop, and conclude lessons in math, science, and social studies. Arts specialists can suggest prints, songs, videos, and books. Numerous arts-based websites are suggested, including those of organizations that have exciting resources. ArtsEdge is a recommended starting place.

Arts Elements and Concepts

All of us can enjoy the arts without instruction. Enjoyment, however, can be little more than entertainment, which evaporates quickly. Arts integration targets deep engagement. This does not happen without explicit teaching of arts concepts (elements and symbols) and skills that form the language of each art. Basic arts literacy enables us to talk about, respond to, and create with the arts. "Without a basic symbolic vocabulary art remains impenetrable. We need to teach how to look at the 'thing.' How an oak in a painting suggests strength and longevity, or olive as peace" (Lockwood, 2005). Students lacking arts literacy become frustrated, along with the teacher, when they try to "read" art, even in picture books. Mini-lessons on a few words and concepts free students to tap brain schema. Arts language allows them to notice more and talk about what they see. Classroom teachers do not need a vast background. They can learn alongside students and gradually add arts knowledge. To do so, many teachers use their planning period to sit in on lessons of school arts specialists. This also models for children an openness to learn and risk taking—essential teacher dispositions for successful arts integration. This initiative also lays the groundwork for planning with arts specialists to integrate the arts.

Visuals Mnemonics.
The brain is constructed to attend to visual images. We have 30 times more visual nerve fibers than auditory and 30% of the cortex is devoted to visual processing, compared to 3% for hearing (Lindstrom, 1999). Classroom visuals can increase learning 400 percent (3M Corporation research, 2001). Arts charts, word walls, banners, and big books are important aids. Teachers who are tight on space use ceiling tiles or install inexpensive roll-up shades. Arts visuals are used in question generation and serve as independent "fix-up" references to reflect on performances and products.

The Ready References in the following chapters summarize basic arts concepts, elements, media, tools, processes, styles, genre, and forms. Teachers can also consult local arts curricula, the INTASC website, and the MENC *National Standards for the Arts* (*www.menc.org*), which include an arts glossary.

Blueprint III: Collaborative Integrated Arts Planning

Learning depends on accessing and forging brain connections. Arts integration planning seeks connections across grade levels and among disciplines to make instruction more brain compatible and more life-like. In particular, the arts are connected to literacy and expand the number and kinds of communication tools students can use. Teachers plan with this arts communication focus and seek out overlapping concepts and skills from separate disciplines. The search is for mutual relationships among big ideas, key concepts, and critical skills. When complementary connections are found, they are used because there is a natural fit. For example, composition is equally important in writing and in art; proportion is critical to math and music. Ready Reference 3.5, later in this chapter, lists shared vocabulary.

Planning Overview

National and state documents provide a framework for curriculum planning. Standards don't have to mean conformity. No child is helped if we narrow the curriculum, establish rigid criteria, and teach only to tests. More consistent with the moral principles of our country is using alternative means to important ends. The arts provide diverse paths by which students can reach important educational destinations. Arts integration engages students with motivation and literacy difficulties and narrows achievement disparities between students from low- and high-income brackets.

The most common paradigm is for arts-based units to be collaboratively planned by

Collaborative planning at Ashley River Creative Arts.

teachers, with arts specialists as consultants. Units can be planned around any center, including artworks, artists, and arts processes, but frequently they center on science and social studies and involve long-term projects. This is logical since these are the two major content areas; math, reading, and the language arts are primarily skills used to process content. While particular processes are used in social studies and science, the content, or conceptual underpinnings, have mostly to do with understanding relationships among (1) people and (2) the natural world, respectively. Even literature, at its core, is fundamentally an exploration of science and social studies issues.

After outlining a unit, sequenced daily lesson plans are made. Clear arts-based lesson plans feature learning objectives that specify what students will know and be able to do in the arts, as well as in the connected academic area.

Pronged Focus.

Lessons that use the arts as teaching tools are planned by determining how the arts can support another curricular area. This involves planning to teach important concepts and skills *about* the arts as well as content in other curricular areas. The goal is to use the arts, not abuse them. While there may be several integration prongs, there has to be at least one significant arts teaching point that complements a focus in the other discipline. From the pronged focus, student objectives are written that explain what students should know and be able to do by the lesson conclusion. To make it easier to assess, objectives are written using observable verbs that describe learning evidence (Planning Page 3.3, later in chapter).

Questions to Guide Planning.

Teaching through the arts involves students living and learning through the arts. To make this a reality, curriculum planners recommend using important concepts, big ideas, and "essential" questions to structure integrated units (Drake & Burns, 2004; Jacobs, 1997/2002; Wiggins & McTighe, 2005). The goal is to engage students in CPS to discover important perspectives. The result is deeper understanding. The planning entails continuous questioning:

- What do we want students to KNOW, DO, and BE by the end of the unit (Drake & Burns, 2004)?
- What are important "secrets of the universe" (patterns, themes, truths) we want students to investigate?
- How can standards for different disciplines be connected in meaningful ways?
- How can lessons be introduced to pique student interest?
- How could the unit be made more appropriate for students?
- How does the unit create new perspectives? How would an artist view the problems? A scientist? A mathematician?
- How is the concept of diversity advanced?

- How is the integrity of each discipline maintained in integration? How may the arts contribute to unit foci?
- How does the unit use authentic materials and methods?

Standards and Benchmarks.

National standards list what students should know and be able to do in each curricular area. Standards have now been developed by professional organizations for every curricular area. Nearly every state has used national standards to create state documents as well. Many local districts have further designated "benchmark" behaviors that describe appropriate learning progress by grade level and/or by developmental stage. These documents are important guides in planning units and lessons. In addition, most states are trying to align achievement testing with standards so that teachers will no longer have to be stretched between what's on the test and what's in the standards. The assumption is that if teachers target the standards, students will be more likely to reach them, and matched tests will show progress.

Teachers need to have standards documents available as they plan, realizing that all standards are not equally important and the number of standards is weighty. Integration is an efficient way to address many standards that duplicate across disciplines. For example, arts-based units readily align with English/language arts standards (Ready Reference 4.4) and frequently fit with science and social studies. Many schools also find particularly meaningful connections among math standards and music, and math and visual art. *Note:* North Carolina has created a kind of *Cliff Notes* of useful standards. *Reference Guides for Integrating the Curriculum* can be purchased at: *www.ncpublicschools.org.*

Standards represent important goals, but they don't comprise all that we want children to know, do, and be. Drake and Burns (2004) point out that teachers actually give priority to character traits (what students should *be*) and those aren't common in standards. Teachers explicitly or implicitly add value-based end goals as they plan (e.g., students will work cooperatively, have empathy, be honest). Arts integration targets standards but uniquely develops cognitive abilities, social skills, and emotional dispositions that are assumed, but not always written into academic standards. Ready Reference 1.1 summarizes "Unique Contributions of the Arts."

Many school districts now follow the lead of the professional organizations when it comes to designing units. The National Council of Teachers of English, International Reading Association, National Council of Teachers of Mathematics, National Council for the Social Studies, and the National Science Teachers Association all advocate life-centered unit and project approaches. For example, the Ohio state arts education model features "life-centered learning" (Ohio Department of Education, 1996, p. 1). Check the websites of most state departments of education for arts initiatives and partnerships.

The National Standards for the Arts.
This document (1994) was developed by the Consortium of National Arts Education Associations (CNAEA) and is a necessary tool for classroom teachers. It specifies the knowledge base, skills, and some affective achievements expected of students in each of the arts in grade groupings of K–4, 5–8, and 9–12. Teachers with minimal background in specific arts disciplines will find many questions clarified about what to teach. For example, the standards for K–4 dance call for students to "accurately demonstrate non-locomotor/axial movements (such as bend, twist, stretch, and swing)," and "create a sequence with a beginning, middle and end" (CNAEA, 1994, pp. 23–25). Once teachers understand concepts such as *nonlocomotor* and *three-part sequence*, they can envision how movement can be used in math, literature, social studies, and science. Included is a glossary of arts terms. View the standards at the MENC website (*www.menc.org*). Each arts chapter of this book includes a summary of the general standards for that arts area.

Ways Schools Plan and Organize.
Integration uses several aliases such as interdisciplinary, multidisciplinary, and transdisciplinary (Drake & Burns, 2004; Jacobs, 1997), but in any design, there is a unifying center. Generally, academic disciplines, along with arts areas, are examined for their connections to the unit center. Often teachers proceed in creative ways (Freeman, Seashore, & Warner, 2003; Horowitz, 2004). For example, at North Carolina A+ Schools, units were planned by cutting the state curriculum into sections, laying them out across the room, and then discussing how to use the pieces for a theme. Most integrated unit planning includes scanning standards to find clusters that can be grouped. Drake and Burns (2004) recommend using different colored highlighters to code overlapping standards. For example, both arts and academic standards address communication and research skills that can be taught in almost any unit. Code those red!

The following planning models all use a unit structure. Most culminate in student performances and exhibits that may occur weekly and happen at the end of each unit. For example, Normal Park Museum Magnet in Chattanooga is a field-based school that works with museum professionals to plan school exhibits that "open" each 9 weeks. Exhibits are created to demonstrate learning connected to local museums. Joyce Tatum, the museum liaison, points out that "as a museum school, we are a museum."

Big Ideas and Important Questions.
One of the joys of 21st-century teaching is that we seem to have edged beyond "covering material." Increasingly educators co-plan based on broad important ideas and processes that cause lessons to fly. They reject a focus on tallies of facts, dates, and isolated skills that cause lessons to flounder. Why? Every human being wants to know secrets and truths about people and the world—how to succeed and be happy. Research confirms that directing students' attention to learning for understanding, rather than grades, is superior (Guthrie, 2004). Themes from literature, generalizations in social studies, and axioms of science offer paths to big ideas. For example, *Charlotte's Web* is more than the tale of a pig and a spider. It plumbs friendship at a deep level to reveal truths such as "Good friends stick by you during tough times" and "True friends see good in you that you don't see." Friends live in our hearts because they positively alter our existence. Literature and the other arts offer tools to grapple with big ideas, especially how struggle hones the spirit, how wisdom is achieved, and where beauty is found.

Teachers access this power through units planned around significant issues that are explored in depth using an inquiry approach. Jacobs (1989/1997) offers a practical way to do this kind of planning. She recommends mapping the curriculum. First, a big calendar is made of what each teacher presently teaches, month by month and by grade level. This allows vertical and horizontal analysis. Teachers then examine what others are doing and where integration possibilities are most natural. Units are then developed around three or four essential questions that lead students to investigate important ideas.

Themes Versus Topics.
In the past teachers worked hard to develop units around topics such as plants, quilts, and dinosaurs. These often produce dramatic products like giant papier mâché dinosaur sculptures, elaborate plant dances, and colorful wall-sized class quilts. As arts integration has evolved, however, there has been more emphasis on depth rather than flash. Units that are a simple string of activities, loosely associated with a topic, are questioned. Edelsky, Altwerger, and Flores (1991) recommend units that use a line of inquiry—a chain of tasks that grow out of important questions connected to themes (e.g., "How can we get rid of drug dealers on the playground?"). Units are not "loaded with activities" and resources are not used to "rev up lagging interests but to satisfy already heightened curiosity" (pp. 64–66).

Themes take topics further. For example, in literature, patterns and cycles that repeat in the lives of people—dead and alive, real and fictional—reveal themes like "If you keep trying, you will succeed" and "Evil beings lose in the end." Teachers first study the material and then generate full sentence theme statements. Next comes writing starter questions. This does not mean students are only to be led to preidentified themes or that the teacher solely creates questions. The larger goal is for students to discover their own "truths." Students choose to wrestle with problems and think deeply when they are internally driven to find out why. The arts contribute to this process by actively engaging them and providing problem-solving tools to use in the search for "big thoughts."

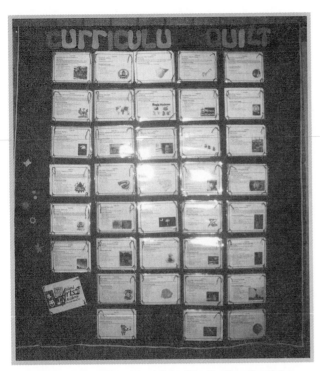

Curriculum quilt at Hilton Head School for the Creative Arts.

Drawing upon unique prior experiences and interpretations, even young children can synthesize personally relevant themes. They do so, too, when teachers ask questions such as, "What did you learn? What was this mostly about? What did this tell you about people or the world?" and "What will you remember forever from this book or song?"

Good lessons allow students to *create* understanding and develop skills connected, but not limited, to standards. See more examples of themes or enduring understandings at websites of both the Virginia Department of Education (*www.pen.k12.va.us*) or the Michigan Department of Education (*www.michigan.gov/mde*).

Unit Centers or Bodies. The most common organization in arts integration is the unit. Concepts and skills that have relevance across disciplines are clustered (e.g., shapes and forms in art and math, patterns, and cycles in dance and science, change and constancy in social studies and literature). The unit center may also be a person such as an artist or author. A genre or form can be the center of study, as can a core work. For example, a core unit using the book, *Sarah, Plain and Tall* (McLachlan), offers plentiful opportunities to examine themes such as "Families can be structured in a variety of ways" or "The role of mother in a family is central," using the arts to create understanding. The arts can be the center, too, and the arts are often integrated with other arts, as happens in real life. For exam-

ple, Beethoven used the poem "Ode to Joy" for his Ninth Symphony.

In sum, five common unit centers are (1) author, artist, or person; (2) genre or form; (3) problem or topic; (4) single book, poem, or song; and (5) event or trip. As the Unit Planning Web depicted in Planning Page 3.1 shows, whatever unit center a teacher selects, the nine "legs" of the planning web—the content areas and disciplines—remain the same: science, social studies, mathematics, reading and language arts, literature, music, dance, drama, and art.

Planning Page 3.2 summarizes a unit development process that begins with standards and topics and moves to targeting big understandings and important questions.

Student Interests and Questions. In addition to these centers, most teachers use student interests and questions, to different degrees, in any unit. In *inquiry-based integration*, student interests and questions form the centers of study (Short et al., 1996). Any unit should actively engage students. Instead of a cute teddy bear unit, a unit on "Inventions and discoveries result from happy accidents" has more substance. Units on core thinking about problem-solving processes, such as CPS, are also common and result in interdisciplinary learning across science, social studies, math, and literary. Processes and skills, however, need content—texts about which to read, write, and make art. That's where literature, science, social studies, and arts "texts" come in.

Unit Length. A unit may be a part of a day, like Ms. Lucas's plant unit, or form an entire integrated day. The unit may last a few days or a month or be a focus for an entire year. For example, schools choose topics like "celebration" and "diversity" as yearlong, schoolwide focus points. Ashley River teachers post current unit titles on their doors. At Hilton Head Creative Arts, a "curriculum quilt" shows all the units for the whole school. Some units are project-based, and most arts-integrated units involve long-term work over several weeks that culminates in a display or performance. Field-based units may connect to a single site, like a museum, or several sites like Normal Park Museum Magnet that partners with seven museums.

Types of Collaboration. The goal is for students to learn targeted understandings and skills in academic areas *and* in the arts. Teachers and arts specialists work together to find genuine, not forced, connections. Teachers and drama specialists might brainstorm or create a Venn diagram between reading comprehension and drama to discover that both areas focus on taking points of view of characters. This suggests that comprehension and drama are natural partners to teaching point of view. In this case collaborative planning would be about aligning the processes and content of the arts with important literary themes. If the target material

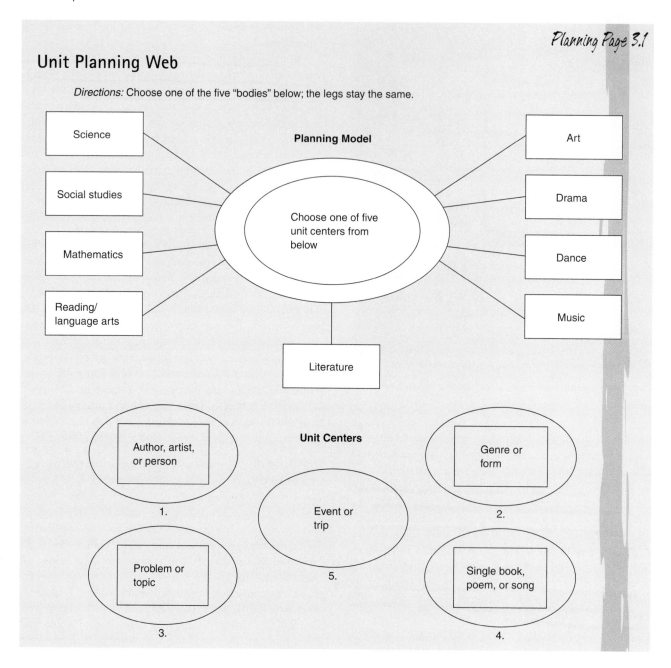

Unit Planning Web

Directions: Choose one of the five "bodies" below; the legs stay the same.

Planning Model

Science

Social studies

Mathematics

Reading/
language arts

Choose one of five unit centers from below

Art

Drama

Dance

Music

Literature

Unit Centers

Author, artist, or person

1.

Genre or form

2.

Problem or topic

3.

Event or trip

5.

Single book, poem, or song

4.

was the *Three Little Pigs,* the drama would have to go beyond pantomiming general pig behaviors. The following are ways teachers and arts specialists work together during planning and subsequent teaching:

Co-planning/parallel teaching. Individual teachers or groups co-plan with arts specialists around a unit center. They find overlapping concepts like "cycles," "balance," or processes that are shared. In this model, instruction happens separately; classroom teachers use arts ideas from the planning, and arts teachers address "nonarts" material—all fo-

cusing on the common connection. The music teacher may develop first graders' phonological awareness by teaching the song "Down by the Bay," followed by having students substitute beginning sounds of words to make new rhyming lyrics. During the same unit, the classroom teacher would work with phonological awareness using songs and other resources suggested by the music teacher.

This type of arts integration is only meaningful when teachers show students that arts experiences are connected to key unit ideas. Being explicit facilitates transfer and creates a sense of cohesion that is a goal of integration.

Unit Development Process

This process is recursive as teachers consult back and forth during the planning steps.

1. *Academics and arts standards;* other goals (e.g., character traits)
2. *Five unit centers or bodies (foci)*
   - *Concept, topic, or problem:* Examples are courage, family, Africa, Civil War, often science/social studies-based.
   - *Core work:* A single book, poem, painting, or play
       Person: Life and works of author, artist, or scientist
   - *Genre:* Study of a form (examples: fairy tales, landscapes)
   - *Person:* Real or fictional person (e.g., picture book artist)
   - *Event or experience:* Examples: field trip, residency.
3. *Important understandings: By the end of the unit, students should know/understand . . .*
   - Write three to five full theme statements to form a complete thought. Example for topic unit on families: *Families can be structured in different ways with each member taking important roles to contribute to its success.*
   - List three to five key questions: *What family roles are necessary? Who determines what each person does? How and why?*

- **NOTE:** Additional understandings and questions need to be solicited from students as the unit develops; these become important foci for learning, too.
4. *Key concepts that support understanding/problem solving*
   - *Examples: family, roles, needs, power*
5. *Skills and processes: By the end of the unit students should be able to . . .*
   - *Examples:* generate questions, visualize, give alternative perspectives, summarize/synthesize, prioritize/evaluate
6. *Arts connections* (co-planned with arts specialists)
   - What arts content, skills, and processes overlap or connect?
   - How will the art form(s) contribute to the understandings, concepts, and skills?
   - What arts materials and tools are needed?
   - How will the arts be a part of assessment?
7. *Multifactored assessment:* What assessments? By whom? How? When? (Connect to standards, goals, and objectives.)
   - Portfolios, performances, and exhibits
   - Rubrics, checklists, self-assessment
8. *Timeline*
9. *Lesson plans:* Two-pronged with objectives for academics and art(s). Where will arts be involved and how? Introduction/development/conclusion? (See plans in each arts chapter.)

Co-planning/coteaching.   Classroom teachers and arts specialists plan together and coteach lessons. Specialists include arts teachers within the school and artists brought in as consultants or for residencies. One advantage of this model is classroom teachers directly observe artists using strategies.

Grade level planning/arts consultants.   Classroom teachers receive professional development in arts content and processes and plan arts-based units or lessons with grade-level teams. Teachers then teach their own arts-based lessons but can consult with others undergoing the same effort. School-based arts specialists are available for consultation during planning and teaching (e.g., questions, materials, and strategies).

Artist residencies.   Artist residencies are used to give students arts experiences the faculty can't provide. Residencies are collaboratively planned so that work directly supports academic and arts curricular goals. Teachers are present during arts experiences so they can expand their arts teaching repertoire and extend student experiences after the residency. (See Blueprint X: "Arts Partnerships for Planning Residencies.")

Schoolwide Units.   Discoveries, patterns, problem solving, creativity, and dreams are examples of topics that have united a whole school in integrated studies that last from one month to an entire year. One school studied a core work, a George Seurat painting, for 5 weeks as a part of a social studies project (Short, 2001). A multicultural focus might serve as a selection criterion for the theme "All cultures solve problems in similar, but unique ways." A schoolwide extended study may also focus directly on the arts. For example, the topic of communication could be expanded to the theme "The arts are vital ways all human cultures try to understand and express thoughts and emotions." To plan these units, arts specialists meet with grade level teams to plan, just as in any unit. Often topics are recycled every 2 or 3 years. See "Birthday Buddies" in the Appendix for this yearlong integrated arts project.

Arts with Arts Integration. Aspects of each art discipline can serve as the focal point of study with other arts areas pulled in. For example, a visual art unit on the "nature and effects of color" would be well served by children's literature that explores color in books like Baylor's (1992) *Guess Who My Favorite Person Is,* the poetry in O'Neill's (1989) *Hailstones and Halibut Bones,* creative movement in response to colors, and music that stimulates color imagery or songs about color.

Field-Based Arts Integration. School trips to an art museum or to hear a concert are not unusual. What is unusual is meaningful integration of field events. Single or multiple trips can serve as unit centers or be important adjuncts (e.g., students at Normal Park Museum Magnet makes multiple field visits to sites). Field experiences can be the focus or a tool to reach a focus. Their meaningfulness depends on pre-during-post trip planning that ties the trip to arts and academic standards and goals. Trips have to be then timed and aligned with appropriate unit content. Finally pretrip lessons are needed to prepare students, and follow-ups help make the most of the experience. Assessment is needed, too. Without all this preparation and follow-up, field experiences can become little more than social time. The Appendix offers a planning tool with before, during, and after field trip strategies.

Blueprint IV: Aesthetic Learning Environment

The "place" of learning deeply affects learners. John Dewey pointed out that if classrooms are not "aesthetic," they are "anesthetic." Picture anesthetic classrooms with stark, dirty walls—students slumped in their seats, sullenly glaring at the blackboard. Teacher talk dominates, especially giving directions and orders. Silence and control hold sway over the messy, noisy work of problem solving. Such circumstances can numb children (Rabkin & Redmond, 2006).

Arts integration seeks to do the opposite—to energize by using the physical and psychological climate as major teaching tools. Aesthetically stimulating schools and classrooms provide settings that provoke curiosity, surprise, and a sense of mystery. The design of a classroom and the mood, created by teacher personality, combine to create a positive context. Murals line walls, clouds are painted on ceiling tiles, plants abound, along with bright carpeted areas, background music, couches, pillows, grouped desks, and displays of children's art (at eye level). There is minimal teacher-made and store-bought decoration. Boxes of children's books, organized by units, genres, and levels, dot the room. Most importantly, an intensity emanates from the joy of discovery. Classrooms buzz with activity as students move about. Teachers laugh, sing, and express delight when students take risks.

Stendhal Effect. Computer artist David Addington reported this reaction to a dramatic presentation: "I sat in the theatre paralyzed after the play *Boom Boom Room.*" This physical response to beauty is called the *Stendhal Effect,* after 18th-century novelist Henri Beyle who used the pseudonym Stendhal. Stendhal observed that the arts have the power to stun—to raise the hair on the back of the neck, to elicit sighs and profound sobs. Like Addington, I have had a few Stendhal Effect experiences. Once in Florence's Academie Museum, I was caught off guard by Michelangelo's towering sculpture of David. I audibly gasped—and I wasn't alone.

The arts are forms of beauty that intrigue, refresh, and excite passion. They give hope by reminding us that there is lovely potential in everyone. When students are surrounded by art, "their eyes drift across the paintings and sculptures"; behavior changes as they are calmed by music (Lockwood, 2005). They listen more actively and notice more details. Just being in the presence of art gives a sense of history and social context. The result: a "deep love and appreciation" of art and an understanding of how beauty can affect the senses (Lockwood, 2005).

The best way to understand more about how and why to immerse students in an aesthetic environment is through example. The following example is a special "museum magnet" in Chattanooga, Tennessee.

School Snapshot:
Normal Park Museum Magnet

Normal Park isn't a normal elementary school. First, there is a museum-quality gallery on the school's main floor with student exhibits changing quarterly. Then there are the sculptures and woodcarvings by noted local artists displayed throughout the campus, along with large colorful murals and 3D sculptural arches. This "museum magnet" was named the top magnet school in the nation in 2005. The school was recognized for its efforts to increase diversity and academic achievement and involve parents and the community through its special form of arts integration.

Working with seven local museums, Normal Park's curriculum connects museum study visits with science and social studies standards-based units. Favorite past units have centered on the human body, healthy choices, the rain forest, and Egypt.

Museum professionals act as consultants to design high-quality exhibits that grow out of the curriculum. A strong indicator of the program's success is the jump in standardized test scores since converting to a museum magnet in 2001. The fifth grade boasts 100% proficiency—the highest level on the state test. What's more, Normal Park teacher Jenifer Zeigler claims that 100% of the parents say their children want to come to school. "Attendance problems just don't exist," she adds.

Every 9 weeks the students work to visually show what they have learned in units. Principal Jill Levine says students are motivated to have real audiences. On opening night visitors are greeted with punch and cookies, and students from the P–5 school act as docents. They are trained to conduct informative tours of the student work.

Grade-level teams plan the units, and arts specialists collaborate to teach the unit's big ideas, key concepts, and skills using arts strategies.

Ms. Zeigler says, "Using the school environment as a learning tool is a plus because it allows students to take ownership." ✳

Aesthetic or Anesthetic?

In school after school, a frequent comment among parents and teachers is that children look forward to the joys arts-based inquiry brings. Kids don't want to be absent because they'll miss a chance to docent in the school gallery or the Friday Reader's Theatre. It isn't just the opportunities the arts bring that cause this reaction, it's an invitational climate that flows from the teachers' personalities and philosophies. Artful teachers celebrate differences, embrace cultural and ethic uniqueness, and immerse students in a relationship of respect. Respect builds trust. Trust creates the comfort necessary for risk taking and experimentation—essentials for creative problem solving. When aesthetic values set the stage for learning, students are more engaged.

Small Changes.

Teachers can take a cue from Eisner (1997) who advises that the "subtle is significant." Spaces should be arranged with attention to order, balance, harmony, and color. Even small changes have large effects. Grouping desks implies that collaboration is expected. Open spaces indicate movement is part of the plan. Centers and stations with buckets of brushes, baskets of arts-based books, and worktables give a sense that hands-on learning is valued. Arts-based classrooms look more like living rooms—comfortable sanctuaries and pleasant places filled with plants, fresh flowers, bright curtains, and framed student artwork. Imagine beautiful background music and pools of light from small lamps that illuminate reading areas. Think of the wonderful smell of potpourri. These simple changes make the environment more stimulating to the senses—more aesthetic.

Start with the "Known."

Disney's many parks are examples of arts-based places that assume everyone loves the arts and can participate, regardless of age or ability. Teachers in arts-based schools understand this. An aesthetic classroom climate is founded on the belief that all students have untapped arts capabilities. Even young children know how to modify their voices, facial expressions, and body posture to assume roles as sister, brother, friend, and student. They know how to "read" musical elements in their mothers' voices. These expressive elements say more than the words themselves. They know colors for sad, shapes that symbolize happiness, and lines that are scary. Every student arrives at school equipped to think through the arts.

Displaying Art.

Interesting art does the same thing for the classroom that it does for homes and offices. In particular, framed student art enriches the classroom and gives honor and respect to the artists, especially if they are taught to make "museum labels" for their work. Students are also challenged by artwork of peers, and such aesthetic displays can activate interest in visiting local museums.

Background Music.

At Hymera Elementary School (Hymera, Indiana) a CD player sits right inside the front door. As at many other schools, background music plays in classrooms, halls, and the cafeteria to craft a positive atmosphere. Teachers are implementing multiple intelligences theory that includes music as a way of knowing—a unique way to think and feel. Current brain research also supports using music to stimulate brain activity. Since distinct regions uniquely respond, it is hypothesized that the elevated brain activity generated by music boosts learning.

Student Contributions.

When students are invited to make the classroom a place that celebrates the arts, they feel a sense of ownership. They become enthusiastic about the transformative power of aesthetic places. Get ready for fresh flowers, air freshener, and lots of music. In my own classroom one student brought in a CD of pianist George Winston, which started a run on instrumentals. Next came Wynton Marsalis (trumpet) and then classical guitar (Andrea Sergovia). The finale was a visit by a father who is a classical guitarist. The third graders were enthralled with guitar music so different from what they had heard before. "It's like an angel's harp," said one girl. "Except he's a man with long fingernails," a boy pointed out. When students contribute artifacts of their lives, they can become important springboards to additional study that develops pride and expertise.

Children learn what they live (Nolte, 1959). As the well-known poem by this title explains, if we want children to be curious, joyful, sensitive, courageous, and hopeful, we structure environments that encourage those characteristics. Teachers who operate from an aesthetic frame of reference make heightening the senses a priority.

Blueprint V: Literature as a Core Art Form

Literature is currently the most readily available arts material in our schools. It is the most frequently integrated art form. Unfortunately, literature isn't always treated as an art form. During the past two decades, high-quality literature has become the primary material to deliver literacy instruction, sometimes at the expense of using it to engage aesthetic sensibilities. Because literature spans every curricular topic, every literary genre, from poetry to science fiction, is now used throughout academic areas. In this book, literature is included as one of the five major arts so the next two chapters focus on how to integrate literature throughout the curriculum. Literature is also a significant source for integrating the arts of music, dance, drama, and visual art throughout the curriculum in the form of "arts-based" literature.

Arts–Based Literature.   A special body of literature is *about* the arts. This includes fiction and nonfiction books, stories about artists, and ways to make music, visual art, drama, and dance. All picture books are automatically arts-based, regardless of their content, because visual art is equal to the text in presenting the message. Arts-based literature is a key material to integrate the arts into science and social studies units. For example, biographies of artists and musicians fit into studies of every historical time period, and their work gives unique insight into values, ways of life, and issues of the time. Every classroom needs a collection of arts-based books students can choose from during independent reading times and as references for work during units. Teachers often organize the books using crates or book boxes for each arts area, or they color dot them as a code. Arts-based read-alouds have become a fixture in many schools, like Ashley River Creative Arts.

Subsequent chapters offer arts-based literature recommendations, and the Appendix has an extensive arts-based bibliography.

Blueprint VI: Best Teaching Practices

Meaningful arts integration ultimately rests on *how* lessons are taught. General "best practices" of teaching are the means by which any instruction is delivered. Shelves of books have been written on the subject, but there is no single set of best practices. There are "legitimate practices" within the bounds of research-based principles, professional wisdom, and shared values (Ferrero, 2005, p. 23). Arts-based lessons rely on these practices, which are filtered and adapted using the perspective of what works in the arts. In general, arts-based best practices take an inquiry approach that puts problem solving at the center (Ready Reference 3.4). While teachers may coteach lessons with artists or school arts specialists, most often they work solo on the classroom stage.

Ready Reference 3.4   Best Teaching Practices for Arts Integration

1. *What you teach is who you are.* Teachers show "arts confidence" and display enthusiasm and passion for the arts.
2. *Inside-out motivation.* Intrinsic motivation is activated by focus on understanding, interests, choices, clear goals, and group work.
3. *Engagement and active learning.* Arts strategies are used to engage the head, hands, and heart in problem solving that transforms ideas.
4. *Creative problem solving.* The CPS process is center stage in teaching how to use the arts as communication vehicles. The arts are given equity in the literacy curriculum.
5. *Explicit teaching.* Mini-lessons clearly focus on the why-what-how-when-where of arts concepts and skills. Transfer is explicitly addressed by teachers and arts specialists.
6. *Apply-practice-rehearse.* Teachers coach students using specific feedback during practice so higher-quality work results.
7. *Aesthetic orienting.* Teachers slow it down and teach students to observe carefully to ground interpretations in evidence. Diverse people, ideas, and approaches are accommodated through orchestrated teaching that balances wholes and parts.
8. *Process and product.* Arts processes are emphasized over products. Examples are used more often than models. Dictated art is avoided.
9. *Management: behavior, time, and materials.* Expectations and limits are clear. Flexible time blocks and predictable routines structure learning, but there is time for personal interest and to explore using authentic arts materials that unlock thinking.
10. *Independence and self-discipline.* Students become increasingly independent as they gain control of body, voice, and mind and learn persistence. They establish work habits and use fix-ups.

This section highlights best practices that serve as pedagogical guideposts for arts integration.

What You Teach Is Who You Are

There is no doubt that teachers with particular dispositions are attracted to arts integration. These teachers readily assume multiple roles as directors, coaches, performers, and audience members in their own classrooms. To do so they need personally uplifting and provocative arts experiences to stay fresh. Teachers like Judy Trotter at Ashley River Creative Arts say they can't turn creative problem solving off. The unique architecture of local buildings and the beauty of backyard nature are transformed into sources of arts-based lessons. Teachers end up writing down teaching ideas in the dark at films, plays, and concerts.

Enthusiasm and Passion. Enthusiasm is one of the most desirable teacher attributes. Students of every age rank it above subject matter knowledge. Arts integration demands both. The etymology of enthusiasm explains that it originally meant to be "in god" (theo) or "in spirit." Teachers who are possessed of a creative and artistic spirit exhibit a passion that draws students. They share their own arts experiences and tell personal stories of creative efforts, including how obstacles are overcome through persistence. These examples help dispel the myth that artistic and creative individuals are innately talented and don't have to work hard.

Arts Confidence. A teacher who says "I can't sing" or "I'm not good at drawing" is writing the arts off. It's like saying, "So what—it's not important anyway." Ms. Lucas reminds us that no teacher claims to not be able to read or do math. A commitment to weaving the arts throughout the curriculum brings many benefits. It also brings the obligation for teachers to approach the arts respectfully, with a can-do, will-do, want-to-do attitude. Sometimes that's scary, but it's done in the belief that meaningful arts integration is worth it. So, no put-downs, please, especially arts self-deprecation.

Inside-Out Motivation

In real life, people choose to engage in creative acts because producing and consuming the arts is inherently motivating. It is not necessary to bribe students with points and stickers in arts-based lessons. The arts are their own reward (Booth, 2003). A survey of attendees at a September 2005 South Carolina statewide conference rated using the intrinsic motivation of the arts as the number one practice for successful arts integration (*www.lander.edu/scaae*).

Certain conditions trigger internal motivation (Guthrie, 2004). The arts align beautifully with these. That's why students choose to do arts problem solving when they resist similar thinking during reading and writing. The six most important factors behind internal motivation are (1) understanding, (2) interest, (3) choice, (4) meaning and purpose, (5) goals and expectations, and (6) the group effect.

Understanding. Arts integration works because the arts add modes of understanding/comprehension and expression. Research confirms that students persist, produce higher-quality work, and enjoy learning more when teachers focus on understanding, not on getting grades or points (Guthrie, 2004). Teachers undermine intrinsic motivation when they urge students to work for higher grades and coupons. We need to stress learning for understanding as we work with uptight students and nervous parents.

Interest. The arts draw attention and sustain interest. They make us ask, "How did she do that?" and want to give it a try. Arts integration uses this power. Teachers teach *to* interests and develop new interests. Interest accounts for some 25 times the variance in comprehension, so it seems reasonable to first find out what students are interested in (assessment). Next comes connecting to interests and creating new interests. The Appendix includes an Interest Inventory example.

Choice. The role of choice in motivation was made clear in a factory experiment with button controls for noise. Only one group had buttons. That group liked work more, missed less work, and was more productive than the no-button group. Interestingly, no one in the button group ever used the buttons—they just had the choice. The arts offer multiple communication choices, but the quality of choice offered is important. The urge to investigate is not be activated if selections are low level. It is unlikely that being given a choice of planets on which to write a report will be seen as authentic (Starko, 1995).

Meaning and Purpose. Even young children have a strong desire to know why. Purposes motivate. A study done in a public area with a copy machine showed the power of purpose. Confederates approached people and asked to "cut in" to make copies. People often allowed them. But when a reason like "My boss is waiting and I'll get in trouble if I'm late!" was added, allowance percentages climbed into the 90s. Purpose setting cannot be ignored. In addition to telling purposes, it is effective to ask students to generate them. Purposes give relevance and meaning to learning, especially if they connect to student lives. For example, students need to know why they are using strategies such as SCAMPER (Ready Reference 2.5) in math. Teachers should take time to explain why and make real-life connections.

Goals and Expectations. Goals are broad ends. They are destinations for which there are multiple paths. The arts expand the number of paths to academic goals, but students need to know the expectations up front if they are to be motivated. It makes sense to discuss what will be assessed and how. Good teachers make goals clear and involve students in personal goal setting.

The Group Effect.   Constructivist philosophy and social interaction theory propose that the social effect of working with groups is significant. The most successful groups (1) feel they need each other, (2) think each person can make a contribution, and (3) know how to share leadership and do creative problem solving. Successful groups continually reflect on what worked or is working and how they can work together better (Daniels & Bizar, 2005). The social power of the group yields a greater quantity and quality of ideas. Students gain perspectives not possible in solo work.

The arts have a long tradition of quality group work such as choirs, dance ensembles, and drama troupes. In arts integration problem solving is almost always done in groups. Partners plan pantomimes, small groups create murals, and class members switch off as audience members, performers, and exhibitors. Teachers help by giving time limits, focus, cues, frames, and most of all, lessons on how to do CPS.

Groups who take risks together are more confident about sharing their efforts with an audience. The motivational power of the audience is well established. Arts integration taps this power by making performances and exhibits key features. When students think others will hear their songs or watch their dances, they become more concerned about quality. This doesn't mean arts problem solving should be done just for audiences. It does mean students benefit from performing, even for classmates. Students also benefit from learning how to be a part of an audience—how to be active listeners and show appreciation.

Engagement and Active Learning

Students are more motivated, remember more, and achieve mastery sooner when they are mentally, emotionally, and physically engaged.

Head–Hands–Heart.   The arts are deeply cognitive. They focus on problem solving in new ways. They are undeniably emotional and value-laden—some say they are also spiritual. Finally, arts making calls for use of every body part.

Engage, Then Inform.   In artful lessons teachers use the arts to get attention and spark interest before they delve into information. Arts strategies cause students to become purposefully active. This engagement causes them to seek information, not resist it. Arts engagement strategies often are used in the lesson introduction, but should be used throughout lessons to sustain engagement. Teachers engage

by creating intellectual unrest, which sets creative problem solving in motion. They pose problems, provoke curiosity, and ask questions. Deciphering cartoons and other visual art is used. Engagement is also triggered by surprise, novelty, riddles, mindbogglers, and physical warm-ups that challenge students to use logic and leaps of imagination to "get it." Note: All the Seed Strategy chapters include an Energizers and Warm-Ups section.

Humor strategies are also common engagement tools because (1) humor is naturally motivating, (2) the source of humor is problems, (3) to "get it," you have to make novel connections, and (4) producing and understanding humor is an art. Humor art, like cartoons, requires no grade, points, or outside reward and can set off further creative problem solving. Original cartoons and riddles can synthesize ideas from any subject (Cornett, 2001). For example, at one elementary school, students studied cartooning and then illustrated sentences types. Characters in each panel spoke in declarative, exclamatory, or interrogative sentences.

Generic engagement strategies, such as Think–Pair–Share (TPS), can be used alongside arts strategies. For example, after asking a question, give think time. After a minute or so, partner for sharing. Every Pupil Response (EPR) can also be used. For example, ask for "thumbs up" to show students have a response; wait for most to signal, if it is important.

Transformation.   Passive listening to a lecture or watching a video is not the best path to understanding. Head–hands–heart directed learning rests on the belief that if you don't think, feel, and act, you don't learn. The arts are not about sponging up. Subject area material is transformed through the arts as any topic or question is problem solved and re-presented through visual art, drama, music, dance, and poetry. It is each student's job to use head, hands, and heart to solve the problem of how to understand and express ideas in personally meaningful ways. The arts are transformation tools.

Creative Problem Solving (CPS)

All arts-based lessons focus on all or some part of CPS, outlined in Chapter 2. This process is how we construct meaning in any form. It is an inquiry process that expects unpredictable answers and products. It is how art is created and understood. This process orchestrates all higher-order thinking for a clear purpose—solving problems. Teachers should teach the process throughout the school year. This includes posting the process. For an example of how one school has adapted the process, see "Transfer" under Explicit Teaching.

Setting the Stage.   The classroom is an ideal haven for students to experiment and make mistakes, to "give it a try and see what happens." Risk taking can be celebrated, even when the results don't work: "I'm glad you tried to write a poem without rhyme. I hear you saying you don't like the poem. Is there a part you do like? How could you use that part?" These questions acknowledge the courage it takes to do something different. Creative risk taking can also be studied through stories about real people, some of whom may have initially appeared foolish. For example, Monet and Stravinsky were publicly ridiculed for their avant-garde approaches. Use the newspaper to find examples and create an add-on bulletin board to honor risk takers.

Connections.   The brain works by making and accessing neural connections to create meaning. The arts are all about connecting, especially through metaphor and analogy. When we ask, "What is this like?" we set the stage for students to call up known images to understand new ideas. Artful teaching stretches students to make unusual comparisons and not just use "hard as rock" clichés.

Activating prior knowledge causes the brain to physically change as it connects new to the known. Teachers can ask, "What letters do you know in the word?" or "What chunks?" to help children figure out unknown words. Arts-based lessons include questions such as "What do you know about shapes? Colors? Jazz? Charlie Chaplin?" Students can also brainstorm key ideas (e.g., "balance" in visual art, dance, math, and writing) to activate the known or use the KWL strategy: students list what they *know*, what they *want* to know, and, finally, after the lesson is finished, what they *learned* (Ogle, 1989).

Visual Literacy.   It is nearly impossible to think about the past or plan for the future without mental images. This is our internal visual art. Best teaching practice is informed by this fact. Explicit teaching about why and how to picture in your head and use imagination (note the root word is *image*) can triple understanding. For example, ask students to visualize a concept like *dog*. Prompt them with the arts elements: add color, shape, and texture. Next, interview students about what they see. What *dog* means to one will be different from everyone else. Our dog experiences are different and we all think about "dogness" by visualizing our background. Understanding is also stimulated by other perceptual senses: hearing, touching, and moving that are integral to the arts.

Empathy.   The word *empathy* was originally coined to label a distinct response to arts involvement. Empathy is more cognitive than sympathy and more emotional than critical distance. Arts-based lessons provide the context for developing this high-level perspective in which we stand in the shoes of others, seeing as they must, feeling as they might. Empathy, alone, solves many problems. In artful classrooms teachers develop empathy by giving students experiences with diverse art forms and asking questions like "How did

the artist who made this think and feel? What would you say/do if you were _____?" Drama activities in which students actually assume roles are examples of strategies that promote empathy.

Inquiry and Questioning.   It seems only logical that "encouraging children to be explorers and questioners, rather than passive acceptors, cannot help honing creativity, thinking and learning" (Starko, 1995, p. 114). Inquiry approaches focus on engaging students in investigations of problems for which there is no one right answer. Teachers activate inquiry when they:

- Ask open/fat questions: "When does it look right, feel right? What makes it good? Beautiful?" Students then share and compare ideas. Integrity is increased when students know they need evidence for their answers.
- Ask students to pose questions: "What questions do you have about this song?"
- Use questions to direct future study. Time is structured for independent or group research (Short et al., 1996).

"Question of the day" and "Answer of the day" are routines that encourage inquiry. These should come from students. For example, one student wanted to know how much trash the school threw away. Students interviewed custodians and cafeteria workers and surveyed kids about how much they left on their plates. A PowerPoint presentation with colorful graphs was used as students assumed roles as reporters (drama) to present findings.

Booth thinks students are made to "feel dumb" when teachers begin with questions about titles and facts (e.g., Who wrote Beethoven's Fifth?). He believes "right or wrong is just too simplistic a way to assess the value of ideas" and can damage the relationship between students and teachers (p. 23). Fat questions like "What makes you think that?" "How do you know that?" "What do you see?" "What have you discovered?" and "Why?" cause more thinking than closed ones that call for yes or no answers. Open questions call for personal meaning making. Closed questions have a single right answer—no meaning making, just recall.

Even a dull closed question such as "Who was the first president of the United States?" can be made interesting when changed to "What do you know about the first president of the United States?" Better yet, "Show me what you know about the first president of the United States," which yields pantomimes of tree chopping, horse riding, posturing, and even lying in a funeral pose. Fat questions stimulate integrated thinking because they ask for ideas to be retrieved, synthesized, and transformed. A good habit is to use questions that begin with "What if? Why? How?" Avoid yes-no queries that start with *who, could, would, should,* and *when.* Couple questions with a wait time of at least 5 seconds to get more responses of better quality.

Explicit Teaching

Howard Gardner, architect of multiple intelligences, believes students need more than "opportunities" to paint, to pot, or to dance. He describes this as a "ploy that makes little sense as students crave arts knowledge and skills that expand their understanding and expression capabilities" (1989, p. 141). Without instruction Gardner warns that student work will be "either derivative from the mass media, or show a vestige of a good idea but lack the technical means to express it properly." The consequence: Students may have a creative spark, but not the basic skills to take the idea further. Opportunity without tools is not opportunity at all.

I Do, We Do, You Do, Re-Do.

An important way to ensure students that clearly grasp concepts and gain facility with skills is to be explicit. Explicit teaching lets students in on the purposes of lessons and the agenda at the outset. It often happens in short 5- to 10-minute mini-lessons and consists of teaching why (purposes), what (actual content or skills, including labels), and how (demonstration, with several examples). Special educator professor Chuck Novak teaches the mnemonic "I DO (teacher sets purpose, shows, and explains), WE DO (scaffolded practice together with coaching), and YOU DO (independent practice, rehearsal, reflection) to explain explicit teaching. RE-DO enables students to revise based on feedback.

Clear teaching about arts concepts and skills is absolutely necessary to quality arts integration and is the responsibility of both classroom teachers and arts specialists. Explicit teaching includes teaching the *why* or purpose of learning, the *what* and demonstrating the *how*. The *how* includes scaffolded practice, followed by rehearsal to gain independence.

For example, if students are expected to use dance to understand and express the meaning of *The Three Bears,* they first need explicit teaching of dance elements. The teacher might begin with questions about how people communicate through their bodies—to say hello and goodbye, to show confidence or confusion. Next, the teacher could ask students to explore body, energy, space, and time using a visual of the BEST dance element (Ready Reference 10.2) to prompt thinking and demonstrate examples. Specific emotions might be danced together like showing happiness with just fingers or toes. Students might next be asked to show happiness with different body shapes and moves. During this group practice the teacher would describe BEST elements students used appropriately and ask questions like, "What's another body part you could use?" The teacher

might coach students to try different levels and speeds to discover the effects. Finally, students could be grouped to select an emotion to dance from the beginning, middle, or end of the story. Dance criteria, such as use of variety and ability to sustain focus, would be discussed in advance to help students plan movement with quality in mind.

Transfer.

How can teachers cause thinking learned in one context, like the arts, to transfer to other academic contexts? To begin with, transfer is not a "one-way" street. There should be a reciprocal and respectful relationship between the arts and other academic areas in which "one subject challenges the other" (Rooney, 2004, p. 11). Explicit teaching for transfer (e.g., telling and showing how dance composition ideas can be used in writing) by classroom teachers and arts specialists is a commonsense idea. It involves being direct about the connections between what is being learned in the arts and how that learning can be transferred to other curricular contexts and vice versa. For example, in the *Learning Through Music* model, explicit teaching is used to teach a variation on CPS—five essential processes in every lesson: (1) listen/describe, (2) question/investigate, (3) create/transform, (4) perform/demonstrate, and (5) reflect/connect/self-assess (Davidson, Cloar, & Stampf, 2003). Clearly these are ways to think and learn that have high transfer potential because they are integral to any deep learning.

Two-Way Transfer.

A bus transfer allows a rider to use one ticket to get to more than one place. It is a great idea because you get more for your money. Transfer of learning is similar. Students can get to multiple destinations from one lesson.

It is readily apparent that a fundamental concept like proportion is "no less authentic and indigenous to music than it is to math" (Scripp, 2003, p. 129), but standards are not set up with cross-referencing. Teachers need to seek out connections and teach fundamental shared concepts across domains to maximize lesson effects. If math is taught well, it seems likely that music would be integrated to support counting and fractions. The concept of proportion can be taught in a math-only manner but is given more depth and breadth if also learned through visual art, music, and dance. It should work two ways. Classroom teachers and arts specialists both need to teach for transfer. For example, music teachers can easily teach pitch and rhythm by drawing on number awareness, sense of proportion, and other mathematical understandings (Scripp, 2003). It seems antiquated to persist in thinking about teaching and learning using no-way or one-way transfer models. Integration transcends parochial thinking and accepts that any concept or discipline can be understood from the perspective of another. Math isn't taught to get results on math tests. Visual art isn't just about creating an exhibit. Of course, this demands a new kind of teacher preparation, and this book is about that kind of preparation.

Teaching specific creative and artistic meaning-making strategies, like SCAMPER, in the context of math, science, social studies, reading, and writing helps students understand why they are learning them. Just being explicit about the need to make the effort to create can cause a transfer of creative thinking skills. Pausing to point out impromptu use of creative strategies during lessons raises the level of explicitness. Displaying the CPS process (Ready Reference 2.5) and directing students to use it as a resource are also important.

Apply, Practice, Rehearse

Arts integration focuses on applying knowledge and skills to accomplish problem solving. Application solidifies learning. Rehearsal or repeated practice of introduced material helps students gain confidence and own their learning. One of the greatest problems in our schools is not giving appropriate and adequate amounts and numbers of practices. Without practice, it is almost impossible to achieve competence. Competence puts us in control of our own lives.

Coaching. Coaching has long been used in the arts. This kind of scaffolding helps students as they work alone or in groups. The teacher makes suggestions, but does not give answers. Thought-provoking and leading questions are used. For example, during drama the teacher will coach students to stay focused and concentrate to show they are staying in character. She also asks "what-if" questions to stretch thinking.

Descriptive Feedback. Of particular importance is coaching with descriptive feedback, not just praise. "Good! Great! Awesome!" are vague, overused, value-laden words. Their genuineness can be doubted. People tend to believe specifics. Specific truthful comments on work gives valuable guidance and causes students to feel important. It takes time, thought, and attention to generate such feedback. Consider the difference between "Super job!" and "Rudy, you used many different facial expressions in your pantomime. That showed you were staying in character." Imagine how you'd feel if a teacher said you'd get an A or a certificate on Friday—if you were good all week. I'd want to know exactly what the teacher meant by "good" first. Then I could decide whether I wanted to "be good" and whether I wanted to be good just to "be good" or be corrupted by focusing on what I'd get for being good. The point is that it is important to use specific language when giving feedback. This liberates students and sets them on a path to creating higher-quality work. Basic arts elements offer a focus to describe what students make, do, and say. In

addition, using the child's name and emphasizing positive progress connects feedback to goals.

Aesthetic Orienting

The power of the arts to stimulate aesthetic knowing should not be neglected. One good way to harness that power is to get into the habit of initially soliciting emotional responses. For example, instead of first using picture book art to predict problems and events, ask students to look closely at a page and share how it feels. Ask volunteers to speculate how artists cause viewers to react with feelings. The arts have tremendous potential to engage emotions and increase sensitivity and empathy. Teachers can activate emotional intelligence and give it direction: "How does this make you feel?" and "Why?" questions are good aesthetic tools to give this orientation.

Observe, Interpret, Reflect. It nourishes the soul to pause to examine a spider web glistening with dew or listen to the principal whistle as she walks down the hall. Taking time to gather data gives depth to interpretation. Aesthetic understanding is developed when teachers slow it down. We can teach students to listen closely, look at details, and notice patterns. We can coach them to sense emotions in music and art and figure out how artists cause these reactions. Eventually students learn to refrain from instant judgments that occur when they react with "unexamined prejudices" (Booth, 2003, p. 22).

Meaning making using the prism of the arts is not a fast way to teach. The artist in us will not be hurried. It takes time for students to explore shapes they can make with their bodies and translate newfound shapes into messages about science. When movement is used to show understanding of verbs like *hunker down* or *slink*, students experience aesthetic knowing. At such times teachers need to step back, watch, listen, and then give descriptive feedback and piggyback on students' ideas to stretch them. Integrating the arts requires habits of the heart and mind that help remove "get it covered quickly" guilt.

Careful observation is the foundation of coming to a sense of what makes quality work. Observe-interpret-reflect is a recommended plan of action to increase aesthetic knowing. It also is a wonderful guide for teachers as they assess because the focus is on gathering evidence. As teachers, we need to relax and carefully observe our students and ourselves.

Delight in Diversity. Artful teachers emphasize that every person works and learns differently. Alternative views and new perspectives are sought. Teachers press students to transform ideas and show understanding in many different ways. The arts are featured in those "different ways." For example, the meaning of a word like *pule* can be shown through body actions, art materials, sounds, and musical instruments. Teachers show delight when students surprise everyone with novel ideas. Teachers affirm them by saying, "I hear what you are saying," "I never thought of that," and "What an unusual idea!" Such comments show a value for the unique through supportive, honest description—not vapid praise. Teachers need to speak the truth: "Marla has an idea no one else has mentioned" and "Joe's idea is different from anyone else's." Questions can affirm, too. "What are some other answers? What's another way we could do this?" convey strong messages. Of course, it isn't just what is said, but how it is said. It's a good idea to periodically tape a lesson and reflect on the music of your voice.

Integrated Versus Isolated.   The National Assessment of Educational Progress (NAEP) shows that students do well with literal comprehension. Unfortunately, students have great difficulty with implicit messages—making sense, rather than just getting an explicit main idea. This suggests they lack the content or thinking skills to get beyond the obvious. Isolated teaching of comprehension skills hasn't worked (Pressley, 2002). The arts, however, are proving to be promising tools and contexts to move students beyond literal thinking.

Artistic thinking is high-level cognition coupled with deep respect for emotional ways of knowing. In particular, the arts rely on CPS, which orchestrates, rather than isolates, a broad range of thinking skills. Basic arts background gives students the knowledge to ask questions, pursue interests, make choices, interpret, express new meanings, and judge worthiness. These processes are special provinces of the arts because problem solving is at the core. For example, arts concepts help in forming provocative questions: "What colors does Eric Carle use? How would his books feel differently if he used more pastels?" Basic arts knowledge enables teachers and students to be more creative because concepts can be combined in an infinite number of ways to create more art and make new interpretations. It is harder to use general ideas, like "integrating art," than to plan using specifics like collage or 3D art.

Balancing Wholes and Parts.   Attention to the whole, while noticing component parts, is an important lesson the arts teach. Fragmenting learning into isolated skill or concept lessons does not yield a satisfied feeling and can lead to dissatisfaction with school and learning. To truly understand, students must be helped to perceive pictures, poems, and songs as wholes, while attending to the patterns and pieces that contribute to making the entirety possible.

Eisner (1997) explains this concept using map reading. A map must be perceived as a whole design, not a collection of discrete pieces. It must be understood that each nation is situated within a continent. Where a continent is situated on the globe is as important in understanding geo-graphical space as where a city is within a nation. This descends down to the house level. Pieces are meaningless without context. This applies to isolated skill teaching with worksheets and fact drills with flash cards.

Brainstorming is a good thinking skill to illustrate this point. It is inefficient to practice brainstorming apart from real problems. Brainstorming, predicting, summarizing, and evaluation are important only when used for genuine purposes. That is why students are taught to use the CPS to make meaning about important ideas in science and social studies. CPS is an incredible organization of higher-order thinking skills, but it is only valuable when it is applied. Thinking or comprehension taught in isolation just doesn't stick (Pressley, 2002).

Process and Product

Students and teachers need to understand that the arts are fundamentally processes we used to solve communication problems. This idea is developed over time using questions and activities that cause students to use unique arts processes. For example, "How can you use your body to communicate confusion? What lines and shapes communicate confusion? How can confusion be understood with musical elements?" If students and parents don't understand the importance of using diverse communication processes in real life, they won't buy into the deep value of arts integration. Ready Reference 3.3 lists topics for short mini-lessons to develop this concept.

The rule of thumb for arts is to emphasize arts thinking and doing over end products. However, performances and displays are important features that show the results of problem solving. This process emphasis is demonstrated when student artwork is exhibited in school galleries that change monthly, while discussing and making art happen every day. The goal is not perfect dance technique or expertly executed lines in yearly plays. Visual art becomes integral to prewriting and as a post-writing response. Sketching is used as an alternative way to journal. Creative movement and dance, singing, and close listening to music all make up daily life in an arts-based classroom. Art making isn't focused on making something cute to decorate the walls or give to mom. The arts are used to make sense and express meaning, not just entertain and impress. Children learn to please the inner audience as they work for deep understanding and seek quality work.

The bottom line is the thinking that goes into the work is what is more important. We should avoid look-alike products and swear off using teacher-made patterns to trace. Stereotyped images of suns, birds, and people are signs the philosophy of arts integration is shallow. So is an emphasis on learning specific dances rather than using dance elements to think. Copying is low-level thinking; imitation may be a compliment to the originator, but we want children to be the originators.

Dictated Art.

Art educator Peggy Jenkins (1986) calls coloring books, fill-in patterns, and outlines "dictated art." Following directions is not art making. Overemphasis on exact directions can cause loss of belief in one's creativity and reduce sensitivity and independent thinking. There is little or no emotional outlet. Children become conformists who stereotype colors of people and shapes of animals. They get the wrong idea that there is a "right" way. Children can become confused and rigid as they struggle to "stay in the lines."

Examples and Models.

The word *model* has come to imply something to copy. While we don't want copying, students do need examples. Albert Schweitzer said examples aren't the important thing, they're everything to understanding; there is a mountain of difference between examples and models. If a teacher shows a collage as a model, presents step-by-step directions, and leaves the model up, students are likely to copy it. A teacher who uses collage as a meaning-making tool will show several examples and present options for creation. Students are coached to create their own meaning by gleaning ideas from a variety of sources. This provides tools without squashing creativity.

Management: Behavior, Time, and Materials

Arts integration requires a combination of clear expectations, flexible time blocks, and predictable routines. Students learn to work responsibly and skillfully with arts techniques, tools, and materials.

Structure and Limits.

Arts-based learning is not loosey-goosey, do-your-own-thing work. In the world outside of school, work is defined by expectations. Creative thinking is ratcheted up by expectations of quality work on authentic problems, given the pressures of time and limited resources. Arts integration thinking aligns with this idea of setting up boundaries to increase CPS and quality work. Consider the difference between "take 1 minute and be creative" and "you have 1 minute to think of ways to use this pencil to make the fan stop humming." Students need to learn to work within limits and focus on problem solving. They should also be taught that use of materials is contingent upon following rules. Criteria for creative work need to be discussed so students understand what "quality" may entail. For example, a dance needs a beginning, middle, and end and variety to communicate and be interesting. These boundaries boost creative thinking. Higher-quality work results, and students are more proud of their efforts.

Personal Projects.

It isn't difficult to set aside time, at least once a week, for interest work. Such short- and long-term projects provide important opportunities for in-depth study. At a simple level, students can develop collections (e.g., rocks, cards, pictures) that can spur study and be arts-making resources (e.g., poems about rocks). Collections and personal investigations cause students to take pride in growing their expertise and individuality.

Explore and Experiment.

Creative ideas don't just pop out of nothingness. You have to mess around, and that makes a mess. Students need to know this. Time needs to be spent playing with art media, observing the work of others, brainstorming, reading, and listening to music for nugget ideas. Exploration time is not "doing nothing." Time is always needed to explore whenever something new is introduced. Exploring and experimenting are start-up strategies that include seeing where the materials take you. Students need to have fun first. Then, when they are feeling good, they will be ready for specific directions and expectations. *Note:* "Use great idea" folders to save sketches, notes, pictures, and words.

Real-World Stuff.

We were looking for a new house recently. We found one on the Internet. My brother-in-law, Bob, sent us 60 pictures and a four-page report on the property. It's not enough. Being there is what it takes. Live concerts, theatre performances, real art (not reproductions), authentic arts materials, tools, and techniques are without equal. Teaching has to include simulations, but expanding use of primary sources and getting students' hands dirty gives more life to learning.

Students want to play significant roles outside of school. This implies we should use real-world materials in school and lay off reliance on workbooks, drill sheets, and thick texts. Primary source material such as diaries, autobiographies, and actual paintings make learning more interesting because they are real-life objects. In addition, students should be taught the methodology of researchers (e.g., data gathering through surveys) rather than passively reading about the work of others. Note that this is an early step in CPS.

Unlocking.

Students can never have enough tools, techniques, and kinds of media. Each new art makes a contribution to expression and may be the one that will be the spark. We recently had an art exhibit at our local museum by a man who didn't begin painting until he was nearly 70. He had cerebral palsy, was wheelchair bound, and for most of his life was not able to express himself because he could not talk. One day an art therapist attached a stylus to a headband. A paintbrush was attached, and Ralph Bell proceeded to paint every day for the rest of his life—more than 1,000 paintings. Students need to hear these kinds of stories to realize that much is locked inside each of us waiting to be released through the arts.

Independence and Self-Discipline

It is time-consuming, frustrating, even painful, to watch students struggle to do what we could do for them so quickly. It is easier to just draw a horse for the child who can't. The question is, what is the goal? If the goal is to end up with a great horse picture, perhaps the teacher should do it. This is rarely the goal. An important goal is to have students experience the pride that comes when they persist and do the work themselves. If it is done for them, they may be grateful, but they can't be proud. That's the *tri* in triumph.

Controls.   A frequent mantra in arts-based schools is to control your mind, body, and voice. This doesn't mean shut up, sit still, and follow directions. Students are taught the ranges of ways they can manage thinking, imagination, body parts and motion, and voices to solve problems and communicate meaning.

Persistence.   Well-intentioned teachers and parents shield children from frustrations necessary to achieve independence. The "learned helpless" syndrome is the result. Students need to struggle, with support. It is helpful to talk about hard work we've attempted with successful and unsuccessful results. We can share efforts at creative production, focusing on effort, not the product. We absolutely need to dispel the notion that great ideas just pop out. A balloon must be filled before it pops. So it is with people and CPS. Creative thinking rests on pumping in knowledge and skills, and then great ideas do seem to just pop up. Few artists hit the jackpot on the first or second try; they serve as biographical examples of how persistence pays off.

Fix-Ups.   Most important is teaching students self-help "fix-ups" and other strategies to deal with problems. Posting problem-solving steps, arts elements charts, and book response choices gives students independent resources. We can also explicitly teach strategies like set work aside and come back later, stop and get input from another source, use music to relax, examine past work for ideas, and make use of mistakes, brainstorm, or web. A general classroom expectation is that students should "try something" before asking for help. Teachers can then attend to help signals (like a red flag stuck in a ball of clay on a desk) by asking, "What have you tried? What do you know? What could you try? What has worked before?" How pitiful for children to have no way to cope except to passively wait for someone to come and do it for them.

Work Habits.   Independence is also built through clear expectations (#1 Best Practice). General expectations and responsibilities should be outlined and practiced beginning the first day. These include classroom rules (see Appendix for examples), cues for attending (e.g., teacher claps a rhythm), process for making space for drama, materials use and cleanup, cooperative group behaviors, and peer critique procedures.

Blueprint VII: Instruction Design

Both research and learning theories support predictable, but flexible, instructional design using time structures, regular routines, and rituals that implement arts integration philosophy. Routines and structures are used in the classroom and school schedule to ensure that the arts are institutionalized in school life. Structures include how lessons are introduced, developed, and concluded. Routines range from energizers to start lessons to cleanup procedures and wrap-up rituals. Time for long-term projects and pursuit of personal arts interests is built into the schedule as well, through clubs and centers.

Instructional Design

Effective lessons share a general organization that is used in arts-based instruction: introduction, development, and conclusion (IDC).

IDC.   Just as a good meal or a well-written paper has a beginning, middle, and end, so does an effective lesson. A short **introduction** prepares students for learning and allows teachers to assess students' background. The mood of the lesson is set, and the purposes or focus of the lesson is made clear so students feel the lesson is meaningful. Teachers may begin with a provocative question or introduce vocabulary through a riddle or "mystery bag" containing items related to key lesson concepts. The introduction should be brief but, if skipped, students may never tune in and remain uninvolved in subsequent lesson segments.

In the **development** the teacher presents or demonstrates. A sense of the whole is developed, perhaps through storytelling, sharing artwork, or listening to a piece of music. A skill or strategy may be presented to use with a problem or question previously introduced. Students explore and discuss, practice, and apply skills, strategies, or media use in this stage.

Finally, in the lesson **conclusion,** students are expected to go beyond mere imitation of demonstrated skills and pull together problem solutions, showing they have learned and used personal creativity, artistry, and higher-order thinking. The conclusion provides the satisfaction of completion and is an important part of continuing learner motivation.

Introduction, development, and concluding strategies are the workhorses of teaching (see the integrated lesson plan in Planning Page 3.3). The arts are natural motivators, attention getters, and interest generators so they fit naturally in introductions. For example, Picasso's *Guernica* might be displayed to generate questions or reactions to war. Drama activities could be used introduce a unit dealing with "cycles

Two-Pronged Lesson Plan

Two-Pronged Focus: What specific skills and concepts are to be taught? Prongs include (1) arts content (concepts and skills) to be taught and (2) core academic content.

Student Objectives: What important student behaviors will be developed and assessed/evaluated? (tied to the focus prongs)

Teaching Procedure: How will the arts and other strategies be used to help students problem solve? (I–D–C organization)

Introduction

1. *Attention/focus:* Eliminate distractions and use signals.
2. *Interest:* Present questions, a riddle, mystery, or problem.
3. *Set mood:* Use vocal variation, music, lighting.
4. *Set purpose:* Focus on understanding. Connect to life.
5. *Review and relate:* Activate background with prediction and anticipation activities, fat questions, brainstorming, or webbing (also yields assessment data).
6. *Make ground rules and expectations clear.*
7. *Energizers and warm-ups:* Engage head-heart-hands.
8. *Vocabulary:* Elements and important concepts may be introduced using visuals, context, and movement.

Development

1. Teacher presents, shows, and provides an experience to engage students in problem solving.
2. A story may be told or piece of artwork displayed.
3. A skill or strategy may be presented to use with a problem or question previously introduced.
4. Students explore, discuss, experiment, practice, and apply in this stage.
5. Students may plan and rehearse as the teacher coaches while circulating around the classroom.

Conclusion

1. Students "show they know." Students are expected to go beyond mere imitation of a demonstrated skill or idea. They are to pull together a problem solution, apply new knowledge and skills, and show they have learned and used personal creativity and artistry. This may involve a performance for peers.
2. Self- and peer-assessment, as well as teacher assessment, occurs through a debriefing activity.
3. End with a calming activity (e.g., fantasy journey, journal entry).

Assessment

1. Return to the objectives to gauge student progress. Items may be added to a portfolio to connect work to stated portfolio goals (standards).

or patterns" by involving students in mime of everyday activities done in the morning, afternoon, and evening. "The Star Spangled Banner" could be examined as a source of feelings and messages to start a unit on American history. The arts are equally valuable as responses to learning in a lesson conclusion. By writing songs and poems, making art, and performing skits and dances, students show what they know. Fourth graders wrote this song after studying the chemical effects of humor on the body (to tune of "Ghost Busters"): When you're all alone and your smiles are gone, who ya' gonna' call? GRIMBUSTERS! When you're feelin' blue and you don't know what to do, who ya' gonna' call? GRIMBUSTERS! They'll make you laugh 'til you cry. Give you a natural high. So, who ya' gonna' call? GRIMBUSTERS!

In general, most lessons proceed in a whole–part–whole manner, giving opportunities to experience the arts aesthetically before examining the parts and pieces. This is accomplished by artful teachers who create individual variations on the lesson framework previously described. Planning Page 3.3 is a framework for integrated planning. More plan examples appear in subsequent arts chapters.

Energizers and Warm-Ups. We wouldn't think of going to a fine restaurant and starting the meal with filet mignon. We shouldn't begin an arts-based lesson without a starter, either. Divergent thinking needs to be unlocked, muscles need to warm up, and voices need to be prepared. Energizers don't need to be lengthy, but they are essential to activating CPS and giving focus. They attract attention, boost concentration, relax, and stimulate CPS. Energizers are usually a part of a lesson introduction, but they can be used at any point to enliven or focus attention. They take the form of questions, movement, tongue twisters, games, chants, poems, songs, and word play.

Each of the arts Seed Strategy chapters describes activities to warm up for creative work. Many collections of energizers are also available, such as *Playfair* (Weinstein) and books by Viola Spolin and David Booth. Focus Ball is one example.

It is a mirroring activity for concentration. A leader puts her hands together, as if holding an invisible ball. Students mirror as the ball is slowly raised, lowered, made larger and smaller.

Opening/Closing Routines.

We all know the best way to diet, exercise, or learn is to set up an ongoing schedule. One of the most effective ways to ensure that the arts are a living part of the class is to establish daily arts routines in which students assume the roles of researchers and presenters. Ms. Lucas used such routines in the Classroom Snapshot. Opening arts routines include everything from artist of the day to arts journaling. Any of these may be part of a classroom circle meeting. Closing routines can include some of the same morning routines or ones suited to wrap up (e.g., singing an ending song together as cleanup happens). After-lunch rituals are common, especially arts-based read-alouds and journaling to music. Generally, each takes a few minutes. Students can sign up or be selected to lead routines as they do for classroom jobs. Other routines are:

Word of the Day (WAD).

Students or the teacher choose an interesting word (e.g., *baroque, scumbling, onomatopoeia*) and display it. A 1-minute lesson on the word is then presented. The "word expert" can sing or say the word, use it in context, mime or show pictures, use objects, explain or show examples, or give nonexamples. The class is asked to think of ways to use the word and is challenged do so throughout the day. In "Beat the Teacher" the class tallies the times the WAD words are used.

Pattern Finds.

Any material can be used to engage students in finding high-frequency symbol patterns, both graphic (visual) and aural/oral. Discovering the importance of redundancy is a learning breakthrough that empowers students. Once they realize that artists, authors, musicians, dancers, and actors use many of the same ideas over and over, they feel it's OK for them to do so. As an example, in the riddle "What is the name of the boy who hangs on the wall?" (Answer: Art), students might find phonic patterns like the diphthong "-oy" in *boy*. Others might find patterns writers use to create visual images with words like "hangs on the wall." Students learn how words can be spelled the same, but have different meanings and pronunciations determined by context (Ready Reference 3.5 on multiple meaning words). Repeated elements can be found in music (refrains), art (geometric shapes), dance (nonlocomotor moves), and drama (facial expressions). Patterns occur at note and letter levels and make up the large structures called *genres* (e.g., a literary genre such as science fiction or a musical genre such as jazz).

Performances and Exhibits.

Students need to be able to predict that their learning will be synthesized into a culminating event. Expectations of these events drive learning. Students experience satisfaction and pride for work well done and are motivated by the force of the audience. A level of anxiety energizes performers and exhibitors as they await reaction and hope for a positive reception. Performances and exhibits are also experiences that bond students and give a

---

Ready Reference 3.5 Multiple Meaning Arts Words

The following are examples of shared arts vocabulary. Teach the multiple meanings to increase understanding and to show links between the arts and other curricular areas.

act	energy	make	plot	space
action	focus	middle	prop	stage
back	frame	mind	rate	step
bend	freeze	mold	read	stretch
block	front	mood	role	theme
body	hard	motion	round	time
bright	high	move	rhythm	turn
circle	level	opening	set	voice
cold	light	pattern	setting	volume
color	line	pitch	shade	walk
curtain	loud	place	shape	warm
direction	low	play	soft	write
draw				

sense of belonging. The most powerful performances grow out of student ideas. Students take leadership, and performances aren't overly teacher directed. Weekly performances include Poetree Presentations (see Chapter 4), and Reader's Theatre (RT), which is frequently tied to guided reading groups. In my classes students regularly prepared RT scripts by adapting poems and other reading material to script form. Every Monday students knew they were responsible for Poetry Performances (Ready Reference 5.3). Many schools schedule grade level and schoolwide events at the ends of units that include everything from art exhibits to PowerPoint presentations. A school art museum is becoming common with changeover exhibits every month or so, complete with exhibit openings. Performances and exhibits are memorable events all of us recall as we look back on schooling.

Grouping. Arts integration draws upon grouping practices to meet student needs. Large group work happens each day, but a great deal time is also scheduled for small group work. Classrooms are organized with tables and grouped desks to encourage collaboration. There is generally space for the teacher to do guided instruction with small groups as other groups work together, sometimes at centers and stations. Groups are sometimes pulled together for common needs, but common interest is also a high-placed criterion. The goal is for students to learn to work in diverse groups. Younger children need to work in pairs and smaller groups at first. Most students benefit from working in groups of four to six, whether it is for a book discussion or to plan a drama. See ideas for facilitating groups under Blueprint VI: "Best Practices."

Centers and Stations. Centers allow students to work independently with materials. In this book *station* refers to a narrowly focused area (e.g., a computer station might have software to explore unit themes or topics). A center is a space that has independent learning options from several sources (e.g., art materials, CDs, props, game boards, and other activities all related to a unit topic, such as "Reoccurring Patterns and Cycles in Our World").

Arts-based centers. All arts-based learning is problem centered. "How can you show _____?" through drama, dance, music, or visual art is a central question. The arts make visible the invisible. Centers offer opportunities for students to independently explore possibilities with drama props like hats and scarves, pictures of dance steps and shapes, a variety of CDs and homemade rhythm instruments and art-making tools and materials. None of these items is expensive or hard to come by and they are examples of materials that invite expression of ideas and feelings in alternative ways.

An Arts-for-Life Center is a general center that includes inspirational quotes about the arts and artists. One classroom job can be writing Arts-for-Life quotes in a special area of the chalkboard. Definitions of art can be found and created by students as they explore the idea of using the arts as learning tools. An arts timeline with birthdays of artists and other significant arts events can be a part of this center. Alongside the 1839 invention of the camera can be pictures and notes collected by students. Teachers can include a map to pin homes of artists. The center may house arts-based books organized by genres such as informational, biography, poetry, and fiction. See the Arts-Based Literature Bibliography in the Appendix.

Clubs and Projects. Regular formats for students to pursue arts-based interests are crucial. This can be time within the school day to do art making or listening to music at a center or station. At many schools there is daily or weekly time within the school day or after school for arts clubs. At Ashley River Creative Arts fourth and fifth graders comprise the Drama Troupe. Recently they performed "Goldilocks" in Spanish and in English. (All children take Spanish beginning in first grade.) Every day at 2:10 there is break-out time for specials. Beyond Drama Troupe, students may join an Art Guild, Chorus, Clay Club, Photography Club, Suzuki violin, and ballet. Students learn choice and responsibility. "It is like an after-school program, but within the school day," explains Assistant Principal Cathy Middleton. Storytelling clubs are also popular for students to share original or found stories.

Children get a sense of belonging in a club that represents their interests. Under the direction of an interested teacher they learn ideas, skills, and tools that allow club interests to grow artistically. Students learn how to use puppets, music, and other props in storytelling and develop oral dramatic skills so important in life in and outside of school. *The Power of Story* (Collins & Cooper, 1996) is a recommended resource for teachers who'd like a short book on storytelling. Also see Storytelling in Chapter 9.

Blueprint VIII: Adaptations for Diverse Needs

The arts can be used to motivate all students and are particularly rich sources for differentiating instruction. Arts integration expands options students can use to communicate through arts processes and materials, including use of multiple intelligences and multisensory methods.

Meaningful arts integration demands that arts connections be appropriate to student needs. The theories and stages described in Chapter 2 are resources to help decide whether certain arts content or processes are right for individuals and groups. In addition, teachers must accommodate for special needs of students and work with arts specialists to make adaptations. Developmentally appropriate ideas are presented in each chapter, and there is a chart in the Appendix.

Student Needs: 10 Ways to Diversify Instruction

Arts advocate Jane Remer has a motto: "All the arts, of all cultures, for all the children and youth, of all cultures." It's a beautiful dream. To make the dream a reality, educators can use the power of the arts to engage students. Overriding the concept of integration, however, is the need for any model or strategy to be differentiated for the range of student needs. Painting all students with the same brush will not create masterpiece lessons.

The word *individualization* itself holds a key. It is made of the chunks: in=not, di=two, vid=see, ual=one, tion=process. This translates into "the process of not seeing or treating two people as if they are one." This viewpoint helps educators address issues related to inclusion as well as delight in the strength and creativity diversity adds to humanity.

The following are general strategies to differentiate curriculum and instruction. They are a synthesis of common categories. The strategies are based on the belief that every child needs "particular" accommodations to ensure progress toward independence. Often the changes are minor.

Chances for student success increase when teachers adjust the PARTICULAR: place, amount, rate, target objective, instruction, curriculum, utensils, levels of difficulty, assistance, and response (Ready Reference 3.6).

1. Place (Learning Setting).
Change the nature of and size of the learning space. Use carrels, centers, music, different desk arrangements, carpet, and cushions. Lower or brighten lighting.

2. Amount (Time and Materials).
Give more or less time (e.g., to explore materials). Use more repetition, examples, and feedback. Give additional practice. Break into smaller steps. Reduce or increase the number of things to be learned.

3. Rate (Frequency).
Slow or quicken the pace. Give more breaks. Create more or less structure by changing the intensity of teacher direction during lessons.

4. Targets (Lesson Objectives).
Make objectives very clear. Use graphing and check-off sheets for goal attainment. Alter goals and the means for a student to reach the targets. Decide what a child can realistically achieve (know and be able to do). Connect to students' interests and lives.

5. Instruction (Teaching Strategies).
Use appropriate kinds and amounts of explicit instruction (model, demonstrate, examples, coaching, feedback, scaffold). Engage students cognitively, emotionally, and physically (hands on/brains on/hearts on). Use open questions, Every Pupil Response, and projects. Organize lessons from whole to part. Use inductive and deductive teaching. Set up routines to provide security, but encourage student choices. Use multiple intelligences, the arts, and multisensory approaches that cause students to be active in processing through visual, auditory, kinesthetic, and tactile modes.

6. Curriculum (Scope and Sequence of Experiences and Materials).
Use easier reading materials or adapt by highlighting main ideas, tape recording, and rewriting. Change order. Give choices within limits. Use hands-on materials such as games, computers, and art media. Use LADDM (Literature, Art, Drama, Dance, Music) throughout the curriculum.

7. Utensils (Media and Tools).
Use visual and auditory aids. Teach problem-solving tools and strategies, such as

---

 **PARTICULAR Adaptations for Student Needs**

Use these 10 areas of adjustment to make instruction more appropriate for the intellectual, physical, and emotional capabilities of students. See Appendix for adapting for students with special needs.

Place   (learning setting)
Amount   (time and materials)
Rate   (frequency)
Targets   (lesson objectives)
Instruction   (teaching strategies)
Curriculum   (scope and sequence of experiences and materials)

Utensils   (media and tools)
Level of Difficulty   (complexity)
Assistance   (scaffolding)
Response   (ways to show learning)

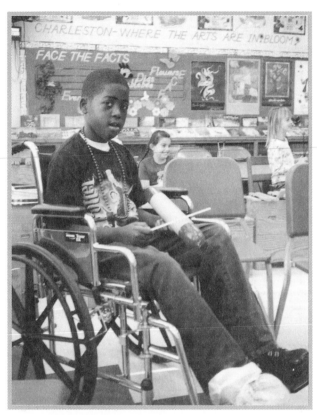

Anthony playing a rhythm instrument.

ways to figure out unknown words or what to do when you don't understand. Teach shortcuts and mnemonics. Use cue sheets and cards. Focus attention on details and patterns to help make meaning. Teach why and when to use strategies and how.

8. Level of Difficulty (Complexity). Make the lesson easier or harder to challenge appropriately. Highlight text essentials. Allow notes during tests. Alter structure or supervision.

9. Assistance (Scaffolding). Use peer tutoring, one on one, and small groups. Make the lesson agenda clear, and use prompts and cues. Coach toward independence by teaching fix-ups and directing attention to connecting known to the unknown, finding patterns, and using mnemonics.

10. Response (Evidence). Give students ways to show they know in a variety of ways. Use projects that call for a product or piece to perform. Distinguish among assessment, evaluation, and grading. Give exemptions (e.g., from oral reading).

Interventions for Special Needs Populations

The subject of the arts is the subject of life. The arts provide avenues to understand ourselves, make meaning of the world, express talents in unique ways, and create empathy for those different from ourselves. Through the arts, children discover common bonds with people. This understanding and awareness are the essence of the arts and can build a feeling of kinship. In a world where quality of life depends on the quality of our relationships with others, the arts can lessen feelings of alienation and be great levelers. No one is considered greater or lesser than another in his or her creative expressions and aesthetic tastes. With this in mind, we can think about similarities among diverse populations of students and stress commonalities, not just differences. We are all human with basics needs: to be respected, to belong, to achieve, and to communicate. Suggestions are given in the Appendix for planning adaptations for students categorized by special needs. These ideas should be used in conjunction with the 10 PARTICULAR ways to differentiate.

Blueprint IX: Assessment for Learning

> *Isn't it ironic, the state doesn't test what really makes us special. They don't even know how.* (Roberts, 2004)

At a recent conference, a speaker quipped, "If the government has its way, there will be no child's behind left." Indeed, the *No Child Left Behind Act* mandated expectations that have caused some schools to fixate on one kind of assessment, standardized tests. Intimidated schools constrict the curriculum to teach TO tests, even though 61% of the public disapproves of this tactic, and research shows early gains are not sustained (Herman & Baker, 2005; Rose & Gallup, 2005). Furthermore, overly directing students to test performance can decrease motivation, reduce achievement, increase drop-out numbers, and reduce the graduation rate (Allington, 2002; Guthrie, 2004; Stiggins, 2002).

Popular metaphors about assessment concerns crop up regularly. For example, "Just weighing a pig doesn't fatten it up," and "Opening the oven too soon causes a cake to fall." The high-stakes environment is based on simplistic notions and can lead to hopelessness. High-stakes tests can blow up a child's future. Assessment methods in arts integration give hope. Arts-based schools follow research that shows the best schools don't spend much time on test preparation. Instead they teach for understanding (Allington, 2002, 2005: Guthrie, 2004).

Assessment is as necessary in the arts as it is in any other curricular area. Arts assessment has traditionally been interwoven with the processes of creating art, which increases the quality of work. Unlike heavy-handed testing that has overtaken schools, the arts have historically relied more on self-assessment and peer critique during work, as well as of finished products. Criteria for good work evolves continually and is collaboratively created by artists, not imposed by onlookers. As a result, we have grown to expect a degree of excellence in the arts that is comparable only to perfectionist expectations about products such as airbags.

Definition and Purposes

Assessment is a process of gathering information. Assessment is distinct from evaluation and grading (see Chapter 14). The main reasons we assess are to: (1) motivate students to learn, (2) plan and adapt instruction, (3) track student progress toward standards and goals, including in the arts, and (4) evaluate the program. The purposes of assessment should determine *what* is assessed and *how*. The first three purposes are the focus of this book. Arts-based program assessment is beyond my scope, but a recommended resource is the South Carolina ABC schools website that features *Opportunity to Learn Standards* converted into clear evaluation tools (*www.winthrop.edu/ABC/*).

Evidence Driven

Twenty-first century assessment is correlated with national, state, and local standards and benchmarks. Standards are goals about what students should know, do, and be (Drake & Burns, 2004). Good assessment gives students multiple ways to show what they know, what they can do, and who they are BEcoming. Information is gathered about where students are in a learning progression; experiences are then designed to move students forward. Assessment is used to plan "what next?"

Issues

If teachers don't understand the purposes of assessment or don't know how to assess, they can become anxious or dismiss assessment as a waste of time. It is tempting for both teachers and artists to focus on student arts products more than the quality of the learning that produced them. Artists may dwell on "formal or technical understanding or easily tested outcomes" (Baker et al., 2004, p. 32); Arts integration is more about process. Then there is the myth that assessing artistic work somehow crushes creativity. Teachers may misconceive arts assessment as "subjective and therefore problematic" (p. 32). Artists generally don't see it this way. They have the vocabulary to talk with students in constructive ways and can help develop criteria to increase quality of work. Examples of "high-placed criteria" follow.

Finally, there is the issue of what is most important to assess. We can't create rubrics and checklists for everything. Standards help prioritize, but teachers need to judge their relative value; all standards are not equal. Many important goals are left out, such as character traits. Goals about honesty, initiative, and sense of humor trump many standards. Decisions need to be made about weight given to different criteria within rubrics as well. Teachers must resolve these issues, and there is no one right way. Teachers and artists should be the point in the debate about what makes quality.

For/Of

Arts integration gives priority to assessment *for* learning, not just *of* learning. The focus is on how assessment can alter learning, not just measure it. Assessment *for* learning is formative and ongoing (e.g., giving feedback on a paper so a student can rewrite it). Assessment *of* learning is summative—it describes the final result. Summative assessment happens after work is complete; assessment data isn't intended to change the work. At integrated arts schools, formative assessment is embedded in lessons. Everyone is involved, especially students who do self-reflection that creates ownership and suggests goals for personal improvement.

Assessment for learning rivals one-on-one tutoring in effectiveness, especially with low-performing students. It is a strong motivational tool that increases quality of work because relationships between effort, feedback, and achievement are emphasized (Stiggins, 2002). Criteria for good work are made clear using work samples, rubrics, and checklists. Students track their own progress and make changes, based on feedback, to increase quality. Assessment for learning features:

1. *Criteria for quality work are determined at the outset.* Students are clear about what is expected in advance of work. Front loading sets up motivation to learn and bonds students and teachers to work for excellence. Students see that feedback is intended to better their performance, not just grade it.

Criteria are best developed with students by discussing what "good work" might look like. Several exemplars of work, as well as examples of weak work, give a picture of possibilities—not of work to be copied. Artwork and videos of dance, music, and drama performances can be analyzed against criteria for good work. These boundaries focus and increase problem solving so students create more thoughtful solutions.

2. *Assessment criteria are fluid.* While criteria are specified, there is room for discoveries during learning. When these are found, criteria are modified.

3. *Continuous specific, doable feedback is given during and after learning.* This makes it more likely that students will sustain motivation and meet criteria. Questions like "What is working?" and "What do you need to do?" ensure that students understand feedback. Peers should give feedback as well, and students need to do regular self-assessment.

Assessing Assessment

Four characteristics stand out in describing effective assessment.

1. *Focus on strengths and needs.* Identifying weaknesses (what students don't know or can't do) is ineffective and mean-spirited. It is better to find out strengths and go right to meeting needs using strengths. To do so teachers use diagnostic tools such as an interest inventory early in the year.

2. *Authentic.* Information must be gathered in a context and manner that shows what students really know and can do. Paper-and-pencil tests are criticized for being inauthentic because they are unable to capture complex thinking, such as CPS. Valid assessments must be humane and doable. Through their implementation they must uplift, not defeat. In arts integration the challenge is to create assessment tools and processes as creative and diverse as the arts themselves.

3. *Multifactored.* No single observational checklist, nor one anecdotal note, can create a portrait of a child's growth. Multiple and varied assessments can give insight into student thinking during work and document growth over time. Culminating projects and portfolios can combine with traditional tests. The opportunity to have multiple means to show learning motivates students, especially those who have a track record of failure on tests. The arts add ways to assess and arts-based assessments can enhance learning.

4. *Continuous.* Data is collected in many ways and from a variety of sources, especially observation, in an ongoing manner. Self-reflection and peer feedback is integral to lessons. For example, in dance, teachers punctuate lessons with debriefings to discuss what's working, what's not working, and how to make it work. Drafts and work samples are collected that lay out concrete evidence of progress. Teachers use sticky notes on a clipboard to jot down observations so they can be easily transferred to student folders.

Assessment Tools

A cornucopia of formal and informal assessment tools is available, but not all are congruent with arts-based philosophy. True-false, fill-in, and multiple-choice tests can't show how a student uses CPS with artistic materials the way a long-term project will. Formal tools, like standardized tests, are mostly used for summative data on students and for program evaluation. As teachers, our most useful tools are informal because they yield specifics, not just percentiles or grades. Students can also use many of these tools to reflect and set goals. Informal tools focus on assessment for learning, which changes what is taught and how in response to needs. The Appendix includes examples of the following:

Checklists. Used to track concepts and skills to be learned during activities. A checklist of tasks allows students to independently track their progress.

Rubrics. There are a variety of types of rubrics. All make a gradient of performance clear, using some rating scale like 1–4. Some districts write school grade rubrics to make criteria for each letter grade understandable. Internet resources are:

- *school.discovery.com/schrockguide/assess.html*
- Educscapes: *www.eduscapes.com/tap/topic53.htm*
- *rubistar.4teachers.org/index.php*

High-Placed Criteria. Rubrics and checklists should focus on key concepts and processes shared by arts and academic areas:

- Using the arts to communicate ideas and feelings
- Showing ownership of work with original ideas
- Attention to details and patterns
- Using art vocabulary to describe and give evidence
- Participation (e.g., concentration, staying in role)
- Persistence in problem solving
- Making connections, especially unusual ones
- Participation (e.g., staying in role, concentration, focus)
- Using and articulating CPS
- Appropriate and creative use of artistic tools and techniques
- Explaining artistic choices
- Working collaboratively, listening, and giving suggestions

Benchmarks. Even when using a rubric, it is helpful to benchmark by "attaching quality to a small, rank-ordered body of student work and then using them for comparison in making judgments about a larger body of work" (Baker et al., 2004, p. 28–30). Students can do this as well. A study of arts-integrated lessons found that collaborative discussions using benchmarks of learning dramatically changed how teachers and artists viewed and used assessment (Baker, et al., 2004).

Performance-Based Assessment. Some argue that understanding can only truly be assessed, and for that matter, even achieved, through performance; students must do something that puts understanding to work (Perkins, 1998; Wiske, 1997). Quality and quantity of progress in the arts has long been demonstrated through performances, exhibitions, and portfolios. Learning is made visible through the arts as work is assessed using criteria for excellence connected to academic areas. In arts integration the arts are both assessment tools and areas that are assessed. Arts–based assessment yields clearer indicators of the kind and degree of learning and is a more comprehensive means of documenting growth.

Projects. Long-term projects often culminate in exhibits and performances that synthesize learning and involve audiences. Project-based units focus on struggling with authentic problems. Project criteria are developed with students in advance. The process to create the product is CPS.

Exhibits. Class museums and displays are a visual means for students to show learning. A school or class museum may just be a special wall. Mounting and framing student art shows it is valued. Museum information plaques should accompany work and contain the artist's name and birth date, the title of the work, the media used and surface, and the date the work was completed. Students can also prepare catalogs to go with exhibits for visitors to learn about the art and artists. These artifacts of learning are judged against prespecified criteria.

Portfolios. Showing capabilities with collected work has long been used in the arts. Work samples give evidence of progress toward criteria. For example, dated entries on audiotapes of oral reading show fluency growth. Drama responses and dances can be photographed and videoed so students can view, reflect, and set improvement goals. Students learn to self-evaluate using much the same criteria the teacher uses.

Not every piece of work should be kept; work that shows something important is the focus. Keeping just the good work does not allow students to see progress over time. Date work and connect items to specific goals. Work should be revisited to celebrate progress and past successes. Some schools now use digital portfolios, especially in the upper grades. A set of guidelines for arts folios is in the Appendix.

Anecdotal Records. Teachers make informal notes as students engage in activities and as they observe products. See an example for dance in the Appendix.

Student Self-Assessment. Student reflection on learning criteria gives a sense of how the real world operates. From the mechanic to the doctor, there are expectations that each worker will continually reflect on

performance and make necessary adjustments. Students should examine successive drafts of work to monitor change. Here are questions to prompt reflection about the CPS process. There are more in the Appendix. These can serve as discussion or writing prompts:

What were you trying to do?
Where and how did you get your ideas?
Why did you do what you did (decisions)?
What did you try that you've never tried before?
How is this connected to other learning? Arts?
What was most difficult?
What worked? What will you do next?
What did you learn most? What did you like best?
What three to five words describe your work?
How did this compare with other work you've done?
What advice would you give to someone else?

Peer Feedback. Students need to be taught *why* and *how* to respond to performances and exhibits of classmates. The art of noticing has to be practiced so students can make evidence-based comments about what they see and hear. Direct them to describe using specific arts concepts and their feelings: It made me feel _____. I wonder _____. The Learn–Wonder–Like (LWL) strategy can be used to jot down responses. Students should be taught that asking questions is a form of feedback, too. Role-playing giving and receiving feedback is good practice and develops empathy as students feel the effects of thoughtless remarks.

Individual Conferences. Personal conferences give valuable insight into children's thinking and convey the message you care about working toward goals. Short conferences of 3 to 5 minutes allow students to discuss goals and show progress. Students may be asked to bring a piece of artwork and explain how CPS was used or to read aloud to check fluency. Checklists, notes, rubrics, and work samples in the child's folio can be reviewed.

Interest Inventories. Interest has astounding effects on learning, but in interviews about memorable school experiences Starko (1995) did not find a single student who remembered being allowed to study a personal interest. We cannot make all lessons interest-based, but we can shift the balance in that direction and make achievement based on motivation more likely.

Teachers can inventory interests in many ways. One is to ask students to divide a piece of paper and list "Interests and Talents" and "Problems and Questions" (also used by writers and artists to find topics). Inventories can be done orally: put questions on cards and draw them out for discussions. To use movement, make a circle and ask students to step in (twist or slide) in response to interest categories. Use the inventory in the Appendix for ideas.

Blueprint X: Arts Partnerships

Partnerships form a web of mutual support based on common needs and goals. The following have goals and needs that connect to learning through the arts: school arts specialists, teaching artists, community arts organizations (local and state), arts councils, museums, community orchestras, colleges and universities (arts and education departments), national arts organizations and alliances, businesses, and governmental organizations like the National Endowment for the Arts (NEA) and the National Endowment for the Humanities (NEH). Some community agencies provide "in kind" support, like space. In Chattanooga, Tennessee, museum professionals help design school exhibit spaces. Many schools partner with businesses and arts organizations to pursue funding for professional development and artist residencies. Ford, Rockefeller, Getty, and Annenberg foundations have been funding arts integration programs since the 1960s (Fineberg, 2004). The Council for School Corporate Partnerships (*http://corpschoolpartners.org*) has guidelines for partnerships. The International Network of Performing and Visual Arts Schools (*http://artsschoolsnetwork.org*) is a source for partnership models. Local universities are potential partners, especially as more offer courses on arts integration and want to place students in schools for practicum experiences.

Direct Service

Partnerships with school-based arts teachers, independent artists who contract to do residencies, and arts organizations that have school outreach programs focus on direct service. This means they work directly with teachers.

Arts Specialists

Licensed arts teachers, professional artists, teaching artists, and professionals in community arts organizations are potential arts partners. Teachers should personally seek out these people.

Connecting with Arts Teachers. School-based arts specialists are the closest sources to help plumb connections. Most are extremely supportive of arts integration, if they understand it is not intended to replace sequential arts instruction. Teachers often begin by sitting in on arts classes to learn more about the arts and about students' arts intelligences. This may mean giving up a planning period. Some schools have reorganized so planning time is before or after school to make this happen, which also makes planning with arts specialists more workable. At most schools planning happens during lunch conversations and impromptu hall meetings.

Committed teachers find a way using phone calls, e-mails, and other means. Of course, it is ideal when the schedule facilitates planning time. Some schools use paraprofessionals for duties and negotiate early release for students as often as once a week. Progressive schools have redefined the role of arts teachers to include "arts coaching." Arts teachers have a reduced teaching schedule so they have time to plan with teachers, observe, and coteach integrated arts lessons.

Some schools are fortunate to have specialists in drama and dance as well as music and art. Physical educators often embrace creative movement and can direct teachers to natural connections, (e.g., math and dance). Arts teachers often are willing to synchronize with lessons and units in the regular classroom if teachers prepare a curriculum map or calendar—a month-by-month list of units in science, social studies, reading, language arts, and math. Arts teachers especially like to co-plan with teachers if the goal is two-way integration. Arts teacher should be able to expect classroom teachers to support their units as well. An example is Duxberry Elementary School in Columbus, Ohio, where teachers supply specialists with lesson topics, units, and goals for the coming grade period. Specialists do the same for teachers, and teachers solicit ways to follow up on arts classes to extend learning.

Artist Residencies. "I used to be the cream on the cake and all of a sudden, I'm the cake! I am part of the actual work, not as much a flash in the pan, but part of a long-term partnership" (artist quoted in Freeman et al., 2003). Artists have four goals for getting involved in partnerships (Waldorf, 2002).

1. *Artistic:* Instill a passion for the arts, and help students learn new ways to think.
2. *Educational:* Enrich and develop students' learning skills and confidence; expand teacher's instructional strategies.
3. *Social:* Promote equity, diversity, and community.
4. *Personal:* Develop teaching skills and further their careers.

Artists feel they can make important classroom contributions to thinking and communication skills. They are usually receptive to overtures to plan with teachers to better understand academic teaching, assessment, and classroom management. Ineffective arts integration happens when artists come in without planning and/or students are not prepared. There are horror stories about artists who come late, can't control the class, don't connect to the curriculum, do things that are inappropriate for students, and focus on being center stage, instead of involving students. Artists complain that teachers are sometimes not ready, have dirty classrooms, don't understand the arts/learning connection, talk negatively about kids in front of the class, and may leave or sit in the back of the classroom, not participating (Fineberg, 2004).

Ashley River Creative Arts features five to six artist residencies a year. They are funded through sources like the PTA and the South Carolina Arts Commission. Each is 1–2 weeks. Recently, a textile artist did a residency in fifth grade on molas to go with a social studies unit. In K–2 classes, artist Laura Rich told African folktales that went with units on animals (kindergarten), emotions (first grade), and weather (second grade). With fifth graders, she added script writing and performances using drumming and songs.

How are these residencies made integral? Everyone has to be clear about roles, goals, procedures, materials, schedule, and room preparation. A written agreement needs to be negotiated that addresses these questions and establishes what the artist will be paid, how, and when.

Checklist: The planning discussion should include:

- Philosophical beliefs about arts integration
- Learning goals, purposes, and standards/courses of study
- Generating big ideas/themes and questions for unit topics
- Specific unit/lesson objectives
- CPS process using artistic tools, techniques, and materials
- Search for connections between the unit and the artist's art form. If there is not a natural fit, stop here.
- Sequence of lessons and materials
- Roles of teacher and artist; active teacher participation
- Composition of the class (economic, social, and developmental levels) and special needs of students
- Best teaching practices (Ready Reference 3.4)
- Preparing students and introducing the artist
- Management of small and whole groups
- Classroom discipline, especially how to prevent problems and resolve conflicts (see "Discipline" in Appendix)
- Assessment plan to determine what students learn
- Follow-up ideas for the teacher to extend learning

The written agreement should be signed and include:

- Description of specific expectations related to goals
- Schedule: exact dates and times
- Location: room arrangement
- Materials needed
- Emergency planning: fire drills, snow days, illness (include e-mail, cell phone, home phone, and school phone)
- Assessment of student learning (what and how)

Teaching Artists. Many artists have little or no background in teaching or in child development. It is appropri-

ate to ask for and contact references. Artists bring invaluable knowledge and skills to the planning, teaching, and assessment, but they are accustomed to doing CPS, not teaching it. They need to understand that the bulk of a residency is about teaching students to problem solve using the arts, not for them to demonstrate personal artistry. Have this discussion up front. Give artists a copy of the CPS process (Ready Reference 2.5) to establish a common language and discuss the focus on arts learning processes versus products/performances. Resist capitulating to the "hysterical demand for polished performance" and emphasis on representational artwork (Fineberg, 2004, p. 59).

Some teaching artists also now work with teachers in a coaching relationship. This includes professional development, classroom demonstrations, and assistance with planning. In the Kennedy Center's Changing Education through the Arts (CETA), arts coaches teach classes, observe teachers implementing arts-based lessons, and provide feedback (Amy Dumas, 2005 interview). A new journal, *Teaching Artist Journal*, edited by Eric Booth, is dedicated to helping artists make the transition to teaching artists. The Kennedy Center's publication *Creating Capacity* also offers ideas for preparing artists for teaching (*www.kennedy-center.org*). If your district is affiliated with the Kennedy Center Partners in Education, you can check with administrators about workshops.

Teacher Spotlight:

Teaching Artist

Kim Keats is a Hilton Head Island teaching artist who says she started as a "guest artist" who just demonstrated artwork. Her role evolved as she began to help teachers learn to create art, especially fiber art. She now does staff development for teachers and team planning, and she recently completed a yearlong residency connecting quilt making and ecology. She co-planned with an English/language arts teacher around an ecology theme and taught monthly lessons with kids on thinking through symbols. The teacher continued the work in between Kim's lessons. She coached the middle school students through the CPS process, and the result was a magnificent quilt that narrates the natural history of South Carolina "From the Mountains to the Sea." The quilt now hangs in the Coastal Discovery Museum. Student wrote throughout the project, which gave them a deep understanding of how visual art expands communication. Their writing became more "detailed and vivid" as they went back and forth between words and art (Interview, September 2005). Why did Keats become a teaching artist? She says it goes hand in hand with doing your own work. "As a teacher you are always learning. This is conducive to producing art yourself. I teach what I love."

Arts Agencies/Organizations

There is no substitute for taking initiative to find partnership possibilities in the community. Local and state arts councils are good clearinghouses and all have websites. Ask about school outreach and make an appointment to discuss the kinds of arts expertise you are seeking. Take along a copy of the school standards and a curriculum map to show the calendar of units. Be ready to explain the concept of teaching and learning through the arts at the heart of arts integration. Other sources are AAA, travel agents, and real estate brokers, who often have packets that detail cultural opportunities. See the Appendix.

Arts Directory

Specialized arts knowledge and skill may be close at hand. A school/community survey can locate people who may be willing to do single visits or may be capable of an arts residency. Circulate a short form to adults requesting names and contact information for arts resources. Encourage people to list themselves. The teacher next door may own every piece of big band music ever written, or the principal may play the African slit drum. Students can be surveyed, too. At Normal Park Museum Magnet all parents agree to 18 hours of work at the school; volunteers can be tapped for artist talents, too. Finally, ask the PTA to assemble the directory.

Student Spotlight:
What Kids Think

A group of Libba Allen's fifth graders are in the hall working on a pictogram. They explain how arts integration has changed them.

"You get more of a perspective on what you want to be when you grow up," says one boy.

Another chimes in, "We get exposed to more things and different."

"Thanks to drama I got into the School of the Arts," a third adds.

"My mind is more at ease," offers a fourth boy.

"Yeah, it stretches you, especially your mind. I love all the arts," says a tall girl.

They return to the pictogram. It is to be a collage of favorite football teams. The lone girl reminds them they need symbols that everyone can understand and "not just the Georgia Bulldogs." The boy accepted at School of the Arts insists that they use lots of detail. Each listens and responds with comments like, "That's a good idea," and "We could try that."

"We need to include everyone," a short boy explains. "Let's get pencils so we can sketch and talk out ideas." *

Conclusion

The spirit of Creative America has spurred us to say and write and draw what we think, feel and dream . . . to celebrate through dance, in songs, in paint and on paper, the story of America: of who we are, where we have been, and what we hope to be. (Hillary Rodham Clinton)

This chapter describes a blueprint to show how arts integration is planned and implemented. The Blueprint's 10 building blocks are interlocking and form the scaffolding for specific strategies described in subsequent chapters.

Resources

See the Appendix for study materials, including more websites.

Videos

Jacobs, H. (1993). *Integrating the curriculum* (series). Alexandria, VA: Association for Supervision and Curriculum Development (ASCD).

Jacobs, H. (1999). *Curriculum mapping: Charting the course for content.* Alexandria, VA: ASCD.

Erickson, H. (2002). *Creating concept-based curriculum for deeper understanding.* Thousand Oaks, CA: Corwin Press.

Website Samples from Appendix:

Americans for the Arts: *www.artsusa.org*

Arts Education Partnership: *http://aep-arts.org*

ArtsEdge: *http://artsedge.kennedy-center.org*

National Endowment for the Arts: *http://arts.endow.gov*

Very Special Arts: *www.vsarts.org*

Children's Literature References

Baylor, B. (1992). *Guess who my favorite person is?* New York: Atheneum.

Booth, D. (1993). *Dr. Knickerbocker and other rhymes.* New York: Ticknor and Fields.

Cole, J. (1993). *Six sick sheep: 101 tongue twists.* Long Beach, CA: Beech Tree.

Cole, J., & Calmenson, S. (1990). *Miss Mary Mack and other children's street rhymes.* Long Beach, CA: Beech Tree.

McCully, E. A. (1992). *Mirette on the high wire.* New York: Putnam's.

MacLachlan, P. (1986). *Sarah, plain and tall.* New York: Harpertrophy.

Nolte, D. (April, 1959). Children learn what they live. *Torrance Schools Board of Education Newsletter.* Torrance, CA.

O'Neill, M. (1989). *Hailstones and halibut bones.* New York: Doubleday.

Polacco, P. (1994). *Pink and say.* New York: Philomel.

Seuss, Dr. (1937). *And to think I saw it on Mulberry Street.* New York: Vanguard.

Weinstein, M., & Goodman, J. (1980). *Playfair: Everybody's guide to noncompetitive play.* San Luis Obispo, CA: Impact Publishers.

Yolen, J. (1981). *Sleeping ugly.* New York: Coward, McCann & Geoghegan.

Integrating the Literary Arts

Questions to Guide Reading

1. WHY has literature become the most integrated art form?

2. WHY should literature be integrated?

3. WHAT should teachers know to integrate the literary arts?

4. HOW are these areas addressed in literature integration: planning, class environment, literature best practices, instructional design, student needs, and assessment?

5. HOW can teachers partner with literary arts specialists?

It's not what we read, but what we remember that makes us readers. (Inez Tennenbaum, South Carolina State Superintendent)

This chapter has a three-pronged focus: *why* literature should be integrated, *what* teachers need to know about literature to integrate it meaningfully, and *how* to plan and implement literature integration. The research and theories from Chapter 2 and the Arts Integration Blueprint from Chapter 3 are applied to the literary arts—the arts of reading and writing literature. The concept of literature as a discipline or content in its own right and as a tool for teaching and learning is a key chapter focus.

Literature at the Core

Arts integration is a hands-on minds-on approach. Teachers intentionally and creatively use inquiry and other active problem-solving strategies key to comprehension instruction (Kamil, 2004; Moats, 2004). Daily read-alouds, independent reading, and guided groups are common routines. The material used most often for these mega-strategies is literature. In addition, many science and social studies units no longer revolve around a textbook. Literature is center stage and is used to enliven historical eras and give faces to the facts of science. Math is not exempt. Authors have discovered that math makes for a great storyline.

In the opening Classroom Snapshot, Amy Weiss uses arts-based read-alouds to "hook and hold" students (McTighe & Wiggins, 2005). Her artful teaching causes students to transform the content of a chapter book using creative problem solving (CPS). The book was selected because of its fit with a social studies unit on families. Ms. Weiss uses at least a half dozen literacy/arts strategies. Count for yourself.

Classroom Snapshot:
Social Studies/Arts-Based Read-Alouds

Students are seated in learning circles on a worn oriental carpet. There are stacks of red and blue cushions in the center.

"Diamond people, come and pick up four wallpaper books," Amy Weiss announces.

Six students rush to the cushions and rummage through blank books with wallpaper covers. There's momentary commotion as "diamonds" return to their groups.

"Do we get to keep these?" asks one girl.

"Yes! What do you think they're for?" Ms. Weiss asks mischievously. Hands go up. "Phil?"

"To write or draw in?" Phil asks.

"You are right on. These are **Lit Logs** for a core book unit. There's at least a page for each chapter I'm going to read to you, starting right now."

Ms. Weiss flips the overhead on. **"Write Right Away"** (WRA) is written on a transparency.

"We've done this kind of writing before. What do you remember?" Hands go up. "Rich?"

"WRA means just write whatever you think about."

"Exactly. What else do you remember?"

"It gets your brain going," says a tiny girl.

"It's just like a quick write," another girl adds.

"It helps you think because you start with what you know and then think about more as you write. We did it in social studies when we started states and capitals."

"You are right, Shaena, we did use it

Reading the art of a picture book.

in social studies," Ms. Weiss says. "Our WRA today is to prepare your brains for the first chapter." Ms. Weiss pulls the transparency down. "Read this title with me." They chorally read, "The Day I Was Born."

"Think about anything your parents or grandparents have told you. Two people in here were adopted, so you might write about when you were first brought home," Ms. Weiss explains. "Open your Lit Logs and write today's date and the title—like I'm doing on the overhead. We'll write about 5 minutes. Questions?"

"Do we need to write in a paragraph?" a girl asks.

"Remember, with WRA, it doesn't matter. This is writing to get ideas out. Write in any form, even a list. Other questions?"

Seeing none, Ms. Weiss begins to write. Ms. Weiss uses the **public writing** strategy to show how to experiment during writing. She crosses out words, circles others, and uses a caret to insert. Some students watch at first and then start writing. Some look up periodically.

After 5 minutes, she says, "Find a place to stop." She waits and adds, "Let's use **Pairs Share.** In your pairs, either read what you wrote or pick out ideas to tell."

Pairs link up. One boy explains how he was a preemie and stayed in the hospital a month. Some read aloud. Ms. Weiss circulates listening, smiling, questioning, and commenting. She seems genuinely interested.

"OK, let's come together. Who heard a story that should be shared with everyone?" she asks. Students volunteer their partners, and one girl tells about the surprise of twins. A boy explains that his partner was born in Korea, but his

adopted parents were at the hospital. After a few minutes, Ms. Weiss makes a transition.

"Think about what the core book I'll be reading might be about. Remember, good literature usually has problems at its core." After a wait time period, she nods and hands go up. She moves to chart paper and picks up a marker. "Arman?"

"It could be about getting born and the problem of no one wanting you." Ms. Weiss writes his idea on the chart."Tim?"

"Maybe it's about a new baby, and the other kids are jealous."

Several more problems are predicted and listed. She then shows the cover of the book *Sarah, Plain and Tall* (Maclachlan). A few children make "oo-oo" sounds.

"How many have read this book or seen the movie?" Two children raise their hands. Both saw the video.

"Sandy and Mechelle know the plot, so they already know some connections to our Write Right Away. Get in a comfortable spot, and I'll read Chapter 1. Try to make different connections. Afterward we'll discuss what is important in the chapter."

Kids scurry to find spots on the rug. Some stretch out. Others grab cushions. Ms. Weiss sits in a rocking chair. When all are settled, she begins to read. She uses **expressive reading.** Her voice is soft at first, and she changes pitch to distinguish characters. Sometimes she reads slowly and pauses. Other times she reads fast. It is almost like she is singing. When she gets to the point where the father says he has received a letter, she stops, lays the book down, and walks over to a board.

"And I have received a response," Ms. Weiss says in a deep voice. She is using **Teacher in Role** to pretend she is Jacob, the father. Ms. Weiss takes an envelope from the class message board. It is a stamped letter. She opens it and reads it aloud, still in the character of Jacob. It is a letter from Sarah Elizabeth Wheaton. When she finishes, she puts it in the envelope and walks back to her chair. The class is silent with expectation. Ms. Weiss picks up the book and finishes the chapter. She reads the last line, "Ask her if she (pause)." The class chimes in "sings!"

Ms. Weiss returns to the **"Best Guess"** prediction chart, and students do thumbs up or down about whether each prediction was confirmed or rejected. The class then brainstorms important ideas in the chapter as Ms. Weiss scribes students' ideas on a web: "Missing someone." "Grief." "Wanting to remember." "Being a family." "Loving each other." "Hope." Next, she asks them to do a **Quick Mime** to pretend they are "missing someone." At their places they use facial expressions and body shapes. She reminds them that drama and dance require concentration. She points to a chart on the wall that lists **Dance Elements** in the categories of body, energy, space, and time (BEST).

"Get a personal space. Reach out and make sure you have room. Let's explore this idea more through dance elements. I'll count to three. On three, freeze in a shape that shows 'missing someone.' She counts and the room fills with statues. Many are bent over, and some are curled in a ball on the floor. Ms. Weiss describes different body shapes and levels they are using. "When I touch you, come alive, look around, and describe body shapes and levels you see." She touches five children. They, in turn, describe curves, angles, and levels of peers. They explore **Frozen Shapes** three more times. Then they debrief.

"You showed unusual thinking. How did the shapes feel?"

"I felt the memory of losing somebody in my arms and my whole body!" a girl in a black T-shirt says.

"What else?" Ms. Weiss asks.

"I saw lots of us ball up, almost like you have a stomach ache," a boy adds.

"Yeah! I felt like that," another boy piggybacks.

Ms. Weiss uses Frozen Shapes with other ideas from the web. She then leads the class to create a **Dance Machine** on the theme "Family members each have a different role." Students reflect on Chapter 1, focusing on character actions. One comes up and rolls dough. Another sweeps. A third sits and writes. Eventually, all join the Machine.

"When I say *family*, add a sound, and when I say *stop*, just freeze," Ms. Weiss announces. "Ready, *family*." There is a cacophony of giggles and noises.

"I see people really concentrating on body shape and moves," she comments. Giggles subside. The class focuses on being a family machine. Ms. Weiss calls, "stop."

Students return to the Lit Logs to write about an idea in Chapter 1 that means something to them personally. Ms. Weiss writes, too, but this time in her own wallpaper log.

By the end of this core book unit, the Lit Logs are full of chapter responses and include artwork. Examples of Ms. Weiss's chapter strategies follow. See the Seed Strategy Index for descriptions.

Chapter by Chapter Arts Integration Strategies:

1. *Before:* Write Right Away (WRA) "Day You Were Born" to activate past experiences. *After* reading: Quick Mime and Frozen Shapes to explore concepts related to theme. Dance Machine on "family" (Big Idea for social studies unit).

2. *Before:* Pretend and Write to Sarah as a character (point of view drama). *After:* Compare lists and letters with Sarah's and write back to Sarah. Start Class Museum.

3. *Before:* Chain 7 poem using an important idea (theme). *After:* Hot Sock game with key concepts (drama energizer).

4. *Before:* Character map Anna. *After:* Listen to "Sumer Is Icumen In" and teach song by rote. Sing in a round.

5. *Before:* Character One Liners (drama). *After:* Somebody-Wanted-But-So plot map (Schmidt, in Macon, 1991).

6. *Before:* Mini-lesson on poetry elements. *After:* Web examples/effects of assonance, consonance, imagery, rhyme, repetition, hyperbole, metaphor, and simile.

7. *Before:* Acrostic poem about a character. *After:* Revise poem. Make poem posters with colored pencil.

8. *Before:* CAP prediction using key words: overalls, argument, strange clouds, tears, barn, wait, eerie, hail, drive, glass. *After:* Rainstorm (music energizer).

9. *Before:* Colored pencil sketches of key book moment. *After:* Tableau of favorite book scene. View video and do Venn diagram (literary elements).

What Are the Literary Arts?

At one point, J.K. Rowling's first three Harry Potter novels occupied the top three spots on the New York Times hardback fiction best-seller list. This caused such heartburn among the literati that a best-seller list of children's books was created so that Rowling's books could be banished to it. (George Will, November 11, 2001)

When the sixth book in the Harry Potter series was released, it broke publishing records. The initial run in the United States was 10.8 million copies. Nearly 3 out of 4 kids ages 11 to 13 have read at least one of the books (Hallett, 2005). Harry Potter is a literary phenomenon. What is it about Rowling's books that has turned many nonreaders into readers and causes youngsters to carry them around before they can read them?

Art is both process and product. The process used to make any art form is creative problem solving (CPS). It is the process Rowling used, as did Shakespeare. It is set in motion by the desire to combine ideas and feelings in new ways. The process yields many products: paintings, songs, dances and, when words are used, literary art. Literature is literary art. It is made, like all art, to convey thoughts and emotions, but the intent is to use words imaginatively. Literature is structured in diverse ways into *genre* that range from fables to science fiction, play scripts to alphabet books. The subject matter of literature can literally be anything. A controversial aspect of any art is its role as a vehicle for truth. Authors are artists who share their truths through the word arts of story and poem.

Arts Integration Blueprint

Chapter 3 introduced the Arts Integration Blueprint. Ready Reference 3.2 shows its 10 building blocks. The first has to do with *why* arts integration should be implemented—philosophy based on research and theory. Next comes *what* teachers should know (arts literacy) and *how* to plan, create an aesthetic environment, use literature and best practices, design instructional routines, adapt for diverse learners, assess, and partner with arts specialists. The Blueprint is applied to integrating the literary arts in this chapter.

Blueprint I:
Philosophy of Arts Integration

> *I now enjoy Tolstoy and Jane Austen and Trollope as well as fairy tales and I call that growth; if I had had to lose the fairy tales in order to acquire the novelists, I would not say that I had grown but only that I had changed. A tree grows because it adds rings; a train doesn't grow by leaving one station behind and puffing on to the next.* (C. S. Lewis, 1980)

Why Integrate Literature?

In Part I, research on and theories about learning, cognition, motivation, developmental stages, multiple intelligences, and creativity were presented to support integrating literature and the other arts. The focus on research and theories (Research Update 4.1) continues in this section, but is accompanied by beliefs and testimonials connected to arts integration philosophy. These reasons are used to justify giving literature a place of privilege in literacy and in science and social studies units.

Russell (1994) writes that the study of children's literature is the study of childhood and human aesthetic, intellectual, and social development. He argues it should be studied to "bring the advantages and the joys of reading to all children, for without reading the ideas of the past would be lost forever, and we would be forced naked into the world" (p. 16). The following are more reasons to "clothe" students in literature.

Literature Brings the Engagement Power of the Arts to Bear on Literacy. The search for why some never get the reading habit has been long and intense. The findings suggest that when interesting literature is integral to instruction, students read more and comprehend at higher levels (Guthrie, 2004; Research Update 4.1). Good books do more than teach the skill of reading. The Harry Potter phenomenon gives testimony to the effects of literary artistry on children's reading behaviors. For many students this series has motivated them to read above grade level and to persist in the face of an intimidating number of pages. They don't do this to rack up points. Harry has affected many children aesthetically and has made them into book lovers or "bibliophiles." Thank you, Ms. Rowling.

Reading Good Literature Causes Active Meaning Construction. Before I read *Black Beauty* in second grade, it had never occurred to me that someone would intentionally hurt an animal. For months the images haunted me—and helped me form a value for living things. Like all art, good literature offers the opportunity to construct personal meaning. Think of great books you've read. Did they

Rockin' with Harry Potter.

Research Update 4.1   Literature-Based Instruction

- A seven-year study demonstrated the effects of interest on reading achievement. Sixteen low-income K–6 students were tracked. Kids started carrying around Harry Potter books by second grade. By fifth or sixth grade they had read them all. Fourteen of the sixteen students achieved or surpassed benchmarks for reading level (Hallett citing Barone 2005, p. 47).
- Second graders in a literature group had superior performance to those in a control group (basal only) on measures of story retelling, story rewriting, and original writing (Morrow, 1992).
- A year long qualitative literature-based case study of second graders showed students grew in overall reading performance. They were highly engaged with books; developed skill in word identification, fluency, and comprehension; and grew in written composition. This qualitative study supports the efficacy of teaching reading and language arts strategies within a literature-based framework (Baumann & Ivey, 1997).
- Literature approaches, supplemented by short, special "decoding lessons," were favored over other approaches in a study using 50 classrooms and 1,000 second graders. Treatment groups were superior to control groups in achievement gains and attitudes toward reading (Eldredge & Butterfield, 1986).
- In New Zealand a literature-based program for first graders had such impressive successes that the Department of Education began nationwide staff development to prepare all teachers to use literature in this manner. Since then the program has become widely popular in the United States under the title Reading Recovery (Holdaway, 1982; Pinnell, 1986).

- Sixty-three first graders matched with more than 2,000 books scored 93% on a state proficiency test (13 points higher than the Utah state standard and 4 months earlier than "normal"). Reading scores were in the 99th percentile for the group, and all but four scored above grade level (Reutzel & Cooter, 1992).
- Boys at the W. J. Maxey Training School for Boys (Lake Whitmore, Michigan) were given hundreds of paperbacks to read and were released from making book reports. They showed significant gains over a control group on measures of self-esteem, attitudes toward reading, reading comprehension, verbal proficiency, and anxiety (Fader & McNeil, 1976).
- Children in literature-based reading programs read as many as 100 books in a year. In programs without literature, students read an average of seven minutes during reading class and only one or two reading textbooks a year (Anderson, Hiebert, Scott, & Wilkinson, 1985; Hepler, 1982).
- New York City second graders from low socioeconomic backgrounds and a history of academic difficulties were taught using trade books. Books were read aloud, time was given for free reading, and students were involved in responses about the books' meanings. At year-end they significantly outscored a control group that used traditional reading materials. Comprehension and vocabulary were measured with standardized tests. This study was replicated with the same results (Cohen, 1968).
- Students involved with multicultural literature showed less negative attitudes toward those different from themselves (Pate, 1988; also see summary in *Social Education,* April/May, 1988).

not teach something—facts and main ideas that connected to your life? Did the authors not use words to build visual and emotional bridges between you and the book. Perhaps you had an experience I had reading Paterson's *Bridge to Terabithia.* Not only were the characters believable, the premise engaging, and the plot forceful, but her use of language left me envious; I caught my breath and grieved with Jess when Leslie died. When I closed the book, I felt changed. I was cognitively and emotionally altered. I felt if I looked in a mirror I would not see my same face. This experience is called *bibliotherapy.*

Visual imagery.   Unlike television, books trigger greater brain activity that includes the personal creation of visual images (Jensen, 2001; Norton, 2005). Personal meaning making through visualizing is satisfying and mentally active, not pas-

sive. Excessive television may even cause brain atrophy and impair ability to visualize, which is crucial to enjoyment and comprehension of books. The National Center for Educational Statistics reports disturbing correlations. Students who watch 1 hour of television per day average a score of 224 on the National Assessment of Educational progress. Scores fall to 196 with 6 or more hours (1992–2000). That's a 30-point difference. Students need to be engaged in generative activities like reading, writing, and drawing.

Literature Builds Empathy and Respect for Others.

The world changes according to the way people see it and if you alter, even by a millimeter, the way a person looks at reality, then you can change it. (James Baldwin)

Baldwin sees literature as "indispensable," especially in our fight against xenophobia. For decades we've had success stories about using literature to broaden cultural attitudes (Hansen-Krening, 1992). Books bring us close to characters of every race, religion, and creed, lessening our fear of the unknown. Given the chance to "walk a mile in the moccasins of others," learners develop empathy. Beyond sympathy, empathy uses aesthetic senses to perceive and understand another's viewpoint. Empathy unites emotion and intellect and is much needed in this time when "getting along" is among our greatest concerns.

Respect for diversity begins with respect for self. Through literature, students discover commonalities among themselves and other peoples, along with differences. In so doing, they begin to connect with those of others. For example, hard work is valued in all cultures and is a character trait that pays off in most stories. Thus, in the African trickster stories of the lazy spider, Anansi, laziness gets him nowhere and earns him a bad reputation among the other animals.

Literature Deepens Understanding. Good literature deals with universal concerns—big questions about surmounting obstacles. Sometimes the problems are with relationships; other times they grow out of conflict between nature and other humans. Appealing literature parallels our interest in discovering what life is about. Award-winning children's author Katherine Paterson and psychiatrist Robert Coles have called this the search for the "secrets of the universe." From early myths, which explain life's mysteries by gods and goddesses, to one of the newest genres, science fiction, we have a literary bank to help us consider what we are and imagine what we might become. Through artistic storytelling, we find friends in characters that share our fears and meet heroes who show us how to confront fear. We can travel back in time or forward to the future. Books take us places we may never physically go, and yet who has read *Charlotte's Web* and not felt wrapped in the coziness of the barn, imagined sitting on the stool, watching Charlotte and listening to the sounds author E. B. White evokes?

Grandeur of truth. Good literature reveals truths, often beautifully, and in so doing satisfies our need to know. Through literature we are persuaded to think about large life questions: What is good? Right? Wrong? What is my place in the world? What contribution can I make? Literary themes are meanings created from engagement with this thought-provoking, emotional art form. Fine stories and poems provide students with tools to pleasurably gain information and to apply moral and ethical standards to problems they will eventually confront.

Literature Gives Comfort and Insight (Bibliotherapy).

> *You think your pain and your heartache are unprecedented in the history of the world, but then you read. It was books that taught me that the things that tormented me most were the very things that connected me with all the people who were alive, or had ever been alive.* (James Baldwin)

Just as the disciples asked Jesus why he spoke in parables, so we ask why teachers should use story and poem to teach. From the words of the master teacher comes the answer. Stories give us a palatable way to understand ourselves—to realize we are not unique, nor alone, in our suffering. Such insight gives solace. The process of reaching that point is bibliotherapy, using books to promote insight and give comfort. Stories are thought to "heal the soul" when a person encounters the right one at the right time (Allen, 1999; Cornett & Cornett, 1980). As they vicariously experience a character's joys and struggles, readers come to deeply empathize, to "become" the character.

While teachers are cautioned not to begin without careful study, anytime a book is used to give comfort, a degree of bibliotherapy naturally takes place. A good book offers distance from the scheduled, stressful lives many children lead. Teachers interested in appropriate books and strategies to involve students in the process are encouraged to consult references such as *The Bookfinder*. In the meantime, use of fine literature will automatically have bibliotherapeutic effects. This is particularly true when teachers use approaches, such as Rosenblatt's (1985) "reader response," that calls for personal connections to stories and poems.

Literature Provides for Aesthetic Needs, Which Increases Motivation. Literature provides for aesthetic needs for beauty, pleasure, awe, and joy that are as basic as the need for food and shelter. These needs are just higher up Maslow's pyramid (1970). When literature is treated as an art form, first, it engages the force of art to motivate. Motivation is cognitive commitment to "extending one's aesthetic experience" (Guthrie, 2004, p. 382). It is a sense of engagement in an important task, and it gives energy and direction.

Like other art, books can motivate through the Stendhal effect (Chapter 3), but children do not automatically gain aesthetic joy from books. Those with reading difficulties may have trouble suspending belief, which inhibits imagination (Purcell-Gates, 1988). Children who start school lacking read-aloud experiences may see only a troublesome decoding task ahead as they confront a page. A level of fluency is needed to savor books; halting word identification is no fun. Supportive strategies such as choral reading, taped books, and partner reading allow readers to relax and participate in meaning making. Even fluent readers benefit from strategies that help release ideas, make connections, and draw conclusions. Chapter 5 has examples such as Exciting-Puzzling-Connecting and Bridges. Also see Blueprint VI: "Best Teaching Practices" in this chapter.

Literature Extends Higher-Order Thinking Needed for Problem Solving.

Good books move us from an egocentric, single perspective into complex abstract thinking (see Chapter 2 on Piaget). At the core of literature is conflict. Even in simple nursery rhymes, conflict drives the plot. It may be introduced and resolved quickly as in Little Miss Muffet. In three short lines she encounters a problem and solves it. Children use higher-order thinking skills (HOTS) to make sense of such literary problems. Techniques such as "put your thumb up when you find the problem" engage analytic thinking and helps them understand that, here again, the CPS has been set in motion. Children can be guided further to gather data and brainstorm solutions as they read and hear stories (see, for example, the Moral Dilemma strategy in Chapter 9). Hypothesizing and predicting increase active engagement in the problem solving necessary in family living and workplace success.

Other HOTS triggered by literature include empathizing to take new perspectives, evaluating character actions, and making personal connections from themes. For example, when students retell Cinderella from the stepmother's point of view, they learn that problems have many sides. Point of view (POV) is a life-linked skill. For example, after reading Yolen's *Owl Moon,* second graders discussed the problem of an endangered species, the spotted owl. They assumed roles as loggers and said they needed to earn money to feed and clothe their families. This shows how young children can abstract life themes from literature. Teachers facilitate life-literature connections when they (1) use think-alouds to demonstrate the process (Lehr, 1991), (2) present literature to learn about life, (3) participate as inquirers, not experts, and (4) offer choices to respond to literature (Tompkins & McGee, 1993, p. 15).

Literature Stimulates Moral Thinking.

Teaching values is a sensitive area, but no one denies that children must learn right from wrong. They need to come to understand and behave using common values for honesty, initiative, responsibility, and so forth. Value-free lessons are virtually impossible, especially in the arts since the content is personal perspectives. Literature, too, is value laden. Authors intentionally and unintentionally weave their beliefs into their words.

Literature integration offers a chance for students to use personal values to think about and respond to conflicts inherent in stories. From Aesop's fables to *Goosebumps,* authors create characters that act in ways that reveal the author's take on right and wrong. Great literature does this

subtly. Plot-driven mediocre books leave us entertained, but without increased insight. The point is that values are natural and important, and we can respect diverse values while engaging students in literature discussions that inevitably give rise to moral dilemmas. Futhermore, when students discuss with classmates of different backgrounds, they have a chance to sort out thoughts and feelings and gain expanded viewpoints. In this chapter and the next, discussion and response strategies are described that target discussions to stretch thinking using a variety of strategies. Students can learn to question and comment using evidence in the story (text-based discussions), connect experiences others may not share, and do creative extrapolations of "what if?" *Note:* For help with censorship issues, go to the website of the American Library Association (*www.ala.org*).

Literature Is Part of Our Cultural Heritage.

History and culture have long been passed on through story. Storytelling is an ancient art that grew from the need to make sense of the world. Our rich treasury of literature is the result of a continuous search for truth and a celebration of the human need to create and consume art. On the surface Lewis Carroll's "Jabberwocky" is wonderfully alliterative nonsense. We smile and enjoy the pure sound of it. Then we wonder at Carroll's creativity to show how sense and nonsense collide. His feelings for words are illuminated, his command of his craft revealed, and we think differently about what makes sense.

Through poems and stories, children become privy to the bittersweet lessons of history. From the view of our ancestors' shoulders is revealed a landscape of possibilities: Dreams can set a life's course, and good can drive evil underground, often through the courage of a single individual like Rosa Parks. No history text will ever make us feel the pain of war as acutely as Crane's *The Red Badge of Courage.* No science book will ever reveal the poetry of the universe the way Seymour Simon's picture books do. No lecture or character-building activity can bring home moral lessons more effectively than the world's collection of folktales. And who has read Jules Verne's *Twenty Thousand Leagues Under the Sea* and not marveled at how his imagined inventions became reality these many decades hence?

Literature Improves Literacy.

High correlations link amount of literature experience with linguistic development. Reading aloud to children increases vocabulary and gives opportunity to assimilate complex sentence patterns into speech and writing (Chomsky, 1972; Purcell-Gates, 1988). Good readers emerge from families that read to them, a lot, at least from age 3. Such children grow to value reading more and plan to read throughout life (Sostarich, 1974; Trelease, 1995). The rhyme, rhythm, and repetition of Mother Goose attune the ear to language sounds. Dr. Seuss's creative distortions of rimes and onsets, vowels and consonants introduce the music of language and presents phonological concepts essential to reading. Children who start school with hundreds of read-alouds under their belts (up to 5,000 hours) know that "book language" is different from regular talk. People don't normally go around saying things like "he sailed off through night and day and in and out of weeks and almost over a year to where the wild things are" (*Where the Wild Things Are*).

Story structure.   Through "lap reading" children hear expressive language. They also come to understand how stories are structured using the building blocks of plot, character, and theme. This concept is the bedrock for understanding any story and doing original writing. Even preschoolers can discover motifs, like the recurring patterns of "threes" in fairy tales (e.g., three pigs and three tries) and the presence of very bad and very good characters. They come to expect good to triumph and can get annoyed with modern versions that spare evildoers. Reading aloud also helps children develop the "concept of reading," which poor readers often lack. Invisible people speaking through print is pretty strange, but without making this connection to reading, children remain foggy about why they should learn to read. No clear purpose equals no real motivation.

Writing.   The kinds of books children read dramatically affect their writing. Artists are quick to say they "ape the greats." Children need to see themselves as artists creating word art when they write. They need to learn strategies used by authors and artists to represent ideas. Students who read books with well-developed literary elements seem to do this naturally. They write with higher quality and use more complex sentences, variety of literary forms, and poetic devices such as rhythm, rhyme, and repetition (Dressell, 1990; Tompkins, 2003). For example, 5-year-old Sarah heard Wanda Gag's *Millions of Cats* and was moved to write her own book about sister Liza going in search of a dog. Mimicking, but modifying, Sarah's character returned with "billions and zillions and pavilions of dogs."

Good Books Are a Vehicle for Teaching Social Studies, Math, and Science.

It is no coincidence that within the word *history* is the word *story*. The most exciting history teacher I know now lives in the mountains of North Carolina. In retirement he continues to do what he did his whole teaching career—tell compelling stories about men and women who changed the world. History would be a jumble of lifeless facts without its stories, as would science, math, art, theatre, and dance. Integrating literature throughout the curriculum literally means bringing in the stories that give life to numbers, verbs, dates, and names. Teachers can teach important academic content in a more engaging way through fiction and nonfiction. For example, sixth graders who read his-

torical fiction recalled more history than those who used the social studies text (Levstik, 1986).

How can quality literature be found to make successful connections? Available source books and websites categorize picture books on nearly every topic or skill. Other sources match fiction and informational books to social studies and science. Ready Reference 4.6 lists sources. Additional sources by content area are offered in Chapter 5. The Appendix includes a categorized arts-based bibliography.

Literature Combats Illiteracy and Aliteracy.

Illiteracy afflicts about one fifth of American adults, rendering them incapable of reading newspapers, job applications, and food labels. Millions more *can* read, but don't. These "aliterates" never developed a love of stories, poetry, or plays—what David Russell calls "belletristic reading." Bookless individuals suffer a poverty of mind and spirit; they miss reading experiences that can change a life, like that of actor Walter Matthau:

> The book that made the greatest difference in my life was *The Secret in the Daisy* by Carol Grace. . . . It took me from a miserable, unhappy wretch to a joyful, glad-to-be-alive human. I fell so in love with the book that I searched out and married the girl who wrote it. (Sabine, 1983 p.136)

Materials matter.

I lik reding, but not workshits. (Doug, second grader.)

Educational researcher Marilyn Adams likes to say in her talks, "If they can do the worksheet, they don't need it. If they can't, it won't help them." Boring unnatural texts are not part of the solution to the literacy problems of one in five children. Standardized tests are currently the hot ticket to gauge literacy progress. What do they show? Vocabulary and comprehension are learned well when good literature is plentiful and opportunties to write imaginatively are frequent. Students gain up to 4 years in reading in 1 year when literature is the core of the reading program. In addition, attitudes toward reading are more positive when trade books replace basals and workbooks (Five, 1986; Reutzel & Cooter, 1992; Tunnell & Jacobs, 1989). The results of using literature-based approaches in special education are also encouraging (Allen, Michalove, & Shockley, 1991; Roser, Hofman, & Farest, 1990). That's important because the bulk of learning disabilities are literacy based.

Matthew Effect.

One of the most well-established findings in reading research is that reading comprehension is an outgrowth of a wide range of purposeful, motivated reading activities. (John Guthrie, 2004)

Students who read the most read the best. It's that simple (Allington, 2005). There's even an educational label—the Matthew Effect, a biblical allusion to the "rich get richer" verse. It's alarming that less than 1 percent of children read in their spare time, and good readers read 10 times more than poor readers. In one first-grade study, low readers averaged 16 or fewer words per week versus high readers who read 1,933 words (Samuels, 2002). Another grim statistic from the American Library Association is that only 5 percent of the population checks out library books. In 2005 the National Center for Educational Statistics reported that the number of 17-year-olds who say they hardly ever read a book rose over 100% in 20 years. Of course, many people buy books and read magazines or newspapers. These statistics just remind us to not assume that because we teach students *to* read, they will automatically enjoy it.

Good books cause children to develop tastes for genres and authors. They come to relish literature as an art to be savored. Literature integration helps fight illiteracy and aliteracy because it has the capacity to stimulate the senses, challenge the intellect, and touch the heart. A childhood spent in vicarious experiences with Pooh, Max, and Harry makes it likely that books will be lifelong close companions.

Blueprint II: Arts Literacy: Literary Content and Skills

> *When I was ten, I read fairy tales in secret and would have been ashamed if I had been found doing so. Now that I am fifty I read them openly. When I became a man I put away childish things, including the fear of childishness and the desire to be very grown up.* (C. S. Lewis, 1980)

Much of what we call civilization and culture is stored in art created by past generations. Some records of human history remain only in shadowy cave drawings and haunting stone sculptures. We prize these artifacts for their extraordinary beauty, but also for insights they offer about our past. Unfortunately, huge quantities of music, dance, and literature were lost forever because they could not be recorded. Literature began as oral art. Our early ancestors must have huddled around flickering campfires telling stories of heroes on noble quests, adventures of clever animals, acts of foolish peasants, and the search for perfect love. Mixed with dance, mime, and song, literature is believed to have its source in these tales. The ancient stories that survive do so because of retelling. Some of the vast oral tradition is preserved in fables, rhymes, proverbs, and parables. Primitive societies used them to both entertain and instruct, just as we do today.

What Teachers Need to Know

Literary knowledge needed for meaningful integration includes background in:

- History and definitions of children's literature
- Literary elements
- Genres of literature
- Selection sources for good literature
- Authors and artists of children's literature
- *National Standards for the English Language Arts*
- Literary meaning-making strategies (read/write)
- Approaches to teaching literature

History of Children's Literature.   Today, written literature is taken for granted. Thousands of books are published in the United States each year, and more than 5,000 are considered children's literature. How did we come to have such a surfeit of this specialized literature? All art reflects the milieu in which it was created, and so it is with children's literature. Attitudes toward children and schooling evolved in response to political, social, religious, and economic forces. In between Aesop's Fables and Harry Potter lie centuries of changing beliefs about childhood and education, mirrored in stories and poems. Until "childhood" was recognized, there was no literature specifically for children (Darigan, Tunnell, & Jacobs, 2002).

Imagine children eavesdropping by ancient hearths to hear tales meant for adult ears—journeys plagued with horrific beasts with magical powers. Children appropriated these stories with animal characters, fast action, and swift justice. Even Aesop's fables were not originally meant for the young. Early books, like oral stories, were also assimilated. For example, *Robinson Crusoe* (1719) was written for the general public, but its captivating characters and high adventure caused children to usurp it. We now think of it as children's literature. Nineteenth-century children also gobbled up Stevenson's *Treasure Island*. The story's realism created an appetite for this genre. We continue to delight in new genres divined by creative authors. It is odd to imagine that genres such as science fiction did not always exist.

Like most art, children's literature has evolved a dual purpose: to offer aesthetic enjoyment and to instruct. At times the didactic purpose has overshadowed the aesthetic. Authors and publishers still struggle to maintain balance for an audience so vulnerable to the power of art.

Definitions and Characteristics: Chariots of Hope.
What distinguishes children's literature from other literature? Two features stand out: (1) It is intended for a young audience, and (2) unlike adult literature, it nearly always holds out a degree of hope. There is even hope when Charlotte dies because her spider children will continue her legacy. Most art offers

 **Literary Elements**

Theme: the unifying truth or universal message in literature.
   Key question: What is the story or poem really about? (Go beyond a topic to a complete truth statement.)

- Explicit themes: messages directly stated.
- Implicit themes: indirectly stated truth statements.

Plot: the order of events set in motion by a problem or conflict.
   Key question: What happened?

- Four types of conflict: between (1) character and nature, (2) character and society, (3) character and another character, or (4) within a character.
- Types of plot patterns: (1) linear 3-part: introduction-development-conclusion (includes climax and denouement); (2) cumulative: events build on one another; and (3) episodic: mini-stories tied together.
- Plot variations: cliffhangers, flashbacks, foreshadowing.

Character: person, animal, or object taking on a role.
   Key questions: Who is it about? Who wants something? Who has a problem? Who changes the most?

- Ways characters revealed: (1) descriptions, (2) their actions, (3) their speech and thoughts, and (4) what others think and say.
- Types: protagonist/antagonist, round or flat/stock, dynamic or static, foil, stereotype.

Setting: the time and place.
   Key questions: When and where does the story take place?

- Types of settings: scenery backdrop or integral.

- Aspects: place or location, time or time period, weather.
- Primary world: real world.
- Secondary world: a created world used in fantasy.

Point of view: the vantage point from which a story is written.
   Key question: Who is telling the story? How?

- First person point of view: uses "I" to tell the story.
- Omniscient or third person: all-knowing, using third person.
- Limited omniscient: omniscient but only a few characters.
- Objective: events reported with no interpretation.

Stylistic or poetic elements: words for artistic effect.
   Key question: How are words used in special ways?

- Figurative language is the use of words to stand for other things: imagery, personification, metaphors, connotation and denotation, motifs, archetypes, symbols, and allusions.
- Mood is the feeling created. Mood is related to the tone.
- Irony is saying or doing the opposite of what is meant.
- Humor is the simultaneous juxtaposition of sense and nonsense to produce a surprising result.
- Sound and musical features of style include rhyme, rhythm, repetition, alliteration, consonance, assonance, and onomatopoeia.

---

some hope, even if it's just hope born of expanded perspective. Children's literature just seems to have a greater degree. Here are definitions to help clarify. Children's literature is …

- "an art form, as are painting, sculpture, architecture, and music" (Russell, 1994, p. 212).
- "all instances in which language is used imaginatively … Literature speaks of the mysteries of the human condition, although in books for children, treatment of these themes is adjusted according to the age-related interests and capacities of the audience" (Cullinan, 1989, p. 8).
- "the main characters themselves are often children, and often more emphasis is placed on the actions than on the thoughts of the characters … The book becomes a child's book when children read, enjoy, and understand it" (Glazer, 1997, pp. 5–7).

Literary Elements.   The elements of plot, theme, character, point of view, and style (Ready Reference 4.1) are used to write and understand literature. Decisions by authors create memorable writings in our literary tradition as well as forgettable works. How so? These elements are just tools in the creative process. It's artistry that makes the magic. By giving students tools, techniques, and materials to work with, we provide them with the means to read and write creatively. Literary elements are indispensable in understanding the unique features of literary genre and subgenre. Teachers need a thorough grounding in these literacy elements to teach students how to understand, respond to, and create good writing.

Theme.   Theme *is* the unifying truth in literature. When we read and write stories and poems, private meanings are constructed. These messages form literary themes, value-laden statements that tie a story together. To find them, ask, "What is the story really about?" Go beyond topics. For example, *Charlotte's Web* is about the topic of friendship. To pull a theme together, ask, "What about friendship?" One answer is "Good friends stick by you during tough times." This is a theme statement. Writers use two types of themes:

Explicit themes are directly stated. These are present as morals in fables. In other genres, authors may state themes, but often imply them. An explicit theme from *Charlotte's Web* is "Life is always a rich and steady time when you are waiting for something to happen or to hatch" (White, 1952, p. 176).

Implicit themes are not directly stated but are truths that can be inferred by reading closely and considering the characters' actions and outcomes. The previous theme about the topic of friendship is implied.

Themes can be further drawn out by asking, "What does the author seem to believe?" If the writer implies, "We only show courage when we are afraid," then characters, plot, and other elements should unite around this idea. Theme is not a retelling; it is a value-based conclusion.

Plot.   Plot is the order of events. The question "What happened?" gets at the plot. The action is usually set in motion by a problem that causes conflict. Conflict is tension between opposing forces. Robert Newton Peck calls this the "two dogs and one bone" idea. Conflict motivates characters to act and keeps our interest. Four types of conflict are:

1. Between character and nature: *Tornado* (Adoff)
2. Between character and society: *Charlotte's Web*—Wilbur wants to live, but society dictates he become bacon.
3. Between characters: *Jacob Have I Loved* (Paterson)—conflict between sisters.
4. Within character: *Sam, Bangs and Moonshine* (Ness)—about a child who tells lies.

The *climax* is the high point of the plot. Tension breaks, the problem begins to be resolved, and conflict lessens. The denouement is the conclusion. These plot aspects usually come together in patterns (see Plot Lines strategy in Chapter 5). Plot patterns may be straightforward or more complex.

Linear plot patterns begin with the introduction of a problem. In the middle the plot is developed by rising or increased action, and there may be several events and consequences. In the conclusion, the action peaks (climax), and the problem is resolved. *Cinderella* is an example.

Cumulative plot patterns have repeated phrases, sentences, or events that keep adding up or accumulating, as in *The House That Jack Built*.

Episodic plot patterns are like several mini-stories tied together. Each episode entails complete linear plot development. An example is Lobel's *Frog and Toad*.

Creative variations in plot patterns are made using *cliffhangers,* unresolved suspense usually at the end of a chapter, and *flashbacks,* which create suspense and interest through "look-backs" at previous times. This complicates the plot and halts forward progress; events are out of chronological order of the main plot. *Foreshadows* hint about something to come later. They add excitement by heightening anticipation. For example, White foreshadows the conflict with the question "Where's Papa going with that ax?" *(Charlotte's Web,* p. 1).

Characters.   Characters are persons, animals, or objects taking a role. Diverse characters show us the many sides of being human, both the dark and light. Through identification with characters, we vicariously live a slice of another life. This gives perspective. Only with close friends do we share the kinds of secrets literary characters allow us to know. These are the Pooh bears and Cats in the Hat we grow to love. They make us laugh and weep and become heroes that inspire dreams. Characters, especially in folktales, decide to behave bravely or badly and then reap punishment or reward. The realization that choices create triumph or failure gives children a sense that they have a measure of control over their lives. Through character motives, actions, and dialog, the theme is uncovered. Knowing how writers create characters helps children unravel them and create their own characters. Here are the secrets. Characters are shown by: (1) descriptions, (2) actions, (3) speech and thoughts, and (4) what others think and say.

Protagonist: the main character (hero). This is the character who changes the most (e.g., Wilbur in *Charlotte's Web*).

Antagonist: the character who creates problems for the protagonist ("between characters" conflict pattern). Mr. McGregor in Potter's *Peter Rabbit* is an example.

Round: well-developed character with both positive and negative traits (e.g., Max in *Where the Wild Things Are*).

Flat or stock: has little or no development, is one sided, all good or bad (e.g., the Prince in *Cinderella*).

Dynamic: characters who cause events to occur and make a substantial change during the story (e.g., Peter Rabbit).

Static: characters who do not change; may be round or flat (e.g., Charlotte in *Charlotte's Web*).

Foil: character with traits opposite to protagonist. Foils contrast with the main character and are usually flat (e.g., Beauty's sisters in *Beauty and the Beast*).

Stereotype: character who exhibits expected traits of a group. Stereotypes are destructive when they use narrow and negative images, such as having all Native Americans take scalps.

Setting.   Setting is the time and place, when and where. Setting is the backdrop or "scenery" for the characters to act out the plot. *When* the story happens may be now or in the past or future. *Where* it happens can be unimportant, as in folktales ("a kingdom far away"), or integral, such as the cabin on the Oklahoma prairie in *Out of the Dust* (Hesse). In fantasy, setting is important because the reader must believe in a new world. In realism the setting can act as an antagonist, as in survival stories such as *Hatchet* (Paulsen), where a boy fights the Canadian wilderness. If the title of the story includes the setting, then it is probably more than a backdrop; for example, in *The Little House in the Big Woods* (Wilder) the setting helps create mood and adds plot tension. The big homey barn in *Charlotte's Web* creates a different mood than the bustling fair where Wilbur must perform to save himself. The setting can also be a symbol of the story. For example, one setting of *Walk Two Moon* (Creech) is a car that, like the main character, is controlled by others and on its way to a mysterious destination. With its hard exterior and comfortable interior, the car is a safe place within a larger, frightening time. The car also foreshadows another vehicle in the book—a bus.

Aspects of setting.   Setting encompasses place or location, time or time period, and weather. The *primary world* is a realistic world used as a setting for fiction (realistic or fantasy). An example is the "real" world of Winnie in *Tuck Everlasting*. The *secondary world* is a "created" world in fantasy. An example is the "living forever" time warp in which the Tuck family is trapped.

Point of view (POV).   Point of view is the vantage point from which a story is written. The angle may be through the eyes of one character or many. Writers may combine or alternate the following POV.

First person: The narrator uses "I" to tell the story, usually from one character's POV, which increases reader identification. It is used a lot in realistic fiction.

Omniscient: Omniscient means "all knowing." The narrator sees and hears all and can tell about what's inside characters' minds. It is as if the author has a godlike power to be in on everything. The story is told in third person (he, she, it) from above the action. Many children's books use this POV because it allows the reader to know many characters. White uses it in *Charlotte's Web*.

Limited omniscient: This is the same as omniscient, but targets just a few characters.

Objective: The third person is used, but there is no subjective interpretation of what characters feel or of events. The author is like a video camera recording action.

Stylistic/Poetic Elements.   Style is how an author crafts words. In both prose and poetry, carefully selected words determine what we know and feel about character, theme, setting, and plot. When used with artistry, the reader may not notice poetic devices of alliteration or figurative language that add impact. When dialect is used skillfully, it seems important and natural. Seriousness is created with unemotional language and short sentences. Flamboyant words, nonsense, and sentences that defy conventional structure seem humorous. Words are used in all these ways in literature:

Figurative language.   This term means how words are used to stand for other things. It includes:

Imagery—appeals to the senses. It triggers concrete images that engage a reader or listener like "The morning light shone through its ears, turning them pink" (*Charlotte's Web*, p. 4).

Personification—giving human traits, such as feelings, actions, and speech, to animals or objects. For example, "The streams and ditches bubbled and chattered with rushing water" (*Charlotte's Web*, p. 176).

Metaphors—comparisons that create mental images by connecting the familiar with the less familiar. Novel thinking and deep understanding results. Simile is a type of metaphor using "like" or "as" to make an explicit comparison. For example, Charlotte is "about the size of a gumdrop" (p. 37).

Denotation and connotation—denotation is the dictionary definition, while connotation is using words in a nonliteral, but understandable way. Saying "the car was a lemon" uses connotation to imply a negative meaning.

Motifs—recurring patterns of images or events. Familiar openings and closings of folktales are motifs: "Once upon a time" and "They lived happily ever after." Huck, Hepler, and Hickman (2001) list six folktale motifs: (1) a long sleep or enchantment *(Rapunzel)*, (2) magical powers *(Jack and the Beanstalk)*, (3) magical transformations *(The Frog Prince)*, (4) magical objects *(Anansi and the Moss-Covered Rock)*, (5) wishes *(The Three Wishes)*, and (6) trickery *(The Three Little Pigs)*. Common *plot* motifs are (1) a cyclical pattern of a young character leaving home, having a dangerous journey, and coming home wiser *(Peter Rabbit)*, (2) journeys with obstacles and encounters with monsters *(Jack and the Beanstalk)*, (3) helpless characters (often female) rescued from dire circumstances *(Cinderella)*, and (4) miraculous events that help a hero end up happy *(Cinderella)*. These are frequent in traditional literature.

Archetypes—relate to motifs but go deeper. They are ancient universal symbols. They trigger unconscious and conscious feelings using images, situations, events, plots, characters, and themes. They occur worldwide in myths, folktales, religious ritual, songs, dances, and art. Common archetypes are (1) seasons (spring for rebirth and beginning, summer for celebration, autumn for tragedy, winter for death/despair), (2) hero on a quest (Odysseus) or hero rescues helpless maiden, (3) colors and shapes (circle for cycles, white for death or purity), (3) settings (forests for danger/the unknown, moving water for a journey). Water signals birth, baptism, and transformation. In *Tuck Everlasting* the forest, water, and seasons are used as symbols, along with the cycle of life pattern (Frye, 1957).

Symbols—represent someone or something else. They are more recent and not as universal as archetypes. Companies use symbols as logos to cause associations, such as WalMart's smiley face. In *Charlotte's Web*, the web symbolizes how life and death are interwoven. Symbols exist to fill in where words leave off and are used a lot in visual art.

Allusions—indirect references to something well-known. We allude to "building a house of straw" from *The Three Little Pigs* to refer to foolish decisions.

Mood. Mood is a feeling created by many literary elements. Style contributes to mood when language creates the emotional state of the story (e.g., humorous or mysterious). Mood is related to tone, which is feeling infused by style devices such as word sounds and imagery.

Irony. Irony is deliberately saying the opposite of what is meant. By juxtaposing opposite but balanced ideas, a story can be more interesting. For example, Wilbur says, "I'm less than two months old and I'm tired of living" (*Charlotte's Web*, p. 16).

Humor. Humor is problem based and usually juxtaposes sense and nonsense to produce surprise. Events can be juxtaposed to create humor as when Jake and Alex talk about "woolly legs," and "being fat," in Jukes's *Like Jake and Me*. Jake thinks they're talking about his wife, but Alex is talking about a spider. Homophones and double meaning words are used in puns and riddles. Poetic language and surprising word use also creates humor. For example, the goose's speech in *Charlotte's Web* ("poking-oking-oking") is humorous because sounds are repeated, but make sense, too. If a goose could talk, it would sound just so.

Sound and musical features. These features of style include:

Rhyme—the repetition of phonograms (sound-spelling patterns that start with a vowel as in *ack*, *ick*) often at the ends of lines of poetry. (see rhyme patterns under poetry).

Rhythm—a pattern of sounds. Includes beat and accent.

Repetition—repeated use of sounds and words.

Alliteration—repetition of beginning sounds in a series of words. For example, "six sick sheep" /s/.

Consonance—repetition of consonants any place in a series. For example, "little fat kitten" /t/.

Assonance—repetition of vowel sounds any place in a series. For example, note the vowel sounds in "soul" and "hole" in "Concentrated is my soul in my molar hole when I have a toothache" (Sigmund Freud).

Onomatopoeia—use of words that sound like their meanings such as *zip* and *clap*.

Genre: Literature Forms with Similar Traits. In human history, millions of pieces of art and music have been created and millions more stories and poems. To begin to fathom this immense creative storehouse, it is necessary to group it. Literature is classified by *age* of intended audience (baby books), *topic* (humor, travel), *problems* (disease, aging), and *length* (novella, short story). Each has a purpose useful in planning lessons. Going further, however, we find divisions of a different sort. Poetry and prose represent distinct bodies of writing, with poetry among the oldest valued writing and a genre all its own. Prose also covers a wide range of forms, subject matter, and style; it can be narrative or expository, fiction or nonfiction. Fiction can be subdivided into traditional literature, realistic, fantastic, historical, and contemporary. What is left is nonfiction, which includes informational books from alphabet books to biography. Literature is created, by humans who defy classification; much fits into more than one area. For example, picture books in every genre are enjoyed by adults as well as children.

The overall goals of literature integration are to (1) teach students to create meaning independently and (2) provide rich aesthetic literary experiences. Genre knowledge (Ready Reference 4.2) makes the following contributions to these goals:

1. Teachers can better plan for breadth to develop flexible literary "tastes."
2. Categories for thinking—prediction frameworks to use before and during reading—aid comprehension. Genres set up story structure scaffolds that explain how characters act.
3. Genres expand the possible forms students can use for writing. These patterns can be tools to write in different genre and even to invent new genre.

Poetry. Poetry is different from prose in its use of (1) compact and emotional language; (2) rhythm, rhyme, and other sound patterns created by alliteration and repetition; and (3) metaphor and other figurative language.

Children respond to qualities of poetry long before they are conscious of their impact. Through nursery

 ## Nine Genres and Example Subgenres

Poetry: Couplet, limerick, concrete or shape, diamante, haiku, free verse

Traditional: Folktales, Mother Goose rhymes, proverbs and parables, fables, myths and legends, tall tales

Fantasy: Animal, toy and tiny-being tales, modern folk and fairy tales, science fiction, high fantasy, time fantasies, horror

Realistic fiction: Contemporary stories about sports, animals, survival, school, and family; also includes historical fiction, mystery; often occur in a series

Informational: Factual writing about art, music, dance, theater, ecology, psychology, sexuality, and technology; also includes alphabet books, counting books, concept books, biography, and autobiography

Picture books: Combine visual art and text, but can be wordless stories (all art); available in all genres

Humor: Combines sense and nonsense using structures such as jokes, riddles, tongue twisters, spoonerisms, hink-pinks, Tom Swifties, palindromes, and chants

Predictable: Can be in any genre; follows a highly repetitive pattern that appeals to young children

Multicultural: Can be any genre, but presently is dominated by folktales from diverse worldwide and international groups, with emphasis on Native Americans and those groups who have immigrated (by choice or force) in large numbers to the United States (Asians, Mexicans, Africans)

---

rhymes, Dr. Seuss, and other word play, babies learn to enjoy language. Poetry attracts attention, makes us want to move, and gives comfort. The joyous language play of preschoolers is sustained when teachers know quality poetry to use and have strategies to meaningfully integrate it throughout the day. This includes knowing kinds of poems children enjoy and how interests can be broadened.

Poetry elements are used in every genre and are included in the literary element of style (Ready Reference 4.1). Poets use these structures and elements to give life to words.

Verse is a line of poetry or a stanza, particularly one with a refrain. Verse is also refers to light-hearted poems.

Stanza is a grouping of several lines together.

Meter relates to repeated patterns like beat and accent.

Rhyme scheme is usually coded. For example, abab is a four-line poem with lines 1 and 3 rhyming and 2 and 4 rhyming.

Blank verse is unrhymed iambic pentameter (Shakespeare uses it). An iamb is the accent pattern "dah DAH," as in "Do what?" Iambic pentameter is five iambs.

Free verse doesn't use traditional meter or stanza patterns.

Lyrical poetry is flowing, descriptive, and personal; it follows no pattern and can be set to music—hence the word *lyric* in both music and poetry.

Narrative poetry tells a story. It usually has no refrain. Hiawatha is an example. *Ballads* are narrative poems with short stanzas, with or without music.

Sonnets are 14 lines long, often in iambic pentameter, and with the rhyme scheme abab cdcd efef gg.

Interest. Student interest in poetry usually declines without teacher intervention (Kutiper, 1997). Teachers can maintain and expand interest with narrative poetry that uses rhyme, rhythm, and humor. Light verse can be used as a bridge to more diverse poetry that extends perception of "good" poetry beyond rhyming and cute. Through aesthetic experiences children learn that poets use this genre to express strong ideas and feelings using many word tools and many forms that may or may not use rhyme.

Writing poetry. Poetry patterns are scaffolds anyone can use to experiment. Ready Reference 5.2 lists ones appropriate for children. By using CPS strategies, such as data gathering and brainstorming, students learn to generate ideas before writing, and experiment with word images. Initially this should be a collaborative writing with the teacher. Search and discovery lessons show students how to find topics other poets use and see how poem patterns are varied and sound patterns created by more than rhyme (e.g., assonance). Ready Reference 4.3 lists well-known poets.

Traditional literature. Folktales reveal truths that endure over time and across cultures. The names of the creators of most are now lost; they are anonymous rhymes, fairy stories, myths, legends, and tall tales that predate the printing press. But the "old stuff" remains popular, along with modern versions, such as "feminist" tales like Yolen's *Sleeping Ugly.*

Folktales are passed down orally. (*Note:* Folklore is the beliefs and customs of a society.) This subgenre includes fairy tales, cumulative stories, and talking beast, noodle

Ready Reference 4.3   Well-Known Poets

Children's Choices are listed each year in the October issue of *Reading Teacher* (*http://reading.org*).

Excellence in Poetry Award

Every three years the National Council of Teachers of English has recognized a poet for a body of work. Recipients are: Mary Ann Hoberman (2003), X.J. Kennedy, Eloise Greenfield, David McCord, Aileen Fisher, Karla Kuskin, Myra Cohn Livingston, Eve Merriam, John Ciardi, Lilian Moore, Arnold Adoff, Valerie Worth, Barbara Juster Esbensen. The Newbery Medal has gone to two poetry books: *A Visit to William Blake's Inn* (Willard) and *Joyful Noise: Poems for Two Voices* (Fleischman). *Horn Book Magazine* and the *Bulletin of the Center for Children's Books* regularly review poetry.

Websites

The Academy of Poets (*http://poets.org*) includes information about many poets, poems, lesson plans, and additional links. Other good sites are: (1) Internet School Library Media Center (*http://falcon.jmu.edu/~ramseyil/poechild.htm*) and (2) Scholastic (*http://teacher.scholastic.com/*).

Children's Favorites

These poets are known in these categories:

Humor: Edward Lear, Lewis Carroll, Shel Silverstein, William Jay Smith, and John Ciardi (all at *http://poets. org/*)

People, Place, and Problems: Myra Cohn Livingston: *http://falcon.jmu.edu/~ramseyil/livingston.htm;* David McCord: *http://factmonster.com/ipka/A0760972.html*

Animals: T.S. Eliot: *http://poets.org/;* William Blake: *http://poets.org/;* Jack Prelutsky: *http://teacher. scholastic. com/writewit/poetry/*

Nature: Robert Frost: *http://poets.org/;* Byrd Baylor: *http:// falcon.jmu.edu/~ramseyil/baylor.htm;* Paul Fleischman: *http://indiana.edu/~reading/ieo/bibs/fleisp.html*

Emotions: Langston Hughes: *http://poets.org/;* Cynthia Rylant: *http://falcon.jmu.edu/~ramseyil/rylant.htm;* Alfred Noyes: *http://poets.org/*

---

head, and fool stories. Point of view is omniscient and characterization is flat and static and often includes archetypes: a wicked stepmother or cunning animal (Frye, 1957). Settings are vague, with time and place referred to as "long ago" or "in a land before time."

Fairy tales include magical objects, spells, wishes, and transformations. Characters are either ordinary humans or humanlike animals transformed because of kindness or sacrifice. The plots involve unfortunate heroines rescued by true love, and characters are often flat and static. They contain stock characters such as witches and giants. Themes involve good overcoming evil, perseverance, and hard work. The style uses conventional openings and closings, repetition, and archetypes like the colors red, white, and black, dark forests, and water.

Cumulative tales have a unique plot structure; characters or objects are added in a chain. Animals occur often and sometimes rescue humans. These tales frequently include food, such as large vegetables, as in *The Enormous Turnip* (Tolstoy).

Talking beast stories have anthropomorphized animals. There is usually a lesson at the end, much like a fable. The conflict involves a confrontation between characters who are flat—good or bad, stupid or clever. An example is the *Three Little Pigs.*

Trickster tales have a character who outsmarts others. Tricksters often take animal forms, such as B'rer Rabbit in the Uncle Remus stories or Anansi in African tales.

Noodlehead or fool tales involve characters who are stupid or clever, good or bad. Foolish decisions result in silly consequences. These tales are full of absurdity and can be like a roller-coaster ride, but by the end everyone is happy.

Examples of folk and fairy tales are:

Aardema, V. (1975). *Why mosquitoes buzz in people's ears.* Dial.
Climo, S. (1989). *The Egyptian Cinderella.* Crowell.
Trivizas, E. (1993). *The three little wolves and the big bad pig.* Macmillan.

Fables are brief stories with stated morals or themes. The most well-known are Aesop's fables from Greece. Main characters are one-dimensional personified animals that are strong or weak, wise or foolish. The plot centers on one event and the setting is a barely sketched backdrop. Conflict is between characters. Lobel's *Fables* is a contemporary example.

Nursery rhymes include Mother Goose rhymes and other light verse, chants, and songs. They are usually short and full of action and memorable characters, like Old King Cole and pencil-thin Jack Sprat. Themes have to do with everyday worries and struggles like single parents with children to feed. Like much original traditional literature, they are full of violence and death, from drowning to decapitation. Beautiful lines are also found, such as "Over the hills and far away" and "One misty moisty morning when cloudy was the weather." Recommended collections are:

De Angeli, M.(1954). *Margaret De Angeli's book of Mother Goose and nursery rhymes.* Doubleday.

dePaola, T. (1985). *Tomie dePaola's Mother Goose.* Putnam.

Myths feature gods and heroes with supernatural and magical powers. Myths explain natural phenomena, such as the origin of the world and seasons. Pourquoi (French for "why") tales explain how the tiger got its tail or how Native Americans got horses (Yolen's *Sky Dogs).* Settings are barely sketched.

Legends are usually based in facts about a person who did something important. Over time the character achieves hero status and the great deed is embellished. DePaola's *The Legend of the Indian Paintbrush* is an example. *Epics* are long narratives or poems about legendary figures. "The Iliad" and "The Odyssey" are Greek epics, and Beowulf is a Norse epic.

Tall tales are based on actual people. Exaggeration is the distinguishing feature. Tall tales are relative newcomers to traditional literature, with the most well known from North America, including Paul Bunyan, Pecos Bill, Johnny Appleseed, and John Henry.

Fantasy. This is a modern genre that features the impossible. It has timeless quality that has provided us with such diverse classics as *Alice in Wonderland* and *Charlotte's Web.* In fantasy imaginary worlds come to life. The setting is integral—time and place significantly affect plot action. Readers suspend belief and feel these strange worlds exist. For example, in the subgenre of science fiction, a spaceship may house an entire community as in *Star Trek.* Themes are lofty, dealing with truth and goodness. Good destroys evil, usually through struggle and suspense. Sometimes characters have supernatural traits. A few are round and dynamic (e.g., the hero), but most are flat and static, firmly on one side or the other of the "dark." POV is often omniscient to give needed background. All this is especially true of high fantasy and science fiction. The plot is usually linear and features impossible events and magical objects. Usually the hero is forced into a quest and pulled into some threatening world. Trials forge the hero's character, but a protector often helps out. When the hero's spirit is finally honed, she or he goes home. Campbell's (1996) *Hero with a Thousand Faces* is a classic book about these common traits. The subgenres of fantasy overlap and include:

Animal fantasy uses personified animals like Charlotte who protects the hero pig. Well-known examples are:

Grahame, K.(1961). *The wind in the willows.* Scribner's.

Selden, G.(1960). *The cricket in Times Square.* Farrar, Strauss & Giroux.

Toy or tiny beings are the peculiarity of this subgenre. Pinocchio comes to life to grow a long nose. Inch-high borrowers live under the floor and snatch things in Norton's *The Borrowers.* Other favorites are:

Banks, L.(1980). *The Indian in the cupboard.* Doubleday.

Van Allsburg, C. (1981). *Jumanji.* Houghton Mifflin.

Modern folk and fairy tales use the elements of oral tales, but are written works with identifiable authors. Examples are:

Calmenson, S. (1989). *The principal's new clothes.* Scholastic.

Thurber, J. (1943). *Many moons.* Harcourt Brace Jovanovich.

Fantastic events, situations, or imaginary worlds use exaggeration, the ridiculous, and imagined settings. In Dahl's *James and the Giant Peach,* an unhappy child travels inside a huge peach, and in the Never Land of Barrie's *Peter Pan,* one never grows up. Other well-known examples are:

Carroll, L. (1985). *Alice's adventures in Wonderland.* Holt.

Sendak, M. (1983). *Where the wild things are.* Harper & Row.

Van Allsburg, C. (1985). *The polar express.* Houghton Mifflin.

Time warp fantasy distorts time, so Tom can enter a special garden from the past in Pearce's *Tom's Midnight Garden.* Recommended examples are:

Babbitt, N.(1987). *Tuck everlasting.* ABC-Clio.

Banks, L. (1981). *The Indian in the cupboard.* Doubleday.

Rohmann, E. (1994). *Times flies.* Crown.

Science-fiction fantasy is set in the future and relies on science fact and fictional inventions, often extensions of modern technology. An example is L'Engle's *A Wrinkle in Time.* Other examples are:

Farmer, N. (1994). *The ear, the eye and the arm.* Orchard.

O'Brien, R. C. (1971). *Mrs. Frisby and the rats of NIMH.* Atheneum.

High fantasy is a subgenre with characteristics of romance. The forces of good and evil collide in ultimate confrontations. Popular examples are:

Lewis, C. S. (1950). *The lion, the witch, and the wardrobe.* Macmillan. (Narnia series).

Rowling, J. K. (1998). *Harry Potter* (series). Scholastic.

Horror stories speak to our urge to be a little afraid—under safe circumstances. The *Goosebumps* series is a popular example, as is Schwartz's *Scarey Stories.*

Realistic fiction. These stories mirror reality and are very popular among children. The content can be controversial. Some books deal with death, drugs, AIDS, homosexuality, and gangs. However, tame series like the Hardy Boys are still popular.

Realism uses a variety of plot patterns, including flashbacks, that stretch out problem resolution. First-person child-narrator POV is common, especially in young adult books, which gives immediacy and helps with reader identification. Other POV are found, however. Themes usually relate to modern life with the real-world settings. Characters are life-like and fully developed with conflicting emotions and motives.

Contemporary realism is set in current time. The settings are like places in the lives of children. DiCamillo's Newbery winning book, *Because of Winn-Dixie* is an example, as are: Bunting, E.(1994). *Smoky nights.* Harcourt Brace Jovanovich. Jukes, M. (1984). *Like Jake and me.* Knopf.

Historical fiction is a subgenre of realism with a setting in the past and in specific regions of a country (the South, Appalachia). These stories allow readers to vicariously live history and appreciate others different from themselves. For example, Polacco's *Pink and Say,* set in the Civil War, gives historical information, but uses invented dialogue to forge emotional connections to real people and events. Historical fiction should only be used to teach history if (1) it has an authentic setting and accurate details and (2) makes clear it is fiction (i.e., aspects are invented). Historical fiction often reflects as much about the time in which it was written as about the time written about. This means readers need to keep the viewpoints at the time of the publication in mind. A good example of this is Twain's *Huckleberry Finn* in which language is used that was acceptable at the time. The 1998 Newbery winner, *Out of the Dust,* is a fine example.

Informational books.   These factual books are about people and natural phenomena. They allow us to learn about life literally and aesthetically. The story is important, but so is accuracy of information and of illustration. A picture book example is *Seabiscuit* (Sheta & McElwee).

General informational books are how-to and "all about it" stories about a process or topic in the sciences, social studies, arts, and so forth. This genre is the place to look for resources on authors and artists. For example, *Talking to Faith Ringgold* is a picture book that shows how to think about and make art.

Concept books give information in simple form by showing relationships between objects and actions. Basic facts about colors, shapes, and letters are presented, often with striking art and humor. Many are art-based like *Mouse Paint* (Walsh) and *So Many Circles, So Many Squares* (Hoban).

Biography is a factual account of someone's life written by another person. *Autobiography* results when someone writes about his/her own life. For a biography to be authentic, facts need to be documented and no characters, dialogue, or scenes are invented. Biographies may deal only with a part of a life, but some attempt a complete recounting. Either way, a good biography gives a sense of wholeness

within a certain time and place. Famous actors, inventors, artists, composers, dancers, and sports icons are the focus, usually with the plot centering on overcoming obstacles. The best brings the person to life and presents a balanced picture, rather than an unrealistic, one-dimensional character. Texts are often extended by illustrations, as in Freedman's *Lincoln, a Photobiography.*

Real-life characters are role models who give opportunities to "try on" occupations and lifestyles so children need honest representations of both genders and faces and races of the world. The potential for solid information giving about different people makes biography an important way to increase tolerance in our youth.

Biographical fiction is both realistic and fanciful. Based on fact, it includes invented dialogue or events. Some degree of fictionalizing occurs in most children's biography, but should be pointed out to children. Many videos, DVDs, and audiotapes of authors and artists are available with biographical books (e.g., Nichol's *Beethoven Lives Upstairs).*

Picture books.   Art and text each play an integral role in conveying meaning in these books. In some cases, the artwork tells the whole story (wordless books). Picture books are written in diverse genre, from poetry to biography, but in contrast to other genre, they are classified by appearance. For today's children bombarded with visual images, picture books are an important fine art experience. More flexible viewpoints emerge when children learn to examine diverse picture book art that uses a range of styles and media.

Book parts.   Picture books are good tools to teach "book parts" like title and half title pages, borders that may be used to tell a side story, and gutters that connect two pages and are important in double-page spreads. Endpapers are immediately inside the front and back covers of a book and are often used to set mood with art. Of course, art styles and media used by the picture book artists are key teaching points. See Chapter 6 for information on teaching art concepts using picture books.

Tremendous change has occurred in picture book art during the past 50 years. Illustrations now portray positive multicultural images and make art integral to the story rather than a decoration. Baby board books, pop up, and other toy books continue to be popular. An important award to know is the Caldecott Award *(www.ala.org).* It was created in 1936 to recognize the picture book genre. Picture books are available for all ages. Even wordless picture books exist for all levels; for example, *The Silver Pony* (Ward) is a wordless chapter book. Other examples of popular wordless books are Day's *Good Dog, Carl* and the *Anno* series.

It is important to examine illustrations to see if they date otherwise timely content. Examine how the art interfaces with the mood and tone of the story. Question the degree to which the art …

1. Elaborates on the setting, plot, characterization, and theme? How do art elements like color, line, shape, and texture do so?
2. Foreshadows events and show action?
3. Shows detail? Are the details accurate and nonstereotypical?
4. Uses media (collage, photography, etc.) to develop setting, plot, characterization, and theme?
5. Creates a mood appropriate to the art's style?
6. Interacts with the actual print on the page?
7. Plays an integral role in the book? (Norton, 2003)

Humorous literature.   Humorous books and poems top the lists of children's favorites so this category is not to be laughed at. Laughter is an important safety value and blasts us with new perspectives. When used to uplift and elevate, not denigrate or devastate, humor can enrich and energize (Cornett, 2001). Humor bibliographies can be located by using the sources in Ready Reference 4.6. Examples of books of pure humor, such as word play, jokes, riddles, and tongue twisters, are:

Mauterer, E. *(2005). Laugh out loud: Jokes and riddles from Highlights.* Boyds Mills.
McMillan, B. (1982). *Puniddles.* Houghton Mifflin.
Rosenbloom, J. (1986). *Silly school jokes and riddles.* Sterling.
Schwartz, A. (1974). *A twister of twists, a tangler of tongues.* Deutsch.
Terban, M. *(1985). Too hot to hoot (palindromes).* Clarion.

Predictable books.   With release of research showing children more easily read with materials using a repetitive structure, teachers have clamored for such literature. These books also provide patterns for writing. Unique features are:

Repeated phrase, sentence, or refrain.   These stories often have a musical or poetic quality. In Martin's *Brown Bear, Brown Bear,* a rhythmic question is repeated, "Brown Bear Brown Bear, What do you see?" In Barrett's *Animals Should Definitely Not Wear Clothing,* the title repeats.

Word play and rhyme.   These books have predictable word patterns or poetry elements (e.g., couplets or internal rhymes) as in Cameron's *I Can't Said the Ant* and Gwynne's *The King Who Rained* (idiomatic expressions).

Predictable plots.   In Charlip's *Fortunately,* a boy has both fortunate and unfortunate events in his life.

Cumulative.   These stories have a series of words or events that repeat and build to a climax. The process is then usually reversed, as in Wood's *The Napping House.*

Concept books.   These informational books on the alphabet, numbers, colors, shapes, and days often are predictable (e.g., Anno's *Counting Book* and Elting's *Q is for Duck*).

Multicultural and international literature.   I recently saw a picture of a fourth-grade class in Los Angeles. The names and faces reinforced the image of the United States as a nation of many cultures. The term *multicultural* often refers to minorities outside the sociopolitical mainstream, including African Americans, Asian Americans, Native Americans, and Hispanics (Bishop, 1992). But multicultural literature and art include works from regional and religious groups, too (e.g., Appalachian, Moslem). Multicultural and international books (first published in other countries) exist in every genre and are increasingly well represented by picture books, such as the 1997 Caldecott winner *Golem,* a Jewish folktale. As a symbol of our growing respect for the culture of minority groups, this area is set apart as a separate literary category (Faltis, Hudelson, & Hudelson, 1997).

All children need to read and see images of all types of people. Children's cultural differences need to be acknowledged, and multicultural literature offers validation. Multicultural literature is now available about most centers of civilization. Concerns persist about stereotypical language and images, inappropriate retellings, and the small number of books published on some cultures. It is important to examine how well characters and culture are portrayed and to consider accuracy, amount of detail, and the extent to which language or text perpetuate stereotypes (Norton, 2005). The International Board on Books for Young People (*www.ibby. org*) publishes a quarterly journal, *Bookbird: World of Children's Books,* to help teachers find appropriate literature.

African American.   Traditional literature has its roots in cultures, such as Swahili, Mali, Zulu, and Ashanti. Many stories were brought by slaves to America and retold, some mixed with Caribbean stories. These tales flourished and evolved; for example, Anansi, the trickster spider from the Ashanti, became "Aunt Nancy" in some tellings. Brer Rabbit stories, collected by Joel Chandler Harris in the 19th century, were traced to the African tradition of cunning animal characters. This literature is rich in themes about perseverance, beauty, and generosity and has engaging language. For example, Bryan uses chanted verse in *Beat the Story Drum, Pum-Pum,* a collection of pourquoi tales. Set in Zimbabwe, *Mufaro's Beautiful Daughters: An African Tale* (Steptoe) is a Cinderella tale and a Caldecott honor book. Noteworthy traditional and contemporary books are:

Hoffman, M. (1991). *Amazing grace. Dial* (realistic fiction).
McKissack, P. (1988). *Mirandy and Brother Wind.* Knopf (fantasy).
Myers, W. D. (1997). *Harlem.* Scholastic (poetry).
Naidoo, (2000). *The other side of truth.* HarperCollins (realism).

Native American.   There are more than 300 tribes in North America from the plains and eastern woodlands, to the southwestern deserts. Together with Canadian cultures, these groups have a vast store of art and ritual, and a nearly 30,000-year history of storytelling (Norton, 2005). Despite distinct differences, there are common patterns: (1) creation myths (how the world arose from chaos), as in Bruchac and London's *Thirteen Moons on a Turtle's Back;* (2) family myths about kinship; (3) hero myths (young hero is a trickster until he gains virtue, usually through a quest), such as *Anpao: An American Indian* Odyssey (Highwater), which is an award-winning collection of myths; and (4) rites of passage myths (involve crossing in and out of a dream state) (Bierhorst, 1976). Contemporary and traditional examples are:

Endrich, L. (1999). *The Birchbark house* (Ojibwa/historical fiction). Hyperion.
Goble, P. (1990). *Iktomi and the ducks: A Plains Indian tale.* Orchard.
Rafe, M. (1992). *Rough-faced girl* (a Cinderella tale). Putnam.
Seattle, C. (1991). *Brother Eagle, Sister Sky: A message from Chief Seattle* (Suquamish). Dial.

Hispanic American/Latino.   Spanish-speaking children are the largest and fastest-growing second-language learners in the United States (Faltis et al., 1997). Unfortunately, *Hispanic* literature can be hard to find. This stems from confusion over the many settings to which the term *Hispanic* alludes: islands of Caribbean and Puerto Rico, South America, and Mexico. Some prefer the term *Latino* (Norton, 2005). Noteworthy books are:

Ancona, G. (1998). *Barrio: Jose's neighborhood.* Harcourt Brace.
Bernier-Grand, C. (2005). *César: Sí, se puede! (Yes, We Can!)* Marshall Cavendish (poetry about Cesar Chavez).
Carling, A. (1998) *Mama and papa have a store.* Dial.
Farmer, N. (2002). *The house of the scorpion.* Simon & Schuster.
San Souci, R. (1998). *Cendrillion: A Caribbean Cinderella.* Simon & Schuster.

Asian American.   This literature includes stories and poems from Japan, Vietnam, China, India, the Philippines, and Pacific Rim countries. Examples are scarce and books may stereotype characters devoid of individual traits (e.g., *Five Chinese Brothers*). Positive examples are *Yeh-Shen: A Cinderella Story from China* (Louie, 1982) and Yep's *The Rainbow People*, a collection of folktales from Chinatown. Fine examples are:

Demi, T.-S. H. (trans.). (1994). *In the eyes of the cat: Japanese poetry for all seasons.* Holt.
Huffman, J. (trans.). (1999). *The cat who lived a million lives.* University of Hawaii Press (Japan).

Park, L. (2001). *A single shard.* Houghton Mifflin (Korean).
Say, A. (1993). *Grandfather's journey.* Houghton Mifflin (Japan).
Whelan, G. (2000). *Homeless bird.* HarperCollins (India).

Other areas of diversity.   Many religious cultures are increasingly represented in children's books. Examples are:

Bell, H. (2003). *Flame.* Simon & Schuster (Persian legend).
Highwater, J. (1994). *Rama: A legend.* Holt (Hindu).
Macaulay, D. (2003). *Mosque.* Houghton Mifflin (Islamic).
Rylant, C. (1986). *A fine white dust.* Bradbury (Protestant).
Wisniewski, D. (1997). *Golem.* Clarion (Jewish).

International books are from or about other countries. An example is Fox's *Possum Magic* (Australia). A growing group of fine books is being translated. Noteworthy ones are:

Bjork, C. (1987). *Linnea in Monet's garden.* R & S (Sweden).
Gallaz, C. (1985). *Rose Blanche.* Creative Education (France).
Maruki, T. (1982). *Hiroshima no Pika.* Lothrop, Lee & Shepard (Japan).

Blueprint III: Collaborative Planning

In Chapters 1–3 the concept of teaching *with, about, in*, and *through* the arts was introduced. This idea of levels of integration should guide literature integration. The goal is to co-plan to get beyond entertaining with books and artificial writing assignments. To do this, students need to learn how to *use* literary knowledge for writing and reading. Beyond the *about* and *in* is teaching *through* literature. This involves using literature and literary writing as tools in science, social studies, math, music, art, drama, and dance. Unit structures and planning models described in Chapter 3 are used in literature integration.

National Standards: Literary Arts

In 1996 the National Council for the Teachers of English Language Arts and the International Reading Association collaborated to develop student goals for reading, writing, speaking, and listening. The result is a set of broad statements of what students should know and be able to do. The standards are being used at both state and local levels to develop curriculum and construct assessments. Ready Reference 4.4 lists the National Standards for the English/Language Arts.

 **Standards for the English/Language Arts***

Overall focus: Literacy growth through experience and experimenting with literacy activities; reading and writing and associating spoken words with their graphic representations.

Goals: Students will …

1. *Read a wide range of print and nonprint texts* (fiction and nonfiction, classic and contemporary works, multicultural literature, genre characteristics and purposes).

2. *Read a wide range of literature from many periods in many genres* (understand aspects of human experience, compare and contrast literature from different periods).

3. *Apply a wide range of strategies to comprehend, interpret, evaluate, and appreciate texts* (draw on their prior experience and interactions with others, use word meanings, and their understanding of text features).

4. *Adjust use of spoken, written, and visual language: vocabulary development, variety of audiences for a variety of purposes.*

5. *Employ a wide range of strategies as they write: writing process, patterns from books read, different audiences and purposes.*

6. *Apply knowledge of language structure, language conventions, media techniques, figurative language, and genre to create, critique, discuss print and nonprint texts* (literary elements, art elements, patterns of writing, analysis of literary devices used to create style).

7. *Conduct research on issues and interests by generating ideas and questions and by posing problems: gather, evaluate, and synthesize data from a variety of sources; use literary experiences to solve problems; seeks out books for personal information.*

8. *Use a variety of technological and informational resources: libraries, databases, computer networks, and video.*

9. *Develop an understanding of and respect for diversity in language use, patterns, and dialects* (multicultural literature, including poetry sharing).

10. *Participate as knowledgeable, reflective, creative, and critical members of a variety of literacy communities* (discussions and conversations, oral sharing of poetry, author's chair, evaluate literary and artistic merit of a book).

11. *Use spoken, written, and visual language to accomplish their own purposes* (oral interpretation of poetry, writing in different genre, book making, connect life events, respond through other art forms, read for enjoyment, storytelling, develop literary preferences).

*Copyright 1996 by the International Reading Association and the National Council of Teachers of English. Adapted from 12 Standards, as applicable to integrating the arts. Ideas that follow standards represent the author's interpretation.

The Standards are starting points for literature integration because they make clear the focus possibilities for units and lessons. State and local standards and courses of study also give information about key concepts and skills expected of students, generally divided into grade groupings.

Integrated Units

Integrated units (1) focus on life-centered themes and questions, (2) are adapted for student interests and needs, and (3) make the arts integral. Discipline-based methods and content are combined into a meaningful whole so students learn about justice, power, and human rights. Textbooks offer explanations, but the arts—in this case, literature—offer the lives of people. For example, in a core book study using a biography of Benjamin Franklin, students are shown the context of his discovery of electricity—what he was doing at the time, where he lived, what he was worried about, and who his friends were. Biography puts face and feelings to

facts and allows readers to vicariously go through the invention process with Franklin. Readers become detectives, mining for clues about how things got to be the way they are today.

Unit Structures

Literature-based units can be planned for time blocks ranging from several days a month, or a yearlong study for a schoolwide unit. Common unit centers are: (1) core or single literary work such as a poem or story, (2) a literary genre, (3) a person, usually an author or poet, (4) a topic/issue, and (5) an event. For example, *Sarah, Plain and Tall* (Maclachlan) was the core work for the opening Classroom Snapshot. Any genre can be a focus, with works studied to discover shared genre traits. An author and/or artist of picture books are frequently the organizer for a unit on a person. A topic or real-life issue, usually connected to science or social studies, is often used as an organizing center (Chapter 3 has examples). Finally, event-based units may start or culminate with an author visit, play made from children's literature, or a film (e.g., *Because of Winn-Dixie*). An author–artist unit planning web appears in Planning Page 6.1. Information sources and guidelines for artist–author studies appear in Planning Page 4.1.

All unit centers are developed using the process outlined in Chapter 3 with focus on writing theme statements and important questions to guide study. See Ready Reference 2.5 for the process. Planning Page 3.1 shows nine-legged planning to integrate curricular areas. Planning Page 4.2 shows how one teacher planned a core book study on *Millions of Cats* starting with themes about making choices.

Field Trip or Literary Event

The most common literature event is a visit by a children's author or book illustrator. Scheduling and preparing for author visits is discussed under Blueprint X: "Arts Partnerships." Literature-focused field trips include visits to art museums to compare art with picture book art, public li-

---

Planning Page 4.1

Author–Artist Study Sources

Websites:
Link to popular author and illustrator sites through:

University of Calgary:
www.acs.ucalgary.ca/~dkbrown/authors.html#atoj

Kathy Schrock's Guide for Educators:
http://www.lib.lsu.edu/hum/lit/authors.html

Carol Hurst's site:
www.carolhurst.com

Reference librarians can give access to Thompson Gale's research website:
www.gale.com

Popular Author-Artist's Websites:

Barbara Cooney:
www.carolhurst.com/authors/bcooney.html

Tomie dePaola:
http://tomie.com

Leo and Diane Dillon:
http://falcon.jmu.edu/~ramseyil/dillon

Susan Jeffers:
http://susanjeffers.com/home/index.cfm

Ezra Jack Keats:
http://lib.usm.edu/~degrum/keats/main.html

Robert McCloskey:
http://falcon.jmu.edu/~ramseyil/mccloskey.htm

Maurice Sendak:
http://falcon.jmu.edu/~ramseyil/sendak.htm

Alice and Martin Provensen:
societyillustrators.org/permanent_collection/provensen.html

Chris Van Allsburg:
http://eduplace.com/author/

David Wiesner:
www.houghtonmifflinbooks.com/authors/wiesner/home.html

Book Sources

Dictionary of literary biography, American writers for children. Vols. 22, 42, 52, 61. Gale Thompson.

Hopkins, L. (1995). *Pauses: Autobiographical reflections of 101 creators of children's books.* HarperCollins.

Locher, F. (ed). *Contemporary authors: A biographical guide to current writers in fiction, general non-fiction, poetry, and journalism, drama, motion pictures, television, and other fields.* (122 volumes). Gale Research.

McElmeel, S. (1992). *Bookpeople: A multicultural album.* Libraries Unlimited.

McElmeel, S. (1993). *An author a month (for dimes).* Teacher Ideas Press.

McElmeel, S. (2004). *Children's authors and illustrators too good to miss.* Libraries Unlimited.

McElmeel, S. (2005). *Authors in the kitchen.* Libraries Unlimited.

Roginski, J. (1989). *Behind the covers: Interviews with authors and illustrators of books for children and young adults.* Libraries Unlimited.

Something about the author: Facts and pictures about contemporary authors and illustrators of books for young people. (1971–2006). Vols. 1–50. Gale Research. Online at: *www.gale.com/ebooks.*

A state-by-state guide to children's and young adult authors and illustrators. (1991). Libraries Unlimited.

Sixth book of junior authors and illustrators. (1989). Wilson.

Something about the author autobiography series. (1986–1987). Vols. 1–4. Gale Research.

Twentieth century children's authors, 4th ed. (1995). St. James.

CPS for Comprehension

These problems to pose with students require "thinking through the arts" to make meaning from the story. The focus is on themes/big ideas in *Millions of Cats* by Wanda Gag.

Music Problems

1. Fluency: Change pitch, stress, tempo, and volume for the refrain. Try crescendo and decrescendo, solo, and group voices.
2. Word choir: Each chooses an important word from the story and decides how to say it. One student is the conductor and points to each indicating how to say the word (e.g., piano, forte, repeatedly, choral). Variation: do with emotion "sounds."
3. Put to music: Create a melody for the refrain. Decide how to sing it (1) when the Old Man first sees all the cats, (2) when the cats eat and drink up everything, and (3) when the Old Woman sees them coming. Change musical elements to show character emotions.

Visual Art Problems

1. Picture It: Choose an important moment in the story. Visualize all the colors, shapes, textures, types of lines you imagine. Write or orally describe.
2. List emotions related to the beginning, middle, and end. Choose an important emotion and think of several colors, shapes, and lines associated with it. Make art that shows your thinking.
3. Select one page to study closely. Tell why you chose this art. Talk or write about the details you observe: What do you see (types of lines, shapes, lack of color)? How does the art make you feel? How did Gag make the art (techniques, media)? Why did she organize it the way she did (composition)? What is communicated in the art that was not in the words of the story?

Drama Problems (OW=Old Woman; OM=Old Man)

1. Use pantomime (body shapes and moves, facial expressions, gestures) to show… three things the Old Woman did while the Old Man was away or three things the cats did before the Old Man arrived.
2. Use pantomime to show how OM and OW felt at the beginning, when the OM saw all the cats, when the OM was trying to decide, and how the cats felt when the OW said they should decide.
3. One liner: Take a role (change voice using musical elements) of a character and say a sentence to show thinking and feeling at an important moment. Use your body to show the character. Don't say who you are and don't be obvious in what you say.
4. Tableau: Work with a group to create a frozen picture about the meaning (theme). Create a "composition" with your bodies and faces. Variation: Take turns "coming alive" and say something.

Dance Problems

1. List ways characters moved in the BME. Examples: trudge, climb. Explore each using different BEST elements (e.g., trudge fast, slow, high, low, lead with different body parts).
2. Transformation: Create a dance that shows an important change from beginning to end (e.g., emotional). Start the dance in a frozen shape to show the emotion. Plan dance movements to a count. End the dance to show contrast from the beginning.

Poetry Problems

Write a poem about important ideas or emotions in the story. Adapt a Poem Pattern (lune, syllable, bio, haiku, etc.). Example: CLERIHEW (ABAB): Old Woman and Old Man/ Were very lonely/ The solution they planned/ Left one cat only.

---

braries to hear stories or talks about special collections, newspaper offices to understand news publishing, and studios of artists or writers. Of course, field trips can be an event that connects to any unit, from fairy tales (e.g., a play based on *Cinderella*) to death rituals (e.g., cemetery field trip). Use the Field Trip guidelines in the Appendix to make sure trips are meaningful and integral to learning.

Special Connections

What's a hornbook? Ever heard of a battledore? Both are early forms of children's books and provide child view en-

trees into early American history. Of course there is science in bookmaking, including how inks, paper, the printing press and other machinery, were invented. Then there is math. For example, Poe used mathematical formulas in his poem *The Raven*. Don't ignore the economic influence of children's books from book selling to publishing and advertising, and, of course, careers in writing.

Two-Pronged Lesson Plan

The concept of an integrated arts lesson framework, with at least a two-pronged focus (an art form and another curricular area) was introduced in Chapter 3. This framework includes a predictable teaching sequence: introduction, development, and conclusion (IDC). This structure used to plan and teach lessons that integrate literature with other curricular areas. Planning Page 4.3 shows an example.

Literature and Social Studies (Third Grade)

Two-Pronged Focus: (1) Literary elements/concepts: point of view (POV), informational genre (authentic versus fictionalized biography). (2) Social studies big idea: The historical record depends on who is "telling the story."

Standards: 3, 6, and 11 (Ready Reference 4.4).

Student Objectives: Students will be able to…
1. Give the POV of books using examples.
2. Give reasons why an informational book is authentic or fictionalized and tell why knowing this is important.
3. Explain how POV is important in life.
4. Use POV to write about an event from two perspectives.

Materials: Four copies of the following books:
Yolen's *Encounter* (Columbus's landing in 1492 reported from the point of view of a native islander).
Columbus's diary entries in *The Log of Christopher Columbus.*
Dyson's *Westward with Columbus* (third-person informational).
Ocean music (any CD of waves), copy of Hoban's *Look Again.*

Teaching Procedure: (S= student, T= Teacher)

Introduction
1. Thumbs up if you know a Cinderella story. Group and give each a role: mice, stepsister, stepmother, father, neighbor, king. Use teacher in role to interview. Ask, "What happened?" Ask about the answers. Why were they different?
2. Show visual: "POV is point of view." Show pictures in *Look Again* and ask S to guess what they are (close-ups of ordinary objects). Ask S to relate this to POV. Ask volunteers to describe the classroom from the POV of a bug on the ceiling, a kindergartner, the principal, an eighth grader.
3. Ask how POV and perspective make a difference in real life.
4. Tell S they'll be using POV and perspective to think about our social studies unit on "exploration and discovery" and that Writing Workshop will be about this the next week.

Development
1. Ask what S know about Columbus. Record comments on chart.
2. Show covers and a few pictures from the three books. Use Predict–Prove strategy. Focus on POV each might take. Show rest of POV chart with the different types and examples.
3. Explain that the books are fact-based, but sometimes authors make up dialogue or characters to make a story interesting. Show "Informational genre: Authentic biography and fictionalized transparency" and explain. Tell S they will buddy-read during Independent Reading using a choice of the Columbus books. The goal is to find out the POV and clues about whether the book is authentic or fictionalized. Number off in 2s. Number 1 comes and picks book and gets with partner to do 15 minutes of reading. Give Evidence Chart to pairs to record findings.
4. Pull together in three groups based on three books. Use Evidence Charts to share and elaborate. Circulate to give feedback and ask questions to prompt evidence from books (actual details).
5. Assemble whole group and ask a person from each of three groups to report findings on POV and subgenre decisions. Compare with predictions on chart. Add new information about Columbus.

Conclusion and Informal Assessment
1. Ask students to TOT (tell one thing) learned about POV and authentic versus fictionalized biography. Ask each student to write down something they think will happen in the book (the buddy reading will continue) and a question they have about Columbus. Collect questions.
2. Tell S to begin thinking about a real event, at school, home, in the news, that they can write about using a different POV. Ideas will be webbed at the start of the Writing Workshop. Point out books written from different perspectives (e.g., *The True Story of Three Little Pigs* by A. Wolf).

Blueprint IV: Aesthetic Literary Environment

Teachers who love literature show it. Their classrooms are stocked with books from every genre and reading level. Book nooks are lined with pillows. Sofas and rockers make the classroom more like a "living room." Teachers bring in claw-foot bathtubs, telephone booths, and Conestoga wagons. They build lofts to give intriguing places to read. The chalk tray becomes a display for "books of the week" with enticing advertising slogans or questions: "A dog with an attitude. Read: *Officer Buckles and Gloria*" (Rathman). Special pages can be tabbed as "sneak peaks." Book displays, connected to units, promote choices for independent reading, too. Poem charts are pinned on clotheslines, ready for poetry routines. Poetry Walls are filled with posted favorites. Poem Pockets, made from library pockets and shoe bags, invite student to choose one or add one, as they collect poems for personal anthologies.

Literature Collections

We tend to "own" what we help create, so kids need to participate in the design of the classroom. Invitations to share well-loved poems and stories from home, as well as posters and quotes that celebrate books, extend ownership. In addition, students can root out writers and readers in their families to "make public" how literature is alive outside of school. Children are proud to find uncles and aunts and dads who write poetry and deserve the title "bibliophile."

Even if the school has a wonderful library, the classroom is closer. When literature collections exist in classrooms, students read 50% more than those in classrooms without collections (Morrow, 2003). A classroom needs several hundred trade books. If the school doesn't provide these, teachers can collect books in inexpensive ways: send home a letter asking for used books (list criteria), go to tag sales, buy from book clubs like Scholastic and Trumpet (teachers get bonus books), or ask the PTA to conduct an old-fashioned book drive (set limits on what can be contributed). Of particular importance is obtaining multiple copies of books for core book studies. This means enough copies for small groups to read the same book (six to eight copies) or class sets. In addition, teachers need to accumulate "text sets" of literature around yearly units. For example, text sets of a 15–25 books, stories, and poems are created for topics like weather and for genre studies of fairy tales. No teacher starts off with such book wealth, but by targeting one or two units a year, the collection grows.

Books are commonly stored in colorful crates designated by genre or topic. Many teachers now color-dot books for readability level, but levels should be treated flexibly. Interest, happily, can overthrow any leveling system and enable children to exceed assessed expectations.

Blueprint V: Literature as a Core Art Form

What makes literature art? So many books, genre, and elements mean many decisions about writing and reading. The decisions can't just hinge on finding any books. The goal is to integrate artful literature so students are immersed in aesthetic experiences with words. This leads to considering what makes quality. As with any art, evaluation is difficult and to some extent personal. It is important, however, to establish criteria for judgments. The school media specialist and the children's librarian at the public library are specialists who can help cull the best from thousands of books. Equally important is for students to learn to present informed opinions using anchor ideas. Here are three concepts to start:

1. Creativity
2. Unity and balance
3. Taste

Creativity

Are literary elements used in original ways? Remember from Chapter 2 how a creative idea is not "entirely new," but a twist or substitution. The key is whether the author makes a creative leap to mold and shape new characters, context, and plots from verbal clay. Is there energy or a spark to the work that makes it seem alive? Does it create a sense of rejuvenation and hope? Are there strong universal themes, motifs, and archetypes? Are they varied to create a story or poem that seems to be both a new invention and a close friend? Or is the plot tired, the style clichè, and the characters dull?

Unity and Balance

Do the literary elements work in concert to make an integrated whole? Characters may be believable and fascinating, but they need a plot that intrigues and an appropriate setting. Beautiful words that go nowhere soon frustrate even the most poetic soul, and a well-drawn setting without compelling characters to act in it seems a frill. Finally, as in all fine art, good literature should be provocative—a creative invention that disturbs our universe. Enduring truths should be unveiled about people and the world, without ramming them down our throats. We must feel that the story has united the elements and allows readers to make discoveries rather than be victimized by didacticism.

Taste

A book can be high in creativity, unity, and balance and still not be beloved. Judging art always includes personal taste, which has to do with what we like, feel comfortable with,

What Makes Good Literature?

Directions: Evaluate a piece of literature using these criteria. Rate from 1=very evident to 5=not evident. Indicate 2, 3, or 4 for ratings in between. NA is not applicable.

Plot

_____ 1. Gains momentum from the conflict.

_____ 2. Conflict is clear and believable.

_____ 3. Does not depend on coincidence.

_____ 4. Original versus dully predictable.

_____ 5. Suspense raised by withholding obvious problem resolutions.

_____ 6. Subplots and/or flashbacks enhance without complicating.

_____ 7. Climax has action or hints at conflict resolution.

Theme

_____ 1. Universal truths can be understood on more than one level.

_____ 2. Contains subthemes that support main theme.

_____ 3. Causes reader to confront a problem or see life as it might be.

_____ 4. Avoids imposing values, prejudices, and opinions.

Characters

_____ 1. Revealed through:
  _____ a. Physical description
  _____ b. Actions
  _____ c. Speech and thoughts
  _____ d. Others' thoughts and words

_____ 2. Developed more through action than description.

_____ 3. Believable, original, and consistent (age, background, ethnicity).

_____ 4. Protagonist changes or grows.

_____ 5. Novel use of foils and flat characters.

_____ 6. Avoids stereotypes.

Setting

_____ 1. Sets stage for action with details and background.

_____ 2. Time and place developed by references to well-known sites or through language use.

_____ 3. Details are appropriate to the time and place.

Point of View

_____ 1. Strongly influences how characters are revealed.

_____ 2. Contains objectivity appropriate to the reader's maturity.

Style

_____ 1. Language is matched to characters and intended readers.

_____ 2. Language is artistic and creative.

_____ 3. Used effectively to create mood.

Notes:

Conclusions:

What are your overall reactions?
How well written is this piece of literature?

---

and just plain suits us at the moment. Series like the *Bobsey Twins* are judged to be mediocre and formulaic by critics. But they are as popular now as they were in the 1950s and are joined by *The Babysitter's Club* and *Goosebumps* books. Adults risk alienating children by forcing books of "quality" on them. It's much like expecting everyone to want a house designed by Frank Lloyd Wright because his is great architecture, without regard for the homeowner's taste.

Ready Reference 4.5 has additional criteria. Modify this format for children or ask them to contribute to an ongoing list on what makes a book, story, or poem great.

Selection Sources

Ready References 4.3, 4.5, 4.6, and 4.7 list key selection sources for teachers. The following are also important tools to find good literature: (1) for units (core book, author or genre study, topic or event-based); (2) connected to student interests, including bibliotherapy aids; and (3) to match reading levels.

Award-Winning Literature. The American Library Association (*www.ala.org*) gives the two most well-known

 **Selection Sources for Literature**

Use to find bibliographies for genre and topic studies, author and artists units, read-alouds, bibliotherapy, and age groups. Check Teacher Resources at the end of the chapter.

Websites

American Library Association:
www.ala.org/ala/alsc

Children's Book Council:
www.cbcbooks.org

The Center for Children's Books:
ccb.lis.uiuc.edu/collection_development.html

Books

A to zoo: Subject access to children's picture books, 4th ed. (2001). Bowker.

Accept me as I am: Best books of juvenile nonfiction on impairments and disabilities. (1985). Bowker.

Adventuring with books: A book list for pre-K and grade 6. (1997). NCTE.

Award-winning books for children and young adults. Scarecrow (annual publication).

Best books for children: Preschool through 6. (1990). Bowker.

Beyond picture books: A guide to first readers. (1989). Bowker.

Books kids will sit still for: The complete read-aloud guide, 2nd ed. (1990). Bowker.

The bookfinder: A guide to children's literature about the needs and problems of youth aged 2–15. (1989). American Guidance.

Books to help children cope with separation and loss 2nd ed. (1983). Bowker.

Children's books: Awards and prizes. Children's Book Council.

Children's books in print. Bowker (annual edition).

Choosing books for children, rev. ed. (1990). Delacorte.

The elementary school library collection: A guide to books and other media. (1992). Brodart.

Exciting, funny, scary, short, different, and sad books kids like about animals, science, sports, families, songs, and other things. (1984). ALA.

Hear no evil, see no evil, speak no evil: An annotated bibliography for the handicapped. (1990). Libraries Unlimited.

A Hispanic heritage: A guide to juvenile books about Hispanic people and cultures. (1991). Scarecrow.

Horn Book guide to children's and young adult books. Vol.7, No. 2 (1996). Horn Books.

The literature of delight: A critical guide to humorous books for children. (1991). Bowker.

More notes for a different drummer: A guide to juvenile fiction portraying the disabled. (1984). Bowker.

Pass the poetry please. (1987). HarperCollins.

Science and technology in fact and fiction: A guide to children's books. (1989). Bowker.

---

children's book awards. Go to the ALA site to get the most up-to-date list of winners. Carol Hurst's Children's Literature website (*www.carolhurst.com*) is also excellent. Access lists of all awards at her site plus book reviews, author/artist links, lesson plans, and bibiliographies of books by grade levels and curricular areas.

Newbery Medal Award (1922+). Presented by the ALA to the U.S. author of the most distinguished contribution to children's literature published during the preceding year. An award winner and runner-up honor books are chosen. Recent winners are *Kira-Kira* by Cynthia Kadohata in 2005 and *The Tale of Despereaux: Being the Story of a Mouse, a Princess, Some Soup, and a Spool of Thread* by Kate DiCamillo in 2004.

Caldecott Medal Award (1936+). The ALA awards this medal to the artist of the most distinguished picture book published in the United States in the preceding year and recognizes honor books as well. Only U.S. residents or

citizens are eligible. Recent winners are *Kitten's First Full Moon* by Kevin Henkes in 2005 and *The Man Who Walked Between the Towers* by Mordicai Gerstein in 2004.

Coretta Scott King Awards (1969+). These commemorate Martin Luther King, Jr., and his wife, Coretta, for promoting peace and brotherhood. They are restricted to African American authors and illustrators whose books made outstanding inspirational and educational contributions (sponsored by the ALA). Recent winners are *Remember: The Journey to School Integration* by Toni Morrison *Ellington, Was Not a Street* by Ntozake Shange (illustrated by Kadir Nelson) in 2005, *The First Part Last* by Angela Johnson, and *Beautiful Blackbird* by Ashley Bryan in 2004.

Carnegie Medal (1937+). The British Library Association gives this to the author of the most outstanding children's book first published in English in the United Kingdom.

Hans Christian Andersen Award.   This international award is given every two years and is sponsored by the International Board on Books for Young People. A living author is honored along with, since 1966, a living illustrator whose complete works are important contributions.

Mildred Batchelder Award (1968+).   This ALA award goes to the most outstanding of books originally published outside the United States in a language other than English and then translated.

Orbis Pictus Award (named for the world's first picture book).   The National Council for the Teachers of English give this award to an author for excellence in children's nonfiction published in the United States.

Awards Bibliographies.   Use these to find recommended books based on certain criteria. *Children's Books: Awards and Prizes* from the Children's Book Council (CBC) summarizes most awards, even ones given by other countries and states in the United States. For example, Ohio gives the Buckeye Book Award each year based on nominations by children and teachers.

Authors and Artists.   Sources for biographical and other information, especially for units that focus on these special people are listed on Planning Page 4.1.

Favorites.   Children's Choices are lists of "best books" selected by children. The list is published annually in the October *Reading Teacher* (International Reading Association, *www.ira.org*).

Children's Literature Canon.   Classic literature is "news that stays news" (Ezra Pound) and includes books that have endured the test of time; they continue to delight and inform audiences. The significance of the theme, credibility of the characters, reality of the conflict, and a style that engages are why some books remain in circulation. This relates to the discussion about human needs to know, belong, feel safe, and experience. Horn Book (*http://www.hbook.com*) publishes a list of such children's classics, as does the Children's Literature Association (*www.ebbs.english.vt.edu/chla/*). On nearly every list are Aesop's fables, Andersen's fairy tales, Mother Goose rhymes, Perrault's fairy tales, *Charlotte's Web, Little Women, Winnie the Pooh, The Wizard of Oz,* and *The Adventures of Huckleberry Finn.*

Poetry Sources.   Ready References 4.3 and 4.7 list selection sources for good poetry for units (including core units that focus on a poet or type of poetry) and to match poetry/poets with student interests. Included are (1) lists of children's favorite poems and poets, (2) collections of particular poets and anthologies (which contain works of many poets), and (3) poetry awards.

Poems.   These are enduring favorites to use with children:

Eleanor Farjeon's "Cat"
Ogden Nash's "Adventures of Isabel"
John Ciardi's "Mummy Slept Late and Daddy Fixed Breakfast" and "Why Nobody Pets the Lion at the Zoo"
Ann Hoberman's "A Bookworm of Curious Breed"
Karla Kuskin's "Hughbert and the Glue"
Irene McLeod's "Lone Dog"
Laura E. Richards's "Eletelephony"
Judith Viorst's "Mother Doesn't Want a Dog"
Shel Silverstein's "The Unicorn" and "Sick"
Jane Yolen's "Homework"
Langston Hughes's "Dreams"
Jack Prelutsky's "Willie Ate a Worm Today," "Oh, Teddy Bear," and "The Lurpp Is on the Loose"

Popular poets.   The humorous poetry of Shel Silverstein and Jack Prelutsky dominates children's choices (Kutiper & Wilson, 1993). Other popular poets are: David McCord, Aileen Fisher, Myra C. Livingston, Eve Merriam, Lilian Moore, Arnold Adoff, Valerie Worth, John Ciardi, Eleanor Farjeon, Ann Hoberman, Langston Hughes, Edward Lear, Vachel Lindsay, Ogden Nash, Karla Kuskin, Irene Rutherford McLeod, Laura E. Richards, Judith Viorst, Paul Janeczko, and Jane Yolen (Kutiper & Wilson, 1993; Norton, 2003).

Arts-Based Literature.   Literature is an art form generated by the same creative process as any other art. Literature is also a storehouse of information about music, visual art, drama, and dance and the artists who create these arts. Arts-based literature comes in all genres: biographies of artists, information and how-to books, and fictional stories with artist characters and/or arts-related themes. Picture books are automatically arts based with the winning combination of visual art and literary art. Together, books, stories, and poems that are related to arts, in any way are called *arts-based*. Each of the arts chapters includes examples of arts-based books for that particular art. There is also an arts-based bibliography in the Appendix.

There is also literature about literature. Stories and biographies about writers, the writing process, and actual books make up "literature-based" literature. These are important resources in growing students' understanding of how the literary arts are made and the people who made them. Examples include *What's Your Story? A Young Person's Guide to Writing Fiction* (Bauer) and *If You Were a Writer* (Nixon). Many books feature protagonists who read and write, such as Duvoisin's *Petunia*. Carol Hurst lists more at: *www.carolhurst.com*.

Poetry Book Examples

Single Poet Collections

Adoff, A. (1979). *Eats.* Lothrop, Lee & Shepard.

Fleischman, P. (1992). *Joyful noise: Poems for two voices.* HarperCollins.

Greenfield, E. (1988). *Under the Sunday tree.* Harper & Row.

Koontz, D. (2001). *The paper doorway: Funny verse and nothing worse.* HarperCollins.

Livingston, M. C. (1986). *Earth songs.* Holiday House.

Moss, J. (1989). *The butterfly jar.* Bantam.

Pomerantz, C. (1982). *If I had a paka: Poems in 11 languages.* Greenwillow.

Prelutsky, J. (1984). *The new kid on the block.* Greenwillow.

Silverstein, S. (1974). *Where the sidewalk ends.* Harper & Row.

Silverstein, S. (2005) *Runny babbit: A billy sook.* HarperCollins.

Stepanek, M. (2001). *Heartsongs.* Vacation Spot Press.

Anthologies

(many poets under one cover)

A jar of tiny stars: Poems by NCTE award-winning poets. (1995). Boyds Mills Press.

Bryan, A. (1997). *Ashley Bryan's ABC of African American poetry.* Atheneum.

Carlson, L. (Ed.). (1994). *Cool salsa: Bilingual poems on growing up Latino in the US.* Holt.

de Regniers, B. S., Moore, E., White, M. M., & Carr, J. (1988*). Sing a song of popcorn: Every child's book of poems.* Scholastic.

Kennedy, K. J., & Kennedy, D. (1999). *Knock at a star: A child's introduction to poetry.* Little, Brown.

Nye, N. (1992). *This same sky: A collection of poems from around the world.* Four Winds.

Prelutsky, J. (1983). *The Random House book of poetry for children.* Random House.

Prelutsky, J. (1986). *Read aloud poems for the very young.* Knopf.

Prelutsky, J. (1999). *The 20th century children's poetry treasury.* Knopf.

Worth, V. (1994). *All the small poems and fourteen more.* Farrar, Straus & Giroux.

Poems in Picture Book Form

Adoff, A. (1973). *Black is brown is tan.* Harper & Row.

Atwood, A. (1977). *Haiku vision.* Scribner's.

Baylor, B. (1977). *Guess who my favorite person is.* Scribner's.

Frost, R. (1988). *Birches.* Henry Holt.

Hopkins, L. (1993). *Poems of Halloween night: Ragged shadows.* Little, Brown.

Johnson, J. (1993). *Lift every voice and sing.* Walker.

Lobel, A. (1984). *A rose in my garden.* Greenwillow.

Longfellow, H. W. (1990). *Paul Revere's ride.* Dutton.

Noyes, A. (1981). *The highwayman.* Oxford University Press.

Blueprint VI: Best Teaching Practices

Here are ways the arts integration teaching practices from Chapter 3 are used in literature integration. Ready Reference 3.4 is an overview of all 10.

What You Teach Is Who You Are

There is no substitute for a teacher who personally loves to read and write. Charlie Brown reminds us that it is never too late to learn, but sometimes it is too early. Some teachers don't become bibliophiles until college when they take courses in creative writing and children's literature. A literary arts knowledge base is essential, but the enthusiasm of a teacher wraps knowledge in a compelling package. Teachers who have experienced the power of books to give joy and meaning have a passion to pass on. If you don't currently have the passion, pick out a couple books recommended in this chapter and give them a chance to work their magic. Also, start hanging around teachers who have the passion. It really is contagious.

Writing and Reading Role Models. Fresh ideas do not flow from a mind fixed on right answers. If children are to interpret literature aesthetically and make heartfelt connections and responses, they need to be around teachers who demonstrate this behavior and invite these kinds of reactions. If they are to write with passion, they need to be have teachers who write with them about topics they know and care about.

Literature integration is about motivating students through the inherent power of the arts. The focus is on interests, choices, meaning, and purpose.

Interest: The Mighty Motivator. No amount of points or pizza coupons will ever match the force of interest in increasing the appetite for reading. Interest accounts for more than 25 times the variance in reading comprehension (Barr, Kamil, & Mosenthal, 1996; Guthrie, 2004). People simply read more and better when materials are interesting. Abundant fiction and nonfiction is now available on any subject, from sports to fantasy to cooking. The Appendix has a sample Interest Inventory, and selection sources in Ready Reference 4.6 are designed to help match readers with interests. We need not rely on predeveloped interests, either. Arts integration is about expanding horizons. Interest builds as students are deeply engaged through head, hands, and heart involvement with good books. We can capitalize on the familiar and make the unfamiliar familiar using strategies like daily arts-based read-alouds and routines like "book ads." These short commercials introduce books to develop new interests.

Choice. Why should students travel lockstep through the same stories all year long? Why must everyone write a sequel to a book or a letter to a character? They shouldn't, but teachers need a repertoire of choices before they can offer them to students. This book has a plethora of choices. More than 100 alternatives to book reports can be found in the Appendix under "Book Report Alternatives." Ready Reference 5.1 lists "Writing Choices A–Z," and Ready Reference 5.2 gives choices for writing poetry through "Poem Patterns." The CPS process is all about choice. Brainstorming, data gathering, and SCAMPER can generate more choices.

Undergraduates have fresh memories of being forced to do book reports and claim that these dull assignments single-handedly made many not want to read. A primary theme of this text is the need to implement MI theory and motivation research on alternative ways to understand and express thoughts and feelings. A strong implication is to give choices of what to read and alternative ways to respond.

Active Engagement. The literary arts are naturally "brains on." They provoke thinking and emotional response. The most profound literature engagement happens when the other arts are combined with literature to add more thinking and hands-on learning. This can happen before, during, and/or after reading and includes well-crafted discussions. Arts-based literature lessons occur throughout the curriculum in mega-routines like daily read-alouds, independent reading, small group meetings, and other routines under Blueprint VII: "Instructional Design." Ready Reference 4.8 lists discussion questions.

One well-known tool to activate thinking is KWL, for "Know, Want to know, Learn" (Ogle, 1989). KWL causes students to seek information. Here's how. Divide a chart into three columns: K for Know, W for Want to Know, and L for Learned. The first two columns are used before reading or writing. Students list what they already know about a topic. Then they list what they want to learn. The class then reads to learn more and writes ideas in the third column that connect to the W. Writing can be drafted or arts responses made based on what was learned. *Variation:* The acronym AQUA can also be used for columns and stands for: Already know, Questions to answer, and Answers found.

Creative Problem Solving (CPS). When literacy instruction is literature-based, the major portion of instructional time is devoted to discussing, creating, sharing, and performing children's literature. The goal is a daily time block of about 2 hours to read, write, talk about, and listen to good stories and poems—uninterrupted. Students are involved in the concentrated search for truths found in implicit and explicit literary themes. They are taught that reading and writing are complementary. As with arts literacy, both are about composing meaning. Of particular importance are strategies good readers commonly use before, during, and after reading (Pressley, 2002). Writers call this prewriting, drafting, and revising/editing, but it is the same kinds of thinking, with different labels. This process parallels the introduction, development, and conclusion phases of a lesson plan. What's more, all these sequences align with CPS. The labels really are only important as tools to help students learn to manage thinking as they solve problems. It is simpler to teach one generic "creating meaning" process and show how to apply it to reading and writing. In this book the CPS is that process and is summarized in Ready Reference 2.5.

Reading/writing process and CPS. Here is an example of CPS applied to the reading process. A good reader starts with the general problem of how to make sense. This sets purpose and serves to motivate through interest. Perhaps the reader is worried about a friend who has lung cancer. The reader begins by searching for information sources. She may surf the Internet or leaf through books to hypothesize and predict. The reader generates questions she wants answered. Before in-depth reading she will gather bits and pieces from overviews and previews of materials. She may read small sections to get a sense of the writing style. At first any material may be accepted, but the reader becomes more selective as she reads on. The reader chooses potential books and scans to find the relevant sections. Then the reader studies these sections carefully or skims to get the gist.

The reader continually returns to her initial problem and begins to prioritize ideas that seem most important. The reader sifts and sorts, visualizes and organizes. She shifts in and out of perspectives using empathy for her friend. Periodically she pauses and tries to make connections, asking, "What does this mean?" and "Does this make sense?" The reader may reread to clarify. Some general categories begin to emerge—possible causes, symptoms, and treatments. The reader may stop and call the friend to get more details about

 **Discussion Questions for Literature**

Guidelines

1. Ask open questions that can be supported with text evidence.
2. Ask students to read aloud sections to support answers.
3. Choose one or two important questions to discuss in depth.
4. Have students stop and write down ideas before discussing. This adds reflection *before* and focus *during* the discussion.
5. Connect text-text, text-world, and text-students' lives. This increases comprehension and promotes aesthetic responses.
6. Read for pleasure, first, to increase aesthetic response. Then reread to find evidence for selected questions.
7. Post questions like the following for students to choose from.

Look at the title and a few pictures; then ask:

- What do you think this is about? Who? When and where (characters/setting)?
- What might be the problems in a book with this title (theme)?
- How does this make you feel (aesthetic response)? Why?

Read a bit; then ask:

- What did you notice so far?
- What's the big question? How do you know (theme)?
- What's the problem? How might it get solved? (conflict/plot)
- What kind of person is this character? How do you know (character)?
- What should the character do (critical/moral thinking)? Why?
- What's happening? Why? What are the important things that have happened (plot)?
- Whose story is this (point of view)?
- What do you notice in the pictures (color, texture, shape, line, perspective)? How does this affect the story?
- What will happen? Why? What would you like to find out?

Read more; then repeat from above or ask:

- What do you now know/feel that you didn't know before (POV/empathy)?
- What questions got answered (confirm/reject predictions)?
- What is confusing (clarification)?
- What events are important? How do you know (critical thinking)?
- What words or language stands out (style)? Why?
- How does this story make you feel (illustrations, mood)?
- What does the dialog tell you about the main character?
- What pictures are you making in your head (visualize)?

After the entire reading ask:

- What happened? Why? What were the problems? How were they solved (plot; cause/effect)?
- What did you like? What were your favorite parts? Why (critical thinking)?
- What was this story really about (themes/key concepts)?
- How is this story like something in your life (connections)?
- Was it right that . . .? Why or why not (critical/moral)?
- Was . . . believable (seem real) character? Why (evaluation)?
- What was special or important about . . . (inference)?
- What did . . . believe/value (inference)?
- What will you remember about this story next week? Next year?
- How is this story like others you've read (connections)?
- What was special about the illustrations (aesthetics)?
- What is special about how the author writes? How did the author make the story interesting (style)?
- Why did the characters do what they did? What does the story tell you about people and behavior (conclusions)?
- Did the story end the way you predicted? Why or why not?
- How did the characters change in the story (characterization)?
- Why did the author write this story (conclusions)?

the diagnosis or go back and forth between websites and books. This problem solving may go on for an hour or days. At some point the reader decides that she has made as much sense as she can. Final conclusions are synthesized. The reader may then share her results or simply be satisfied to have a greater understanding of the problem.

Notice that the final solution to this particular reader's problem may be similar to other readers, but not identical. Because the reader had a specific purpose for reading and used CPS, the result will be a personally constructed understanding. The ways this reader visualizes and connects, organizes and concludes will be a one-of-a-kind transformation. Students who expect that their meaning making will be unique are more likely to be actively engaged. Owning the problem is critical to motivation, as is belief in finding new solutions. This previous example was for reading nonfiction. There are variations in the process for fiction. For example, reader stance is weighted more in the direction of enjoyment, and the meaning making would be more focused on pulling themes from characterization, plot events, and setting.

Personally Constructed Meaning.   Reading that uses CPS results in diverse forms of meaning: writings, collages, and musical compositions. Choices about the HOW to show meaning transform meaning. The CPS process remains basically the same, but thinking through writing or other art forms brings a unique dimension to understanding. For example, the reader worrying about her friend's cancer may use her final synthesis of information to restart the entire CPS process. One creative solution becomes the start of another cycle. The problem may still involve worry over the friend's cancer, but the anticipation of an "artistic" product now uses more than information to console. The reader may choose to write a song or a piece of poetry. This kind of connecting and transforming is common in the arts. Think of films like *Philadelphia Story* (HIV victim) or the ballad *My Darling Clementine* (the drowning of a lover). Poems have been inspired by every known human emotion and tragedy from terrible loss ("On Flanders Field" on World War I) to courage ("Charge of the Light Brigade"). What compels poets, musicians, and dancers to make this kind of art? The answer is complex, but the initial motivation has to do with sensing a problem and a deep need to construct personal meaning.

Limiting Choices.   A creative effort can be overwhelming. One problem is unlimited choices. This holds for the many meanings hidden in literature and the possible ways to express ideas in writing. One way to ease this stress is to use strategies such as timed writings, unstructured free writes to release what is already known. For example, suppose a child is to use a form of writing to respond to a book. A good place to begin is to make two lists: (1) possible types of writing and (2) important moments or ideas in the book. From these lists, the student can then make more choices. If a student picks a letter form and wants to write about when Jack chose to go up the beanstalk the third time, then those two things can be squeezed for what is known about letter writing and that moment in the story.

Risk Taking.   Our words have the power to give hope and encourage risk taking. FFOE thinking (Ready Reference 2.5) during CPS can be encouraged through comments like "You showed *fluency* with so many ideas," "It shows *flexibility* to use the fable structure to write when one has never written before," "That's an *original* interpretation," or "The details you added made me see your point" (*elaboration*). These are a joy to give because they uplift students. Students also develop the courage to risk from encouraging messages like "I think you're on the right track with writing a haiku on *Charlotte's Web*. It is about nature so you made a meaningful connection."

Explicit Teaching

In Chapter 3 the idea of explicitly teaching basic elements of art forms was explained. This is direct teaching about why, what, how, when, and where to use concepts and skills. It happens through demonstrations and scaffolded practice, with feedback. In the area of literature, explicit instruction can focus on: (1) the CPS for reading and writing, (2) literary elements, and (3) genre structures and traits, which give students the tools to read in more depth and write with greater variety.

Students need to be explicitly taught how to use CPS with reading and writing. Without scaffolded practice with CPS, they can become reluctant learners. I saw this in our Reading Center during interviews. Children routinely declared they weren't good readers because they didn't know how to "pronounce all the words" or couldn't "read fast." Struggling readers and writers are doomed if they don't know that reading and writing are for creating meaning through problem solving.

Reading and writing are not simply literal acts of sounding out and spelling correctly. Children need clear goals to give context for decoding tools like phonics. What goals? One is an accurate concept of the orchestrated strategies good readers and writers really do in life to make sense—the CPS process.

Wholes and Parts.   Teaching nitty-gritty literary elements and genre traits can be dull and irrelevant if students don't understand why and how they can be used to create personal meaning. Literary arts components don't have to be memorized, nor do they have much value in isolation. Explicit teaching includes showing reasons in meaningful contexts and explaining why to learn the elements. In general, the process of teaching literary concepts begins with experiencing literature. This means reading aloud stories and poetry, as well as daily time to read independently. Once students have enjoyed poems, fables, and mysteries in an aesthetic manner, they are ready to learn their inner workings. This kind of instruction can be summarized with a teaching sequence that goes whole–part–whole. It begins with reading and oral sharing of literature, moves to explicit teaching about elements and traits, and returns to the whole again to generate new works or reread with new perspective.

Big Books, Charts, and Banners.   Literary elements and genre characteristics should be reinforced with visuals. Students may collaborate to make big books, breaking down the work by specific pages (e.g., one page on characters, another on theme). Pages can include examples from literature, definitions, and artwork. Genre charts are made using large roll paper to grid: traits of a genre down the left side and actual book, poem, or story titles across the top. The chart is filled in as students discover trait examples.

Songs and other mnemonics can also be written by students to transform literary concepts elements. Second graders wrote this song about literary elements to the tune of "Frère Jacques": "Plots and themes (2X). Make a story (2X). Add in characters (2X). Play with words. That makes style."

Mini-lessons.   Five to 10 minutes of explicit instruction is enough to target specific information or skills needed to read and write literature with more artistry. The next Seed Strategy chapter offers ideas for literary elements, genre characteristics, and authors and illustrators.

Aesthetic Orienting

High engagement of the senses happens when teachers slow it down so literature can be savored. Students can be taught to observe carefully, notice how words make them feel, respond to images, and ground interpretations in evidence. Zoom in/zoom out teaching orchestrates and balances wholes and parts.

Reader Response Theory.   Children's literature grew out of a storytelling tradition that thrives because of artful words. Children who are taught to enjoy the music of poetry and vicariously experience the thrill of book journeys are primed for a literary life. Unfortunately, in an effort to milk this capacity of literature to boost skills, its aesthetic potential can get trampled.

Louise Rosenblatt developed Reader Response Theory to explain how readers can take an efferent or aesthetic stance as they read (1985). Efferent reading dwells on getting information—just the facts. This was the focus of most literature instruction in bygone days. Rosenblatt's work has

been influential in giving parity to aesthetic reading and reorienting instruction to broader based reader engagement. She believes readers and writers are involved aesthetically when they attend and respond to sounds and images associated with words—to experience emotional, as well as denotational, word properties. Teachers stimulate this response when they direct students to listen to and read aloud chosen words and phrases for the purpose of enjoying language. Students are asked to notice the music of words. "Why would the author use such words?" and "How do these words make you feel?" are questions that invite aesthetic response. Students learn to use language to prompt mental images; not just literal ones, either, but richly embellished pictures drawn from background experiences. Children need time to experience the capacity of books to stir the imagination with "what if" questions, and give fresh perspectives on problems. Picture books add a concrete visual art dimension to the aesthetic experience. They extend appreciation when attention is drawn to their diverse art styles.

Aesthetics First.   The practice of engaging aesthetic responses before focusing on information is particularly important for literature discussions and when students share personal writing. This shows the value for literature as an art form, first. It allows students to express feelings and attitudes using emotional intelligence, which tends to overshadow other intelligences if not given an outlet. Student integrity is developed when they learn to support responses with evidence or reasons.

Critical Approach.   In this approach teachers teach literary elements and genre characteristics that help students notice more. This aligns with artistic habits of careful observation of details and patterns both to data gather for CPS and to increase aesthetic experience. In the critical approach students learn literary concepts and language that enables them to voice ideas and opinions and tools to write their own pieces. The goal is to teach students to understand, respond to, and express themselves through the literary arts using both aesthetic and efferent stances. Here are balanced questions: How did the story or poem make you feel? Why? What was the mood of the story? How did the author create the mood? What struck you about how the story was written? How were words and pictures used to create a feeling in the book? How would the story be different if the author had chosen to write in another genre? Here is a visual literacy example using the critical approach with picture books.

Visual Literacy.   We are most fortunate to have fine art readily available in picture books. Numerous awards aid teachers in selecting books for art study. See Blueprint V: "Literature as a Core Art" and Ready Reference 4.6. Teachers who teach children to "decode" the art increase both understanding and enjoyment. This begins with the Look Closely art strategy in which students take time to discover. Visual art elements (Chapter 6) are used as prompts to stretch observation. Students are asked to share the emotional impact of the art and speculate about how the artist caused feelings. Questions such as, "How does this picture make you feel?" and "What do you see" are starters. Even primary students can see how color is used to balance a composition. They are delighted to learn that artists intentionally use line to lead the eye and make the reader turn each page. They enjoy noticing repeated shapes that move the eye around and give a sense of rhythm. With a bit of Internet research on book illustrators (publishers' websites), teachers can collect useful information about how these artists work. The Appendix and Ready References 4.8, 6.10, and 8.8 list questioning strategies. Ready Reference 7.5 has picture book ideas. Keep in mind that picture books have a story, but they are called *picture* books.

Stretching Time

Discussions that go beyond plot retellings take lots of time. Arts-based responses to literature mean time to plan, rehearse, and perform. Where does it come from? When teachers meaningfully integrate the arts, school time is not expanded, time use is changed. Two of the important sources are discipline and motivational time hogs. Students who are aesthetically engaged are more interested. They savor words and linger over pictures. This is the path to the intrinsic rewards of literature. Poignant moments happen in arts-based literature lessons. Students "re-member," or become members again of the human family, held together by common beliefs and history, both of which are revealed in literature. Engaged students are motivated and

are not discipline problems. Motivating through coupons, stickers, and points, may seem fast, but their effect does not last.

Independence and Self-Discipline

Teachers can easily show ways to respond to and write literature, but they must then go one step more and expect these tools to be used. The teacher who asks "What have you tried?" when a student complains, "I don't know what to write" or "I can't figure out this word" is setting an expectation for independence. Independence is not acquired easily, but the arts can help. Students need to understand that the teacher is not going to do it for them and be taught self-help strategies. For example, beyond "sound it out," they need fix-ups like spell aloud, chunk, and use synonyms. For writing, students need spelling fix-ups such as use a synonym, circle and go on, and put down a few letters. A tool to help students judge a book's readability is the rule of thumb or five-finger method: Open to one page in the middle and read. For each unknown word, raise one finger. If you get to the thumb, the book may be too hard. A caveat is in order. A book may be too difficult, but a child's interest can compensate. Ohlhausen and Jepsen (1992) explain book selection by likening it to Goldilocks' decisions. Students decide if a book is too hard, easy, or just right.

Blueprint VII: Instructional Design: Routines and Structures

Daily rituals and routines institutionalize literature integration. When teachers get in the habit of using arts-based literature strategies to introduce, develop, and/or conclude lessons, they guarantee head-heart-hands engagement. It becomes routine to intentionally teach students to concentrate, focus, and engage CPS problem solving. In particular, the lesson introduction sets the stage with energizers and warm-ups.

Energizers and Warm-Ups. Just as in any arts area, we need to help students get ready to read and write about literature. Chapter 5 describes a dozen energizers and warm-ups to engage the CPS. Check all Seed Strategy arts chapters since other arts energizers work for literature. Here is one example.

Riddle of the day. Riddles trigger higher-order thinking, especially CPS, and contain attractive language for quick lessons on patterns

Principal's weekly discussion group.

(e.g., spelling/phonics). Riddles are basically a question and an answer, and students can easily write their own about any content. Here is a sequence: (1) Write the riddle in a special place. (2) Put blanks for the answer. Fill in a few letters, especially consonants, to guarantee success. For example, "What do you call a boy that hangs on the wall?" ___ ___ ___ (3) Chorally read the riddle, pointing to the words. (4) Students guess letters, *not* the answer! Letters are written as guessed. (5) When most are guessed, students signal if they know. If so, the answer is said chorally; if not, add more letters until everyone is "in the know." (6) Students find patterns and interesting words (e.g., silent ee, double vowels, verbs, homographs). Oh, by the way, the answer is ART.

Opening and Closing Routines.

Most teachers used predictable routines to start and end the school day. Energizers can also be used at these times. Chapter 3 featured some of Ms. Lucas's many arts-based routines. Here are other favorites.

Spotlights. An author/artist spotlight is a mini-unit on a children's author or book illustrator using the "few minutes a day" plan. A special easel or chair can actually be lit using a flashlight. If the spotlight were on Ezra Jack Keats, a student might share a fact about him, talk about a picture from *The Snowy Day*, or read a passage. Variations: with Laugh a Day, students share humor like a joke, riddle, poem, cartoon, or hink pink. Humor uses both creative language and art, so it can be squeezed for insights about sounds, images, multiple meanings, and unusual connections. Poem a Day (PAD) is daily arts-based poem sharing. Ready Reference 5.3 lists ways to do Poem Performances.

Writer's chair. Students share original writing in this routine. The class gathers around a special chair in which the writer sits. The writer reads aloud from his manuscript, and students practice good audience etiquette: active listening, giving descriptive feedback, and asking open questions. This strategy helps children feel that writing is more than an assignment; it becomes a way to share emotions, ideas, and their CPS. For example, students may write a fantasy using learned genre traits. *Variation:* Use a reader's chair to share favorite books or poems and an artist's chair for artwork.

Book ads. These are like ads done on *Reading Rainbow* or *Cover to Cover*. The purpose is to interest classmates in a book. First, teachers demonstrate and then invite students to sign up. Children see so many TV ads that they readily have good ideas. Ads are usually only 2 or 3 minutes and typically include (1) a short introduction (attention getter, tell title/author, display a few pictures, read chapter titles or book blurb, or share author facts), (2) a short excerpt, perhaps of some dialog, and (3) a conclusion (ask for predictions about the book and invite the audience to read to find out if they are right). Students may choose to make an audiotape or video or write a jingle or slogan. Ads are more interesting if props and music are used. For example, I like to play the beginning of Beethoven's Fifth Symphony and read the first couple of pages from Rylant's *All I See* as a book ad. Ads can also be as book responses to show student comprehension.

Reading and Writing Workshop.

Reading/Writing Workshop is a block of time during which students mostly read and write. Usually the workshop begins with explicit teaching using a mini-lesson that targets something students need. Mini-lessons last 5 minutes or so. For example, a teacher may demonstrate spelling fix-ups or how to generate metaphors to make writing interesting. Students then read and write independently for 30–45 minutes. Students may be at any of the three writing and reading stages in their work (e.g., before-during-after) with some doing responses to books and other brainstorming to generate ideas to get started. During workshop times, students may read with a partner, write in Lit Logs, and work at learning centers. Teachers circulate to coach as students work, schedule groups for guided reading and writing, and do individual conferences. Throughout the workshop students are guided by the expectation they are to document their progress with work evidence. In arts integration that work is usually connected to upcoming performances or exhibits.

Arts-Based Read-Alouds.

According to the National Reading Panel (2000), "instructional methods that generate high levels of student involvement and engagement during reading can have positive effects on reading comprehension" (p. 4, 124–125). Daily read-alouds have that kind of engagement potential. When this powerful teaching strategy is made artful by coupling it with arts-based strategies, the result is *arts-based read-alouds*. From picture books to chapter books, arts-based read-alouds have become important platforms to teach the most difficult and most important kind of comprehension—higher-order thinking, which includes critical thinking and synthesis of ideas (Cornett, 2006; Kamil, 2004).

Struggling readers, in particular, have great difficulty understanding exactly what reading is. Some teachers skip teaching this. They assume children understand that reading is meaning making using clues from the abstract "art" of letters. That's unfortunate. Read-alouds, however, seem to fill the gap. Reading aloud makes the invisible visible.

Teacher read-alouds are standard events in most literacy blocks these days. Arts-based read-alouds are a variation during which the teacher reads aloud *to* and *with* children, with focus on providing an aesthetic experience. Like independent reading, arts-based read-alouds may include arts-based children's books. Any literature, however, may be introduced, developed, or concluded with arts strategies that involve problem solving. Planning Page 4.2 shows arts responses to *Millions of Cats*.

EAR: Fluency.   An essential purpose of arts-based read alouds is for students to hear expressive reading—making music from print. Interpreted meaning of printed text is vividly portrayed using variations in pitch, dynamics, tempo, stress, and pause. In literacy circles this is called *fluency,* which boils down to expression, accuracy, and rate (EAR). In a book like *Tuck Everlasting,* literary language, unlike normal talk, is heard that may very well be above students' reading levels, but at their interest levels. "She was a great potato of a woman" is just one metaphor Babbitt uses to paint mind pictures. Read-alouds also bond groups like singing does. Read-alouds are a daily routine that should include pre–during–post arts-based responses, such as those Amy Weiss used for *Sarah, Plain and Tall* in the Classroom Snapshot earlier in this chapter. In addition, pausing to discuss words and inviting students to chime in with predictions increases involvement. Predictions can be mimed and sketched as well as verbalized.

Independent Reading.   Research confirms that the amount of time spent reading is the main determinant of reading achievement (Guthrie, 2004). Research supports budgeting time each day for student independent reading (Krashen, 2005). Common names for this routine involving reading choice books are: SSR (sustained silent reading), SQUIRT (silent quiet independent reading time), and DEAR (drop everything and read). Whatever it is called, students need to just plain read (JPR) and not just have lessons about reading (Allington, 2005; Trelease, 2005). Full participation of everyone is important; the teacher acts as a role model. Here are guidelines:

1. Plan 10–20 minutes (shorter with primary children).
2. Students need to be ready and have an extra book in case they finish. Student can repeat readings of books for fluency.
3. Everyone should be comfortable and stay put. Buddy reading can be used, especially with young children who need the support of a partner (or books on tape).
4. Soft background music may be played to set mood.
5. After reading, plan time for writing and arts-based responses. Generic questions can be used: What was the most exciting or interesting part? What were special words? How did the pictures make you feel and why? Ready Reference 4.8 lists examples.

A variation involves giving a choice related to units. For example, students all read a biography to prepare for writing a biography. While it is important to have "free reading" every day, some days can be designated to promote arts-based reading. This, too, is made more relevant by offering choices that connect to units. For example, set out 5–10 books about musicians who lived during a period the class is studying.

Literature Discussions.   Allington (2005) insists that even a little conversation makes a huge difference in students' language development and motivation. This is based on longitudinal research on the amount of talk heard by children whose parents were professionals, versus working class or poor. Students raised by parents with professions start school having heard 30 million more words.

Discussions are naturally rewarding because they are social and intellectually engaging. They should be a daily part of the schedule and have the feel of conversations. Discussions can connect to read-alouds or any unit work. Once students learn how to discuss, they become highly motivated. Discussions have unmatched potential to increase comprehension because talking out thoughts and listening to others generates a web of meanings. These discussions are not ping-pong question-and-answer sessions between teacher and students and should not be dull plot retellings (Cornett, 1997). They are "grand conversations" among people who all know the plot and wish to seek meaning together (Eeds & Wells, 1989). The leadership shifts away from the teacher. Here are ideas to prepare students to participate in and lead discussions.

Discussion guidelines.   The goal is to eventually have discussions in which all come away with new perspectives. To begin, develop rules.

1. Come prepared. Read the book to participate. (Give note-taking frames for during reading like LWL: learn, wonder, like).
2. Aim for the goal of creating meaning by sharing perspectives.
3. Support interpretations and opinions with evidence from the book.
4. Restate others' ideas before you present an opposite interpretation.
5. Try to learn something you hadn't considered before.
6. Show active listening with "body talk" and by responding to others with positive comments.

Even adults are reluctant to speak up if they don't feel prepared or that their point of view will not be respected. It is helpful to give students options to organize thoughts. Here are some ideas to help:

- *Discussion cards.* Give students an index card to jot down ideas to discuss. Categories include: important events, puzzling things, exciting parts, emotional parts, things characters say, and special words.
- *EPC charts.* Give a frame with the categories of exciting part, puzzling part, and connecting part (Cornett, 1997). Use three large circles or three columns. During reading, students note pages that fit these categories. They star one or two to discuss. *Note:* Connections can relate to personal experiences, another book, or the world.

- *Read-alouds.* Students choose part of the story or poem to read aloud to start the discussion. They tell why they chose it (e.g., important event, use of language, connected to their lives). Students should rehearse so that reading is fluent. Suggest that the section contain a whole idea and discuss time limits to prevent monopolizing.

Organizing discussions. Here are start-ups for teacher-led discussions, adaptable for student-led discussions.

- *Use role play rules.* For example, "Show me being an active listener." "Use your face and body to make me believe." "Now show me a poor listener." Practice giving feedback, paraphrasing, and asking clarification questions.
- *Sit in a circle so everyone can see.* Try the fishbowl technique: Volunteers come into an inner circle to discuss while an outer circle listens in. At stop points, the outer circle follows up on comments heard and asks questions. For example, "I liked what Mimi said because I did not think that the boy might have died" (Lowry's *The Giver*) or "I would like to ask Tom why he thought the mother committed suicide" (Creech's *Walk Two Moons*). Next, circles exchange positions. This teaches listening as well as speaking.
- *Use write right away.* Give students 3–5 minutes to write about a question the leader cares about, but can't answer. Choose a question for which there are clues in the story.

During the discussion. Encourage all to participate. Start with volunteers or call on any student—be prepared is the first rule of coming to the circle. Use "no hands up" to make it more conversational. Weave a more complex web of meaning with questions such as "What do the rest of you think about Bobby's idea?" "Did anyone have the same idea?" "Is this a new idea for anyone?" "Who has an opposite idea from Bobby's?" and "What in the story supports Bobby's idea?" Periodically stop and recap important ideas that have been shared so far.

Discussion conclusion. To bring the discussion to an end, ask students to share (1) the most important points made, (2) what made sense, (3) what someone said that was a new idea, and (4) how people had like ideas. The "tell one thing" strategy can be used, with a pass option to allow face saving. Usually this is "pass and come back," since by the full round all ideas have been expressed and it is acceptable to repeat ideas.

Ready Reference 4.8 lists discussion questions. Post examples so that students have choices and have examples to create questions. Emphasize that good questions are ones they care about and are for which they don't have answers.

Performances and Exhibits. Chapter 3 introduced the idea of using performances and exhibits to drive learning. Literature-based performances include Reader's Theatre (RT), in which students present expressive oral reading of original scripts or those of others (see Chapter 9). Weekly poetry performances are another common routine. For example, every Friday is PoeTree Day in Rebecca Hofmeister's fifth grade. Students write or find poems, rehearse all week, and then perform. They make poems sing with their voices, and they dance the poems, too. Using techniques such as antiphonal reading, character voices, and sound effects gives life to poetry. After each poem is shared, it is ceremoniously hung on a "PoeTree" made from a tree branch set in plaster of Paris. After the performance the class sings:

> Oh Poetree Oh Poetree
> How funny are your verses
> They make us laugh
> They make us grin
> They make us feel all good within
> Oh Poetree Oh Poetree
> Thank you for your verses

Ms. Hofmeister's class is quick to talk about what they think makes poetry. For example, they list: "cool words, especially the sounds," "the ways poetry makes you feel happy or serious," "not so long like whole stories, but still there is a story," and "makes you think differently because you see pictures in your head." Ready Reference 5.3 lists ways to perform poetry.

Centers and Stations. A center can be a shoebox of activities or an elaborate bulletin board–table combination. Centers and stations can be placed around the room's perimeter or in corners, with desks around an open space for circle meetings and movement. A daily block of time is usually set aside to work at choice stations, and time is scheduled for assigned work, too. Center and station visits can be organized with a class chart of names down the left side and a symbol for each center across the top. Laminate the chart so that students can check off and erase as needed.

Common literary arts centers and stations include:

Book nooks. Crates of arts-based books and headsets for listening to music while reading, taped books, and author interviews. Teachers frequently use Book Nooks as required visits during guided reading rotations.

Writing center. A variety of papers, writing tools, and computers. A "real-life" Writing Center has examples of common writing forms—invitations, friendly letters, notes of apology and job applications. Ready Reference 5.1 lists writing forms. An alphabetized set of folders, tabbed with writing forms, is useful in this type of center. Stocked with art supplies to mount, frame, and bind finished writing products, the center is a "must visit" each day.

Book response center.   Arts materials, music, hats, scarves, and other props available for student responses.

Fluency station.   Repeated reading, taping, and graphing progress (rate, accuracy). This is especially important for beginning readers who need more practice. Fluency, in turn, increases enjoyment of literature. By rereading the same story or poem, students become familiar with plot and characters, gain confidence, and increase comprehension. Through repeated readings, beginners realize that words have meaning and can be said in different ways to give personal interpretation. Thus, vocabulary grows. Students self-evaluate by listening to themselves using EAR criteria: expression, accuracy, and rate.

Humor center.   Funny literature from every genre from joke books to poetry. Included are blank wallpaper books and cards to make joke books or riddle rings. This was my students' number one choice among centers.

Centers can also be set up for each arts area or changed to reflect units or projects (e.g., "Life Struggles of Artists, Authors, and Musicians" or "Exploring Space Through the Arts"). See more guidelines for centers and stations in other chapters.

Flexible Small Groups.   Real writers talk with others to get feedback, generate directions, and get angles on ideas. In real life, people pair up to discuss books and join book clubs. At family gatherings, grandparents tell stories that embarrass grown aunts and uncles but further bond the family together with laughter and memory. The social nature of literature and writing is a force to put to motivational use. Leveled guided reading groups should not be the only small groups students experience. Students need chances to work in groups based on interests as well as needs. Four or five book choices can be presented as "book ads" and then offered as choices. Students can write choices in order on slips of paper, and groups can then be organized. Interest grouping fills the need to belong, facilitates exchange of points of view, and develops collaborative skills. The key is flexibility. Avoid keeping students in the same ability groups, a narrow-minded practice that rests on a false assumption that people need to have equal skill levels to work together.

Blueprint VIII: Adaptations for Diverse Needs

PARTICULAR is a framework of 10 ways to differentiate curriculum and instruction to accommodate students' needs and build on strengths. It involves adapting place, amount, rate, target objective, instruction, curriculum materials, utensils, level of difficulty, assistance, and/or response possibilities (Ready Reference 3.6). Lesson formats to track the use of multiple intelligences in literature and writing instruction can be individualized to meet interest, age, and stage differences. In general, literary development proceeds along a continuum from sound to sense and simple to complex literary forms. See the Developmental Stage Continuum in the Appendix. Here are broad guidelines to assist in literature differentiation. Note that humor, animal, and action oriented books are enjoyed by all ages and stages.

Developmental Stages

Preschool–K.   Rhyme, rhythm, and repetition (sounds of language) are important. Children enjoy and understand stories and rhymes with simple plots, short dialog, clear images, and action that builds quickly to a climax, followed by a satisfying ending. A blend of fantasy and reality is preferred. Humor and animal stories are popular (e.g., Dr. Seuss stories and Brett's *The Mitten*).

Grades 1–2.   Traditional literature, how and why stories, magic, and fantasy are popular. Predictable books empower children to read and write their own versions at this age.

Grades 3–4.   More sophisticated folktales, with problems and decisions made by characters, are enjoyed, as well as stories about the use of reason and judgment, scary tales, myths, legends, tall tales, and fables. Chapter books are appealing because they seem more grown-up. Interest grows in informational books.

Grades 5–6.   The search for personal identity has now begun and children question things more. They enjoy more elaborate tales (grandfather tales), fables, fantasy, humor (e.g., Jack tales), myths (Greek and legends), informational books, biography, mysteries, and ghost stories. Realistic fiction becomes popular.

Matching Books and Students

The most important match between children and books is interest. Interest sets motivation in motion. Without interest books matched for "reading level" become just another task. See an Interest Inventory example in the Appendix.

Leveled Books and Readability.   Children have degrees of reading ability, but materials have readability. Matching the two is another way to adapt. Several models are currently used to level books. No system can exactly match a book to a specific child so levels should be coupled with teacher judgment. Most use criteria such as:

- *Vocabulary:* "decodability," repetition of words/phrases, length of words, affixes, and multisyllabic words.
- *Conceptual difficulty:* ideas behind words and background assumed by the author.
- *Type of language:* sentence structure and length, and punctuation.
- *Predictability:* of language plot, theme, characters.

Also considered are length, font size, and layout of pages and the illustrations. Reading Recovery uses numbered levels, while Pinnell and Fountas (2005) use the alphabet.

Metametrics developed *The Lexile Framework* (1995), which uses numerical ratings. For example, *Sarah, Plain and Tall* is 540 lexiles and our 1040 tax manual is 1240.

The website *www.ChildrensBooksInPrint.com* lets you search more than 550,000 titles by 5,000 plus subjects, age, and Lexile® levels, as well as by a specific series, characters, or awards. This extensive resource also offers 167,000 full-text reviews and more than 13,000 annotations. This can be purchased from Bowker.

Blueprint IX: Assessment for Learning

In Chapter 3, assessment was defined with focus on several purposes. In particular, the use of assessment to motivate learning was aligned with the philosophy of arts integration. The ideas presented here relate to literature and expand the discussion in Chapter 3. The Appendix has example assessment tools, including portfolio guidelines.

Portfolios. Portfolios of student writing have become a staple in elementary and middle schools. In addition to writing samples, students show literary growth through logs of books read, charts that show the distribution of reading across genres, and lists of favorites (characters, words, books, authors). Literature Log entries and other written responses to literature can be included to document growth toward goals and objectives. Ready Reference 4.4 lists English/language arts goals.

Exhibits and Displays. Displays of student-made books, in different genre, and of arts-based literature responses are important items to include in a school museum. Many book response projects are arts activities, and the overlap between visual art and literature allows the "mini-gallery" for art projects to function as a way to share excitement about books. Displays of poetry anthologies that children write or collect are another example of a way to

show off growth and make an event out of assignment completion (e.g., have an opening for each new gallery display, with appetizers, beverages—the works!).

Books children write. It is not unreasonable to expect all children to write and bind many books in a school year. These can be class collaborative books, coauthored books, and single-author works. The project nature of writing and book making motivates students and is a concrete progress indicator. Books can be pocketed and placed in the class library. Autographing parties can mark the "publication" of each new book. Chapter 7 has bookmaking and binding ideas.

Individual Conferences. Key assessment information is gathered during times when students "show they know" in a one-on-one setting. It is ideal to have at least a 5-minute conference weekly with each student to review the portfolio, discuss progress, and set goals (e.g., plan book responses or review books each child wants to read). Conference time can be used to discuss books and listen to a child orally read to graph fluency progress (wpm and accuracy). It is helpful to keep a conference notebook, with a page for each child, to note goals and progress made toward each goal.

Blueprint X: Arts Partnerships

Many teachers and librarians share goals that can be accomplished through literature integration. A good librarian knows sources for excellent trade books for any unit or a genre study. Our local library offers a phone-order service. Call up with a unit request, and they pull 30 books to keep a month. To find literary arts specialists, create a directory by surveying teachers, students, and parents about favorite books and writing experiences. There are poets, novelists, and genre experts hidden among the faculty, staff, and parents. These specialists may be available to co-plan or teach.

In addition to the information on partnering with arts specialists in Chapter 3, here are suggestions to optimize school visits by children's book authors and illustrators.

Author/Artist Visits

Today, the writers and illustrators of children's literature are celebrities who draw admiring audiences at conferences. There are even picture books about visits such as Pinkwater's *Author's Day* and Fitch's *The Other Author Arthur*. Authors travel to schools for residencies lasting a day, or longer for local authors. An author or artist visit is such an exciting occasion, it may even be the basis for an "event" unit that culminates with the visit. As with any arts event, planning is everything. Here are tips for working with children's writers and artists for an in-school residency. Two recommended references are McElmeel's *ABCs of an Author/Illustrator Visit* (1994) and Saunders's *The Author Visit Handbook* (1999).

1. Check *www.smartwriters.com* for a list of speakers.
2. Google the author or artist to check out information.
3. Plan early (a year ahead). Contact the publisher through the website to plan arrangements with an appearance coordinator. Don't hesitate to ask for references.
4. Investigate fund raising possibilities with the PTA. The publisher may sell quantity amounts of books at a discount so they can be resold at a profit.
5. Plan objectives. Use the standards in Ready Reference 4.4 and in your local district. Expect students to have an aesthetic experience and learn information/skills.
6. Spell out everything in a contract: date, time, schedule, equipment, and expectations. Plan a budget to cover the fee, travel, food, and so forth. (Budget at least $500 a day plus expenses. Even local authors rarely are free and should be offered some honorarium.)
7. Confirm the agenda. In writing describe: the number of presentations and length, room arrangement, group sizes, types of presentation, request for autographs, and advance book orders.
8. Request publicity materials from the publisher. Ask for biographies in quantity, black and white pictures, book lists, posters, bookmarks, and jackets. Ask if there is a DVD or any material showing the author working or perhaps an interview. Nationally known author/illustrators may have been filmed, or there are CDs/tapes available of them. Teacher guides for books may be printed for free from some websites. Send a press release to the local newspaper. The publisher may have a form.
9. Prepare the students: Do an author–artist study. Check out the author's website. Read lots of books and generate questions. Have students respond to books through writing, art, drama, dance, and music. Their arts transformations will deeply connect them to the books and make personal meaning making richer.
10. Rehearse what the students are to do and how they are to interact with the author/artist. Role play audience etiquette.
11. Follow up the visit with "what did you learn" response activities. This includes thank-you notes from students, but also arts responses like poems, artwork, songs, or videos of dances or dramas.
12. Note that phone interviews aren't usually free. Generally, $50–$75 for a half-hour is expected. You need a speaker phone for the whole class to benefit.

The following websites have more information on planning an author/artist visit:

Children's Book Council:
www.cbcbooks.org/contacts/visits/.html.

Scholastic:
http://teacher.scholastic.com/products/tradebooks/authorvisits/

Teacher-Librarian Magazine:
http://teacherlibrarian.com

Student Spotlight:
Creating Third Space

Integration is all about creating new meanings through the arts, what Deasy and Stevenson (2005) call the "third space." When students become deeply involved in the arts the boundaries between them and texts dissolve. Learning becomes so much fun. This chapter ends with one of those third space moments. It is from Ms. Smith (fifth grade, Lady's Island Elementary):

The students rewrote a section of *James and the Giant Peach* in script form. We broke into four groups and each took a set of pages so we could make one play. As they were writing, they asked me if they could make it funny. I told them, "sure!" The results were the following lines:

James: We need strong string. I don't think we can do it.
Grasshopper: James, we have plenty of string. We can wake the silkworm up and made him spin.
Spider: What about me, what am I chopped liver?
Ladybug: (giggling) No, chopped spider.

Conclusion

Social, religious, and economic forces continue to influence the evolution of children's literature. Children are now expected to be independent earlier and, some say, are hurried into adolescence. With many overscheduled and overstressed, it is increasingly important that we tap the power of literature to slow them down and give joy. This chapter has offered ideas for meaningful literature integration that balances aesthetic enjoyment with information and instruction. Specific literature examples for the Arts Integration Blueprint give teachers means to increase connections between student interests and books and to collaboratively plan standards-based units.

We must continue to guard against potential abuses of literature, as we implement research on its power to motivate children to read, write, and learn in curricular areas. Literature, like all art, needs to be primarily regarded for its aesthetic contributions, and not simply as a tool to achieve literacy. The next chapter is the first of five Strategy Seeds chapters with ideas starters to plan literature integration.

Resources

See Chapter 5 and the Appendix for additional materials.

Recommended Websites

Children's Literature Web Guide: *www.acs.ucalgary.ca/*

Kathy Schrock's Guide: *http://school.discovery.com/ schrockguide*

Vandergrift's Children's Literature Page:
http://scils.rutgers.edu/~kvander/ChildrenLit/index.html

Professional Organization Websites:

American Library Association (ALA): *www.ala.org*

Children's Book Council (CBC): *http://cbcbooks.org*

International Reading Association (IRA): *www.ira.org*

National Council of Teachers of English (NCTE): *www.ncte.org*

National Writing Project: *www.writingproject.org*

Teachers and Writers Collaborative: *http://www.twc.org*

Audio/Visual Sources

Booklist Online: *www.ala.org/ala/booklist/booklisthtm.*

Weston Woods: *http://teacher.scholastic.com/products/westonwoods/*
(Videos about authors, artists and children's books)

Journals

(Research, Articles, Reviews, Author profiles)

Bookbird (International Board on Books for Young People)
Booklist and *Book Links* (ALA))
Bulletin of the Center for Children's Books
Children's Book Review Index (Gale Research)
Children's Literature in Education (APS Publications)
Horn Book Magazine (Horn Book, Inc.)
Language Arts (NCTE)
The New Advocate (Christopher–Gordon Publishers)
Reading Teacher (IRA)
School Library Journal (Bowker)

Children's Literature References

Adoff, A.(1977). *Tornado.* New York: Delacorte.

Anno, M, *Anno series of books.* New York: Philomel.

Barrett, J. (1989). *Animals should definitely not wear clothing.* New York: Aladdin.

Bauer, J. (1992). *What's your story? A young person's guide to writing fiction.* New York: Clarion

Bishop, C. (1996). *Five Chinese brothers.* New York: Putnam.

Brett, J. (1989). *The Mitten: A Ukrainian folktale.* New York: Putnam.

Bruchac, J., & London, J. (1992). *Thirteen moons on a turtle's back.* New York: Philomel.

Bryan, A. (1987). *Beat the story drum, pum-pum.* New York: Aladdin.

Cameron, P. (1961). *I can't said the ant.* New York: Putnam.

Charlip, R. (1984). *Fortunately.* New York: Simon & Schuster.

Christopher, J. (1967). *The white mountains.* New York: Simon & Schuster.

Conger, D. (1987). *Many lands, many stories: Asian folktales for children.* Rutland, VT: Charles E. Tuttle.

Crane, S. (2002). *The red badge of courage.* New York: Atheneum.

Creech, S. (1994). *Walk Two Moons.* New York: HarperCollins.

Dahl, R. (1983). *James and the giant peach.* New York: Puffin.

Day, A. (1985) *Good dog, Carl* San Diego, CA: Green Tiger.

DiCamillo, K. (2000). *Because of Winn-Dixie.* Cambridge, MA: Candlewick.

Dyson, J. (1991). *Westward with Columbus.* New York: Scholastic.

Elting, M. (1980). *Q is for duck.* New York: Houghton Mifflin.

Fitch, S. (2002). *The other author Arthur.* East Lawrencetown, Nova Scotia: Pottersfield.

Freedman, R. (1987). *Lincoln: A photobiography.* New York: Clarion.

Gag, W. (1928). *Millions of cats.* New York: Coward-McCann.

Gwynne, F. (1970). *The king who rained.* New York: Trumpet.

Hesse, K. (1998). *Out of the dust.* New York: Classic Press.

Highwater, J., & Scholder, F. (1992). *Anpao: An American Indian odyssey.* New York: HarperCollins.

Hoban, T. (1971). *Look again.* New York: Macmillan.

Hoban, T. (1998). *So many circles, so many squares.* New York: Greenwillow.

Hunt, I. (1994). *Across five Aprils.* New York: Silver Burdett.

Jukes, M. (1987). *Like Jake and me.* New York: Knopf.

Keller, C. (1985). *Swine lake: Music and dance riddles.* Upper Saddle River, NJ: Prentice Hall.

Lowe, S. (1992). *The log of Christopher Columbus.* New York: Philomel.

Lowry, L. (1993). *The giver.* New York: Bantam Doubleday Dell.

Maclachlan, P. (1985). *Sarah, plain and tall.* Santa Barbara, CA: ABC-Clio.

Marshall, J. (1973). *George and Martha.* Boston: Houghton Mifflin.

Martin, B. (1992). *Brown bear, brown bear, what do you see?* New York: Henry Holt.

Munsch, R. (1980). *The paper bag princess.* Toronto: Annick.

Ness, E. (1971). *Sam, Bangs & moonshine.* New York: Henry Holt.

Nichol, B. (1994). *Beethoven lives upstairs.* New York: Orchard.

Nixon, J. (1998). *If you were a writer.* New York: Aladdin.

Norton, M. (1953). *The borrowers.* New York: Harcourt Brace.

O'Neill, M. (1989). *Hailstones and halibut bones.* New York: Doubleday.

Paterson, K. (1977). *Bridge to Terabithia.* New York: Crowell.

Paterson, K. (1980). *Jacob have I loved.* New York: Crowell.

Paulsen, G. (1999). *Hatchet.* New York: Aladdin.

Pinkwater, D. (1998). *Author's day.* Madison, WI: Demco Media.

Rathman, P. (1995). *Officer Buckles and Gloria.* New York: Putnam.

Ringgold, F., Freeman, L., & Roucher, N. (1996). *Talking with Faith Ringgold.* New York: Crown.

Rockwell, T. (1973). How to eat fried worms. New York: Franklin Watts.

Schwartz, A. (1992). *Scarey stories boxed set.* New York: Harper Trophy.

Scieszka, J. (1991). *The true story of the 3 little pigs.* New York: Viking.

Sendak, M. (1963). *Where the wild things are.* New York: Harper & Row.

Steptoe, J. (1987*). Mufaro's beautiful daughter: An African Tale.* New York: Lothrop, Lee and Shepard.

Tolstoy, L. (2002). *The enormous turnip.* San Diego, CA: Harcourt.

Verne, J. (1997). *20,000 leagues under the sea.* New York: Random House.

Walsh, E. (1989). *Mouse paint.* San Diego, CA: Harcourt.

Ward, L. (1973). *The silver pony.* Boston: Houghton Mifflin.

White, E. B. (1952). *Charlotte's web*. New York: Harper & Row.

Wilder, L. E. (1971). *Little house in the big woods*. New York: Harper Trophy.

Willard, N. (1981). *A visit to William Blake's Inn: Poems for innocent and experienced travelers*. San Diego, CA: Harcourt.

Wood, A. (1984). *The napping house*. New York: Harcourt Brace.

Yep, L. (1992). *The rainbow people*. New York: HarperCollins.

Yolen, J. (1987). *Owl moon*. New York: Philomel.

Yolen, J. (1990). *Sky dogs*. San Diego, CA: Harcourt.

Yolen, J. (1992). *Encounter*. San Diego, CA: Harcourt.

Yolen, J. (1997). *Sleeping ugly*. New York: Coward, McCann & Geoghegan.

5 Seed Strategies for Literature and Poetry

Questions to Guide Reading

1. What Seed Strategies can be used to introduce literature lessons and/or teach literary concepts?

2. What Seed Strategies help to integrate literature with science, social studies, math, and literacy?

3. How can literature and poetry be integrated with other arts?

This chapter includes specific ideas for integrating literature throughout the curriculum. The strategies are intentionally undeveloped and are to be used to prompt creative lesson planning. They are not recipes. Adaptations are necessary to meet student needs and curriculum standards.

All Seed Strategies assume teachers know about literary elements and principles for teaching literature—the focus of the previous chapter. Most Seeds are adaptable for at least K-6 using the PARTICULAR ideas in Ready Reference 3.16. The chapter opens with a look at how one teacher has taken drama seed strategies and developed them to work with parts of speech.

Classroom Snapshot:
Verbs, Literature, and Pantomime

Stacey Sturgell's room is arranged in a U. A couch with a red pillow is along one wall. Reading Words hang on a clothes-line. A collage of nouns covers one wall and words cover the windows. The chalk tray is lined with books for daily DEAR time. A sign reads "Control your voice, body and mind."

Stacey sits in a director's chair. Her second graders are seated on a colorful rug. She smiles, "Eyes up here," she says and points to a sign that reads, "A verb shows action."

"Today's read-aloud is about verbs. Listen and be ready to plug in actions *To Root to Toot to Parachute*" (Cleary). She reads using **oral cloze** to increase engagement; she stops before words and waits for students to supply verbs. She also uses **inserted questions,** like "What do you notice about verbs?"

Stacey's reading is expressive; she uses a variety of pitches, volumes, stress, and tempos. Her vocal dynamics make the reading sound musical, which is an essential for fluency. She also accurately pronounces and adjusts rate to purpose.

After the read-aloud, Stacey asks what they know about **charades.** Some have played this drama game with Mr. Jordan, the drama teacher. They say charades requires no talking. It's pantomime. They seem ready to show what they know about verbs.

Stacey holds up a basket with blue cards and gives one to each child. "Put on your creativity hats!" she says. "I want each person to think of an action word or _____ (students say 'verb') and write it on the card." Stacey pulls out a purple card.

"Here is my **example.** Get ready to be **close observers.** Put your thumb up if you know the verb." Stacey mimes rubbing her fists in her eyes and stretches her mouth downward. She counts to three for all to say, "cry." She laughs and gives another example. This time she stands up, then sits down and reaches to her right. With her thumb and forefinger she quickly pushes down. Only one child puts his hand up. His other hand is over his mouth suppressing a giggle. Stacey winks at him.

"Watch again. Notice what I do from the very beginning." This time she pretends to pull down her pants and

The classroom as a living room—sofas and rocking chair for free reading.

does the quick action with her hand. Most hands immediately go up. The whole class is laughing.

"One, two, three," she counts. They yell, "Flush!"

"So, verbs are words that show_____?" Stacey waits. Hands go up. She holds up one, two, then three fingers as a signal.

"Action! Action! Action!" is the choral chant.

"Right. Now, I want you to think of interesting verbs to pantomime. Remember that **creative thinkers** don't use their first idea. Brainstorm in your groups. Put your verb on one side and your name on the other. You have 3 minutes."

Stacey groups students in fours. She cues them with 30 seconds left.

"Criss-cross applesauce. Eyes up here" Stacey says and the students scurry to pretzel sit on the carpet.

She draws out a card. "Okay, John, remember to show with your face and body. Audience, remember to look closely and notice details. John, when you are ready, say **'begin.'"**

John stands still and focuses on a spot above his classmates' heads. He says "begin" and starts to raise and lower both arms. He slowly spreads his fingers and tilts from side to side. Thumbs go up. **"Curtain,"** he says. John looks around and chooses a boy.

"Flying?" John nods and smiles. The class applauds.

"Oops, remember soft," Stacey says, as she claps with two fingers.

"What did John do that helped?" she asks. Students mention the flapping and his "concentration like an eagle."

"What are other ways to show flying?" she asks, and a girl shows with one hand a plane-like movement. Stacey smiles broadly, **"That was really different.** That's what we

want, people who think of unusual ways to show ideas." She draws more cards and students take turns miming. Throughout, she **coaches** them to "use control of body and mind" and show meanings in different ways.

After about 10 minutes the kids are distracted by a roach crawling up the wall. Stacey announces, "This is South Carolina and there are bugs. Let's name him!"

Someone calls out "Charley!" so Stacey says, "So Charley is crawling up the wall. What is the verb?" "Crawling!" they respond. Stacey whispers, "If you can hear me, tiptoe to your desks. The verb is tiptoe."

When students are seated, Stacey explains she will leave the **verb basket** up front. They can add to it from today's reading.

"Even from science or social studies?" one boy asks.

"Especially science or social studies!" she responds.

"Can we do this again, then?" a girl asks.

"Of course, how about this afternoon?" Stacey asks.

"Yeah!" is the class response. A boy adds, "Let's skip recess!"

Note: More books by Brian Cleary are: *A Mink, a Fink, a Skating Rink* (nouns); *Hairy, Scary, Ordinary* (adjectives); and *I and You and Don't Forget Who* (pronouns).

Chapter Organization

Seed Strategies are organized into four sections, but many can be used in any area. The sections on Energizers, Elements, and Genre Traits are included to help build knowledge and skill base students need to meaningfully participate in integrated lessons. *Note:* Meaningful arts integration does not happen unless lessons include at least one arts focus and one focus in another curricular area.

I. Energizers and Warm-Ups

Energizers and warm-ups are used to prepare students for creative thinking. There are Energizers and Warm-Ups at the start of each Seed Strategy. Consult other chapters for more ideas for concentration and relaxation.

Tongue Twisters and Lip Blisters. In addition to favorites such as "Bugs Black Blood" and "Swiss Wrist Watch," there are new ones in books such as *Six Sick Sheep*

(Cole, 1990). "Aluminum Linoleum" and "Zip zap zot" gets everyone puckered and giggling, relaxed and ready to be creative. The Internet also has tongue twisters on any topic.

Chants, Action Poems, and Songs.

Many collections are available, such as Cole's *Miss Mary Mack* and Booth's *Dr. Knickerbocker.* Ask students to echo line by line. Display words on a transparency and add actions. For example, with Dr. Knickerbocker the chant suggests actions: "Let's put the rhythm in our hands" (clap clap).

Uncle Charlie.

Leader thinks of a category and gives clues by saying "Uncle Charlie likes _____ but not_____." For example, "Uncle Charlie likes pepper but not salt." Guessers reply, "Uncle Charlie likes _____" and gives an example that fits. The leader then says, "Yes, you can come in," meaning they are right or "No, you can't come in," if they are wrong. Here's another clue: "Uncle Charlie likes butter but not bread." (If you said, "hammers but not saws," you can come in: the category is "words with double consonants."

CPS Process.

See Ready Reference 2.5. For example, SCAMPER a character and take students on a visualization journey: Think about Wilbur. Imagine him turning into a little dog looking up at Charlotte's web. Now change him into a big dog. Now think of Wilbur as a pig with a dog body. Make this new Wilbur really small. He is trying to talk to Charlotte, but he gets littler and littler. Oops, now he's growing, growing, growing. He is getting giant. Look at Charlotte's expression. Now he shrinks back and Charlotte starts to grow.

Analogy Go Round.

Use this to review a story (adapted from Starko, 1995). The idea is to stretch and twist thinking. Set up a verbal frame to fill in as you go around a circle:

Opposites: Force opposite characters together: *Wilbur* is like *Templeton* because_____. This can be done with any literary element: The *farm* is like the *fair* because_____.
Random combinations: Combine any idea with a literary element: Wilbur is like a *pencil* because_____. Plug in ideas in the first blank and give reasons in the second.
Personal analogies: I am like *Charlotte* because_____.

Word Association.

Form a circle. Leader says any word and person to right says first thing that comes to mind. Connect quickly!

Minister's Cat.

This memory/category game is done to a rhythm. Form a circle. Go around with each student plugging in an adjective, in alphabetical order: "The minister's cat is an *active* cat. The minister's cat is a big cat. The minister's cat is a c_____ cat." Adapt for characters (e.g., Charlotte was an *artistic* spider, *brave* spider).

Who Stole the Cookies?

Leader asks, "Who stole the cookies from the cookie jar?" The group names the person to the leader's right and says, "_____ stole the cookies from the cookie jar." That student responds, "Not I," and the group chants, "Then who?" Leader names a student, who becomes IT, saying "_____ stole the cookies . . ." IT repeats first question and play continues.

Prereading and Writing.

Here are three examples:

Webbing is brainstorming on paper. Put a topic in the center and draw out 3-5 legs. Write connected ideas on them. Fill up the paper. Next, group ideas by circling or coding similar ones. For example, before reading *Jack and the Beanstalk,* web "greed." *Variation:* Web any literary element, genre, or person.

Chain 7 is connected listing. Choose a topic. Write a first word below it that connects to the topic, a second word connected to the first, and so on. Connect the seventh word to the sixth *and* to the topic. For example, for greed: (1) hog, (2) fat, (3) greasey, (4) slimey, (5) green, (6) puce, and (7) ugly. (*Note:* This can sound like poetry when read aloud.)

Cubing (Neeld, 1986) uses six ways to examine a topic. For example, Cube greed: (1) describe it, (2) analyze it (what are its parts), (3) associate feelings, (4) apply it (what can it be used for), (5) argue for it (pro), and (6) argue against it (con). *Variations:* Write six ways on a cube. Roll it and do 1 minute on each side.

Predict–Prove (Stauffer, 1969).

This teacher-directed strategy sets problem solving in motion. Evidence-based guesses are solicited before reading using a book cover or page art. Students then read to confirm or reject predictions so there is active learning throughout the reading process. The basic steps are:

1. Read the title, show the cover, and selected illustrations.
2. Ask for three predictions. *Characters:* Who will it be about? *Setting:* When and where? *Plot:* What problems might be in the story?
3. Record predictions on a chart.
4. Students read the book or teacher reads aloud to students.
5. Students give evidence during think stops to confirm or reject predictions. *Suggestion:* Celebrate both rejection and confirmation.

Mystery Bag.

(prereading). Students try to find connections as the teacher reveals one object at a time from a sack. For example, sticks, red items, and a basket. Take out the easiest last, for suspense. Tell students to not "call out" so everyone sees everything before any guesses are taken. *Variation:* Students make book-related object collections and present their mystery bags.

Character or Story Riddles.   Students write and share riddles with three clues, arranged general to specific. Use these steps: (1) Choose a subject such as *cats*. (2) Use a book title or character and brainstorm words that sound like the syllables: Wil=bur=chill, hill, still, fill, sill; bur=stir, her, purr, sir. (3) Combine syllables to fit the subject: Wil-purr. (4) Make up a question: What did a fan of *Charlotte's Web* name his cat? (Wilpurr)

Write Right Away.   (quickwrites). Students do timed free writes to activate prior knowledge or pull together information (e.g., after a discussion). A time limit of 53 minutes is set. *Example:* 5 minute freewrite on "beauty is on the inside" to introduce *Beauty and the Beast*.

CAP Prediction.   (prereading). Brainstorm List words from an upcoming book that relate to characters, actions, and problems (CAP). Students sort the words into three categories by predicting how they might connect with C, A, or P. Word cards can be used in a pocket chart or coded with the letters.

Word Pairs.   Select an even number of important words from an upcoming book or poem. For example, choose eight words that could make four pairs. Ask students to work in groups to pair words any way that makes sense. Ask groups to explain reasons. Celebrate novel connections.

Rhyme Change.   Nursery rhymes and other chants and poems are great verbal warm-ups for creative thinking. For example: "Hickory Dickery Dock, A mouse ran up my . . ." (students supply rhyme). Change vowel sounds for phonemic awareness development: Dack, Deck, etc.

II. Teaching About Literature: Elements and Genre Traits

This section offers ideas for teaching about the building blocks of literature (elements) and the different structures or literary forms (genres).

Venn Diagrams.   Venn diagrams are used to compare and contrast different aspects of two books or stories: literary or art elements, genre traits, versions of the same story, or books by the same author. Two overlapping circles are drawn. Separate circles are for the individual characteristics of the two things being compared. The overlap area is for commonalities. Example: Venn the main character in the Harry Potter series and Frodo in *Lord of the Rings*.

Big Bingo.   (elements review). Use bulletin board paper cut into 4-foot lengths and folded four times to make a giant bingo board. Group students and give time to write elements in the blanks on the giant card (post Literary Elements). Play by giving a definition and students cover elements with index cards. When a group wins, they read back the labels, paraphrase a definition, and give a story example.

Character: Web, Wheel, and Graph.   *Web.* Write a character's name in the center. Draw and label legs on the web to represent character aspects: speech, thoughts, actions, and appearance and what others think or say about the character (other categories: character's feelings, worries, hobbies, talents, skills, personality). *Adaptations:* For biographies, change the legs to include fitting categories: obstacles faced, significant achievements, special life events.

Graph. Make a graph with boxes at least one inch square and with enough spaces on the X and Y axes to write the names of important characters. List the names twice: on the left side in a vertical column and then at the top across the row of squares. Where two names intersect, students write in how the characters interacted or related.

Sociowheel Put the name of a character in the hub of a wheel. Write the names of three or four characters on the rim. Spokes should connect the hub character to each of the rim characters. On each spoke, write how the hub character is connected to each rim character.

Suggestion: Do on the overhead as a class. *Variation:* Students need two circles, one as big as a coffee can lid and the other an inch in diameter bigger. Fasten the circles in the center with a brad. Students then write the names of characters around the edges of both circles. Line up names and discuss the ways the characters relate. Turn the wheel and a new character pair lines up and discussion proceeds. *Adaptation:* Make one large wheel for the class. Laminate it so that you can change character names.

Character Inventories.   Students fill out a personality inventory on a character. Possible items: Favorite foods? Likes? Dislikes? Favorite books? Films? Hobbies? Encourage students to think beyond literal information in the book. *Variation:* Describe clothes, hands, eyes, or body.

Character Poems.   Use any of the Poem Patterns in Ready Reference 5.2 to write poems about characters.

Character Report Card.   After reading, students complete a report card to grade characters on talent, tact, poise, appearance, honesty, and so forth. With younger students, do this collaboratively. Ask students to justify the grades.

Somebody–Wanted–But–So.   (character, motive, problem, plot). Make a chart with the four words across the top (Macon, 1991). Students draw or write about the main character (somebody) in the first section, what the character wanted (second section), roadblocks or conflict (but), and the resolution in the "so" section.

Plot Lines. Linear, mountainlike, circular, and episodic patterns of events in stories can be drawn using a plot line with events written along it (Tomlinson & Brown, 1996). Roadblocks or obstacles are indicated by bumps in the line. For example:

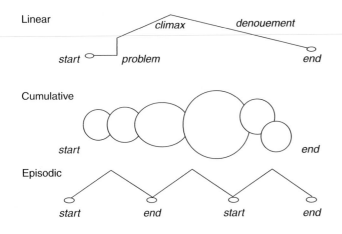

Linear

Cumulative

Episodic

Episode Plot Cards. Key plot events are brainstormed and written on individual cards. Cards are placed in plot order using a pocket chart or clothesline.

Home–Adventure–Home Map. This plot structure is also called the *BME,* for beginning–middle–end (Tompkins & McGee, 1993), or IDC (introduction, development, conclusion). Use after or during reading to structure comprehension by categorizing a plot into three main parts. Students see how a problem initially sets the plot in motion, the middle section is a series of events (the "adventure") that deals with the problem, and end events resolve the problem. Students can also use the map to plan original stories using the home–adventure–home parts. This can also be a planning tool for drama responses or student-led discussions. Ask students to star items on the map they wish to discuss.

Circle or Pie Story Maps. Diagram book events or the plot of home-adventure-home stories on a large circle divided into pie pieces. At the top of the circle, draw a house to show how stories often begin in a homey place. Explain how characters have an adventure, but return home at the end. The events are written or drawn, one at a time, while moving clockwise around the circle. The pie slice below the house is where students begin. When the circle is complete, the story ends in the same place it began. *Adaptations:* Make a large circle pie map on the board or chart paper to do as a class. Use completed maps to retell stories.

Ladder to Success. Ladders are especially good for biography and similar to a lifeline (Tompkins & McGee, 1993). Students list important events in a character's life on

the rungs. Rungs lead up to a climatic event. Earlier events (chronologically) are closer to the bottom.

Setting Sense Web. Write or draw the setting in the center. Label five extending legs: see, taste, smell, hear, and touch. Students brainstorm using the web. For example, What would you see, hear, taste, smell, and touch in the setting of *Peter Rabbit?*

Take a Stand (Themes). Themes derived from a story (Ready Reference 4.1) are written out on the board and numbered. Students stand on a "strongly agree to strongly disagree" imaginary line to show their feelings about the theme as each theme number is called. Students can be interviewed about reasons for where they stand.

Genre Traits.

Chart. Write several story titles, from the same genre, in boxes across the top of a page. The characteristics of the genre are then written along the left-hand side. Story examples are sought to go with each trait. *Example characteristics:* Folktale (1) opening or closing special language, such as "Once upon a time," (2) vague setting—could be anywhere, (3) plot is a simple chronological order, (4) flat or one-dimensional characters (good or evil, foolish or genius), (5) problem involves a journey from home to perform tasks and confront obstacles, and (6) miraculous events.

Web. Write story title in the center. Draw legs out to show the traits of the genre to which the story belongs. Brainstorm story examples. See previous folktale genre characteristics. *Variation:* Do as a class.

Bio Webs. (biography). Write a person's name in the center. Legs are labeled with important events in the person's life. Smaller legs are webbed off main events. *Extension:* Use webs to write biographical summaries.

III. Connecting Literature to Curricular Areas

This section offers prompts to plan lessons that integrate science, social studies, literacy, and math with literature. For ideas on how to use drama, music, visual art, and dance with literature, consult the Literacy sections of each of the Seed Strategy chapters. Also see "Book Report Alternatives" in the Appendix.

Science Focus

Science Standards. All standards can be accessed at the National Science Teachers Association (NSTA) website: *www.nsta.org.*

Good Literature   NSTA and the Children's Book Council identify *Outstanding Science Trade Books for Students K–12* each year. Access the lists from 1973 forward at *www.nsta.org/ostbc/*. Here are examples of recommended books published in 2004 and 2005.

Biographies

Linus Pauling: Advancing science, advocating peace. (Pasachoff). Inspirational story of Pauling's interest in science from childhood to his Nobel Prizes.

Bone detective: The story of forensic anthropologist Diane France. (Hopping). Comprehensive book on this topic.

American women inventors (Camp). Super book about women who created inventions like the square-bottom paper bag.

Earth and Space Science

Are we alone? Scientists search for life in space. (Skurzynski). Explains the search for extraterrestrial intelligence.

Environment and Ecology

Arrowhawk. (Schaefer). Beautiful, disturbing story of a red-tailed hawk shot with an arrow and raptor conservation.

Nature in the neighborhood. (Morrison). Valuable beautiful book about urban animals and plants.

The least of these: Wild baby bird rescue stories. (Harris). Beautiful book about bird rehabilitation and identification.

Archaeology, Anthropology, and Paleontology

Feathered dinosaurs of China. (Wenzel). Describes astonishing fossils of feathered dinosaurs found in China.

Earth and Space Science

Endangered planet. (Burnie). (This is an important book for those concerned about the environment.)

Life Science

The tarantula scientist. (Montgomery). Stunning close-up photos and discoveries about the biggest and hairiest spiders.

Genre Studies.   Certain genres have a special connection to science. General informational books are important resources, but biographies of scientists and inventors are also key literature. For example, Fox's *Women Astronauts: Aboard the Shuttle* (1987) tells the stories of eight women, including Sally Ride. In addition, a science fiction genre study can focus on verifying which science is "real." Poetry can be connected to both informational books and science: for example, the books *Monarch Butterfly* (Gibbons, 1989) and the poem "Chrysalis Diary" in Fleischman's *Joyful Noise* would enhance an insect unit.

Engagement: Informational Books.   Provide generic prompts to note ideas as students read informational books. Brozo (1998) lists these questions: What is …

1. The most interesting or exciting word, phrase, sentence, or picture?
2. An idea, detail, issue, or concept you feel strongly about?
3. A feeling about this idea, detail, issue, or concept? Why?
4. A connection between your own experiences and the ideas, details, issues, and concepts?
5. A place in the book that made you think of something you have experienced, seen, or know about? Why?

Things to Write and Say.   Ready Reference 5.1 lists writing forms that can be used in science. For example, write a letter to a character about what you are learning in science.

Poem Patterns.   Ready Reference 5.2 lists patterns that can be used to write about science topics or processes. For example, write an abab four-line poem about the circulatory system.

Five Ws and H Webs.   After reading an informational book or story, students web who, what, when, where, how, and why to summarize. Add details to answer the five Ws and H questions.

Acronyms and Acrostics.   *Mnemonics* are memory devices that work because the brain seeks patterns and associations. Invite students to play with acronyms, in which letters in a word stand for concept. For example, *McHale* is a mnemonic for the forms of energy (mechanical, chemical, heat, atomic, light, electric). Acrostics are mnemonic sentences. Students remember more when they create their own for science, but here are examples: Nine planets from the sun: "My very eager mother just served us nine pies." (A tenth planet has been discovered, but remains unnamed.) Stages of the cell: "In Paris, men are tall" (interphase, prophase, metaphase, anaphase, telephase). Soil components, "All hairy men want big razors" (air, humus, minerals, salts, water, bacteria, rock, and particles). Zoological groups in descending order: "Keep pets or cats from getting sick" (kingdom, phylum, order, class, family, genus, species).

Social Studies Focus

Social Studies Standards.   You can access all standards at the National Council for the Social Studies (NCSS): *www.socialstudies.org*

Good Children's Literature.   NCSS and the Children's Book Council produce *Notable Social Studies Books for Young People* each year. Access the bibliography at *www.socialstudies.org/resources/notable/*. Here are featured books for 2004.

Ready Reference 5.1   Writing Choices A–Z

Directions: Use this list of writing forms to write about any work of art (literature, song, dance, drama). Any writing can also be done "in character" for drama.

Acceptance speech	Funny word list	Ode
Advertisement	Greeting card	Paradox
Advice column (Dear Abby)	Haiku	Poem (Ready Reference 5.2)
Announcement	Headline	Postcard
Apology	Holler (see call or yell)	Poster
Award presentation	Horoscopes	Propaganda (card stacking, etc.)
Brief biography	Insult	Ransom note
Bumper sticker	Introduction	Remedy
Call or holler	Invitation	Report
Campaign speech	Irony	Résumé
Certificate	Jingle	Slogan
Chant	Journal, log, or diary	Stinky pinky
Cheer	Jump-rope rhyme	Telegram
Cinquain	Letter (business-	Thank-you note
Command	friendly)	Title (book, TV program)
Commercial	Lie	Tom Swifty
Complaint	Limerick	Tongue twister
Compliment	List (to-do, grocery,	Tribute
Contract	wishes)	Triplet or tercet
Curse	Love note	Understatement
Definitions (of unusual words)	Magic spell	Wanted poster
Diamante	Marquee notice	Warning
Editorial	Menu	Weather forecast or report
Encyclopedia entry	Mixed metaphor	Will
Epilog	Nominating speech	Wish
Excuse	Note	Yell (see call or holler)
Fable	Obituary	

Biography
Facing the lion: Growing up Maasai on the African savanna (Lekuton). Personal journey of a young Kenyan man.
The man who made time travel. (Lasky). A timepiece for longitude revolutionizes sea travel.

Contemporary Concerns
September 11, 2001: Attack on New York City. (Hampton). Diverse stories.
Vote! (Christelow). One of the best books on electoral politics for youth.

Geography, People, and Places
Murals: Walls that sing. (Ancona). History of murals and how an artist develops a design.

History, Life, and Culture in the Americas
America the beautiful. (Bates). Each line of poetry is matched with a place in the United States.
Freedom roads: Searching for the Underground Railroad. (Hansen & McGowan). A must-have book on how historians use primary documents.
The printer. (Uhlberg). A deaf printer in the 1940s warns others about a fire.

World Culture and History
Who was the woman who wore the hat? (Patz). Describes experiences of interned Jews.

Economics
The hard-times jar. (Footman). Migrant family saves money in a jar.

Literature and Poetry Strategies

 **Poem Patterns**

Suggestions: Share poems orally first. Ask students to notice details, patterns, and feelings. Brainstorm personal and important ideas, images, and feelings. When writing poetry, encourage varying repetition in lines and words and use of alliteration, rhyme, imagery, onomatopoeia, and metaphor. See "Special Focus: Poetry sharing and writing" on page 146.

Repeated lines: Write repeated lines that start with a stem:
   I wish: I wish the sky would stay red all day. I wish I could touch a cloud.
   Is: Thunder is grumpy. Happiness is yellow and fizzy.
   Color: Red is red hot pepper. (See *Hailstones and Halibut Bones* by O'Neill).
   Five senses: Sounds like _____ / Looks like _____ / Tastes like _____ /...
I used to (think or feel), but now I (think or feel): I used to think poetry had to rhyme, but now I think I can just write my feelings and have a good time.
If/ So or If/Then: If I were a light bulb/I would glow hot and bright/So people could read in bed at night.
Five-line: Each line has a focus: (1) a thing, (2) a person, (3) a special place, (4) a feeling, (5) a sound.
Riddle poems: Give three clues, with the first most general and the third most specific. Example: _____ _____ _____ _____ 1. Easy to carry. 2. Full of words inside. 3. Rhymes with cook.
Lie poem: Each line is something not true (do collaboratively).
Preposition poem: <u>Within</u> the drawer / <u>In</u> a desk / <u>Inside</u> the metal tray / <u>With</u> a row of teeth (stapler).
Concrete or shape: Words are placed on the page to look like the poem's topic (e.g., a swing, tree, a kiss shape for a love).
Couplet: Two lines end in rhyme. Sometimes trees/Have knobby knees.
Triplet: Three lines that rhyme.
Quartet: Four lines with a different rhyme patterns: aabb, abab, abcb, abca.
Clerihew or bio poem: Quartet about a person: Pat Benne/Did marry Kenny/But they are poor/And want money more.
Limerick: Humorous five-lined verse with aabba rhyme pattern. The rhythm pattern is important:

There once was a cat on a porch
He sat in the sun 'til he scorched
His paws and backside
Were both nearly fried
So his friends starting calling him "Torch."

Syllable and word count:
   Haiku: Japanese nature verse using three unrhymed lines. There are 17 syllables in the poem distributed by line as 5-7-5.
   Lune: Three lines with 3–5–3 words in each line.
      A funny man
      Liked to tell silly stories
      About 4H Camp
   Tanka: Five lines with these syllables per line: 5-7-5-7-7.
   Cinquain: Five-line poem that does not rhyme. Number of words per line: 2–4–6–8–2 (subject, adjectives, action, feeling or observation, adjective/ synonym).
   Diamante: Seven-line poem, shaped like a diamond. Line pattern: 1 noun, 2 adjectives, 3 -ing words, 4 word phrases or nouns, 3 -ing words, 2 adjectives, 1 antonym. *Note:* The topic can be changed in the middle to relate to the antonym. For example:
      Halloween
      Spooky Fun
      Running Screaming Eating
      Costumes Candy Bunny Baskets
      Hunting Coloring Singing
      Happy Pastel
      Easter
Found poems: Cut random phrases from magazines, newspapers, or cards. Phrases are arranged until a poem is created (need not rhyme).
Other pattern possibilities: Tongue-twisters, jump-rope rhymes, and advertising jingles.

Genre Studies. While any genre has potential connections to social studies, informational books, biography, and historical fiction have particular links; each can present unit content from a different angle. With historical fiction, students can use informational books to verify accurate versus fictional details. Poetry can be connected with informational books. For example, the narrative poem "The Midnight Ride of Paul Revere" by Longfellow can be paired with a Revolutionary War study.

Culture Unit Maps and Webs. One way to structure a culture unit is to "map" findings students find from various sources. Here are category legs: (1) language, the dialect or actual words used in a book; (2) values, as they contrast with mainstream America; (3) art, music, drama, or dance in the book and what each art reveals about values, customs, etc.; (4) historical facts; (5) customs and traditions; (6) contributions the culture has made; and (7) events and issues associated with the culture.

What-If Writing.

In *Jokes to Tell Your Worst Enemy* (Corbett, 1984), there is a section on "History Rewritten Mother's Way" (e.g., Paul Revere's mother will not let him go out). Use this as a prompt for "what-if" writing about historical events. Discuss the humor and possible serious side effects.

Joke Books.

There is now a collection of jokes and riddles about most important places, events, and people, including nearly every president. Start a Joke of the Day social studies to provoke critical-creative thinking routine. For example, *The Abraham Lincoln Joke Book* (DeRegniers, 1978) is a gem because most are stories and jokes he actually told.

Mystery Person.

After reading a piece of historical fiction or a biography, students choose a book character and find three objects that represent him or her. Objects are then revealed to the class one at a time, with the most obvious one (in its connection to the character) coming last. Students guess who the person is by connecting the three items.

Biography Boxes.

Students fill boxes with objects, pictures, and poems that may have been important to a person. Boxes are shared. Students learn that things used or seen each day are also things famous individuals used. *Variation:* Use with any book character or an artist or author.

Folktale Detectives.

Students study a culture by (1) reading folktales to find out what is valued or (2) exploring how the literature of the world's cultures has common motifs. For example, Venn diagram to compare Snow White and the Queen: young vs. old; happy vs. bitter; inner strength vs. focus on magic and spells. *Suggestions:* Contrast characters and settings in folktales—high vs. low place, young vs. old, bad vs. good (Levi-Straus, 1967).

Book Maps.

Use a biography or piece of historical fiction and draw the setting or a portion of it to show where and what story events take place (Johnson & Louis, 1987). Use these steps:

1. Demonstrate map making. Read aloud a story with simple events and setting, and keep track of characters on a setting drawing.

2. Guide map making. Read aloud another story with simple events and settings with the students tracking where the characters are and the events of the story. Each decides what he or she would like to include in the map and how.

3. Encourage or assign map making for independent reading.

Timelines.

Timelines are visual representations of historical events and can be used to summarize an informational book or historical fiction. Use a horizontal line and make hash marks vertically to record chronologically important dates and events.

Point-of-View Guide.

Before reading a historical or informational book, pairs interview one another about characters that will appear in the book (e.g., settlers, explorers, or any persons). Interviewers ask five Ws and H questions and write down responses. *After* reading, students review interviews and compare and contrast with book information. To develop comparisons, students can role-play a press conference or TV talk show.

Lifelines.

The goal is to record significant events in a person's life by carefully rereading for important information (Tompkins, 1990). Use long shelf paper. A line is drawn down the middle. Dates of important events are put chronologically on the line, marked by hash marks. Beside, above, or under each date a title, description, and/or picture of each event is shown. Photocopied pictures can be used or students may create illustrations.

Literacy: Reading and Language Arts Focus

Literacy/Literature Standards.

All standards can be accessed at the National Council of Teachers of English (NCTE) and the International Reading Association (IRA) at *www.ncte.org* or *www.ira.org*.

Lit Logs.

Literature Logs (wallpaper books, composition books, or a notebook section) increase active engagement for independent reading. Students date entries, note stories read (titles and pages), and write reactions or questions about the plot, characters, and style. They may retell plot events, make predictions, write a poem, and/or free write about feelings. *Variation:* Logs may be exchanged to write peer responses, or the teacher may collect and write comments. If students write in each others' Logs, they need to be taught how to respond positively. Model using an example Log entry on the overhead.

Prequels and Sequels.

After reading a story, students write what may have happened before the book was written or after the end. Encourage students to attend to details and literary elements to use a similar style, appropriate characters, and a fitting plot. Emphasize consistency as well as plausibility in the plot.

Class Newspaper.   News articles, weather forecasts, advertisements, interviews, police reports, comics, classifieds, and obituaries can be created about any literature. For example, a *Charlotte's Web* Newspaper might involve students in writing forms used in different parts of a newspaper including the five Ws and H structure of articles. The newspaper could be a culmination of a core book unit or developed chapter by chapter (e.g., do cartoons for one chapter, classifieds for another, and obituaries at the end).

Real-Life Writing.   Ready Reference 5.1 shows many forms in which people write. Students can use these to write about any topic or book they have read. *Example:* Tribute to the Big Bad Wolf.

Word Walls.   Word walls make visible a critical element of literature—words. They boost interest in seeking out words to post (use cards or sticky notes). A word wall becomes a source for new writing ideas and an aid for unknown words, too. Words can be webbed, individually or as a class, and expanded using common affixes (-ed, ing, s, er). For example, the word *range* can be webbed or expanded into: ranger, arrange, arrangement, arranging, deranged, and rearrange.

Word Sorts.   Students list interesting words found *during* reading on cards. Afterward, pairs categorize the words. Possible categories are characters or people, setting, time, problems or conflict, main idea or themes, and plot or actions. *Adaptations:* (1) Present a list of words from the story or poem *before* reading. Students group words as a prediction activity. (2) Post a chart listing literary elements. Students jot down a key word for each element as they read.

Vacabutoons.   Students create cartoons to show the meanings of words. See the book by this title by Sam Burchers (1996).

Buddy Reading.   Use this variation for independent reading. Partners share a book in these ways: take turns reading aloud, read chorally, or read silently. They agree to stop at points to discuss (1) exciting or puzzling parts and (2) connections to their lives, the world, or other books. They can use the five Ws and H questions to question each other and strategies like fat questions, explicit (right there) or implicit (between the lines) questions. See Ready Reference 4.8 for questions to post as choices. For older students, pair to discuss parts read silently using strategies such

as EPC (see "Discussions" under "Instructional Design" in Chapter 4).

Partner Writing.   Students read a story and then write to a friend about it. Possible entries are a letter, a note about what they liked or didn't like and why, or a mini book review (appropriate for intermediate students who've read book reviews; consult *Book Review Digest* in a library or get reviews from journals such as *Horn Book* or *School Library Journal* as examples). For example:

Dear Jenny,
>I want to recommend *Walk Two Moon* to you. The book really makes you think because there are lots of flashbacks. It is sort of like a mystery because you only get clues to what is going on and then you find out the truth at the very end.
>
>   The author makes you love the characters—especially the grandparents. This book made me cry, but I felt like it made sense at the end. It also made me treasure my parents and grandparents.
>
>   Your buddy, Lou

Bridges.   (based on Berthoff, 1981). Draw a vertical line down the middle of a page; this is the bridge. The left-hand side is used to write down words, phrases, sentences, or passages students find interesting or important *during* reading. On the right side, students bridge the ideas from the left column to their own experiences by writing connections. *Variation:* Use to prepare for discussion by asking students to write questions in the right column. These can be prioritized by starring important ones. Follow with time to write about how the discussion changed their thinking.

Anticipation Guides.   (prereading strategy). Display 3-5 theme-related statements for a book students will read. They rate their agreement or disagreement or use true-false and discuss reasons for ratings. Next, students read to confirm or change ratings. *Adaptation:* Do rating as a follow-up to stimulate discussion of a book. Example from *Like Jake and Me*:

Directions: Rate from 1–Strongly Agree to 5–Strongly Disagree.

1. Everyone is afraid of something.
2. It is important for people to feel needed by other people.
3. Boys should not dance because that is a girl thing.
4. If people talk about something, they will understand each other.

Story-map Yourself.   Teach the grammar or structure of stories by having students map their own lives. Map sections are: Who? (main character is the student), When and where? (setting), Problems? Goals? Plot (key events to reach goals), Plot resolution (what the student hopes will happen). *Variations:* A variety of maps can be used: (1) web with three legs labeled beginning, middle, and end; (2) bubbles for each literary element; (3) E-shaped charts with the theme along the vertical line, key events on the beginning, middle, and end on the horizontal lines, and characters in the open spaces.

Sentence Frames.

Frames are response prompts. The structure jump-starts thinking. Frames can be used *after* any book or lesson or as general writing prompts. Repeat the frame as many times as desired (e.g., three times for each). The following are mostly based on children's books.

1. Fortunately_____ Unfortunately_____
2. Someday_____
3. Why_____? Because_____
4. _____ is the hardest when _____and is the easiest when_____
5. I used to (think or feel)_____, but now I (think or feel)_____
6. When I _____ I look or feel like _____ because _____
7. I seem to be _____, but really I am _____
8. The important thing about _____ is that _____ It's _____, It's _____, And it's _____ But the most important thing about _____ is it _____
9. I am _____ I saw _____ I heard _____ I smelled _____ I tasted _____ I felt _____
10. When I was young_____

Letters.

(Tierney, Soter, & O'Flahavan, 1989). Use Cleary's *Dear Mr. Henshaw* or *Dear Mr. Blueberry* (James) as an introduction to writing letters to an author or artist. In letters students can include questions about how characters were created, what ideas or feelings they have about books, and why the artist chose to use a certain art media or style. As an alternative students could write a letter to the editor. First present an issue to the class that will appear in an upcoming book. Students take a stance and give reasons to defend it. They then write a letter to the editor. Next, they read the book. *Note:* A creative book in which actual letters are delivered to characters is *The Jolly Postman's or Other People's Letters* (Ahlberg, 1986). The letters can form the basis for drama or writing (e.g., writing other letters in roles).

Take-offs.

This type of writing involves adapting a pattern to make a new story. Predictable books like Williams and Chorao's *Kevin's Grandma* provide a take-off framework. For example, Zolotow's *Someday* is a series of episodes that all begin with the word *someday*. Books can be illustrated and bound.

Word Collections.

Students list interesting words found *during* reading. Groups decide whether each word describes or relates to the main character and, if so, how. For example, use words from *Lindbergh's View from the Air*: nature, season, pasture, nestled, transformed, perspective.

Twenty Questions.

Adapt this game for literature by having a student or panel assume the role of a character. The audience then asks "yes or no" questions, but the question cannot be "Is your name_____?" The goal is to guess the identity in 20 or less questions. *Variation:* Form teams to guess and alternate. Periodically ask students to put thumbs up if they know the identity. Coach for better questions by asking, "What would be a question you could ask to find out an important detail?"

Math Focus

Math Standards.

All standards can be accessed at the National Council of Teachers of Mathematics (NCTM): *www.nctm.org*.

Good Literature.

Teachers often feel that math is harder to integrate with literature and writing than other areas. But there are now many math-based pieces of literature. In addition to the Anno books, here are two favorites:

Lionni, L. (1960). *Inch by inch*. Astor-Honor. (length, capacity, area, and volume)
Scieszka, J., & Smith, L. (1995). *Math curse*. Viking. (many math concepts)

NCTM has reviews of more than 550 titles with analyses of books' content and accuracy, illustrations, style, and any included activities. Order: *The Wonderful World of Mathematics: A Critically Annotated List of Children's Books in Mathematics, Second Edition* at the website *www.nctm.org*.

Here are examples of math-based children's literature:

Anno, M. (1992). *Anno's counting book*. HarperCollins.
Capie, K. (1985). *The biggest nose*. Houghton Mifflin. (length, area, volume)
Ellis, J. (2004). *What's your angle Pythagoras?* Charlesbridge.
Hopkinson, D. (1993). *Sweet Clara and the freedom quilt*. Knopf.
Levy, J. (2004). *Journey along the Erie Canal*. Powerkids Press.
Schwartz, D. (1985). *How much is a million?* Lothrop, Lee & Shepard.
Tang, G. (2003). *Math-terpieces*. Scholastic.
Tompert, A. (1990). *Grandfather Tang's story*. Crown. (tangrams)
Evans, E., et.al. (2002). *Mathlinks: Teaching to the NCTM 2000 standards through children's literature*. Libraries Unlimited.
Various authors. (2004). *Math literature series*. Math Publication Solutions.

Math/Literature Websites and Resources.

Elaine Young's Math 3213: *http://sci.tamucc.edu/~eyoung/literature.html* (101 math-related books by math concept and grade level).

NCTM lesson plans. For five example plans that connect math and children's literature, go to: *http://illuminations.nctm.org/index_o.aspx?id=83.*

Math Poetry.

Many types of poetry depend on math concepts for their construction (e.g., counting syllables, words, and lines in haiku, diamante, and limericks). Show students different poem patterns (Ready Reference 5.2) to use to write math poems (e.g., a haiku about numbers in nature: A two-eyed giraffe/Uses four legs to reach high/And eat with one mouth).

Story Problems.

Use math-based literature to create story problems. For example, in Carle's *The Very Hungry Caterpillar* the caterpillar eats a certain number of things each day. How many total items did he eat?

Chapter Books.

Students create a math character and write a story with several chapters. In each chapter the character solves another math problem. The problems can be related to math skills and concepts previously taught (D. Smith, Lady's Island Elementary School).

Graphing Plots.

Teach students the concept of graphing by measuring the excitement level or "good news–bad news" event in a story (Johnson & Louis, 1987). Here's how:

1. Prepare a graph. The vertical axis is labeled "excitement level," with the top line "high," and the bottom labeled "low" (or use "good news/bad news"). The horizontal axis is labeled using numbers assigned to the different events.
2. Present the graph. Use the overhead to show how graphs work. Brainstorm story events. List these on the board.
3. Complete the graph. Number the event list in chronological order. Event numbers are then placed along the horizontal axis and "rated" by placing a dot at the level decided. Dots are then connected.
4. Ask students to graph. Pairs create graphs for another story. *Variation:* List favorite stories and graph how much students like them.

Math Shape or Concept Books.

Students choose a geometric shape or a concept (addition, fractions, etc.) and write stories in which their shapes or concepts are characters. Informational books can also be created with pages that explain the math concept. Books can be illustrated and bound. *Variation:* Show the video *Dot and the Line,* a romance between these two shapes. *Note:* These are also art elements.

Math Copycat Books.

Use math-based children's books as frames to write copycat books. For example, McMillan's *Counting Wildflowers,* Carle's *The Very Hungry Caterpillar,* or Sendak's *Chicken Soup with Rice* can be used as frames.

Picture Book Math.

Give groups stacks of picture books and ask them to find the math necessary to make a book by finding facts in these categories: number of pages (often 32), size of pages, words per page (or in whole book), and so forth.

Sequence Story.

Write or tell a story with each line beginning with a number, in consecutive order. For example, "*One* day Mary was sleeping when the doorbell rang. *Two* men were at the door. *Three* fingers were missing on one man's hand. *Four* minutes passed before Mary decided what to do." Teams can work to try to get as far as possible.

Special Focus: Poetry Sharing and Writing

Poetry is sound and sense. Words seem to sing when rhyme, rhythm, and repeated sounds combine. Nothing starts us thinking through poetry like a sensory experience. Read aloud, "Easy Pickin'?" and think about the sound patterns and the sense.

> Cobbler pie cereal toppin'
> There's no stoppin', easy pickin'
> Blackberries
>
> In the thicket
> Stickers prickin'
> Splinters stickin'
> Blackberries
>
> Tricky pickin'
> Fingers prickin'
> Sticky pickin'
> Blackberries
>
> Finger lickin'
> It's addictin'
> Oh so wicked
> Blackberries
>
> Time's a tickin'
> Neck's a crickin'
> Getting' sickened
> Blackberries
>
> Cobbler pie cereal toppin'
> There's no stopping, easy pickin'
> Blackberries

Poetry is particularly important to literacy instruction because it gives most children their introduction to the in-

Ready Reference 5.3   Poetry Performance Strategies

Directions: These are ways to perform poetry.

Choral or unison. Do all together.

Cumulative. One or two start and gradually more voices come in. Everyone reads the last line.

Antiphonal. Two opposing groups. For example, high and low, loud and soft.

Line-a-child. Each student reads one line.

Refrain with groups. Repeated lines are done by a chorus.

Character voices. Assume a character and use appropriate voice.

Narrative pantomime. Do actions the poem suggests as narrator reads or recites.

Sign language. Use finger spelling or American Sign Language to perform.

Background music or art. Play music or show art as poem is read.

Cloze. Use sticky notes and cover predictable words. Students then guess.

Reader-responder. Reader reads one line and responder orally improvises. For example, *Mary had a little lamb.* Responder: *I bet her husband was surprised.*

Reader's theatre. Set poem up like a script with names and parts.

Use props. Add musical instruments, puppets, objects.

Sound effects. Assign sounds to be made when certain words are read.

Question and answer. Find poems in question and answer form. For example, Q=Who has seen the wind? A=Neither I nor you (Christina Rossetti). Everyone gets a Q or A and reads when it makes sense. *Note:* Students can then write their own Q & A poems.

Actions. Children dance or mime certain words or phrases.

Memorize and recite. Change volume, pitch, tone, rate, pause, and stress to do oral interpretation.

Q-U (cue you): Read your line on cue card after you hear your cue. For example,

Q: Mary had a little lamb.
U: Its fleece was white as snow.
Q: Its fleece was white as snow.
U: And everywhere that Mary went . . . .

Call and response (echoic). Students echo leader's oral interpretation line by line.

Canon or round. Read like a round. Different groups start at different times.

Ostinatoes. Repeat a word or phrase that is important, for example, "Who has seen the wind?" (Repeat *Wind-Wind* or chant throughout reading.)

---

toxicating music of words (Mother Goose rhymes, Dr. Seuss). This section is a brief overview of how to make poetry a daily part of arts-based literacy, math, science, and social studies instruction. There is also an abundance of poetry *about* math science and social studies. Poetry performance strategies in Ready Reference 5.3 are some ways to bring poetry to life. Poetry writing strategies in Ready Reference 4.7 can be used to transform subject matter concepts. Poetry naturally connects with other art forms using strategies such as poem prints (art strategy) or setting poetry to music. Consult Ready Reference 4.7 for recommended poets and poems. Blueprint II: "Arts Literacy: Literary Elements" in Chapter 4 discusses poetic elements.

General Principles for Poetry Integration

As with any arts area, the emphasis in poetry integration is on the process of sharing, responding to, and creating poetry, not perfect performances or products. Here are other general poetry integration principles:

- Poetry is sound. Nothing is as important as sharing poems orally, using a variety of strategies.

- Poetry is sense. Students need to hear poetry before discussing it. No one knows all that a poem means, so encourage many responses and go light on interpreting *for* students.

- Creating and sharing poems gives a sense of control over language. This confidence leads to reading and writing growth.

- Encourage risk taking. The strange, the silly, and the far-fetched can be freely explored with poetry. Rules about grammar, punctuation, and capitalization just don't apply.

- Help students discover what makes poetry. For example, it usually is compact, emotionally intense, full of sound patterns (rhythm and rhyme, onomatopoeia, alliteration) and figurative language (metaphor, imagery).

- Teach the musical qualities. Rhyme, rhythm, repetition, onomatopoeia, and alliteration are what make poetry seem musical.

Ongoing Poetry Routines

- PAD (poem a day) is the routine of actively *doing* poems using poetry performance strategies (Ready

Reference 5.3). Poem charts can be used to enlarge poems so everyone can see.

- PoeTree: A small branch is placed in a pot filled with plaster of paris. From the limbs, students hang copies of poems they find, adapt, or write. (Hopkins, 1987).
- Poetry anthologies: Students collect favorite poetry by writing their own, trading, and copying poems from source books. Personal anthologies are made into books or organized in recipe boxes under categories such as animals, humor, weather, people, places, holidays, and feelings.

Poetry Sharing and Performance

- Warm up the face and voice. See Energizers and Warm-ups in Chapters 9 (drama) and 11 (dance).
- Encourage repeated sharing of the same poems to increase enjoyment and attune the ear to special use of words.
- Organize choral reading to take advantage of the power and support of the group. Teach choral reading using lessons on musical dynamics: sing together; do rounds; group the class into twos, threes, or fours and give each a musical phrase, ostinato, or refrain.
- Use musical signals for start, stop, slow, fast, loud, and soft. Conduct poems in the style of an orchestra maestro (see Chapter 13).
- Teach rhythm and beat by encouraging clapping, snapping, and tapping of feet, or divide the class in half, with one group chanting a phrase or refrain while the other claps the beat. Challenge by giving the second group a different, syncopated refrain to the same simple beat.
- Coach students out of shyness. Focus thinking on the images in the poem, adding simple gestures and movements, trying different voices, or reading louder and slower.
- Ask students to give each other feedback on what worked well.

Memorizing Poetry

- Memorizing is a valuable, ongoing activity if students are allowed to choose poems and given options for performance (e.g., partners, tape recordings, use of visual aids, props, or puppets).
- Warm up memory and imaging skills with daily routines such as The Minister's Cat or I'm Going on a Trip that require remembering and repeating ideas. Memory lists can be used by having a category each day. For example, list all the red things in your house.
- Start simple with one line to memorize. The class can then recite with each one doing his or her line. A longer

poem with a refrain can be used with students learning just the refrain while the teacher reads or recites the rest.

- Use the build-it-up method: Teach the first line of a poem, then recite it and add the second line, then add the third, and so on until the whole poem is memorized.

Composing Poetry: Written and Oral

- Start with oral sharing: Children learn to listen and speak before they learn to read and write. See Ready Reference 5.3.
- Coach students to write about concrete things, using specific details (especially the five senses).
- Sharpen the powers of observation: (1) Ask students to describe an object in the room, then one not in the room; go for details. (2) Ask them to describe an object in the room using only three words. (3) Offer a series of nouns, such as cat, tree, and sky and ask for possible varieties using adjectives.
- Provide a line and challenge students to expand using details. For example, "The man walked down the street." (Expand and elaborate by inserting words and adding phrases.)
- Teach imagery: Use categories, such as places, feelings, animals, colors, flowers, noises, smells, vehicles, weather, and so forth. Keep lists in an idea book for writing.
- Teach metaphor: (1) Ask students to look at a familiar object or the sky. (2) Ask what it looks like. What it *is* like. What it reminds them of. Use Cubing (see Energizers). (3) Make two lists of nouns and compare something from one list to something on another. (4) Offer a choice of objects; then ask students to write a detailed objective description of it. Then have students write a poem made up of one-line comparisons to something. For example, A_____ is like a _____ because _____.
- Use Poem Patterns (Ready Reference 5.2) to give structures to adapt. For example, for the "I wish . . ." pattern, ask each student to write a line that includes a color. The class shares the poem using line-a-child. Another example: Select an object or person. Each student says one line about the subject. Encourage students to use senses (e.g., I see, I hear, It feels, . . .).
- Teach the concepts of line, syllable, and counting syllables: Cut up a poem into lines. Have students reassemble it. Put separate lines in a pocket chart or have students each hold a sentence strip with a line as the class reads it. Count lines in poems. Count syllables by feeling the Adam's apple as words are said. Exaggerate and stretch syllables for emphasis.
- Teach about rhyme: Read a poem, leaving out rhyming words. Pause for students to provide (cloze strategy). Use contests: Groups try to recite the longest list of

rhymes). Use challenges: (1) Write a silly poem using as many rhyming words as possible. Start by picking a word and ask for three to five rhymes. Next, write a poem using those as end words. Repeat with three pairs of different rhymes. (2) The orally composing poems in rhymed couplets. Give the first line, and the students supply the second, back and forth. (3) Memorize four-line nursery rhymes. Take out the familiar rhyme words and ask for new ones. Explore combinations and discuss what happens. (4) Write original quatrains using different rhyme patterns: aabb, abab, abcb, abca.

- Teach rhythm and beat: Start with songs, keeping time with hands, feet, or rhythm instruments. Overemphasize the beat in choral recitations. Replace the words with numbers or scat phrases such as "doo-wop."

Poetry Art. Students examine a piece of art to note the mood, use of media, style, and art elements. Give students examples of poetry patterns (cinquain, haiku, limerick; see Ready Reference 5.2). Write collaborative pattern poems and then individual ones based on art. Alternative: Students write poems and then create art to go with poems. For example they can print or stomp over the top of the poem, collages around poem edges, or watercolors with poems across the bottom.

Poem Match. Students find or write a poem that connects to a work of art. See Writing Choices from A to Z in Ready Reference 5.1. In addition, see Poem Patterns in Ready Reference 5.2. Art and poetry can be shared during docent talks and displayed together in a class museum.

Visual Poetry. Create concrete poetry written in the shape of the subject. For an example of a whole book with this type of poetry, see Froman's *Seeing Things: A Book of Poems*.

Onomatopoeia Poems. Create sound poems by using objects or rhythm instruments. Begin by exploring sounds with different objects. Work in groups to plan a five-line poem that builds from one sound up to five sounds. Decide which sound will be line 1, which two sounds will be line 2, and so on. Encourage thinking about rhythm patterns, accent, tempo, and dynamics. Students can rehearse their sound poems, present them, and then write them down using onomatopoeic words. For example,

Ding
Bang Bang
Shush Shush Shush
Rattle Rattle, Clap Clap
Ding Bang Shush Rattle Donk

Poetry Collections. Collect poems about music (e.g., Shel Silverstein's "Ourchestra") for individual and class anthologies. Display special poems on posters and perform with rhythm instruments.

Poem Pantomimes. Pantomime possibilities exist in many poems. For example, de Regniers's, "Keep a Poem in Your Pocket" is about what a poem can do for you. Students mime as the poem is read (narrative pantomime). Beyer's "Jump or Jiggle" poem describes the ways different animals walk, Crane's "Snow Toward Evening" describes a calm, peaceful snowy night, and Hillyer's "Lullaby" is a poem about a rowboat drifting along. In Miller's "Cat," movements are described in detail. *Note:* Poetry is hard to edit because of rhyme and rhythm. Select poems for narrative pantomime carefully.

Reader–Responder. Do in partners. Reader reads one line and responder orally improvises by saying whatever comes to mind. Continue throughout the poem. For example, reader: "Jack and Jill went up the hill." Responder: "I wonder how high the hill was."

Choral Reading. Choral reading invites experimentation with words and musical elements (volume, tempo, pitch, pause, and stress) that build fluency. Options include: (1) leader reads a line and class echoes; (2) leader reads a section and class reads a refrain or creates an original refrain; (3) solo readers read sections and whole group reads the rest; or (4) two groups take turns reading. (See the poetry performance strategies in Ready Reference 5.3.) Do multiple repeated readings for increased fluency.

Classroom Snapshot:
Arts-Based Read-Alouds

Literature integration was introduced in Chapter 4 using an arts-based read-aloud. This Snapshot brings us back to the use of this literature integration strategy and leads into the next chapter on integrating visual art. Notice how the teacher uses inserted questions to keep attention and cause students to think about deep meanings. Afterward, she **coaches** students through the **problem-solving process** with more **open questions** to create a composition. The thinking process includes the same pre-during-post steps as written composition, but art materials are used. In particular, notice how Ms. Petros directs attention to **details** and focuses on **experimentation** and diverse products.

"Today I'm going to read *Sweet Clara and the Freedom Quilt* (Hopkinson)," Fannie Petros says. "I want you to look and listen closely so you can make your own quilts."

Fannie begins to read in a soft southern dialect that is her own. She uses **inserted questions** to keep attention and engage. They are all fat questions with multiple answers, like "Why was she away from her mama?" She takes time to show each picture and asks **what they notice**. She weaves information about the artist into the story.

An inclusion teacher periodically offers extended explanations about key concepts such as "big house." She also asks open questions like "What is she going to do?" "Why would she make a map?" "What would she do with a quilt?" and "Why are they trying to get to Canada?" The teacher is there for an autistic girl, a boy with learning disabilities, and another student with language delays. To this last question a red-haired girl answers, "To be free." A girl with braids says, "To escape slavery." And a boy with glasses answers, "For happiness."

Fannie reads with lots of **vocal dynamics**—she pauses, stretches words, and changes pitches. All of these musical elements of fluency make the story come alive.

"What does it mean to 'get big with listening'?" she asks at one point.

A boy in a sweatshirt says he thinks it is "listening hard."

A girl responds, "It helps you get somewhere."

Fannie reads on and asks, "What was the underground railroad?"

"A secret place," says a boy with large blue eyes.

A boy elaborates, "It was going from house to house and to boats and houses to get away."

After the read-aloud, students choose partners.

"Choose wisely," Fannie advises. "Work with your 3D pattern blocks to experiment. Think of how many ways you can make a North Star."

"It can be anyways," pipes up a small boy.

"That's right. Let's look at examples of the many ways. See these. Some repeat so they have a _____." Fannie waits and students fill in with "pattern."

"What else do you notice?"

"Different colors.

"Kinds of shapes."

"I see patterns," says a girl,

"So, why are we doing the North Star?" Fannie asks.

"For the Freedom Train Riders—to point the direction to freedom," exclaims a boy.

"OK, choose where you will sit and start to experiment with your 3D pieces," Fannie says.

Students begin to partner and work with the soft rubber shapes of all sizes and forms. Fannie circulates and responds to inquires with comments like, "You choose. Make them your own way. Yes, repeat the pattern, but make yours different. Nobody should be copying. Use your own imagination."

Students confer about possible arrangements and periodically call out shape names.

"Hexagon, cool!" says one boy.

After about 10 minutes Fannie shows students how to use construction paper to transfer their rubber shapes "draft" into final draft form. ✳

Conclusion

In the long history of man, countless empires and nations have come and gone. Those which created no lasting works of art are reduced today to short footnotes in history's catalog. Art is a nation's most precious heritage, for it is in our works of art that we reveal to ourselves, and to others, the inner vision which guides us as a Nation. And where there is no vision, the people perish. (Lyndon B. Johnson, at the signing ceremony for the National Foundation on the Arts and Humanities Act of 1965)

This chapter is a compendium of Seed Strategies to jump-start planning for literature integration throughout the curriculum. The ideas are to help prime the pump for creative thinking as teachers plan arts-based lessons and integrated units.

Resources

See the Appendix for more resources.

Children's Literature References

Ahlberg, J. (1986). *The jolly postman's or other people's letters.* Boston: Little, Brown.

Aliki. (1986). *How a book is made.* New York: Harper & Row.

Ancona, G. (2003). *Murals: Walls that sing.* Singapore: Marshall Cavendish.

Anno, M. (1977). *Anno's counting book.* New York: Crowell.

Bates, K. (2004). *America the beautiful.* New York: Little Simon.

Bruchac, J., & London, J. (1992). *Thirteen moons on turtle's back.* New York: Philomel.

Burnie, D. (2004). *Endangered planet.* Boston: Kingfisher.

Camp, C. A. (2004). *American women inventors.* Berkeley Heights, NJ: Enslow.

Carle, E. (1984). *The very hungry caterpillar.* New York: Putnam.

Christelow, E. (2004). *Vote!* New York: Clarion.

Cleary, B. (1996). *Dear Mr. Henshaw.* New York: Avon.

Cleary, B. (2001). *To root to toot to parachute.* Minneapolis, MN: Carolrhoda.

Cole, J. (1990). *Miss Mary Mack.* New York: Morrow.

Cole, J. (1993). *Six sick sheep.* New York: Morrow.

Corbett, S. (1984). *Jokes to tell your worst enemy.* New York: Dutton.

DeRegniers, B. S. (1978). *The Abraham Lincoln joke book.* New York: Random Library.

Fleischman, P. (1988). *Joyful noise: Poems for two voices.* New York: Harper & Row.

Footman-Smothers, E. (2003). *The hard-times jar.* New York: Farrar, Straus and Giroux.

Fox, M. (1987). *Women astronauts: Aboard the shuttle.* New York: Julian Messner.

Froman, R. (1987). *Seeing things: A book of poems.* New York: HarperCollins.

Gibbons, G. (1989). *Monarch butterfly.* New York: Holiday House.

Hampton, W. (2003). *September 11, 2001: Attack on New York City.* Cambridge, MA: Candlewick.

Hansen, J., & McGowan, G. (2003). *Freedom roads: Searching for the underground railroad.* Peterborough, NH: Cricket.

Harris, J. (2005). The *least of these: Wild baby bird rescue stories.* Portland OR: West Winds Press.

Highwater, J. (1977). *Anpao: An American Indian odyssey.* New York: Lippincott.

Hopkinson, D. (1993). *Sweet Clara and the freedom quilt.* New York: Knopf.

Hopping, L. (2005). *Bone detective: The story of forensic anthropolist Diane France.* New York: Franklin Watts/Scholastic.

James, S. (1991). *Dear Mr. Blueberry.* New York: M. K. Mcelderry.

Keller, C. (1985). *Swine lake: Music and dance riddles.* Upper Saddle River, NJ: Prentice Hall.

Krull, K. (1995). *Lives of the artists.* San Diego CA: Harcourt Brace.

Lasky, K. (2003). *The man who made time travel.* New York: Farrar, Straus and Giroux.

Lemaosolai-Leukton, J. (2003). *Facing the lion: Growing up Maasai on the African savanna.* Washington, DC: National Geographic.

Lindbergh, R. (1996). *View from the air: Charles Lindbergh's earth and sky.* New York: Puffin.

Lionni, L. (1963). *Swimmy.* New York: Pantheon.

Louie, A. (1982). *Yeh-shen: A Cinderella story from China.* New York: Philomel.

Lowe, S., & Sabuda, R. (1992). *The log of Christopher Columbus.* New York: Philomel.

McCully, E. (1992). *Mirette on the high wire.* New York: Putnam.

McKissack, P. (1988). *Mirandy and brother wind.* New York: Knopf.

McMillan, B. (1982). *Puniddles.* Boston: Houghton Mifflin.

McMillan, B. (1986). *Counting wildflowers.* New York: William Morrow.

Montgomery, S. (2004). *Search for the golden moon bear: Science and adventure in the Asian tropics.* Boston: Houghton Mifflin.

Morrison, G. (2004). *Nature in the neighborhood.* Boston: Houghton Mifflin.

O'Neill, M. (1989), *Hailstones and halibut bones: Adventures in color.* New York: Doubleday.

Palocco, P. (1994). *Pink and say.* New York: Philomel.

Pasachoff, N. (2004). *Linus Pauling: Advancing science, advocating peace.* Berkeley Heights, NJ: Enslow.

Rockwell, T. (1959). *How to eat fried worms.* New York: Yearling.

Schaefer, L. (2004). *Arrowhawk.* New York: Henry Holt.

Schwartz, A. (1972). *A twister of twists, a tangler of tongues.* New York: Harper & Row.

Sendak, M. (1962). *Chicken soup with rice.* New York: Harpercrest.

Skurzynski, G. (2004). *Are we alone? Scientists search for life in space.* New York: National Geographic Society.

Terban, M. (1985). *Too hot to hoot.* New York: Clarion.

Uhlberg, M. (2003). *The printer.* Berkeley, CA: Peachtree.

Wenzel, G. C. (2004). *Feathered dinosaurs of China.* Watertown, MA: Charlesbridge.

White, E. B. (1952). *Charlotte's web.* New York: HarperTrophy.

Williams, B., & Chorao, K. (1991). *Kevin's grandma.* New York: Dutton.

Yolen, J. (1992). *Encounter.* New York: Harcourt Brace.

Yolen, J. (1997). *Sleeping ugly.* New York: Coward, McCann & Geoghegan.

Zolotow, C. (1989). *Someday.* New York: HarperTrophy.

6 Integrating Visual Art Throughout the Curriculum

Questions to Guide Reading

1. Why should visual art be integrated (research and philosophy)?

2. What visual art literacy do classroom teachers need for meaningful integration?

3. How can the Arts Integration Blueprint be used to implement visual art integration (planning, learning environment, arts-based literature, best practices, instructional design, adaptations, and assessment for learning)?

4. How can teachers partner with literary arts specialists?

The arts escalate consciousness. (Elliot Eisner)

The headline is "Cops Study Vermeer," and it's no joke. New York City police officers are now trained to solve crimes by looking at art. It's all in the details. Art educator Amy Herman instructs the NYPD to analyze and notice the who, what, where, why, and when of art from Rembrandt to Renoir—and do it quickly. She teaches them to systematically look from foreground to background to get a sense of the whole scene. Officers practice drawing inferences and conclusions based on what they see. One captain found grand larceny and felony assault in El Greco's *The Purification of the Temple*. A detective explained that crime and art are both solved by noticing little things (Bryon, 2005). The same classes are also taught to medical students to help in diagnostic work. So what about classroom teachers?

Visual Imagery and Literacy

A room hung with pictures is a room hung with thoughts. (Sir Joshua Reynolds)

Visual communication is one of the "new literacies" of the 21st century. Why? It is nearly impossible to think without visual images. Einstein said he did most of his thinking in images, but had difficulty putting those images into words. He explained, "The way I do it is I visualize a structure in my imagination, maybe it's complex, maybe it's simple. And I rotate it, and I put different combinations together. And I can sit all day doing this" (quoted in Shaw, 2000, p. 210).

Educators have reawakened to how visual learning is central to communication (Tompkins, 2004). Mental visual art, in particular, is recognized as a requisite for thinking used in creative problem solving (CPS) (Ready Reference 2.5). This is not a new idea. Historically, religious frescoes and paintings in churches throughout the world educated the print illiterate. According to stained glass artist Dee Mays, the word *story* came to be applied to levels of buildings because stained glass window stories were built up and up as generations added more.

Cognition

There is a growing respect for how art involves more than use of the hands. Any artwork is a window into an artist's experiences in a particular time and culture. Through guided art examination students make this discovery. They learn to think beyond the literal when they gain new ways to see. For example, they learn that cubism expresses thoughts and feelings without representing any thing. Through art making students experience the joy of making meaning with hands-on materials.

Unfortunately, art is more often seen as a means to decorate, not to communicate. A cultural bias for verbal communication persists, particularly in school, despite the intensely visual nature of the world. Visual images are pervasive, but teachers may give minimal attention to decoding their messages, even though picture books are center stage in most literacy programs. Scarce instruction in visual literacy crops up in stereotyped use of colors, shapes, and symbols in children's art. Middle schoolers may still depict the sun as a circle with sticks coming off or draw birds as joined commas. Research shows children are capable of more complex perception. When classroom teachers act on a broadened definition of literacy, students are taught to read visual symbols and use them to express understandings. The result is work that has more variety and detail and is more satisfying to the child artist.

Cityscape mural at Ashley River Creative Arts.

Details

Meaning is made from details. Think of the way we know people by their particular features. Visual art thrives on such particulars. Artists strive to make each work unique, sometimes with a slight change in color or line; Mona Lisa would communicate something very different if da Vinci had raised the line of her mouth. Eisner (2005) urges a greater focus on details. One key reason is the cause-effect relationship between acute visual perception and ability to write well. He isn't alone. As one teacher explains, "I think that concentrating on the details in the artwork gave them the eye and the patience to go back into their writing again . . . the art helps the writing and the writing helps the art" (Baker et al., 2004, p. 7).

The teacher in the opening Snapshot joins others who now teach students to develop the artist's eye (Starnes & Siegesmund, 2004). He causes his students to take time to notice and connect to past experiences, which increases comprehension (Pressley, 2002). This is in contrast to teaching that emphasizes coverage rather than in-depth study of a work—artwork in this case. Uniqueness and commonality are treated simultaneously in Mr. Novak's lesson.

Classroom Snapshot:
Fantasy Unit with Chagall

Every child is an artist. The problem is how to remain an artist once he grows up. (Pablo Picasso)

The artist easel is draped with a black cloth. Mr. Novak is sitting on a low chair. This is the morning literacy block scheduled for reading–writing workshop approach. His fourth and fifth graders read a variety of genres and write in diverse forms for 2 hours.

"What is this?" Mr. Novak asks.

"The **mystery bag,**" the class responds.

"Right. You know the routine. First item." Mr. Novak pulls a yellow rubber duck from the bag. Students giggle.

"**Look closely.** Think about the colors, what it means, how it makes you feel." He pauses. "Next item." Out comes a yellow ball.

"Oh, oh," one boy raises his hand, "I know."

"Keep looking. We have two more items. Charles, glad you are making **connections.**" Mr. Novak struggles to reveal a floppy teddy bear. Charles looks puzzled.

"Last item. Think about how the items are related." He pulls out a child's tutu. More giggles.

"I see several thumbs up. Take a few more seconds. Look closely. Make connections. OK, Michael."

"Things from our past."

"Why do you say that?"

"Because they are little kids' stuff—soft and man-made."

"Yes. You're right. Who else? Sonya?"

"They are happy things. They remind me of having fun when I don't have to go to school." The class laughs.

"What do you think of Sonya's idea? Aspen?"

"I agree they make you feel happy and I agree with Michael about the past. I think it goes together. Soft toys and pleasant memories." Several shake their heads to agree.

"Charles, you had an idea early on. What were you thinking?"

"I thought you were just doing 'yellow' or 'plastic.' Then you brought out the teddy bear. The yellow part fits because it is an uplifting color."

After a few more minutes, Mr. Novak unveils the bottom half of the shrouded print.

"Cool," one boy says.

"What is it?" someone else says.

"Look closely. What do you see?" asks Mr. Novak.

"Really weird stuff. Is that a tree?"

"I see two people and one is green with white lips."

"Look, a cross. He has on a ring, too."

"The nuts or flowers are exploding. See the splattered paint!"

"Wow, those are strange shapes, like a moon eclipse. But it's red. Look there's a ring with an apple on it. Maybe this artist didn't have a lot of toys and had to play with this stuff."

"It's not a person on the right. Look. It's more the shape of a snout or something. Maybe he played with a pig!" The class laughs.

"You are really noticing colors, shapes, and images. What else? How does this make you feel?"

"It has bright yellow so it's happy. There is the cross. Maybe he's religious."

"But the guy is green. Of course, when you're a kid, colors don't matter. Maybe a kid painted this?" Kristen asks.

The class continues with many more discoveries until Mr. Novak asks them to get ready to see the rest. The class gets still. Many lean forward. Slowly he pulls cloth up. Little by little the print is revealed. The kids gasp.

"Make connections," Mr. Novak urges them.

"This is crazy. The people and houses are upside down. The woman is milking a cow in the head of a horse!"

"But the colors are really interesting. It's like a dream. Things can be anything in your dreams," says a girl who hasn't spoken before.

The discussion is animated as students make more discoveries. Comments converge on ideas about dreams, toys, happy memories, and childhood. One child actually uses the term "abstract" and another mentions "collage." About 15 minutes into the lesson, Mr. Novak explains that a Russian Jew named Marc Chagall painted it in 1911. He was inspired by pleasant childhood memories and folktales. Mr. Novak asks about their memories of stories from childhood. They list fairy tale titles and Disney films.

Mr. Novak moves into the lesson development by asking what makes fantasy. Students call out characteristics, such as "something not real" and "dreamlike places and events," and he writes them on the overhead. He then explains they are starting a genre unit on fantasy. He asks them why Chagall might have painted fantastic images in *I and the Village*. The students return to the "good feelings and freedom" ideas from earlier. He then asks about *Charlotte's Web* (White) and how it relates. Students comment on the elements of fantasy in the story (e.g., animals talking) and also how most of them heard it read aloud in second grade. It was a good memory from their childhood.

In the lesson conclusion Mr. Novak asks why people might write, read, or paint fantasy. There are many responses: for entertainment, relaxation, to make money, to be creative, to get ideas out, to feel good. He brings out a **text set** of fantasy books: *Tuck Everlasting* (Babbitt), *Able's Island* (Steig), *The Borrowers* (Norton), *Bunnicula* (Howe & Howe), and *The Indian in the Cupboard* (Banks). He says they'll be able to choose one book to study fantasy and find more specific characteristics. He puts them on the chalk tray for browsing. Students are to rate their choices by the end of the day. Five **book circles** will form for discussion. He explains they will also be creating their own fantasy using writing and art.

Postscript:

The fantasy unit lasted a month. Students met daily to discuss books. Mr. Novak held **"What do you see?"** discussions of other fantasy paintings, like Henri Rousseau's *The Dream*, and students explored the artists' motives and ways for creating these works. The unit culminated in a museum display of student paintings. All were framed. At an "exhibit opening," students acted as docent guides for students and adults who came to tour the museum (part of the hall). ✴

Arts Integration Blueprint

In Chapter 3 a plan for arts integration was described using the teaching levels *with*, *about*, *in*, and *through* the arts. The Arts Integration Blueprint (Ready Reference 3.2) uses this continuum. It goes further to describe ways to achieve curricular goals and standards with customized instruction. The 10 building blocks attempt to balance using art as a teaching and learning tool (arts for learning sake) while respecting art as a discipline itself (arts for art's sake) (Booth, 2003). The Blueprint begins with why arts integration should be implemented (philosophy based on research and theories). Next comes what teachers should know (arts literacy) and how to plan lessons, create an aesthetic environment, use arts-based literature and best teaching practices, design instructional routines, adapt for diverse learners, assess, and work with arts specialists. The Blueprint is applied to visual art in this chapter.

Blueprint I: Arts Integration Philosophy

> *Every genuine work of art has as much reason for being as the earth and the sun.* (Ralph Waldo Emerson)

Why Should Teachers Integrate Art?

Research on integrating visual art is summarized in Research Update 6.1. Research combines with theory and professional wisdom to inform beliefs. The following are philosophically based reasons used to argue for visual art integration.

Art Is a Primary Vehicle for Symbolic Communication.

There is a story about Picasso doing a portrait of a man's wife. When the man saw the painting, he complained it did not look like her. "Do you have something that does?" Picasso asked. The man opened his wallet and pulled out a photo of his wife. "Awfully small, isn't she?" Picasso remarked. Most learning in any discipline relies on *representation*, not literal images. Think of drawings in the dictionary, photographs in history texts, and plastic models in science. These images do not show everything. Maps, charts, and diagrams are abstractions that show "significant properties" (Arnheim, 1989, p. 30). "A human figure carved in wood is never just a human figure, a painted apple is never just an apple. Images point to the nature of the human condition" (p. 26).

Humans are prewired to think though visual symbols, which are used from early childhood. The child who sees a "fingernail" in the night sky is using metaphor to compare a known image with something inexplicable. Unfortunately, this visual capacity can wither if not developed (see brain research in Chapter 2). Students need to be taught how to use natural communication potential that transcends language. For example, a discussion might center around how a single tree, against a desolate background, conveys a sense of loneliness that would take paragraphs to describe. Even then, words would not entirely capture the range of emotional and cognitive messages one image can. Students can be taught to look closely and observe how artists use color, shapes, and line in nonliteral ways. In this way they learn to use an innate ability to think symbolically.

Students who learn to "read" art become literate in profound ways. They learn to decode visual symbol systems

---

Research Update 6.1   Visual Art and Achievement

- Seventh grade "reluctant readers" took a more active role in reading when they were engaged in visual art. Drawing pictures of visual impressions formed while reading, illustrating books, and visually representing key details of nonfiction texts improved reading skills (Deasy, 2002).
- **New York City.** Nine- and 10-year-olds in a "visual thinking" curriculum developed reasoning skills by using visual evidence when they were taught to "read" art. This translated into better "reading" of evidence in science (Deasy, 2002).
- **California.** When sixth graders' understanding of history was assessed through drawing as well as writing, they were able to show more of what they knew. This was true for both language proficient and English limited students (Deasy, 2002).
- Studies support that visual thinking using color tools increases the cognitive processes of problem solving, organizing, and memory (Longo, 1999).
- **Needham, Massachusetts:** Since integrating art into the curriculum in 1983, test scores for average third-grade students in Eliot Elementary, a racially mixed school, have increased to the 99th percentile

(*www/newhorizons.org/strategies/arts/cabe/oddleifson.html*).
- **Rocky Mountains:** Writing skills showed significant improvement when drawing and drama strategies were used in the primary grades (Moore & Caldwell, 1993).
- **CBS This Morning** (February 28, 1997): Students with learning disabilities gained 1–2 years in developmental levels after 8 weeks of special drawing instruction. The program has been found to increase reading, writing, math, and language skills up to 20 percent in other schools (Brookes, 1996).
- Reading and math scores were significantly higher for 96 students in eight visual-art-enriched first grades. The students scored an average of 77 percent at grade level, as compared to 55 percent for the control group (Gardiner, 1996).
- Visual arts students scored an average of 47 points higher on the math and 31 points higher on the verbal section of the SAT (College Board, 1999–2000). See more information about SAT scores at: *www.collegeboard.org/prof/*. Click the "search" button and enter "national report."

and use new tools to represent their ideas and feelings. When taught how to peel away layers and unwind bits of any visual message, students can have the "ah-ha" experience. Insight from visual art is highly motivating, deep comprehension that children can have long before they have print fluency with reading materials.

Art Involves Sensory Rich Thinking.

> *A painter takes the sun and makes it into a yellow spot. An artist takes a yellow spot and makes it into a sun.* (Pablo Picasso)

Images are stored in the brain's visual cortex and sounds in the auditory cortex. But the visual cortex is 30 times larger. That explains the results of the following study. Subjects were shown 10,000 images, each for 5 seconds over 5 days. On the last day they were shown a random sample of 160. Subjects were 73% accurate in choosing ones previously shown from pairs (Standing, 1973). The eyes contain "nearly 70% of the body's sensory receptors and send millions of signals every second along the optic nerves to the visual processing centers of the brain" (Wolfe, 2001, p. 153). The capacity for long-term memory of images is unlimited.

Visual perception is a cognitive event; interpretation and meaning are indivisible from seeing. Art is also hands on and tangible. We touch materials to make art using color, line, and shape. When we view art, both kinesthetic and tactile senses are activated by brushstrokes that go up or down or are heavy or light. What we see is a function of perception—a painting can evoke the sounds and smells of a summer boat ride or a raucous party. As the senses are stimulated, we respond mentally, physically, and emotionally. The symbols used in art are sensory-rich and form a language that beckons us to consider new perspectives and use prior knowledge to make personal meaning.

Art Activates Emotions and Motivates.

At the start of the 21st century we seem to have a new respect for the centrality of intuition in understanding. *Emotional Intelligence* author Daniel Goleman (1995) claims, "A view of human nature that ignores the power of emotions is sadly shortsighted . . . intelligence can come to nothing when the emotions hold sway" (p. 4). The roots of both the words *emotion* and *motivate* have to do with motion. Emotions cause us to take action that can result in positive or negative consequences. While art involves the intellect, it activates affective ways of knowing, too. It is an outlet for ideas and feelings. It is a safety valve that can allow emotional catharsis. Jenkins (1986) calls this "externalizing" what we feel and know (p. 15). Both viewing and doing art can give emotional release. This is evident in art therapy sessions when clients report feeling relaxed and joyous. Delight can arise from something as simple a making a line curve in a special way or as complex as the emotions stirred by the famous *National Geographic* cover photo of a stunning green-eyed Afghani girl.

Art Develops an Aesthetic Frame of Reference.

> *I come here every day on my coffee break because it is some kinda purdy.* (Landscaper, Sapphire Valley Golf Course, North Carolina)

Aesthetic sensitivity involves a sharpening of the senses, an awareness or appreciation of experiences (Feeney & Moravcik, 1987). It is a perceptual process that results in "a stimulating and harmonious" experience (Lowenfeld & Brittain, 1975). Thomas Moore (1998) uses the old-fashioned word *beauty* to describe this reaction. He argues that beauty is a source of imagination "that never dries up." A thing may be absorbing, but "may not be pretty or pleasant. It could be ugly, in fact, and yet seize the soul as beautiful in this special sense" (p. 278). Some pieces of art are so arresting that they "lure the heart into profound imagination" (p. 278).

Aesthetic responses lie at the heart of living. Aromas, sounds, colors, tastes, and textures fill our environment and stimulate responses. Brain research shows that smell, for example, is directly processed by the brain with long-lasting effects. Broudy (1979) contends all thinking and action depend on aesthetic thinking, especially image making, which gives the imagination "the raw material for concepts and ideals" (p. 63). Aesthetic experiences are primary sources of understanding vital to every child's education.

While children may not have language to express aesthetic awareness, they often are at a higher level of aesthetic development than we think. Think of the expressions of wonder and delight at flowers, butterflies, or pictures—gasps and sighs that show heightened sensitivity. Innate responses to beauty can be enlarged to think about art using diverse cultural concepts.

Michael Parson's research (1987) on the stages of aesthetic development is summarized in Ready Reference 6.1. It is presented to describe a progression that is not intended to be prescriptive, but gives teachers a basis to plan with an expanded vision of what's possible.

Art Develops Higher-Order Thinking.

Even infants are capable of high-level thought involving attention to visual details in faces (Wingert & Brant, 2005). Young children also use higher-order problem solving during art *making*. Their drawings of people and trees show how they shrewdly analyze and translate observations using basic shape patterns. These are more than mechanical imitations of what is seen; they are expressions of what children *know*. For example, preschoolers make stick drawings of people with huge heads. They are showing that they have concluded that the head is an important feature.

Ready Reference 6.1   Aesthetic Development Stages

Stage 1: Favorites.   Children delight in virtually all paintings, especially the colors. They like to pick favorites and talk about personal connections.

Stage 2: Subject matter.   Focus on representational art; it's better if it is more realistic. The artist's skill is admired.

Stage 3: Emotions.   Concern is for emotional stimulation, the more intense the better. Now the person has more than a personal preference and has developed an appreciation for how an artist causes the viewer to respond with emotion.

Stage 4: Style and form.   The viewer now understands that art is socially and culturally influenced and is important because of its meaning-making capabilities. Art is viewed as an important communication vehicle, with a primary power to give meaning. Color, texture, space, and form are analyzed as the person judges the competence of the artist to create new perspectives.

Stage 5: Autonomy.   Judgments are made on a personal and social basis. Art is viewed now as an important means of helping us consider the human condition and life itself through the questions it raises and the ideas and feelings it evokes. The work is used to seek truth and shared meaning with others in a kind of "conversation about life."

Source: Adapted from Parsons, Michael, J. (1987). Talk about a painting: A cognitive developmental analysis. *Journal of Aesthetic Education, 21*(1), 37–55.

When given materials and tools to create art, children will experiment and use imagination. When taught how to use materials and tools, they work with greater satisfaction and depth of problem solving. This can be as simple as showing how to paint with different strokes and amounts or the effects of dripping and splattering. After short demonstrations students are ready to explore to create a product, or just experiment, period.

Teachers who expect students to be independent, to generate rather than imitate, engender greater thinking. In contrast, teachers distort art when they give black line pages to color or directions that mimic painting by number. Art pedagogy abandoned these practices long ago, but a still few still lag behind. The result is a series of look-alike products that show kids can follow directions. These products do not reflect higher-order thinking. Furthermore, the work is not authentic art.

Higher-order thinking is developed through confrontation with problems. Artists and authors give us cues to create meaning, but children need to be taught to arrive at their own conclusions. Teaching can advance or thwart this development. This is obvious when students are given distorted ideas about what art is and how it comes to be. For example, if students think art must always look like something, they can lose faith in their abilities to create art. Some begin to refuse to try, for fear their art will not be like a "real" artist's. Arnheim (1989) reminds us that realism is not the end all for art and is even rejected by some cultures; depicting the pharaohs realistically would have suggested they were human and could have gotten you killed.

CPS orchestrates higher-order thinking for a specific purpose—to solve problems. Ready Reference 2.5 shows how all levels are coordinated. Some teachers also use a taxonomy to construct questions. The most well-known is that of Benjamin Bloom (1956) who divided cognition into levels. Recently, one of his students reordered his taxonomy and placed "creative thinking" (synthesis) at the top. I like the idea of creativity being at a high level, but what is equally important is teaching students *how* and *when* to synthesize as they make meaning. Here are the original Bloom levels with question and direction examples.

1. *Memory:* just the facts (literal). (What are the primary colors?)
2. *Interpretation:* read between the lines and add your own experiences to infer. (Explain *in your own words* how to create shades and tints.)
3. *Application:* put a skill to use. (Use what we've been learning about mixing colors to make different skin tones.)
4. *Analysis:* examine pieces to develop understanding. (Look closely to discover the repeated elements in this art.)
5. *Synthesis:* put pieces together to make a creative whole; requires invention and imagination. (How can you use collage materials to show what you learned about the environment?)
6. *Evaluation:* make a judgment based on the goodness or badness, rightness or wrongness using some criteria. (What do you think about this piece of art? Why do you think as you do?)

Students are also now taught to use this model to generate their own questions and to respond in any art form. For example, a synthesis-level art project could demonstrate what was learned from a science unit on ecology. The goal is cause students to think above the memory or literal level and coordinate higher-order thinking skills (HOTS) to solve problems.

Art Strengthens Self-Concept and Confidence About Being Unique.

Art is an extension of a person, an expression of who I am and what I am. (Sabe and Harrison)

In a two-year study of teachers who integrated visual art, McDermott (2004) found that children who struggled in regular classrooms were often successful using art. He concluded art did not "make them feel vulnerable but provided them with countless ways for thinking about and expressing their ideas" (p. 13). Expression is a primary goal of integrating art, and expression is linked to understanding. Students gain confidence as they make and do. They can use knowledge about science, culture, and narrative in artwork without "one answer" looming over them.

Art doing and viewing adds another way for children to communicate and expand perspectives. The focus on novel thinking in a noncompetitive context allows students to vie with internal standards of what makes sense. That's why students are often more willing to experiment in art—creativity is more openly valued. Through imaginative problem solving during art, students make personal discoveries. When art is coupled with other areas of study, students can associate positive art feelings and transfer art thinking (e.g., art composition skills used for writing). Art offers ways to manage emotions, images, and even the environment, which yields a sense of confidence. This is the theme of a Jewish folktale about a tailor who makes "something from nothing," bringing joy to himself and his family (see Gilman's picture book version, *Something From Nothing*).

Art Promotes Respect for Diversity.   The aphorism "God is in the details" reminds us how much small things matter. Art reflects culture, so it is an ideal source for studying the details of the values and customs of the world's peoples using visual images and objects that grab attention. Students are motivated to find out more when they are shown portraits, landscapes, still lifes, sculptures, and architecture. Teachers can simply ask what such art shows about the people who created it. A cultural print or artifact can also be a tool to reveal how people address problems in multiple ways. For example, art often shows the unique details of cultural dress, but all humans need some kind of clothing.

Art integration supports culturally responsive teaching. Children have more opportunities to express themselves freely, and teachers view knowledge as flexible (McDermott, 2004, p.13). Children are free to "use their own cultural lenses to construct and share their knowledge of the world" (p. 13). McDermott found that in art lessons children learned more collaboratively, and teachers celebrated efforts, regardless of performance levels. As they share work during times like art docent talks or artist chair, students come to realize no one's work is the same and that difference is exciting.

Art Develops Focus, Concentration, Responsibility, and Self-Discipline.   No teacher wants to spend most of his or her time managing behavior. During art children choose to engage. They paint, work with clay, and draw on IBooks. Such materials are self-motivating, but students learn that using them is contingent upon disciplining oneself to use them appropriately. Visual art integration can cause children who may resist learning to want to give it a try; the learning context contrasts with the "right answers" focus in math and spelling (McDermott, 2004).

For parents and teachers who decry the inability of children to stay on task and complete work with pride, art offers a viable means of developing important social and character traits. Students learn that nothing can be created without sticking with work to completion. As peers admire the work of those who are self-disciplined, insight is gained into what it takes to be successful. Students see that those who take risks, handle materials responsibly, and complete work are seen as responsible and given additional privileges.

Art Naturally Integrates Curricular Areas.

Art is to society as dreams are to a person. (Laliberte and Kehl)

Look around and find the art of life—furniture, clothes, cars, and dishes. Chair designs, from the throne to the beanbag, show how sitting signals relationships and status. Chair materials also reflect advances in science. Art shows how we create to survive and thrive. Art reflects life—in and out of school.

In school, art making and written composition can be good partners. The lessons of art have to do with exploring, experimenting, and organizing using tools and materials—the same thinking that produces writing. Artists do rough drafts, such as da Vinci's "cartoons" for paintings, and refine products through revision and editing. Teachers also use art to prompt writing. For example, students keep sketchbooks of writing possibilities. Sketchbooks are also used to record science observations, which is a common use of art in the science world. Essential properties of a topic may be best captured through art making first, offering a strategy to break writer's block.

Art offers an alternative way of knowing. It is an intelligence that can be used in any curricular area. For example, it is impossible to think about plants in the same way after seeing Georgia O'Keeffe's paintings. Heart, head, and hands are used to create, evaluate, understand, and respond to art. It is dreary to imagine studying without art—books without illustrations or maps, no globes or models of the atom.

Looking through the aesthetic lens of art develops new viewpoints. Examining art about plants, historical events, or people yields insights into science and social studies not available otherwise. Art pieces can be an introduction to, or an elaboration of, knowledge gained from reading texts. An aesthetic frame of reference gained from visual art experiences can unveil the beauty embedded in all disciplines.

Art Is a Way to Assess.

Art is a private feeling made into a public form. (Judith Rubin)

Assessment is gathering information about student learning. Unfortunately, the most important thing we want them to learn is to think, which is invisible. Visual art makes the invisible visible. Art gives a look inside the private world of thoughts and feelings. Teachers do need to be cautious about inferring meanings from child art. Excessive use of black may mean the black crayon was simply nearby. Given that caveat, we can examine artwork for signs of cognitive, emotional, and physical development. For example, when circle, vertical, horizontal, and diagonal lines appear in drawings, this shows that children are ready for handwriting instruction.

Just as a child's writing gives clues to thinking, artwork provides growth evidence, particularly about those who lack verbal fluency. A child may be able to express ideas with paint or clay not possible through words. Art can also stimulate passionate tales of events. Think about what is shown about the language development of 5-year-old Liza in this story based on her drawing of an erupting volcano:

> The town was afraid. They could hear the insides making growling sounds. Then it happened. The lava broke out and ran all over the people. It was blood red because it was hot rock. Hot hot rock. So hot it burned up the people. But see here. This is a people bird. The people were burned to ashes but the ashes molded into lava birds that could fly so high no volcano could ever touch them again. The end.

Blueprint II: Arts Literacy: Content and Skills

Every artist dips his brush into his own soul. (Henry Ward Beecher)

Integration occurs when two or more ideas a[re com]bined for mutual benefit. All parts retain their wor[th; a] synergism is created in which the sum is greater than the parts. Classroom time is maximized. Teachers, however, must have a knowledge base *about* visual art to teach *through* it. One source of the visual art literacy classroom teachers need is the 2002 standards produced by the Interstate New Teacher Assessment and Support Consortium (INTASC: *www.ccsso.org/intasc*). These standards are consistent with those of the National Board for Professional Teaching Standards. Teachers should also consult the full text of *National Standards for the Arts* (for K–12 students) available at *http://menc.org.*

What Do Teachers Need to Know to Integrate Art?

In K–6, the basic visual art content and skills include studying: (1) the historical, social, and cultural role of each art in our lives; (2) communication through art forms by creating, exhibiting, and responding to art; and (3) valuing art and developing aesthetic sensitivity (the roles of beauty and emotion in life). What classroom teachers need to know to integrate art at the *about* and *in* levels is summarized in this section. Two good websites for definitions of art concepts are *http://artlex.com* and *www.artcyclopedia.com.*

Purposes: Defining Art.

Art is the imposing of a pattern on experience, and our aesthetic enjoyment in recognition of the patterns. (Alfred North Whitehead)

Art is visual communication. It was one of the earliest ways humans expressed and understood each other and still serves this basic purpose. But the concept of what "art" is can be hard to grasp. Mostly the problem has to do with quality issues. The word *art* implies something "good" and gets into aesthetic tastes. Discussions aimed at defining art can be lively, but should not be avoided just because there are no right answers. Students can be guided to discover characteristics of what makes something art. For example, present three items like a toy, a shell, and a painting (use a reproduction, if necessary). Ask students to list what they see and decide which are art and why or why not. Make this a weekly routine to create depth of understanding. Seek more art examples that call for adding or subtracting from the list of traits.

Processes.
Visual art can be created or *made* or *viewed* using cognitive and emotional processes.

Art making.
The overall art-making process is creative problem solving. Artists decide about subject matter, style, media, and materials to create a composition. The

composition is made using art elements in varying ways by applying principles of design. The elements and processes teachers need to know are described in this section, mostly in the Ready References.

Visual literacy.

> *I shut my eyes in order to see.* (Paul Gauguin)

Visual "decoding" and expression skills are now included in literacy standards in most districts. To become visually literate, students need to be taught how to read visual images and use art tools to make meaning. Teachers also need to teach basic art concepts to ensure that art is not simply an added amusement. As with the other arts, visual art needs to be experienced as a whole before it is broken down into component parts. Students are motivated to learn elements, media, or styles if they have had positive art making and viewing experiences. Elements can be introduced informally, using labels as natural opportunities arise—teachers point out lines, shapes, textures, and colors in picture book art or in nature. Displays of art elements are important references. Instruction in using art basics can prevent student tendencies to abandon art expression in upper grades.

Viewing art.   People look at art to try to understand and to enjoy it. This later is often called *appreciation*, but appreciation rests on understanding. The goal of teaching art viewing is to show how to read clues to what the artist is saying. Many grow to enjoy art they didn't like when they are taught how to decode visual information and thus understand. This is especially true for art abstracted from reality and nonrepresentational art not intended to depict "things." Teachers can tap into these ways to understand art:

History of the artwork.   It is meaningful to integrate artworks about a time in history or art created at a certain time with social studies. Teaching about the artist's background gives a context for when and where the art was created. Students can be asked to predict the place and time based on close looking at the subject matter. Groups can also be given a variety of art postcards to arrange chronologically according to predictions from close examination of details.

Art criticism.   Criticism involves closely examining the art (elements, style, media, and composition) to construct meaning. The focus is on how the art is "portrayed," not on doing what critics do with films (Wachowiak & Clements, 2005). Students learn to problem solve art when asked, "What do you see? What is it about (subject matter)? How did the artist make this (media/techniques)? What arts elements and design ideas were used? Where might the artist have gotten ideas?"

Aesthetics.   The ideas behind the art including tastes and preferences, are involved in aesthetic thinking. For example, right now my community is having a big aesthetic discussion about whether the sculpture for a new waterfront park should be realistic (dolphins) or fanciful (mermaids). The debate is heated. Students can be drawn into these kinds of stimulating discussions with focus on the questions "Why do you think _____?" and "How do you know _____?"

Social, Economic, Cultural, and Historical Factors. Time, culture, and social norms affect art making and understanding. Nothing is made in a vacuum. This fact of art is one of the reasons it can be so naturally integrated with social studies. Art is made about any topic in the curriculum and learning is enriched by its presence. Meaningful visual art integration is facilitated by putting artworks in context. A web of understanding is constructed by discussing clues in art that reveal factors that influenced its creation. This can be a highly motivating discovery process that engages students in analysis of details to support their conclusions.

People: Artists.   Children find the childhoods of famous artists compelling, and studying artists is a natural connection to the literary genre of biography. Timelines about artists' lives emerge when teachers provoke students' interests about the time when the person lived. Maps and globes become important tools to locate places where men and women created the world's art treasury. Since styles of art reflect the society in which they are created, students can come to understand the economic and social circumstances under which new styles were born. For example, the chaotic turn into the 20th century was the context for the birth of abstract art, cubism, and dada.

Our most robust role models are always real people. Students gain courage to take risks from the personal struggles of real artists and see that being creative doesn't mean starting cold. For example, Picasso copied African masks and Degas worked from photographs. Both then twisted, combined, reshaped, and stretched the ideas gathered from these sources.

Artists take many roles, including painter, sculptor, architect, animator, curator, critic, historian, and of course, teacher. Art-related careers should be included in any career education study. Over time teachers come to know many artists from Mary Cassatt to Frida Kahlo; these people can be the focus of a unit, or their work can be integrated into other units. A list of names and sources for artist information is listed in Ready References 6.2 and 6.3. Check Chapter 4 for sources for picture book artist-author studies. Presented later in this chapter, Planning Page 6.1 shows a planning web for a unit on Chris Van Allsburg.

 **Picture Book Artists**

Planning Page 4.1 lists other sources for artist studies.

Artists Commonly Studied

Brown, Marcia	Macaulay, David
Carle, Eric	McDermott, Gerald
dePaola, Tomie	Peet, Bill
Dillon, Leo and Diane	Polacco, Patricia
Dr. Seuss	Potter, Beatrix
Fox, Mem	Ringgold, Faith
Keats, Ezra Jack	Sendak, Maurice
Kellogg, Steven	Van Allsburg, Chris
Lobel, Arnold	Yolen, Jane

The Caldecott Award is given yearly by the American Library association for picture book art. All Caldecott artists are listed at *www.http://www.ala.org*. **Horn Book** publishes interviews with all Caldecott winners (*www.hbook.com*)

Websites for Videos/DVDs on Picture Book Artists:

Example Video:
Eric Carle, Picturewriter (making collage)

Artist/Author Videos:
http://www.scils.rutgers.edu/~kvander/authorvids.html.

Weston Woods:
http://teacher.scholastic.com/products/westonwoods/index.htm.

 **Well-Known Artists**

Use this as starter sources for studies of artists and works.

Websites with Artist/Works Information
http://Artcyclopedia
http://school.discovery.com/schrockguide/
http://educationindex.com/art/
http://famousPainter.com
http://gardenofpraise.com/art.htm
http://loggia.com/index.html (comprehensive site)
http://nwrel.org/comm/topics/arts.html
http://princetonol.com/groups/iad/lessons/middle/ index.htm (comprehensive site).

Artists with One Example (* = top ten at: *www.kidsart.org*)

Albert Bierstadt, *The Rocky Mountains Landers' Peak*
Pieter Bruegel the Elder, *Children's Games*
Sandro Botticelli, *The Birth of Venus*
Michelangelo Buonarroti, *The Creation of Adam* (Sistine Chapel ceiling)
*Mary Cassatt, *The Boating Party*
Paul Cezanne, *Apples and Oranges*
Marc Chagall, *I and the Village*
John Singleton Copley, *Paul Revere*
Salvador Dali, *The Persistence of Memory*
Edgar Degas, *Little Fourteen-Year-Old Dancer*
Albrecht Durer, *Young Hare*
Vincent van Gogh, *Starry Night*
Paul Gauguin, *Vision After the Sermon, Hail Mary*
Francisco de Goya, *Don Manuel Osorio Manrique de Zuniga*
El Greco, *View of Toledo*
*Winslow Homer, *Snap the Whip*
Pieter de Hooch, *Woman Peeling Apples*
Edward Hopper, *Nighthawks*
Vassily Kandinsky, *Improvisation 31* (Sea Battle)
Paul Klee, *Senecio* (*Head of a Man*)

Frida Kahlo, *Self Portrait with Cropped Hair*
Jacob Lawrence, *Parade*
Roy Lichtenstein, *Wham*
René Magritte, *The Eye*
Henri Matisse, *The Swan*
Joan Miro, *People and Dog in the Sun*
Piet Mondrian, *Broadway Boogie Woogie*
Claude Oscar Monet, *Impression: Sunrise, Bridge Over a Pool of Lilies*
Grandma Moses, *Through the Old Covered Bridge*
Edvard Munch, *The Scream*
*Georgia O'Keeffe, *Red Hills and Bones*
Pablo Picasso, *Mother and Child*
Jackson Pollock, *Painting, 1948*
Raphael, *St. George and the Dragon*
Rembrandt van Rijn, *Self Portrait*
*Remington, *The Smoke Signal*
Renoir, *A Girl With a Watering Can*
Diego Rivera, *Pinata*
Norman Rockwell, *Marbles Champion*
Henri Rousseau, *Woman Walking in an Exotic Forest*
Georges Seurat, *La Grande Jatte*
Gilbert Stuart, *George Washington*
Henry Tanner, *The Banjo Lesson*
Henri Toulouse-Lautrec, *At Moulin Rouge*
Jan Vermeer, *The Love Letter*
Leonardo da Vinci, *Mona Lisa*
Andy Warhol, *Campbell's Soup Can*
James McNeill Whistler, *Arrangement in Black and Gray*
Grant Wood, *American Gothic*
Andrew Wyeth, *Christina's World*
N.C. Wyeth, *The Giant*
Wang Yani, *Baboons*

Art Media: Materials and Techniques. Architect Frank Lloyd Wright said that he "could feel in the palms of his hands the Froebel blocks." It was in early childhood when these shapes "had become instinctive to him, giving him his first strong perception of the meanings of volume and form" (Bill, 1988, p. 29). No teacher's words or any book can ever substitute for work with actual art tools and materials. The kinesthetic–tactile intelligence activated in these encounters may indeed trigger a life devotion.

Teachers with a repertoire of strategies beyond "draw a picture" can offer students options, which increase and change their responses; media use changes the message of art. For example, "violence" in a cartoon comes across differently than when it is expressed in a marble sculpture. Students learn a broad range of communication tools from knowledgeable teachers. Materials and tools open doors. For example, Ken Robinson says Paul McCartney probably wouldn't have been much without the guitar. Alternative materials motivate and interest is piqued by increased choices. Ready References 6.4 and 6.5 list materials, tools, and ideas. These are basics:

- Assorted brushes, chalk, pencils, water-based markers, crayons, and paints (tempera, watercolors, and paint crayons)
- Different kinds, sizes, and colors of paper, including brown kraft paper, sketchpads, and construction paper.

- Clays for sculpting and modeling (e.g., Crayola's Model Magic)
- Glues and pastes, especially white glue
- Scissors appropriate for children
- Collage materials such as shells, buttons, pebbles, and lace
- Boxes and tubes for construction and papier mâché bases
- Cleanup supplies
- Workspace (easels and tables covered with shower curtains)

Actual Art.   To meaningfully integrate visual art, teachers need art for children to look at. This includes reproductions/prints, art postcards, arts-based books, cartoons, photographs, 3D examples, and cultural artifacts such as masks, pottery, and fiber art. Ready References 6.5, 6.8, and 6.9 give examples of picture book art categorized by art concepts.

Other useful items to collect are art quotes, facts about artists, and art-related songs and music. Many materials are available cheaply. Give friends, other teachers, school staff, and parents a list of items to save (e.g., paper towel tubes to use for "looking closely"). Stores that sell wallpaper may donate sample books. These make quick book binders for writing and can be used in collage. Paper and photography companies often give away paper products.

Picture files are valuable tools and practically free. Collect magazines, calendars, postcards, greeting cards, old photos,

---

 **Art Materials and Media Techniques**

Directions: Use these ideas to integrate art making throughout the curriculum.

Bookmaking: pop-up, accordion, big books, mini-books

Calligraphy and block lettering: embellished lettering or letters simply cut from standard-sized blocks (e.g., construction paper)

Collage: design made by pasting or gluing assembled materials on a surface

Craft: handcrafted item such as pottery or quilt

Diorama: shadow box made with shoe box to create a scene

Display: arrangements around a concept or theme

Drawing: linear art made with pencil, charcoal, pen, crayon

Enlargement: use overhead projector to make images larger

Fiber art: fabrics, yarn, string, and so forth

Fresco: paint on wet plaster

Intaglio: process of engraving

Lithography: Plate printing method (Pictures are drawn on a plate. The plate is submerged in water. The ink adheres to the chalk or paint. Heavy pressure prints the design.)

Mask: paper bag, tag board, balloon with papier mâché

Mixed media: paper, wire, paint, fabric all used in one artwork

Mobile: three-dimensional art that moves, usually suspended

Montage: combination of several distinct pictures to make a composite picture

Mural: large wall art

Painting: tempera (pigments in egg base), acrylic (made from polymer), watercolor, oil (pigments in oil base)

Pastel: chalk art

Print: pull a print or "stamp" with found objects

Puppet: bag, hand, finger, stick, sock, box

Rubbing: paper is placed over objects and crayons or markers are used to bring up images

Scratchboard: black crayon or ink is placed over another color such as silver or multiple colors; sharp tool is used to scratch surface and reveal color

Sculpture: three-dimensional art made from wood, clay, metal, found objects, plaster, or papier mâché

Wash: translucent watercolor used over another medium

These books can be used to teach about a medium children can then use. Most are well-regarded "classics" that should be easy to find. A good overall reference is Molly Bang's *Picture This: How Pictures Work* (2000, Seastar).

Collage

Bunting, E. (1994). *Smoky night.* (Ill. by D. Diaz). Harcourt Brace Jovanovich.

Day, N. R. (1995). *The lion's whiskers: An Ethiopian folktale.* Scholastic.

Hughes, L. (1995). *The block.* Metropolitan Museum of Art.

Crayons and Colored Pencils

Brown, M. (1982). *The bun. A tale from Russia.* Harcourt Brace Jovanovich.

Lionni, L. (1970). *Fish is fish.* Knopf.

Van Allsburg, C. (1986). *The stranger.* Houghton Mifflin.

Drawing

Barrett, P., & Barrett, S. (1972). *The line Sophie drew.* Schroll.

dePaola, T. (1989). *The art lesson.* Trumpet Club.

Johnson, C. (1955). *Harold and the purple crayon.* Harper & Row.

McCloskey, R. (1942). *Make way for ducklings.* Viking.

Fiber Art

Hall, D. (1980). *The ox-cart man.* Viking.

Kroll, V. (1992). *Wood-Hoopoe Willie.* Charles Bridge.

Roessel, M. (1995). *Songs from the loom.* Lerner.

Mixed Media

Bang, M. (1985). *The paper crane.* Greenwillow.

Burningham, J. (1989). *Hey! Get off our train.* Crown.

Young, E. (1989). *Lon po po. A Red Riding Hood story from China.* Philomel.

Mural

Gerstein, M. (1984). *The room.* Harper & Row.

Winters, J. (1991). *Diego.* Random House.

Painting

Agee, J. (1988). *The incredible painting of Felix Clousseau.* Farrar, Straus & Giroux.

Cooney, B. (1982). *Miss Rumphius.* Viking. (acrylics)

dePaola, T. (1988). *The legend of the Indian paintbrush.* Putnam.

Dunrea, O. (1995). *The painter who loved chickens.* Farrar, Straus & Giroux.

Locker, T. (1984). *Where the river begins.* Dial. (oil)

Roalf, P. (1993). *Looking at painting: Children.* Hyperion.

Pastels/Chalk

Dewey, A. (1995). *The sky.* Green Tiger.

Howe, J. (1987). *I wish I were a butterfly* (Ill. by E. Young). Harcourt Brace Jovanovich.

Van Allsburg, C. (1985). *The polar express.* Houghton Mifflin.

Pen and Pencil/Ink

Gag, W. (1956). *Millions of cats.* Coward, McCean & Geoghegan.

Macaulay, D. (1977). *Castle.* Houghton Mifflin.

Mayer, M. (1974). *Frog goes to dinner.* Dial.

Van Allsburg, C. (1981). *Jumanji.* Houghton Mifflin.

Viorst, J. (1972) *Alexander and the terrible, horrible, no good, very bad day* (Ill. by R. Cruz). Atheneum.

Photography

Angelou, M. (1994). *My painted house, my friendly chicken.* Clarkson-Potter.

Brown, L. K., & Brown, M. (1996). *Visiting the art museum.* Dutton.

Desalvo, J., Stanley, C., & Olive, J. (photographers). (2001). *CowParade Houston.* Workman.

Freedman, R. (1987). *Lincoln. A photobiography.* Clarion.

Johnson, N. (2001). *National Geographic photography guide for kids.* National Geographic Society.

Kissinger, K. (1994). *All the colors we are.* Redleaf.

Printmaking

Carl, E. (1987). *The tiny seed.* Picture Book Studio.

Haley, G. E. (1970). *A story, a story.* Atheneum.

Lionni, L. (1963). *Swimmy.* Random House.

Waber, B. (1996). *"You look ridiculous," said the rhinoceros to the hippopotamus.* Houghton Mifflin.

Sculpture (Three-Dimensional Art)

dePaola, T. (1982). *Giorgio's village.* Putnam. (paper sculpture)

Haskins, J. (1989). *Count your way through Mexico.* Carolrhoda. (papier mâché)

Hoyt-Goldsmith, D. (1990). *Totem pole.* Scholastic. (wood carving)

Prokofiev, S. (1985). *Peter and the wolf* (Ill. by B. Cooney). Viking. (paper sculpture)

Watercolor

Asch, F. (1995). *Water.* Harcourt Brace.

Bunting, E. (1990). *The wall* (Ill. by R. Himler). Clarion.

Le Ford, B. (1995). *A blue butterfly. A story about Claude Monet.* Doubleday.

Potter, B. (1902). *The tale of Peter Rabbit.* Warne.

Yolen, J. (1987). *Owl moon* (Ill. by J. Schoenherr). Philomel.

Weaving

Allen, C. (1991). *The rug makers.* Steck-Vaughn.

Castaneda, O. S. (1993). *Abuela's weave.* Lee & Low.

Miles, M. (1971). *Annie and the Old One.* Little, Brown.

and restaurant place mats to use for art making and study. For example, students can sort pictures into categories such as subject matter, media, style, artist, or art elements. In doing so they use vocabulary and thinking skills such as comparing, contrasting, and classification. Pictures can prompt both art and writing or actual art-making materials (e.g., for collage). Picture files can also be used for drama and storytelling. Collect interesting words and phrases that provoke images, such as headlines and advertisements. Sort pictures into labeled folders (words and phrases, styles, subject matter, cultures, people, holidays, emotions, places, dance, and movement). Mount or use plastic sleeves. Write drama/oral expression and writing strategies on each folder. Finally, make a table of contents. Poems, quotes, and cartoons about art and artists can also be collected and used in routines or on bulletin boards, or as inspiration to make poem or quote books. Ready References 6.10, 7.1, and 7.2 list ideas for art-based discussions that can be used with pictures.

Visual Elements and Concepts.

A line is a dot that went for a walk. (Paul Klee)

Art specialists think art viewing and making is teachable and dispute that instruction about art elements endangers creative invention. Nearly everyone has the capacity to understand art language used to express ideas and feelings, and "neither children or accomplished artists state, to their own satisfaction, what they want to say unless they have acquired the means of saying it" (Arnheim, 1989, p. 57). The goal is not to "foist technical tricks" on students beyond their ability. Art knowledge should be taught on a "need-to-know" basis considering developmental levels and task demands. Visual concepts are learned best, as all communication is, in a meaningful context. Isolated concept and skill lessons don't take. In addition, children should discover as much as possible, rather than be told. Ready Reference 6.6 lists art elements.

Design principles.   Artists have to decide how to arrange and organize their work to create a coherent whole that says what they want to say. This is similar to what writers do. Ready Reference 6.7 summarizes the principles and concepts teachers need to know to do mini-lessons and question and coach students, while Ready Reference 6.8 lists children's books to support those lessons.

 ## Visual Art Elements

Line: a horizontal, vertical, angled, or curved mark, across a surface (e.g., long, short, dotted)
Shape: the two dimensions of height and width arranged geometrically (e.g., circles, triangles), organically (natural shapes), symbolically (e.g., letters)
Color: (hue=color names), primary, secondary, and complementary; warm (red/yellow) and cool (blue/green)
    Value: lightness (tints) or darkness (shades) of colors
    Saturation: vibrancy/purity vs. dullness of color

Space: (2D) the area objects take up (positive space) and that surround shapes and forms (negative space). In depth illusions are created by techniques such as perspective and overlapping
Texture: way something feels or looks as it would feel (e.g., slick, rough)
Form: 3D (height, width, and depth) shown by contours (e.g., sphere, pyramid, cube)

Ready Reference 6.7   Art Concepts and Design Principles

Composition: arrangement of the masses and spaces
    Foreground, middle, and background: the areas in a piece of art that appear closest to the viewer, next closest, and farthest away
Structures and forms: 2D—art with length and width, such as paintings or photography; 3D—art also has height/depth, such as sculpture
Balance: weight of elements distributed symmetrically or asymmetrically
Emphasis: areas that are stressed and attract the eye

Variety: no two elements used are the same
Repetition: elements used more than once (e.g., shapes, lines) create pattern and texture
Contrast: opposition or differences of elements (e.g., created by light colors next to dark)
Rhythm/motion: sense that there are paths through the work
Unity: the sense there is a whole working together
Light: illusion created with lighter colors

Ready Reference 6.8 Art Concepts and Children's Books

These are examples of arts-based children's literature. Many could fit under more than one category.

Art Elements

Adoff, A. (1973). *Black is brown is tan.* HarperCollins. (skin tones)

Crews, D. (1995). *Sail away.* Greenwillow. (Air-brushed shapes show pattern through repeated images of objects.)

Crosbie, M. J., & Rosenthal, S. (1993). *Architecture colors.* Wiley. (Colors are photos of architectural features. Series includes *Architecture Shapes* and *Architecture Counts.*)

Ehlert, L. (1994). *Color zoo.* HarperCollins. (wordless book with holes that form shape-changing abstract animals)

Heller, R. (1995). *Color! Color! Color!* Grosset & Dunlap. (rhythmic language; acetates that overlap to show mixing)

Jonas, A. (1989). *Color dance.* Greenwillow. (Children dance with cloth that overlaps to create new colors.)

Pinkwater, D. M. (1977). *The big orange splat.* Scholastic. (Creative man paints his house different colors.)

Polacco, P. (1988). *Rechenka's eggs.* Philomel. (Patterns are everywhere in this Ukrainian story about Pysanky eggs.)

*Sendak, M. (1964). *Where the wild things are.* Harper & Row. (Expressive lines are used in this story about a naughty boy.)

Shalom, V. (1995). *The color of things.* Rizzoli International. (Colors are drained from a town, and children paint them back.)

Shaw, C. G. (1988). *It looked like spilt milk.* Harper Trophy. (Free-form shapes turn into ordinary objects.)

Yenawine, P., & the Museum of Modern Art. (1991). *Colors.* Delacorte. (MOMA artwork illustrates this concept book. Series includes *Lines, Shapes,* and *Stories.*)

*Yolen, J. (1988). *Owl moon.* Philomel. (A walk on a snowy moonlit night depicted with color contrast and perspective.)

Style

Brown, A. (2000). *Willy's pictures.* Candlewick. (surreal qualities given to great paintings; pullouts of original art)

Say, A. (2000) *The sign painter.* Houghton. (Edward Hopper–style paintings)

Subject Matter

Blizzard, G. S. (1992). *Come look with me: Exploring landscape art with children.* Thomason-Grant. (from series: *World of Play, Animals in Art,* and *Enjoying Art with Children*)

Cheltenham Elementary School, Kindergarten. (1994). *We are all alike . . . We are all different.* (Scholastic portraits)

Locker, T. (1994). *Miranda's smile.* Dial. (An artist tries to paint his daughter's portrait.)

Artists/Culture

Everett, G. (1991). *Li'l sis and Uncle Willie.* Hyperion. (African American artist William H. Johnson's art)

Lepschy, I. (1992). *Pablo Picasso.* Baron's Education Series. (Biography focuses on difficulties as a child. From series *Children of Genius, which* includes *da Vinci* [1984].)

Lewis, S. (1991). *African American art for young people.* Davis. (12 artists: quilter, sculptor, painter, and found art)

Lionni, L. (1991). *Matthew's dream.* Knopf. (A young mouse becomes a painter in this tale of a career in art.)

Lord, S. (1995). *The story of the dreamcatcher and other Native American crafts.* Scholastic. (photography, beadwork, and mask making)

McDermott, G. (1993). *Raven: A trickster tale from the Pacific Northwest.* Harcourt Brace. (traditional art forms and shapes)

*Ringgold, F. (1991). *Tar beach.* Random House. (Culture: African American autobiography; painted and quilted fabrics)

Rodari, F. (1991). *A weekend with Picasso.* Rizzoli. (fictional weekend with the artist, photographs/artwork)

Turner, R. M. (1993). *Faith Ringgold.* Little, Brown. (biography of quilt maker, background for Ringgold's *Tar Beach*)

Wallner, A. (2004). *Grandma Moses.* Holiday.

Art Forms/ Media

McLerran, A. (1991). *Roxaboxen.* Lothrop, Lee & Shepard. (Children build houses from stones, old pottery, and crates.)

Micklethwait, L. (1994). *I spy a lion: Animals in art.* Greenwillow. (animals and details in famous art)

Paul, A. W. (1991). *Eight hands round.* HarperCollins. (American quilt patterns and explanations of origins)

Pfister, M. (1992). *The rainbow fish.* North-South Books. (Beautiful fish finds happiness; scales are made with foil.)

Polacco, P. (1990). *Thunder cake.* Putnam. (clothing and quilts full of patterns)

Venezia, M. (1991). *Paul Klee.* (Biography starting in childhood. From series *Getting to Know the World's Greatest Artists.*)

Wilson, F. (1969, 1988). *What it feels like to be a building.* Preservation. (architectural features made with people)

---

*Caldecott Award books.

Ready Reference 6.9 Art Styles in Children's Books

Cartoon Style: Simple Lines and Use of Primary Colors

Schulz, C. (2001). *Peanuts: The art of Charles M. Schulz.* Pantheon.

Schwartz, D. M. (1985). *How much is a million?* (Ill. by S. Kellogg). Scholastic.

Seuss, Dr. (1957). *Cat in the hat.* Random House.

Spier, P. (1980). *People.* Doubleday.

Expressionism: Leans Toward Abstract, Focuses Emotions

Bemelmans, L. (1939). *Madeline.* Viking.

Carle, E. (1984). *The very busy spider.* Philomel.

Ehlert, L. (1989). *Color zoo.* Lippincott.

Le Tord, B. (1999). *A bird or two: A story about Henri Matisse.* William B. Eerdmans.

Livingston, M. C. (1985). *A circle of seasons.* (Ill. by L. E. Fisher). Holiday House.

Martin, B., Jr., & Archambault, J. (1989). *Chick chicka boom* (Ill. by L. Ehlert). Simon & Schuster.

Williams, V. B. (1982). *A chair for my mother.* Mulberry.

Folk Art/Naive: Nontraditional Media/Untrained Artists

Aardema, V. (1975). *Why mosquitoes buzz in people's ears* (Ill. by L. Dillon & D. Dillon). Dial.

Hall, D. (1979). *The ox-cart man* (Ill. by B. Cooney). Viking.

Polacco, P. (1988). *Rechenka's eggs.* Philomel.

Provenson, A. (1990). *The buck stops here: The presidents of the United States.* Harper & Row.

Xiong, B. (1989). *Nine-in-one Grr! Grr!* (Ill. by N. Hom). Children's Book Press.

Impressionism: Dreamlike Quality, Relies on Light

Bjork, C. (1985). *Linnea in Monet's garden* (Ill. by L. Anderson). R&S.

Howe, J. (1987). *I wish I were a butterfly* (Ill. by E. Young). Harcourt Brace Jovanovich.

McCully, E. (2000). *Mirette and Bellini cross Niagara Falls.* Putnam.

Zolotow, C. (1962). *Mr. Rabbit and the lovely present* (Ill. by M. Sendak). Harper & Row.

Realism: Represents Reality in Shape, Color, and Proportion

Holling, H. C. (1969). *Paddle-to-the-sea.* Houghton Mifflin.

McCloskey, R. (1969). *Make way for ducklings.* Viking.

Turkle, B. (1976). *Deep in the forest.* Dutton.

Viorst, J. (1972) *Alexander and the terrible, horrible, no good, very bad day* (Ill. by R. Cruz). Atheneum.

Zelinsky, P. (1997). *Rapunzel.* Dutton.

Surrealism: Distorts Images; Fantastic Quality

Bang, M. (1980). *The grey lady and the strawberry snatcher.* Four Winds.

Brown, A. (1998). *Willy the dreamer.* Candlewick.

Sciezka, J. (1989). *The true story of the three little pigs by A. Wolf* (Ill. by L. Smith). Viking.

Van Allsburg, C. (1981). *Jumanji.* Houghton Mifflin.

Winter, J. (1988). *Follow the drinking gourd.* Knopf.

Artistic styles.　Another area of art that can be integrated is the study of the unique styles artists create. Higher-order thinking skills are honed as students analyze and evaluate style traits. Discriminating and appreciating diverse styles also enlarges understanding and tolerance. Ready Reference 6.9 lists examples from picture books. *Note:* The Arts-Based Bibliography in the Appendix has books about artists and styles. For example, see *Talking with Artists* (Cummings, 1992) with interviews of children's book illustrators. Check out sources for videos and software in Planning Page 4.1 and Ready Reference 4.6.

Subject matter: What art is about.

The source of art is not visual reality, but the dreams, hopes, and aspirations which lie deep in every human. (Arthur Zaidenberg)

Subject matter groupings help students understand art and give options for original art making. For example, a response to the characterization in a piece of literature might be a portrait. Here are common classifications:

- Portrait: person(s)
- Cityscape: city view
- Landscape: outdoor scene
- Seascape: view of a body of water
- Interior: inside view of a room or building
- Still life: arrangement of nonliving objects
- Abstract: focus on color, shape, line, and texture

Art elements, design principles, styles, media, and subject matter need to be taught explicitly using mini-lessons. These art concepts can also be used to generate questions and make learning games. Chapter 7 describes Seed Strategies for visual art concepts using word sorts, games, and questioning.

Discipline-Based Art Education (DBAE).

Walling (2001) writes, "For much of the 20th century visual art education centered on one overriding goal, helping students realize 'creative self-expression.'" (p. 626). He calls this a "self-limiting philosophy" (p. 626). In the 1980s, the Getty Center created an influential curricular model that recommended decreased emphasis on art making and an increased focus on teaching art history, aesthetics, and art criticism. The model retained hands-on art but stressed art inquiry. The rationale was grounded in the belief that art education, based entirely on creating art, does not give a sense of the place of art in life and the world. The Getty curriculum raised questions about the lack of visual and artistic literacy among students who could complete 13 years of school with little opportunity to reflect on the immense bank of world art. Today it is accepted that a balanced program of art experiences is needed. Ready Reference 6.10 offers questions and strategies to guide those discussions. While children's cognitive growth (e.g., language and conceptual development) is greatly facilitated by exploration through drawing and other artwork, even young children benefit from opportunities to examine and discuss their art and that of others (Alexander & Michael, 1991; Gardner, 1990; McWinnie, 1992). Curriculum ideas are presented at the Getty website: *www.getty.edu/education/search/curricula.html.*

Blueprint III: Collaborative Integrated Art Planning

Visual art integration planning is about finding mutually supportive connections between visual art and other academic areas. This entails teaching *about* art and involving students *in* using art knowledge to solve problems. Children do not grow in visual art literacy if they are simply told to draw pictures after reading something or look at pictures without guidance. Opportunity, without instruction, does not do justice to art as a discipline and cripples children's use of visual communication. A critical integration question is "What did my students learn *about* each discipline being integrated?" not just "What subjects were used in the lesson?" This does not mean every teacher must be able to draw well. It does mean teachers need basic knowledge and skills to use visual art language and present examples of art-making options. This also does not mean students shouldn't have free time to make art. Children are regularly given free time to read, but they are also taught *how* to read. Children need to be taught *how* to read art and express through visual language, too.

Unit Planning

Chapter 3 summarized the ways specialists and classroom teachers plan arts-based integrated units. Planning Page 3.2 shows the unit development process. Important points are:

- Academic and arts standards are used, along with other goals.
- Assessment and instruction are aligned to standards and goals.
- Mutual connections are sought.
- Unit centers are developed with statements and questions.
- Student interests and questions are accommodated.
- Project work is common and culminates in displays that are central assessment pieces.
- Field-based units focus on visits to special sites, like museums, and involve work with arts professionals.
- Sequenced, two-pronged lesson plans are made.

Standards. The National Standards for the Arts includes a visual art section. This is an important planning tool for lessons and units. Standards help teachers incorporate learning *about* and *in* art into lessons in other subjects. Ready Reference 6.11 shows the main visual arts standards. View the full document at *http://menc.org*. See examples of state versions of these standards, with lesson examples and assessment ideas at state departments of education websites. Connecticut's is a good place to start.

Finding Art Connections. What does art have to do with science, social studies, or math? Consider these connections:

Social studies. Since the focus of social studies is relationships among people, an integrated unit can include or center on the lives of artists, artworks, styles, societal influences, cultures, and careers in art. Any culture can be studied through visual art since art has been produced by every culture. Economics might be studied through the phenomenon of blockbuster museum exhibits or the multibillion dollar art auction business. Remember, kids are intrigued by big numbers!

Science. Art and science were interchangeable in Leonardo da Vinci's world. He wrote about art and drew science. He applied the science of color, explored anatomy, and invented machines (Walling, 2001, p. 631). Science depends on the scientific method, which uses creative problem solving, so this is a mega connection. Science and art both include the study of pigments, the science behind color, the chemistry of art materials, the physics of art forms (e.g., sculpture and mobiles), the creation of optical illusions, and the photographic process. Thomas Locker, a contemporary artist, integrates science and art in books like *Cloud Dance* and *Water Dance* that contain exquisite

 **Art Discussion Questions and Strategies**

Directions: Use to teach students to decode artwork and engage in personal connections and storytelling. *Note:* Phillip Yenawine is shown using these kinds of strategies with students in the video *What Do You See?* (Chicago Art Institute).

1. *Concrete to abstract.* Young children have difficulty with questions like "Why might the artist have painted this?"(motives or intentions) and understanding symbols such as colors that represent seasons. Try such questions and if they have trouble, use more concrete ones. *Note:* Children need time to examine abstract art and often prefer it to detailed realism.

2. *Plan ahead.* Create a *line of questioning* that leads to a point. Help students see something they would not have seen otherwise. Go for the "Ahhh" or aesthetic response.

3. *Ask open questions:* What do you see? What's this about? What does this tell us about people? What story does this tell? These activate CPS and use higher-order thinking. Assure students that there is no one interpretation of art. Ask for honest responses.

4. *Give time to look.* Encourage curiosity and engagement by guiding students to look carefully. Set an amount of time to observe details and not talk.

5. *Speak at children's level, but don't paternalize.* Relate to their experiences and try to include each child, at least with eye contact. Vary your voice. Smile and make eye contact to sustain attention.

6. *Use wait time and every pupil response (EPR) signals.* More students respond and they have longer and more thoughtful answers if you ask, wait 3 to 5 seconds, and then ask for a signal, such as thumbs up. Wait for everyone for certain questions so that all feel they are expected to be active. Then call on selected students.

7. *If the question doesn't work, rephrase.* Keep trying!

8. *Be sensitive to interests.* Take advantage of unexpected teachable moments to follow through on curiosity.

9. *Respond to children's answers.* Use active listening behaviors. Don't rush or interrupt. Give them time to speak.

10. *Compliment honest and appropriate answers.* Use descriptive feedback, not just praise.

11. *If a wrong response is given, don't embarrass.* Say something like "That's an interesting idea. Who has a different idea?" Use dignifying techniques: Ask the student to explain why he thinks so; ask for ideas of others; try to cue toward accurate answers, so responders save face. *Note:* This only is necessary in obvious situations such as when a student says a Rembrandt painting is by Degas. In this case you might say, "This was done by a Dutch artist but not van Gogh. Do you know another Dutch artist who may have painted this?"

12. *When an answer is partly correct.* Rephrase the question; use the correct information to create another question: "Yes it is true that _____, but let's look again and see if we can find _____."

13. *Follow through on responses:* Ask for evidence for ideas. A sequence is:
    Question: What season of the year is it?
    Answer: Winter.
    Follow-up: How does the artist show this?
    Ask students to tell more about their thinking. Paraphrase responses and ask if you've done so accurately. Ask other students to respond (e.g., What do the rest of you think about Joan's point?).

14. *Encourage student questions.* Make requests such as "What questions do you have?" or invite students to write questions. Put them in a hat and draw them to help students feel safe.

15. *Plan small-group discussion.* Give a few minutes to discuss together: Partner and talk about what choices the artist made to create this work. This allows shy students to participate and prepares all for a large-group discussion. Start with pairs or trios with immature students and work up to groups of 4–6.

16. *End the discussion.* Ask students to tell something they learned, what someone said that made sense, something that was surprising, or what interesting ideas they heard.

---

paintings of nature with activities that promote scientific inquiry.

Literacy. The basic processes for decoding and encoding in visual art and the language arts are the same. The former doesn't use words, however, while the language arts do. Visual literacy is now accepted as a requirement for effective communication. There is mutual benefit when visual art and the language arts are integrated. For example, art vocabulary (e.g., labels for art elements) adds to general vocabulary for reading, writing, speaking, and listening. Students develop all levels of thinking needed for comprehension when they are engaged in art criticism. These are all natural and meaningful art/literacy connections. *Note:* Planning Page 7.1 shows a guided literacy/art lesson.

Ready Reference 6.11   National Standards for Visual Arts

Overall focus: Create, express, and respond through visual media, expression of feelings and emotions, new ways of communicating and thinking, application of knowledge to world problems, historical and cultural investigation, and evaluation and interpretation of the visual world.

1. *Understanding and applying media, techniques, and processes.* Example: Communicate ideas and experiences through visual art. Use materials safely.
2. *Using knowledge of structures and functions.* Example: Explain art messages and what an artist does to convey meaning.
3. *Choosing and evaluating a range of subject matter, symbols, and ideas.* Example: Explain possible content for artwork and ways to show meaning in different ways.

4. *Understanding the visual arts in relation to history and cultures.* Example: Examine how aspects of culture and history are expressed in works of art.
5. *Reflecting upon and assessing the characteristics and merits of their work and the work of others.* Example: Explain purposes for art and how people's experiences influence their art.
6. *Making connections between visual arts and other disciplines.* Example: Find similarities and differences between making visual art and writing. Make art throughout the curriculum to show understanding.

Source: Content Standards (material in bold type) excerpted from the *National Standards for Arts Education,* published by Music Educators National Conference (MENC). Copyright © 1994 by MENC. Reprinted with permission. The complete standards are available from MENC, 1806 Robert Fulton Drive, Reston, VA 20191 (telephone 800-336-3768).

Literature.   Art and literature are naturally connected through picture books. Art strategies can be used before reading a book, during reading, or in response to a book. For example, art strategies can stimulate visual imagery using the actual words of an author. Natalie Babbitt's description that "Mrs. Tuck was a great potato of a woman" can be mined for color, texture, shape, and line. Students can make their versions of this image with collage, drawing, or soft sculpture materials.

Math.   Art and math are integrally related. For example, linear perspective is math based, and both art and math focus on geometric shapes. Planning Page 6.2 is an example of a math and arts integrated lesson using the two-pronged plan format.

Arts.   Art and music share many elements, including rhythm and pattern. Think of looking at art and imagining what you hear. Music can inspire art, and vice versa. Art is used in theatre sets and actors' costumes. Art and dance share elements such as lines that move and shapes that create a composition. Dancers have been an inspiration for art (e.g., Degas's ballerinas).

Arnheim (1989) points out that good work in biology or mathematics is done when the student's natural curiosity is awakened, when the desire to solve problems and to explain mysterious facts is enlisted, and when the imagination is challenged to come up with new possibilities. In this sense, scientific work, the probing of history, or the handling of a language is every bit as "artistic" as drawing and painting.

Unit Types.   Any of the five unit types can be used to integrate visual art: (1) author or artist, (2) genre or form, (3) problem or topic, (4) book, poem, or song, or (5) event or trip (Planning 3.1). Visual art can be the body/center of a unit or one of the legs of the Planning Web. When planning any unit, remember to web ideas, align activities with art and other academic standards, plan initiating or starting events, sequence lessons to develop the unit, and create a culminating event to wrap it up (Planning Page 3.2).

Artist studies.   A common classroom unit that integrates visual art is the artist/author study. The focus is usually creators of picture books. Students engage in art criticism of illustrations, research biographical information, and learn how the artist does creative problem solving to create a unique style. Other arts and subject areas are used to explore the person being studied. Sources for information on artists and authors appear in Planning Page 4.1. Planning Page 6.1 depicts a planning web for an author/artist study. Here are guidelines to plan an artist/author unit. Ready References 6.2 and 6.3 list artists that may be the focus.

Guidelines and ideas.   involve students in the following research, as much as possible.

1. Collect materials about artists. Check publisher's websites and sources in Planning Page 4.1. Books such as *Something about the Author* (Hedblad, 1998) have biographical information, audio and videotapes sources, quotes, and interesting facts.

Unit Web for Artist–Author Study

Chris Van Allsburg
12+ picture books

Center circle: Wife is an elem. tchr. Sculptor - likes to build things. No art classes in high school. Took college art "on a lark." Detail oriented. Pictures → stories. Teaches college art now. Artists he admires: Edward Hopper, René Magritte, Balthus. Studied as a child. "What if..."

Science
- "What if..." in scientific investigation
- Experimenting
- problem-solving
- Wreck of the Zephyr
- Polar Express
- time as a variable
- environmental issues
- Just a Dream
- The Stranger
- seasons — Polar Express
- Fact vs. fantasy — Determining truth or fact
- "What are mysteries" in science?
- animals — wild vs. domesticated, insects
- "What could happen." — Polar Express, Stranger

Art
- Symbols — dog (pay homage), cat (Cecil)
- What do you see? (discussions)
- Strategies — make board game, make alph. bk., cartoon pics w. captions
- Compare with — Balthus, Magritte, Hopper
- use of borders
- cartooned as a child
- lots of detail
- Style — surrealism, pointillism, chiaroscuro
- mood
- Art elements — perspective, odd scale/size, color b+w especially in landscape, texture
- Materials — pastels, pen + ink, charcoal

Drama
- Storytelling from pictures — before / after
- Z was zapped — convert to RT
- interviews
- Verbal — "What if..." conversation time
- Pantomime — "What if..."
- "What if dances" — Detail dances

Dance
- Non-loco / frozen sculptures

Music
- "Ants Go Marching"
- Dreams — sea chanties (Wreck of the Zephyr)
- Songs — Music — mood / mysterious
- Instruments — bell, Violins (Wretched Stone), VA plays recorder
- Compose — find background music for books
- Sounds to go w. rdgs.
- used in film "Jumanji" — What if songs

Soc. St.
- artist training
- book illustrator
- Career — financial
- Geography — Ben's Dream
- History — Ben's Dream
- Selecting
- Social Values — What's important?, text, art
- Economics — bookmaking, book pub.

Math
- math
- measurement — In stories?, patterns
- details
- shapes
- geometry in art
- angles — perspective, VA info. "homage"
- Themes?
- Patterns?

Rdg./LA
- Vocabulary — art terms, words in stories, odd names
- Comprehension — Lit. response options, Story map, Retelling, Discussion etc., student led
- Write poetry — poem patterns, "What if...", Imaginary place
- Write — diary or log, fantasy, book/film review, time variation, setting — landscape, imaginary vs. real
- Read — Reviews + Interviews, 12+ books, Books that are ch. lit.
- Websites
- Info. on author
- Something about the Author

Literature
- Genre — Info = alph. bk, fable, Folktales, Fantasy, picture bk., fairy tale, tall tale
- Archetypes & Motifs — water / dreams, sleep, cycles, magical objects, journey → quest
- Poetry Alive strategies
- Poetry — Dreams, Silverstein's "What if...", Mysteries, Puzzles, Animals, The shrinking of Treehorn
- Book Connections — Imogene's Antlers, Flat Stanley, The Big Orange Slot
- Lit. elements — Mood — text "thru" art, Characters — flat, Plot — cliffhangers — Ants, journey structure
- Themes — Art allows us to express feelings + ideas words cannot. There are things that are unexplainable. Imagination + dreams give us insight. Devil or God is in the details.

2. Make an artist "map" with categories such as: name and vital statistics, books illustrated or main artworks awards, art information, childhood, hobbies, interests, how and why the person creates, quirks, and quotes about or from the person.
3. Read a biography or autobiography. Aliki's *How a Book Is Made* is helpful to learn about artists and bookmaking.
4. Locate where artist lives on a map.
5. Use art criticism questions to discuss the book art.
6. Experiment with the artist's media and styles. Invite a local artist to demonstrate or visit an artist's studio.
7. Find other art and books in the same media and style.
8. Arrange a conference call with the artist. Make contact through the publisher's website and expect a fee.
9. Write a letter or e-mail the artist.
10. Do a presentation on the artist and his or her work. Consider "becoming" the artist and do this in first person.
11. Make a display, posters, or brochure on the artist.
12. Write and bind a book about the author or artist.
13. Interview a local author/artist about the art process.
14. Create artist/author blurbs for class books.
15. Visit a local printing or publishing company.

Field trips with a visual art focus.   Opportunities for art-related field trips abound with virtual trips on the Internet to the Louvre or Museum of Modern Art in New York City. Most museum sites have extensive resources for teachers.

The Smithsonian Institution is the world's largest museum complex. Find activities and information at *http://www.si.edu.*

Hirshhorn Museum and Sculpture Garden's site includes an education section with interactive features (create a sculpture): *www.hirshhorn.si.edu/education/interactive.html.*

Kidsart's website lists top museum sites for students: *http://www.kidsart.com/tt0101.html.* On the list are the National Gallery of Art in Washington, D.C., and the Minneapolis Institute of Arts. The Museum of Fine Art (Boston) and Children's Museum of Indianapolis have wonderful sites, too.

Additional museum websites for students are listed at: *http://princetonol.com/groups/iad/lessons/middle/for-kids. htm# MUSEUM.*

Art connections can be made to most field trips; for example, art such as Picasso's *Paul as Harlequin* or Chagall's *The Blue Circus* can be painted with a circus field trip. Walking trips to examine local architecture of churches, monuments, or cemeteries are chances to build art vocabulary, gather data for an art project, and develop community pride. Just a trip around the block can provide rich images to categorize by colors, lines, shapes, and textures. See Field Trips Guidelines in the Appendix for doing pre-trip, during trip, and post-trip plannng.

Museum trips.   Here are guidelines to make sure students get the most out of a museum visit.

Before the visit: Use Ready Reference 6.12 as a guide to possible activities. Ask if the museum provides materials to prepare and if there will be a docent to guide. Try to get postcards of art children will see. Do sorts, matching, and discussions of elements with the cards.

Study art elements, practice looking at paintings, study artists and forms you'll see, and make a list of what you want to find out together. Plan curriculum connections. For example: math (shapes/size), social studies (portraits/landscapes/events), and science (landscapes/nature/animals). Some recommended books are Brown's *Visiting the Art Museum* and the following:

Browne, A. (2003). *The shape game.* Farrar, Straus & Giroux.

Hooper, M. (2000). *Dogs 'night in the art museum.* Millbrook.

Micklethwait. L. (1993). *I spy two eyes: Numbers in art.* Greenwillow.

Weitzman, J., & Glasser, R. (1998). *You can't take a balloon into the Metropolitan Museum.* Dial.

During the visit: Give students specific things to look for and do. Have students take roles and do close looking, storytelling, and sketching. Students may want to buy postcards to start a personal collection.

After the visit: Follow up with activities to find out what students learned. Ask them to write about favorite paintings or do art response projects (media, styles, forms) and drama. Continue with postcard activities (see Chapter 7).

Projects.   Art-making projects are highly motivational and are a common part of unit study. Projects offer concrete assessment information about learning, as well. They are usually interest and discovery based and may be done in small groups (e.g., murals). Students use CPS and begin with exploration of a problem. The Italian Reggio Emilia schools shape the entire curriculum around hands-on projects that are shared or displayed. A project can involve any media and subject matter and take any of the forms described under "art literacy." The anticipation of a culminating exhibit can drive a unit or an entire school, like Normal Park in Chattanooga, Tennessee.

Two-Pronged Lesson Planning.   Meaningful integration entails the use of lessons with two or more prongs: art and math focus, art and language arts focus, art and dance, and so forth. Planning Page 6.2 shows an art/math example.

Museum Scavenger Hunt

Use before the trip and for activities during the visit.

Ask Students to Find Examples of Art with . . .

- Striking use of colors (e.g., complementary)
- Strong use of line
- Ways artists create texture
- Obvious use of light (white?)
- Different moods
- Shapes and masses (e.g., geometric, organic)
- Subject matter: still life, landscape, portrait, abstract, seascape, cityscape, interior
- Examples of perspective: atmospheric, linear, overlapping
- Lots of detail and ones without
- Unity, as sense of wholeness
- Patterns, motifs, or repeated elements
- Unusual arrangements or compositions
- Media examples: sculpture (materials), watercolor, acrylic, oil, tempera, collage, fabric art
- Different time periods
- Different frames (e.g., oval, fancy gold frame) and the effect

Things to Look for . . .

- What's in the background?
- Eyes: Where do they look? Do they follow you?
- Hands: details? where, why, and how placed? folded?
- Brushstrokes (e.g., scumbling is dry brush painting)
- Edges: lost and found, contours and shadows

Things to Say to Students . . .

- Take a few minutes to look. I'll meet you in the next gallery.
- Look up close, middle, and far away. Find the magic view spot.
- Look closely at details. Go beyond the obvious.

Example Questions

- What is going on in the art?
- What is the mood? How does it make you feel?
- What do you see? Colors? Shapes? Images?
- Where does the artist want you to enter the work? What is the focal point?
- Where does your eye go first? Why? Next?
- Decode or read the painting. Squint. See the shapes and colors. What stands or pops out?
- Use your senses. What do you see? Feel? Smell? Hear? Music? Taste?
- What do you notice about the brush strokes? Why did the artist do this? What is the effect?
- What story did the artist want to tell?
- Find examples of "beauty of the masses."
- What is the subject matter: Landscape? Seascape? Still life?
- Portraits: What about the background? How does it affect the composition? What is the essence of the person? What do you notice about hair? Hands? Eyes?
- What adjectives or nouns can you connect to the art?
- What is the time of day? How do you know?
- Nudity: Why is it used? (e.g., shows timelessness because clothes date; symbol of superiority or nothing to hide; beauty of human curves)
- What about edges? Hard? Lost?
- What did the artist choose to do? What arrangement? What purposes?
- What does the title have to do with the work?
- How does the artist use color to move your eyes?
- What did the artist want you to think or feel?
- How are _____ and _____ alike and different?
- What if _____ was changed? (e.g., size, color, materials)

Blueprint IV: Aesthetic Learning Environment

> *Though we travel the world over to find the beautiful, we must carry it with us or we find it not.* (Ralph Waldo Emerson)

Art-enriched contexts surround students with art and invite them to look closely. Whole schools now strive to create an aesthetic classroom environment for learning (Deasy & Stevenson, 2005). The school campus becomes the site for outdoor and indoor sculpture gardens and flower gardens inspired by Monet's own. There are opportunities to respond to color, texture, line, and shape. As the accompanying Teacher Spotlight shows, however, the individual classroom remains the site of most learning; each teacher creates a unique classroom canvas.

Sylvia Horres's Classroom

A banner proclaims, "Painting the Past: Style of Grandma Moses." Displayed are 15 watercolors by first graders. Not one has a simple band of sky at the top or a mere ribbon of

Art/Math Lesson Plan Grade 4

Two-Pronged Focus: (1) Art elements of shape, pattern and repetition, abstract, and asymmetrical. (2) Math concepts of pattern and geometric shapes.
Art Standards: 1, 2, 3, and 5 (Ready Reference 6.11)
Student Objectives: Students will know and be able to:

1. Use five elements of shape and repetition to create a pattern.
2. Orally label geometric shapes (rectangle, circle, triangle, square).
3. Write examples of how shapes are a part of life and why pattern is important.

Teaching Procedure: The teacher will . . . (S = Students)

Introduction

Post discussion rules: looking closely, use of art materials. Tell S we'll do two silent activities. They are to figure out how they are related.

1. Mystery bag: draw out fabrics in different patterns (dots, plaid, stripes) and tell them to look closely to find what they have in common.
2. Without talking, put five elements of shape word cards in pocket chart (Brookes, 1996): circle, dot, straight line, curved line, and angled line. Gesture for S to draw these. Circulate, smile, and nod as S follow directions. Repeat with eight word cards that have a series of elements to make a pattern (dot, dot, horizontal line, horizontal line, curved down line, curved up line, triangle, triangle).

Development

1. Ask: *How were the mystery bag and the drawing activities related? If necessary, scaffold by holding fabric up to cards. What did both have?*
2. Tell S the goal is to learn the five elements and use them to create an abstract work of art.
   Show two prints: Kadinsky's *The White Dot* and Wyeth's *Due North*. Explain the difference between a reproduction print and an original work of art.
3. Ask: *How are these two artworks alike and different?* Probe for five elements. When they are named, write them on the board.

4. Tell S that Wyeth's work is called realistic because we recognize what it is and Kadinsky's work is called abstract because the focus is on color and elements of shape, not on representing things in a real way—the feel is more important. Label each work.
5. Divide into small groups to find examples of elements of shape, geometric shapes, and patterns (repeated elements). Give each group a clipboard to record.
6. Reassemble and take reports by randomly calling on S.
   Ask: *Why did you find so many examples? Where are there shapes outside of school? Why are patterns made? Used? How do patterns affect people?*
7. Tell about making abstract art: Important to experiment, fill up the space with elements, shapes, patterns. Give paper, markers, and 10 minutes to explore. Play tranquil New Age background music.
8. Reassemble and ask S to tell one thing they discovered about materials, elements, and patterns. Ask if these drawings are realistic or abstract, and why.
9. Do directed abstract activity: Say (1) draw two lines that go to the edges of the paper, (2) draw three dots, (3) draw four curved lines, and (4) draw a circle that touches another line. Fill in all the spaces with colors or collage materials.

Conclusion/Assessment

1. Circulate and give descriptive feedback about elements and concepts as S work.
2. Do art docent talks in fishbowl arrangement, with docents telling elements, shapes, pattern, and how they got ideas. Audience members ask one question or give a comment. Use a writing frame to wrap up: The five elements of shape are _____. Five geometric shapes are _____. When elements are repeated, they form _____. Patterns in my life are (1) _____ and (2) _____.
3. Frame art and put up in class gallery.

---

green grass along the bottom. There are no "joined comma" birds. The space on the paper is completely filled with rolling hills that meet skies of pink, purple, orange, and green—defying any notion that primary children are limited to thinking the sky is blue. There are foregrounds, midgrounds

and backgrounds in each painting, created by roads that narrow in the distance.

Student desks are arranged in sixes, indicating group work is the norm. A set of addition problems, depicted with Picasso-like eyes, bears the title, "Picasso Math." The windows are covered with poetry. An abundance of books fills crates, arranged by levels and topics. There are also manipulatives, calendars, plants, and word webs for Chinese New Year. A large Venn diagram contrasts words for "apple" versus "pumpkin" with shared concepts in the center. Phases of the moon are displayed with black and yellow shapes.

Immersion

Walt Whitman knew little about the brain compared to what we know today. And yet, when he wrote about a child who went forth each day and became the object he looked upon, he poetically expressed what research now confirms: The images that enter the brain become the basis for the images we create and the people we become. Children need to see beautiful images. The same consideration needs to be given to classroom design as is put into our home environments. Broken blinds, dirty floors, mismatched furniture, and peeling paint indicate apathy and imply a low priority for aesthetics.

Children feel and behave better in places that please the senses. Cleanliness is a given. Color schemes need to complement one another. Light should be soft, not glaring white, to relax and make learning pleasant. Storage areas are needed to organize tools and materials. Framed art, live plants, music, pleasant smells, fresh air, and art displays all heighten aesthetic response. Positive attitudes are created and spirits uplifted. While there is no one best aesthetic environment, consider these questions (Jensen 2001; Koster, 1997):

- Is there plenty of soft, natural light?
- Are there carpeted and uncarpeted areas that are visually pleasing, inviting, and functional?
- Are learning centers balanced with open areas?
- Are walls and furniture neutral so there is an illusion of space? (Bold primary colors negatively affect some children.)
- Are walls a neutral backdrop to display art?
- Is student art displayed respectfully?
- Do displays seemed planned or hurriedly put together?
- Is artwork displayed on easels? Is it changed regularly?
- Are art displays at students' eye levels?
- Are bulletin boards teacher made, with cutesy art and cutouts that limit aesthetic response and reinforce stereotypes?
- Are holiday decorations stereotypical? Is cultural art trivialized by displaying it only for holidays?
- Are there focused displays with a few select items at a time?
- Is there organization and order for supplies and books?

Color.   Most people have color preferences, perhaps because the body needs what color gives. We see color by absorbing light through our eyes, where it is converted to energy. Even people without sight feel it. The light energy stimulates the pituitary and pineal glands, which regulate hormones. Red stimulates, warms, and increases heart rate, brain activity, and respiration. Pink soothes and relaxes. Orange makes us hungry and reduces fatigue. Yellow jars memory and boosts blood pressure and pulse rate. Green calms and makes us feel hopeful. We associate it with spring and new beginnings. Blue relaxes by lowering blood pressure, heart rate, and respiration. It makes us feel cooler (Friedmann, 2004, p. 2). Paint colors matter. Pink is currently used in prisons (and Iowa State's opposing team's locker room) and hospitals. Classrooms are painted blue for calming purposes. Shades and values matter too, so do more research before beginning.

Exhibit Space.   An aesthetic classroom needs a place to display artwork. A bulletin board or cork strip can be used for quick displays. A clothesline or drying rack with clothespins or clips can also serve to exhibit completed projects, if art is arranged with some plan. Not all kids want their work up and this should be respected. Some prefer to keep art in a portfolio or scrapbook for personal use rather than public consumption.

Respectful Art.   Children enjoy what is familiar and may shrink from the strange. But if they are to become accepting of dimensions of beauty, they need immersion in all its variations. Classrooms should contain art in many styles showing people of different ages, races, ethnicity, sexes, and skin colors. Art should reflect different places and time periods—images of people going about life in ways that may seem foreign and yet show how basic needs for food, clothing, shelter, knowledge, love, and beauty are universal. Respect for diverse peoples is encouraged when art shows people in dignified, contemporary situations, not just historical garb. Overuse of art showing half-naked Native Americans wearing feathers is inaccurate, to say the least.

Stultifying Art.   Commercial cutouts, cute cardboard pinups, and coloring book art should be avoided because they blunt thinking. Just as damaging are traceable patterns and punch outs of ethnic groups and races dressed in historical costumes, suggesting they are less advanced and still live this way. Think how absurd it would be to shows Americans in Pilgrim outfits as if these are "typical" Americans. Images of Japanese people in kimonos and Eskimos in igloos are limiting, if not balanced with contemporary images. Original art sculptures, fine art prints, postcard prints, and coffee table-type art books are sources of the full range of authentic cultural art.

Art Sources

Students see art and artifacts brought from home (pottery, quilts, photographs) as intriguing sources of aesthetic stimulation and family heritage. Aesthetic sensibilities can be cultivated by planning quiet times to pass around objects for close examination. A "beauty center" stocked with student finds can include shells, leaves, and rocks and serve as discussion starters about the special "magic" feelings possible when you see a field of sunflowers or touch a new baby's velvety hand (Koster, 1997).

Blueprint V: Literature as a Core Art Form

Visual Art–Based Literature

We are blessed with technology that pairs literature with exquisite visual art. In our homes we proudly display pricey coffee table tomes. In schools we have magnificent picture books. Hundreds of books make powerful statements about art's central place in life.

Caldecotts.   The Caldecott Award is presented yearly by the American Library Association (ALA) for excellence in books that contain pictures that are more than illustrations. These are pictures that make aesthetic statements. These books are readily available in schools and are important sources for visual art integration. There are books in most art media and styles. Access the full list of Caldecotts at *www.ala.org.*

Art-Based Literature.   Ready Reference 6.8 lists annotated children's book examples to show the variety of art topics available. These are also valuable resources for units. For example, to introduce artists and art elements:

Anholt, L. (1998). *Picasso and the girl with a ponytail.* Barron.
Johnson, C. (2003). *Harold and the purple crayon: Harold takes a trip.* Piggy Toes Press.
Lionni, L. (1975). *A color of his own.* Pantheon.
Winter, J. (1998). *My Name Is Georgia.* Silver Whistle.

The Appendix has a bibliography of art-based literature. Planning Page 4.1 lists sources for information about artists.

Picture Book Art Integration.   Picture books are now available on nearly any curricular topic. In their short history (about 70 years), they have become a mainstay of the literacy curriculum and are often used as core material in science, social studies, and math lessons. For example, during a Civil War unit, a picture book such as Polacco's *Pink and Say* can give both an aesthetic experience and historical information. *Mirandy and Brother Wind* (McKissack) is a lovely book about a special dance in the African American culture using dialect. Seymour Simon's books are a stunning blend of photography and science.

Any fine picture book can serve as material to develop language and visual literacy skills by using the "What do you see?" strategy described in Ready Reference 6.10. Art strategies to explore picture book art are given in Ready Reference 7.7. *A to Zoo: Subject Access to Children's Picture Books* (Lima, 2005) is a reference that is a bibliography of just picture books, categorized by author, title, and subject or topic. Ready Reference 4.6 lists other print and web based sources.

Reading picture book art.   Here are general guidelines for teaching with picture books.

1. Teach art concepts so students have words to think and talk.
2. Take time to "decode" illustrations. Use magnifying glasses and paper tubes to isolate and examine line, color, and other elements as well as the media, style, and mood. Discuss how the book would be different if the art wasn't included or was in a different style (e.g., cartoon versus impressionistic).
3. Compare the art in versions of the same story. Many folktales, such as *Little Red Riding Hood,* are available in picture books. Do Venn diagrams on chart paper or the overhead.
4. Ape the greats. Use the CPS process (Ready Reference 2.5) to experiment with various media and styles used by artists and try out unusual book formats like pop-ups and shape books.
5. Plan artist-centered units. By examining a body of artwork produced by artists such as Maurice Sendak, Tomie dePaola, or Patricia Polacco, students become versed in the concept of style, grow to understand various styles, and view the creative process closely. Aesthetic development occurs as preferences form, but students can't like what they don't know.

Two recommended references on using pictures books for visual literacy are *The Potential of Picture Books: From Visual Literacy to Aesthetic Understanding* (Kiefer, 1994) and *Picture Books for Looking and Learning: Awakening Visual Perceptions Through the Art of Children's Books* (Marantz, 1992).

Picture book detectives.   Children are more attuned to details than adults and enjoy doing "look closely" with magnifying glasses to find small, surprising aspects of art. For example, artists may insert repeated "side notes" (Chris Van Allsburg puts his dog in most books). Ask students to examine book art to find what the art tells about the following elements.

- Setting: where and when
- Characters: especially body shapes and parts such as hands and faces; look for how characters change from the beginning

- Plot: pictures show events not in the text, even subplots or asides (as in Gilman's *Something from Nothing),* or foreshadow events and create tension with hints and clues)
- Style: use of exaggeration, humor; how mood is created
- Point of view: where the viewer enters the picture

In addition, books can be examined to find (1) whether the story is extended through art or only literally illustrates the text and (2) book parts (endpapers, gutters, borders, double-page spreads, where the story begins in the art).

Questions such as "What does the artist do that surprises you?" and "How does the book make you feel and why?" help children discern aesthetic differences. This can be done with two books: compare details that artists use and the amount of action or movement in the art. Teach students that subtle changes make significant differences: A well-placed bit of line or a small shadow can say so much.

Picture book responses.   Making art is an important way for students to respond to any book. Art can also accompany any writing. It is important, however, for students to learn diverse ways to respond through art. Ready Reference 6.4 lists many media and forms that can be used to respond to picture books. Also see the "Book Report Alternatives" in the Appendix.

Students can also respond to important ideas in any literature by creating art using any of the subject matter that connects: landscape (outdoor scene in the story); portrait (a character in the story); cityscape (view of a city in the story); interior (inside a room or building in the story); seascape (a view of a body of water in the story); still life (nonliving objects in the story arranged on a surface); or abstract (color, shape, line, and texture to express feelings).

Blueprint VI: Best Teaching Practices

Elementary art was not motivating for me because of lack of choice. (Gloria Dalvini, professional watercolorist, Beaufort, South Carolina)

Arts integration takes a discovery orientation that captivates students who ordinarily find schooling uninviting; the "uncommon" is at the core of creating, understanding, and responding. This bent for seeking the unusual increases active involvement and engagement. The questions "what if" and "why not" become forces to propel teachers and students to break out of ineffective traditional modes. Teachers pose questions for which they do not know answers. Students are prompted to "try it" and learn from mistakes. Mistakes are

"re-viewed" as avenues to new understandings and used in the same way watercolorists let the paint direct them. Materials exploration becomes a spark to "see what happens" and then make something of it. Inspiration is oblivious to the perspiration that forms when students are so involved in the work of creativity that they lose track of time and groan when recess is announced. How is this achieved? Much is a result of good teaching. Ready Reference 3.4 summarizes best arts integration practices. Here are elaborations of practices that particularly apply to visual art.

Teacher Roles: Guide and Director

Classroom teachers often lack confidence about their own art abilities and may have limited personal experiences. Lack of confidence manifests itself in rigidity: using precut assembling tasks, painting by number, coloring in the lines, and tracing. The goal is not necessarily student-made art that "looks like something." This book is intended to give enough philosophy, research, and knowledge for readers to reject destructive notions that focus on convenience, tradition (that's the way it's always done), and entertainment. These reasons are not grounded in contemporary child development views and are not what most educators choose for their own sons and daughters. We lay the foundation in the elementary school. That foundation must be strong. Here are signs it is made of straw:

Teachers should NOT . . .

- Model step-by-step directions to copy rather than create.
- Use commercial display materials that are cute and convenient.
- Use stencils/cutters to trace or punch out letters and shapes.
- Make the bulletin boards, rather than having students do them.
- Encourage staying in the lines and stereotypes (e.g., blue sky).
- Do art *for* students or have "artistic" students do it.

Other danger signs include students saying, "I can't do it" or "I can't draw" when art activities are introduced. These comments indicate they have little confidence in their own creativity and don't understand that the focus is on the process, not the product. When children know few ways to express themselves (e.g., stick drawing), it is clear the teacher has not done his or her job in teaching options for materials, techniques, and tools. Finally, when students say that they hate certain styles, like abstract art, without studying them, it is clear teachers have not taught them to understand before they judge.

Creative Problem Solving and Authentic Art

Teachers who are committed to arts integration have a "what-if" perspective. They invite students to experiment, gather ideas, pose potential solutions, reflect, evaluate, and feel the joy of discovery (see the CPS in Ready Reference 2.5).

But CPS creates dissonance and pressing students to deal with it can be exasperating, even for master artists like Georgia O'Keeffe. She spent her early years teaching college in Texas. One day she became frustrated when trying to get her students to think for themselves. She went to the board and wrote, "Would all the fools in this class please leave!" One student immediately asked, "Then who will teach us?" To her credit, Ms. O'Keeffe laughed. Children's author Katherine Paterson reminds us in *Sign of the Chrysanthemum* that "it is only through fire that the spirit is forged." We should not back away from engaging students in CPS. Ready Reference 2.7 gives boosters to massage the process to make ideas more forthcoming.

Visualizing.
Visualization is part of CPS. It uses five distinct mental actions: (1) transfer long-term memories into temporary visual memory, (2) zoom in to identify details, (3) embellish images, (4) rotate image, and (5) scan visually with your mind's eye (Bruer, 1999). Teaching students to create visual images as they read is one of the few strategies known to increase comprehension (Pressley, 2002). We remember in images, not words, what we see, hear, feel, and experience; our mental pictures are actual reconstructions of the neural pathways originally formed during the experience (Siegel, 1999). That's why we say things like "I see what you are saying."

One strategy to develop mental imaging is called *guided visualization*. Students are asked to make mental pictures as a story is read or told. For example, before a plant unit, teachers might describe a trip through a plant. The five mental actions can be evoked with vivid and accurate adjectives. Students can be directed to zoom in on details and elaborate by changing colors, shapes, and textures. The images may be turned upside down or sideways. These are personal pictures, created meanings that motivate students to read and learn more.

Explicit Teaching

Children may be distracted, at first, when they are made aware of what they have been doing unconsciously as they make or look at art. Consciousness is necessary, however, if they are to grow and develop. Mona Brookes (1996), founder of Monart, makes a convincing argument that symbolic art development and the ability to create representa-

tional art are entirely different. She shows how instruction in realistic drawing does not hinder symbolic natural expression. Without instruction, however, she says most children do not automatically discover how to draw realistically. Many abandon drawing by their teens (see more in Chapter 7). Indeed, many adults say they can't draw; they think "drawing" means representing an image realistically and expertly. Interestingly the same level of quality is not demanded to claim reader status as is demanded for "artist" status. We are shocked by print illiteracy and should be shocked by arts illiteracy.

Art-Making Guidelines.
Students do not discover the range of communication possibilities for art by just exploring. Most need explicit instruction in how to use a variety of media, tools, and techniques (Ready References 6.4 and 6.5) and different surfaces (e.g., fabric, wood). Chapter 7 has more art making specifics. Here are general guidelines.

- Provide several examples as references, not models to copy.
- Use an "explore–practice–express" sequence. Exploration piques interest in learning to use tools and materials. Consider a sequence of (a) time to explore, (b) time for practice with feedback, and (c) actual use of materials.
- Demonstrate basic ways to use materials and tools before exploration, especially if there are safety issues. At times, materials and tools can be put out without an introduction to discover possibilities. We do want doers, not just viewers.
- Repeat use of the same materials and subject matter to allow depth of experimentation. This leads to more confidence and skill. The focus remains on involving students in making art.
- Limit direction giving, which creates impatience.
- Give clear feedback: "You have used four shapes" is more effective than "Good shapes!" Describe what students are doing. Use art vocabulary. Focus on what is being learned. "Good job!" and "Great!" teach nothing.
- Also, don't interrupt with comments when students are concentrating and involved.
- Do not insult by asking, "What is it?" Instead, offer comments and ask about art elements or the process: "How did you do this? I see you are trying to put the wash over the candle drawing." Ask about artistic decisions: "Why did you do it this way?" Challenge them to predict: "What do you think will happen if . . . ?" or "How could you . . . ?"
- Expect appropriate behavior. Art making should be a time for concentration. Play music without lyrics (see Chapter 12) and make rules about quiet. Brookes

(1996) believes children must be taught the pleasures of silence because they rarely experience it. She says it takes time for children to be comfortable with quiet, but stresses that it is necessary for concentration.

- After students finish, invite them to do docent talks about their work and explain their CPS process.
- Invite students to write or tell stories about their art, find music that goes with it, or create musical compositions.
- Have students sign their own art, like artists (who usually don't write anything except their signatures *on the art*). Students can then title or write about the art on separate paper at their developmental spelling levels.
- Connect art to students' lives. Instead of isolated art activities or art used as a reward for finishing work, integrate art using the *with, about, in,* and *through* model. Use art in routines and content units in science and social studies.

Teach How to "Read" Art.   Just as the language art of reading is not just "caught" and has to be "taught," so it is with visual art. Students need to be taught art language and concepts so they can understand and discuss their work or that of others. The elements of art are its alphabet or "code." Students learn to decode art through explicit and incidental teaching of basic art elements and concepts. Explicit teaching is described in Chapter 3 and includes teaching what, how, when, and why through demonstration and coached practice. Explicit teaching is accompanied by charts, class word walls, and other visuals that can quadruple retention. Post memory aids to help with concepts like the spectrum—ROY G. BIV is an acronym for red–orange–yellow–green–blue–indigo–violet.

Personal Words.   Students also need personal arts vocabulary references and records. Art "word walls" made with file folders, arts dictionaries using blank books, and word rings (cards punched and hooked on metal shower curtain rings) reinforce vocabulary and build feelings of pride and ownership. These tools help students gain independence with reading art texts. Children are particularly proud when they learn to read book art and use art terms to discuss illustrations in science and social studies books, often better than their parents.

Evaluative Judgments/HOTS.   Students don't automatically know how to make good judgments, especially when looking at art. Without instruction, they tend to want to stop at loving or hating a work. These reactions halt thinking. Children need to be taught to take time and describe what they see and the feelings the art evokes. They can be coached to create stories (interpretations) from art. Art criticism is teachable, even to primary students. "Think-alouds" can be used to model critique that rests on giving evidence for opinions. Ratings of judg-

ments (1 to 5 scale) of "goodness," or how much a work is liked, can be used, too, and then discussed. These practices create an expectation for reflection, first. Respect for considered thinking can be taught so breezy conclusions are soon seen as just that. Ultimately, students need to grasp that to appreciate art means to understand it, not that you have to like it.

Aesthetic Orienting

A first-rate soup is more creative than a second-rate painting. (Abraham Maslow, quoting a client, 1968)

Teachers need not be able to draw realistically or sculpt well to help children do so. Artistic teachers are those who set up an aesthetic classroom, ask provocative questions, respond with descriptive comments, and model how to listen, look, and feel the world's beauty. Here are four other strategies.

Aesthetic Scanning.   Norton (2003) describes "aesthetic scanning" as a scaffolded sequence in which students look closely at picture book art to describe the emotions, meanings, organization, and how the art was created (pp. 140–141). Show students that by taking time to notice details, new discoveries can be made about everyday things. Use cardboard tubes or magnifying glasses to examine fabrics and art for details. Colored transparencies and transparency frames make interesting "windows" to focus attention. Books such as Hoban's *Look Again* can be inspirations to analyze the visual world by looking at parts of plants, animals, and clothes. Hoban overlays frames over photographs to cause viewers to see only a tiny piece of a whole, such as a seed or a tail. A similar effect can be achieved using note cards or sticky notes to mask part of a picture (e.g., mask half of a print and predict images, colors, and shapes). Model use of descriptive language such as "I see rounded shapes or a muddy brown color" and ask students to describe using the "I see . . . and . . . structure."

Aesthetic Aromas.   The perfume industry knows well the power of smell to affect behavior. We avoid nasty smells and seek out attractive aromas. A classroom with fresh flowers, potpourri, and fresh air provides for aesthetic sensing and creating. Encourage students to share discoveries about good smells through discussions, journals, and on group-made charts. Give feedback to stretch language and encourage use of descriptive words; for example, "You have a lemony clean smell!"

Aesthetic Sounds.   Easy rhythm instruments can be made to explore the differences in sounds. For example, put beans in a butter tub or make sand blocks by gluing sandpaper to old cassette tape cases. Record environmental sounds and create art to go with the sounds. At times, play music as students make art. Discuss art in terms of the sounds associated with it (e.g., a seascape or landscape). Write sound poems about art, like this onomatopoeia example about a schoolday: "Ring/ha ha ha/patter patter/slam/creak/ring ring/ achoo/gobble crunch slurp/scribble/sigh/whew/ ring/trip-trap, trip-trap/honk toot roar."

Texture/Touch Aesthetics. Here are ways to develop tactile perception so students grasp the concept of texture in artwork.

1. Ask students to describe feelings as they finger paint, use collage, and try chalk using different pressures. Model this, saying, "When I press hard, the line is darker and thicker."
2. Make feely bags. Put them at a station or use for circle times; students reach in and either describe the item's nature or use it in an add-on story. For example: "There was once a thin bendy creature who wore paper clothes"(stick of gum).
3. Ask students to bring items for topical displays on rough, soft, silky, cold, or hard.
4. Go on texture walks to find thin, thick, and heavy items. Use items for "found things" collages or table displays.
5. Make texture books (e.g., fabrics, foils, papers) by gluing items to card stock and fastening with brads or make big books with text from students.

Process and Product

> *Dictated art is not art but a contradiction of it.* (Blanche Jefferson)

Integration includes looking at and understanding art as well as making it. A balance is needed between creation and appreciation, impression and expression, viewing and doing. All of these draw on mental and physical processes. Students are taught to look at art using seeing and thinking processes that result in conclusions (mental products). In making art there are processes for working with media, tools, and techniques to create tangible products. Balance is needed, with a tilt toward process for children P-6. It can be achieved by assuming an inquiry or studio attitude so children have ample time to explore. This is parallel to writing workshops that budget time to "mess around" with new materials and ideas. Students can use the time to do what most of us did when we first used computer drawing tools—scribble and experiment. Children need to have permission to do the same if the CPS is to proceed. Once students gain confidence with tools and materials, they want to do art making. Criteria for quality products can then be introduced to motivate work toward excellence.

Process and product are balanced similarly when the focus is on understanding the work of others through close looking investigations. Artists and their works are examined, art is placed in contexts, and there is opportunity to reflect and refine aesthetic thinking. Memorizing names and dates of artworks is not useful. Nor is copying ideas. The hub of these discussions is the thinking process. Like adults, children do "borrow" ideas. Urge them to adapt these for their own work and learn art terms to describe aesthetic qualities (e.g., color, texture). This knowledge is a valued product. Thus process and product are again balanced, with weight given to the former.

Dictated Art. If black outlined material is occasionally used, it should not be called "art." Teachers should, at minimum, encourage some CPS: add lines, use unconventional colors, tear off sections, paste materials on, add captions or titles, and scrunch the paper to give it texture. The question is, Why use the outlines to begin with? Giving blank paper for free drawing isn't great teaching, but is preferable because children have to make more decisions. Instructional choices should be measured by their ability to move students toward independent problem solving. Dictated art does little to prepare students to live in a democratic country whose citizenry values freedom, independence choice, and individuality.

Blueprint VII: Instructional Design: Routines and Structures

Visual art integration becomes a way of life when it is institutionalized through predictable routines. Teachers can make it a habit to use visual art strategies to introduce, develop, and/or conclude lessons (see IDC in the teaching procedure, Planning Pages 3.3 and 6.2). Here are other ways teachers organize to visual art integration.

Energizers and Warm-Ups

Visual art energizers and warm-ups can be used in lesson introductions to activate visual thinking. They stimulate the senses and prepare students for using the CPS. Of particular importance is teaching students to think like an artist, which includes strategies to spark ideas and overcome blocks. Mr. Novak used the Mystery Bag energizer in the opening Snapshot. There are many other examples in Chapters 7, 9, 11, and 13.

Daily Routines and Rituals

The goal is for students to take responsibility for routines that start and wrap up the day. For shy students, use a puppet (named "Art" with a smock and beret) to speak to the group. Daily riddles, poems, and songs about art and artists can be found or cowritten. For example, Barbara Streisand's song "Putting It Together" is about making art. Examples of routines to start or end the day include docent talks, Print of the Day, and I Spy.

Docent Talks.   The word *docent* simply means "teacher" and has long been used in the art world. Art docents give museum tours to teach about art and artists. When students do docent talks, they present a piece of art (original or that of an artist). Students tell about the media used, aspects of the creative process tried, what they learned by experimenting and making mistakes, etc. Classmates then respond with descriptive feedback about what they see or how the piece makes them feel, or they may ask the docent questions. A special artist's chair can be used to share information.

Print of the Day.   In this opening routine a piece of art is displayed. A question(s) is posed for students to think or write about: What title would you give this art (main idea)? What words describe how it makes you feel (adjectives)? How did the artist cause the feeling (cause-effect)? What catches your eye first (priorities)? What can you find that no one else will (details)? How would a mathematician describe this art? What would a scientist see (point of view)? These questions cause students to do both critical and creative thinking. After a few minutes, discuss in pairs or small groups or as a class.

Teachers may use the same art all week with a different question each day. Teachers can also give the title, before showing the art, and ask for predictions about art elements such as colors, lines, shapes, and media (categorical and hypothetical thinking). Students should be asked to give evidence for responses to emphasize justifying conclusions. The "full reveal" follows and close looking confirms or disproves predictions.

I Spy.   Students are prompted to notice details and patterns in art. A large magnifying glass adds fun. Start by saying something like, "I spy four geometric shapes or three primary colors" as a challenge to look closely. Students examine details of the composition and volunteers "show they know" with the magnifier. A student is chosen to then lead the I Spy challenge work well.

Art Discussions

Art-based discussions focus on criticism and aesthetics. They can take place daily, connected to read-alouds, guided reading groups, or social studies and science. The goal is engaged meaning making accomplished through problem solving. Any material can be used, including student art and picture book art. Art prints are available from companies such as Shorewood or the National Gallery. Many are just a dollar. Calendar art goes on sale for up to 75 percent off in January. Invite students to bring in prints, sculptures, and paintings to use as well.

The first step is to "look closely." Students learn to concentrate and take time (most people average less than 10 seconds looking at museum art). Start by asking students to describe the art. "What do you see?" is the main question (subject matter and art elements). Follow with these:

1. How did the artist make this? (media/techniques)
2. What arts elements and design principles were used?
3. Where/how might the artist have gotten ideas?

Next, ask for interpretations: "What does this mean? Why do you think the artist did that?" Finally, ask students to create stories about the art; interpretive and creative discussions are more engaging than focusing on identification or description.

In the Partial Picture Preview variation, a section of the art is shown and students are asked to predict the content of the covered portion. Another effective strategy is to ask groups to choose a section on which to focus (e.g., background). Groups can then serve as "experts" on their sections. Another strategy is to ask students to imagine what happened one minute after the art piece was finished. This can evolve into a writing or drama activity. Besides using a magnifier to see more brush strokes, shapes, and colors, use a flashlight or laser pointer to highlight areas.

Eventually, students see how artwork done by others expresses diverse messages and gives insight. Group discussions move into more meaningful areas. Students become comfortable expressing their concerns under safe, structured circumstances where unique perspectives are valued and learn to lead discussions. Ready Reference 6.10 has how-to discussion ideas and there are more guidelines in Chapter 4 and the Appendix.

Stations and Centers

Centers and stations provide opportunities for independent work that extends a lesson or a personal interest. A center does not have to be elaborate. Continuous centers or a station (a place with a single focused activity) might include:

Book-Making Station.   with wallpaper, fabric, and other materials to bind student-made books.

Puppet-Making Station.   with examples of different types of puppets and materials to make them (see the types in Ready Reference 7.4).

Books About Art and Artists.   in a book nook center with shelves or areas with children's literature related to other arts areas.

Art-Making Corner.   Art opportunities need to change every few weeks. One month the corner can be a collage center with small containers of feathers, buttons, and a variety of papers. Then transform the space into a sculptor's studio with modeling clay, play-dough, and simple tools (popsicle sticks or plastic knives). Watercolors, pastels, markers, watercolor crayons, and a posted list of ideas to try should be available. See possibilites in Ready Reference 6.4. Include a few books that show how artists use different media and styles (Ready Reference 6.9).

Multicultural Arts Center.   Include many examples of different kinds of art and actual artifacts. This is a place to include a picture file of art to examine for different styles or media.

Masterpiece Corner.   Display art prints at children's eye level on easels, which adds a feeling of importance, because easels are special art furniture. (Find easels at flea markets for as little as a dollar.) Use the ideas previously given for the art discussion routine. For example, display a question with a print as a journal stimulus: "Why do you think the artist chose to paint this?" Postcards, matching the large print, can be used to make comparisons or to set up as a matching station. Or buy two copies of the same print and cut one up so students can attend to art details by matching pieces with the whole. Provide information about artists and share books about artists when displaying a work of art. Krull's *Lives of Artists* is a source, and others are given in the Appendix under Arts-Based Children's Literature.

Note: Be sure to tell students that prints and posters are not the original art so they understand the real thing may be much larger and look different. Students are usually interested in the dimensions of original art and locations where they might travel to see it in a gallery.

Beauty Center.   A small table can be designated for students to display items they consider beautiful. This simple area can send students on a year-long search and invite endless discussions. Students can also be shown how to make personal Beauty Boxes with collections of pictures and objects that evoke pleasant responses. Box items can prompt writing and start discussions about individual concepts of beauty.

Blueprint VIII: Adaptations for Diverse Needs

Children who are encouraged to draw and scribble stories at an early age will later learn to compose more easily, more effectively, and with greater confidence. (U.S. Department of Education, *What Works: Research About Teaching and Learning* (1986))

Visual Art and Child Development

Children's early drawings are no longer seen as poor attempts at art, anymore than babbling is considered bad speech. It is clear that art reflects cognitive, affective, and physical development. Children's drawings reveal how they think, their emotional state, and fine and gross motor development. Symbolic drawing development grows in stages, similar to growth in verbal communication. Beginning with the basic art element of line, art development can be seen in toddlers who use art tools to extend fingers to make marks. Small steps lead to giant leaps and general abilities become increasingly refined. Artistic developmental signs show the cognitive and physical growth necessary to write; drawing tools are writing tools, too. Art lines and shapes are the same as those used in handwriting—circles, horizontal, vertical, slant, and curved lines.

Meaningful Scribbles.   Kellogg (1969) broke the ground in recording children's art development. She spent 20 years collecting more than 1 million samples of children's drawings that unveiled a universal artistic journey. The early developmental sequence moves from random scribbles to more controlled scribbling and then to formation of enclosed shapes that show increased understanding of spatial relationships. Shapes evolve into symbols, like mandalas and suns, used to create people shapes. Ready Reference 6.13 shows the stages. Lowenfeld and Brittain (1987) extended Kellogg's work through the adolescent years and theorized that children make advances naturally, without being taught to draw. By age 9, base lines and skylines appear, and "x-ray drawings" show understandings about the unseen. By age 12 many begin to abandon spontaneous drawing.

Developmental Stages or Waves.   Gardner (1990) postulates that development occurs in waves rather than stages. Waves of knowledge rise and then spill over into other intelligences. For example, children draw animals and make the sounds of the animals as they draw, which pulls musical intelligence into the visual-spatial. More commonly, general stages are used to *describe* children's development; they should not *prescribe* what they can or can't do (Wachowiak & Clements, 2005). It is impossible to categorize a child using age or grade characteristics; even identical twins are different because of their experiences. Children are products of genetics and their experiences—nature and nurture. This must be remembered as descriptors are used to plan for strengths and accommodate needs. It also is important to understand that later is not better. Artists like Pablo Picasso and Henry Miller worked to recapture art thinking from their childhoods and that produced masterful art. See Appendix for more about Developmental Stages.

Ready Reference 6.13 From Scribbles to Pictures

Note: Children's drawings reflect growth in thinking (cognition) and in physical control (gross and fine motor) over materials and art tools.

Ages	Benchmarks
1–2 years	*Random scribbling.* Exploration of tools and materials, showing increasing fine and gross motor control. Single and multiple dots and lines (vertical, horizontal, diagonal, and wavy) produce some 20 basic scribbles that eventually include loops, spirals, and circles. Examples:

2–7 years	*Shape making.* Scribbles begin to be intentionally used to make basic shapes or diagrams. Children combine shapes and use overlapping. Eventually, the shapes form aggregates (three or more diagrams together). Examples:

3–5 years	*Symbol making.* Lopsided geometric shapes are made. Mandalas and suns are drawn and evolve into human figures. At first, arms and legs stretch from the head. Eventually, torsos emerge and human figures are drawn with more and more completeness. Examples:

Sources: Based on Kellogg (1969) and Lowenfield and Brittain (1987).

Human development is more spiral than sequential, with a gradual building during which children may skip or reverse stages depending on things like how familiar they are with materials (p. 33). We all tend to regress to "messing around" when we try a new tool, just to see how it works. Patterns of development are more obvious in early years before culture and education do major sculpting of children's minds. Education matters. Different cultures emphasize different aspects as well (e.g., realism not as important in some). As in all development, interests play a powerful role and further individuate development. In general the stages begin to become muddied as diversity increases. Predicting becomes more and more difficult.

In visual art "observed knowledge" is a big player in development. Instruction alters the quality of the development of the ability to see and to do art. As more and more detail emerges, we can infer the child has keenly observed art elements in the world. Each piece of art is tangible evidence of connections forged in the child's brain. Instruction is everything. Without teaching, students can stall in their development, lose interest, and get frustrated. Finding your medium is one of life's mysteries and some never do. Imagine Michelangelo without marble or Alexander Calder without mobiles. It is hard to predict how specific children will respond to media/tools (e.g., clay vs. drawing). Diverse experiences are vital.

General patterns of artistic growth. Artistic development parallels cognitive, physical, and socioemotional growth outlined by theorists such as Piaget, Erikson, Maslow, and Gardner (see Chapter 2). In general it proceeds in the following directions.

General to specific. or wholes to parts, with increasing attention to detail. For example, drawing starts with tadpole-like and stick figures using geometric shapes and moves to bending limbs, curved and sausage limbs, joints, and use of overlapping and foreshortening. At first, figures float with no base. Proportion/size is used by young children to show what is most important (e.g., big head). Stereotyped colors for grass and sky are still common in primary grades, but color is used expressively, too, to show emotions.

Uncontrolled to controlled. from exploration of media and tools to skilled use of lines, shapes, and colors to represent ideas.

Known to seen. At first people are drawn with general traits children "know," not what they really look like (Wachowiak & Clements, 2005). As children develop, they notice more. What they see changes what they know. While older children are more conscious of "feelings," younger children do use color, lines, and shapes expressively.

Me to others. Children become increasingly group/peer oriented, with steady growth of interest in the community and the world.

Single to multiple perspectives, with increasing use of evidence to draw conclusions. As children become more logical and more systematic, they gain ability to self-evaluate.

"Abstract" to realistic, first with images that represent the "known" and show feelings. These evolve into realistic images, which peaks about age 11. *Note:* Paul Klee and others try to recapture early "naïve" perceptions.

Gender awareness. Children increasingly show more boy/girl details, like hair and clothes, in their art.

Art preferences grow from art that connects to personal interests, to preference for realism, and finally to diverse understandings and tastes that reflect experiences (i.e., understand expressive art and use art in more expressive ways).

The brick wall. Art educator Mona Brookes (1996) offers an explanation for why some youngsters stop drawing. Children naturally produce symbolic drawing, based on what they "know," not what they "see." It develops in a predictable way like all communication. Young children create symbols for animals, people, and trees and talk to themselves as they draw, often telling a story. For example, "Here is my cat, Tigger. Charles taught her to sit up and dance like a bear." Symbolic drawing usually culminates in abstract stick-figure images.

About age 8 or 9, children give up symbolic drawing and want to draw realistically so others recognize the images. Brookes and others argue that this realistic drawing skill doesn't usually happen without instruction (Brookes, 1996; Wachowiak & Clements, 2005). To show the impor-

tance of instruction, Brookes gave children prompts to "draw a person," which produced stick-figure images. After one lesson on analyzing shapes and attending to detail, the drawings showed dramatic differences. Brookes teaches a drawing alphabet with five elements of shape to "analyze and break down what is seen" so they can "see with an educated eye" (p. xxx). While children can be taught to do realistic work, she emphasizes that they should be free to do symbolic drawing (1996).

Writing parallels. Writing development is similar to drawing development. Spelling/handwriting begin with scribbles and "pretend writing." Spelling proceeds from gross approximations, using just beginning and ending sounds to represent words, to greater accuracy. Details of words, especially the middles or the spellings for the schwa sound, are the last to develop. For example, the word *bird* evolves from B to BD to BRD to BerD to bird. Educators recognize the need for visual pattern instruction to teach conventional spelling. Children need the same to grow in their use of art symbols.

Early Primary K–2 Suggestions.

Art discussions. Younger children are more concrete and less product oriented. They like bright colors and may prefer abstract or simplified representational art. Students can describe the subject matter but have trouble with style and composition. They like to pretend and take roles in art and do "what-if" discussions. Teach concepts like cool/warm colors using matching (paint chips) and mixing. They can usually connect personal experiences to art and learn arts vocabulary.

Art making. Students are interested in topics like animals, games, toys, and weather as art subjects, and they can tell stories about their art. Keep directions short and supervise work by coaching. Let students repeat subjects and try new tools like sticks to engrave. Use big paper and coach them to fill the page. Show them how contrast is created with light/dark shapes. Involve students in cooperative murals, printing with erasers, clay, found objects, hands, and feet. Use clean Styrofoam trays for incised relief prints. Show students how to pinch, poke, stretch, coil, and ball clay. Use the subtract versus add method for stable sculptures.

Primary/Intermediate Grades 3–4 Suggestions.

Students are being drawn toward realism but abstract art coexists, so art doesn't have to "look right" to them. This is a transition period during which students rely on what they know, but this is now being informed by what they see. They are able to focus more and are interested in other cultures, life processes, plants, and animals.

Art discussions. Students can look at art longer and use more arts vocabulary. They can compare and contrast art and recognize style, media, and forms.

Art making.   Children now are more deliberate and like to plan their art. Shapes are more in proportion, and they like to use action. They can be taught color mixing for tints and shades and use of the color wheel. Students can be shown how to use diminishing size and overlap and how to create a horizon. Sketch trips help students see distance, overlap, pattern, and texture in the world. Contour drawing with fat soft pencils is recommended. Use everyday objects and direct attention to the environment for radiating lines, colors, patterns, and emphasis in nature. Teach how to make collage by tearing, pleating, and curling for texture and use tissue paper for topics like dreams, moods, and sounds. Use collages to teach postive/negative shapes. Continue with prints made with vegetables, clay, and found objects, and work with clay pinch pots.

They now can do some self-evaluation of their work so help them consider criteria like variety and filling page.

Upper Grades 5–6 Suggestions.   "Identity versus role confusion" is the main crisis (Erikson, 1950) at this stage, and students have self-doubts that can carry over into art. Making art may decline if they believe they are no good at it. Students become self-critical, but this can be put to good use to engage them in identifying strengths and needs in their own work. They tend to conform and want to "do it right," so teachers need to show diverse examples of "good art" and ask students what they notice. They will experiment with tools, techniques, and media in a supportive environment.

Students need to be taught more art vocabulary, tools, and skills, or they remain static or even regress. Aesthetic discussions help to stretch the concept of good art so they do not overly focus on realism. Students need freedom to use their more developed individual interests. Students are gender and group focused. They are interested in heroes, history, community, and environment. They need personal time to reflect and concentrate using sketch journals.

Art discussions.   Students can discuss compositional features, style, mood, and symbols and compare and contrast works by form and meaning. They like to learn tricks of the trade like the speech bubbles and stars to show violence in comics. They need more arts vocabulary to see more for discussions. They are impressed by size and cost of art and why the artist did what he did. Interest in the surreal (macabre/bloody) emerges. Metaphoric images are understood (e.g., isolation represented by a single flower). The preference for super realism doesn't peak until about age 11, so stretch them by asking for evidence for preferences to expand thinking.

Making art.   Students can use perspective, shadows, movement, and overlap. Challenge them to create unity. Continue contour drawing. They have more advanced color awareness so direct attention to the environment and show more mixing. Collages can be used to teach positive and negative space in 3D. Students can be taught to score to indent paper to tear. Printing remains important and students can do linoleum prints.

General Preferences.   Children prefer realistic works, especially in upper elementary. Use single subjects with young children and more complex compositions with older students. Subject matter is the primary factor in children's preferences, and there is a strong difference between boys and girls. They may react negatively to abstract art or works showing objects they don't like, such as dead animals. Alternatively, if a primary child likes dogs, he will probably like dog art. The second most important factor is color. Primary children prefer lots of contrast and color. Older students prefer more tints and shades (Wachowiak & Clements, 2005).

Differentiating Instruction

At all stages children have certain common needs; they are more alike than different. For example, all children benefit from learning in an aesthetic environment from a teacher who uses best practices. All students need to be stretched to make visual discoveries and, in general, achieve more when there is an inquiry stance to learning and teaching.

Children also have differences. Chapter 3 presented a set of 10 strategies to differentiate instruction, called PARTICULAR. These are some ways to meet developmental and special needs of students:

Place: Set up work areas with fewer distractions.

Amount: Use projects that require a few simple steps for children who need success.

Rate: Go more slowly with directions and allow more time to finish.

Target objectives: Make the goals clearer by showing more examples.

Instruction: Give more explicit instruction with clear art language; build in more repetition through questioning and choral responses.

Curriculum materials: Use more visual aids (e.g., color wheel, elements chart with symbols, and personal elements charts for each desk to help remember all the things to try).

Utensils. Use a children's rotary cutter for those who cannot handle scissors. Tape paper to the table so that it won't move. Use scented paint and markers for those who have limited sight. (Scents can be added, like lemon.) Attach drawing and painting tools to head gear or tape to a hand to improve control. Thicken paint and use shorter and larger brushes. Use collage materials that can be arranged and rearranged. Start with larger pieces or objects that are easy to grasp. Wrap crayons and markers with masking tape or foam curlers to provide better grips.

Level of difficulty: Build in more time to explore materials so that students feel more in control.

Assistance: Use the "guided hand technique" to help students get the feel of drawing or painting (put your hand over theirs or theirs over yours); allow students to work with a partner.

Response: Consider different ways students can respond other than the project selected. For example, give materials choices, rather than all make a paper bag puppet from collage materials. Consider stages, interests, background, and unique needs when designing art-making or art-looking lessons.

The Appendix offers more suggestions for working with students with special needs.

Websites

The Federal Citizen Information Center *http://kids.gov/ k_ arts.htm* offers links and clear information about developmentally appropriate art lessons.

This University of Florida site details developmental stages: *www.arts.ufl.edu/art/rt_room/teach/young_ in_art/intro.html.*

Arts Education Partnership (*www.aep=arts.org/ publication.htm*) offers a downloadable publication on developmental stages called *Young Children and the Arts: Making Creative Connections* (1998).

Blueprint IX: Assessment for Learning

Chapter 3 described four purposes of assessment that are congruent with arts integration philosophy. The most important is using assessment to motivate and modify learning and teaching. All the guiding principles and characteristics of good assessment apply to visual art integration (i.e., continuous, multifactored, authentic, and focused on strengths and needs). Because visual art has obvious "products," it is important to keep in mind that the thinking and working processes are still the focus of assessment.

Exhibits.   Displays of artwork are important for their motivational power and to show evidence of learning. In addition to 2D art exhibits, designated tables or cases for completed projects are ideal ways to make learning public. By expecting students to have three-dimensional work others will want to see, we change how they think and plan. That's the assessment *for* learning idea. Meaningful displays include titles with works "tagged" so that others understand their significance, much like a museum plaque. Teachers and students use criteria for art displays to direct the process for creating work and focus attention on what makes quality work. Such criteria are needed for the visual environment of the whole school. Refer to the Blueprint section on aesthetic environment for ideas and consider asking a museum professional to collaborate on designing exhibit space for schoolwide displays. The Appendix offers examples of assessment tools, and a rubric is included at the end of the final Classroom Snapshot in this chapter. Two points, more specific to visual art, are discussed next.

Task Completion.   While the emphasis of visual art integration is on process, it is important that students finish work, which demonstrates persistence and commitment. It is difficult for teachers and students to judge artwork unless it is completed. The satisfaction of success is withheld, too, if effort is not made to reach closure. Self-discipline is developed by working through problems and frustrations with support. Therefore, it is important to insist an art project, once undertaken, be carried as far as possible, especially if it is self-chosen. This is not an unwarranted imposition. Anybody who has watched children "spend long periods of time on some challenging piece of construction or deconstruction knows that there is no end to patience, once the goal is sufficiently attractive" (Arnheim, 1989, p. 34). Task completion is expected in other curricular areas to show evidence of learning and should be a goal that is assessed in visual art.

Student Portfolios.   Student growth, both artistic and otherwise, can be documented by setting up a portfolio for each student. Most are organized around a few goals, attached to the front of a container, that are aligned with visual art standards (national/state/local). Clear goals serve to motivate students to want to reach them. Two basic goal categories are (1) knowledge and skills to make art and (2) knowledge and skills to read/understand art. These parallel "comprehension" and "composition" goals in reading and writing.

Progress in using art vocabulary, media, and tools should be tracked. Arts teachers with hundreds of students cannot do this kind of assessment. At integrated arts schools classroom teachers are increasingly taking this on because they realize the power of assessment to motivate learning. For example, several schools in Chattanooga have designated a few visual art goals for each grade level by working with arts specialists. Teachers set up student art folios that are mostly maintained by students. For large art samples, a container is made using packing tape to bind together two large pieces of cardboard and connecting strings to tie it shut.

Items placed in the collection are dated and titled. A note is attached about the media and the assignment to explain how it is connected to one or more of the goals. Teachers conference with students using these portfolios, and there are regular times for students to share folios with peers and others. See details on arts folios in the Appendix on assessment.

Program Evaluation.   For checklists to assess the visual arts component of arts integration, go to *www.winthrop.edu/ABC/*. South Carolina ABC Schools have converted the Opportunity to Learn Standards into a useful format for this purpose.

Blueprint X: Arts Partnerships

Life is a great big canvas and you should throw all the paint you can on it! (Danny Kaye)

Potential visual arts partners with classroom teachers include the school art teacher, local artists, teaching artists, museum professionals, and gallery owners. There are a wide range of artists in any community, from sculptors and jewelry makers to quilters, potters, and newspaper photographers. Videographers/camera people from the local television station may be available for at least a guest spot.

Artist Dee Mayes works on stained glass project.

Collaboration between classroom teachers and art specialists are only fruitful if all participants feel there is a common need and each person plays an important role. While the classroom teacher will know the students better, the specialist knows more about art, which brings expertise and depth to art integration efforts. Meaningful integration rests on the knowledge and commitment of the teachers and arts specialists and the ways in which available resources are connected and then sequenced.

A successful collaboration begins with planning together. Chapter 3 outlined guidelines for collaborative planning in the Arts Integration Blueprint. In particular, the information in Section III: "Collaborative Planning," and Section X: "Arts Partnerships," regarding planning residences needs to be reviewed. The unit development process (Planning Page 3.2) is a helpful guide.

The focus of any planning should be on standards and goals and finding natural connections between visual art and other curricular areas. Clusters of standards that overlap visual art and other curricular areas can be found by "scanning" for common processes and content. This should happen, to some degree, even for a guest appearance.

If specialists are from outside the school, they may not be aware of safety concerns related to toxicity of materials and fumes from markers and sprays. This needs to be discussed. Also discuss the appropriateness of art subject matter. Nudity in art may be a problem for a particular school context.

Teachers should remember that specialists may not have a wide range of teaching strategies and need to understand that children need active involvement through questions, visual aids, and demonstrations rather than a lecture. Discuss a lesson introduction that begins with questions or a demonstration. Planning Page 6.3 shows a unit planned by a stained glass artist and a fourth grade teacher around shared concepts about communication.

Community-based programs may offer trained volunteers to teach lessons about artists and subject matter or to do art projects. Arts Go to School is often based in a museum, and volunteers are trained as docents to go into classrooms. An example in operation is at the Ella Sharp Museum (*www.ellasharp.org*) in Jackson, Michigan. Springfield Museum of Art in Springfield, Ohio, has a similar program (*www.spfld-museum-of-art.org*). Contact museums nearby about school programs or discuss starting one of the above with education curators.

Hollie's Stained Glass 9–Day Plan

Hollie Steele, Grade 4, Battle Academy; Dee Mays, Stained Glass Artist, Chattanooga, Tennessee

Big Ideas

1. The more ways we have to communicate, the better we can express our thoughts/feelings and understand others. We use more than words to communicate.
2. Art, reading, and writing share the same CPS process and many of the same words and concepts.
3. You can read thoughts and feelings in art.
4. People affect each other's lives.

Essential Questions

1. How is the visual art process like/different from the language arts? Why are both called *arts*?
2. Why are all the arts important to communication?
3. What makes a good reader/writer/artist?
4. How do other people's stories help us to plan our lives?

Shared vocabulary/concepts: BDA (before, during, after)/BME (beginning, middle, end) reading sequence/ plot, "stories" (in stained glass and reading), symbols, compare-contrast, line, strategy, biography
Reading vocabulary: almanac, indentured servant
Art vocabulary: mosaic, tile, grout, shape, texture
Materials: Books: *Molly Bannacky* by Alice McGill, *Dear President Jefferson*. Materials: glass, white paper, grout, Elmer's All Glue

Timeline (9 days) Teaching Procedure (S = Students).

Day 1: Art Preview of *Dear President Jefferson* (first African American almanac writer and mathematician, Benjamin Bannacker). Ask S to tell what they see. Ask how art elements make them feel. Ask what the message of the art is and how it is we can read it without words. Read aloud, stopping to ask about art messages. Explain biography. Ask about why we need to know about people who made an *impact* (a word on TN test) in our lives. Brainstorm people who have made an impact on their lives.

Day 2: Focus on the book's sequence/plot. Ask S to make mental pictures of something that happened in the beginning, then middle, and then the end (BME). Partner to share, then ask for volunteers to describe one of each. Prompt: What colors, shapes, lines, and textures do you image? Post an Arts Vocabulary Chart for reference. Ask about (1) importance of images in reading and art and (2) sequence the writer must have used to write the book: pre, during, post. Choose one person from the brainstorm. Begin interview and writing biographies about a person in their lives. (Homework: Interview person)

Day 3: Do an Art Preview and read aloud *Molly Bannacky.* Synopsis: *English milkmaid tips her pail, which is considered stealing. She is saved from death because she can READ, but is banished to the American colonies. She earns her freedom, starts a farm, and buys a slave whom she teaches to read. They fall in love and marry. One of her grandsons is Benjamin Bannacker, whom she taught to read.* Ask why reading is important. Discuss what good readers do before, during, and after (BDA) reading. Compare with the writing process. Continue writing biographies.

Day 4: Ask S what they know about stained glass and how these relate to picture book art. Give examples of symbols (heart, cross) and ask for examples. Explain that letters and numbers are symbols. Ask what letters symbolize. Explain the sequence to make stained glass. Brainstorm and design, on a large paper, images and symbols from the BME of *Molly Bannacky.* Continue biography writing.

Day 5: Revise designs and create larger symbols to show the sequence. Prompt S to think about Art Concepts and the Design Principles of balance and unity. Groups color-code the design for colored glass placement. Focus on juicy descriptive images in biographies. Use books for examples: *Maniac McGee, George Washington Socks, Molly Banacky.*

Day 6: Stained glass artist, Dee Mays, will tell the background of stained glass: glass in churches told stories, and they were built on top of one another (origin of "stories" for building). She will help S glue the paper to a clear glass window. The S will begin gluing the pieces of colored glass to the other side of the clear glass.

Day 7–9: S will finish gluing. Finish the biographies and share in the Author's Chair. Ask S to compare and contrast the processes for writing, reading, and making the stained glass. Ask: What happened BDA? Ask: How do each deal with images? Ideas? Feelings?

Classroom Snapshot:

Problem Solving Through Visual Art

In this chapter many strategies have been introduced as tools to achieve meaningful visual arts integration. All of the pieces are best understood when they are put together in a lesson. Each art-based lesson is unique, but here is another example to expand the image of what's possible. It is from the classroom of Robin Fountain at Ashley River Creative Arts in Charleston, South Carolina.

A large print of *Starry Night* hangs on the wall of the first room. Students are using imaginary paintbrushes to get the feel of the strokes van Gogh must have used. On the chalk tray two books are displayed: *Under the Quilt of the Night* (Hopkinson) and *Follow the Drinking Gourd* (Winter).

Don McClain's "*Starry Night*" **song is playing**. Robin holds up the picture book, *The Starry Night* (Waldman), which has end papers of a child's version of the painting. She reminds the students that they have talked about the lines and colors van Gogh used. Now she asks them to **look closely** at the lines.

"He changed the positions," notices one boy.

"But they go together," adds another.

"Those are good observations. I want you to keep thinking and looking, like we've been doing for two weeks."

"I see short curvy lines and dashes," says a blond girl.

"Show me with your imaginary brushes," Robin says.

The class begins to dab in the air with small strokes and quick comma-like movements. Robin takes time to look at each student and give **descriptive feedback**.

"Our focus has been the night sky. Today you will be able to create your own night sky with oil pastels. You will be working on your background—not the foreground. This is not a cityscape. Think about what you want in your night sky using your own ideas about color. Later you'll be able to do a foreground."

"Any colors?" asks one student.

"Yes! **Everybody's needs to look different.**"

Robin asks the students what they remember about how to use oil **pastels** as she passes out large blue paper. The boxes of pastels are in the center of desks pushed together.

Robin changes to a CD from World Playground. It is **"international music"** with a steady beat and a fast tempo. The song "Tqure Kunda" is from Senegal.

Students begin to dab and circle, using long and short strokes. Robin circulates giving more feedback, encouraging students to fill up the space and noticing the use of a wide range of colors. The song "Three Little Birds" (Jamaica) comes on and the children sing along as they make their art.

"If you can't hear the music, you are too loud," she reminds them and then begins to sing along herself. She is standing under a poster that reads, "Control your voice, body, and mind."

Robin explains that the next step will be for the students to tear black construction paper to create the foreground. Just as with previous Grandma Moses artwork, these pieces will be evaluated using a **rubric**. The students know in advance what they need to include. It is that balance of freedom with boundaries that structures a problem-solving context in which children are motivated to strive for excellent work.

Robin's Art /Social Studies Rubric.

Grandma Moses painted her past so the paintings were student images of their pasts. Students self-evaluated using these criteria: (1) perspective, (2) horizon, and (3) three things from the past: games, animals, and clothes.

Conclusion

Art is the lie that enables us to realize the truth. (Pablo Picasso)

This chapter introduced visual art integration throughout the curriculum. The Arts Integration Blueprint included a rationale for integrating visual art (*why*). In particular, art is viewed as much more than an act of the hand: It is an unmatched communication vehicle. As children return to artwork to revise it or use art as a source for ideas, they use the same thinking skills needed in written composition. When children learn to draw and talk about their work, they see that marks have meaning. Cognition is restructured.

The chapter also included *what* visual art literacy teachers need to have and teach to accomplish meaningful art integration. General principles for planning, teaching, and collaborating with visual art specialists completed the chapter focus—the *how*. The next chapter is a categorized collection of starter ideas that extend the focus of *how* to a more specific level to help teachers plan lessons with a visual art component.

Resources

The Appendix lists resources for further study, including more websites. Chapter 7 lists resources, including sources for print and posters and multicultural art.

Websites

American Art Therapy Association: *http://arttherapy.org.*

Education World: *www.educationworld.com/arts/* comprehensive site.

National Art Education Association: *www.naea-reston.org/.*

Videos

Art's place. (1994). Princeton, NJ: Films for the Humanities.

Lively art of picture books. Weston, CT: Weston Woods.

Picture thoughts. (1994). Columbia, MD: Hamilton Associates (critical thinking about art with children; 60 min.).

Traditional expressions. Santa Cruz, CA: Multi-Cultural Communications (multicultural art projects).

What do you see? Art Institute of Chicago (how to discuss art).

Novak, M. (1994). *Mouse TV.* New York: Orchard Books.

Stevens, J. (1995). *From pictures to words.* New York: Holiday.

Children's Literature References

Aliki. (1991). *How a book is made.* New York: HarperCollins.

Babbitt, N. (1975). *Tuck everlasting.* New York: Farrar, Straus & Giroux.

Banks, L. (1980). *The Indian in the cupboard.* Garden City, NJ: Doubleday.

Brown, L. K., & Brown, M. (1992). *Visiting the art museum.* New York: Dutton.

Cummings, P. (1992). *Talking with artists.* New York: Bradbury.

Gilman, P. (1992). *Something from nothing.* New York: Scholastic.

Heller, R. (1995). *Color! Color! Color!* New York: Grosset & Dunlap.

Hoban, T. (1971). *Look again.* New York: Macmillan.

Hopkinson, D. (2002). *Under the quilt of the night.* New York: Atheneum.

Howe, D., & Howe, J. (1999). *Bunnicula.* New York: Atheneum.

Krull, K. (1995). *Lives of the artists.* New York: Harcourt.

Le Tord, B. (1999). *A bird or two: A story about Henri Matisse.* Grand Rapids, MI: William B. Eerdmans.

Lionni, L. (1995). *Matthew's dream.* New York: Knopf.

Locker, T. (2002). *Water dance.* New York: Harcourt.

Locker, T. (2003). *Cloud dance.* New York: Harcourt.

McKissack, P. (1998). *Mirandy and Brother Wind.* New York: Knopf.

Nixon, J., & Degen, B. (1995). *If you were a writer.* New York: Simon and Schuster.

Norton, M. (1991). *The borrowers.* San Diego: Harcourt Brace Jovanovich.

O'Neill, M. (1989). *Hailstones and halibut bones—Adventures in color.* New York: Doubleday.

Paterson, K. (1973). *Sign of the chrysanthemum.* New York: Crowell.

Polacco, P. (1994). *Pink and say.* New York: Philomel.

Steig, W. (1976*). Able's Island.* New York: Farrar, Straus & Giroux.

Waldman, N. (1999) *The starry night.* Honesdale, PA: Boyds Mills.

White, E. B. (1952). *Charlotte's web.* New York: Harper & Row.

Visual Art Seed Strategies

Pyramids, cathedrals and rockets exist not because of geometry, theories of structures, or thermodynamics, but because they were first a picture—literally a vision—in the minds of those who built them. (Eugene Ferguson, historian)

The chapter opens with a Classroom Snapshot of a teacher using visual art to develop students' higher-order thinking. Notice how she developed several Seed Strategies.

Classroom Snapshot:

Problem Solving Through Art/Math

Creation begins with a vision. (Henry Matisse)

Ceiling tiles in Ashley Sires's room feature children's books, like *Ramona Quimby, Age 8* (Cleary). On an easel is *Math-terpieces* and *The Grapes of Math* (Tang), along with Picasso prints. Students are writing in composition books when the morning television newscast comes on. The principal interviews students and forecasts daily events. The opening routine includes a calendar activity for patterns and predicting. Then the student teacher, Deana, takes over. She uses the overhead to do a **warm-up** that links math and haiku.

"Haiku is 5 plus 7 plus 5 syllables for a total of _____? Thumbs up when you know." Most students put thumbs up. On her signal they call out "17."

"Today we are doing more work with shapes," Deana explains. "What ones do you remember?"

Students call out pyramid, cone, and cube.

"How many sides on a cube?" she asks.

"Six!"

"And what are they called?"

"Faces."

"Right. I'm going to show you some art by famous artists," Deana holds up *Math-terpieces*.

"Oh, Vincent van Gogh," a boy says.

"What shapes do you see?"

The students list many, including circles.

"How did he create the circles?"

"Swirling and curving," a girl suggests.

Deana turns to an abstract with red squares and lines. It is by Mondrian. She repeats the "What do you see? What do you feel? How did he do that?" sequence of **open questions** and then connects it to a previous field trip to Cyprus Gardens.

"Let's make a **web.**" She creates a drawing with spokes for the five senses and extends the "What did you see?" to smell, hear, feel, and taste. Students list a dozen ideas—lots of animals like alligators and butterflies. One boy connects to Monet's bridge painting.

"Today we are going to look closely at a Picasso painting. Scoot up to see more." She calls teams to the rug.

"This is *The Three Musicians.* Why would I show it to you today?"

"Just to make us happy."

"You are right that art makes us feel things," Deana says. **"What do you see that causes that?"**

"Lots of shapes," says a boy in a T-shirt.

"Tell me exactly. Look closely."

Students inch forward and **brainstorm.**

"Why is it called *The Three Musicians?*" Deana asks. They say the obvious: There are three people and they have instruments.

"**Look closely.** What are the instruments?"

"A guitar!"

"Oboe?"

"Piano."

"OK, now look at the people. How are they different?"

"I see trapezoids!"

"Look at the quadrilaterals."

"I see a dog, now."

The students begin to point. An inclusion teacher interjects that "Many people are counting sides."

"Show us a hexagon," Deana invites and a boy jumps up to run his finger around the six sides.

"How about five sides?"

"Pentagon!" several say.

Deana next reads from a biography of Picasso that makes the point that artists paint according to their moods. She asks, "What does this make you think?" and a boy immediately says, "Blue period!"

"Yes, when Picasso's friend died, he painted lots of blue pictures. Then he fell in love so what do you think he painted?"

"Pink."

"Red."

"Why do you think that?"

"Because they are happy colors."

"They make you feel warm inside."

"They do. He went on to a stage using lots of cubes. This is his cubist period." Deana shows an abstract of Picasso's friend.

"Look at this!" says a girl. "It's a broke-up face."

"Exactly. He broke up the cube. Now look at a different painting of three musicians."

"It feels countryish."

"It is so brown. There aren't many geometric shapes."

"Picasso's is more like a jazz musician," comments a boy.

"Why do you think that?" Deana asks.

"Because it is more adventuresome. It is more alive."

Making pattern snakes.

"Great connections. Now, I'm going to **give you a problem."**

"Good!" says a boy. Deana smiles.

"I want to you to use the pattern blocks differently than ever before. Look on the five senses web. Your challenge is to create cubist art that shows Cyprus Gardens."

She passes out black paper and asks, "Where will you start?"

"Experimenting with shapes," a girl responds.

"What else can you do to problem solve?"

"Gather other ideas. We can look in *Math-terpieces.*"

"We can add more to the web."

"Yes. Try lots of patterns. Don't take your first idea."

Deana puts a crate of rubber shapes in the center of each group. There is already a toolbox of glue and scissors in the center. Students eagerly begin to experiment.

Later, students will write haiku to go with their cubist art, all related to Cyprus Gardens. ✺

Chapter Organization

> *Art is not what you see, but what you make others see.* (Edgar Degas)

Deana is beginning her teaching career under the tutelage of a teacher who is a veteran of arts integration. She has already learned how to adapt many art seed ideas to fit lessons. This chapter includes such undeveloped prompts to help plan for integrating visual art to meet standards and

Integrating math, art, and literature.

student needs. These Seed Strategies need to be thought about in the context of the previous chapter that described basic principles for visual art integration.

The Seed Strategies are generic. They are not geared to particular ages or grades. Most can be adapted for grades K–6 by using the 10 PARTICULAR ideas in Ready Reference 3.6. The seeds are organized into sections, but many fit in more than one section. The separate sections on Energizers and Elements and Concepts are provided to prepare for meaningful meaning construction using visual art media, tools, and techniques.

I. Energizers and Warm-Ups

The purpose of energizers and warm-ups is to ready students mentally and physically for creative problem solving. They cause students to relax, gather and release ideas, and focus. Many of them can be used to introduce any lesson that intends for students to be engaged in CPS—in other words, nearly every lesson.

Art Walks. Take walks to find art and beauty in nature. Use clipboards to note colors, textures, and shapes. Return to the same spots to find differences during the year. Stop to sit in special places to listen to sounds. Tell students to close their eyes and picture what they hear. Prompt with visual art vocabulary. After walks, sketch or paint the experience.

Scribble and Doodle. Tell students to draw lines, dots, and circles of all shapes and sizes to fill up the entire paper. Encourage overlapping and working both rapidly and freely.

Eyes Warm Up. Tell students to warm hands by rubbing them together. Lightly place warm hands over eyes for a minute. *Variation:* Students close eyes and imagine colors and shapes mentioned by the teacher.

Visual Gym. Teacher suggests a series of images to sketch or imagine. *Example:* Describe angles, curves, dots, circles, triangles, ovals, colors, and textures. See *Put Your Mother on the Ceiling* (Mille).

SCAMPER (Eberle, 1971). This acronym represents a set of verbs for brainstorming. First display the verbs and practice using a piece of art or any problem. The verbs are: Substitute, Combine, Adapt (change), Modify (minify or magnify), put to other uses, Eliminate, and Rearrange or reverse. For example, ask: What surfaces can be painted on? What if you made the image upside down? What if you took a part of the picture and made it huge? Tiny? *Variation:* Show how artists have used SCAMPER (e.g., Picasso's bull's head made from a bicycle seat and handle bars).

SFTW. (See–Feel–Think–Wonder). This develops observational skills and higher-order thinking. Show a piece of art related to a lesson. A picture from any book, especially picture books, works. Students write or tell what they *see* (focus on art elements and subject matter), *feel* (ask what causes the feelings), *think* (connections to their lives or other art or topics), and *wonder* (questions the art brings up). An oral or written frame can be used: I see . . . I feel . . . and so on.

Mirror Image. Give any line drawing and ask students to draw the mirror image. Try an abstract scribble (e.g., a jagged line).

Five Shape Elements. Give teams 1 minute to find circles, dots, and straight, angled, and curved lines in the room. Count and graph. *Variation:* Search for one shape element for 1 minute.

Shape Match. Give each group a set of word or picture cards with the five shape elements: circle, dot, and curved, straight, and angled line. Display any art and ask groups to turn over one card and find an example in the art. Share and continue.

Doodle Log. Instead of writing in journals, students can doodle about favorite words, their day, and so on. Doodle logs can also be used when students finish projects early (contributed by Ohio art teacher, Misty Kaplafka).

Songs and Chants. Compose art songs with students to remember art concepts and elements. For example, for primary colors and mixing, "There was an artist who had some paints—red and yellow and blue. And with the paints he made his art—red and yellow and blue. Here a red, there a blue, now it's purple—what a hue!"

Art Poems.   Collect poems about art or poems that inspire art making. A classic collection on color is O'Neill's *Hailstones and Halibut Bones.* Designate a color of the day and perform using the Poetry Performance ideas in Ready Reference 5.3.

Riddles.   Find or create riddles about art, artists, styles, and particular works. Start with an answer such as "Picasso." Take each syllable in the word and think of other soundalikes. Then, make up a question: "What pig artist liked to make abstract paintings?" Answer: Pigasso.

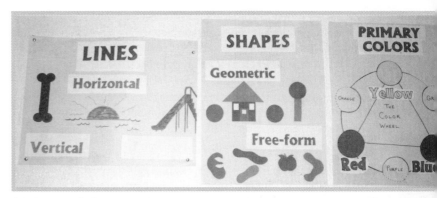

Art elements display.

Make a Mess.   Give time to explore new materials and techniques before creating a product. During exploration students make discoveries and gain confidence and control. Take time to share discoveries.

Brain Squeeze.   Before making art or doing interpretations, take time to squeeze ideas. For example, "What are things we can look for in art?" Ideas can be recorded in web form or on a list.

Mystery Bag.   Introduce a piece of art or an art project by finding three to five objects that connect to it in some way. Pull each out of a bag and ask students to solve the mystery for how they relate. Mr. Novak used this in the Chapter 6 Classroom Snapshot.

Twenty Questions.   Use an art concept or an object in a bag that represents an idea (e.g., texture). Students ask questions to discover it. All questions must be able to be answered with yes or no, for example, "Is it something about landscape?" "Is it something you mix?" Students can't guess the item until all 20 questions are asked.

Senses Stations.   Stimulate the senses before making or viewing art by setting up areas for students to:

Taste: Close eyes and try salt, sugar, lemon (use sticks).
Touch: Feely boxes with sandpaper, silk, foil.
Sight: Magnifying glasses, tubes, kaleidoscopes.
Smell: Perfumes, potpourri, oils, candles.
Hear: Environment sounds, sea shells, bags to shake.

Look Back.   When students have trouble coming up with ideas, suggest they look through past art for an idea to redo differently. A part can become a whole piece; a tree or shape in the background can be the subject of a new work.

Browsing.   Keep files of magazine pictures, cards, photos, and book covers for students to look through to trigger art making.

Picture Book Starters.   Use book art for ideas about how to use different media, styles, and subject matter. For example, in Bunting's *Smoky Night* collage, materials are used and many Eric Carle books are collages made from his "painted papers."

Collections.   Use scrapbooks, photo wallets, albums, or clear shoe bags to organize items that grab aesthetic attention. Beans, sand, and pebbles can be layered in jars to study the effects of pattern. Student collections serve as conversation starters and for art making or as writing prompts.

Postcards.   Use art postcards to have students do sorts and finds. For example, groups can sort by subject matter (e.g., portraits, landscapes), styles, and art elements (e.g., color, texture). Connect sorts to units: sort by cultures, animals, and plants.

Open sorts.   Students are given random postcards and they create categories to group them.

Student collections.   When a teacher is enthusiastic about collecting, students often catch the spirit. Students can collect and make art postcards with index cards and original art or magazine art (e.g., ads for fine art appear in magazines such as *Architectural Digest*). Postcards are indispensable and inexpensive collections. Art postcards are also wonderful to remember birthdays or as cards to send notes to parents.

II. Teaching Art Concepts and Elements

Color in a picture is like enthusiasm in life. (Vincent van Gogh)

This section includes ideas for teaching specific art knowledge for viewing and doing art. Pair these ideas with Best Practices from Chapter 6.

Concentration.   Play this memory game using 10 pairs of art cards that can be matched (e.g., two pieces by

Renoir). Small groups lay out cards face down. Use a pocket chart for large group play. Each person gets a turn to flip two cards and make a match. If successful, the player keeps the cards and plays again. If not, she must replace the cards face down. The play passes to the next person, who tries to remember where cards are. To reinforce art learning, students must name the artist or style or "say something true" about each card turned over.

Art Elements Mnemonics.

Use a grid (paper divided into 8 to 10 sections). Label each box with an art element: color, line, shape, etc. Students then do a drawing that serves as a mnemonic for each element. *Variation:* Do on large paper with groups collaborating.

One-Minute Find.

Call out an art element and give groups one minute to find examples (e.g., kinds of lines in the classroom). Ask them to count ones found and/or write answers. *Variation:* Graph results.

Big Book or Poster Elements.

Displays of art elements and concepts are useful references during art viewing and making. The class can make big books, posters, or individual books with titles such as *The Facts about Color.* Use poster board for the covers of big books; roll bulletin board paper can be folded and stapled with a long-arm stapler for pages.

Word Charts.

The goal is to find unusual and descriptive words to expand concepts behind art elements and add words to charts. For example, for textures, words such as *rough, smooth, silky,* and *bumpy* may be added to the chart. For patterns, words like *checked, striped, borders,* and *dotted* are likely.

Hot Sock.

Make a set of cards with art elements or concepts. Tie a sock in a knot. Sit in a circle with IT in the center. IT closes his eyes and throws the sock, which is a "hot potato" no one wants. IT calls "stop" at any time. The person caught passes the sock to the right, and that person holds the sock while IT reads one card. The caught person must name a set number of items in the category (four to six) while the sock is passed from person to person around the circle. The goal is for IT to finish before the sock gets back around; otherwise a new IT goes to the center. *Variation:* Use with any categories or alphabet cards.

Elements Exploration.

Start with lots of newsprint and one color of paint. Invite students to bring brushes from home (e.g., sponge, baster, bottle washer). Give a series of directed explorations: Paint different lines: angled, curved, lying down, angry, calm, excited, thick. Create different shapes: dots, circles, triangles, uneven, loose, happy. Take one shape and paint it different sizes. Group the same shapes. Paint a group of shapes that are the same size.

Change colors and color code "same" shapes or same sizes. Outline shapes in a lighter or darker color. Try painting slowly. Try using very little paint to dab. Smear a lot on. Give feedback as students work. Afterward, ask what they discovered about art elements. *Adaptation:* Ask students for exploration ideas.

Game Boards.

Make all-purpose game boards using file folders or pizza cardboard. Laminate and print information needed on a board. Make separate cards for different concepts. For example, create art question or concept cards (colors, shapes, lines, styles). Students play by naming as many ideas in a category and move the number of spaces designated by a spinner or dice.

Bubbles.

Explore shape and color with bubbles: Mix 1 tablespoon of dish detergent, 5 tablespoons of water, and 1 tablespoon of glycerine. Blow bubbles and catch on paper painted with wet tempera. Explore organic and geometric shapes with bubbles made through straws, pipe cleaner wands, plastic berry baskets, funnels and plastic from soda six packs.

Statues.

Look at famous statues and discuss their emotions and why statues exist. Look closely to see how different body parts are arranged. Have students assume a statue pose and when tapped, say a one liner about what he or she is thinking or feeling.

Questions.

Use open questions to stimulate close looking and deep thinking: What is special about. . . ? What is happening? What does this make you think about? How did the artist make this? How do you think the artist felt when she created this? Why? Find–trace–point to elements or concepts, e.g., (biggest, brightest). Ready Reference 7.1 has more questions and activities about art elements.

Compare and Contrast.

Create a large Venn diagram to record likenesses and differences between paintings. For example, compare and contrast the elements, media, style, and subject matter of two paintings called *First Steps,* one by van Gogh and one by Picasso.

Experts.

Cover half of a painting or ask small groups to choose a focus section (e.g., foreground, background). Groups serve as "experts" on their section and report to the whole group.

Photographs.

Class pretends to pose in a group photograph that might happen or happened in literature (e.g., family at the fair in *Charlotte's Web*). Students decide about the composition, background, and so forth. Pose and freeze. Students say a one liner in character about thoughts when tapped (drama). *Variation:* Photograph the compositions.

Art Elements Questions and Activities

Line:

- What kinds of lines do you see? Straight, curved?
- How do the lines make you feel? Tired, busy, relaxed?
- Which are repeated? Why do you think?
- Which lines are strong? Which are faster?

Activities: Students pick a line and follow its movement with their hands or draw in the air. Use a flashlight to "trace" a line or students can make light chalk lines on the floor to get the feel of lines. Use lines as a stimulus for dance or movement: shape your body in angles, move in a zigzag, make curves with different body parts.

Shape:

- What kind of shapes do you see in the painting?
- How do the shapes create a pattern?
- Which are organic? Geometric?

Activities: Students make a shape with their arms, fingers, or bodies. Ask them to look for a shape in the room and find that shape in the art. Paint or draw all kinds of lines (e.g., wavy, zigzag). Go on a shape walk to find shapes within shapes (e.g., windows, roofs, cars).

Texture:

- If you could touch the objects in the art, how would they feel?
- How has the artist made the textures appear real?

Activities: Ask students to touch the floor, face, and chairs and describe how each feels. Tell them to cup their hands to make a fist telescope to isolate an area of a painting. Ask about the kinds of brush strokes the artist used.

Color:

- How has the artist used color? How does it make you feel? Why?
- How would the painting be different if_____ was changed to_____?
- Name all the colors. What colors are used the most?
- What are some unusual uses of color?
- What happens when white is used?
- What happens when colors are put next to each other, for example, red and green?

Activities: Close your eyes and think of a color in the painting. Imagine yourself turning into that color. How do you feel? Find complementary colors, primary colors, and examples of hues, tints, and shades. Get paint chips from paint stores to show hues. Brainstorm color names using paint chip titles as idea starters.

Space and Composition:

- Why and how has the artist created a foreground, midground, and background?
- Introduce perspective. How is the space broken up? Where do you think the artist was standing? Why?
- Where does your eye go next in the painting? Why?
- Squint and look at a picture. What masses stand out?
- Why are some things smaller, blurrier, overlapped? How did the artist do that?

Activities: Choose a small part of a picture and magnify it by drawing just that part much larger. Use paint or markers. Create a tableau (frozen picture) of a painting by asking students to assume the same positions as figures or become a tree, pond, or hills.

Light and Shadow:

- What is the possible light source? From what direction is it coming? How has the artist created volume (modeling gradations of light and dark)?

Activities: Imagine the painting in a different light. Ask how the feel of the painting would change. Use a flashlight to shine light in different directions on an object and ask what they notice.

Perspective:

- How does the artist show that some things are closer and others are far away?

Activities: Look at objects from different angles and distances (e.g., stand on a chair); use microscopes or a magnifying glass.

Emotion and Mood:

- How does the painting make you feel? Why? How do you think the artist felt about his or her subject?
- What do you hear? Taste? Smell?

Activities: Show with face and body shape how the art feels. Make a list of feelings and how to create them (e.g., sad shapes and colors).

Food Alternatives.   Food tools, such as potatoes for printing, are commonly used. However, it is important for children to distinguish art materials from food—for safety reasons and for aesthetic purposes. Instead of pasta, consider using buttons, shells, or pebbles in collages or cut up straws to string pieces. Sponges or Styrofoam can be cut in creative shapes for printing (precut sponges are not recommended because this is dictated art).

Subject Matter: Questions and Activities.   Ready Reference 7.2 lists ways to involve students with art subject matter.

Square Foot Display.   Students can learn to organize and compose from arranging flowers, furniture, or collected nature items. Give each a square foot of space for a choice display. Labeling displays involves students in summary/synthesis thinking.

Sing a Picture.   Display a landscape, seascape, or cityscape and brainstorm sounds associated with different parts. Encourage creative thinking about what "might be." Come to agreement on sounds for five or six parts of the art. Discuss the pitch, dynamics, and how many times the sound will be repeated. The teacher then points to an area of the art and students make the sounds, sustaining them or repeating them, as decided. Try harmonizing sounds or doing the sounds in round form. *Variation:* Use prints with several people and break students into groups to find songs or create songs for characters to sing. Come back together for groups to perform.

Parent MiniPage.   Parents often don't know how to respond to children's art and don't know why and how to encourage art making. Here are suggestions to share with them:

- Don't ask, "what is it?" because that's insulting.
- List what you see in your child's art (e.g., colors, shapes, lines).
- Explain how the art makes you feel or think.
- Ask your child to "tell about the art."
- Ask how the art was made. Emphasize process and the effort.
- Make art projects alongside your child.
- Keep a folder of your child's art and date the pieces.
- Set up a special place or table to do art.
- Visit museums and other special art displays. Stop to talk about what you see and feel.
- Regularly share what you think is beautiful and tell why. Invite your child to talk about what is beautiful to him/her.

Art Bags.   Use large zip lock bags to send home a piece of art, a book related to it, and a related artifact or object. Invite students to check these out to share with their families. For example, a spring bag can have prints or postcards of Monet's garden art, the book *Linnea in Monet's Garden* (Bjork), and flower seeds to plant.

III. Using Different Media

This section begins with ideas to prevent problems by planning ahead for art making.

General Tips

Before doing art projects, be sure to prepare for contingencies. Here are a few tips:

- Make student cleanup a routine part of projects. Make this expectation clear in advance.
- Stain removal: Try toothpaste to get crayon from clothing.
- Collect egg cartons or ice cube trays. Use half for different paint colors and the other half for mixing. Alternative: Use washed juice cans, cut in half, and set in student milk cartons for stability. *Note:* Don't give out all possible colors. Students need to explore mixing.
- Collect a variety of paint tools. Use Q-tips to make "dot art" similar to Seurat's style. Students can also paint with rolled newspaper "brushes."
- Use baseball-size clay balls to store markers. Poke holes so each looks like a multi-holed bowling ball. Let clay harden.
- Use clear plastic shoeboxes and bags to store materials.
- String a clothesline to hang art. Hang straw beach mats and use drapery hooks to hang anything that you can punch a hole in and put over the hook. Use plastic drying racks that have clothespins on each arm as a way to display or as mobiles.
- Use old shirts to cover clothes. Cut off long sleeves and button backwards. Garbage bags can also be used: slit and then cut arm and neck holes. Warn children about putting bags over their heads.
- Trim paintbrushes with scissors to keep them fresh.
- Use warm iron to flatten curled art.
- Mount or frame student art to give it a finished look. Transparency frames make quick frames. Save the tabs off soda cans to tape hangers on the back of pictures.
- Students should do most of the work (e.g., don't cut out shapes for them). If there is too much preparation, it is probably not an appropriate art activity for children.

Mixing Colors: Color Triangles

To show primary colors and the secondary colors made from them, draw a large triangle with the three points: red (top point), yellow (next point moving clockwise), and blue. Draw an upside down triangle over the first triangle

Ready Reference 7.2   Reading Art Subject Matter

Direct students to take time to stop and look at art for at least 30 seconds. Meaningful experience depends on learning to look longer, notice details, respond personally, ask questions, and think about possible messages from the art. Guide students to discover how art reflects the time period and culture that produced it. For example, 20th century art reflects values for originality and individuality in a world of mass production and imitation.

Landscapes *are about the land.*

- What is the mood? Season? How do you know? If you were there, how would you feel?
- Where do you enter the work of art? Why did the artist create this position for you to take?
- What did the artist do to make you feel a part of the scene?
- Do you feel like an onlooker? If so, how did the artist keep you at a distance?
- Look closely to see if there are people. If so, how are they related to the landscape?
- Does the landscape seem real or imaginary? Why? Does it describe or capture an actual look of a place, or does it give more of the feeling of a place (expressive)? Why?
- What title would you give this work? Why?
- Walk into the painting. What do you see, hear, feel? What could you do there?
- Think of a special place you have been. What made it memorable? If you could artistically re-create this setting, what medium would you use (oil paint, watercolor, pastels, charcoal, pencil, collage)? What would you emphasize? Why?

Portraits *are of people but show more than what a person looks like.* Artists use a "visual vocabulary" to communicate this. Consider this special artistic vocabulary as you look at a portrait. (See Ready Reference 6.1 Visual Art Elements and Concepts.)

- What does the artist tell about this person? How does this person feel?
- *Clothing:* What clues does the person's dress give?
- *Facial expression, posture, and gestures:* What does the person's body language say? What do the eyes, eyebrows, mouth, throat, forehead, and angle of head seem to tell? Where is the person looking? How does this affect you? How is the person positioned? Why? What is he or she doing with his or her hands? Take the position yourself. How do you feel? Would you want to meet the person? Why or why not?
- *Background and accessories:* Where is the person? What clues does the environment provide about the person? What might the specific objects in the setting mean?

- *Size and medium:* Is the portrait life-size, or is it smaller? How does the size change how you feel? What media and materials do you think the artist used? What if the materials were different? How would marble give a different feeling than paint?
- *Details:* Start at the head and slowly observe. Pretend you are the person and walk, sit, and stand. Be the person and say one thing in role.
- Look at real people through a tube or frame to see shapes of eyes, lips, and head. Observe groups of people: How close are they? How are they grouped (line, circle, random)?

Still lifes *are paintings of inanimate (nonliving) objects.*

- What attracts your eye? What do you discover that you didn't notice at first glance?
- What is the most important part of the painting?
- How does the artist make it seem that there is light on surfaces?
- What kind of lifestyle do the objects represent? Why might the artist have chosen these objects? What might the objects represent (symbols)?
- What objects could you use to make a still life (e.g., toys, fruit, school items)? Why? How would you arrange them? What would you want to say in a still life?

Abstract art *goes beyond showing the visible world to allow expression through color, line, and shape. Images are "abstracted" from what they represent.*

- What is your first reaction? How did the artist cause you to react like this?
- What are you curious about? Why do you think the artist chose to create an abstract work?
- How does the work's abstractness change how it makes you feel?
- How would you describe the personality of the art? What contributes to it? How does it cause you to stop and think?
- What meaning or feelings do you think the artist intended? What does it mean to you?

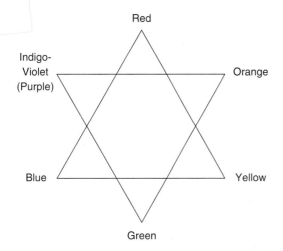

to create a star. Label these points (moving clockwise from top right) orange, green, and purple (the last is also called indigo–violet). By combining two adjacent points on the star you get the color in between (e.g., red and yellow make orange). Students can make color triangles for their desks.

Other Mixing Hints. Always start with the lighter color and add the darker. (1) White paint tints or makes lighter and creates pastels. White is used a lot, so buy double. To tint, start with white and add color to it, a bit at a time. (2) Black shades or makes darker or duller. Add a small amount of black to a color (e.g., black to white makes gray and black to red makes brown). (3) Skin colors can be made with black, brown, yellow, red, and white. Start with lighter and add darker colors to create shades; for example, blend white chalk with orange crayon. Remember that skin can be almost any color and most artists use many colors, even in a single face. (4) Use a clear pie pan on the overhead to drop food coloring to show mixing. Turn out the lights and let the colors fill the room. (5) Color sugar with food coloring and layer in jars. (6) Show how to mix colors on a color wheel. (These can be purchased at art supply stores.) (7) See children's literature in Ready Reference 6.8 for books about mixing colors (e.g., *Color! Color! Color!* by Heller and *Colors* by Felix.

Drawing and Rubbing

> *To draw you must close your eyes and sing.* (Pablo Picasso)

Human beings seem born to draw. Drawing is linear art made with any tool that can make a mark; it is also a precursor to writing. Rubbings are made by placing paper over objects such as coins, shells, wire, or any texture and then using crayon, marker, and so forth to bring up the lines from the textured surfaces underneath. Scratch art or etching is scraping away a surface to reveal a lighter color. Resist con-

sists of using a wash of paint over something that resists it (e.g., crayon).

Tools and Media. Fingers, sticks, toothpicks, and straws can be used, along with pencil, charcoal, marker, pen, crayon, pastels or chalk, and shaving cream. Children can draw on a blank surface, in paint or any medium, such as glass wax sprayed on windows. (Color glass wax with tempera paint, or add food coloring to hand lotion or toothpaste, for a drawing medium. Note: Food color stains.)

Computer Technology. Computers have revolutionized the making of both commercial and fine art. Computers are used in two ways. First, teachers and students can create and manipulate images (art making, including planning and producing two-dimensional virtual objects). A sketch can be scanned and then, using a program like Adobe Photoshop, the image is manipulated. In addition, use computers to investigate visual art (art history criticism, aesthetics). Interactive CD-ROMs and the Internet offer text and images, even virtual tours of museums—often with sound and video clips that elaborate on the historical period with music and interviews. Check websites such as *www.virtualfreesites.com/museums.museums.html*.

Surfaces. Experiment with a variety of papers, cloth, sandpaper, bags, towels, wrapping paper, paper doilies, graph paper, or chalkboard. Draw on T-shirts with fabric markers or crayons (cover with a paper bag and iron on warm to fix crayon). Scratchboard can be made by using light crayons first and then covering with heavy black or dark crayon. Scratchboard can also be purchased with silver on top and black underneath. Use a nail or stick to etch.

Drawing Ideas. Buy or make sketchbooks to capture ideas. Encourage "looking closely" and sectioning off an area (e.g., if it's a portrait, try looking at the face in fourths). A squiggle on a paper, traced hands and feet, or thumbprints can be starters to create animals, objects, people, or abstract art. Draw to music or draw without looking down while a "model" is studied. Some artists have success drawing upside down.

Crosshatching. Using this technique, artists draw fine black lines parallel to one another and then cross them. Crosshatching can be light or heavy, adding depth and texture.

Shape elements. These elements can be taught directly and used to analyze any image and produce a realistic drawing of most anything:

1. Dots (oval, round, elliptical, and kidney shapes)
2. Circles in different shapes (oval, round, elliptical, and kidney) and that are "empty" rather than "colored in" like dots
3. Straight lines

4. Curved lines
5. Angled lines (Brookes, 1996, p. 59)

Drawing Figures. Start with a focal point: eye, hole, or center. Look closely and analyze. Notice dots, circles, straight lines, angled lines, and curved lines. For *overlapping,* draw things in the front, first, and then draw things farther away. If a mistake happens, make something out of it by repeating it, adding to it, or transforming it. Break people down into circles and tube shapes—the head is an egg shape and the neck is a tube. Grid off face to position eyes, nose, and so on.

Crayon Ideas for Varied Crayon Effects. Peel and break crayons, use them on their sides, or tape several together. Encourage mixing of colors and creation of hues of one color by changing amounts of pressure. Blend white chalk with orange or brown crayon for skin tones. Rub crayon drawings with a cloth to give them a gloss. For *crayon resist,* try painting over crayon drawings with tempera, watercolor, or food color. Use black construction paper for the background and paint over crayon drawing with white paint. An alternative is to use white crayon or a candle to draw on white paper and then wash over with paint to reveal the image. This seems like magic!

Chalk Ideas. Encourage children to break chalk, use it on its side, or dip it in water (once dipped, it is ruined for regular use). Try wetting the paper with a little sugar water and then using chalk. The chalkboard and sidewalks have great surfaces because of their size and texture. Tape the end of chalk to keep hands clean.

Cartooning. Examine books like Hoff's *Sammy the Seal,* Stevenson's *Could Be Worse,* Griffith's *Grandaddy's Place,* and Steig's *Caleb* and *Kate.* List what is noticed about shapes and lines. Start with simple shapes in classroom. *Emphasize* no copying.

Painting and Painting Tools

You paint what you are. (Andrew Wyeth)

Types of Paint. Acrylic, oils, tempera (comes in liquid, powder, and blocks), watercolors, watercolor crayons, and even melted crayons can be used to paint. (Turpentine melts crayons. Consider safety issues before using this. Always ventilate.) Refillable paint markers with felt tips can be an alternative way to use tempera. Paints can be made by combining food color and egg or adding food color to shaving cream, liquid starch, hair gel, or even Vaseline. Explore stains and paints made from tea, mustard, berries, bleach, shoe polish, or just water.

Tools. Use a variety of brushes: toothbrushes, hairbrushes, combs, and brush curlers. Fingers, feet, hands, feathers, rags, old deodorant rollers, sponges, squeeze bottles, sticks, Q-tips, cotton balls, and straws can be used as paint tools. Newspaper can be rolled into tubes and used as a throwaway brush. Chalk can be dipped into tempera to create interesting effects.

Painting Surfaces. Paint can be applied to wood, canvas, fabric, paper plates, windows, doilies, transparencies, plastic sheets, cookie sheets, or wallpaper. (Many stores will donate old wallpaper books to schools.) Rocks can be painted, too; just add liquid white glue to the paint to help it stick. Frescoes are created by using paint on wet plaster. Ceiling tiles in the school can be painted with tempera or acrylic plants using a theme (e.g., celebration). The class may collaborate on a theme or topics, as well. *Note:* Students should sketch out ideas. Use masking tape to divide off sections for group work. In some classrooms, tiles are painted based on children's books or are painted to look like clouds.

Techniques. Have a brush for each color, and encourage experimentation with mixing: add white to tint and black to shade, and use the color wheel to mix secondary and tertiary colors from the primary colors of red, yellow, and blue. Introduce *scumbling* by showing how to use thick paint over dried paint (i.e., dry brush). Explore dabbing, spatter painting (use a ruler to flip a brush), blob painting (place blob on paper and fold), and straw painting (blow blobs by using a straw). Add salt, Epsom salts, flour, oatmeal, sand, sawdust, or soap flakes to give texture or thicken (salt gives a bubbly effect). Liquid starch, corn syrup, or detergent can be added to change how paint spreads. Soap helps tempera adhere to glossy surfaces.

Hand painting includes pounding and dabbing with the fingers, fist, or side of hand. When sponge painting, clip a clothespin to the sponge for a handle. Bleach can be applied to construction paper or bright cotton fabric, but don't let children work with bleach. To tie-dye, fold cloth or knot and then dip in bleach or dye. For marbling, mix linseed oil and tempera powder (children should not breathe this) to a thick cream. Put a half-inch of water on a cookie sheet and drop the mixture on to it. Carefully lay a sheet of paper on top and lift up, dry, and flatten with warm iron.

Painting Tips. Watercolors can stain clothing. Keep a bucket of soapy water and towels handy for cleanup. Never have children mix dry tempera powder because it is easily inhaled.

Printmaking

Prints are made using techniques to produce many copies (e.g., woodcut, linoleum, silk screen). Monoprints produce only one print. Prints can be pulled from a surface (e.g., a n which students have fingerpainted) or stamped with found objects: erasers, vegetables (carrots, potatoes), woodcuts, linoleum cuts, or any form that is raised. Real flowers can be pounded into paper to make a monoprint.

Tools. Collect objects for printing: pieces of carpet, wire, mesh, bubble wrap, corrugated cardboard, fingers (use watercolors), feet, hands, sponges, erasers, corks, wood block, and nature (leaf prints). Cut print shapes from clean Styrofoam trays, rubber-tire inner tubes, or shoe insoles, and glue to blocks for a handle. Vegetables and fruits can be used, but take care that kids don't confuse food and art materials. *Note:* Soles of feet can be painted and used to print animal bodies. Knuckles can be used to print rows and patterns, for example, a border of small pumpkins (idea from teacher A. Wirz, Lady's Island Elementary School).

Surfaces. Print on paper, fabric, wood, clay, or even paper towels.

Techniques. Place folded newspaper under the printing surface to cushion. Put paint in shallow tray (e.g., cookie sheet or paper plates). Have a separate container for each color. Use a brayer (roller) to paint onto the item with which you will print. Too much paint will smear image. Make repeated patterns with vertical or horizontal prints. Overlap, twirl, and swirl to create designs. A print can also be made by outlining an image in white glue. Let it dry. The raised glue can be rolled with paint and used to print. Alternatively, roll paint by gluing raised items or yarn on paper towel tubes and then coating the items with paint. Any carved item (see three-dimensional art) can be used for printmaking.

Children can make giftwrap, greeting cards, T-shirts, and stationery using printing or stenciling. Stencils can be cut from plastic or paper (e.g., fold paper in half, cut out a shape, open and use as a paint stencil—not much paint is needed). When stenciling, use a sponge or round brush to dab on paint. Use various thicknesses to create a more interesting image.

Collage

The word *collage* derives from the French word *coller*, which simply means to paste on. Pablo Picasso and George Braque invented collage and used it in their abstract cubist works in the early 1900s. Collage consists of assembling materials and then ordering them. Children enjoy the tactile nature of collage, and this medium invites an experimentation attitude—realism is not the goal. Collage can be stimulated by any topic or theme (e.g., seasons, plants, school, etc.). Encourage a variety of shapes and sizes, both torn and cut. Protect desks with newspapers.

Materials. Just about anything can be used, from stones, sticks, and other found nature objects to string, yarn, ribbon, or buttons to make a collage. Collage can be made from any type of paper including sandpaper, foil, construction, cardboard, newspaper, tissue, wallpaper, greeting cards, and magazines. Wetting crepe paper and colored paper can produce interesting effects, but the bleeding can stain clothes. Children's own old paintings can be torn or cut up. Paper doilies offer possibilities for texture. Broken and shaved crayon pieces create a mosaic effect, as can small squares of other construction paper shapes. Sprinkle shavings on paper, fabric, T-shirts, or old sheets; then cover with newsprint and press with a warm iron. Consult references for pictures of mosaics before beginning. Bits of fabric can be used, as well as pasta. For colored pasta, just combine food color and 1/4 cup alcohol. Put in a covered container and shake (don't have children do this!). Colored rice, sawdust, or sand can be made by using tempera paint; don't let students use dry paint because it is easily inhaled. Teachers should do the mixing. Collages can be sprinkled with sugar or salt to create sparkle and increase texture. Be sure to sprinkle over wet glue.

Backgrounds. Use roof shingles, cardboard, poster board, plastic lids, styrofoam, and sandpaper as surfaces on which to arrange and glue. Leaves, crayons, and colored tissue can be pressed between wax paper using a warm iron (cover with newsprint so iron doesn't get sticky). For a thicker base and more texture, made a dough by combining half salt and half flour and adding water. Objects can then be pressed into the dough and coated with thinned white glue. Use a shoebox or egg carton lid, or styrofoam tray to hold the pressed-out dough. Plaster of Paris can also be used. Just mix according to the directions and press objects such as shells or buttons into it. Food coloring can be added to the plaster. It sets up fast, in about 15 minutes.

Collage Glue. White glue is usually best. It can be thinned with water when working with colored tissue or used as an overall coating for finished work, as in decoupage. Paste can be made from flour and water. Add oil of peppermint or wintergreen to prevent spoiling. Have popsicle sticks or Q-tips available for students who don't want to use fingers. Have wet sponges or towels available to wipe off glue.

Artistic Techniques: Enlarge, Simplify, Crop

Many artists make small things very large or simplify a subject down to basic geometric forms (e.g., triangle or circle). Georgia O'Keeffe is an example. She also cropped pictures (cut them off so only a part of a flower showed). Show examples of these techniques and allow students to experiment with enlarging, simplifying, or cropping objects, plants, animals, and so forth. To enlarge, make a transparency of anything and display on an overhead projector. Pull the projector back to make the image bigger. For example, basic fairy tale character shapes can be traced on transparencies. Next, tape large paper to the wall and project each transparency to use as sketch bases. Sketch outlines should be used in original ways—don't turn this into a big coloring book activity! Students can also trace each other's bodies to get outlines for large-people paintings.

Displays and Bulletin Boards

Bulletin board space should be primarily for displaying student work, and students should be involved in planning the design. Interactive displays can be made by adding question cards or flip cards to lift for answers. Teach basic calligraphy techniques and how to cut block letters to create labels (versus using commercial cutters). See the Appendix for books on calligraphy. Block lettering uses the idea that any letter can be made from a block of paper—just cut straight lines. Begin by cutting as many blocks as letters needed. Blocks can be any size. Then imagine the letter and make straight cuts. Don't worry about "hole" letters like *B* and *R*. Cut through joining areas because they'll be glued or stapled down.

To frame or finish off a bulletin board, make a border with ribbons or leaves. Here's how to cut a border the old-fashioned way, like paper doll strips: First, pull off about 3 feet of large paper from a roll of bulletin board paper. Roll into a tube and cut slices about 2 to 3 inches long using a paper cutter. Creatively cut a pattern along one of the longer edges (zigzag or scallops). Open the strip and staple onto the bulletin board.

Posters and signs can be made to advertise any content. Take time to examine ads for ideas students can adapt through CPS like that used in SCAMPER (Ready Reference 2.5).

Murals

Murals are large wall paintings. In school, murals can be any big composition and are usually created by groups. Murals help children learn to cooperate and take pride in group work. Group planning and sharing are essential aspects of mural making.

Murals are made from a variety of media, from crayons to collage. The easiest are ones where students each add an item (e.g., a nature collage mural or a print of a foot or hand). Students can learn how to plan full scenes relevant for science, social studies, or literature. Check out community murals on the Internet (*www.tcom.ohiou.edu/community/murals/*).

Mixed Media

Use paper, wire, paint, fabric, and any other materials in one artwork. Banners, murals, and even portraits, landscapes, or abstracts can be made with any imaginable combinations. Children's books such as Bunting's *Smoky Nights* and Ringgold's *Tar Beach* show examples.

Fiber Art.   Cloths and yarns can be used to create art with texture and pattern. Fabric art connects well with social studies: clothing of cultures and time periods and careers (knitter, weaver, quilter, tailor, seamstress). There are wonderful pieces of children's literature that deal with fiber art; for example, weaving is central to *Annie and the Old One* (Miles). For a science connection, explore natural dyes, such as carrot tops for a green–yellow, onion skins for an orange dye, and tea for brown or orange. Colored drink mixes can serve as dyes, too. An adult can use an ordinary Crock-Pot to heat. Be sure to wear rubber gloves and rinse with cold water to set the dye. *Note:* See Judy Chicago's dramatic fiber art, *The Dinner Party*, at her website: *www.judychicago.com/judychicago.php?p=gallery*.

Crafts.   Crafts include handcrafted traditional art such as pottery, weaving, and quilt making.

Color Window Quilt or Banner.   Give each child a zip lock bag, colored tissue paper, and cellophane. Children cut, tear, and arrange their piece and then the bags are taped together with clear, wide tape. Make into window banners or quilts.

Class Quilt.   Everyone's quilt background should be the same size to start off. Origami paper works and other media can be added. (See examples of random patterns used by quilters like the ladies at Gee's Bend: *www.quiltsofgeesbend.com/quilts/*.) Subject matter can vary. For example, each student can make a personal quilt piece about herself. In math, quilts can be used to explore geometric shapes (squares, triangles) and for counting. Experiment with printing, lettering, and collage. Encourage students to avoid the obvious: This need not be representational art; it can be abstract. Use chalk to mark placement on large bulletin board roll paper. (I tape two long pieces together side by side.) Glue finished quilt pieces. Wipe off chalk. Create a border using steps explained previously under displays and bulletin boards. Students can make cartoon-type "speech bubbles" telling about their creation process to post with the finished quilt.

Literature Quilts.   Quilts are particularly adaptable as art responses for books. Each student can each make a square for a class book quilt. Encourage use of diverse art materials and styles. The subject matter could be a book everyone has read, a favorite book, an author–artist study, or a genre.

Self-Portrait Banner.   Materials: white paper, white fabric (12 × 12 inches), pencil, chalk, water, mirror, permanent black marker, and masking tape. Directions: (1) Look in a mirror and examine your face closely. Sketch each half, really thinking of shapes and line. Outline in black marker. Add whatever you want to represent you (e.g., hat or symbols). (2) Put fabric over paper and tape down. Trace black outline with marker. Wet fabric—do not soak. (3) Use chalk to put in color. When dry, spray with nonaerosol hair spray. (4) Sew or glue all portraits into banners or a quilt.

Photography

> *Good art is not what it looks like, but what it does to us.* (Roy Adjak)

Now that disposable and digital cameras are readily available, classroom photography is easy. Teach a few important aspects of composition with a series of tasks (Cecil & Lauritzen, 1994) and then discuss the results: (1) Take the same person or object close up and far away. (2) Take a person or object with a lot of light and then with shadows or less light. (3) Take pictures of different subject matters: people, places (land, water, interiors of houses), animals, and action shots. (4) Create a still-life arrangement and photograph it. (5) Photograph the same person or object in the center of the picture and then off center (more to the left, right, top, or bottom).

Students can sort pictures depending on what they judge works best. Display with captions created by students on poster board. *Variation:* Students take a series of pictures of people, places, and events and then write a story that pulls the photographs together. Story and pictures can be made into a book.

Three-Dimensional Art

3D art can be made from assorted materials, including found objects, papier mâché, paraffin, and soap using the add or subtract methods. 3D art projects give tactile stimulation and an emotional outlet through touch because of the versatility of the materials.

Materials. Clays and doughs (see recipes in Ready Reference 7.3) and firing clay (from earth used for pottery) can be used. See Baylor's *When Clay Sings* for clay examples. Wood, paraffin, and soap can be used for carving, as well as materials from recipes. Papier mâché is also inexpensive and versatile (recipe follows).

Tools. Fingers, spoons, nails, sticks, cutouts (not cookie cutters), rolling pins, and things to press in to give textures (e.g., potato masher) are all possibilities.

Techniques. Use each of these methods to sculpt: add, subtract, punch, slap, pound, pinch, and stack. Children will naturally use clays and doughs to make cylinders and then balls and then pancake shapes. Modeling and plasticine clays hold their shape well but need to be warmed to make them pliable. Let children know they must knead the clay to warm it, which to develops finger strength.

Papier mâché. This is molding and sculpting material that is cheap and yields delightful shapes to paint or collage. Cut or tear up newspaper into 2-inch-long strips. Use thinned white glue or wheat (wallpaper) paste and dip strips. Run strips between fingers to remove excess. Let dry. Start with bases such as a Styrofoam tray and boxes. Move to more difficult curved and rounded shapes such as balloons and cardboard tubes.

It is easier to have one group at a time work on papier mâché because of the mess. Begin with a project in mind, rather than explore as you would in other media. Be sure to do cleanup immediately because the mix becomes hard and makes floors slippery. Shower curtains are useful to cover work surfaces.

Puppet heads can be made by starting with a base as simple as a wad of newspaper on top of a paper tube reinforced with masking tape. Spaghetti or candy boxes can be covered with papier mâché, painted, and used for puppets (make sure children can get fingers or hands inside). Papier mâché can be bought from sources such as Dick Blick (800-447-8192, *www.dickblick.com*) or J. L. Hammett Co. (800-333-4600, *www.hammett.com*).

Mobiles. These 3D artworks move. Show Alexander Calder's mobiles for ideas. Use sticks, hangers, or picture frames to suspend items from wire, yarn, cord, or ribbon. Mobiles can be made from found objects or by attaching created items. Encourage experimentation with balancing the weights of objects.

Other sculptures. Stick sculptures can be made by using a clay ball as a base and pushing in toothpicks, buttons, shells, and other similar objects. Sand molds are made by pressing objects into damp sand (lids, pencils, buttons, shells). Pour a thin mix of plaster of Paris (like salad dressing) about 1/2-inch deep into the depression. Put a pop-can tab or paper clip in the mixture to make a hanger.

Soap. To make soap clay for carving, mix 3/4 cup soap powder and a tablespoon of water. Whip until stiff. This can be used to coat projects to create a snow effect or molded (with wet hands). It dries hard and can be painted.

Paper. Crepe paper sculptures can be made by tearing paper, soaking 1 to 2 hours, pouring off the water, and adding wheat paste. It dries hard and can be sanded.

Yarn. Soak yarn in white glue and then wrap it around a balloon, as sparsely or densely as desired. When dry, break the balloon.

Vermiculite. Combine vermiculite (get at a plant store) and plaster. Add water and stir until thick. Pour into a mold or small box. Tear the box away when dry and carve with a table knife, nail, or blunt scissors.

Diorama or shadow boxes. These are scenes made by using a shoe box or other container to create a stagelike setting with 3D objects that are made or found.

 **Recipes for Clays, Doughs, and Pastes**

Clays and Doughs

Soft Dough
(stays soft if stored in a plastic bag)

Ingredients: 1 c water, 1/4 c salt, 1 tbsp vegetable oil, 1 tbsp alum, 1 c flour (nonrising), food coloring (optional—stains skin and clothing!)

Bring water to a boil. Add salt and food coloring. Remove from heat and add the oil, alum, and flour. While it is still hot, mix and knead for 5 minutes. *Note:* If you add food coloring, it is best to do so at the beginning or add to dough after mixing using a few drops at a time and folding dough over color to mix. To change the texture, add cornmeal, sawdust, coffee grounds, sand, or other grainy items.

Goop:
Mix one part cornstarch and one part cold water.

Baker's Clay
(makes one cup): (used to make ornaments or jewelry)

Ingredients: 4 c flour, 1 c salt, 1/2 c warm water, food coloring (optional—will stain skin and clothing!)

Mix ingredients, kneading until smooth (5 minutes). Add more flour as needed. *Note:* If you add food coloring, do so a few drops at a time and fold dough over color to mix. Dough should be used the day it is made. Add 1 teaspoon alum and put in plastic bag to keep longer. The dough can be baked at 300°F until hard, approximately 20 to 60 minutes depending on the thickness. For Christmas ornaments, make holes for hanging before baking. Clay can be painted with felt tips on enamel or use half tempera and half white glue. Spray with fixative when done.

Soda-Starch Clay
(makes one cup)

Ingredients: 1 c baking soda, 1/2 c cornstarch, 2/3 cup warm water, food coloring or tempera paint (optional—will stain!)

Mix ingredients in pan until thickness of mashed potatoes. Stir to boiling. Pour on a cool surface and knead when cool. Add coloring during kneading. Store in plastic bag until ready to use. Shape beads by using a drinking straw to make holes. To speed dry, bake 10 minutes at lowest oven setting or 30 seconds on medium in a microwave. *Note:*

Make a day or two ahead. Make batches in different colors. You can use crayons, paint, or marker to paint this clay. Set with clear nail polish or shellac.

Salt-Starch Clay

Ingredients: 1 c cornstarch, 1/2 c salt, 1/2 c water

Mix and cook over low heat until it hardens. Salad oil delays drying.

Sawdust Clay

Ingredients: 2 c fine sawdust, 1 c wheat paste (wallpaper), 1/2 to 1 c water, 1 tsp alum to keep from spoiling

Mix to bread dough consistency. Let dry slowly. Keeps in plastic bag or refrigerator. *Note:* Good for making puppet heads and relief maps. Can be painted with tempera.

Pastes

Cornstarch Paste
(makes 1/2 pint)

Ingredients: 1/4 c corn starch, 3/4 c water, 2 tbsp sugar, 1 tbsp vinegar

Mix cornstarch and cold water in pan. Add sugar and vinegar. Stir constantly and slowly heat until it clears and thickens. Cool before using. Paste can be stored in the refrigerator several weeks if kept sealed. *Note:* Cornstarch paste has a pleasant smell and texture. It is not too sticky and is a safe, almost colorless paste that dries clear. It forms a stronger bond than flour paste and can be used for lightweight items such as fabric, yarn, rice, and thin cardboard. This is one of the stronger homemade pastes, but it must be cooked ahead of time. It is hard to remove when dry; it requires soaking and scrubbing.

Flour Paste
Add water to flour until it is thick but spreadable. *Note:* Children can make this. It can be used on most kinds of paper, and it is safe and does not stain clothes. The texture is different from school paste, so it makes an interesting change. It wrinkles thinner papers and makes a relatively weak bond, so it is not recommended for collage. It washes off easily when wet, but requires soaking and scrubbing if dry. It cannot be stored and should be used when first made. Add oil of wintergreen or peppermint to resist spoiling.

Architecture. Teach basic shapes such as the cube, arch, sphere, cone cylinder, pyramid, rectangular solid, and triangular solid. Then take a neighborhood walk to find examples in buildings. Books like McLerran's *Roxaboxen* can

be used to motivate students to think about construction as art making. Arches can be made with boxes and blocks, and cardboard tubes make a base to construct columns that can become corinthian, doric, or ionic with some papier

Ready Reference 7.4 Puppet and Mask–Making Ideas

Finger puppets: Cut off fingers of cheap work gloves to make individual puppets. Students can glue on materials or use fabric paints. *Alternatives:* Use small candy boxes (like Milk Duds boxes) as a base. Students can also create figures from paper or cardboard and attach "finger rings" to slip the puppets on.

Glove puppets: Each child needs one glove. Each finger becomes one character to be created from a story. Five characters are possible or some fingers can be objects in the story.

Stick puppets: Attach a popsicle stick, tongue depressor, ruler, or wooden dowel to a character made of paper, papier mâché, or cloth. *Variation:* Find sticks from trees to use as a base.

Shadow puppets: Cut character body parts from construction paper and hinge arms, legs, and so forth together with brads. Lay on overhead projector and move body parts to tell story.

Paper bag puppets and masks: Use small paper bags to create a character's face or body using paint, collage, markers, and so on. The puppet's mouth can be placed at the fold so that it looks as if it is talking. Yarn, grass, and twigs can be added for hair and paper or cloth for clothes. Use grocery bags to make puppet masks that students wear on their heads—cut eyes, mouth, and nose holes.

Sock puppets: Students sew or glue scraps of fabric, yarn, and pipe cleaners on socks. The sock can also be cut at the toe to create a mouth or held so that a mouth is created by a fold.

Paper plate puppets: Paper plates can be used for puppets and for masks. Students add materials to create a character and then tape sticks or rulers to the back for handles. *Variation:* Use plastic coffee can lids instead of paper plates as the base.

Papier mâché heads and masks: Use the recipe for papier mâché and apply to a ball of newspaper, attached to a toilet paper tube with masking tape. When dry, paint and attach other materials to create a character. A fabric body can be glued or sewn using a generic body pattern made from two pieces of cloth or paper.

To make a mask, papier mâché over a balloon. When dry, paint, trim and cut holes for eyes, nose, and mouth. Can be a full head or cover just the face.

Object puppets: Find and adapt objects that relate to a story and lay them on top of a box (used as a stage) or table as the story is told, for example: a covered thread spool (tuffet), a plastic spider, a tiny doll (Miss Muffet), or a toy spoon. Check craft stores for a variety of tiny objects, often in packages with multiples. *Variation:* Painted rock puppets: collect rocks and paint to represent characters. Display and manipulate as story is told.

Clothespin puppets: Use old-fashioned clothespins as the base to create characters. Clip to a ruler to give extra height.

Envelope puppets: Use large or small envelopes as the character base. Combine several envelopes for a different effect.

Pipe cleaner puppets: Bend, cut, and combine pipe cleaners to form puppets. Create a handle from one pipe cleaner.

Paper cup puppets: Use Styrofoam or paper cups as the creation base. Use cups of different sizes and combine cups for creative effects, for example: create taller puppets with several cups.

Card puppets: Use index cards as bases. Attach to sticks or use on a flannel board by gluing coarse sand paper or felt to the back. Card puppets can be placed in a pocket chart as a story is told.

Tagboard masks: Cut tagboard into ovals big enough to cover a face. Make four 1-inch slits, one on each "corner" so that the mask is given contour. Use masking tape to secure. Draw ovals for the eyes and a space to cut out a mouth. Paint and use collage materials to decorate according to a variety of cultures (display books with pictures of masks for data gathering).

Plaster gauze masks: The face is covered with Vaseline and then gauze, soaked in plaster, is applied and allowed to set up. (Keep nose, mouth, and eye areas clear.) Mask is removed and painted with acrylics or tempera. (Make sure students aren't claustrophobic.)

---

mâché, glue, and paint. This is a particularly relevant art connection to studies of communities and countries. There's a post office or government building with Greek columns in nearly every American city. Terms that relate to architecture, such as *arch, beam, column, post,* and *lintel* can be taught to give students conceptual anchors. The Pittsburgh History and Landmarks Foundation's *Int-*

roduction Architecture is available online at: *www.phlf.org*. It includes excellent drama, dance, and field-based sketching, mask and mural activities for teaching basic architectural concepts.

Puppets and masks. Ready Reference 7.4 describes ways to make puppets and masks with readily available materials.

Bookmaking

Pop-up, accordion, big books, minibooks, sewn book, and shape books can be made to bind up student writing and artwork. Many books are available on making and binding (e.g., use wallpaper to cover or "sew" with yarn through hole punches). Example resources are *The Elements of Pop-up* (Carter) and *Read a Book, Make a Book* (Norris).

Animal Flip Books. This book type combines animal parts to create new creatures. Students draw or find magazine pictures of animals and insects that have distinct heads, bodies, and legs. Pictures should be similar in size. Each animal is a page in the book that needs to be fastened together so that body parts are in approximately the same place on each page. Each page is then cut into thirds: head, body, legs. By turning the different page parts, new animals are created and can be named. This can evolve into creative writing by setting up categories for students to use to invent a description of their new creature: habitat, food, habits, and movements. For younger students, body parts can be placed on cards and assembled on a table. *Variation:* For older students, use a grid, listing or depicting animal or insect heads across the top of a page, and bodies down the left side. By finding the intersection of the X and Y axes, students create new visual combinations (e.g., X (heads) for goat, cow, llama, cat, and Y (bodies/legs) for dolphin, turtle, snake, duck.

Big Books. Big books are enlarged copies of favorite books, poems, or chants about the size of poster board. To construct a big book as a response to a book, lesson, or unit of study:

1. *Paper:* 18-by-30-inch white chart paper and 12-by-18-inch white construction paper will be needed, plus two pieces of poster board at least 18 by 30 inches, and clips, metal rings, or cord to secure the cover.

2. *Art materials:* Glue, markers, crayons, wallpaper sample, and other collage materials.

3. *Type of book:* Replica or new version? To make this decision, select a predictable story or poem with obvious patterns or rhyme (see list of predictable books in Chapter 4 under "Genre"). Reading the book or poem several times invites children to chime in. Prepare for writing by brainstorming ideas. Students then dictate a rough draft, which the teacher writes on a large chart or older students write independently. Then the story or poem is reread and revised.

4. *Text:* Words are printed on white construction paper and glued on the larger sheets of paper. The text should be divided evenly across the pages of the book so that there is room left for artwork.

5. *Illustrations:* Students can use materials, styles, and techniques. Encourage experimentation with the styles of various artists.

6. *Title page with the copyright year and the names of authors and artists:* Design a title page and, if the book is a replica, a statement such as "Retold and illustrated by Mr. Walker's class." If the big book is an adapted version, use a statement such as "Based on Charlotte Zolotow's book, *Someday.*" Make a dedication page for the beginning of the book, a page about the authors, and a reader comment page at the back.

7. *Cover:* Students design a front and back cover, and it is glued to the poster board.

8. *Page sequence:* Have students order the pages, and put the book together with front cover, title page, copyright page, dedication page, story, page about the authors, comment page, and back cover. Use rings, cord, or metal clips to bind.

IV. Connecting Visual Art to Curricular Areas

This section gives seed ideas to connect visual art and science, social studies, math, and literacy.

Science Focus

The full science standards document can be accessed at the National Science Teachers Association (NSTA) website: *www.nsta.org.*

Art News. John Mieyal, professor of pharmacology at Case Western Reserve in Cleveland, says the arts are important communication tools. He shows his students how to doodle, cartoon, and diagram to explain how substances affect human biology and might be used for medicinal purposes (Jack, 2005).

Art and Nature. First, students examine how an animal, plant, or natural object are shown in different ways by artists. Present three to five pieces of art that contain an image. For example, use dog images and ask what dog information is shown in each, how each picture feels different, and why the artists showed the dogs as they did. Picture book art can be used. Compare art with science facts gathered. Example: Compare Gag's *Millions of Cats* and Pinkwater's cat in *The Wuggie Norple Story.*

Nature Collage. Plan art walks to collect natural items to display or use in collages. Examples: twigs, leaves, stones, bark, and feathers. Add museum tags to displays.

Fish and Bird Art. Students choose a fish or bird and research (1) where it lives, (2) what it eats, and (3) how it moves. This information is then connected to how the fish or bird looks (color, shape, size of body parts). Students next create a new fish or bird by thinking of answers to the three questions and using a variety of art media. New animals are named. Students can do oral presentations and display work in the class museum.

Food Mural.   Students work in teams to research a food's origin. Use paint and collage materials to construct a mural to show how food ends up on the dinner table. For example, show how wheat is planted, harvested, processed, baked, wrapped, and delivered to stores.

Sketch Invisible Animals.   Examine water under a microscope or with hand lenses and sketch living organisms. Show students how to do quick sketches with pencils to capture important details. Emphasize close looking to draw specifics. Sketches can be enlarged into full drawings or paintings. *Note:* In the video *The Lively Art of Picture Books* (Schindel, Weston Woods), Robert McCloskey sketches ducks. *Variation:* Invite a local visual artist to demonstrate sketching before this activity.

Habitat 3D.   Use boxes to create dioramas of animal habitats (land or water). Add clay sculptures, tempera paint, found objects, and papier mâché in construction. Emphasize the importance of showing how the habitat would enable the animal to survive (food, shelter, etc.). *Variation:* Create habitat mobiles—one per animal.

Habitat Hat.   Students research different habitats to discover unique characteristics. See *www.fi.edu/tifi/units/life/habitat/habitat/html* for ideas. Students then bring in magazine pictures (wildlife magazines are a good source) and "found" objects (shells, sticks, etc.) to affix to hats. Use old hats or paper hats as a base. Provide raffia, construction paper, tempera paint, and glue (teacher C. Kotarsky, Lady's Island Elementary School).

Museum Scavenger Hunt.   During a museum visit give pairs or teams a scavenger hunt form on which to record "finds" in these categories: animals, plants, and other images related to space and land forms. Make spaces to note title, artist, date, media, and a place to comment about subject matter (facts/feelings) for each piece of art.

Pounded Flowers.   Do this in the spring. Collect a variety of fresh flowers. Discuss their names and how they look similar and different. Students then place the flowers on light-colored construction paper and cover them with clear plastic wrap. Pound each flower with a hammer until the color is embedded in the paper. Frame and display.

Scientific Drawings.   Examine the drawings of Beatrix Potter and Robert McCloskey, both of whom studied animals and plants carefully to render their images. Students can then choose to do a careful scientific drawing, focusing on important details. Use photos or actual plants for close looking. *Variation:* Examine the drawings of Audubon at *www.nytstore.com* (go to "fine art," "Audubon").

Nature Sculptures.   Use types of clouds (e.g., stratus, cumulus) to inspire soft sculptures. See the recipes in Ready Reference 7.3.

Science of Color.   Groups each need a prism to investigate color. Paint or use crayons to record observations and discover the pattern (ROY G. BIV: Red, Orange, Yellow, Green, Blue, Indigo, Violet). Follow up with data gathering the how and why of the spectrum.

Nature Collections and Displays.   Students create displays from "found" nature, including seasonal collections like a fall display of leaves, twigs, stones, and dried flowers. Label each using museum tags with common and Latin names (make up for creative thinking). *Note:* killing insects for displays is inappropriate.

Rock Paintings.   Students select fist-sized rocks. Add white glue to tempera paint or use acrylics to make paint that will stick. The paintings can be abstract or students can carefully study the rock shape to see what images are suggested (e.g., mouse, cat). Display abstract and representational works for ideas. *Examples:* Show Matisse, Miro, and van Gogh prints for ideas about colors and lines. Be sure to tell students that Michelangelo believed the image was in the stone waiting to be freed; he did not impose his image on the stone.

Step into the Painting.   Invite students to think like scientists. Display and discuss the scientific process. Focus on observing details and asking questions. As a group brainstorm observations from a piece of art (e.g., a landscape). Look closely with magnifying glasses. Focus on the content and how the painting might have been made. Give five Ws and H questions as a frame for student questions.

Grow a Head.   Use knee-high hose to make living heads. Fill hose with a teaspoon of grass seed and then a mixture of soil and sawdust. Tie snugly with a string. Paint on face with fabric paint. Put head in a shallow dish and pour water over it. Place in a sunny area and watch the grass "hair" grow. Ask students to record daily observations in a science journal (e.g., measurements, colors, textures).

Garbage Art.   Use clean trash that students collect to make collages that promote looking at throwaways differently. Emphasize experimenting with how to group items on cardboard and use patterns. Encourage tearing, scrunching, and even using pieces of plastic and glass for mosaic effects (take care about sharp edges). *Variation:* Combine with painting, fabrics, and nature materials.

Foot Painting.   Put on music and ask students to listen to its rhythm and mood. Spread out large paper. Use shallow trays of tempera. Tell students to roll up pant legs. Start with a choice of a few colors. Students create art by paint-

Visual Art Strategies

ing with their feet—to the music. Discuss the effects of different feet (e.g., ridges on footprints).

Everyday Objects. Check out an unusual book that uses ordinary things as unit centers: *Inquiry-Based Learning Using Everyday Objects: Hands-on Instructional Strategies That Promote Active Learning in Grades 3–8* (Alvardo, A., & Herr, P., 2003, Thousand Oaks, CA: Corwin Press).

Social Studies Focus

The full social studies standards document is available from the National Council for the Social Studies (NCSS): *www.socialstudies.org.*

Make Me a World. Papier mâché, used over a balloon base to create personal globes, can accompany individual research projects related to countries, continents, and oceans. Paint with tempera and label major areas. (See previous papier mâché directions.) Hang with string from ceiling. *Variations:* (1) study history of globes and students choose to make a globe in a style from a time period; (2) use in science to make planets.

Signature Art. Part of social studies involves coming to respect individual differences. Show a facsimile of signatures (e.g., *Declaration of Independence*). Give students paper and choices of tools and media. Allow time to write signatures many different ways. Display products and discuss differences in size, color, lines, and shapes. Focus on what makes each name so different and the effect on a viewer.

Paraphs. These are special designs John Hancock and Queen Elizabeth I added to their signatures to prevent forgery. Download examples of paraphs at *http://art.lex.com.* Discuss how art often has its roots in functional needs of people (e.g., antique tools are displayed for decorative purposes; showhorse trainers teach horses to "dance" using steps originally needed in ranching). Give students large paper to experiment with creating personal paraphs.

Group Composition. Learning cooperative behavior is a key goal of social studies so any art project that expects students to take individual responsibility and come together to create a whole work is appropriate. For example, all these are collaborative art: murals, class topic quilts (state, city, transportation, etc.), group sculptures such as totem poles, or constructing with cardboard boxes, tubes, or papier mâché around a topic such as inventions. *Note:* Art need not be representational to convey important messages.

Multicultural Art. Any country or culture can be studied through its art forms. Assemble prints, pictures, and artifacts. Ask students to observe the art elements details and patterns. Ask about what the figures are doing and why. Ask about the emotions conveyed by the art and why the artists showed

what they did. Students can research pieces of art (media, techniques) and then experiment with these. Emphasize the values portrayed in each art form by asking, "What does this show about the people?" *Note:* Mixing skin tones was described earlier. *Variation:* Each child begins a personal collection of art from a culture or ethnic groups using magazines, advertisements, and postcards. Display in a class museum.

Artifacts. Artifacts are tools or ornaments made by humans using design principles and art elements. Many were originally for functional purposes. Artifacts can be coordinated with units and used for art interpretation, art making, writing, and drama. Invite students to contribute to a display of artifacts from their own lives. Discuss the five Ws and H about family artifacts. Label each with a museum tag. Compare with historical artifacts that reveal aspects of everyday life of a people. Baskets, carvings, quilts, pots, and jewelry give us hints about the values and needs of cultures and the artists.

Holidays. Many are concerned about how the "holiday curriculum" trivializes social studies. The problem lies in the superficial ways in which holidays are studied and the lack of connections to standards. Stereotypical and dictated art abound and need to be avoided. Instead of tracing hand turkeys and coloring Pilgrim and Indian heads at Thanksgiving, it is more meaningful to engage students in using a variety of art media to express ideas and feelings about major themes. For example, (1) meals are rituals used to celebrate events in many cultures, (2) people offer food as a gift to show appreciation and love, and (3) there are many ways to give thanks. Use any art form, medium, tool, and technique to allow students to express these understandings. The more unique each student's art is, the better. Personal construction of meaning that has fealty to basic facts is the goal.

Mandalas. The mandala is a circular shape that has been used in all cultures for eons. The circle is a satisfying and comforting shape and mandalas come in all sizes. First, motivate students to search for examples of circles or find art compositions with circular patterns from various cultures and contemporary art. Search for the circle image in daily life, including advertisements such as the Coke sign. Brainstorm circular things in nature, such as the sun and moon or the cycle of seasons. After this data gathering, students are ready to create original mandalas. This broad idea can be interpreted in any way, from round abstract artworks to poster-sized realistic works containing multiple circular-shaped images. Any material may be used. Young children especially enjoy collage mandalas. Discuss final products by asking students to become "art docents" to tell about why they made their choices of media and how they arranged their compositions. Focus on how each mandala feels and what causes the emotional effect.

Update Art. Do a modern-day version of an artist's work to make it reflect the current time rather than an historical time. For example, change the background or dress of portraits (e.g., *Mona Lisa*). *Note:* This has become a popular idea especially using Grant Wood's *American Gothic*.

Class Flag. Examine the flags and symbols of countries. Discuss how and why they use the colors, shapes, designs, materials, and lines they do. Divide into groups to create a class flag to represent what's important about the class. Make fabric, paper, paint, and collage materials available for design.

Famous People Sculptures. Students choose a person who has made a significant contribution to history (explorer, president, artist, activist). Brainstorm what students would like to know with focus on the five Ws and H questions. Students are charged to find details about how the person looked, moved, talked, and dressed, what she or he ate, valued, and achieved. Students then construct sculptures from papier mâché or make puppets (use paper bags, papier mâché heads, stuffed hose, or stuffed plastic bags to make heads; Ready Reference 7.4). Crayola's Model Magic is a bit pricey, but works well. Sculptures can be used for "expert presentations" or panels done in role.

Famous Sculptures. Partners take turns sculpting each other using famous poses from historical paintings or sculptures (e.g., *Washington Crossing the Delaware, The Thinker*). *Variation:* Half of the class assumes a famous pose while the other half pretends to be museum visitors who tour in pairs and use dialogue to show what they see, how they feel, and who they are.

Draw to Music. Listen to music about a relevant place, person, or topic (e.g., *Grand Canyon Suite* or *American in Paris*). Write or draw to the music and then share what and how the music communicated important messages.

Sound and Show Compositions. Students prepare a sound and art presentation around a choice social studies topic, such as a culture or country. They may work in groups or pairs to find a piece of music to play as they present art on transparencies, PowerPoint, or an easel as the song is played. Art can be student made or "found art."

Literacy: Reading and Language Arts Focus

The full standards literary/literature standards document is available from the National Council of the Teachers of English (NCTE) and the International Reading Association (IRA) at *www.ncte.org* or *www.ira.org*.

Guided Art and Literacy Lesson (GALL). In this generic lesson, the structure of visual art is the literacy material to develop listening, speaking, reading, and writing

skills. Thinking skills used in the CPS process serve as the framework. The lesson is teacher directed and uses introduction, development, and conclusion steps. Students can learn to direct GALL lessons if steps are posted and practiced (Planning Page 7.1).

Planning Page 7.1

Guided Art and Literacy Lesson (GALL)

Introduction

See and feel. Students closely examine a work of art for a period of time (e.g., 2 minutes). Ask: What do you see? Look closely for details. How does it make you feel? Why? No talking at this stage. Display "Art Concepts and Elements" to prompt thinking. *Example art: I and the Village* by Chagall.

Predict. Students hypothesize/predict possible messages the artist intended. Ask students to tell (1) what they saw/felt and (2) what it might mean. The teacher can scribe for young children using chart paper or overhead. *Example:* The artist has everything going in different directions, so he may be trying to say he is confused.

Development

Data gather. Read about the artist and/or the work of art. Teachers may read to the students or show a video. *Example:* Read Greenfield's *Marc Chagall*.

Evidence. Students give evidence to confirm or reject predictions. Emphasize that "being right" is not the goal. Do in pairs, small groups, or whole group. *Example:* Prediction about confusion is rejected because Chagall was being playful and childlike. He focused on dream qualities.

Conclusion

Write. Students respond in writing (Ready Reference 5.1). *Example:* Write a letter to Chagall or a story about his dream. The story could start at the top of the picture and move to the bottom.

Artmaking. Students do an art response connected to the original art (Ready References 6.5 and 6.11). *Example:* Watercolor paintings of dreams or a class mural of good memories done in Chagall's style.

Publish. Students' responses are made public through displays, oral sharing, and bookmaking (e.g., class big book).

Variations: Any piece of art can be used for tableau and can be danced. Students can take the role of an artist and explain thoughts and feelings about making the art. Music can be found that "fits" the art and played during a close viewing.

Picture Books.   Ready Reference 7.5 lists many ways to teach arts and language arts with picture books.

Cinco Parts of Speech.   Look closely at a piece of art. Number your paper 1 to 5 and list: (1) nouns you see; (2) verbs and actions; (3) adjectives; (4) adverbs; and (5) a sentence using the ideas you've generated. *Note:* Abstract art works well.

Listen and Draw.   Partner students and give one a secret object. They sit back to back as one describes the object while the other tries to draw it. Encourage students to tell size, shape, and color and focus on use of visual details. *Variations*: Do by arranging sets of objects or with one partner describing a drawing while the other draws (e.g., a geometric or organic shape).

Note Sketching.   Imagery facilitates memory and is a powerful way to learn words and concepts. For example, students can draw or make mental pictures of words versus memorizing dictionary definition (Wolfe, 2001). Show students how to take notes using a split-page format: Make a vertical line to separate paper into one third and two thirds. Take notes on the two-thirds section. Stop periodically and sketch out important ideas on the one third.

Artist Birth Mates.   See the Appendix for a complete description of the year-long research project that matches each student with an artist born on his or her birthday.

Artists Like Me.   After studying an artist, have students write about all the ways the artist was like them. Suggest categories such as feelings, family, physical characteristics, interests, places lived (source: Misty Kaplafka, Ohio art teacher).

Art Stories.   Choose any art print(s) as a prompt for group or individual stories. Use portraits for characters, a landscape for the setting, and an abstract or nonfigurative work for problem/conflict ideas. Teach students to establish the problem quickly and be descriptive about the setting and characters. *Variation:* Use for circle storytelling followed by individual writing.

Ready Reference 7.5   Picture Books Art Strategies

1. *Ape the Greats.* Explore picture book styles and media using Ready References 6.5 and 6.9. Experiment using an artist's media and styles. Adapt using SCAMPER (Ready Reference 2.5).
2. *Predict from art.* Before reading show one or two pictures. Prompt to look closely. Ask for predictions, using only the pictures, about (1) Who? *characters,* (2) When and where? *setting/time,* and (3) What might the problems be? Ask for evidence from the art. Record ideas on a chart divided into three columns so students can confirm or reject.
3. *Clothesline prediction.* Use two copies of the same book. Take one apart and cut off the text. Display the pictures before reading. Ask students to put them in the order they think will happen. Coach students to come to an agreement about an order. Use a clothesline to pin pictures up in order. Next, read the book and check picture order. Rearrange as necessary. *Variation:* Partner students to write or tell a story to go with the pictures before reading.
4. *Experts.* Each child or group selects a picture. The goal is to notice everything by looking closely. Small magnifying glasses make this more fun, or use toilet paper tubes. Prepare cue sheets that give categories to observe: art elements, media, style, decisions the artist made, composition (arrangement). Expert panels report.
5. *Blow-up art.* Many books are available as big books so the art is easy to see. Use the *art discussion strategies* in Ready Reference 6.10 with any picture. Another option is to make color transparencies of selected pages. Stewig's series, *Reading Pictures* (1988), has lesson plans and poster-sized art from picture books.
6. *Partial picture preview.* Cover a portion of one picture and ask students to examine the remaining part. Ask "What do you see?" and other open questions. Ask students to predict the covered portion. *Variation:* Look at pictures in a mirror (reverse image), upside down, or from far away to discover new colors and shapes. Composition can be studied by squinting to see the masses, instead of the details. Students can hypothesize why the artist made the choices he or she did.
7. *Style match.* Compare art done in the same style as the book (e.g., impressionistic, folk art. Ready Reference 6.9). Example: compare and/or create a Venn diagram based on the work of Monet and Emily McCully's art in *Mirette on the High Wire* (light, color, shapes, and edges).
8. *Scavenger hunts.* Students search picture books for specifics: media, style, borders, perspective (within and among books). Set up a bingo-type format. *Note:* Students need access to many books and must know the art elements. This activity can last a day or a week or turn into an ongoing routine.

(continued)

Ready Reference 7.5 Picture Books Art Strategies *(continued)*

9. *Wordless books and LEA.* Language experience approach (LEA) is a classic strategy to teach reading and writing. Use it with wordless books: Ask students to dictate a story that goes with the pictures (or write their own). Finished stories become the reading material for lessons (e.g., play I Spy to locate high-frequency phonic patterns) and for independent reading. *Suggestion:* To build independence and keep attention, ask students to spell aloud when you take dictation from them.

10. *Book parts.* Teach about how book parts such as: endpapers, set the mood, and gutters should not break up pictures across double pages. Examine the effects of borders. Teach title page, half-title page, and credits to increase visual literacy.

11. *Compare–contrast books.* Use a Venn diagram to record likenesses and differences between the same story written and illustrated by two different picture book artists. This provides an opportunity to work on the higher-order thinking skills (HOTS) of analysis.

12. *Create characters.* Combine the body, head, and legs from different characters in picture books to make new characters. Either cut up picture books or use the art as an inspiration for drawing (not copying). Write a story to go with the new creatures.

13. *Make a picture book.* Students can write/illustrate picture books in any genre: alphabet, concept, predictable, or fairy tales. Encourage use of a variety of media and styles.

14. *Frame favorites.* Treat picture book art as art. Cut books apart, make color copies, write to publishers for posters or prints, or use publishers' catalog pictures to create framed art. Create a gallery.

15. *Concentration/memory.* To play concentration, make 6 to 10 pairs of cards with the artist's photo and one example of his or her art. Paste all on same-sized cards and turn upside down to play. The goal is to remember the location and pick up pairs. Get pictures and book art from publishers' catalogs and book covers. E-mail publishers for photos and examples of book art.

16. *Set the scene.* Re-create a book scene with tableau (frozen picture drama). Students may want to use props, costumes, and so forth. *Example:* Make whole room into a water scene from *Swimmy* (Lionni).

17. *Puzzles.* Cut up pictures and give each child a piece. Each child studies his piece to try to find as much as possible about it. Assemble to see the whole picture. Do before or after reading a book.

18. *Special days.* Everyone picks a book with a special trait (e.g., pop-up, alphabet, special endpapers, borders). Each child studies the book so that she can present the focus in 1 minute.

19. *Storytelling.* Cut up several picture books. Students combine the mixed-up art to make a new story. Make sure there are pictures of characters and settings. *Variations:* Do storytelling in a circle with each student picking a picture and adding. Groups can take picture packs to write or tape their stories. An alternative recording idea is to storymap stories students told or will tell.

20. *Collages.* Use old picture books as source material for collages (e.g., by media such as cartoons and watercolor, subject matter such as portraits and landscape, or topics such as plants and animals).

Talking Art. Each student writes something a person in a piece of art might be saying. Give each student a blank piece of paper and show how to cut cartoon-type speech bubbles. Bubbles are displayed around the art.

Learn–Wonder–Like. Students pretend they are going to meet the artist of a particular work. In preparation they generate a list of comments and questions about what they *learned*, *wondered*, and *liked* about the art. *Variation:* Do in a talk show format.

Fine Art Storytelling. Review the literary elements (Ready Reference 4.1). Use an art print as a stimulus to tell a story. Pass the print around a circle with each student adding to the tale. *Variation:* Use several portraits and a landscape (or seascape or cityscape) to set up the characters and setting.

Parts of Speech. Display parts of speech categories. Under each category, ask students to find verbs, adjectives, and the like related to a piece of art. This can be done in small groups, with each group taking a part of speech.

Word Squeeze. Look closely at a piece of art to find all the colors, shapes, places, textures, lines, feelings, actions, things, and so forth. Make columns on a piece of paper and brainstorm words for each. Tell the students to squeeze the art like a sponge to find things no one else sees.

Seeing Systematically. Give each student a magnifying glass or cardboard tube (or use fist) to examine a piece of art. Tell them to look at the art systematically: foreground–background, top–bottom, left side–right side, edge–center. This can be guided with 1 minute on each area. Afterward, students free-write and then prioritize most important ob- servations. *Variations:* Students create titles for the artwork. Focus on capturing the main ideas/feelings.

Name a Color.   List all the color names students know. Divide into groups to find new words for the colors (e.g., cerise for red) using the dictionary, thesaurus, and other ref- erence materials. Follow with doing a piece of art to ex- periment with making new colors through mixing. New colors can be named by students.

Walk into a Painting.   Students pretend to physically enter a landscape, seascape, or cityscape. Take them on a guided journey through the work. Afterward, students write or tell how they felt and what they saw, using all five senses.

Art Ads.   Teach the most common propaganda devices: bandwagon, glittering generalities, celebrity endorsement, common folks, and everybody's doing it. Break students into groups to create a 1-minute ad to sell a piece of art using the techniques. These can be written or presented orally.

Artist Interview.   Ask students to brainstorm questions to ask an artist about a particular piece of art (sculpture, col- lage, painting). Example question starters: I was wondering why . . . , I am wondering how . . . , I am puzzled about . . . . Set up pairs to interview each other by alternating being the artist and interviewer. *Variation:* Use student-made art for the interviews.

Mini-Museum.   Students need a sturdy box to create a display of collected items that relate to a book, story, or poem. Items may be made or found that connect to char- acters, setting, and theme. Museum tags are added to items with a title, approximate date, and material for each. Set up museums as stations to be visited by groups, with creators serving as docent guides to talk about the items.

Wanted Posters.   After showing examples of wanted posters and portraits, each student selects a book character and creates a poster. A portrait is drawn by examining the general shape of the face and measuring distances between eyes, nose, mouth, and so forth. At the bottom of the poster, students write a description of the character, the place and time last seen, and a contact person. Rewards or other no- tifications may be added. (Parts of the text may be reread for accurate details.)

Stretch-to-Sketch.   Students interpret what happened to characters and the roles each played by making sketches (quick rough drawings) (Harste, Short, & Burke, 1988). Each character can be sketched in several story actions to summarize the events. Students present their drawings by

explaining interpretations and discussing how others [saw] the same things and why. Drawings can be compared and contrasted.

Art Prediction Cards.   Two copies of a book or a pho- tocopy are cut apart. Pictures are pasted on tagboard and displayed in "bookological" order. Students observe pic- tures, without talking, to get clues about the upcoming story. Then ask students to use literary elements to discuss the pictures. Ask "What can you tell about the setting? Characters? Plot? Mood? How do you know?" The story is then read. Afterward the pictures can be reused for retelling. *Variations:* (1) Students write captions for pictures. (2) Be- fore reading, present cards out of order and ask students to agree about a predicted order; read the story and then re- arrange the cards.

Quickdraws.   Before reading, students sketch about a topic that relates to the upcoming book (Tompkins, 1997) to activate visual imagery. They use the images while read- ing to confirm, reject, and modify ideas during active mean- ing construction.

Sketchbooks.   Each child has a sketchbook to draw in before, during, or after reading or listening to literature. Sketchbook responses can be brought to discussions to or- ganize sharing. Prompts for sketches include characters, set- ting, most exciting points, special objects or symbols, plot, theme, and even style sketches related to special words. For example, the sun is described as a "sliding egg yolk" in *Tuck Everlasting*. Sketches can also be used as writing prompts (e.g., write a poem or paragraph about a sketch).

I Spy (observation/vocabulary).   Set this up as a game as in the *Where's Waldo* books. Say "I spy . . ." to start. Ask students to find special elements to finish the phrase. En- courage them to look closely for big shapes, little shapes, curvy lines, light, and dark and to try to find action and de- tails. Use with abstract art to stretch thinking. See the *I Spy* art series (Marzollo) which focuses on finding something in masterpieces, such as letters, animals, and toys.

Art Match.   Show a variety of shapes and colors on sep- arate cards (e.g., construction paper shapes and colors). Dis- play an art print and ask students to find and name the same shapes and colors in the art. Ask how patterns are created (by repeating shapes and colors).

Memory Game.   Tell students to study a piece of art carefully for a time period. Then cover it up. Ask them to list everything they remember. Do this individually or in groups, orally or in writing. Uncover the painting and check for accuracy of observations. *Note:* Repeat and ex- tend the time each time to stretch observational skills.

nce 7.6 Artist Experts

... or becoming an expert on any artist.

Read abo... ...

1. Life of the artist: biographical information such as birth, death, marriage, children, friends
2. Who and what most influenced the artist
3. Time period in which the artist lived
4. Country or countries where the artist lived
5. Style in which the artist worked or school of art to which the artist belonged
6. Influence the artist had on the world of art (for what the artist is known)
7. Other artists of that period
8. Medium(s) the artist used
9. A particular work of art the artist did, for example, the most famous or controversial
10. Art criticism about the artist and his or her work

Write ...

1. Letters: to artists or someone in the art; to museum curator to request information about a work of art
2. Biographical sketches of artists
3. Story about a great artwork (see *Girl in Hyacinth Blue*—adult example, Vreeland, 1999)
4. Story about how the work of art came to be
5. Menu that might be served during the time the art was created
6. Report on the customs of the time of the artist
7. Report on the clothing styles of the time of the artist
8. Description or criticism of a piece of art
9. Report about the period of art
10. Paragraph hypothesizing what the artist would do if she were alive
11. Script for play or scene about the artist's life
12. Comparison of the work of two artists; Venn diagram
13. Timeline of the artist's work
14. Book for children about an artist, medium, or style (see bookmaking ideas in this chapter)

Word Walls (vocabulary). Designate a space for students to put up artistic words (with special shapes and meanings). Sticky notes can be used or make any card into a sticky note with removable glue sticks. Words can be alphabetized or grouped by color, shape, media, and style.

Word Webs. This is similar to a word wall. Put each art category in the center of large paper. Attach lines or yarn radiating from each category. Students add to the webs by finding examples in artwork. They can draw or write the idea on the web. Students can underline and write their initials beneath personal contributions. For example, a "line" web category would include: zagged, straight, curved, or thin.

Art Chair (creative thinking/reflection). Teach the CPS process (Ready Reference 2.5). After making art, ask students to write or tell about the parts used. Written papers can be divided into CPS sections: attitude, problem definition, data gathering, experimenting, and so forth. Present as Artist Chairs in which students sit in a special place to share and be interviewed.

Dialogue Journals and Logs. These can be done individually, as dialogues between two students, or as team journals. Topics to write back and forth about include: What do you think about the painting? How does it make you feel? What does it make you think about? What mood do you think the artist was in when he or she created this work of art? Why did the artist entitle the work of art as he or she did?

Compare and Contrast. Different messages are conveyed through the use of different media (e.g., sculpture, poetry, dance). Compare and contrast two pieces of art that evoke similar feelings and messages. How does each artist create the response? What do both artists do that is similar? For example, look at art about courage, love, family, war, suffering, or nature.

Storyboard. Picture book artists often begin with a storyboard—brief sketches or mock-ups of how the finished book might look. To make a storyboard create a series of drawings (in order) that tell a story and glue them on a poster board.

Art Prewrite. Students create any type of art or collect art (postcards, pictures, pottery) to use as topics for writing. The art is "squeezed" for writing ideas by brainstorming. For example, web the five Ws and H questions related to a piece of art. Any of the things to write and say in Ready Reference 5.1 can be used (caption, letter, list).

Artist Experts. Ready References 7.6 and 7.7 offer reading/ writing ideas for becoming an expert on any artist.

Ready Reference 7.7   # Artists Alive!

Students pick an artist and do the following to bring the artist to life.

- *Collection:*
  Start finding and saving works of art by the artist (e.g., prints, calendar art, postcards).
- *Ape the greats:*
  Use the colors, mood, style, and techniques of the artist to create adapted works of art.
- *Update:*
  Make a modern-day version of the artist's work (e.g., change the costumes).
- *Vary it:*
  Do another version of the art (e.g., van Gogh's, *Starry Night*—do Sunny Day, Rainy Day, Stormy Night, Foggy Night, or Snowy Night).
- *Guests and experts:*
  Invite a local artist, museum curator, or college professor to speak about the artist or interview them.
- *Art gallery:*
  Visit a museum and see the real thing.
- *Artist's studio:*
  Visit the place where an artist works; ask to shadow the person for a day.
- *Video:*
  Watch a video of the artist's life (e.g., *Lust for Life* about van Gogh).
- *Art show:*
  Have an event to display the artist's work and students' work together.
- *Mini art gallery:*
  In the hall, classroom, or a special place in the school, include works by famous artists and students' works of art.
- *Painting of the week:*
  Students select a favorite from among several works of art and display with "speech bubbles" telling things they know, think, or feel about it.

Visual Art Strategies

Math Focus

Access the full math standards at the National Council of Teachers of Mathematics (NCTM) website: *www.nctm.org*

Quilts.   Create class geometric quilts using traditional patterns found in folk art or by observing patterns in the environment (dots, checkerboard, and stripes). Each student uses a square of paper (about 10 by 10 inches) to plan. Patterns can be painted or made from cut paper, fabric, newspaper, or thin plastic. Squares are then glued onto a large piece of bulletin board roll paper (black makes a good background). A border can then be added. *Variations:* Students can be limited to just one shape to experiment with variations on it (e.g., triangle combinations).

Origami Art.   Japanese paper folding involves the study of shape, line, symmetry, and angle. Special origami paper in a package with variety of colors works well and is available from any art supply store. There are many resource books (LaFosse, 2003) on simple origami shapes, such as bird shapes, and the children's book *Sadako and the Thousand Paper Cranes* (Coerr) would be a wonderful story addition to this art–math project.

Color Recipes (Measurement).   Pair students and give each pair an eyedropper and three small cups of tempera (red, yellow, and blue; use ice cube trays cut in half). Students then experiment to create colors. They record the number of drops to create each color. Ask pairs to name their new colors. *Variation:* Give students one primary color and a cup of white and black. Experiment with recipes for shapes and tints (numbers of drops).

Art Auction.   Students prepare information about pieces of art to "sell" the works. Each student takes a turn at selling and auctioning. Give each a sum to spend at the auction.

Story Problem Art.   Students create art to go with story problems that they are given or they can write and illustrate original ones. Problems can be exchanged for solving. *Suggestions:* Teach basic drawing shapes. See previous drawing and sketching ideas.

SCAMPER.   Students are given a shape to manipulate using Eberle's SCAMPER steps: substitute, combine, adapt, minify or magnify, put to other uses, eliminate, and reverse or rearrange. They create a piece of art to show the things they did with geometric shapes (triangle, square, or circle). Use any media.

Count Me In.   Groups are given a piece of art to examine for numbers of things. Give a time limit and then share as a group (e.g., 11 curved lines, 8 right angles, 14 red flowers).

I Spy Math.   Find the math in any piece of art (print, collage, sculpture) or picture book. List geometric shapes, patterns (anything repeated), types of lines, and use of symmetry. Discuss any parts that give a feeling of infinity and how it is accomplished. Use a large magnifying glass.

Symmetry.   Each student gets one-half of a picture from a magazine or print. By carefully studying the half, the student tries to duplicate it on the opposite side.

Making Math Art.   Use art that is very geometric, such as that of Mondrian or Escher, and ask students to discuss how the artist might have made it and why. Have students try their own geometric math art by repeating shape patterns.

Step into the Painting.   Students become mathematicians and tell or write observations based from a math point of view. Encourage thinking about how the painting might have been made and the content of the work. Before beginning, list specific math vocabulary/concepts students may use. Example: I see a four-sided work that has a triangular composition. There are five figures with the male figures being greater than the female in size.

Infinity Art.   Show examples of Seurat's dot art (pointillism) and ask students to look closely to discover how the images are made. Discuss how the dots make up sets to create a whole image. Students can make their own dot art using Q-tips to paint.

Teacher Spotlight:

My First Year in Arts Integration

How do teachers phase into arts integration? Here is a first-person account from a first-year teacher (Lady's Island Elementary).

"I have conscientiously worked to tie art and the other curricular standards together. I am seeing a huge difference in my fifth graders' retention of information and interest level.

In science we classified animals as vertebrates and invertebrates using the art form of collage. We also made camouflaged butterflies and hid them in the classroom. The ones with the best camouflage were not found at all. This was a wonderful demonstration of understanding. The students also invented animals and drew special adaptations for survival.

In social studies students researched Indian tribes and used authentic techniques to make crafts. We've done a lot

with drawing of historical events, too. Recently, we studied cartooning, and the students drew political cartoons. Some were better than the newspaper! One was a Pilgrim shooting airplane-shaped bullets at a turkey who had the head of Osama bin Laden.

In math students made drawings about square numbers. They had to internalize the concept to depict their number. They also created "measurement monsters" to learn measurement equivalencies, such as 2 cups equal 1 pint. Students wrote number sentences that described themselves and included self-portraits.

In English/language arts students wrote and illustrated four framed comic strips, each with a different type of sentence: declarative, interrogative, exclamatory, and imperative. The process was amazing. Not only did they have to write each type of sentence, but it had to be creative and funny! We've also illustrated poems (me, too, actually) and made simple masks to act out stories for the kindergarten children.

It has been an amazing year, and it is just October!"

Conclusion

Art is either plagiarism or revolution. (Paul Gauguin)

I think Gauguin's idea has great relevance for teachers. We are constantly borrowing ideas from anywhere we can get them. The Seed Strategies in this chapter are the result of years of collecting. This particular cache of nuggets can initiate planning visual art connections with other curricular areas. When these are used within the context of the Arts Integration Blueprint and transformed by individual teachers to fit their students, these ideas can become revolutionary.

Resources

See the Appendix for further study, including more websites.

Multicultural Art Sources: Artifacts

Braman, A. (1999). *Kids around the world create! The best crafts and activities from many lands.* New York: Wiley.

Kohl, M., & Potter, J. (1998). *Global art: Activities, projects, and inventions from around the world.* Beltsville, MD: Gryphon House.

Terzian, A. (1993). *The kids' multicultural art book: Art & craft experiences from around the world.* Charlotte, VT: Williamson.

Art Institute of Chicago: *www.artic.edu/* (beadwork, weaving)

Christian Children's Fund: *www.christianchildrensfund.org/*

Museum of Modern Art: *www.moma.org/* (Chinese brush paintings)

Oxfam America: *www.oxfamamerica.org* (worldwide handmade items)

Save the Children: *http://savethechildren.org* (Africa and Asia)

Southwest Indian Foundation: *www.southwestindian.com*

Sources of Prints and Posters

Art Institute of Chicago, The Museum Shop (800-621-9337)
National Gallery of Art: *www.nga.gov*
Print Finders: *http://printfinders.com* (914-725-2332)
Sax Visual Arts Resources (800-558-6696)
Crystal: *www.crystalpublications.net*
Shorewood Prints (203-426-8100)
UNICEF (800-553-1200)

Software

Software is continuously being released. Visit a rating site, such as *www.epinions.com/* to find current recommended products.

Children's Literature References

Ahlberg, J., & Ahlberg, A. (1986). *The jolly postman*. Boston: Little, Brown.

Ai-Lang, L. (1982). *Yen Sen: A Chinese Cinderella story*. New York: Philomel.

Baylor, B. (1987). *When clay sings*. New York: Macmillan.

Bjork, C. (1987). *Linnea in Monet's garden*. New York: R&S Books.

Bruchac, J., & London, J. (1992). *Thirteen moons on a turtle's back*. New York: Philomel.

Bunting, E. (1994). *Smoky night*. San Diego, CA: Harcourt Brace.

Carter, D., & Diaz, J. (1999). *The Elements of pop-up*. New York: Simon & Schuster.

Cleary, B. (1992). *Ramona Quimby, age 8*. New York: Harper-Collins.

Coerr, E. (1977). *Sadako and the thousand paper cranes*. New York: Putnam.

Felix, M. (1993). *The colors*. Mankato, MN: Creative Education.

Gag, W. (1928). *Millions of cats*. New York: Coward, McCann.

Greenfield, H. (1991). *Marc Chagall*. New York: Abrams.

Griffith, H. (1992). *Granddaddy's place*. New York: Morrow.

Heller, R. (1995). *Color! Color! Color!* New York: Grosset & Dunlap.

Hoff, S. (1999). *Sammy the seal*. New York: HarperCollins.

Lionni, L. (1973). *Swimmy*. New York: Random House.

Marzollo, J. (1998). *I spy*. New York: Scholastic: Cartweel.

McCully, E. A. (1992). *Mirette on the high wire*. New York: Putnam.

McLerran, A. (1992). *Roxaboxen*. New York: Puffin.

Miles, M. (1971). *Annie and the old one*. Boston: Little, Brown.

Mille, R. (1997). *Put your mother on the ceiling*. Highland, NY: Gestalt Journal Press.

Norris, J. (1999). *Read a book, make a book*. Monterey, CA: Evan-Moor.

O'Neill, M. (1989). *Hailstones and halibut bones*. New York: Doubleday.

Pinkwater, D., & dePaola, T. (1988). *The Wuggie Norple story*. Palmer, AK: Aladdin.

Ringgold, F. (1991). *Tar Beach*. New York: Crown.

Steig, W. (1986). *Caleb and Kate*. New York: Farrar, Straus & Giroux.

Stevenson, J. (1987). *It could be worse*. New York: Morrow.

Tang, G. (2001). *Grapes of math*. New York: Scholastic.

Tang, G. (2003). *Math-terpieces*. New York: Scholastic.

Willard, N. (1981). *A visit to William Blake's inn*. New York: Harcourt Brace Jovanovich.

Zolotow, C. (1989). *Someday*. New York: Harper & Row.

Integrating Drama Throughout the Curriculum

Questions to Guide Reading

1. Why should drama be integrated (research, theories, philosophy) through the curriculum?

2. What should teachers know about the drama to integrate it.

3. How should drama integration be implemented?

4. How can teachers partner with drama/theatre specialists?

*H*obart Elementary is the second largest elementary school in the nation. Ninety percent of its 2,000 students come from households with incomes below the poverty level. All are from immigrant families, primarily Hispanic and Asian. None speaks English as a first language. But Rafe Esquith's fifth graders read far above grade level. Their test scores are in the top 5 to 10 percent of the country. How does he do it? Mr. Esquith immerses them in Shakespeare—his plays, life, and times. The yearlong study ends in April with a full production. One year, it was *Hamlet*, the next *The Taming of the Shrew* (Trudeau, 2005).

Drama in Education

Drama is life with the dull bits cut out. (Alfred Hitchcock)

Theatre and drama have a long history of relationships with human behavior and education. Primitive peoples pan-tomimed rituals to cast out demons; Aristotle thought theatre gave audiences a catharsis to release emotions. Medieval priests used theatre to explain Christianity to the masses. Drama in schools, however, didn't come on the scene until the early 20th century. Progressive educators emphasized students *doing* rather than just reading and memorizing. Like Hitchcock, they wanted the dull bits cut out. John Dewey and others looked to the arts as tools to make learning active. Drama proved a natural.

Now 21st-century research suggests that the problems of many students could be prevented with high-quality dramatic work (Arts Education Partnership, 1998). Findings that connect reading, writing, and drama are particularly strong. Drama also stimulates motivation to learn by engaging students in real-life problem solving (Deasy, 2002).

In the opening Classroom Snapshot, Sarah Lane puts this research into practice. She has been teaching sixth grade for 7 years and he is a vivacious teacher. She began integrating drama after a staff development project 2 years ago. Now she uses drama daily with focus on the problem-solving process. This lesson showcases performance as well. She combines several drama strategies, such as one-liners and teacher in role to teach toward standards in social studies and theatre/drama.

Classroom Snapshot:
Social Studies Through Drama

Good teaching is one-fourth preparation and three-fourths theatre. (Gail Godwin, *The Old Woman*, 1937)

Ms. Lane's class is in the middle of an environmental issues unit on how humans have changed the environment. They have been reading about problems with the coral reef in the Bahamas.

Sarah holds up a yellowish-red piece of coral. "I'm going to pass this around and you can each say a **one-liner** about it. You can **pass** and we'll come back, if you wish."

They are in a circle and and she starts with a boy on her left. He takes it and grins as he explores the surface.

"I'm hard and I'm dead," he says and passes it on.

"They're killing us by polluting our home," the next boy says.

A small girl takes the coral and says, "I pass."

It takes about 5 minutes to go around the room. The last boy says, "I could make a lot of money if I could just find a way to get around the authorities." Sarah then nods to the girl who passed earlier. The girl reaches for the coral.

"Without the coral reef, our country will not survive. When we kill it, we kill ourselves," she says softly.

The class observes a moment of silent reflection on her comment before Sarah speaks.

"It was interesting how you took on so many different roles. Shana, you seemed like a very concerned Bahamian. **What did the rest of you notice?**" Hands go up.

"The sadness in her voice," says a boy.

"She looked sincere," anther boy comments.

"Some people spoke like they were the coral. That was really cool. I'd never have thought of doing that," a girl says.

Others comment about how classmates showed feelings with words and how the coral was held.

Sarah then moves on and summarizes main topics they've been studying: the Bahamian economy, lifestyle, and its people's relationship to the reef. She asks what she has left out, and several comment about the destruction of the reef and the tourist trade. Sarah then explains what will come next.

"We now want to really go into detail about the interaction between people and the environment. We're continuing our study by becoming characters and using voice and body to make us all believe in your ideas."

Sarah picks up a **Mr. Mike** from the table. "Imagine you are a Bahamian citizen who has a specific interest in the reef. Think of all the points of view you have read about. We are just getting ready for a live **telecast** to inform everyone in the Bahamas about the issues."

She explains that **half** will be the **audience** and half the **panel.** All will have a chance to speak.

Drama specialist, Jeff Jordan, directs an emotion pantomime.

"Let's set up. Five minutes to show time. Panel members take these chairs. Audience, get into in two rows."

It seems chaotic as students make decisions, but in a minute all but two chairs on the 10-seat panel are taken.

"Great work. OK, only 2 minutes to show time. I'll be asking panelists to introduce themselves and make a short statement about their position. Audience members, you can respond with remarks and questions."

Sarah pushes a button on a CD player. She flips the lights out. Bahamian rhythms fill the room and the **lights** go on. She holds up the mike.

"Welcome to *Bahama Today.* I'm Sarah Lane and I'd like to welcome our panel of guests and audience members who are here to discuss the issues surrounding the coral reef. We'll begin with our panel members. Please introduce yourselves and tell us why you have come."

Sarah hands the mike to the panel member nearest her. The panel proves to be a diverse group ranging from fishermen to a politician. Some are vehemently opposed to government interference, and others are passionate about saving the reef. Sarah next opens it up to the audience.

"Please stand, give your name, and tell why you have come," she tells them.

Audience members direct comments to specific panelists and ask questions. All but two participate. After about 10 minutes, Sarah sums up remarks and ends with, "I'd like to thank our guests for coming and remind viewers to watch every day at this time to learn more about current issues on *Bahama Today.*"

She starts the music and flips out the lights. The music plays a bit longer before she turns on the lights.

"Let's talk about what just happened," she says. After a half-minute of no response Sarah backs up.

"I think you are still processing all this. Let's do a **Write Right Away** to **debrief.** Use the next page in your journal and let's go for 2 minutes."

Students get pencils and journals. Sarah moves to an overhead and begins to jot down her observations. At first a few watch her. She uses sentence fragments and key words. Eventually, all begin to write. She gives them nearly 5 minutes and then asks them to find a place to stop.

"Please form groups of three or four with people nearest to you and take a few minutes to share what you wrote. Read or just tell it."

Sarah waits until everyone is in a group and **circulates** as students talk.

"You think that you made the politician too stereotyped? **Why do you say that?**" she asks a boy who has critiqued his own performance.

She comments and asks **clarification questions** such as "What do you mean by _____?" and "Are you saying _____?"

The room is full of discussion. After about 5 minutes, Sarah brings them back together.

"I could tell you understood the importance of using **details** and **examples** to create believable characters. It sounds like many of you are planning to find out more specifics before I spring another drama on you!" The students laugh.

"Let's do more group work to think about the issues and what just happened on the TV program. We'll use groups of family, friends, or neighbors that viewed the telecast. Assume a role in your group and discuss the show. Count off in fives."

Sarah directs each group number to a certain area. The room is carpeted, so most sit on the floor. There is a general commotion. She dings a **push bell** and says, "When I ring again, begin to talk in your group. Ready," she dings. Ten minutes pass before she rings and says "Freeze." She moves to a group and knocks on a desk. She is back **in role**, this time as a "newcomer."

"Hi everybody. Sorry I'm late. I just watched the TV show on the reef. What are you doing?"

A boy summarizes the gist of their discussion. It turns out they are fishermen sitting on a wharf. Sarah becomes a fisherman, too. They commiserate about the hardships placed on them by the government. A girl in the group brings up concerns about the long-term survival of the reef. This takes about 2 minutes. Then Sarah steps out of role and compliments them on the diversity of roles they chose.

She concludes the lesson by making an assignment, due at the end of the week. Students are to **write, in a role,** to show different perspectives on the reef issue. It can be a letter, newspaper article, editorial, diary entry, or even a song. The students seem excited and ask questions about whether they will get to share what they write. Sarah seems genuinely delighted with this idea.

"Especially if it is a song," she grins. ✸

Arts Integration Blueprint

I'm watching *Whose Line Is It Anyway?* as I do most nights. It's total improvisation, and there are always great laughs from the theatre games they play: Weird Newscasters, Party Quirks, Scenes from a Hat. Right now, Colin Mochrie and Ryan Stiles are using props in as many ways as they can think of in a minute. My favorites are the "Do it as if" challenges Drew Carey gives them to sell CDs or narrate a silent movie segment. I'm entertained, but it goes beyond that. I'm amazed at the capacity of humans to do creative problem solving. And yet, we all do it every day as we take different roles and figure out how to make our lives work. Role taking is at the heart of it all.

Drama is now in the lead among the arts in showing potential to increase students' learning, especially literacy (Deasy, 2002). Why is drama so influential? Some answers are in the Philosophy section of the Blueprint.

Chapter 3 introduced the Arts Integration Blueprint (Ready References 3.1 and 3.2). The Blueprint scaffolds meaningful arts integration around the questions *why* should the arts be integrated, *what* should teachers know (arts literacy), and *how* to plan lessons, create an aesthetic environment, use arts-based literature and best teaching practices, design instructional routines, differentiate instruction, assess, and cooperate with specialists. The place of drama in the Blueprint is the subject of this chapter. Drama integration usually begins first with teaching *with* the drama—doing simple activities here and there. Drama and theatre literacy allows educators to move into teaching *about* and *in* drama. Using drama as a teaching and learning vehicle *through*out the curriculum is the goal. The levels build on one another and quality depends on attention to each of the 10 major aspects of the Blueprint.

Blueprint I: Philosophy of Arts Integration

The best drama uses as much truth as possible. (Dorothy Heathcote)

Why Should Teachers Integrate Drama?

Teachers who incorporate drama into daily learning say they are giving students safe havens to try different roles on for size. They report increased motivation and substantial effects on learning in science, social studies, math, and language arts. If doesn't stop there. Research Update 8.1 shows drama results in schools across the country. The following is a summary of reasons to integrate drama, grounded in beliefs and research.

Drama Increases Motivation, Concentration, and Focus.

Drama grabs attention with its novelty. There is a sense of occasion when performance is anticipated, even it is one half of the class presenting to the other half. The topics of drama are highly interesting because they derive from real-life problems. When used to introduce a lesson, drama causes students to speculate, tap into feelings, and want to learn more. A problem from an upcoming lesson can be explored through pantomime or verbal improvisation, causing interest to be piqued and prediction thinking to be activated. All this is highly motivating.

Pantomime and verbal role taking fill a basic need for activity—mental, physical, and aesthetic imagining. Activity is a source of motivation. Drama integration includes explicitly teaching students to actively concentrate, focus, and control their bodies and voices. They learn specific tools to focus and "make others believe" by staying in character. Many intelligences are used, including verbal and bodily kinesthetic. All the senses and emotions are engaged. This happens in the social setting of a classroom of peers so it would be surprising if students were not attentive.

Drama Stretches Perspective Through "In-Role" Practice.

> *Art is the only way to run away without leaving home.* (Twyla Tharp)

Dorothy Heathcote explains that there is a difference between the real world and the "as-if" world. In the latter, "we can exist at will. Brecht calls this 'visiting another room'" (Robinson, 1990, p. 8). According to Heathcote, our actions are controlled in these rooms by how free we feel to experiment. "If we needed a reasonable reason for including the arts in schools, surely it is here in these two rooms" (p. 8).

Drama capitalizes on children's natural desire to pretend and take roles during play. Through drama, the number of roles students can assume is expanded and so is their perspective. Students can rehearse life roles in which they will make decisions as parent, friend, or boss. These dramas often center on universal questions using strong themes within great literature: How do humans respond when they are given success,

rather than earning it? What is the nature of real happiness? How must we deal with evil? During drama, children examine different viewpoints and try them out. In an accepting atmosphere they feel free to sort out beliefs and values. In this way, drama shapes ideas and feelings allowing students to make sense out of their concerns. For example, in science, students may assume the role of experts in debates about problems, like the growing resistance of certain bacteria to antibiotics. During a career education unit they might pantomime significant aspects of careers they have investigated.

Drama Increases Reading Comprehension and Writing Fluency.

Preservice teacher education and professional development for practicing teachers now consider training in drama integration particularly important because of its power to increase reading, writing, and general language skills. Studies clearly show that children who dramatize stories have higher comprehension scores than those who only read the story (Deasy, 2002; Henderson & Shanker, 1978). Textbooks are given life when teachers involve students in dramatizing events in science and social studies. Students who dislike reading put forth effort to comprehend because drama participation depends on having information. If students know they will be pantomiming significant actions of a character from a text, they have a point of concentration. They are reading so they will be able to **do.** Most exciting is the transfer potential. One research finding is that students who use drama to understand one story transfer those thinking skills to unfamiliar texts (Catterall, 2002).

Vocabulary increases as students hear and read words related to drama activities. Writing is more descriptive. Students write more and with greater proficiency, which is a result of clearer thinking about how to organize and develop ideas (Deasy, 2002).

Drama Expands Speaking and Listening and Nonverbal Communication.

> *After three months, desperate to reach him, she asked him to play a character in a story and he began to speak in role. At the end of the year the class was asked to complete the sentence, "Drama is a gift to me because . . ." The formerly silent boy wrote: "Because it makes me brave enough to say what I want to say."* (Lushington, 2003)

Drama gives voice because it engages a different kind of thinking. We are freed to say things in role that we wouldn't normally say. Verbal communication needs to be altered by the roles we take in specific situations in life. Drama unties the tongue that may get tangled if not made supple through practice. The scene is set with a question like, "What should the father and the boys do to get the mother

Research Update 8.1   Drama and Academic Achievement

- Many studies show positive effects of drama on language development, including written and oral story recall, reading achievement, reading readiness, oral language development, and writing (Deasy, 2002).
- Drama-involved students outscored noninvolved students in reading as of eighth grade. The difference favoring drama/theatre students grows steadily. By 12th grade nearly 20% more are reading at high proficiency (Fiske, 1999).
- *Critical Links* presented 19 studies that support using drama to develop literacy skills such as reading comprehension. REAP and Project Zero combed through 400 drama studies (REAP, 2000).
- Elementary children involved in dramatic play seemed to increase tendencies to be thorough and explicit in story retellings (Deasy, 2002).
- When drama was used as a rehearsal for writing, letter writing and narrative writing were significantly improved (Moore & Caldwell, 1993; Wagner, 1988).
- First and second graders who participated in drama to re-create a story previously read aloud had greater story comprehension than a control (Deasy, 2002).
- Ten weeks of in-class drama coaching in a remedial third–fourth grade transformed reading instruction and improved students' attitudes and success in reading. Dramatic training and expression allowed students to see themselves as active readers and experience a sense of achievement (Deasy, 2002).
- Fifth-grade remedial readers who used drama as a learning tool consistently scored higher on the Metropolitan Reading Comprehension Test and outperformed a control (Dupont, 1992).
- Fifth and sixth graders who participated in a yearlong improvisational drama program had greater expressive and interactional language. Expressive language showed higher-order thinking such as speculating, predicting, and evaluating. Interactional language was found in peer exchanges and brought up moral issues. "Drama puts back the human content into what is predominantly a materialistic curriculum" (Deasy, 2002).
- Students with learning disabilities involved in drama show improved behavior and oral expression. They acquired social skills such as courtesy, self-control, focus on classroom work, and ability to follow directions. These benefits were sustained when tested 2 months after the project ended (Deasy, 2002).
- A program involving drama activities, including role playing, improvisation, and writing stories, enabled elementary students to achieve significant gains in vocabulary and reading comprehension. Students also reported improved attitudes relating to self-expression, trust, self-acceptance, and acceptance of others (Gourgey, Bousseau, & Delgado, 1985).
- Students from lower-income households who were highly involved in theatre outscored in reading proficiency peers who were not involved in theatre. The 9% advantage of eighth graders involved in theatre grew to a 20% advantage by the 12th grade (Fiske, 1999).
- Sixteen studies of students K–12 showed that drama positively affects the ability to take on the roles or perspectives of others—that is, to increases empathy (Kardash & Wright, 1987).
- Use of creative drama activities positively affected student achievement in a variety of areas, such as reading, oral and written communication, and interpersonal and drama skills (Kardash & Wright, 1987).
- Positive relationships were found between oral language growth (speaking) and use of creative drama in fourth, fifth, and seventh graders (Stewig & McKee, 1980).
- ESL (English as a second language) students who were involved in drama exhibited significantly greater verbal improvement than a control group not involved in drama (Vitz, 1983).
- Economically disadvantaged African American and Hispanic students in grades 4–6 who participated in a dramatics program showed improved reading achievement and more positive self-concepts (Gourgey et al., 1985).
- Drama increased interaction among students with and without mental handicaps in a study comparing fifth graders who either were involved in drama or noncompetitive games (Miller, Rynders, & Schleien, 1993).
- Sixty Head Start students who received regular and frequent drama and sign language instruction had higher language scores than a control group. They participated in drama and sign for four days a week (Arts Education Partnership, 1998).
- About 40% more of "no-drama" students felt that making a racist remark would be acceptable. Only about 12% of students involved in theatre thought so. The advantage favoring students involved in theatre is statistically significant (Fiske, 1999).

to come home?" after the problem is introduced in Brown's *The Piggybook*. Possible solutions are explored as students talk through the problem, assuming roles as the slob-like father and kids. It seems like play, but serious thinking is produced.

Students involved in drama activities develop increased fluency, not only in language, but in nonverbal communication through use of the body and face. They learn to match words and actions as they do focused work in pantomime or speak in different roles. This prepares them for the real world in which "I hear what you say but I believe what you do" rules. Students learn how a small gesture, body posture, or a person's gait can communicate hesitancy, excitement, or fear. The importance of becoming attuned to verbal and nonverbal communication is born out in research on muggers. They pick out victims by "reading" their body language. A limp or stagger shows vulnerability. In sum, drama causes student to extend both the range of ways they send messages and their ability to understand them.

Drama Stimulates Creative Problem Solving (CPS).

> *You can't depend on your judgment when your imagination is out of focus.* (Mark Twain)

Consider the difference between pantomiming a squirrel gathering nuts versus miming a squirrel gathering nuts with something sticky on its paws. The first mime might be fun, but the second demands more thinking. There is conflict. The actor must think of "all the ways" to solve the problem. It is not surprising that students involved in rich drama experiences increase their CPS skills. Drama integration changes the classroom from a place where students are told what to think into active experiences to think independently.

During drama, students must imagine, make hypotheses, test out solutions, evaluate ideas, and redefine problems. What are all the ways to show how Jack felt as he climbed the beanstalk each time? How can we show the meanings of words, such as *pule* or *contrite*, using body, face, or one line spoken in a role? What if Cinderella didn't want to marry the prince because she fell in love with the doorman? These questions are invitations to think about "what if" and experiment with possibilities. Studies show drama can boost verbal and visual creative thinking in diverse students from the young to the disadvantaged (Deasy, 2002; Karioth, 1967). The seeds are sown for children to grow into adults who look at problems more flexibly—from alternative viewpoints and with respect for diverse solutions.

Drama Can Enhance Psychological Well-Being.

> *Improvisation is a way of achieving identity.* (Alfred Nieman)

Drama allows students to express feelings under the protection of pretend. This safety permits them to experience therapeutic release of pent-up emotions. Through drama, students learn that people feel a range of emotions they can express appropriately. It is liberating for a child to realize she is not the first person to dislike another and that negative feelings can be channeled in positive ways. In addition, self-confidence grows as students learn to control their bodies and their words to express ideas and feelings. Positive self-image emerges from repeated successes in drama problem-solving situations. This is particularly true for special populations of students who have participated in drama (Deasy, 2002).

Drama Develops Empathy. Multiple studies show how drama causes students to understand character motivations and come to identify with characters at a deep level (Deasy, 2002; Lushington, 2003). This happens as students get deeply involved in their roles through using sense of smell, taste, touch, vision, hearing, movement, and even the sense of humor. When these combine with emotions and imagery, perspective is enlarged and empathy is achieved. Empathy goes beyond sympathy. It involves "becoming" another person, feeling what another feels and thinking what another thinks.

For example, during a Civil War study students demonstrated deep involvement with in-role "I statements" from different perspectives: "I saw smoke puff out of cannons so thick it looked like they were belching dragons." "I heard the nurse crying and I knew the man in the cot next to me had died of his gut wound." "I smelled burning grass as we torched the town." "I felt the stiffness in my good leg as I hobbled the final mile on a stick." "I couldn't stop laughing when I saw my wife come out on the porch as I walked up the dirt road of our farm." This kind of lived-through experience results in new viewpoints not possible through logic alone. By walking a mile in another's shoes, students develop tolerance and respect. There is less urge to hate or destroy those who behave, think, or feel differently.

Drama Causes Reflection on Moral Issues and Values. As in life, the core of drama is conflict. Drama permits students to become conscious of their values and those of others as they work through curricular and social problems. New values and beliefs become the end products of dissonance and problem resolutions worked out through role taking. Schaffner says drama "puts back the human content into what is predominantly a materialistic curriculum" (quoted in Deasy, 2002, p. 50).

During drama, values are not to be imposed by the teacher. They are explored and discussed as students confront issues about rightness, wrongness, goodness, and badness in literature, math, science, and social studies. This doesn't mean the teacher is value neutral; on the contrary, all teachers should clearly support universal values for honesty, truth, hard work, courage, integrity, and respect for others. Lessons are rarely valueless. So teachers can't teach without addressing values. Drama places this sensitive and important area in a workable context. Religious issues and religion itself become focal points, especially in coming to understand cultures; imagine trying to comprehend the Middle East without studying the religions of its people.

Drama Builds Cooperation and Other Social Skills.

Teachers may complain, "My students can't work in groups." The world of work and family however demands cooperation. No teacher would argue that students who can't read shouldn't be taught to read. Cooperation can be taught as well, just not by telling. Students learn active listening and problem solving by working in groups.

Drama is a group art. Actors depend on one another and work together. Drama sets up ideal circumstances for team building—misfits and loners, along with the popular and the gregarious, must collaborate. Research shows drama increases peer interaction, social relationships, and conflict resolution skills (Deasy, 2002).

At first, students work in pairs and trios and work up to larger groups. Initial dramatic work is more teacher-directed with greater controls present. For example, students work at a desk space. As students gain experience in planning scenes, they learn give and take, when and how to listen, and to speak up. They also gain respect for the unique ideas of classmates.

Awareness of social problems grows, too, as students research hunger, poverty, and homelessness in preparation for roles. Finally, as audience members for theatre performances, students gain social awareness as actors invite them into a staged world to vicariously live through plays dealing with social issues of every sort. Heathcote and Bolton (1995) explain that drama causes students to participate in the real world more fully because they have "played in the imagined."

Drama Contributes to Aesthetic Development.

Reason can answer questions but imagination has to ask them. (Albert Einstein)

Drama and theatre give the Stendhal Effect, the "ah" experience of being touched or moved (Lushington, 2003). Maslow calls these experiences "aesthetic" and places the need for them at the top of his pyramid. However, aesthetic needs for beauty and deep understanding are never completely filled. Chuck Tuttle, at the Chattanooga Theatre, says, "Drama integrates everything." We never get enough of the beauty-making power of music, art, dance, and literature brought together in theatre.

Drama is the key component of theatre. The *National Standards for the Arts* set goals for students to understand the art of theatre and to learn about dramatic structure involving conflict and characters. Students deepen sensory awareness and learn to express themselves through the artistic use of pantomime, dialogue, and improvisation.

Drama Is an Avenue to Other Areas of the Curriculum.

Drama is a learning tool grounded in informed exploration and discovery. It draws on innate abilities and desires to assume roles and pretend. We associate actors and acting with drama, and it is the action that makes drama so captivating. Children want to do. We should welcome student action; we don't need more passive citizens. But we don't want children to grow up taking action without information and reflection. Drama gives students a chance to act, but with a preparation and a safety net to catch them when decisions are unwise. This net is the conscientious planful teacher who is knowledgeable about drama strategies and willing to adapt them for specific student needs.

Drama motivates students to learn the bones of the body and the levels of government. It becomes a meaning-making tool to shape a sea of curricular skills and facts. Specific information is seen as relevant as students take roles as nurses, mayors, parents, and scientists to solve problems. Fascinating details of history, like school dunce caps, no longer distract because they are treated as clues to important themes (Mantione & Smead, 2003). Students explore character motives and actions that define and their relationships to one another and to the world.

Drama Makes the Invisible Visible for Assessment.

Concepts such as the structure of a cell or the movement of electrons are abstract. They are better understood when made concrete. Drama make ideas and feelings observable and audible using body, face, and voice to "externalize" what is known. Drama shows what students know and can do. It can be used to preview or review a lesson so teachers can observe student performances for formative or summative purposes.

Assessment needs to be authentic and give accurate information about how students think. Concepts and skills learned in any subject area can be demonstrated through pantomime and verbal dramas. Once externalized, the teacher and students can scrutinize the work together, using criteria derived from curricular goals. For example, students can be asked to write to a friend, in the role of Charles Drew, to explain scientific work. This kind of written role taking causes students to achieve depth of understanding through personal involvement. It also yields a document that shows the degree of knowledge acquired about scientific concepts.

Drama Is Fun-damental.

Over the door of a school in Richmond, Virginia, is a stone carving that reads, "Thou Shalt Have Fun." While many educators feel uncomfortable justifying inclusion of anything in curricula just because it is fun, we can never forget that fun is fundamental to happiness. One goal of education has to be to help students be happy (Noddings, 2005). Fun and entertainment can help us forget, enable us to cope by giving respite from problems, and provide enjoyment—a state of elation, upliftedness, or joy that gives energy and hope.

We cannot dismiss the importance of fun in learning, and drama is definitely fun. The word *play* is linked to theatre and drama. We go to plays and in theatre "the play is the thing." In drama, *play* is also a verb. Drama harnesses our natural motivations to play and shows students how to shape experiences (Lushington, 2003). Students have fun taking roles, solving problems, doing interesting things, learning new skills, working with people, meeting challenges, moving around, and making discoveries. Compare these aspects of fun with what we want to happen each day at school. There isn't much difference between good education and fun.

Blueprint II: Arts Literacy: Content and Skills

What Do Teachers Need to Know to Integrate Drama?

> *I believe that every child I meet understands deep, basic matters worthy of exploration but they may as yet have no language for them. One of the languages they may develop is through dramatic work.* (Dorothy Heathcote)

Successful arts integration depends on teacher knowledge and skill. Even if there is a drama specialist on staff, classroom teachers need basic drama/theatre literacy and a repertoire of strategies to teach students how to create and express meaning. INTASC (2002) is one source of what teachers need to know and be able to do in the arts. Those standards can be accessed at *www.ccsso.org/intasc*. Of course, the necessary level of teacher knowledge is governed by what students are expected to know and do. That falls under the *National Standards for the Arts* (Ready Reference 8.4) presented later in this chapter.

These two standards documents are two sources for drama/theatre arts knowledge base addressed in this section that includes:

- Definitions of and background on drama and theatre
- Drama elements
- Drama processes/skills
- People: roles and careers
- Styles, forms, and genres (kinds) of drama and theatre (e.g., tragedy, comedy, musicals)

- Noteworthy works sources
- Approaches and teaching strategies
- Special curricular connections and the *National Standards for the Arts*

Classroom Drama: History, Definitions, and Pioneers. How did drama become integral to the curriculum? Here is a brief look at the people who made it happen. What they created, decades ago, is now called "classroom drama." Unlike Mr. Esquith's theatre approach, it balances performance and process.

Winifred Ward: Performance focus. During the early 20th century Winifred Ward started a program in Illinois schools that combined children's literature with drama. She used movement, pantomime, dialogue, and characterization activities. She believed performance was vital to child development and could be supported by simple to complex drama work. Her work is so respected that she is now called the "mother of creative drama." In the decades after Ward's successes, other teachers and researchers in America and the United Kingdom were drawn to drama's educational potential to influence learning.

Brian Way: Process focus. Not everyone agreed with Ward about the importance of performance. Brian Way and others focused on the drama *process*. Way uses student personal experiences to lead them to self-discovery and encourages teachers to "sneak" drama into the classroom, even for 5 minutes each day. His approach opposes teacher demonstration because he argues that acting skills are unnecessary for drama participation. Life events are used as the stimulus, with few performances and little focus on evaluation.

Dorothy Heathcote: Problem-solving approach. It took a British woman to unite process and performance. Heathcote is now respected as the world's "preeminent classroom drama expert" (Catterall in Deasy, 2002, p. 58). In her approach students are engaged in problem solving about life experiences. They reflect, analyze, and test out conclusions in the safe circumstances of an imagined, but authentic, context. Students are thrust into a sink-or-swim situation, with a teacher–leader as a significant participant. Students are involved in (1) learning the craft, history, and place of theatre in our lives, (2) using an "as if it were" drama to motivate study, (3) making plays, and (4) performing for audiences. Heathcote's approach has been center stage in designing classroom drama that connects to curricular areas.

Cecily O'Neill: Real-world reflection. O'Neill shares Heathcote's philosophy and has extended it for American educators. "Drama lessons that rely on games and exercises to the neglect of the creation of dramatic roles and context are lacking what is, for me, the essential activity of drama" (O'Neill in McCaslin, 1990, pp. 293–294). The goal is not to have students escape from the real world, but to reflect on it.

Viola Spolin: Focus on seeing and doing.   Spolin (1999/2001) has the distinction of authoring two of the most popular books among drama educators and teachers. She emphasizes getting participants to see and do, not just imagine or feel. Her goals are to have students lose all inhibition and learn intuitively. Her books of theatre games, also used in actor training, still top most favorites lists.

Geraldine Siks: Embedded in language arts.   Siks (1983) placed drama in the categories of both art and the language arts, where it is found today in most curricula. Her major focus is on students' creative and expressive skills. Students learn to be audience members, players, and playmakers. Most importantly, students learn to problem solve through taking different roles.

Defining classroom drama.   Putting on rehearsed plays a few times a year is product oriented. The focus of this book, and most drama integration, is process drama—the use of drama concepts and skills to cause students to restructure content information by transforming it. Scripts may be memorized occasionally, but process drama is used daily. It is a mainstay teaching tool. This chapter concentrates on creative or classroom process drama use throughout the curriculum.

According to drama educator Ruth Heinig (1993), *creative drama* is the term most widely used in the United States to describe drama integration. Creative drama is more structured than the dramatic play in which children naturally engage. Other terms such as *improvisation*, *role playing*, *informal drama*, *drama in education (DIE)*, *process drama*, and *educational drama* are used in Great Britain and other countries, some of which have a particular emphasis. For example, DIE invites students to project themselves into a "moment in time"; they learn more about a topic after first exploring it through drama (Heinig, 1993, p. 4).

The American Alliance for Theatre and Education (AATE) defines creative drama as "an improvisational, non-exhibitional, process-centered form of drama in which participants are guided by a leader to imagine, enact, and reflect upon human experiences" (*www.aate.org*). In contrast, theatre is performance: The emphasis is on a spectacle for an audience. Drama and theatre share basic structures, but "theatre is concerned with communication between actors and audience; drama is concerned with the experience of the participants, irrespective of the audience" (Way in Rosenberg, 1987, p. 31). Way even worries that the creativity of young children may be undermined by emphasis on viewing formal theatre.

Creative classroom drama is participant and process centered, with a teacher or leader guiding students though explorations of personal experiences, social issues, and pieces of literature. Children improvise action and dialogue and use drama elements during the process. They creatively use voice, body, and space to make others believe in a mood, idea, or message. They assume "pretend" roles to generate creative problem solutions. Unlike role playing for therapeutic reasons, classroom drama's purposes are artistic, emotional, social, and academic.

Drama Elements.

Imagination is more important than knowledge. (Albert Einstein)

Drama is a slice of every person's struggle to deal with conflict. As with every art, it has its own special "language" used to create and express/perform ideas and feelings. Drama does share much with literature. Characters (1) encounter problems (2) in a specific setting and (3) take action to resolve the problems. The big difference is that drama brings characters to life in the form of actors. The setting (when and where) is the space where the characters play out the action for an audience. Students learn to study motives and show these to make characters seem real. Vocabulary and conceptual knowledge is increased as students figure out how to take roles and convince, convert, coax, sell, feud, or bargain.

Characters.   Actors portray human and nonhuman roles and initiate and carry out the plot (action). The main character must be believable and care about what happens. This is the hero or protagonist who must face life, make decisions, and accept consequences. In drama, characters are created through (1) actions, (2) words, and (3) what others say or how they react. When characters talk with each other, they use **dialogue.** Pantomime is free, creative, and mindful movement with no talking. It is used to express ideas and feelings through actions using the face and body.

Conflict.   As with literature, there must be a conflict or problem that motivates characters to make decisions and take action. Conflict sets plot in motion and should create suspense and tension. There are four types of conflict: (1) between a character and natural forces, like the weather, (2) between a character and societal rules or institutions (the farm rule that runt pigs are slaughtered in *Charlotte's Web*), (3) between a character and another character, such as the other girls against a poor Polish girl in *The Hundred Dresses* (Estes), and (4) within a character as with Ramona who constantly struggles against her proclivity for misunderstanding situations. A fifth type of conflict may also occur, especially in science fiction, between a character and technology as in *The Wretched Stone* (Van Allsburg), a tale about problems created by a mesmerizing rock with a blue glow, like a TV screen.

Ready Reference 8.1   Drama Elements

Also see Ready Reference 4.1 on Literary Elements.

Actors assume roles of characters.
Space is where the action happens.
Audience views the action and sometimes interacts with the actors.
Conflict sets the plot/action in motion and creates suspense and tension. Five types:

1. Between a character/nature
2. Between a character/societal rules or institutions
3. Between a character and another character
4. Within a character (internal conflict)
5. Between a character and technology

Characters/actors initiate and carry out the plot (action). Must be believable and care about what happens.
   Created through: actions, words, and what others say or how they react. When characters talk with each other, they use dialogue. When no words are used, drama takes the form of pantomime.
   Protagonist: main character or hero, who must face life, make decisions, and accept consequences.
Plot is the sequence of events set in motion by a problem or conflict. The structure is beginning, middle, and end.
Setting consists of the "created" time and place for action in a specfic space.
Mood is the feel created by the setting (time, lighting, music, place), pace, characters' use of words and body, etc.

Plot.   The sequence of events set in motion by a problem or conflict creates the plot. The simplest plot structure has a beginning, middle, and end in a linear pattern. Action rises to a climax and falls as problems are resolved.

Setting.   Time and place provide a context for action which make up the setting. In drama this is a space with both imagined and real objects.

Mood.   The feel of a piece is called the mood. It is created by the setting (time, lighting, music, description of the place), pace, and characters' use of word and body.

Ready Reference 8.1 summarizes the elements of drama.

Drama Skills and Processes.
Drama is used to create and express meaning, just like music and visual art. The main medium, however, is the body, mind, and voices of people. The processes used to create drama work from the inside of a person to the outside or the reverse. For example, anger can be produced by pounding on a table until the emotion "seeps" in. What is shown during drama with the body, face, gestures, and words reflects thoughts and feelings taken in through the senses. To make drama, a person must concentrate, sense, perceive, imagine, and think; the physical body and speech communicate these inner processes.

Students need certain skills to create and understand drama. What's more, creative and artistic work depends on being in an environment that offers freedom with limits. In such a context students need practice with the building blocks of the art form—drama in this case. Drama elements are tools, as are skills and processes. All serve to assist in creative problem solving that results in new personal meanings.

Ready Reference 8.2 summarizes basic drama skills and processes that focus on learning to control mind, body, and voice when taking roles during acting. But drama doesn't stop with acting. Students are involved in reading scripts (e.g., reader's theatre) and writing scripts based on real and imagined experiences. The script form is also an option for transforming any curricular material. Students are involved in designing spaces (backdrops, sets) and simple costumes (e.g., scarves, hats), directing, and researching to gather information. Because drama is mostly a group endeavor, students learn collaborative problem solving and how to give and receive feedback. Of particular importance is learning to adapt behavior based on self-evaluation.

Finally, while drama is process oriented, performance happens often in the form of peer audiences. Pairs perform for pairs or small groups perform for other groups. Sometimes groups perform for the rest of the class, and occasionally performances happen for outside audiences, especially other classes. This means students need to learn audience etiquette—how to attend, listen, and respond appropriately to performances.

Styles, Forms, and Genre.
Theatre embodies drama but is different in that theatre is a spectacle created for an audience. Classroom drama is process oriented and may or may not become a spectacle. The kinds or forms of drama and theatre include: (1) improvisation using body, mind, and voice; (2) pantomime—nonverbal, creative, mindful movement to express ideas and feelings with the face and body; (3) reader's theatre; (4) storytelling; and (5) plays and scripts.

Just as with literature, theatre and drama can be tragic or comic, fiction or nonfiction. Any genre of literature can

Ready Reference 8.2   Dramatic Skills and Processes

Acting skills: taking roles, pretending, improvising using:

Body: controlling and using the body to respond and express ideas and feeling. Includes use of appropriate energy, displaying sensory awareness, gestures, and facial expressions.

Mind: using different kinds of thinking and feeling, especially:

Focus: concentration, staying involved, making others believe in the realness of the character, following directions.

Imagination: creative problem solving that results in unique ideas, elaboration on ideas, and spontaneous thinking.

Voice: speaking clearly and fluently using appropriate variety in volume, rate, tone and pitch, pause, stress; ability to improvise dialogue.

Script writing: transformation of personal experiences or curricular material into script form.

Designing spaces and costumes: basic sets and costumes.

Directing: organizing peformances.

Researching: data gathering for background.

Evaluation: giving feedback, using suggestions, self-evaluating, and adapting own behavior.

Social skills: cooperation, conflict resolution, active listening, and responding.

Audience etiquette: attending, listening, and responding appropriately to performances.

---

be transformed through drama. Of course, the pinnacle of theatre is live performances. While not everyone can regularly take in a Broadway play, most communities have live theatre. Teachers who integrate the arts owe it to themselves to see live theatre including special genres, like musical theatre which was born in America. Next best are the spectacular films we've all become accustomed to, in every genre from film noir to westerns. Television also offers some excellent drama.

People.   People take a vast range of roles in drama and theatre beyond acting. Career opportunities can be integrated into many units and include playwright, director, set and costume designer, sound and light technician, critic, historian, filmmaker, and teacher. Noteworthy people in the field can be foci of study as well. Of course, William Shakespeare appears on every list.

Noteworthy Works Sources.
Books by Dorothy Heathcote, Viola Spolin, and Ruth Heinig are "must-have" practical sources of works and teaching ideas. Consult a children's drama specialist at your school or a local college for sources of scripts. Here are a couple to get started.

Aaron Shephard's website *www.aaronshep.com/rt/ RTE. html* offers free scripts. His newest book is *Stories on Stage* (2005). He also published *Folktales on Stage: Children's Plays for Reader's Theatre,* which includes 16 scripts from many cultures. Another reader's theatre website is *www.cdli.ca/CITE/ langrt.htm.* Wolfman's *Stories for Reader's Theatre* (2004) includes multicultural scripts with favorite tales like *Millions of Cats.*

Jenning's *Theatre for Young Audiences: Twenty Great Plays for Children* (1998) is an example of an anthology based on books like *Charlotte's Web.* One of the websites to order play scripts is: *http://childrenstheatreplays.com.*

Approaches and Teaching Strategies.
The approaches of Dorothy Heathcote and others each represent diverse goals for drama, teacher roles, stimuli for drama, and activities in which students are engaged. In this book, ideas from all these approaches previously described have been culled for their appropriateness to meaningful integration. On the process/performance teeter-totter, process is the heavier party for integration purposes. Performance is used primarily, like any assessment product, to motivate.

Basically, in classroom drama the teacher's role is to guide students, through questioning and coaching, to define problems, improvise solutions, try out ideas, reflect, and evaluate. Drama knowledge is taught, as students need tools to transform science, social studies, math, and literacy material into dramatic forms. While classroom drama is not focused on performing, teachers plan time for group sharing, at times, especially within the class. Classroom drama can be simple or complex; Spolin's theatre games and simple pantomimes are accepted as valuable drama work, as is Ward's story drama and Heathcote's in-depth explorations for personal meaning and perspective.

Successful drama integration usually starts with a few minutes a day. Eventually drama can be meaningfully used in science, social studies, language arts, and math. Gradual, thoughtful implementation ensures that justice is done to both drama/theatre (as an art) and the basic content and skills in core curricular areas. At some points teachers may have the luxury of being able to do drama lessons for an hour or longer. Most connect drama to units over the course of the entire study, like Sarah Lane. They use drama in the same way reading and writing are used as vehicles for communicating ideas and feelings about learning. In any case, the goal is to design lessons that are more than a series of isolated activities.

Blueprint III: Collaborative Planning

> *Drama . . . can be a mirror, a magnifying glass, a microscope or a searchlight.* (Cecily O'Neill)

Meaningful Connections

Some insist drama can be used to teach any subject more effectively (McCaslin, 1990). That's not enough. Early in the planning for drama-based units and lessons, teachers search for natural connections so that both areas are enhanced by the integration. The goal is **two-way** transfer. Here are some examples of natural links.

Literacy. Drama and the language arts (speaking, listening, reading, and writing) share many goals. These include becoming skilled at verbal and nonverbal communication. Educators now consider drama and theatre to be central to the English language arts curriculum. Why? Incontrovertible evidence shows that significant involvement in drama/theatre improves literacy skills (Deasy, 2002; Deasy & Stevenson, 2005; Palmarini, 2005). Drama can increase writing prolixity and reading comprehension and improve oral expression. The inference is that dramatic knowledge and skill can be increased by pairing it with literacy instruction. Some areas, like playwriting, cannot disconnect drama and language arts literacy.

Literature. Literature and drama share most of the same elements from a focus on using tension or conflict to propel the plot to characters and setting. Their natural compatibility and both drama and literature understanding can be increased through integration.

Science and Social Studies. Since the Progressive Education movement began, integration of drama with other curricular areas has been popular. Dorothy Heathcote clearly demonstrates how learning can be given depth and breadth through drama integration, especially in science and social studies (see the videos, "Dorothy Heathcote Talks to Teachers–Parts I and II," each about 30 minutes). In lieu of putting on plays with memorized lines, Heathcote helps children make sense of their world by causing them to reflect on life experiences.

Other Potential Connections. Some connections seem obvious—history of theatre and drama, science and math of theatre (e.g., stage construction, makeup), economics of theatre productions, and psychology (e.g., drama therapy). Not to be ignored are the vast connections to multicultural understanding gained from the works of playwrights and filmmakers. Then there is the concept that all of life demands skilled shifting in and out of roles, and varying use of body, thinking, and voice to suit specific circumstances. It could be argued that drama and life are inseparable, with success hinging on mindful and artful role taking.

The National Standards for the Arts: American Goals

When a teacher signs a contract in a school district, he agrees to teach to standards and goals adopted by the board of education. Standards and goals in curriculum frameworks help teachers know **what** to teach, but do not explain **how** to teach. Teachers are hired with the expectation that they know current instructional methodology for planning, teaching, managing/disciplining, and assessing. Teachers are also expected to be able to select materials and adapt lessons for diverse student needs. For arts-based schools, that means teachers need a level of arts literacy and knowledge of best practices in each art form to teach through the arts.

Standards, and benchmarks that lead up to them, are desired goals, not material to be "covered" (McTighe & O'Connor, 2005). This implies teachers should plan with standards in hand but be selective. Meaningful integrated units and sequenced lesson plans are customized for specific students, and many go much beyond the standards. Districts expect teachers to specify connections between lessons and standards; the Planning Pages in this book provide examples. In addition, it is just good teaching to make lesson goals and objectives clear to students at the lesson outset; it is wise to communicate goals/standards to parents, too.

The *National Standards for the Arts* (Ready Reference 8.3) can be viewed at *http://menc.org*. For examples of state-level arts standards, go to the websites for the department of education. Many have useful documents, including Ohio, Kentucky, South Carolina, and North Carolina. Connecticut includes theatre/drama standards and gives sample lesson ideas and assessment alternatives (*www.state.ct.us/sde/dtl/curriculum/currkey3.htm*).

Ready Reference 8.3 National Standards for Theater (K–8)

Overall focus: Learn about life, pretend and assume roles, develop socially, interact with peers, bring stories to life, direct one another, improvise, write, act, design, compare forms, analyze, evaluate, understand the world (history, cultures).

1. *Script writing by planning and recording improvisations based on personal experience and heritage, imagination, literature and history (K–4), and by creation of improvisations and scripted scenes based on personal experience and heritage, imagination, literature, and history (5–8).* Example activities: Create classroom dramatizations; improvise dialogues to tell a story.

2. *Acting by assuming roles and interacting in improvisations (K–4) and by developing basic acting skills to portray characters who interact in improvised and scripted scenes (5–8).* Example activities: Clearly describe characters; use concentration and body and vocal elements to express characters; dramatize personal stories.

3. *Designing by visualizing and arranging environments for classroom dramatizations (K–4) and by developing environments for improvised and scripted scenes (5–8).* Example activities: Use art media and techniques to make settings; organize materials for dramatic play.

4. *Directing by planning classroom dramatizations (K–4) and by organizing rehearsals for improvised and scripted scenes (5–8).* Example activities: Plan a class play; use drama elements and skills; play the roles of director, writer, designer, and actor.

5. *Researching by finding information to support classroom dramatizations (K–4) and by using cultural and historical information to support improvised and scripted scenes (5–8).* Example activities: Find literature to adapt for classroom drama (books, poems, songs, any material usable for plays); research time periods and cultures for dramatic material.

6. *Comparing and connecting art forms by describing theater, dramatic media (such as film, television, and electronic media), and other art forms (K–4). Comparing and incorporating art forms by analyzing methods of presentation and audience response for theater, dramatic media (such as film, television, and electronic media), and other art forms (5–8).* Example activities: Compare how the different arts communicate ideas; describe visual, aural, oral, and kinetic elements of theater.

7. *Analyzing and explaining personal preferences and constructing meanings from classroom dramatizations and from theater, film, television, and electronic media productions (K–4). Analyzing, evaluating, and constructing meanings from improvised and scripted scenes and from theater, film, television, and electronic media productions (5–8).* Example activities: Evaluate performances using specific criteria; explain characters' wants and needs.

8. *Understanding context by recognizing the role of theater, film, television, and electronic media in daily life (K–4). Understanding context by analyzing the role of theater, film, television, and electronic media in the community and other cultures (5–8).* Example activities: Web ideas for why theater is created; attend performances and discuss what is learned about culture, history, and life from theater.

Source: Content Standards (material printed in bold type) excerpted from the *National Standards for Arts Education*, published by Music Educators National Conference (MENC). Copyright © 1994 by MENC. Reprinted with permission. The complete National Standards and related materials are available from MENC: The National Association for Music Education, 1806 Robert Fulton Drive, Reston, VA 20191 (800-336-3768).

Unit Planning

Ready References 3.4 and 3.5 outline the steps to plan arts integrated units and lessons. The first phase is collecting documents that clarify, in this case, what students should know and be able to do in drama and theatre. This includes local, state, and national standards. While drama and theatre are not the same, the National Standards include drama concepts and skills under the category of theatre. Ready Reference 8.3 lists eight standards related to drama that students are expected to meet. All the drama strategies and activities in this book relate to one or more of these standards.

Standards documents and local courses of study provide sources for drama content and guide teachers in choosing drama skills that mesh with other units being planned. The goal is for students to grow in their drama knowledge and skill. Abuse occurs when students know no more about drama at the end of the lesson than they did at the beginning. "Peppering" lessons with role taking is not sufficient (Palmarini, 2005, p. 3).

Unit Centers.   Any of the five integrated unit centers or bodies can be used to teach school district requirements in math, reading and language arts, science, and social studies, as well as in the arts of music, art, drama, dance, and literature. Drama-based lessons and units can focus on one or more of traditional subject areas. For example, a literature-based study of an author/illustrator like Byrd Baylor can use drama and the other arts along with math, science, social studies, and reading/language arts as "legs" to support the unit. Drama would be a learning tool in such a unit, just as any other leg. An adaptation of this idea is to envision a unit with drama as the body with the focus on:

1. a person (actor, playwright, director, author, artist)
2. a particular genre or form (improvisation, reader's theatre, comedy)
3. a problem or topic (e.g., censorship)
4. a book, poem, song, or play (e.g., *Hamlet*)
5. an event, such as a trip to see a play at a local theatre.

The major concepts and skills in math, science, social studies, literacy, and the other art forms are used as support legs. Planning Page 6.1 shows an example of a unit planning web. Ready Reference 8.6 shows drama strategies planned during a literature-based unit on author/artist Patricia Polacco and her books.

Accommodating interests. Well-planned units designed to draw on interests and drama hold great promise in this area. In Heathcote's approach, drama-based lessons begin with identifying a point of great interest, tension, or conflict in a unit under study. To get to this point, she begins with discussions to elicit students' ideas, which yields a lesson focus. She then usually takes the role of a character, herself, and engages students in roles, although she frequently steps out of role to clarify directions or redirect thinking. Current events, moral and ethical problems, universal themes and questions, and the cognitive and affective domains become grist for the drama mill.

Theatre events. Going to see a play is the most common event at the center of a drama unit or an initating or culminating event. Live theatre experiences have countless values, not the least of which is the opportunity for children to be introduced to an aesthetic form of entertainment they can enjoy for the rest of their lives. Without school trips to see live performances, many children only experience in-house assemblies. There is a sense of occasion in going to the theatre—ritual and ceremony that children need to grow aesthetically.

Field trips to see children's theatre have the potential to develop aesthetic sensibilities, promote educational aims, and offer chances for social awareness and skill development. Just as with other field trips, theatre experiences should be selected to align with curricular goals and be an integral part of a unit. Lessons are needed to prepare for the trip and follow up the play. See Field Trips in the Appendix for before, during, and after teaching guidelines. With regard to theatre and drama, students need to understand:

- Live performances are different from videsion dramas, largely because the audience sevent and there is a feeling of spontaneity. the audience gives to the actors, the more the actors can give back to the audience.
- There is an expected audience etiquette in a theatre. This ensures everyone can enjoy the performance and the actors are respected. Discuss talking, rattling paper, kicking seat backs, and other problem behaviors. Students need to be taught when to applaud, when to stand, what an ovation means, and what happens if you arrive late to a play.
- The play will have characters, plot, conflict, and setting. Introduce special vocabulary like *set, costume, stage left,* and *stage right.*
- Theatres are set up in different ways. Discuss the seating sections like orchestra and balcony.
- Discuss the style or form of the production. Is it musical theatre? Comedy? Will there be monologues?
- *Note:* Cue sheets or "look-fors" help students know ahead of time what is coming. They can then experience a sense of discovery about the set, costumes, and characters. Ask for materials ahead of time for this kind of information. If not, check the Internet for background.

After the play, it is helpful to have a discussion, and, just as in good literature discussions, it is important to encourage a variety of viewpoints. Some useful questions include: "What did you see? How did it make you feel? What in the play made you feel that way? What was important in the play? What was it really about? What was missing? What was the playwright trying to say?" Of course, this is a perfect time to do some drama activities related to the play. For example, ask students to do tableaux of important scenes.

Two-Pronged Lesson Format. All units are delivered through a sequence of lessons. One way to ensure that drama is made integral is to use the two-pronged format. Planning Page 8.1 offers an example. Of course, lessons may integrate several art forms so two prongs is a minimum. Teaches must decide, in the case of multiart integration, which arts will be the focus for teaching *about* and *in* the art. Everything can't be taught and assessed in every lesson.

Blueprint IV: Aesthetic Learning Environment

Aesthetic classrooms and schools create a supportive learning environment through physical and psychological means. Some schools, like Lady's Island in Beaufort, South Carolina, managed to remodel to accommodate drama and dances spaces. But a stage can be any open space. Classrooms

Drama and Science (Primary Grades)

Narrative pantomime is used in this lesson during a unit on habitats that began a week ago.

Two-Pronged Focus: (1) Drama elements and skills: *pantomime* with focus on control, display of sensory awareness, use of gestures and face, and responding to nonverbal communications of others; focus and concentration; following directions. (2) Science concepts: components of habitat and effects on animals.

Theatre Standards: 2, 5, and 7 (see Ready Reference 8.3)

Student Objectives: Student will be able to:

1. Use body and face to show specific components of habitats (food, water, shelter, and space).
2. Concentrate and focus to control body and respond to others; follow oral directions (cues).
3. Predict responses of animals who are missing basic habitat components.

Teaching Procedure: The teacher will: (S=Students)

Introduction

1. Use the Focus Ball strategy to help S focus and concentrate.
2. Ask S to list names of animals and places they live—from previous lessons. Record ideas on a chart (language experience strategy: ask them to spell chorally to help with phonics). Ask what *habitat* means and clarify, as needed.
3. Tell them today's lesson is about parts of habitats and what happens when a part is missing. Explain *narrative pantomime* will be used to show animals in their habitats. Ask what makes drama (drama elements/skills posted). Ask which drama uses no words (pantomime).
4. Do a series of Show Me Quick pantomimes with focus on use of face: happy, thinking, worried, hungry. Repeat with whole body (at desk area). Divide class in half. Each half gives the other feedback on what they did that showed concentration and focus.

Development

1. Put first habitat card in pocket chart: food. Read chorally and ask about foods in different habitats. Use a few S examples and stop and pantomime different animals eating those foods. Give descriptive feedback on use of body and face (shapes, movements, sizes) to show the animal. Repeat with water, shelter, and space components.

2. Explain that narrative pantomime is when someone tells a story while others use their faces, bodies, and imagination to show the story. Review rules about start and stop signals. Tell everyone to find a personal space in the room.
3. Give each a card with an animal name. No one knows it but there are duplicates. Say "When I say 'start,' everyone is to explore ways to show their animal in a variety of ways, such as shape, moves, and size. Stay in your personal spot. At the 'freeze' signal, everyone should stop. Start. Give feedback on focus, concentration, unusual ideas. Repeat in *slow motion*.
4. Use signals for the *narrative pantomime* (read slowly):

    You are hungry. You begin to look for *food* in your habitat. You find the kind of food you eat. Slowly you eat your meal. After a while you start to get full and begin to slow down. In an area nearby, you hear a sound and you become afraid. Your body shows you are scared. You look for *shelter* and move there. You watch carefully and you wait, being very still, until you know you are safe. The coast seems to be clear. You are feeling good because you are safe and full of food. You move around your habitat *space* showing you are satisfied. Because you ate so much, you are thirsty. You see *water* nearby and move there and begin to drink. The water is very cold. After a long cool drink, you begin to feel lonely, and you look for another animal like you. You move around noticing how other animals move to see if you can find another of your species. You greet your fellow animal when you find him or her. It has been a long day and you are getting tired. You move slowly to a place of shelter. You begin to get ready to rest. Slowly you drift off to sleep.

Conclusion/Assessment

1. Ask S: What did you think about? What worked? What problems? How did you find another similar animal? Collect cards and repeat with new animals.
2. Brainstorm what might happen if a habitat part is limited, like space. What if humans build a road through the habitat? Ask what information S needs to show the parts of habitat and animal behavior better. List ideas on the chart.
3. Let S choose an animal to read more about habitat needs (books on display). Tell them we'll do a drama Tuesday using what they find; this time the animals will have inadequate habitat components, so there will be problems (conflict).

can be arranged with desks in a U shape or desks can be grouped so that there is an open area. If not, there is always "push back the desks" or go outside. A carpeted area can be created for free or inexpensively by asking local carpet stores to donate samples. Double-sided carpet tape can be used to secure squares. However the space is set up, it needs to be there. Giving space for drama shows that it is a priority. Drama is too important to not make space.

In addition to space, some basic materials are needed. Drama is actually pretty cheap. Scarves, hats, paper, socks—these are all simple objects that can be used as props for improvisation. An old trunk filled with these kinds of objects makes a class treasure chest. A video camera and tape player are wonderful to capture drama so students can enjoy and do self-assessment. Cameras are often shared by groups of teachers in arts-based schools.

Most classroom ethos is determined by the teacher whose mood "makes the weather." A teacher can crush or liberate creative thinking without a single word. The medium of drama is the person. It is risky to put yourself out there. In a classroom where the teacher creates an inviting climate and openly values creative thinking, students will take chances that make for good problem solving and great drama. The aesthetic environment discussed in Chapter 3 lays a foundation for dramatic work to emerge. Students who have a teacher who is always ready to think of "what if" and do "let's pretend" have the drama advantage. Ready Reference 2.5 summarizes the CPS and 2.6 and 2.7 list creative boosters and blockers.

Blueprint V: Literature as a Core Art Form

Every genre of children's literature offers potential dramatic material. Biography can be particularly useful because the characters are real people in conflict-filled situations.

Drama and theatre-based books are available in every genre and on any topic imaginable. There are informational books on acting, puppetry, storytelling, reader's theatre, and the history of theatre. Then there are timeless pieces of fiction like the picture book, *Crow Boy* (Yashima), in which a teacher puts a boy on stage and this event changes his life. Of course there are dozens of books for children related to Shakespeare and his plays. Other examples of drama/theatre-based children's books are:

Blackwood, G. (1998–2003). *Shakespeare…* (series). Dutton.
Blume, J. (1981). *The one in the middle is the green kangaroo.* Yearling.
dePaola, T. (2005). *Stagestruck.* Putnam.

Hoffman, M. (1991). *Amazing Grace.* Dial.
Park, B. (2004). *Junie B., First grader: shipwrecked.* Random House.
Robinson, B. (1972). *The best Christmas pageant ever.* Harper & Row.
Sendak, M. (1976). *Maurice Sendak's really Rosie; Starring the nutshell kids.* Harper & How.
Suskin, S. (2004). *The art of broadway theatre.*
Van Allsburg, C. (1987). *The A was Zapped: A play in twenty-one acts.* Houghton Mifflin.

The Appendix includes an Arts-Based Bibliography with more examples of drama/theatre-based books, including books recommended for pantomime and verbal activities. An annotated sampling appears in Ready Reference 8.4.

Blueprint VI: Best Teaching Practices

Drama educator Nellie McCaslin (1990) believes the attributes of any good teacher are the characteristics most needed to integrate drama: sense of humor, high standards, good discipline, imagination, respect for the ideas of others, sensitivity to individuals, ability to guide rather than direct, and a focus on sharing, rather than showing. In the end, the imaginative teacher creates her own methods by adapting ideas like the Seed Strategies in the next chapter. Adventuresome teachers go further to readily combine drama with dance, music and visual art. The following are general drama principles that elaborate on best practices introduced in Chapter 3.

What You Teach Is Who You Are

Toronto teacher Matt Duggan says, "I used to think I wouldn't ask my students to do anything I was uncomfortable doing when I was a kid. Then I realized I was a very uncomfortable kid, so there was not a lot we'd be able to do" (as quoted in Lushington, 2003, p. 1). Duggan's sense of humor makes him a prime candidate for arts integration. He knows he has to stretch himself to stretch the kids. Teachers can show enthusiasm and commitment to drama as an art form in easy, but significant ways, especially through their own use of body, voice, and imagination. This includes intentionally using personal facial expressions, eye contact, gestures, and body postures as teaching tools. Daily read-alouds become designer lessons when teachers vary vocal dynamics, pitch, tempo, stress, and pause. Teachers can draw attention to the effects of voice and body by asking questions like "How did I use my voice?" and invitations to compare the effect with reading in a monotone.

Ready Reference 8.4   Literature for Drama

See more at the end of Chapter 9 and in the Appendix.

How-to Books

Caruso, S., & Kosoff, S. (1998). *The young actor's book of improvisation: Dramatic situations from Shakespeare to Spielberg, Vol. 1.* Heinemann.

Friedman, L. (2001). *Break a leg!: The kid's guide to acting and stagecraft.* Workman.

Kohl, M. (1999). *Making make-believe: Fun props, costumes and creative play ideas.* Gryphon House.

Stevens, C. (1999). *Magnificent monologues for kids.* Sandcastle.

Literature for Pantomime

Adoff, A. (1981). *Outside/inside poems.* Lothrop, Lee & Shepard. (poems about feelings)

Berger, B. (1984). *Grandfather Twilight.* Philomel. (old man raises the moon in the sky)

Bunting, E. (1992). *The wall.* Clarion. (a boy and father visit the Vietnam War Memorial)

Carle, E. (1969). *The very hungry caterpillar.* Philomel/Putnam. (caterpillar becomes a butterfly; challenge to use a variety of actions to eat; good for flannel board or puppet)

Carroll, L. (1989). *Jabberwocky.* Abrams. (good for imagining ways to move, e.g., *gyre*)

Chaconas, D. (1970). *The way the tiger walked.* Simon & Schuster. (animals imitate tiger's walk)

Charlip, R. (1980). *Fortunately.* Four Winds. (narrative mime)

Cole, J. (1987). *The magic school bus inside the earth.* Scholastic. (field trips in a microscopic bus; series)

dePaola, T. (1975). *Strega Nona.* Prentice Hall. (Strega Nona has a magic pasta pot; good crowd scenes)

Emberley, B. (1967). *Drummer Hoff.* Prentice Hall. (cumulative story good for mechanical movements)

Gerstein, M. (1984). *Roll over!* Crown. (animals roll out)

Giff, P. R. (1980). *Today was a terrible day.* Penguin. (mime problems at school)

Johnson, C. (1955). *Harold and the purple crayon.* Harper & Row. (boy has drawing adventures)

Kahl, V. (1955). *The duchess bakes a cake.* Scribner's. (many characters to mime)

Keats, E. J. (1962). *The snowy day.* Viking. (mime boy's actions)

Kuskin, K. (1982). *The philharmonic gets dressed.* Harper & Row. (orchestra members get ready; follow conducting drama)

McCully, E. (1992). *Mirette on the high wire.* Putnam. (girl learns to walk the highwire)

McDermott, G. (1975). *The stonecutter.* Viking Penguin. (Japanese folktale; no dialogue)

Mendoza, G. (1989). The hairy toe. In G. Mendoza (Ed.), *Hairticklers.* Ten Speed. (choral refrain)

Parish, P. (1963). *Amelia Bedelia.* Harper & Row. (a maid takes instructions literally; many sequels about misunderstanding)

Paulsen, G. (1987). *Hatchet.* Bradbury. (boy survives 54 days in the wilderness)

Pinkwater, D. (1993). *The big orange splat.* Scholastic Trade. (interviews, and pantomime possibilities)

Ringgold, F. (1991). *Tar beach.* Crown. (girl imagines flying)

Rossetti, C. (1991). Who has seen the wind? In K. Sky-Pock (Ed.), *Who has seen the wind?* Rizzoli. (mime leaves)

Rounds, G. (1990). *Lizard in the sun.* William Morrow. (life from the animal's perspective)

Rylant, C. (1988). *All I see.* Orchard. (boy makes friends with a painter; pretends to paint many things)

Seuss, Dr. (1940). *Horton hatches the egg.* Random House. (Horton is "faithful, 100 percent"; chorally chant motto)

Seuss, Dr. (1961). *The Sneetches.* Random House. (machine mime)

Small, D. (1985). *Imogene's antlers.* Crown. (girl grows antlers and family tries to cope)

Spurdens, D. (1984). *BMX.* Sterling. (stunts, riding)

Tolstoy, A. (1968). *The great big enormous turnip.* Franklin Watts. (cumulative tale about trying to pull up a huge vegetable)

Ungerer, T. (1986). *Crictor.* Harper & Row. (Madame Bodot's pet boa protects her from burglars)

Van Allsburg, C. (1988). *Two bad ants.* Houghton Mifflin. (two ants have adventures)

Wood, A. (1984). *The napping house.* Harcourt Brace. (cumulative)

Zemach, M. (1976). *It could always be worse.* Farrar, Straus & Giroux. (crowded family brings animals into their house)

Literature for Verbal Activities

Aardema, V. (1975). *Why mosquitoes buzz in people's ears.* Dial. (African tale shows the domino effect from misunderstanding)

Aardema, V. (1981). *Bringing the rain to Kapiti Plain.* Dial. (African Nandi cumulative tale like "The House That Jack Built")

Bayer, J. (1984). *My name is Alice.* Dial. (do sequence drama)

Bemelmens, L. (1939). *Madeline.* Viking Penguin. (Madeline lives in a Paris convent)

Bennett, J. (Ed.). (1987). *Noisy poems.* Oxford University Press. (many sounds)

Bodecker, N. M. (1974). *"Let's marry," said the cherry.* Atheneum. (short, rhymed couplets)

Cameron, P. (1961). *"I can't," said the ant.* Coward-McCann. (a broken teapot creates a problem for kitchen inhabitants)

Chess, V. (1979). *Alfred's alphabet walk.* Greenwillow. (Alfred sees things like a "herd of hungry hogs hurrying")

Day, A. (1985). *Good dog, Carl.* Green Tiger. (an intelligent dog babysits a squirmy child; almost wordless; sequels)

dePaola, T. (1983). *Legend of the bluebonnet.* Putnam. (Comanche tribe is saved by the sacrifice of a girl's warrior doll)

Gag, W. (1928). *Millions of cats.* Coward-McCann. (old man goes on journey and gets more than expected; repeated chant)

Galdone, P. (1968). *The Bremen town musicians.* McGraw-Hill. (animals encounter a band of robbers and gain wealth)

Haley, G. (1970). *A story—A story.* Atheneum. (African tale about spider who gives the sky god animals to own all the stories)

Heide, F. P. (1971). *The shrinking of Treehorn.* Holiday House. (boy notices he is shrinking, but no one else does)

Isaacs, A. (1994). *Swamp angel.* Dutton. (tale about big girl)

Kellogg, S. (1971). *Can I keep him?* Dial. (boy has a conversation with his mother about a pet)

Marshall, J. (1972). *George and Martha.* Houghton Mifflin. (stories work well for QU reading and interviews)

McDermott, B. (1976). *The Golem: A Jewish legend.* Lippincott. (rabbi creates a clay figure; good for debates and interviews)

McGovern, A. (1967). *Too much noise.* Houghton Mifflin. (old man tries to stop noise in his house; use for expert panels)

Munsch, R. (1980). *The paper bag princess.* Annick. (a princess rescues a prince; use for interviews)

Rathmann, P. (1995). *Officer Buckle and Gloria.* Putnam. (dog does tricks)

San Souci, R. (1989). *The talking eggs.* Dial. (girl gets riches while greedy sister is punished)

Say, A. (1993). *Grandfather's journey.* Houghton Mifflin. (good for interviews about home)

Scieszka, J. (1989). *The true story of the 3 little pigs by A. Wolf.* Viking. (use for POV storytelling)

Slepian, J., & Seidler, A. (1990). *The hungry thing.* Scholastic. (a beast's sign reads, "Feed Me")

Steptoe, J. (1987). *Mufaro's beautiful daughters.* Lothrop, Lee & Shepard. (African Cinderella tale)

Tresslet, A. (1964). *The mitten.* Lothrop, Lee & Shepard. (lost mitten is a haven for animals)

Turkle, B. (1976). *Deep in the forest.* Dutton. (three bears story with a twist)

Van Allsburg, C. (1984). *The mysteries of Harris Burdick.* Houghton Mifflin. (great for storytelling)

Van Allsburg, C. (1986). *The stranger.* Houghton Mifflin. (stranger suffering from amnesia stays with a family)

Viorst, J. (1972). *Alexander and the terrible, horrible, no good, very bad day.* Atheneum. (boy details everything that goes wrong for him in one day; repeated lines)

Wiesner, D. (1991). *Tuesday.* Clarion. (almost wordless picture book about flying frogs)

Winter, P. (1976). *The bear and the fly.* Crown. (bear family has a nagging fly)

Wood, A. (1985). *King Bidgood's in the bathtub.* Harcourt Brace Jovanovich. (king invites everyone to come in)

Young, E. (1989). *Lon Po Po: A Red-Riding Hood story from China.* Philomel. (sisters outwit a wolf)

Teacher in Role. Role taking is at the core of drama. Teachers may assume a variety of roles, in any curricular area, to engage students in response. For example, become a bystander for a history or science moment and ask for clarification about what's happening. Students get used to spontaneously responding in role as the teacher becomes a next-door neighbor or a town official. If young children are confused by mixing pretend and reality, just tell them you are in role or use a prop like a hat or name tag to signal.

Teacher in role allows the teacher to be in charge of the time and direction of the action. Questioning controls the amount of time and the depth of problem solving. Relationships are forged as the teacher is seen as a fellow risk taker, a "player" who is a part of the drama. A sense of mystery or urgency, belief, and commitment are engendered by the teacher's attitude and involvement.

Heinig (1993) explains that teachers who assume roles, extend belief, stimulate thinking, provoke discussion, direct problem solving, and break down barriers between themselves and students (pp. 265–280). The goal is to be low key and not overplay or stereotype a role. Other generic roles teachers can assume are helpless characters: "I don't know and need help," authority figures (challenger), messengers, one of the crowd, devil's advocates (boss, expert, chief), or antagonists (p. 277). Props may be used but are not necessary. My favorite is an on-the-scene television reporter. A plastic mike is a must for this one.

Motivation. Drama is naturally interesting and involves the students in every aspect of CPS. Group work and choices abound as students readily seek understanding in every curricular area—not for points, either. Drama captures the essence of play and play is self-motivating.

Role of the audience. When children are proud of their work, they want to share. The desire to perform as a source of motivation is too valuable to ignore. It deepens learning, too, when students see how groups treat the same drama problem differently. A good strategy is to divide the class in half. One half then performs while the other half views, interprets, and responds. Then reverse roles. With small groups, take turns presenting. For example, two groups can present a pantomime at the same time while the rest of the class is the audience.

Before students perform, the audience needs to be clear about its role. Discuss with students how it is polite to listen attentively, not talk during the performance, be respectful and responsive, and applaud at the end. Additional audience engagement happens when the teachers let the audience know they'll be expected to give feedback to the actors. Display questions they can choose from to respond at the end. For example, What worked? What made the characters believable? (Be sure to focus on the positive.)

To firm up the role of the audience, it is a good idea to take a few minutes and have everyone role-play. For example, narrate as students pantomime:

> You take your seats. You show that you are excited to see the performance. The curtain opens and you carefully examine the set. The scene is a sad one. Then a character does something funny. Another character does something wonderful and you applaud. The scene ends and you applaud. The scene has been particularly good, so you stand and applaud. Now you take your seat and think about several things you'd like to tell the actors about their performance.

In addition to the daily replaying for classmates, a variety of audiences should be sought. Consider a standing invitation for parents to visit and not just for "special" events. Cooperate with fellow teachers to increase performance options. Seek out unconventional audiences—invite the custodians, cooks, and secretary. Take performances on the road to nearby nursing homes and senior service centers. The important idea is not see the yearly play or concert, for which students rehearse weeks and weeks, as the only time an audience is in order.

Creative Problem Solving

Drama relies heavily on CPS, so it is important for teachers to understand the process and influences on this higher-order thinking. Use the resources in Chapter 2 to boost creative thinking, and to learn what squelches it. See Ready References 2.5, 2.6, and 2.7. One specific strategy that boosts CPS is using visual imagery to solve problems. These are pretend field trips.

Virtual field trips. Through the power of pretend, students can take vivid virtual trips or mental journeys. Just as radio and storytelling trigger mental images of places, characters, and events, so can the teacher's voice. These mind journeys allow students to visit other countries, ecosystems, and even different time periods. Students' imaginations and creative thinking are stretched as they conjure up internal pictures. Simulated field trips can be used to introduce a unit or lesson or as a follow-up. Here are guidelines to construct virtual field trips.

- Write, tell, or choose trip stories that provoke rich sensory imagery. Look to your science, social studies, or literature curriculum to obtain ideas for suitable topics.
- Have students clear away distractions from their desks, close their eyes, and be comfortable.
- Use your voice to calm students; speak slowly and softly and use pauses. Read or speak at a steady pace.
- Give students time to create the images in their heads using the senses of sight, hearing, smell, taste, and touch.
- Limit the trip to 5–10 minutes.
- After the trip, ask students to mentally review the high points. They can share what they experienced in small groups or do a Write Right Away, sketching, one-liner, or partner storytelling of a key moment.
- As a whole group synthesize what was learned (e.g., in social studies, science, or literature) from the trip.

Examples instead of models. Just as in art or dance, students need to take a CPS orientation for drama. This means they understand that there are many ways to express feelings and ideas using body, voice, and imaginative thinking. For example, "Think of all the ways to use pantomime to show a feeling like greed or shyness. What body parts could be used and in what ways? (Use BEST elements, Ready Reference 10.1, to stretch and twist thinking.) What facial expressions can be used? How could these feelings be shown in pairs or trios?" Teachers should form a habit of asking for examples, rather than giving them, which helps students learn independent thinking.

Discussions and questioning strategies. Nearly every chapter features Ready References on questioning, with example questions and general guidelines for discussions. Discussions are primary contexts for creative problem solving, but their effectiveness depends on questioning strategies. This is relevant to discussions held before, during, and after drama, in small and whole group circumstances. Discussions may take place to clarify key concepts or special language or words or to stretch thinking. While yes–no, "closed" questions have a place, open, or fat, questions generate more participation and a greater range of answers, which is the goal of CPS and meaning making in general. Questions that get at universal themes are most likely to engage students. For example, before a drama ask "Why do characters disobey their parents as in *Peter Rabbit* or *Little Red Riding Hood?*" The problem of understanding disobedience is then explored through drama. Frames can be used to extend thinking during and after drama as well. For example, ask students to complete these sentence stems related to the subject matter under study: "I wonder . . ." or "What if . . . ." Ready Reference 8.8 lists more "all-purpose" fat questions.

Explicit Teaching

Gustav Meyrink's (1994) fable "The Curse of the Toad" is about a millipede who loved to dance. It challenges us to consider the effect of bringing to a conscious level what we do unconsciously. An old toad who hates the millipede tests this effect. He asks the millipede,

> Tell me then, oh most honorable one, when you walk, how do you know which foot to lift first, which is the second, and the third, which comes next as fourth, fifth, sixth—whether the next is the tenth or the hundredth, what meanwhile the second is doing, and the seventh: is it standing, or moving; when you get to the 917th, whether you should lift the 700th, put down the 39th, bend the 1000th or stretch the fourth? . . . But the millipede was glued to the ground, paralyzed, unable to move one single joint. He had forgotten which leg to lift first, and the more he thought about it the less he could work it out. (p. 54)

It may be of concern that children's joy in pretending might be disturbed by instruction in specific elements and tools of drama. Might we not paralyze them as the toad did the millipede by imposing cognition on intuition? Children readily engage in "let's pretend" but drama integration involves more than spontaneous play. Just as we support a toddler's innate desire to walk, so we can and should extend the urge to pretend.

We can build on innate dispositions to role-play using explicit instruction in the drama/theatre literacy base outlined previously. This involves direct instruction in what drama is and what we can use to make drama. In addition, children need time for discovery learning. Usually explicit instruction is done in short mini-lessons, followed right away by opportunities to use new knowledge. Explicit instruction includes demonstration, coaching, feedback, and teaching the elements and skills of theatre and drama. Of special importance is teaching ways to identify conflict (the core of drama) in literature, songs, and paintings and in life. For example, ask students to identify the problem and discuss what decisions must be made to solve it. From there students can learn to use pantomime and verbal improvisation to explore solutions.

Special note: Most children understand the difference between pretend and reality, but it is useful to explicitly teach this and tell or ask about the difference. Students need to see drama as "pretend" time that allows practice of skills needed in real life. Ready References 8.1 and 8.2 list drama elements and skills.

Organize and Structure. As students explore the elements of drama, they need to be taught to use a three-part, beginning–middle–end (BME) format. This begins with teaching students to construct scenes that have these same three parts as stories have. Another structure for planning is: Who? Where? What problems, conflicts, or obstacles? What actions or feelings? A planning sheet with BME or the questions just listed can focus student work.

Management: Time, Space, Students

Drama activities are exciting. Students are often out of their seats, moving and talking as they solve problems in role. The stage needs to be set for classroom drama. Space needs to be organized, desks rearranged quickly. Teachers need ways to get attention, give directions, and move activities along. Here are basic pointers.

Rules and Expectations. We need to know and respect the rules and limits at home, at work, and in the stores where we shop. Ground rules and expectations for drama are needed, as well. Explain limits on space, time, and speed. For example, "Stay at your desk or in your personal spot. Walk in place. I'll count to five. Do this in slow motion." State expectations in straightforward language without sugar coating or paternalism. It is helpful to use cue words: first, second, before, finally, and so forth. After giving directions, ask "What questions do you have?" and then signal to begin work.

Distractions. Before beginning, desktops should be cleared, as should any area where the drama will happen. Keep props to a minimum or don't use them. If props are to be used, don't put them out until they are needed.

Goals. To make sure students understand what is to be done in a small group or individually, it is important to practice an example or two with the whole group. This goes for any teaching, not just drama.

Signals. Signals are valuable cues to help organize and get the action going—or stop it. For example, say "places," "curtain," "lights," or "home" to start a drama. Lights, sounds, music, a drum, bell, or tambourine are effective signals, too. EPR (every pupil response) signals after questions or directions teach students to control their own actions and learn to direct others. Ready Reference 8.5 lists attention-getting signals used by teachers for drama and other activities.

Transitions. Make transitions by calling groups or rows or by creative categories such as eye color, patterns of clothes, or birthdays. It is helpful to cue students that a transition is coming up by announcing the time left: "You have 1 minute to finish planning."

Grouping. Larger groups and larger spaces require more planning and controls. Start with smaller amounts of time

 **Attention Getters and Signals**

This list was generated by classroom teachers in Ohio.

1. Whisper directions.
2. Flick lights.
3. Play a favorite tape or CD.
4. Use tambourine, chimes, piano chord, or any pleasant sound.
5. Have children echo what you say. *Examples:* "Jambo Jambo" ("Hello Hello" in Swahili) or use a tongue twister (aluminum linoleum).
6. Ask children to echo a rhythm pattern, sign, or movement.
7. Start a chain reaction: Say to one student "Would you tell the person next to you to. . . ."
8. Say, "I'm looking for someone who is . . . (fill in a behavior like 'in a curved shape')."
9. Write a message in large letters on the chalkboard.
10. Write directions on large cards. *Example:* "Look at me and smile."
11. Say, "Let's listen . . . to hear grass grow, clock tick."
12. Say, "I'd like to see . . . the color of everyone's eyes."
13. Have a secret code word (e.g., foreign language, special vocabulary, or phrases such as "chicka boom chicka rucka").
14. Tell students to close their eyes and make mind pictures.
15. Say, "Think what is stopping you from listening right now."
16. Count aloud backward from 10 (invite students to join in).
17. Agree on a class signal to get attention if . . . the ceiling was about to fall in, there was a fire, etc.
18. Tell a joke or riddle. Knock knocks work.
19. Call students' names who are ready to listen.
20. Have a nonverbal signal. *Examples:* touch pocket or ear, hold up two fingers, thumbs up.
21. Give a direction with universal appeal. *Example:* "Sit down if you ever wanted a 2-hour recess," "Freeze if you like money," or "Raise your hand if you'd like some ice cream."
22. Give points to students who are listening. Use a clipboard, board, or overhead.
23. Write the names of five students who are ready on the board.
24. Sit in a particular place or use a particular stance.
25. Do something different. Attire can attract attention (e.g., "Did you notice that _____ is wearing _____?")
26. Say, "If you can hear my voice, _____ (behavior)."
27. Call and response sequences: T=Guaca Guaca, S=Guacamole; T=Peanut, or S=butter; or T=Bread, S=jam
28. Use a group reinforcer. *Example:* Use cloze blanks on the chalkboard and say, "I need to see people ready to earn another letter in '_____' (letters spell out a goal like *extra recess*)."
29. Make up a class chant: "We're ready, we're ready as ready can be. In just five seconds, chicka rucka chicka bees."
30. Use sign language for directions such as sit down and line up. See *Joy of Signing* (Riekehof, 1987).
31. Ask students to close their eyes and imagine, for example, the sun setting or the ripples moving out from a stone thrown in a pond.

---

and space. Have students work in pairs, before trying larger groups. Pantomiming in slow motion teaches self-control and calms students.

There is not as much teacher control when students work in small groups, but group work is crucial to dramatic problem solving and an essential workplace and family skill. Students learn to work in groups by working in groups. Create pairs, trios, and quads by counting off. At times give a choice based on interests or ability to work together. Instead of "Find a partner," say "Find a partner who is your same height" or "Find two people you can cooperate with." This helps students learn to distinguish between friends and those they can best work with.

Avoid cliques by rotating groups. Learning circles can also be the basis for group work. Another option is to give each child a color or symbol (circle, square) and group by symbols. Group decision making is developed by asking students for their ideas. Once they understand the variety of choices in drama, ask them to set time and space limits. Suggest the amount of rehearsal needed and discuss whether to present to an audience or not.

Participation.   When drama is first introduced, invite volunteers instead of forcing participation; forcing can increase reluctance and be contagious. Students want to know what they are volunteering for, so explain the general idea. For example, "I need three people who know how to walk in place." The goal is to involve all students. One way is to use the unison strategy. Unison means simultaneous "all-at-once" participation. Time is used effectively and no one is waiting for a turn, which creates boredom and prompts mischief. Students feel the comfort created by safety in numbers. Maximum involvement can be achieved through double casting (have two or more children perform the same role). For example, have three wolves in *The Three Little Pigs.*

Discipline for Independence

The root of the word *discipline* is disciple. A disciple is not forced to follow a leader; she chooses. Drama-based lessons are intended to build this kind of relationship between teacher and students. Self-discipline and independence grow as students choose to follow such a teacher. They make more effort and persist because they are drawn into the magic circle of possibilities a teacher can create. They feel respected and give trust and respect in return. "She never believed I couldn't" was a tribute I once heard given to such a teacher.

Independence grows from learning how to control body, mind, and voice and ways to extend use of all three. Drama does this. It begins with clear expectations so students learn to focus, concentrate, and know the rewards of putting forth best efforts.

Control techniques used by drama specialists are now popular tools many classroom teachers use. They have been adopted wholesale in some schools. For example, Browne Academy in Chattanooga, Tennessee, uses drama teaching artist Shaun Layne's controls for schoolwide discipline. Drama teacher Jeff Jordan has done the same for Ashley River in Charleston, South Carolina (e.g., "Criss-cross applesauce" is used in every classroom as a signal).

Here are important guidelines. The Appendix also has a summary of Discipline, Prevention, and Intervention Strategies. Chapter 10 includes additional discipline and management ideas, especially related to personal space and time limits.

- When a rule is broken, acknowledge the student's feelings to help save face. For example, "I see that you want to be in Susan's group." Then restate the rule. Next, implement a logical consequence, not a punishment. "In this class we work in different groups. Work with this group or at your desk alone."
- Consequences should be clear from the lesson start, along with a review of rules. Chapter 10 has rule examples.
- Not everyone can be made happy. Try to ignore whiners. Small infractions aren't worth attention, and some behaviors are to get attention.

- Watch for signs of need for attention, and give it frequently for positive behavior.
- Drama is fun and interesting. Don't cajole into participating. Start with those who want to participate; others will follow.
- Acknowledge failures and be honest. This helps model how to handle problems. Start over with a revised procedure. Students need to see drama as an experiment. It is not predictable.
- Veteran teachers know that "giving the eye" and being physically close are often enough to get students back on task. Circulate as students work and look them directly in the eye.
- Follow through with consequences. Don't threaten and don't hesitate. Stop the activity if students are not on task. Don't keep going if only part of the class is involved. Review consequences periodically. Some teachers post them.
- Use private conferences with repeat offenders and difficult children as soon after the lesson as possible. Public humiliation is unethical. If offenders must be removed, return them to the activity ASAP. Often a 2-minute time-out is as effective as total removal. Of course, admission back should be contingent upon agreeing to follow the rules.

Drama to Teach Rules.   Drama is a tool to teach just about anything, including classroom rules. Students can create improvised scenes (Chapter 9) that show cooperation, active listening, compromise, respect for alternative opinions, and other desirable behaviors. Direct them to make sure scenes have a beginning, middle, and end. Scenes can be set up by first identifying characters, a setting, and a problem situation. Challenge students to think about "what-if" situations: What if some people didn't do their share of the work in a group project? Remind students to use CPS, which includes brainstorming ways to settle arguments. Students may choose pantomime or verbal drama. For example, students created a pledge based on the Golden Rule using a frame to structure thinking: "Because I like to _____, I will _____. Because I don't like _____, I will _____. Because I want _____, I will _____." Here is their final product:

We, the sixth grade class of Overlook Elementary, want to have our opinions heard, so we promise to listen to others. We like to be treated with respect, so we will not disrespect others. We do not like to be touched in unfriendly ways, so we will not touch anyone with fighting on our minds. We want to work in groups, so we will cooperate and get work done together. We hereby so promise all the above on this day in September 2003.

Blueprint VII: Instructional Design: Routines and Structures

Classrooms run smoothly because of predictable routines and organizing structures. Within these frameworks there is great variability. One framework is the lesson itself, with a predictable introduction, development, and conclusion. What happens in each lesson segment is unpredictable.

Structuring Lessons

The two-pronged integrated arts lesson framework introduced in Chapter 3 is a predictable structure. It can be used creatively to help students gain skills and learn concepts related to drama and other curricular areas. As discussed previously, integrated arts lessons need to include at least one arts concept—drama in this case—to ensure that the integrity of the art form is not lost when drama is integrated with another curricular area. When you teach a few concepts, students can go into some depth and become comfortable with the possibilities of each skill or element (e.g., pantomime). Direct or explicit instruction using the introduction, development, and conclusion structure is used in the example plan in Planning Page 8.1.

Note: After doing a drama, take time to comment on things you saw or heard during the lesson. No names are necessary, since the focus of drama is on the group working together. The conclusion should be a time for students to reflect and do self-evaluation: What worked? Didn't work? Why? What did you like? What did you learn? New ideas? What would you do differently? Teachers may also wish to invite students to repeat activities with a novel twist, even two or three times, if interest in this kind of exploration is shown during the discussion.

Lesson Introductions.   The purpose of the introduction is to motivate and ready students for learning. Here are common introduction strategies:

- Remove visual or auditory distractions and get attention.
- Establish mood and set a climate for creative exploration (see Ready Reference 2.7 for Creativity Boosters).
- Build on prior knowledge and past experiences.
- Stimulate interest. Interest can account for 30 times the variance in understanding. Web, ask questions, and do warm-ups to build interest.
- Coach students to concentrate and focus, to "make us believe," and not be hams.
- Make sure students know the content. If they are to do a drama about pollution, they need background from a variety of experiences. They need knowledge to inform the drama.

Lessons can sink or swim based on the introduction. This is the point in time where students need to perceive purpose. Take time to discuss the real-life connections of drama (e.g., roles we take every day) and develop the concept that the arts are forms of literacy. Use the mini-lesson topics in Ready Reference 3.3 to start. Students need to understand that drama is an enjoyable art form used for serious learning purposes. At first they may not understand why social studies time is used for drama; they may not see the arts as communication tools, parallel to reading and writing. Through discussions and reaching the point in drama where empathy and insight are experienced, students do begin to understand. For example, students unfamiliar with using drama acted silly when first pantomiming the Trail of Tears March of the Cherokees. In time, with coaching and more information about the dire circumstances of the migration, students were able to feel how hopeless, tired, and discouraged the Indians were after walking day after day through bad weather, starving and sick. See the generic lesson plan on Planning Page 3.3 for more ideas. Ready Reference 8.6 gives examples of drama problem solving for comprehension.

Energizers and Warm-Ups.   Students get used to the routine of starting lessons with short activities that can relax or rev up. Energizers are such brief activities that create a climate for risk taking, give focus, and facilitate concentration, imagination, cooperation, and self-control. Here are samples for the body: (1) make circle movements that slowly travel head to toe, (2) walk across the room in different ways, at different levels, or in a variety of "as-if" situations, and (3) direct students to pretend they are balloons blowing up and then collapsing (add sound effects, if you like). See the energizers and warms-ups in Chapter 9 and in all Seed Strategies chapters. In addition to the energizers and warm-ups in the next chapter, check out these websites: *www.teachingonline.org/drama3.html* and *www.learnimprov.com*.

Routines and Rituals.   Routines and rituals establish habits of mind and body. Here are routines schools and teachers use.

- Create a morning school television show with students taking roles as newscasters, weather reporters, and interviewers.
- Use drama energizers and warm-ups to start/end the day and lessons.
- Use humor strategies to relax students so that they feel comfortable taking risks to be creative.
- Present reader's theatre scripts one day each week (Chapter 9).
- Make special times to discuss drama and theatre in real life like roles people play, actors on TV, and why they are effective.

Ready Reference 8.6 Drama Problem Solving for Comprehension

These are drama strategies planned to deepen comprehension of Patricia Polacco books. They are divided into pantomime and verbal improvisation. These activities assume prior teaching about drama elements and skills.

1. ***Pink and Say: Pantomime tableau of key scenes***
   Prioritize the most "tension-filled" scenes. Group students and give time to make a frozen picture. For example, create a tableau of Pinkus helping Sheldon to safety or when the boys were being pulled apart after the Confederate soldiers discovered them. Frozen characters can choose to "come alive," stay in character, and answer questions or say a one-liner. For example, "We are very scared and don't know if we will live or die." Adaptation: Do behind a white sheet with a light to make body language more dramatic.
   Verbal: Television show. Students portray important book characters on a discussion panel for a television show. The audience questions them about what happened and how they felt. For example, "How did it feel serving your country during the Civil War?"
   Verbal: Newsbreak. Students become newscasters and do short newsbreak interruptions to update the class on what is going on in the Civil War. Interviews from characters can be included. This connects with a social studies lesson, with students sharing feelings, as well as facts about events.

2. ***The Bee Tree: Narrative pantomime*** Students mime as narrator reads: "You are a bee. Show how you fly to

a flower and land. Show how you begin to gather pollen. Show how the pollen is sticky. Fly back to your beehive. Put down the pollen and go to sleep for the night."
   Verbal: Character interviews. Students pair up. One is the interviewer and the other is a story character. Students focus on using a character's language and style of speaking. The interviewer asks five Ws and H questions. Switch roles and repeat.

3. ***My Ol' Man: Pantomime comic strip.*** Break into four groups. Each group chooses one scene from the beginning, middle, or end. The comic strip will be four different frozen pictures or tableaux. Give groups 5 minutes to plan. Group 1 poses for the first frame, holds 10 seconds, and then moves to the next scene, and so on. When finished, say "Curtain."
   Verbal: Interview. Pair off with an A and a B. B becomes a newspaper reporter who just heard about this amazing man who is out of a job but keeps his hopes alive with the help of a magic rock. A is the extraordinary man. B interviews A to get facts to write a good news story (use 5 Ws and H questions.) Switch roles. Variation: Students actually write the news stories.

- Put up a marquee to announce noteworthy films or plays.
- Share theatre experiences. Have a "critic's corner" for students to post movie evaluations.
- Maintain an ongoing Web of Roles People Play (e.g., pictures, words in collage form).
- Do morning drama, like charades to review yesterday's learning. Do drama (e.g., one-liners) to summarize at the end the day.
- Sing action songs and do poems to start or end the day (see Poetry Performances in Ready Reference 5.3).

Clubs

More and more arts-based schools have drama-based clubs like the Drama Troupe at Ashley River Creative Arts. Storytelling clubs, reader's theatre groups, and playwriting clubs are other interest-based groups students can choose, if the structures are there. Some clubs meet within the school day, and others meet after school. All clubs need a sponsor. This may be a teacher, parent, or interested community member.

Blueprint VIII: Adaptations for Diverse Needs

Drama specialists are an invaluable source for differentiating instruction and should be consulted, if at all possible. General information about developmental stages is included in Chapter 2 and the Appendix. Teachers can use the basic principles for adapting instruction for at-risk students and those with special needs presented in Chapter 3. Ready Reference 8.7 gives examples of adaptations. Drawing on students' abilities rather than focusing on disabilities is a key idea when considering any instructional modification.

Drama is unique in its ensemble focus: The emphasis is on partner or group work. Group work can be particularly enjoyable for students with special needs. If reluctant or shy children are not forced to participate in uncomfortable ways they grow to want to be involved because they see peers having fun. Puppets and props also help children feel safe.

Ready Reference 8.7   PARTICULAR Ways to Differentiate Drama

Place: Limit and define the space for doing drama (e.g., desk area).

Amount: Do fewer activities or shorter ones.

Rate: Go slower or faster to meet student needs.

Targets: Change the goals, make them clearer or shorter.

Instruction: Use more teacher direction. For example, use narrative pantomime to start and consider taking a role.

Curriculum materials: Use familiar stories or student experiences for drama activities.

Utensils: Use visual aids such as nametags or headbands to help students understand the roles.

Levels of difficulty: Generally, pantomime is easier than verbal improvisation, and individual drama activities directed by the teacher are easier than group work. Perhaps the material is too conceptually difficult and needs to be altered. If students act silly, it may be they don't know what to do or feel they can't do what is expected. Humor is often used to cover embarrassment. Consider adapting the level of difficulty.

Assistance: For example, children with hearing impairments need to see your face and mouth as you speak. Ask students what to do to help themselves. Don't force shy children to participate because this may increase reluctance. If students don't seem to be able to end the drama, tell them to plan an ending before presenting, ask the audience for ideas, or you take a role and end it.

Response: Alter what you expect in the conclusion. For example, you may have planned for students to present small group work to the whole group, but group work has been satisfying enough.

In general, nonverbal (pantomime) activities are easier than verbal activities. Solo or individual drama strategies done in unison are recommended before small group work. (The exception is older students who have body concerns that make an introduction to drama through pantomime awkward for some.) It works well to start with common ways pantomime is used in daily life—nonverbal communication to show how something is too hot or cold, to greet others, or to show excitement. Space should be managed, as appropriate to student needs, by beginning with limiting students to small areas, like their desks, and then moving to large areas as they show readiness to handle more. Large areas such as cafeterias, gyms, or playgrounds may have echoes, signal a recess attitude, and cause chaos if students are not properly prepared.

As with any creative problem solving, it is productive to use whole-group, teacher-directed drama strategies before breaking students into small groups. This helps set expectations about the kinds of thinking and behaving that will be expected in the small groups. The rule of thumb is to order activities from easy to more difficult and from low content to more content dense (e.g., move from personal interests to subject area concepts and ideas application). Humor used at the start of a lesson relaxes students and activates creative thinking for serious work (the tension and conflict in drama) later in the lesson. Finally, students often see adaptations that teachers don't, so it is important to invite their ideas.

Blueprint IX: Assessment for Learning

Assessment *for* learning, versus *of* learning, emphasizes formative feedback *during* lessons. Formative assessment boosts motivation and increases the quality of student work. It is particularly influential in boosting achievement of lower-performing students (Leahy et al., 2005). In research in six countries, including the United States, students "achieved in 6-7 months what otherwise takes a year" (Leahy et al., 2005, p. 19).

The arts have a long history of using formative assessments. Drama and theatre specialists, in particular, rely on coaching, or formative feedback during drama rehearsal. In the classroom this entails coaching students to use drama elements and skills and work toward other knowledge and skills in the Standards. Summative assessment happens at the conclusion of work, too, when there are culminating performances or products like readers' scripts. Student progress in using drama as a learning medium is also demonstrated and celebrated using portfolios, videotapes, and displays.

Coaching: Formative Feedback

Formative assessment focuses on giving students the information they need to move forward. This can happen through written feedback, but in drama specific oral comments, sometimes called *side coaching,* are often used as students work. The line between assessment and instruction blurs as coaching is used to remind about directions, goals, and assessment criteria; (2) talk students through an activity, and (3) maintain control. It is also used to help the audience (usually peers) understand what a group is doing, and fill in awkward silences. Coaching does not mean giving lots of directions. It involves offering suggestions and questions as scaffolds. It is a way to challenge students to use their bodies and voices in new ways. (See BEST in Ready Reference 10.1 for movement possibilities.)

Questions. Coaching creates depth of understanding and higher-quality expression of ideas and emotions. Questions are often used like "What could you do to show the character's age or how the character feels?" Teachers ask many "what if" questions to stretch and direct. For example, "What if the weather changed?" "What if someone got sick?" "What if things got out of control and you couldn't stop the process?" "What if the world stopped rotating? What if dinosaurs still lived?" To help students prepare scenes, ask:

- What does your character want? How can you show this?
- Tell me more about . . . (explore the emotion or thinking of the character).
- What does the place have to do with how the character feels or acts?
- What else might you try?
- How could this problem be solved?
- What do you want the audience to see and feel?
- How could props, lighting, and/or music be used?

It is worth the extra time to cue carefully and coach as students work. The effects are clear in their development of skills and confidence.

Descriptive Feedback. It is especially important to note the unique and different ideas students devise. Do so by infusing "I statements" like "I see," "I notice," and "I wonder." Refrain from phony praise. Ask students to isolate part of a drama, such as just one movement in a pantomime, and solicit peer feedback. For example, ask a student to repeat just the part where she was grasping the beanstalk before beginning to climb it. Ask other students what they see. This habit of doing (showing with hands, face, and posture) and then asking for student observations uses a discovery or inductive method that promotes reflective thinking.

Focus and Concentration. Teachers and parents lament children's short attention spans. Concentration is a specific drama skill and a criterion that belongs in a rubric for most drama activities. Concentration can be taught, and drama is a valuable teaching vehicle to do so. Here's how a coached session might go. Begin by asking students what helps them concentrate and what distracts them. Ask them to focus with body and face and give descriptive feedback. As students work on a drama problem, continue with feedback: "Fred is really concentrating. He is remembering to keep his body bent like an old man." When children reach the creative flow state described in Chapter 3, they will be totally involved. Signs include feeling time go quickly, spontaneously adding details to drama, and asking to repeat activities. One class of third graders so enjoyed a narrative pantomime of *The Wretched Stone,* they asked to replay it instead of having recess. When students ham it up or show off, they are not genuinely involved. Discuss this before it happens. Several activities in the energizers and warm-ups strategies section of Chapters 9–11 target concentration and focus.

Observation Records

Drama is sometimes tricky because so many teachable moments and important assessment information emerge. One of the best forms of assessment is teacher observation of what students show they know throughout the process. A clipboard with sticky notes, each with a child's name, works well to jot down evidence of lesson objectives. Notes should be dated and given to students to put in their folios.

Rubrics and Checklists

Teachers can use rubrics and checklists. Students need to be involved in using these tools for self-assessment and peer feedback, as well. Rather than squelch motivation, deep thinking creativity with grades and traditional tests, teachers can discuss general assignment criteria before work is begun, which gives students more focus during work. For example, a rubric for a drama performance would include criteria for the main area of "ability to inhabit a character": body posture and gestures, movement, facial expressions, eye contact, and variety in use of voice (volume, tempo, pitch, etc.). Because drama is being used as a teaching vehicle, additional criteria about *using* drama would help show transformation of learning. For example, using historically accurate information about Clara Barton in drama could be one criterion in a unit on individuals who made a big difference. Ready Reference 8.9 shows a drama skills checklist. Other assessment examples are provided in the Appendix.

Peer Feedback

After drama presentations, students need to debrief and it helps to give them structures to facilitate articulation of thoughts and feelings. For example, students can simply tell

 **All-Purpose Fat Questions**

Post questions so students learn to use different kinds to discuss and reflect on their work. Teachers should model use of open/fat questions and show how they cause more discussion. These questions help students think more deeply and facilitate oral expression.

- What worked?
- What did you enjoy?
- What would you change?
- How was the ending? What was the best moment? Why?
- How did you work with others?
- How did you show involvement?
- How did you get your idea? Where did you gather ideas?
- Why did you do what you did?

- What were you trying to do?
- What did you try that you've never tried before?
- What did you learn most?
- How is this connected to other things you are learning?
- What ideas did you use from what we've been learning about drama (elements, skills, concepts)?
- What did you learn? What was this mostly about? What did this tell you about people or the world? What will you remember forever?

what they saw or heard, describing honestly, using posted drama elements and skills. They can also use sentence stems to express their feelings: "I liked . . ." or "It made me feel . . . ." The liked–wonder–learned (LWL) strategy can be used after a drama to record responses in three columns. Students also need to learn to ask questions of others as a form of feedback. Because receiving feedback is hard for some, it helps to role-play giving and receiving feedback. This also shows students how rude or thoughtless remarks can make a person feel. Sensitivity and empathy are important to constructive feedback.

To help teach students discuss and reflect on their drama work, Ready Reference 8.8 has questions for students to use as guides.

Program Evaluation

Check out the checklists for theatre and drama in the *Opportunity to Learn Standards* at: *www.winthrop.edu/ABC/*.

Blueprint X: Arts Partnerships

Arts Agency Collaborations

There are now collaborations among a variety of arts organizations and schools across the country. See the School Registry in the Appendix for contacts. The Kennedy Center Partners in Education lists sites in most states. Check out the partnerships to see if your school is a member. Another example is Shakespeare & Company, based in Lenox, Massachusetts, which is a theatre company that has partnered with public schools for 20 years (*www.shakespeare.org/*). Many organizations provide workshops for teachers

on a low- or no-charge basis. Contact local museums or arts councils to see if they are involved in partnership projects or interested in getting started. See Chapter 3 and the Appendix for more information. Local workshops conducted by artists and classroom teachers engaged in arts integration are becoming more common. Keep an eye out for advertisements.

Strong partnerships need two basic elements: shared goals and time to plan (Booth, 2005). Local college theatre departments and community theatre organizations all are interested in growing audiences so they may be potential partners for schools. They may not understand the concept of arts integration, however. This is where classroom teachers need to work as adult educators as they seek out partnerships. Teachers need to try to entice specialists into co-planning and perhaps working with students as well. Drama and theatre specialists can help find connections with other disciplines and show how to make them without damaging the integrity of the art form.

Arts Education Partnership *(http://aep-arts.org)*

A mission of this national organization is to facilitate partnerships between schools and arts organization. Go to the site for publications like *Learning Partnerships: Improving Learning in Schools with Arts Partners in the Community.* The publications can be downloaded.

Teaching Artists and Artist Residencies

Professional actors, playwrights, and other drama and theatre specialists may be available through a local arts council or college or by contacting artists in your community. Children's theatre groups may be willing to be involved in your

Ready Reference 8.9   Drama Skills Checklist

Name _____   Date _____

Directions: Evaluate using 1, 2, 3, 4, 5, with 1 indicating no evidence and 5 indicating very evident. Add notes and discuss.

_____ **Use of body:** ability to coordinate and control body, use of appropriate energy, display of sensory awareness and expression, use of gestures and facial expressions, communication through pantomime, interpretation of others' nonverbal communication

_____ **Verbal expression:** speaking clearly and using variety in volume, rate, tone and pitch, pause, emphasis, inflection, fluency, ability to improvise dialogue

_____ **Focus:** concentration and staying involved, making others believe in the realness of the character, following directions

_____ **Imagination:** creative thinking, unique ideas, elaboration on ideas, spontaneity

_____ **Evaluation:** giving constructive feedback, using others' suggestions, self-evaluation, adaptation of own behavior

_____ **Social skills:** working cooperatively in groups, listening and responding to others

_____ **Audience etiquette:** attending, listening, responding appropriately to others' performances

---

classroom, and Theatre in Education projects are another dimension worth investigating. It is important to realize that artists often have little or no background in teaching or child development. Before bringing an artist into a school or class, it is important to meet ahead of time to prepare. See the checklists in the Arts Partnerships section of the Blueprints in Chapter 3 and 4.

Of course, the best potential for partnership is with a drama teacher. More and more schools are fortunate to have a drama specialist. Carolee Mason, a Canadian drama specialist of 27 years, finds herself increasingly acting as a resource for colleagues. For example, a veteran math teacher asked her for drama activities to alleviate math anxiety. "He saw a change in the classroom culture and an improved comfort level that enhanced the learning environment" (quoted in Lushington, 2003, p. 1).

Specialists usually welcome invitations to plan with teachers, especially if integration is viewed as going both ways; at times the drama teacher should be able to ask for support for her unit focus on a theme or topic. Classroom teachers can make it easy for a specialist to assist in integration by providing a month-by-month listing of units and lessons in science, social studies, reading, and language arts, so math specialists can make suggestions. In addition, teachers can invite specialists to do the same with a list of topics they plan to develop. Classroom teachers can also ask for ways to follow up on drama classes or extend drama work. It is highly recommended that generalists sit in on drama classes to learn more about drama and about ways students can make meaning using drama. The drama teacher in the following spotlight will give you a sense of what's possible.

Teacher Spotlight:

Poetry with a Drama Specialist

Jeff Jordan has been at Ashley River for 10 years. He has a master's degree in speech/theatre from the University of South Carolina and taught theatre in Columbia, South Carolina. He first came to do a drama residency and was "overwhelmed by the school." He states, "Jayne Ellicott (the principal) gives us the freedom to give students a true artistic experience." He is passionate when he declares, "The arts expand the curriculum, while tests narrow it."

His schedule is: Grade 1, once a week; Grades 2–4, twice a week; and Grade 5, once a week. As a specialist he thinks a key part of his role is to listen and offer suggestions to classroom teachers. He tries to mesh drama/theatre when it "fits meaningfully into units." For example, "in third grade there is a huge folk/fairy tale unit, so I teach script writing and audition techniques," he explains.

"I like drama because Mr. Jordan is my teacher," explains a first grader. In the opinion of Ashley River second graders he is a "good teacher with super warm-ups and a great actor who loves to teach." The third graders say they know he loves Ashley River and likes to write and read stories. The fourth graders point out that Mr. Jordan "makes us laugh." He makes them feel "it's OK to make mistakes, but he wants you to concentrate and try your best." They like it that he has taught them to take risks. The fifth grade calls Mr. Jordan the "drama king."

Pantomiming emotions: Controlling body, face, and voice.

Drama Specialist in Action

The essence of all art is to have pleasure in giving pleasure.
(Mikhail Baryshnikov)

The floor is brightly carpeted. There are no desks. A huge puppet stage is in one corner. One folding chair and a desk are pushed in a corner. Pictures of students cover a bulletin board. Kids are seated "Criss-cross applesauce" in personal spaces on the floor.

"How many heard the storm last night?" Jeff Jordan asks. Most hands go up.

"Remember our school is Ashley River . . ."

Students chorally finish with "Creative Arts!"

"What are all the arts, then?" he asks. Students call out the list.

"OK, artists create! Right? So we are going to create movable poetry."

As if on cue, they begin to recite a poem they all know. Jeff coaches then to put in more voice, body, and facial expressions to show the feeling of the poem.

"Don't just say it like you are a choral robot," he teases. "If you were the director, what tips would you give to improve this?" Students immediately offer ideas:

"Bouncing voice!"

"Say it with feeling and energy."

"Don't be rigid and boring."

"Make your voice sound like your movement."

"Do your best."

"So, what if I said 'thunder'", Jeff asks.

A boy stands right up and with a low pitch says, "Thunder," making his body large with a broad stance. A few students giggle.

"Clap it back to me," Jeff demands, and the whole class claps his rhythm and is attentive once again.

He plugs an upcoming artist residency by Laura Rich and tells the class her focus will be on movement poetry and weather. Today is a warm-up for her work. He explains they will first write and then perform their poems.

They begin with the **"actor's warm-up."** Jeff directs them to reach and stretch as if they are pushing up a bar.

"Shake out your hands. Put your imaginary bar at chest level and push and pull it back. Shake out. Shake. Now isolate. Shake one hand. Two hands. Both knees. Shake shoulders, stomach, face. Now do your whole body. Do not touch others. Do not fall down."

"OK, back to last night's storm. We are going to do **weather statues,** first. Think about being different. If you see low people, then you go high, etc. Action, and . . . freeze!"

Some students are in spread out on the floor. Others are posed on tiptoes with arms in jagged positions. No one looks the same. Mr. Jordan wanders among the statues **coaching** them to "Focus. Concentrate." He stops to describe facial expressions and body positions.

"On **3-second cue,** let's do *rainstorm.* 3-2-1." Students spring to life in new positions until Mr. Jordan calls, "Freeze." Again he **circulates and gives feedback.** This time he clicks his finger near a few faces and compliments those who keep concentration.

"Cut. OK, 5-second cue for *lightning.* 5-4-3-2-1." This time students are energized to make large sweeping movements. Mr. Jordan repeats his coaching. Then they relax and he gives them a 4-second cue for *sunshiny day.* This time he reminds them that directors look for people who can hold their concentration. They then do snow and finally hurricane.

"Criss-cross applesauce. Hands in lap. In your place," Jeff calls. Students return to seated positions on the floor. He explains they are going to do prewriting. He reads three poems written by students. After reading "Clouds" he asks, **"What did you notice?"**

"No rhyming," comments one boy.

Jeff responds, "Right, poems don't have to rhyme. What images?"

When there are no responses, he rereads "clouds like cotton candy" and asks them to picture this in their heads. He repeats the line several times. **"What do you see and feel?"** Students now call out "sticky," "puffy," "pink," "fluffy," "sugary," and "towering." Next Jeff reads, " 'When clouds cry'—that is personification!"

A boy with a shirt that reads "Mikey" says, "Once we saw a cloud that looked like a hammerhead shark!"

"You could do a poem on that image," Jeff says with a smile. He then reads a rainbow poem and asks more questions about images and feelings. There are many responses. Finally, he announces, "The Storm." He directs them to **listen closely** to the last line. He reads slowly, softly at first. His voice builds with the storm. Students do not take their eyes off him.

At the conclusion Jeff asks for observations, feelings, and other **"noticings."** Words like *suspenseful, scary, dramatic, dark,* and *swirling* are suggested.

"These are pretty short," one boy observes.

"Yes, good noticing. Nobody said that before!" Jeff says as if he is genuinely delighted.

"Now, you need to think about a weather moment and describe how the weather feels. Use your whole body to think of how the weather moment feels—like we did before. Then add words that describe the feelings and movements."

Students pass out clipboards and blank paper. "Write first. Add the title later," Jeff advises. "Don't worry about spelling—sound it out, yeah, yeah, yeah," he sings Beatles-style and they giggle. One girl suggests they can use the dictionary, but Jeff suggests they do that after they get their ideas roughed out.

Jeff circulates as students work and gives feedback. "Arthur is starting with question. Mario has three lines already." He urges them to write fast and in 5 minutes most have filled a page.

The lesson has been fast paced and intense. One girl has written: Balmy air surrounds me.

Full of heavy wet wind.
I try to breathe
I feel like I'm suffocating.
The hot humid weather
Is summer in South Carolina.

When There Is No Drama Specialist

By starting a school directory of persons with drama background and skills, teachers have found drama expertise in nearby places. The teacher next door may have had courses in children's drama or may act in community theatre. A parent may have skills to do a workshop on nonverbal communication. Circulate a form to all adults in the school requesting names and contact information for people who could be used as drama or theatre resources. Encourage people to list themselves. Students, parents, and community groups can also be tapped for potential skills. Use the Internet to locate home pages of drama and theatre organizations at the local and state levels. Selected Internet websites are listed in the Appendix for starters. Don't forget to contact the theatre department in nearby colleges to find out about student internships or other ways college students might serve as drama resources.

Classroom Snapshot:
Science Through Drama

This chapter ends with day's end in Amy Walker's third grade at Ashley River Creative Arts. A four-person group stands at the ready with props: paper plate sun, tambourine, and green crepe paper.

"Remember to present your skits like your audience is first graders who know nothing about photosynthesis. **Audience**—watch and listen so you can give feedback and ask questions. Action!"

On cue the narrator reads and a paper plate becomes a rising sun. Crepe paper transforms into plant leaves slowly emerging from a striped T-shirt. The tambourine player accompanies in the background, and is featured in solos during several dramatic moments in photosynthesis. The actors freeze, the audience claps, and the actors bow.

"What did they do that worked?" Ms. Walker asks.

"The narrator was loud."

"They worked as a team."

"Jerry—uh—I mean, the accompanist, was into it!"

"How do you mean?"

"Well, he showed the feel of it—like when he got faster or just stopped and then was slow and in the background. It created a mystery, sort of."

"What questions do you have?" Ms. Walker then asks.

"What type of food does a plant make?" asks a girl.

The narrator answers, "Sugar."

Other groups present their photosynthesis mini-dramas. One uses sound effects for water. Another uses a rain stick. Each performance adds new images to target science concepts. As both audience and performers, students listen closely to each other, observe, wonder, question, and learn. When applause erupts, there are smiles all around.

Out of nowhere come flags made with paper, fabric, paints, collage materials—each one on a twig stick. The flags bear symbols like masks, palettes, violins, and unicorns. Many have seven stripes. Why seven?

"Because there are seven specials at Ashley River," explains a tall girl. "The unicorn is our mascot."

"Remember our American Revolution test is on Friday. Let's chant the 13 colonies."

On the board is written the **mnemonic,** "Granny Smith never vacuums cats, dogs, people, newts, nannies or navigators, maybe rude monkeys." Ms. Walker points to each word as students **chant,** "Georgia, South Carolina, North Carolina, Pennsylvania, Virginia, Connecticut, Delaware, New York, New Hampshire, New Jersey, Massachusetts, Rhone Island, and Maryland."

"And who loved his flag?"

"Jasper," students shout chorally.

"How do we know?"

"Because he saved the flag at Fort Moultrie."
"Why do you think he did that?" Ms. W asks.
This time only three hands go up. She calls on each.
"For the group, the other soldiers."
"To get everyone to keep trying."
"To give them hope."
"Hurray! Let's wave our flags to say we want everyone in our class to have hope," Ms. W joins in the flapping frenzy as students hurry out to head home

Conclusion

Our doubts are traitors, and make us lose the good we oft might win, by fearing to attempt. (William Shakespeare)

This chapter on why and how to integrate drama throughout the curriculum has been an effort to give courage to attempt. Solid research, clear theories, and a fund of professional wisdom justify the use of this powerful teaching and learning tool. To make drama integration meaningful, however, classroom teachers do need drama and theatre literacy, and this chapter outlined the nature of this knowledge, as well. The Arts Integration Blueprint provides a skeleton for planning, teaching, and assessing. Essential to bringing drama to life is collaborative work drama specialists to customize lessons for specific students. They also know good Shakespeare quotes.

Resources

See the Appendix for additional materials, including websites.

Additional Website

http://knowitall.org (search "Writing")

Software and Games

Play Write, IBM Educational Systems (software)
Puppet Maker, IBM Educational Systems (software)
Kid on Stage, Music for Little People (games)

Videotapes

Creative dramatics: The first steps. Northwestern Film Library, 614 Davis St., Evanston, IL. 60201.
Max makes mischief (30 min.). University Park: Pennsylvania State University. (unit on *Where the Wild Things Are*) Available from the Instructional Media Center, National–Louis University, Evanston, IL. 60201:
* *Dorothy Heathcote Talks to Teachers—Part I and Part II.*
* *Dorothy Heathcote Building Belief, Part I and II.*
More Heathcote videos: AV Centre, University of Newcastle, Framlington Place, Newcastle upon Tyne NE2 4HH, England.

Children's Literature References

Brown, A. (1990). *The piggybook.* New York: Knopf.
Estes, E. (1994). *The hundred dresses.* New York: Harcourt Brace Jovanovich.
Van Allsburg, C. (1991). *The wretched stone.* Boston: Houghton Mifflin.
White, E. B. (1952). *Charlotte's web.* New York: HarperTrophy.
Yashima, T. (1955). *Crow boy.* New York: Viking.

Drama and Storytelling Seed Strategies

Questions to Guide Reading

1. How can drama Seed Strategies be used to introduce lessons?

2. What Seed Strategies can be used to teach drama concepts?

3. What Seed Strategies help to integrate drama with science, social studies, math, and literacy?

4. How can storytelling be integrated throughout the curriculum?

This chapter is mostly a compendium of idea prompts to help teachers brainstorm for drama integration. The ideas are in seed or kernel form. This means they are undeveloped, but they can initiate lesson planning. Seed Strategies should be selected based on their potential to make a "meaningful fit" with student needs, lesson objectives, and curricular standards. All teaching strategies must be adapted. No one idea can be used, even by next-door teachers at the same grade level, without making changes. Seed Strategies are not "leveled," and most can be customized to make them appropriate for primary and intermediate grades.

The Special Focus section in this chapter is on storytelling. It gives an overview of purposes, procedures, and Seed Strategies.

In the opening Classroom Snapshot a teacher uses many drama Seed Strategies to develop vocabulary using a book connected to a Civil War unit.

Classroom Snapshot:

Vocabulary Meanings Through Drama

Second-grade teacher Martha Kearney is using a **sock puppet.**

"Say that like the president would say it," orders the puppet.

"I'll declare war!" shout the students.

The sock puppet speaks in a soft southern dialect that is Martha's own. "Workers were brought over here from _____."

She uses the **oral cloze strategy.** Students immediately show they are making sense because they say "Africa" in unison.

"and sold them as slaves when they arrived in _____."

Some say "America," others "the South" and "the United States."

The puppet is shaking its head. "There are many right answers."

"So, what is the North's point of view?" the puppet asks.

"No slaves," says one boy.

"What is the South's?" she continues.

A girl with freckles says, "The slaves got what they needed, and the masters got what they needed."

"So what was the problem?" the puppet asks.

"The slaves were sad," a boy comments.

"What are some better words than *sad*?" asks the puppet.

"Miserable!" says a blond boy.

"That is a descriptive word," says the puppet. "I have to leave now. Goodbye."

Martha marches the puppet to the closet. The class waves and calls out, "Goodbye" and "See you tomorrow." When she turns back around, the teacher has a large card with *miserable* printed on it.

Ashley River students pantomiming emotions.

"Yesterday we learned about a slave who felt miserable. Why?"

Hands go up, but Martha waits. She finally calls on one student.

"His master was going to sell him," explains a boy.

"Show me *miserable*," Martha coaches them to use their bodies and faces to show through **pantomime.** She takes time to describe how students use their mouths, heads, and arms. This **descriptive feedback** causes them to increase concentration.

"OK, when he was running away, how did he feel?"

"Scared!"

"Give me a synonym for *scared* that begins with /f/."

"Frightened!"

"Yes! Show me the meaning of *frightened*."

Students curl up and cover their faces as Martha describes the range of use of body parts and facial expressions they create.

"If I was the director of a play, show me why I should choose you to be one of my actors." Students respond with more focus, and some try to exaggerate their facial expression to show more fear.

"You are all hired! Now, he was _____." She holds up a card with the word *exhausted*. "When I say 3, everyone read it, 1-2-3."

"Exhausted!"

Martha lowers her volume and seems to take on the meaning of the word herself. "Why was he so exhausted?"

"He was tired from running."

"All the fear was wearing him out."

"OK, on 3 again. Show me *exhausted* and freeze."

Students do **frozen pantomimes** to convey the word meaning.

"On 2, sit up," Martha directs. She counts and then continues, "Then he made it to the safe house, but he became _____." She holds up another vocabulary card, *confused*.

The students immediately read the card chorally.

Martha now looks confused with her eyebrows and eyes squinted together. "Why was Louis confused?"

A boy who hasn't said anything before raises his hand. "He thought he was free when he crossed the river. But, he wasn't."

"Show me *confused*," she says. Students scratch their heads and look around with eyebrows together. Again, Martha gives feedback.

"Then he had a time when he was _____." The card reads *embarrassed*.

The students chorally read. Then she asks why Louis was embarrassed. Students describe Louis's clothes, and a boy finally summarizes the nature of the clothes as "women's."

At this point Martha tells them to stand up. She selects one student and tells him that he is a "kind man," and she will take the role of Louis. **In role,** she asks, "Why would you want me to wear a woman's clothes?"

"This will help you get away," says the "kind man."

"OK, everyone, get a partner. If you are a one, raise your hand. You are the kind man. Twos, you are Louis. When I say 'begin,' I want you to talk to each other. Louis people, you start. Begin."

Pair Dialogue

As the pairs begin to interact, Martha circulates and coaches, "Say that with more feeling, " she urges one girl. The girl does and the teacher smiles. After a few minutes they reverse roles.

"You are all now going to be Louis. Think of how you feel in your surroundings in the slave quarters. Use your whole body. Concentrate. Close your eyes and picture in your head. I'll read the next part."

Martha reads from the chapter book *Long Journey Home* (Lester). The book has six stories on freedom. The one she reads is about a slave named Louis who is deciding what to take with him. During the remainder of the reading she **inserts mimes** to get students to "show" how they feel. At one point she reads about Louis walking slowly to the door. She tells students to walk to their seats like Louis.

Martha coaches several students to "stay in character." She continues to read as she walks around the room. One boy points to a painting of the North Star at an appropriate moment in the story, others mime actions at their seats, as suggested by the text.

Martha's voice is soft as she asks, "How are you feeling?"

The students almost whisper as they call out, "frightened," "thankful," "relieved," and "confused."

"Everyone, show me *relieved*," she says. Students sigh and slump. She then reads on, but pauses and spontaneously converts the text into **narrative pantomime** material.

"You have been running and running, and your chest is burning in pain. Show me this pain," she coaches.

The second graders grimace, clutch their chests, and hold their heads.

"Hold that feeling. Captains, please pass out the writing journals," she says. Five students get up. They will spend 10 minutes **writing in character** about what they have just experienced.

Chapter Organization

You will find Martha Kearney's strategies, plus many more Seed Strategies in the five sections of this chapter. Many can be used across curricular areas. The sections on Energizers, Pantomime, and Verbal strategies are provided to give ideas to engage students and teach specific drama elements and skills. This builds a knowledge and skill base so drama can be used as a vehicle to make meaning. These are followed by science, social studies, literacy, and math drama Seed Strategies. Storytelling follows the curricular seeds.

Drama Reminders

All drama-based strategies are made more effective when teachers:

- Plan for meaningful integration by teaching the unique aspects of drama, as well as using drama as a learning vehicle.
- Focus on student problem solving through drama, not just doing the teacher's ideas. Drama is not about imitation of a model. Best dramas result when students feel free to create surprising ideas.
- Do explicit teaching of drama content: Name the strategy, tell its purpose, ask open questions, and give examples, time to experiment, and descriptive feedback.
- Coach students to "make me believe"—to focus, concentrate, and stay in role by controlling mind, body, face, and voice.
- Teach start and stop signals.

- Ask students for new ways to repeat the drama to make it better.
- Teach the basics of being good audience members.

I. Energizers and Warm-Ups

Energizers and warm-ups are short strategies used to motivate or relax, or increase concentration and focus. They stimulate thinking in specific ways that prime the brain for creative thinking using body, face, and voice. Most energizers trigger higher-order thinking and require self-control. Energizers from other chapters, especially dance, can be used for drama integration.

Greetings! Everyone mills around until leader says "Greet." Everyone starts to greet people in different ways. The leader can suggest roles or dispositions: Pretend you are long-lost friends or are from another culture (e.g., Japan, France).

Wiggle Worms. (Focus). Students find a personal space. The teacher mimes opening a jar of worms and tells students to get ready to grab them. Toss the worms and direct students to catch and eat and become the wiggle worms. On "freeze" cue, students stop. Repeat with half the class being the audience who gives feedback. Then reverse halves. (Source: Jeff Jordan, Ashley River)

Hand Study. (Focus/Observation). Partners take turns examining each other's hands. Tell them to see and feel everything that makes hands unique. *Variation:* Use as a "get to know you" activity: This is Joe and he has very thick hands with short fingernails. His hands are tan as if he works outside a lot.

Play Ball. (Focus/Concentration). Form a circle. Leader holds an imaginary ball (show size with hands) and calls someone's name before it is thrown, saying, "Sue, basketball." The receiver then says, "Thank you, basketball." Play continues, with receiver calling a name and throwing the pretend basketball. After a few rounds the leader introduces a second ball, saying, "Joe, beach ball," and Joe responds, "Thank you, beach ball." Continue to add more balls. At the end, call "stop" and ask everyone with a ball to hold it. The audience guesses the kind of ball by its size and how it is held.

Concentration. (Visualizing). Make a tray of items. Direct students to study the items by picturing them in their heads. Cover the tray. Students list all they remember. *Variation:* Students close their eyes and an item is removed or rearranged. They figure out the change. Use small wipe-off boards so all can write the missing item and show boards.

Line Up.   Students line up: alphabetically, by birthday, by height, and so forth. Once in line, they interview those around them to find out three things about one another. *Variation*: Give directions to group in North, South, East, or West locations. *Example:* Redheads take the North wall.

Tongue Twisters and Tanglers.   (Fluency warm-up). First say each twister slowly as a group. Next, practice individually and in pairs or go around a circle. Make into a game where play begins over if a person mispronounces. Examples are: A hot cup of coffee from a proper copper coffee pot. Aluminum linoleum. Bugs black blood. Six sick sheep. Unique New York. Find more in *Six Sick Sheep* (Cole). Follow-up: Students collect and create twisters. Organize alphabetically in a recipe box. Put up a Twister Master chart to keep track of ones they say three times without error. Challenge with longer twisters such as "Peter Piper" (Schwartz's *A Twister of Twists: A Tangler of Tongues* offers the history of this classic).

Finger Plays.   (Focus). Teach finger plays such as "The Itsy Bitsy Spider." There are many collections and Little Richard has a wild CD of them. Here is an untraditional one for focus. Seat everyone on the floor and say: I relax and focus (point to self with thumb and lay hands in lap). I gather in the good (gather with hands brought in). I push out the bad (push outward with both hands). I celebrate the joy all around me (raise hands, spread fingers, and do silent cheer).

One Word at a Time.   A person says one word to start a sentence. The next person says a word, and so on. This requires concentration to make a long "sensical" sentence.

Sound and Action Stories.   (Close listening). A narrator tells a story while children echo lines and do actions. "Going on a Bear Hunt" is an example, and is accompanied by a walking rhythm. Between sections give time to mime. When the bear is seen, actions are reversed—double time. Another example of a sound/action story appears in Ready Reference 9.2.

Scavenger Hunt.   (Team work/categories). Give groups items to find in a time limit. For example, "In 5 minutes find a silky item, a book with an r-controlled word, something that moves, and something that can be used to create." Items can be collected or written down. *Variation*: Use the five senses to organize searches: "Find something that looks like _____, sounds like _____, feels like _____."

Word Change.   Sit in a circle. First person says a sentence like "Mary had a little lamb." Next person repeats the sentence, but changes one word: "Mary had a little goat." Keep going all the way around. Challenge: Reverse and return the sentence to its original form.

Partner Search.   (Close listening). Make cards with sounds or song titles and pass them out. For example, do five different titles on five sets of cards for 25 students. The goal is to have groups form by finding those who are singing the same song or making the same sound.

Two Facts and One Lie.   Students list three facts about themselves. One item should be false. Students read aloud items. The audience applauds to show which one they believe is the lie. *Note:* Discuss how to use creative ideas without being obvious.

Animal-Car-Flower.   (Categories). This helps students get to know one another. Students write down the three categories and an example that applies to them. For example, "My name is _____ and I identify with a cat because _____, a Jeep because _____, and roses because _____." *Variation:* Change categories to water, land, buildings, music, furniture, fruit, etc.

Reverse Web.   (Team builder). Students form small groups. Use large paper and have everyone write. *Directions:* Draw a circle in the center with a leg coming out for each person. Write a name on each leg. In the center, write/draw things the group has in common. The more unusual the better (e.g., all like broccoli).

Pass and Pretend.   (Visual imagery). Sit in a circle. Pass around an ordinary object (scarf). Students use it in a creative way by imagining what it can become. For example, a scarf could be rocked like a baby. Encourage focus on details of action (see Invisible Object Mime). *Variation 1*: Do without a prop and ask students to imagine an object and pantomime using it. First person passes it to the next, who must use the same object and then transform it into something else. *Variation 2*: Pass a straw and say, "This is not a straw, it's a _____" and then demonstrate how it has transformed.

Character Voices.   (Fluency). Make character cards. Then make a list of random sentences: "Hi, how are you?" "Can you tell me how to get to the nearest hospital?" "We've really been having bad weather lately." "I'm so tired." Students each draw a card and say the sentence, in character. Others tell what message and feelings they heard and clues to who it is. For example, Santa might "ho-ho-ho" in between his words or phrases.

Laugh Contest.   (Focus/Control). A panel tries to resist laughing as one classmate has a go at telling jokes, making faces, and the like. Discuss school-appropriate humor before doing this!

Belly Laughs.   (Team builder). Everyone lies on the floor with his head on someone else's belly. At a signal, someone says "ha" and the "ha" travels around the circle. When it gets around, someone else starts a different laugh (e.g., "he he").

Noiseless Sounds. (Focus). Brainstorm ways to pantomime sounds without making any noise: laugh, applause, choke, sneeze. *Variation*: Ask students to divide the sound into three consecutive pantomime actions (e.g., steps in a sneeze). Groups practice and present to the whole class.

What's Different?. (Concentration). Pair students and label as A and B. A faces B and concentrates on details of B's appearance. Leader signals and pairs turn back to back. B makes a change. Pairs turn around, and A gets three guesses to figure out "what's different." Then it's B's turn.

Bell Tolls. (Category game). This requires fast thinking and movement. Give each student a half-inch piece of masking tape. Make a circle with an IT in the center. Each person stands on the tape. IT begins by saying "The bell tolls for all those who _____" and plugs in a category (play an instrument, know Picasso's first name). Anyone who fits the category must move and try to get a new spot while IT tries to get a spot. The person without a spot is the new IT. At any point in the game, IT can shout "tornado" and everyone must move to a new spot, not right next door. Adapt for any unit (e.g., knows the capital of Maine).

Name Sock. (Learn names). Make two balls by knotting up socks. Stand in a circle and explain the purpose is to learn names. Ask each student to say his name. The class echoes. The leader then models how the game works by saying her name and the name of another person to whom she then throws a ball. That person says her own name, another person's, and throws to that person, etc. When things are going well, the leader throws out a second sock ball. *Variation*: Students each take an alias (e.g., book character, famous person).

Hot Sock. (Fluency). Make a set of alphabet or category cards and use a knotted sock. Sit in a circle with IT in the center. IT closes her eyes and throws the sock. At will, IT says stop. Person caught with the sock passes it the person to the right who holds it. IT draws a card and reads it. Sock is now passed person to person around the circle while the "caught" person names five items in the category. *Example*: Five things that start with B.

Voice Stunts. (Focus). Form groups of four. Give groups a phrase. For example, "To be or not to be," "Zig-zag-zog," or "Slip-slap-slop." Each person says one word in the phrase and play goes around the circle, or IT can pass using eye contact or pointing.

Stunts and Tricks. (Confidence). Students perform stunts. For example, rub stomach and pat head at same time, balance balloon or pencil on the end of your nose, stand with left shoulder and side of left foot snug against a wall and try to raise right leg. See Goodman's *Magic and the Ed-*

Following the "Drinking Gourd" stars

ucated Rabbit and Randi's *The Magic World of the Amazing Randi* for more ideas.

Boring Words. (Fluency). Brainstorm a list of dull words (e.g., *cardboard*, *the*, *dust*, *box*). Practice saying them changing volume, rate, pitch, pause, and stress to make them interesting. *Variation*: Collect boring phrases and sentences for this activity.

Ways to Celebrate. Use a variety of ways to celebrate good ideas. *Examples*: standing ovation, pat on the back, firecracker mime, or mime and say together, "Pat, pat, pat, on the back, back, back, for a job well done. Altogether now . . . REPEAT."

II. Pantomime Strategies

Pantomime is acting without words. It demands that participants take roles and pretend. When students are taught to think through mime, they learn to imagine and simulate places, events, and emotions that may never be experienced firsthand (e.g., walking on the moon). Mime can be as simple as "becoming" a teapot and pretending to tip and pour. Frequently it is used to show something in the process of transforming, such as a seed becoming a plant or a character becoming increasingly frustrated as he tries to whistle. In arts integration mime is used to show understanding of concepts, like the difference between water and ice using body shape and movement. Pantomime can also develop into complex performances such as a reenactment of Columbus's travails on his voyage to the New World.

Simple or complex, mime triggers CPS and makes visible the results. Conscious change of body shapes, movement, and facial expression are used to show emotion, age, size, weight, temperature—or any other sensory area. Pantomime is a form of drama that young children naturally exhibit before they learn to speak. It gives a communication alternative to shy students or children with limited oral expression skills to express ideas and feelings.

The teacher's role is to set up problems that cause students to think through body and face action. A good place to begin is real-life roles that call for movement. For example, in pretending to cook, it would be important to show mixing, stirring, and pouring. Teachers should examine curricular content for natural opportunities to take roles and do meaning making through pantomime. Students are most successful when teachers start with easy structures like narrative pantomime and short experiences confined to small spaces, like the desk area. Student work is enhanced by coaching during mime, saying "I see _____" or ask-

ing children to describe in detail what they see peers using. Common problems, like students who want to make pantomimes into guessing games, should be anticipated: Limit number of guesses, ask students to focus on describing pantomime details that give the best information, and ask for evidence to support guesses.

This section includes types of pantomimes adaptable for use throughout curricular areas. Check Ready References 9.1 and 9.4 to think about actions that connect to concepts in science, social studies, or math. The goal is give students additional ways to show they know—to make learning visible. Each of the activities demands CPS and should result in transformation of understandings about concepts. Many of the pantomime ideas are excellent for review and all cause students to extend thinking beyond simple recall of information.

Invisible Objects. Use a "mystery" bag or basket. Tell students to think of objects related to a unit they are studying, (e.g., from colonial times or ones that might be used by fairy tale characters). Each student pretends to pull out an item and shows its shape, size, weight, texture, temperature, and a way it can be used. Guessers put thumbs up. IT calls

Ready Reference 9.1 ## A-to-Z Pantomime Possibilities

Directions: Brainstorm things to mime about a topic. Use this list to give examples and to create original pantomimes in any curricular area. For example, pantomime verbs (action words) in language arts to show word meanings.

- Actions: clean, travel, eat, ignore, cough, nudge, videotape
- Animals: moving, eating, sleeping; different categories (e.g., insect, bird, mammal)
- Book chapters: actions in each chapter
- Character actions: spider writes in web, Jack climbs beanstalk
- Emotions or feelings: happy, angry, disgusted, surprised, embarrassed
- Foods: being gathered, prepared, eaten
- Getting ready: for school, to go to the beach
- Hobbies or vacations: juggling, jumping rope, tennis
- Holidays or festivals: wedding dances, party decorating
- Jobs, occupations, careers: bricklayer, seamstress, carpenter
- Machines that move: computers, mixers, vacuum, mower
- Musical instruments: being played, carried, cleaned
- Objects: holding and placing objects (fruit, animals, food)
- Making objects: shoes, quilt; shapes (e.g., types of Greek columns)
- Pairs: takes two to fold a sheet, play tennis
- People: famous celebrity or politician poses/actions, inventors inventing, common roles (mother, police officer)
- Pets: how to care for, play with, train
- Places: beach, cave, closet, rooftop, edge of cliff
- Plants: changing, growing, blooming, dying
- Processes: nesting, cooking, building, manufacturing
- Rituals and customs: greetings, farewells
- Sensory responses to items: what if . . .? (good smell, scary sound)
- Sports: how to dress for, play, waiting your turn
- Things you: like to do, don't like to do
- Tools: use of, cleaning, carrying
- Toys: using, storing
- Vehicles: scooter, inline skates, tricycle
- Walking: change characters, circumstances, mood, destinations, levels, pathways, speeds
- Weather: response to conditions or pretend to be a kind of weather
- Wise sayings: for example, "you can lead a horse to water but you can't make him drink"
- Word categories: antonyms, homophones, three syllable

on selected peers. To become IT, a student must describe mime actions that were most "telling" and name the item. To help make an object look real, coach children to take time to:

1. Slowly study it (size, shape, texture, temperature).
2. Reach out as if to touch it (move toward it to show how you will take hold).
3. Take hold (imagine your hands on it, then feel it).
4. Use it as you would if it were really there.
5. Stop and slowly replace it.
6. Let go slowly and move away.

Afterward, tell students to isolate a part they did the best and demonstrate, or ask them to give each other feedback on which steps looked most real and why.

Number Freeze. Students number off in fives. Give a setting or context (e.g., the farm in *Charlotte's Web*). Teacher calls a number and these students pantomime an action done in the designated setting. The next number is then called, and this group mimes while the others act as the audience. Audience members can be invited to tell specifics they observed, followed by "naming" the action.

Quick Change. Generate a list of emotions caused by events in units or stories. For example, "disappointed you can't go to the ball." Give a series of "Show me with your face and body" directions using the list. For example, "Show me exhausted from marching through mud."

Mirrors. (Concentration). Brainstorm people or characters. Students line up in two facing lines or in a double circle. Partners face each other. Partner A pretends to be a book character or real person and looks into the mirror. B becomes the mirror. The goal is to align actions so that an observer can't tell the "real" from the "reflection." Start in slow motion. *Example*: Student A pretends to be an evil stepsister getting ready for the ball. Reverse and B chooses a character.

Pantomime Solo. Students work individually but mime in unison with the group, each in a personal space (Heinig, 1993). The teacher controls the action by coaching and narrating. For example, "You are Little Miss Muffet looking for a place to sit and eat. Remember, you've been frightened by a spider in this garden before." Give signals to start and end, such as flick lights or countdown.

Number Mime. Ask students to do multiple pantomimes. For example, "Think of three things Goldilocks might have done while going through the woods and number them, one, two, and three in your mind. When I say a number, you mime your idea." Coach to "make me believe" with details.

Pair Pantomime. Brainstorm actions requiring two people (e.g., playing checkers in colonial times). Partner students. At a count, or with a time limit, students mime as many as they can. Literature example: Prince putting the slipper on Cinderella. *Suggestion:* Do one action in slow, regular, and then in quick time to increase self-control. *Variations:* Mime famous pairs like the Wright brothers. Add conflict in repeat playing to increase CPS (e.g., Cinderella's feet smell).

Break It Down. (Analysis/Sequence). Students list a series of actions in an event or a place (e.g., sneeze). Break each into three to five parts to pantomime in order. For example, wrinkle nose, suck in breath 3× throwing back head, throw head forward, wipe nose. *Variation:* Add conflict (e.g., can't get to the choo).

Think Back Pantomime. Students recall actions of characters or actions from science, math, or social studies (e.g., sewing the first flag). Tell them to choose one. When you say "begin," repeat it in place until the stop signal. Replay and ask students to use the BEST (dance) elements to make creative changes. *Extension*: Ask students to line up and replay by plot order or get into groups (beginning, middle, end of story, importance, etc.).

Emotion Pantomimes. Start with an example of an emotional situation. *Example*: You are home alone and you hear strange noises. Ask students to recall emotional moments in literature or other areas of study, times when character had strong feelings. Give a start signal for students to use face and body to mime examples. Give feedback on use of details to show action/emotion using "I see . . ." frame. Split the class into actors and audience to share. Reverse so that all have a chance to observe and discuss what works. *Variation*: Add a problem or conflict to increase interest and creative thinking.

What If: Obstacle Pantomimes. Brainstorm actions of characters or people from units (e.g., write in a web). Do a group pantomime of the ideas. Next, divide into small groups and ask groups to add a problem, obstacle, or conflict to one action. Small groups then pantomime (e.g., Charlotte is very sleepy).

Kalamazoo. (Adapted from Heinig, 1993). Divide class into two groups to decide on a pantomime category (e.g., jobs, animals, toys). Tell them to line up facing each other. Group 1 says "Here we come," and group 2 responds, "Where are you from?" Group 1, "Kalamazoo." Group 2, "What do you do?" Group 1, "Here's a clue." Group 1 then pantomimes while group 2 guesses. A time limit can be set.

Chain Pantomime. One person starts a pantomime in the center of the room. Others join as they guess the general topic (guessers can whisper answers to the teacher). For example, for a weather unit a student might mime towering cumulus clouds. Others would join and mime other types of clouds.

Categories Pantomime.

Brainstorm types of words and examples (e.g., homophones, antonyms, rhyming words, silent e words). Form groups of four. Call out a category. One person in each group pantomimes original examples while the rest number their papers and write what they think is mimed, in order. Call time. Groups check with leader and new leader is chosen. Call next category. *Variation:* Use categories related to any current unit. Possible categories are:

Things that are: vertical, high, twisted, fast.
Example (in order): elevator, clouds, pretzel, electric fan.

Five Senses Pantomimes.

Brainstorm things to do in five sense categories or categorize from a book or unit. Students pantomime. *Variation:* Add a problem. For example, you are eating a chicken sandwich, but you bite into something hard.

Song Pantomimes.

Many songs have characters and actions that can be mimed, such as boat rowing, stars twinkling, or ants marching. Give groups song lyrics and ask them to find all the actions and think of unusual ways to be in a role miming the action.

Action Pantomime.

Brainstorm actions (verbs) or ways to move from current units. (See BEST dance elements in Ready Reference 10.1 and Locomotor and Nonlocomotor Action Bingo in Chapter 11). Put words in a basket. Each person picks one and "becomes the move," while others guess its name. This can be done in pairs (e.g., all *A* people "twist" while *B*s observe and switch).

Safe Fights.

Drama, literature, and history are full of conflict. It is a good idea to prepare for one kind of conflict that students often want to pantomime—fights. Ask students to practice showing different moves in personal spaces without touching anyone (e.g., punch, stab, claw, slap). Do in slow motion or to a count. Get into pairs. In slow motion, practice with one person responding. Emphasize no touching or falling down. Use start and stop signals.

QU Plot Pantomime.

(Adapted from Heinig, 1993). Ask students to list key events in a story. Put events in order. Type a copy of the list so that each YOU (U) has a Cue (Q) to look for. Write a starter Q to set the pantomime in motion. Make two copies of list and cut one into strips to pass out to students. Keep full copy of the QU sheet to keep track of the action. Double or triple cast so everyone is involved. Here is an example of a full copy based on *Charlotte's Web.* Cut so each strip has a Q and a U. Give each student a strip.

Q: The leader says, "A Day in the Barn"
U: Pretend to be Charlotte spinning her web
Q: When Charlotte spins her web
U: Mime Wilbur eating out of his trough
Q: Wilbur eating out of his trough
U: Pretend to be Fern and come in and sit on a stool to watch
Q: Fern comes in and sits on her stool
U: Pretend to be Templeton sneaking around
Q: Templeton sneaking around
U: Applaud

Variation: Use to review content under study (e.g., steps in a science experiment).

Charades.

This is a favorite pantomime game. Form two teams. Each takes a turn. Traditional categories are book, song, television show, film, and famous person, but any category can be used: one-, two-, or three-syllable words, rhyme pairs (hink pinks such as "sad dad"), synonyms, antonyms, words beginning with a letter or sound, homophones (sum–some, red–read), quotes, proverbs, famous pairs (e.g., peanut butter and jelly), states, countries, and so forth. Students can create cues to start the game: sounds like (pull ear), short word (show size with fingers), long word (show with two hands moving apart), syllable numbers (show with fingers), movie (pretend to roll film), book (use hands to show open book).

Imaginary Place.

(Heinig, 1993). The goal is to create a setting by stocking it with appropriate items. Mark off space with masking tape. Students pantomime bringing in items and placing them. Pairs work together for big items. Audience is coached to tell what they see and guess what is mimed. Challenge students to use the items they add in some way, plus a previous item, to fix visual images. For example, two students bring a stove into a restaurant, so the next player brings in a refrigerator. After placing the fridge, the student may check the oven temperature before exiting. Periodically, review all items and their placement. Use settings from history and literature.

Count–Freeze.

Give students a category to pantomime (Ready Reference 9.1). Tell students you will count to 10 as they pantomime. They are to freeze on 10. *Variation:* Do in pairs or trios, and count at different speeds. Example categories: things you do at school, in threes or twos. Literature example: "The Mouse at the Seashore" (fable): things the mouse might have done on his journey in the morning, afternoon, and evening. Give time of day and students mime.

Time Mime.

(Control). Students mime at different speeds from slow to fast. For example, "To slow count, move as if you are under water." Play slow mood music or a piece such as "Clair de Lune." For fast motion pantomime, tell students to move like a fast-forwarded video. Play Scott Joplin songs or a fast piece such as the "Spinning Song." Use this idea to replay any pantomime at different speeds.

Nursery Rhyme.   (Mime). Sing or recite nursery rhymes. Divide into groups and have each group plan which rhyme to say and mime, or just mime, for others to guess.

Transformations.   Brainstorm characters or things that change (e.g., young to old, seed to plant). Ask students to break down phases and do in slow motion. Add music. For example, become a fairy tale character and change, on a slow count of 10, into another character (e.g., beast into a prince).

Tableau/Frozen Picture.   (Tortello, 2004). Pairs or small groups are given a scene to depict and asked to freeze in appropriate positions (e.g., a tension-filled moment in a story). Audience may be asked to describe what they see, what it means, and what makes them believe in the picture. They may also wish to ask questions of members of the tableau, especially ones about their feelings and motives. Students may select their own scenes from science or social studies as a unit review. *Variation 1*: Ask students to create three different tableaux to a count. For example, "Remain the same character but move into three different positions as I count 3.2.1." *Variation 2*: Tell students to freeze, then move, and then freeze on cue to bring the tableau to life. Give audience members a role (e.g., if the scene is Wilbur winning the blue ribbon, ask the audience to tell what they see as if they are farmers, Templeton, Charlotte, or the owner of the slaughterhouse. This emphasizes point of view). *Variation 3*: Frozen scenes may be performed as silhouettes by using a light behind a taut sheet. Stand close to the sheet to present a clear image and turn lights off. Use colored gels on the lights for interesting effects.

One-Liner Tableau.   Students re-create, in tableau, scenes from photographs, portraits, cartoon strips, and the like. A series or cartoon strip can also be performed. Tableaux can be created for scenes before or after a scene in a painting or photo to stretch thinking. After students are "set," teacher taps them one by one and each says a one-liner of what they are thinking or feeling. *Variation*: When they are tapped, students come to life, do an action, and then freeze. *Note*: Large, old picture frames can be used to "pose" for tableaux. Take photographs of tableau poses.

Tableau Captions.   Use book titles, newspaper headlines, current events, advertisement slogans, quotes from famous people, or phrases from units as prompts for frozen picture tableau. For example, "Why does she always get to sit up front?" or "Mars Lander Hits Hard." *Variation*: Create three different tableau frames.

Sound–Motion Machine.   Choose a category to pantomime (e.g., a chapter in MacLachlan's *Sarah, Plain and Tall* has these movements: rolling a marble, sweeping, riding a horse). Each student chooses a repeatable movement related to the category. One person starts the pantomime, and others join in until all are moving in a space. On signal, everyone adds a sound. *Variation*: All members of a machine must be touching to show they are a connected whole.

Prediction Pantomime.   Technically, all pantomimes should be creative, but prediction pantomime offers more room for improvisation. Instead of interpreting actions, this pantomime idea involves more "what-if" thinking. For example, stop reading a story at a poignant point and ask students to pantomime predictions of what might happen next. Emphasize thinking about possibilities. For example, "I want to see three things Cinderella might do after she gets home after the first night. I'll count to signal. Let's begin. One." *Variation*: Do half of an experiment or stop partway through a video and ask students to mime an event they anticipate.

Pantomime and Action Songs.   Numerous songs offer actions to mime as the group sings, such as "If You're Happy and You Know It." *Variation*: Write your own with actions (e.g., if you're happy and you know it laugh out loud, smile a while, show your teeth, grin a lot). Other examples: "Little Bunny Foo Foo," "Grand Old Duke of York," "My Hat It Has Three Corners," and "This Old Man, He Played One." The *Serendipity Encyclopedia* (Coleman, 1997) has many. See the music chapters and the Arts-Based Bibliography in the Appendix.

Improvised Scene.   Pick a scene with two or more characters. Start with simple plot outlines. For example, "Let's try the scene when Miss Muffet gathers the things she needs to eat and then finally sits down on her tuffet." Coach, as needed (e.g., "And then she had to find something to carry it all in"). Remind students to use signals to start and stop scenes. *Variation*: Give groups a scene to plan from the beginning, middle, or end of a story. Each group presents a scene. Provide rehearsal time. *Variation*: Add dialogue, using steps on page 256, or captions.

One Minute After Scene.   Ask students to imagine what happened one minute after a piece of art was finished. Divide into groups to plan the scene. Groups then present to the whole class.

Planning Character Improvisation.   Read a story and stop after the conflict is introduced. Break into groups to discuss these questions, which are the same categories contained in a literature storymap:

- What does the character want or need (goals or motives)?
- What is the problem or conflict?
- What stands in the way of the character getting what he or she wants?
- What actions can the character take to deal with the problem (plot)? Where might the character be (place)?
- What might the character say (e.g., a one-liner about the problem)?

Note: It helps to give students a planning sheet with the questions. Permit work in groups to plan a scene with a beginning, middle, and end to deal with the questions. A good way to structure is to create a one-liner about the problem to end the scene.

Character Meetings.

Each student chooses a character from a story everyone knows. Partners then have conversations, in character, about their lives, problems, and so forth. Invite pairs to share conversation highlights with the class. *Variations*: (1) Use in social studies with historical characters. (2) At a signal, characters freeze and audience suggests an emotion. When conversation begins again, characters must use the emotion.

Improvised Story Drama.

Create a play from any story without a script to memorize. Use quality stories with lots of action and believable characters. Dialogue can be improvised during the story playing using these steps:

1. Read or tell a story and tell students to listen for dialogue, special words, and refrains and to get the gist of the story.
2. Afterward, review the plot and proceed to cast, adding characters, and even crowds so that all can participate. Plan sound effects, music, and the space to be used (e.g., at desks or open space?).
3. Decide who will narrate(s) and how to start and end the drama.
4. Play the story with the teacher coaching. If there are problems in the replaying (e.g., if students don't know how to end), assume a character role and facilitate, or be the narrator and tell a conclusion with students following your lead. Circle or cumulative stories work well to begin (e.g., Henny Penny), as do episodic plots, such as Marshall's *George and Martha* books (Heinig, 1993).

Song Skits.

Play a piece of music connected to a unit (e.g., "The Star-Spangled Banner"). Students develop a scene with a beginning, middle, and end to show how the composer thought of the music or song. Remind students to include conflict in the beginning, and the end of the scene should resolve the problem. Coach them to use start and stop signals and to make events believable.

Narrative Pantomime.

In this pantomime, a narrator reads or tells a story as students mime. Narrative pantomime is teacher directed so it gives a degree of security to students new to drama. It is usually based on familiar material from previous units or stories and is useful for introducing basic story structure (beginning, middle, end) and literary elements (plot, setting, characters, conflict, resolution) because the students must physically engage with each of these concepts.

Material.   Most stories can be adapted for narrative pantomime. Select stories with lots of action, a clear climax, and quiet ending. Beware of too much description and literary devices such as flashback. Recast the story in the second person, "you," to cause students to more easily take the role of a character. Edit stories by eliminating dialogue and extraneous description. Action can be added by changing descriptions to actionable text (e.g., instead "It was a hot hazy day" change to "You wipe your brow and squint as you look across the hazy horizon"). In some stories there is a repeated sound, word, or phrase that is hard to resist, so invite choral response. For example, in Robert Munsch's *Thomas' Snowsuit* there is repetition of the word, "No!" A pause for students to add the word increases engagement. (This book can easily be converted to a narrative pantomime.) For chapter books or long stories, isolate one event to mime. For example, choose one chapter from *Because of Winn-Dixie* (Dicamillo, K.) or *Junie B. Jones and the Stupid Smelly Bus* (Park). Remember to convert the text to "you" while reading, rather than use the first person.

Narrative pantomimes can be written or told by the teacher or students. It is important for students to understand that interesting narratives have a beginning, middle, and end and need conflict or tension. It is also important to keep events in order because it is difficult to mime a nonsequential narrative such as "You wake up. You get up and brush your teeth. First you turn on the water and then you put paste on your toothbrush." Use the BEST dance elements in Chapter 10 to put variety into the actions of any pantomime.

To introduce narrative pantomime, read the story aloud first. Ask students to listen for actions as they enjoy the story. During the pantomime, the narrator needs to read expressively and give the class time to mime. If time is short, students can mime a story they haven't heard, but try to anticipate possible problems.

Props, costumes, and scenery are not necessary. Imagination can supply all that is needed. If students are excited about developing pantomimes further, music may be added. In addition, teachers and students can add characters or actions by imagining others who might enter the story. An example of a narrative pantomime written by a teacher is provided in Planning Page 8.1. Components of habitat were taught through narrative pantomime in a previous lesson.

Stories of journeys, trips, or cycles of events (e.g., caterpillar turning into a butterfly or "day in the life of . . ." structures) work well for narrative pantomime. Van Allsburg's *The Z Was Zapped*, Van Laan's *Possum Come a-Knockin'*, Berger's *Grandfather Twilight*, Keats's *A Snowy Day*, and Chaconas' *The Way the Tiger Walked* are stories that need only minor changes to become usable texts. Ready Reference 8.4 provides an annotated bibliography for narrative pantomime, and there are more in the bibliography in the Appendix.

Pretend to Paint. Students imagine they have tiny paintbrushes and not much space to paint. Narrate a pantomime in which you tell them to keep painting, but the size of the brush and the space keeps getting bigger and bigger. Music can be used to accompany this (e.g., "The Blue Danube" waltz).

Narrative Pantomime with Ballads. As students sing or listen to a story sung through a ballad, invite them to interpret actions with pantomime. Example: Davey Crocket.

Group Stories. *Strega Nona* (dePaola), *Clown of God* (dePaola), and *Lentil* (McCloskey) are examples of children's literature with crowd or group scenes. These stories can be used for narrative pantomime and for easing students into dialogue. Do this by freezing scenes and asking members to give a one-liner about who they are or what they feel at the moment. From there students can move into writing dialogue for groups.

III. Verbal Improvisation Strategies

Improvisation involves creating ideas spontaneously by "thinking on your feet." It can be done using pantomime or, as discussed in this section, using words. Verbal improvisation engages all types of thinking in the CPS process. In particular it is frequently used to: review a lesson, make predictions at a stop point, and encourage in-depth analysis of material. The following strategies are organized from easy to more difficult.

Sound-Effects Stories. Students can add simple sound effects with their voices or musical instruments (e.g., sim-

ple rhythm instruments) as the teacher reads or tells a story such as *Too Much Noise* (McGovern) or *Night Noises* (Fox). Read the story aloud and ask students for sounds they heard. Plan how and who will make the sounds. Specific groups can be responsible for certain parts with the whole group involved at other points. *Suggestion*: Use an imaginary volume-control knob and practice controlling loudness before doing the story. Other stories with refrains or repeated lines are Viorst's *Alexander and the Terrible, Horrible, No Good, Very Bad Day*, Peck's *Hamilton*, and Hutchins' *Don't Forget the Bacon*.

Sound Stories. Find or write a story or poem that contains repeated words (e.g., character names) (Heinig, 1993). Brainstorm sounds that would work for repeated words and list them on the board. Each time repeated words are read, students respond with a sound. To prepare, rehearse the sound that go with each cue word. For example, Jack-"oops" and sad face, Jill-giggle and play with curl. Many stories and poems are set up to use sounds; for example, "Laughing Time" in William Jay's book by the same title, has animal names to elicit a variety of laughs such as hee-hee, ho-ho, hee-haw. McGovern's book *Too Much Noise* and Murphy's *Peace at Last* are other good ones. *Variation*: Add actions to sounds. There is an example sound story in Ready Reference 9.2.

Volume Control. Brainstorm sound categories (e.g., short vowels, city sounds, kitchen sounds, sounds from any story or unit content). IT stands in front, calls a sound category and "turn ups" the volume or "turns it down" using an agreed-upon cue. For example, use move hand to low or high position. *Variation:* Do in pairs or small group, instead of whole class.

Don't Laugh. (Fluency/Control). Form groups of five or six who stand in a circle. One is IT, who points at someone and asks a funny question. Person to the right of person questioned must answer. Everyone tries not to laugh. Go fast. *Example:* Would you eat blue food?

Pair Sound Effects. Brainstorm sounds from a context or event (e.g., ocean, storm, grocery store). Partners choose to be *A* or *B*. *A* makes sounds and *B* stand behind *A* and makes actions that coordinate. Reverse roles. Everyone participates simultaneously, but a few can volunteer to replay examples for whole class. Discuss choices.

One-Liners. (Props or pictures). Students change their voices (volume, rate, pitch, pause, stress) to take a role and respond to a picture or object. If a picture is used, students can become characters or objects in it. If an object is used, students choose to be a person who would use the object.

Ready Reference 9.2   Sound Story Example "Stolen Tarts"

Directions: Brainstorm and then rehearse sounds and actions the audience can add. During reading, pause after underlined words for response. Here are examples:

Heart:	Thump thump on chest with fist
Queen:	Blow kisses
King:	"Find him!" and point finger
Knave:	"Tee hee!" while smiling and shaking head
Tarts:	"Yum" and rub tummy
Soldiers:	Stomp feet

Long ago in the Land of *Hearts* there was a terrible theft. It was on St. Valentine's Day that the *Queen* of *Hearts* baked some *tarts* to celebrate the national holiday. She baked raspberry, lemon, and custard *tarts* as a gift for the man to whom she had given her *heart*—the *King* of *Hearts*. The *Queen* placed her *tarts* on the windowsill to cool. While the *Queen* straightened up the royal kitchen, the *Knave* of *Hearts* sneaked up to the window. The *Knave* grabbed all the raspberry *tarts*. When the *Queen* saw the *tarts* were gone, she cried, "What *heart*less fellow has taken my *tarts*?"

The *Queen* went to the *King* for help. Quickly he dispatched his *soldiers* to find the thief and the missing *tarts*, saying, "Find him!"

It wasn't anytime before the *soldiers* returned with the *Knave* and what was left of the raspberry *tarts*. The *King* ordered that the *Knave* have no *tarts* to eat for a whole year. The *Knave* of *Hearts* knelt before the *Queen*, asked for forgiveness, and crossed his *heart* to promise he would never steal her *tarts* again. It was a *heart*warming ending.

Each student says a related one-liner. Others tell how the actor best showed his/her identity. For example, after reading "Little Red Riding Hood," pass around a red cape. Students use the cape and say a line to reveal who each is from the story. *Note:* Students can create picture collections using magazines, cards, Internet, etc. Invite contributions to a Class Prop Box for units (e.g., weather items and pictures).

Conflicting Messages. (Fluency/Expression). Students say a one-liner differently from what the words seem to convey (e.g., "I am happy" spoken with great sadness).

Say It Your Way. (Fluency/Expression). Students say a sentence in a role or in a mood. Others try to guess their identity. Create role cards with character or person names. Students draw cards and rehearse reading the sentence many ways (e.g., angry, sad, confident). Coach to emphasize different words to change meanings: *Who* is my friend? Who *is* my friend? Who is *my* friend? Who is my *friend*? Here other examples:

- I don't like your attitude.
- Everyone just left.
- She has a terrible headache.
- We only have five left.
- Remember to check each answer.
- Where do you think you are going?
- Turn out the light.
- Close the door.

Character Talk. (Fluency/Expression). This is a good review strategy. Students write important sentences or phrases from stories or any unit material on cards. Mix cards in a basket. Students draw cards and read aloud as the character who said it. Discuss the context of the line.

Sentence Frames. (Fluency/Expression). Each person orally completes this frame: "I am . . . and I want . . . ." The goal is to not give names, but a role they play and a goal. Coach students to change volume, rate, pause, pitch, and stress. Each response should be different in content and expression. After each student says the frame the group can echo, "She is _____ and she wants _____." *Suggestions*: Use book characters or famous persons. See more sentence frames under Reading and Language Arts in Chapter 4.

QU (Cue–You) Reading. (Listening, fluency). Sequence readings can be made from literature, poetry, or any subject matter. Jokes and riddles are perfect because of the reader–response or question–answer format. Prepare a set of cards that each have a Q (cue) statement and a U (you) statement. Students rehearse their U (highlight this) with meaningful expression, and study the Q (the listen for). For example, Q=Mary had a little lamb. U=It's fleece was white as snow. Be sure to keep a master copy of the entire reading. *Suggestion:* Type the original and use the copy function to repeat the U line as the Q for the next reader. Cut QU lines apart. *Suggestions:* Adapt stories such as *If You Give a Mouse a Cookie* (Numeroff), *Pierre: A Cautionary Tale* (Sendak), or *The True Story of the Three Little Pigs by A. Wolf* (Scieszka). Poetry written in the first person, like Silverstein's "Sick," works well (Ready Reference 9.3). See also QU pantomimes previously described.

Ready Reference 9.3   # QU Sequence Reading Example

Directions: Cut apart QU (cue-you) statements for each person or group. Distribute and give rehearsal time. The leader starts by reading the first Q. A person with U reads next, and it continues as readers hear their cues. (Based on *Mirette on the High Wire*, McCully, 1992.)

Q: Bellini's story.
U: I was a man in hiding—hiding from myself.

Q: I was a man in hiding—hiding from myself.
U: I just needed to rest.

Q: I just needed to rest.
U: Gateau's boardinghouse on English Street seemed as good a place as any.

Q: Gateau's boardinghouse on English Street seemed as good a place as any.
U: I did worry about the other guests seeing me.

Q: I did worry about the other guests seeing me.
U: It never occurred to me that I was being watched by much brighter eyes.

Q: It never occurred to me that I was being watched by much brighter eyes.
U: Mirette! The spunky redheaded daughter of Madame! Mais oui!

Q: Mirette! The spunky redheaded daughter of Madame! Mais oui!
U: She was not to be denied once the enchantment of the wire overtook her.

Q: She was not to be denied once the enchantment of the wire overtook her.
U: I saw her take her falls. I thought she'd give up.

Q: I saw her take her falls. I thought she'd give up.

U: But Mirette had the courage a young heart and a new dream give.

Q: But Mirette had the courage a young heart and a new dream give.
U: I did not want to be her teacher because I did not want her to discover my secret.

Q: I did not want to be her teacher because I did not want her to discover my secret.
U: I recognized the agent when he checked in.

Q: I recognized the agent when he checked in.
U: It was inevitable Mirette would learn my hidden fear.

Q: It was inevitable Mirette would learn my hidden fear.
U: Mirette's belief in me was greater than my fear of myself.

Q: Mirette's belief in me was greater than my fear of myself.
U: I bought the length of hemp and went to work. I worked automatically preparing for the walk.

Q: I bought the length of hemp and went to work. I worked automatically preparing for the walk.
U: But I could not move when I felt the wire touch my feet.

Q: But I could not move when I felt the wire touch my feet.
U: That child's face shattered the cage around my heart. Dear Mirette.

Q: That child's face shattered the cage around my heart. Dear Mirette.
U: Bravo for the children! They make us remember what it means to be alive.

Conflicting Motives.   Brainstorm a list of motives or reasons for the actions of characters or people and examples of what they do. Put motives on cards. Ask for two volunteers—*A* and *B*. *A* draws a card (e.g., to get *B* to sit down) and leaves the room. B draws a different motive (e.g., to get *A* to say the word, "No."). *A* and *B* are brought back and given a context (e.g., "You are in the grocery store and you meet an unpleasant neighbor.") Neither partner can verbally give away his or her motive. Audience observes how *A* and *B* interact, who accomplishes the goal first, and how.

Dialogue Cards.   (Fluency). Collect words, phrases, sentences, and headlines from magazines, newspapers, ads, and greeting cards. Paste each on a card. Give each student a card face down. Pair students and tell them to choose to be *A* or

B. Turn over cards. A begins the dialogue using the card. *B* must respond and incorporate his or her card. *Variation 1*: Do a chain activity. Everyone lines up and (1) just reads card expressively or (2) goes in order but improvises verbal response that connects to previous person by using card. *Variation 2*: Separate question and answer cards (make sure there is an equal number). Distribute randomly. Number questioners, who then read in order. Whoever thinks they can answer with a card has a go at it.

Emotion Conversation.   Each student chooses a character or person from current study. Roles can be from the same book or different (e.g., a real person from current events and a fictional character). Pair as *A* and *B*. Leader calls *A* or *B* and pair starts a conversation, each in role. Say "freeze" and ask the audience to tell the emotions of the characters. Say "action" and continue the conversation. *Variation*: Freeze and audience suggests a new emotion characters must assume (e.g., angry, surprised, elated).

Character Monologues.   Sit in a circle. Students become a character or person from recent study. Each makes an announcement, a wish, or a complaint. (Ready Reference 5.1). Audience put thumbs up if they know the character.

Car Wash.   Form two facing lines. Students assume character roles or are given a topic. Two end people walk between the lines. As they pass, students say one-liners to them. Then the next two go and so forth. For example, when reading aloud *Officer Buckles and Gloria* (Rathman), stop at the point where Officer Buckles feels like a fool. Students each think of good things about the dog. Walkers become Officer Buckles and pass through the car wash hearing "voices" comment on his friend.

Television Shows.   Adapt game and talk show formats. Examples: *I've Got a Secret, Jeopardy, Wheel of Fortune, Concentration, Password,* or *Oprah*. The show adaptations work best after a unit of study (e.g., *Oprah* discussion/interview format on endangered species).

Discussions.   A discussion becomes a dramatic encounter when students take roles (e.g., characters, famous persons, objects). Use the questions in Ready References 4.8 and 8.8, as well as suggestions for discussions in Chapter 4. Students can also brainstorm in the role. See Chapter 2 for brainstorming guidelines.

Empathy Roles.   Each student takes the role of a character or person everyone knows. The teacher begins a discussion or interview with an open question concerning a key moment, problem, topics, or theme. It is best if an important question is used (e.g., moral dilemma). Each student enters the discussion in character and remains in character throughout. The teacher can call on students for ideas or students can volunteer. Example based on *Sarah, Plain and Tall* (MacLachlan): "We're here to discuss the issue of advertising for a husband or a wife in the newspaper. I'd like to find out what each of you think. Please introduce yourself and give your opinion." *Variation*: Students prepare by writing down who they are, what they want, and how they act and feel. Name tags can also be used.

Panels.   Everyone can be the same or different characters who present views on an issue. Panels begin with opening statements, and then the audience asks questions. *Variation 1*: Students take roles of consultants, experts, or advisers on a topic. For science and social studies, students should research to plan for their roles. *Variation 2*: Set this up as a press conference.

The Chair.   A volunteer sits in a chair. Another volunteer takes a role and begins a conversation. The seated person must figure out who the other character is and respond accordingly. For example, volunteer is Thomas Jefferson, and student in the chair is George Bush. This is adaptable for literature, social studies, and science and works well for current events. *Variation*: Partners sit back to back. Pairs each take the role of a book character, an occupation, or family role. On signal, they face and the first to talk sets the situation. The second person must figure out who his or her partner is and respond in role.

Elevator.   Students are in small groups. The place is a jammed elevator. Students think about who they are, problems they have, and how they feel. On signal, the group starts a conversation. *Variations*: Brainstorm contexts from stories, time periods, and locations under study. Any public place works. Students can be book characters, persons in paintings, scientists, or historical figures.

Interviews.   Teacher assumes the role of interviewer and students take a character role. Students are questioned in talk show style and use voice and body to convey who they are. A good starter interview question is "What happened?" Example, the teacher is a TV host interviewing (1) characters in *Charlotte's Web* right after the first word appears in the web, (2) animals from fables like Lobel's "The Mouse at the Seashore," or (3) unpopular characters, such as a wolf, who present a point of view. If a panel is used, members can be questioned by the class, who also take roles (e.g., news reporters). *Suggestions*: Interviewers should introduce themselves (e.g., "I am …and I want to know.…"). Use microphone prop. Be sure to coach students to stay in role. *Variation*: Interviews can be done in pairs with one student as interviewer.

Show Time.   Use to review a unit of study. Groups write and present commercials, news updates, songs, and the like that summarize important points. Remind students to include key information, not empty glitz. This provides a good opportunity to teach propaganda devices such as bandwagon or glittering generalities. Limit time to 2-3 minutes. *Examples:*

Newsbreak: "We interrupt this program to let you know that animals have been found to have four components in their habitats. Without water, shelter, food, and adequate space, animals cannot survive. We learned today that habitats are shrinking and our world may soon lose valued animal populations. More on this breaking story on Live at Six."

Commercial Break: "High/bad cholesterol? Stressed? Tired? You need the Laughter Prescription! With only 15 laughs a day, you can get your minimum daily requirement and be on the road to an energetic happy life. Learn to laugh your way through life. Call 1-800-JOKE."

Note: Inventions make great advertisements (e.g., cotton gin for social studies or a graphing calculator in math).

Book Ads. Individuals, pairs, or small groups set up a scene based on a problem from a book they will advertise. The scene must end, however, before the problem is solved. End each commercial with "If you want to know what happened, you have to read this book." *Variation:* Create commercials using music, songs, slogans, and props. Limit time to 1 minute—TV time is expensive!

Debate. Divide class in half and assign each a side in an argument. Give time to plan. At signal, begin debate with a person from each side stating a position. Alternate back and forth until all viewpoints have been heard. Rebuttal time can then be given to each side. To encourage alternative viewpoints, ask opponents to summarize each side's points at the end. Teachers should (1) moderate and can assume a role (e.g., police officer called to a "crime scene" in *Little Red Riding Hood*) and (2) comment, question each side, and open it up for audience questions. Can be done in pair. For example, one side says Little Red should be taken away from her parents because of negligence; the other side takes the opposing position. *Variation:* Do as expert panels (e.g., experts on wolf behavior).

Improvised Scenes. (See pages 255–256.) Give short scenes to play from familiar stories. First students plan a beginning, middle, and end and start and stop signals. Emphasize the need to build in conflict by presenting a problem that is resolved by the end. Examples: (1) stepsisters and stepmother in the coach, going to the ball worried about mysterious girl who charmed the prince, or (2) animals who saw the transformations of other animals are talking after Cinderella leaves for the ball. They want to get transformed, too.

As soon as possible, prompt students to think of their own scenes. Suggest they choose from important moments or emotions in a story. In science or social studies, consider significant events (e.g., when Philo Farnsworth gets the first television picture). Sources for improvised scenes include current events, children's literature, wordless picture books, and "famous last words." Events, processes, and procedures from science, social studies, and math are also good resources. Focus on "let's suppose" and "what if" (e.g., switch characters, settings, or circumstances of any story or historical event). Create card sets for settings, characters, problems, and props for an endless number of combinations of characters, problems, and places. Examples for Who? Problem? and Where?

1. Hurried shoppers. A robbery happens. Grocery.
2. Hungry mosquitoes. On the beach when Columbus first lands.
3. Five children. Hot summer day on the porch. Dad brings out two double popsicles.

Start a discussion to develop characters, the setting, plan of action for the problem or conflict, and resolution. A planning frame can be given to write down ideas about who, where, what problems, what to do or actions, solutions, and conclusion. Eventually, students learn to plan independently in small groups.

Remind students to: (1) structure scenes with a beginning, middle, and end; (2) plan how to show what the characters want; (3) develop conflict (have characters persuade, argue, obstruct, or bargain); and (4) plan a reasonable resolution. Help students feel the importance and tension by giving time limits. Use signals to add clear structure (e.g., to begin and end the scene) and music to create mood. See coaching in Chapter 8.

Follow up with a discussion of what worked. Scenes can also be replayed with a twist (e.g., teacher may take a role or students may be engaged in a written response such as a 5-minute quickwrite). Ready Reference 9.4 lists ideas for scenes.

I Heard It First. Brainstorm a list of songs that are famous, such as the Hallelujah chorus and "The Star-Spangled Banner." Students then break into small groups and plan a scene about the first time the music or song was ever heard by an audience and their reactions. Scenes should have a beginning, middle, and end.

Ready Reference 9.4   # Improvised Scene Source Material

Directions: Use as a starter idea bank for scenes.

- Characters: lizard, baker, potter, wise woman, fortune teller
- Places: island, beach, cave, treehouse, barn, boarding house, jungle
- Character conflicts/motives: argue, convince, persuade, defend, plot, debate, tease, deny, confess, accuse, beg

- Rituals: graduation, inauguration, parade, eulogy, pledge
- Actions: eat, clean, drink, work, bathe, run, cook, swim
- Conditions or problems: ill, dark, nervous, hot, embarrassed, odor, stress, wet, lost, lonely, noisy

Role Play.   Role playing is used in every drama. It involves considering a situation from another's viewpoint. Because of the added perspective understanding of any subject is enhanced. In general, use role playing to put students in problem situations so that feelings, values, and viewpoints can be explored. A particular kind of role playing, called *sociodrama*, focuses on real-world problems of the present and future.

To create a role play:

1. Choose problems or topics about which students know something.
2. Define the specific situation that requires the characters to take some action (e.g., factory owner whose factory is polluting a river and an EPA agent who must enforce regulations about river pollution. The two are brought together by a government agent).
3. Give the audience a role (e.g., questioners at a break point or evaluators of the different positions taken).
4. Plan an introduction to set up the scene.
5. Replay same scene with different groups to get a variety of versions.
6. Discuss what students noticed about the drama aspects as well as the content of the scenes.

IV. Connecting Drama to Curricular Areas

This section offers examples of pantomime and verbal activities that show how drama can be used as a teaching tool to enhance academic learning. Once again, these are beginner Seed Strategies to prompt thinking about meaningful arts integration.

Science Focus

Science standards can be accessed at the National Science Teachers Association website: *www.nsta.org*.

Project Wild.   *Project Wild* has hands-on, activity-oriented lesson plans for science. In addition to drama, music, art, literature, and creative writing, activities are suggested to develop science concepts. More information about *Project Wild* is available online (*www.projectwild.org*). *Project Wet* is also available.

Animal Sounds.   IT makes the sound of an animal, and the group pantomimes shapes and actions of the animal. *Variation*: IT makes sounds from everyday world (e.g., clock ticking or phone ringing), and the group creates actions to pantomime that context.

Nature or Animal One-Liners.   Use pictures of natural forms (e.g., mountain, tree, stream, animals). Each student says a sentence, in role, to show known facts and use new vocabulary. For example, "My stalactites are growing up a lot today" (cave).

Environmental Debate.   Divide students into two teams to research a side on an environmental issue. For example, "Should whales be hunted?" Students assume roles as debaters. Each side presents an opening statement and then gives pros or cons in a time limit. After each side presents, give time for rebuttal and a summary statement.

Famous Science Scenes.   Break into groups to do tableaux (frozen pictures) of special moments in science, such as Alexander G. Bell's first telephone call, the Wrights' flight at Kitty Hawk, or Armstrong walking on the moon.

Animal Charades.   Brainstorm (before or after a unit) ways to classify animals (wild, domesticated, herbivores, carnivores, insects, mammals, aquatic, land based). Small groups work to list animals in each category. (Record on a chart for younger children.) Each student then picks an animal to pantomime. Coach to think of how the animal sleeps, moves, eats, and where it lives. Set up pantomimes to be presented in this order: start frozen, then move, and then freeze. Teams can write their animal or category guess on a wipe-off board and display at signal. The mime confirms correct guesses. Mimes can also be planned and presented by small groups.

Emphasize science content by asking for reasons why the animal belongs in a category. To stress the drama aspect, ask students to give feedback on what the mime did to make them believe it was a particular animal. Limit number of categories for less mature learners. Other science categories are: land forms, states of water.

Close Observation.   Take time to purposefully watch mammals, insects, or fish on a video or in real life. Ask students to observe and use specific verbs and adverbs to tell how they move and why (e.g., to get food, to avoid predators). If animals are in groups, ask how they are organized (e.g., bird flight patterns). Next, students decide which animal to pantomime and how to use their observations. Give time to rehearse. Present group pantomimes to class. The audience should be asked to describe what they see, not just guess the animal.

Special Props.   Challenge students to use simple props to feel as animals do. For example, try to eat rice with your mouth as birds do or try to drink like a cat or dog from a tub of water. Use props to get the feel of snakes shedding their skins or birds in a nest (e.g., use garbage bag with end cut open; use leaves or build nests).

Animal Panels.   Groups choose an animal to research. Each group becomes an expert panel, in the role of their animal. Each tells facts, feelings, problems, pros and cons, etc., of being a dog, cat, or fish. Audience members can ask questions of the panel.

Social Studies Focus

Social studies standards are available from the National Council for the Social Studies (NCSS): *www.socialstudies.org*.

Moral Dilemmas. (Use historical fiction or biography). Students stop reading at a point where a character has to make a decision. Small groups take the role of the character and discuss the dilemma in first person, saying "I felt" or "I think" statements. Information from the story is used to propose possible actions. Groups reassemble to summarize the discussion or role play of one of the courses of action. *Note:* The dilemma should not have one clear right answer; this forces students to consider several options. For example, Avi's *Night Journeys* has many points where a stop and discuss in role would be appropriate. Procedure pointers: Stop when a problem has been found and ask students to describe the problem:

- What is it?
- Who has the problem?
- What are the general circumstances of the problem?
- What is the goal for solving the problem?

  Small groups then brainstorm problem solutions:

- What possibilities would be legal and safe for all?
- What is the best solution (consider cost, safety, length of time, and legal, moral, and practical issues)?

  Try out the solution:

- Role play whether the problem gets solved.
- What does this say to you for the future?

Read the rest of the story and compare solutions with the one in the book (based on the work of Lawrence Kohlberg; adapted from Johnson & Louis, 1987).

Portrait Conversations. Pair students to plan a conversation between two portraits of famous historical figures that might hang side by side in a gallery. Look closely to examine the works for clues about time period, values, cultural aspects, message, and the like that give ideas for dialogue. These can be written or oral. *Variation:* Ask students to plan dialogue for figures in an historically based painting (e.g., *Washington Crossing the Delaware* or *The Signing of the Declaration of Independence*).

Famous Portrait Monologues Use portraits of famous figures (e.g., U.S. presidents). Students research persons in the art and prepare 1-minute monologues about the times,

problems, values, economics, and customs. Monologues are presented in character in the first person.

What's My Line? Based on a 1950s television show, this drama focuses on finding out occupations of panelists. Panelists can all have the same occupation or the same role (e.g., all might be signers of the Declaration of Independence). The audience can only ask yes or no questions and is given a time limit or a set number of questions (e.g., 5 minutes or 20 questions). The teacher acts as moderator and allows the audience to take turns questioning. To deal with monopolizers, use the rule that when a panelist answers "no," someone else takes a turn to question.

Biography Drama. Groups read biographies from an historical period and note actions to pantomime, special events, important scenes, and special lines of dialogue. Students plan with biography groups. For example, they might improvise dialogue for the scene leading up to Patrick Henry saying "Give me liberty or give me death." *Suggestion:* Focus on actual words the person used and conflicting positions the person took (e.g., Jefferson owned slaves).

Literacy: Reading and Language Arts Focus

In Los Angeles and other school districts primary classrooms are required to spend 3 hours a day in reading instruction. It seems reasonable, given the drama research, that "such long stretches" should be punctuated with "language-directed dramatic activities" that have been shown to inspire increased participation, especially among students learning English as a second language (Catterall, 2003, p. 105).

Literacy/literature standards are available from the National Council of the Teachers of English (NCTE) and the International Reading Association (IRA) at *www.ncte. org* or *www.rdg.org*.

Research. Theatre and drama are language rich and naturally engage students in verbal communication. The commonalities shared between drama and the language arts account for strong effects of drama in research studies (Deasy, 2002). Students involved in theatre and drama spend time researching characters and settings, writing scripts, and interpreting lines. Nearly all pantomime and verbal strategies can be adapted for literacy lessons. Here are examples.

Emotional Vowels. Form a circle. IT goes in the center and chooses an emotion. IT then expresses the emotion, but can only make a vowel sound (A, E, I, O, or U). (Designate short or long vowels, schwa sound or diphthongs like oy or ow.) The class echoes. Students then signal to name both the emotion and vowel sound. IT calls on peers until a correct answer is found and that person becomes IT.

Antonym Pantomimes. Make a card set with two antonyms on each card. A student draws a card and pantomimes one word. The audience must guess the opposite. This can be done in small groups with a set of cards for each group. *Suggestion*: Students should not call out guesses, but should wait until the pantomime is done, write out a guess, and, on signal, hold it up. *Variation*: Do with synonyms, homonyms, and homophones.

Antonyms Partners. Pairs become opposite emotions, heights, sizes, weights, and so on. Pairs present and audience guesses antonyms.

Daffynitions. Teams of four to five students find unusual words. Each team member writes a definition for the word, but only one member writes the correct definition (use the dictionary). Each team stands and members orally read definitions in turn, trying to convince the audience that each has the correct one. The audience can applaud, afterwards, to vote on which they believe is correct. *Variation*: Use unusual objects instead of words.

Rhyme Change. Nursery rhymes, chants, and poems are adaptable to word play activities that serve as verbal warm-ups and stimulate creative thinking. Here is an example: "Hickory Dickory Dock, A mouse ran up my . . ." (students supply rhyme). All vowel sounds can be practiced (phonemic awareness) with variations like Hickory Dickory Dack, Hickory Dickory Deck, and so forth.

Spelling Mime. Students mime each letter in a word or a thing that starts with each letter. *Example*: CAT = cup plus apple plus typing. Groups can present a word with each member doing a separate letter.

Story Captions. Brainstorm a list of important scenes or events in a story. Give each a caption. Put on slips and drop in a basket. Tell students to find personal spaces. Read one caption and on "begin," cue students freeze using their faces and bodies to show the feelings and message of the caption. Examples: "Cozy in the Barn" (*Charlotte's Web*) and "Proud of My Twig House" (*Three Little Pigs*). *Note*: Can also be used with nonfiction from science and social studies. *Extension*: The captions can be used as prompts for art making to expand comprehension of story mood and events.

7 Up. (Vocabulary development). Brainstorm "up" combinations: stand up, sit up, get up, wake up. Put in a hat. Form groups. Team captains draw from a hat and mime for their group. Do as a relay with captains tagging next group member to get a slip from the hat.

Pretend and Write. Either assign roles or let students choose a role from a piece of literature, song, or painting.

Next, each writes a letter, chant, note, or any form, in role (see Ready Reference 5.1 for writing options). Example: Choose a family member from *Sarah, Plain and Tall* (Anna, Caleb, or Jacob) after Chapter 2. Write a letter to Sarah introducing yourself and asking her questions. Students switch letters and become Sarah to write a reply. *Variation*: Do as a guessing game. Discuss how to give clues, without coming right out and giving the person's name or family role. *Note*: Students don't sign letters.

Pretend and Write: Dear Abby. Show examples of the column "Dear Abby." Students then write a "Dear Abby" letter using a problem from a book. Partners exchange and, in the role of Abby, write a reply. *Example* (after the first chapter of *Sarah, Plain and Tall):*

Dear Abby,
  My father is a widower and I think he really needs a wife. My brother and I also need a mother. What should we do? Worried daughter

Dear Worried Daughter,
  Why don't you talk to your dad about how you feel? Be honest. This will let him know you think it is OK to look around. Abby

Pretend and Write: Journals. Students become a real or fictional character and keep a daily journal. The point is not to write about real events, but about what could have happened, or feelings caused by events. In the case of historical fiction or biography, students can extend the journal's authenticity by doing research on characters. *Variation*: For chapter books, provide time for entries after each chapter to document the change in the main character's thoughts and emotions in reaction to experiences. Students can pair up and read each other's journals to get different perspectives.

Pretend and Write: Letters. Focus is on using conventional letter-writing form, the writing process, grammar, and spelling. Students take a role of a character and write a friendly or business letter to another character or real person. Contents and purposes will vary. Students can pair and write back to sender, taking the role of the receiver.

Point of View Roles. Students choose a character in a story or are assigned roles. Students read or listen to the story and answer questions in role in writing or orally. For example, using *Mirette on the High Wire* (McCully), students can be asked to imagine they are a touring artist staying at the rooming house. Answer these questions (before the high wire act at the end):

1. What have you noticed about the man? How does he make you feel?
2. What do you think about his friendship with Mirette?

3. Why do you think he stays to himself so much?

Masks: Six Dramatic Roles. According to Temple (1991), story characters fill one or more of six roles and may also change roles. Use these roles to create masks and puppets for retellings and improvisations of stories (see Ready Reference 7.4 for puppet/mask ideas):

1. The Lion Force: main character
2. The Sun or Object: what the Lion Force wants
3. Mars, the Rival: tries to keep the Lion Force from getting what she or he wants
4. Moon, the Helper: helps Lion Force achieve desired goals
5. Earth, the Receiver: benefits from Lion Force's actions
6. Libra, the Judge: decides if Lion Force may have the Sun or Object

Character Sculptors. In pairs, one person becomes the clay. The others then "sculpt" the person into a character with specific emotions and actions concentrating on body shape and levels.

Showtime. After reading a book, form groups to create a commercial, jingle, news update, or newsbreak to convey something important about the book. Number groups for order of performance. Give 10 minutes to plan. The whole group comes back together and the show begins.

Reader's Theatre or Radio Plays. Like a radio broadcast, RT is "theatre of the mind." It is widely acclaimed as a fluency tool in literacy (Hudson et. al., 2005). Readers sit or stand while doing oral interpretive reading from a script. They try to create the illusion of dramatic action in the minds of the audience. The focus is on using the voice expressively; props are usually not employed. RT is particularly suitable for intermediate students, but can be adapted for younger children by choosing shorter scripts and reading to them as they follow along on the first go-through. Adapted short poems are a good place to begin. For example, see Wolf's *It's Show Time!: Poetry from the Page to the Stage* (poem scripts).

Reader's Theatre is an appropriate use of oral reading because it is audience oriented and students rehearse before the presentation versus cold round-robin reading that has been deemed detrimental to children. Other values of RT are diverse. (1) It integrates listening, speaking, and reading and can include writing when students create their own scripts. In addition to literature, biographical material such as letters, diaries, or speeches can used, which helps to show students how to adapt material into script form. They can move later to original script writing. (2) The ensemble or group nature of RT encourages cooperation and other social skills. (3) When readers assume character roles, they learn to empathize with a variety of feelings and viewpoints, which yields insights about people and the world. (4) Self-confidence is increased as students share exciting stories that evoke positive audience responses. (5) No lines are memorized and the focus is on one of the key pillars of reading fluency. To use Reader's Theatre:

- Find or create scripts for students' interests, abilities, and curricular connections. Several companies and Internet sites publish scripts, and literature anthologies often contain stories in script form. The Institute for Readers Theatre in California has a script service. Also, see the list of more than 40 titles at *www.amazon.com*, which ranges from holiday scripts to fractured folktale scripts.
- The script can be read to students for the first reading, read silently by students, or orally read by students in small groups.
- Groups are formed according to the characters outlined in the scripts. Groups can prepare different scripts or perform the same script and then discuss their different interpretations.
- Students need time to rehearse. Emphasize the need to vary volume, rate, pitch, pause, and stress to convey meaning. Students should highlight their parts and mark words they think should be stressed. Nonverbal communication with the face, some gestures, and even body posture can be added. The focus remains on oral interpretation, however.
- Scripts should be placed in folders or binders so that students can hold them without distracting the audience with page turning. Students may sit on high stools or stand. Stools of varying heights can be used to suggest character relationships.
- Staging ideas: Readers can start with their backs to the audience and turn around as each part is introduced. Characters with major roles might stand to the far left and right, if they don't interact with one another. Characters with similar ideas can be grouped. With younger students it helps to use hatbands or name tags so the audience can keep track of characters. Lights can be used to signal scenes.
- The point of Reader's Theatre is not to create a visual spectacle, but students may shift position on stage (e.g., to indicate joining a group). Readers may stand when they read and then sit, or spotlights might be used. Props should not be used, unless essential, since it is awkward to handle a script and a prop. Sound effects and music can be added, since these are part of creating the "radio play" effect.
- Invite students' creative ideas by asking "What else could you try?" and "What are other ways to have the audience get the message or feeling?"

- The narrator should make eye contact with the audience to draw them in. Other characters may look up when not reading or when they can during reading.
- Make sure audience members are clear about their important roles as active listeners. Review appropriate audience responses before presentations start. After the readings, invite performers and audience members to discuss what worked, what they learned, what they noticed about use of voice to establish character, what the most important parts were, and so forth.
- Follow up presentations with invitations to write different script endings, trade scripts with other groups, videotape, or even perform for other groups (e.g., a touring troupe to visit other classes).
- An example of a Reader's Theatre script, converted from an old English tale, is offered in Ready Reference 9.5.

Math Focus

Math standards can be accessed from the National Council of Teachers of Mathematics: *www.nctm.org*.

Story Problems.   Give small groups the same story problem. The goal is to plan how to role-play the problem and end the scene by showing the answer. Each group presents its version. The audience gives feedback on what worked for each scene and after all the scenes, they compare and contrast.

Daily Math.   Brainstorm a list of times people use math every day (e.g., cooking, giving change, sewing). Pairs plan a 1–2 minute pantomime of an example. Pairs perform and the audience describes what they see and tell the math idea. *Variation:* Allow players to each say one sentence in role.

Math One–Liners.   Sit in a circle. Pass around a geometric shape or a visual of a math concept (e.g., symbol for greater than). As each student receives the shape or symbol the goal is to say one line in that role. *Example:* "I'm always right," "Three is not a crowd for me," and "I always have an angle" (triangular shape). *Variation:* Add pantomime, when possible (e.g., greater than symbol).

Math Improvisation.   Make a set of cards with math-related situations. Give each group a card to plan a scene. Scenes should have a beginning, middle, and end and a problem. An example card might have (1) Who? 3 men, (2) What? a quart of milk, and (3) Where? a 10-story building on fire (problem).

Fraction Mime.   After introducing fractions, use an open space to have the class become a "whole" and then divide up to solve problems: Become two equal halves, become fourths, become thirds. When numbers are uneven, ask students how to deal with the "extras."

Break It Down.   Pairs become an "answer." They plan combinations to mime. *Example:* 27=20 wiggling fingers plus 4 blinking eyes plus 2 ears plus 1 wrinkled nose.

 **Reader's Theatre Script Example**

Cast: Narrator, Girl, Old Man

Narrator: A GIRL once went to the fair to find a job as a maid. A funny-looking OLD MAN agreed to hire her. When they arrived there, he said he had to teach her new names for things in the house.

Old Man: What will you call me?

Girl: Why master, or mister, or whatever else you wish, sir.

Old Man: No, you must call me "master of all masters." And what would you call this?

Narrator: The OLD MAN pointed to his bed.

Girl: Why bed, or couch, or whatever you wish, sir.

Old Man: No, that's my "barnacle." And what do you call those?

Narrator: He pointed to his pantaloons.

Girl: Breeches, or trousers, or whatever else you wish, sir.

Old Man: No, you must call them "squibs and crackers." And what do you call her?

Narrator: The Old MAN pointed at his cat.

Girl: Cat or kit, or whatever you wish, sir.

Old Man: No, you must call her "white-faced simminy." And now this, what would you call this?

Girl: Fire or flame, or whatever you wish, sir.

Old Man: No, no. You must call it "hot cockalorum." And what is this?

Narrator: He went on, pointing to the water.

Girl: Water or wet, or whatever you wish, sir.

Old Man: No, "pondalorum" is its name. And what do you call this?

Narrator: Asked the MAN as he pointed to his house.

Girl: House or cottage, or whatever you wish, sir.

Old Man: You must call it "high topper mountain."

Narrator: That very night the GIRL woke her master up in a fright.

Girl: Master of all masters, get out of your barnacle and put on your squibs and crackers. For white-faced simminy has got a spark of hot cockalorum on his tail, and unless you get some pondalorum, high topper mountain will be all on hot cockalorum!

Source: Based on "Master of All Masters" English folktale (Jacobs, 1890).

Drama and Storytelling Strategies

Talking Math. Children choose to become a math concept. They form expert panels to present. The audience questions them using the five Ws and H questions (e.g., panel of squares or the number 1).

Math Commericals. Students prepare ads to sell particular math concepts or skills: fractions, time, division. The goal is to convince the audience they need this math form.

Number Talk. Give each student a number from 1–5. Pairs or groups have a conversation, but each can only use the number of words designated.

Special Section: Storytelling, an Integrated Art Form

> *You are the vessel for the tale.* (Heather Forrest, storyteller)

Storytelling has much in common with drama and theatre. Both rely on conflict to develop characters, plot, and themes. Storytellers take on roles and imaginatively use voice and body to bring words to life. At its core, storytelling is a dramatic vehicle. In the 1920s it was Winifred Ward's course in storytelling that led to creative drama (Collins, 1997). Storytelling also frequently includes use of movement and dance to suggest characters, mood, and places. Storytellers may invite movement responses from the audience as well. Many tellers also sing, play musical instruments to accompany stories, and invite the audience to sing along. The "visual art" of storytelling has much to do with the colorful mental pictures tellers paint for listeners using rich descriptive language. Storytelling is an art form that naturally integrates the arts. And, like other arts, storytelling is now being tapped for its learning potential. This Community Snapshot shows how that is happening at the initiative of one arts organization.

Community Snapshot:

Storytelling Collaboration

The first weekend in May each year more than 8,000 students descend on downtown Jackson, Michigan. It's Storyfest! Teachers bring students to storytelling sessions conducted by national tellers such as Donald Davis, Charlotte Blake-Alston, Heather Forest, Eth-No-Tec, and Jay O'Callahan. Stories range from personal/family to historical tales.

"It is a community event that brings children and adults together," explains Virginia Lucas, former Storyfest chair. In addition to the school schedule, adult performances on Fri-

day and Saturday night bring hundreds of families to the 1930s vintage Michigan Theatre.

Lucas can't say enough about the artistry of the storytellers, but her description of the response of families reveals why she believes storytelling is important. "It is just amazing to hear them tell their own family stories before they even leave the theatre! Storytellers give us words in context. It is this gift of learning how to use words in context that makes us literate." Saturday morning is "interactive storytelling" for young children and their parents. Teachers attend workshops to learn to use storytelling throughout the curriculum.

Since 2005, Storyfest has focused on storytelling's role in literacy development. "Oral storytelling shows children how to think in 'frames,'" says Lucas. "We need concepts like beginning, middle, and end to understand stories—oral and written." During storytelling students learn to use thinking skills such as prediction, inference, and drawing conclusions. These higher-order skills can be used during storytelling long before children have print decoding fluency.

Young children engaged in storytelling also hear patterns and the rhythms of language in an enjoyable context. Lucas says children "listen to sounds of words and learn to create their own images." She worries that too much television creates dependence on sources outside themselves for visual images.

Jackson Storyfest is an example of a community-school-arts collaboration. With its focus on literacy, one goal of Storyfest is to develop the listening and speaking skills that are the foundation for reading and writing. Students also learn how to be participating audience members during live performances.

Storyfest is funded through grants from corporations like Target and Sam's Club. Lucas works all year with local businesses and individuals to raise the approximately $20,000 the festival costs. "The festival could not operate without the dedication of volunteers," she says. To learn about Jackson Storyfest, visit *www.jacksonstoryfest.org.*

Why Storytelling?

Storyteller Rives Collins believes human beings are "storytelling animals" and explains how storytelling is a natural, common, and ancient human activity. Written accounts of storytelling date back as far 4,000 years to Cheops, the Great Pyramid builder. In every culture people love to tell and listen to stories. From the griots of Africa to Navajo shaman and French troubadours, storytellers have preserved history. They continue to educate, enlighten, and enliven our lives.

We tell stories to prepare and reassure ourselves. We invent fantasy stories to amuse others, to make sense of the world, and to build relationships. We ask others, "Remember the time . . . ? "How was your day?" "What did you do at school?" "What do you think will happen?" We intuitively put great store in the power of stories. From biblical parables to creation myths and tall tales, stories engage us as no other words can. For example, someone stating, "We learn from our mistakes" has a different impact than hearing this story with a similar theme:

> A young man who wished to be wise went to a sage high on the mountain.
>
> "How can I become wise?" the young man asked respectfully.
>
> The old man looked thoughtful and replied, "Have wisdom."
>
> "But how do I get wisdom?" asked the young man.
>
> "Develop good judgment," the sage answered.
>
> "But how can I get good judgment?" the young man cried.
>
> "Experience," said the sage wisely.
>
> "And how do I get experience?" said the young man in frustration.
>
> "Bad judgment," said the sage.

According to S. H. Clark in *How to Teach Reading in Public Schools* (1899):

> If teachers should succeed in developing the state of mind that would cause the pupils to go to the printed page as they would go to the feet of one who has a story to tell, we should be willing to ask nothing else of them as a results of all their teaching.

Storytelling Is Valuable Because It ...

- *Is brain food.* Storytelling is a holistic activity that involves a balanced diet of cognitive and emotional knowing.

Social/Emotional

- *Builds community.* Listeners are brought together in cultural tales that include relevant symbols and traditions. We learn people are more alike than they are different.
- *Bonds.* A special relationship is created between listeners and tellers that is different from reading aloud in which the book can create a distance or barrier. Storytelling seems more intimate, as if the teller is sharing something of herself.

Cognitive

- *Increases knowledge.* Listeners learn in a way that doesn't feel like a "taught" lesson. Everyone loves to learn, but we resist didactic teaching. Stories give information, opinions, and new perspectives in an invitational way.

- *Stimulates higher-order thinking.* Young children internalize the structure or grammar of story before they can read. They predict, analyze, synthesize, and evaluate as they listen.
- *Teaches problem solving.* Listeners hear provocative ideas that show how others solve problems in creative ways.
- *Stimulates creativity.* Students want to respond by writing or do other activities that allow imaginative expression.

Literacy

- *Triggers visual imagery.* Storytelling causes listeners to make their own mental images—a kind of personal movie. Visual imagining is used frequently by fluent readers.
- *Increases vocabulary.* Students hear diverse dialects and unusual language that sensitizes them to the power of words to create images and provoke emotions.
- *Improves listening comprehension.* Understanding is built on listening, which is thinking about what is heard. Listening comprehension comes before reading comprehension.
- *Increases oral skills.* When listeners become tellers, they using oral communication skills.

Motivation

- *Whets the appetite.* Students become interested and want to hear more. They seek out similar stories to read and write.
- *Develops empathy and identity.* Listeners come to like specific characters, see their points of view, and realize they share values, tastes, and ways of living.
- *Helps us cope.* Listeners come to better understand life, to make sense of conflict, and see that there are patterns, such as in relationships between good and evil.
- *Is superb entertainment.* Storytelling engages listeners so that they feel uplifted and renewed.

Storytelling Strategies and Resources

There once was a rabbi who was a gifted storyteller. Everyone felt he gave each story just to him. A man finally asked, "How is it we all hear the same story but you touch each of our individual hearts?" In response, the rabbi told about a girl who shot arrows. Wherever an arrow stuck, she pulled it out and painted a bright bull's eye around it. "It is you that paints the target," the rabbi said, "inviting the story into your heart" (Collins, 1994).

Where can you get good stories like this to tell? What are pointers from professional storytellers? The ideas in the following sections are good starters. Ready References 9.6 though 9.8 summarize pointers, and 9.9 is an example story plot skeleton. Use these resources to find stories, learn to tell them, and involve students in storytelling. Here are Seed Strategies to get started:

Ready Reference 9.6   ## Choosing Stories to Tell

Like love, knowledge, and fairy dust, stories are best when shared. (From *The Woman Who Flummoxed the Fairies*)

Choose stories that . . .

- Fit your personality. Select stories you care about, are important to you, and you feel compelled to tell. Remember, we are the stories we tell.
- Appeal to our better nature: ones about courage, love, laughter.
- Reveal an aspect of the human condition (impatient, restless).

- Evoke emotions that leave the audience enriched.
- Have the force of language. Powerful words evoke visual images. They are beautiful and specific.
- Are culturally authentic and fair to the original sources.
- Are audience appropriate. Consider who will hear them. Consider audience characteristics (age, stage, time, place, occasion, interests).
- Start strong and end in a satisfying way. Try to get attention to start and end with a punch.
- Are short. Work up to longer ones.

Note: Plan to read 10 to find 1 that suits you!

Ready Reference 9.7   ## Learning Stories to Tell

- Visualize each event and character in relation to the climax. Rerun the story in your mind's eye like a movie.
- Use a whole-to-part process: read or listen to the whole story several times before beginning to learn the parts.
- Focus on plot (storyline) first. Map out the sequence of images and events. Don't memorize. *Note:* Stories have a general structure that answers the questions who? what? where? why? and how? Think about the beginning, middle, and end. Some tellers make a plot skeleton (Ready Reference 9.9) or make a map, chart, or events. Notecards or an outline of events can help, too. Heather Forrest uses a series of connected circles she calls "steppingstones." Another option is a series of stick drawings of events to use as rehearsal device.
- Get a powerful first sentence to capture attention.
- Memorize the opening and ending to give yourself a frame in which to work. Also memorize any special phrases or refrains. Rehearse, but don't memorize, the rest. Use improvisation—the kind we use in real life to give directions or excuses and in conversation.

- Practice out loud. Use a tape recorder to listen to yourself. Tell it to the mirror. Videotape and critique your facial expression and gestures. Tell to a friend and then to a group. Own it by repeated retellings.
- Exaggerate gestures and vocal dynamics during practice to extend yourself. For example, open your mouth wider and increase volume to reach the "back row." Go into exta detail, count to three during a pause, say some parts very fast. Later you can tone down and select what you want to keep.
- Develop the characters. Imagine what they would wear, what their hands look like, how they would stand and move, and how their voices would sound. Interesting characters are created through detail (words, gestures, facial expressions, body use).
- Select words that paint pictures, describe feelings, and elaborate on details. Add sound effects where appropriate.
- Puppet and props. If you are using these, keep them out of sight until they are needed.

Opening Rituals. Collect and create opening rituals from stories. For example (T: teller and A: audience):

- *Call and response:*
T: Knock knock.
A: Who's there?
T: A story.
A: A story who?
T: A story for you.

OR

T: When I say hi, you say ho, HI.
A: Ho.
T: Hi.
A: Ho.
T: When I say stop, you say go. Stop.
A: Go.
T: I will.

 Pointers for Telling a Story

Dress so your appearance complements and does not distract. Choose a location without distractions. A circle creates an intimate climate.

Introduction

- Keep it short.
- Establish mood with your demeanor (posture, face, dress, gestures, tone of voice).
- Invite the audience to imagine and participate—to be together in a "mind space."
- Relax the audience with a smile or humor. Example: knock-knocks build rapport with young children.
- Use a ritual, for example, light a candle, close your eyes, touch fingers of both hands together as if you are holding a ball and bow your head. Use a call and response like "When I say CRICK, you say CRACK" (West Indies).
- Motivate the audience to listen. Use a hook.
- Use poems, rhymes, games, riddles, and tongue twisters to get attention.
- Pass around an object or picture and ask questions. Example: What does this make you think of or feel?
- Use eye contact with audience members in different locations so that everyone feels you are telling the tale to them.
- Be as physically close to your audience as possible.
- Personalize the story to the audience and place.

Throughout

- Remember, there is elegance in simplicity. Use only what you need.
- Show enthusiasm with your voice, eyes, body, gestures, and tempo.
- Use gestures, facial expressions, and movement to help define characters, create the setting, and set mood.

- Mentally picture the story so that you can make it live.
- Make word pictures by using language that evokes all five senses. Help the audience savor language by using words that are unique to the story. For example, when telling *The Baker's Scent,* storyteller Heather Forrest says, "The smell rose up like a hand and went down the street collecting noses" (Jackson, MI, Storyfest, 1994).
- Share the power with your audience by involving them.
- Increase suspense. Pause is waiting with a purpose. Pause to allow listeners to imagine and predict, to savor a moment. "The pause is like the big space that makes the beauty in Japanese paintings" (Heather Forrest).
- Give a sense of the place and the mood using voice, body, and descriptive words.
- Make each telling different to keep it spontaneous.
- Imagine being your own audience to give new perspective.
- Vary your voice for interest. Change the volume, rate, pitch, and pause (e.g., whisper, yell). Each character should have an idiolect. Use dialects as appropriate.
- Articulate and enunciate clearly. Refrain from using fillers such as "uh" and "um."
- Ignore interruptions.

Ending the Story

The last sentence should have a finality to it so that listeners feel satisfied and understand the tale is completed. There needs to be a signal for applause. You may want to use a closing ritual, for example, "Snip, Snap, Snout, This tale is told out."

- *African ritual:*
  T: A story. A story.
  A: Let it come, let it go.

- *From the Sudan:*
  T: This story is the truth.
  A: Right.
  T: This story is a lie.
  A: Right.
  T: This story is both truth and lie.
  A: Right.

- *Candle lighting:* Turn on a small battery candle and say, "By the flame of the story candle we are freed to travel in our minds to other times and places."

- *Beginnings:* A long time ago back before yesterday and use-to-bes. Long, long ago. In a time before time. Once upon a time.

Audience Participation.   Storytelling is always participatory, because the audience co-creates through imagination—especially visualization. Here are ideas to increase audience engagement:

1. Stop and ask for ideas, for example, "What kind of fabric might the tailor use?"
2. Increase curiosity with a pause (e.g., "Nothing I'm going to tell you is true (pause) all the time").
3. Use a cloze-pause for the audience to supply a refrain, phrase, or word (e.g., and the witch sang, "Bubble bub-

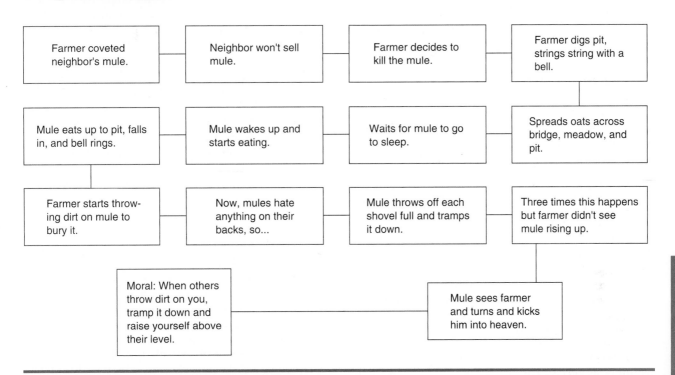

Ready Reference 9.9 ## Plot Skeleton for "Fable of the Farmer and Mule"

ble pasta pot, boil me some pasta nice and hot," from Tomie dePaola's *Strega Nona*). Or "Once upon a time there were three bears who got up one morning and made some. . . ."

4. Sound effects: audience supplies these creatively or "as rehearsed" before telling.

5. Add sign language to stories that an audience can mimic. *Joy of Signing* (Riekehof, 1987) is a clear reference.

6. Cumulative stories: Stories such as *This Is the House That Jack Built* (Taback) involve lists that repeat and build. Invite the unison response or have sections of the audience respond.

7. Story stops: Invite the audience to group mime or improvise dialogue with a partner. For example, from *Little Red Riding Hood:* (1) Stop where Red first meets Wolf and ask audience to show how she felt using facial expression and body shapes/moves. (2) Pair so everyone is a Wolf with a Red and tell them to have a conversation at a signal. (3) Stop and ask audience to give Red advice about what she should do after meeting the wolf. (4) Stop and interview the audience as if they are story characters.

8. Questioning: Stop and ask the audience, "What do you know so far?" after the conflict has been introduced.

After the story, ask, "What images do you have in your head?" that is less judgmental than, "What did you like best?"

9. Whisper a line to one person, who passes it on until it circulates around the room. This works for special surprises. For example, "And when he woke up on the end of his nose was a . . ." (whisper "huge bologna").

Vocal Expression. Brainstorm all the different ways to use voice in telling stories. For example, storytellers talk slowly, very fast, high pitch, scared, giggly, using regional accents and dialects. Choose a paragraph or sentence out of the newspaper or a book. Have each student read or say it aloud using three different voices.

Talk with Your Body. Practice ways to send a message using body gestures. *Examples*: I'm tired. I'm bored. I'm afraid. It's freezing in here. Ask students to create original body sentences and pantomime. Do as pairs to get more participation. *Variation*: Try to show emotions without using the face (use mask).

Follow the Leader. This circle activity encourages using the body to communicate. IT mimes going on a walk (in place) and encountering a variety of obstacles (e.g., a crack in the sidewalk, a short wall, a fence with a gate, a puddle). The rest of the class imitates actions. Limit the obstacles to three, and then everyone guesses and a new IT can be chosen. *Variation*: Invite students to find actions in stories to mime. Start an ongoing chart (e.g., opening, reading, and closing a book; throwing types of balls; peeling and eating a banana).

Painting Word Pictures.   This increases use of details. Sit in a circle. Give students a simple sentence. Go around, with each person repeating the sentence, adding description. For example: The woman walked down the road. The bent old woman walked down the narrow road. The spry old woman walked frantically down the long hot road.

Riddle Stories.   Riddles are a comfortable way to break into storytelling because they are short and they get an obvious audience response. Hundreds of joke and riddle books are available on nearly every topic from computers to insects. Here's a favorite: Two legs was sitting on three legs with one leg in his lap. In comes four legs and snatches one leg. Up jumps two legs and picks up three legs and throws it at four legs and gets one leg back. *Note*: Ask audience for guesses and then repeat more slowly so they "get it." (Answer: 1=chicken leg, 2=man, 3=stool, 4=dog.)

Food Stories.   Food and stories go together. Ask each person or group to learn a story with a food connection. Stories are told and then everyone feasts. This works well with ethnic stories and folktales. *Examples*: Stone Soup, *Little Red Hen* (bread), *Three Wishes* (sausage).

Circle Stories.   Sit in circle and use an opener, for example, "Once long ago when time was just getting started. . . ." Each person adds just one word or how ever many you want. The goal is to introduce a problem and resolve it after a designated number of rounds. Suggestion: Post a Story Structure chart to remind students about: setting, characters, problem, plot actions/events, resolution. *Variation:* Use to review any subject. For example, "In science we've been studying about Mars and. . . ."

Key Word Storytelling.   Choose a list of 5–10 words important to an upcoming reading assignment. Pair students to tell a story that uses all the words. In one study students remembered 90% of 120 words using this method versus 13% by the control (Wolfe, 2001).

Story Challenge.   Give three words, phrases, objects, or pictures that must be used (do circle story, partner, individual, etc.). Example phrases are: a thorny rose, lightning strikes, one lost sneaker. Remind students that stories have a beginning, middle, and end and involve a problem. *Variations*: Use a phone book to get names for characters,

spin a globe for a setting, and draw from a "problem box" (problems that children generate).

Jigsaw Stories.   Tell a story to the group. Next, cut it up into parts so that each student has a section. Individuals rehearse their parts. Then the group assembles to tell the whole story. Number the sections the first time you try this.

Alphabet Stories.   Sit in a circle. Person 1 begins the retelling and must start with a word that begins with the letter *A*. The next person picks up the story, but must use the letter *B,* and so on. *Example*: A family of three bears lived in a dark wood. Bears need special furniture, and these three bears had chairs and beds to fit them. Chair Maximum was for Papa Bear, Chair Medium was for Mama Bear, and Chair Mini was for Baby Bear. (Thanks to second graders in Ohio, for this example.)

Literature Frames.   Use a children's book that has a predictable structure as a verbal frame (e.g.*, When I Was Young in the Mountains,* Rylant). Partner students and have them tell about when they were young, using the stem "When I was young . . . ." *Variation*: Do this in a Ping-Pong manner. Each student tells one line, and passes the turn by making eye contact with a student.

Retell Favorites.   Students choose to paraphrase a family story. For shy students, invite them to use objects, props, or puppets. *Variation*: Each child makes a prop box of items to draw out as the story is told. This also helps students remember the story.

Partner Retelling.   Students pair off and tell a favorite story. Partners must remember each other's stories. At a signal, all change partners and retell the story they just heard. This is excellent for listening skills. *Variation*: All students hear the same story and then partner to tell it to each other. Partner A begins and, at a signal, stops and B must pick up the story line.

Personal Story Prompts.   Have students choose or draw randomly a stem to use as a starter (e.g., "The funniest thing that ever happened to me was . . ." or "The most embarrassing moment I've ever had was the time . . ." or "The most memorable person in my family . . .").

I Am Stories.   Brainstorm with students roles they play, such as brother, sister, friend. In groups, ask students to use the stem "I am . . ." and tell all the roles they play. They should feel free to add interesting details (e.g., "I am the shortest person in a family of six people, three of whom are my brothers") (Collins, 1997).

Rerun and Respond.   After a story has been told, invite students to rerun the story in their heads. They may use art, music, drama, dance, or creative writing responses to transform the rerun. *Example*: Rerun and think of three gestures and two sound effects to add. Students can also do a partner retelling (described previously).

Round-Robin Retelling.
This is a kind of circle story. Students can retell picture books, fairy tales, and so forth. One person starts and passes on the story line. A ball of yarn with knots every yard can be passed and used as a cue. *Variation*: Retell from a different POV than original story, for example, Little Red Riding Hood from Grandmother's viewpoint. Use in science or social studies to retell events from different viewpoints.

Backwards Stories.
This is a Round-Robin Retelling, but the story is told from the ending to the beginning. This really demands concentration and thorough story understanding.

Prop Stories.
Many stories have an object that can be used as a puppet or visual aid as the story is told. Young children especially love this, and older children are more comfortable telling stories if they can use a prop to focus the audience's attention. Here are example titles of stories/books with obvious props: Albert Lamorisse's *The Red Balloon*, Ruth Orbach's *Apple Pigs*, Robert Kraus's *The Tail Who Wagged the Dog*, Byrd Baylor's *Everybody Needs a Rock*, and Eric Carle's *The Very Hungry Caterpillar*.

Art Story Map.
Provide students with portraits, landscapes, and nonrepresentational art (e.g., abstract), and ask them to choose one of each. Students create (write or tell) a story using portraits for characters, a landscape for the setting, and an abstract work for a story problem. Remind them to establish the problem quickly and be descriptive about the setting and characters. Share stories with art displayed. *Suggestion*: arts postcards are inexpensive and easy to use for this.

Story Ballads.
Ballads tell tales through lyrics and music. First, share examples. Next, work with students to convert a familiar story to a ballad by using rhythm instruments and singing parts. Action words can be used as the stimulus for mime or skits during the ballad. Rehearse. *Suggestion*: Videotape the end product. *Variation*: After whole-group efforts, try small-group ballad writing.

Puppet Shows.
Students plan a story adaptation, stage, and props to retell through puppets. For example, write a Reader's Theatre script (Ready Reference 9.5). Help students map out the story using events in the beginning, middle, and end. Then decide who will make each character, scenery, and so forth. Chapter 7 describes 10 types of puppets. Stages can be made by using a push rod in a doorway to hang a curtain. Presentations can be made using the overhead projector (shadow puppets). Rather than memorize a script, encourage improvisation. As with all performances, rehearsal is needed to practice with puppet manipulation and oral expression.

Storytelling Sources and Resources

An excellent place to begin to search for stories and more storytelling ideas is the National Storytelling Network (NSN), which offers workshops, periodicals, and a directory of storytellers. Check the website, *www.storynet.org/NSN/*.

As stories are selected, be aware that it is nearly impossible to explore many cultures without controversy. The stories of most cultures focus on good overcoming evil (devils, witches, etc.), often employing violence. Western culture peculiarly emphasizes happy endings. Many traditional folktales have been sanitized to take out violent acts and dark characters. However, scholars feel this lessens the impact of the story and denies children's need to cope with the "shadow" (see, e.g., Bruno Bettleheim's (1989) classic, *The Uses of Enchantment*).

Printed versions of multicultural folktales and fables can be found in the 398.2 section of the public library. Check both the children's and adult areas. Simplified versions are an excellent source from which students can explore improvisation with storytelling.

Here are some places to start to find stories to tell:

- Children's literature, especially picture books
- Fables (Aesop, Lobel, Thurber) and folktales
- Your own ethnic or cultural traditions
- Family stories
- Retellings of stories you've heard others tell
- Bible or religious stories
- Historical events
- Contemporary news
- Childhood stories

Anthology examples:

Chase, R. (2003). *Grandfather tales*. Boston: Houghton Mifflin.

Gross, L., & Barnes, M. (1989). *Talk that talk: An anthology of African-American stories*. New York: Simon & Schuster.

Hamilton, V. (1993). *The people could fly: American black folktales*. New York: Knopf.

San Souci, R. (1989). *Short and shivery: Thirty chilling tales*. New York: Doubleday.

Schram, P. (1993). *Jewish stories one generation tells another*. Dunmore, PA: Aronson.

Schwartz, A. (1986). *More scary stories to tell in the dark*. New York: Harper & Row.

Yolen, J. (1988). *Favorite folktales from around the world*. New York: Pantheon.

Teacher Spotlight:
Science and Drama

This Spotlight returns to the focus of this chapter—using drama as a teaching tool.

The first graders are on the floor. Some are balled up. Others are on their sides. A few have their heads covered with their arms. The teacher, Liza Dean, **coaches** students to show being woodland animals in a hibernated state.

"Think of how you would feel if you had been asleep a long, long time—all winter. Think of how you will hold your head and move your arms and legs. When I say "begin," I want you to wake up. When I say **"freeze,"** you freeze. Ready, **BEGIN."**

Twenty-plus children begin to stretch limbs, rub their eyes, yawn, and wriggle. At first they move slowly. "I am going to count to 3 and then you will freeze. Ready. 1-2-3, " says Liza. On "3" the classroom grows silent and is filled with statues. Some are at the floor level. Some are at a medium level. A few are at a high level.

Why is Liza using **narrative pantomime** in a science unit? She thinks the drama strategies of moving and frozen pantomime, used after reading, causes students to become thoroughly engaged in **problem solving**, which is the foundation of comprehension. "It causes them to visualize and become a part of the action," she explains. "It is an important way to increase comprehension skills." She points out that is hard to think without making pictures in your head. **"Visual imagery** is necessary to cognition, but it must be explicitly taught."

Liza explains the philosophy of her school. "We encourage each student to be different—to move in ways that make sense to them and to use their faces to show the emotions each of them thinks relate best to what we are studying. The arts are about difference, not sameness."

What about standards and tests? "Of course, we also look at the arts standards and expect students to learn techniques and concepts about the arts. We want to 'use' the arts, not 'abuse' them," she explains.

How are basics like vocabulary and phonics taught in arts-based lessons?

"Better!" Liza exclaims. "The arts are teaching and learning tools. The goal for using drama in this lesson was for students to show understanding of specific science concepts by thinking through body shapes, actions, and facial expressions. First graders can show more than they can say or write." ✳

Conclusion

Life beats down and crushes the soul and art reminds you that you have one. (Stella Adler)

This chapter is a compendium of Seed Strategies to stimulate drama integration throughout the curriculum. Storytelling was a special focus. Both drama and storytelling are arts that give life to learning.

Resources

See the Appendix for more materials, including websites.

Activity Books

Erior, P. (2000). *Drama in the classroom: Creative activities for teachers, parents and friends.* Fort Bragg, CA: Lost Coast Press.

Heinig, R. B. (1986). *Creative drama resource book for grades 4 through 6.* Upper Saddle River, NJ: Prentice Hall. (K–3 book also available)

Heinig, R. B. (1992). *Improvisation with favorite fairy tales.* Portsmouth, NH: Heinemann.

Heller, P. (1995). *Drama as a way of knowing.* York, ME: Stenhouse.

McClasin, N. (2005). *Creative drama in the classroom and beyond.* New York: Allyn & Bacon.

Rooyackers, P. (1997). *101 drama games for children: Fun and learning with acting and make-believe.* Alameda, CA: Hunter House.

Rubin, J., & Merrion, M. (1996). *Creative drama and music methods: Introductory activities for children.* North Haven, CT: Linnet Professional.

Pollock, J. (1997). *Side by side: Twelve multicultural puppet plays.* School Library Media No. 13. Lanham, MD: Scarecrow.

Schafer, L. (1994). *Plays around the year: More than 20 thematic plays for the classroom.* New York: Scholastic.

Walker, L. (1996). *Readers theatre strategies development through Readers Theatre, storytelling, writing and dramatizing!* Colorado Springs, CO: Meriwether.

Winters, L. (1997). *On stage: Theatre games and activities for kids.* Chicago: Review Press.

Zipes, J. (2004). *Speaking out: Storytelling and creative drama for children.* Oxford, UK: Routledge.

Children's Literature References

Avi. (1994). *Night journeys.* New York: Beech Tree.

Baylor, B. (1974). *Everybody needs a rock.* New York: Scribner.

Berger, B. (1984). *Grandfather twilight.* New York: Putnam.

Carle, E. (1984). *The very hungry caterpillar.* New York: Putnam.

Chaconas, D. (1970). *The way the tiger walked.* New York: Simon & Schuster.

Cole, J. (1993). *Six sick sheep: 101 tongue twists.* New York: Beech Tree.

dePaola, T. (1986). *The clown of God.* New York: Harcourt Brace.

dePaola, T. (1989). *Strega Nona.* New York: Harcourt Brace.

DiCamillo, K. (2000). *Because of Winn-Dixie.* Cambridge, MA: Candelwick Press.

Forest, H. (1990). *The woman who flummoxed the fairies.* San Diego, CA: Harcourt Brace Jovanovich.

Fox, M. (1989). *Night noises.* San Diego, CA: Harcourt Brace Jovanovich.

Goodman, J. (1981). *Magic and the educated rabbit.* Paoli, PA: Instructo/McGraw-Hill.

Hutchins, P. (1978). *Don't forget the bacon*. New York: Puffin.

Jacobs, J. (1890). *English fairy tales.* London, England: David Nutt.

Jay, W. (1990). *Laughing time*. New York: Farrar, Straus & Giroux.

Keats, E. J. (1962). *A snowy day*. New York: Viking.

Kraus, R. (1971). *The tail who wagged the dog*. New York: Windmill.

Lamorisse, A. (1967). *The red balloon*. New York: Doubleday.

Lester, J. (1972). *Long Journey Home*. Scholastic.

MacLachlan, P. (1985). *Sarah, plain and tall*. New York: Trumpet Club.

Marshall, J. (1973). *George and Martha: Encore*. Boston: Houghton Mifflin.

McCloskey, R. (1978). *Lentil*. New York: Viking.

McCully, E. (1992). *Mirette on the high wire*. New York: Putnam.

McGovern, A. (1966). *Too much noise*. Boston: Houghton Mifflin.

Munsch, R. (1988). *Thomas' snowsuit*. Toronto, Ontario: Annick.

Murphy, J. (1992). *Peace at last*. New York: Dial.

Numeroff, L. J. (1985*). If you give a mouse a cookie*. New York: HarperCollins.

Orbach, R. (1981). *Apple pigs*. New York: Putnam.

Park, B. (1992). *Junie B. Jones and the stupid smelly bus*. New York: Random Library.

Peck, R. (1976). *Hamilton*. Boston: Little, Brown.

Randi, J. (1989). *The magic world of the Amazing Randi*. Holbrook, MA: Adams.

Rathmann, P. (1995). *Officer Buckles and Gloria*. New York: Scholastic.

Rylant, C. (1992). *When I was young in the mountains*. New York: Dutton.

Schwartz, A. (1974). *A twister of twists, a tangler of tongues*. London: Deutsch.

Scieszka, J. (1991). *The true story of the 3 little pigs*. New York: Viking.

Sendak, M. (1962). *Pierre: A cautionary tale*. New York: Harpercrest.

Taback, S. (2002). *This is the house that Jack built*. New York: Putnam.

Van Allsburg, C. (1987). *The z was zapped*. Boston: Houghton Mifflin.

Van Laan, N. (1992). *Possum come a-knockin'*. New York: Knopf.

Viorst, J. (1972). *Alexander and the terrible, horrible, no good, very bad day*. New York: Atheneum.

Wolf, A. (1993). *It's show time!: Poetry from the page to the stage*. Asheville, NC: Poetry Alive!

Integrating Dance and Movement

Questions to Guide Reading

1. Why should dance/movement be integrated (research, theories, and philosophy)?

2. What do classroom teachers need to know to integrate dance and movement (dance literacy)?

3. How can dance be integrated (planning, environment, literature, instruction, adaptations, assessment)?

4. How can teachers partner with arts specialists?

Nobody cares if you can dance well. Just get up and dance.
(Martha Graham)

Dance is big right now. Fox TV has a hit in *So You Think You Can Dance,* and ABC offers *Dancing With the Stars.* Films like *Take the Lead* and *Shall We Dance?* inspire Banderas, Gere, and Lopez fans to take lessons. Membership in the U.S. Amateur Ballroom Dancers Association has doubled, and dance studios are thriving. A recent documentary, "Mad Hot Ballroom," which portrays NYC fifth graders vying for a trophy, is the 10th highest grossing documentary ever. The Learning Channel debuted *Ballroom Bootcamp* in 2005. Tango, waltz, samba, and salsa are all popular on college campuses from Harvard to Witten-

berg University in Ohio (*The Beaufort Gazette,* September 4, 2005).

Dance is also gaining much needed momentum in our elementary and middle school classrooms. As the saying goes, it's hard to keep your brain in gear once your bum goes numb. The more serious we get about standards, enduring understandings, and essential skills, the more we need the force of dance to engage students. *Hands on* was in the education lexicon before *heads on* and *hearts on*. Dance is hands on, feet on—*whole body on*. But dance isn't just physical. Like all the arts, dance is about creative problem solving—thinking on your feet. Can dance be a meaningful vehicle to learn science, social studies, math, and literacy?

Two Ways

In the opening Classroom Snapshot, teacher Wrenn Cook takes on the challenge. Wrenn is a dance expert who believes integration goes two ways—using dance in the regular classroom and bringing traditional subject areas into dance lessons. She shows how important science content can be taught using a simple dance format that moves from a warm-up to engaging students in transforming skeletal information into choreographed dances. Notice her use of descriptive feedback and how she coaches students to problem solve with emphasis on original adaptations.

Classroom Snapshot

Science and Skeleton Dances

The desks are pushed to the edges of the room. Twenty-four third graders are standing in a circle. Music with a steady beat and moderate tempo plays loudly enough to hear and feel the rhythm, but softly enough to hear the teacher. Ms. Cook is guiding them through a "skull to phalanges" **warm-up.** Students isolate and move particular body parts.

"Let's tilt our skulls forward and return to center, forward and return to center," she says.

Students **chant,** "Skull-skull, skull-skull" to the beat.

After several **repetitions,** Ms. Cook proceeds to the jawbone. Students giggle as they try to say "mandible-mandible" while opening and closing their mouths.

"We look like my goldfish!" says one boy; they all start imitating gills. Ms. Cook **redirects focus** by moving on to clavicles and sternum until the warm-up has touched on every bone, head to toe.

More Than Imitation

"Now it's your turn. We'll go clockwise around the circle. **Create a new movement** for a bone. Corinne, show us a different way to move our skulls." Ms. Cook suggests.

Lion dancers at Ashley River Creative Arts.

Corinne tilts her skull side to side. The students and Ms. Cook follow suit, chanting, "skull-skull." For "ulna," a boy does a "karate chop" in which he strikes one forearm against the other in a downward motion.

"That's right, Kevin, ulna-ulna. See how he uses the pinky finger side of his lower arm? What lower arm bone is on the thumb side?" Ms. Cook asks. The students show her.

"That's right! The radius. Let's do Kevin's movement using the radius, instead of the ulna."

Students contort to touch their radius bones to opposite arms, until one **discovers** that upward chopping is easier.

"**Great solution!** Let's all do that together. Let's alternate arms. Radius right, radius left, radius right, radius left."

The warm-up lasts 10 minutes and has served as a review of content points from the previous day's lesson. By the time they reach the phalanges, students' eyes are bright and cheeks slightly flushed. They are fully alert.

"Everyone really stayed focused. Have a seat where you're standing." Ms. Cook gives out a Skeleton Dance handout. It lists seven "commands," beginning with "Touch some phalanges to a patella."

Creative Problem Solving

"Here is your choreography problem," Ms. Cook pauses. "Each group is challenged to create a group dance about the skeletal system." She explains they are to come up with movements for all the commands. The goal is to create an interesting dance composition for an audience. She points out **"Choreography Tips"** on the handout that lists ideas for how to use dance elements to create visual interest.

"Try to find **unexpected ways** to dance the commands and to choreograph transitions from one segment to the next," she explains.

"Let's talk about the first command, 'Touch some phalanges to a patella.' Someone show me one way that a dancer could do that." Antonio jumps up and poses with the fingers of each hand touching each kneecap.

"That's one, Antonio! Now someone show us **a different way** to touch phalanges to a patella." A girl balances on one leg, touching her toes to the knee of the leg.

"Great balance, Danielle! What other ways can we touch phalanges to a patella? You don't have to make a still shape—you can move." Students have **multiple solutions,** and all show they understand phalanges and patella.

"I see you understand what to do. I can't wait to see your skeleton dances!"

At this point Ms. Cook shows them the evaluation **rubric** and invites questions to make sure they understand. She divides them into six preselected groups of four. They are **heterogeneous** and mix gender, race, and ability levels.

Ms. Cook circulates as the students start problem solving. She listens and **coaches** with questions and information.

"Hey, I know! While moving our pelvis right and left, we could jump up and down on the metatarsals, then we could switch," says one student.

Skeleton dance: waving metacarpals in the air.

Cook watches closely, checking for accuracy and **making notations** on the rubric for the task. At the conclusion, students are asked to **comment**.

"I really liked how Tyler's group went down to the floor when they had to touch the lumbar vertebrae to the floor," a girl says.

"Jamica's group was really together when they did the part about waving their metacarpals," a boy says.

Ms. Cook notes use of **science vocabulary** and compliments them on observational skills. Students begin to push their desks back. A boy asks if they can perform the skeleton dances for a **"real" audience.**

"Yes, let us do it," they all begin to plead.

Ms. Cook promises to look into having the students perform at the upcoming school science fair.

"If you get to work right away on your science reading assignment," she explains.

With that, students smile and get out their science books to read more about the skeletal system. The lesson has lasted about 50 minutes. Dance has been the vehicle for science and acted as a motivational force.

Wrenn Cook's unit plan and rubric appear in Planning Pages 10.1 and 10.5. 💥

"Okay. Then maybe we could each do a **solo**, and everyone else **freezes in a shape** until their turn," a boy responds.

Some immediately begin **inventing** and practicing movement. Others first talk through a plan from beginning to end. Ms. Cook mediates with a group who can't agree. They work out a compromise. When one group asks if they can perform two commands simultaneously, Ms. Cook asks to see the movement they are considering. They perform a **complex sequence.** They accurately use the required bones, and she congratulates them for their originality. Another group adopts a narrative form. Ms. Cook responds with delight when they show a comedic section from their story dance.

After about 20 minutes, most are ready. Ms. Cook **cues them** that they have 5 more minutes to finish the choreography and rehearsal. She reminds them they need to memorize their dances since they can't use handouts during the **performance.** As students refine their dances, Ms. Cook plays **two music selections** and asks groups to choose one to accompany their dance. She plays each again so students can rehearse with both and pick a best fit.

Peformance and Assessment

Finally they are ready. Students sit at the end of the room facing an area designated as the "stage." As they watch the dances, some exclaim, "Cool!" or "Awesome!" in response to the choreographers' creative choices. They laugh at some funny parts and nod knowingly as they recognize movements for specific commands. As each group performs, Ms.

Teaching With, About, In and Through

Most classroom teachers would agree that they could learn to do what Wrenn Cook did in the Snapshot. While she had the advantage of knowing dance elements and ways to coach students through simple choreography (dance making), Wrenn had to study the science content to make a meaningful fit. Classroom teachers just do the opposite when they integrate dance. That is what this chapter is about—how to go beyond a bit of creative movement here and there or teaching a folk dance, like the Irish jig, during a culture study. To teach *through* dance demands a level of dance literacy. This chapter summarizes what to teach *about* and how to involve students *in* dance so that they can learn *through* it.

Relax! You Need Not Be a Dancer Yourself

Our bodies and how we move them say so much. So much, in fact, that muggers choose victims by watching how people move: They look for tentative, irregular, undirected walking. Movement is a powerful communicator that fascinates and repels, delights and disgusts. And yet, unlike the use of words, movement has heretofore not been a full partner in the core communication curriculum. This reticence about dance is paradoxical. Our society is riveted on movement, especially sports. But daily use of kinesthetic ways of knowing is less prominent in the classroom. Perhaps movement is so basic, we take it for granted that students know how to use it skillfully to communicate thoughts and feelings. Some do, but most don't. Teenagers, in particular, are unaware of what their exaggerated swaggers and awkward shuffles say. We suffer for those young people who lack confidence in how to manage their bodies.

Dance and creative movement are frequently the art forms teachers feel least prepared to integrate. The look of one's body is important in our culture. Beautiful, intimidating body images bombard us daily through the media, and we have become very body sensitive. It is not surprising teachers are sometimes uncomfortable using creative movement, especially if they're not sure exactly what that means. Teachers do not want to appear awkward or have their bodies targeted for student ridicule. But students often feel the same way, especially after the primary grades.

How can we get over it? Most important is to start with a foundational truth: We all love to move. It feels good to walk, run, stretch, wiggle, and shake. We can search out ways movement affects daily life. This establishes a life link. It is also vital to make the learning link: We remember what we do more easily than what is told to us or what we read. Next, we can find strategies to put kinesthetic ways of knowing into action in creative and artistic ways.

It has to begin with the teacher. Teachers need to be actively engaged in their own lessons. Dance integration is not about demonstrating specific dances, however. The goal is to cause students to problem solve through movement. When and if teachers decide to include structured dances (e.g., folk dancing in social studies), they can choose to demonstrate such dances or invite guests to do so, perhaps in collaboration with the physical education teacher. The school's arts resource directory may also list dancers who are willing to teach specific dances.

Arts Integration Blueprint

There are shortcuts to happiness, and dancing is one of them. (Vicki Baum)

In Chapter 3 the Arts Integration Blueprint was introduced. Ready Reference 2.5 gives an overview. These 10 building blocks begin with WHY arts integration should be implemented (philosophy based on research and theories).

Next comes *what* teachers should know (arts literacy) and *how* to plan lessons, create an aesthetic environment, use arts-based literature and best teaching practices, design instructional routines, adapt for diverse learners, assess and work cooperatively with arts specialists. The Blueprint is applied to integrating dance in this chapter.

Blueprint I: Philosophy of Arts Integration

Nothing is more revealing than movement. (Anonymous)

When one looks at the image of a rising arch or tower in architecture or at the yielding of a tree bent by the storm, one receives more than the information conveyed by the image . . . . The body of the viewer reproduces the tensions of swinging and rising and bending so that he himself matches internally the actions he sees being performed outside. And these actions . . . are ways of being alive, ways of being human. (R. Arnheim, 1989)

A philosophy is a set of beliefs. Educational beliefs grow from research, theories, and professional experience. Research Update 10.1 summarizes research relevant to thinking about dance integration. That research and the theories in Chapter 2 were used to synthesize these 13 reasons to integrate dance.

Why Should Teachers Integrate Dance and Movement?

I dance because it brings me closer to my creator. Morgan Grant (Saginaw dancer)

Dance Is Primary Form of Communication.

If I could tell you what I mean, there would be no point in dancing. (Isadora Duncan)

The importance of movement in communication cannot be minimized. If you saw *Meet the Fockers,* you know where this is going. Babies as young as nine months have been taught to sign and can learn an average of 70 gestures, long before they have 70 words in their speaking vocabularies. Children can coordinate more behaviors in their hands before those in their throat and mouth (Hochman, 2005). Researchers claim teaching baby sign frees kids to express feelings and desires. Some developed a 12-point IQ advantage and higher reading scores.

Research Update 10.1   Dance and Achievement

- After 20 dance sessions, first graders who participated in the dance-reading curriculum scored higher in the area of phonetic knowledge and skills than 350 who did not (MacMahon, Roe, & Parks, 2003).
- At-risk first-grade students who were taught basic letter and sounds through creative movement improved more in those reading skills than did a control group. "The development of linguistic abilities mirrors the development of dance phrase making . . . dance can help children discover the 'music' of language" (Deasy, 2002, p. 10).
- Teenagers serving time in detention facilities benefited from twice-weekly dance classes. "Patience, and sometimes even compassion, can be social by-products of aesthetic engagement" (Deasy, 2002, p. 13).
- Music or dance opportunities offered compelling social benefits for underprivileged students, including providing an emotional safe haven; giving the feeling they were special; acting as assimilation tools for recent immigrants and other new kids; and bolstering

friendships as they entered new situations. These art opportunities "helped most achieve success both in and outside of school" (Fiske, 1999, pp. 77–78).
- Students with disabilities who participated in a 12-week dance program showed significantly higher scores for creativity (fluency, originality, and imagination) than those in adaptive physical education programs (Jay, 1991).
- Third-grade science scores on tests about the water cycle were raised to 97 percent when dance was used as the vehicle. Previous year's students scored below average on the test (Baron, 1997).
- In Seattle, Washington, third graders who studied language arts through dance increased Metropolitan Achievement Test scores by 13 percent in 6 months (Gilbert, 1977).
- The College Board reports that for the 1999 school year, students with 4 or more years of dance background scored 27 points higher on average math and verbal scores. For more about SAT scores, go to *www.collegeboard.org/prof/*.

Body language was the first language humans probably used and retains first place as children develop. Even for adults, nonverbal language has primacy over the verbal, especially when the two conflict. For example, imagine someone saying, "I'm delighted to be here" with a sneer on his face. It is fun and effective to ask students to demonstrate examples of "when words and actions conflict" to make this point.

Dance is a means of showing what we know. It enables children to express thoughts and feelings that otherwise are inexpressible. The kinesthetic mode is the one through which our earliest learning happens. Movement can be a universal language, like the upraised shaking fist. And yet, you can get into a lot of trouble assuming the OK sign means the same thing in Italy as it does in the United States. Hanna points out that "dance has many dialects" (1999, p.19).

Dance Calls for Creative Problem Solving (CPS) and Imagination.

Great ideas originate in the muscles. (Thomas Edison)

How many ways can you move across the room? What are all the body parts you can use to make circles? What are all the ways cats move? Leaves? Water? How can you show the idea of *addition* using dance? What are words that describe movements? When teachers ask fat questions such as these,

they set up opportunities for creative problem solving. Teachers who encourage risk taking and experimentation, and who give children time to explore ways to use movement to communicate thoughts and feelings, are freeing unlimited powers of the imagination. That power can be put to use to solve problems in any subject matter under study.

CPS begins with finding problems and then gathering information to solve them. Every dance activity should focus on this idea of exploring movement to unleash creative and artistic thinking. In the regular classroom, this means having students come to understand key concepts about dance and acquire basic communication skills used in this kinesthetic way of knowing. Fleming points out that dance is "the cheapest and most available material to use for creative experiences. It does need space but not as much as we have traditionally thought"(1990, p. 5).

Dance Is Integral to Real Life.

Consider how many times . . . you handled a basketball compared to the number of times you skipped to music. (Ruth Murray)

John Dewey's idea that school should not be preparation for life, but part of life, fits here. Dance has pride of place in religion and ethnic identity (Hanna, 1999). It is an integral part of the rituals and ceremonies of our lives—weddings, inaugurations, proms, and holidays. States like North and South Carolina have state dances (clogging and shagging). Square dancing has been proposed as our national dance (Hanna, 1999). Dance needs to be as integral to the classroom world as it is in the world beyond school walls.

It is intriguing to consider the response of audiences to entertainment phenomena such as "Lord of the Dance" and "Riverdance." Just as athletic games draw huge crowds, dance attracts entertainment dollars—another real-life connection. Certainly, part of the attraction of sports is the movement aspect. We enjoy watching the light airy moves of Michael Jordan or the elegant golf swing of Tiger Woods. While sports is not the same as dance, there is a connection. In sports, as in dance, the body is used as a tool. Certain individuals go further to make their sport into an art form; they take their moves to a level of beauty that awes and inspires.

Dance Develops Responsibility and Instills a Value for Hard Work.

> *In life as in the dance: Grace glides on blistered feet.* (Alice Abrams)

Dance often involves group work. Students develop responsibility when they are a part of a group in which their ideas and cooperation are needed and when they are taught how to be responsible. But they need to be taught how to respond in a group and to group members. Responsibility means "having the ability to respond." Teachers need to model active listening behaviors, such as paraphrasing another's ideas and asking for clarification, and nonverbal responses, such as nodding and use of eye contact.

Students involved in formal dance study learn the rigor required to develop skills in ballet, tap, or jazz. Any dance demands concentration on the body, energy, space, and time elements. Students who choose such study must commit to a regimen of regular practice. They quickly see that struggle and hard work are needed to master new ideas. Why do they choose pain and hard work? One student put it this way, "It was mind over movement for me. I really liked the challenge to get my body to do what I wanted. I was inspired by dancers who could do amazing moves. I wanted to stretch myself." There certainly is a pride that comes from conquering obstacles, the thrill of performance, and the reinforcement given by significant others in the audience.

Dance Increases Sensitivity, Respect, and Cooperation.

When a class is engaged in group problem solving through movement, students begin to see how everyone has a different view of a situation. There are numerous ways to express thoughts and feelings about the cycle of life and death through movement; no one body shape or locomotor movement is right or wrong. The emphasis is on finding original ways to think and feel about what is being learned. Students soon see that other students think of things they wouldn't have come to know working alone. Two bodies and heads are better than one. Students delight in the artistry of fellow classmates as they witness the inventiveness of peers. A graceful slide or a humorous foot dab executed at the right moment can provide a moment of insight—oohs and ahs, laughter, and even awe. In a more structured vein, partner and circle dances require students to help each other in an enjoyable context. Students feel intrinsic motivation to learn under these circumstances.

Dance Increases Focus and Concentration.

Students involved in solving movement problems or exploring movement have to focus on making their bodies work to control body parts and energy. Teachers who use dance as a learning tool stress the use of self-regulation by starting with small and easy movement problems and increasing the difficulty over time. They cause students to concentrate by structuring dances with beginning, middle, and end segments. They give positive descriptive feedback to those who show they can stay on task and show involvement.

Dance integration includes teaching students to appreciate pleasant feelings that come from being quiet and still. Students learn to feel sensations of inner peace and pride in controlling body parts and shapes. Self-discipline develops as they learn to manage movement, gradually at first and then for increasing lengths of time and with more variety. Eventually students learn to express ideas and emotions through dance in original ways as they become more self-regulated and can make their bodies respond as desired.

Dance Develops Self-Control and Confidence.

> *Graceful movement is just the right amount of energy for what you're doing.* (Michael Ballard)

One of the first things strangers notice about a good friend of mine is her posture. She sits and stands very erect. She walks with fluidity and grace. The ways she holds and moves her body communicate that she is a leader—and she is. A former department chair at a college, she now heads up several community groups, including the Jackson, Michigan, Storyfest.

Famed dancer Jacques D'Amboise explains that by learning to take control of your body, "you discover that you can take control of your life" (quoted in Hanna, 1999, p. 29). He speaks from personal experience. His mother enrolled him in ballet school to get him off the streets of Harlem. Today he runs the National Dance Institute that partners with New York schools.

As students learn to control their bodies, endurance and strength develop, enabling them to feel more poised. Satisfaction with one's body and self-confidence increase as students attain mastery of body parts and movements that extend their range of expression. We all want to feel good about our bodies. Dance can develop self-assurance as students have successful experiences in solving problems creatively through dance. For example, teachers can ask students to show different ways to walk across the room or how George Washington might have stood as he was installed as the first president. Students might look at a painting of President Washington and try to hold his pose. Students may go further to try to walk as Mr. Washington would, right after the scene in the art.

Dance Is Integrated Brain–Body Work.

I see the dance being used as a means of communication between soul and soul—to express what is too deep, too fine for word. (Ruth St. Denis)

Gardner (1996) includes dance under body-kinesthetic intelligence, and neurologist Mark Hallett (1999) claims that using the body maximizes brain use. Any athletic work at peak performance can use close to 100% of the brain, which dispels the myth that humans never use more than 10%. Dance is athleticism with artistry. The added dimension of the aesthetic permits creative and inner self-expression, crucial for happiness and satisfaction.

Dance is highly intellectual, with a mind–body connection that "activates far more brain areas than traditional seatwork" (Jensen, 2001, p. 72). The whole person is involved in dance construction.

During dance, students use multiple intelligences, not just kinesthetic intelligence. Patterns and counting are essential, so math and logic are used. Spatial intelligence is used to visualize floor patterns and choreograph. We dance to music, responding to the rhythm and melody. Dance has its own vocabulary to construct stories, so it draws on verbal intelligence. It is interpersonal when you dance with or work with others (e.g., choreographers) and intrapersonal in that it involves reflecting on personal development. Finally, dance includes naturalistic knowing because it is based on moves in nature, and dances often have nature themes (Nelson, 1998).

Through dance we communicate what we think, feel, and value. When students dance ideas from science, social studies, or math, they gain new views on subjects, because the physical body is engaged, which activates more areas of the brain. "Dance provides a primary medium for expression involving the total self (not just a part, like the voice) or totally separated from the physical self (like painting or sculpture)" (Fleming, 1990, p. 5). Savvy teachers help chil-

dren become "whole" people through the integration of the arts. Dance integration, in particular, involves more holistic learning than other arts because of the brain-body connection.

Dance Is Healthy.

My heart lifted my feet, and I danced. (Nathan of Nemirov)

An ad from the American Heart Association displays a silhouetted child in front of a TV. The boldface caption reads, "Caution: Children Not At Play." Obesity levels of children have risen dramatically as youth mimic the passive television viewing habits of adults. On the average, they now spend about 4 hours a day viewing versus doing. Some spend more and the more they watch, the lower their test scores. What about during the school day? How much learning time is spent using the body in active physical ways? How much of the ballooning statistics about "hyperactive" kids has to do with children's bodies rejecting "sit still" classrooms?

Dance is exercise, and exercise makes us healthy. It increases blood circulation and muscle tone. Dance burns up calories. Like any exercise, dance triggers the brain to produce endorphins, natural pain killers, and catecholamine, an alertness hormone. No wonder children enjoy dance; they are out of pain and full of energy. West Virginia schools are taking advantage of the motivational power of dance to make children active. The popular video dance game "Dance Dance Revolution" is now provided to kids by the Public Employees Insurance Agency (Barker, 2005).

Dance is another kind of therapy or emotional release to alleviate stress. A University of Illinois study shows complex physical learning may even compensate for prenatal alcohol exposure (Smith, 2003). Dance used before, during, or after a lesson can increase physical readiness for cognitive learning by activating more brain areas.

Dance Satisfies the Aesthetic Need for Beauty.

There is hardly a sight more beautiful than a graceful human being. When students have opportunities to view dances and participate in dance creation, they increase their aesthetic sensitivity. Creative dance emphasizes the expressive and imaginative potential of children, so dance can also add beauty to our students' lives. Maslow (1970) believes the need for beauty is high level and must be met for a person to feel fulfilled or "self-actualized." Beauty uplifts us and can give hope in the way a potted flower on a rotted window sill can. It creates a sense that life is worth living. Captivating ethnic dances, such as the hora from Jewish culture, stretches children's concepts of beauty and offers information about how diverse groups celebrate. What's more, it is harder to hate people who give gifts of beauty in the forms of dance, art, and music. The spectacle of a cultural dance performance is a powerful bridge. Even more powerful is sharing in the dance making!

Dance Is a Path to Cultural Understanding and Expression.

> *Sometimes dancing and music can describe a true image of the customs of a country better than words in a newspaper.* (Gene Kelly)

All art forms are vehicles for the ideas and values of their creators. Dance, like any art, reflects the time and place in which it is created. This makes dance an important means of coming to understand values and customs of other cultures (Hanna, 1999). For example, Batoto Yetu is a Harlem dance company that uses dance to pass on African cultural history to children. They believe this understanding builds respect and hope (*This Morning,* CBS, April 11, 1997).

Social studies units are particularly appropriate contexts for using dance. Students feel the mood and values of those who created dance forms in contrasting periods of history. For example, the 400-year-old dance form ballet reflected Medici court life, while clogging gives clues to mountain life in North Carolina. Dances reflect changing values, tastes, economic conditions, and social trends. From the limbo to the lambada, there is rich material in these dances to reveal what groups think and feel. Through dance investigations, historical events can be understood from a different point of view. For example, Native American ghost dancers in the 19th century created dances to celebrate the return of the lands taken by the U.S. government. The dancers tried to conjure up the powers of their ancestors and created such a fervor among tribes that the government eventually forbade the dance. When ghost dancing continued, U.S. soldiers attacked and killed a camp of dancers, including many children. Students can view dances (live or on video—see PBS website) and analyze them for the messages they send.

Dance Is a Cross-Curricular Learning Tool.

Students involved in dance learn effective ways to use the body as a language. Dance elements become conceptual anchors students can use across disciplines to show understanding. Most vocabulary meanings can be danced, especially verbs, adverbs, and emotion words like *contrite* and *ferocious*. Choreography involves composing and gives options to organize thoughts; it parallels written composition. In science and social studies dance is now used in schools across the country to both learn and demonstrate understanding of processes such as making fossil fuels, planet rotation, life cycles, and the decay process. Students use their bodies to gain deep understanding of key concepts such as dependence, interrelationships, and cause–effect. All of

these examples show how dance can extend self-expression capacities. As students learn the dance elements of body, energy, space, and time, they simultaneously learn to analyze and categorize their thinking. Many concepts, such as rhythm, space, and shape, are used in music, drama, and the visual arts as well. Other dance concepts such as balance can be extended to areas such as physics.

Dance Gives Joy.

> *The place of the dance is within the heart.* (Tom Robbins)

Imagine a group of people dancing. Eyes sparkle. They smile and laugh as energy explodes in whirls and wiggles. People constantly surprise themselves as they discover ways bodies can be made to move to a musical beat or an internal rhythm. It is hard to be still.

Dancing can also give the feeling of being "high" or uplifted, just as any creative activity can. Dance and creative movement are entertaining to do and view. Nothing is more interesting than people watching. What is it that attracts attention? How people walk, how they hold their head and body, how they get from one point to the next, how they move to music—all these images captivate us because they say so much about each person. Perhaps that's part of why generations have been influenced by Elvis Presley's hip and leg moves and Michael Jackson's moon walking. Elizabeth Wall, a Richmond, Virginia, principal, explains that students changed when dance was integrated at her school. They expressed "a sense of humor and as attitudes and values changed, self-control developed . . . . They looked forward to school" (Fleming, 1990, p. 32).

Blueprint II: Arts Literacy: Content and Skills

> *Dance is music made visible.* (George Balanchine)

Meaningful integration is defined by the quality and degree to which teachers teach dance concepts and skill, as well as how they use dance as a communication tool. This is analogous to teaching children *to* read and write so they can both understand what they read and express ideas and feelings through writing. Children need to know dance vocabulary and how to construct dance phrases, sentences, and whole works. In dance this composition process is called *choreography*, but it is basically the same as writing any complete work. There should be information and artistry in the introduction, development, and conclusion framework.

What Do Teachers Need to Know to Integrate Dance?

The pursuit of dance literacy for integration purposes begins with teachers personally experiencing creative dance. This book can't give that experience. There is no substitute for actually dancing. Hopefully the following information will give enough of a picture to motivate readers to seek out experiences to experiment with the language of dance.

The dance literacy level needed by teachers is contingent upon the dance literacy now expected of students. Ready Reference 10.5 lists the *National Dance Standards* (K–8) for students. Standards for what classroom teachers should know and be able to do in dance were developed by the Interstate New Teacher Assessment and Support Consortium and can be downloaded from the website *www.ccsso.org/intasc*.

In elementary and middle school dance literacy basically involves studying (1) the historical, social, and cultural role of dance in our lives; (2) communication through dance by creating dance, understanding dance language, and performing; and (3) valuing dance for its aesthetic contributions. Classroom teachers need to know:

- Definitions of dance
- Purposes and roles of dance
- Dance elements
- Dance processes
- Genre, forms, and styles
- People of dance
- Sources for dance-related materials
- Teaching approaches

Definitions of Dance.

> *Dance is not about something. Dance is something.* (Mary Joyce, 1994)

It does seem that animals dance. Dogs can be trained to twirl and jump, as can bears and cats. My nephew is a horse trainer and the range of moves he teaches the horses resemble dance, with steps, rhythms, even changing levels. But do animals dance?

In every art form the question is "what makes it?" Dance is no exception and follows the other art forms in emphasizing intention. Dance is movement aware of itself. It transcends just taking steps and is distinct from pantomime (drama). It is communication through movement that intends to express ideas and feelings for aesthetic purposes. Dance is artful movement.

Most people expect children to master control of their bodies, but they may not understand how dance is a part of this. Dance takes students further by adding another vehicle for creative problem solving—the body. The same inno-

vative thinking that produced hip-hop is used to invent in the worlds of science and business. The crossovers are exemplified in the many dancers who have become successful in other fields.

Note: The word *dance* remains a touchy term in some communities, so some schools call it *creative movement*.

Dance versus movement.   As I type this sentence, I am moving. This is not dance. And yet I can take my hands from the keys and begin to play with "typing movement." Now I experience the feel of my fingers moving and the shape of my hands on an abstract level. I can use other body parts to create the lightness of touch and the irregular rhythms of typing. I can do this with my toes, torso, and hips. The movement is no longer done to accomplish a task but to explore how kinesthetics is a way of knowing and feeling.

Movement becomes dance when there is focus on expressing thoughts and feelings; this goes go beyond using physical means to get a job done. Dance is an art, and art is not created nor understood for just function. Even a sequence of skilled gymnastic movements performed to music does not make a dance. "There must be something present that pertains to the spirit of the performer, and the movement must communicate that spirit" (Murray, 1975, p. 18).

Creative movement and dance.   Dance involves becoming conscious of movement. Dance consciousness starts with awareness of body parts: close your eyes and focus on body parts, starting with your head and moving slowly down to your toes. Born of modern dance, creative moment had a heyday in the middle part of the 20th century. Based on natural movement rather than a specific dance genre such as ballet, creative movement became popular in physical education classes. This is logical because dance is movement and, like dance, physical education uses movement to solve problems. The difference is that dance uses kinesthetics to solve problems creatively. The expression of feelings is integral to the process.

In the political fervor over low test scores, dance is being reconsidered as a necessary cog in the wheel of education. The research summarized in Research Update 10.1 has done much to cause a reawakening, as has Gardner's theory of multiple intelligences. Educators are being brought back to the future as Gardner and others show how bodily kinesthetic intelligence is essential to learning. Revelations from the nascent field of neuroscience suggest the arts are the most productive ways to stimulate high achievement over the long haul of schooling (Jensen, 2001).

Purposes and Roles.   The purpose of dance, like all the other art forms, is fundamentally to communicate. The intention of communication in the arts is not only to share information, however. Dance focuses on expression of feelings and values and intends to cause aesthetic response.

Even the early ballets, like *Swan Lake* and *The Sleeping Beauty*, were used to provide ethical instruction in court behavior, in beautiful form (Hanna, 1999).

In the young United States dance was considered a vehicle to acquire social grace and get some exercise. The 20th century brought new educational philosophies, like that of John Dewey. Dance in education was given a boost by progressive educators who emphasized moving and doing. A new focus on self-expression triggered an evolution in emphasis, from ballet to folk to modern dance (Hanna, 1999). Martha Graham forever altered our concept of what dance could be. Isadora Duncan and others took creative expression through dance further. Creative movement became creative dance that uses natural, even everyday movements. People began to see that dance could be more than learning to execute the five codified positions of ballet.

Today we still enjoy the beauty and messages of ballet. We also enjoy and learn about cultures from world dances and are amazed at the athleticism of dancers like Pilobolus. Social dances from salsa to street dancing permit a wide range of creative expression. The diversity of tastes and preferences and inventiveness of our country is apparent in the dance menu from which we select. These can be used as teaching and learning tools in our classrooms.

Dance Literacy. William Safire points out that we have certain words that bridge the gulf between spoken and unspoken language. These mega-words overarch our thinking. Words like *expression, understanding, communicating,* and *knowing* are not limited by words (1991). We use these mega-words to describe the most important things we want to happen in learning, and they absolutely describe what happens in the arts.

The study of dance is rich in expression, but it is not devoid of words. Dance has its own "vocabulary" used to create dance phrases and sentences. These, just as in written language, can become full compositions of meaning. Martha Graham, the single greatest figure in modern dance, was hailed in her obituary for "creating a language" with movement (Hanna, 1999, p. 52). She used a special vocabulary that included "percussive contractions and releases and dramatic stories" (p. 15).

Dance Elements.

Technique—bodily control—must be mastered only because the body must not stand in the way of a soul's expression. (La Meri)

Several systems are used for categorizing dance meaning-making concepts. This is the symbol system of dance that can be consciously used to create movement for specific purposes and contexts. The following is a simple system of remembering dance elements that is useful for classroom teachers and students. (Thanks to Randy Barron, dance educator affiliated with the John F. Kennedy Center for the Performing Arts, for this idea.) It is easy to remember because it is organized around the acronym BEST: body, energy, space, and time. Ready Reference 10.1 summarizes BEST.

Ready Reference 10.1 **BEST Dance Elements and Concepts**

B=Body, E=Energy, S=Space, T=Time

Body

Parts: head, neck, torso (hips, abdomen, shoulders, back), arms and elbows, hands and wrists, fingers, legs, knees, and feet (ankles and toes)
Shapes: curved, twisted, angular, small-large, flat-rounded
Actions or moves:

- Nonlocomotor: stretch, bend, twist, rise, fall, circle, shake, suspend, sway, swing, collapse
- Locomotor: walk, leap, hop, jump, gallop, skip, slide

Energy

- Attack: smooth or sharp
- Weight: strong or light
- Strength or tension: tight or loose and relaxed
- Flow: sudden or sustained, bound or free

Space

Level: low, middle, and high
Direction: forward, backward, sideways, up, down
Size: large and small
Place or destination: where we move to
Pathways: patterns on the floor or air (e.g., circular)
Focus: where the dancer looks

Time

Rhythm: pulse or beat
Speed: time or tempo
Accent: light or strong emphasis
Duration: length
Phrases: dance sentences, patterns, and combinations (e.g., twist, twist, twirl, and freeze)

Choreographic Principles:
Repetition, contrast, unity, variety, balance, patterns, and transitions used to make dance

Body parts, shapes, actions.   We use all body parts to communicate, both those outside and inside. Think of the ways to move just your little finger or the effect on the body when you tighten inner muscles. Body shape includes ways to form body parts to create everything from pleasant round and curved shapes to sharp angry angles and pointed shapes. Then there are all the ways to move in place or through a space. Stationary actions are called *nonlocomotor* and include stretch, bend, twist, rise, fall, circle, shake, suspend, sway, swing, and collapse. Movement through space is called *locomotor movement* and includes actions such as walk, run, leap, hop, jump, gallop, skip, and slide.

Energy is the force a person uses and signals the mood the dancer intends. It includes the person's attack (smooth or sharp), weight (heavy or light), strength or tension (tight or loose), and flow (sudden or sustained).

Space is the personal or shared area in which the body is used. Space is filled up by changing levels (low, middle, and high), directions, size, place or destination, and pathways (how to get to a destination—directly or in an indirect way). Focus or concentration, or where a person is looking, is also included.

Time is another element used during movement. It includes rhythm (pulse, beat), speed or tempo, accent or emphasis (light or strong), duration (length), and phrases (dance "sentences," or patterns and combinations of all dif-ferent kinds of movements). For example, "three different middle-level slow, wringing shapes" is a phrase that may create a message about discomfort or struggle.

Dance Processes.

The activity is the art. (Mary Joyce)

Choreography is dance making—creating, composing, and improvising movement to make meaning. Choreography involves planning and performing—or getting others to perform your designs. When students learn to make dances about concepts in science and social studies, they are in-volved in intense creative problem solving (CPS) as they apply choreography principles, like using repetition, con-trast, unity, variety, balance, and pattern. They learn to or-ganize and structure their thinking using BEST elements to create dance phrases and sentences and organize them into themes with variations. Like in music, dance can use "call and response" and take a narrative structure and tell a story. It is possible to learn to write the plan for any dance down using a notation system invented by Hungarian dancer Rudolf Laban (Ready Reference 10.2).

Dance can also be viewed live or on video or film. To understand and appreciate what the dance is saying requires knowing how to "read" the language of dance. This involves

Ready Reference 10.2   Qualities of Movement

Rudolf von Laban (1879–1958) was a dancer and a movement scientist. He studied the elements that create "qualities of movement" and discovered how mood is cre-ated by combining eight actions, using different degrees of effort and amounts of space. The eight actions are charted here against "sustained or sudden, strong or light, direct or indirect." For example, wringing is a twist-ing and turning movement that can be sustained or sud-den. It can be strong or light and involves several body parts going in different directions (versus direct move-ment toward a target).

Use this chart to coach students to use different amounts of effort and space with the eight actions. This kind of exploration expands thinking through dance/movement.

3 Choices:	Sudden/Sustained?	Strong/Light?	Direct/Indirect?
8 Actions:			
Wring			
Thrust			
Slash			
Float			
Glide			
Press			
Flick			
Dab			

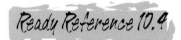

Dance Forms and Styles

African	Country/western	Irish	Social
Asian	Courtship	Jazz	Square
Ballet	Creative	Jitterbug/swing	Street
Ballroom	Electric slide	Minuet	Tap
Belly	Flamenco	Polka	Theatrical
Caribbean	Folk and national	Reels	Turkey trot
Charleston	Fox trot	Religious/liturgical	Twist
Circle	Hip hop	Salsa	Waltz
Clogging	Indian	Shag	Warrior

Ready Reference 10.4   Well-Known Dancers

Martha Graham (modern dance)	Natalia Makarova (ballet)
Jacques D' Amboise (ballet)	Isadora Duncan (modern dance)
Mikhail Baryshnikov (ballet)	Ben Vereen (many styles)
Gene Kelly (modern)	Gregory Hines (many styles)
Fred Astaire (ballroom)	Alvin Ailey (modern dance)
Rudolf Nureyev (ballet)	Rudolf Laban (modern dance)

noticing how the dance elements are used and responding to the effects created by dancers' bodies. Understanding is thus increased, which results in increased appreciation and deeper aesthetic knowing.

People of Dance.   Teachers need to know some of the people who have made dance what it is today. Units can focus on a particular dancer or dance as either as a reflection of a time period or culture (Ready Reference 10.3). Dances and dancers can also change thinking of a time or culture. We see that today with the influence of hip-hop music and dance on youth. That influence can be positive or negative. Either way, it needs to be acknowledged that it happens before we can direct influence. Suppressing any communication just makes it more seductive for children.

Dance offers a range of career opportunities from dancer to choreographer, dance critic, dance historian, and dance teacher. All of these options belong in a career education unit. Ready Reference 10.4 lists examples of dances and dancers that can be integrated.

Genre, Forms, and Styles.   Throughout history people have loved to invent dances. Today we are blessed with a gourmet menu to choose from as we seek personal enjoy-

ment or plan innovative ways to teach. From ballet, tap, and jazz, we can find values, beliefs, and lifestyles recorded. In folk dances we find cultural insight, as we can with fad dances. As the Macarena and electric slide slip from the scene, in comes hot hot salsa. Ready Reference 10.3 lists dances that can be integrated into social studies, understood through health science and math, and read for their messages.

Sources for Materials

Once you have some space, dance is pretty cheap to integrate. It is helpful, over time, to accumulate music CDs, DVDs/videos, pictures of dances and dancers, books, and other material to use as references and in lessons. For example, jazz as a reflection of the time in which it was invented cannot be understood without seeing it. Check the websites at the end of the chapter for places to start on the Internet and some video sources.

Music for Dance.   Although there is a close association between music and dance, music is not necessary for dance integration. It is useful for warm-ups, movement exploration, or free dance (Joyce, 1994). Children's songs that just give movement directions to follow are like coloring

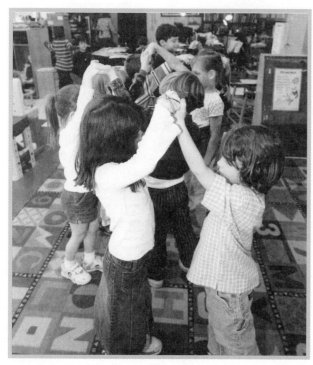

Learning history through dance: minuet.

books—they do not encourage creative thinking (Stinson, 1988). When music is used, choose music for dance that promotes creative, not stereotyped, movement and is rhythmic but not too complicated. Shorter selections of simple classical music (Brahm's Fourth Symphony, Debussy's "Clouds," Wagner's "Forest Murmurs," and Copeland's "Billy the Kid") work well, as do children's songs that suggest, but don't dictate, movement, such as those by Ella Jenkins. Electronic and loud music promotes bump and grind movements inappropriate to school. Go through your personal collections of tapes and CDs and look for music that:

- Makes you feel like moving or dancing.
- Has a predictable structure; it feels like it goes somewhere.
- Has a clear quality (could invite marching or delicate movements).
- Has no lyrics, is instrumental (no words), or words that aren't important to the quality (e.g., Enya).
- Has different tempos and moods.
- Uses a variety of instruments (saxophone, piano, violins, drum, etc.).
- Includes folk music from different countries, ethnic groups, or time periods (e.g., Putamayo's "A World Instrumental Collection").
- Is classical sounding, especially soloists and chamber ensembles (e.g., Chopin). Symphonies can overwhelm.

Consider CDs from these musical artists:

Bobby McFerrin ("Circlesongs")
Chuck Mangione
Cirque du Soleil
Enya
Gabrielle Roth and the Mirrors
George Winston
Gotan Project
Kenny G
Latin Colors of the World
Mickey Hart ("Planet Drum")
Paul Winter
Tomita
Windham Hill
Wynton Marsalis
Yanni

See categories of music especially helpful for classroom teachers in Chapter 12. One resource is *Music for Creative Dance Vol. 1–4* available at *www.ravennaventures.com.*

Dancing songs. Many songs are naturally connected to movement (e.g., "The Grand Ole Duke of York"). Many action or movement songs, singing games, and song dances are available. Hap Palmer, Little Richard, Ella Fitzgerald, and Steve and Greg all have produced movement-oriented collections on tape and CD. Special songs with dances include twist music, hokey pokey, chicken dance, and the pony. Richard Simmons's workout tapes have examples as well. It is important to keep in mind that teaching specific dance steps or moves is not the goal. These are good for warm-ups mostly, and students should be encouraged to create, not just imitate. To really stretch the imagination, ask students to move in ways that contrast with the song (e.g., what would not fit with a lullaby?).

Teaching Approach

Dance integration has little to do with teachers directing students to mimic, step by step, until a dance is learned. It has to do with directing creative movement explorations that can become whole compositions when a sequence of movements is ordered into a beginning, middle, and end. The classroom teacher's purposes are best served by a focus on using dance for problem solving. This begins with guided discovery about the nature of movement. This open-ended approach embraces a variety of acceptable solutions. Creating dances and learning about dance aspects should be planned times for students to feel the joy that results from trying out their own ideas to solve dance puzzles.

At times dance integration does include students learning structured folk or social dances. But the mainstay of a classroom teacher's repertoire of dance strategies is not demonstrating combinations of memorized steps. If dance is to be a useful and joyful meaning maker, the focus needs to be on using dance language in creative ways to express thoughts and feelings. This symbol system, like those of all communication forms such as verbal language, math, art, and music, consists of teachable elements—tools for meaning making.

Dance Isn't Pantomime.   Pantomime is often confused with creative dance. Pantomime does use movement without words, but it is a drama form in which people take roles and pretend to be something or someone. Pantomime can become imitation rather than creative movement.

Teachers need to be clear about the different purposes and processes of dance versus pantomime. Movement is more abstract in dance. The focus is on the moving itself, not on pretending to move *like* an animal or plant. If teachers say "move like a cat," students usually pantomime stereotyped paw and claw movements. For a dance frame of thinking the same direction can be given with a changed focus: Show me the shape of a cat's body, how it walks, how its muscles move. How would it walk backwards or on a low level? These directions cause students to kinesthetically explore options for the concept of cat movements. When dance is used for problem solving, students are urged to consider the movement possibilities *of* an idea, rather than *in* the idea itself. This is particularly important when teaching new concepts in science or social studies. The goal is an extended perspective that results from creative problem solving by kids, not mimicry.

Contrasting pantomime and creative dance may seem like splitting hairs, but the teacher who makes the distinction can extend thinking tremendously. For example, when using dance with songs, poems, or children's literature, students are given another dimension of meaning making. Miming Max's wild rumpus in *Where the Wild Things Are* is not dance. It is a worthy way for students to become part of the story and think about characterization. But children can learn to go beyond to work on ways to express anger (the emotion that got Max sent to his room) using a full range of body parts and moves. A concept important to the book's theme is extended through movement. The teacher needs to decide if the goal is to "become" or "be" the character (drama) or probe the movement extensions of important ideas and feelings in a lesson (dance).

Blueprint III: Collaborative Planning

Meaningful dance integration is not a "program of little dances once a year for an audience taught under pressure and presented in the school auditorium" (Murray, 1975, p. 19). The words *integral, integrity,* and *integration* come from the same root that has to do with "essentialness." For integration to have integrity, the arts must be an integral part of learning. This implies that classroom teachers and specialists have dual responsibility for planning, teaching, and assessing both arts and academic content and skills. Co-planning is where it all starts. Planning with specialists helps set the stage for the arts to be more than decoration and entertainment. Dance specialists can put dance in historical and cultural contexts and keep the focus on artistic ways of thinking and doing. Specialists are also good resources for dance-specific "best practices."

Planning Page 3.2 summarizes the unit development process. It begins with examining standards and goals.

National Standards for Dance

The *National Standards for the Arts* is a national consensus document that includes dance standards. These standards have been used across the country to frame state and local standards. The Standards address the question, what should be taught in dance? They are structured around movement-centered and audience-centered goals that suggest sequenced, developmentally appropriate competences for students. The goal is for students to learn basic movements and dance vocabulary so they can understand and create dance composition. Dance Standards are grouped by grades 4, 8, and 12 and were used in the construction of the arts section of the National Assessment for Educational Progress (NAEP).

Standards, goals, objectives, and outcomes in curriculum frameworks only help teachers know *what* to teach. They do not explain *how*. They are meant to serve as a "template without stifling local creativity" (Hanna, 1999, p. 62). The seven Dance Standards students are expected to meet are summarized in Ready Reference 10.5. A full copy of the Standards is available from Music Educator's National Conference (*http://menc.org*). All the strategies and activities in this section of the book and the next chapter relate to one or more of these standards.

For examples of arts standards developed at the state level, go to the website of the department of education in your state. Other states you can use as sources are Kentucky, Ohio, Wisconsin, South Carolina, North Carolina, and Connecticut.

Complementary Connections.   Notice in Wrenn Cook's Unit Plan (Planning Page 10.1) how she listed both dance standards and science standards. Collaborative planning between specialists and classroom teachers focuses on finding overlap. Standards can be scanned and clustered to find connections, but teachers are encouraged to think broadly.

There are obvious connections between history, cultures, and dance, but there are sociology, economic, and

Ready Reference 10.5   Seven National Standards for Dance

Overall focus: Develop self-image, self-expression, and discipline, body awareness, movement exploration, and creative problem solving, appreciation of self and others, cooperation and collaboration, use of musical rhythms, performing for an audience, respect for diversity, and celebration of cultures.

1. *Identifying and demonstrating movement elements and skills in performing dance.* Example: Perform locomotor movements, create shapes, personal space, pathways, move to beat and tempo, show concentration, describe actions and dance elements.

2. *Understanding choreographic principles, processes, and structures.* Example: Create dances with a beginning, middle, and end structure. Improvise and create new movements. Use partner skills such as leading and copying. Create dance phrases.

3. *Understanding dance as a way to create and communicate meaning.* Example: Explain how dance is different from sports and everyday gestures. Discuss what a dance is communicating. Present original dances and explain their meanings.

4. *Applying and demonstrating critical and creative thinking skills in dance.* Example: Find multiple solutions to movement problems. Observe two different dances and discuss differences and similarities. Apply aesthetic criteria to observed dances. Demonstrate appropriate audience etiquette.

5. *Demonstrating and understanding dance in various cultures and historical periods.* Example: Perform folk dances. Share dances from own heritage. Put dance into historical periods based on style and elements. Analyze for values conveyed.

6. *Making connections between dance and healthful living.* Example: Set personal goals for a dancer. Discuss healthy practices. Create and use dance warm-ups.

7. *Making connections between dance and other disciplines.* Example: Create a dance to explain a concept from another discipline. Respond to dance by making a painting, song, or writing about messages it conveys.

Source: Content Standards (material printed in bold type) excerpted from *National Standards for Arts Education*, published by Music Educators National Conference (MENC). Copyright(c)1994 by MENC. Reprinted with permission. The complete National Standards are available at http://menc.org.

psychology links as well (e.g., dance therapy). Wrenn's Classroom Snapshot, which opened this chapter, gives an example of one of many science/dance connections, but weather is full of movement, as are pulleys and levers (weight and balance). Imagine studying gravity by exploring strength, energy, and force using the body. There is much to be understood through exploring the actions that created fossil fuels: time, heat, pressure, no air, and NO movement. Dance and math of dance share many natural links like counting and patterns. Dance is also a communication system, so students can learn how to "speak" its language and use dance elements to compose. There is even a dance writing symbol system, called Laban Notation, that students can use to record original dances. During co-planning look to life in general for dance connections. This potential is often the path to motivating students and convincing them of dance's curricular importance. The goal is authentic connections, not finding ways to make dance another guy on the corner in a mattress suit selling bedding. Planning Pages 10.2 and 10.3 offer examples of connecting dance to health and math.

Arts with Arts Integration

Not to be ignored is integrating dance with the other arts. The arts share a common core of ideas that should be integrated with one another, not just with traditional academic areas. For example, much of visual art involves movement (e.g., draw). Music, art, drama, and dance possess parallel elements such as line and shape. Dance can put sounds and feelings into motion. Students can dance a painting or paint the dances they create. When teachers show how the arts are interwoven, students develop more complex webs of knowing about the world. For example, shape can be explored by painting to music on big paper. Ready Reference 3.5 lists a few of the concepts shared across disciplines.

Unit Centers.   In Chapter 3, five different integrated unit cores were explained. The core or unit body can be extended using the nine academic and arts legs (Planning Page 3.1). For example, a teacher or team might plan integrated lessons and units using one or more of the traditional subject areas as a unit body, or a unit may be a study of a per-

Skeleton Dance Unit Overview

This unit of study is designed for Dance, Grade 3, and can be taught solely within the dance curriculum or as a collaboration between the dance specialist and third-grade classroom teacher.

Unit Goals

1. To develop skillful use of the body by applying underlying principles regarding skeletal alignment and joint movement.
2. To use knowledge of the skeletal system for analytical and creative purposes in dance.

Dance Standards

The Roman numerals relate to the National Standards available at *www.menc.org.*

   I. A/B, H, I, J (extensions I. F, G, K)
  II. B, D, G (extensions A, E)
 III. (extension)
  IV. A (extension E)
   V. A, B (extension C)
  VI. B (extension C)

Third-Grade Science Standards

Students will . . .

   I. A.2.b. Recognize bones, joints, and muscles in the arms and legs of the human body as structural adaptations responsible for movement.

Preassessment (Prior Knowledge)

Before introducing this unit of study, students should have participated in lessons based on dance elements. They should have participated in enough improvisation activities to be comfortable with movement exploration.

In addition, they should have had prior experience in working with partners or in small groups to complete brief composition tasks.

If the classroom teacher already has introduced the skeletal system in the context of the science curriculum, then components of this unit can be shortened or deleted, retaining those concepts and activities that are specifically related to dance.

Lessons

1. Our Bones Help Us Dance
2. Name the Bones
3. Getting Our Bones and Joints Ready to Dance
4. Create a Dance About Our Bones

Bibliography

Frank, M. S., et al. (2000). *Harcourt science.* Orlando, FL: Harcourt.

Meeks, L., & Heit, P. (1999). *Totally awesome health.* Blacklick, OH: Meeks Heit.

Children's Literature

Balestrino, P., & Kelley, T. (1989). *The skeleton inside you.*

Barner, B. (1996). *Dem bones.*

Hvass, U., & Theinhardt, V. (1986). *How my body moves.*

Simon, S. (1998). *Bones: Our skeletal system.*

Anderson, K. C., & Cumbaa, S. (1993). *The bones and skeleton gamebook: A challenging collection of puzzles & projects.*

Source: Wrenn Cook, Columbia College, Columbia, SC.

---

son, genre, or core work and the arts; math, science, social studies, and literacy become the legs that support and move the unit along. Dance and movement would be used as learning tools in such a unit, just as any other leg.

Teachers are encouraged to think creatively and plan units that focus on (1) a dancer or choreographer, (2) a dance (jazz, ballet, tap), (3) dance questions (e.g., Why do people dance? How do dances emerge?), or (4) a core dance work (e.g., minuet and early American history) or even a dance-based children's book such as *Sometimes I Dance Mountains* (Baylor et al.). Math, science, social studies, reading and language arts, and the other art forms would be the support legs. Involving students in research on dancers and

dance genre enables them to connect literature, social studies, and other art forms as they search for the whys and hows that motivated the creation of dance throughout human history. Planning Page 6.1 shows planning for an author-artist study. Examine how dance is used.

Topics to be explored through dance can also be solicited from students (feelings, interests, questions, and concerns). These can develop into whole units or a single integrated lesson. To create the dance connection, students are asked to list movements that correspond to the topic. Movements can be explored in unison and then in small groups and can grow into full compositions with a three-part "frozen shape-moves-frozen shape" structure dance using BEST elements.

Dance and Health (Fifth Grade)

Two-pronged focus: (1) circulatory system, (2) dance elements

Dance standards: 1–4, 6–7 (Ready Reference 10.6)

Student Objectives: Students should be able to:

1. Show dance phrases that express differing heart-beats (rhythms).
2. Show movement qualities that express changes in the circulatory system (e.g., flow).
3. Use body shapes and personal space to show heart's shapes and movement.
4. Maintain focus.
5. Work cooperatively in groups.

Teaching Procedure: The teacher will: (S= students)

Introduction

1. Signal for attention and tell S to sit in personal space.
2. Remind S about posted rules.
3. Use riddle routine (riddle about heart on board).
4. Ask what they remember about circulatory system. Use visual of circulatory system.
5. Show how to take pulse and move to beat. Use slit drum.
6. Ask "What if . . .?" and "Show me . . ." beats and rhythms during rest, anger, etc.

Development

1. Read aloud fantasy journey and ask S to show with body shape and focus what is described (about heart changing rhythms).
2. Choral read and move to "Dr. Heart" chant to show heartbeat and blood flow. Repeat and increase rate.
3. Pause to ask about flow (sustained movement) and rhythm or beat (percussive).
4. Play "Tranquility" tape and ask S to create a sustained or percussive movement to go with it.
5. Group S to create a dance with a beginning-middle-end to show flow and beat. Challenge S to include creative use of the "circle."
6. Circulate and give descriptive feedback as S work.

Conclusion

1. Divide class so one-half observes while others dance.
2. Audience gives feedback about concentration, percussive versus sustained beats, and shapes (e.g., circles to represent cycle).
3. Repeat chant.
4. Ask what they learned.

Assessment and Evaluation

1. Observe S and use checklist with range of criteria from "clear" to "not present" based on objectives 1 to 5.

Note: Stinson (1988, p. 51) recommends staying away from the topic of "superheroes" because of aggressive actions. Also, avoid stereotyped movements such as sitting "Indian style" or doing "war dances" during Native American studies.

Two-Pronged Lesson Plans.

I now know that a reading experience involves more than just books and words. It involves the child's life and interest as a source, his mind for thinking, his voice for verbalization (stories, poems, songs), his hands for writing, and his whole body for a deeper understanding through creative movement and dance. A child must sense and respond for true learning and understanding." (Loretta Woolard, fourth-grade teacher, quoted in Fleming, 1990)

Planning lessons that integrate dance begins with deciding that important concepts and skills will be taught about both

a subject and about dance. The planning begins with meaning: selecting topics and problems and then deriving themes and questions to investigate. To use dance successfully, the lesson focus should be full of movement possibilities—actions and shapes should readily come to mind. A topic of "fruits and vegetables," for example, may have more possibilities for sensory explorations than for movement. If a topic involves mostly pantomime or pretending in role, it is harder to extend to dance. For example, getting dressed involves zipping, buttoning, and tying. All of these movements are so specific that teachers need to stretch to open them up to additional movement possibilities: "Think of such things as tying yourself into a knot or buttoning your hand to your knee" (Stinson, 1988, p. 51).

When dance is integrated, teachers need to be honest about using it in respectful ways and not trivialize it. Both dance and the subject it is integrated with should be treated as areas of substance. For example, a circle-cycle dance cre-

Dance and Math (Third Grade)

Two-Pronged Focus: (1) fractions and problem solving; (2) dance elements: body shapes, levels, and choreography

Dance Standards: See Ready Reference 10.5.

Student Objectives: Students will:

1. Use high, middle, and low levels and body shapes that are curved, straight, angular, and twisted to show: (1) equivalent fractions and (2) fractional parts of wholes and sets that have been divided into as many as 16 parts.
2. Maintain focus.
3. Work cooperatively in groups.

Materials: Two charts, fraction problem cards

Teaching Procedure: The teacher will: (S= students)

Introduction

1. Signal for S to group into regularly assigned squads. Remind students about posted rules.
2. Tell objectives of lesson for fractions and dance.
3. Play inspirational music and do warm-up routine.

Development

1. Show charts of four body shapes and three levels. With each S in personal space, call a shape and level in which to freeze (e.g., curved low or straight high).
2. Show fraction chart to review: whole, 1/2, 1/3, 1/4, 1/5, 1/8, 1/16. Ask S to show each (e.g., show 1/2 by dividing into two groups). Do for each, letting S figure out how to arrange themselves.

3. Ask about equivalent fractions (review from previous lesson). Give examples: 1/2 = 2/4. Group to work in squads to show a fraction problem through dance. Ask how they could create a three part dance for 1/2 transforming to 2/4 starting with frozen shapes/levels, adding movements, and then ending with a frozen shape. Brainstorm and try their ideas.
4. Break into squads and give each a fraction problem card.
5. Circulate and give feedback as S work.

Conclusion
Performances

1. Divide class so one-half observes while others dance.
2. Audience observes to figure out fraction problem.
3. Audience gives feedback on what worked.
4. Reverse groups and repeat.
5. Ask what they learned about dance and fractions.

Assessment and evaluation

1. Teachers/self/peer evaluation checklist with criteria (objectives).
2. Use from "clear" to "not present" based.
3. Photograph students to aid assessment.

Source: Adapted from Mr. Crabb and Mrs. Peterson, Lady's Island Elementary School, Beaufort, SC.

---

ated to a steady beat for a lesson on the circulatory system truly helps students feel the heart pumping and beating, the blood moving, and how the whole system operates on a cyclical basis. Planning Page 10.2 shows such a lesson. Also see Planning Page 10.3 that shows a math and dance lesson.

Dance-Based Field Units. Figure skating is now the most popular Olympic event in terms of audience viewing. This is not surprising since it combines athleticism with artistry that engages emotions like no other competitive event. This artistry happens to be a kind of dance. Unfortunately, most of us just watch on television, and miss the emotional impact of a live performance.

A fifth kind of dance-based unit focuses on an event, usually a field trip to see a live dance performance. "Arts-based field trips aren't isolated experiences, but part of what

we've been learning," says Mary-Mac Jennings, first-grade teacher at Ashley River Creative Arts. "When we went to see 'Peter and the Wolf,' the children couldn't stop talking about how the dancers were doing what they had learned."

Dance concert attendance is an invaluable opportunity for children to see skilled amateurs and professionals perform dances from traditional ballet to the South Carolina shag. Concerts by local companies, including those at colleges, as well as national touring events such as "Riverdance," expand students' personal visions of career possibilities. They also offer the educational opportunity to disband negative cultural and gender stereotypes associated with dance. Nothing is more powerful than live performance to show children the athletic connections to dance and to help them see strong men and women with the skills, artistry, and confidence to use movement expressively.

Without school-sponsored trips many children experience only in-house assemblies, few of which will be devoted to dance. Just as with other field trips, however, dance expeditions should be carefully selected and planned to align with curricular goals. Critical to maintaining the integrity of dance excursions is the three-part structure discussed in Chapter 3: (1) prepare students for the trip, (2) help them become mentally focused during the trip, and (3) follow up with debriefing about what was learned. Live performances are different from video or television dramas because the audience shares in the event. There is a feeling of spontaneity that causes the performers to respond to the energy of the audience. Here is a short checklist to help prepare:

1. Make clear expectations for audience etiquette so that everyone enjoys the performance and the dancers are respected. A discussion of behavior consequences is important. This means the teacher must know the expected behaviors for the site being visited. It is useful to ask students to role-play how to act before, during, and after the concert.

2. To set the purpose make sure students know how the trip is integral to the unit; ask them to generate questions they want answered during the trip. Cue sheets (i.e., worksheets listing things to notice during the performance) help students anticipate what is coming. Ask for materials to help prepare cue sheets for the class so they can experience a sense of discovery about the moves dancers make (e.g., "That was a triple lutz!"). Concept mini-lessons that focus on key terms such as *choreographer* or the use of music, sets, and costumes help students become mindful viewers.

3. Give guidelines about what students are expected to learn from the field trip and hold them accountable. If students know there is to be an assessment (not just a test, either), they are more focused on the trip's purpose and less on socializing. Review study sheets and general questions before the trip that are to be used when the class returns. For example: What is one thing you could follow up on and find out more about? How did the experience make you feel? Why? What did the trip have to do with what we've been studying? Show the most important thing you learned about _____ using art materials, drama, music, or dance and movement. Write a poem about the trip. Write a letter convincing me that trips like these are important in school. Write a thank you note to _____.

4. Children will need reminders during performances. Nonverbal signals can be seen across a theatre and reinforce the concept that communication can be without words. It is particularly helpful to use sign language for "sit down," "line up," and "listen." See books of sign such as Riekehof's *The Joy of Signing* (1987).

5. It is important for teachers to participate as learners and viewers, as well as managers of their classes. Teachers should be models of good audience etiquette.

6. Take time to debrief after the dance, even on the bus. Encourage discussions about a variety of points of view. Ask, "What did you notice? How did it make you feel? What in the dance made you feel that way? What was it really about? What was missing? What was the choreographer trying to say?"

Field trips to concerts are not unusual. What is unusual is the meaningful integration of these trips. Meaningful integration begins with planning. See the more detailed Field Trip Guidelines in the Appendix.

Observation and Discovery Trips. Field trips don't have to mean a bus trip. Students often get so excited about trips that they can't get serious about learning. We can take only a few field trips, but short, close-to-school trips can be practice for larger trips and are very valuable. For example, a walk around the block to discover how people move as they do their work or play can give insight into the Body, Energy, Space, and Time dance elements used in everyday life. Observation walks to see how plants and animals move can be a rich foundation to refine students' use of verbs to describe movements.

Blueprint IV: Aesthetic Learning Environment

I remember a student who was in trouble for frequently getting up to sharpen his pencil. When asked why his pencil tip broke so often he replied, "It doesn't. I just need an excuse to move." Hopefully, the curtain has closed on rigid classroom procedures that require children to sit still most of the day on hard chairs.

An environment that promotes dance depends on two main factors: teacher attitude and space. Teachers show they value dance in many ways. Most important is the second factor: Dance requires space. Some schools now have designated areas for dance shared by teachers, but dance integration mostly happens in classrooms. Many teachers permanently rearrange the room in a U shape with desks in groups so an open area is left. Others just become efficient at getting students to push back the desks.

What else is common in a dance-rich environment? First of all, the space needs to be safe, as do the materials. Here are other ideas to consider:

*   Space has no protruding objects.
*   Floors are responsive (concrete is unsafe).
*   Musical instruments should be available, especially rhythm for dance accompaniment and ones that represent other cultures.
*   Music CDs and CD player should be on hand.

- Useful props include scarves, streamers, elastic bands, bean bags, balloons, and rubber-backed carpet squares.
- DVD player can be used to view dance-related videos.
- Dance-based books should be readily available.
- Display areas should feature dance photos, dance elements, and Word Wall of dance/movement-related words (student collected).

The *Opportunity to Learn Standards* were created to help schools plan for arts learning. One section is about facilities and materials. South Carolina educators have converted the standards into a useful checklist that can be downloaded for dance and the other arts at *www.winthrop.edu/ABC/*.

Blueprint V: Literature as a Core Art Form

There are dance-based books in every genre, from biography to folktales, including books about dancing and dancers. For example, *I Feel Like Dancing: A Year with Jacques*

D'Amboise and the National Dance Institute (Barboza) can be paired with the award-winning video by the same title. Find dance-based books to link with historical units by using the list of dancers and dances in Ready References 10.3 and 10.4. Find picture books using references like *A to Zoo* listed in Ready Reference 4.6.

Any literature that includes movement or movement imagery has potential for dance and creative movement as well. For example, *Sometimes I Dance Mountains* (Baylor et al., 1973) has a lovely poetic text that can stimulate many movement explorations before, during, or after the book is read, and rhythm instruments can be added. Isadora's (1976) *Max* can be used to relate dance and sports. Carl Sandburg's "Lines Written for Gene Kelly to Dance To" is a poem that asks the famous dancer to dance such ideas as the alphabet and the wind. The entire poem offers wonderful possibilities. Try it with a musical background like Leroy Anderson's "Sandpaper Ballet." (Say a line, turn up the volume, fade down, say the next line, and so on.) Ready Reference 10.6 presents an annotated sampling of dance-based children's literature.

Invite students to find books about dance or ones with movement. Set up a permanent display that highlights

Ready Reference 10.6   Dance–Based Children's Literature

Ackerman, K. (1988). *Song and dance man*. Random House. (grandpa relives his vaudeville days)

Archambault, J., Martin, B., & Rand, T. (1986). *Barn dance*. Henry Holt. (animals of the farm gather together with a skinny little boy for a hoedown in the barn)

Barboza, S. (1992). *I feel like dancing: A year with Jacques D'Amboise and the National Dance Institute*. Crown. (three students spend a year at the Institute)

Bierhorts, J. (1997). *The dancing fox: Arctic folktales*. (18 Inuit folktales)

Gauch, P., & Ichikawa, S. (1992). *Bravo, Tanya*. Philomel. (girl loves to dance in the meadow but can't in ballet class)

Glassman, B. (2001). *Mikhail Baryshnikov: Dance genius*. Gale Group.

Glover, S., & Weber, B. (2000). *Savion!: My life in tap*. Morrow.

Gray, L. (1999). *My mama had a dancing heart*. Scholastic.

Jonas, A. (1989). *Color dance*. Greenwillow. (three dancers show how colors combine through an overlapping scarf dance)

Lobel, A. (1980). "The camel dances." Fables. Scott Foresman. (a camel loves to dance ballet and performs for her friends)

Malcolm, J. (2000). *Drat! We're rats!* Starcatcher.

McKissack, P. (1988). *Mirandy and Brother Wind*. Knopf. (Mirandy tries to capture the wind as her partner for a dance contest)

Patrick, D., & Ransome, J. (1993). *Red dancing shoes*. Tambourine Books. (girl is given shoes that allow her to dance)

Pavlova, A. (2001). *I dreamed I was a ballerina* (Edgar Degas, Illus.). Simon & Schuster.

Staples, S. (2001). *Shiva's fire*. HarperCollins.

Van Laan, N. (1993). *Buffalo dance: A Blackfoot legend*. Little, Brown. (story of traditional ritual before buffalo hunts)

Wallace, I. (1984). *Chi Chiang and the dragon's dance*. Atheneum. (boy gains respect when he performs the dragon's dance)

Walton, R. (2001). *How can you dance?* Penguin Putnam Books for Young Readers. (rhyming text connects dance to life)

Waters, K., & Cooper, M. (1990). *Lion dancer: Ernie Wan's Chinese New Year*. Scholastic. (boy describes his first Lion Dance performance)

Wells, R. (1999). *Tallchief: America's prima ballerina*. Viking.

Wood, A., & Rosekrans, H. (1986). *Three sisters*. Dial. (pig wants to be a dancer until she takes her first class)

dance literature (e.g., use a clear plastic book pocket to display a book and change weekly).

The Appendix includes a bibliography of dance-based literature.

Blueprint VI: Best Teaching Practices

I just dance, I put my feet in the air and move them around. (Fred Astaire)

What You Teach Is Who You Are

Any teacher who values creativity and movement can learn to integrate dance. Teachers who feel uncomfortable about dancing in front of students need to understand that modeling dances is not necessary to meaningful integration. The goal of integrating dance and movement is not to get students to mimic. Students can be asked or directed to move in certain ways without any demonstration. Lack of a "model" can even cause more creative problem solving than when students are shown steps.

Most important is for teachers to show enthusiasm and interest in dance. That begins with seeing teaching from the "what-if" vantage point of an artist. Next comes a bit of confidence to investigate movement possibilities in lessons—not just how something moves, but how it might move under different circumstances—while maintaining a focus on curricular targets.

Of course teachers need to work toward a level of dance literacy. That is a given in any area. More importantly, we need teachers who value the "imaginative rather than imitative uses of movement" (Fleming, 1990, p. 77). Dance knowledge doesn't go far without know-how and enthusiasm. As Martha Graham said, nobody cares how you look, just get up and dance.

Start Small.
Rather than beginning with a whole unit using dance, teachers should try a lesson or two. For example, start with a health lesson on body parts or the shapes bodies can make using different muscles. Look for teachable moments in any language arts lesson to connect body language and verbal communication. The key is to make sure first attempts are successful, for you and for students. Another way to begin is to integrate energizing warm-ups to introduce the day or lessons. See Chapter 11 for ideas.

Inside-Out Motivation.
Dance is intrinsically motivating. Attaching dance to any lesson makes it interesting. Best practice dictates we go further and clearly explain how dance contributes to understanding and extends expression possibilities, which brings us to the SFP.

We Get What We Expect.
Hundreds of studies have examined the influence of teacher expectation, or the self-fulfilling prophecy (SFP). The conclusion is that a demonstrated belief in students' creative potential makes it much more likely they will rise to the occasion. For example, teachers need not limit dance making to the common three-part sequence of (1) beginning frozen shape, (2) movements, and (3) a frozen ending shape. This is a solid structure to begin with, but students soon can, and should, innovate. Teachers show they expect stretching to create variety by coaching students to try out ways to organize and structure dances. Just as there are many ways to write a sentence and many types of writing forms, so it is with dance. Students should be reminded that new dances are constantly created. They'll probably know more examples than you do. At any rate, coach them to try movements at different speeds and at different levels to stretch thinking. Give feedback to show delight in original ideas that flow from minimal prompting.

Teachable Moments.
Once students are comfortable with the general purposes and ways of integrating dance and movement, teachers can be alert to moments with movement possibilities. There are obvious occasions. When it starts to snow, BEST elements can be explored for blizzards, snowflakes, and sleet. Movements can be abstracted and explored from current events (e.g., storms on the sun that resulted in magnetic "belches"). Invite students to be on the lookout for ideas that can be danced in any unit under study.

The Group Effect.
In the opening Classroom Snapshot, Wrenn Cook's students begged to perform their skeleton dances for audiences beyond their peers. Students have an innate desire to exhibit progress through dance performance. Audiences are a powerful motivator. Consider inviting parents and grandparents for regular Friday performances that synthesize learning for the week. Some schools have combined this with kids lunching with parents in the cafeteria.

Of course, there is always the split audience idea of dividing the class in half and taking turns performing. This puts students in both "do and view" roles. Remember to ask audiences to expect to give descriptive feedback after performances. This gives the audience a more active role and gives performers needed feedback. As students learn good audience social skills they gain in their ability to do this kind of analysis and evaluation.

Engagement and Active Learning

Dance engages head, hands, and heart in problem solving. Students are called upon to use their own ideas to transform important concepts through movement. This causes students to cognitively restructure information, and they are in turn transformed themselves.

Engagement.   When two people become engaged, they make a commitment. This is a choice. We can't make students engage, but we can set up circumstances under which they will likely choose to do so. Physical energizers are excellent tools (see next chapter). They get students up and moving. Another effective engagement habit is to ask students to show, instead of tell.

Show Versus Tell.   Opportunities for dance expression can be woven throughout lessons. For example, many students would not be able to verbally define "cycle" but could use their hands, head, and body posture to do so. When students are asked to show, describe, and relate (e.g., connect to their lives), they begin to form more meaningful links. If this becomes just pantomime, coach students to use different body parts or change energy or time to convey the dimensions of the concept.

Creative Problem Solving

> *You are lost the instant you know what the result will be.* (Juan Gris)

Pilobolus ("sun-loving fungus") is a dance ensemble that appears on television commercials and was profiled on *60 Minutes.* Using grace, tension, strength, and endurance, the dancers demonstrate themes related to aquatics, animals (e.g., seahorses and spiders), and gravity using their bodies in surprising ways (*www.pilobolus.com*). These dancers remind us that the most creative ideas come from people who are not bound by conventions. Creative problem solving depends on flexibility, risk taking, and openness to possibilities. The greatest football coaches have used CPS with dance. For example, Notre Dame's famed coach Knute Rockne was inspired to pattern backfield formations for his "Four Horsemen" after watching a dance performance (Boston, 1996). Lesson planning is a daily opportunity to do creative thinking. Dance integration puts the CPS process center stage as students learn to use dance thinking to connect and imagine ideas, conduct inquiry, and grow in new perspectives. Teachers do need to show students how the CPS described in Chapter 2 (see Ready Reference 2.5) is used in both dance making and understanding dances they view. This begins with creating conditions for creative problem solving. By the way, Pilobolus has an incredible human alphabet book (Kane).

Freedom with Structure.   Paradoxically, creativity is often enhanced by limitations. Creative dance is no exception. Freedom alone does not ensure creative thinking. Freedom with structure and focus does. Students need to know the restrictions on space, time, touching others, following directions, obeying signals, and using props that produce creative dance. When rules are clear and consistently applied, students learn self-discipline and are helped to think divergently about the specific context in which they are working. None of us can move "any way we want, any time we want" in our homes or at work. Purposeful movement done with concentration on a specific problem is the goal; even in free-time dance, guidelines about space and other issues are needed.

Who's Dance?   To help students understand the importance of using CPS to make dance, instead of mimicking steps modeled by a leader, try this. Play a familiar piece (e.g., "Dance of the Flowers"). Model teacher-invented movements and give time for students to imitate. Repeat the dance until students can do it in unison. Next, play another piece of music and ask students to invent movements. Use music that *suggests* flowers or plants (e.g., Enya's "In Memory of Trees"). Ask students to practice. Then split the class in half to do performances. The audience gives descriptive feedback. After both halves perform, ask about the thinking and feeling between the two ways to learn.

Questions.   Teachers pose questions like "What if?" and "How could you . . .?" to set CPS in motion. Just about any idea can be related to dance by asking questions involving the BEST elements and then connecting elements (locomotor moves in different shapes or levels). Ideas are also given depth by use of contrast: Ask students to do the opposite or show a nonexample. Sustained or continuous movements of the circulatory system can be contrasted with the bound movements of the digestive system such as food being swallowed (moving in clumps).

Visual Imagining.   Most of how we think involves visual images. But imagery is limited to what is stored in the brain, so it, like pantomime, can restrict thinking through dance. One way to avoid the downside of imagery in dance is to use CPS to explore dance elements. For example, explore many ways to move body parts first, and then invite students to "become" through drama. This helps expand the initial imagery.

Similes, metaphors, and other image-based language can be powerful helpers to stretch imaginations for movement: "Show me you are as solid as igneous rock" or "Let me see you shrink as small as an atom." Ask for images that lead to movement, too: "Stretch our body as if it is being pulled by magnets on either side of you. Use as many body parts as you can." Comment on images that spring from movement: "You're in a round shape. What else do you know that is round in our environment?" This use of imagery enriches concept development through movement, rather than reinforce stereotyped behavior. Finally, images can be used as a basis for movement: "What kind of movements might a starfish do?" instead of "Pretend you are a starfish and move around." It is a subtle but significant difference in thinking.

Experimenting with Elements. Skill and artistry is gained as control grows. "Move any way you want to the music" assumes that students know many ways to move. But they may, in fact, have limited experiences, especially on a conscious level. The goal of integrating dance and movement is to help students expand communication choices. Once students know many possibilities for using their bodies to respond to music, or another stimulus, teachers can give time for free creative movement without students feeling awkward. Embarrassment stems from not knowing what to do or doing the "wrong thing." We can teach children many ways to move and that there really aren't "wrong" moves—although some moves are not school appropriate! Sequence and balance are the secrets here.

Explicit Teaching

Effective dance integration rests on teachers developing student dance literacy and clearly explaining that what they learn in dance can be used in other subjects. Explicit teaching occurs in 5–10 minute mini-lessons that deal with the why-what-how-when-where of important dance concepts and skills. Demonstrations are followed by scaffolded practice in problem solving using controlled use of the body. See Chapter 3 for more information on explicit teaching.

By giving children clear dance language and a predictable lesson structure, they acquire the skills to succeed and feel safer about taking risks. Explicit instruction to teach basic elements of BEST (Body, Energy, Space, and Time) should be accompanied by visual aids such as charts. Lessons should target just one or two dance elements or ideas so that students can go into some depth and explore possibilities of each. Dancing about images such as happiness or sadness or inviting free dance before the elements are grasped can be stumbling blocks to student success. Students may simply get silly (humor is used to cope) or even withdraw if they lack needed tools.

Mnemonics. Dance memory aids are fun to create and should also be posted. Students enjoy co-writing songs and poems for class big books or posters. Here is an example a first grade co-wrote, called the "BEST Dance Rap:"

> Body, Energy, Space, Time
> Change Your Levels
> Change Your Lines
> Keep Your Focus
> Move and Freeze
> Make New Shapes
> Balance, but Watch Your Knees!

Transfer. If learning in dance is to transfer to other curricular areas, students must be shown the connections and have chances to practice them. Transfer should be explicitly addressed and is the responsibility of both teachers and arts specialists since it should work two ways.

Free Dancing? Undirected versus directed or explicit lessons are an issue throughout education today. In dance integration there are particular concerns about preparing students for success by using explicit teaching. Here's the problem: If dance integration is initiated by playing music and telling students to do any dance they wish, many students will be embarrassed about moving at all. Others will engage in rigid, and sometimes vulgar, movements they've seen Britney Spears or Michael Jackson use. For this reason, it is recommended that free dance be made available after teaching dance elements. Information about movement options makes all the difference, as does warm-up time to explore ways to communicate through the language of the body. This sequence assures student success and builds confidence. Students focus more on what their bodies can do and how it can be done. Cognitive and physical processes are thus engaged.

Aesthetic Orienting

Anyone who says sunshine brings happiness has never danced in the rain. (Anonymous)

Aesthetic response develops over time and with experience (see Chapter 6). This special form of understanding is facilitated when teachers slow it down, teach students to observe carefully, and expect interpretations to be grounded in evidence. In dance this usually occurs after class performances during which students discuss what they observed—usually dance concepts. The focus is not on right or wrong movement, but students should be urged to talk about movements that are more pleasing or surprising and ones that work better than others to get across the dancers' intentions. In response to all performances, students learn that applause is a part of good audience etiquette.

Questioning. Open or fat questions are a mainstay in creating an aesthetic orientation to making and understanding dance: How many ways? What's another way? What if? What is the shape of _____? How might _____ move? How does that affect the feel? These types of questions direct students to think about how to create variety and interest through details. Alert students to these kinds of questions so that they can also begin to ask them of one another and to respond to teacher questions. (See the Special Features section in the front of the book for a list of all the Ready References on questioning.)

Apply–Practice–Rehearse

It takes practice to learn the range of ways the body can be used to communicate. Dance integration cannot be meaningful without daily time for students to practice using dance elements, with feedback. This is where the line between teaching and assessing becomes blurred as teachers coach students using specific feedback. The result is quality work results.

Process or Product

The dominant purpose for creative dance and movement is the doing of it—the process, not the product. This cannot be overemphasized. To show to students how important kinesthetic learning is, do a bit of action research. Give half the class a set of numbers to learn (8-3-9-6-11-23-87-92). Send them out of the room to study for 10 minutes. With the remaining group, tell them to study kinesthetically by creating dance movements to remember the number sequence—a movement to go with each number. Have them practice the number movements in order, saying the numbers with the movements for 10 minutes. Bring the whole class back together and give them a test to write the number sequence. Ask students to grade their own papers and then compare the scores of the two groups. Regardless of the scores, ask students to tell how they learned and how it felt. (Usually the dance group does better and enjoys the studying more.)

Make/Do/View. Using dance as a teaching tool involves planning for students to create, perform, and respond aesthetically to dances they see. The viewing gives ideas for the making and doing of dance, and doing dance makes students more astute viewers. For example, by learning to "read" peer dances and video dance performances, students can develop a discriminating awareness of movement as an artistic medium. Choreography is the creative composing of original dances, an additional way to express ideas and feelings using dance thinking.

Products. While there is a place for structured dances in the regular classroom (e.g., when studying Ireland, a guest might teach the Irish jig), this is not desired nor feasible daily or even weekly. If dance is to be used as an important learning tool, the emphasis needs to be on process strategies to help students make meaning kinesthetically, creatively, and artistically. This does not mean that dance products won't result from movement explorations. In fact, when students become adept at using dance to understand and express themselves, there will be many times when they will create dances for science and social studies. The pride in these creations compels many students to want to perform for audiences.

Management: Behavior, Time, and Materials

Dance integration proceeds more smoothly and enjoyably when expectations and limits are clear. Class control during creative movement comes from teaching students the discipline of dance—how to control their bodies as they move. There is no magic trick or perfect set of techniques to make a class behave. A lot of management has to do with a kind of presence the teacher exudes—a demeanor that conveys "I'm in charge but we can work together and enjoy learning." The Appendix gives some time-tested techniques and habits used by teachers to establish discipline and interventions for common problems. Here are a few basics, particularly for dance making:

Show Enthusiasm. The mood of the day is often set by how the teacher greets the class in the morning. Use sign language or other kinesthetic ways to say "Hello, glad to see you." The book *The Joy of Signing* (Riekehof, 1987) is an excellent reference.

Start Small. Plan short lessons of about 10 minutes at first. If classroom management is an issue, begin with students staying at their desks or help them learn about movement in a personal spot marked with a sticky colored dot or piece of masking tape on the floor. Personal dots or spots can serve as "home base," which can be signaled at any time to control or stop movement.

Noise. Dance involves movement and some noise. Start with this expectation and make it clear to the principal and other teachers, who may not understand what you are doing. As students gain knowledge about the purpose and nature of dance, they will take it more seriously. As confidence and self-control increase, students will be less noisy because they will be more involved.

Space. When you need more space, move the lessons outside, in the gym, or in the cafeteria. Larger spaces can actually increase anxiety and cause some students to become overstimulated. In any space, students need to know dance used to make meaning is not free play or recess.

Grouping. For random small groups, ask students to find others whose names begin with the same letter or who are wearing a particular pattern (stripes, circles). Readjust initial groups to even out numbers, if necessary. This causes students to think in categories and take time to examine details.

Ground Rules. Rules can be taught by explaining, posting them, role playing, and games. One idea is to draw a huge hand on a poster and call it your Rules of Thumb or High Five rules. Write rules on the fingers and use a raised hand as a signal to think about the rules. Here are common rules teachers use: (1) follow directions: obey cues and signals, (2) respect others (e.g., personal space), (3) be responsible, (4) participate actively (enthusiasm), and (5) concentrate (no talking during movement). Take time to have students role-play each rule. Role-play nonexamples, or the opposite, so that there is no misunderstanding. It's easy to practice rules in a game format. For example, play "home base" by telling students the goal is not to be the last one to get in their personal spot when they hear "home base." Directions can be given in the form of a challenge to create interest: "Before I count to eight, see if you can get into a perfect circle." Another helpful habit is to invite students to participate, rather than order them to do so: "I'd like to invite all of you to try to make a shape on a low level that you think no one else will think of."

Concentratration and Focus.

Concentration is helped by removing distractions and limiting the space for dancing. Masking tape or imaginary lines can be used for this purpose, too. Beyond that, concentration and focus are teachable. We can't expect students to attend if they don't know how. A game structure works well. For example, "Frozen Shape" challenges students to make a shape in their personal space and hold it for so many counts. Students enjoy trying to increase the hold time each day and can graph their efforts. This is also a chance to compliment original shapes students create, especially stable ones that have a base and are balanced. See the energizers in the Seed Strategy chapters for more ideas.

Rule-Breaking Consequences.

A hierarchy of consequences, appropriate to the transgressions, should be made clear to students. Students are confused by inconsistent teachers. They perceive them as unfair. A consequence hierarchy can be as simple as (1) a warning (verbal or nonverbal); (2) a 1-minute time-out; (3) a 5-minute time-out and conference with the teacher after the lesson; and (4) loss of a chance to participate in the lesson that day and a phone call to parents. A teacher must be as good as her word: Follow through, immediately, when a problem occurs. Students will not believe or respect the teacher who continually threatens and warns without taking the promised action. Of course, hitting another child or disrespect for the teacher calls for a high-level consequence right away (number 4!) and probably would involve the principal. Post general consequences with the understanding that a teacher must do what is necessary to ensure the class is learning. Discuss consequences explicitly during the same time the rules are introduced, usually in the first week of school. Inform parents about rules and consequences at the start of school. Finally, there is no substitute for good judgment and common sense.

Signals.

Every teacher needs signals to get attention, start and stop action, and make transitions. A drum or tambourine is a good investment because it can be used to get attention and for start and stop signals. One favorite attention getter is to start the class with students echoing a rhythm. This causes them to feel different rhythms usable in dance exploration as well. Patterns can be clapped or drummed: 1-2-3, 1-2-3-4, or 1-2-3-4-5-6-7-8. By changing the stress, students can feel and think about the effect of energy/emphasis in dance or

any form of communication. Don't forget to set signals for silence (raised hand palm out) and for "noise" (two hand "taking"), and practice each several times until they are automatic. See *The Joy of Signing* (Riekehof, 1987) for ideas. Start and stop signals will need to be used to structure dance performances, too (e.g., say "curtain," "show time," "close your eyes," "positions," and "lights" as cues).

Feedback.

Compliment students with descriptive feedback, and ask students to give each other feedback to create a positive community feeling. Many students initially feel uncomfortable about dance so it is important to create many positive associations with early dance efforts.

Blueprint VII: Instructional Design: Routines and Structures

Dance integration means using movement as a basic communication tool. Dance offers ways to understand and express ideas that will remain locked inside our students if movement is not taught as a meaning-making option. Dance is made integral when it becomes a predictable part of lessons and the school schedule. Dance and movement are used to start the day or period and in the introduction, development, and conclusion of lessons and units.

IDC Lesson Framework

It helps to think of a lesson as a performance. It needs an introduction, development, and conclusion to be complete. The IDC orchestrates teaching strategies to reach the lesson objectives. That means the lesson begins with students understanding how dance will play a role in learning science, math, or social studies. Here are basic ideas for a dance-based IDC.

Introduction.

Lessons begin with attention getters, warm-ups, and other focus strategies. Teachers may tell or ask students how the lesson goals and objectives relate to real-life uses and contexts. Early on it is effective to ask for examples, rather than telling, so that students do as much or more thinking than the teacher. Basic dance elements may be reviewed or explicitly taught directly at this time, telling the name of the element, using visuals, and repeatedly asking students about target dance concepts throughout the lesson.

Development.

This is a time for students to experiment and explore: Ask how, what, and where questions about the dance elements. Ask students to move in place and then in space. Try the movement with different body parts and then with different locomotor movements. Change levels, directions, time and speed, and energy. Ask students to combine elements. For example, walk at a low level slowly or with energy. Teachers need only model a movement to help clarify thinking. The goal is not to get students to simply imitate, except in the case of teaching specific folk or ethnic dance step sequences.

Conclusion. The conclusion of the lesson involves students showing what they have learned. They may be asked to demonstrate movements, write, or tell one thing (TOT) learned. A "memory minute" can be a time for everyone to close their ideas and review the lesson or a relaxation exercise to preserve the aesthetics of the lesson. At this point students should be able to put what they've learned to artistic use in a simple form. If students are to create a dance for classmates to observe, structure is essential. A frozen shape–movements–frozen shape sequence is a basic structure students can use to create dances and involves creating a beginning, middle, and end. Encourage students to build in level changes that will make dances more interesting. Ask students to freeze the starting shape so that you and their peers can give descriptive positive feedback on what the shape says and how it feels. Students can be asked to give each other feedback on the element focus and what the dance communicated after a dance sharing. Finally, closure is achieved and important assessment information can be gained from asking students to explain what was learned about dance in general and the lesson focal points, including other subject matter content in the lesson.

Routines and Rituals

Simple props, such as a tambourine or bell, are important tools for teachers to use as start and stop signals. Students enjoy using rhythm instruments to beat out rhythms for dance. Wooden spoons and oatmeal boxes work well for this. Whistles are not the best musical instrument for signaling because they tend to demand and alarm, like a scream, rather than create an aesthetic mood. Don't forget that the human voice is a perfect vehicle to accompany or signal. If it is comfortable, sing or hum a rhythm for students (left and right and left and right and stop) or use a special word or phrase to signal for attention or as a start-stop. For example, try famous dancers names as signals: "Isadora Duncan" rolls off the tongue and kids enjoy echoing it.

Start and Wrap-Up. Creative dance is a great way to start each day. Dance puts students in a positive frame of mind and body for learning. Begin with easy movement warm-ups such as the ones in Chapter 11. Play music as students come in that invites clapping or tapping or using the whole body. From there, children can be given more space. There are recommended books of dance strategies and activities in the bibliography. For example, Gilbert's (1992) *Creative Dance for All Ages* is full of activities useful to energize and warm up.

Transitions. Good instructional design includes strategies for transitions and ways to dismiss by groups. Music, a rhythm, or a sign may be used to signal time to move. To dismiss groups, use strategies like Ticket Out: Students have to tell or do something on their way out the door. A movement example is "All those who _____ (e.g., know what sway or sustain mean) may 'slither' up for our reptiles lesson".

Lessons That Flop

Many lesson failures occur because the teacher isn't clear about the lesson objectives: what exactly should students know and be able to do by the end that they couldn't do or didn't know at the start? Inadequate preparation or lack of structure can also doom a lesson. By using a lesson framework, much of this problem can be alleviated. Here are other suggestions.

1. *Structure lessons so that behavior expectations are crystal clear.* Chaos derives from loss of clarity about goals and uncertainty about how to achieve them. This doesn't imply a rigid structure, but a general organizational scheme is needed. An enormous variety of strategies and activities can then be selected within any structure. For example, think of all the ways to introduce a lesson using pictures, questions, objects, songs, or a movement challenge. Keep in mind that too many directions confuse students and that dance is kinesthetic. Get students moving as soon as possible.

2. *Learning to integrate dance involves trial and error.* When something is not working, teachers should feel free to alter strategies in the lesson plan while maintaining the dance and other curricular focus. It is important to be flexible within the parameters of research-based concepts of (1) effective teaching, (2) learning theory, and (3) the philosophy and principles of arts integration. Chapters 1–3 provide an overview of these areas.

3. *Dance construction by the children should not be considered essential to every integrated lesson.* Teachers who do not feel well prepared in dance may initially confine teaching to movement exploration, such as more teacher-directed dance element experimentation. Eventually, students spontaneously begin to construct dance sequences, if they are given experiences that focus on problem solving through movement exploration, invention, and improvisation. Teachers should not rush into having students compose dances. They should feel proud to see that students are enlarging their repertoire of movements and are gaining poise in use and confidence about their bodies.

4. *Consider preplanning dance-based lessons.* Do so by using the BEST elements to create questions and directions for students. Once movement possibilities have been

squeezed from the topic or theme, it is time for the introduction, development, and conclusion of the lesson. Teachers need to decide on whether they will expect a dance structure as a culmination or if they will just be using warm-ups or isolated dance strategies throughout a lesson. In either case, assessment should be planned to gauge learning in dance and the target curricular area. See Planning Page 10.4 for preplanning a literature lesson and other dance-based plans.

Planning Page 10.4

Preplan for Integrated Dance/Literature

1. *Choose standards for dance, literature, and student needs.*
2. *Choose one of five "bodies" for lessons/units:* (1) problem/ topic, (2) person, (3) core work, (4) genre/ form, or (5) event. Decide the content focus for the dance exploration. Decision: core book, *Where the Wild Things Are.*
3. *Determine themes possibilities:* No one likes to feel powerless. We all like to be in control.
4. *Brainstorm BEST elements to find best fit.* Decisions: (1) Energy: flow (bound versus sustained) and using concentration on speed (fast and slow) to develop feel of control (inside self); (2) Body: all parts, shapes doing nonlocomotor and locomotor with "powerless qualities" (e.g., floppy, jerky, uncertain).
5. *Plan questions and directions to cause "exploration" literature themes using dance.* Example: How did Max feel when he had to stay in his room (out of control)? Use your hand to control your foot without touching it, like there is an invisible string attached. Use a finger to control your knee, your elbow. Bend over and hang loose, dangle your fingers and arms. Explore loose and controlled with body parts. Take steps forward and backward as if pulled by an invisible force. Walk across the room using an uneven rhythm that shows you are not in control. Collapse to floor level in a loose way. Move all body parts with lots of control and flow. How does this feel differently? Start at head and move to feet doing controlled, sustained, and slow moves and then faster. Do same with controlled and bound, slow and then fast.
6. *Plan composition criteria:* In small groups, make a dance that compares powerlessness with self-control. Start with a frozen shape. Put 5 to 10 moves in your dance. Have a frozen ending shape. Be sure to include a different variety of levels and shapes in your dance.
   (Go to Integrated Lesson Plan framework form in Ready Reference 3.3) to plan IDC.

Four Corners Stations

This is a unique adaptation of the learning station idea and can be a daily routine. Designate a specific movement problem for the four corners of the room. Small groups go to each corner and solve the problem. For example, Corner 1=warm-ups to a music CD; 2=stretch station, 3=wiggle station, 4=walk in place station. At a signal, students rotate to next station.

Clubs

Our children see the arts as part of everyday life. We have girls and boys who sign up for Ballet Club or Clay Club. Our kids think everybody learns this way. (Mary-Mac Jennings, Ashley River Creative Arts)

Many schools now offer time for interest-based clubs during the school day. For example, Columbus School in Berkeley, California, has a dance discovery club (Fleming, 1990). When choice club time is a part of the school structure, students benefit greatly. They try out many arts that can become lifelong pursuits. In the case of dance, that can range from tap, jazz, ballet, or pop dance groups to folk dances.

Blueprint VIII: Adaptations for Diverse Needs

In the dance, even the weakest can do wonders. (Karl Gross)

The Appendix includes a general developmental continuum with guidelines that are important to use when planning appropriate lessons for primary and intermediate students. In general, physical development, like other development, proceeds from general to more specific. Children ages 5–12 are in transition but usually have increasing balance, strength, and endurance. Instruction and experiences are everything to development. They determine rate of growth and range. Children are more likely to get hurt or hurt others because of carelessness, not because their bodies and muscles are not ready to move. Diligent use of ground rules, signals, and other rituals helps prevent collisions with objects or other children. In general,

- Clear the space of dangerous objects—anything that could be slipped on or that protrudes.
- If the students take off their shoes, have them remove theirs socks, too, to prevent slipping.
- Begin slowly and watch for signs that a student may lack self-control. Students need time to work with different body parts in place and across space to see the results of physical actions. They also need time to release energy.

- Some students will need individual attention, but this needs to be provided in a way that does not embarrass.

Adaptations for Special Needs

The 10 ways to differentiate introduced in Chapter 3 (Ready Reference 3.6) were to change the place, amount, rate, target objectives, instruction, curriculum materials, utensils, levels of difficulty, assistance, and response. These changes can help match lessons to students' stages (e.g., older students may laugh a lot at first because they are unsure of themselves and are so conscious of changing bodies; laughing is a natural way to deal with problems). Amount and rate can be adjusted by starting with basic dance warm-ups and doing a thorough job of teaching the BEST elements one at a time so that students are comfortable. Target objectives, materials, and response may need to be adjusted for students with physical disabilities; for example, students in wheelchairs, with limited use of the body, might be given the role of beat keeper or be in charge of start and stop signaling. The Appendix has a chart of additional adaptations for students with special needs.

Blueprint IX: Assessment for Learning

Increasingly, the artists and teachers began to see that the more powerful the art, the greater the evidence of learning. (Baker and colleagues, 2004)

Arts integration emphasizes assessment *for* learning that is focused on student strengths and needs, authentic, continuous, and multifactored (see Chapter 3). This is called *formative assessment*, and it mostly happens during the learning process so it has more effect on achievement. This means most assessment of dance-based lessons occur as students problem solve through movement. Teachers observe students in process and use rubrics and checklists to make notes. Feedback is given immediately to increase the quality of work. It becomes routine for students to self-assess during and after lessons, and peer feedback is encouraged throughout work.

Assessment of dance-making performances does happen. There is a dual purpose. Performances are assessed for aesthetic qualities, and use of dance knowledge and performances are used to show learning in science, social studies, and math. Assessment criteria reflect both prongs: academics and arts. Dance skills and concepts must be united in the minds of the teachers (Baker et al., 2004). For example, at Ashley River Creative Arts, most units result in performances or exhibits called the "Unit Celebration."

General Criteria: Observing Dance and Dance Making

As with language arts, dance is receptive (knowing through "reading" observations and using other senses) and expressive (showing thoughts and feelings) sides. The *Dance Standards* should be used to create criteria, at least in these two basic areas that are also referred to as responding and creating/performing. Here are some of the important criteria that appear in rubrics for dance-based lessons:

- Flexible persistence; decides what's not working and how to make it work (Baker et al., 2004)
- Connecting dance with other areas (e.g., written composition)
- Conscious use of CPS
- Aesthetic noticing; describes meanings and emotions in physical gestures and shapes
- Working collaboratively
- Dance has beginning/middle/end
- Effective entrances/exits
- Variety: body parts, shapes, levels, energy, space
- Interesting transitions

Feedback

Clear and focused descriptive feedback (not just vacuous praise) is needed throughout dance making. Wrenn Cook demonstrated this in her skeleton dance lesson as she pointed out what the students did. She also coached them to stretch their imaginations by using "what-if" type of questions. Her Skeleton Dance Rubric appears in Planning Page 10.5.

Anecdotal Records

Catterall (2003) explains that "paper and pencil tests on literacy and numeracy give us but a slim slice of the information pie. We need close and expert observations of learners" (p. 113). Teachers should rely on observation to see if students are progressing toward lesson targets. Jot down notes about specific student behaviors on cards or sticky notes that can be added to portfolios. Use a clipboard to make quick observation notes easier. This kind of assessment captures authentic evidence during the lesson process, as opposed to fabricated "virtual reality" assessments.

Group Debriefing

An effective teaching habit is to take a few minutes at the end of lessons to discuss what students learned that was most important. Responses can be written on a chart to give them value and linked to lesson objectives. At the same time, words and ideas can be added to an ongoing Arts Word Wall or other cumulative class charts.

Planning Page 10.5

Skeleton Dance Choreography Rubric

Rating: Needs Improvement=0–1, Good=2–4,
Excellent=4–5

Criteria
Science Information

1. All or most commands were not accurate.
2. More commands were accurate than not.
3. WOW! This group really knows the skeletal system. Every command was obeyed with 100% accuracy.

Dance elements (space, movement qualities/ dynamics, time)

1. No attempt or almost no attempt was made to create interest through the use of space, dynamics, and time elements.
2. The group sometimes used dance elements to create interest.
3. WOW! The group found a number of ways to use dance elements to create an interesting dance.

Originality

1. Little or no attempt to find unique ways to satisfy the commands or to use dance elements.
2. This group found somewhat creative ways to satisfy the commands and to use dance elements.
3. WOW! This group came up with creative and unexpected ways to satisfy the commands and to use dance elements.

Teamwork/Rehearsal

1. Group had some trouble working together. They either did not complete the task or didn't use their time well.
2. Group completed the task and had some time remaining for practice.
3. WOW! This group worked really well together to choreograph and to rehearse their dance. "Practice makes perfect," and this dance was perfectly performed!

Self-Assessment

After lessons students need time to write and discuss questions such as:

How did you challenge yourself physically?

What did you try? What worked?

What choices did you make?

What did you learn about dance/choreography that you did not know before?

Portfolio Entries

To document growth in dance literacy, these items can be included in an Arts Folio (see Appendix).

- Charts and personal checklists of dance elements
- Anecdotal observation notes from teacher and peers about BEST elements use
- Photos and videos of dance making
- Journal entries or other reflective pieces based on assessment criteria

Students can pair up to share folios with focus on what they liked, what they would change, and what they had learned.

Explicitly tell students about their progress. Use charts and checklists to show them what they have learned. Add new dance information to large class webs about dance or use KWL (Know-Want to Know-Learn) charts.

The Appendix includes examples of informal assessment tools to use with integrated dance lessons. For program evaluation, check out the *Opportunity to Learn Standards* checklists (*www.winthrop.edu/ABC/*).

Blueprint X: Arts Partnerships

Consult Chapter 3 for a list of potential art partners and guidelines for setting up artist residencies. The Appendix includes a School Registry to help find schools near you that are partnering with organizations, agencies, or individual artists. Of course, an on-site dance teacher is the most likely partner, and more and more schools are hiring them. Although creative dance broke with physical education in the 1980s, many PE teachers have an interest and background in creative movement and make excellent partners. Local dance teaching artists may be contacted through local arts agencies.

Initiating Collaboration

Teachers interested in partnering for dance integration should initiate conversations with the physical education teacher or, if the school is fortunate to have one, the dance teacher. Local college faculty are other sources to ask for advice about dance and movement strategies that could be used in the regular classroom. It is a good idea to make an appointment to talk in more depth. A positive way to begin is to ask to observe dance and movement lessons. If a dance specialist is on staff, give him or her a list of units, concepts, and skills to be taught during the month. Specialists can be asked to provide the same information to the classroom teacher so that both can look for possible links. Once a working relationship begins to develop, specialists can be asked to do lessons with students that connect to classroom lessons. Classroom teachers need to expect to reciprocate or extend specialists' lessons.

Planning. How is collaboration with specialists made a reality? Teacher Mary-Mac Jennings explains that Ashley River Creative Arts starts with a daylong planning meeting each spring. The whole school plans together, focusing mainly on the science and social studies units for the next year. "This is incredibly valuable," she says. Teachers also meet with arts specialists once a month. As a planning/accountability device, one column from teachers' lesson plans is "on file" in the office. This column shows how the arts are used in each unit. Ms. Jennings likes this idea because it "keeps everyone focused and aware."

Keep the beat!

Residencies

Artist residencies are an important part of the arts integration model in many schools. At Ashley River each year, every grade looks forward to the 1 or 2 weeks when artists come into classrooms. This year Ms. Jennings is planning for a local musician/dancer to come for a week of mornings. "The residencies keep everyone excited. We love having artists come and we look forward to the student performances that the artists facilitate." Residencies are usually paid for by grants from South Carolina and the PTA raises matching funds. See the guidelines in Chapters 3 and 4 for residencies.

Teacher Spotlight:
Mary-Mac's Minuet

Mary-Mac Jennings is currently teaching her kindergartners to do the minuet. "I just went on the Internet and got the directions and found a CD with music that fit. Of course, I adapted it for my children." Ms. Jennings teaches at Ashley River Creative Arts Elementary, where nearly all content and skills are taught through the arts. The academic connection to the minuet is math, and the focus is on patterns. "They are also learning to listen for changes in the music so listening skills are involved," she explains.

What does Ms. Jennings recommend for teachers just starting to integrate dance? "Just do it!" she exclaims. "Talk with teachers who are integrating the arts, visit if you can, plan with others. Don't feel like you have to have all the ideas and get it right. There is no right."

What other dance-based lessons are ahead? "This year the spring insect unit will culminate in insect dances based on the dance learning begun in the winter. One thing builds on another," she adds.

Conclusion

When we teach a child to draw, we teach him how to see. When we teach a child to play a musical instrument, we teach her how to listen. When we teach a child how to dance, we teach him how to move through life with grace. When we teach a child to read or write, we teach her how to think. When we nurture imagination, we create a better world, one child at a time. (Jane Alexander, chair for the National Endowment for the Arts)

This chapter has introduced integrating dance throughout the curriculum using the Arts Integration Blueprint. Research and educational theories were reviewed and combined to explain the beliefs underlying dance integration. The dance literacy classroom teachers need was outlined to answer the "What teachers should know" question. The *how* question was addressed using essential building blocks of collaborative planning, aesthetic environment, use of literature as a core art, best practices, instructional design, differentiating instruction, assessment, and forming arts partnerships. In Chapter 11, Seed Strategies for teaching dance basics and integrating dance throughout the curriculum are organized into curricular and multiarts integration categories.

Resources

See the Appendix for more study materials, including websites. Chapter 11 has activity book recommendations.

Professional Organizations

National Dance Association: *www.aahperd.org/nda/*

National Dance Education Organization: *www.ndeo.org*

DVDs, Videos, CDs

Anne Green Gilbert's site *www.creativedance.org* (click on workshops, then resources for people, places, and props).

BrainDance. AGG Production. *www.creativedance.org. Teaching Creative Dance,* AGG Production (85 min.).

Creative movement: A step towards intelligence. (1993). West Long Branch, NJ: Kultur (80 min.).

Dana, A. (1991). *All-time favorite dances.* Long Branch, NJ: Kimbo Educational.

Dance and grow. (1994). Scotch Plains, NJ: Dance Horizons (60 min.).

He makes me feel like dancin'. (Award-winning documentary on National Dance Institute: *www.nationaldance.org.* NDI also offers a teacher/choreographer's handbook).

Move 'n Groove Kids (2002). PBS: *www.pbs.org* (26 min.). (many videos available on dance and dancers).

Children's Literature References

A to zoo: Subject access to children's picture books (4th ed.). (2001). Bowker.

Barboza, S. (1992) *I feel like dancing: A year with Jacques D'Amboise and the National Dance Institute.* New York: Crown.

Baylor, B., Sears, B., & Longtemps, K. (1973). *Sometimes I dance mountains.* New York: Atheneum.

Isadora, R. (1976). *Max.* New York: Simon & Schuster.

Kane, J. (2005). *The human alphabet.* New York: Roaring Brook Press.

Rylant, C. (1994). *All I see.* New York: Scholastic.

11

Dance Seed Strategies

Questions to Guide Reading

1. How can dance Seed Strategies be used to introduce lessons?

2. What Seed Strategies can be used to teach dance concepts?

3. What Seed Strategies can be developed to integrate dance with science, social studies, math, literacy, and the other arts?

Remember, Ginger Rogers did everything that Fred Astaire did, backward and on high heels. (Anonymous)

In the opening Classroom Snapshot, Cyrus Longo takes several Seed Strategies and develops them for a science lesson. He uses energizers and warm-ups, a focus on BEST dance elements, and student creation of unique three-part dances to transform concepts about water. He also uses many best practices, including CPS, open questions, EPR, and coaching with feedback.

Classroom Snapshot:

States of Water Through Dance

Note: A small sign on Mr. Longo's desk says, "Who can turn a child's mouth into a smile? Who can turn a child's walk into a dance? A teacher."

The desks are pushed back, and 27 fourth graders are in their "personal **space bubbles**." **Nature music** conveys the subtle rhythm of rushing water and crashing waves. Mr. Longo's voice is quiet but easily heard as he begins the warm-up.

"Okay, **stretches.** Reach over your head. Now one arm higher and alternate back and forth. Let's go for eight counts: 1–2–3–4–5–6–7–8. Both arms up and drop to your sides. Relax. Reach out with both arms, in front. Let your hips tilt so your back and arms are parallel to the floor. Now relax your back and curve it so you can dangle your head and hands. Let's slowly roll up with your head coming up last. **I'll count down from 8.**"

There is a unison sigh and students wait for the next direction. Mr. Longo takes them through warm-ups for **specific body parts**, working from top to bottom: head, neck, torso/core (shoulders, hips, back, abdomen), arms and elbows, hands, fingers and wrists, legs and knees, and feet and ankles.

"Ready, **shake out!** Right arm. Left arm. Whole body. Take a deep breath and slowly let it out. Take another. Hold it. Very slowly release it without letting your body slump. I see straight bodies out there. Good concentration. Now, sit in your space, eyes up here."

The warm-ups take about 5 minutes. Mr. Longo begins his introduction to the science lesson.

"Put your **thumb up** if you can tell me about the water cycle."

Almost everyone responds. Students talk about where water is found on Earth, how much water there is, what causes pollution, and what makes water. When a boy lists three forms of water (ice, liquid, and steam), Mr. Longo asks what causes these states. The students seem uncertain.

"It's fine if you're not sure about what causes water to be in a solid, liquid, or gas because that's what our lesson is. **Let's start with what you do know.** In your space, when I say "three," show me a body shape that feels like water in

Cheering and chanting vocabulary at Ashley River.

solid form. Ready 1–2–3. Yes! I see stiff bodies and straight lines. Without losing your shape, try to look around. **What do you notice?**"

"Everyone is compact."

"I see angles."

"Sarah, what do you mean by angles?"

"Like James has his arms and legs bent in straight. I think forty-five degree angles, aren't they?"

"Good observation!"

"I'll count again. This time, every time **I say "three" change** your solid shape in some way. Try a different level or direction. Look at the **Dance Elements Chart.** Okay, ready? 1–2–3. 1–2–3. 1–2–3. Wow! You really thought of lots of hard shapes. How did you do it?" Lots of thumbs go up.

"I wanted to do what you said, but be different. I tried to feel really solid, but change to a high level and use new body parts," explains a tall girl.

"I thought about how it feels inside a piece of ice. I used more energy to hold my molecules together," says a boy.

"Hey, I'm getting cold. B-R-R-R," jokes Mr. Longo and the class laughs. "But why is ice cold?" he asks.

The class tells what they know about temperature and its effects on water. Mr. Longo then uses the comment about molecules and asks what they think the distance is among the molecules in ice. They concur that they "felt" close together.

Mr. Longo takes the students through **dance explorations** of liquid water and finally water vapor. He increasingly focuses his questions and **descriptive comments** on the molecular structure of the three states and how each feels when they make their individual shapes. After about 10

minutes, he tells the students to get into small groups. Students were previously assigned and know where their group space is.

"Your problem is to create a dance using movements related to all three forms of water. Remember, you're not pretending to be water, but communicating about the states showing possible movements. How will the dance be organized?"

"A **beginning, middle, and end.**"

"A starting shape, movement, and an ending frozen shape."

"Creative ideas!"

"Thanks for reminding us, Gloria! Yes, making a dance uses the scientific method. Start by brainstorming ways water gets from one form to another and movements to show these changes. I'll come around as you work."

Students huddle in groups of four. Mr. Longo waits as they get started. After a few minutes, he **circulates** to listen in on a group. He has a **clipboard** with yellow sticky notes all over it and jots down as he listens.

"Ice melts when it gets warmer—above 32 degrees. We could show melting by starting high (she tiptoes and reaches up) and slowly getting lower and spreading out."

"We could be part of a rigid ice sculpture with lots of angles. We need to be really close together." Everyone giggles.

"What about when we melt and spread out. We'd be liquid. Somehow we need to show getting hotter, so we can evaporate."

"We could be being cooked to boiling. Wow. You'd really have to move fast and jump around. Look at my fingers boiling!" Gloria demonstrates with wild finger movements. The others join in, and a boy declares, "Look, my foot is boiling!"

Mr. Longo smiles and moves to another group. They are discussing cloud movements and how to show water moving from a gas to precipitation (liquid). He asks what the difference is between precipitation and condensation, and they spend a few minutes differentiating the terms. A third group is working on water appearing as frost and is experimenting with "quick-freeze" movements.

After about 10 minutes, Mr. Longo announces they have **5 minutes** to decide a starting shape, how to use movements related to the three states of water, and an ending shape. He **coaches** them to think about how to use the space in the room. He tells them to sit in their groups when they are ready.

Each of the four groups **performs** their dances. The rest of the class takes the part of the **audience.** Each dance takes 3 or 4 minutes. After each performance Mr. Longo asks the audience to "tell what they saw," and he compliments students who give **specific observations** about shapes, movements, and connections to the states of water.

The lesson ends with a **debriefing** in which Mr. Longo asks them what they learned about states of water. Finally, students rearrange their desks and take out Science Learning Logs to write for 5 minutes about states of matter. There is a reading assignment on the board about the water cycle in their science text, and students begin to read as they finish their logs.

Mr. Longo explains that there is little in the reading that hasn't already come up in the lesson. Some students need the print reinforcement, and he claims he's too traditional to do away with the textbook completely.

Mr. Longo circulates and gives each student a yellow sticky **note with an observation.** Each student takes out a folder and sticks it inside where there are several others.

"I'll never forget the three water states and where the molecules are," one girl writes. "I like to learn this way because you just remember science better and it is fun." ✳

Chapter Organization

The Seed Strategies in this chapter are organized into three sections, but many overlap and can be adapted for any curricular area. The third section focuses on integrating dance with other arts.

All seeds need to be developed for integration purposes. They are just idea starters. The energizers and the section on dance elements are provided to prepare students for problem solving and teaching dance basics. Choose seeds as they fit with curricular objectives and adapt them using the 10 PARTICULAR ways to differentiate from Chapter 3. Consult the Appendix for adaptations for students with special needs. Finally, Seed Strategies are intended to stimulate CPS by teachers; however, students should be invited to adapt strategies and lead activities, as soon as possible.

I. Energizers and Warm-Ups

Energizers and warm-ups can be used to get attention, set mood, warm up the body for movement, and stimulate creative problem solving. If used regularly, many build focus, concentration, control, and following-directions skills.

Brain Dance. Gilbert (2005) recommends a warm-up sequence for the whole body, which involves breathing deeply and touching and moving all body parts; head to toe and back to core; head-tail separate and together; upper/lower body parts; body sides isolated, cross-lateral midline and upper/lower body; and moving off balance. See the website *www.creativedance.org*.

Inhale/Exhale/Stretch. Direct students to slowly inhale, reach up and overhead and to floor with knees bent. Exhale. Repeat to each side. Roll head and shoulders forward and backward, bend arms, do socket rolls, touch head to shoulders, touch knees, touch toes, sit and twist and bend, do slow windmills, toe presses, heel to toe slowly, clasp hands behind and stretch shoulders, spine stretches, squat and press forward (exhale), bend one leg and repeat (exhale). Slow, nonrhythmic mood music can be used. Nature sounds on CDs and tapes work well.

Slow Breathing. Tell students to do all these slowly: Breathe in through your right nostril and out the left. Become as high and large as you can and then exhale and shrink as small as possible. Breathe in and exhale, making a single sound (e.g., short vowel sound). Suck in breath through clenched teeth and breathe out through your nose. Breathe to the rhythm of music. Place hands on abdomen and breathe in and exhale.

Watch My Hand (Concentration). Partner students. One is the "hand" and the other must follow partner's hand with his eyes. Leader should change levels and directions. At signal, partners reverse roles.

Hang Loose. Use an object to represent the concepts of "relaxed and tense" or "loose and tight" (e.g., piece of yarn versus pencil). Call out a body part and ask students to make it tight and hard, then loose and soft.

Wiggle and Giggle (Concentration). Ask students to giggle with a foot, a knee, and on up the body to the head. Shaking and wiggling with controls (signals, numbers) develops focus.

Foot to Foot (Weight Shift). Ask students to "Move foot to foot (most basic locomotor step). Go smaller, larger, faster, slower. Expand to "leap with body curved forward.""

Hand Warm-Up. Direct everyone to make a fist and then show one, then two, then three, then four, and then five fingers. Repeat. Do other hand and then both. Change tempo.

Hug Yourself. Call out a body part to hug (e.g., hand hugs, finger hugs). Encourage creative thinking. *Variation:* do as partners.

Who Started the Motion (Observation). Stand or sit in a circle. One person leaves the room while another is selected to be IT. IT leads others through different motions, such as waving hands or tapping feet. Player #1 returns and watches to figure out who is starting the movements as the leader begins each new one. Give three guesses.

Head, Shoulders, Knees, and Toes. First practice singing this song. Repeat, stand in a circle, and touch body parts mentioned in the song.

Body Touch Rhythm. Use a rhythm or chant (e.g., "Touch your head, head, head . . . touch your toes, toes, toes"), as students do choice creative moves.

Walk Different Ways. Give directions to walk: in place—slow and fast, forward, backward, and sideways. Work on posture and alignment: Call out "tiny steps, giant steps, on heels, on tiptoe, in place, backward, forward, as lightly as possible (an element of force), or slowly (an element of time)." *Variation:* Students throw scarves, balls, hoops, or ropes and try to catch with body parts. Can be done to music.

Freeze (Self-Control). Play music or use a tambourine. Tell students to move in a specific way until the sound stops and then freeze. When the music begins again, they move in their frozen shapes. For example, "When the drum begins, walk in place to the beat."

Magic Shoes. Students imagine they have on magic shoes that allow them to walk in special ways (e.g., on water, on air). *Variation:* brainstorm ways to walk. Write on cards and draw and draw hat. Call out with a creative change (e.g., speed, level, shape, energy).

Body Directions. Give a series of directions, such as, "Show me 'up' with your body, now 'down.' How can you make your body go way up? Way down? How high can you get? Show me halfway down. Make yourself as small as you can. Now great big. Pretend your feet are glued to the floor. Now move your body up and down."

Noodle-Freeze (Following Directions). Direct students to move in loose and relaxed ways, first in one spot, varying the speed and levels. At a signal, students freeze in a shape. *Variation:* Students say a one-liner about their shape (e.g., "I feel like I'm melting").

Five-Shape Concentration. The goal is to create, number, and remember five shapes. Leader then says "one" and students make the first shape. On "two," a second shape is made. This continues through "five." Then the leader calls numbers at random, and students make the shape for that number.

Slow-Mo Concentration. Students pick an everyday movement and do it slowly (e.g., sweeping, bending over, reaching). Groups perform by dividing class in half. Audience gives feedback on focus and concentration.

Circle Back Rub (Relaxation). Students form a circle, facing sideways. Each student touches the shoulders of the person in front. Leader says "go" and each person rubs the back of the person in front. Leader says "switch," and all turn and repeat.

Lightning Concentration. Form circle and join hands. Leader squeezes a rhythm to both the right- and left-hand partners. The rhythm is passed around until it collides in one person. That person shouts "lightning" and becomes the leader.

Paranoia (Concentration). Students spread out to fill up space. On signal (e.g., drum beat), they walk around the room filling up the space, leaving no holes. The leader then calls "one" and everyone finds someone to follow, not letting the person know he's being followed and still trying to fill up the space. Then call "two" and students follow a second person. Finally "three" is called. The leader then alternates numbers.

Popcorn. On signal, students walk around, filling up space. At the signal "one," each person picks a person to track with his eyes. Whenever they come near that person, they jump. Next the leader says "two" and a second person is tracked, while still tracking the first. When the second person is passed by, students freeze for a second. Everyone now walks around jumping and freezing. Finally, the leader says "three," and a third person is identified. When that person is passed, students say "popcorn." Continue until "freeze" signal.

Imagination Journey (Concentration). Narrate a series of movements. For example: Put your feet into warm water and wiggle your toes. Now put your legs in and swish them around. Make circles in the water. Slip farther into the water and sway your hips back and forth. You are up to your waist. Slowly walk in place. Feel the weight of the water. Raise your hands up out of the water and stretch them over your head. Jump up and down. Feel the water. Sink down up to your neck. Let your arms float on top of the water. Press your hands down in the water to your sides and then raise them up. Put your hands on your hips and twist, twist, twist. Now rotate your head forward, to left and back, then right and around again. Oops, the water splashes up your nose. Wiggle your nose and blow the water from your lips. With your toes, pull the plug. The water slowly drains out. You shiver as it moves below your armpits. As it reaches your thighs, you raise your knees up and down, up and down. Finally the water drains out. You twirl around and sit down.

Mood Setting. Use music to relax before movement. Allow students to move or not move. Artists like Enya and George Winston work well. Example: Enya's "In Memory of Trees" CD.

Sound to Motion. Use sound effects tapes, rhythm instruments, bells, and environmental "found sounds" to invite creative thinking. Ask students to show motions for a series of sounds (e.g., strong? high? low? direction changes?).

Energizers and Warm-Ups for Cooperation. **Add on.** Form four or five lines with students standing, side to side. At one end a person starts a movement, and the next picks it up and adds to it. The movement travels down the line until the end. The starter person then moves to the end and a new starter begins. *Note:* Each line will be doing its own thing.

Movement chain. Stand in a line or U shape. On signal, people on the two ends start a movement or a rhythm and send it around until it reaches the end. End people then go to the center of the line, and new end people start movements or rhythms.

Don't cross the line. Pairs face each other and grasp shoulders. They imagine a line between them. Each starts pushing but cannot cross the line. The goal is to push hard, but not push each other over. Repeat back to back or side to side.

Buddy walk. Pairs lean back to back against each other. First, they silently walk around. Then they try to sit on the floor and rise up again. Can also be done side by side.

Back-to-back dancing. Pairs slightly lean against each other and begin dancing with music. Use slow music at first. Each must try to sense what moves to make to stay together.

Co-op musical chairs. Remove chairs, as in the traditional version, but all find a place to sit when the music stops and must help everyone sit somewhere. No one is eliminated.

Sheet music. Use an old sheet and tell children to hold on around the edge. Put several balloons in the center and put on a CD with slow tempo music. The goal is to keep balloons afloat, while keeping the beat of the music.

Shrink and stretch. Group forms a circle stretching out so only fingertips touch. Move out as much as possible without losing touch. At the signal "shrink," the circle moves in to take up as small a space as possible. Then leader says "stretch," and so forth.

Balloon balance or bust. Small groups join hands and form circle. A balloon is given to each, and the object is to keep it in the air without dropping each other's hands.

Stuck together. Pairs hold a note card between two body parts (e.g., head to head with card in between). Another card is then added, and so on, until one card falls. Can be done in small groups with one person in the center and others joined to the one person with a card in between. At signal, center person moves and group must follow without dropping cards. *Variation:* do without cards. Leader calls two body parts to touch.

No holes. Group spreads out to fill up all space. On signal (e.g., drum beat), everyone walks around trying to keep the space completely filled. When leader signals "stop," all must freeze. If there is a hole, leader points to it and someone must fill it up.

Body count. Everyone walks around filling up the space. Leader then calls out a combination (e.g., three heads and two hands). Students quickly find others to create this combination of touching body parts.

Spider web. Everyone must be touching someone else in an appropriate spot. When leader signals, everyone moves slowly around the room, always touching someone (e.g., with a foot, hand, shoulder). At stop signal everyone must be touching (i.e., connected by the human web).

II. Dance BEST Elements and Concepts

Ideas in this section are to teach basic dance concepts. BEST elements appear in Ready Reference 10.1.

Personal Space. Students find a personal spot. They explore their personal space, not moving from the spot, by making shapes at low, middle, and high levels. Combine with force, time, and leading with different body parts (e.g., bend slowly, leading with shoulder). *Variation:* Use carpet squares or hula hoops to define personal space.

Space Bubbles. Use imaginary bubbles or hula hoops. Students imagine that the hoops are big bubbles around them. Ask them to explore the limits. Ask them walk around and do moves and steps without touching other's bubbles. Use drum or count to change time, space, energy.

No Words (Dance Communication). Use only gestures and motions to give directions: "Come forward, turn, sit." Partners then create their own movement directions. Remind students not to show, but tell with movements. *Challenge:* Repeat without using hands. Afterward, discuss the role of gestures and movements in communication.

Follow the Leader. Students imitate actions or words of the leader. For example, wiggle hips at a low level or punch elbows at a high level. Use the BEST elements for ideas. Leader passes the lead to another who takes over.

Simon Says. Play "Simon Says" using BEST element (Ready Reference 10.1) and Laban combination (Ready Reference 10.2). For example, "Simon Says" use your body to show a circle. Relate to units (e.g., time lesson: move clockwise in a circle).

Cumulative Name Game.   Form a circle and ask each student to create a movement to match the syllables in her name. The leader demonstrates using a unique level, body part, and move. *Example:* Su'-san: starting at low level and slither up to high level saying "Suuuu-san!" After each student demonstrates her or his name move, everyone mimics it. *Challenge:* To learn names, repeat everyone's move from the beginning each time.

Step In.   Use this movement activity to review any content. Students form a circle. The teacher gives movement directions. *Example:* "Take two steps in if you know the capital of Ohio. Step back one if you know the state bird." *Variation:* Brainstorm ways to get into the circle. Use BEST dance elements for ideas. After modeling, students take over.

Famous Dances.   Students research a famous dance (e.g., minuet). Expert panels present their findings and take questions from the audience. *Variations:* (1) Experts demonstrate dance aspects. (2) Research dancers (Ready Reference 10.4).

Musicals and Dance.   Watch a musical (e.g., "Mary Poppins"). Discuss how dance is used. What does dance communicate about the story and characters that would be missing without the dance?

Balance Pantomime.   Brainstorm times when balance is important (e.g., walking on a wall, crossing a creek on stepping stones). Ask half to pantomime, while other half observes and gives feedback. Reverse. Discuss differences between mime and dance.

Ball Bounce.   Direct students to bounce an imaginary small ball (e.g., a tennis ball). Change to a beach ball, basketball, and so on. Tell them to show the size and hardness of the ball with their bodies. Change energy and speed.

Movement Words Hunt.   Challenge students to find words that are either locomotor or nonlocomotor moves (Ready Reference 11.1). Here are examples: *Locomotor:* walk, leap, jump, drag, slide, scoot, skip, crawl, dash, float, pounce, prance, spin, swoop. *Nonlocomotor:* twist, swing, rock, sway, collapse, curl, dodge, explode, grab, lean, lift, point, poke, press, push, quiver, rise, shake, shiver, sink, squirm, turn, writhe.

Card Draw and Move.   Students call out ways to move. Write them on cards. Groups sort cards into locomotor and nonlocomotor. Next, students list adverbs that qualify each (e.g., walk slowly, fast, with force, in a "shape," using a lot of space, in a rhythm). Form circle. Put cards in two piles and draw one from each and do it.

Movement Bingo.   Use the words from Ready Reference 11.1 to play bingo. When someone wins, everyone does the moves to check.

I'm Stuck.   Narrate series of sticky situations using different body parts; You are clapping your hands when they suddenly won't come apart. You try to get them to separate. Finally, they pop apart. You reach up to scratch your face. Now your hand sticks to your face. You try different ways to pull your hand off, but it is hard. Blop! It comes off. You start to walk around when your left foot sticks to the floor. You try to make the best of it. You move around with your left foot glued down.

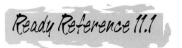 **Locomotor and Nonlocomotor Moves**

Put these on cards for a pocket chart and use them to play Movement Bingo, do warm-ups and expand vocabulary development.

Walk: shift weight from one foot to the other with one foot always on the ground.
Run: same as walk, but there are moments when neither foot touches the ground.
Gallop: this is a step leap with the same foot always leading in an uneven rhythm.
Leap: like a run but you are in the air longer with both feet off the ground.
Skip: combines step and hop in an uneven rhythm, and the lead foot alternates.
Jump: weight changes from both feet to both feet.
Hop: requires weight change from one foot to the same foot.

Shake: a wiggle done in place.
Bend: close up your joints.
Stretch: open up your joints.
Push: use your body to move against a resistance.
Pull: use your body away from a resistance.
Twist: rotate in a direction up to the body's limit.
Turn: spin around, whirl, and twirl.
Rise: come up to a higher level.
Sink: move down to a lower level.

Other action words: zoom, slither, scatter, explode, crumple, melt, and tiptoe.

Body Moves and Steps.

Use these activities to explore types of moves and steps:

Leap: Pretend to leap over real or imagined objects (e.g., a log or a rubber swimming pool).

Hop: Use a hoop. Hop in and out. Hop all the way around the hoop. Change tempo.

Jump (in different ways): with feet together, then apart, alternate these, land on one foot.

Run: Explore with imagery. Run on hot sand, to the finish line, to catch a bus, and so on.

Slide: Slide as if the floor was slick or warm. Slide like you are tired or in a hurry.

Step hop: Clap a one-two beat. Students step on beat 1 and hop on beat 2. Try it to music.

Stretch ("as if"): you are waking up, yawning. Challenge to stretch out long and then wide.

Bend: Do real-life bends (e.g., tie shoes or pet a dog).

Sit: Try to sit, kneel, and lie down without use of hands.

Shake: Ask for real-life shaking and practice these (e.g., a bowl of jelly or baby's rattle).

Turn, twist, lift: Practice turning with feet at different levels and speeds.

Rock and sway: Sway like the wind. Gradually increase the force so that it becomes rocking. Sway while walking, slowly, faster, larger, smaller, and so forth (Pica, 1991).

Laban Effort Actions.

Practice these eight actions changing body parts, amounts of energy, and/or the timing (sustained versus quick): Punch, slash, wring, press, dab, flick, float, glide. Lead with different parts of body (e.g., glide with your shoulder, flick with a hand, punch with a

Fourth position—arms en haute.

shoulder). Finally, give three Laban actions and students create a dance with five moves. Use the three-part frozen shape-movements-shape sequence. Partner and have students teach each other their dances.

Shake and Shape.

On a signal, everyone shakes and wiggles a body part. When leader says "freeze," all must stop. Begin again. Ask students to give descriptive comments about frozen body shapes.

Shape Go Round (Adapted from Celeste Miller).

Form a circle. One child goes into the center and makes an emotion shape at a low, middle, or high level. The next comes in and connects to the shape. When the people sculpture is set, the first person leaves. A third comes in and so on. *Variation:* Do with two at a time or three. Challenge students to enter and exit consistent with the target emotion.

Movement Problems.

Start a movement such as arm swinging. Ask problem-solving questions such as "How can you make it smaller? Show me. Now larger. Move the swinging to whole body and then back to just arms. What are the effects of these movements?" Ask half the class to do while others observe. Then reverse. Ask fat questions such as "What did you see? How did it feel?"

Across the Floor.

Divide into teams and do as relay. Call a move (e.g., walk, run, leap, jump, skip) or a combination. When ITs touch a target, the next team member moves.

Walks.

Students walk to drum beats (e.g., half-time, double-time, walk time, march time). Next, students explore walking by talking them through a sequence: "Walk in place. Now walk around the room without bumping into people. Cover the whole room. Walk with toes first. Walk as if you just got a compliment, were embarrassed, have a stomach ache, are worried, have a heavy load." Vary walks in low, medium, and high levels using music (e.g., jazz).

Imagination Walk.

Students line up and take turns walking to a destination as others observe and describe. Each walks a different way across the room. Repeat and add energy, change time, use space and body differently, repeat phrases.

Jump–Turn–Freeze.

Students walk around and keep an eye on one person. They should not follow the person. Next, add a second person and then, after a while, a third person to the list of others that each student is trying to watch. Students are to keep walking. Then say, "When you pass the first person, JUMP!" Continue for a while and then add TURN for the second person and finally FREEZE for the third.

Three Levels.

Students create a shape and then freeze in low, middle, and high levels on a count or signal.

Get Moving: Pathways.   Everyone spies a destination and moves there in a straight pathway and back home, then a curvy pathway and back home, using as little space as possible. Use start/stop signals.

Adopt a Dance.   Each student chooses a move or step and gives it a "unique touch." Sustain until you make eye contact with someone and then adopt their dance.

Dance Machine.   Each student chooses a move that can be repeated. One student goes to the center and begins his or her move. One by one all "add on" by touching on some plane and repeating his or her move until all are "one" machine with a variety of moving parts. Machine can be around an idea (e.g., a book or chapter in a book, a concept or feeling).

Pass-It-On Moves.   One person in the circle starts a move and others imitate until the moves get all the way around to the starter. The next person to the right then starts a move, and so on. Do to music.

String Shapes.   Each person stands in elastic loop (one yard of tied together elastic). Make movements while holding onto the elastic. Ask students to then move to music while creating a variety of shapes with the band.

Responding to Accent.   Clap a phrase accenting the first beat (e.g., think of "I love you" with accent on three different words). Clap the same phrase accenting the last beat. Children move to the phrase, showing the accent by a change of movement (use after time element is taught).

Video Response.   Watch a video (e.g., a musical with dance in it such as "Oklahoma") that ties into a lesson and has a dance connection. Direct students to watch for specific dance elements (BEST) and how they are used to communicate an idea or feeling. This can be a jigsaw cooperative learning activity. *Variation:* Show an animal film like *March of the Penguins* to analyze movements. Compare with a dance video like *Dying Swan* (Ann Shea, Chattanooga).

Ribbon or Scarf Dancing.   In a large space, allow experimentation with dancing to music with the scarves or ribbons. Tape 2 feet of ribbon to the end of a pencil to create a wand for each student.

Shape Rope.   In personal space, students each hold up a rope high and drop it. Tell them to observe how the rope landed and make the same shape with your body. Continue dropping the rope in different ways.

Balancing Moves.   Ask students to stand in their spots and do particular moves (e.g., stand on one foot, on tiptoes, twist), while balancing a book on their heads.

Energy Boost.   Ask for things that move slowly, strong, quick, weak, light. Combine ideas by asking, "What moves slowly and lightly?" Students try each combination.

Statues.   Students assume a choice shape. On signal they change to another shape. Say "memorize your body." Do at different speeds. Do three shapes and put together as a shape or statue dance. *Variation:* Move freely around the room until "freeze" signal. Students stand still in a shape and do not move until "thaw" signal. Leader should give descriptive comments on shapes (e.g., levels, space).

Movement Sentence Add-On.   Do in circle, First student creates a sentence (e.g., three moves or steps) and next person imitates, but adds on something. Do in small groups.

Four Square Feedback.   Divide notebook paper into four sections labeled BEST. As groups present dances, the audience writes what they saw and felt in a square for each. Encourage specific ideas about each BEST element. Afterward, comments are shared.

Dance Freeze.   After learning dance elements, put on music without lyrics (new age or classical) for students to free dance. When the music stops, each freezes and gives a one-liner about a dance element he or she is using. *Example:* "I am at a high level because the music was fast and made me feel happy."

III. Connecting Dance to Curricular Areas

This section describes example Seed Strategies to prompt thinking about using dance to explore concepts and skills in science, social studies, math, and language arts. Courses of study and curriculum guides are useful in identifying suitable dance material, and Ready Reference 11.2 offers several ideas, largely related to science. Look for content that has "movement possibilities."

Solicit topics for dance exploration from students, too. Ask for movement ideas related to categories such as feelings, weather, celebrations, cooking, weddings, birthday parties, funerals, shopping, and work. Explore movements in unison and then in small groups. As a culminating activity, ask students to plan a dance based on a subject area concept. Suggest the dance have a beginning, middle, and end. Use the *three-part freeze-move-freeze* structure to get started.

Science Focus

Science Standards.   All standards can be accessed at the National Science Teachers Association (NSTA) website: *www.nsta.org*.

Dance Webbing.   Choose a science topic such as seasons (Ready Reference 11.2). Web kinds of movement associated with it. Use BEST dance elements of body, energy, space and time to expand the movements. *Example:* falling leaves twist,

Ready Reference 11.2 # Environmental Sources of Dance Making

Directions: Think and do movements that show:

Body systems: respiratory, circulatory, digestive, nervous
Body actions: eat, walk, run, hug, hop, skip, sit
Seasons and cycles: life cycles (e.g., butterfly)
Growing things: small to large movements, slow, sustained
Weather: contrasts in nature (e.g., force of tornado versus gentleness of a breeze)
Plants: sizes, shapes, ways they grow
Animals and insects: cats creep, stretch, sneak, roll, slink, ball up, leap
Places or environments: movements at beach, mountains, desert

Machines and mechanical actions: pulleys and levers, tools
Electricity and magnetic forces: north and south poles, pull, repel
Space and solar system: rotate, use of space, size, shape, pathways
Gravity: force, pull, weight
States of matter: solid, liquid, gas
Causes and effects: temperature, wind
Energy: fire, steam, solar, nuclear
Technology: computer, elevator
Inventions and objects: crepe paper, cotton balls, rope scarves, elastic

---

turn, and float at high levels down to the ground (low level). Break into groups, and group chooses one idea to explore further. Reassemble to show top three dance moves.

North Pole, South Pole (Magnetic Force).
Students walk as if the floor is a giant magnet. Then suggest that the ceiling is the magnet. Call out the pull on different body parts. Suggest they walk as if the body is an opposite pole of a magnet.

Environmental Dance.
Choose a category from Ready Reference 11.2 to explore. *Example:* Pairs experiment with movements related to pollution and create a dance phrase or sentence to a count of 8 that shows something about pollution. *Variation:* students first write down a main point they've learned about the environment. Use these as captions to create dance sentences.

Environmental Walk.
Brainstorm places in the environment. Leader calls out a place and students walk (in place) based on the conditions (e.g., hot sand on beach, thick forest, marsh, rocky path). *Variations:* (1) Do in small groups and each perform. Audience describes the conditions they observed. (2) Add an environmental problem that would change walking conditions (e.g., oil spill on beach, broken glass trash on a prairie). Explore showing conditions with different body parts.

Dancing Animals.
Play various types of danceable music. Encourage students to warm up by moving as different animals, concentrating on moving at different levels, and with a variety of body parts.

Places to Sit.
Experiment to find the effect of sitting in different places such as a bicycle, horse, swing, airplane, step.

Discuss the science/health behind designing places to sit and work (ergonomics). Students then decide on a frozen sitting position they can hold. Coach them to use a variety of shapes and levels. On signal, half the class freezes and other half views and comments, as they would at a museum exhibit. Reverse roles. *Variation:* Combine with photos and art, such as Rodin's *Thinker.*

Tool Dance.
Brainstorm tools used for eating, gardening, building, schoolwork, etc. List movements associated with tools. Try them at different speeds and levels. *Example:* Shovel-push in, dig, lift, throw, pat down. *Variation:* Pairs choose a tool and create a dance phrase. Do to a count.

Sound Movement Collages.
Sounds of the body, city, nature, animals, machines, children's names, and names of states and cities can all suggest movement. Brainstorm a category and then stretch it for movement possibilities. Encourage students to think of the shape, size, rhythm, and energy of the words. Break into groups and ask each to make a collage (an assemblage of items glued together) of sounds and movement. Groups can then create a freeze–move–freeze dance and perform. This activity can be followed by an actual visual art collage around the topics danced.

Mechanical Movements.
Brainstorm things that move in nonorganic ways (e.g., jerky moves of robot or computer). In pairs or small groups, explore moving different body parts at varying levels using mechanical movements.

Machine Dances.
Create a whole or small group dance based on BEST elements of machines. *Examples:* elevator, escalator, or computer. (See description of "machine" earlier.)

Insect Dances. Each student or group chooses an insect to explore through movement. Each performs a "freeze–move–freeze" dance: Start frozen, do three to five moves, then freeze in a shape. Dances can include movements related to eating, life cycle, environmental changes, and their effects. Coach for variety in using BEST elements.

Real-Life Sounds. Brainstorm sounds in categories: body, city, nature, animals, machines, chants, rhymes ("Pease Porridge Hot"), songs ("Row Row Row Your Boat"), and nonsense phrases (e.g., "slip, slap, slop"). Student's names, names of states, cities, work chants ("heave heave ho, yo yo, heave heave ho") are also sources. Explore the rhythm, size, shape, and energy of sounds. Stress original moves that no one else does.

Inventions Dance. Use common items such as tissue, boxes, paper clips, ropes, and elastic bands to create a dance of inventions. Movement with the object should be explored, not pantomimed. *Example:* Experiment with ways to move with a tissue using BEST elements.

States of Water. Students dance molecular movement in a solid, liquid, or gas. Lead students through small-group explorations to move as if melting, condensing, and evaporating. Explore changing from a solid to a liquid and then to a gas. Use different parts of the body, energy, space, and time. Finally, ask each group to create a freeze–move–freeze dance that shows concepts about molecular movement and structure.

Animal Movement Exploration. Students show different animal movements (e.g., different ways to walk, stretch, and sleep). Coach them to show movement of breath, bones, and muscles. Do movements to a count of 10 to increase concentration and focus.

Endangered Species. Pick an endangered animal and explore ways it moves and under different circumstances (tired, hungry, scared). Use "what-if" questions to explore possibilities. Use children's literature for ideas, such as *The Girl Who Loved Wild Horses* for horse actions.

Heartbeat. Ask students to feel their own heartbeats. Show them how to take a pulse. In the classroom space, direct students to move to their own heartbeats using a variety of shapes and moves. Ask "what-if" questions: "You got really scared? Tired?"

Body Painting. Pretend each body part is a paintbrush and explore a variety of brushstrokes (e.g., broad and sweeping, quick and short, slow and thick). *Variation:* Explore movements associated with any career.

Bird Flight. Groups create a dance based on different types of bird flight. Include different formations (space and pathway) birds use, changes in speed and level, and changes in leaders. Think about different body parts. Dances should have a beginning, middle, and end.

Weather Dance. Students are frozen in a shape. Weather changes are announced by narrator, and students respond by changing levels and shapes for snow, light rain, and raging hailstorm. Begin by restricting movement to one spot and then move to locomotor. *Variation:* Convert to a relay dance in which all start frozen and then begin to move, one at a time, until all are moving. Then reverse the action. This works well if the weather event starts small and slow, escalates, then slows and stops.

Art Alive. Make action come to life from a painting by creating a freeze–move–freeze dance that explores concepts of gravity, balance, momentum, muscles, and use of light and shade. For example, use "fighting" art like *Dempsey and Firpo* or *Stag at Sharkey's* by artist George Bellows.

Life Cycle. Students dance each phase of the life cycle of an animal or plant separately by using BEST elements. After each phase, have them put it together in a dance. Stress that movements can convey feelings. Sounds can be added.

Constellations. Groups form frozen shape of constellations. Small groups then move across night sky to night sounds. *Variation:* Small groups rotate in and out of the "stage" space or come in low, move to high formation, and back to low across the night sky.

Horse Dancing (From Todd Lyon, Horse Trainer). Invite a horse trainer to speak and demonstrate the commands and moves horses are taught (e.g., Tennessee Walkers). View a video, if possible, and discuss horse "dance" routines using BEST elements. Create a chart that lists special vocabulary (e.g., trot, gallop, canter, pace).

Social Studies Focus

Social Studies Standards. All standards can be accessed at the National Council for the Social Studies (NCSS): *www.socialstudies.org*.

Dance Possibilities. Ready Reference 11.3 uses BEST to give ideas for dances possibilities in social studies.

Real-Life Rituals. Brainstorm movement in life (e.g., greetings, farewells). Divide into pairs and portray each in various ways using different body parts, moves, steps, space, energy, and time.

Get to Work. Brainstorm ways people work: picking, washing, sweeping, raking, fixing. Each person or small group creates a work dance based on a real or imaginary prop associated with work (e.g., broom) and moves in creative ways. Music can be added. Dance should have a beginning, middle, and end.

Ready Reference 11.3   # Social Studies Movement Possibilities

Directions: Choose any topic and then experiment with all movement associated with it.

Big Questions: "How did it used to be and why? Why is it like it is today and what can I do about it?"

- Brainstorm and then explore BEST dance elements related to: economic development, citizenship, communities, cultures and diversity, customs, directions, global understanding, governments, holidays, land and water formations, legends, occupations, housing, population density, rituals, and transportation

- Everyday actions (cook, wash)
- Map skills and geography
- Social interactions (sharing, cooperation, respect, trust)
- Physical environment (e.g., use of natural resources)
- Thinking skills: cause and effect, sequencing, gathering data, discovering relationships, making judgments, drawing conclusions

Trio Community Dances.   Trios form and each member develops a shape and moves using a community concept or problem (e.g., loneliness, sharing). Members teach their part to their group. The final dance consists of members doing the dances of all members in a sequence.

Ceremonies.   Invent a ceremony related to daily life within the classroom. Create a dance to accompany it and use high, medium, and low levels in the dance, such as a start-the-day ceremony.

Military Moves.   Research military moves used in different countries (e.g., pivot, straight leg Nazi march). Learn terms and moves such as left flank, right, center, offense, and defense (Joyce, 1994).

Magic Wand.   Display a full-length portrait such as a narrative scene from history with several figures in it. Students assume figures' positions. When touched by a magic wand, they move in ways the figure might move. Coach them to become conscious of how to bend and walk, the use of curved and straight lines, and positive and negative space. Leader can add emotions and motives: "Move as if you are in a hurry."

Country or State.   Students show "terrain" using changes in levels as narrator describes a tour of a place. Students can also show the size of the state or country in relation to other countries or states as leader calls them, for example, Texas vs. Rhode Island. *Variation:* Students show what they know about a place (products, industries, climate, or plant life) by interacting with them through movements and imagination.

Create a Folk Dance.   Select a folk song like "Home on the Range" and ask groups to create movements for one line. Distinguish between pantomime and dance by focusing on BEST elements (Ready Reference 10.1) to explore possibilities. Sing the song and each group teaches its dance sentence.

Historical Event.   Brainstorm movements that would have been part of a special event such as the signing of the Declaration of Independence. Do in slow motion, changing rhythm and space. Create the mood of the moment with your body.

Holiday and Season Dances.   Brainstorm movement qualities of Halloween characters (stiff movements of a skeleton) or create a "giving" dance for Thanksgiving (focus on rituals and feasts), or "loving shapes" to rhythms for Valentine's Day. Spring dances can focus on rising and stretching and other growing movements.

Current Events Dances.   Use teachable moments and brainstorm movement possibilities. For example, the Olympic Games or national elections can inspire sports dances or dances related to the opening or closing event.

Foreign Language.   Dance terminology can be an entrée into a culture or country study. For example, ballet was born in Italy, but grew up in France so its "language" is French: plie means "to bend" (root for pliers) and revele means "to rise." Pas de chat means "step of the cat" (think of when ballerinas shake their toes).

Folktale Dance.   Focus on an event in a folktale. For example, for Gag's *Millions of Cats*, dance shapes and sizes cats might have taken when the old man found them.

Sports Dance.   Create dances using sports moves. Ask students to plan warm-ups and then move into motions of the actual game. Choose music to go with the movements and organize final explorations into a freeze–move–freeze dance.

Folk and Ethnic Dances.   Discuss different ways dances have been used through history (ceremonies, prayers, celebrations) and how forms of dance have evolved, using common movements for expressive purposes. View a whole

Dance and Movement Strategies

dance or steps from another culture or time period. Discuss what is represented (rituals for marriage, weather, seasons).

Folk dances are usually appropriate for upper primary and intermediate students. Begin with short dances based on a step such as walk in time to music and walk in a circle. Horas and kolas of the Middle East are basically a series of steps and variations on the steps performed without partners in a circle. Some demand challenging footwork. Common dances include the polka, waltz, schottische, and mazurka (Ready Reference 10.3).

When teaching traditional dance steps, it helps to use a "I do, we do, you do" sequence: All face the same direction. Show the whole dance, then practice in unison until all have the basics. Involve children in identifying step components and then join steps to create a whole work or even a new step. Steps do need to be mastered before doing dance figures in which they are to be used. Mix up partners frequently so no one feels "stuck." (This process deviates from total teacher direction requiring only student imitation.)

Variation: Create original dances around the same topics. For example, an Irish jig. First play Irish folk tunes and/or show a video (e.g., *Riverdance*). Ask open questions about the BEST elements and the feel of the dance. Group students to choreograph their own jig with focus on feet and legs. Hands are held behind the back. Encourage them to kick to the beat, but create new steps, turns, and so forth.

Literacy: Reading and Language Arts Focus

Literacy/Literature Standards. All standards can be accessed at the National Council of the Teachers of English (NCTE) and the International Reading Association (IRA) at *www.ncte.org* or *www.ira.org*.

Phonics Shapes.   Ask students to make:

- Soft shapes for soft *c* and *g* words and hard shapes for hard *c* and *g* (e.g., city, giraffe; cat, go, gone).
- Sustained movements for vowels (can be held continuously). Example: Make your body long or short depending on the sound you hear in hat, hate/cot, coat. Vowel digraphs can be shown in pairs with one person becoming "silent."
- Bound moves for consonants that make "stop" sounds (*b, p, t,* hard *c, k, d,* hard *g, j, v*) and sustained for consonants such as *s, l, r, m,* and *n.* For consonant blends, partner to show blending.

Letters of the Alphabet.   Pairs make letters using high, medium, and low levels. Stress original ideas and ask students to explain their interpretations. *Variation:* Students

make a shape of an object that starts with the letter. Change levels and speeds.

Rhyming Words.   Give a spelling pattern (-ack,-ick,-ot,-eek,-op). Read a poem that contains the pattern or read a list of words, some with the target. When students hear a word that rhymes with the pattern, they do a creative movement or make different shapes. *Suggestion:* Rehearse possibilities. Post chart of words like *bend, twist, reach,* and *push out* to extend thinking.

Syllables.   Ask students to change BEST dance elements according to number of syllables. Say words aloud. For example, "Hippopotamus has five syllables so make five shapes as I say each syllable." Vary the elements (e.g., time, energy) during word repetitions.

Spelling.   Teacher gives a word and students spell it by moving in a floor pattern to "write it" using a chosen pathway to shape the letters. *Variation:* Pairs call words to each other.

Antonyms.   Brainstorm movement words and opposites, such as smooth-jerky, tight-loose. Then (1) call a word and students do it at different levels and speeds, (2) call a word and students do its opposite, or (3) partner doing the word and the other its opposite. Use with different levels, qualities, and tempo.

AB Antonym Dances.   Brainstorm movement antonyms (e.g., high-low, fast-slow, smooth-jagged, left-right). Next, guide exploration of meanings of word pair using BEST. For example, show me fast with your foot, hand, and head. Small groups then choreograph an AB dance using one pair of antonyms: A=a movement phrase or sentence with the first word, as the B section uses the second word (should show contrast with the "A" section in as many ways as possible). Perform dances with audience/class giving "what worked" comments, afterwards.

Word a Day.   Pick a movement word. Students squeeze the word for possible meanings by exploring it through movement and finding synonyms and related words (e.g., jump-bound, vault).

Word Walls and Webs.   Develop vocabulary through movement by asking students to look for action and movement words in their reading. Put up a large sheet of paper. Ask students to add to the Dance Word Wall web. At any point, these words can then be used for movement (e.g., slither, sneak, ambulate, dodge, dragged, plod, saunter, amble, trot). *Variation:* make a dance word collage.

Compare and Contrast (Comprehension).   Contrast movements such as strong–light, tight–loose, explosive–smooth, up–down, and wide–narrow by asking students to jump all these ways. Compare ways to do the same move: walk, stride, pace, shuffle.

Cause-Effect. Pairs face each other. One is the cause and the other is the effect. Cause moves and the effect must respond appropriately (e.g., if cause steps forward, effect must move to keep from being stepped on). Encourage creative effect responses.

Classification. Call out a category to classify a movement. Students explore all they can do in that category (e.g., quick at low level, quick bending, quick twisting, quick reaching). *Variation:* Students take turns demonstrating three different moves or actions and group must figure out what all have in common.

Parts of Speech. Explore adverbs by asking students to move different ways. For example, do locomotor/nonlocomotor moves/steps merrily, sadly). Web words from a story, put on cards, and explore different ways (e.g., run slowly, crawl sneakily). Combine into dances, with a beginning, middle, and end, about a chapter or event in a story.

Gestures. Brainstorm everyday nonverbal communication used to greet or respond (e.g., wave, beckon, stop). Explore how to do these different ways (e.g., fast, slow, different body parts, levels).

Story Tableau. Small groups use body shape and space to show a story concept (e.g., grief, celebration, loneliness). Freeze in the shape. On signal, each person unfreezes and does moves to a count (e.g., count of 3 or 4).

Verbal Dance. Students create a freeze–move–freeze dance, but actually talk out loud as they dance, changing voice to match movements. For example, "low level, low level, flick fingers, flick toes, jump jump, twirl, high level, punch, shrink, collapse."

Dance a Story. Stories abound with characters and situations with movement potential. To be dance, not drama, only the essence of the character or situation is used. A literal movement translation results in pantomime (drama), not dance. Stories can be danced or pantomimed; both call for targeting an event or image, rather than a whole story. This example combines dance and drama based on McCulley's *Mirette on a High Wire.* Put masking tape on the floor. Groups take turns balancing in different ways: one foot, tiptoes along the line, with dance movements exploration. Those waiting pantomime the crowd watching and reacting.

Character Dance. Any story character can be explored through movement by considering ways a character might move. For example, how would Wilbur in *Charlotte's Web* move if he was happy? Hungry? Afraid? Tired? How is his movement different from Charlotte's or Templeton's? How does body shape show something about a character? On signal, students dance in character. Divide the class in half so that one-half can observe and comment. Reverse. *Example:* Do three moves Charlotte might use in a spider dance.

Character Walk. Each student walks around the room as a famous person or character, varying normal level, posture, rhythm, gate, and so forth. When leader says "change," each person tries another walk variation.

Theme Dance. Any theme from a poem or book can be danced by first brainstorming ways to express the theme with body parts, movements, energy, and use of space and time. For example, the theme "Courage comes out of fear," can be danced in a frozen shape, movements, and frozen shape (three-part dance) planned and performed by small groups that each present a very different interpretation.

Key Topic Dance. Brainstorm important words or topics in a poem or book. Next, list web movements, shapes, levels, energy, and so forth that could be used to convey the topic. Give small groups the choice of a topic or word to plan a dance or a series of movements to show it.

Dance Poetry. Read a poem about dance and ask students to listen for movement possibilities. For example, encourage showing different ways to use the body and space to express the joy of dance in these poems: "Dancing Pants," "Dancin' in the Rain," and "Danny O'Dare," by Shel Silverstein. Make Poem Charts of dance poems for repeat dancing.

Poetry in Motion. Read aloud a poem for enjoyment, first, and then ask students to interpret movement as the poem is reread. Narrate movement or excerpt words and sentences for students to speak and dance. Music or percussion instruments can be used to highlight poem action. Example poems are "Push Button" by Shel Silverstein, "Jump or Jiggle" by Evelyn Beyer, "The Swing" by Robert Louis Stevenson, and "Jump-Jump-Jump" by Kate Greenaway. Jump rope rhymes are also wonderful ways to energize with rhythmic words. See collections such as *Miss Mary Mack and Other Children's Street Rhymes* (Cole) and Booth's *Doctor Knickerbocker and Other Rhymes.*

Line by Line. Read aloud a poem, first. Next, give each student or group a line to explore the movement possibilities of the line (e.g., rhythm of the words, emotions, images). Encourage more than pantomiming. The poetry can then be danced line by line as a narrator reads, or groups can plan to perform just one line.

Write About a Dance. After any dance or creative movement, students write about what they did and felt. The BEST elements give writing focus. The writing can be in the form of a story, informational piece, or a poem (Ready Reference 5.1) about the dance. Here is a diamante based on observed shapes.

Shapes
Round Angled
Changing Size and Levels
Dance Shapes Show Feelings
Frozen Moving Forms
Pointed Curvy
Shapes

Story Tension. Discuss tension in a story and how characters go about relieving it. Ask, "What point is the climax or most intense part?" Students then show with the body the tension.

Characters Alive! Use a painting or picture from a book with several characters in it. Groups become the characters by posing as a frozen picture. They then "come alive" and do three dance moves consistent with the characters. Coach students to do locomotor moves and use low, medium, and high levels. Finally, they return to original frozen positions.

Math Focus

Math Standards. All standards can be accessed at the National Council of Teachers of Mathematics (NCTM): *www.nctm.org*.

Math/Dance Connection. Math is basically the study of quantitative relationships. Dance is also concerned with relationships among shape, time, and size. Through dance, students can come to understand basic math concepts such as add, subtract, divide, and duration (second or minute). Higher-level math skills require sequential thinking, examining situations for important details and patterns. Dance also involves these types of thinking, so dance and math can reinforce one another.

Two Guys Dancing Math. This dance duo does school performances and residencies (one "guy" is college professor). Check out their 2001 book *Math Dance*, by Karl Schaffer and Erik Stern (publisher: MoveSpeakSpin; website: *www.mathdance.org*).

   Math moves possibilities. Brainstorm moves in math, including estimating, adding, multiplying, dividing, patterns, geometric shapes, fractions, lines, curves, and subtracting. Give each group one concept. Each decides at least three different ways to show their math concept through movement.

Geometric Shapes (Following Directions). Everyone walks around filling up the space. When a leader calls a shape, all freeze in that shape (circle, triangle, square). Leader gives feedback for unusual ideas (use of energy or space). *Variation:*

Students partner to make the shape. Do also with letters of the alphabet.

Telling Time. Use masking tape to make a large clock on the floor. Children move around in the 12 hour spaces by stretching arms to a person in the middle of the clock as the teacher calls a time. Explore different times: recess time and lunch time and ways to move around (fast, slow, hop, slide).

Shape Dance. Many folk dances are done in a circle, square, or line. Invite a guest to teach one and relate it to the math concept. Challenge students to find other math ideas in the dance (e.g., counting, parallel lines, sequencing—first, second, third).

Get the Facts! Call out math problems to solve by jumping, hopping, or walking along a number line. Give a different way to move each time (fast, slow, low, halting, flowing). Sounds, chants, and instruments can be added.

Angles and Degrees. Tape a large rectangle on the floor so that every student can stand on the tape. Give a series of directions related to the rectangle: Take three straight forward steps in. Now step back to the perimeter. Turn 45 degrees right. Stick out left arm. What's that angle? (acute) Face forward on the perimeter. Turn 90 degrees left. Stick out your left arm. What is the angle from the tape? (right) Corner people, change positions. What does the line they are walking do to the rectangle? (makes two triangles) How could we show 180 degrees? 360 degrees?

Math Glue. Everyone moves around in slow motion. Teacher says "glue 2" and students find others to stick to in that number (everyone must keep moving in slow motion). Teacher then calls "unstick" and continues with a new number.

   Twos and threes. Teach number groups by calling out a way to move and giving the pattern. For example, "Hop in twos with a pause after the two hops." Make into dances of moves grouped into twos and threes.

   Angle dance. Students create a dance that illustrates angles (right, oblique). Each dance should have a beginning, middle, and end and can be locomotor or nonlocomotor. Use freeze–move–freeze form.

Math Dance. Students choreograph a dance to teach to others by creating instructions in math terms. For example, to do the "math hop," take two steps forward, slide right, hold for four counts, and hop three times.

Number Shapes. Teacher signals and students make their bodies into shapes of numbers. They may need to work together. Challenge them to make these shapes combine with time, space, and force.

IV. Multiarts Focus: Dance Integrated with Other Arts

This book focuses on integrating the arts with core curricular areas. And yet this is not the only important integration plan. The arts have much in common with one another and should be used in concert to work toward both academic standards and arts standards. It is also important to integrate the arts with each other to magnify the unique impact the arts can have, as described in Chapter 1 (Ready Reference 1.1).

Art Dance Connection. Much of visual art involves movement (e.g., draw, paint) and art and dance possess parallel elements such as line and shape. Dance can awaken the kinesthetic sense and put feelings into motion. Students can dance a painting or paint the dances they create. The kinesthetic center of dance can motivate children to want to move. The need to express through movement can extend to scribbles, drawing, and painting. Relate dance elements to other art forms and the language arts to make connections and develop thinking structures. For example, explore shape in art and dance by painting to music on big paper. Find line, pattern, rhythm, and images expressed in art, music, and so forth. Movement possibilities include explorations of lines, shapes, and directions.

Choreograph to Music. Play a piece of music and ask students to listen closely to the tempo, mood, and rhythm. Discuss and repeat listening. Brainstorm ways to show the important parts of the music with dance. As a whole or in groups, create a dance to go with the music. Devise a symbol system to note how to perform the dance (e.g., circles, lines, and squares to show movements).

Dynamics! Use a drum, finger cymbals, and other percussion instruments. Ask students to change the size of body actions according to the sound (e.g., loud makes large movements). Use a variety of instruments to help students understand how timbre can change and still have a loud or soft sound.

Body Melody Match. Select a familiar song. Explain that the body may show melodic pattern. As children sing or listen, ask them to move up or down in a space to illustrate the shape of the melody.

Sing with Your Hands. Post and teach the Kodaly hand signs to add kinesthetics to hearing the scale. See Chapter 12 for the hand movements called Curwen signs that show the scale from "do" up.

Sign Language. Teach songs in sign language or add signs to any song. See Riekehof's (1978) *The Joy of Signing*.

Art in Motion. Show art with physical motion in it. Discuss how motion is shown and why a particular step is sometimes "frozen" by the artist (e.g., which part of a sneeze would you depict?). Re-create the artwork as a dance. Freeze as shown, move to a count, and freeze again. *Variation:* Create dances that show what happened before and after the moment in the artwork.

Sculpture or Architecture Dances. Display pieces of sculpture or pictures of buildings or furniture. Ask about space, curves, and movements and how each might move if it came to life. Ask students to show the size, energy, and flow with their bodies.

Artists That Move. Set up a station with art books or assign students to locate art that includes movement (e.g., Matisse and Degas). Discuss or write journal entries about how artists show movement through line, shape of body, and use of space.

Dance a Painting. Display a print and ask brainstorm shapes, movements, and emotions (note the word *motion* in this word). Direct attention to the foreground, middle ground, and background in subjects such as landscape, seascape, and still life. Divide into groups. Each decides a way to dance the painting, using a beginning–middle–end structure. The goal is not to pantomime but stretch for ideas: What movements came before this moment in the art, during, and after? What is just outside the subject matter (e.g., other people, movements)? After students prepare, take turns presenting. Background or mood music can be added.

Paint a Dance. Use large paper to capture a dance after doing it. This can begin on a small scale with just painting or drawing certain movements (e.g., curved lines, circles, shaking, turning).

Negative and Positive Space. On signal, students make body shapes. Start with "fixed spot" shapes before locomotor. Stress the use of different levels. At freeze signal, all stop and look for "holes" in people's body shapes, made with arms, legs, or fingers. Ask students to squint to see hole shapes—the negative space. *Variation:* partner. Person *A* makes a shape with holes (negative space) in it, and person *B* then makes a shape that interacts with the negative space.

Emotion or Color Dance. Make cards with emotions (pictures or words) or colors. Groups choose three cards and put them in an order (beginning, middle, end) to create a dance. Encourage students to repeat actions and use variety.

Dances can be accompanied with readings of color poems such as those in O'Neill's *Hailstones and Halibut Bones*. Appropriate "emotion" music can be used, too.

Teacher Spotlight:

From Ballet to Fifth Grade

Libba Allen is an animated woman who has been teaching at Ashley River for more than 20 years. She has seen the dream of the school's first principal, Rose Maree Myers, grow into a reality.

Ms. Allen, who now teaches fifth grade, was initially hired because of her background in ballet. "Rose Maree thought ballet had given me discipline. She is a very detail-oriented person, and she convinced us we could do it."

The "it" that Ms. Allen refers to is arts integration. "This approach gives students an outlet to express themselves," she says. She describes examples such as using pictographs in math and writing based on student photographs or art stimuli. Her students keep science journals in which they draw their observations about things like the terrarium/aquarium in her room.

Ms. Allen is particularly proud of the photography lab at AR, constructed from a $50,000 grant. The grant also provided professional development for teachers to learn photographic skills.

Like other teachers at arts-based schools, Ms. Allen acknowledges that considerable time is involved in planning for arts integration. The students are "out" for 80 minutes a day, however, so teachers have a good block of planning time.

It is worth it? "All students can excel!" Ms. Allen exclaims passionately. "The arts give them the expressive tools to do so." And she had the discipline from ballet to make it happen. ✳

Conclusion

An ulcer is an unkissed imagination taking its revenge for having been jilted. It is an unwritten poem, it's an undanced dance, it's an unpainted watercolor. It is a declaration that a clear spring of joy has not been tapped and that it must break through muddling on its own. (John Ciardi, poet)

This chapter is a compendium of starter ideas to use in dance integration. These Seed Strategies can be adapted and developed to create integrated lessons for science, social studies, math, and liter-

acy lessons. Used in combination with the Arts Integration Blueprint explained in Chapter 10, these strategies can get the curriculum *moving* in the right direction.

Resources

See the Appendix for further study, including more websites.

Dance Activity Books

Alison, L. (1991). *A handbook of creative dance and drama*. Portsmouth, NH: Heinemann.

Bennett, J. P. (1995). *Rhythmic activities and dance*. Champaign, IL: Human Kinetics.

Berthoz, A. (2000). *The brain's sense of movement*. Cambridge, MA: Harvard University Press.

Choksy, L. (1987). *120 singing games and dances for elementary schools*. Upper Saddle River, NJ: Prentice Hall.

Fleming, G. A. (1990). *Children's dance*. Reston, VA: American Alliance for Health, Physical Education, Recreation and Dance.

Gilbert, A. (1992). *Creative dance for all ages*. Reston, VA: National Dance Association.

Hanna, J. (1999). *Partnering dance and education: Intelligent moves for changing times*. Champaign, IL: Human Kinetics.

Joyce, M. (1994). First steps in teaching creative dance to children (3rd ed.). Mountain view, CA: Mayfield.

Landalf, H. (1997). *Moving the earth: Teaching earth science through movement for grades 3–6* (Young Actor Series). Lyme, NH: Smith & Kraus.

Malam, J. (2000). *Song and dance*. New York: Franklin Watts.

McGreevy-Nichols, S. (1995). *Building dances: A guide to putting movements together*. Champaign, IL: Human Kinetics.

Pica, R. (1995). *Experiences in movement with music, activities, and theory*. Albany, NY: Delmar.

Rowen, B. (1994). *Dance and grow: Developmental dance activities for three- through eight-year-olds*. Pennington, NJ: Princeton Book.

Stinson, S. (1988). *Dance for young children: Finding the magic in movement*. Reston, VA: American Alliance for Health, Physical Education, Recreation and Dance.

Children's Literature References

Booth, D. (1993). *Dr. Knickerbocker and other rhymes*. Boston: Tickner & Fields.

Cole, J. (1999). *Miss Mary Mack and other children's street rhymes*. Minneapolis, MN: Sagebrush.

Gag, W. (1928). *Millions of cats*. New York: Coward-McCann.

Goble, P. (1978). *The girl who loved wild horses*. Scarsdale, NY: Bradbury.

McCully, E. (1997). *Mirette on a high wire*. New York: Putnam.

Oneill, M. (1989). *Hailstones and halibut bones*. New York: Doubleday.

12 Integrating Music Throughout the Curriculum

Questions to Guide Reading

1. Why is music considered an integral teaching tool (research, theories, and philosophy)?

2. What kind of music literacy do classroom teachers need to have to integrate music meaningfully?

3. How is music integration implemented (planning, learning environment, arts-based literature, best practices, instructional design, adaptations, and assessment for learning)?

4. How can teachers partner with music specialists?

Where words leave off, music begins. (Heinrich Heine)

In the News

Sweetwater school district is 8 miles from the U.S.-Mexico border. It is "one of a growing number of schools using mariachi to engage Hispanic students in school" (Brown, 2005).

Artists, inventors, and scientists routinely play music to jump-start creative problem solving (CPS). Music kindles emotional responses and fires up cognition, often in the form of mental images. Music can make time seem to speed by. It makes the drudgery of exercise palatable. We are energized by Sousa marches and Dixieland jazz; the fast tempo causes us to tap, sway, and smile. Rock and roll makes us want to dance. Baroque music (e.g., Bach or Vivaldi) arouses feelings of grandeur. Chopin and other Romantic composers can trigger dreamy images; Puccini's operas exude a passion that nearly hurts.

Humans insatiably seek the aesthetic effects of music. Concerts sell out, joggers run with iPods, and music is piped throughout airports. CD players are basic car equipment. Teenagers on a family trip feel abused if not allowed to listen to favorite CDs. Lawyers sing in their offices as workers sing in farm fields. Nurses whistle and musicians play on street corners. Families gather to sing "Happy Birthday" or watch *American Idol*.

Boosted by multiple intelligences theory and research that connects music and learning, classroom teachers have joined in. They now use all styles of music, from Mozart to nature sounds, to start the day, as transitions, and to relax or rouse after lunch. Arts integration goes even further. Music is made integral to daily learning in the way it is integral to daily life. Compelling evidence supports this full integration into the curriculum. Jensen (2001) states, "If this were a court case, the ruling would be that music is valuable beyond a reasonable doubt" (p. 14).

In the opening Classroom Snapshot, Bernadette Chilcote applies the research. She couples the teaching of reading with both a listening and creating music experience. Music is used strategically to expand vocabulary, comprehension, and fluency. These children are doing the hard work of learning to read, willingly. Music is part of what makes them want to learn.

Classroom Snapshot:
Music-Based Literacy

"Criss-cross applesauce!" Ms. Chilcote is on the floor with her first graders. They sit up for a "close listening" to a CD

Bowing away in the Ashley River garden.

based on *Follow the Drinking Gourd* (Winter, 1988), yesterday's picture book read-aloud. The **lyrics** to the song are today's reading material. Their teacher tells the children to **focus on the voices** to see what they **notice.**

"Listen for how these voices and the **musical instruments** make you feel," she says.

A man and woman sing, "Follow the Drinking Gourd" (Harris). After the first verse, Ms. Chilcote pauses the CD and asks, "What musical instruments do you hear? How did the music feel? What else did you notice?" She waits until many hands are up before she calls on anyone.

"The man's voice is deeper," says a curly-haired boy.

"Her voice is beautiful. Like an angel," says a small girl.

"High-pitched," explains another boy.

Other students notice the instruments and guess there is a guitar because of the "strumming" and "plucking."

"Those are great words, *strumming* and *plucking*," Ms. Chilcote comments. "**Let's say them** three times like they sound." Tongues vibrate on the /str/ and smack on the plucking. Students become serious when she asks them about the feel of the song.

"I think they are afraid they'll get caught," a redheaded girl whispers.

"Yes, it feels like it has to be a secret or they'll die," the boy next to her adds.

Ms. Chilcote nods to each responder. **She follows up** with "What makes you think that?" and "Why do you think so?"

The class does a **close listening** to the entire song, and then the teacher asks how the **song lyrics connect** to the picture book from yesterday. She holds up the cover.

"The book has pictures but no singing," notes a boy.

"The song is in it, though," points out another.

"**Show us where,**" Ms. Chilcote hands another copy of the book to him, and he flips to a page and points.

"Here," he points to a line that has "follow the drinking gourd in it." "Here, too," he continues and turns the page.

"The song is in the whole book," a girl concludes.

Ms. Chilcote turns to the back of the book. "What is this?" she asks as she shows the music for the song. Three hands shoot up and she smiles broadly, "John, first, then Lynn and Morgan."

"It's how to play the notes!"

"It's the sheet music—what you read."

"Yeah, I can read these notes on the staff!"

"Wow," says the teacher. "So we can read words and read notes to make music. It's another kind of reading."

She then asks about other books from the social studies unit. Some talk about the "sadness" of the time. One child says that the "world is better without slaves and we all have freedom."

In a version of **repeated reading,** Ms. Chilcote distributes copies of the lyrics and the children use their fingers to **follow along.** They do two more **close listenings,** but now they sing along. It is a lot of reading for first graders, but most are on track, especially for the refrain, "Follow the drinking gourd! Follow the drinking gourd. For the old man is a waiting for to carry you to freedom, If you follow the drinking gourd" (Winter, 1988, p. 45).

The lesson ends with Ms. Chilcote explaining how they will be able to show their comprehension of the song using art materials. Students cut the lyrics into verses. She points to a chart on the wall that says "How to Make Art."

"You'll have lots of **choices** for how you use the art elements to show what you think and feel about the verses," she says.

"I want to make mine blue for sadness," says a girl.

"I'm using brown and black with jaggedness, like for ripped pants and scaredness," responds the girl next to her.

"Everyone will have a different one," their teacher reminds them. "It's important to remember to **use our freedom.**"

Arts Integration Blueprint

In Chapter 3 the Arts Integration Blueprint was introduced as a scaffold for arts integration. Ready Reference 3.2 lists the 10 building blocks. The first has to do with *why* arts integration should be implemented (philosophy based on research and theories). Next comes *what* teachers should know (arts literacy) and *how* to plan lessons, create an aesthetic environment, use literature and best teaching practices, design instructional routines, adapt for diverse learners, and assess and work cooperatively with arts specialists. The Blueprint is applied to music in this chapter. First, some research.

Music Research: It's Only Natural

There is growing interest in how the arts affect the brain (see Chapter 2). Music has been a particular focus, especially when used in classrooms (Research Update 12.1). The overall conclusion is that if a child's environment is rich in music, the brain's structure will be more complex. Let's review important findings.

We Are Hardwired for Music. The brain is predisposed to detect patterns and sounds. Every child begins life immersed in rhythm, the most basic element of music. The steady beat of the mother's heart attunes the baby to patterned sound. Voices, with unique rhythms and timbre, enter the world of the womb. The unborn child physically responds, showing an innate desire to listen and a preference for consonant versus dissonant sounds. Early on, the tiny fetus reacts to phonemes (the smallest sound units in language) such as the percussive consonant sounds of /t/, /p/, and /f/. As the growing child eavesdrops, the brain grows, absorbs, and makes connections (Begley, 2004; Jensen, 2001; Wolfe, 2001). Phonemic awareness later will form spoken language that is the foundation for reading.

Regions of the Brain Dedicated to Music Overlap with Other Areas. A review of studies on the "Mozart Effect" (music used to increase learning) shows that areas of the brain used for spatial reasoning (mentally visualizing, moving, and relating objects) are also used to process music

---

Research Update 12.1 Music and Academic Achievement

- In a Tucson, Arizona, school (2002), classical music plays all day in hallways to calm and relax students. This is one part of Opening Minds through the Arts (OMA) that targets at-risk students. OMA students score significantly higher than non-OMA students on measures of words, pictures, and listening (Kippelen, 2002).
- Test scores continue to rise at the Conservatory School even though students spend less time on reading and more time on music. Literacy-challenged students usually receive tutoring in reading using music (Scripp, 2003).
- The ability to process musical symbols and representations is a "leading predictor" of learning in other subjects. Musical pitch was found to be more predictive of math ability and rhythm more predictive of reading. "This cannot be considered random or irrelevant" (Scripp, 2003, p. 122). Website: *http://nec-musicined.org.*
- Ford Elementary School in Lynn, Massachusetts, now ranks number one in the state on standardized tests for third-grade reading. This change is attributed to the Learning Through Music experimental program for students with the lowest reading and math scores. Students are given an hour a day of music reading and computer-enhanced composition work (Scripp, 2003).
- Kindergartners who listened to music and watched an educational video scored higher on the DIBELS test than those who just watched the video. Students also had less off-task behavior while listening to music (Register, 2004).
- First graders who received music listening instruction had significantly higher reading scores than a control (88th percentile versus 72nd) (Weinberger, 1998).
- A strong relationship was found between awareness of pitch and ability to sound out in reading (Weinberger, 1998).
- Fourth-grade "emotionally disturbed" students improved their writing quality and quantity when they listened to music (with headphones) versus writing in silence (Deasy, 2002).
- First graders in Pawtucket, Rhode Island, involved in a special music program performed significantly better in math and reading than a comparison group without the music (Chan, Ho, & Cheung, 1998).
- Interest in learning is up and so is attendance at Bugg Elementary (Raleigh, North Carolina), a school where test scores were below average. Students listen to Gustav Holst's symphonic suite "The Planets" in science and learn about fractions as they study musical notation. The goal: boost reading and math scores.

(Deasy, 2002). Some music brain circuits reside near or overlap somewhat with math, in particular (Begley, 2004). Physicist Gordon Shaw, known for his research on the Mozart Effect, believes music uses many of the same higher brain functions as both science and math do (2000). Language and music seem to share some neural circuits as well. This suggests learning functions in the brain are more integrated than previously thought.

Music Uses the Whole Brain.

Music is processed in both the left and right hemispheres and activates cognitive, affective, psychomotor, visual, and auditory systems depending on "whether you are reading music, playing an instrument, composing a song, beating out a rhythm or just listening to a melody" (Wolfe, 2001, p. 161). Brain scans show that virtually the entire cortex is active when musicians play. Different areas perform different functions, from directing movement to thinking to feeling to remembering (Weinberger, 1998). Multiple brain sites are synchronized by firing patterns that oscillate across the brain, enhancing efficiency and effectiveness (Jensen, 2000).

Music Involvement Changes the Brain.

For example, the corpus callosum that connects hemispheres is enlarged in musicians (Begley, 2004). The younger the child is when music lessons begin, the more cortex develops (Begley, 1996). Music also triggers different brain states: harp music for theta (half awake), Muzak and smooth jazz for alpha (relaxes alertness), and upbeat and pop for beta (alert) (Jensen, 2000). Rhythms enhance visualization (e.g., rain forest recording). Listening to music for as little as 1 hour per day can cause the brain to reorganize. Different types of music do different things. More complex music (like Mozart's "Sonata for Two Pianos in D Major" or Haydn's symphonies) may create greater brain "coherence" (Jensen, 2000; Malyarenko et al., 1996).

Music Affects Mechanisms for Emotion, Memory, and Language.

Music activates areas of the brain related to emotion by changing levels of chemicals such as epinephrine, endorphins, and cortisol, which causes the "flight or fight" reaction to an event (Wolfe, 2001). The brain responds to musical patterns, increasing memory of content embedded in or coupled with music.

Music Affects People Differently.

Music activates different areas of the brain in musicians and nonmusicians, and which areas are activated depends on what is listened to and for (e.g., melody in the right hemisphere, lyrics in Wernicke's areas, rhythm in Broca's area) (Jenson, 2000).

Blueprint I: Philosophy of Arts Integration

> *A man should hear a little music, read a little poetry, and see a fine picture every day of his life.* (Goethe)

Why Integrate Music?

The beliefs about the values of music integration grow out of brain research and research that links music and academic achievement. The latter are summarized in Research Updates 12.1 and 12.2. In addition, some philosophical beliefs are linked to theories, like multiple intelligences outlined in Chapter 2. Finally, accumulated professional experience informs beliefs. These sources yield the following 11 reasons to integrate music.

Music Is a Significant Part of Life.

> *Alas for those who never sing, but die with their music in them.* (Oliver Wendell Holmes)

Thirty-thousand-year-old bone flutes have been found in France (Jensen, 2001). Ancient drums have been unearthed at other sites. These ancient artifacts show that music has been with us from our beginnings. It is used to amuse and relax, to pass on history and values, to inspire and to glorify achievements. Parents instinctively sing and rhythmically rock fussy babies, but they just as readily spice up broccoli with spontaneous songs: "Here comes broccoli. It's so green. Yummy yummy tree trunks. Open up to eat."

Imagine a day without music. Out would go the radio, the CDs, and much of television. Life would be dull. Music elements are embedded in life. A simple sentence like "Turn out the lights" is altered as the speaker changes the pitch, tempo, volume, and emphasis. The command "Turn *out* the lights" becomes a seductive whisper "Turn out the li-i-i-ghts?" It's all in the music.

The economic impact of music on our lives is staggering. In the 2000 U.S. census, more than 130,000 persons listed their livelihoods as musicians or composers; that figure does not include dozens of related careers, such as teachers and music store owners. More than 1,500 orchestras generate employment for thousands more. We spend billions each year on concerts, CDs, MP3 players, and music DVDs. One Rolling Stones concert tour grossed more than $27 million. Phone ring tones are a $3 billion business.

Much of school motivation comes from connecting learning to life outside the school walls. Music is out there. We need to bring it in and make explicit its life values.

Research Update 12.2   Effects of Music

- Preschoolers given 8 months of keyboarding and singing showed enhanced spatial-temporal (abstract) reasoning. A control group given computer lessons showed no improvement. Spatial-temporal reasoning is important in subjects such as mathematics and science (Rauscher et al., 1997).
- Various approaches to music instruction were found to increase spatial-temporal reasoning; traditional music notation led to the strongest results (Deasy, 2002).
- In a sample of 25,000 kids from every region of the United States, 20% of the 12th-grade class could do high-level mathematics. However, among low-SES students involved in instrumental music, fully *one third* performed at high levels of math (Catterall, 2003). *Note*: Low SES associates with low performance in nearly every published study.
- Fifty-seven studies showed arts experiences increased self-concept, language, cognitive development, critical thinking, and social skills. Of special note was the positive effect of music participation on self-concept (Trusty & Oliva, 1994).

- College students who listened to Mozart had temporary increase in spatial reasoning (Shaw, 2000). But in another study, complex rhythms, even a rhythmic rain forest background proved to be three times better than Mozart (Jensen, 2001, citing Parsons et al.).
- Math performance improved in a study in which one group studied math with a Mozart sonata and scored an eight-point increase over a control group (Campbell, 1997; *www.musica.uci.edu*).
- Juvenile delinquent males improved in self-confidence versus delinquent males of the same age who were given instruction but no guitar performance (Deasy, 2002).
- The College Board reports students with 4 years of music coursework scored an average of 49 points higher on the combined verbal and math portions of the SAT. The more years students spend in music, the higher the scores (MENC: *www.menc.org/information/advocate/sat.html*).

Music Is Natural.   Babies make their own music as they intuitively babble songs. Babies can grow into children who seek music to gather information and sort out feelings. A new industry of private music schools, such as Kindermusik, International, and Music Together has sprung up in response to brain research and child development studies. They provide early music listening and music making experiences that attune children to phonemes (sound units)—awareness necessary for speaking and reading. Research shows that poor phonemic awareness is at the root of many reading problems; children need to hear sound nuances to decode.

Music Is a Vital Communication Vehicle.

Music is the shorthand of emotion. (Leo Tolstoy)

Communication is understanding and expressing ideas and feelings. Music does both, in unique ways. For example, in a pedestrian tunnel at Chicago's O'Hare Airport, neon art rhythmically pulses along the ceilings and walls as synthesized music plays. Lyrics softly urge "keep walking, keep walking." The message is understood and everyone chooses to comply.

It is also clear that musical listening experiences and chances to make music stimulate imaginative thinking and sharpen problem solving. Music is one of the eight ways of knowing counted as a distinct human intelligence (Gardner, 1999). Music is highly cognitive. For example, Campbell (1997) reports that music majors have the highest rate of admission to medical school. Music involves thinking to produce it and thinking to understand it. It enhances cross-lateral brain activity and time in the "zone" or "flow." Even young children readily create music. They make up songs and adapt hand-clap and jump-rope rhymes. These sound experiments stimulate creative thinking.

From early childhood we sing to understand and express feelings. Mozart's "Twinkle, Twinkle Little Star, How I wonder what you are" enables preschoolers to ask questions beyond their vocabularies (Page, 1995). "Me" egocentrism eventually morphs into a world of "we" as children discover peers; song preferences change to focus on understanding relationships with others.

Music is highly emotional communication. There are music pieces and songs to reflect our deepest emotions from love to despair. We are flooded with vivid "you are there" emotions when we hear songs from our past, especially teen and young adult years.

Music Boosts Attention, Memory, and Recall. Armstrong (1993) reports that an educated Iatmul in New Guinea can learn between 10,000 and 20,000 clan names. Music makes this possible. Names are chanted using the pattern-seeking inclination of the brain. Learning through music can seem effortless because we unconsciously *entrain* to patterns, just as we entrain as we walk with someone by adjusting our gaits. Heart rate and body cycles entrain to rhythms around us (Armstrong, 1993; Page, 1995). Brain waves imitate external rhythms, too.

Advertisers deftly use the mnemonic effect. Jingles compel us to buy products: "You deserve a break today, so get out and get away." Sometimes these ditties, with their "rent it—eat it—buy it" messages invade our thinking and we are powerless to quash them. This is because the brain looks for associations (Wolfe, 2001). Most Americans first experience musical mnemonics when learning the alphabet. Children repeatedly sing to Mozart's "Twinkle, Twinkle Little Star" melody (also used for "Ba Ba Black Sheep"), and the letters are thus placed into memory. The combination of enjoyable repetition is a winning musical format. Not every song works. Lyrics have to have "positive message and resonate emotionally with kids"(Jensen, 2000, p. 90). For background music Jensen suggests jazz or Baroque with 65–80 beats per minute to enhance concentration.

Music Promotes Physical and Mental Health. Since drumbeats were first heard in Africa, the soothing properties of music have been known. Music is used across cultures to alter mental state by changing brain chemistry (Jensen, 2000). Stress hormones are reduced and the immune system is boosted. Music can also lower heart rate.

Music therapists have used music for more than 50 years for illnesses ranging from anorexia to drug addiction and mental retardation. One study found that daily music significantly increased healing antibodies. Blood pressure, heart, and respiration rates went up and down with the tempo of music. One man, whose life support was to be ended, awoke and said the dulcimer music drew him back (*Springfield News Sun*, 1997, p. 1.) Pleasant colors and images are triggered by musical sounds (chromesthesia), and songs can provoke cathartic effects such as sobbing. Faster musical rhythms induce smiling, even laughing because they trigger the release of endorphins, the body's natural opiates, and change brain waves (e.g., Parkinson's patients regain cadence rhythms for walking).

Business and industry use this power of music not only in advertising but to increase workplace productivity. For example, music is intentionally used to create positive mood and energize employees, which increases attendance. Listening to music is also a "form of mental priming" that promotes multitasking by the brain (Scripp, 2003, p. 134).

Music Bonds People Together.

Music cures a lot of loneliness. (Anonymous)

Educators at the singing schools of Hungary believe music increases sensitivity, harmony, and cooperation through its emotional appeal and group participation—choirs are big there. Singing brings people together in shared emotions.

Creating "harmony" is a social and personal skill as well as a musical achievement. Shared music is communication that can bridge gaps between generations and mend fences among disparate groups. For example, Union and Confederate soldiers, weary from fighting each other by day were known to join in songs across the night. In singing classrooms the learning community is made stronger as an invisible web of group spirit is woven, which is often the specific purpose of patriotic and folk songs and marches (Page, 1995). Songs sung around campfires on chilly nights bring people into an envelope of communal sound. Then there are the young lovers who bind themselves together with "our song."

Americans have a rich tradition of singing that often surprises foreign visitors, especially our standing before sports events to unite in "The Star-Spangled Banner." SING! is a $600,000 project to promote more singing across America. In 2007 a film will be released to promote family singing and encourage nationwide songfests (contact Ralph Burgard at *ralph@burgard.net*.

Music Expresses Cultural and Personal Identity.

Without music life would be an error. (Nietzsche)

Music has been called the "universal language of mankind." Music is so important that the act of music making is considered a gift. For example, it is a high tribute to have a song written especially for you. Music shows up in our most important ceremonies and traditions from birthdays to New Orleans style funerals. Music is central to most religions. Study the music of a culture to find out what people celebrate and fear and how they grieve.

Teenagers become passionate about "our music" as bodies and brains go through sweeping changes. During adolescence, music commonly becomes a means to carve out individual identity. Even Mozart, at age 16, wrote a great symphony to "grapple with the torment of being a teen" (Lockwood, 2005). Today rap and hip-hop styles are popular and influence youth, with some children much farther into this music world than parents fathom. *Note:* Some researchers think heavy metal or gangsta rap may stimulate the brain's seizure center.

Music Records and Reflects History.   Recorded history is replete with songs and music that tell tales of heroes, passions, and wars. It is impossible to think of the civil rights movement without recalling songs of marchers or not to associate World War II with Glenn Miller's big-band sound. Songs and chants with attractive rhythms, satisfying repetition, and unforgettable melodies instill lessons from the past, celebrate victories, and lament disasters. Information and values are passed along in hymns, military chants, and folk and pop songs. Composers are inspired by historical events giving us well-known songs like "God Bless America," written by Irving Berlin at the brink of World War II.

Throughout history, each tribe and group has crafted a unique musical identity. Today, diverse music represents our diverse human family. In the United States we embrace every genre and style from folk to classical, rock and roll to rap. Blues? Jazz? All are readily available at the local mall or on the Internet.

Music Is a Coping Device.

> *God made music so we could pray without words.*
> (Anonymous)

Music "sustains people under the most degraded circumstances" (Booth, 2003, p. 20). Slaves sang to endure and, in a manner, controlled suffering. Others sang "Follow the Drinking Gourd" to find the path to freedom using the stars in the night sky. Music gives solace during wrenching moments such as funerals, lost loves, and fear ("I whistle a happy tune"). We hum and rock to give physical and mental peace; we sing lullabies to calm cranky children. Singing and humming ease the passing of time and make unpleasant work more pleasant.

Music Increases Social/Motivational Behaviors.
Music can be enjoyed without instruction but to sing or play an instrument well demands skill and discipline—attention, know-how, practice, and the desire to improve (Hope, 2003). There is growing evidence for the positive influence

of music on social-emotional development and behavior. Musical activities require self-discipline, respect, empathy, dealing with frustration, and collaboration (Scripp, 2003).

Pride is a powerful fuel for the learning engine. By learning to sing or play an instrument, children develop confidence, posture, and poise. Through musical achievements they gain insight into important connections between sustained effort and satisfaction. When children see that significant adults share pride in their hard work, this self-discipline grows and can be transferred to other areas of life. From Bill Clinton's saxophone experiences to current Arkansas Governor Mike Huckabee's guitar playing comes testimonials to this effect.

Music Has the Power to Make Us Happy.   Einstein claimed that he got the most joy from his violin. He said he even thought in music. To be happy is an educational goal not to be dismissed (Noddings, 2005). Music is one of the ways in which our "cognitive skills remind our emotional self that life is joyful" (Scripp, 2003, p. 31). Music can change the feel of learning. Music is a form of beauty that can transform any environment, charging us with aesthetic responses. Students and teachers immersed in music are uplifted and energized. Students who are guided to develop diverse musical tastes have more options for using music as a special way of knowing, expressing, and enjoying.

Music has great power, but that power can and has been abused. Music integration should include discussions about the downside to music euphoria. Music can harm with hateful lyrics that provoke aggressive responses. Any art form that demeans a person or group should be questioned.

But back to the main point: Music is fun, and fun is a fundamental motivation to learn. Happy children learn better. As the song says, "Hava Nagila" ("Let Us Be Happy" was written by a 12-year-old Jewish boy 100 years ago).

Music Is a Vehicle for Learning Throughout the Curriculum.   There is a special term for using music as a learning tool: *musicogeniceupadia*. The motivational power of music can be combined with its communication potential to cause students to want to learn and to learn more. Play and music both arise from the instinct to create and express, so it isn't surprising that music raises interest in subject matter. Musical sounds charge the brain, stimulating whole-brain involvement.

Through songs and music, students increase general vocabulary, fluency, and understanding. Music develops listening skills, and listening is a main pillar of learning. We really don't need cause-effect "scientific" results that show music can increase test scores. There is strong evidence that music promotes intrinsic motivation, disciplined work habits, and collaboration—all of which are necessary for achievement.

Music gets attention. It has the potential to increase time on task and qualitatively improve thinking during learning, which improves both efficiency and retention (Campbell, 1998). As Jensen (2000) notes, "The more educators use music to assist in learning other material, the more quickly and accurately the material will become embedded" (pp. 74–75).

Blueprint II: Arts Literacy: Content and Skills

> *The woods would be very silent if no birds sang except those that sang best.* (Henry David Thoreau)

Classroom teachers who effectively use music as a learning vehicle throughout the curriculum have a basic level of music knowledge and skills. A minimum level of music literacy is prescribed by the level expected for students. The *National Standards for the Arts* addressing music are listed in Ready Reference 12.8. In general students are expected to know (1) music's historical, social, and cultural role in life; (2) communicating through music by learning to read/understand music, creating original music, and performing; and (3) the aesthetic aspects of music.

What Do Teachers Need to Know to Integrate Music?

The Interstate New Teacher Assessment and Support Consortium (INTASC) recently developed standards for what classroom teachers need to know about the arts. The music section can be downloaded at: *www.ccsso.org/intasc*. In this section of the Blueprint, music literacy needed by classroom teachers is outlined in these areas:

- Definitions of Music
- Purposes and Roles
- Music Elements and Concepts
- Music Processes
- Musical Instruments
- Genre, Forms, and Styles
- People
- Music Materials
- Teaching Approaches

Defining Music. The world is full of sound. Even birds and whales seem to sing. Is that music? What about the whirring of a fan or the babbling of a brook? The question

"What is music?" has no one answer but should be part of an ongoing conversation about the arts (Ready Reference 3.3) for daily topics. There is agreement that sound must be organized in time and space to make music. It would seem to be highly dependent on the ears, too. However, Beethoven and others who acquired deafness continued to compose, and today most schools for the deaf include marching bands and choirs (Jensen, 2000). Indeed we perceive rhythm and beat with the entire body, and producing and understanding music requires both cognitive and emotional perception.

But what is the difference between sound and music? Compare an African drumbeat and the patter of a baby's feet. Both have rhythm. Both evoke emotional response. But the drumbeat is an intentional organization of sounds for the sake of making sound. The sounds evoke feelings and emotions through the use of rhythm, tempo, melody, harmony, pitch, and repetition. These basic elements are used to create images and ideas in a musical form. Music can be thought of as sound patterns over time intended to express moods, ideas, or feelings.

Purposes and Roles.

> *It gives a soul to the universe, wings to the mind, flight to the imagination, a charm to sadness, gaiety and life to everything. It is the essence of order and leads to all that is good, just, and beautiful, of which it is the invisible, but nevertheless dazzling, passionate, and eternal form.* (Plato on music)

Music is a form of communication. It is used to understand and express thoughts and feelings, just like reading, writing, speaking, and listening. However, music, like all arts, goes beyond to intend to provoke aesthetic knowing and response. The goal of music isn't just to give or receive information but to give a sense of beauty. Music is created through creative problem solving (CPS); within it is wonder, yearning, curiosity, and new connections. We marvel at musical inventing that stretches the possibilities of sound (e.g., as DJs "scratch" turntable sounds).

Music Elements and Concepts.

> *I am music. I make the world weep, laugh, wonder and worship.* (Goethe)

Musical elements alone do not create music, but they are building blocks. These elements create a common language teachers can use to engage students in deeper listening and give students scaffolds to create music. In other words, these are tools to meaningfully integrate music.

Tempo. Tempo is the time or speed—how fast the music is. Tempo is usually labeled using Italian words. From slowest to fastest they are: largo, lento, adagio, andante, moderato, allegretto, allegro, vivace, presto, and prestissimo. *Ritardando* means to slacken the tempo, and *accelerando* means to quicken.

Rhythm. Rhythm is movement of sounds through time. In songs the words usually match the rhythm. Try saying and clapping the words "happy birthday to you." Now do the same with "She'll be comin' round the mountain when she comes." Feel the different rhythm?

Beat and accent. Beat has to do with a steady underlying rhythmic pulse, such as a clock ticking. The accent is where the strongest emphasis is placed as in the waltz: *one* two three, *one*. Everything we sing or say has a rhythm that can be varied by changing the tempo, beat, and accent.

Meter. Meter is the beat and accent groupings of rhythms (e.g., triple meter=3/4 [waltz] or songs like "Happy Birthday").

Tempo, rhythm, beat, and accent show the strong connections between math and music. There is a numerical pattern of beats over a length of time.

Notes. Rhythm is represented by a series of notes ranging from whole (usually 1 beat per measure) to quarter notes (4 beats per measure) to 8th, 16th, and even 32nd. In order to understand music, one must also understand math concepts of time and fractions and be able to count beats.

Syncopation. Syncopated rhythms are uneven, as in jazz. The beat remains steady, however. Try to say "Charlie Parker Played Be Bop" by syncopating it to "Charrrr-lie Parrr-ker Played Be Bop." (Parker was a reknowned jazz saxophone player.)

Pitch. Pitch is the high or low tones in the sound pattern.

Timbre. Timbre (pronounced "tambur") is the same as tone color and has to do with the unique qualities of a sound (e.g., voices or sounds made by plucking or blowing instruments). Each sound has a timbre that enables you to hear whether you've dropped your keys or a pencil. Children enjoy experimenting with timbres using body parts, sticks, and rulers.

Dynamics. Dynamics is the volume or relative loudness or softness of the sound. Dynamics give emotional intensity. The Italian words *forte, piano, pianissimo,* and *crescendo* appear in music to indicate dynamics or how loud the music should be played.

Texture. Texture is the layering of instruments and/or voices to create a thin or full feeling. Melodies, rhythms, and timbres can be combined to create textures. We can create texture by combining voices, as in singing a round like "Frère Jacques." Orchestral music is an example of a full texture.

Melody. Melody is the tune. It is a series (more than one) of musical tones or pitches falling into a recognizable pattern (e.g., in "I'm a Little Teapot," the motions show melodic direction). Melodies may be based on major or minor scales, but you do not need to know what a scale is to make a melody. When we sing words, they become melodies.

An octave is the distance between the first and last notes of our Western scales of eight notes (think of Do Re Mi Fa So La Ti Do) or between any pitched note and the next note with the same name (eight notes higher or lower). Most of our folk songs use the eight main notes of the Western scale. The five other notes that come between the scale notes are called *sharps* and *flats*; think of the black keys on a piano.

Harmony. Harmony is the blending of tones or sounds (e.g., chords). When two or more pitches are blended simultaneously, harmony is made. Children often know about barbershop quartet harmony.

Form. Form is the structure, shape, or pattern of a piece of music or a song, such as AB (binary form, as in "Fish and Chips"), ABA (ternary, as in "Happy Birthday"), and ABACA (rondo form). The *A*s and *B*s are separate themes. The order of repetition is the key and largely determines the form of a piece of music. Musical styles and genre are closely related to form (e.g., jazz versus opera).

Ostinato. Ostinato is simple rhythmic or melodic content repeated over and over to accompany a song. Ready Reference 12.1 summarizes music elements and concepts.

Music Processes. All communication is basically either receptive (taking in information and feelings) or expressive (giving out). Both making music and listening to music involve cognitive, emotional, and aesthetic processes. Using these divisions music is made or expressed (1) by composing or creating original pieces or songs, or (2) performing works of others. You don't need to be a music specialist to involve children in creating music with simple instruments and writing their own songs. Daily singing is invaluable.

Music is received, understood, and appreciated by reading the sheet music/lyrics and/or listening. Classroom teachers can learn to guide music listening, as Ms. Chilcote did in the opening Classroom Snapshot. Reading musical notation can be a joint venture of the specialist and classroom teachers.

Reading music. A non-Western perspective sees everyone as a music participant. This view helps us consider how music can become more integral to learning. If music is a natural extension of the human spirit, it should have a place in every discipline that examines people's courage, creativity, inventiveness, and resiliency. Reading music goes further to allow participation in a range of activities from using

Ready Reference 12.1   Music Elements and Concepts

The basic elements of music are defined here.

Tempo (time): Adagio is slow and allegro is fast.
  Rhythm: movement of sounds through time (matches words, not beat). Includes underlying beat.
  Meter: groupings of beats and accents.
  Syncopation: uneven rhythms as in jazz
Pitch: highness or lowness of a sound.
  Tone: a sound of well-defined pitch, represented by a note.

Timbre: tone color or unique qualities of sound.
Dynamics: volume or relative loudness or softness of the sound; gives emotion. Forte=loud, Piano=soft, Crescendo=volume goes up, Decrescendo=volume goes down.
Texture: layering of instruments and/or voices to create a thin or full feeling.

Other Concepts

Melody (tune): a series (more than one) of musical tones falling into a pattern; includes pitch.
Harmony: the blending of sounds, such as chords; two or more pitches simultaneously.
Ostinato: simple rhythmic or melodic content repeated over and over to accompany a song.
Notation: symbols for tones written on a staff.
Form: structure, shape, or distinct patterns; related to style and genre.
Composition Principles: unit, variety, repetition/contrast, balance, tension/release.
Composition Forms: call/response, verse/refrain, theme/variation, Cannon, AB, ABA, Rondo (ABACA).

---

hymnals to playing music from a score. With that said, Ready Reference 12.2 is for those with absolutely no experience but a desire to know some basics.

Musical Instruments.

The first musical instrument humans undoubtedly used was the voice. It is the one most used today. The other instruments are broken into families: strings, brass, woodwinds, and percussion. Of course, today we have electronic instruments, including software to compose on the computer. Instruments from different cultures are important additions to units and can be demonstrated, shown in pictures, and heard on recordings, as students study uniqueness among peoples. Check websites for pictures and sites where instruments can be heard. Teachers may not be able to stock many kinds of instruments, but sounds can be explored through "found," homemade, or inexpensive ones. Hopkins's *Making Simple Musical Instruments* lists easy ones made from everyday items. Examples include:

- Sound makers (sticks, stones, shakers)
- Percussion or rhythm: anything that can be struck, scraped, or rubbed (tambourines, triangles, wood blocks, bells, maracas)
- Melody instruments to make tunes (bells, xylophone, tone bars, glasses of water, bamboo flutes, rubber bands)
- Harmony instruments (autoharp, guitar, dulcimer)
- Orchestral and band (violins, trumpets, organs, accordions, harmonicas, Indian sitar)
- Orff xylophone (wooden) and the metallophone (metal); have removable bars. Ask the music teacher about Orff instruments.

Genre and Music Styles.

Jazz tickles your muscles, symphonies stretch your soul. (Paul Whiteman)

The terms *genre* and *style* are sometimes used interchangeably, but style generally refers to the distinctive way in which musical elements are used. For example, periods of musical development (e.g., Baroque) have a unique style. Style can also refer to media to make music (e.g., keyboard style).

It would take more than one course in music history to become familiar with all music genres and styles. Teachers with a music history background start integration with a definite advantage, but most teachers actually know more than they think they do. For example, everyone is familiar with classical music from cartoons, such as Bugs Bunny, and advertisers frequently sneak Bach or Beethoven to sell a product. Films such as *Platoon* and *Ordinary People* introduced millions to composers such as Vivaldi and Pachelbel.

Teachers new to music integration are encouraged to begin with genre and styles they know and enjoy so that they can transfer their enthusiasm to students. Once integration is under way, teachers can branch out and explore, along with students. Ready Reference 12.3 lists genres in alphabetical order.

Ready Reference 12.4 clarifies some of the eras or periods of music commonly used to classify Western classical music (music with lasting significance). "Classical" is also one of the periods. The example works listed are just that, examples. They are offered as a place to begin as teachers at-

Ready Reference 12.2   Reading Music: Quick Reference

1. Each note is represented by these letters of the alphabet: ABCDEFG (no note letters above G).
2. Notes are written on a staff, which has five lines and four spaces. Each line represents a note, as does each space. The staff looks like this:

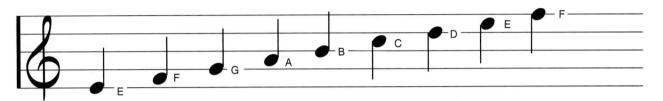

3. To remember the notes on the lines, the phrase "Every Good Boy Does Fine" can be used. For the notes in the spaces, use the acronym FACE (treble clef only).
4. Notes can go above or below the five-line staff by adding ledger lines. To figure a note on a ledger line, just keep using the A–G sequence; for example, the ledger line (one above) the top staff line would be A because the top staff line is F; the next space is G and, again, the next ledger line would be A.
5. If music has two staffs, one is for the higher notes and the other the lower notes. (It gets confusing to keep adding more and more ledger lines so this is easier.) The top staff is the treble or G clef and has this special sign: ♭ The bottom staff is the bass or F clef and has this sign: ♩:
6. On a piano, middle C is in the center of the keyboard. To figure out the white notes on either side of it use the A–G sequence. The black keys are the sharps (#) and flats (b). A sharp raises a note a half-tone (makes it higher) and a flat lowers it a half-tone.
7. The staff is divided into measures or bars (vertical lines) and can have any combination of notes and rhythms. Special symbols convey notes worth different counts or number of beats. For example,

8. The time signature is two numbers (looks like a fraction) at the start of the staff that tells you the number of beats in a measure (bar) and what kind of note gets one beat (e.g., 3/4 means 3 beats to a measure and the quarter note gets one beat).

Ready Reference 12.3   Music Genre and Style

Barbershop	Dixieland	March	Ragtime
Baroque	Environmental	Motown	Rap
Big Band and Swing	Folk Songs	Movie Themes/Soundtracks	Reggae
Bluegrass	Hip-Hop	Musicals	Rock and Roll
Blues	Jazz	New Age	Romantic Era
Choral	Latino	Opera	Soul
Classical	Lullaby	Pop	World Beat
Country	Madrigal		

Ready Reference 12.9   Music Eras and Composers

Selected Periods, Composers, and Example Works

Baroque

1650–1750 *Ornate, flamboyant with predictable forms* (*Note:* good for background)

Bach (1685–1750), German: *Brandenburg Concerti* and 22 preludes and fugues
Pachelbel (1653–1706), German: *Canon in D Major*
Vivaldi (1678–1741), Italian: *Four Seasons*
Handel (1685–1759), German: *Messiah, Water Music,* and *Royal Fireworks Music*

Classical

1750–1820 *Emotional restraint and simplicity*

Haydn (1732–1809), Austrian: *Clock Symphony, Surprise Symphony, The Creation, The Seasons*
Mozart (1756–1791), Austrian: Operas (*Don Giovanni, Marriage of Figaro, The Magic Flute*), *Jupiter Symphony, Coronation Concerto for Piano, A Little Night Music*
Beethoven (1770–1827), German: nine symphonies

Romantic

1820–1870 *Dreamlike and emotional, may suggest a story or concept*

Schubert (1792–1828), Austrian: *Unfinished Symphony, The Great Symphony*
Schumann (1810–1856), German: *Spring Symphony, Papillons* (butterflies)
Mendelssohn (1809–1847), German: *Scottish Symphony* (No. 3) and *Italian Symphony* (No. 4), *Songs without Words*
Chopin (1810–1849), Polish: all his piano works
Strauss (1804–1849), Austrian: waltzes
Liszt (1811–1886), Hungarian: *Hungarian Rhapsodies*

Rossini (1792–1868), Italian: operas (*The Barber of Seville, William Tell, Cinderella*)
Verdi (1813–1901), Italian: operas (*La Traviata, Rigoletto, Falstaff, Aida, Otello*)
Puccini (1858–1924), Italian: operas (*La Boheme, Tosca, Madame Butterfly*)
Berlioz (1803–1869), French: *Symphony Fantastique, Romeo et Juliette*
Tchaikovsky (1840–1893), Russian: *Symphonies 4–6, Swan Lake, The Sleeping Beauty, The Nutcracker, 1812 Overture*
Brahms (1833–1897), German: *Symphonies 1–4*
Wagner (1813–1883), German: operas (*Tristan and Isolde, The Flying Dutchman, The Valkyries*)

Post-Romantic/Twentieth Century

1890–1930 *Focuses more on mood and experimentation with music "without melody"*

Mahler (1860–1911), Bohemian: *Songs of the Wayfarer, The Song of the Earth, Symphony of a Thousand* (No. 8)
Debussy (1862–1918), French: *The Sea (La Mer), Prelude to the Afternoon of a Faun*
Prokofiev (1891–1953), Russian: *Peter and the Wolf, Romeo and Juliet*
Sousa (1854–1932): all his marches
Strauss (1864–1949), German: *Don Quixote, Macbeth,* operas (*Salome, Elektra*)
Stravinsky (1882–1971), Russian: *The Rite of Spring, The Firebird, Petrushka, The Soldier's Tale*

Others to Know

Bernstein (1918–1990): *West Side Story*
Bizet (1838–1875): *Carmen, Symphony in C Major*
Copeland (1900–1990): *Fanfare for the Common Man, Applachian Spring*
Rimisky-Korsacov (1844–1908): *Sheherazade, The Snow Queen*
Williams (1932–): *Jaws, E.T., Raiders of the Lost Ark, Superman.*

---

tempt to increase music background. Dates are included for those interested in plotting birthdays on a timeline to go along with social studies. Celebrating artist birthdays is also a routine to integrate the arts (see Birthday Buddies in the Appendix).

Twentieth- and 21st-century American music has much to offer, too: 1930s Latin; 1940s big band; 1950s rock and roll; 1980s punk rock and New Age; and country music in the 1990s. To get up on rap and hip-hop, check out books

like Stanley's *Rap, the Lyrics: The Words to Rap's Greatest Hits* and Toop's *Rap Attack 2: African Rap to Global Hip Hop.*

People.   Music people take on many roles: composer, musician, singer, conductor, sound engineer, critic, and teacher. Students need to know the range of careers available and add a "real person" element to songs and musical works. A number of videos can be viewed alone or with children's books they accompany. The most well-known is *Beethoven Lives*

Upstairs (picture book has the same title). Most biographies give students an opportunity to learn something of the struggles and inspiration behind success that propelled these people to reach such heights. Studying real people who lived in a particular time and place allows students to see how context influences artistic work. Students can identify with the troubles and triumphs of composers and other people who have made music an integral part of their lives. It gives hope and comfort for children to see they share life experiences with famous artists. Again the goal is to weave in the lives and works of musicians from different backgrounds to give a wider view. Expanded viewpoints gives students more forms to use as they create original musical variations.

For ideas about genre, styles, composers, songs, and other potential questions about what to teach, you may want to consult *The Music Teacher's Book of Lists* (Ross & Stangl, 1994). Ready Reference 12.4 lists people in the music world to get started. Consider making your own A–Z Singers and Musicians list by involving students in the search and selection. Sadie's *New Grove Dictionary of Music and Musicians* (1988) is a great reference for finding background on people, music, and songs, including "Happy Birthday." For folk songs try Sing Out Coorporation, which publishes *Sing Out! The Folk Song Magazine,* started by Pete Seeger (*www.singout.org/*).

Music Materials: Sources. The goal is to use music from a variety of periods, cultures, and genres as appropriate to units and students. Children's concept of what is "good" is malleable, so this is the time to stretch not narrow. Choose music that touches you, stimulates curiosity, is accessible, and has lasting value and enduring meaning. Use music you are drawn to over and over. The music specialist will usually be responsible for a sequential music curriculum, leaving the classroom teacher free to explore genres from gospel to opera according to preferences, student interests, and unit connections. Start small by collecting background music, music to introduce units, and songs to sing.

Materials collection. To begin music integration teachers need some basic materials.

Books: Song collections, biographies of musicians, finger plays, chants and rhymes, how to make instruments, and other music-based children's literature (see Appendix).

Poems, quotes, cartoons: See Livingston's *Call Down the Moon, Poems of Music.*

Pictures: Musicians and instruments, including art prints.

CDs, tapes, and videos: Start a discography of music to use in units. See Ready Reference 12.5 for music ideas for

---

 **Music Resources**

See Activity Books at the end of Chapter 13.

Websites

Music Educators National Conference:
www.menc.org

Education Planet:
www.educationplanet.com
> (comprehensive site with links to books, music, and lesson plans)

Songs for Teaching:
www.songsforteaching.com
> (lyrics, sound clips, songs for every subject, including "Dirt Made My Lunch, and Oh Bacteria," "Action Preposition Blues," "The Verb Rap Song," and "From Your Seat" for children with physical challenges)

Instrument Encyclopedia:
www.music.umich.edu/research/stearns_collection

Songs of the Century:
http://en.wikipediq.org/wiki/songs_of_the_century
> (365 classic songs selected from the 20th century)

Children's Music Web:
www.childrensmusic.org
> (public domain music, monthly recommendations/artist webs, custom CDs)

MIDI information:
http://midi.org/

Music Maker:
www.iknowthat.com/com/L3?Area=Music&Cook=

Multicultural Organizations Websites

American Folklore Society (Journal of Folklore):
http://afsnet.org/

Center for Southern Folklore:
www.southernfolklore.com

Country Music Association, Inc.:
www.cmaworld.com

Smithsonian Institution:
www.smithsonianglobalsound.org/
> (digital downloads of multicultural music)

The World Music Institute:
www.worldmusicinstitute.org

units. Be sure to consult with the music teacher. She or he will have references by curricular topics, dates, and holidays.

Construction materials (to make instruments): tubes, boxes, beans, sticks, tubs. See Chapter 7 for papier mâché.

Music and Songs to Know.

This song will live forever. (Kate Smith, 1938)

The great singer said that right before she sang Irving Berlin's "God Bless America." That was the first time it was ever publicly sung. It's always touchy to start listing books or topics everyone should know, but music "that will live forever" is a good criterion for starters. The Music Educators National Conference (MENC) is on a campaign to "Get America Singing . . . Again" and has compiled a list of songs music teachers feel all Americans should know and treasure as part of our national common culture (Ready Reference 12.6). It includes folk songs, Negro spirituals, patriotic songs, a Jewish celebration song, a Japanese folk melody, and many old favorites. In addition, you may want to survey your own community and involve students in compiling a "favorites list." Ready Reference 12.7 includes favorites from teachers and children from across the country.

Music Approaches.

The human voice is the most readily available and most important musical instrument for children to explore . . . accompaniment can distract the children's attention from the musical elements of pitch, volume, and timbre, produced by the voice alone. (Zoltan Kodaly)

In real life, music is everywhere, all day, every day—on our iPods, on the radio, in the mall, and in the hums and whistles of people around us. Music is more than a pleasant background. It is a powerful tool. Classroom teachers are now providing significant experiences that used to be reserved for music class. Music has become as integral to inside school as it is to outside life.

Knowledge of specific approaches to music teaching helps classroom teachers communicate with specialists and expands their own strategy repertoire. The following summaries give background on what specialists do and put integration into perspective as classroom teachers start using music as a teaching tool. A common thread in most is the active involvement of students in making and responding to music using movement. All these approaches connect music to a wide array of curricular areas, from language arts to

---

Ready Reference 12.6   Top 40 Songs to Know

Recommended by Music Educators National Conference (www.menc.org)

Amazing Grace
America (My Country 'Tis of Thee)
America the Beautiful
Battle Hymn of the Republic
Blue Skies
Danny Boy
De Colores
Dona Nobis Pacem
Do-Re-Mi
Down by the Riverside
Frère Jacques
Give My Regards to Broadway
God Bless America
Green, Green Grass of Home
Hava Nagila
He's Got the Whole World in His Hands
Home on the Range
If I Had a Hammer
I've Been Working on the Railroad

Let There Be Peace on Earth
Lift Ev'ry Voice and Sing
Michael (Row Your Boat Ashore)
Music Alone Shall Live
Oh! Susanna
Oh, What a Beautiful Mornin'
Over My Head
Puff the Magic Dragon
Rock-a My Soul
Sakura
Shalom Chaverim
She'll Be Comin' Round the Mountain
Shenandoah
Simple Gifts
Sometimes I Feel Like a Motherless Child
Star-Spangled Banner
Swing Low, Sweet Chariot
This Land Is Your Land
This Little Light of Mine
Yesterday
Zip-a-Dee-Doo-Dah

Ready Reference 12.7 Favorite Songs (Not in Top 40)

Alouette
Alphabet Song
The Ants Go Marching
Baby Bumble Bee
Be Kind to Your Web-footed Friends
Bear Song
A Bear Went Over the Mountain
Bingo
Boom Boom Ain't It Great to Be Crazy
Camptown Races
Chicka Boom
Clementine
Do Your Ears Hang Low?
Down by the Bay
Down in the Valley
Found a Peanut
Go In and Out the Window
Good Night, Ladies
Greasy Grimy Gopher Guts
Green Grass All Around
Hambone
Have You Ever Seen a Lassie?
Head, Shoulders, Knees, and Toes
Hokey Pokey
I Know an Old Lady
I Wish I Were
If You're Happy
I'm a Nut
In the Good Old Summer Time
It Ain't Gonna Rain
It's a Small World
John Brown's Body
Kum-Ba-Ya
Little Skunk's Hole

Loop de Loo
Make New Friends
Miss Mary Mack
My Aunt Came Back
My Bonnie Lies Over the Ocean
Ninety-Nine Miles from Home
Noble Duke of York
Oh, Chester
Old Hogan's Goat
Old MacDonald
On Top of Old Smoky (Spaghetti/Pizza)
One Bottle of Pop
Over the River
Peanut Butter Song
Polly Wolly Doodle
Pop! Goes the Weasel
Popeye, the Sailor Man
Rise and Shine
Singing Bee
Six Little Ducks
Skip to My Lou
Take Me Out to the Ball Game
Ten Little Indians
There's a Hole in the Bottom of the Sea
There's a Hole in the Bucket
This Old Man
Turkey in the Straw
Twinkle, Twinkle
Up in the Air, Junior Bird Man
Waltzing Matilda
When the Saints Go Marching In
Yankee Doodle
You're a Grand Old Flag

---

social studies. Generalists can investigate each further by talking with specialists in their schools and visiting music-based websites.

Eurythmics.   In the 1890s, Swiss educator Émile Jacques Dalcroze proposed a theory called *eurythmics*. He believed control of balance and body movements, along with the use of the senses, prepared children to attend and concentrate, skills necessary for school success. He observed that sensory-based learning relaxed muscles, while maintaining alertness, and helped to open learning channels for concentration. In eurythmics, music and movement are inseparable; the body is used as a natural instrument for the study of rhythm. Dalcroze showed how any musical idea could be transformed

into movement, and any movement could be translated into a musical idea. To start off, students "become" the music as they listen and move to it. Later they study musical symbols and instruments. Unfortunately, Dalcroze was dismissed from the Geneva Conservatory for encouraging students to remove their shoes. We have him to thank for helping to advance the idea of body-kinesthetic learning widely accepted today.

Orff.   Dalcroze was joined by Carl Orff in Germany, who also linked music and movement. (Music and dance were not connected until the 20th century, because music was considered high art, while dance was thought common.) Orff developed a music education program that worked off the idea that feeling comes before understanding. He stressed the thrill of music making through chants, rhythms, and language. The Orff method employs rhymes and proverbs as a basis for teaching rhythm, phrasing, and musical expression. Orff's instruments, created for children with no technical facility, are widely used in American schools to experiment with musical sounds.

Kodaly.   Zoltan Kodaly was a Hungarian composer and early childhood expert who believed singing should be the basis of a music program. His work provided impetus for the singing schools in Budapest, Hungary. These schools are still highly regarded as some of the best in the world. Kodaly thought children should learn many simple songs, sing in tune, and do listening activities to develop aural skills. He contended that children can learn complex musical ideas in games, and all can become musically literate (read and write music) by developing concepts in experiential ways rather than through rote teaching. Kodaly believed quality musical listening enhanced concentration, focus, and thinking. He reasoned that language, reading ability, and coordination are developed as musical sound patterns are discerned.

Kodaly's methods are based primarily on singing nursery songs and doing traditional circle games that include movement. Eventually, children learn musical terms, and they read music using folk songs. Skills are developed through a sequential curriculum for sight reading and singing. The Kodaly system of hand signs are often used by music teachers to help children sing and gesture the notes of the scale: *do* is a fist in knocking position; *re* is a palm outstretched down and tilted up; *mi* is palm down; *fa* is thumb down; *so* is a handshake; *la* is with the first two fingers and thumb making a downward U; *ti* is pointing the index finger up (Choksy, 1974). For more information on Kodaly, visit the website: *www.oake.org/*.

Blueprint III: Collaborative Planning

Music integration uses the models and theories for thinking about curriculum and instruction in Chapters 1–3. Ideally, integration is planned collaboratively using the different co-planning/coteaching options discussed in Chapter 3. Most models rely on unit teaching and are planned with attention to:

- Academic and arts standards, along with other goals
- Mutual connections between academic and arts areas
- Five unit centers
- Aligning assessment and instruction with standards
- Student interests and questions
- Culminating performances and/or exhibits
- Sequencing lessons and writing two-pronged plans.

Nine National Standards for Music K–8

Ready Reference 12.8 summarizes the music standards for elementary and middle school students. These are a part of the *National Standards for the Arts* discussed in Chapters 1 and 3. Both the music standards and academic standards are needed to plan meaningful integrated lessons that teach *about, in,* and *through* music. These standards and other curriculum frameworks help teachers to know what to teach, but they do not explain teaching methodology or integration strategies, nor do they give ideas about materials. These are discussed throughout this Blueprint. Chapter 13 is a compendium of Seed Strategy starter ideas. All the strategies and activities in this chapter relate to one or more of the music standards. Consult your local and state courses of study for ideas tailored to the specific needs of your community. For examples of arts standards developed at the state level, visit the department of education websites in states like Connecticut, Kentucky, Ohio, North and South Carolina, Virginia, and Wisconsin.

Respected, Not Trivialized

Meaningful arts integration targets teaching for two-way transfer. This means finding ways music can assist in learning traditional subjects and the reverse; music knowledge and skill is increased by studying social studies, math, and so on. Collaborative planning seeks mutually beneficial connections between academic areas and, in this case, music. The question is, can music play a meaningful role in the unit? Perhaps another communication form, such as like drama or writing, may be a better fit. When natural clusters are found, there has to be a commitment to more than music exposure. To teach *through* music involves teaching *about* music and involving students *in* using music knowledge to problem solve. Opportunities to sing or listen to music, without instruction, do not do justice to music as a discipline and limit children's enjoyment, understanding, and expressive skill development.

An important integration question is "What did my students learn *about* each discipline being integrated?" not just "What subjects were used?" While classroom teachers need not be able to sing or play an instrument *well,* all need basic knowledge and skills to use music language and present examples of music possibilities. This does not mean students shouldn't have time to sing or listen to music just for enjoyment. Students are regularly given free reading time, but they are also taught *how* to read. Students need to be taught *how* to read music and express themselves through the language of music, too.

Complementary Connections

In the late 1990s Project Zero investigated evidence of critical links between music and academic achievement in math, language arts, and general cognitive development.

Ready Reference 12.8   Nine National Standards for Music (K–8)

Overall focus: creating, performing, responding to music (sing, play instrument, move to music, create own music, read and notate, listen to, analyze, evaluate, and understand historical and cultural heritage, which is basic human expression).

1. **Singing, alone and with others, a varied repertoire of music.** Example activities: Learn songs from different cultures, traditional American songs, songs from different genres (lullabies, gospels, rounds, work songs). Observe conductor's cues during singing (change dynamics, sing expressively, use appropriate posture and rhythm).
2. **Performing on instruments, alone and with others, a varied repertoire of music.** Example activities: Echo short rhythms (clap, stamp, etc.). Play rhythm instruments while others sing.
3. **Improvising melodies, variations, and accompaniments.** Example activities: Use "sounds" to create songs with a beginning, middle, and end. Improvise rhythm and ostinato accompaniments.
4. **Composing and arranging music within specific guidelines.** Example activities: Make and use instruments with songs. Find background music to go with poetry or literature readings.
5. **Reading and notating music.** Example activities: Recognize 2/4, 3/4, and 4/4 meter signatures. Read pitch (do re mi . . .) with hand signals.
6. **Listening to, analyzing, and describing music.** Example activities: Do close critical listening to identify music elements and characteristics of styles and genre.
7. **Evaluating music and music performances.** Example activity: Explain personal preferences and why using musical terms.
8. **Understanding relationships between music, the other arts, and disciplines outside the arts.** Example activities: Compare and contrast concepts across art forms (texture, line, rhythm). Connect ways music intersects with reading and language arts, science, social studies, and math.
9. **Understanding music in relation to history and culture.** Example activities: Explain how music expresses culture and history. Investigate musical careers. Use appropriate audience behavior.

Content Standards (material printed in bold type) excerpted from the National Standards for Arts Education, published by Music Educators National Conference (MENC). Copyright © 1994 by MENC. Reprinted with permission. The complete National Standards and additional materials are available from MENC; The National Association for Music Education: *www.menc.org.*

Analyses of large collections of studies leaves little doubt that there are strong associations with learning, music, and other subject areas (Scripp, 2003). Teachers and music specialists will find many connections. To begin with, there are songs and pieces of music *about* each area, including songs specifically written to teach math facts, states and capitals, and bones of the body. This bountiful area just skims the surface, however, of meaningful music integration. Consider these connections:

Literacy and Music.   Reading music involves the same kinds of decoding skills needed to read print—turning abstract symbols into sound. In print reading those symbols include the letters that represent the 44 phonemes (sounds) in English. In music written symbols have also been created to record sounds (e.g., pitch and rhythm). Reading aloud is similar to singing lyrics. Both require use of music elements to create fluency. Scripp (2003) reports that there is a special association between rhythm and reading (p. 138). Of course musical messages can also be "read" by listening, just as we listen to a story versus reading one. The listening process is similar, but there is a different "language" for each.

Composition.   We compose our thoughts and express them verbally through speaking and writing. Music composition happens when people spontaneously sing original songs, hum melodies, or use an instrument to try out musical ideas. Some composers actually try out the music in their heads and go right to writing it down using musical notation. Children who compose songs, collect favorite songs, and respond to music in journals are writing— another language arts area. The patterned nature of music makes it useful in spelling as well. Students can be taught to tap out word rhythms like "en-cy-clo-ped-i-a" or sing the spelling of words (Disney tune). This draws on musical mnemonics. Students can also create original word melodies using the universal notes of G, E, and A or any tune. Small groups can each be given a word to spell using rhythm, tempo, and dynamics to create word melodies.

Vocabulary.   Hundreds of words specific to music overlap with many areas of life. Consider just two: *line* and *score.* Then there are the millions of words in song lyrics.

Comprehension.   To understand a written or spoken message, it is necessary to problem solve, using all levels of thinking to create meaning. Meaning increases enjoyment. Music is understood and appreciated in the same way.

Literature. Music and song share many structures with literature. For example, themes, songs, plots, and characters are most evident in forms like opera and ballads. Poetry, in particular, shares the following with music and song: rhyme, rhythm, beat, pitch, volume, speed, stress. All literature is more or less a written conveyance of the author's images of how words, phrases, and sentences would sound (i.e., music elements of language, like dialect, are imagined and represented).

Math. Mathematical and music reasoning share a focus on the concept of proportion—fractions in the context of whole, half notes, and distances of notes within scales. Other shared concepts are order, sequence, patterns, counting relationships, hierarchies, and systems thinking. Keyboard training has been shown to have a "significant effect on children's ability to classify and recognize similarities and relationships between objects" (Rauscher et al., 1997). In particular, there seems to be a strong connection between pitch skills and math (Scripp, 2003). Graziano, Peterson, and Shaw (1999) documented how proportional math was enhanced through music training.

Counting songs have long been a part of early childhood and for good reason: Through the strategic use of music, teachers improve skills in measuring, counting, graphing (the five-line staff is a graph), fractions, problem solving, time, and spatial reasoning. See the music-based bibliography in the Appendix for collections of math songs such as Baker's (1991) *Raps and Rhymes in Maths* (probability and time). For a three-way multicultural-math-music connection the math basis of cultural music can be studied. For example, German songs are often grouped into threes, while Australian songs frequently have grouped beats into twos and fours and are organized using eighth notes. Japanese music is often based on a scale of five notes, rather than the eight-note scale used in Western cultures. Finally, mastering a musical instrument develops mathematical understanding and vice versa (Hope, 2003).

Science. Music shares many processes with sciences such as measurement, inquiry, observation, experimentation, discovery, and classification. The science of sound (acoustics) is a fit. Of course there are hundreds of pieces of music about science, ranging from Debussy's "La Mere" to John Denver's "Rocky Mountain High."

Social Studies. Music and social studies fit well together because of the historical and cultural basis of music. Traditional songs and folk music, passed from generation to generation, help teach the rules and values of cultures. Each culture puts its own signature on its music, so Indian ragas cannot be mistaken for American country. In many cultures work songs are still an integral part of life. Music and dance are believed to have power to coax plants to grow (Page, 1995). Hundreds of high-quality multicultural materials are now available, including CDs and videos. See Page's (1995) *Sing and Shine On! A Teacher's Guide to Multicultural Song Leading*, and check out *www.songsforteaching.com*. Look under social studies.

Songs can be an interesting and informative introduction to an era. For example "America" was first written as a poem by Katherine Bates after a trip out west in 1892. Her poem, inspired by the beauty of the country, became popular. People sang it to 75 different melodies, including polkas and marches. Eventually a church hymn written called "Our Mother Dear Jerusalem" was coupled with the poem, and it is this melody we know today.

Arts with Arts. Music shares many concepts and processes with the other arts, including timing, coordination, gesture, composition, pattern, shapes, line, and color. These concepts are inseparable in areas like musical theatre and ballroom dance.

Unit Centers

Planning Page 3.1 shows common integrated unit structures that center on five different bodies and are supported by nine legs (four traditional subjects plus the five arts). Ideally teacher teams co-plan with music specialists around the unit bodies: (1) topic or problem, (2) genre or form, (3) single work (poem, book, song), (4) person, and/or (5) event. For example, they might collaborate on a study of a musician, such as Charlie Parker, using the picture book *Charlie Parker Played Be Bop* (Raschka) as a key resource. All the arts, as well as math, science, social studies, and literacy would be legs to support the body. Students would read and write about Mr. Parker, study the conditions of the early 20th century that influenced his music, learn the math of syncopated rhythms, and so on. Music would be used as a learning tool, just as any other leg, as students do critical listening to his works.

Alternatively, teachers may choose a particular music genre, like gospel, as a body. Units may be planned around problem solving initiated by questions that arise during other learning like "What causes all these kinds of music to be created?" A core work unit is another option with book, poem, or song as the unit center. Again, music may be the body (e.g., song) or a support leg. For example, a sixth-grade class did a core study of Hesse's *Out of the Dust* (1998 Newbery Award). Not only did they vicariously experience the life of a teenager during the 1930s Dust Bowl, but they found significant themes about music in the main character's life. Songs her family might have sung were brought into the unit, including work and wedding songs and funeral music. Planning Page 6.1 shows a planning web for integrated unit with some music ideas in it. For other arts-with-arts unit ideas, see Burz & Marshall's *Performance Based Curriculum for Music and the Visual Arts* (1999).

Music Event Units. Music performances may be brought to the school or music-related field trips may be planned. These are important unit adjuncts or can be the centerpiece of a study, using the event as the starter or culmination. Opportunities to hear the local symphony or a special concert can be pivotal in children's musical development and their lives. Many communities now have arts coordinators who contact schools to schedule trips and provide pre- and post-performance lesson ideas. The Appendix provides a checklist for plan-

ning arts-based field trips. In addition, Chapters 8 and 10 include ideas that apply to music events. See the sections on preparing students for live performances and using simulated mind trips to take students to places they cannot go physically.

Check the websites of the local and state arts council and use the phone book to find other music resources in the community. Meaningful field trips can be made to music stores and local colleges. For example, combine a lesson on running a business with a trip to a music store. Easy field trips can be a part of many units, including listening walks to collect sounds in the cafeteria or on the playground. Planning Page 12.1 suggests a literature unit incorporating music.

Planning Page 12.1

Literature Through Music (Grades 1–2)

Two-Pronged Focus: (1) music making and (2) literature interpretation (rhythm of words/alphabet).
Music Standards: 1,2,3,7,8. (Ready Reference 12.8)
Literature Standards: 1,3,4. (Ready Reference 4.4)
Student Objectives: Students should be able to:
1. echo rhythms and pitches of words
2. perform on cue
3. suggest ways to show meaning with instruments
4. tell one way to improve
Materials:
Chicka Chicka Boom Boom by Bill Martin/John Archambault, Alphabet, Musical instruments: piano, Orff percussion instruments
Teaching Procedure: (S=students)

Introduction
1. Play "Twinkle Twinkle" on the piano and ask S to name the tune. Explain that the alphabet song melody was written by Mozart. Show picture. Display alphabet and play again with all singing the alphabet.
2. Do Echo Me (expressively): (1) Chicka chicka boom boom (clap), (2) Skit skat skoodle doot (pat on lap), (3) Flip flop flea (use low middle and high pitches and pat lap, clap hands, and snap fingers, (4) Coconut tree (say and put rhythm in shoulders). Repeat 3 times.
3. Read book and invite practiced responses.
4. Tell S they will bring the book to life with music and a theme song. Ask what you would hear if CCBB was a movie if you closed your eyes (moods: happy, sad music).

Development
1. Sing theme song using sol-feg syllables.
2. Ask three Ss to play a steady beat on xylophone, metallophone, and contra bass bars and all sing together with accompaniment. Repeat to find silent beats (holes) in melody. Add snaps for these and S to do glockenspiels (for rests).
3. All sing and keep the steady beat. Ask about silent beats (rests) and teach to snap on whole rests.
4. Ask what the alphabet does. Teach glissando (sliding sound) to show going up the alphabet tree (xylophone).
5. Perform first verse with new instruments. Ask for changes to make it better. Ask about how to show crash at end. Ask about adding a middle section.
6. Divide into four groups: (1) Chicka chicka with hand drums/tambours (say and play); (2) Skit skat with tambourines; (3) Flip flop flea with Chinese temple blocks or wood blocks with three different sounds; (4) Coconut tree using congos or unpitched drums. Add Wheeee with a vibraslap.

Conclusion
1. Full performance rehearsal. Direct and read book with inserted song. Ask for other places to add instruments and actions.
2. Final performance. Ask what worked.

Assessment
1. Students match up the four chanted sounds with their rhythmic notation.
2. Observation and record keeping on individual computer checklist.

Source: Ann Cheek, Ashley River Creative Arts Elementary.

Lesson Sequence.   Lessons must be ordered in a unit—what will be taught first, second, third, and so on. The flow of lessons is established by thinking about how one will lead into another. For this reason, it is important to think about which lesson will be the introduction and which will wrap up the unit. The culminating lesson generally involves presenting projects that synthesize learning from the entire unit. For example, students might write and perform original "scat" songs to show they understand jazz concepts like syncopation, but also overlapping language concepts like onomatopoeia, rhyme, and repetition.

Two-Pronged Integrated Plans

Once the overall unit design has been planned and an order of lessons determined, teachers get down to nitty gritty daily lesson planning. Integrated plans need a minimum of two prongs—one focus on an academic area and another on an art form. Lessons can have more than two, and the two can be both arts prongs. The prongs are not just what will be used, but what will be taught and assessed, so two is plenty. That doesn't mean you can't incorporate many art forms into instruction, but you can't teach in depth and assess everything in one lesson.

See the lesson format using a two-pronged focus and student objectives in Chapter 3. Refer to the detailed discussion about dividing the teaching strategies into introduction, development, and conclusion. Keep in mind that if students are expected to create a song, structure is important; for example, adapt lyrics to a familiar tune or, in the case of the Charlie Parker book, write new words to use in place of be bop, fisk fisk, and other "scat" words. Plans need to include strategies for transition, use of space, materials, and even ways to dismiss groups: "Your ticket out today is. . . " or "All those who can/know . . . may . . . ." Planning Page 12.1 shows a two-pronged plan created by a music specialist.

Start Small and Grow.   Rather than plan a whole unit on music or even one with significant use of music, novice teachers are encouraged to try single lessons (e.g., teach the history of a song, such as "Row, Row, Row Your Boat" and use the lyrics for reading material). The key is to make sure first attempts are successful, for you and for your students. Begin by integrating energizing music warm-ups to introduce the day. For example, teach a new song every Monday. Explore the language arts connections by using a song chart and the "I Spy" strategy in which students tell types of words and language structures they see in the song. Ease toward more meaningful integration by using a Music Elements chart to discuss songs and accustom the class to discovering music connections in other subjects.

Blueprint IV: Aesthetic Learning Environment

South Carolina: Students have their regular independent reading time to Baroque music like Bach's *Brandenburg Concertos*, Handel's *Water Music*, and Vivaldi's *Four Seasons*.

California: The relaxing sounds of New Age music waft through the halls and cafeteria of an arts-based elementary school. A teacher boasts about the bus drivers who also play music to set mood and control behavior. Drivers and students negotiate radio stations and CDs, contingent on students using desired "bus etiquette."

Illinois: An elementary principal, who is a John Phillip Sousa fan, plays marches over the intercom every Monday as students and teachers arrive. They report they can't help but walk to the beat.

The goal of music integration is not to create more Mozarts, but he and other musical geniuses did grew up in rich music environments. We are all formed by the sounds around us. As evidence, consider how babies the world over babble in the phonemes of the language they hear. Children grow to like and value the sounds that surround them. Arts integration takes advantage of this by providing diverse musical experiences. Such variety broadens interest and builds respect for people's diverse musical expressions.

Immersing students in a musically rich environment is an important path to increasing aesthetic knowing. Aesthetic thinking takes us into a different state of awareness; we experience full sensory perception, concentration, imagination, reflection, consideration, questioning, even confusion as we perceive sounds or images that are pleasing or displeasing (Goldberg, 1997). This includes attuning to the sound patterns created as people and machines go about their work, and nature is a limitless source. It also means learning how music can have both positive and negative influences. In one study male felons cited rap as their top musical preference. Other studies show heavy metal and rap listening correlate with lower grades, behavioral problems, early sex, arrest, and drug use (Took & Weiss, 1994).

A critical factor in creating an aesthetic environment is music immersion. *Immerse* means to totally cover or involve. Background music plays a major role.

Background Music: Research

Music has been used to enhance mood in a number of studies and even cause a change of mind (whether a painting is liked or not). The type of music is important; sad music caused

 **Ready Reference 12.9**   **Background Music**

Music affects people differently so try different pieces to find a fit with your class.

General

Baroque Music (Mozart, Bach, Handel, Vivaldi, and Pachelbel) which is 60 bpm (resting heart rate)
Also try: Beethoven, Berlioz, Debussy, Chopin, Liszt
Jazz: George Benson, Kenny G., Duke Ellington, Issac Hayes
Environmental: ocean, waterfall, rain forest, Indian ragas

Beginning of the Year

The King and I (Getting to Know You)

Start the Day

Handel's Hallelujah Chorus
Beatles (Good Morning)
Bobby McFerrin (Be Happy)
Disney (Hakuna Matata)
Richie Valens (La Bamba)
Movie themes: Superman, Chariots of Fire, Rocky
Village People (YMCA)

Calm/Relax

Piano, harp or classical guitar, jazz
Yo Yo Ma
Pachelbel's Canon
Concertos by Bach
Disney (Fantasia)
Brian Eno (Music for Airports)
Artists: David Kobialka, Georgia Kelly, Michael Jones

Memory

Lozanov "Superlearning" (research on 4/4 time)
Mozart, Beethoven, Bach, Vivaldi, Pachelbel, Handel, and Haydn

Imagination and Creative Thinking

Jazz (Miles Davis, David Sanborn)
New Age (Windham Hill, Ken Davis, Tony O'Conner)
Beethoven, Tchaikovsky, Liszt

Hungarian Rhapsodies
Fantasia (Disney)
Debussy (Claire de Lune)
Indian ragas
Mozart (Musical Joke)
Prokofiev (Peter and the Wolf)

Transitions

Vince Guaraldi (Peanuts theme)
Mozart, Hadyn

Celebration

Tina Turner (Simply the Best)
Three Dog Night (Celebrate)
Chili Pepper (Hot, Hot, Hot)
Queen (We Are the Champions)
Kool and the Gang (Celebration)
Handel (Hallelujah Chorus)
Otis Day and the Knights (Shout)

Energizing (75 bpm+ in major key, rhythmic)

Mother Goose Suites
Flamenco from Spain (e.g., Fire and Grace)
Cossack from Russia
Polynesian drums
Isley Bros (Shout)
Little Richard
Jerry Lee Lewis (Great Balls of Fire)
Beach Boys (Fun, Fun, Fun)
Jive Bunny and the Mixmasters
Pete Seeger

Wrap Up

Sound of Music (So Long, Farewell)
William Tell Overture
Louis Armstrong (Wonderful World)
I've Been Working on the Railroad

Sources: Music for learning is available from Learning in New Dimension, Box 1447, San Francisco, CA 94114.

subjects to rate art as more depressing (Jensen, 2000). Music has boosted mood and survival rates in Alzheimer's patients and those with mental illness (Wigram & Backer, 1999).

Purposes.   In general, background music is used to promote good feelings about school, to motivate and energize. It is also used to heighten awareness and increase concentration and focus. Background music is used to relax before

tests and to create mood and give background for reading, writing, and making art. Ready Reference 12.9 lists music for different classroom purposes.

Relaxed Alertness.   Appropriate background music played for 20 minutes at a time can induce an alpha state of relaxation (Jensen, 2000). The research and work of A. A. Tomatis in France and Georgi Lozanov (1978) in Bulgaria

cifics on how to enhance learning through mu-
found that relaxation caused by specific music
mind alert and able to concentrate. For example,
concertos by Bach and Pachelbel's *Canon* have been played
as information about a topic is presented verbally. The most
conducive music is Baroque music, such as that of Mozart,
Bach, Handel, Vivaldi, and Pachelbel, which matches the average resting heart beat of 60 beats to the minute. This creates a relaxed alertness that can enhance test performance
(Cockerton, Moore, & Norman, 1997; Giles, 1991).

Imagination and Creativity. Artists, scientists, and
writers routinely use music to stimulate divergent thinking.
See Ready Reference 12.9 for music recommendations like
"Crystal Meditations" (Don Campbell). Music with dolphin, whale, and bird calls and sounds of nature blended
with woodwinds and piano and strings are good for stimulating imaginative thinking.

Guidelines. Background music should be played daily.
Music greets students as they come in and is played during
art making, silent reading, and writing times. Students learn
to adapt. At the Conservatory Lab Charter School in
Boston, high-quality background music is important to the
mission. "Students have learned to subdue their voices and
be respectful of others, and yet they still remember the music. They have increased their social-emotional skills, too, by
altering their behavior in order to get choice music played"
(Scripp, 2003, p. 134).

Repeated exposure to excellent music develops listening skills measured by comprehension tests. For example,
several variations on Mozart's "Twinkle, Twinkle Little
Star" were played, and students learned to listen and analyze
at the same time—counting the variations. Discussions
about what causes the differences in the variations increased
comprehension.

Rhythms of the brain tend to echo the rhythms of music. This propensity toward entrainment means music is selected for specific reasons and student needs. In general,
Jensen (2000) recommends music that is:

- Purposefully selected (e.g., to calm or excite, to stimulate for challenging task, to relax)
- Predictable and repetitive; use major key (for productivity)
- Instrumental, especially single instruments (less distracting)
- Low volume
- Simple structurally (e.g., Baroque and jazz; movements
  are adagio or andante; orchestras can overwhelm)

Besides Background Music

Here are other ideas from schools throughout the United
States to increase aesthetic knowing through music.

Music Lending Library. Sets of CDs and tapes, similar
to a class library of books, are made available for checkout.
Parents and PTAs often will contribute to this project. CDs
are sometimes paired with a song-based book and placed in
a zip lock bag for take-home purposes. Simple directions
are included about what to listen for or to do repeated read-
ing/ singing of lyrics. This is an excellent fluency development tool because singing adds music to words, and music
increases the emotional effect of words.

Music Journals. Journaling includes prompts to write
about how music is a part of life. Specific pages are designated for an ongoing listing of favorite songs, musical
pieces, musicians, or even music jokes (What do you get if
you divide a tuba in half? Answer: a one ba).

Quotes and Poems. Music poems and quotes are collected and posted. Livington's *Call Down the Moon* is a lovely
collection of poetry about music. Teachers who use routines
like poem a day or a quote a day include music-related ones.
Repeated poetry readings allow for students to really focus on
the musical qualities of poems (e.g., rhythm, beat, dynamics).

Blueprint V:
Literature as a Core Art Form

Is Wynton Marsalis's *Jazz ABZ: A Collection of Jazz Portraits*
(2005) an alphabet book for kids or an informational book
for jazz lovers? Since he uses poetry patterns (from tanks to
haiku), maybe it is poetry. As discussed in Chapter 4, humans
resist classification. What is for sure is that this is a music-
based picture book (photography) so it has many connections and uses throughout the curriculum. His book joins a
growing list of arts-based literature.

Never has more high-quality literature been available.
A plethora of books is specifically devoted to music (e.g.,
multicultural song collections) and a variety of genre of
music-based children's books (e.g., picture book fiction).
When literature is viewed from the lens of music, it seems
more books than not are linked. Seeking the connections
increases the awareness of music's importance and adds another avenue to find quality material for units.

Music-based literature is now center stage in arts integration (Cornett, 2006). *Charlie Parker Played Be Bop* is a striking picture book appropriate for any age. If it is read while
playing a tape or CD of "Night in Tunisia," it becomes a magical lesson with messages about history as well as genre and
styles (thanks to Duxberry Elementary teachers for this idea.)

Biographies are particularly important for in-depth accounts and introduce students to people with whom they

Music-Based Literature by Topic

Abilities and Disabilities

Keats, E. J. (1964). *Whistle for Willie*. Viking.

McCloskey, R. (1940). *Lentil*. Viking.

White, E. B. (1970). *The trumpet of the swan*. Harper & Row.

Animals

Brothers Grimm. (1988). *The Bremen-town musicians*. McGraw-Hill.

Hurd, T. (1987). *Mama don't allow: Starring Miles and the Swamp Band*. Harpercrest.

Karas, G. (1994). *I know an old lady who swallowed a fly*. Scholastic.

Prokofiev, S. (1961). *Peter and the wolf*. Franklin Watts.

Steig, W. (1994). *Zeke Pippin*. HarperCollins.

Creativity and Imagination

Isadora, R. (1979). *Ben's trumpet* (jazz). Greenwillow.

Rylant, C. (1988). *All I see*. Orchard Books.

Cumulative and Repetitive Stories

Dodd, M. (1988). *This old man*. Houghton Mifflin.

Emberley, B. (1967). *Drummer Hoff*. Simon & Schuster.

Karas, G. (1994). *I know an old lady who swallowed a fly*. Scholastic.

Martin, B. (1989). *Chicka chicka boom boom*. Simon & Schuster.

Raffi. (1987). *Down by the bay*. Crown.

Dance and Movement

Gray, M. (1972). *Song and dance man*. Dutton.

Isadora, R. (1976). *Max*. Macmillan.

Martin, B. (1986). *Barn dance!* Henry Holt.

Fairy and Folk Tales

Lewis, R. (1991). *All of you was singing*. Atheneum.

Whitehead, P. (1989). *The Nutcracker*. Stoneway Books.

Families and Friends

Griffin, H. (1986). *Georgia music*. Greenwillow.

Pinkwater, D. (1991). *Doodle flute*. Macmillan.

Williams, V. B. (1984). *Music, music for everyone*. Greenwillow.

Language Arts

McMillan, B. (1977). *The alphabet symphony: An ABC book*. Greenwillow.

Marsalis, W. (2005). *Jazz ABZ*. Candlewick.

Nursery Rhymes and Lullabies

dePaola, T. (1984). *Mary had a little lamb*. Holiday House. (rounds)

Beall, P. (1996). *Wee sing sing-alongs* (with tape or CD). Price Stern Sloan.

School

Giff, P. (1992). *Meet the Lincoln Lions band*. Dell.

Science, Nature, Health

Jenkins, E. (1989). *Rhythms of childhood* (with tape or CD). Smithsonian/Folkways.

Papp, C. (1988). *Follow the sunset: A beginning geography record with nine songs from around the world* (with tape or CD). Entomography Publications.

Social Studies

Ryan, P. (2002). *When Marian sang*. Scholastic.

Spier, P. (1973). *The Star-Spangled Banner*. Doubleday.

Winter, J. (1988). *Follow the drinking gourd* (slavery). Knopf.

Sound Effects

McGovern, A. (1992). *Too much noise*. Demco Media.

Spier, P. (1990). *Crash! Boom! Bang!* Doubleday.

Sports

Isadora, R. (1976). *Max*. Macmillan.

---

might identify. Biographies also add the human element to both science and social studies. For example, Krull's *The Lives of Musicians* gives short bios with interesting facts and a perspective on the time in which each musician lived. Planning Pages 12.2 and 12.3 offer titles focused on music and curricular topics. Ready Reference 12.10 lists artists who record for children. More examples appear in the Arts-Based Bibliography in the Appendix.

Aliki. (2003). *Ah music!* HarperCollins. (informational book)

Music–Based Books by Categories

Aliki. (2003). *Ah music!* HarperCollins. (great informational book about music)

Picture Books Based on Songs

Fox, D. (1987). *Go in and out the window* (various styles). Metropolitan Museum of Art.

Hurd, T. (1987). *Mama don't allow: Starring Miles and the Swamp Band.* Harpercrest.

Karas, B. (1994). *I know an old lady who swallowed a fly.* Scholastic.

Keats, E. (1987). *The little drummer boy.* Aladdin Books.

Mattox, C. (1990). *Shake it to the one that you love the best.* JTG.

Pearson, T. (1984). *Old MacDonald had a farm.* Dial.

Winter, J. (1988). *Follow the drinking gourd.* Knopf.

Orchestras and Bands

Johnston, T. (1988). *Pages of music.* Putnam.

Koscielniak, B. (2000). *The story of the incredible orchestra: An introduction to musical instruments and the symphony orchestra.* Houghton Mifflin.

Kuskin, K. (1982). *The Philharmonic gets dressed.* Harper & Row.

Moss, L. (1995). *Zin! zin! zin!: A violin.* School & Library Binding.

Moss, L. (2002). *Music is.* School & Library Binding.

Williams, V. (1984). *Music, music for everyone.* Greenwillow.

Musical Genre and Styles

Bryan, A. (1991). *All night, all day: A child's first book of African-American spirituals.* Atheneum.

Fleischman, P. (1988*). Rondo in C* (classical). Harper & Row.

Gray, M. (1972*). Song and dance man* (vaudeville). Dutton.

Hart, J. (1982*). Singing bee! A collection of favorite children's songs.* Lothrop, Lee & Shepard.

Martin, B. (1986). *Barn dance!* (country). Henry Holt.

Raschka, C. (1992). *Charlie Parker played be bop.* Orchard Books.

Musical Instruments

Turner, J., & Schiff, R. (1995). *Let's make music!* Hal Leonard (book/CD; how to use recycled items; multicultural)

Wiseman, A. (2003). *Making music: How to make and use 70 homemade musical instruments.* Storey Books.

Collections of Songs/Singing Games (See Chapter 13 bibliography)

Barkman, A. (1987). *Rise and shine* (with tape or CD). Moody.

Cote, P. (1995). *Do your ears hang low? Fifty more musical fingerplays.* Scholastic.

Fox, D. (1987). *Go in and out the window.* MMoA.

Glazer, T. (1992). *Eye winker, Tom Tinker, chin chopper: Fifty musical fingerplays.* Doubleday.

Hart, J. (1982). *Singing bee! A collection of favorite children's songs.* Lothrop Lee & Shepard.

Jenkins, E. (1989). *You'll sing a song and I'll sing a song* (tape or CD). Smithsonian.

Raffi. (1990). *Baby Beluga* (with tape or CD). Crown.

Seeger, M. (1987*). American folk songs for children* (with tape or CD). Cambridge Rounder.

Careers in Music

Fleischman, P. (1988). *Rondo in C.* Harper & Row.

Gmoser, L. (1997). *Great composers.* Smithmark.

Isadora, R. (1979). *Ben's trumpet* (jazz). Greenwillow.

Johnston, T. (1988). *Pages of music.* Putnam's.

Krull, K. (1993). *Lives of musicians.* Harcourt Brace Jovanovich.

Mitchell, B., & Smith, J. (1988*). America, I hear you: A story about George Gershwin.* Carolrhoda.

Humor

Keller, C. (compiled). (1985). *Swine lake: Music and dance riddles.* Prentice Hall.

Boynton, S. (2002). *Philadelphia chickens* (CD). Workman. (singing critters in a rollicking musical)

Cohn, A. (1993). *From sea to shining sea: A treasury of American folklore and songs.* Scholastic.

Griffith, H. (1986). *Georgia music.* Greenwillow. (music's role in a grandfather/granddaughter relationship)

Kuskin, K. (1982). *The Philharmonic gets dressed.* (delightful picture book)

Ready Reference 12.10   Musical Artists Who Record for Children

Peter Alsop	Gemini	Sarah Pirtle
Linda Arnold	Red Grammer	David Polansky
Fran Avni	Greg and Steve	Barry Louis Polisar
Pamela Ballingham	Bill Harley	Raffi
Joanie Bartels	Chris Holder	Rosenshontz
Steve Bergman	Janet and Judy	Phil Rosenthal
Marcia Berman	Ella Jenkins	Kevin Roth
Heather Bishop	Kathi and Milenko	Nancy Rumel and Friends
Kim and Jerry Brodey	Kids on the Block	Pete Seeger
Rachel Buchman	The Kids of Widney High	Sharon, Lois, and Bram
Janice Buckner	Lois LaFond	Paul Strausman
Frank Cappelli	Francine Lancaster	Marlo Thomas and Friends
Tom Chapin	John McCutcheon	Tickle Toon Typhoon
Rick Charette	Marcia Merman	Uncle Ruthie
The Children of Selma	Mary Miche	Bill Usher
Jon Crosse	Eric Nagler	Jim Valley
Charlotte Diamond	Hap Palmer	The Weavers
Jonathan Edwards	Tom Paxton	Weird Al Yankovic
Terrence Farrell	Peter, Paul, and Mary	Patty Zeitli

Blueprint VI: Best Teaching Practices

What You Teach Is Who You Are

> *Before teaching anyone else, I must teach myself.* (Sylvia Ashton Warner)

"She loves music more than anybody," the students say of Mrs. Engle. Their teacher says it all started because she played big band records to get in a positive mood for teaching. That was in the 1960s. One morning she was in a rush and left a record on when her fifth graders came in. They were shocked, but begged to hear more. Mrs. Engle was surprised the kids liked the "old stuff," but it became a routine to start the day with music. It lasted 42 years. This spunky lady credits much of her career longevity to using music.

Classroom teachers don't need to be able to sing *well*, play an instrument, or read music to start music integration. Being a Mozart fan is not required. What is needed is a commitment to the philosophy of arts integration and a willingness to learn. Put music into perspective. It is a way of knowing—an intelligence every person possesses.

Arts integration begins with where teachers are as people—starting with whatever music experience and interest each has. That's why continuing to grow one's musical intelligence is essential to successful music integration. The choices are many: attending concerts, singing in a choir, taking music lessons, or just becoming a more dedicated music collector.

"I Can't Carry a Tune in a Bucket!"   To start off, it's more important that classroom teachers sing with enthusiasm than to worry about singing quality. Music teachers claim that most everyone can learn to carry a tune, with practice. Teachers who take the risk to sing with and to students add a strong dimension to integration. If teachers play an instrument, they can play for their students to provide a model and allow students to broaden their view of "teacher." (Think of the response to Bill Clinton playing the sax on *Saturday Night Live*.)

Inside-Out Motivation.   Anyone reading this sentence has experienced the aesthetic motivation music provides. It is saying the obvious to point out that music is self-motivating. Children innately want and need to create, explore, and imitate sounds. They enjoy activities involving sound discrimination, classification, sequencing, improvisation, and organization of sounds into songs and music.

Teachers capitalize on the intrinsic motivational power of music whenever they pair meaningful music experiences with other curricular areas. A further way to establish meaningfulness (essential to inside-out motivation) is to connect music to life. Teachers do this by showing how music is used in daily rituals from waking up to the radio to jogging with an MP3 player. Students can also log or web music in their lives for one day or imagine a single day without music. Class music surveys can uncover places music happens and the many types of music classmates know.

An excellent teacher habit is to routinely ask how songs and music are linked to topics in math, science, and social studies. Musical intelligence can be activated by posing questions like, "What kind of music would show how it felt when they signed the Declaration of Independence?" or "What pop songs do you think Benjamin Franklin would have liked?" Ask students how the use of music changes the classroom and learning (e.g., motivation and concentration) to help them own their learning.

Expectation.   The motivational force of teacher expectation has been documented in hundreds of studies. The self-fulfilling prophecy (SFP) has been confirmed for music, too. When participants were told that music would enhance learning, it did. In contrast, when a group was told the music would detract, it did (Dibben, 2004).

Audience effect.   Music integration can also tap the motivational power of the audience. As Ashley River music teacher Ann Cheek puts it, "It is just awesome. Regardless of how small their part is, everybody gets to be on stage. It is a validation that they are an important piece of the puzzle. They know we need everybody involved." She explains that a musical production involves all of the arts, so it compounds the motivational force of many art forms.

Harmful effects.   Music also can have negative effects and these need to be discussed. For example, Scheel and Westefeld (1999) detail connections between heavy metal music and adolescent suicide. Motivation comes from a focus on understanding; students need to know that the typical teenager has 40 percent hearing loss caused by music played at more than 90 decibels over a sustained time.

Engagement and Active Learning

Musicogeniceupadia works because music making, music reading, and listening engage the mind, emotions, and body. The bulk of music-based instruction has to do with providing curriculum-based singing and listening experiences. Music is used as a starter to introduce units (e.g., listen/sing "The Star Spangled Banner" and teach its history at the start of a study of the War of 1812) or as a lesson response (e.g., teaching song writing about curricular topics).

Singing with Students.   Students do not mind if the teacher does not have a fine singing voice if genuine enthusiasm is expressed. Making the effort to sing with students builds relationships and community—staples for discipline.

Since classroom teachers are not perceived as specialists, students accept amateur efforts as natural and normal, especially if teachers sing throughout the grades at the school. With experience and commitment to music integration, all teachers can learn to sing without embarrassment, without being limited by the Western notion that only the talented should sing out. Remember Thoreau's point that the forest would be a very quiet place if only the talented birds did the singing.

Language Arts.   Singing naturally integrates the language arts of listening, speaking, and reading (Douglas & Willatts, 1994; Kantrowitz & Leslie, 1997; Lamb & Gregory, 1993). To sing, we must hear in our heads, in the same way we hear musical elements of words when reading silently: Which words are to be stressed? What rate? What volume? Singing also emphasizes diction, or clear enunciation of words. Because we usually sing words, vocabulary is built through singing. By pointing out lyrics on a large chart or the overhead, students make the speech-to-print match essential for reading success.

Children enjoy singing the same songs repeatedly, which builds competence and confidence. Teachers usually begin with songs they know (Ready References 12.6 and 12.7) and then continue to learn new songs (e.g., ones with limited voice range and notes), often suggested by a music specialist. A repertoire of a dozen action songs (e.g., "Little Bunny Foo Foo") is a good goal. These serve many purposes, including acting as sponge activities when there are schedule delays. Use the Ready References to start a class songbook with lyrics to use as reading material. Consider taping singing at different points in the year and giving a tape to each child as an end-of-year gift.

Teaching Songs.   Classroom teachers do need to be able to teach songs. To learn a song, students must be motivated to learn and do close listening to hear specific pitches, grasp the tempo and underlying beat, and identify the rhythmic patterns. Teachers need to help them do this and put it all together in a whole. Here are guidelines. Also see Ready Reference 12.11.

1. Consider developmental levels. Keep songs for younger students simple—easy lyrics, limited melody (not too high or too low), and a catchy beat. See books like Jarnow's (1991) *All Ears: How to Use and Choose Recorded Music for Children*.

2. Combine singing with movement. Teachers who move when they sing demonstrate the increased enjoyment from combining the two. Singing accompanied by appropriate facial expressions is more engaging. Sign language can also be used to add movement. Riekehof's *Joy of Signing* is a reference, or you may improvise hand signs and motions. Clap, tap, or use rhythm instruments to keep a steady beat. Use the beat to invite movement. In collaboration with the

Ready Reference 12.11 Teaching Songs

Rote Method

1. Motivate and stimulate interest. For example, give background on the song. (See *New Grove Dictionary of Music* for ideas.)
2. Sing the song or play a recording. The singing should be in your normal voice, not too high pitched. The range should be appropriate for the students. Teacher enthusiasm is critical at this step, so show it.
3. Ask students to describe what they heard using music terms (e.g., repetitions, rhythm).
4. Echo sing. Teacher sings a line or phrase and students echo. Go through the whole song. Continue to build up by repeating previous phrases and adding on. If the song is difficult, slow down, but keep a steady beat. If there are unusual words, try echoing the whole song in a speaking voice the first time. Repeat this step as much as necessary.
5. Display the lyrics on a chart, overhead, or pocket chart.
6. Sing through many times. Ask students for ideas on how they can improve and target an element (e.g., dynamics, enunciation).

Rounds

1. Use the rote method to teach the whole song. When it is mastered, go to the previous step 5.
2. Instruct the students to sing softly so that they can hear each other. Establish start and stop hand signals so that you can direct each group. Keep a steady beat.
3. Start with just two parts to keep it simple, with each group singing through twice.

---

music specialist, move up to singing rounds and creating harmony.

3. Stay on a specific key. The ideal range for children is usually from about middle C up to G. If songs are pitched too high or low, they have trouble matching the pitch. Usually, students who sing out of tune are not hearing the notes clearly and may need to have a note or phrase isolated for practice. Use the amount of repetitions needed for success. Almost all children can learn to sing well if they are taught to take time to listen closely. Even middle school students who have not done much singing can succeed if the teacher coaches them to listen so that intonation is accurate. Suggest they try to hear the notes in their heads before singing. If students aren't perfect singers immediately, remind them that singing in tune, like all skills, comes with practice. Rent the film *The Chorus* about a classroom teacher who transforms the lives of juvenile delinquents by spending the time it takes to teach them to sing. It is a superb French film for adults.

4. Start with favorite songs. See recommended lists in the Ready References or the *Music Teachers' Book of Lists* (Ross & Stangl, 1994). Consult the music basal in the district and check with specialists for ideas, especially for folk and patriotic songs.

5. In general, it is recommended that students learn to sing without accompaniment so they listen to themselves and develop their voices—no karaoke at first. One easy way to begin is with "call and response" songs in which students simply echo. Keep a steady beat and clap or snap rhythms to echo. Students can also become leaders. Here is a favorite chant for call and response: Teacher: Acka lacka ching (Students echo); T: Acka lacka chow (S echo); T: Acka lacka ching ching chow chow (S echo); T: Booma lacka booma alack sis boom bah (S echo); T: Reading Reading-Rah Rah Rah (substitute any phrase) (S echo).

6. Teach new songs slowly. Use many repetitions. Nonsense syllables such as "la," "ti," and "tah" can also be used to explore the singing voice. Give frequent encouragement and be supportive of efforts; singing requires risk taking. Explain that everyone can sing well in their own range if they listen carefully and do their best. To teach a round, make sure students master the whole song first, or the song will fall apart during the round. Music is a skill learned through the three Ps: practice, practice, and practice. Neural pathways and muscle tone develop with multiple repetitions.

7. Explicit teaching using model, imitate, and repeat is the most typical sequence for songs. Students should hear the whole song first, before seeing the lyrics, which puts the focus on an enjoyable aesthetic experience. Give direct instruction line by line or phrase by phrase. Finally, sing the whole song several times to increase fluency and enjoyment. *Note:* Some music educators recommend starting with the parts and building up to the whole song, rather than having students hear the whole to begin with. Both whole-to-part and part-to-whole methods involve listening to a part of a song and then echoing the teacher for the bulk of the lesson. As parts are mastered, the song builds up until students can sing the entire song well. Ready Reference 12.11 summarizes steps.

8. Sing daily. Post lyrics *after* students hear a new song so they initially do close listening. Write words large enough to see. Pocket charts enable one line to be put up at a time. Sing songs to start the day and to clean up (e.g., "Kum Ba Yah" works). Instead of giving directions, sing or chant; use the universal melody of "na na na NA na"—think of the childhood taunt—and sing, "Line up and go home."

9. Teach songs from diverse cultures for holidays, traditional songs, and others that go with units. See the Appendix for Arts-Based Children's Literature (music section) and the Ready References in this chapter and the next for recommendations. Students and their families are also sources of songs and music (consider co-constructing the curriculum with your students). Help students learn songs that make up a cultural bank, including songs from their own culture.

Song Writing.   Teachers harness the mnemonic power of music by teaching how to put curricular information into songs, raps, and chants. When students write original songs about content areas, they transform information which entails elaborate thinking. Warren's (1991) *Piggyback Songs for School* is one collection of songs about science, math, and social studies concepts. Use these as examples for students to write their own, which is better for learning than memorizing somebody else's song. Memorizing is low-level thinking. Song writing proceeds like any writing. Check the poetic devices in Chapter 4 for help and be sure to discuss how song lyrics aid memory (*why* they work). Co-writing lyrics to familiar melodies can ease students into seeing how music can be used to transform curricular concepts and skills. Simple rhythm instruments can be made or found to perform songs.

Music Listening.   Children are inundated with music. We need to ensure that music chosen for school gives exposure to music they would not otherwise hear. Of course, worthy music is a subjective concept, but it is important to develop criteria for quality. For example, if music lyrics are to be examined, then the words should be audible and clear. Some orchestral music can overwhelm students and elicit exaggerated responses. Consult music specialists and use the bibliographies in this chapter and in the Appendix to help find quality music.

Listening goes beyond hearing. Listening is understanding and can be taught. When it comes to music, there is a great deal for students to understand. Within music, with and without lyrics, there are messages in the form of images, stories, and emotions. Directed music listening helps move students beyond hearing. For example, two versions of any song can be played with listening for specifics that cause the variation. Deeper listening is developed through discussions that focus on important details.

Teach for Transfer.   Arts integration seeks to maximize learning by bringing the motivational and communication power of the arts to bear on other curricular areas. This purpose needs to be explicitly addressed with students by showing connections. For example, demonstrate how reading comprehension involves adding musical elements to printed words by experimenting with the music of reading and talking. Read aloud this sentence, "George Washington was the very first president of the United States of America." Now, try again and change the dynamics (volume). Try again and change tempo (speed). Once more and change pitch and tone. Finally, try changing the rhythm (group phrases differently and add a regular beat, e.g., 1–2–3–4).

Students enjoy manipulating musical elements using words and discover how words really convey very little without the added music. Take time to ask how different versions of the same sentence mean different things based on how the person interprets them through added music elements. Discuss how different words, phrases, and sentences feel different based on how they are said and read. The habit of playing with musical elements of language will increase comprehension and help students speak in more interesting ways and more effectively communicate what they want to say.

Musical Instruments.   Classroom teachers combine art and music when they show how to make and play simple instruments. Instruments extend expression of ideas and feelings with everything from songs to poems. Any story or writing form can be performed with Orff instruments or simple shakers, bells, or drums. For example, parts of speech can be emphasized using particular instruments. See previous instrument examples.

Creative Problem Solving

Just as in the other arts and in language arts, creative problem solving is used when students write original songs, play music, and listen to music. The process needs to be explicitly taught (Ready Reference 2.5), which is exactly what they do at New England Conservatory Lab School. To make the process kid-friendly, teachers there post and teach five CPS processes for learning with, about, in, and through music (Scripp, 2003):

1. Listen: observe, discriminate, decipher, perceive, describe
2. Create: invent, transform, improvise, produce, compose
3. Perform: demonstrate, interpret, follow through, work with deadlines, memorize, achieve fluency and mastery of skills
4. Inquire: question, investigate, analyze, discover
5. Reflect: make connections, self-assess, establish goals, revise work

Arts with Arts.   Integrating the arts is about helping students discover interrelationships that exist in our world and using CPS to make meaning through all art forms. To achieve this goal, students need to be shown how the arts share common aspects. Basic elements cut across art forms (rhythm, line, shape), and all art forms are created through the creative problem-solving process. We can ease students into the risk taking necessary to do higher-order thinking to create, perform, and respond in the arts by setting the stage with expectations. For example, begin to collect and share anecdotes about the struggles and failures most famous artists endure before achieving any measure of success. Share stories about the reactions to highly innovative ideas; Igor Stravinsky's "Rites of Spring" caused a riot when it was first played because it didn't conform to what people thought was good music. When students learn how people are often uncomfortable with the unfamiliar, they can learn to be more open to difference and thus grow in flexibility and tolerance.

Explicit Teaching

While the Mozart Effect got a lot of press about using the potential of background music to increase learning, we now know the effects are temporary. Scripp (2003) explains that "Far more studies tell us that making music and becoming literate in music—being able to read, interpret, and write music—make a greater and more sustainable difference in enhancing learning in other subjects" (p. 122). Becoming literate in music depends on explicit teaching.

Classroom teachers usually cooperate with the music specialist to teach music elements and concepts as needed for lessons and units. The music teacher often takes the lead in areas like teaching the reading of music notation. Classroom teachers can both lead and follow in other areas like song writing and teaching basic music elements to do close listening to music.

Explicit teaching of musical elements is particularly important and proceeds using the guidelines laid out in Chapter 3: teach *why* to know the elements, *what* they are, and *how* to use them to listen and make music. This is done in a I DO, WE DO, YOU DO sequence with the teacher first demonstrating, followed by group practice and individual practice. During practice the teacher coaches students to increase success.

Whole to Part.   Music elements and other specific concepts and skills are best taught as needed in a context. For example, a favorite song might be sung, and then the teacher would explicitly teach an element or two to better understand the music. The lesson would conclude with singing the song again. This whole–part–whole sequence is recommended for introducing all arts: (1) experience the art form as a whole, (2) work on the skills or individual parts, and (3) put it all back together again.

Knowledge of basic musical elements enables students to understand music better and can assist them in music making. During integrated activities, basic elements are needed to talk about the music of cultures under study or music elements in songs and poems. Elements are labels for words, and words contribute to general vocabulary development; so by teaching elements, students develop language and conceptual anchors to explore ways music can be thought about and created. There is a sampling of strategies to develop concepts about elements in Chapter 13 under "Basic Elements and Musical Concepts."

Visual Displays.   Music elements charts offer students a permanent reference to make, think about, and discuss music. Chapter 3 has other ideas for word walls, charts, and banners. Common mnemonics should also be posted. For example, "Every good boy does fine" is a time-tested mnemonic for musical notes on the staff lines for the treble clef. STAB (soprano, tenor, alto, bass) helps us remember the voices in a quartet. Arts content, just like any other content, can be learned through arts strategies. Students enjoy co-writing songs and poems for class big books or posters about music concepts.

Reading Music.   The special skills of reading and notating music notation (symbol system that represents elements of rhythm and pitch—the fundamental building blocks of music) may be beyond the classroom teacher's capabilities to start off. It is worth trying to learn to read some music, and a few basics are listed in Ready Reference 12.2. According to Scripp (2003), the research shows the importance of students gaining skill in "reading notes, letters, and numbers at the same time" (pp. 137–138). He calls these "complementary multiple representations" that allow students to solve problems that result in improved test scores in math and reading.

Aesthetic Orienting

To read Schiller's poem "Ode to Joy" is to know one kind of beauty, yet to hear it sung by a great chorus as the majestic conclusion to Beethoven's Ninth Symphony is to experience beauty of an entirely different kind. (Bruce Boston, 1996)

One of the goals of music integration is to learn how to get more personal enjoyment from music. Aesthetic-oriented teaching gives students tools to further understand sensory experiences; with understanding comes the possibility for more pleasure. This begins with discussion about how music is an expression of our humanity and culture and a way of expressing and understanding ourselves.

Stretching. We have a tendency to disdain the strange. If we are serious about teaching tolerance, flexibility, and respect for diversity, music is a powerful tool to stretch the concept of the familiar. Here are some suggestions. First, don't give students the chance to say they don't like unfamiliar music. Start right in and have them listen with a purpose—to identify instruments they hear, voices, the beat, and so on. Next, ask them to *describe* what they heard as best they can, but not to evaluate it for preferences yet. Then, give students many opportunities to hear a piece over and over (at least three times, with different purposes) so that they become familiar with it. This simple strategy is effective in expanding musical taste. Make the strange familiar.

Close Listening. There are many reasons to provide critical and creative music listening experiences. Listening to music stimulates the right and left brain hemispheres, triggers cognitive and emotional processes, and enlarges us as whole persons. Music is primarily an art form created for enjoyment, so students need to experience it for the pleasure it brings. This implies we should give time to just listen and just sing. Even when students are to do critical thinking (analysis and evaluation) of a piece of music, it is helpful to let them experience the music as a whole, as an enjoyable art form, before breaking it down for study.

To increase critical listening give students a "listen for" or purpose (element, instrument, style, or genre) and do repeated listening to selections to develop abilities. Try this: Distribute cards with pictures of instruments, and ask children to hold up the card that corresponds with the instrument when they hear its timbre. Take in-room trips to the windows to stop and listen closely to the sounds outside or stop and listen to school and body sounds and rhythms. Ask students to label sounds they hear as fast or slow or high or low. Describe and model sounds made with instruments, and ask students to describe them. Develop the concept of how sounds express emotions. Ask students to make sounds that are tired, happy, or fearful. In general, develop sensitivities to the role that sound plays in how they feel about a place.

Live Music. Nothing substitutes for the real thing when it comes to developing aesthetic understanding. If you don't play an instrument, invite friends to do so. Children need to see cellos and violins played up close. They benefit from chances to talk with drummers and trumpeters after performances.

Preferences. It is natural to develop music preferences. Teachers should share the music they love and invite students to do the same. Students can come to understand that aesthetic preferences are legitimate reasons for making decisions and are worth discussing. Aesthetic discussions are not intended to change preferences, but to broaden understanding. Just as we can never have too many friends, we should never confine ourselves or our students to what we and they already know. Aesthetic orienting is about continually trying out new music that may become another one of our favorites.

Management

Chapters 3, 8, and 10 described specific ways teachers manage time, materials, and student behavior that are apropos to music integration. Music is often used as a signal to start and stop activities. A drum and a tambourine are recommended tools. Rhythmic words can be chanted as attention getters: "Mozart, Beethoven, Manalow, Bach. Get cleaned up and beat the clock." Even a name or word that has musical powers can be used as the attention getter of the day: "Rimsky-Korsakov." Basic rhythms are routinely clapped or snapped to get attention and to signal transitions. See Ready Reference 8.5 for more ideas.

Practice and Independence

Even music geniuses devote long hours to practice. Why? They are self-motivated to develop both skill and artistry. Arts integration isn't about developing prodigies, but it is about developing skill and self-discipline that set the stage for artistry. One specialized example of how practice leads to independence comes from the Suzuki program at Ashley River Creative Arts. While all schools wouldn't choose to offer Suzuki, all educators should know why it is highly successful.

Practice—Suzuki Style. Shinichi Suzuki applied observations about how German children gained early language fluency to teaching music. The hallmarks of the Suzuki process are: daily close listening to music, repeated imitation of sounds, and encouragement through feedback and praise. Practice sessions are short, just 3–5 minutes to start, but they must be daily. Suzuki teacher Debby Mennick insists that a nurturing environment and following the Suzuki protocol ensure every child can learn to play the violin. The goal is to develop musical ability by growing skills in concentration, memory, analytical thinking, problem solving, physical coordination, confidence, and self-esteem. A trained ear and love for beautiful music is the result—as well as ability to play the violin.

At Ashley River students have two 40-minute Suzuki classes per week. One is a master class that must be attended by a parent or "home teacher." This class has no more than three students who each receive an individual lesson observed by the other students and parents. The group learns by observing and serves to encourage and motivate individuals to play pieces. The home teacher/parent learns how and what to teach and, if absent, must send a cassette tape to record the class. A child who comes without a parent can observe, but will not have a lesson. More than three absences can result in discontinuing the child from the program; such is the importance placed on consistency and daily practice.

Blueprint VII: Instructional Design: Routines and Structures

Arts routines are institutionalized into the daily schedule of Mary-Mac Jennings, a kindergarten teacher at Ashley River Creative Arts. Every morning begins with music and movement. "All of our phonemic awareness is done with songs like 'Willoughby Wallaby' where children's names are substituted." She uses lots of Mozart and particularly likes "Beethoven's Wig," which includes lyrics written to classics like "The Fifth Symphony." Mary-Mac also recommends old favorites like "Shake the Sillies Out" for morning music and movement.

Putting predictable routines and rituals in place early in the school year makes a substantial contribution to music integration and enables students to assume increasing responsibility. Once students understand how music will happen weekly, daily, and within lessons, they can predict, conduct, adapt, and suggest new routines, much like Mrs. Lucas's class did in the Classroom Snaphot in Chapter 3.

Lesson Introductions

Music is used to introduce specific lessons by selecting songs and pieces that relate. For example, the lesson may begin with listening to Japanese flute music to set the mood for a reading of *Crow Boy*. Students can be asked to discuss how the music feels and what it shows about the composer's background. After reading, the same music can be replayed and connected to the story. Do a repeated listening several times so students develop skills for close listening. Teachers also use music as a background *during* lessons. See "Read to Music" Seed Strategy in Chapter 13 under Literacy.

Daily and Weekly Routines

Teachers use a variety of daily or weekly routines that are music based. Here are examples.

Suzuki master class lesson at Ashley River Creative Arts.

Start the day. Background music and singing familiar songs are common day starters. Songs can be sung with or without posting lyrics and the routine should be varied. If visuals are used, song charts should be easy to read. Some teachers and students create a collaborative collection of favorite songs, and each student ends up with a personal collection. Singing can be followed with a study of language patterns. Teachers often use the lyrics as the primary material for explicit phonics and spelling lessons (e.g., use personal copies for students to find patterns). Students should be invited to bring in tapes and CDs to begin the day, during recess, or during silent reading and writing times. Any opening music listening or singing can be given more depth by focusing on music elements and/or information about the music (composer, genre, etc.). See Ready Reference 12.11 and the Appendix for more on teaching songs and songbook titles.

Disc jockey of the day. A student is in charge of the CD player and/or music instruments used for background at the start of the day, transitions, and wrap-up.

Music critic. Students listen to a piece of music or song and give their opinions (backed up by evidence). TV shows like *American Idol,* which captivate millions, are discussed in light of the pros and cons of judges, winners, and losers.

Circle discussions. Teachers often begin the day with a circle meeting. Music can be part of this kind of sharing and discussion. Music-related newspaper articles, television shows, and radio programs can be connected to units under study. Songs and music used in advertisements can be discussed to develop the concept of using music to focus, set mood, and make ideas memorable. See Ready Reference 3.3 for conversation starters.

Composer of the day.   A few facts about the composer and a musical piece or song are shared in this routine. This is more effective if the composer is connected to a current unit, but musicians' birthdays can be celebrated as they come up by playing music examples. Some schools do this schoolwide on the morning TV show (source: *www.classical. net/music/composer/dates/comp4.html*).

Wrap-up.   The pairing of music with other tasks creates an opportunity to respond to common work in uncommon ways. For example, music and songs can be used as a part of cleanup rituals. Here's a song used by a fourth-grade teacher for that purpose (to the tune of "I've Been Working on the Railroad"): "We've been working in this classroom, all the live long day. We've been working in this classroom—it's a mess now, wouldn't you say? Can't you see the clock a ticking? Soon the bell will ring. Let's get this place in order. Clean up as we sing." This teacher also plays fast tempo music like the "William Tell Overture" to get chores done before dismissal. (*Note:* Marching to a cadence is used similarly in the military for tedious drills.) In this way the day also ends on a positive note.

Energizers and Warm-Ups

Numerous music energizers and warm-ups can be used to prepare students for risk taking and creative thinking. They activate or relax and tap into interests. Since performing music is also a physical activity, the body often needs to be prepared as well. Energizers and warm-ups cause students to use both body and mind. Chapter 13 suggests energizers and starter ideas for teaching musical concepts and elements. Many of these can also be used as warm-ups as can Seed Strategies from other arts chapters. For example, drama verbal strategies and dance rhythm strategies link with music. In general, think about doing song sharing, poems, chants, and rhythms that take a few minutes and cause both mental and physical engagement. One example follows.

Name rhythms.   Call a child's name and beat out the rhythm using syllable patterns and accent. Ask students to echo. The teacher can also beat out the rhythm of a name and the owner echoes and becomes the leader. For example, "Virginia" would be four claps with the second ac-

cented. Relate this to poetry meter patterns. See the "word rhythms" in Chapter 13.

Centers, Stations, Displays

Music Displays.   Students can become more aware of music in everyday life if there is a special table to display ordinary objects with music potential (keys, pencils, boxes, and bottles filled with beans). Displays can include any music-related items, each tagged with a plaque prepared by students to show title, use, etc.

Music-Based Book Displays.   Teachers now include a special crate of music-based books or a labeled space in book nooks and other free reading areas. Heightened awareness about music-based books can be coupled with the book ad routine (see Chapter 4). Students may be in charge of supplying a special section of the chalk tray with books they find about music. Once a spot is established, students can display personal books or library books. A question can be posted above each book to entice readers: "How *does* an orchestra get dressed?"

Instruments Center.   Inexpensive instruments can be found at tag sales or made from common materials (see Arts Literacy section). Ask parents to donate old guitars, drums, flutes, and so on. This is a popular center, especially during inside recess.

Listening Centers.   Stations with headphones are particularly useful in integrating music because students can independently listen to CDs connected to units (e.g., environmental sounds that can be classified or identified). Students can also choose listening centers during free time. There they can help select music for start of the day or other routines. Alternatively they can just choose relaxing music. Musical selections should be available along with information about the composers or styles. Children can also match musical selections with composers as a follow-up to "close listening" done as a group to discern genre and traits. This kind of activity has the potential to spur a lifelong interest and further expand musical tastes.

Schoolwide Structures

Schools sometimes choose yearly themes that almost always include music. Every country or culture has specific music that may become a monthly schoolwide focus for singing and listening. This may include broadcasts on the morning TV show.

At many arts-based schools, children may choose to join a diversity of music groups. For example, at Ashley River

Creative Arts the last 40 minutes of every day is reserved for clubs and groups, including a chorus and the Piped Pipers percussion group.

Blueprint VIII: Adaptations for Diverse Needs

> *If you can talk, you can sing. If you can walk, you can dance.* (Zimbabwe aphorism)

Nature and Nurture

We are born with music in us. The natural inclination for music is there, but the brain is plastic. Environment and instruction make all the difference, but even children from impoverished environments usually start school with some musical background. Many have well-established preferences since music is often associated with powerful social contexts. This result is sometimes a passionate attachment to specific artists, styles, or genres. Personal musical tastes develop through the process of acculturation: if parents sing and play many kinds of music, children are more likely to sing well and develop diverse tastes. Atypical of American culture, some cultures expect everyone to sing or play an instrument. For example in Polynesian culture, harmony is highly valued, and most children sing well. In other cultures each child's first rattles and bangs are celebrated and converted into musical rhythms (similar to how American parents expand babblings of "ma-ma" into "Mother, yes, I am your mother") (Page, 1995).

Musical Development

Children progress through stages of musical development that parallel other development. See the Appendix for general stage characteristics. Primary teachers need to know that children come with natural musical background that can be tapped in lessons throughout the curriculum.

Preschool. Even toddlers bounce and rock to music and love to play with sounds. Preschoolers can learn simple songs, and by age 3 the brain has developed so rhythm improves. Kids can't get enough of marching, clapping, tapping, and swaying. They are ready for simple keyboard practice, kazoos, and recorders. By age 4, children understand rhythm, tempo, volume, and pitch and can create their own songs with improvised lyrics. They love songs that suggest actions, such as "Head, Shoulders, Knees, and Toes," and enjoy fingerplays, rhythm instruments, and creative movement. Folk songs, marches, and easy pop songs work well.

Primary Grades. Here are some guidelines for ages 5–8.

- Able to sing and echo rhythms and melodies during call and response songs
- Out of tune is normal; pitch awareness develops with modeling
- Some music preferences, like silly songs and lots of rhythm (Sousa marches)
- Open to diverse musical genres from classical to hip-hop
- Ready for music lessons on recorder, keyboard, or violin between the ages of 3 and 8, but the sooner the better
- Able to compose music, so give opportunities to both sing and compose (e.g., on a keyboard) (Habemeyer, 1999; Upitis & Smithrim, 2003)
- Recommended musical artists for this age group include: Hap Palmer, The Kids of Widney High, Rosenshontz, Pete Seeger, Steve and Greg, Marlo Thomas and Friends, Tickle Tune Typhoon, Peter Alsop, Heather Bishop, Tom Chapin, Ella Jenkins, Kids on the Block, and Disney tunes

Intermediate Grades. (Ages 9–12). There is increasing variation in children because of experiences and instruction. Preferences are more pronounced. Considerations for this age/stage include:

- Promote music lessons; competence on an instrument is still possible (Jensen, 2001, p. 19). Vocal training can begin around age 12.
- Plan singing in groups, such as musicals, choirs, and quartets.
- Emphasize nonmusical benefits: memory, creativity, relaxation, enjoyment, self-discipline, and satisfaction.
- Provide positive musical role models.
- Recommended musical artists include: Bill Harley, Janet and Judy, Mary Miche, The Weavers, and Weird Al Yankovic.

Classroom teachers have a lot to build on as they integrate music. Begin with what children already know. Start with their strengths and interests and use ideas for differentiating instruction (Ready Reference 3.6). Literacy instruction, in particular, can be coupled with music and songs children enjoy. For example, ask children to dictate lyrics to a favorite song and use the chart for reading/singing to build fluency. Songs are naturally motivating and provide rich material to teach high-frequency words and phonic and spelling patterns. After singing, play "I Spy" using any language concept from letters to parts of speech. With more mature students, use school appropriate songs to teach sentence structure (grammar), usage, alliteration, and so forth.

Blueprint IX: Assessment for Learning

Arts integration has blossomed at an interesting time in the evolution of assessment. On the one hand, assessment traditions in the arts have informed cutting edge thinking in assessment; the use of portfolios, exhibits, and performances are arts tools that are being incorporated into assessment plans in non-arts-based schools as well as arts-based. The increased effort to balance the use of formative (during learning) with summative assessment (final work) is another assessment pattern that has long been used in the arts; critiques and coaching are time-honored ways to increase quality of work. It isn't surprising that integrated arts schools have embraced assessment *for* learning, as opposed to overemphasis on assessment *of* learning. (For a discussion of the difference, see Chapter 3.)

What is surprising is the slowness with which the arts themselves have been included in assessment. Perhaps this is attached to the lingering misconception that assessment may somehow limit creative development. Indeed, the opposite is true. Progressive teachers and schools are finding ways to give feedback to students as they engage in music and the other arts to increase the quality of learning. That includes boosting engagement in creative problem solving, which usually increases happiness with the learning process.

Two-Pronged Planning

In the case of arts integration, assessment must be at least two pronged. We need to support learning in traditional academic areas and in the arts. This is planned from the outset using a lesson plan format in which curricular objectives and arts objectives are specified with assessment planned for both, during and at the end of work.

Feedback

The most important formative assessment is observation (using criteria) that is shared in the form of feedback. Students benefit from feedback from the teacher and peers to increase use of music concepts and skills. For example, a teacher can say, "You have great volume. You are breathing from your diaphragm!" This reinforces a singing skill that can be carried forward.

Both students and teachers need evidence that all the work put into music integration is paying off. Classroom teachers can cooperate with music specialists to provide such evidence. For example, Ashley River music specialist Ann Cheek records each child's status on music objectives according to "beginning, developing, or applying levels." Progress is tracked on concepts such as melody, rhythm, timbre, and creative expression. She does individual reports by using print merge on her computer.

There have been discussions in previous chapters of performances and cumulative portfolios. Both of these are relevant to music growth. Portfolios can include: original songs, video and audio recordings, checklists of progress, journal entries, and other writing about music. Tests and quizzes can be included as well, as appropriate to the goals and standards (see music standards in Ready Reference 12.8). The Appendix includes 10 assessment examples and explanation of how to set up and manage arts folios.

Interest Inventories

Assessing music interests and preferences gives valuable diagnostic information for teachers to adapt lessons. Much can be learned about music background through conversations as well and through observation and talks with parents. A sample Interest Inventory is included in the Appendix.

Program Evaluation

For specific checklists to examine the quality of music education, go to the South Carolina ABC schools website. The *Opportunity to Learn Standards* have been formatted in a usable way. The address is *www.winthrop.edu/ABC/*.

Blueprint X: Arts Partnerships

Brooklyn, New York. PS 314 used to be on the state's list of worst schools. Not any more. The school partnered with the Metropolitan Opera for arts-based units. Students attend dress rehearsals, use the plots and settings to learn history (e.g., *Aida*) and literature (e.g., *Faust*), and write their own operas.

When classroom teachers partner with music specialists, there is incredible potential. Even a small encounter can make a difference. I recently met a teacher in Chattanooga, Tennessee, who has been teaching for 31 years. In the conversation, Arlene Sneed explained:

> I was an at-risk child. When I was in the sixth grade, Norman Woodall, the Hixson High School band director, came to show musical instruments. If I had been absent, I would not be who I am today. That one day literally changed my life. Learning to play a musical instrument gave me the confidence, discipline, and determination to pursue the education I needed to get here.

Partnering doesn't have to mean a residency, even though this arrangement is desirable. Teachers should seek out community partnerships using the resources in Chapter 3, especially the local arts council. Musical guests can be sought out in the form of local singers and musicians who may be able to perform music connected to units in science, social studies, and the like. Often students find potential candidates in their families. Arlene Sneed's experience reminds us it is worth the effort to try to find musicians for even one-shot visits.

Music Teachers

Of course the music teacher is the specialist most likely to partner with classroom teachers. Ashley River music teacher Ann Cheek has a sizable lending library of music-based children's literature available to teachers. She also burns CDs for them and is a part of the planning teams for units.

Technology

A developing speciality area in music is the use of technology. Ten years ago teachers rarely looked to technology for help in music integration. There is now music software to learn to read music and understand music history. Music-computer specialists can show teachers how to involve students in creating original musical compositions with software which often requires a MIDI or musical instrument digital interface. This is an electric musical keyboard that plugs into a computer. There is also software that does not require a MIDI nor any amplification. Books like *The Musical PC* review software.

CD-ROMs can now be purchased that allow students to see and hear orchestras playing and get background information on composers or instruments. Social studies, math, reading, and language arts experiences are automatically integrated in this type of software experience. Consult sources in your own locale.

Classroom Snapshot:

African American Music and History

Teacher Sylvia Horres brings this chapter back to where it started: a regular classroom teacher using music in an integral way.

Ms. Horres is seated in a canvas director's chair. Students sit pretzel style on the carpet around her.

"Remember, there is no one right answer!" she tells the class as she shows a page from a picture book about Booker T. Washington. The book is *More Than Anything Else* (Bradby), and Sylvia is doing an introduction for her daily read-aloud. This month it is connected to a social studies unit on African American History.

"Look closely at what is in his hands," Ms. Horres coaches them.

"Maybe they are pictures of his family and he misses them," says one boy.

"What makes you say that, Sam?"

"Well, because he looks so sad. His head is way down."

"So, what might this book be about—just from our close look at the pictures?"

A girl with lots of curls responds, "Maybe it is about getting freedom." The teacher again **asks for evidence** from the picture. There are more student observations, each followed by Ms. Horres's request for evidence to support their hypotheses.

"Reading a book for the first time is like watching a movie at a theatre," she tells them. "I want you to just view and listen. Think about our predictions and find out details you want to discuss later. Especially, enjoy!"

The class is focused as the teacher reads this moving story about a boy's desire to learn to read. Of course, it isn't exactly like watching a movie because Ms. Horres is skilled at using **inserted questions** to actively engage students in making meaning from the pictures and the story. She asks about theme with questions like "Why is it important for him to learn to read?" She also focuses on idioms and metaphors such as "he jumped into another world" by asking what this means, how it feels, and why the author didn't just "say it straight."

Ms. Horres reads expressively. She is a model of **fluency**. She "makes music" with her voice, varying the volume, tempo, pitch, and rate to cause the words to seem like song lyrics. It is obvious that she believes reading aloud is an art; this is no unrehearsed performance.

At one poignant moment in the story she stops and asks, "What does 'taking the sounds of my name and draw them on the ground' mean?" The room is quiet. It is as if a sacred act has been described. In a whisper one boy says, "He is writing his letters." There is a respectful **wait time** and then Ms. Horres asks,

"What do you think this boy might have done with his life?"

"He got to be free?" asks another hopefully.

"He did. But, how could reading make him free?"

"Maybe he became an author and writing let his ideas be free," thinks a boy.

"What a **beautiful** way to say it, Germaine. Now I have to tell you that this is not a fiction book. It is *nonfiction*. It is about a real person and his name was Booker."

Sylvia turns to the computer behind her that is hooked to a TV monitor. She clicks to display a picture from the **Internet** and tells the rest of the story of Booker's life, including setting a context for "blues music in troubled times."

At the end of the storytelling, Ms. Horres asks the students to **connect** books they've read that had to do with slave songs and secret messages. In particular, they remember *The Drinking Gourd* and how the song gave directions for escaping slaves.

"Today we're going to learn more songs, not just ones with secret codes, but music about how black people felt after they were free. This is sad music about their troubles. What colors are sad?"

"Blue!" say two boys at once.

"You got it. This is 'blues' music. Let's listen to some."

"Yeah!" shout the students.

"**Listen for** two things: How people use their voices and the instruments they are using now that they are free. Who remembers our **movement rules**?"

"Body controlled," says one girl.

"No talking," says another girl.

"What else?"

"Just feeling the music and moving for yourself," a boy adds.

"Yes. Find your place in the room and freeze." Ms. Horres starts the CD. Students sway to mellow blues sounds. She also moves and coaches students to use their arms, legs, feet, head, and hips. After a few minutes the teacher counts to 3, and the students freeze.

"How did you feel when you were dancing?" she asks.

Students say they felt tired, sad, drowsy, sleepy, worn out, and hungry. Ms. Horres starts a **vocabulary web** of words on chart paper and asks students to "spell for me" as she writes.

She asks how the music **caused** the feelings and students say it was slow. Sylvia tells them this is the **tempo** of the music. She also asks what they noticed about the voices and the instruments. Students think they heard horns "stretched out," and the voices were "flowing," some deep and some high pitched.

Walk to Read is almost over. Ms. Horres tells the students to move like the blues to line up. As they exit, she asks them to each tell one thing they learned. Quickly 17 students offer 17 different ideas from "blues is sad music" to "Booker liked books." Tomorrow they will continue, but today they are returning to homeroom. In this way, grade-level teachers each develop specialty arts-based lessons taught to all students at that grade level during the unit.

Text Set for African American Unit

When Marion Sang
(Boy's Choir of Harlem)
God Bless the Child
(CD/Billy Holiday lyrics)
Ella Fitzgerald
If I Only Had a Horn
Perfect Harmony
No Mirrors in My Mama's House
Ben's Trumpet
I See the Rhythm
More Than Anything Else

Barefoot
Back Home
A Lesson for MLK, Jr.
Five Bold Freedom Fighters
Amazing Grace
The Sounds That Make Jazz
Little Stevie Wonder (with CD)
A Blue So Blue

Conclusion

What's more, the teachers are positive about it and the parents are happy. (Larry Scripp, 2003)

Scripp is talking about music-based learning. Every child deserves to grow up with music woven into the fabric of learning, not as an isolated event that happens every other Tuesday. This chapter explains *why*, as well as *what* classroom teachers need to know to make this a reality. *How* music may be integrated was presented in the Arts Integration Blueprint sections. In the next chapter more specific ideas are given to teach music elements so that students can use music as a way of learning. There are also Energizers and Seed Strategies for integrating music throughout curricular areas.

Resources

See the Appendix for study materials, including more websites. Chapter 13 lists recommended music activity books.

Videos

Making music in the classroom (video). (1995). Berkeley, CA: Langstaff Video Project. Cultural songs.

Children's Literature References

Ambrus, V. (1970). *Seven skinny goats.* New York: Harcourt, Brace & World.

Baker, A., & Baker, J. (1991). *Raps & rhymes in math.* Portsmouth, NH: Heinemann.

Bradby, M. (1995). *More than anything else.* New York: Orchard.

Hesse, K. (1997). *Out of the dust.* New York: Scholastic.

Hill, S. (1990). *Raps and rhymes.* New York: Penguin.

Hopkins, B. (1995). *Making simple musical instruments.* Asheville, NC: Lark.

Livingston, M. (1995) *Call down the moon, poems of music.* New York: Margaret McElderry.

Marsalis, W. (2005). *Jazz ABZ: A to z collections of jazz portraits.* New York: Candlewick.

Nichol, B. (1994). *Beethoven lives upstairs.* New York: Orchard.

Raschka, C. (1992). *Charlie Parker plays be bop.* New York: Orchard.

Stanley, L. (Ed.). (1992). *Rap, the lyrics: The words to rap's greatest hits.* New York: Penguin.

Toop, D. (1991). *Rap attack 2: African rap to global hip hop.* London: Serpent's Tail.

Wallace, R. (1993). *Smart-rope jingles: Jump rope rhymes, raps, and chants for active learning.* Tucson, AZ: Zephyr.

Music Seed Strategies

Questions to Guide Reading

1. What Seed Strategies can be used to introduce lessons and/or teach music concepts?

2. What Seed Strategies can help integrate music with science, social studies, math, and literacy?

Teacher Spotlight:

Literature Through Music

Ann Cheek, the music teacher at Ashley River, is famous for her mini-musicals. Each year her students turn books like *Chicka Chicka Boom Boom, Zomo the Rabbit,* and *The Very Hungry Caterpillar* into performance pieces. They use musical instruments, often bought through a box top program. "Last year we raised $3,000 to buy two glockenspiels and a computer," Ms. Cheek reports. (See *www.boxtops4education. com.*) She especially focuses on Orff instruments, noting that "Orff pedagogy has taught me how to work with poetry and speech to teach music."

Ms. Cheek is passionate about integration. "Without the arts, you are missing a whole important part of life and history." She challenges anyone to try to understand the Great Depression without Woody Guthrie's songs. "This Land Is Your Land" cheered up a nation. "In life things aren't separated," she insists. "The arts should be integral to life inside school, too." Ms. Cheek explains that music is another di-

mension to express yourself and shows the evolution of a culture. "Americans play the harmonica, banjos, and other folk instruments, and we also enjoy music at the 'high end' of culture—orchcestras and operas," she says.

Literacy

"We need to model a love of reading," Ms. Cheek says as she gestures to her large music-based classroom library for free reading. She especially enjoys integrating children's literature into music lessons, and the room is filled with children's books for units of study. Ann explains that music involves learning specific content and skills, just like any other form of literacy. "Classroom teachers can integrate aspects of the arts, but specialists are needed to go into the kind of depth that eventually creates music literacy," she recommends. Ms. Cheek brings in every area of the curriculum to music and is ready to be a resource for classroom teachers. Teachers sing her praises for everything from burning CDs for them to helping them understand music concepts.

Math and Music

On the bulletin board is the Pizzarondo. It shows whole, half, quarter, eighth, and sixteenth notes used to teach fractions to all grade levels. "They learn the relative value of notes," Ms. Cheek explains. She shows how each represent a fraction of a pizza. When she teaches the Pizzarondo, she uses manipulatives with layers so she can show how whole notes relate to the other notes. Students sing as they pull felt pizza pieces off of the big pizza, singing "Make me a pizza if you can. . . ."

Chapter Organization

This chapter presents Seed Strategies to prompt creative lesson planning using music. The Seed Strategies are organized

Making music at Ashley River Creative Arts.

into three sections: energizers and warms-ups, music elements, and curricular areas, or ideas for science, social studies, literacy, and math. Many Seeds fit in more than one section, and some use multiple arts, not just music.

I. Energizers and Warm-Ups

Energizers are used to get attention, increase focus, and start creative problem solving. They also are used to warm up the voice and body. Also see the energizers and warm-ups in chapters on dance, drama, art, and literature.

Morning TV Show.   Use a schoolwide broadcast to spotlight/play different genres of music each morning, followed by 30-second genre reports. Lots can be learned about jazz on the 2-minute-a-day plan.

Mood Music.   When students enter the room, have music playing that creates the mood for upcoming work. *Example:* Play nature sounds related to a science lesson. Stop the CD and ask students to listen again to notice sounds, instruments, patterns, etc.

Sing the Scales.   Warm up voices by singing major and minor scales, with or without words or instruments. Major and minor scale music can be purchased at music supply stores. *Variation:* sing using short or long vowel sounds.

Tongue Twisters.   Warm up students' voices for singing with tongue twisters. See more examples in Chapter 9. Here is one for singing: "Tip of the tongue, the teeth, and the lips." Say it three to five times. *Variation:* Sing the scale using one vowel sound, like short a.

Theme Song.   Select or do a collaborative writing of a class song. Sing together as a daily routine. *Example:* Sing "High Hopes," about an ant moving a rubber plant. *Variation:* Change songs for each social studies or science unit.

Say It Different Ways.   Form a circle. IT says a sentence, which is passed around with each person changing the volume, rate, pitch, accent, and rhythm patterns. *Example:* "The rain in Spain falls mainly on the plain."

Clap Rhythm.   List suggestions of favorite poems or songs. Then, instead of singing, clap the rhythm by syllables. Do as a call and response or echo. *Variation:* Clap the beat instead of the rhythm.

Echo Me.   A leader claps, slaps, snaps, or clicks a series of rhythms that are echoed by the class. Use children's names: divide them into syllables and accent (e.g., Clau´ di a). Adapt for phrases or topics such as days of the week, months of the year, animal names, or plants. Challenge by turning rhythm patterns into a round: Divide the class in half with a leader for each half to start the pattern at varying times.

Name Echo.   Stand in a circle. Leader says her name and class echoes using the exact volume, pitch, dynamics, tempo, etc. Student to right then does the same. Class echoes. *Variation:* Do as a cumulative name echo, repeating from the first name.

Name Songs.   Sing songs that call for use of student names. *Examples:* "Willoughby Wallaby Woo" or "Name Game." *Variation:* Adapt songs like "My Aunt Came Back" to student names.

Question and Answer Songs.   Many songs involve people asking and answering questions, such as "Baa Baa Black Sheep" and "Are You Sleeping?" Divide the class in half and direct one-half to sing questions and other half the answers.

Happy Birthday.   Partners sing "Happy Birthday" or another song to one another as if it really mattered. Make this an "ode to joy" or celebration of each other (Booth, 2003, p. 24).

Join In.   Form small groups to listen to a musical selection. Challenge each group to create a movement pattern involving clapping hands and tapping their feet as the music is replayed. Then stop the music. Have group 1 do its movements when the music starts. Keep adding more groups until all groups are doing their movements.

Musical Memories. Students close their eyes and imagine different sounds as they are described (e.g., crickets chirping, wind chimes, jingle bells, song on keyboard). Give time to create the sound images. After each, ask the student to describe the images.

Celebrate. Use a rhythmic chant or cheer to celebrate class and individual efforts. *Example:* Pat pat pat/ on the back back back/ for a job well done (3X). Add patting movement.

Tempo Change. Students get into their personal spaces. Music is played with varying speeds. They move in response to music (can be in place or locomotor). Use slow, fast, staccato (choppy), or legato (smooth) or music that has accelerando. For "Beep Beep" (the Little Nash Rambler song), divide into groups according to vehicles (six in a van, four in a car, two on a motorcycle, etc.). Vehicles "drive" around as this '50s song accelerates.

Ann Cheek, music teacher, using Solfege.

Rhythm Mirror. Form a circle with an IT in the middle who begins a rhythm or movement. Others must mirror. IT passes the rhythm on by staring at one person, who slowly takes over and changes places with IT. The class observes and begins to mirror the new rhythms and actions when they feel the exchange is complete.

Rhythm Sync. Group forms a circle. When leader says "begin," everyone makes an original rhythm using hands, feet, or voice. Slowly, by listening to each other, the group becomes one rhythm. Then individuals slowly begin new rhythms, and a new group rhythm emerges.

Exchange. Two lines form on opposite sides of the room. The first pair at one end starts. Each person in the pair begins a unique rhythm and walks toward her partner. As they pass, the two exchange rhythms. Then the next pair goes and on down the line. Focus on unusual rhythms.

Rhythm Pass. Do in groups of four to six. Pass a rhythm around a circle. *Example:* With a 1-2 rhythm all slap knees, palms down on downbeat, and then palms up. IT slaps hand of right neighbor on 2, and neighbor passes and so on until the pass is complete and the group is back to each slapping own knees on 1. The last person to receive the pass becomes IT.

"Head, Shoulders, Knees, and Toes." First, sing the song through. Then add motions. Practice at a slow tempo. Finally, ask students to stand in a circle and do movements as they sing, gradually substituting body parts with hums, but continuing the actions: Touch head, touch shoulders, touch knees, touch toes, and so forth. Sing at different volumes and tempos.

Shoe Beat. Everyone sits in a circle and removes one shoe. Agree on a song or rhythm pattern to do together during which shoes are passed, left to right, and held. For example, "Mary had a little lamb" could be "pass–pass–hold." If you don't keep the rhythm, the shoes pile up on you!

Balloon Movement. Put on classical music (e.g., Haydn pastoral) and give small groups a balloon to waft to the beat. Be sure to discuss behavior expectations and explain how the activity is about concentrating to stay on beat.

Knock and Respond. When someone knocks on a door to the rhythm "da-da da-da-DA," we know to reply "da-da." Create original rhythms by having partners make up ones to demonstrate. Challenge the group to learn new knock and respond patterns.

Rhythm Circle. Stand in a circle with IT. IT creates a rhythmic phrase that is passed around the circle to the right until it returns to IT. The person to right is then IT.

Add on Songs. Collect songs that invite improvised verses such as "If You're Happy and You Know It" and "The More We Are Together." "Down by the Bay" requires adding original rhyming words. A funny example of a copycat song is "On Legs You'll Find Two Legs Behind" to the Scottish tune "Auld Lang Syne."

Pizzarando: Math and music.

plicated, with whistles, clicks, claps, and slaps, slower and faster. At any point the leader can "pass it on," and another person becomes leader.

Hum Melodies. Choose a song students know. Hum the first line. Keep humming until someone guesses. Everyone sings the words as soon as the song is named. Then have a student take a turn at humming a song. Example songs are "I've Been Working on the Railroad" and "Row, Row, Row Your Boat."

Listening Phones. Use PVC pipe to make "phones" for students to hear their own voices. Use two curved pieces to make the earpiece and voice piece. Cut a 3-inch straight piece for the handle.

Name Harmonies. Pair children with long and short names. Pairs take turns beating out their names in rotation and together. Rhythm instruments or body parts can be used. *Variation:* Student pairs sing their names in harmony.

Name Duet. Pairs explore combinations using just their names (e.g., Dan-Amber, Dan-Dan-Dan, Amber-Dan-Amber-Dan-Amber-Dan). Vary by changing the tempo of one name, the other, or both. Change the combination of tempo and volume in different ways. Explore harmonies created by beating out both names or varying volume and tempo.

Name Melody. Students work in pairs or small groups to create a melody for each person's name or put all the names to a tune.

Cumulative Counterpoint Melodies. Make a list of songs everyone knows, such as "Row, Row, Row Your Boat." Form small groups. Each student chooses one song to hum using a syllable, such as "la la" or "ti ti." An IT starts humming. Then the student to the right starts humming on top of IT's song during the second time around, the third person adds on, and so on. Humming overlapping melodies at the same time, without words, teaches counterpoint.

Kazoo Melodies. Make Kazoos from combs by folding paper over them or use empty candy boxes (e.g., small Milk Dud boxes). A leader plays a melody on a kazoo. Others echo on kazoos.

Environment Sounds (Pitch). Tape common sounds. Ask students to signal if the sounds are high or low or in between high and low. Examples are a door bell, mixer, and computer hum.

Bingo Scavenger Hunt. Set up a blank bingo page on which students write musical concepts. (List categories and examples on the board, such as musical genre and styles, composers, singers, instruments, elements, and particular songs. At a signal, students begin to search for peers who know about each concept. The goal is to write names under each music word until bingo happens—across, down, or diagonally.

Hum Groups. Type four song titles on slips of paper. Repeat the titles until you have enough for everyone. Students draw a slip and on a signal sing or hum the melody while trying to find others singing the same melody. Fellow hummers remain together until everyone is grouped. *Example:* "Row, Row, Row Your Boat."

BGIM. Start each Monday with a celebration song. *Example* (tune = "You Are My Sunshine" or "This Land Is Your Land"): Be glad it's Monday. Day after Sunday. Be glad it's Monday, all day today. Be glad it's Monday. It's such a fun day. Be glad that Monday's here to stay.

II. Music Elements and Concepts

These Seed Strategies develop a music knowledge and skill base needed for use of music as a learning tool.

Rhythm Symphony. The leader creates a rhythm and the group echoes it. Keep going, getting increasingly com-

Guess Who Panel (Timbre). A panel of five students comes to the front. All students close their eyes. Leader taps one panel member on the shoulder. Tapped person says "Who did that?" Students open their eyes and guess who spoke. Each time a name is guessed, ask "How did you know?" Coach for answers that describe the uniqueness of voices. Repeat but have students sing "Who did that?" Stress that each speaking and singing voice is unique.

Old MacMajor. Use the tune of "Old MacDonald" to learn the key signatures (idea from music teacher Aurelia Cornett):

"Old Macmajor had some keys e-i-e-i-o. And in these keys there were some sharps e-i-e-i-o. With a one sharp G and two sharps D and the key of A has one, two, three. Old Macmajor had some keys e-i-e-i-o. Old Macmajor had some keys e-i-e-i-o. See how easy it can be e-i-e-i-o. Four sharps give up the key of E and A has three and two in D and there's just one in the key of G. Old Macmajor had some keys e-i-e-i-o."

Name That Instrument (Timbre). First students experiment with rhythm instruments to become familiar with their sound qualities. Label each instrument (e.g., tambourine, shaker). Then tell them to close their eyes as an IT plays one. Stress that each instrument has a unique sound, even though some sound similar. Take guesses along with reasons. *Variation:* Use a tape or CD of orchestral instruments or other music instruments (guitar, banjo).

Dynamics Dial. Dynamics has to do with volume. Make a volume dial out of cardboard or use an old clock. Label "soft" to "loud" on the dial with the musical symbols *pp* (very soft), *p* (soft), *mp* (medium soft), *mf* (medium loud), *f* (loud), *ff* (very loud), and *mfz* (loudest). Invite students to sing a familiar song as someone turns the dial or volume button. The children should sing accordingly. For example, if the dial said "pp," children sing very, very softly. *Variation:* Teach hand signals to show dynamics. Make them up or use ones from books such as *Joy of Signing* (Riekehof, 1987).

Conducting Dynamics. Use with any musical instruments (Orff, homemade, or found sounds). Ask students to play very soft, soft, loud, and very loud. Challenge to start softly and gradually play louder (crescendo) and vice versa (decrescendo). Invite students to conduct. Students play louder as the conductor raises her hands and softer as she lowers. Have the conductor try fast raising to practice sudden dynamic changes.

Pretend to Conduct. Let students pretend to conduct using conducting patterns. Teach start and stop signals, and then practice actual patterns, learning "downbeat" and "up-beat." Orchestra members can use different sounds as their instruments (e.g., click, hum, pop, hiss, whistle, etc.). Basic conducting patterns are:

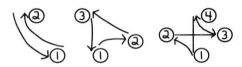

Musical Elements in Art. After teaching the elements of music, use a piece of art and ask students to find these same elements. For example, folk art and folk music can be compared. Find rhythm in art, texture, tempo, style aspects, and dynamics (areas that are louder or softer).

Sound Textured Story. Read a story that has repeated language. Cumulative stories work, as do sound stories (see Chapter 4). Next, assign repetitive words and ask students to think of different ways to say words or add sound effects. For example, every time the word *hen* is heard, students say "cluck cluck cluck" or strike triangles. Involve everyone using unison, duos, trios, or individual sounds. Discuss how textured layers are created as sounds enter and reenter. Ask students to compare sound textures to fabric textures (e.g., rough, soft).

Thick and Thin Voices (Texture). Use poems or stories and assign different numbers of students to participate in solo and choral readings of parts. Ask how it sounds when more people are reading compared to fewer. Label as "thick" and "thin" sounds. Repeat using singing voices. Relate to using individual versus multiple instruments by playing recordings of the same song or music done by an orchestra versus a single instrument.

Barbershop Quartet (Harmony). One person sings the main melody while others harmonize or echo the tune to make a barbershop quartet. Some good songs for quartets are "By the Light of the Silvery Moon," "Sweet Adeline," "Down by the Old Mill Stream," and "Down by the Bay." (This is a good time to introduce the terms *soprano*, *alto*, *tenor*, and *bass* and the acronym STAB to remember them.)

Cannons and Rounds (Harmony). Start by speaking in rounds. Students can also sing with a CD that features rounds. "Row, Row, Row Your Boat" is a popular round. Once they can sing along, they are ready to sing on their own. Movements can be created for each line and performed while singing, which helps students keep track of where they are. After each group practices and knows its lines, all groups can also sing simultaneously.

Picturing Song Form. Play a variety of musical pieces. Discuss repetitive patterns and similar and contrasting sections.

Target one piece. Ask students to raise a hand when the first line or phrase is heard. Label this A and draw a picture of an object that begins with A. Have students raise the same hand if the next line is similar and draw another A object on the board. If the line is different, have them raise the other hand and draw an item that begins with B. Continue until there is a complete picture to represent all the phrases. Sing again and have students raise appropriate hands as symbols are designated. For example, "Mary Had a Little Lamb" would be "ABAC."

Instrument Pantomime.   After reading a book such as Isadora's *Ben's Trumpet* or Raschka's *Charlie Parker Played Be Bop* (saxophone), brainstorm types of instruments. In small groups, one student pantomimes playing different instruments, when the leader signals. Group members write down their guesses. Change players in the groups at the end of one minute and start again.

Musical Rainbow.   Add food coloring to each of eight glasses filled with different amounts of water. (Each should have about one inch more than previous glass.) The eight notes will make a beautiful rainbow when put in order. 1 is clear; 2 is red; 3 is orange; 4 is yellow; 5 is green; 6 is blue; 7 is purple; 8 is clear. *Note:* red plus yellow makes orange. Blue plus yellow makes green. Red plus blue makes purple. Under each glass, put a paper with the number of the tone that the glass plays.

Musical Form Books.   Read a book based on a song (e.g., Raffi's "Shake My Sillies Out"). Sing the song. Ask students how form (pattern) is illustrated in the story or song. Give children phrases of a favorite song to illustrate to creating a class book. Children draw a picture for each line of the song. If a line repeats, they should draw the same picture. The final book will show the song's form.

Repeat a Beat (Ostinato).   Make a sound and repeat it a number of times: tap the window, click your tongue, or repeat a syllable (dum dum dum). Tell students to listen carefully and to count how many times they hear the sound. Then they repeat the sound exactly. Let students take turns making a sound while others count and echo the pattern.

Poem Ostinati.   First students memorize a poem. Explain the concept of ostinato (something repeated over and over). Then ask one group to recite the poem, while another group recites an ostinato (a line or word that repeats). The ostinato may be a line they have created, the title of the poem, or a selected line from the poem. After students have practiced the last two activities, break the class into three groups. Two groups perform the poem as a spoken round, while the third group performs the ostinato. An example poem is Silverstein's "Listen to the Mustn'ts" (repeat "mustn'ts"). *Variation:* Use rhythm instruments to create ostinati.

Staff Walk (Notation).   Make a large musical staff on the floor (masking tape). Students walk horizontally across a certain space of the staff without touching a line, or do this with the lines on the staff. Everyone says or sings notes touched as they walk. *Variation:* Throw bean bags on lines or spaces of the staff and name the notes.

Syllable Sing (Critical Listening).   This helps hear note tones, phrasing, and rhythm. Choose a jingle from a commercial or a familiar melody. Sit in a circle and ask each student to sing only one syllable. Go around until it is blended. *Variation:* Use whole words or phrases to help hear ostinati (repetition).

Instruments Notation.   Find everyday items, or "found sounds," that make music. Even body parts can be used. The goal is to write music for each sound. First, pairs choose two found sound instruments and decide ways to notate (make symbols for) timbre, pitch, and volume. For example, jingle bells might be small dots to show the high, light sound. Next, pairs write the numbers 1 to 8 across the top of the paper and the names of two instruments at the top of the left margin. Next, put symbols for each instrument under the numbers to show when each should be played. When both are to be played, place them under the same number. Loudness can be shown by drawing a symbol larger or smaller. Pairs then perform.

Music Concentration (Notation).   Draw music symbols and different kinds of notes on the chalkboard. Students take turns naming each symbol to remember it. Students then close their eyes while a symbol is erased. They open their eyes and try to guess what symbol was erased. As more are erased, students are to name the most recent deletions, as well as the previous ones. Correct answers are reinforced by writing the answer back on the board. *Variation:* Ask for examples or an explanation of each concept.

Musical Notation.   Use a favorite song. First, speak the lyrics while clapping the rhythm (e.g., "Happy Birthday"). Decide where long, short, and silent sounds occur (not vowels). Invent symbols to record musical sounds (e.g., circles, squares, or lines for notes). The symbols should show if the melody goes up or down and if the notes are long or short in time; for example, use small circles for short notes and large circles for long notes. Chant the lyrics again while pointing to symbols. Ask students again how to represent high and low sounds in the melody, as well as symbols for rhythm. Repeat and then ask children to create symbols to address tempo and dynamics. Sing the complete song while pointing to the symbols.

Body Sound Compositions (Notation and Composition).   Ask students to demonstrate sounds that can be made with their hands, fingers, feet, tongue, lips, cheeks, and other body parts. Pairs create a composition using various combinations. *Variation:* Put sounds and actions to any favorite musical recording.

Jives (Rhythm).

Hand and body jives allow exploration of rhythm. Examples include "Shimmy, Shimmy Cocoa Puff" and "Hambone." Basically, you slap and brush your hands to a rhythm. See Mattox's *Shake It to the One That You Love Best*.

Two-Part Rhythm.

One group chants and claps a steady beat to the nursery rhyme "Hot Cross Buns," while another group chants "One a Penny, Two a Penny" over and over.

Rhythm Box Beats.

Each student needs an empty milk carton or shoe box and a wooden spoon or big pencil. The inside of the box or carton is struck, one side at a time, in the same order to create a 1–2–3–4 beat (common in music). Try at different tempos and put to music by playing along with four-beat songs (see the time signature on sheet music). Next, strike the box using other music beats: 1–2 or 1–2–3 (waltz time).

Follow the Leader.

Use rhythm instruments, homemade or purchased (sticks, tambourines, drums, cymbals). Leader plays different rhythms. Everyone echoes the rhythm on his or her instrument (e.g., "ta-tum ta-tum ta-tum tum tum").

Make It Italian (Tempo, Dynamics).

Use the following Italian words used in music to expand vocabularies and spice up class activities and directions. *Variation:* Teach the effect of speed on singing and on any task. Use a metronome and sing a familiar song at each tempo, such as "Happy Birthday." Discuss changes in pitch, enunciation, and the like.

Largo = broad (40–60 beats per minute)
Lento = slow (60–66 bpm)
Adagio = at ease (66–76 bpm)
Andante = walking (76–108 bpm)
Moderato = moderate (108–120 bpm)
Allegro = quick/happy (120–168 bpm)
Presto = very fast (168–200 bpm)
Prestissimo = fast as possible (200–208 bpm)

Singing Speeds.

Play examples of accelerando (e.g., Strauss's "Acceleration Waltz," the '50s song "Beep Beep," and Brahms's "Hungarian Dances"—they get faster and faster). Try singing any song using accelerando. Add dynamic changes like crescendo and decrescendo (get louder and get softer) or use staccato (choppy) and legato (very smooth). *Variation:* Students create three different shapes and remember them. Repeat the shapes to the different tempos marked by the metronome. Discuss how tempo changes movements (e.g., sustained versus bound).

Instrument Categories.

Collect pictures of orchestral instruments. Ask students about people (family members) who have similar, but unique voice sounds. Explain this is also true for instruments. Show pictures grouped in families (percussion, strings, woodwind, and brass). Shuffle cards and have students regroup them by similar sound. Reinforce efforts based on sound groupings (some may group by size, material, etc.). Explain how instruments are grouped by: (1) sound similarity, (2) the way they are played, and (3) the material from which they are made.

Instrument Rummy.

Make a deck of 52 cards, with pictures of instruments (percussion, strings, woodwind, and brass replace the four groups of face cards). Each player gets 5 cards. Place remaining cards on the table. The object is to acquire sets of four common instruments (string, brass, woodwind, and percussion). The first player draws from the pile and chooses to keep the card or discard it face up. The player with the most instrument sets at the end is the winner.

Homemade Jam.

Have a jam session with student-made instruments. Put on music and play along. *Variation:* Create a parade using all the instruments. (Titles of instrument-making books can be found in the Appendix under Arts-Based Children's Literature.)

Musical-Style Party.

Have a party where students come dressed as country, jazz, rock, opera, or other type of musicians. Students may choose a specific musician, such as Elvis Presley or Louis Armstrong. *Variation:* Invite students to imitate a favorite musical artist by lip syncing Clay Aiken, Alvin and the Chipmunks, Garth Brooks, or The Beatles (combine with the "style party"). *Note:* Be sure to discuss school-appropriate costumes and artist imitation.

Music Response Options.

Students can use their musical intelligences to respond to a book or unit of study using a variety of activities. Nineteen ideas are given in Ready Reference 13.1.

III. Connecting Music to Curricular Areas

There is nothing more integrated than real life. Here is an example of the life-saving power of music.

Colorado Springs. Five-year-old Jasmine saved her mother's life because she knew a song. Her mother started having a seizure. Jasmine knew how to call 911 because of a CD the Colorado Symphony Orchestra distributes to children. The "Safety Hop" CD has hits like "Buckle Up," "Under the Smoke," and, yes, "Call 911" (to the tune of "My Boyfriend's Back"). Jasmine said she remembered the lyrics and just did what the song said. So far, more than

Ready Reference 13.1   Music Response Options

Use these ideas to respond to a book or area of study.

1. *Songwriting.* Write a song about the characters or people, plot, theme, or setting (place or time period). Use a familiar melody.

2. *Sing it, rap it.* Choose an important part of the story or event to put to music (sing it, rap it, or write a poem. Ready Reference 5.2 lists Poem Patterns).

3. *Background music read-aloud.* Choose a part and add rhythm instruments or music that suits the mood.

4. *Scavenger hunt.* Find music and songs that relate to story emotions, topics, themes, time period, or culture.

5. *Song list.* Make a list of songs the main character would like to listen to or sing. Use these to plan an operetta.

6. *Match instruments.* List musical instruments associated with characters, parts of the plot, setting, or a topic (e.g., a plant or animal). Example: What instrument would the wolf sound like in *Three Little Pigs?*

7. *Diagram the story plot.* Choose musical elements to re-create the action. For example, show rising action with faster rhythm and climax with loud music.

8. *Rhythm plus.* Make a list of special words and phrases. Put them to a rhythm or even create a melody. Think about which words or phrases could be repeated over and over (ostinato). Example: Cats here, cats there, cats and kittens everywhere (*Millions of Cats*)!

9. *Word choir.* List words or feelings for characters, plot, or theme. Groups line up and a category is given (e.g., a character). The "director" then points to each student, who must make a sound or say a word about the char-

acter and continue as long as the director indicates. The director indicates dynamics, tempo, and so forth. All can be cued to respond solo or in unison.

10. *Opera.* Sing the story. Make the story into an opera. Rewrite words so they can be sung (libretto).

11. *Musical instruments.* Make musical instruments (kazoo, drum, shaker, etc.) that characters might play or that represent characters. Reread story and when each character enters, students play a short rhythm or melody.

12. *Make a mix.* Create a tape or CD mix of songs and music for a favorite character.

13. *Musical mobile.* Use items that relate to the book or topic that will make sounds as they move.

14. *Music fans.* List musicians characters would prefer.

15. *Rock band?* If the characters in the book formed a band, what would it be called? What kind of music would they play?

16. *Jingle writing.* Write an advertising jingle to sell the book.

17. *Sound collage.* List all the sounds in the book. Make a sound collage by re-creating the sounds and organizing them on a tape.

18. *Singing words.* Practice reading a section, sentence, or phrase aloud, adding music elements to make the print sing (e.g., change dynamics, tempo, or pitch).

19. *Lip sync.* Find a song that a character would sing; for example, what might Jacob sing to Sarah in *Sarah, Plain and Tall?*

25,000 CDs have been distributed (*Early Show* on CBS, Interview, April 6, 2005).

You don't have to be in a symphony to write songs that have important information in them. In these Seed Strategies, you'll find a composition process and several examples of songs written by students in collaboration with their teachers.

Webbing.   There are many ways to meaningfully integrate music. Webbing is an all-purpose brainstorming strategy that helps locate connections between music and other areas. Choose any topic and web all the kinds of music associated with it. Web to plan lessons or as a starter for student research. In the latter, break students into groups with each selecting one or several kinds of music to explore in depth. Culminate with group sharing.

The following are starter ideas for integrating music with science, social studies, literacy, and math.

Science Focus

Science Standards.   A complete listing of standards can be accessed at the National Science Teachers Association (NSTA) website: *www.nsta.org.*

Music Month.   March is the official music month, so plan a musical focus for each day: a composer, song, genre, or fact.

Science Summary Songs.   Students summarize important science concepts by writing lyrics using familiar or original melodies. See songwriting steps under "Literacy: Reading and Language Arts" in this chapter. Invite groups to create additional verses. *Examples:*

1. "Four Oceans" (Tune: "Bingo")
   There is a planet with four oceans, and this is what we call them
   Atlantic, Pacific, Indian, Arctic (3X)
   And that is what we call them.

2. "North, South, East, and West" (Tune: "Oscar Meyer Weiner")

   North, south, east, west are directions
   Go north to find lots of ice and snow. BRRRR
   Go south and the temperature changes
   This is where the warm breezes blow. WHEW
   Go east to find the Atlantic Ocean
   And there you see great big towns
   Go west and cross the Rocky Mountains
   Keep going 'cause you're Pacific bound.

3. "Metamorphosis" (caterpillar). (Tune: "Farmer in the Dell")

   The butterfly lays eggs. The butterfly lays eggs.
   REFRAIN: Changes o' changes, Metamorphosis.
   Caterpillars hatch from eggs, caterpillars hatch from
        eggs. REFRAIN
   Caterpillars eat leaves. Caterpillars eat leaves.
        REFRAIN and so on.

4. "Two Hundred Bones" Rap (tap each bone to the rhythm):

   Skull head bone, head bone, head bone.
   Skull head bone, head bone, YEAH!
   Ribs, vertebrae, pelvis, pelvis. Ribs, vertebrae, pelvis,
        BONES!
   Clavical-collar bone, scapula–shoulder bone.
   Bones Bones. Two hundred bones REPEAT (in
        decrescendo).
   Humerus, radius–ulna arm bones. Humerus, radius
        ulna, Yeah!
   Femur, tibia–fibula leg bones. Femur, tibia–fibula, Yeah!
   Two hundred bones in the body, body. Two hundred
        bones in the body, Yeah!

   Variation: Students find additional bones to add. (Thanks to teachers at Duxberry Elementary for this idea!)

Musical Season Stories. Play seasonal music without words, and pantomime events from the season. For a spring story, students may mime a flower blossoming. Students may also practice writing about the process of a flower growing from a tiny seed sprout afterward. Vivaldi's *The Four Seasons* works.

Science Symphonies. Many pieces of music celebrate or describe aspects of our world or universe. Collect examples to listen to and discuss what they depict through tempo and timbre of instruments. *Examples:* "La Mer" (The Sea), "Grand Canyon Suite," "Flight of the Bumble Bee," "Water Music," "Theme to 2001." *Variation:* Discuss how science is shown in songs such as John Denver's "Rocky Mountain High" or "Country Roads." Gustav Holst's "The Planets" can be used with an invitation for students to write an "Earth" one since Holst did not include it.

Vibration Study. Vibrations pass through the eardrum, hammer, stirrups, and the water of the cochlea and are sent as an electrical nerve signal to the brain. We also hear sounds because sound is conducted through our bones. Ask students to cover their ears and hum to hear the sound coming through the bones. Students can try as many different timbres as possible with a pencil, hands, and the like.

Musical Weather Reports. What would a rainy day sound like? Towering cumulus clouds? Thunder and lightning? Hurricane? Help students create and present weather reports in which the meteorologist makes the sounds as the type of weather is mentioned. *Variation:* Write or find songs about the weather to introduce or conclude weather reports. *Example:* "April Showers" from Disney's *Bambi*. Poetry can also be used (e.g., Rain, rain go away). Try creating a full operetta based on a weather report and songs.

Bird Song Survey. In the spring, go on a close listening walk for bird songs. Tape each song. Match with bird pictures on return to class. Discuss differences in melodies, pitches, and rhythms and the different timbres of each bird. *Variation:* Use musical notation to write down bird songs or ask a music teacher to help do so. Students can also write lyrics to bird songs, similar to the "bob white" we use to make the quail song. Ask "What does it sound like the bird is saying?"

Sound Sorts. Students sort musical instruments by different attributes, including materials used to make them, sounds they make, construction to produce sounds, or orchestra groups. Students should be encouraged to find a variety of ways to categorize.

Science and Sound. Explore acoustics by inviting a speaker from a sound system company, or a conductor who can show and explain a score (a graph of frequencies, intensities, and volume).

Rainstorm Simulation. This is a rhythm activity. Sit in a circle with eyes closed. A leader begins by rubbing palms together. Person to right picks it up until the whole class is participating. Then the leader switches to finger snaps that moves around the circle. Next is thigh slaps, then foot stomps, with periodical "claps" of lightning. Reverse the order to show the storm dying out.

Nature Sounds Orchestra. Students imitate or tape sounds in nature, such as a bird whistling, dog barking, water splashing, and the wind. Combine sounds to create a nature orchestra. *Note:* The Word Choir Seed Strategy can be used. *Variation:* Compose environmental rhythms song; rap or chant by using these sounds—live or taped: door shutting, stirring with a metal spoon, clock ticking, typing, and fan whirring.

Sound Mobiles. Study the reasons behind how sound is created. Make mobiles from silverware or other objects that will create music as they move. Use string or wire to tie objects to a stick, pipe, or hanger.

Sound Collage. During a study on sound (how it travels) students can choose magazine pictures that show items that produce sounds (animals, machines, people, etc.). Arrange on a large piece of paper, overlapping to make a collage. As collages are shared, students can point at a picture while the class makes the appropriate sound.

Social Studies Focus

Music and the other arts are primary carriers and extenders of this history. (Hope, 2003)

Social Studies Standards. A complete list of standards are available from the National Council for the Social Studies (NCSS): *www.Socialstudies.org*.

States and Capitals Chant. Use drums or sticks to develop a basic beat and compose a mnemonic for chanting cities and states (e.g., Columbus, Ohio; Philadelphia, Pennsylvania; Atlanta, Georgia; Sacramento, California).

Continents Song. Use familiar tunes to summarize factual information (e.g., the names of the seven continents). *Example:* ("She'll Be Comin' Round the Mountain"): There are seven continents on the earth (2X) We have seven great big land forms, seven great big land forms (2X) There are seven continents on the earth.

There are North and South America. Australia, Africa and Europe. Then there is Asia and Antarctica. Asia and Antarctica. Asia and Antarctica make it seven.

Music and Culture. Explore a culture by listening to its music and songs. Discuss what the music shows about the culture (values, ideas). Possible questions:

- How does the music feel? What does it sound like?
- Who makes the music?
- How is music made?
- What instruments are used?
- Why would a culture create this kind of music?
- When was the music made?
- What kind of music is this? How is it like other music?
- How has music in the culture changed over time?

Variation: Challenge students to create an imaginary culture and answer questions about its music.

Summary Songs. Song writing is a valuable way to synthesize information and it is most effective when students write their own compositions, as opposed to memorizing songs of others. Why? "The person doing the work is the one growing the dendrites" (Wolfe, 2001, p. 187). Here is a song written after a field trip to the Hunley Submarine

(Lisa Trott, Ashley River Creative Arts, Charleston, South Carolina). (Tune: "Yellow Submarine")

> In the town where I was born
> There sat a sub beneath the sea
> And its tale is really hip
> It fired and sank a Yankee ship.
> The first time the sub went down
> Eight men from Erin, they did drown
> Then the next stop in the drink
> Horace Hunley, he did sink
> But this third and famous trip
> Took Captain Dixon and a ship
> *REFRAIN: We all lived in the Hunley submarine*
> *The Hunley submarine, the Hunley submarine*
> *We all drowned in the Hunley submarine*
> *The Hunley submarine, the Hunley submarine*
> It took eight men to to turn the crank
> The sub moved forward but then it sank
> Inside was small and very cramped
> An in the end, was very damp.
> REFRAIN
> The Hunley sat for many years
> Then up we came, with many tears
> Now folks know we did our best
> A proper burial, I hope that's next
> REFRAIN

Multicultural Song Book. Students collect songs from different cultures and countries by making notebooks of lyrics and sheet music and mixes using CDs and tapes. *Variation:* Each student or group selects one culture for which to find songs or music. Each student's contribution is put into a class collection.

How Instruments Began. Use this idea with a unit on early human history. Explain how our ancestors did not have the kind of musical instruments we have today. Music was made about their feelings and experiences using available materials. They plucked, blew through, and struck using bones, rocks, wood, and shells. Invite students to design an instrument using plucking, blowing, or striking of a familiar item in their environment. *Variation:* Each student researches an instrument played in the manner of the one made and presents findings.

Musical Classifieds (Newspaper Unit). Students create ads about instruments, musicians, or musical needs. *Example:* Lost—large musical instrument, percussion type. Black and white in color on main part. Last seen standing on three legs. Students read aloud and guess instrument. *Suggestion:* Make at least three clues for classifieds, with the first clue general and the last one the most specific.

Music Current Events.   Start a "Music in the News" weekly routine. Invite students to find music-related stories and/or write songs based on news events using familiar tunes. *Note:* Many folk songs are old tunes with new lyrics (e.g., civil rights songs were based on spirituals).

Multicultural Music and Dances.   Analyze songs as historical records of how people felt, thought, and acted. Research the significance of songs—how music has influenced history (e.g., France's "La Marseillaise" or the Mexican American workers' "De Colores"). Other possibilities include: Native American music, Irish jigs, civil rights music, tribal mountain music, Western cowboy tunes, patriotic songs, and African tribal music. Guide students to understand that music (1) helps create identity and (2) expresses a people's values and passions. For example, the Apache song "I Walk with Beauty" (based on a Navajo poem) expresses a concept of beauty with all things living in harmony. (See Burton's *Moving Within the Circle: Contemporary Native American Music and Dance.*)

Song Sources.   Review purposes of songs and various types (lullabies, work songs, sea chanteys, patriotic songs, etc.). Ask for examples of social and historical events that use certain types of songs, such as birthdays and weddings. Read about an event and brainstorm types of songs that people or characters might sing, play, or compose. Ask students to explain their reasons. This is also a good time to share picture books that are based on songs (e.g., "The Star-Spangled Banner" or "Follow the Drinking Gourd"). Discuss how some songs were once work songs ("I've Been Working on the Railroad" and "Erie Canal") that we now sing for enjoyment and to remember history.

Song History.   Here's an important one to know: Before March 3, 1931, "America the Beautiful" was the national anthem. In 1916, President Wilson issued a presidential order for all Army and Navy bands to cease playing it and instead play "The Star-Spangled Banner." The world of music pointed out that it made no sense to force people to sing a song that was almost unsingable. So, what provoked Wilson to make the change?

On September 14, 1814, Francis Scott Key was on a British warship that was bombarding Fort McHenry. Key was on a diplomatic mission, which deprived him of liquor, when he wrote some song lyrics to the tune of a British drinking song, called "Anacreon in Heaven" (Anacreon is the Greek god of wine). He supposedly said that no sober person could actually carry the melody. When Wilson knew the United States would have to enter the Great War, his wife declared that "America the Beautiful" was too peaceable and nonmilitary for a country about to declare war.

Music Time Line.   Read about composers of different time periods and place contributions on a time line. Add other significant events (composers' birthdays, song or music events). *Variation:* Make a time line of periods (Middle Ages, Renaissance, Baroque, Classical, Romantic, and 20th century) and find example music pieces/songs for each. Combine pictures of artwork, clothing, architecture, dances, or theatrical productions from the time. Discuss how all art reflects societal changes and investigate the materials and technology available at the time or in the area.

Community Sing.   Start the day or week with a Community Sing. Singing together is a way to bond a group and is used in most cultures. Write or sing patriotic, camp, folk, or appropriate contemporary songs. A collaborative class anthem can be written to share student beliefs about school and learning, and special songs can be found or written to celebrate people, seasons, or special events, such as Secretary's Day. *Variation:* Ask the music teacher for examples from different cultures or use the 42 songs recommended by Music Educators National Conference.

History Through Music.   Find songs and music that reflect the environment and times, for example, music or songs about specific historical events and values ("Battle Hymn of the Republic"). Examine a period song to discover its origins and how it expressed the attitudes, worries, and values of the time. *Example:* "Dixie" had to do with a currency issued by a southern bank. Dix is the French word for 10.

Introduce a Time Period.   Play music to introduce a social studies unit. Ask: "What do you hear? What does it tell you about this time? How does this music sound different from contemporary music? Why?"

Cultural Contrasts.   Use a Venn diagram (two overlapping circles) to compare music from countries, cultures, and ethnic groups with music that is familiar to students. Use music elements to categorize likenesses and differences. *Variation:* Contrast two songs about the same topic (e.g., war).

Literacy: Reading and Language Arts Focus

Literacy/Literature Standards.   A complete listing of standards are available from the National Council of the Teachers of English (NCTE) and the International Reading Association (IRA) at *www.ncte.org* or *www.ira.org*.

Common Connections.   Music and literacy have a lot in common. For example, music involves decoding, fluency, comprehension, and composition. Songs include lyrics with all manner of vocabulary and structures that can be used as central reading materials. Songs are available at every "reading level" and have a powerful advantage because they are interesting and participatory. Music and poetry also share many traits such as rhythm and repetition that appeal to student's somatic (body) perception. No sound 21st-century literacy program is without a body of music and songs to directly teach and reinforce key literacy concepts and skills.

Literacy Through Songs. Ready Reference 13.2 gives ways to use songs to teach reading, writing, speaking, and listening skills.

Guided Music and Literacy Lesson. Music and listening, speaking, reading, and writing are integrated in this special guided lesson. This is a variation on the two-pronged plan format, but it still includes an introduction, development, and conclusion. The instructional steps are to listen closely and think, predict, read, share, write, music response, publish. These can be posted so that students can eventually guide small- or whole-group lessons. The guided music and language arts lesson teaching steps are outlined in Planning Page 13.1.

Singing Words. The teacher leads students in singing, chanting, cheering, clapping, and snapping letters and syllables in spelling or vocabulary words. Use forte, piano, crescendo, and other terms to change the volume and speed of each word. *Variation:* Do body spelling to background music with a beat. (Idea from Fannie Petros, Ashley River Creative Arts).

Word Rhythms. Students find examples of phrase patterns in names of classmates, song lyrics, place names, and so forth. Each of the patterns can also be played with rhythm instruments.

1. Iamb: dah DAH: Do what? (Iambic pentameter is 5 iambs "I like to eat my peas without a fork.")
2. Trochaic: DAH dah: Rudy, Eileen
3. Anapestic: dah dah DAH: Virginia
4. Dactylic: DAH dah dah: Claudia (Double dactyl: Gloria Zittercoff)
5. Spondaic: 5 DAH DAH: Go there.

Echo Me. Explore oral interpretation using the musical concepts of dynamics, pitch, tempo, beat, accent, and rhythm. Recite the alphabet or a nursery rhyme in a normal manner. Repeat and talk fast or slow, use a high-pitched voice or deep, bass voice. Break everything into distinct separate syllables or put the accent on every third word. Challenge students to echo you exactly. For example, "Mary Had a Little Lamb" could become a mystery or a

---

 **Singing for Literacy**

Directions: Make song charts by printing lyrics on poster board or chart paper. Overhead transparencies can also be used so that students can clearly see the lyrics.

- **Echoic read** lyrics to work fluency elements (EAR, for expression, accuracy, rate); expression includes changes in volume/dynamics, pitch, pause, and stress.
- **Repeat reading** of lyrics to build fluency.
- **Speech-to-print match** by pointing at lyrics and lines as they are sung. Use creative pointers (e.g., conductor's wand).
- **Put each song line on a sentence strip.** Students must put them in order.
- **Students write out songs** they already know by heart to practice composing, spelling, and handwriting.
- **Sing a word** is another way to stretch its sounds to help with phonemic awareness.
- **Song cut-ups** allow students to sort words, phrases, and lines into categories (parts of speech, syllables, alphabetical).
- **Song big books** give each student or a group a line to illustrate and make a book page.

- **Cloze for comprehension** by using sticky notes on a song chart or whiting out words on individual song copies. Students "sing" to figure out what's missing.
- **Ballads** (songs that tell stories) can be mapped according to literary elements (characters, plot, theme, style).
- **Word finds** can be created for students to find high-frequency words or spelling patterns (silent *e*, *r*-controlled, phonograms, etc.) in lyrics and highlight or circle the targets.
- **Song adaptations** by collaborative writing of new verses (e.g., "Down by the Bay," "My Aunt Came Back") gives practice with rhyming words.
- **Song books** are created when students make a favorite song into an individual book by illustrating each line of the song. See bookmaking options in Chapter 7.
- **Song anthologies** are collections of students' favorite songs (lyrics/ sheet music) in a notebook or file. These can be bound and given as gifts.

Guided Music and Literacy Lesson

Two-Pronged Focus: Choose from (1) music elements and concepts and (2) reading and language arts skills and concepts.

Standards: 6, 8, 9 (Ready Reference 12.8)

Student Objectives: Students should be able to . . . (list specific music and literacy outcomes here).

Teaching Procedure: The teacher will ask students to . . .

Introduction

1. *Listen closely:* Play a piece of music/song for a few minutes so students can hear and feel everything it seeks to convey. No talking at this stage.
2. *Predict:* Students write predictions about what the composer is trying to convey. Teachers can scribe for younger children.

Development

1. *Gather data:* Read about the musician and/or the work. Teachers may read to the students.
2. *Present evidence:* Students give evidence to confirm or reject their predictions about the work. Emphasize that the goal is to find the truth, not to be right. Can be done in pairs, small groups, or whole group.

Conclusion

1. *Write:* Students write a response. Focus on important ideas learned about the music or composer. Provide examples of writing forms students may use (Ready Reference 5.1).
2. *Music response:* Give musical response options lesson, such as replay music and free write, move, or paint (Ready Reference 13.1).
3. *Publish:* Student responses are "made public" through displays, oral sharing, singing, and book making (e.g., class big book).

proclamation by varying the delivery. Also try dialects and foreign accents.

Sound Substitution. Phonological and phonemic awareness can be developed through singing songs and changing the sounds of letters. For example, a favorite is "I Like to Eat, Eat, Eat Apples and Bananas." The song is sung over and over changing the vowels to short and long sounds like "I like to oat oat oat, opples and bononos."

Sing to Spell. Add the mnemonic power of music to spelling by using recognizable tunes. Any five-letter word can be spelled to "You Are My Sunshine." Use "Happy Birthday" to spell six-letter words and "Twinkle, Twinkle Little Star" for seven-letter words.

Sing Letter Sounds. To develop particular letter and sound skills in reading, have students hum melodies using only the target sound. For example, hum "Happy Birthday" just using the /s/ or /b/. This also can be done to teach short vowels. For example, sing "Happy Birthday" with just the short *a* sound. *Variation:* Songs such as "Apples and Bananas" invite students to substitute long and short vowel sounds.

Sing the Vowels. Professional singers warm up by singing vowels because vowels are made with the throat loose and open, allowing more sounds to come out. Consonants stop sounds. For example, in a speaking voice: "Happy birthday to you." In a singing voice: "Haa py Birrrthday to youuouou." Children can learn the differences between the sounds of vowels and consonants by singing. This is particularly helpful with students who have trouble hearing individual phonemes since this stretches sounds and increases phonemic awareness.

Finger Plays and Songs. Finger plays and songs can be used to develop vocabulary, reading skills, sequencing, rhyming, and, of course, musical form (e.g., "Five Little Squirrels" and "Five Green and Speckled Frogs"). Suggested sequence: (1) Students listen to the song, without accompaniment. (2) Repeat listening with a focus (e.g., listen for words that start with /f/). (3) Sing together using printed lyrics. (4) Repeat several times, and (5) cut song apart for sorting and ordering (e.g., sequence lines, sort vocabulary by syllables, rhymes). (6) End with repeat singing. *Note:* If using finger plays, model possible movements during Step 1 and invite new ideas from students. Step 2, everyone does the finger movements.

Word Choirs. Ask for volunteers to form a choir line. Give a topic such as happiness. When a leader points to each choir member he must say or sing a word or make a sound related to the topic. For example, students say "play, laugh, or love" for happiness. Create directing signals for students to say or sing their words or sounds and hold or sing at different pitches. Teach students how to conduct word choirs. Word choirs can relate to any unit, such as growing things or other cultures. See previous conducting signals.

Song Character Interviews. Students listen to a song in which several characters occur. Students each choose one character and listen again to find out about the character from the music and lyrics. For example, "Three Blind Mice" has mice, the farmer's wife, and other characters that could be inferred (e.g., farmer, neighbors, representative of the humane society). The teacher takes the role of an interviewer and uses a prop mike to ask the characters questions (e.g., Who are you? What do you want? What are your problems? What will you do about your problems?). This can be done in pairs, with students taking turns interviewing one another.

Read Arounds.   After reading a story, each student chooses one sentence from the story and rehearses to read it aloud (adapted from Tompkins & McGee, 1993). Each student then reads the line using the oral expression elements of volume, rate, pitch, pause, and stress to interpret meaning. Afterward, students discuss why they chose their lines (e.g., the special sound or sense in the passage). *Variation:* Use each line to make a class big book with each page having one line and art.

Song Writing.   Use the steps in Ready Reference 13.3. Here is the final version of a song created to remember the most common prepositions.

78 Prepositions (Tune = "Yankee Doodle")

Out from under in between over of into through
About above across against along at after but by
Next of out outside till to
Round since than unlike
Up upon within without
Toward to till since throughout
Among around as by before behind below besides
Beyond except down for from in onto like near
   next off on
Plus regarding opposite
Past down underneath
Unto considering than despite
During inside concerning

(Source of prepositions, *The Bedford Handbook for Writers,* 4th ed.) For additional resource material on songwriting, try Wiggins's (1991) *Composition in the Classroom: A Tool for Teaching.* See the Arts-Based Bibliography in the Appendix for more resources, including books about rap music.

Interviews.   Small groups list questions to ask musicians, songwriters, conductors, and so forth. Guests are invited to visit and students interview using planned questions.

Singing Commercials.   Divide into teams and give each a magazine with picture advertisements. Teams create a song to promote the product in their picture. They may select from familiar tunes or write lyrics to an original melody. Teams then present their commercial jingles.

Musician Expert (research skills).   See Ready Reference 13.4 for this long-term project.

Hootananny.   Have weekly sing-alongs using song collections made by students. Add new songs to a class list as they find new favorites. Put some lyrics on posters or transparencies and invite students to create personal song books. Use song posters and songbooks as resources for teaching or reinforcing reading skills and concepts. For example, ask students to find words (play I Spy) that fit a specific phonic pattern (vowel digraphs, rhymes, high-frequency phonograms, or rimes). In addition, fluency is increased by doing repeated readings or singing lyrics.

Music and Emotions.   Play a piece such as Vivaldi's *The Four Seasons.* Ask students to use their faces to show the feelings of the music. *Variations:* (1) Use art materials to show

---

 **Song Writing**

Use these basic steps to show students how to write original songs. This is an adaptation of a strategy for teaching reading and writing, called the *language experience approach,* in which students work under the guidance of a teacher and then work independently.

1. Choose a topic (e.g., prepositions).
2. Brainstorm words and feelings related to the topic. The teacher can serve as a recorder using a chart or the overhead projector. Ideas can be webbed. Use dictionaries and other resources for more ideas.
3. Students organize ideas. Phrases can be dictated to the teacher as she scribes or students can work in small groups.
4. Look at other songs for structure. Lyrics are put in an order. Students decide the form, rhythm, melody, and tempo. For example, will there be a background beat?

Rhythm instruments? Which lines or words are to be repeated? How fast, slow? What melody? (If students just use the universal melody—the three notes G, E, A—they can make many songs. They all know this because it is the taunt used worldwide: Na na na na na.) Let students know that composers often repeat melodies (listen to pieces to discover this).
5. Make final revisions.
6. Perform: Tape, do live sharing, use visuals to accompany.

Ready Reference 13.4   Music Experts

Students work individually or in groups to research a song, composer, musician, or musical style. Panels present and audience members (other students) ask questions. *Variation:* (1) Groups work on the same composer and everyone is the same person on the panel (i.e., simultaneous casting). (2) Panel members become a person or people who may have lived during the time. To become experts, students can do the following:

- *Collection:* Find works by the person (e.g., tapes, CDs, sheet music). Include pictures.
- *Mini-biography:* Students write one-page bios on a musician. *Variation:* Obituary or tribute writing.
- *Song tribute:* Write a song about the musician.
- *Ape the greats:* Use the mood, style/genre, and techniques of the music as a frame to create adaptations (e.g., add verses, write new lyrics, or original work in the style of the artist).
- *Update:* Make or find a modern-day version of the work (e.g., *Hooked on Classics* versions of the classics).
- *Guests and experts:* Invite a local musician, singer, college professor, or conductor to speak about a musician. Prepare questions to interview the guest speaker.
- *Concert:* Attend a live performance or find a DVD.

- *Musician's studio:* Visit the place where a musician works (e.g., a concert hall). Ask to shadow a musician for a day.
- *Video/DVD:* Watch a video of the musician's life (e.g., *Beethoven Lives Upstairs*) and take notes.
- *Music show:* Have an event to display the musician's work. Set up classroom stations to listen to tapes or CDs.
- *Mini-display:* Set up a display in the hall, classroom, or special place in the school. Include works by famous musicians and students' works (e.g., compositions, pictures, information about the musician).
- *Vary it:* Do another version of a piece of music (e.g., use just a part of a song or piece of music to play or sing; write different lyrics to a song).

Culmination: A class performance with each student choosing 1 minute of his/her expertise to share in any form.

---

the feelings of the music (e.g., colors, lines, shapes). (2) List or write about the feelings.

Music Response Journals (Listening). Students keep journals about thoughts and feelings triggered by music. They can write while listening to a selection or after listening. Specific ideas: (1) Write song title (real or created). (2) Sketch instruments heard. (3) List adjectives to describe sounds or emotions. (4) Write a story that suits the music. (5) Write a description or write about visual images stimulated by the music (latter is called *chromesthesia*).

Cloze Telegrams. Students complete telegrams or secret messages by writing the correct musical note on the staff using music paper (request from music teacher) or a staff on the board. This helps with spelling as well as musical notation. Individual wipe-off boards also work for this and everyone can show their note at a signal. For example, Moz__rt pl__ys __ concert __t Town H__ll (a missing). Sousa promot__d to Marin__ band dir__ctor (e missing). *Variation:* If instruments are available, students can play the missing notes.

Operettas. An opera is a story told with music. Introduce opera using books such as Englander's *Opera! What's*

All the Screaming About?, Price's *Aida: A Picture Book for All Ages,* or Rosenberg's *Sing Me a Song: Metropolitan Opera's Book of Opera Stories for Children.* Listen to examples, then choose a familiar story. Compose or find songs for main scenes. Students can use familiar tunes or compose new ones. When actual words from the story are sung, they are called a *libretto.* Songs can be sung without accompaniment, or instruments or recorded music can be added. Lead characters can sing their dialogue and some parts may be spoken. *Example:* The Three Pigs Opera with songs about leaving home, fear, strong foundations, evil, and bad judgments. *Example:* When a pig is afraid sing "Whenever I Feel Afraid" (from "The King and I"). Teach students to write cues in dramatic opera form (e.g., Enter Big Bad Wolf, shifting eyes from side to side, or Trees [chorus] sing). *Note: Into the Woods* is musical based on fairy tales. Disney created several, such as *Beauty and the Beast.* Currently there is a Broadway musical based on a spelling bee.

Sing Literature. Read-aloud books that are based on music or a song. Invite students to "sing" lines from the story. *Example: Charlie Parker Played Be Bop* has many possibilities. *Variation:* Read stories with related music playing in the background. *Example:* Play Tchaikovsky while reading the *The Nutcracker.*

Read to Music.   Find music that can be played in the background as a story is read or told. *Example:* "Claire de Lune" works for the beginning of Yashima's *Crow Boy,* while Ma Mere (Debussy) gives emotion to the end of the story. Ask students how reading to music changes the read-aloud. *Variation:* Invite students to find background music for scenes in books.

Song Story.   Students select a song and brainstorm who might have written it and why. Work in groups to write a story that explains how the song came to be. *Variation:* Students research song origins using references such as the *New Grove Dictionary of Music and Musicians.*

Read All About It.   Students choose to read about the life of the musician or singer (biographical information: birth, death, marriage, children, friends):

- Who and what most influenced the artist
- Time period in which the artist lived
- Country or countries where the artist lived
- Style in which the artist worked
- What the artist is most known for, including particular works
- Criticism about the artist and his or her work
- Other artists of that period

Write All About It.   Students choose to write a:

- Letter to the musician
- Letter to the music publishing company to request information about a song, piece, or the musician
- Biographical sketch of the musician
- Story in a modern setting that includes the music
- Description of the music or song
- Menu during the time the music was created
- Report on the customs of the time of the artist
- Report on the clothing styles of the time of the artist
- Story about how the music came to be composed
- Report about the period of time
- Paragraph hypothesizing what the musician would do if he or she were alive today
- Play or poem about the musician's life
- Comparison of the work of two musicians
- Time line of the musician's work
- Book for children about a musician, style, or genre of music

Music Dictionary.   Students make personal dictionaries of musical elements, concepts, song titles, and composers. Use wallpaper for covers and encourage students to illustrate entries. *Note:* Many music words overlap with other vocabulary (e.g., consider the many meanings of the word *line*).

Song Charts.   Create song charts for reading material by writing lyrics on poster board or large newsprint. Use sticky notes on the charts to cover certain words to practice fig-

uring out concealed parts. Cut apart charts and put song line strips in a pocket chart or make big songbooks from the charts. *Variation:* Give each student or group a line from a song to illustrate for a class big book.

Class Song Books.   Create class anthologies of favorite songs, composer fact sheets, song fact sheets, and even riddles about music. For example, brainstorm ideas and make a chart of favorite songs. Have each student sign up to write up the lyrics and research the song. Sing or read from the book each week. Have students make individual songbooks, song collections, or tape collections to go with their interests and needs (e.g., moods, study music). *Note:* Relate this to the iPod's popularity.

Musical Poetry.   Use chants, street rhymes, and jump rope rhymes for language arts. Ask students to describe musical elements in poetry. Encourage students to make up movements and add homemade or found sound rhythm instruments (see collections such as Cole and Calmenson's [1990] *Miss Mary Mack*).

Song Scavenger Hunts.   Use songs as content to find language patterns, or conduct a week-long hunt to find songs in certain categories (e.g., ones with lots of B words, with rhyme or alliteration, about books).

Musical Chair Story.   Put on music. Everyone starts writing a story and writes until the music stops. Each person then passes his or her story to another and music begins again. The goal is to write a complete story in a designated number of passes.

Experts.   Students choose to do research on a musical instrument or music in a particular culture. They then make a presentation to the class on their findings.

Read to Music.   First read aloud a poem or story without a music background. Next, read with music. Ask students to tell how the two were different and relate this to music in films or television shows. Invite students to find appropriate music to go with a story or poem. *Example:* Play "Claire de Lune" to read the beginning of Yashima's *Crow Boy.*

Compare and Contrast.   Compare versions of the same song, for example, "Peter and the Wolf" or Mozart's "Twinkle, Twinkle Little Star." Use a Venn diagram to note differences in musical elements and instruments.

Language Mentors.   Music is a language with a special symbol system. Encourage students who wish to learn to read and speak (sing and play) this language by pairing them with a mentor. Invite students to share their prowess with the class.

Culture and Language Through Song.   Teach students to sing a familiar song in the language of the country under study (e.g., "Frère Jacques" or "Allouette" from France).

Math Focus

Math Standards.
A complete listing of standards are available from the National Council of Teachers of Mathematics (NCTM): *www.nctm.org*.

Math Music Connections.
Music and math have a lot in common. Music is constructed using patterns and is organized sequentially. Notes have different fractional values, and every piece of music has a time signature. Math and music even share similar vocabulary (e.g., measure, count). Music concepts like crescendo and decrescendo rely on the ability to think about math concepts like "less than" and "greater than." Just as in math, the relationships of the parts to the whole is critical.

Scale Numbering.
Number the notes on the musical scale from 1–8 with do = 1, re = 2, mi = 3, fa = 4, so = 5, la = 6, ti = 7, and do = 8. Sing the scale with numbers instead of syllables. Invite students to construct math problems by singing them. *Example:* Sing "ti minus re = sol." *Variation:* Give students a series of numbers to sing according to the scale match (e.g., 1155665 would come out "Twinkle, Twinkle Little Star"). Challenge students to sing backwards and present their own number song phrases for the class to decode by singing.

Data Collection and Graphing.
Students listen to music and record names of instruments and tally the times each is heard. Students then are shown how to create bar graphs of results. *Suggestion:* Discuss the effects of the instrument quantities.

Patterns.
Teach a song like "Are You Sleeping?" Ask students to listen for the repeated pattern. Show ways to represent the pattern through shapes and numbers. For example, the different pitches of the lyrics that can be represented with the numbers 12311231 to show the sound goes up up up down, up up up down, etc. Ask students for other ways to represent the pattern (e.g., letters, shapes, hand signals). *Transformation:* Ask students to change the sound pattern in some way and sing the results.

Fraction Pies or Pizza.
Since music is based on subdivisions of time into fractions, students can cut pies into fractions and use musical notation to label the pieces. For example, divide pies in half with a picture of a half-note on each slice.

Song Graphs.
Students graph the notes of 2 or 3 songs by color coding the songs. Put the scale (do-re-mi-fa-so-la-ti-do) along the X axis and a number of notes along the Y axis (e.g., graph the first 10 notes). Students then color in the boxes. *Note:* Some boxes will have more than one color. *Example:* Graph the first 10 notes of "Row, Row, Row Your Boat," "Twinkle, Twinkle Little Star," and "Happy Birthday."

Musical Math.
Give math problems for students to apply music knowledge (adapted from Athey & Hotchkiss, 1995). For example:

Take the number of keys on a piano: 88
Add the number in a quartet: 4
Add the number in a trio: 3
TOTAL = 95

Use these musical concepts to construct problems:

1. Solo/quarter-note/quarter-rest
2. Duet/half-note/half-rest
3. Trio/dotted half-note/number of valves on a trumpet/legs on a grand piano
4. Quartet/whole note/whole rest/number of strings on a violin
5. Quintet
6. Number of strings on a guitar/sextet
7. Septet
8. Octave/octet

Note Math.
After students have learned the symbols for whole, half, quarter, eighth, and sixteenth notes, they can solve and create note math problems. *Example:* A whole note minus a quarter note = _____ ?

Word Problems.
Students listen to a piece of music, list instruments heard and number of times each was heard. Next, students write a word problem. *Example for addition:* I heard (musical instrument) beats. I heard (music instrument) beats. How many beats were heard altogether?

Number Lyrics.
Students sing familiar songs replacing lyrics with numbers. This can be as simple as singing "Twinkle, Twinkle Little Star" and starting with "One, two, three, four . . ." or as challenging as singing odd numbers, even numbers, or by 10s or 5s. *Variation:* Use the tune to "San Fermin" to sing numbers or months in Spanish.

Mnemonic Songs.
Use the memory power of music to help learn basic mathematical processes. *Example:* Here is a "Long Division Rap" written by sixth graders in Hayes, Kansas, to help them remember the process.

> I'm Dr. D, and I'm on the scene
> With my division rap that's oh so mean
> It goes divide, multiply, subtract, and bring down
>   (repeat)
> Now you can do it wrong or you can do it right
> But if you do it wrong you'll be here all night
> I say, divide, multiply, subtract, and bring down
>   (repeat)

Rhythm and Sound Math.
Students use rhythm instruments or body sounds to present addition and subtraction problems. For example, *AB* pairs present with *A* doing

2 beats and student *B* doing 4 bells. Class responds with six claps or snaps.

Numerals and Counting.   Prepare flashcards from 1 to 10 to use with "Ten Little Indians" (change to pumpkins, if desired). Play steady beat for 4 measures, then 2 measures—ending with fast sixteenth notes. Ask students about the difference between slow and fast sounds (rhythm, division of beats, steady beat). Repeat for students to signal for fast sounds.

Next, sit in a circle and review numerals 1–10 with flashcards. Teacher plays slow steady beat again, and students pass cards around the circle clockwise. When children hear fast beats they hold up cards, instead of passing. Practice. Next, everyone sings the song and students hold up the right card when the number is sung. Practice. Sing numbers going down from 10 as teacher plays beat and cards are passed around. Everyone holds cards high when the sixteenth notes are heard. Then the song begins again and cards are passed. Each child holds up a new card when the song is sung again. *Variation:* Sing in another language to reinforce counting, (uno, dos, tres inditos, quatro, cinco, seis inditos . . .). Or, use number words instead of numerals (idea from Amy Golden, New York City music teacher).

Water Music (Measurement).   Use 10 clear glasses. Students measure the side of each glass and subtract 1 inch from the top. Divide this measurement by 10. Use a crayon to mark 10 sections on each glass. Fill glasses with water to the lines. Label the first glass 1, the second glass 2, and so on, until the 10th glass is labeled 10. With a teaspoon, gently tap the first glass near the rim. Listen for the sound. As the numbers get higher and water increases, the tones get lower. Have students tap out phone numbers to listen for pitches, and create other addition and subtraction problems to play.

Add On.   Use songs like "Down in the Valley" and start singing with two children. Then those two each select a partner and there are four, those four select, etc. The song "Wishy Washy" starts with two sailors and one boat, then four sailors and two boats, etc. Ask children to figure out how many will come next (idea from Debbie Fahmie, Florida music teacher).

Counting Songs and Chants.   Teach counting songs and chants to help students learn this skill (e.g., "One potato, two potato," "The Ants Go Marching"). Some of these songs are also good for marching to a one-two beat. See Arts-Based Bibliography in the Appendix under "Music" for book titles.

Musical Quilt.   Read about how quilts are made. Examine patterns and geometric shapes. Discuss how quilts portray feelings or events. Tell students they will be composing a song quilt. Decide on an experience, event, or emotion. Divide into small groups. Each group contributes a line to a song. Select a traditional folk tune to accompany the lyrics that children create. Next, children write lyrics on a fabric square or colored paper (e.g., origami paper) using permanent markers. Assemble quilt and sing the squares as a leader points to each.

Shape Composition.   Students need 15 to 20 pieces of paper in geometric shapes (multiple numbers of three to five different shapes cut ahead, or they can cut triangles, squares, circles, and diamonds). Review shape names. In groups, students lay out a pattern they like and then decide on a sound for each shape. Homemade rhythm instruments may be used. Groups rehearse and then perform their composition (e.g., square for drum, circle for shaker). Think of how this pattern would sound:

Rhythm Instruments.   Many resource books show ways to make rhythm instruments that can be painted and decorated. For example, place papier mâché over a light bulb, let it dry, and then tap it to break it. Paint and you have a shaker. Rainsticks can be made by inserting toothpicks up and down a wrapping paper tube (it helps to make the holes ahead with a small drill). Fill tubes with rice or small beans and plug the ends. Sticks can then be painted or covered with collage materials.

- Body percussion: rub palms, snap fingers, clap hands, slap knees, tap fingers, tap toes, stamp, click tongue.
- Sand blocks: plastic tape cassette holders wrapped with sandpaper (two per student).
- Shakers: papier mâché a light bulb. Paint with tempera. Break.
- Shakers: potato chip cans filled with beans or rice.
- Shakers: old keys or a ring.
- Drums: oatmeal box, coffee can, large plastic tubs (from ice cream or slaw).
- Strikers: large wooden knitting needles or large metal or wooden spoons, PVC pipe sections.
- Vocals/ostinati: doo wop/shu-wop; dum diddy diddy; shu-boom shu-boom; chicka chicka boom boom; bu-bu-bu-bubblin'; a do run run run a do run run.

Artist Spotlight:

A Master Creative Problem Solver

Classroom teachers sometimes think music integration is particularly difficult. One problem is having the right music materials. This closing Spotlight is on a real-life artist who had the same problem. It is about the great violinist Itzhak

Perlman, and it happened in 1995 during a performance at the Lincoln Center in New York City.

Mr. Perlman had polio as a child and now wears braces on both legs. He uses crutches to walk. When he was introduced for this performance, he slowly made his way across the stage, one step at a time. When he reached his chair, he carefully sat down and laid down his crutches. Then he undid one leg clasp and then the other. He tucked one foot back, and stretched the other forward. Finally, he bent down, picked up his violin, put it beneath his chin, nodded to the conductor, and began.

After he had played only a few bars, there was a loud bang. One of the violin strings had broken. The whole audience knew what Mr. Perlman had to do—go through the whole struggle with clasps and crutches to get another violin or replace the string.

But he didn't. After a moment he took a deep breath and closed his eyes. When he opened them, he signaled and the orchestra began again.

The audience was stunned. They knew it is impossible to play a symphonic piece with just three strings. On that night Itzhak Perlman refused to know this. He recomposed in his head and coaxed sounds from the remaining strings that seemed unbelievable.

When he finished, the audience was absolutely silent. Then, as if on cue, everyone stood up and applauded wildly. People cheered and whistled. It went on and on. Mr. Perlman mopped his brow and smiled. Finally, he raised his bow. The applause stopped and the audience waited for him to speak. When he did his voice was soft.

"You know, sometimes it is the artist's task to find out how much music you can still make with what you have left" (Author Unknown).

Conclusion

Many of us go to our grave with the music still inside of us.
(Anonymous)

This chapter is a compendium of dozens of ways to get the music out. Used in conjunction with the Arts Integration Blueprint described in Chapter 12, teachers should be more prepared to approach teaching like Itzak Perlman did—to take risks and to make music with what they have.

Resources

See the Appendix for additional materials, including websites.

Music Resource Books

Barrett, J., Veblen, K., & McCoy, C. (1997). *Sound ways of knowing.* Thomson Learning. (Excellent resources throughout)

Beall, P. (1996). *Wee sing sing-alongs.* Price Stern Sloan. (American folk with tape/CD)

Birkenshaw-Fleming, L. (1989). *Come on everybody let's sing.* Gordon Thompson Music.

Choksy, L., & Brummitt, D. (1987). *120 singing games and dances for elementary schools.* Prentice Hall. (games and dances)

Cohn, A. (Ed.). (1993). *From sea to shining sea: A treasury of American folklore and songs.* Scholastic.

Davidson, L., & Norton, A. (1999). *The learning through music handbook.* New England Conservatory.

Durell, A. (1989). *The Diane Goode book of American folk tales and songs.* Dutton.

Eddleman, D. (Ed.). (1999). *Great children's songbook: A treasure chest of music & activities.* Carl Fischer Music Publisher.

Eston, R., & Economopoulos, K. (1998). *Pattern trains and hopscotch paths: Exploring pattern.* Dale Seymour.

Flohr, J. (2005). *The musical lives of young children.* Prentice Hall.

Goodkin, D. (1985). *Sally go 'round the sun.* Doug Goodkin.

Hackett, P. (1998). *The melody book* (3rd ed.). Prentice Hall. (excellent diverse collection of 300 songs with easy instrumental accompaniments)

Krull, K. (1992). *Gonna sing my head off!* Knopf. (folk songs)

Metropolitan Museum of Art Staff. (1987). *Go in and out the window: An illustrated songbook for young people.* Henry Holt.

Miche, M. (2002). *Weaving music into young minds.* Delmar/Thomson Learning. (includes a CD; practical ideas and resources, websites, connections to top names in children's music like Raffi, Red Grammer, and Tom Chapin)

Mitchell, L. (1991). *One, two, three-echo me! Ready-to-use songs, games, and activities to help children sing in tune.* Parker.

Mitchell, L. (1992). *The music teacher's almanac: Ready-to-use music activities for every month of the year.* Parker.

Schiller, P., & Moore, T. (1993). *Where is Thumbkin?* Gryphon House. (activities based on songs)

Sporborg, J. (1998). *Music in every child's classroom: A resource guide for integrating music across the curriculum K–8.* Libraries Unlimited.

Stanley, L. (Ed.). (1992). *Rap, the lyrics: The words to rap's greatest hits.* Penguin.

Wright, T., Neminovsky, R., & Tierney, C. (1998). *Timelines and rhythm patterns: Representing time.* Dale Seymour.

Yelton, G. (Ed.). (1991). *The musical PC.* MIDI America.

Multicultural Books/Music

Barchas, S. (1999). *Bridges across the world* (with CD). High Haven Music.

Bryan, A. (1991). *All night, all day: A child's first book of African-American spirituals.* Atheneum.

Campbell, P. (1994). *Roots and branches* (with CD). World Music Press. (background information and songs from more than 25 countries)

Floyd, M. (Arr.). (1991). *Folksongs from Africa.* Faber Music.

Gritton, P. (1991). *Folksongs from the Far East.* Faber Music.

Gritton, P. (1993). *Folksongs from India.* Faber Music.

Lewis, R. (1991). *All of you was singing* (African American). Atheneum.

Lipman, D. (1993). *We all go together: Creative activities for children to use with multicultural folksongs.* Oryx Press.

Mattox, C. (1990). *Shake it to the one that you love best: Play songs and lullabies from black musical tradition.* Warren Mattox.

National Gallery of Art. (1991). *An illustrated treasury of songs.* Rizzoli International. (songs, ballads, folk songs)

Page, N., & Clark, K. (1995). *Sing and shine on!* Heineman.

Seeger, P. (2004). *Rise up singing! Singout.* (collection of folk songs including the round "Hava Nagila")

Toop, D. (1991). *Rap attack 2: African rap to global hip hop.* Serpent's Tail.

Walter, C. (1995). *Multicultural music: Lyrics to familiar melodies and authentic songs.* T. S. Denison.

Book Sellers and Sources for Recordings and Media

Alcazar's Kiddie Cat 902-244-8657, Box 429, Waterbury, VT 05676 (large catalog of children's music recordings and videos)

Anthology Record and Tape Company, 135 West 41st St., New York, NY 10036 (African and Asian)

Canyon Records, 4143 North 16th St., Phoenix, AZ 85016 (Native American music)

Cellar Book Shop, 18090 Wyoming, Detroit, MI 48221 (Philippines, Asia, the Pacific, Australia, and New Zealand)

Children's Book and Music Center, 800-443-1856, 2500 Santa Monica Blvd., Santa Monica, CA 90404 (folk and world music, offers preview service)

Children's Small Press Collection, 313-668-8056, 719 N. Fourth Ave., Ann Arbor, MI 48104 (small publisher, many classroom resources)

Dove Music, Box 08286, Milwaukee, WI 53208 (Spanish American)

Floyd's Record Shop, Post Drawer 10, Ville Platte, LA 70586 (Cajun and Creole music)

G.P.N. Media, 764 Pleasant Ave., Tulare, CA 93274 (videos and instruments from Africa, South America, and Japan)

Homespun Tapes, Box 694, Woodstock, NY 12498 (folk, jazz, yodeling)

Ladyslipper, 919-683-1570, Box 3130, Durham, NC 27705 (music by women artists)

Music for Little People, 800-836-4445, Box 1460, Redway, CA 95560 (audio and video recordings and musical instruments)

Original Music, RD 1, Box 190, Lasher Rd., Tivoli, NY 12583 (world music, hard-to-find titles).

Shorey Book Store, 110 Union St., Seattle WA 98104 (Northwest Indian music and culture)

Sing Out, Box 5253, Bethlehem, PA 18015 (publishes *Sing Out! The Folksong Magazine on North American Music* and *Rise Up Singing!* an excellent collection; reprints of songs)

Tower Records, 800-522-5445, 692 Broadway, New York, NY 10012 (all recordings in print)

World Around Songs, Route 5, Burnsville, NC 28714 (series of song books on nearly every culture)

World Music Press, P.O. Box 2565, Danbury, CT 06813 (multicultural books, recordings, videos)

Instrument Sources

Carroll Sound, Inc., 351 West 41st St., New York, NY 10036 (drums, percussion, ethnic instruments)

House of Musical Traditions, 7040 Carrol Ave., Takoma Park, MD

Jag Drums, 88 Hibbert St., Arlington, MA 02174 (ewe barrel, donno, and brekete drums; marimbas)

John's Music Center, 5521-A University Way N.E., Seattle, WA 98105 (ethnic and Orff instruments)

Knock on Wood Xylophones, RD 2 Box 790, Thorndike, MA 04986

Lark in the Morning, P.O. Box 1176, Mendocino, CA 95460 (American and European folk)

Peripole, Inc., Browns Mills, NJ 08015-0146 (ethnic and Orff instruments)

Rhythm Band, Inc., Box 126, Fort Worth, TX 76101-0126 (ethnic instruments and materials)

Children's Literature References

Burton, B. (1993). *Moving within the circle: Contemporary Native American music and dance.* Danbury, CT: World Music.

Cole, J., & Calmenson, S. (1990). *Miss Mary Mack and other children's street rhymes.* Long Beach, CA: BeechTree.

Englander, R. (1983). *Opera! What's all the screaming about?* New York: Walker.

Isadora, R. (1991). *Ben's trumpet.* New York: Harpertrophy.

Mattox, C. (1990). *Shake it to the one you love best: Play songs and lullabies from the black musical tradition.* El Sobrante, CA: Warren Mattox.

Price, L. (1990). *Aida: A picture book for all ages.* San Diego, CA: Harcourt Brace Jovanovich.

Raschka, C. (1992). *Charlie Parker plays be bop.* New York: Orchard.

Rosenberg, J. (1989). *Sing me a song: Metropolitan Opera's book of opera stories for children.* New York: Thames & Hudson.

Yashima, T. (1976). *Crow Boy.* New York: Puffin.

Epilogue

If you can see things out of whack, you can see things in whack.
(Dr. Seuss)

This quote refers to humor, but Dr. Seuss could have been talking about school reform in America. Many educators and arts advocates have judged schooling to be out of whack with real life. Their solution is arts integration.

Arts integration taps the vast potential of the arts to transform teaching and learning—to put education back in whack. Mounting research connects the arts to academic achievement, but more importantly the arts are strongly linked to cognitive and motivational growth that underlie success in school and life. We know students become more active meaning makers as the arts engage "head, heart, and hands." The arts are unique communication vehicles—tools that permit understanding and expression of ideas and feelings that are beyond words.

Classroom teachers are center stage in arts integration. Drawing upon the artist within, they invent, stretch, and twist ideas to solve learning problems. They move out of a zone of comfort to the edge of teaching possibilities. Teachers involved in arts integration say it's worth it. They know they can change the future—one child at a time. What they believe is expressed poetically by Hiam Ginott (1985):

I am the decisive element in the classroom. It is my personal approach that creates the climate. It is my daily mood that makes the weather. As a teacher, I possess tremendous power to make a child's life miserable or joyous. I can be a tool of torture or an instrument of inspiration. I can humiliate, humor, hurt or heal. In all situations, it is my response that decides whether a crisis will be escalated or deescalated and a child humanized or dehumanized.

Bibliography

A+ Schools Program. (2001). North Carolina A+ Schools Program. In *The arts and education reform.* Greensboro, NC: University of North Carolina.

Alexander, K., & Michael, D. (Eds.). (1991). *Discipline-based art education: A curriculum sample.* Santa Monica, CA: Getty Center for Education in the Arts.

Allen, J., Michalove, B., & Shockley, B. (1991, March). I'm really worried about Joseph: Reducing the risks of literacy learning. *Reading Teacher, 44,* 458–472.

Allen, M. (1999). *What are little girls made of? A guide to female role models in children's books.* New York: Facts on File.

Allen, R. (2004, Spring). *The arts give students a ticket to learning.* Retrieved from *http://www.ascd.org.*

Allington, R. (2002, June). What I've learned about effective reading instruction. *Kappan, 83* (10), 740–747.

Allington, R. (2005, February). *What really matters for struggling readers.* Keynote, South Carolina Reading Association, Myrtle Beach, SC.

Anderson, R. C., Hiebert, E., Scott, J., & Wilkinson, I. (1985). *Becoming a nation of readers: The report of the Commission on Reading.* Washington, DC: National Institute of Education.

Anderson, R. C., et al. (1986). Interestingness of children's reading materials. In R. Snow & M. Farr (Eds.), *Aptitude, learning and instruction.* Hillsdale, NJ: Erlbaum.

Annenberg Institute for School Reform at Brown University. (Fall 1998). How the arts transform schools: A challenge for all to share. *Challenge Journal, 3*(1). Retrieved from *http://www.annenberginstitute.org/Challenge.*

Annenberg Institute for School Reform. (2002). *Opportunity and accountability: Arts environment as models of equity.* Retrieved from *http://www.annenberginstitute.org.*

Annenberg Institute for School Reform. (2003). *The arts and school reform: Lessons and possibilities from the Annenberg Challenge Arts Projects.* Providence, RI: Author.

Armstrong, K. (2004), *History of God: The 4000 year quest of Judaisim, Christianity and Islam.* New York: Gramercy Books.

Armstrong, T. (1993). *7 kinds of smart.* New York: Penguin.

Armstrong, T. (2000; 1994). *Multiple intelligences in the classroom.* Alexandria, VA: Association for Supervision and Curriculum Development.

Arnheim, R. (1989). *Thoughts on art education.* Los Angeles: Getty Center for Education in the Arts.

Artistic employment in 2000. (2000, May). Research Division Note 78. Washington, DC: National Endowment for the Arts.

The arts in every classroom. (2005). Video series from Annenberg/CPB channel. Viewed at *http://www.learner.org.*

Arts Education Partnership. (1998). *Young children and the arts: Making the creative connection.* Washington, DC: Author.

Arts Education Partnership. (1999). *Learning partnerships: Improving learning in schools with arts partners in the community.* Washington, DC: Author.

Arts environments as models of equity (proposal). (Undated). Providence, RI: Brown University. Downloaded from *http://www.annenberginstitute.org.*

Arts Project and The Grove/Tanglewood Model Arts Project. (2005, May). *Summary report* (Unpublished document). Greenville SC: Greenville County Schools.

Aschbacher, P., & Herman, J. (1995). The humanities program evaluation. In *The arts and education: Partners in achieving our national education goals.* Washington, DC: National Endowment for the Arts.

Athey, M., & Hotchkiss, G. (1995). *A galaxy of games for the music class.* West Nyack, NY: Parker.

Au, K. (2002). Multicultural factors and the effective instruction of students of diverse backgrounds. In A. Farstrup & S. J. Samuels, *What research has to say about reading instruction.* Newark, DE: International Reading Association.

Baker, R., Boughton, D., Freedman, K., Horowitz, R., & Ingram, D. (2004, April). *Artistic production as evidence of learning in interdisciplinary contexts.* American Educational Research Association, San Diego, CA.

Barboza, S. (1992). *I feel like dancing: A year with Jacques d'Amboise and the National Dance Institute.* New York: Crown.

Barker, A. (2005, April 11). W. Va. Health study tried video dance game as weight loss for kids. *Beaufort Gazette,* 3C.

Barlow, J. (2002, August 7). Complex physical learning may compensate for prenatal alcohol exposure, study shows. *Innovations Report.* Urbana, IL: University of Illinois, Retrieved from *http://www.innovationsreport.com.*

Baron, R. (1997, February). *Scientific thought in motion.* Presentation at The Kennedy Center, Washington, DC.

Barr, R., Kamil, M., & Mosenthal, P. (Eds.). (1996). *Handbook of reading research,* Vol. 2. Mahwah, NJ: Erlbaum.

Barron, F. (1969). *Creative person and creative thinking.* New York: Holt, Rinehart, & Winston.

Barton, P. (2005, July 23). Huckabee builds a case for arts in school. *Arkansas Democrat-Gazette* (Little Rock), A1.

Baumann, J. F., & Ivey, G. (1997). Delicate balances: Striving for curricular and instructional equilibrium in a second grade, literature/strategy-based classroom. *Reading Research Quarterly, 32,* 244–275.

Beck, I., & McKeown, M. (2002). Comprehension: The sine qua non of reading. In S. Patton & M. Holmes (Eds.), *The keys to literacy* (p. 54). Washington, DC: Council for Basic Education.

Begley, S. (1996, February 19). Your child's brain. *Newsweek, 127*(8), 55–61.

Begley, S. (2000, July 24). Music and the mind. *Newsweek.* Retrieved from *http://www.keepmedia.com/pubs/Newsweek/2000/07/24.*

Begley, S. (2004, June 18). Math whizzes do excel at music, but is link merely a coincidence? *The Wall Street Journal,* B1.

Berthoff, A. E. (1981). *The making of meaning.* Montclair, NJ: Boynton/Cook.

Bettleheim, B. (1989). *The uses of enchantment.* New York: Vintage.

Bierhorst, J. (1976). *The red swan: Myths & tales of the American Indian.* New York: Farrar, Straus & Giroux.

Bill, B. (1988). *Many manys: A life of Frank Lloyd Wright.* London: Heinemann.

Bishop, R. (1992). Multicultural literature for children. In V. Harris (Ed.), *Teaching multicultural literature in grades K–8.* Norwood, MA: Christopher-Gordon.

Bizar, M. (2005). *Teaching the best practices way.* Alexandria, VA: Association for Supervision and Curriculum Development.

Blythe, T., & Gardner, H. (1990, April). A school for all intelligences. *Educational Leadership*, 33–36.

Bloom, B. (1956). *Taxonomy of educational objectives*. New York: Longman.

The bookfinder: A guide to children's literature (Vol. 1). (1994). Circle Pines, MN: American Guidance.

Booth, E. (2003, Summer). Arts for art's sake and art as a learning tool: Achieving a balance. *Journal for Learning Through Music, 2,* 19–22.

Booth, E. (2005, Winter). The teaching artist. *The Teaching Artist, 1*(2), p. 2.

Boston, B. (1996). Educating for the workplace through the arts. Reprinted from *Business Week,* October 28, 1996. Columbus, OH: McGraw-Hill.

Bransford, J. D. (Ed.). (1999). *How people learn: Brain, mind, experience, and school.* Washington, DC: National Academy of Sciences.

Brookes, M. (1996). *Drawing with children.* New York: Putnam.

Broudy, H. S. (1979). How basic is aesthetic education? Or is it the fourth R? *Language Arts, 54,* 631–637.

Brown, P. (2005, April 24). Sousa? Many students march to mariachi instead. *New York Times,* final section, p. 1.

Brownlee, S. (1997, February 17). What science says about those tender feelings. *U.S. News and World Report,* 58–60.

Brozo, W. (1998). *Readers, teachers and learners: Expanding literacy across the content areas.* Upper Saddle River, NJ: Merrill/Prentice Hall.

Bruer, J. T. (1999). In search of brain based education. *Kappan, 80*(9), 648–654.

Bryon, E. (2005, July 27). To master the art of solving crimes, cops study Vermeer. *Wall Street Journal,* 1.

Burchers, S. (1996). *Vocabutoons.* Punta Gorda, FL: New Monic.

Burgard, R. (1997). *Schools as communities: Public education and social cohesion.* Washington, DC: National Endowment for the Arts.

Burnaford, B., Arnold A., & Weiss, C. (Eds.). (2001). *Arts integration and learning: Chicago arts partnerships in education.* Mahwah, NJ: Lawrence Erlbaum.

Burnaford, G., Arnold, A., & Weiss, C. (2002*). Renaissance in the classroom: Arts integration and meaningful learning.* Mahwah, NJ: Lawrence Erlbaum.

Burton, J., Horowitz, R., & Abeles, H. (1999). *Learning in and through the arts: Curriculum implications.* New York: Teachers College Press, Columbia University.

Burton, J. M., Horowitz, R., & Abeles, H. (2000, Spring). Learning in and through the arts: The question of transfer. *Studies in Art Education, 41*(3), 228–257.

Burz, H., & Marshall, K. (1999). *Performance-based curriculum for music and the visual arts.* Thousand Oaks, CA: Corwin.

Caine, R., & Caine, G. (2005). *12 brain/mind learning principles in action.* Thousand Oaks, CA: Corwin Press.

Cambourne, B. (2002). Holistic, integrated approaches to reading and language arts instruction: The constructivist framework of an instructional theory. In A. Farstrup & S. J. Samuels (Eds), *What research has to say about reading instruction.* Newark, DE: International Reading Association.

Campbell, D. (1997). *The Mozart effect.* New York: Avon.

Campbell, J. (1996). *Hero with a thousand faces.* New York: MJF.

Campbell, P., Brabson, E., & Tucker, J. (1994). *Roots and branches: A legacy of multicultural music for children.* Danbury, CT: WorldMusic.

Carter, D., & Diaz, J. (1999). *The elements of pop-up.* New York: Simon and Schuster.

Catterall, J. (1995). *Different ways of knowing: 1991–1994 National Longitudinal Study final report.* Los Angeles: The Galef Institute.

Catterall, J. (1998). *Involvement in the arts and success in secondary school.* Washington, DC: Americans for the Arts.

Catterall, J. (2002). Research on drama and theatre in education. In R. Deasy (Ed.), *Critical links: Learning in the arts and student academic and social development.* Washington, DC: Arts Education Partnership.

Catterall, J. (2003, Summer). Education policy implications of recent research on the arts and academic and social development. *Journal of Learning Through Music, 2,* 103–109.

Catterall, J., Chapleau, R., & Iwanaga, J. (1999). The Imagination Project at UCLA. In E. Fiske (Ed.), *Champions of change.* Washington, DC: Arts Education Partnership.

Catterall, J., Chapleau, R., & Iwanaga, J. (1999). Involvement in the arts and human development: General involvement and intensive involvement in music and theater arts. In E. Fiske (Ed.), *Champions of change: Impact of the arts on learning.* Washington, DC: The Arts Education Partnership.

Catterall, J., & Waldorf, J. (1999). Chicago arts partnerships in education: Summary evaluation. In E. Fiske (Ed.), *Champions of change: The impact of the arts on learning.* Washington, DC: The Arts Education Partnership.

Cecil, N., & Lauritzen, P. (1994*). Literature and the arts for the integrated classroom.* White Plains, NY: Longman.

Chan, A. S., Ho, Y. C., & Cheung, M. C. (1998). Music training improves verbal memory. *Nature, 396*(607), 128.

Chauvet, J., Deschamps, E., & Hilliare, C. (1996). *Dawn of art: The Chauvet Cave: The oldest known paintings in the world.* New York: Abrams.

Choksy, L. (1974). *The Kodaly method.* Upper Saddle River, NJ: Prentice Hall.

Chomsky, C. (1972). Stages in language development and reading exposure. *Harvard Educational Review, 42,* 1–33.

Cockerton, T., Moore, S., & Norman, D. (1997). Cognitive test performance and background music. *Perceptual and Motor Skills, 85,* 1435–1438.

Cohen, D. (1968). The effect of literature on vocabulary and reading achievement. *Elementary English, 45,* 209–213, 217.

Coleman, L. (1997). *Serendipity encyclopedia.* Grand Rapids, MI: Serendipity.

Collins, R. (1994). Story told at Storyfest, Jackson, MI.

Collins, R. (1997). Storytelling: Water from another time. *Drama Theatre Teacher, 5*(2), 6.

Collins, R., & Cooper, P. (1996). *The power of story.* Upper Saddle River, NJ: Prentice Hall.

Connor, S. (2003, December 8). Glaxo Chief: Our drugs do not work on most patients. *Independent,* 1.

Consortium of National Arts Education Associations. (1994). *National standards for arts education: What every young person should know and be able to do in the arts.* Reston, VA: Music Educators National Conference.

Cooper, R. (1998). *Socio-cultural and within-school factors that affect the quality of implementation of school-wide programs* (Report No. 28). Baltimore, MD: Center for Research on the Education of Students Placed at Risk (ERIC ED426173).

Cornett, C. (1997, March). Beyond plot retelling. *Reading Teacher,* 527–528.

Cornett, C. (2001). *Learning through laughter, again.* Bloomington, IN: Phi Delta Kappa.

Cornett, C. (2006, November). Center stage: Arts-based read alouds. *Reading Teacher, 60*(3).

Cornett, C., & Cornett, C. (1980). *Bibliotherapy: The right book at the right time.* Bloomington, IN: Phi Delta Kappa.

Cortines, R. (1999). Introduction. In L. Longley (Ed.), *Gaining the arts advantage: Lessons from school districts that value arts education.* Washington, DC: President's Committee on the Arts and the Humanities.

Csikszentmihalyi, M. (1990). The domain of creativity. In M. A. Runco & R. S. Albert (Eds.), *Theories of creativity* (pp. 190–212). Newbury Park, CA: Sage.

Cullinan, B. (1989). *Literature and the child* (2nd ed.). New York: Harcourt Brace Jovanovich.

Cunningham, A., & Shagoury, R. (2005, October). The sweet work of reading. *Educational Leadership,* 53–57.

Dacey, J. S. (1989). *Fundamentals of creative thinking.* Lexington, MA: Lexington Books.

Daniels, H., & Bizar, M.(2005). *Teaching the best practices way.* Alexandria, VA: Association for Supervision Curriculum Development.

Daniels, H., Darby, J. T., & Catterall, J. S. (1994). The fourth R: The arts and learning. *Teachers College Record, 96,* 299–328.

Darby, J., & Catterall, J. (1994). The fourth R: The arts and learning. *Teachers College Record,* 299–328.

Darigan, D., Tunnell, M., & Jacobs, J. (2002). *Children's literature: Engaging teachers and children in good books.* Upper Saddle River, NJ: Pearson.

Davidson. L., Claar, C., & Stampf, M. (2003, Summer). Strategies for school change through music and the arts. *Journal of Learning Through Music, 2,* 64–76.

Deasy, R. (Ed.). (2002). *Critical links: Learning in the arts and student academic and social development.* Washington, DC: Arts Education Partnership.

Deasy, R., & Fulbright, H. (2001, November 24). The arts' impact on learning. *Education Week, 34,* 38.

Deasy, R., & Stevenson, L. (2005). *Third space: When learning matters.* Washington, DC.

deBono, E. (1991). *Six thinking hats for schools: 3–5 resource book.* Logan, IA: Perfection Learning.

DeMoss, K., & Morris, T. (2002). *How arts integration supports student learning: Students shed light on the connections.* Available at *http://www.capeweb.org/rcape.html.*

Dewey, J. (1899). *The school and society / The child and the curriculum.* Chicago: University of Chicago Press.

Dewey, J. (1997). *How we think.* Mineola, NY: Dover Press.

Dibben, N. (2004). The role of peripheral feedback in emotional experience. *Music Perception, 22,* (No. 1), pp. 79–115.

Donohue, K. (1997). *Imagine! Introducing your child to the arts.* Washington, DC: National Endowment for the Arts.

Doughty, R. (2002). *Arts education in South Carolina: A brief retrospective.* Greenwood, SC: South Carolina Alliance for Arts Education.

Douglas, S., & Willatts, P. (1994). Musical ability enhances reading skills. *Journal of Research in Reading, 17,* 99–107.

Drake, S., & Burns, R. (2004). *Meeting standards through integrated curriculum.* Alexandria, VA: Association for Supervision and Curriculum Development.

Dreeszen, C., April, A., & Deasy, R. (1999). *Learning partnerships: Improving learning in schools with arts partners in the community.* Washington, DC: Arts Education Partnership.

Dressel, J. H. (1990). The effects of listening to and discussing different qualities of children's literature on the narrative writing of fifth graders. *Research in the Teaching of English, 24,* 397–414.

Duma, A. (2005, April). Phone interview with Director of Teacher and School Programs, The Kennedy Center.

Dupont, S. (1992). The effectiveness of creative drama as an instructional strategy to enhance reading comprehension skill. *Reading Research and Instruction, 31*(3), 41–52.

Eberle, R. (1971). *SCAMPER: Games for imagination development.* Buffalo, NY: Development of Knowledge.

Edelsky, C., Altwerger, A. B., & Flores, B. (1991). *Whole language: What's the difference?* Portsmouth, NH: Heinemann.

Edwards, K. L. (1994). *North American Indian music instruction: Influences upon attitudes, cultural perceptions and achievement.* D.M.A. dissertation, Tempe, AZ: Arizona State.

Eeds, M., & Wells, D. (1989). Grand conversations: An exploration of meaning construction in literature study groups. *Research in the Teaching of English, 23,* 4–29.

Efland, A. D. (2002). *Art and cognition: Integrating the visual arts in the curriculum.* New York: Teachers College.

Eisner, E. (1983). *Beyond creating.* Los Angeles: Getty Center for Education in Art.

Eisner, E. (1992, April). The misunderstood role of the arts in human development. *Kappan,* 591–595.

Eisner, E. (1997, November). *The arts and imagination.* Keynote delivered at the Imagination Celebration Conference, Columbia University, New York.

Eisner, E. (1998). *The kind of schools we need.* Portsmouth, NH: Heinemann.

Eisner, E. (2000). Ten lessons the arts teach. In *Learning and the arts: Crossing boundaries.* Retrieved from *http://www.giarts.org/pdf/Learning.pdf.*

Eisner, E. (2002a). *The arts and the creation of mind.* New Haven, CT: Yale University Press.

Eisner, E. (2002b). What can education learn from the arts about the practice of education? *Journal of Curriculum and Supervision, 18,* 4–16.

Eisner, E. (2005). An introduction to a special section on the arts and the intellect. *Kappan, 87*(1), 8–10.

Eldredge, J. L., & Butterfield, D. (1986). Alternatives to traditional reading instruction. *Reading Teacher, 40,* 33–37.

Ellis, R. D. (1999). The dance form of the eyes: What cognitive science can learn from art. *Journal of Consciousness, 6,* 6–7.

Ellison, L. (1992, October). Using multiple intelligence to set goals. *Educational Leadership,* 69–72.

Erikson, E. (1950). *Childhood and society.* New York: Norton.

Evans, J., & Moore, J. E. (1985). *How to make books with children.* Monterey, CA: Evan Moore.

Fader, D., & McNeil, E. (1976). *The new hooked on books.* New York: Berkeley.

Faltis, C., Hudelson, S., & Hudelson, S. (1997). *Bilingual education in elementary and secondary school communities: Toward understanding and caring.* New York: Allyn & Bacon.

Farstrup, A., & Samuels, S. J. (2002). *What research has to say about reading instruction.* Newark, DE: International Reading Association.

Fauth, B. (1990). Linking the visual arts with drama, movement, and dance for the young child. In J. Stinson (Ed.), *Moving and learning for the young child.* Reston, VA: American Alliance for Health, Physical Education, and Dance.

Feeney, S., & Moravcik, E. (1987). A thing of beauty: Aesthetic development in young children. *Young Children, 42*(6), 7–15.

Ferrero, D. (2005). Pathways to reform: Start with values. *The Best of Educational Leadership,* 21–26.

Fineberg, C. (2002). Integrating the arts into the wider curriculum. In *Planning an arts-centered school: A handbook.* New York: The Dana Foundation.

Fineberg. C. (2003). *Planning an arts-centered school.* New York: Dana Press.

Fineberg, C. (2004). *Creating islands of excellence: Arts education as a partner in school reform.* Portsmouth, NH: Heinemann.

Fiske, E. (Ed.). (1999). *Champions of change: The impact of the arts on learning.* Washington, DC: The Arts Education Partnership and The President's Committee on the Arts.

Five, C. (1986). Fifth graders respond to a changed reading program. *Harvard Educational Review, 56,* 395–405.

Fleming, G. A. (Ed.). (1990). *Children's dance.* Reston, VA: American Alliance for Health, Physical Education, and Dance.

Florida, R. (2004). *The rise of the creative class.* New York: Basic Books.

Fogarty, R. (1991). *The mindful school: How to integrate the curricula.* Palatine, IL: Skylight Publishing.

Fogg, T., & Smith, M. (2001). The artists in the classroom project: A closer look. *Educational Forum, 66,* 60–70.

Ford Foundation. (2005, Winter). *Deep in the heart of Texas.* Retrieved from *http://www.fordfound.org.*

Freeman, C., Seashore, K. R., & Werner, L. (2003). *Methods of implementing arts for academic achievement: Challenging contemporary classroom practice.* Minneapolis: University of Minnesota, Center for Applied Research and Educational Improvement.

Friedmann, S. (2004, April 4). How colors affect feelings. *Beaufort Gazette, 2.*

Frye, N. (1957). Theory of symbol. In *Anatomy of criticism*. Princeton, NJ: Princeton University Press.

Gallagher, K., & Booth, D. (Eds.). (2003). *How theatre educates.* Toronto, ON: University of Toronto Press.

Gardiner, M. (1996). Learning improved by arts training. *Scientific Correspondence in Nature, 381*(580), 284.

Gardner, H. (1973). *The arts and human development.* New York: Wiley.

Gardner, H. (1983; 1993). *Frames of mind: The theory of multiple intelligences.* New York: Basic Books.

Gardner, H. (1989, Winter). Zero-based arts education: An introduction to ARTS PROPEL. *Studies in Art Education,* 71–83.

Gardner, H. (1990). *Art education and human development.* Los Angeles: Getty Center for Education in the Arts.

Gardner, H. (1993a). *Creating minds.* New York: Basic Books.

Gardner, H. (1993b). *Multiple intelligences: The theory in practice.* New York: Basic Books.

Gardner, H. (1999). *The disciplined mind.* New York: Simon & Schuster.

Gazzaniga, M. (2005). *Arts and cognition.* Washington, DC: Dana Foundation.

Gelman, R. (1979). Preschool thought. *American Psychologist, 34,* 900–905.

Getzels, J. W., & Jackson, P. W. (1962). *Creativity and intelligence.* New York: Wiley.

Gilbert-Greene, A. (1977). *Teaching the 3 Rs through movement experiences.* New York: Macmillan.

Gilbert-Greene, A. (1992). *Creative dance for all ages.* Reston, VA: National Dance Association.

Gilbert, A. (2005). *Brain-compatible dance education.* Available at *http://www.creativedance.org.*

Giles, M. (1991). A little background music please. *Principal, 71,* 141–167.

Ginott, H. (1985). *Between teacher and child.* New York: Avon.

Given, B. (2002). *Teaching to the brain's natural learning systems.* Alexandria, VA: Association for Supervision and Curriculum Development.

Ginsberg, H., & Opper, S. (1969). *Piaget's theory of intellectual development.* Upper Saddle River, NJ: Prentice Hall.

Glazer, J. (1997). *Introduction to children's literature* (2nd ed.). Upper Saddle River, NJ: Prentice Hall.

Goldberg, M. (1997). *Arts and learning.* White Plains, NY: Longman.

Goldberg, M., Bennett, T., & Jacobs, V. (1999, April). *Artists in the classroom: A role in the professional development of classroom teachers.* American Educational Research Association Montreal, Quebec, Canada.

Goldberg, M. R., & Phillips, A. (2000). *Arts as education.* Cambridge, MA: Harvard Educational Review.

Goleman, D. (1995). *Emotional intelligence: Why it can matter more than IQ.* New York: Bantam.

Gopnik, A., Kuhl, P., & Meltzoff, A. (1999). *The scientist in the crib: Minds, brains and how children learn.* New York: William Morrow.

Gourgey, A., Bousseau, J., & Delgado, J. (1985). The impact of an improvisational dramatics program on student attitudes and achievement. *Children's Theater Review, 34*(3), 9–14.

Graziano, A., Peterson, M., & Shaw, G. (1999, March). Enhanced learning of proportional math through music training and spatial-temporal training. *Neurologial Research, 21*(2), 139–152.

Greene, M. (1997, February). Why ignore forms of art? *Education Week,* 4–5.

Greene, M. (2001). *Variations on a blue guitar: The Lincoln Center lectures on aesthetic education.* New York: Teachers College Press.

Gregorian, V. (1997, March 13). 10 things you can do to make our schools better. *Parade Magazine.*

Griss, S. (1998). *Minds in motion.* Portsmouth, NH: Heinemann.

Grossman, P., Wineburg, S., & Beers, S. (2000). Introduction: When theory meets practice in the world of school. In S. Wineburg & P. Grossman (Eds.), *Interdisciplinary curriculum: Challenges to implementation* (pp. 1–16). New York: Teachers College.

Gunzenhauser, M. G., & Gerstl-Pepin, C. I. (2002). Guest editors' introduction: The shifting context of accountability in North Carolina and the implications for arts-based reform. *Educational Foundations, 16,* 3–14.

Guskey, T. (2000). *Evaluating professional development.* Thousand Oaks, CA: Corwin Press.

Guthrie, J. (2000). Contexts for engagement and motivation in reading. In M. Kamil, P. Mosenthal, P. Pearson, & R. Barr (Eds.), *Handbook of reading research* (Vol 3). New York: Erlbaum.

Guthrie, J. (2004). Motivating students to read. In P. McCardle & U. Chhabra (Ed.), *The voice of evidence in reading research.* Baltimore, MD: Brookes.

Habemeyer, S. (1999). *Good music, brighter children.* Rocklin, CA: Prince.

Hall, G. E., & Hord, S. M. (1987). *Change in schools: Facilitating the process.* Albany, NY: State University of New York.

Hall, G. E., Loucks, S. F., Rutherford, W. L., & Newlove, B. W. (1975). Levels of use of the innovation: A framework for analyzing innovation adoption. *Journal of Teacher Education, 26*(1), 52–56.

Hall, J. (2005). Neuroscience and education. *Education Journal, 84,* 27–29.

Hallet, M. (1999, May). *Gray matters: Sports, fitness and the brain.* (Interview on National Public Radio).

Hallet, V. (2005, July 25). The power of Potter. *U.S. News and World Report,* 45–49.

Hanna, J. (1992, April). Connections: Arts, academics and productive citizens. *Kappan,* 601–607.

Hanna, J. (1999). *Partnering dance and education.* Champaign, IL: Human Kinetics.

Hansen, L., & Monk, M. (2002). Brain development and structure of learning. *International Journal of Science Education, 24*(4), 343–356.

Hansen-Krening, N. (1992). Authors of color: A multicultural perspective. *Journal of Reading, 26*(2), 124–129.

Harris, L. (1992). *Americans and the arts VI/Nationwide survey of public opinion.* Washington, DC: Americans for the Arts.

Harste, J., Short, K., & Burke, C. (1988). *Creating classrooms for authors.* Portsmouth, NH: Heinemann.

Hart, A., & Mantell, P. (1993). *Kids make music!* Charlotte, VT: Williamson.

Hart, B., & Risley, T. (Spring 2003). The early catastrophe: The 30-million word gap. *American Educator.* Retrieved from *http://www.aft.org/American_Educator/spring2003/catastrophe.html.*

Hartzler, D. (2000). *A meta-analysis of studies conducted on integrated curriculum programs and their effects on student achievement.* Unpublished dissertation, Indiana University, Bloomington.

Heath, S.B., with Roach, A. (1999). Imaginative actuality: Learning in the arts during the nonschool hours. In E. Fiske (Ed.), *Champions of change: Impact of the arts on learning.* Washington, DC: The Arts Education Partnership and the President's Committee on the Arts and Humanities.

Heathcote, D., & Bolton, G. (1995). *Drama for learning.* Portsmouth, NH: Heinemann.

Hebert, D. (2005). *Getting to the top: Arts essential academic learning requirements.* Seattle, WA: New Horizons for Learning.

Hedblad, A. (1998). *Something about the author.* Detroit: Gale.

Heinig, R. B. (1993). *Creative drama for the classroom teacher.* Upper Saddle River, NJ: Prentice Hall.

Henderson, L. C., & Shanker, L. C. (1978). The use of interpretive dramatics versus basal reader workbooks. *Reading World, 17,* 239–243.

Hepler, S. (1982). *Patterns of response to literature: A one year study of a fifth and sixth grade classroom.* Unpublished doctoral dissertation, The Ohio State University, Columbus.

Herman, J., & Baker, E. (2005, November). Making benchmark testing work. *Educational Leadership, 63*(3), 48–54.

Hetland, L., & Winner, E. (Eds.). (2000, Fall/Winter). The arts and academic achievement: What the evidence shows. *The Journal of Aesthetic Education, 34* (34), Champaign, IL: University of Illinois Press.

Hochman, D. (2005, February 25). Their fingers do the talking. *Life Magazine,* 8–11.

Holdaway, D. (1982). Shared book experience: Teaching reading using favorite books. *Theory into Practice, 21,* 293–300.

Hope, S. (2003, Summer). Questions and challenges concerning music's role in education. *Journal for Learning Through Music, 2.*

Hopkins, L. (1969). *Books are by people.* New York: Citation.

Hopkins, L. B. (1987). *Pass the poetry please.* New York: Harper & Row.

Horowitz, R. (2004). *Summary of Large-Scale Arts Partnership Evaluations.* Washington, DC: Arts Education Partnership.

Hubel, D. (1988). *Eye, brain, and vision.* New York: Freeman.

Huck, C., Hepler, S., & Hickman, J. (2001). *Children's literature in the elementary school* (4th ed.). Dubuque, IA: McGraw-Hill.

Huckabee, M. (2005). *Initiative on the arts in education 2005–2006.* Education Commission of the States. Retrieved from *http://www.ecs.org.*

Hudson, R., Lane, H., & Pullen, P. (2005, May). Reading fluency assessment and instruction: What, why, and how? *Reading Teacher, 58*(8), 702–713.

Impact of Arts Education on Workforce Preparation. (2002). National Governor's Association. Retrieved from *http://www.nga.org/.*

Ingram, D., & Riedel, E. (2003). *Arts for academic achievement: What does arts integration do for students?* Minneapolis: University of Minnesota, Center for Applied Research and Educational Improvement.

Ingram, D., & Seashore, K. R. (2003). *Arts for academic achievement: Summative evaluation report.* Minneapolis: University of Minnesota, Center for Applied Research and Educational Improvement.

International Association of Visual and Performing Arts High Schools. (2000, February). Annual meeting, Mobile, AL.

Interstate New Teacher Assessment and Support Consortium (INTASC). (2002, June). *Model standards for licensing classroom teachers and specialists in the arts.* Washington, DC: Council of Chief State School Officers. Retrieved from *http://www.ccsso.org* (click on "Projects").

Intrator, S. (2004–2005). The engaged classroom. *The Best of Educational Leadership.* 2–5.

Isaksen, S. G., & Treffinger, D. J. (1985). *Creative problem solving: The basic course.* Buffalo, NY: Bearly Limited.

Jack, C. (2005, July 18). *Arts in school can have lifelong impact. Plain Dealer,* (Cleveland, OH) D1.

Jacobs, H. (Ed.). (1989). *Interdisciplinary curriculum: Design and implementation.* Alexandria, VA: Association for Supervision and Curriculum Development.

Jacobs, H. (1997). *Mapping the big picture: Integrating curriculum and assessment, K–12.*

Alexandria, VA: Association for Supervision and Curriculum Development.

Jacobs, J. (2002). *Children's literature.* Columbus, OH: Merrill/Prentice Hall.

Jarnow, J. (1991). *All ears: How to use and choose recorded music for children.* New York: Viking.

Jay, D. (1991). Effect of a dance program on the creativity of preschool handicapped children. *Adapted Physical Activity Quarterly, 8,* 305–316.

Jenkins, P. (1986). *Art for the fun of it.* New York: Simon & Schuster.

Jennings, C. (1998). *Jenning's theatre for young audiences: Twenty great plays for children.* New York: St. Martin's Press.

Jensen, E. (2000). *Music with the brain in mind.* San Diego, CA: Brain Store.

Jensen, E. (2001). *Arts with the brain in mind.* Alexandria, VA: Association for Supervision and Curriculum Development.

Jewitt, C., Kress, G., & Ogborn, J. (2001). Exploring learning through visual, actional, and linguistic communication: The multimodal environment of a science classroom. *Educational Review, 53*(1), 5–19.

Johnson, T., & Louis, D. (1987). *Literacy through literature.* Portsmouth, NH: Heinemann.

Joyce, M. (1994). *First steps in teaching creative dance to children* (3rd ed.). Mountain View, CA: Mayfield.

Kamil, M. (2004). Reading comprehension. In P. McCardle & U. Chhabra (Eds.), *The voice of evidence in reading research.* Baltimore, MD: Brookes.

Kantrowitz, B., & Leslie, C. (1997, April 14). *Readin', writin', rhythm. Newsweek,* 71.

Kappan. (2005). Themed issue on art and the intellect, *87*(1).

Kardash, C., & Wright, L. (1987, Winter). Does creative drama benefit elementary school students? A meta-analysis. *Youth Theater Journal,* 11–18.

Karioth, E. (1967). *Creative dramatics as an aid to developing creative thinking abilities.* Unpublished doctoral dissertation, University of Minnesota.

Keirstead, C., & Graham, W. (2004). *VSA arts research study: Using the arts to help special education students meet their learning goals.* Portsmouth, NH: RMC Research Corporation.

Kellogg, R. (1969). *Analyzing children's art.* Palo Alto, CA: Mayfield.

Keppel, P. (2003, Summer). Teaching musicians the art of possibility: Observations on a master class by Ben Zander. *Journal for Learning Through Music, 2,* 28–30.

Kiefer, B. (1994). *The potential of picture books: From visual literacy to aesthetic understanding.* Upper Saddle River, NJ: Prentice Hall.

Kippelen, V. (2002, March). *The halls are alive.* Retrieved from *http://connectforkids.org.*

Koster, J. (1997). *Growing artists.* Albany, NY: Delmar.

Krashen, S. (2005, February). Is in-school free reading good for children? Why the National Reading Panel (NRP) is still wrong. *Kappan, 86*(06), 444–447.

Kutiper, K., & Wilson, P. (1993). Updating poetry preferences: A look at the poetry children really like. *Reading Teacher, 47*(1), 28–35.

LaFosse, M. (2003). *Origami activities: Asian arts and crafts for creative kids.* North Clarendon, VT: Tuttle.

Lakshmanan, I. (2005, June 22). For Venezuela's poor, music opens doors. Retrieved from *http://www.boston.com/news/world/latinamerica.*

Lamb, S. J., & Gregory, A. H. (1993). The relationship between music and reading in beginning readers. *Educational Psychology, 13,* 19–26.

Larson, G. (1997). *American canvas.* Washington, DC: National Endowment for the Arts.

Leahy, S., Lyon, C., Thompson, M., & William, D. (2005). Classroom assessment: Minute by minute, day by day. *Educational Leadership,* 18–26.

Learning and the Arts: Crossing boundaries. (2000, January). *Proceedings from an Invitational Meeting for Education, Arts and Youth Funders,* Los Angeles. Retrieved from *http://www.giarts.org/Learning.pdf.*

Lehr, S. S. (1991). *The child's developing sense of theme: Responses to literature.* New York: Teachers College Press.

Levine, M. (2002). *A mind at a time.* New York: Simon and Schuster.

Levi-Straus, C. (1967). *Scope of anthropology.* London: Cape.

Levstik, L. (1986). The relationship between historical response and narrative in a sixth-grade classroom. *Theory and Research in Social Education, 14,* 1–15.

Lewis, C. S. (1980). On three ways of writing for children. In S. Egoff et al. (Eds.), *Only connect readings on children's literature.* New York: Oxford University Press.

Lewis, R. (2002, September). I made it by myself. *New Horizons for Learning.* Retrieved from: *www.newhorizons.org.*

The Lexile Framework. (1995). Durham, NC: Metametrics.

Lima, C. (2005). *A to zoo: Subject access to children's picture books.* New York: Simon and Schuster.

Lindsey, G. (1998–99, Winter). Brain research and implications for early childhood education. *Childhood Education, 75*(2), 97–100.

Lindstrom, R. (1999, April 19). Being visual: The emerging visual enterprise. *Business Week:* Special Section.

Lockwood, S. (2005, March). *The window: Saving creativity in Teens.* Seattle, WA: New

Horizons Learning. Retrieved from *http://www.newhorizons.org*.

Longley, L. (Ed.). (1999). *Gaining the arts advantage: Lessons from school districts that value arts education*. Washington, DC: President's Committee on the Arts and the Humanities.

Longo, P. (1999, November 8). Distributed knowledge in the brain: Using visual thinking networking to improve students' learning. Boston: Learning and the Brain Conference.

Lowenfeld, V., & Brittain, W. L. (1975). *Creative and mental growth*. New York: Macmillan.

Lozanov, G. (1978). *Suggestology and outlines of suggestopedy*. New York: Gordon & Breach.

Luftig, R. (1994). *The schooled mind: Do the arts make a difference? An empirical evaluation of the Hamilton Fairfield SPECTRA 1 Program 1992–93*. Oxford, OH: Miami University, Center for Human Development.

Lushington, K. (2003, December). Lighting the fire of imagination through theatre and drama in Ontario schools. Retrieved from *http://www.code.on/Pages/dramaarticle.html*.

MacKinnon, D. W. (1978). *In search of human effectiveness*. Buffalo, NY: Creative Education Foundation.

MacMahon, S., Roe, D., & Parks, M. (2003). Basic reading through dance program: The impact on first-grade students' basic reading skills. *Evaluation Review, 27*, 104–125.

Macon, J. (1991). *Responses to literature*. Newark, DE: International Reading Association.

Malyarenko, T. N., Kuraev, G. S., Malyarenko, Y. E., Khvatova, M. V., Romanova, N. G., & Gurina, V. I. (1996). The development of brain's electric activity in 4 yr. old children by long-term sensory stimulation with music. *Human Physiology, 23*, 76–81.

Mantione, R., & Smead, S. (2003). *Weaving through words: Using the arts to teach reading comprehension strategies*. Newark, DE: International Reading Association.

Marantz, S. (1992). *Picture books for looking and learning: Awakening visual perceptions through the art of children's books*. Westport, CT: Greenwood.

Mardirosian, G. H., & Fox, L. (2003). Literacy learning intervention for at-risk students through arts-based instruction: A case study of the imagination quest model. Presentation at the Learning Conference 2003: What Learning Means, Institute of Education, University of London.

Marron, V. (2003, Summer). The A+ schools program: Establishing and integrating the arts as four languages of learning. *Journal for Learning Through Music, 2*, 91–97.

Marzano, R., Pickering, D., & Pollock, J. (2001). *Classroom instruction that works: Research-based strategies for increasing student achievement*. Alexandria, VA: Association for Supervision and Curriculum Development.

Maslow, A. (1968). *Toward a psychology of being*. Princeton, NJ: Van Nostrand.

Maslow, A. (1970). *Motivation and personality*. New York: Harper & Row.

Mason, C., Thormann, M., & Steedly, K. (2004). *VSA arts affiliate research project: How students with disabilities learn in and through the arts*. Washington, DC: Very Special Arts.

McCardle, P., & Chhabra, U. (Ed.). (2004). *The voice of evidence in reading research*. Baltimore, MD: Brookes.

McCaslin, N. (1990). *Creative drama in the classroom* (5th ed.). New York: Longman.

McDermott, P. (2004). Using the visual arts for learning: The case of one urban charter school. *Second Annual Ethnography in Education Research Forum, 27–28*.

McElmeel, S. (1994). *ABCs of an author/illustrator visit*. Worthington, OH: Lippincott.

McTighe, J., & O'Connor, K. (2005, November). Seven practices for effective learning. *Educational Leadership, 10–18*.

McTighe, J., & Wiggins, G. (2004). *Understanding by design: Professional workbook*. Alexandria, VA: Association for Supervision and Curriculum Development.

McWinnie, H. J. (1992). Art in early childhood education. In C. Seefeldt (Ed.), *The early childhood curriculum*. New York: Teachers College Press.

Mello, R. (2004, March). When pedagogy meets practice: Combining arts integration and teacher education in the college classroom. *The Journal of the Arts and Learning, 20*(1), 135–164.

Meyrink, G. (1994). The curse of the toad. In *The opal and other stories*. Riverside, CA: Ariadne.

Miles, M. B., & Huberman, A. M. (1994). *Qualitative data analysis* (2nd ed.). Newbury Park, CA: Sage.

Miller, H., Rynders, J., & Schleien, S. (1993). Drama: A medium to enhance social interaction between students with and without mental retardation. *Mental Retardation, 31*(4), 228–233.

Mitchell, C., & Weber, S. (1998). Picture this! Class line-ups, vernacular portraits, and lasting impressions of school. In J. Prosser (Ed.), *Image-based research: A sourcebook for qualitative researchers* (pp. 197–213). London: Falmer.

Moats, L. (2004). Science language and imagination in the professional development of reading teachers. In P. McCardle & U. Chhabra (Eds.), *The voice of evidence in reading research*. Baltimore, MD: Brookes.

Moore, B., & Caldwell, H. (1993). Drama and drawing for narrative writing in primary grades. *Journal of Educational Research, 8*(2), 100–110.

Moore, T. (1998). *Care of the soul: How to add depth and meaning to your everyday life*. New York: HarperCollins.

Morrison, C. (2003, February 24). Arts-in-education efforts. *The Asheville Citizen-Times*, B1.

Morrow, L. (2001). Literacy development and young children: Research to practice. In S. L. Golbeck (Ed.), *Psychological perspectives on early childhood education* (pp. 253–279). International Reading Association Journal.

Morrow, L. (2003). *Handbook of research on teaching the English language arts*. Mahwah, NJ: Lawrence Erlbaum.

Morrow, L. M. (1992). The impact of a literature-based program on literacy achievement, use of literature, and attitudes of children from minority backgrounds. *Reading Research Quarterly, 27*, 250–275.

Murfee, E. (1995). *Eloquent evidence: Arts at the core of learning*. Washington, DC: The President's Committee on the Arts and the Humanities.

Murray, R. L. (1975). *Dance in elementary education: A program for boys and girls* (3rd ed.). New York: Harper & Row.

Music therapy at Case Western Medical School. (1997, June 7). *Springfield New Sun, 1*.

Nash, J. M. (1997, February 3). *Fertile minds*. Time, 48–49.

National Art Education Association (2002). *Authentic connections: Interdisciplinary work in the arts*. Reston, VA: Author.

National Center for Education Statistics. (2000). Retrieved from *http://nces.ed.gov*.

National Center for Education Statistics. (1997). *Highlights of the NAEP 1997 arts assessment report card*. Washington, DC: U.S. Department of Education, NCES. Retrieved from *http://nces.ed.gov/nationsreportcard/pdf/main1997/1999486.pdf*.

National Reading Panel. (2000). *Teaching children to read: An evidence-based assessment of the scientific reading literature and its implications for reading instruction*. Washington, DC: National Institute Child Health.

Neeld, E. C. (1986). *Writing* (2nd ed.). Glenview, IL: Scott, Foresman.

Nelson, C. (2001). *The arts and education reform: Lessons from a four-year evaluation of the A+ Schools Program* (Executive Summary). Winston-Salem, NC: Kenan Institue for the Arts.

Nelson, K. (1998). *Developing students multiple intelligences*. New York: Scholastic.

New American Schools. (2003). The Leonard Bernstein center for learning. Retrieved from *http://naschools.org*.

New York City Board of Education. (1992–1993). *Chapter I developer/demonstration program: Learning to read through the arts*. New York: Office of Educational Research.

No Child Left Behind Act of 2001, Pub. L. No. 107-110. (2001). Retrieved from *http://www.ed.gov/nclb/ landing.jhtml*.

Noddings, N. (2005, September). What does it mean to educate the whole child? *Educational Leadership, 63*(1), 8–13.

Norton, D. (2003). *Through the eyes of a child: An introduction to children's literature* (6th ed.). Upper Saddle River, NJ: Merrill/Prentice Hall.

Norton, D., & Norton, S. (2005). *Multicultural children's literature.* Upper Saddle River, NJ: Merrill/Prentice Hall.

Ogle, D. (1989). The know, want to know, learn strategy. In K. Muth (Ed.), *Children's comprehension of text: Research into practice.* Newark, DE: International Reading Association.

Ohio Department of Education. (1996). *Ohio's model competency-based program: Comprehensive arts education.* Columbus, Ohio: Author.

Ohlhausen, M. M., & Jepsen, M. (1992). Lessons from Goldilocks: Somebody's been choosing my books but I can make my own choices now! *New Advocate, 5,* 31–46.

O'Neill, C., & Johnson, L. (1984). *Dorothy Heathcote: Collected writings on education and drama.* Cheltenham, UK: L Stanley Thomas (Publishers) Ltd.

Oppenheimer, T. (1999, September). Schooling the imagination. *Atlantic Monthly, 284*(3), 71–83.

Oreck, B., Baum, S., & McCartney, H. (1999). Artistic talent development for urban youth: The promise and the challenge. In E. Fiske (Ed.), *Champions of change.* Washington, DC: Arts Education Partnership.

Osborne, A. (1963). *Applied imagination* (3rd ed.). New York: Scribner's.

Page, N. (1995). *Sing and shine on! A teacher's guide to multicultural song leading.* Portsmouth, NH: Heinemann.

Paige, R., & Huckabee, M. (2005). Putting arts education front and center. *Education Week, 24*(20), 40, 52.

Palmarini, J. (2001, Summer). The REAP report. *Teaching Theatre,* 12–20.

Palmarini, J. (2005, Winter). The teaching artist. *Teaching Theatre, 16*(2), 1–6.

Parsons, M. J. (1987). *How we understand art: A cognitive developmental account of aesthetic experience.* Cambridge, NY: Cambridge University Press.

Patchen, J. (1996, September). Overview of discipline-based music education. *Music Educator's Journal,* 19–25.

Pate, G. (1988). Research on reducing prejudice. *Social Education, 52*(4), 287–291.

Peck, R. (1988). *Secrets of successful fiction.* Seattle: Romar.

PEN. (2004, March 4). *Public Education News Weekly NewsBlast.*

Perkins, D. (1998). *The intelligent eye: Learning to think by looking at art.* Santa Monica, CA: Getty Center.

Perkins, D. N. (1987–1988, December/January). Art as an occasion of intelligence. *Educational Leadership,* 36–42.

Perrin, S. (1994, February). Education in the arts is an education for life. *Kappan,* 452–453.

Piaget, J. (1950). *The psychology of intelligence.* New York: Harcourt Brace.

Piaget, J. (1952). *The child's conception of number.* New York: Humanities Press.

Piaget, J. (1954). *The construction of relativity in the child.* New York: Basic Books.

Piaget, J. (1980). *To understand is to invent.* New York: Penguin.

Piazza, C. (1999). *Multiple forms of literacy.* Upper Saddle River, NJ: Merrill/Prentice Hall.

Pica, R. (1991). *Moving and learning.* Champaign, IL: Human Kinetics.

Pinnell, G. (1986). *Reading recovery in Ohio, 1985–86: Final report.* Columbus, Ohio: The Ohio State University.

Pinnell, G. & Fountas, I. (2005). *Leveled books, K–8: Matching texts to readers for effective teaching.* Portsmouth, NH: Heinemann.

Posner, M., & Rothbart, M. (2005). Influencing brain networks. *Trends in cognitive science, 9*(3), 99–103.

The power of the arts to transform education. (1993). Los Angeles: J. Paul Getty Trust.

President's Commission on National Goals. (1960). *Goals for Americans.* New York: The American Assembly, Columbia University.

Pressley, M. (2002). Metacognition and self-regulated comprehension. In A. Farstrup & S. J. Samuels, *What research has to say about reading instruction.* Newark, DE: International Reading Association.

Project Zero. (2000). *Reviewing education and the arts project (REAP), Executive summary.* Cambridge, MA: Harvard University. Retrieved from *http://www.pz.harvard.edu/Research?REap/REAP.*

Psilos, P. (2002). *The impact of arts education on workforce preparation: Issue brief.* Washington, DC: National Governors' Association, Center for Best Practices. Retrieved from *http://www.nga.org/.*

Purcell-Gates, V. (1988). Lexical and syntactic knowledge of written narrative held by well-read-to kindergartners and second graders. *Research in the Teaching of English, 22,* 128–160.

Rabkin, N., & Redmond, R. (2005, January 8). The art of education. *Washington Post,* A19.

Rabkin, N., & Redmond, R. (2005, April 13). Arts education: Not all is created equal. *Education Week, 24*(31), 46–47.

Rabkin, N., Redmond, R. (2006). The arts make a difference. *Educational Leadership, 63*(5).

Rauscher, F., Shaw, G., & Ky, K. (1995). Listening to Mozart enhances spatial-temporal reasoning: Towards a neurophysiological basis. *Neuroscience Letters, 185,* 44–47.

Rauscher, F., Shaw, G., Levine, L., Wright, E., Dennis, W., & Newcomb, R. (1997). Music training causes long-term enhancement of preschool children's spatial-temporal reasoning. *Neurological Research, 19,* 2–8.

Rauscher, F. H., & Shaw, G. L. (1993). Music and spatial task performance. *Nature.* Cited in *Why to Learn Music;* retrieved from *http://www.uwgb.breznayp/music.htm.*

REAP (Reviewing Education and the Arts Project). Project Zero at Harvard University (2000). *Journal of Aesthetic Education, 34*(3).

Register, D. (2004, Spring). The effects of live music groups versus an educational children's television program on the emergent literacy of young children. *Journal of Music Therapy, 41*(1), 2–27.

Reimer, B. (2004). New brain research on emotion and feelings, dramatic implications for music education. *Arts Education Policy Review, 106*(2), 21–28.

Remer, J. (1996). *Beyond enrichment.* New York: American Council for the Arts.

Reutzel, D., & Cooter, R. (1992). *Teaching children to read: From basals to books.* Upper Saddle River, NJ: Prentice Hall.

Riccio, L., Rollins, J., & Morton, K. (2003). *The sail effect: Development of a model for measuring the effectiveness of the arts as an instrumental element in overall academic and social development for students in an arts-infused elementary school.* Washington, DC: WVSA Arts Connection.

Richards, J. C., Gipe, J. P., & Moore, R. C. (2000). *The challenge of integrating literacy learning and the visual and communicative arts: A Portal School focus* (ERIC ED 442784).

Richmond-Cullen, C. (2005). Congressional Testimony on April 28, on behalf of Pennsylvania Department of Educations and Americans for the Arts.

Riekehof, L. (1987). *Joy of signing.* Springfield, MO: Gospel.

Ritter, N. (1999). *Teaching interdisciplinary thematic units in language arts.* Bloomington, IN: ERIC Clearinghouse on Reading, English, and Communication.

Roberts, T. (2004, September 29). The discipline of wonder (Editorial). *Education Week,* 31.

Robinson, K. (2000). *Learning and the arts: Crossing boundaries.* Retrieved from *http://www.giarts.org/pdf/Learning.pdf.*

Robinson, K. (Ed.). (1990). *Exploring theater and education.* London: Heinemann.

Rooney, R. (2004). *Arts-based teaching and learning: Review of the literature.* Rockville, MD: Westat. Retrieved from *http://www.vsarts.org/x954.xml.*

Rose, L., & Gallup, A. (2005, September). The 37th annual Phi Delta Kappa/Gallup Poll of the public's attitudes toward the public schools. *Kappan,* 41–54.

Rosenberg, H. (1987). *Creative drama and imagination: Transforming ideas into action.* New York: Holt, Rinehart & Winston.

Rosenblatt, L. (1985). Viewpoints: Transaction versus interaction—a terminological rescue operation. *Research in the Teaching of English*, *19*, 98–107.

Roser, N. L., Hofman, J.V., & Farest, C. (1990). Language, literature, and at-risk children. *Reading Teacher, 43*, 554–559.

Ross, C., & Stangl, K. (1994). *The music teacher's book of lists*. West Nyack, NY: Parker.

Ruppert, S. (2006). *Critical evidence: How the arts benefit student achievement*. Washington, DC: National Assembly of State Arts Agencies and Arts Education Partnership.

Russell, D. (1994). *Literature for children: A short introduction* (2nd ed.). New York: Longman.

Sabine, G., & Sabine, P. (1983). *Books that made the difference*. Hamden, CT: Libraries Professional.

Sadie, S. (Ed.). (2001). *New Grove dictionary of music and musicians*. New York: Grove.

Safire, W. (1991, April 29). On language. *New York Times Magazine*, 16.

Samuels, J. (2002). Reading fluency. In A. Farstrup & S. J. Samuels, *What research has to say about reading instruction*. Newark, DE: International Reading Association.

Saunders, S. (1999). *The author visit handbook*. Portsmouth, NH: Heinemann.

Schacter, D. (2002). *Searching for memory: The brain the mind and the past*. New York: Basic Books.

Scheel, K. R., & Westefeld, J. S. (1999, Summer). Heavy metal music and adolescent suicidality: An empirical investigation. *Adolescent, 34*(134), 253–273.

Schmidt, B. (1991). Story map. In J. Macon (Ed.), *Responses to literature*. Newark, DE: International Reading Association.

Scripp, L. (2003, Summer). Critical links, next steps: An evolving conception of music and learning in public school education. *Journal of Learning Through Music, 2*, 119–140.

Schwen, M. R. (1995). Theatre as liberal arts pedagogy. *Liberal Education, 81*(2), 32–38.

Seaman, M. A. (1999). *The arts in basic curriculum project: A ten year evaluation. Looking at the past and preparing for the future*. Columbia: University of South Carolina.

Seashore, F. (2001). *Arts survive: A study of sustainability in arts education partnerships*. Cambridge, MA: Project Zero, Harvard Graduate School of Education.

Seashore, F., Werner, K., & Werner, L. (2003). *Methods of implementing arts for academic achievement: Challenging contemporary classroom practice (pp.ii–iii)*. Minneapolis, MN: Center for Applied Research and Educational Improvement.

Seidel, S. (1999). Stand and unfold yourself. A monograph on the Shakespeare and Company research study. In E. Fiske (Ed.), *Champions of change*. Washington, DC: Arts Education Partnership and the President's Committee on the Arts.

Shanahan, T. (2004). Critique of NRP Panel Report. In P. McCardle & U. Chhabra (Eds.), *The voice of evidence in reading research*. Baltimore, MD: Brookes.

Shaw, G. (2000). *Keeping Mozart in mind*. San Diego: Academic.

Shaywitz, S. (2004). Neurological basis for reading disability. In P. McCardle & U. Chhabra (Eds.), *The voice of evidence in reading research*. Baltimore, MD: Brookes.

Shephard, A. (2005). *Stories on stage*. Olympia, WA: Shepard.

Short, G. (2001). Arts-based school reform: A whole school studies one painting. *Art Education, 54*, 4–11.

Short, K., Schroeder, J., Laird, J., Kauffman, F., Ferguson, M., & Crawford, K. (1996). *Learning together through inquiry*. Portland, ME: Stenhouse.

Siegel, D. J. (1999). *The developing mind: Toward a neurobiology of interpersonal experience*. New York: Guilford Press.

Siks, G. (1983). *Drama with children*. New York: Harper.

Simmons, T., & Sheehan, R. (1997, February 16). Brain research manifests importance of first years. *The News & Observer*. Retrieved from *http://www.nando.net/nao/2little2late/stories/dayl-main*.

Smith, S. (2003, April 2). Why not dance? *Chicago Tribune*, 2.

Smutny, J. (2002). *Integrating the arts into the curriculum for gifted students* (ERIC ED470524).

Soep, E. (2005, September). Critique: Where art meets assessment. *Kappan, 7*(1), 36–63.

Sostarich, J. (1974). A study of the reading behavior of sixth graders: Comparisons of active and other readers. Unpublished doctoral dissertation, The Ohio State University, Columbus.

South Carolina Arts Commission. (2002, April). *The enonomic impact of the arts in South Carolina*. Columbia, SC: Author.

Spilka, R. (2002). Approximately "real world" learning with the hybrid model. *Teaching with Technology Today, 8*(6). Retrieved from *http://www.uwsa.edu/ttt/articles/spilka.htm*.

Spolin, V. (1999). *Improvisation for the theater: A handbook of teaching and directing techniques*. Evanston, IL: Northwestern University Press.

Spolin, V. (2001). *Theater games for the lone actor*. Evanston, IL: Northwestern University Press.

Standing, L. (1973). 10,000 pictures. *Quarterly Journal of Experimental Psychology, 25*, 207–222.

Starko, A. (1995). *Creativity in the classroom: Schools of curious delight*. White Plains, NY: Longman.

Starnes, D., & Siegesmund, R. (2004). *Literacy: An integrated visual arts student learning delivery system*. Atlanta: EMSTAR Research.

Stauffer, R. (1969). *Directing reading maturity as a cognitive process*. New York: Harper & Row.

Steiner, D. (2003, Summer). Making music work for education. *Journal for Learning Through Music, 2*, 9.

Sternberg, R. J. (Ed.) (1988). *The nature of creativity* (pp. 429–440). New York: Cambridge University Press.

Sternberg, R. J., & Lubar, T. I. (1991). Creating creative minds. *Kappan, 72*, 608–614.

Stewig, J. (1988). *Reading pictures*. New Berlin, WI: Jenson.

Stewig, J., & McKee, J. (1980). Drama and language growth: A replication study. *Children's Theater Review, 29*(3), 1.

Stiggins, R. (2002, June). Assessment crisis: The absence of assessment for learning. *Kappan, 83*(10), 758–765.

Stinson, S. (1988). *Dance for young children: Finding the magic in movement*. Reston, VA: American Alliance for Health, Physical Education, Recreation and Dance.

Strauss, A., & Corbin, J. (Eds.). (1997). *Grounded theory in practice*. Thousand Oaks, CA: Sage.

Stronge, J. H. (2002). *Qualities of effective teachers*. Alexandria, VA: Association for Supervision and Curriculum Development.

Tardif, T. Z., & Sternberg, R. J. (1988). What do we know about creativity? In R. J. Sternberg (Ed.) (1997), *Successful intelligence: How practical and creative intelligence determine success in life*. New York: Dutton/Plume.

Temple, C. (1991). Seven readings of a folktale: Literary theory in the classroom. *New Advocate, 4*, 29.

Thaut, M. H., Moore, D. M., & Peterson, D.A. (2003). Correlates of cortical plasticity in musical template learning. *Journal of Cognitive Neuroscience*. In *Gray matters: The arts and the brain*. Retrieved from *http://www.dana.org/books/*.

Thiessen, D., Matthias, M., & Smith, J. (Eds). (1998). *The wonderful world of mathematics: A critically annotated list of children's books in mathematics*. Reston, VA: National Council of Teachers of Mathematics.

3M Corporation. (2001). Polishing your presentation, *3M Meeting Network Articles*. Retrieved from *http://3m.com/meetingnetwork/readingroom/meetingguide_pres.html*.

Tierney, R., Soter, A., & O'Flahavan, J. (1989). The effects of reading and writing upon thinking critically. *Reading Research Quarterly, 24*, 134–173.

Tishman, S. (2003). *MoMA's visual thinking curriculum: Project Zero investigated the educational impact and potential of the Museum of Modern Art's Visual Thinking Curriculum*. Cambridge, MA: Harvard Graduate School of Education, Project Zero. Retrieved from *http://www.pz.harvard.edu/Research/MoMA.htm*.

Tomlinson, C., & Brown, C. (1996). *Essentials of children's literature* (2nd ed.). Boston, MA: Allyn & Bacon.

Tompkins, G. (1990). *Teaching writing: Balancing process and product.* Upper Saddle River, NJ: Merrill/Prentice Hall.

Tompkins, G. (1997). *Literacy for the 21st century.* Upper Saddle River, NJ: Prentice Hall.

Tompkins, G. (2003). *Literacy for the 21st century.* Upper Saddle River, NJ: Merrill/Prentice Hall.

Tompkins, G., & McGee, L. (1993). *Teaching reading with literature: Case studies to action plans.* New York: Merrill.

Took, K. S., & Weiss, D. S. (1994). The relationship between heavy metal and rap music and adolescent turmoil: Real or artifact? *Adolescence, 29,* 613–621.

Torrance, E. P. (1962). *Guiding creative talent.* Upper Saddle River, NJ: Prentice Hall.

Torrance, E. P. (1973). *Is creativity teachable?* Bloomington, IN: Phi Delta Kappa.

Tortello, R. (2004, October). Tableaux vivants in the literature classroom. *Reading Teacher, 58*(2), 206–208.

Trelease, J. (1995). *The read-aloud handbook.* New York: Penguin.

Trusty, J., & Oliva, G. (1994). The effects of arts and music education on students' self-concept. *Update: Applications of Research in Music Education, 13*(1), 23–28.

Trudeau, M. (2005, April 26). Inner city teacher takes no shortcuts to success. *All Things Considered,* National Public Radio.

Tunnell, M. O., & Jacobs, J. S. (1989). Using "real" books: Research findings on literature-based reading instruction. *Reading Teacher, 42,* 470–477.

Upitis, R., & Smithrim, K. (2003, April). *Learning through the arts:* Kingston, Ontario: Royal Conservatory of Music.

U.S. Department of Education. (2005, March). *Arts education: Improving students' academic performance.* (Televised series viewed at *http://www.connectlive.com/events/ednews/.)*

Valliant, G. E., & Valliant, C. O. (1981). Natural history of male psychological health, X: Work as a predictor of positive mental health. *American Journal of Psychiatry, 138,* 1433–1440.

Venturelli, S. (2001). *From the information economy to the creative economy: Moving culture to the center of international public policy.* Centre for Arts and Culture. Retrieved from *http://www.culturalpolicy.org.*

Vitz, K. (1983). A review of empirical research in drama and language. *Children's Theater Review, 32*(4), 17–25.

Vreeland, S. (1999). *Girl in hyacinth blue.* Denver: McMurry & Beck.

Vygotsky, L. S. (1978). *Mind in society.* Cambridge, MA: Harvard University Press.

Vygotsky, L. S. (1986). *Thought and language.* Cambridge, MA: MIT Press.

Wachowiak, F., & Clements, R. (2005). *Emphasis art* (8th ed.) New York: HarperCollins.

Wagner, B. J. (1988). A review of empirical research in drama and language. *Language Arts, 65*(1), 46–55.

Wagner, B.J. (1998). *Educational drama and language arts.* Portsmouth, NH: Heinemann.

Waldorf, L.A. (2002). *The professional artist as public school educator: A research report of the Chicago Arts Partnerships in Education, 2000–2001.* Los Angeles: UCLA Graduate School of Education & Information Studies.

Wallace, G. (1926). *The art of thought.* New York: Harcourt Brace.

Wallin, N., Merker, B., & Brown, S. (1999). *The origins of music. A Bradford book.* Cambridge, MA: MIT Press.

Walling, D. (2001, April). Rethinking visual arts education: A convergence of influences. *Phi Delta Kappan,* 626–631.

Warren, J. (1991). *Piggyback songs for school.* Torrance, CA: Frank Shaffer.

Weinberger, N. (1998, November). The music in our minds. *Educational Leadership.* 36–40.

Weinberger, N. M. (2003). The nucleus basalis and memory codes: Auditory cortical plasticity and the induction of specific, associative behavioral memory. *Neurobiology of Learning and Memory 80*(3): 268–284. In *Gray matters: The arts and the brain.* Retrieved from *http://www.dana.org/books/radiotv/gm_0902.cfm.*

Welch, N. (1995). *Schools, communities, and the arts: A research compendium.* Washington, DC: National Endowment for the Arts.

Wiggins, G., & McTighe, J. (1998). *Understanding by design.* Alexandria, VA: Association for Supervision and Curriculum Development.

Wiggins, J. (1991). *Composition in the classroom: A tool for teaching.* Reston, VA: Music Educators National Conference.

Wiggins, J., & McTighe, J. (2005). Understanding by design. Alexandria, VA: Association for Supervision and Curriculum Development.

Wigram, T., & Backer, J. (1999). *Clinical applications of music therapy in psychiatry.* London: Jessica Kingsley.

Williams, J. (2002). Reading comprehension strategies and teacher preparation. In A. Farstrup & S. J. Samuels (Eds.), *What research has to say about reading instruction.* Newark, DE: International Reading Association.

Wilson, Egan, K. (1999). *Children's minds: Talking rabbits and clockwork oranges.* New York: Teachers College Press.

Wingert, P., & Brant, M. (2005, August 15). Reading your baby's mind. *Newsweek.* Retrieved from *http:newsweek.com.*

Winner, E. (1983). Children's sensitivity to aesthetic properties in line drawings. In D. R. Rogers & J. A. Sloboda (Eds.), *The acquisition of symbolic skills.* London: Plenum.

Winner, E., & Hetland, L. (2000a.). The arts and academic improvement: What the evidence shows. *The Journal of Aesthetic Education.* Retrieved from *http://www.pz.harvard.edu/REAPhtm.*

Winner, E., & Hetland, L. (2000b, November 1.). Does studying the arts enhance academic achievement? *Education Week, 64,* 46.

Wiske, M. (1997). *Teaching for understanding: Linking research with practice.* San Francisco: Jossey-Bass.

Wolfe, P. (2001). *Brain matters: Translating research into classroom practice.* Alexandria: VA: Association for Supervision and Curriculum Development.

Wolfman, J. (2004). *Stories for reader's theatre.* Portsmouth, NH: Libraries Unlimited.

Wood, K. (1988). Guiding students through informational text. *Reading Teacher, 41,* 912–920.

Yen, W., & Ferrara, S. (1997). The Maryland School Performance Assessment Program: Performance assessment with psychometric quality suitable for high stages usage. *Journal of Educational and Psychological Measurement, 57,* 60–84.

Young, P. (2003, January–February). Don't leave your students playing the blues. *Principal, 83*(3), 220–225.

Zemelman, S., Daniels, H., & Hyde, A. (1998.) *Best practice: New standards for teaching and learning in America's schools.* Portsmouth, NH: Heinemann.

Zull, J. (2005). Arts, neuroscience, and learning. *New Horizons for Learning.* Retrieved from *http://www.newhorizons.org.*

Appendix A

Developmental Stages and the Arts

Use these general guidelines to observe for cues to developmental needs. Forcing children to "move ahead" does not work and can harm. Consult a pediatrician if a child does not seem to be developing appropriately.

Important Points

- Children develop at different rates depending on genetic inheritance and experiences.
- Developmental benchmarks are flexible. They *describe* and should not *prescribe* what a child can do. Any child may be atypical of a description.
- Children learn in an integrated way. It is vital that lessons address multiple areas of development (e.g., cognitive, emotional, social, and physical).
- Development is more spiral than sequential. There is a gradual building during which children may skip or reverse stages depending on their familiarity with activities. It is natural to regress to "messing around" when a new tool is introduced.
- Patterns of development are more obvious in early years before culture and education do major sculpting of children's minds.
- Interest plays a forceful role in individuating development.
- Developmental stages become muddied as diversity increases. Predicting becomes more difficult.
- Instruction alters the ability to see and to do. Use of more detail and variety show the child is keenly observing.
- Without good teaching, a student's interest and development can stall.
- Finding a personal medium is one of life's mysteries. Imagine Disney without film or McCartney without the guitar. It is hard to predict how a child will respond to media/tools. Diverse experiences are vital.

General Patterns

Artistic development parallels cognitive, physical, and socioemotional growth outlined by theorists such as Piaget, Erikson, Maslow, and Gardner (see Chapter 2). In general, it proceeds from:

General to specific. Gross motor to fine motor, wholes to parts, with increasing attention to detail. Physically, children grow increasingly stronger and more coordinated and have more endurance and balance.

Uncontrolled to controlled. From exploration of media/body, tools, and skills to increasing control.

Known to seen. Concentration causes children to notice/see more. What they see changes what they know.

Me to others. Children become increasingly group/peer oriented, with steady growth in interest in the community and world.

Single to multiple perspectives, with increasing use of evidence to draw conclusions. As children become more logical and more systematic, they gain ability to self-evaluate.

"Abstract" to realistic (for art), as they first draw images that represent the "known" and show feelings. These evolve into realistic images, which peaks about age 11.

Gender awareness. Children increasingly are aware of boy/girl differences and tend to conform to cultural expectations.

Primary: Ages 5–7

Young children are egocentric and perceive things as happening to, for, or because of them. They see one point of view or one aspect at a time. Attention span is short, and short-term memory is limited. They are concrete and learn best through physical and multisensory activities.

Characteristics

- Respond to/through the arts, with feelings and emotion
- Motivated by curiosity
- Little concept of age, time, distance, or culture
- Have concern for others and want to comfort
- Assume events are causally related because they occur together
- Give life to inanimate objects (animism—e.g., thinks moon is smiling because of a curved shape); think objects move for a purpose (e.g., trees move to get air)
- Begin spelling, writing, and enjoy telling stories
- Become increasingly independent; try new activities
- Can compare and contrast sounds, pictures, and movements
- Can create original art, songs, stories, and dance
- Can dramatize and dance familiar actions and events
- Can explore, experiment, play, and pretend using art materials, props, music, and movement
- Need encouragement to experiment
- Need an inviting environment, rich in sensory stimulation
- Work with repetition and patterns (e.g., 3s, word play)
- Need frequent rest periods

Potential Problems

- Working in groups
- Understanding why, how, and when questions
- Distinguishing fact from fantasy
- Understanding relationships of parts to whole
- Sorting or grouping by function or dimension
- Making comparisons to achieve understanding
- One-to-one correspondence

Suggestions

- Frequently call children by name and give feedback.
- Use concrete examples and activities. Show rather than tell.
- Ask children to show (arts), not just tell.
- Limit focus of discussions (e.g., target arts elements).
- Use humor. Play with words, terms, and labels. Sing and chant.
- Limit lessons to 20 minutes and use variety.
- Ask children to get a "personal space."
- Make connections to children's lives: "Raise your hand if . . ."
- Refrain from discussing time periods and using the passive voice.
- Ask children to pretend or "be" (drama/role-play).
- Ask about sizes of objects and nearness and farness.
- Allow movement choices and ask the reasons for choices.
- Write and recite poetry and paint pictures that depict themes such as nature, school, and family. Encourage discussion.
- Exhibit children's artwork so it is easily seen.
- Make portfolios to keep favorite stories, photos, and artwork.
- Encourage children to select favorite musical recordings.
- Encourage improvisations and storytelling using imaginary props.

Intermediate: (approximately ages 7—9)

Children want to learn to control techniques, skills, and language/vocabulary. Direct them to "fill up the space" and "use variety to create interest," Children improve quickly when taught such basics. Amenability to instruction contrasts with the previous stage. When given examples of how to use dance or poetic elements, students catch on quickly but need time to practice. Teachers need to be knowledgeable about arts content and skill, thorough and systematic in their presentations, encouraging, and disciplined so that time on task is created.

Characteristics

- Understand past and present; can sequence/order
- Egocentric (until about age 9) but can now see other viewpoints

- Understand relationship between parts and whole
- See a sharp line between good and evil and want justice
- Can sort by function and dimension
- Longer short-term memory, but still limited attention span
- Beginning to perceive differences between the sexes
- Need activity alternated with rest
- Want to be independent; get annoyed at conformity
- Accept defeat poorly; need encouragement and feedback
- Want to excel and love to be challenged
- Learning to abide by rules and play fair
- Place high priority on friends
- Interested in the artist's role in the creative process
- Like to "show they know" (e.g., point out differences between themselves and representations in paintings)
- Interested in textures, colors, characters, sports, humor, and trivia (e.g., Guinness World Records)
- Like to find out why and how things work and collect things
- Like to be physically active
- Make believe and use imagination (e.g., what-if)
- Want attention, and all want a turn
- Work in small groups

Middle Graders: Ages 11—13

Children are trying to find out who they are. They begin to strive to be like friends. The peer group is increasingly important. Cliques form. Girls and boys begin to differ greatly. This is a period of rapid growth during which girls grow quicker. There is more interest in the opposite sex.

Characteristics

- Can make hypotheses without direct experiences; can do some abstract thinking (e.g., "What does this mean?")
- Conservation and reversibility learned
- Like to discuss more complex ideas (e.g., mood, perspective)
- Want to know how and why
- Interested in hearing others' ideas
- Anxious to explore different lifestyles
- Increasingly independent and begin to test rules and limits
- Will choose peers over adults
- Adopt social values; look to adult behavior rather than words
- Link good morals to rewards
- Industrious, like to make things and accomplish goals
- Competitive urge is strong; enjoy team and group activity
- Develop special interests and hobbies

Suggestions

- Partner and use small groups; separate boys and girls at times.
- Ask for evidence to support conclusions (why-how questions after what-where-when questions).

- Limit historical information and connect to daily life.
- Use humor (e.g., riddles and tongue twisters).
- Focus on art and music about animals, children, and friends.
- Ask students to "make believe" and tell or show.
- Ask students to find paintings or other art that fits into categories (e.g., landscapes) or ask for categories.
- Give challenges (e.g., "who can find the most . . . ").
- Ask to pretend they are in artwork, be a character, and say something or create a tableau.
- Give generous feedback. Use student names.
- Ask students to compare and contrast (e.g., music).
- Tell interesting facts about artists and process/media.
- Give responsibility (e.g., group leader) and allow some competition.
- Invite focus on one work to become "experts."
- Ask for alternate ways to express or understand.
- Use a mini-lesson and then ask for application.

- Make clear criteria for quality work.
- Survey interests and connect to students' lives.
- Study careers related to the arts (e.g., museum curator).

Teens: (approximately ages 12+)

Youth begin to develop "individual style" and personal interpretation in artistic interests and expressions. They should have basic arts literacy so they can move on to experimenting and applying ideas in unique ways. Copying and imitating are not considered "creative." From here on, further artistic development is contingent upon increasing involvement with specialists who can challenge young people. Students become frustrated when their efforts do not produce the quality they envision and need help learning to self-evaluate, seek alternative solutions, and set goals.

Appendix B

Adapting Arts-Based Lessons for Students with Diverse Needs

Use these guidelines to increase appropriateness.

- Increase concreteness. Add pictures, props, labels, charts, nametags, etc. Example: Post charts of arts concepts with symbols for *line*, *shape*, and *color*.
- Move from easy to more difficult, shorter to longer. Example: Teach pantomime before verbal improvisation.
- Repeat activities and plan time for exploration. Experiment more with a new material like clay.
- Teach key points explicitly, especially abstract concepts. Increase amount of labeling, modeling, examples, and practice.
- Use more hands-on activities for those lacking verbal skills. Examples: art making, pantomime, use of rhythm instruments (e.g., home-made shakers and found sounds).
- Design challenge so students feel successful. The arts liberate so children can surprise teachers with insights and show more concentration.
- Instead of praising work, use "I see . . ." statements.
- Provide mixed group work in the arts to use "peer power."

Students with Physical Disabilities

- Limit space to make it easier for them to manage.
- Use more verbal activities for those with limited movements.
- Match students with a "buddy" who can quietly explain to those with hearing impairments, help move a wheelchair, or clear an area for those with limited mobility.
- Find ways to involve those in wheelchairs. Expect participation and use touch to calm, direct, and assist.
- Adapt dance and pantomime for a student's most mobile part (e.g., emphasize gestures if hands and arms are mobile).
- Paint mental pictures and give clear details. Describe art materials, tools, pictures, and props. Allow students with visual impairments to explore with touch.
- Place students with hearing impairments close to music to feel the vibrations. Seat students to easily see your face, especially if they can lip-read. A window behind you will cast a shadow on your face.

- Don't exaggerate speech. This distorts sounds students are taught to notice.
- Repeat other students' comments for those with hearing loss.
- Use more visuals: pictures, props, gestures, directions.

Students with Emotional Disabilities

- Some have difficulty with self-control; others are withdrawn.
- A consistent and supportive environment is important. Students need extra feedback and small successes. Start with energizers and warm-ups, to increase comfort.
- Students with short attention spans need to change tasks more often. Be ready to cut an activity short.
- Move in slow increments to increase concentration. Select energizers that increase focus.
- Movement using large muscles is often successful (e.g., dance and drama (especially pantomime) and mural making.)

Students from Diverse Language and Cultural Backgrounds

- All children can participate in dance, art, and drama that call for nonverbal work. The arts are universal languages.
- Cultural connections with holidays, customs and people foster diversity. Use multiethnic music, visual art, and dance activities. Invite guest artists and students to share arts from their cultures.
- Folk literature is universal, and it is a good source of multicultural art. Encourage student storytelling and use these for drama, dance, art, and music responses.
- English vocabulary can be taught through children's literature (e.g., wordless picture books) and cultural songs translated into English. Use dual language nametags or hats for characters during drama (e.g., stepsister, mother).

Children with Speech Difficulties

- Provide a relaxed atmosphere so students have fun and forget about speech problems. Engage with dance, art, and pantomime.
- Use oral activities that have a "play" feel, like energizers.
- Allow students to speak through a puppet and use pictures and props.
- Give opportunities to sing, speak, and hear others use creative and conversational language.
- To lessen stuttering, use rhythmic activities, singing, unison choral speaking, and dramatic role-playing.

Students with Academic Gifts and Talents

- Allow students to bypass basics.
- Academically gifted children are usually ahead of peers in language. They excel in dialogue, improvisation, and writing.
- Allow students to lead arts activities (e.g., narrate a pantomime or direct poetry performances (Ready Reference 5.3).
- Offer long-term projects (e.g., playwriting, puppet shows).
- Locate mentors for more in-depth work (e.g., artists, musicians, composers, dancers, writers, actors).
- Encourage group work even if students want to work independently. Group work in the arts gives chances to learn social skills like cooperation and active listening.

Appendix C

Assessment Tools and Resources

Sample 1: Arts-Based Interest Inventory

Name _____   **Nickname** _____

Birthday _____   **Favorite Color** _____

What are your favorites?

- Foods
- Sports
- TV shows or movies
- Books
- Songs and music
- Hobbies/collections
- Things about school

1. Do you have any pets?
2. What do you enjoy doing with your family?
3. What do you do well?
4. How do you like to spend your free time?
5. Where have you traveled?
6. Do you belong to any clubs or organizations?
7. Do you play or would you like to play a musical instrument?
8. What dances do you know?

9. What museums have you visited?
10. Have you ever been in or seen a live play?
11. What have you written? Any poetry or songs?
12. What types of art do you like, make or look at?
13. Who do you admire? Why?
14. Do you like to act or pretend?
15. Do you like to tell stories? Listen to stories?
16. What makes you laugh? How do you make other people laugh?
17. What artist would you like to meet (musician, dancer, actor, etc.)? What three questions would you ask him or her?
18. What type of literature do you enjoy reading?
19. If you could write a book, what would it be about?
20. What would you like to know more about or be able to do in the arts?

Sample 2: Teacher Self-Evaluation of Integrated Arts Lessons

Reflect on your teaching using these questions. Think of evidence for each. Rate yourself from 1 to 4 with 4 being very evident (use with a videotape and peer observation).

1. How satisfied were you with the overall lesson? Why?
2. To what extent did students learn important concepts and skills in both the art area and another curricular area?
3. What evidence do you have for what students learned in the art form?
4. How did you focus on lesson objectives/criteria for assessment from the start?
5. How was mood set in the lesson? How did you develop interest?
6. How did you engage head-heart-hands during the lesson?
7. What adaptations were made for student needs?

8. How did you show enthusiasm for the art form? How did students respond?
9. How did you cause students to be involved in creative and artistic ways (CPS modeling, open questions, coaching, etc.)?
10. How did the lesson feel? How comfortable were you and the students during the lesson?
11. How were audiences used to increase quality work?
12. What discipline prevention/intervention and management strategies were used and to what effect?
13. What risks did you take?
14. How did you use the 10 Arts Integration Blueprint principles?

Sample 3: Student Checklist of Artistic and Creative Skills

Observe students during arts listening, viewing, and doing. Rate each student behavior using a 1–4 scale, with 4 =very evident and 1=not evident. Next to the rating, date when evident (3+).

Student Name _____

_____   1. Uses the arts to communicate ideas and feelings.
_____   2. Intentionally uses CPS strategies such as SCAMPER and brainstorming.
_____   3. Uses arts vocabulary to describe what is seen, heard, and felt.
_____   4. Uses a variety of arts tools, media, and techniques.
_____   5. Seeks alternative ways to understand and express through the arts.
_____   6. Takes risks to offer personal interpretations.
_____   7. Gives supporting evidence for opinions.
_____   8. Compares and contrasts using prior arts experiences.
_____   9. Builds on previous arts experiences.
_____ 10. Notices details and patterns.
_____ 11. Is open to and respectful of alternative perspectives.
_____ 12. Shows interest in arts reflections and discussions.
_____ 13. Offers both first impressions and revisions of impressions.
_____ 14. Works collaboratively.
_____ 15. Works independently.
_____ 16. Is aware of special strengths in arts areas.

Sample 4: Class Checklist/Drama Rubric

Discuss the rubric at the start of the school year. Encourage self-evaluation throughout the year. Create a class list to regularly rate the degree to which each student shows evidence of these drama skills. Level 1=low evidence. Level 2 =some moderate evidence. Level 3=the highest level. Level 3 is described below.

Level 3

Body: Very able to coordinate and control body. Uses appropriate energy. Displays sensory awareness and expression. Uses gestures and facial expressions skillfully to communicate through pantomime and to accompany verbal work. Responds appropriately to nonverbal communication of others.
Verbal expression: Speaks clearly. Uses appropriate variety in volume, rate, tone and pitch, pause, stress, emphasis, and inflection. Is fluent and can improvise dialogue.

Focus: Can concentrate and stay involved. Makes others believe in the realness of the character. Follows directions.
Imagination: Uses flexible creative thinking to solve drama problems. Contributes unique ideas and elaborates on others' ideas. Shows spontaneity.
Evaluation: Gives constructive feedback and uses suggestions of others. Can self-evaluate and adapt own behavior.
Social skills: Works cooperatively with groups: listens and responds to others.
Audience etiquette: Attends, listens, and responds appropriately to others' performances.

Sample 5: Art Project Self/Peer Evaluation Rubric

Art projects will be graded using these criteria. Your "Reflections" paper will be used, along with your project and any drafts as evidence. Self-evaluate before turning in your work. N=no evidence, 1=little evidence, 2=satisfactory evidence, 3=strong evidence.

Criteria	Rating
Directions followed	____
Information gathered from several sources	____
Risk taking and experimentation (tools, techniques, and media)	____
Original (new to you) ideas used	____
Project completeness	____
Organized reflections with examples	____
Met deadline	____

1. What did you learn most from this project?
2. How did you feel about your product?
3. What obstacles did you have to overcome while creating your product?
4. Would you like to publicly exhibit your art?

Sample 6: Dance: Student Reflection

Student Name _____   **Date** _____

1. How did you feel about the dance making and sharing?
2. What did you contribute to the group work on dance making?
3. What was the most interesting thing about the process of creating the dance or the dance itself?
4. What problems or obstacles came up during the dance creation? How were they solved?
5. How do you take risks and experiment with BEST dance elements?
6. How did you encourage other students?
7. How did you show involvement and concentration?
8. What did you learn that you can now use in the future?

Sample 7: Anecdotal Records for Integrated Dance Lessons

Directions: Place a sticky note for each student on a clipboard. During group planning and during sharing note observations about individuals. Place sticky notes in student portfolios. **Comment on:**

- Collaboration skills
- Risk taking and experimentation
- Positive attitude
- Use of various body parts and moves
- Use of energy
- Use of space
- Use of time
- Concentration
- Dance form: beginning–middle–end
- Creativity (ideas used in new ways)

Sample 8: Music Student Self-Evaluation

Student Name _____   **Date** _____

1. How have you used music to express ideas and feelings in other subjects?
2. What have you learned about making music that has helped you?
3. What have you learned about listening to music?
4. What were your favorite integrated music lessons/projects? Why?
5. What would you like to learn more about in music?
6. How do you feel about singing together in class?
7. How is music related to real life?

Sample 9: Literary Arts Checklist

Name _____   **Date Observed** _____

1. Chooses to read in free time.
2. Has favorite authors.
3. Has favorite genre.
4. Uses literary elements to discuss and evaluate books.
5. Uses books and authors as "models" for own writing.
6. Uses art elements to comment on illustrations.
7. Connects personal experiences to books.
8. Shares feelings and insights about books.
9. Responds to books through a variety of art forms.
10. Participates in book discussions by preparing and by leading.

Sample 10: Haiku/Watercolor Rubric

Directions: Use for self, peer, and teacher evaluation. Rate 1–3 with 3=highest evidence and 1=low evidence. N=no evidence.

Criteria	Rating
1. Used 5–7–5 syllable pattern	____
2. Nature ideas	____
3. Original variations	____
4. Experimentation (words and watercolor techniques)	____
5. Explained choices	____
6. Connected to Japanese culture	____

Arts Folios

Each student needs a container to keep evidence of growth toward grade-level benchmarks in music, art, drama, and dance/movement. This evidence serves as a motivator for students to move toward more independent learning. Students need access to folios to check their own progress and should be able to add dated evidence to document progress. *Note*: Keep a range of work samples, not just "good" work.

Organization

1. Student decorated front cover.
2. Goals (benchmarks) inside cover. By the end of the year each student should be able to. . . (Music, Art, Drama, Dance). Examples:
   - Use vocabulary/key concepts to talk/write about each art.
   - Use techniques/skills to MAKE each art form.
   - LOOK AT and/or LISTEN TO each art form and show understanding (what it means/feels).
   - Show understanding of the special way each art form contributes to culture and history.
   - Show understanding of how each art form is a unique way to express, receive, or respond to thoughts or feelings.
   - Show growth in using creative problem solving (CPS).
3. Dated work examples that show progress towards benchmarks. (*Note:* Only items that relate to the previously listed goals are included.)

   EXAMPLES:

   Arts Vocabulary Evidence (Goal #1)
   - Word rings, webs, and charts (targeted arts vocabulary)
   - Word wall folder/dictionary (e.g., mini word wall on tag board)

   Performances/Exhibitions (Goal/benchmark #3)
   - Checklist of audience etiquette used (self, peer, teacher)
   - Written or art responses that show specific benchmarks
   - Logs of attendance at nonschool sponsored concerts, etc.

Suggestions: Maintaining and Using Arts Folios

1. Start a class ARTS WORD WALL from which students can choose words to learn.
2. Number folios so students can easily keep them in alphabetical order.
3. Glue generic goals to the inside of everyone's folder, but have each child set some individual targets (e.g., self-chosen arts words to learn each week).
4. Explain the goals and folio items will show how much students are learning. Encourage students to focus on the goals and look for evidence to put in folios.

5. Discuss each goal individually at the start of the year. Refer to goals throughout the day (e.g., when you read aloud connect fluency (EAR = expression, accuracy, rate) with drama skills.
6. Use the folios as motivation to learn. *Example:* "I'll be looking for people who are concentrating during the performance. I have my clipboard with stickies to make notes. I'll give you the sticky notes for your Arts Folio."
7. Target four or five students per day/week for observation (e.g., check for focus during drama/dance). Use class observation checklists or individual checklists.
8. Do 1–3 minute individual conferences to review folios. Use an egg timer. Try "doing lunch" with students for conferences.
9. Schedule folio time each week for students to look at work and note progress (e.g., with a partner). Bring the class together for students to share one thing added.
10. Monthly, ask students to look at goals and think about what to do to keep growing. Do in small groups or as a whole class. Direct by giving examples of goals and ways to meet goals. *Example:* "Everyone has a goal to pronounce, spell, and tell/show the meanings of words in drama. I am putting a check on each word on your word ring for each of the three things. You need three checks to show you know the word. How can you learn more words?"
11. Portfolio Presentations: Partner students to share folders once a month. Come together as a whole to share what was learned from partners.
12. Make the folios the focus of parent conferences. Ask students to show their folders and share with parents evidence of progress toward goals.
13. Tie grades to folio evidence by creating a rubric of what needs to be documented to get an A, B, etc. Do this by grading period or as an end-of-the-year rubric with progress reports during the year, as long as students and parents are clear about progress in meeting the year-end grade goals.
14. Let students keep their folders at the end of the year.

Assessment Resources

Internet Resources

Glossary of assessment terms: *www.hbem.com/library/glossary.htm*.

Example standards-based tools: *www.exemplars.com/*

American Association for Supervision and Curriculum Development (ASCD): *www.ascd.org (books, videos, journal)*

Books and Articles

Allen, D. (Ed.). (1998). *Assessing student learning*. New York: Teachers College Press.

Armstrong, C. (1994). *Designing assessment in art*. Reston, VA: National Art Education Association.

Baker, R., Boughton, D., Freedman, K., Horowitz, R., & Ingram, D. (2004, April). *Artistic production as evidence of learning in interdisciplinary contexts*. Annual Meeting of the American Educational Research Association, San Diego, CA.

Beattie, D. (1994, March). The mini-portfolio: Locus of a successful performance examination. *Art Education*, 14–18.

Bellanca, J., Chapman, C., & Swartz, E. (1994). *Multiple assessments for multiple intelligences*. Palatine, IL: IRI/Skylight Training and Publishing.

Blythe, T., Allen, D., Powell, T., & Schieffelin, B. (1999). *Looking together at student work: A companion guide to assessing student learning*. New York: Teachers College Press.

Costa, A., & Kallik, B. (2000). *Assessing and reporting on habits of mind*. Alexandria, VA: Association for Supervision and Curriculum Development.

Danielson, C., & Abrutyn, L. (1997). *An introduction to using portfolios in the classroom*. Alexandria, VA: Association for Supervision and Curriculum Development.

Eisner, E. W. (1998). Reshaping assessment in education: The kind of schools we need. *Educational Leadership*, 132–154.

Iwanicki, E. F. (2001, February). Focusing teacher evaluations on student learning. *Educational Leadership*, *58*(5), 57–59.

Johnson, P. H., et al. (1995, July). Assessment of teaching and learning in "literature-based" classrooms. *Teaching Education, 11*, 359–371.

Khattri, N., Kane, M., & Reeve, A. (1995, November). How performance assessments affect teaching and learning. *Educational Leadership*, 80–83.

Lewin, L., & Shoemaker, B. (1998). Great performances: Creating classroom-based assessment tasks. Alexandria, VA: Association for Supervision and Curriculum Development.

MacGregor, R. (1992, November). A short guide to alternative assessment practices. *Art Education*, 34–38.

Manebur, D. (1994, March). Assessment as a classroom activity. *Music Educators Journal*, 23–47.

Performance assessment topic pack. (2001). Alexandria, VA: Association for Supervision and Curriculum Development.

Popham, J. (2003). *Test better teach better: Instructional role of assessment*. Alexandria, VA: Association for Supervision and Curriculum Development.

Stiggins, R. (2002, June). Assessment crisis: The absence of assessment for learning. *Phi Delta Kappan*, 758–765.

Suskie, L. (2004). *Assessing student learning*. Boston: Anker.

Transforming classroom grading. (2000). Alexandria, VA: Association for Supervision and Curriculum Development.

Wiggins, G. (1997). *Educative assessment*. San Francisco, CA: Jossey-Bass.

Appendix D

Discipline Prevention and Intervention

Prevention

___ Think of the classroom as a living room. Bring in rugs, art, plants, and music.

___ Be the teacher you would want for yourself. Model expectations for attitude, courtesy, respect, and enthusiasm for learning. Use active listening techniques with students.

___ Enjoy the students. Laugh with them and share their humor. No sarcasm.

___ Write down specific positive behaviors on stickies and give to students to keep in a "Positive Post-Its" folder.

___ Post the few rules and consequences that are necessary. Start out firm and allow students to "earn" more and more freedom.

___ Involve students in making rules. Role play: "Show me how you'll look when you are listening," and "Show me a scene of showing respect."

___ Teach with variety and connect to real life. Change methods. Integrate the arts!

___ Give choices within limits (e.g., "When you finish___ you can either ___ or ___").

___ Capitalize on interest to boost success as much as 25 times.

___ Get attention before starting with signals (e.g., a rhythm, chant, sign language). Stop if you don't have attention and state your expectation in a businesslike way (e.g., "I need . . ." use every pupil response).

___ Set up predictable routines: Open and end the day with a poem, song, or riddle. Assign jobs and responsibilities. Post a daily agenda. Tell the lesson focus and goals.

___ Let students know you read books and like to dance, sing, and draw. No one wants to be around blah know-nothing teachers. Vary your voice (no monotone lectures).

___ Ask open questions to get more thought and participation (e.g., "What did you learn about . . . ?" versus "Who was the main character?").

___ Foster intrinsic motivation. Focus on learning for its own worth and its relation to the world. Extrinsic rewards can harm interest so use stickers and stamps sparingly and only as "symbols" of hard work. If you use extrinsics, make them: (1) intermittent and phase out as soon as possible, (2) focused on

privileges versus "things," and (3) show students they are making progress toward goals. Vague certificates at the end of the week are ineffective.

___ Let students choose where to sit until they show they cannot learn in that spot. Show them how to establish personal space.

___ Expect that students will have bad days. Give a coupon to turn in homework late one time a grading period. Allow use of the "pass" option, occasionally, during questioning.

___ Send silent signals. Use sign language to communicate, nod your head, and make eye contact.

___ Remember to start fresh each day. Greet children and make them feel welcome.

Discipline Interventions

___ Use proximity. Stand close and circulate as you teach. Vary the pattern so everyone has a chance to be close. Walk about three steps toward a nonlistener and he or she will usually attend, or stand between inattentive students. Use the two-finger touch technique or touch a student's paper or desk to focus attention.

___ Ignore behavior unless it interferes with learning. Follow up with a private conference with students who perpetually cause problems. Some teachers keep a camera handy.

___ Encourage shy or hesitant speakers. Nod and smile as they speak.

___ Never threaten, but if you promise, carry it out. Be consistent.

___ Do not publicly humiliate. Talk to repeat offenders privately. Focus on what you observed, what you expect, and why. Ask, "What can you do to solve your problem?" Set behavior goals.

___ Lower volume or slow rate or pause to get attention.

___ Elevate with descriptive feedback. Say, "John, you put three different colors on your quilt piece so far" (praise controls and may seem empty).

___ Never gossip about student problems with other teachers. This is unprofessional. Never talk about students in front of other students as if they aren't listening.

____ Ensure that time-outs include a chance to return when the student agrees to follow the rules. Ask what rule was broken and discuss how to behave the next time a similar situation arises.

____ Use hierarchical and appropriate consequences. A warning is a courtesy we all appreciate. Take away one minute or two of recess, instead of a whole recess. Never assign sentence writing as a consequence because writing should not be a punishment. Loss of a privilege is often an appropriate measure.

____ On-the-spot assistance: Make eye contact, move toward the student, and state your expectation (e.g., "Joe, I want you to sit in your chair and start writing"). Give THE EYE. Attack the problem, not the person. Mention names (e.g., "This morning Pat was saying she thought . . . ."). Say a name before asking a question to help a student "tune in."

____ State what you want children *to do* versus *not to do*. Instead of "Don't talk," say "Listen." Address the group as a first step: "There are people who are talking who need to listen."

____ Negative remarks don't solve problems. "Don't talk" (negative) versus "Susan, what do you need to do, and how can I help you do it?" (positive).

Appendix E

Book Report Alternatives

Directions: Use these suggestions to give students choices to show understanding of a book and further investigate interests.

Poetry

Poem match: Find or write a poem that goes with the book.

Poem patterns: Write a cinquain, diamante, or clerihew about the story, a main point, or a character (Ready Reference 5.2).

Poetry alive: Share a poem using a *Poetry Performance* strategy (Ready Reference 5.3): choral, antiphonal, cumulative.

Writing and Speaking

Adjective blitz: List 10 adjectives that describe a character.

Book dedications: Dedicate a book to a character.

Call an author: Plan the questions for a conference call.

Connecting: Write about how the book connects to your life.

Copycat story: Write a story using the same title, theme, or pattern of the book.

Current events: Tell how a character would react to an event.

Decision making: Take a familiar story. Brainstorm what would have happened if a character made a different decision.

Demonstration: Show something you learned from the book.

Diary: Write several diary entries as if you were a character.

Dictionary: Make a dictionary of special words in the book.

Episode cards: Put plot events on cards to tell the story.

Episode or sequel: What happened after the story ended?

Friendship: Explain why you would like a character as a friend.

Grocery list or menu: Create a menu for the characters.

Heinz 57: Describe the book in 57 words.

Humorous event: Write or tell about the funniest part.

Important or interesting: Write or tell about the most important or interesting part.

Interview: Interview someone about a topic in the book, or write an interview between a character and the author or between you and the author.

Library recommendation: List reasons to buy the book.

Lifeline: Make a timeline of the events in a character's life.

Movie: Explain why a book could (or could not) become a movie.

Newspaper: Write stories or ads based on characters and episodes.

Next-door neighbor: Name a character you'd like as a neighbor.

Object talk: Use objects or props to tell the story.

Past to present: Bring a book character from past to present.

Principal recommendation: Tell the principal about the book.

Puzzling or exciting: Write or tell about a puzzling or exciting event.

Scrapbook. Collect and label items related to the book.

Sentence list: List the five most interesting sentences.

Simplify: Rewrite the book for a younger reader.

Summarization: Get the plot down to one paragraph.

Telegram: Summarize the book in 15–50 words.

Venn diagram: Compare to another book (literary/art elements).

Word hunt: List 10 words to describe the book or 10 unusual words in the book.

Write: Write to a favorite character (Ready Reference 5.1).

Music and Dance

Dance moves: Show movements in the story with different body parts.

Dancing characters: List dances a character might do.

Favorites list: List songs or music the main character would like.

Make a mix: Collect music that goes with the book.

Music mesh: List ways music connects to the book, such as songs, music, rhythm, melody, and instruments.

Slow motion: Show a character in slow motion at three moments.

Songwriting: Write a song or rap using literary elements in the book.

Tape record: Tape part of the story using background music.

Three-part dance: Choreograph a frozen shape–moves–frozen shape dance about a feeling or main idea in the story.

Visual Art

Book jacket: Create a book jacket to advertise the book.

Bookmarks: Make a bookmark with book quotes and a blurb.

Bulletin board: Display literary elements in the book.

Can do: Fill a can with quotes and objects about the book.

Cartoons: Draw cartoons of important scenes.

Clay model: Create a character or special object in the book.

Clothesline props: Pin up props/pictures to retell the story.

Collage: Make a collage about the book's theme.

Cooking: Prepare and serve food related to the book.

Diorama: Create a diorama that illustrates the setting.

Flannel board pieces: Use to retell the story.

Greeting card: Create a greeting card about the theme, characters, or setting.

Lost and found: Create a lost or found advertisement.

Map: Make a map of the country or imaginary land in the book.

Media and style: Experiment with the techniques in the book.

Mobile: Make a mobile with characters or objects in the book.

Mural: Create a mural about the book.

Paper dolls: Cut and dress paper dolls of the main characters.

Photography: Take pictures that relate to the story.

Postcard: Create a postcard that describes your book.

Poster ad: Create a poster that sells the book.

Relief map: Create a map of the setting using a dough recipe.

Scroll: Create a scroll to unroll and show important ideas.

Sketch: Draw an action sequence. Make into a flip book.

Stage: Use a box to design a miniature stage setting.

Travelog: Create a travelog using pictures, postcards, and magazine clips to show the settings.

Wordless book: Make a book about the story and use no words. Use any media or techniques.

Drama

Author: Become the author and tell why you wrote this story.

Author's prerogative: Tell how you would change the story if you wrote it.

Be the book: Pretend to be a book and advertise yourself.

Be a character: Tell what you think of the author.

Book review: Be a book critic. Evaluate the text and the art.

Chalk talk: Draw on the board as you tell the main story events.

Character interview: Write an interview between two characters.

Charades: Play charades based on book characters.

Commercial: Do a 1 minute ad for a book.

Dinner date: Invite a character to dinner. Create a menu.

Doll clothes: Dress a doll as one of the book's characters.

Dress up: Create a costume for a character.

Flannel board: Make felt characters and tell the story.

Minor character: Become a minor character and tell the story.

Movie producer: Evaluate the book as a possible film.

Movie version: Compare the movie or TV version with the book.

Panel discussion: Organize a pro and con panel to debate an issue. One person can be the author.

Pantomime: Do a slow-motion pantomime of a character or scene.

Pretend and write: Be a character and write to another character or keep a journal.

Puppets: Make a character puppet. Set up dialogue for the story.

Reader's theatre: Write a script and present the book.

Reporter: Be a TV reporter and report on the book. Choose an exciting part for "Live on the scene . . . ."

Sales talk: Pretend your audience consists of bookstore owners.

Skit: Mime or use dialogue in a skit about an event.

Stump the expert: Have classmates try to stump you with questions about the book.

Television show: Create a game show or news show about the book.

Unpopular position: Choose a character and defend why his or her role in a story should be changed.

Literature

Biography imagination: Pretend you visited the person. Tell or write about your visit.

Character web: Web what the main character looks like, acts like, feels like, and says.

Critical reading: Evaluate the book using literary elements.

Experiment: Do a scientific experiment associated with an informational book about science.

Fairy tales: Read several fairy tales and create your own tale using the common elements.

Folktales: Mix characters from folktales to write a new one.

Genre change: Write the book in another genre.

Historical fiction: Find music that was popular in the period.

Mystery: Put a story object inside a box. Give clues to guess the book.

Plot diagram: Draw the plot organization (linear, episodic, cumulative).

Plot graph: List the events and then graph them on a scale of good news to bad news events.

Point of view: Rewrite from the POV of another character.

Read another book: Choose another by the same author, illustrator, theme, or genre or with the same character.

Appendix F

Artistic Birthday Buddies Project

Birthday Buddies is a year-long integrated project that connects students with artists, musicians, dancers, actors, writers, singers, and composers. First help students find an artist, author, or musician born on their birthdays. Use the Internet, encyclopedias, or references like *Something About the Author* or *Krull's Lives of Musicians.* Then students may choose from these activities:

1. Gather information: biographical facts, unique artistic style, time period when the person lived and worked, geographic area(s), and birth country. *Note:* Videos are now available on many artists, authors, musicians, actors, and dancers.
2. Collect quotes from the birthday buddy, fascinating or funny facts, pictures, and other information (use websites, including publishers' websites for authors).
3. Make a time line of the artist's life and most important works. Include visual images (e.g., pictures, drawings) along the line.
4. Use a map to display the artist's birthplace, cities where she or he worked, and the person's burial site, if deceased. Use a class map for students to pin small flags with artist information.
5. Write: (1) a newspaper story with headlines about the artist; (2) a letter to the artist; (3) a news article in the role of a critic;

(4) a description of the artistic, literary, or musical work including a discussion of a favorite work; (5) a tribute to your birth mate; (6) a poem (e.g., couplet, diamante, haiku) about the person; (7) a dialogue between the artist and you, if you were to meet; (8) a scene about your birth mate visiting your school; or (9) a list of questions to ask the person.

6. Create a birthday card with a poem or riddles about the artist. Make a birthday present (e.g., a piece of art, song, or poem) or a time capsule of items your buddy would want saved for the future.
7. Create an exhibit of the artist, author, or musician's work.
8. Design a hat the artist might wear.
9. Plan a class birthday party. Students come in role and use props or costumes to share in the first person. Designate a special chair to share original work by the artist buddy. The audience should prepare questions. For summer birthdays, pick a day during the school year. For example, select a special date in the life of the birthday buddy such as a first publication, exhibit, or concert date.

Appendix G

Arts-Based Field Trips

Initial Planning

- Get information from the arts organization about the nature of the visit. Some museums, orchestras, and arts centers provide activity packets to "frontload" students for the visit.
- Visit the site prior to the trip. Check about coat racks, restrooms, seating, etc. Ask about food and water availability and regulations about eating packed lunches.
- At the site, take time to generate questions or points for pre-trip lessons. For example, list concepts or questions related to special exhibits at a museum. Pick up printed information and take pictures at the site to share.
- Meet with arts specialists and professionals and plan together. This includes informing museum professionals about standards/goals and the unit to which the field experience connects. Determine what materials students will need if they are to work at the site, such as clipboards, paper, and pencils.

Pre-Trip Activities

At integrated schools in the Dallas, Texas, ArtsPartners program, students do a series of activities before each arts/cultural event. If they are attending a concert, teachers may have students examine pictures of orchestra instruments and listen to recordings of each. Students may then mime instruments by choosing a body shape and making instrument sounds (Idea from program director Donna Farrell). Other pre-trip student preparation activities include:

- Instruct students to generate questions they want answered during the trip.
- Conduct mini-lessons on concepts that build background and put field learning into context. For example, key concepts for an art museum visit include museum, sculpture, and abstract (see Ready Reference 6.12). A trip to a concert needs to be preceded with a mini-lesson on orchestra setup and composition, the role of the conductor, and the difference between a song and a musical piece.
- Make behavior expectations and consequences clear. This means the teacher must know expectations of the site being visited. For example, art museums do not allow people to touch art works or run in the galleries. Teachers need to convey rules to students. It is worthwhile to role-play how to behave, especially how to use appropriate audience etiquette.
- Discuss guidelines about what students are expected to learn during the field trip. Explain how they will be held accountable. If students know there is to be an assessment after the trip, they are more focused on the trip's purpose. This can be accomplished by reviewing study sheets or listing general questions to be discussed after the trip. General questions include: What was the most important thing you learned? What is one thing you could find out more about? How did the experience make you feel? Why? What did the trip have to do with what we've been studying? Extension/assessment activities might include: Write about the trip and what you learned. Show what you learned with art materials, drama, music, or dance and movement. Write a poem about the trip. Write a letter convincing the teacher that field trips like these are important in school. Write a thank-you note.

During the Trip

It is important for teachers to participate as learners and as managers of their classes during the trip. Many times I've conducted student tours at museums only to have teachers stand with parents at the back of the group and talk. Teachers should be models of active learning. This includes scaffolding the experience by asking questions and coaching students to stay focused on pre-trip expectations.

Concluding the Trip

Teachers may wish to debrief students before leaving the site to let hosts know some of what students gained. Students need to be made aware that the teacher will do this so that they can prepare during the visit and not embarrass themselves and their teachers with poor responses.

Responses and Extensions

Field trips can be used to initiate a unit, take place at a special time during the unit, or be a culminating event. Whatever the timing, students should know they will be expected to "make meaning" from the experience by responding. Responses can take many forms and usually involve students in transforming and extending ideas through the arts. Students should be given choices, including letters, journal entries, songwriting, skits, and art making. At Dallas ArtsPartners schools, extensions often tie the experience into another academic subject, such as connecting time signatures or making instruments for math or science. Whatever form activities take, they should be selected to reveal the quantity and quality of the meaning making students did as a result of the visit.

Appendix H

Websites

Organizations

American Alliance for Theatre and Education: *www.aate.com*

Americans for the Arts: *www.artsusa.org*

Arts Education Partnership: *http://aep-arts.org*

ArtsEdge: *http://artsedge.kennedy-center.org*

J. Paul Getty Museum: *www.getty.edu/*

International Reading Association: *www.reading.org/*

The Kennedy Center's Partners in Education:
http://artsedge. kennedy-center.org

Leonard Bernstein Center: *http://artfullearning.com www.nashville.*
org/mc/leonard_bernstein.html

Lincoln Center Institute: *www.lcinstitute.org/*

National Art Education Association: *www.arts.arizona.edu/arted/*

National Assembly of State Arts Agencies (NASAA):
www.nasaa-arts. org

National Association for Music Education: *http://menc.org*

National Dance Educators Organization: *www.ndeo.org*

National Council for the Teachers of English: *www.ncte.org*

National Dance Association: *www.aahperd.org/nda/*

Very Special Arts: *www.vsarts.org/*

Miscellaneous Useful Arts Sites

Arts 4 Learning: *arts4learning.org/*

Arts Wire: *www.artswire.org*

Crayola Arts Education: *www.crayola.com*

Virtual Museums: *www.icom.org/vlmp*

World Wide Arts Resources: *www.wwar.org*

General Clearinghouse Sites

Kathy Schrock's Guide for Educators:
http://school.discovery.com/ schrockguide/

Children's Literature

American Library Association (ALA): *www.ala.org/*

Carol Hurst's Children's Literature Website: *www.carolhurst.com/*

Children's Book Council (CBC): *www.cbcbooks.org/text.html*

Kay Vandergriff's Children's Literature Home Page:
www.scils.rutgers.edu/~kvander/childrenlit/index.html

LibrarySpot: *www.libraryspot.com*

Copyright Information

U.S. Copyright Office: *http://loc.gov/copyright/*

Censorship Policies and Perspectives

American Library Association: *www.ala.org*

National Art Education Association: *www.naea-reston.org/*

National Association for Music Education: *http://www.menc.org*

Funding Information

www.arts.gov/

www.artsschoolsnetwork.org

www.ed.gov/fund/grant

www.grantsalert.com

www.nea.gov/grants

PEN Weekly NewsBlast: *www.publiceducation.org*

Appendix 1

School Registry of Arts-Based Schools

This is a sampling of schools engaged in arts-based education. Some are individual buildings and others are school districts or members of consortia.

Alabama

Selma: *http://selmacityschools.org*

Alaska

Anchorage: Winterberry Elementary: *http://winterberry.org*

Arizona

Peoria: *http://portal.peoriaud.k12.az.us/default.aspx*

Arkansas

See A + schools: *http://aplus-schools.org/*

California

Montclair, Buena Vista Arts Integrated School: *http://omsd.k12.ca.us/buenavista/*

Colorado

Summit: *http://summit.k12.co.us/index.html*

Thompson: *http://thompson.k12.co.us/NSchools/sch_home.html*

Connecticut

Connecticut Commission on the Arts HOT Schools (statewide consortium of schools): *http://ctarts.org/hot/hotnews.htm*

Delaware

Wilmington, Cab Calloway School of the Arts: *http://ccsaarts.com*

Florida

Hillsborough County, Lockhart, Muller and Phillip Shore Elementaries: *http://apps.sdhc.k12.fl.us/*

Georgia

Decatur, Hooper Alexander Elementary: *http://dekalb.k12.ga.us/schools/elementary/hooperalexander/*

Idaho

Meridian, Christine Donnell School of the Arts: *http://meridianschools.org/schools/magnet/art-and-leadership/*

Illinois

Chicago (12 elementaries), contact: *http://capeweb.org/pschools.html*

Indiana

Lafayette, Earhart Elementary School: *http://www.lsc.k12.in.us/earhart/index.htm*

Kentucky

Contact Different Ways of Knowing: *http://dwok.org*

Louisiana

New Orleans, Lusher School: *http://gnofn.org/~lusher/*

Massachusetts

Needham, John Eliot Elementary: *http://eliot.needham.k12.ma.us/*

Minnesota

Minneapolis, Annenberg Challenge *http://mpls.k12.mn.us/aaa*

New Jersey

Newark: *http://nps.k12.nj.us/*

New York

New York City, Waverly School for the Arts: *http://nycenet.edu*

Port Chester, King Street School: *http://portchester.k12.ny.us/king/kinghome.htm*

North Carolina

See A+ schools: *http://uncg.edu/iss/a+schools.html*

North Dakota

See A+ schools: *http://state.nd.us/arts/arts_ed/aplus.htm*

Ohio

Hamilton, Adams Elementary: *http://HamiltonCitySchools.com/ schools/adams/index.cfm*

Oklahoma

Norman, Wilson Elementary: *http://www.wilsonelementary. com/*
Also check for A+ schools at: *http://aplus-schools.org/*

Oregon

Portland: *http://pps.k12.or.us/*

Pennsylvania

Pittsburgh, go to Arts Propel: *http://pz.harvard.edu/Research/ PROPEL.htm*

South Carolina

Go to statewide consortium site: *http://www.winthrop.edu/abc/*

South Dakota

See A+ schools sites at: *http://aplus-schools.org/*

Sioux Valley, Eugene Field A1 Elementary School: *http://sf.k12.sd.us*

Tennessee

Chattanooga, Allied Arts Schools:

http://alliedartschattanooga.org/home.html

Texas

Dallas ArtsPartner Schools at: *http://dallasartspartners.org*

Washington

Seattle, Mclure Middle: *http://seattleschools.org/schools/mcclure/ arts.html*

Washington, DC

Changing Education Through the Arts (CETA): *http://kennedy-center.org*

Wisconsin

Milwaukee, Elm Elementary: *http://milwaukee.k12.wi.us/*

Additional Websites with School Information

Arts School Network: *http://artsschoolsnetwork.org/member_ schools.htm*

Magnet Schools of America includes 500 arts-based schools: *www. magnet. edu*

See dissemination sites at the National Endowment for the Arts: *www.nea.gov*

Appendix J

Arts-Based Children's Literature

For more books with artistic protagonists, go to the Children's Literature Web (*www.ucalgary.ca/~dkbrown/* or *www.carolhurst.com*).

Art

Making Art

Aliki. (1986). *How a book is made.* New York: Harper & Row.

Bang, M. (2000). *Picture this: How pictures work.* New York: SeaStar.

Baumgardner, J.(1993). *60 art projects for children: Painting, clay, puppets, paints, masks, and more.* New York: Clarkson-Potter.

Belloli, A., & Godard, K. (1994). *Make your own museum.* Boston: Houghton Mifflin.

Bolognese, D., & Thornton, R. (1983). *Drawing and painting with the computer.* New York: Franklin Watts.

Bostick, W. A. (1991). *Calligraphy for kids.* Franklin, MN: La Stampa Calligrafa.

Carroll, C. (1996–2004). *How artists see* (series). *New York:* Abbeville.

Carter, D., & Diaz, J. (1999). *The elements of pop up.* New York: Simon and Shuster.

dePaola, T., & Willard, N. (1977). *Simple pictures are best.* San Diego, CA: Harcourt Brace Jovanovich.

Diehn, G. (2002). *Simple printmaking.* Asheville, NC: Lark.

Emberly, E. (1991). *Ed Emberly's drawing book: Make a world.* Boston: Little, Brown.

Fischer, L. E. (1986). *The papermakers.* Boston: Godine.

Graham, A., & Stoke, D. (1983). *Fossils, ferns, and fish scales: A handbook of art and nature projects.* New York: Four Winds.

Haldane, S. (1988). *Painting faces.* New York: Dutton.

Hauser, J. (1995). *Kids' crazy concoctions: 50 mysterious mixtures for art & craft fun.* Charlotte, VT: Williamson.

Hoban, T. (1986). *Shapes, shapes, shapes.* New York: Greenwillow.

Hyman, T. S. (1981). *Self-portrait: Trina Schart Hyman.* Reading, MA: Addison Wesley.

Irvine, J. (1992). *How to make super pop-ups.* Fairfield, NJ: Morrow.

Kohl, M. (1989). *Mudworks.* Bellingham, WA: Bright Ring.

Kohl, M., & Gainer, C. (1991). *Good earth art: Environmental art for kids.* Bellingham, WA: Bright Ring.

Lightfoot, M. (1993) *Cartooning for kids.* New York: Firefly Books.

Marks, M. (1972). *OP-tricks: Creating kinetic art.* Philadelphia: Lippincott.

Muller, B. (1987). *Painting with children.* Edinburgh, Scotland: Floris.

Reid, B. (1989). *Playing with plasticine.* Longbeach, CA: Beechtree.

Richardson, J. (1997). *Looking at pictures: An introduction to art for young people. New York:* Abrams.

Sakata, H. (1990). *Origami.* New York: Japan Publishers, U.S.A.

Schulz, C. (2001). *Peanuts: The art of Charles M. Schulz.* New York: Pantheon Books.

Solga, K. (1992). *Make sculptures.* Cincinnati, OH: North Light.

Stangl, J. (1986). *Magic mixtures.* Carthage, IL: Teaching Aids.

Striker, S. (1984). *The anti-coloring book.* New York: Holt, Rinehart & Winston.

Terzian, A. (1993). *The kids' multicultural art book: Art & craft experiences from around the world.* Charlotte, VT: Williamson.

Webb, P. H., & Corby, J. (1991). *Shadowgraphs anyone can make.* New York: Running Press.

Art as Part of the Book's Theme

Abby Aldrich Rockefeller Folk Art Center. (1991). *The folk art counting book.* New York: Abrams.

Ackerman, K. (1990). *Araminta's paint box.* New York: Atheneum.

Alexander, L. (1982). *Kestrel.* New York: Dutton.

Alexander, M. (1995). *You're a genius BLACKBOARD BEAR.* Cambridge, MA: Candlewick.

Allen, C. (1991). *The rug makers.* Austin, TX: Steck-Vaughn.

Allison, B. (1991). *Effie.* New York: Scholastic.

Angelou, M. (1994). *My painted house, my friendly chicken.* New York: Clarkson-Potter.

Anholt, L. (1994). *Camille and the sunflowers.* Hauppauge, NY: Barron's Educational Series.

Anno, M. (1989). *Anno's faces.* New York: Philomel.

Asch, F. (1985). *Bear shadow.* New York: Simon & Schuster.

Baker, A. (1994). *Brown rabbit's shape book.* New York: Larouse Kingfisher.

Bang, M. (1985). *The paper crane.* New York: Greenwillow.

Barrett, P., & Barrett, S. (1972). *The line Sophie drew.* New York: Scroll.

Bedard, M. (1992). *Emily.* New York: Doubleday.

Bjork, C.(1995). *Living in Monet's garden.* New York: Farrar, Straus & Giroux.

Blood, C., & Link, M. (1990). *The goat in the rug.* New York: Aladdin-Macmillan.

Blumberg, R. (2003). *Shipwrecked: The true adventures of a Japanese Boy.* New York: HarperCollins.

Brenner, B. (1989). *The color wizard.* New York: Bantam.

Brown, A. (2003). *The shape game.* New York: Farrar, Straus & Giroux.

Bulla, C. (1987). *The chalk box kid.* New York: Random House.

Burns, M. (1994). *The greedy triangle.* New York: Scholastic.

Bush, T. (1995). *Grunt, the primitive cave boy.* New York: Crown.

Carle, E. (1984). *The mixed-up chameleon.* New York: Crowell.

Carle, E. (1992). *Draw me a star.* New York: Philomel.

Carlstrom, N. W. (1992). *Northern lullaby.* New York: Philomel.

Castaneda, O. S. (1993). *Abuela's weave.* New York: Lee & Low.

Catalanotto, P. (2001). *Emily's art.* New York: Simon & Schuster.

Cazet, D. (1993). *Born in the gravy.* New York: Orchard.

Clement, C. (1986). *The painter and the wild swans.* New York: Pied Piper-Dial.

Coerr, E. (1986). *The Josefina story quilt.* New York: Harper Trophy.

Cohen, M., & Hoban, L. (1980). *No good in art.* New York: Greenwillow.

Cole, B. (1989). *Celine.* New York: Farrar, Straus & Giroux.

Cooney, B. (1982). *Miss Rumphius.* New York: Viking Penguin.

Coville, B. (1991). *Jeremy Thatcher, dragon hatcher.* San Diego, CA: Harcourt Brace Jovanovich.

Craven, C., & dePaola, T. (1989). *What the mailman brought.* New York: Putnam.

Demarest, C. L. (1995). *My blue boat.* New York: Harcourt Brace.

Demi, L. (1988). *Liang and the magic paintbrush.* New York: Henry Holt.

dePaola, T. (1973). *Charlie needs a cloak.* Upper Saddle River, NJ: Prentice Hall.

dePaola, T. (1988). *The legend of the Indian paintbrush.* New York: Putnam.

dePaola, T. (1989). *The art lesson.* New York: Putnam.

dePaola, T. (1991). *Bonjour, Mr. Satie.* New York: Putnam.

deTrevino, E. B. (1965). *I, Juan de Pareja.* New York: Farrar, Straus & Giroux.

Dobrin, A. (1973). *Josephine's imagination.* New York: Scholastic.

Dubelaar, T. (1992). *Looking for Vincent.* New York: Checkerboard.

Dunrea, O. (1995). *The painter who loved chickens.* New York: Farrar, Straus & Giroux.

Ernst, L. C. (1986). *Hamilton's art show.* New York: Lothrop.

Feiffer, J. (1993). *The man in the ceiling.* New York: HarperCollins.

Fox, P. (1988). *The village by the sea.* Orchard.

Freeman, D. (1987). *Norman the doorman.* New York: Viking Penguin.

Gibbons, G. (1987). *The pottery place.* New York: Harcourt Brace Jovanovich.

Goffstein, M. (1985). *An artist's album.* New York: Harpercrest.

Goffstein, M. (1986). *Your lone journey: Paintings.* New York: HarperCollins.

Grifalconi, A. (1990). *Osa's pride.* Boston: Little, Brown.

Harwood, P. A. (1965). *Mr. Bumba draws a kitten.* Minneapolis: Learner.

Hort, L. (1987). *The boy who held back the sea.* New York: Dial.

Hurd, T. (1996). *Art dog.* New York: HarperCollins.

Isadora, R. (1988). *The pirates of Bedford Street.* New York: Greenwillow.

Jarrell, R. (1964). *Bat poet.* New York: Macmillan.

Jenkins, J. (1992). *Thinking about colors.* New York: Dutton.

Johnson, C. (1955). *Harold and the purple crayon.* New York: HarperCollins.

Kesselman, W., & Cooney, B. (1980). *Emma.* New York: Doubleday.

Knox, B. (1993). *The great art adventure.* New York: Rizzoli.

Koch, K., & Farell, K. (1985). *Talking to the sun.* New York: Metropolitan Museum of Art.

Konigsburg, E. L. (1967). *From the mixed-up files of Mrs. Basil E. Frankweiler.* New York: Atheneum.

Lobel, A. (1968). *The great blueness and other predicaments.* New York: Harper & Row.

Lobel, A. (1980). *Fables.* New York: Harper & Row.

Locker, T. (1989). *The young artist.* New York: Dial.

Lyon, G. (2004) *Weaving the rainbow.* New York: Atheneum.

MacAgy, D., & MacAgy, E. (1978). *Going for a walk with a line.* New York: Doubleday.

MacLachlan, P. (2003). *Painting the wind.* New York: J. Cutler Books.

Markun, P. M. (1993). *The little painter of Sabana Grande.* New York: Bradbury.

Martin, B. (1992). *Brown bear, brown bear, what do you see?* New York: Henry Holt.

Mayers, F. (1991). *The ABC: Museum of Modern Art.* New York: Abrams.

McPhail, D. (1978). *The magical drawings of Mooney B. Finch.* New York: Doubleday.

Micklethwait, L. (1991). *I spy: An alphabet in art.* New York: Greenwillow.

Miles, M. (1971). *Annie and the old one.* Boston: Little, Brown.

Mori, K. (1993). *Shizuko's daughter.* New York: Henry Holt.

Munsch, R. (1992). *Purple green and yellow.* Toronto: Annick.

O'Kelley, M. L. (1983). *From the hills of Georgia: An autobiography in paintings.* Boston: Atlantic Monthly.

O'Neal, Z. (1985). *In summer light.* New York: Viking Kestrel.

Paterson, K. (1979). *Bridge to Terabithia.* New York: Harper & Row.

Paulsen, G. (1991). *Monument.* New York: Delacorte.

Peet, B. (1989). *Bill Peet: An autobiography.* Boston: Houghton Mifflin.

Pinkwater, D. (1993). *The big orange splot.* New York: Scholastic.

Polacco, P. (1997). *In Enzo's splendid gardens.* New York: Philomel.

Raven, M.. (2004). *Circle unbroken: The story of a basket and its people.* New York: Melanie Kroupa Books.

Reiner, A. (1990). *A visit to the art gallery.* New York: Green Tiger.

Rockwell, A. (1993). *Mr. Panda's painting.* New York: Macmillan.

Rodari, F. (1991). *A weekend with Picasso.* New York: Rizzoli.

Rylant, C. (1982). *When I was young in the mountains.* New York: Dutton.

Sanford, J. (1991). *Slappy Hooper: The world's greatest sign painter.* New York: Warner.

Sorensun, M. (2006) *Ambrose and the cathedral dream.* Collegeville, MN: Liturgical Press.

Small, D. (1987). *Paper John.* New York: Farrar, Straus & Giroux.

Spier, P. (1978). *Oh, were they ever happy!* New York: Doubleday.

Spinelli, E. (2001). *Sophie's masterpiece: A spider's tale.* New York: Simon and Schuster.

Steig, W. (1988). *Abel's island.* New York: Farrar, Straus & Giroux.

Tallarico, T. (1984). *I can draw animals*. New York: Simon & Schuster.

Tang, G. (2003). *MATH-terpieces: The art of problem-solving*. New York: Scholastic.

Testa, F. (1982). *If you take a paintbrush: A book of colors*. New York: Dial.

Tuyet, T. (1987). *The little weaver of Thai-Yen village*. Emeryville, CA: Children's Book Press.

Wadell, M., & Langley, J. (1988). *Alice the artist*. New York: Dutton.

Watson, W. (1994). *The fox went out on a chilly night*. New York: Lothrop, Lee & Shepard.

Wilhelm, J. (1988). *Oh, what a mess*. New York: Random House.

Williams, V. B. (1986). *Cherries and cherry pits*. New York: Greenwillow.

Art History and Appreciation

Agee, J. (1988). *The incredible painting of Felix Clousseau*. New York: Farrar, Straus & Giroux.

Alcron, J. (1991). *Rembrandt's beret*. New York: Tambourine.

Behrens, J. (1982). *Looking at children*. Chicago: Children's Press.

Blake, Q. (2003). *Tell me a picture*. Brookfield, CT: Millbrook.

Blanquet, C. (1994). *Miro: Earth and sky. Art for children*. New York: Chelsea House.

Blizzard, G. (1992). *Come look with me: Exploring landscape art with children*. Charlottesville, VA: Thomasson-Grant.

Bohn-Ducher, M., & Cook, J. (1991). *Understanding modern art*. London: Osborn House.

Bonafoux, P. (1991). *A weekend with Rembrandt*. New York: Rizzoli International.

Brown, L. K., & Brown, M. (1986). *Visiting the art museum*. New York: Dutton.

Burdett, L. (1995). *A child's portrait of Shakespeare*. Buffalo, NY: Blackmoss.

Cachin, F. (1991). *Gaughin: The quest for paradise*. New York: Abrams.

Collins, D. R. (1989). *The country artist: A story about Beatrix Potter*. Minneapolis: Carolrhoda.

Conner, P. (1982). *Looking at art* (series). New York: Atheneum.

Contempre, Y. (1978). *A Sunday afternoon on the Island of Jatte*. Paris: Dululot.

Crespi, F. (1995). *A walk in Monet's garden*. Boston: Little, Brown.

Cummings, P. (1992). *Talking with artists*. New York: Bradbury.

Drucker, M. (1991). *Frida Kahlo: Torment and triumph in her life and art*. New York: Bantam.

Galli, L. (1996). *Mona Lisa: The secret of the smile*. New York: Bantam Doubleday Dell.

Gardner, J. M. (1993). *Henry Moore: From bones and stones to sketches and sculptures*. New York: Four Winds.

Goffstein, M. B. (1983). *Lives of the artists*. New York: Harper & Row.

Greenberg, J., & Jordan, R. (1993). *The sculptor's eye: Looking at contemporary American art*. New York: Delacorte.

Greenfield, H. (1991). *Marc Chagall*. New York: Abrams.

Highwater, J. (1978). *Many smokes, many moons: A chronology of American Indian history through Indian art*. New York: Lippincott.

Isaacson, P. M. (1993). *A short walk around the pyramids and through the world of art*. New York: Knopf.

Kinghorn, H., Badman, J., & Lewis-Spicer, L. (1998). *Let's meet famous artists*. Minneapolis, MN: Denison.

Krull, K. (1995). *Lives of the artists: Masterpieces, messes, and what the neighbors thought*. San Diego, CA: Harcourt Brace.

La Pierre, Y. (1994). *Native American rock art: Messages from the past*. Charlottesville, VA: Thomasson-Grant.

LeTord, B. (1995). *A blue butterfly: A story about Claude Monet*. New York: Bantam Doubleday Dell.

Lipman, J., & Aspenwall, M. (1981). *Alexander Calder and his magic mobiles*. New York: Hudson Hills Press.

Macauley, D. (1973). *Cathedral: The story of its construction*. New York: Houghton Mifflin.

Messinger, L. M. (1991). *For our children*. Burbank, CA: Disney Press.

Milande, V. (1995). *Michelangelo and his times*. New York: Henry Holt.

Muhlberger, R. (1993). *What makes a Monet a Monet?* New York: Viking.

Munthe, N., & Kee, R. (1983). *Meet Matisse*. Boston: Little, Brown.

Newlands, A., & National Gallery of Canada Staff. (1989). *Meet Edgar Degas*. New York: Harper.

O'Neal, Z. (1986). *Grandma Moses: Painter of rural America*. New York: Viking Kestrel.

Peppin, A. (1980). *The Usborne story of painting*. Tulsa, OK: EDC.

Pluckrose, H. (1987). *Crayons*. New York: Franklin Watts.

Provenson, A., & Provenson, M. (1984). *Leonardo da Vinci: The artist, inventor, scientist in three-dimensional, movable pictures*. New York: Viking.

Richardson, J. (1997). *Looking at pictures: An introduction to art for young people*. New York: Abrams.

Richmond, R. (1992). *Children in art*. Nashville, TN: Ideals Children's Books.

Roalf, P. (1992). *Looking at painting series: Dancers, Cats, Families, Seascapes, Self-Portraits*. New York: Hyperion.

Rodari, F. (1991). *A weekend with Picasso*. New York: Rizzoli International.

Rylant, C., & Catalanotto, P. (1988). *All I see*. New York: Orchard.

Sills, L. (1989). *Inspirations: Stories about women artists*. Nills, IL: Whitman.

Skira-Venturi, R. (1990). *A weekend with Renoir; A weekend with Degas*. New York: Rizzoli.

Sturgis, A. (1994). *Introducing Rembrandt*. Boston: Little, Brown.

Sullivan, C. (Ed.) (1989). *Imaginary gardens: American poetry and art for young people*. New York: Abrams.

Swain, S. (1988). *Great housewives of art*. New York: Penguin.

Thompson, P. & Moore, B. (1997). *Nine ton cat: Behind the scenes in an art museum*. Burlington, MA: Houghton Mifflin.

Turner, R. (1991). *Georgia O'Keefe*. Boston: Little, Brown.

Walker, L. (1994). *Roy Lichenstein: The artist at work*. New York: Dutton Lodestar.

Wallner's, A. (2004). *Grandma Moses*. New York: Holiday.

Walters, A. (1989). *The spirit of Native America: Beauty and mysticism in American Indian art*. San Francisco: Chronicle.

Winter, J. (1991). *Diego*. New York: Knopf.

Woolf, F. (1993). *Picture this century: An introduction to twentieth-century art.* New York: Doubleday.

Yenawine, P., & Museum of Modern Art. (1991). *Series on Modern Art: Colors, Lines, Shapes, Stories,* New York: Delacorte.

Zhensun, A., & Low, A. (1991). *A young painter: The life and paintings of Wang Yani, China's extraordinary artist.* New York: Scholastic.

Photography

Allen, M., & Rotner, S. (1991). *Changes.* New York: Macmillan.

Arnold, C. (1991). *Snake.* New York: Morrow.

Barrett, N. (1988). *Pandas.* New York: Watts.

Bauer, J. (1995). *Thwonk!* New York: Dutton.

Brown, T. (1986). *Hello, Amigos.* New York: Henry Holt.

Brown, T. (1987). *Chinese New Year.* New York: Henry Holt.

Burton, J. (1991). *See how they grow series: Kitten, Puppy.* New York: Lodestar.

Cobb, V. (1990). *Natural wonders.* New York: Lothrop.

Cousteau Society Series. (1992). *Dolphins, Penguins, Seals, Turtles.* New York: Simon & Schuster.

Doubilet, A. (1991). *Under the sea from A to Z.* New York: Crown.

Eye Openers Series. (1991). *Baby animals, Jungle animals, Pets, Zoo Animals.* New York: Aladdin.

Feeney, S. (1980). *A is for aloha.* Honolulu: University Press of Hawaii.

Freedman, R. (1988). *Lincoln: A photobiography.* New York: Clarion.

Goldsmith, D. (1992). *Hoang Auk: A Vietnamese-American boy.* New York: Holiday House.

Hewett, J. (1990). *Hector lives in the United States now: The story of a Mexican-American child.* New York: Lippincott.

Hirschi, R. (1990–1991). *Four seasons series.* New York: Dutton.

Hoban, T. (1990). *Exactly the opposite.* New York: Greenwillow.

Johnson, N. (2001). *National Geographic photography guide for kids.* Washington, DC: National Geographic Society.

Kuklin, S. (1991). *How my family lives in America.* New York: Bradbury.

Le Tord, B. (1999). *A bird or two: A story about Henri Matisse.* Grand Rapids, MI: Eerdmans.

Lehrman, F. (1990). *Loving the earth: A sacred landscape book for children.* Berkeley, CA: Celestial.

Marshall, J. P. (1989). *My camera at the zoo.* Boston: Little, Brown.

Meltzer, M. (1986). *Dorothea Lange: Life through the camera.* New York: Puffin.

Miller, M. (1991). *Whose shoe?* New York: Greenwillow.

Morris, A. (1989). *Bread, bread, bread.* New York: Lothrop, Lee & Shepard.

Morris, A. (1990). *Loving.* New York: Lothrop, Lee & Shepard.

Oliver, S. (1990). *My first look at seasons.* New York: Random House.

Rauzon, M. (1992). *Jungles.* New York: Doubleday.

Ricklin, N. (1988). *Grandpa and me.* New York: Simon & Schuster.

Robbins, K. (1991). *Bridges.* New York: Dial.

Schlein, M. (1990). *Elephants.* New York: Aladdin.

Stanley, D. (2000). *Michelangelo.* New York: HarperCollins.

Steichen, E. (1985). *The family of man.* New York: Museum of Modern Art.

Waters, K., & Slorenz-Low, M. (1990). *Lion dancer: Earnie Wan's Chinese New Year.* New York: Scholastic.

Wilkes, A. (1991). *My first green book.* New York: Knopf.

Winter, J. (1998). *My name is Georgia.* New York: Harcourt.

Drama

Doing Drama (includes books for pantomime and verbal activities)

Adoff, A. (1981). *Outside/inside poems.* New York: Lothrop, Lee & Shepard.

Alexander, L. (1992). *The fortune tellers.* New York: Dutton.

Bailey Babb, K. (1990). *Beginning readers theatre: Presentation masks and scripts for young readers.* Denver, CO: Skipping Stone.

Bany-Winters, L. (2000). *Show Time! Music, dance and drama activities for kids.* Chicago: Chicago Review.

Barchers, S. (1993). *Reader's theatre for beginning readers.* Englewood, CO: Teacher Ideas.

Bayer, J. (1984). *My name is Alice.* New York: Dial.

Bemelmens, L. (1939). *Madeline.* New York: Viking Penguin.

Bennett, J. (collected) (1987). *Noisy poems.* New York: Oxford University Press.

Bodecker, N. M. (1974). *"Let's marry," said the cherry.* New York: Atheneum.

Bradley, A. (1977). *Paddington on stage.* Boston: Houghton Mifflin.

Cameron, P. (1961). *"I can't," said the ant.* New York: Coward-McCann.

Caruso, S., & Kosoff, S. (1998). *The young actor's book of improvisation: Dramatic situations from Shakespeare to Spielberg,* (Vol. 1). Portsmouth, NH: Heinemann.

Chaconas, D. (1970). *The way the tiger walked.* New York: Simon & Schuster.

Charlip, R. (1980). *Fortunately.* New York: Four Winds.

Chess, V. (1979). *Alfred's alphabet walk.* New York: Greenwillow.

Cole, J., & Calmenson, S. (1990). *"Miss Mary Mack" and other children's street rhymes.* Longbeach, CA: BeechTree.

Corbett, S. (1984). *Jokes to tell your worst enemy.* New York: Dutton.

Cullum, A. (1995). *Shakespeare in the classroom: Plays for the intermediate grades.* Carthage, IL: Fearon Teacher Aids.

dePaola, T. (1979). *Charlie needs a cloak.* Upper Saddle River, NJ: Prentice Hall.

Dunleavy, D. (2004). *The jumbo book of drama.* Tonawanda, NY: Kids Can Press

Dunn, S. (1990). *Crackers and crumbs. Chants for whole language.* Portsmouth, NH: Heinemann.

Eastman, P. D. (1960). *Are you my mother?* New York: Random House.

England, A. W. (1990). *Theatre for the young.* New York: St. Martin's.

Fraser, P. (1982). *Puppets and puppetry: A complete guide to puppet-making for all ages.* New York: Stein & Day.

Freeman, R. (1991). *Makeup art.* Danbury, CT: Franklin Watts.

Friedman, L. (2001). *Break a leg! The kid's guide to acting and stage-craft.* New York: Workman.

Georges, C., & Cornett, C. (1986). *Reader's theatre.* Aurora, NY: Developers of Knowledge.

Gerke, P. (1996a). *Multicultural plays for children: Grades K–3 (Young Actors Series),* Vol. 1. Lyme, NH: Smith & Kraus.

Gerke, P. (1996b). *Multicultural plays for children: Grades 4–6* Vol. 2. Lyme, NH: Smith & Kraus.

Gerstein, M. (1984). *Roll over!* New York: Crown.

Gibbons, G. (1985). *Lights! Camera! Action! How a movie is made.* New York: Crowell.

Giff, P. (1995). *Show time at the Polk Street School: Plays you can do yourself in the classroom.* New York: Yearling Books.

Goffstein, M. (1987). *An actor.* New York: Harper & Row.

Guarino, D. (1991). *Is your mama a llama?* New York: Scholastic.

Hackbarth, J. (1994). *Plays, players, and playing: How to start your own children's theater company.* Colorado Springs, CO: Piccadilly.

Haley, G. (1970). *A story–A story.* New York: Atheneum.

Heide, F. P. (1971). *The shrinking of treehorn.* New York: Holiday House.

Hutchins, P. (1976). *Don't forget the bacon.* New York: Greenwillow.

Juster, N. (1989). *A surfeit of smiles.* New York: Morrow.

Kamerman, S. (1988–1994). *The big book (series): Folktales, Christmas, large cast, skits.* Boston: Plays.

Knight, L. M. (1990). *Readers theatre for children: Scripts and script development.* Englewood, CO: Teachers Idea.

Kohl, M. (1999). *Making make-believe: Fun props, costumes and creative play ideas.* Beltsville, MD: Gryphon House.

Lade, R. (1996). *The most excellent book of how to be a puppeteer.* Brookfield, CT: Copper Beech.

Laughlin, M. K., & Latrobe, K. H. (1990). *Reader's theatre for children.* Englewood, CO: Teacher Ideas.

MacDonald, M. R. (1990). *The skit book; 101 skits from kids.* Hamden, CT: Linnet Books.

Martin, J. (1997). *Out of the bag: The paper bag players book of plays.* New York: Hyperion.

McGovern, A. (1967). *Too much noise.* Boston: Houghton Mifflin.

McGowan, D. (1997). *Math play!* Charlotte, VT: Williamson.

Mendoza, G. (1971). *The Marcel Marceau counting book.* New York: Doubleday.

Murray, B. (1995). *Puppet and theater activities: Theatrical things to do and make.* Honesdale, PA: Boyds Mills Press.

Parish, P. (1963). *Amelia Bedelia.* New York: Harper & Row.

Pollock, J. (1997). *Side by side: Twelve multicultural puppet plays.* Lanham, MD: Scarecrow.

San Souci, R. (1989). *The talking eggs.* New York: Dial.

Schafer, L. & Spann, M. (Ed.). (1994). *Plays around the year: More than 20 thematic plays for the classroom.* New York: Scholastic Professional Books.

Scull, M. (1990). *The skit book: 101 skits for kids.* Hamden, CT: Linnet.

Sendak, M. (1963). *Where the wild things are.* New York: Harper & Row.

Sharmat, A. (1989). *Smedge.* New York: Macmillan.

Small, D. (1985). *Imogene's antlers.* New York: Crown.

Smith, M. (1996). *The Seattle Children's Theatre: Seven plays for young actors* (Young Actors Series). Lyme, NH: Smith & Kraus.

Stevens, C. (1999). *Magnificent monologues for kids.* South Pasadena, CA: Sandcastle.

Straub, C. (1984). *Mime for basic beginners.* Boston: Plays.

Swortzell, L. (1997). *Theatre for young audiences: Around the world in 21 plays.* New York: Applause.

Thaler, M. (1974). *Magic letter riddles.* New York: Scholastic.

Tolstoy, A. (1968). *The great big enormous turnip.* New York: Franklin Watts.

Tresslet, A. (1964). *The mitten.* New York: Lothrop, Lee & Shepard.

Turkle, B. (1976). *Deep in the forest.* New York: Dutton.

Ungerer, T. (1986). *Crictor.* New York: Harper & Row.

Van Allsburg, C. (1984). *The mysteries of Harris Burdick.* Boston: Houghton Mifflin.

Van Allsburg, C. (1986). *The stranger.* Boston: Houghton Mifflin.

White, M. (1993). *Mel White's Readers Theatre anthology: Twenty-eight all-occasion readings for storytellers.* Colorado Springs, CO: Meriwether.

White, W. (1997). *Speaking in stories: Resources for Christian storytellers.* Minneapolis: Augsburg.

Winther, B. (1992). *Plays from African tales.* Boston: Plays.

Wolf, A. (1993). *It's show time! Poetry from the page to the stage.* Asheville, NC: Poetry Alive!

Zemach, M. (1976). *It could always be worse.* New York: Farrar, Straus & Giroux.

About Drama

Aagesen, C., & Blumberg, M. (1999). *Shakespeare for kids: His life and times.* Chicago: Chicago Review Press.

Bellville, F. (1982). *Theater magic: Behind the scenes at children's theater.* Minneapolis, MN: Carolrhoda.

Cullum, A. (1968). *Shake hands with Shakespeare.* New York: Scholastic.

Evans, C., & Smith, L. (1992). *Acting and theatre.* Philadelphia: Stage Step

Walsh-Bellville, C. (1986). *Theater magic: Behind the scenes at a children's theater.* Minneapolis: Carolrhoda.

Drama as Part of the Book's Theme

Berenstain, S., & Berenstain, J. (1986). *The Berenstain bears get stage fright.* New York: Random House.

Best, C. (2006). *Are you going to be good?* New York: Farrar, Straus & Giroux.

Blume, J. (1981). *The one in the middle is a green kangaroo.* New York: Yearling

Booth, C. (1992). *Going live.* New York: Scribner.

Boynton, S. (1993). *Barnyard dance!* New York: Workman.

Brown, M. (2005). *Buster and the dance contest.* New York: Little, Brown.

Burgard, A. M. (2005). *Flying feet: A story of Irish dance.* San Francisco: Chronicle.

Byars, B. (1992). *Hooray for the Golly sisters!* New York: Harper.

Cohen, M. (1985). *Starring first grade.* New York: Greenwillow.

Conlon, J. (1994). *The performers.* Vero Beach, FL: Rourke Press.

Coville, B. (1987). *Ghost in the third row.* New York: Bantam.

de Regniers, B. (1982). *Picture book theatre: The mysterious stranger and the magic spell.* San Francisco: Seabury Press Harper & Row.

dePaola, T. (1983). *Sing, Pierrot, sing: A picture book in mime.* New York: Harcourt Brace Jovanovich.

Freeman, D. (1970). *Hattie: The backstage bat.* New York: Viking.

Gerrard, R. (1992). *Jocasta Carr: Movie star.* New York: Farrar, Straus & Giroux.

Giff, P. R. (1998). *Rosie's big city ballet.* New York: Viking Press.

Gish, L. (1987). *An actor's life for me.* New York: Viking.

Greydanus, R. (1981). *Hocus pocus, magic show!* Mahwah, NJ: Troll.

Hoffman, M. (1991). *Amazing Grace.* New York: Dial Books.

Holabird, K. (1984). *Angelina and the princess.* New York: C. N. Potter.

Howard, E. (1991). *Aunt Flossie's hats (and crab cakes later).* Boston: Houghton Mifflin.

Kroll, S. (1986). *The big bunny and the magic show.* New York: Holiday House.

Lamb, C., & Lamb, M. (1988). *Tales from Shakespeare.* New York: Crown Publishing.

Leedy, L. (1988). *The bunny play.* New York: Holiday House.

Lepscky, I. (1989). *William Shakespeare.* New York: Barron.

Marshall, J. (1993). *Fox on stage.* New York: Dial.

Martin, A. M. (1984). *Stage fright.* New York: Holiday House.

McCully, E. A. (1992). *Mirette on the high wire.* New York: Putnam.

Morley, J. (1994). *Entertainment: Screen, stage, and stars.* New York: Franklin Watts.

Oppenheim, J. (1984). *Mrs. Patoki's class play.* New York: Dodd Mead.

Robinson, B. (1972). *The best Christmas pageant ever.* New York: Harper & Row.

Schreiber, E. (2004). *Comedy girl.* New York: HarperCollins.

Sendak, M. (1976). *Maurice Sendak's really Rosie: Starring the Nutshell Kids.* New York: Harper Row.

Stanley, D., & Venneman, P. (1992). *Bard of Avalon: The story of Shakespeare.* New York: Morrow.

Thee, C. (1994). *Behind the curtain.* New York: Workman.

Tryon, L. (1992). *Albert's play.* New York: Atheneum.

Van Allsburg, C. (1987). *The Z was zapped: A play in twenty-one acts.* New York: Houghton Mifflin.

Yolen, J. (1992). *Street rhymes around the world.* Honesdale, PA: Wordsong.

Yashima, T. (1976). *Crow boy.* New York: Puffin.

Dance

Doing Dance

Barlin, A. (1993). *Goodnight toes! Bedtime stories, lullabies, and movement games.* Pennington, NJ: Princeton Book.

Bennett, J. (1995). *Rhythmic activities and dance.* Champaign, IL: Human Kinetics.

Brady, M. (1997). *Dancing hearts: Creative arts with books kids love.* Golden, CO: Falcrum.

Esbensen, B. (1995). *Dance with me.* New York: HarperCollins.

LaPrise, L. (1996). *The hokey pokey.* New York: Simon & Schuster.

Southgate, M. (1996). *Another way to dance.* New York: Delacorte.

Walton, R. (2001). *How can you dance?* New York: Penguin Putnam Books.

Weiwsan, J. (1993). *Kids in motion: A creative movement and song book.* Milwaukee, WI: Hal Leonard.

Dance in a Book's Theme

Ackerman, K., & Gammell, S. (1988). *Song and dance man.* New York: Knopf.

Allen, D. (2000). *Dancing in the wings.* New York: Dial.

Andreae, G. (2001). *Giraffes can't dance.* New York: Orchard.

Asch, F. (1993). *Moondance.* New York: Scholastic.

Auch, M. (1993). *Peeping beauty.* New York: Holiday House.

Baylor, B. (1973). *Sometimes I dance mountains.* New York: Scribner.

Berenstain, S., & Berenstain, J. (1993). *The Berenstain bears gotta dance!* New York: Random House.

Binford, D. (1989). *Rabbits can't dance!* Milwaukee, WI: Gareth Stevens.

Bornstein, R. (1978). *The dancing man.* New York: Seabury.

Bryan, A. (1987). *The dancing granny.* New York: Aladdin.

Carter, A. (1989). *The twelve dancing princesses.* New York: Lippincott.

Cristaldi, K. (1992). *Baseball ballerina.* New York: Random House.

Daly, N. (1992). *Papa Lucky's shadow.* New York: Margaret K. McElderry Books.

dePaola, T. (1979). *Oliver Button is a sissy.* San Diego, CA: Harcourt Brace Jovanovich.

Edwards, R. (1994). *Moles can dance.* Cambridge, MA: Candlewick.

Elliot, D. (1979). *Frogs and the ballet.* Ipswich, MA: Gambit.

Esbensen, B. J. (1995). *Dance with me (poems).* New York: HarperCollins.

Ferguson, J. (1994). *Alvin Ailey, Jr.: A life in dance.* New York: Walker and Co.

Freeman, D. (1996). *A rainbow of my own.* New York: Viking.

French, V. (1991). *One ballerina two.* New York: Lothrop.

Gauch, P. (1989). *Dance, Tanya.* New York: Philomel.

Getz, A. (1980). *Humphrey the dancing pig.* New York: Dial.

Giannini, E. (1993). *Zorina ballerina.* New York: Simon & Schuster.

Gray, L. M. (1995). *My Mama had a dancing heart.* New York: Orchard.

Greene, C. (1983). *Hi, clouds.* Chicago: Children's Press.

Hoff, S. (1994). *Duncan the dancing duck.* New York: Dial.

Holabird, K. (1998). *Angelina ballerina.* New York: Crown.

Hollinshead, M. (1994). *Nine days wonder.* New York: Philomel.

Hurd, E. (1965). *The day the sun danced.* New York: Harper & Row.

Hurd, E. (1982). *I dance in my red pajamas.* New York: Harper & Row.

Isadora, R. (1976). *Max.* New York: Macmillan.

Isadora, R. (1993). *Lili at the ballet.* Itasca, IL: Putman.

Jonas, A. (1989). *Color dance.* New York: Greenwillow.

Jones, B., Kuklin, S. (1998). *Dance!* New York: Hyperion.

Keats, E. J. (1962). *The snowy day.* New York: Viking.

Kistry, D. (1996). *George Balanchine.* Minneapolis, MN: Lerner.

Komaiko, L. (1992). *Aunt Elaine does the dance from Spain.* New York: Doubleday.

Lasky, K. (1994). *The solo.* New York: Macmillan.

Lionni, L. (1963). *Swimmy*. New York: Pantheon.

Locker, T. (2002). *Water dance*. San Diego: Voyager/Harcourt.

Lowery, L. (1995). *Jitter with bug*. Boston: Houghton Mifflin.

Marshall, J. (1990). *The cut-ups carry on*. New York: Viking.

Mathers, P. (1991). *Sophie and Lou*. New York: HarperCollins.

Mayer, M. (1971). *The queen always wanted to dance*. New York: Simon & Schuster.

McKissack, P. (1988). *Mirandy and Brother Wind*. New York: Knopf.

McPhail, D. (1985). *The dream child*. New York: Dutton.

Medearis, A. S. (1991). *Dancing with the Indians*. New York: Holiday.

Michelson, R. (2005). *Happy feet: The Savoy Ballroom lindy hoppers and me*. New York: Gulliver's Books.

Morrison, L. (1985). *The break dance kids: Poems of sport, motion, and locomotion*. New York: Lothrop, Lee & Shepard.

Mott, E. C. (1996). *Dancing rainbows: A pueblo boy's story*. New York: Cobblehill Books/Dutton.

Noll, S. (1993). *Jiggle, wiggle, prance*. New York: Puffin.

Oxenbury, H. (1983). *The dancing class*. New York: Dial.

Patrick, D. L. (1993). *Red dancing shoes*. New York: Tambourine.

Pinkney, A. (1993). *Alvin Ailey*. New York: Hyperion.

Plummer, L. (2000). *A dance for three*. New York: Delacort.

Richardson, J. (1987). *Clara's dancing feet*. New York: Putnam.

Rockwell, A. (1971). *The dancing stars: An Iroquois legend*. New York: Crowell.

Sanders, M. (2003). *I hope you dance*. Nashville, TN: Rutledge Hill Press.

Scheffrin-Falk, G. (1991). *Another celebrated dancing bear*. New York: Scribners.

Schroeder, A. (1989). *Ragtime turnpie*. Boston: Little, Brown.

Sendak, M. (1962). *Alligators all around*. New York: Harper & Row.

Sendak, M. (1963). *Where the wild things are*. New York: Harper & Row.

Simon, C. (1989). *Amy, the dancing bear*. New York: Doubleday.

Skofield, J. (1984). *Nightdances*. New York: Harper & Row.

Spinelli, E. (1993). *Boy, can he dance!* New York: Four Winds.

Wallace, I. (1984). *Chin Chang and the dragon's dance*. New York: Atheneum.

Waters, K., & Slovenz-Low, M. (1990). *Lion dancer: Earnie Wan's Chinese New Year*. New York: Scholastic.

Wood, A. (1986). *Three sisters*. New York: Dial.

Dance History and Appreciation

Alice in wonderland in dance (videorecording). (1993). New York: V.I.E.W. Video.

Anderson, H. C. (1991). *The red shoes*. New York: Simon & Schuster.

Anholt, L. (1996). *Degas and the little dancer: A story about Edgar Degas*. London: Frances Lincoln.

Bailey, D. (1991). *i*. Milwaukee: Raintree.

Barboza, S. (1992). *I feel like dancing: A year with Jacques d'Amboise and the National Dance Institute*. New York: Crown.

Cinderella: A dance fantasy. (1993). New York: V.I.E.W. Video.

Cocca-Leffler, M. (2001). *Edgar Degas, paintings that dance*. New York: Grossett & Dunlap.

Dood, C., & Soar, S. (1988). *Ballet in motion: A three-dimensional guide to ballet for young people*. New York: Lippincott.

Edom, H., & Katrak, N. (1998). *Starting ballet*. Willington, DE: Usborne.

Fonteyn, M. (1989). *Swan Lake*. San Diego, CA: Gulliver.

Gherman, B. (1990). *Agnes De Mille: Dancing off the earth*. New York: Atheneum.

Glassman, B. (2001). *Mikhail Baryshnikov: Dance genius*. Farmington Hills, MI: Gale Group.

Glover, S., & Weber, B. (2000). *Savion! My life in tap*. New York: Morrow.

Gray, L. (1999). *My mama had a dancing heart*. New York: Scholastic.

Greene, C. (1992). *Katherine Dunham: Black dancer*. Chicago: Children's Press.

Haskins, J. (1990). *Black dance in America: A history through its people*. New York: Crowell.

Hoffman, E. T. (1984). *The Nutcracker*. New York: Crown.

Isadora, R. (1991). *Swan Lake*. New York: Putnam.

Klein, N. (1983). *Baryshnikov's Nutcracker*. New York: Putnam.

Malcolm, J. (2000). *Drat! We're rats!* Sydney, Australia: Starcatcher.

Pavlova, A. (2001). *I dreamed I was a ballerina*. New York: Atheneum.

Schick, E. (1992). *I have another language, the language is dance*. New York: Macmillan.

Staples, S. (2001). *Shiva's fire*. Glenview, IL: HarperCollins.

Verdy, V. (1991). *Of swans, sugarplums, and satin slippers: Ballet stories for children*. New York: Scholastic.

Wells, R. (1999). *Tallchief: America's prima ballerina/Maria Tallchief*. New York: Viking Penguin.

Werner, V. (1992). *Petrouchka*. New York: Viking.

Music

Making Music

Adams, P. (1975). *This old man*. New York: Grossett & Dunlap.

Aliki. (1968). *Hush, little baby*. Upper Saddle River, NJ: Prentice Hall.

Aliki. (2003). *Ah music*. New York: HarperCollins.

Axelrod, A. (1991). *Songs of the Wild West*. Metropolitan Museum of Art. New York: Simon & Schuster.

Bangs, E. (1976). *Yankee Doodle*. New York: Parents Magazine Press.

Bantok, N. (1990). *There was an old lady*. New York: Viking Penguin.

Barbareski, N. (1985). *Frog went a-courting*. New York: Scholastic.

Bolam, K., & Bolam, J. (Arr.). (1992). *Folksongs from Eastern Europe*. London: Faber Music.

Bolam, K., & Gritton, P. (Arr.). (1993). *Folksongs from the Caribbean*. London: Faber Music.

Brett, J. (1990). *The twelve days of Christmas*. New York: Putnam.

Bryan, A. (1991). *All night, all day: A child's first book of African-American spirituals*. New York: Atheneum.

Campbell, P., Brabson, E., & Tucker, C. (1994). *Roots and branches* (with CD). Danbury, CT: World Music.

Child, L. (1987). *Over the river and through the woods*. New York: Scholastic.

Cohn, A. (Compiler). (1993). *From sea to shining sea: A treasury of American folklore and songs*. New York: Scholastic.

Cole, J., & Calmenson, S. (1991). *The eentsy, weentsy spider: Finger-plays and action rhymes*. New York: Mulberry.

Cooney, B., & Griego, M. C. (1981). *Tortillitas para Mama and other nursery rhymes*. New York: Henry Holt.

Corp, R. (Arr.). (1991–1993). *Folksongs from the British Isles, Ireland, America,* series. London: Faber Music.

Cracre, L. (1989). *Arroz con leche: Popular songs and rhymes from Latin America*. New York: Scholastic.

Currie, S. (1992). *Music in the Civil War*. Cincinnati: Betterway.

de Regniers, B. (1991). *Sing a song of popcorn*. New York: Scholastic.

Disney Press. (1991). *For our children*. Burbank, CA: Author.

Durell, A. (1989). *The Diane Goode book of American folk tales and songs*. New York: Dutton.

Emberly, B. (1969). *London Bridge is falling down*. Upper Saddle River, NJ: Prentice Hall.

Fiarotta, N. (1993). *Music crafts for kids: The how-to book of music discovery*. New York: Sterling.

Fleischman, P. (1992). *Joyful noise: Poems for two voices*. New York: HarperCollins.

Floyd, M. (Arr.). (1991). *Folksongs from Africa*. London: Faber Music.

Garson, E. (Compiler). (1968). *The Laura Ingalls Wilder songbook*. New York: Harper & Row.

Gill, M., & Pliska, G. (1993). *Praise for the singing: Songs for children*. Boston: Little, Brown.

Giovanni, N. (1971). *Spin a soft black song: Poems for children*. New York: Hill & Wong.

Girl Scouts of U.S.A. (1980). *Canciones de nuestra cabana: Songs of our cabana*. New York: Author.

Glazer, T. (1980). *Do your ears hang low? Fifty more musical fingerplays*. New York: Doubleday.

Glazer, T. (1988). *Tom Glazer's treasury of songs for children*. New York: Doubleday.

Glazer, T. (1990). *The Mother Goose songbook*. New York: Doubleday.

Griffith, H., & Stevenson, J. (1986). *Georgia music*. New York: Greenwillow.

Gritton, P. (Arr.). (1993). *Folksongs from India*. London: Faber Music.

Hart, J. (1992). *Singing bee! A collection of favorite children's songs*. New York: Lothrop, Lee & Shepard.

Houston, J. (1972). *Song of the dream people: Chants and images of the Indians and Eskimos of North America*. New York: Atheneum.

Johnson, J. (1995). *Lift every voice and sing*. New York: Scholastic.

Kennedy, J. (1983). *Teddy Bear's picnic*. San Marcos, CA: Green Tiger.

Kidd, R., & Anderson, L. (1992). *On top of Old Smokey: Collection of songs and stories from Appalachia*. Nashville, TN: Ideals Childrens.

Koontz, R. (1988). *This old man: The counting song*. New York: Putnam.

Kovalski, M. (1987). *The wheels on the bus*. Boston: Little, Brown.

Krull, K. (1989). *Songs of praise*. San Diego, CA: Harcourt Brace Jovanovich.

Langstaff, J. (1974). *Oh, a hunting we will go*. New York: Atheneum.

Livingston, M. (1986). *Earth songs*. New York: Holiday House.

Livingston, M. (1995). *Call down the moon: Poems of music*. New York: Margaret McElderry.

Magers, P. (1987). *Sing with me animal songs*. New York: Random House.

Mattox, C. (1990). *Shake it to the one that you love best: Play songs and lullabies from black musical tradition*. Everett, WA: Warren.

Metropolitan Museum of Art Staff. (1987). *Go in and out the window: An illustrated songbook for young people*. New York: Henry Holt.

National Gallery of Art. (1991). *An illustrated treasury of songs: Traditional American songs, ballads, folk songs, nursery rhymes*. New York: Rizzoli International.

Oram, H., Davis, C., & Kitamura, S. (1993). *A creepy-crawly song book*. New York: Farrar, Straus & Giroux.

Peek, M. (1988). *Mary wore her red dress and Henry wore his green sneakers*. Boston: Houghton Mifflin.

Philip, N. (Ed.). (1995). *Songs are thoughts: Poems of the Inuit*. New York: Orchard.

Poddany, E. (1967). *The cat in the hat songbook: 19 Seuss-songs for beginners*. New York: Random House.

Rae, M. M. (1989). *The farmer in the dell*. New York: Scholastic.

Raffi. (1987). *Down by the bay*. New York: Crown.

Raffi. (1989). *The Raffi everything grows songbook*. New York: Crown.

Rosenberg, J. (1989). *Sing me a song: Metropolitan Opera's book of opera stories for children*. New York: Thames & Hudson.

Silberg, J. (1989). *My toes are starting to wiggle! and other easy songs for circle time*. Overland Park, KS: Miss Jackie Music.

Smith, N. S. (1996). *Songs for survival: Songs and chants from tribal people around the world*. New York: Dutton.

Spier, P. (1973). *The Star-Spangled Banner*. New York: Doubleday.

Toop, D. (1991). *Rap attack 2: African rap to global hip hop*. London: Serpent's Tail.

Vozar, D. (1995). *Yo hungry wolf? A nursery rap*. New York: Doubleday.

Vozar, D. (1997). *MC Turtle and the Hip Hop Hare: A happenin' rap*. New York: Doubleday.

Walter, C. (1995). *Multicultural music: Lyrics to familiar melodies and authentic songs*. Minneapolis, MN: Denison.

Walther, T. (1981). *Make mine music*. Boston: Little, Brown.

Warren, J. (1991). *Piggyback songs for school*. Everett, WA: Warren.

Williams, V. (1988). *Music, music for everyone*. New York: Morrow.

Winter, J. (1988). *Follow the drinking gourd*. New York: Knopf.

Wirth, M. (Comp.). (1983). *Musical games, finger plays, and rhythmic activities for early childhood*. West Nyack, NY: Parker.

Yokum, J. (1986). *The lullaby songbook*. San Diego, CA: Harcourt Brace Jovanovich.

Yolen, J. (1989). *The lap-time song and play book*. San Diego, CA: Harcourt Brace Jovanovich.

Yolen, J. (1992). *Jane Yolen's Mother Goose songbook*. Honesdale, PA: Caroline House/Boyds Mills.

Making Instruments

Doney, M. (1995). *Musical instruments*. New York: Franklin Watts.

Elliott, D. (1984). *Alligators and music*. Boston: Harvard Common.

Fiarotta, N. (1995). *Music crafts for kids: The how-to book of music discovery*. New York: Sterling.

Hopkin, B. (1995). *Making simple musical instruments*. Asheville, NC: Lark.

Palmer, H. (1990). *Homemade band: Songs to sing: Instruments to make*. New York: Crown.

Music as Part of Book's Theme

Ambrus, V. (1969). *Seven skinny goats*. San Diego, CA: Harcourt Brace Jovanovich.

Angell, J. (1982). *Buffalo nickel blues band*. New York: Bradbury.

Awmiller, C. (1996). *Wynton Marsalis, gifted trumpet player*. Chicago: Children's Press.

Baer, G. (1989). *Thump, thump, rat-a-tat-tat*. New York: Harper & Row.

Baker, K. (1988). *The magic fan*. San Diego, CA: Harcourt Brace Jovanovich.

Bang, M. (1985). *The paper crane*. New York: Greenwillow.

Barnwell, Y. M. (1998). *No mirrors in my nana's house*. San Diego, CA: Harcourt Brace.

Bates, K. L. (1993). *America the Beautiful*. New York: Simon & Schuster.

Baylor, B., & Himler, R. (1982). *Moon song*. New York: Scribner.

Birdseye, T., & Bammell, S. (1988). *Airmail to the moon*. New York: Holiday House.

Blake, Q. (1991). *All join in*. Boston: Little, Brown.

Bottner, B. (1987). *Zoo song*. New York: Scholastic.

Boynton, S. (2002). *Philadelphia chickens*. New York: Workman.

Brandt, K. (1993). *Pearl Bailey with a song in her heart*. Mahwah, NJ: Troll.

Brett, J. (1989). *The mitten: A Ukrainian folk tale*. New York: Putman.

Brett, J. (1991). *Berlioz the bear*. New York: Putnam.

Brooks, B. (1986). *Midnight hour encores*. New York: Harper & Row.

Buffett, J., & Buffett, S. J. (1988). *The jolly man*. New York: Harcourt Brace Jovanovich.

Bunting, B., & Zemach, K. (1983). *The travelling men of Ballycoo*. New York: Harcourt Brace Jovanovich.

Byars, B. (1985). *The glory girl*. New York: Puffin.

Card, O. S. (1980). *Songmaster*. New York: Dial.

Carle, E. (1996). *I see a song*. New York: Scholastic.

Carlson, N. (1983). *Loudmouth George and the coronet*. Minneapolis, MN: Carolrhoda.

Chalk, G. (1993). *Yankee Doodle*. New York: Dorling Kindersley.

Clement, C. (1988). *The voices of the wood*. New York: Penguin.

dePaola, T. (1983). *Sing, Pierrot, sing*. San Diego, CA: Harcourt Brace Jovanovich.

Duder, T. (1986). *Jellybean*. New York: Viking.

Dupasquier, P. (1985). *Dear Daddy*. New York: Bradbury.

Edwards, P. K., & Alisson, D. (1987). *Chester and Uncle Willoughby*. Boston: Little, Brown.

Fleischman, P., & Wentworth, J. (1988). *Rondo in C*. New York: Harper & Row.

Frances, D., & Reiser, B. (2002). *David gets his drum*. New York: Marshall Cavendish.

Freeman, D. (2004). *Manuelo the playing mantis*. New York: Viking.

Freeman, L. (1953). *Pet of the Met*. New York: Viking.

Gatti, A. (1997). *The magic flute*. San Francisco: Chronicle.

Gioffre, M. (1985). *Starstruck*. New York: Scholastic/Apple.

Goffstein, M. (1977). *Two piano tuners*. New York: Farrar, Straus & Giroux.

Gollub, M. (2000). *The jazz fly*. Santa Rosa, CA: Tortuga.

Greenfield, E. (1988). *Nathaniel talking*. New York: Writers & Readers.

Hantzig, D. (1989). *Pied Piper of Hamlin*. New York: Random House.

Hasley, D., & Gammel, S. (1983). *The old banjo*. New York: Macmillan.

Hedderwick, M. (1985). *Katie Morag and the two grandmothers*. London: Bodley Head.

Hentoff, N. (1965). *Jazz country*. New York: Harper & Row.

Hesse, K. (1997). *Out of the dust*. New York: Scholastic.

Hoffman, E. T. (1984). *The Nutcracker*. New York: Crown.

Hogrogian, N. (1973). *The cat who loved to sing*. Palmer, AK: Aladdin.

Hughes, S. (1983). *Alfie gives a hand*. New York: Mulberry Books.

Isadora, R. (1979). *Ben's trumpet*. New York: Greenwillow.

Johnston, T. (1988). *Pages of music*. New York: Putnam.

Keats, E. J. (1971). *Apt. 3*. New York: Macmillan.

Keller, C. (Compiler). (1985). *Swine lake: Music and dance riddles*. Upper Saddle River, NJ: Prentice Hall.

Kherdian, D., & Hogrogian, N. (1990). *The cat's midsummer jamboree*. New York: Putnam.

Kidd, R. (1988). *Second fiddle: A sizzle & splat mystery*. New York: Lodestar.

Komaiko, L., & Westman, B. (1987). *I like music*. New York: Harper & Row.

Krementz, J. (1991). *Very young musician*. New York: Simon & Schuster.

Krull, K. (1995). *Lives of the musicians: Good times, bad times, and what the neighbors thought*. San Diego, CA: Harcourt Brace.

Kuskin, K. (1982). *The philharmonic gets dressed*. New York: Harper & Row.

Lasker, D. (1979). *The boy who loved music*. New York: Viking.

Leodhas, S. N., & Hogrogian, N. (1965). *Always room for one more*. New York: Henry Holt.

Lionni, L. (1979). *Geraldine, the music mouse*. New York: Random House.

Lobel, A. (1966). *The troll music*. New York: Harper & Row.

Martin, B. (1986). *Barn dance*. New York: Henry Holt.

Martin, B. (1989). *Chicka chicka boom boom*. New York: Simon & Schuster.

Maxner, J. (1989). *Nicholas Cricket*. New York: Harper & Row.

McCaffrey, A. (1976). *Dragonsong*. New York: Macmillan.

McCloskey, R. (1940). *Lentil*. New York: Viking Penguin.

McDermott, G. (1992). *Papagayo*. San Diego, CA: Harcourt Brace Jovanovich.

McDermott, G. (1992). *Zomo the rabbit*. San Diego, CA: Harcourt Brace Jovanovich.

Menotti, G., & Lemieux, M. (1986). *Amahl and the night visitors*. New York: Morrow.

Mosel, A. (1989). *Tiki tiki tembo*. New York: Holt.

Moss, L. (1995). *Zin! zin! zin! A violin*. New York: Simon & Schuster.

Moss, L. (2002). *Music is*. New York: Putnam.

Nichol, B. (1993). *Beethoven lives upstairs*. New York: Orchard Books.

Old, W. (1996). *Duke Ellington: Giant of jazz*. Hillside, NJ: Enlsow.

Paterson, K. (1985). *Come sing, Jimmy Jo*. New York: Dutton.

Paulsen, G. (1985). *Dogsong*. New York: Bradbury.

Perkins, L. (2003). *Snowmusic*. New York Greenwillow Books.

Phail, D. (1999). *Mole music*. New York: Holt.

Pinkwater, D. (1976). *Lizard music*. New York: Dodd Mead.

Price, L. (1990). *Aida: A picture book for all ages*. New York: Harcourt Brace Jovanovich.

Purdy, C. (1994). *Mrs. Merriwether's musical cat*. New York: Putnam.

Raschka, C. (1992). *Charlie Parker played be bop*. New York: Orchard.

Ray, M. L. (1994). *Pianna*. San Diego, CA: Harcourt Brace Jovanovich.

Rayner, M. (1993). *Garth pig steals the show*. New York: Dutton.

Reid, B. (1993). *Two by two*. New York: Scholastic.

Ryan, P. (2002). *When Marian sang*. New York: Scholastic.

Schroeder, A. (1995). *Carolina shout*. New York: Dial.

Schroeder, A., & Fuchs, B. (1989). *Ragtime tumpie*. Boston: Little, Brown.

Seeger, P. (1989). *Abiyoyo* (African folktale). New York: Scholastic.

Sharmat, M. (1991). *Nate the great and musical note*. New York: Dell.

Showell, E. (1983). *Cecilia and the blue mountain boy*. New York: Lothrop.

Skofield, J., & Gundersheimer, D. (1981). *Night dances*. New York: Harper & Row.

Stecher, M. (1980). *Max the music maker*. New York: Lothrop.

Steig, W. (1994). *Zeke Pippin*. New York: HarperCollins.

Stevens, B. (1990). *Handel and the famous sword swallower of Halle*. New York: Philomel.

Stock, C. (1988). *Sophie's knapsack*. New York: Lothrop.

Sturges, P. (2004). *She'll be coming around the mountain*. Waltham, MA: Little, Brown.

Taylor, S. (1985). *All-of-a-kind family*. New York: Dell.

Thomas, I. (1981). *Willie blows a mean horn*. New York: Harper & Row.

Treschel, G. (1992). *The lute's tune*. New York: Doubleday.

van Kampen, V., & Eugen, I. C. (1989). *Orchestranimals*. New York: Scholastic.

Van Laan, N. (1995). *Possum come a-knockin*. New York: Knopf.

Voight, C. (1983). *Dicey's song*. New York: Atheneum.

Walter, M. (1989). *Mariah loves rock*. New York: Macmillan.

Walter, M. P., & Tomes, M. (1980). *Ty's one-man band*. New York: Scholastic.

Weik, M. H., & Grifalconi, A. (1966). *The jazz man*. New York: Atheneum.

Wharton, T. (1991). *Hildegard sings*. New York: Farrar, Straus & Giroux.

Wildsmith, B. (1988). *Carousel*. New York: Knopf.

Williams, V. B. (1983). *Something special for me*. New York: Greenwillow.

Wood, A., Woo, A., & Wood, D. (1988). *Elbert's bad word*. New York: Harcourt Brace Jovanovich.

Yolen, J. (2000). *Harvest home*. San Diego, CA: Harcourt-Brace.

Yorinks, A., & Egielski, S. (1988). *Brave, Minsky!* New York: Farrar, Straus & Giroux.

Zolotow, C., & Tafuri, N. (1982). *The song*. New York: Greenwillow.

Music History and Appreciation

The adventures of Peer Gynt: A puppet production (videorecording). (1995). Los Angeles: Laser Light Video.

Ammons, M. (1995). *Music A.D. 450–1995*. Greensboro, NC: Mark Twain Media, Carson-Dellosa.

Anderson, D. (1982). *The piano makers*. New York: Pantheon.

Arnold, C. (1985). *Music lessons for Alex*. New York: Clarion.

Autexier, P. (1992). *Beethoven, the composer as hero*. New York: Abrams.

Bain, G., & Leather, M. (1986). *The picture life of Bruce Springsteen*. New York: Franklin Watts.

Bayless, K., & Ramsey, M. (1990). *Music: A way of life for the young child*. New York: Merrill.

Beck, I. (1995). *Peter and the wolf*. New York: Atheneum.

Bierhorst, J. (1979). *A cry from the earth: Music of the North American Indians*. New York: Four Winds.

Brighton, C. (1990). *Mozart: Scenes from the childhood of the composer*. New York: Doubleday.

Bye, L. D. (1993). *Students' musical dictionary*. Pacific, MO: Bayside.

Bye, L. D. (1988). *Students' guide to the great composers: A guide to music history for students*. Pacific, MO: Bayside.

Carle, E. (2001). *Today is Monday*. New York: Philomel.

Carnival of the animals: A puppet production (videorecording). (1996). Los Angeles: Laser Light Video.

Davis, A. (2002). *Ella Fitzgerald: The tale of a vocal virtuosa*. Westport, CT: Hyperion.

Deitch, K. M. (1991). *Leonard Bernstein: America's maestro*. Lowell, MA: Discovery Enterprises.

Downing, J. (1990). *Mozart tonight*. New York: Messner.

Emberely, R. (1989). *City sounds*. Boston: Little, Brown.

Englander, R. (1983). *Opera! What's all the screaming about?* New York: Walker.

Fonteyn, M. (1987). *Swan Lake*. New York: Harcourt Brace.

Fornatale, P. (1987). *The story of rock n' roll*. New York: Morrow.

Glass, P. (1969). *Singing soldiers: A history of the Civil War in song*. New York: Grossett & Dunlap.

Greene, C. (1992). *John Philip Sousa, the marching king*. Chicago: Children's Press.

Greens, C. (1992). *Johann Sebastian Bach: Great man of music; Ludwig Van Beethoven, musical pioneer*. Chicago: Children's Press.

Guthrie, W. (1998). *This land is your land*. Waltham, MA: Little, Brown.

Hart, M. (1990). *Drumming at the edge of magic: A journey into the spirit of percussion*. New York: Harper & Row.

Haskins, J. (1987). *Black music in America*. New York: Crowell.

Hayes, A. (1991). *Meet the orchestra.* San Diego, CA: Harcourt Brace Jovanovich.

Hayes, A. (1995). *Meet the marching Smithereens.* San Diego, CA: Harcourt Brace Jovanovich.

Helprin, M., & Van Allsburg, C. (1990). *Swan lake.* Boston: Houghton Mifflin.

Jones, K. M. (1994). *The story of rap music.* Brookfield, CT: Millbrook.

Kendall, C. W. (1993). *Stories of women composers for young musicians.* Edwardsville, IL: Toadwood.

Koscielniak, B. (2000). *The story of the incredible orchestra: An introduction to musical instruments and the symphony orchestra.* St. Charles, IL: Houghton Mifflin.

Kroll, S. (1994). *By the dawn's early light.* New York: Scholastic.

Krull, K. (2003). *M is for music.* Orlando, FL: Harcourt.

Lasker, D., & Lasker, J. (1979). *The boy who loved music.* New York: Viking.

Lillegard, D. (1987). *Woodwinds.* Chicago: Children's Press.

McKissack, P. (1991). *Louis Armstrong: Jazz musician.* Hillside, NJ: Enslow.

Meyerowitz, J. (Narrator). (1993). *George Balanchine's The Nutcracker.* Boston: Little, Brown.

Mitchell, B. (1987). *Raggin': A story about Scott Joplin; America, I hear you: A story about George Gershwin.* Minneapolis, MN: Carolrhoda.

Monceaux, M. (1994). *Jazz: My music, my people.* New York: Knopf.

Monjo, F. N., & Brenner, F. (1975). *Letters to Horseface: Being the story of Wolfgang Amadeus Mozart's journey to Italy.* New York: Viking.

The Nutcracker: A puppet production (videorecording). (1995). Los Angeles: Laser Light Video.

Parker, J. (1995). *I wonder why flutes have holes and other questions about music.* New York: Kingfisher.

Peter and the wolf: A puppet production (videorecording). (1995). Los Angeles: Laser Light Video.

Philip, N. (1995) *Singing America: Poems that define a nation.* New York: Viking Press.

Pillar, M. (1992). *Join the band!* New York: HarperCollins.

Previn, A. (Ed.). (1983). *Andre Previn's guide to the orchestra.* New York: Putnam.

Price, L. (1990). *Aida: A picture book for all ages.* San Diego, CA: Harcourt Brace Jovanovich.

Rosenberg, J. (1989). *Sing me a song: Metropolitan Opera's book of opera stories for children.* New York: Thames & Hudson.

Sabin, F. (1990). *Mozart, young music genius.* Mahwah, NJ: Troll.

San Souci, R. (1992). *The firebird* (retold). New York: Dial.

Saport, L. (1999). *All the pretty little horses.* New York: Clarion.

Schulman, J. (Adap.). (1991). *Story of the Nutcracker* (cassette). New York: HarperCollins.

Simon, C. (1992). *Seizi Owaza: Symphony conductor.* Chicago: Children's Press.

Simon, H. W. (1989). *100 great operas and their stories.* New York: Doubleday.

Stevens, B. (1983). *Ben Franklin's glass harmonica.* Minneapolis, MN: Carolrhoda.

The Swan Lake story (videorecording). (1993). New York: V.I.E.W. Video.

Tames, R. (1991). *Frederick Chopin.* New York: Franklin Watts.

Thompson, W. (1991, 1993). *Pyotr Ilyich Tchaikovsky, Claude Debussy, Franz Schubert, Wolfgang Amadeus Mozart, Ludwig van Beethoven, Joseph Haydn.* New York: Viking.

Velasquez, E. (2003). *The sound that jazz makes.* New York: Walker and Company.

Venezia, M. (1994–1995 & various). Series on famous composers and musicians. Chicago: Children's Press.

Ventura, P. (1989). *Great composers.* New York: Putnam.

Weil, L. (1989). *The magic of music.* New York: Holiday House.

Wildlife symphony (video). (1993). Pleasantville, NY: Reader's Digest.

Wilson, R. (1991). *Mozart's story.* London: A. & C. Black.

Wolff, V. E. (1991). *The Mozart season.* New York: Henry Holt.

Zin! Zin! Zin! A violin (video). (1996). Lincoln, NE: The Library.

Seed Strategies Index

Literature and Poetry, 135–151

acronyms/acrostics, 140
analogy go round, 137
anticipation guide, 144
big bingo, 138
bio webs, 139
biography box, 143
BME map, 139
book map, 143
bridges, 144
buddy reading, 144
CAP prediction, 138
chain poem, 157
chants and songs, 137
character inventory, 138
character poems, 138
character report card, 138
character webs, wheels, graphs, 138
choral reading, 149
circle or pie map, 139
class newspaper, 144
creative problem solving, 137
cubing, 137
culture unit, 143
episode plot card, 139
five w's & h web, 140
folktale detective, 143
genre chart/web, 139
genre study, 140,142
genre traits, 139
graphing plots, 146
home adventure map, 139
informational books, 140
joke books, 143
ladders, 139
letters, 145
lifelines, 143
lit logs, 143
math bookmaking, 147
math poetry, 146
minister's cat, 137
mystery bag, 137
mystery person, 143
onomatopoeia poem, 149
opposites, 137
oral cloze, 135
partner writing, 144
picture book math, 146
plot lines, 139
Poem a Day (PAD), 147
poem match, 149
poem mime, 149
poem patterns, 140,142
poetry art, 149
poetry collections, 149

poetry memorizing, 148
poetry performance, 147
POV guide, 143
predict/prove, 137
prequels and sequel, 143
random combinations, 137
reader response, 149
real-life writing, 144
rhyme change, 138
riddles, 138
SCAMPER, 137
sentence frame, 145
sequence story, 146
setting web, 139
sociowheel, 138
somebody wanted, 138
story map, 144
story problems, 146
take-offs, 145
take a stand, 139
things to write, 140
timeline, 143
tongue twisters, 136
twenty questions, 145
uncle charlie, 137
vocabutoons, 144
Venn diagram, 138
visual poetry, 149
webbing, 137
what-if writing, 143
Who Stole . . . , 137
word association, 137
word collection, 145
word pairs, 138
word sort, 144
word wall, 144
write right away, 138

Visual Art, 190–215

animal flip book, 205
ape the greats, 209
architecture, 203
art ads, 211
art auction, 213
art bags, 196
art chair, 212
art elements mnemonics, 194
art match, 211
art news, 205
art and nature, 205
art poems, 193
art prediction cards, 211
art prewrite, 212
art print story, 209
art walks, 192
artifacts, 207
artist alive, 213

artist birth mates, 209
artist expert, 212
artist interview, 211
artists like me, 209
big book for elements, 194
big book making, 205
brain squeeze, 193
browsing, 193
bubbles, 194
cartooning, 199
chalk ideas, 199
cinco strategy, 209
class flag, 208
class quilt, 201
collage, 200
collections, 193
color recipes, 213
color window/banner, 201
compare/contrast, 194, 212
concentration, 193
count me in, 213
crafts, 201
crayon ideas, 199
crosshatching, 198
dialogue journals/logs, 212
diorama, 202
displays/bulletin boards, 201
doodle log, 192
drawing/rubbing ideas, 198
drawing figures, 199
draw to music, 208
elements exploration, 194
enlarge, simplify, crop, 200
everyday objects, 207
experts, 194
eyes warm-up, 192
famous people art, 208
fiber art, 201
fine art storytelling, 210
fish/bird art, 205
five shape elements, 192
food alternatives, 196
food mural, 206
foot painting, 206
game board, 194
garbage art, 206
group composition, 207
grow a head, 206
guided art lesson, 208
habitat hat, 206
habitat, 3D, 206
haiku, 190
holidays, 207
hot sock, 194
I Spy, 211,214
infinity art, 214
learn wonder like, 210
listen and draw, 209

look back, 193
make a mess, 193
make me a world, 207
mandalas, 207
math art, 214
memory game, 211
mini-museum, 211
mirror image, 192
mixed media, 201
mobiles, 202
multicultural art, 207
murals, 201
museum hunts, 206
mystery bag, 193
name a color, 211
nature collage, 205
nature collections, 206
nature sculpture, 206
note sketching, 209
one-minute find, 194
open sort, 193
origami, 213
painting ideas, 199
papier-mâché, 202
paraphs, 207
parent tips, 196
partial pic preview, 209
parts of speech, 210
photography, 194
picture books, 193, 209
poetry art, 149
postcards, 193
pound flowers, 206
print making, 199
puppets and masks, 204
questions, 194
quick draws, 211
quilt or banner, 201, 213
recipes, 203
riddles, 193
rock paintings, 206
SCAMPER, 192, 213
science of color, 206
science/color, 206
scientific drawing, 206
scribble/doodle, 192
sculpture, 202
see–feel–think–wonder, 192
seeing systematically, 210
self-portrait, 201
sense station, 193
shape elements, 198
shape match, 192
signature art, 207
sing a picture, 196
sketch animals, 206
sketchbooks, 211
soap sculpture, 202

songs/chants, 192
sound/show, 208
square foot, 196
statues, 194
step in, 206, 214
story board, 212
story problems, 213
stretch to sketch, 211
student collections, 193
subject matter, 196,197
symmetry, 214
talking art, 210
three-dimension art, 202
twenty questions, 193
update art, 208
visual gym, 192
walk into a painting, 211
wanted poster, 211
word charts, 194
word walls/webs, 212
word squeeze, 210

Drama and Storytelling,
247-275
7-up, 264
action pantomime, 254
alphabet stories, 272
animal-car-flower, 250
animal charades, 262
animal panels, 262
animal sounds, 262
antonym pantomime, 264
antonym partners, 264
art story map, 273
backwards stories, 273
bell tolls, 251
belly laughs, 250
biography drama, 263
book ads, 261
boring words, 251
break it down, 253, 266
car wash, 269
categories mime, 254
chain pantomime, 253
character laughs, 250
character meetings, 255
character monologues, 260
character sculptor, 264
character talk, 258
charades, 135, 254
circle stories, 272
close observation, 262
commercials, 260
concentration, 249
conflicting messages/motives,
    258, 259
count freeze mime, 254
daffynitions, 264
daily math, 266
Dear Abby, 264
debate, 261
dialogue cards, 259
discussions, 260
don't laugh, 257

elevator, 260
emotion conversation, 259
emotion pantomime, 253
emotional vowels, 263
empathy roles, 259
environmental debate, 262
famous portrait monologues, 263
famous science, 262
finger plays, 250
five sense mime, 254
follow the leader, 271
food stories, 272
fraction mime, 266
greetings, 249
group story mime, 257
hand study, 249
hot sock, 251
I am stories, 272
I heard it first, 261
imaginary place, 254
improvisation ideas, 257-262
improvised scenes, 255, 261
improvised stories, 256
interviews, 260
invisible objects, 252
jigsaw stories, 272
Kalamazoo, 253
keyword stories, 272
laugh contest, 250
literature frames, 272
mask, 265
math commercials, 267
math improvisation, 266
math one-liners, 266
mirrors, 253
moral dilemmas, 263
name sock, 251
narrative mime, 249, 257
nature one-liners, 262
news break, 260
number freeze, 253
number mime, 253
number talk, 267
noiseless sounds, 251
nursery rhyme, 255
one-liners, 255, 257
one minute after, 255
one word, 250
painting word pictures, 272
pair dialogue, 248
pair mime, 253
pair sound effects, 257
panels, 260
pantomime ideas, 251-257
pantomime solo, 253
partner retelling, 272
partner search, 250
pass and pretend, 250
personal stories, 272
portrait conversations, 263
POV roles, 264
prediction mime, 255
pretend-paint, 257
pretend-write, 264
Project Wild, 262

prop stories, 273
puppet shows, 273
reader's theatre, 265, 266
research, 263
retell stories, 272
reverse web, 250
rhyme change, 264
riddle stories, 272
role play, 262
round robin retell, 273
QU stories, 254, 258-259
quick change, 253
safe fights, 254
say it your way, 258
scavenger hunt, 250
sentence frames, 258
show time, 260, 265
songs/pantomime, 254-255
sound effects/action stories,
    250, 257-258
sound motion machine, 255
special props, 262
spelling mime, 264
story ballads, 273
story captions, 264
story challenge, 272
story problems, 266
storytelling, 267-275
stunts and tricks, 251
tableau, 255
tableau captions, 255
talk with your body, 271
talking math, 267
television shows, 260
the chair, 260
think back mime, 253
time mime, 254
tongue twisters, 136, 250
transformations, 255
vocal expression, 271
voice stunts, 251
volume control, 257
ways to celebrate, 251
what-if/obstacle mime, 253
what's different?, 251
what's my line?, 263
wiggleworms, 249
word change, 250

Dance and Movement,
307-322
across the floor, 313
adopt a dance, 314
angle dance, 320
angles and degrees, 320
animal exploration, 316
antonyms, 318
art alive, 316
art in motion, 321
artists that move, 321
back to back, 311
balance moves, 314
ball bounce, 312
balloon balance, 311

balance mime, 312
bird flight, 316
body count, 311
body directions, 310
body melody match, 321
body moves/steps, 313
body painting, 316
body touches, 310
brain dance, 309
buddy walk, 311
card draw, 312
cause-effect, 319
ceremonies, 317
character walk, 319
characters alive, 320
choreograph to music, 321
circle back rub, 310
classification, 319
compare-contrast, 318
constellations, 316
co-op musical chairs, 311
country or state, 317
cumulative name game, 312
current events dances, 317
dance a painting, 321
dance a story, 319
dance freeze, 314
dance machine, 314
dance poetry, 319
dance web, 314
dancing animals, 315
don't cross, 311
dynamics, 321
emotion/color dance, 321
endangered species, 316
energy boost, 314
environment dance, 315
environment walk, 315
famous dances, 312
folk dances, 317
folktale dance, 317
follow the leader, 311
foot to foot, 309
foreign language, 317
four square, 314
freeze, 310
geometric shapes, 320
gestures, 319
get the facts, 320
get to work, 316
get moving, 314
hand warm-up, 309
hang loose, 309
"head shoulders," 316
historical events, 317
holiday dances, 317
horse dancing, 316
hug yourself, 309
I'm stuck, 312
imagination journey, 310
imagination walk, 313
inhale/exhale, 309
insect dances, 316
inventions dance, 316
jump-turn-freeze, 313

key topic dance, 319
Laban effort actions, 313
letters/alphabet, 318
life cycle, 316
lightning, 310
line by line, 319
machine dances, 315
magic wand, 317
magic shoes, 310
math dance, 320
math glue, 320
math moves, 320
mechanical moves, 315
military moves, 317
mood set, 310
movement add-on, 314
movement bingo, 312
movement chain, 311
movement problems, 313
musicals, 312
negative/positive space, 321
no holes, 311
no words, 311
noodle freeze, 310
North Pole, 315
number shapes, 320
paint a dance, 321
paranoia, 310
parts of speech, 319
pass it on, 314
personal space, 311
phonics shapes, 318
places to sit, 315
poetry in motion, 319
popcorn, 310
real-life sounds, 316
real-life rituals, 316
response to accent, 314
rhyming words, 318
ribbon dance, 314
sculpture dance, 321
shake and shape, 313
shape concentration, 310
shape dance, 320
shape go round, 313
shape rope, 314
sheet music, 311
shrink and stretch, 311
sign language, 321
sing with hands, 321
Simon Says, 311
slow breathing, 309
sound motion, 310
sound/move collage, 315
space bubbles, 311
spelling, 318
spider web, 311
sports dance, 317
states of water, 316
statues, 314

step in, 312
story tableau, 319
story tension, 320
string shapes, 314
stuck together, 311
syllables, 318
telling time, 320
theme dance, 319
three levels, 313
tool dance, 315
trio dances, 317
twos and threes, 320
verbal dance, 319
video response, 314
walk different ways, 310
walks, 313
watch concentration, 309
weather dance, 316
who started it?, 309
wiggle and giggle, 309
word a day, 318
word hunt, 312
word walls/webs, 318
write about, 319

Music, 359–378
add-on songs, 361, 376
balloon movement, 361
barbershop quartet, 363
BGIM, 362
bingo hunt, 362
bird song survey, 367
body compositions, 364
brainstorm, 367
cannons and rounds, 363
celebrate, 361
clap rhythm, 360
class songbooks, 374
cloze telegrams, 373
commercials, 372
community sing, 369
conducting, 363
continents song, 368
counting songs, 376
cultural contrasts, 369
culture and song, 374
cumulative melody, 362
current events, 369
data collection/graph, 375
dictionary, 374
dynamics dial, 363
echo me, 360, 370
emotions, 372
environment sounds, 362
exchange, 361
experts, 372
finger plays, 371
follow the leader, 365
form books, 364

fraction pies, 375
guess who, 363
guests and experts, 374
guided music/literacy
        lesson, 370
happy birthday, 360
hootenanny, 372
history through music, 369
history timeline, 369
homemade jam, 365
how instruments began, 368
hum groups, 362
hum melodies, 362
instrument rummy, 365
instruments categories, 365
instruments notation, 364
instruments pantomime, 364
interviews, 372
introduce eras, 369
jives, 365
join in, 360
kazoo melodies, 362
knock and respond, 361
language mentors, 374
listening phones, 362
make it Italian, 365
mnemonic songs, 375
mood music, 360
morning TV, 360
multicultural music/dance, 369
multicultural songbook, 368
music and arts, 363
music and culture, 368
music concentration, 364
music memory, 361
music month, 366
music rainbow, 364
music response journals, 373
musical chairs, 374
musical classifieds, 368
musical math, 375
musical poetry, 374
musical quilt, 376
name duet, 362
name echo, 360
name harmony, 362
name melody, 362
name songs, 360
name that instrument, 363
nature orchestra, 367
notation, 364
note math, 375
number lyrics, 375
numerals and counting, 376
"Old Macmajor," 363
operettas, 373
patterns, 375
picturing songs, 363
poem ostinati, 364
question/answer songs, 360

read all about it, 374
read around, 372
read to music, 374
repeat a beat, 364
response options, 365
rhythm and sound
        math, 375
rhythm box beats, 365
rhythm circle, 361
rhythm instruments, 376
rhythm mirror, 361
rhythm pass, 361
rhythm symphony, 362
rhythm sync, 361
say it differently, 360
scale numbering, 375
science and sound, 367
science summary song, 366
science symphony, 367
season story, 369
shape composition, 376
shoe beat, 361
sing letter sounds, 371
sing literature, 373
sing the scales, 360
sing to spell, 371
sing vowels, 371
singing speeds, 365
singing words, 370
song character
        interview, 371
song charts, 374
song graphs, 375
song history, 369
song scavenger hunt, 374
song sources, 369
song story, 374
songwriting, 372
sound sort, 367
sound collage, 368
sound mobiles, 367
sound substitution, 371
sound texture story, 363
staff walk, 364
states and capitals, 368
style party, 365
summary songs, 368
syllable sing, 364
tempo change, 361
theme song, 360
thick/thin voices, 363
tongue twisters, 360
two-part rhythm, 365
vibration study, 367
weather reports, 367
webbing, 366
word choir, 371
word problems, 375
word rhythms, 370
write all about it, 374

A+ schools, 10, 14, 68
academic achievement and the arts; *see also* Research Updates; LADDM areas; research; testing, 10, 11, 14, 34–35, 284, 325, 338
accommodation and assimilation; *see* Piaget
achievement gap, 1, 2, 15, 22, 33–34
active engagement and learning; *see also* engagement, 60
Adams, M., 101
adapting for diverse needs; *see also* PARTICULAR; differentiated instruction, 12
aesthetic; *see also* criticism
    awareness and appreciation, 74, 159, 160, 179, 282, 284, 330, 342
    development, needs and stages, 99, 156, 157, 222
    environment, class and school; *see also* Arts Integration Blueprint; LADDM areas, 11–12, 31, 37, 56–57, 72, 73, 174, 177–78
    orienting, 74, 79–80, 125, 156, 176, 178, 298, 351–352
    scanning, 177
    teaching, learning, thinking, 31–32, 57, 73, 160
    versus anesthetic, 72–73, 174
African-American; *see* multicultural
age-stage appropriate; *see* developmental levels
Alexander, J., 305
aliteracy; *see also* illiteracy, 101
Allen, L., 93, 322
Allington, R., 16
alliteration; *see* poetic device
allusion, defined, 105
alphabetic code; *see* literacy, reading
"America the Beautiful," history, 369
American Alliance for Theatre and Education (AATE), 224
American Library Association (ALA), 102

Americans for the Arts, 13, 406
Annenberg Challenge for Arts Education, 15
antiphonal; *see* poetry performance
Ape the Greats, 101
Apollinaire
archetypes; *see* motifs and archetypes
architecture, 203
Aristotle, 23, 48
Armstrong, K., 6
Armstrong, T., 40
Arnheim, R., 279
art, definition, 7, 159
art; *see* visual art
artifacts, 58
artist-author
    birthdays, 403
    study; *see* unit
    residencies and visits, 58, 71, 91–92, 130–131, 242, 305
artist(ry)
    characteristics; *see also* teacher, artful, 65, 153, 160
    expert, strategy, 212–213
arts
    added education, 7
    and cognition; *see also* cognition; thinking, creative problem solving, 76
    and the brain; *see* brain
    as communication tools; *see also* communication, 4, 7, 85, 12, 16, 30–31, 62–63, 66, 80
    as core disciplines, 21
    as teaching and learning tools, 8, 11, 29, 57
    -based literature; *see also* literature, 120
    -based read-alouds; *see* read alouds
    -based schools; *see* schools; snapshots; Research Updates
    -based reform; *see* reform
    defining; *see* LADDM (separate entries)
    directory, 93, 279
    economic impact of, 326
    elements, concepts and skills; *see* arts literacy

for art's sake/learning's sake, 10, 57, 154
    in human history, 6
    infusion; *see also* integration, 10, 56–57
    integration definition; *see also* integration, 11
    literacy; *see also* LADDM; INTASC, 12, 61–63, 66
    organizations; *see* LADDM, Arts Integration Blueprint (partnerships); websites
    partnerships, 12, 91–93, 242
    processes, skills, forms, products; *see also* Arts Integration Blueprint, arts literacy, 65, 80–81
    rationale; *see also* Arts Integration Blueprint, philosophy; Research Updates, 6, 7, 62, 72
    routines and structure; *see* instructional design
    specialists; *see* specialists; partnerships; teaching artist
    standards; *see* standards
    to introduce, develop or conclude, 83
    unique contributions, 16
    with arts integration, 72, 115, 169, 227, 282, 290, 302, 321, 340, 351, 359
Arts and the Basic Curriculum (ABC), 5, 6, 14, 27, 37
Arts Education Partnership (AEP), 20, 23, 242
Arts for Academic Achievement, 14
Arts Go to School, 186
Arts Integration Blueprint; *see also* LADDM arts areas, 56–93
    adapting for diverse needs, 85–87
    aesthetic environment, 57, 72–73
    applied to each arts area; see Chapters, 4, 6, 8, 10, and 12
    arts literacy, 12, 61–66
    arts partnerships, 10, 12, 91–93

assessment FOR learning, 75, 87–90
    best teaching practices, 12–13, 33, 74–82
    collaborative planning, 57, 66–72
    instructional design: routines and structures, 12–13, 58, 82–85
    literature as a core art, 73–74
    overview/summary of building blocks, 12–13, 62–63
    philosophy of arts integration, 26, 28–33, 46, 60, 80
    questions, 61
ArtsEdge; *see also* websites, 406
Ashley River Creative Arts Elementary, 3, 4, 24, 60, 92, 293, 303, 324, 352, 356, 357, 359–360, 368
Asian American; *see* multicultural literature
assessment; *see also* Arts Integration Blueprint; LADDM; projects and performances; test(s)ing
    and evaluation, 88–89, 292
    anecdotal/observation records, 90, 241, 303, 309, 356
    arts folios; *see also* portfolios, 303, 397
    authentic, criteria for, 78, 89
    benchmarks; *see also* standards, 89
    definition/purposes, 21, 79, 88–89, 185
    effective, 89, 185
    evidence-based, 88, 90
    FOR learning, 12, 33, 75, 88, 185
    formative and summative, 88–89, 240, 303, 356
    grades and grading, 88
    informal tools, examples, 3, 4, 89, 356, 394–398
    multiple intelligences, 41
    portfolios, performances and exhibits, 3, 8, 33, 59, 84, 89–90, 129–131, 185, 277, 296, 304, 397
    program evaluation, 88, 186, 242, 304, 356

423

assessment; *see also* Arts Integration Blueprint; LADDM; projects and performances; test(s)ing *(Contd.)*
  resources, 397
  rubrics and checklists, 4, 8, 33, 88–89, 188, 241, 243, 278, 293, 303–304
  self and peer, 88, 90, 24, 293, 304
Astaire, F., 296
at-risk students; *see also* PARTICULAR Adaptations, 6, 10, 15, 20–22, 27, 33, 36–37, 56, 66, 85, 188, 221, 280, 327
attention (span); *see* concentration
attention getters; *see also* discipline; concentration; signals, 82, 236, 328
audience(s); *see also* motivation
  etiquette, 229, 294
  participation and engagement, 30, 73, 76, 233–234, 341
  types and roles of, 80, 294
authentic learning, 9
author artist study or visit; *see* artist-author; unit

Bach, J.S., 323, 332, 334, 342
balance; *see* integration, meaningful
Baldwin, J., 98, 99
ballet, 285, 322
Baron, R., 285
basic skills; *see* LADDM, arts literacy; literacy
beauty, need for/teaching, 72, 156, 181, 281–282, 329, 330
beginning middle end (BME), 235
Bennett, T., 26, 229
BEST; *see* dance elements
best teaching practices; *see also* teacher characteristics; Arts Integration Blueprint; LADDM areas, 11, 12, 33
bibliophiles, 97, 99, 117
bibliotherapy, 98, 99
big ideas and essential questions; *see also* themes and truths, 9, 11, 12, 58, 66–68, 187, 317
biography; *see also* literary genre, 160
birthday buddies, 403

blank books; *see* writing; book making
block lettering, 201
Bloom's taxonomy; *see also* questions; higher-order thinking, 157
body parts and moves; *see* dance elements
book(s)
  ads or talks, 59, 122, 127
  circles, 154
  leveling; *see also* readability, 130–131
  recommended; *see* awards; science; social studies; literature, math
  making, 58, 125, 163, 205
  nook, 58, 129
  parts; *see* picture books
  report alternatives, 401–402
  sources; *see also* literature, arts-based, 163
Booth, E., 10, 29, 57, 77, 92, 329
Boston, B., 11, 351
brain
  -based teaching/learning, 30, 37–39, 40, 66, 282, 325–326
  development and influences, 38, 40, 182, 329
  research; *see also* music; research; Research Updates, 37, 38, 40, 73, 156, 284, 325–326, 328
brain's-on learning; *see also* engagement, 11, 282
brainstorming; *see also* Creative Problem Solving, 54, 80, 191
Brookes, M., 177, 183
Broudy, H., 156
building blocks, Arts Integration Blueprint, 60
Burgard, R., 328

Caldecott Award; *see* literature awards
call and response (storytelling and songs), 269, 349
CAPE (Chicago Arts Partnership with Education), 6, 15
Casals, P., 8
careers, arts; *see also* workplace; LADDM areas
Carle, E., 65
Carnegie Medal; *see* literature awards
Catterall, J., 40
censorship, 100, 406

centers and stations; *see also* Arts Integration Blueprint, instructional design; LADDM areas, 13, 58, 73, 85, 129, 180, 302, 354
Chagall, M., 154
Changing Education through the Arts (CETA), 15, 92
character(s); *see also* arts literacy, drama elements, literary elements; Seed Strategies Index, 103–104
charter schools; *see also* schools, 11
Cheek, A., 341, 356, 357, 359
Chilcote, B., 323–324
choice; *see also* interest; motivation, 42, 43, 46, 75, 122, 124
Chopin, F., 323, 334
choreography; *see also* dance, 278, 283, 285, 299
chromesthesia, 328
Cinderella story, 6
cinquain; *see* poem patterns
class gallery and museum, 73
class, teacher and school profiles; *see* snapshots; schools
classic(al); *see* music; literature canon, 120
classroom arrangement; *see* aesthetic environment
classroom management; *see* discipline
clays and doughs; *see* recipes
clerihew; *see* poem patterns
climate, learning; *see* aesthetic environment
climax; *see* plot; literary elements
Clinton, H.R., 93
Clinton, W., 329
close looking and listening; *see also* look closely, 352
cloze strategy, 147, 247
clubs, arts-based, 5, 28, 85, 239
cluster or web; *see* Seed Strategies Index, literature; brainstorming
coaching; *see also* descriptive feedback, 8, 31, 45, 74, 78–79, 91, 149, 178, 235, 240, 277, 296
cognition/cognitive; *see also* thinking, 17, 30, 35, 40, 76, 152
cognitive dissonance; *see also* problems, 7
cognitive, affective and psychomotor; *see also* development, 326

collaboration/collaborative planning; *see also* Arts Integration Blueprint; LADDM areas; standards, 4, 5, 9, 11, 12, 19, 37, 57, 68–69, 71, 243, 289
collage; *see* visual art media
Collins, R., 272
color; *see* visual art literacy:elements
coloring books; *see* dictated art
Comenius, 1
communication and the arts; *see also* arts, 12, 16, 17, 19, 33, 34, 78, 92
  effective, 29, 36, 45, 62, 66, 152–153, 158, 162, 177, 303, 379
  receptive and expressive, 303
community (building); *see also* energizers in Seed Strategy chapters, 17, 19
compassion, 19
competence and control; *see also* discipline; confidence, 20, 31
composer of the day, 58, 354
composition; *see also* music; writing; visual art, 18
comprehension and understanding, 8, 17, 18, 31, 68, 80, 153, 156, 168, 177–178, 219, 239, 339
concentration and focus, 17, 20, 31, 158, 177, 219, 241, 281, 300
conferences, with students, 90, 131
confidence and courage, 20, 158, 281–282, 329
conflict, definition and importance, 221, 224
conformity, problems with, 81
connections, importance; *see also* integration, meaningful; higher-order thinking; creative problem solving; collaborative planning, 78, 153, 167–168, 186, 290
connotation and denotation; *see also* figurative language, 105
consequences hierarchy; *see also* discipline, 237, 300
consonance and assonance; *see also* style, 106
constructivism; *see also* Arts Integration Blueprint philosophy, 28, 37, 76

controls, drama; *see also* discipline, 237
Cook, W., 289, 291, 296
cooperation; *see also* groups; motivation, 17, 19, 222, 281
copycat books and songs; *see* writing
copying, problems, 176, 179
copyright information, 406
core book; *see* unit types
Coretta Scott King Award; *see* literature awards
Cornett, A., 363
Cornett, C., 3, 76, 99
Cornett, L., 159
Cornett, R., 81
Cornett, S., 101
correlation; *see* research
co-teaching and co-planning; *see also* collaboration; Arts Integration Blueprint; LADDM areas, 11, 57, 60, 68, 70–71, 289–290, 305
course of study (COS); *see* curriculum; standards
CPS; *see* Creative Problem Solving
Crabb, C., 293
creating meaning; *see* meaning making
Creative Problem Solving (CPS) process, 9, 13, 17, 25, 29, 31, 33, 47–55, 57–58, 63, 65, 74, 76–78, 150, 152, 157, 159, 167, 177, 282
and the reading/writing process, 122
CPS summary, 50
examples for the arts; *see* LADDM areas
Creative Spirit Profile (self-evaluation), 48–49
creativity and creative thinking, 36, 39, 65, 297
definition and influences, 29, 53
theories, models, research, 48
crescendo and decrescendo, in music, 331, 363
critical/creative listening and thinking, 17, 18, 36, 178
criticism/critique; *see also* critical thinking; higher order thinking; creative problem solving literary, 125
visual art critique, 18, 160, 178
Csikszentmihalyi, M., 48, 52

cubing strategy, 54
cueing; *see also* attention getters; coaching, 229, 235, 244, 294
culture(s) and the arts, 17, 158
definition, 18, 19
unit; *see* unit types; social studies; multicultural
curriculum
constriction/narrowing, 22, 34, 66, 87
curriculum and instruction adaptations; *see* PARTICULAR adaptations; at risk; differentiated instruction
alignment and mapping; *see also* standards; unit clusters, 28, 67–69, 91
benchmarks; *see* standards
frameworks; *see* lesson plans; units; schools
goals; *see* standards
quilt, 69

Da Vinci, L., 7
Dalcroze, E., 337
Dallas ArtsPartners, 15
D'Amboise, J., 281
dance
and the arts; *see* arts with arts
and creative problem solving (CPS), 276–277, 280, 284, 286, 289, 297, 308
and culture/real life, 281, 283
and curricular areas; *see* literature math, science, social studies; Seed Strategies Index
and imagery, 297
and movement, 284, 289, 296
and sports/health, 279–282, 285, 293
Arts Integration Blueprint, dance, 279–306
adaptations for diverse needs, 302–303, 392–393
aesthetic environment, 294–295
arts partnerships, 304–305
assessment FOR learning, 303–304
best teaching practices, 296–300
collaborative planning, 289–294, 305
dance literacy: elements and concepts, 283–289
instructional design: routines, 300–302

literature, dance-based, 295, 414–415
philosophy, 279–283
as a teaching and learning tool, 282, 285, 299
as communication, 279, 282, 284–286, 290, 298, 300
BEST dance elements, 285–287, 312–314
careers and people, 287
choreography, 285–286, 299
coaching; *see also* coaching; descriptive feedback, 286, 300
defined, 284
history, 280, 284
integration, meaningful; *see also* integration; Arts Integration Blueprint; Seed Strategies Index, 278
integration, rationale; *see also* Arts Integration Blueprint, philosophy; research, 279–281, 284, 289, 298
lesson plans(ing); *see also* units, 276, 293, 300–302
machine strategy, 96
problems and concerns, 281, 292, 298
processes and products, 286, 289, 299
research; *see also* research; Research Updates, 279
resources and professional organizations, 287, 305–306, 322
Seed Strategies; *see* Seed Strategies Index, dance
and curricular areas; *see also* math; literacy; science; social studies, 314–321
and other arts; *see* arts with arts integration
BEST elements and concepts, dance, 311–314
energizers and warm-ups, 287, 309–311
specialists; *see also* specialists; collaboration; partners, 289, 304
standards; *see* National Standards for Dance; INTASC, 284, 290
styles, genre and forms, 283, 285, 317
teacher(ing); *see also* teacher characteristics, 279, 284, 287, 296, 301

three-part (freeze–move–freeze), 291, 301, 308
units; *see also* units; lesson plans, 287–294
versus pantomime, 289
view and do, 296
vocabulary; *see also* vocabulary, 289–290
Dean, L., 274
DEAR; *see* independent reading
Deasy, R., 6, 10, 11, 13, 35–36, 40
debriefing, 89, 96, 218, 238, 245, 294, 301, 303
Degas, E., 191
democracy, 32
demonstration; *see* explicit teaching
denouement; *see* literary elements
depth and breadth; *see* themes and truths
descriptive feedback; *see also* coaching, 46, 79–80, 124, 177, 188, 235, 241, 244, 248, 277, 281, 296, 300, 303, 356
details, importance; *see also* patterns, 18, 31, 44, 65, 79, 152–153, 218
developmental stages and levels; *see also* learning theories, 29, 47, 130, 156–157, 181–183, 355, 389–391
brain; *see* brain
cognitive, affective, psychomotor, 326
developmentally appropriate; *see also* PARTICULAR adaptations; at risk; best practices, 289, 392–393
Dewey, J., 51, 72, 216, 280, 285
diamante; *see also* poem patterns, 320
dictated art(s)/coloring books, problems, 81, 157, 179, 289
didactic, concept, 102, 117
Different Ways of Knowing program (DWOK); *see also* schools, 14
differentiated instruction; *see also* PARTICULAR adaptations; Arts Integration Blueprint, adaptations, 85–86, 130, 154, 183–184, 239, 392–393
diorama; *see* visual art media
direct or explicit; *see* explicit teaching

disabilities and handicaps; *see also* at risk; PARTICULAR, 392–393

disadvantaged; *see* at risk

discipline; *see also* concentration; attention and classroom management, 2, 4, 10, 17, 74, 81–82, 136, 235–37, 299, 352

rules and controls; *see also* drama; dance, 82, 237, 294, 297, 299

intervention/prevention strategies, 399–400

self; *see also* independence, 36, 281, 329

discovery learning; *see* inquiry

discussion

examples and strategies, 128–129, 180, 234

literature; *see* literature

questions; *see also* questions and questioning, 123, 234

text-based; *see* text

visual art and prints, 180, 183–184

displays; *see also* visuals; songs, 73

dissonance; *see* cognitive; problems; CPS process

divergent thinking; *see also* creative problem solving, 83

diverse perspectives, thinking, values; *see also* POV, 281

diverse populations; *see also* PARTICULAR; at risk, 11, 37, 87

diversity; *see also* cultures, 30, 37, 72, 79, 99, 158, 166

Dixie, song history, 369

docent(s), 58, 73, 154, 180

drama

and creative problem solving (CPS), 218, 221, 234, 239

and other arts; *see* arts with arts

and other curricular areas; *see* math, literacy, science, social studies; Seed Strategies Index

Arts Integration Blueprint, drama, 279–306

adaptations for diverse needs, 239–240

aesthetic environment, 229–231

arts partnerships, 242–246

assessment FOR learning, 222, 240–242

best teaching practices, 231–237

collaborative planning, 227–229, 242

drama/theatre literacy: elements and concepts, 223–227

instructional design routines, 238–239

literature, drama-based, 231–232

philosophy, 218–223

as a teaching and learning tool, 226, 249

as communication; *see also* meaning making, 221–222, 227

careers, 226

defined, 223–224

dialogue, 248

discussions; *see* questions; discussions

forms, pantomime and verbal; *see also* pantomime; Seed Strategies and Seed Strategies Index, 225, 230, 248–249

history, 216, 223–224

integration, meaningful; *see* Arts Integration Blueprint; integration; Seed Strategies Index

integration, rationale; *see* Arts Integration Blueprint, philosophy; research

lesson plans and planning, 229, 230, 238–239

management and discipline; *see also* discipline, 235–237

pantomime; *see* drama forms

process(es) versus performance, 224–226

rationale, integration, 219, 221–222

research; *see also* Research Updates, 216, 219–220

resources and professional organizations; *see also* resources, 224, 246, 274, 406

Seed Strategies; *see also* Seed Strategies Index, drama, 247–275

and curricular areas; *see* literacy, math, science, social studies

energizers and warm-ups, 238, 244, 249–251

pantomime strategies, 239, 251–257

verbal/improvisation, 239, 257–262

specialists; *see also* careers; teaching artist, 226, 244

storytelling; *see* storytelling

teacher's role; *see also* teacher in role, 226, 231, 233

standards; *see* National Standards for Theatre; INTASC, 223, 227–228

troupe, 85

units; *see also* units; lesson plans, 227–229

versus theatre, 225

vocabulary; *see also* drama literacy; vocabulary

drama in education (DIE); *see* drama history

drawing (and rubbing); *see also* visual art media/techniques, 162, 198–199

alphabet, 183

ideas and media; *see* visual art materials/techniques

realistic and symbolic; *see also* symbolic, 177, 183

stages; *see also* developmental levels, 181

drop-outs; *see also* at risk, 22

drugs and drug-free schools, 15, 21, 22

Duncan, I., 279, 285

Duxberry Elementary, 367

dynamics, music, 330

EAR (expression, accuracy, rate); *see* fluency

early childhood, 22, 73

Easy Pickin' poem, 146

Edison, T., 32, 280

effective teaching; *see* best arts teaching practices

effort; *see* persistence; motivation

Einstein, A., 15, 32, 38, 54, 152, 222, 329

Eisner, E., 8, 16, 19, 39, 63, 73, 80, 153

elements and concepts; *see* arts literacy; LADDM; Seed Strategies Index

Ellicott, J., 4, 5

emotions and emotional intelligence, 7, 17, 19, 30, 39, 56, 59, 79–80, 126, 156, 221, 282, 232, 326, 327

empathy, 19, 36, 39, 51, 77, 79, 98, 99, 100, 329

energizers and warm-ups; *see also* Seed Strategies under LADDM areas, 83

engagement; *see also* motivation; interest; hands-on, 7, 8, 12, 14, 19, 29, 31, 36, 45, 66, 68, 73–74, 76, 97, 99, 122, 176, 296–297, 348, 379

English Language Learners (ELL), 10

ensemble; *see* group work

enthusiasm and passion; *see* teacher characteristics

entrainment, 328

environment; *see* aesthetic environment

EPC chart; *see also* discussion strategies, 128

EPR (every pupil response), 76

equity, educational, 36

Erikson, E., 43

stage theory; *see also* learning theories; development, 43

essential questions; *see also* big ideas; themes and truths; questions, 8, 11, 56

eurythmics, 337

evaluation; *see* assessment

evaluative judgments; *see* higher-order thinking; creative problem solving

evidence, importance of, 18, 34

-based teaching; *see also* assessment, 35, 88

examples versus models, 81, 234, 296

excellence; *see* quality work

exceptionalities; *see* at risk; differentiated instruction PARTICULAR adaptations

exhibit/document progress; *see* assessment; performances and exhibits

expectation and self-fulfilling prophecy (SFP), 296, 348

explicit idea or theme; *see* literary elements

explicit teaching, 12, 31, 33, 42, 66, 70, 74, 78–79, 124, 177, 235, 238, 298, 349, 351

explore, experiment and discover, 81, 298

explore-practice-express lesson, 177

expressive and receptive; *see* communication

expressive reading; *see also* reading aloud; fluency, 95

externalize, importance, 33, 156, 222
extrinsic rewards; *see* motivation

fables; *see also* literary genre, 108
Fahmie, D., 376
fairy tales; *see also* literary genre, 108
fantasy; *see* literary genre
fantasy journey; *see* imagination journey
Farnsworth, P., 54
fat questions; *see* questions
feedback; *see* descriptive feedback; coaching
FFOE (fluent, flexible, original, elaborative); *see also* creative problem solving; creativity, 51, 124
fiction; *see* literary genre; genre
field-based learning, 43, 72, 171
  pre-during-post trip guidelines, 72, 404–405
  simulated; *see* imagination journey, 234
  trips, 10, 171, 293, 341
figurative language, 105
fish bowl strategy; *see also* discussion, 129
five finger rule, 126
fix-ups; *see also* independence, 66, 82
flow state; *see also* creative problem solving, 31, 327
fluency; *see also* literacy, 128, 130, 150, 221, 326, 329, 339
focus; *see* concentration; attention getters
focus ball strategy, 84
foil; *see* literary elements, character
folios, arts, 90, 397
folktales; *see* literary genre; genre
form; *see* LADDM elements; genre
formative and summative; *see* assessment
Forrest, H., 267
Fountain, R., 188
fourth R., 16
fragmenting learning; *see* isolated
frames; *see* scaffolds
frameworks; *see* lesson frameworks
free verse; *see* poem patterns
freedom with limits; *see* creativity; creative problem solving

fresco, definition, 162
Frost, R., 48
frozen shapes; *see* tableau, 96
fun, importance; *see also* humor, 222, 298, 329
funding, grants, budgets, 5, 406

Gallup Poll, 22
Gardner, H., 22, 40, 78, 282, 284
gender, awareness; *see* developmental stages
generalists, 17
generalizations; *see* big ideas; themes and truths
genre; *see also* literary genre
  charts, 125
  defined, 106
  study; *see* unit types
Getty Center for Education in the Arts, 167
ghost dancers, 283
gifted and talented; *see* differentiated instruction
Ginott, H., 379
glossary, arts terms, 68
goals; *see also* motivation, 75
goals; *see* integration; Arts Integration Blueprint, philosophy
Goals 2000, 21
Godwin, G., 216
Goodlad, J., 16
Goethe, 326, 330
Golden, A., 376
Goldilocks strategy; *see* five finger rule
good reader and writer characteristics, 102, 122, 124
grades and grading; *see also* assessment, 75
graduation rates and the arts; *see* at risk; drop-outs
Graham, M., 276, 285, 296
Gray, B., 13
Gris, J., 297
group(s) work/grouping; *see also* social; Vygotsky; clubs, 43, 47, 75, 85, 130, 222, 235, 239, 277, 281, 296, 299, 341
Guernica, 7
guided lessons; *see also* explicit teaching, 85, 130, 208

habits, teacher; *see* best teaching practices
haiku; *see also* poem patterns, 190
Hand Middle School, 33
hands-on, brains-on; *see also* engagement, 29, 39, 60, 65, 122

Hans Christian Andersen; *see* literature awards
happiness; *see* humor; fun, 329
Haris Poll, 16
harmony; *see also* music elements, 331
Harry Potter, 96–97
Hava Nagila, 329
head, heart, hands; *see also* engagement, 76, 126, 159, 276, 296, 379
Heathcote, D., 219, 223
Heinig, R. 224
high poverty students; *see* at risk
high stakes; *see* tests
higher-order thinking skills (HOTS); *see also* creative problem solving; Bloom's taxonomy, 16, 18, 21, 33, 35, 45, 80, 100, 156–158, 166, 178, 190
Hispanic-American; *see* multicultural
historical fiction; *see* literary genre
history; *see* social studies
Hitchcock, A., 216
holistic learning; *see also* whole to part, 9, 282
hope, role of arts in, 33, 72, 87, 102, 223, 282–183
Horres, S., 172, 357
hot sock energizer, 194
Huckabee, M., 11, 329
humor, 46, 53, 76, 106–107, 130, 328

I Spy strategy, 180, 355
I statements; *see also* discipline, 399–400
IDC (introduction-development-conclusion); *see* lessons
illiteracy; *see also* aliteracy; literacy, 101
illumination; *see* creative problem solving process
imagery; *see* visualize; figurative language
images, importance; *see also* visualization; thinking, 30
imagination and imaginative thinking; *see also* creative problem solving, 77, 297
imagination journey or trip, 3, 177, 234
immersion; *see* aesthetic environment; Arts Integration Blueprint
improvisation; *see* drama

inclusion; *see* differentiating instruction; PARTICULAR adaptations
incubation; *see* CPS process
independence; *see also* discipline, self, 31, 74, 82, 126, 179, 237, 352
independent reading, 74, 128
individuality, encouragement of, 37
individualization; *see* differentiated instruction; grouping
inductive; *see* inquiry
informational; *see* literary genre
infusion, arts; *see* integration
inquiry learning; *see also* questions, 8, 11, 34, 56, 68–69, 73–74, 77, 167, 179
inside-out motivation; *see also* motivation, intrinsic, 31, 74, 347
instructional design: routines and structures; *see also* Arts Integration Blueprint; LADDM, 12, 82, 84, 238
instruments; *see* musical
intaglio; *see also* visual art materials/techniques, 162
INTASC; *see* standards
integrated
  arts philosophy; *see* Arts Integration Blueprint
  arts-based schools; *see* schools; *see also* Research Updates; snapshots
  lessons; *see* lesson plans; schools; Planning Pages table in front of book
  unit structures and examples; *see* units
integrating the arts with the arts; *see* arts with arts
integration, arts, 8
  definition and characteristics, 8, 11, 12, 159, 167, 289
  effects, 56, 57
  how to; *see* Arts Integration Blueprint; LADDM
  ineffective, 59, 80, 91, 176
  institutionalizing, 126, 179
  levels of and models; *see also* WAIT; schools, 12, 57, 58
  meaningful, 3–4, 9, 10, 12–13, 25, 32, 58–61, 66–67, 69–70, 72, 74, 85, 171, 186, 218, 227, 283, 289–290, 294, 323, 338

integration, arts, 8 *(Contd.)*
models; *see also* Research Updates; schools, 407–408
planning; *see also* collaborative planning; units, 67, 68
principles; *see* Arts Integration Blueprint
rationale and research; *see also* Arts Integration Blueprint; LADDM; philosophy; research; Research Updates; academic achievement, 2, 5, 9, 14, 67
resources; *see also* websites; Appendix, 25, 55, 93, 133, 150, 188–189, 214–215
starting, 13, 57, 66, 226, 296, 299, 332, 342
teacher roles, 32, 37
two-way, 91
intelligence; *see* multiple intelligence
interdisciplinary instruction; *see also* integration; units, 8, 11, 283
interest
importance and teaching to, 8, 19, 28, 31, 39, 46, 81, 107, 117, 122, 130, 162, 291, 329
inventory; *see* assessment, informal tools; Appendix
interior, *see* visual art subject matter
International Reading Association (IRA), 112, 133
Interstate New Teacher Assessment and Support Consortium (INTASC); *see also* standards, 20, 21, 61, 159, 284
interventions; *see* differentiated instruction; PARTICULAR; grouping
intrinsic; *see* motivation
introduction, development, and conclusion; *see* lessons
irony, in literature, 106
isolated teaching, problems, 80, 164

Jacobs, H., 67–68
Jensen, E., 325, 326, 328, 330
Jennings, M., 293, 305, 353
Jesus, 99
Jordan, J., 217, 237, 243

journals and logs, 58
judgment, poor, 79

Kaye, D., 186
Kearney, M., 247
Keats, K., 92
Kellogg, R., 181
Kelly, G., 283, 295
Kennedy Center's Partners in Education, 20, 23, 60
Kindermusik, 327
kinesthetic; *see also* multiple intelligences; dance; physical, 30, 162, 279–280, 282, 284, 299
kitten experiment; *see also* brain research, 38
know-do-be, 6, 57, 88
Kodaly, Z., 336, 338
Kotarsky, C., 206
KWL/AQUA strategy, 122, 304

Laban, R. (Laban notation), 286, 290
LADDM (acronym for literature, art, drama, dance, music), 62
Lady's Island Elementary (LIES); *see also* schools, 26, 229
landscapes; *see* visual art subject matter
language, of the arts; *see also* arts literacy; communication; LADDM, 283, 330
language arts; *see also* literacy; communication, 45, 168, 348
learned helplessness, 82
learning
conditions for, 28
disabilities; *see* at risk, 5
principles, 30
theories, 40–47
Learning to Read through the Arts; *see also* schools, 10
Learning through Music (model), 78
legends; *see* literary genre
lesson(s); *see also* units; Planning Pages in Special Features table at front of book; know-do-be; snapshots and spotlights, schools
effective, 12, 67, 83, 301
guided, 208, 370
introduction, development, conclusion (IDC) framework, 82, 179, 283, 300, 342, 353

isolated skill or concept; *see* isolated skills
mini; *see* mini
plans and planning, examples; *see also* Planning Pages table in front of book, 116, 173, 276, 302
two-pronged integration concept, 12, 67, 83, 171, 229–230, 292, 342, 356
leveled books; *see* books
Levine, J., 73
Lewis, C.S., 102
lexile; *see* book levels
life-centered curriculum; *see* units; real life
like-wonder-learn strategy (LWL) 90, 242
omniscient POV; *see* POV; literary elements
Lincoln Center Institute; *see* professional development
line; *see* visual art elements
listening and speaking, 219, 281, 350
literacy; *see also* communication; arts as communication; LADDM
and creative problem solving; *see also* creative problem solving, 50
and the arts, 4, 6, 9, 10–13, 24, 30, 36, 57, 59, 62, 74, 100, 168–169, 216, 218–219, 227, 263–266, 318–320, 339, 359, 369
as meaning making; *see also* meaning making, 122
block schedule; *see also* independent reading, lessons, guided; read-alouds, arts-based, 4, 32, 122, 127, 153
comprehension; *see* comprehension
defined, 16, 29, 152–153
fluency; *see* fluency
goals, 17
new or 21st century, 152
reading and language arts, 50, 143–145, 208–214, 348
research; *see also* research; Research Updates, 101
skills in songs; *see also* songs, 355
standards; *see also* standards, 318–320, 369
visual, 65, 77, 152, 159–160, 167–168

literary (arts); *see also* literature, 11, 65, 94, 96
literature
and creative problem solving (CPS), 115, 122
and other curricular areas; *see* math, literacy, science, social studies
approaches to teaching, 98, 125
arts-based books, 74, 175, 231–232, 295, 323–324, 344–346, 359, 409–420
Arts Integration Blueprint, literary arts/literature
adaptations for diverse needs, 130–131
aesthetic literary environment, 117
arts partnerships, 131–132
assessment, 131
best teaching practices, 121–126
collaborative planning, 112–116
instructional design: routines, 126–130
literary arts elements and concepts, 99, 102–112
literature as a core art, 117–121
philosophy, 97–102
awards and favorites, 118, 120, 175
canon, 120
collections, 117
definitions, 102
developmental stages; *see also* developmental
discussion; *see also* discussions; 128
questions; *see also* questions, 123
evaluating; *see also* awards, 117–118
genre, 106–107
fantasy, 109
humor, 111
informational/nonfiction, 110
multicultural/international, 111–112
picture books, 110–111
poetry; *see* poetry
predictable, 111
realistic fiction, 109–110
traditional literature, 107–109
goals, integration *see also* standards; Arts Integration Blueprint
philosophy, 106

history and influences, 102
integration, meaningful; *see also* integration; Arts Integration Blueprint, 96, 124
integration, rationale; *see* Arts Integration Blueprint, philosophy; research
lesson planning; *see also* lessons; pre-during-post, 116
music connection, 340–341
professional organizations; *see also* LADDM areas, 133
research; *see also* research; Research Updates, 98
resources, 118–119, 133, 150
Seed Strategies; *see also* Seed Strategies Index, literature
  and curricular areas; *see also* math; literacy; science; social, 139–151
  and other arts; *see* arts with arts integration
  elements and genre traits, teaching, 138–139
  energizers and warm-ups, 136–138
  sources, books/poets, 108, 119
specialists; *see also* specialists; collaboration, 131
standards; *see also* standards, National; INTASC, 143
websites; *see also* websites; resources, 119, 133, 406
lithography; *see also* visual arts materials/techniques, 162
living room; *see also* aesthetic environment, 117
locomotor/nonlocomotor; *see* dance BEST elements
look back and laugh log; *see* humor, 153
look/listen closely strategy; *see also* details; aesthetic; criticism, 13, 79, 162, 179–180, 324
low socioeconomic status; *see* at-risk students
Lowenfeld, V., 156, 181
Lozanov, G., 343
Lucas, V., 267

magnet schools, 11, 72
mangagement; *see* discipline
Marsalis, W., 344
mask, definition and making, 204

Maslow's Needs; *see also* motivation, 45–46, 222
  and arts integration, 46
math
  and the arts; *see also* Seed Strategies Index, 36, 65, 78, 145–146, 169, 190, 213–214, 266–267, 282, 290, 293, 320, 326, 327, 340, 348, 362, 375
  notable books, 145–146
  and spatial reasoning; *see* spatial
  standards; *see also* standards, 145, 213, 320, 375
Matthau, W., 101
Matthew Effect, 101
Mays, D., 152, 187
McCartney, P., 162
meaning
  making/constructing; *see also* visualizing, 7, 9, 18, 24, 29, 31, 33, 39, 47, 50, 58, 60, 69, 79, 115, 153, 156–157, 160, 180, 222, 285
meaningful integration; *see* integration; *see also* Arts Integration Blueprint
meaningfulness and purpose; *see also* motivation, 75, 102
melody; *see also* music elements, 331
meta-analysis; *see also* research; scientific, 35
metacognition; *see* thinking; independence; fix-ups
metaphor; *see also* figurative language, 105, 155
meter; *see* poetic elements; music elements
Meyrink, G., 235
Michelangelo, 72
middle schools; *see* schools
Middleton, C., 85
MIDI (music instrument digital interface), 357
Millions of Cats, 115
mind meld strategy, 54
mini-lessons; *see also* explicit teaching, 57, 64, 66, 78, 125, 127, 235, 298
minorities; *see also* cultures, diversity, 5
mission statement; *see also* Arts Integration Blueprint philosophy, 27, 32, 33
mnemonics (memory aids); *see also* visuals, 6, 125, 298, 328
mobile; *see* visual art materials/techniques

model and demonstrate; *see* explicit teaching
models, use of; *see* examples role, 31, 37, 121, 160
Monart, 177
Monet, C., 58, 65
montage; *see also* visual art materials/techniques, 162
mood; *see also* literary elements; drama elements, 106
Moore, T., 156
moral thinking/values, 100, 221
motifs and archetypes, 101, 105
motivation; *see also* persistence; interest; choice; hope; meaning
  defined, 99
  influences, causes, types, 9, 36, 46, 75, 124, 158, 233, 296
  intrinsic versus extrinsic, 8, 19, 31, 43, 46, 68, 74, 75, 89, 156, 281, 296, 330, 347
  to learn, 9, 14, 73, 219, 329
movement; *see* dance
Mozart, W.A. and Mozart Effect, 325, 329
multicultural; *see also* culture(s); diversity; units, 71, 107, 214
  art (s) sources, 111–112, 215, 282, 320, 358
multiple intelligences, 11, 12, 40–43, 73
  schools; *see also* schools, 43, 85, 282, 323, 327
multisensory teaching (VAKT), 85
multitasking, 9
mural; *see also* visual art materials/techniques; Seed Strategies Index
museum visits; *see also* field trips, 171–172
music
  and the brain/cognitive development; *see also* brain, 40, 325–326, 329
  and child development; *see* developmental stages
  and creative problem solving (CPS), 330, 350
  and culture; *see* culture; multicultural; diversity, 328
  and curricular areas; *see also* literacy; math; science; social studies, 369, 375
  and language, 7, 339
  and life, 326

and other arts; *see* arts with arts
appreciation/listening, 350
approaches, 336
Arts Integration Blueprint, music
  adaptations for diverse needs, 355
  aesthetic environment, 342–344
  arts partnerships, 356–358
  assessment for learning, 356
  best teaching practices; *see also* teaching, 347–353
  collaborative planning, 338–342, 359
  instructional design: routines, 353–354
  literature as a core, music-based, 344–346, 359
  music literacy: elements and concepts, 325, 330–338
  philosophy, 326–330
as communication, 327, 330
as a mnemonic and motivator; *see also* mnemonics; motivation, 328
background, 58, 73, 328, 342–344
brain research; *see also* brain research, 327
composers; *see* musicians
composition; *see also* writing, 339
definition, 330
field trips; *see* field trips
genres, styles, 329, 332–333
history, periods and eras, 326, 329, 334
instruments, 332, 336, 350
integration, meaningful; *see* integration; Arts Integration Blueprint; Seed Strategies Index
integration, rationale; *see* Arts Integration Blueprint, philosophy; research
lesson plans/planning; *see also* music units; lessons, 356, 370–371
listening experiences; *see also* critical listening, 324
negatives and problems, 348
people/careers; *see also* musicians, 334–335
processes and skills, 331
rationale for, 330
reading; *see also* literacy, 331, 333, 351, 369

music *(Contd.)*
  research; *see also* brain; research; Research Updates, 325, 327, 329
  resources and professional organizations; *see also* websites; Appendix, 335, 336, 357, 358, 377
  response options, 366
  routines; *see* Arts Integration Blueprint, instructional design
  Seed Strategies; *see also* Seed Strategies Index, music and curricular areas; *see also* math; literacy; science; social studies, 365–376
  and other arts; *see* arts with arts integration
  elements and concepts, teaching, 362–365
  energizers and warm-ups, 354, 360–362
  software, computer, 215
  songs; *see* songs
  standards; *see National Standards for Music;* INTASC, 330, 338
  teacher knowledge/skills; *see* Arts Integration Blueprint, music literacy; teacher
  units; *see also* units; lesson plans, 340
  therapy, 328
Music Educator's National Conference (MENC), 336
Music Together, 327
musical
  artists for children, 347
  development/tastes and preferences; *see also* development, 355
  intelligence; *see* multiple intelligences
musicians and composers, 335
musicogeniceupadia, 329
Myers, R., 4
mystery; *see also* literary genre
mystery bag strategy, 153
myths; *see also* literary genre, 109

National Assessment of Educational Progress (NAEP), 1, 21, 27, 36, 80
National Council for the Teachers of English Language Arts (NCTE)112, 406
National Dance Institute, 281
National Endowment for the Arts (NEA), 11

national initiatives and legislation; *see also* schools, 20
National Longitudinal Study, 15
National Reading Panel (NRP), 18
National Storytelling Network, 273
Native American; *see* multicultural
natural connections; *see* integration, meaningful
nature versus nuture, 181, 355
needs, basic; *see also* Maslow; cognitive; emotional; physical, 30
networking, 11
Newbery; *see* literature awards
Nietzsche, 328
No Child Left Behind Act (NCLB); *see also* curriculum constriction; testing, 15, 18, 22, 28, 60
nonfiction, divisions; *see* literary genre
Normal Park Museum Magnet School, 11, 68, 72
Novak, C., 78
nursery rhymes; *see also* literary genre, 108

observation; *see* assessment, anecdotal
Ohio's Arts Education Model; *see also* state standards, 67
O'Keefe, G., 177
omniscient/third person; *see* point of view
O'Neill, C., 223
Opening Minds through the Arts (OMA), 6
one-liners, drama, 217
onomatopoeia; *see also* style, 106, 179
open or fat questions; *see* questions
Opening Minds through the Arts (OMA), 325
Opportunity to Learn Standards; *see* assessment, program evaluation
oral expression; *see* drama; fluency; reading aloud
Orbis Pictus Award; *see* literature awards
Orff music education, 337, 359
Osborne, A., 54
ostinato; *see also* music elements, 147, 331

ownership; *see also* motivation, 73

PAD (poem a day), 13, 58
Paige, R., 15
painting; *see* visual art materials/techniques
pairs share strategy, 76, 95
pantomime; *see also* drama, nonverbal
  ideas for, 5, 59, 135
narrative; *also see* drama form, 3, 234
  strategies; *see* Seed Strategies Index; Arts Integration Blueprint
Parsons, M., 156
part-to-whole; *see* isolated skills; whole to part
partial picture preview strategy, 180
PARTICULAR adaptations for diverse needs; *see also* differentiated, 86, 130, 240
partner/buddy reading, 144
partnerships, arts agencies; *see* Arts Integration Blueprint; LADDM areas
pass option, 217
pastels; *see* visual arts materials/techniques
pattern finds strategy, 84
patterns, importance of; *see also* details, 31, 79, 328
pedagogy; *see* Arts Integration Blueprint; best teaching practices; teaching
percussion rhythm; *see* musical instruments
performances and exhibits; *see* assessment; standards; poetry
Permal, I., 377
persistence and resiliency; *see also* motivation, 34, 65, 82, 281
personal space, 2, 96
personification; *see also* figurative language, 105
perspective; *see* point of view; diverse(ity)
Petros, F., 24, 149, 370
philosophy, defined; *see also* Arts Integration Blueprint, 28–33
phoneme(s) awareness, 325, 327, 339, 353
phonics; *see also* literacy; Seed Strategy chapters, literacy, 318
photography; *see* visual art materials/techniques

physical (education); *see* dance; specialists; kinesthetic
Piaget, J., 43
Piaget's stages; *see also* development; learning theories, 43–45
  and arts integration, 45
piano and pianissimo; *see* music elements (dynamics)
Picasso, P., 156, 188, 190
picture book(s)
  and curricular areas, 65
  art, reading, 175
  artists, 161
  characteristics and parts of, 65, 107, 110–111
  teaching strategies, 153, 175–176, 209–210
picture file, resource, 162
Pilobolus (dance company), 285, 297
pitch; *see also* music literacy: elements, 331
planning; *see* collaborative planning; lessons; units
Planning Pages; *see* Special Features table at front of book
Plato, 330
plot; *see also* literary elements; drama elements, 103
  maps and graphs; *see* Seed Strategies Index
  structure and patterns; *see* motifs and archetypes
  types, 104
poem a day (PAD) routine, 147
poetic devices and elements; *see also* style, 7, 103, 107
poetree strategy; *see also* Seed Strategies Index, 129
poetry
  awards and favorites, 109, 120
  definition and features, 106–107
  integration principles and strategies, 147
  patterns, types and forms, 142, 179
  performance, 85, 147
  sharing and writing, 107, 146
  sources, 120–121
poets, award-winning and favorites, 108, 120
point of view (POV); *see also* literary elements, 100, 103, 219
  types, 105
portfolios; *see* assessment
portraits; *see* visual art subject matter
postcards, visual art strategies, 160, 164

Potter, H., 96

practice and rehearsal, importance of, 79, 281, 298, 352

praise, problems; *see* descriptive feedback

predictable books; *see* literary genre

prediction strategies*; see also* KWL, 96

pre–during–post stages; *see also* reading; writing, 122

prejudice, developing, 79

pretending, importance; *see* drama definitions

pride; *see also* motivation, intrinsic; persistence, 281, 329

printing; *see* visual art materials/techniques

prints, art; *see also* discussion; questions, 13, 180, 215

prior knowledge, activating, 77

problem(s) solving; *see also* creative problem solving, 8, 9, 12, 14, 19, 25, 75, 179, 279, 288

process versus product, 74, 77, 88, 179, 299

professional development, 4, 27

professional organizations*; see also* LADDM resources; standards, 67, 406

proficiency; *see* standardized tests

program evaluation; *see* assessment

progressive education, 285

projects and performances; *see also* assessment; units, 8, 25, 28, 39, 81

pronged focus; *see* lesson planning

prose; *see* literary genre; genre

protagonist*; see* literary elements

puppets and mask making, 204

purposes and reasons; *see* meaning; motivation, intrinsic

QU; *see* sequence reading

qualities of movement; *see* Laban

quality work, 79, 81, 87–88

quest or journey; *see* motifs

questions/questioning about art at museums; *see* museum

and questioning; *see also* Ready References, 177, 191, 241, 244

clarification, 218, 281

discussion; *see also* discussion; literature, 234

examples for Bloom's taxonomy; *see* Bloom's taxonomy

frames for, 242

important; *see* essential

inserted, 149

open/close/fat, 4, 13, 77, 149, 154, 160, 190, 194, 242, 280, 298

reflection, 90, 244

wait time; *see also* questions, 76–77

"What-if. . . ?," 64, 176, 241, 296–297

quickwrite; *see* writing strategies

racial, ethnic, and cultural issues; *see* cultural; multicultural

rap, division song, 375

Rathbun, C., 55

Rauscher, F.S., 40, 340

read-alouds, arts-based, *see also* literacy, 3, 74, 100–101, 122, 149, 339

readability, 130

reader response theory, 99, 125, 129

Reader's Theatre (RT), 85, 266

reading
and language arts; *see* literacy; good readers

and music; *see* music; songs

and writing workshops, 127, 153

aesthetic versus efferent, 125

before–during–after strategies; *see* reading process

comprehension; *see* comprehension

decoding art, 62, 65, 160, 178, 197

defined, 18

fluency; *see* fluency

music; *see also* music reading; music literacy, 332–333, 339

phonics; *see* literacy; phonics

pre–during–post; *see also* good readers; BME; creative problem solving, 122

process, 122

Reading Recovery, 98

Ready References (key summaries); *see* Special Features table at front of book, 17

rehearsal; *see* practice

realistic; *see* visual art styles, 155

real-world materials and methods, 81, 280

recipes; *see* visual art materials/techniques

reform, arts–based/whole school, 4, 5, 10, 11, 13–14, 26, 34, 173, 379
steps, 27

Reggio Emilia School, 171

relaxed alertness; *see also* motivation, 343

relevance; *see* meaningfulness

religion and the arts, issues; *see also* diversity, 6, 222, 328

Remer, J., 13

repeated listening and reading, 130, 324

repetition, importance; *see* practice

representational; *see* visual art styles

research; *see also* scientific; LADDM research; Research Update, 11, 14, 15, 34–38

brain; *see* brain

design, 34, 38

quantitative and qualitative, 22

Research Updates; *see also* Special Features table at front of book, 6, 10, 60, 155, 220, 280, 327

reasons to integrate LADDM; *see* Research Updates; Arts Integration Blueprint, philosophy; LADDM areas

residency; *see* artist–author

resiliency; *see* persistence

resources; *see also* integration; websites; LADDM areas Appendix, 406

rhyme, rhythm, repetition; *see also* poem patterns; poetic elements, 7, 106–107

rhythm; *see also* literacy; music literacy, 325

riddle of the day; *see also* instructional design: routines; humor, 126

Riley, R., 28

risk-taking, 32, 43, 46, 124, 238, 280

rituals and ceremonies; *see* instructional design: routines

Rockne, K., 297

role models; *see* models

role-play and taking; *see* drama

Rosenblatt, L., 125

rote method; *see* songs

routines and rituals; *see* instructional design; Arts Integration Blueprint; LADDM areas

ROY G BIV (acronym for spectrum), 198, 206

rubbing; *see* visual art materials/techniques

rule of thumb; *see* five finger rule

rules, expectations, consequences; *see* discipline

safety; *see also* visual art, 294, 302

Sarah, Plain and Tall, 95–96

SAT scores; *see* academic achievement; standardized tests

scaffolding; *see also* Vygotsky, 47, 78–79, 298, 330

Scalafani, S., 22

SCAMPER; *see also* creative problem solving, 51

schema, 44

school registry, 407–408

schools, integrated arts; *see also* Research Updates; snapshots; 4, 6, 10, 11, 14–15, 26, 33, 43, 60, 68, 325, 407–408

school-wide themes; *see* units

Schweitzer, A., 81

science/health
and the arts; *see also* Seed Strategies Index, 8, 59, 65, 67, 139–140, 167, 205–207, 214, 217, 219, 222, 227, 230, 245, 262–263, 276, 280, 282, 284, 289–292, 304, 314, 328, 340, 348, 366

fiction; *see also* literary genre, 109

notable books, 140

standards; *see also* standards, 139, 205, 314, 366

units, 67, 72, 304

scientific method; *see also* creative problem solving, 50, 167

scientific research; *see also* research; evidence, 34

scratch art; *see also* visual art media, 162

scribbles, basic; *see also* developmental stages, 181

Scripp, L., 325, 358
sculpture/3D; *see also* visual art media, 162
Seed Strategies Index, arts (separate), 420–421
self-discipline and control; *see* discipline
sensory awareness; *see* aesthetic
sentence frames/stems, 258
sequence reading; *see also* Seed Strategies Index, drama, 258
setting; *see also* literary elements; drama elements, 103, 105
Seuss, Dr., 65, 379
shade and tint; *see also* visual art media, 198
Shakespeare, W., 246
shape, in art, 183
sharps and flats, 333
Shaw, G., 326
Shea, A., 314
Shepherd, B., 23
show versus tell, 297
sign language, 279, 294
signals; *see* attention getters; cues; discipline
simile; *see* metaphor
simulated trips; *see* field trips; imagination journey
SING!, 328
singing strategies; *see also* songs, 59, 348, 370
Sires, A., 190, 353
sketchbooks, 158
skin colors, making, 198
Smith, K., 27, 336
Smithsonian Institution, 171
snapshots and spotlights
   artist/teaching artist, 127, 243, 276–278
   schools, arts-based, 26, 56, 72
   student, 93, 132
   teacher/class, 3, 24, 55, 58, 92, 94, 135, 149, 153, 172, 188, 190, 216, 214, 245, 247, 290, 305, 307–309, 322, 323–324, 357, 359
Sneed, A., 356
social skills; *see also* cooperation; groups; Vygotsky, 17, 18, 47, 222, 328, 329
social studies
   and the arts; *see also* Strategy Seeds Index, 2, 59, 140–142, 160, 167, 188, 207–208, 214, 219, 227, 263, 282, 289, 316, 340, 348, 357, 358, 368
   movement possibilities, 289, 296, 317

notable books, 141
standards; *see also* standards, 140, 208, 316, 368
units, 57, 59, 67, 72, 94, 142, 247
socioeconomic status, 15
solfege in music (hand signs), 361
song (s)
   teaching, 348–349
   to know, 336–337
   writing/reading, 350, 370, 372
sound story, example of, 258
spatial reasoning, 36, 325, 327
special needs students; *see also* at risk; PARTICULAR adaptations, 392–393
specialists (arts); *see also* LADDM; arts partners; teaching artist; collaboration; co-plan and coteach, 91, 305
SPECTRA arts program, 6
speech difficulties; *see also* PARTICULAR adaptations, 392–393
spelling; *see* literacy; writing
Spolin, V., 224
SSR (sustained silent reading); *see* independent reading
STAB (acronym for soprano, tenor, alto, bass), 351
staff development; *see* professional development
stages; *see* development
standards and standards-based planning/teaching; *see also* math, science, social studies, 9, 13, 20, 66–67, 88, 140, 145
Interstate New Teacher Assessment and Support Consortium (INTASC), 61, 159, 223, 330
National Standards for Dance, 290
National Standards for Music, 338–339
National Standards for the Arts, 21, 68
National Standards for the English Language Arts, 112–113, 143
National Standards for the Visual Arts, 169
National Standards for Theatre, 227–228
Opportunity to Learn Standards, 242, 295, 304
scanning and clustering, 68, 78, 289
standardized tests and scores; *see also* tests, 3, 14, 87

station; *see* centers and stations
statues strategy, 96
Steele, H., 187
Stendhal effect (beauty), 72, 222
stereotype; *see also* characters; literary elements, 176, 287, 293
still lifes; *see* visual art subject matter
story
   definition, 152
   plot skeleton, example of, 217
   structure, aspects of, 101
Storyfest, 267, 281
storytelling, 267–273
   how to choose and tell, 269–271
   reasons for, 6, 100, 267–268
   strategies and resources, 268, 274
strategies, teaching; *see* lesson plans; teaching; best practices; Seed Strategies Index
strengths and needs; *see also* assessment, best practices, 89
stress; *see also* brain influences, 282, 328–329
structure and limitations, importance, 81, 297
struggling learners; *see* at risk; differentiated instruction
Sturgell, S., 135
stylistic elements; *see also* literary elements, 103, 105
SUAVE arts program, 6
subject matter; *see* visual
surrealism; *see* visual art
Sustained Silent Reading (SSR); *see* independent reading
Suzuki, 352
symbolic versus realistic drawing; *see also* developmental stages; visual art styles, 181
symbols; *see also* figurative language; communication, 106, 155, 285
syncopation, defined, 331
synergism, 9
synthesis thinking; *see* Bloom's taxonomy

tableau, drama strategy, 96, 248
Tanglewood Middle School, 56
tanka; *see* poetry patterns
teach with, about, in, and through; *see* WAIT

teachable moments, 296
teacher(s)
   artful/creative, 73–74, 76, 79, 83, 94, 178
   arts literacy/knowledge needed; *see also* Arts Integration Blueprint:LADDM areas; INTASC, 61, 284, 330
   characteristics; *see also* best teaching practices; artful teacher, 6, 11, 29, 34, 66, 73, 75, 121, 177, 231, 280, 294, 296, 299, 330, 338, 379
   directed; *see* explicit evaluation, 176
   in films, 52
   in-role, drama, 217, 233
   integration, knowledge; *see* Arts Integration Blueprint; LADDM literacy
   roles, 176
teaching
   artist, 65, 92, 242
   pedagogical guideposts, 75
   procedure and sequence; *see* whole part whole; lessons
team plan; *see* collaboration; specialists
television, impact, 98
Templar, J., 65
tempo (time); *see also* music literacy, elements, 330
testing, problems with; *see also* curriculum constriction, 34, 35, 87
tests (scores); *see also* standardized; academic achievement, 5, 6, 10, 14, 22, 27, 28, 35, 56, 72, 284, 330
text(s)
   -based discussion, 100
   definition and types, 16, 18, 33, 62
   sets or multiple copies, 117, 154, 358
   texture, see also visual art; music, 331
Tharp, T., 219
theatre; *see* drama
thematic units; *see* units
themes and truths; *see also* big ideas; truths, 69, 99, 103, 219, 279, 292
   literary, types; *see also* literary elements, 99, 103, 117
   school-wide; see *also* units
   questions to reveal, 69, 219

versus topics; *see also* units, 68, 71

theories, learning and teaching, 13, 30–34, 40–55

think aloud strategy, 100, 178

thinking; *see also* higher order; images; visualization, 16, 283

thinking hats; *see also* creative problem solving, 54

third space, 7, 132

Thoreau, H.D., 330

three-dimensional (3D) art; *see* visual art materials/techniques

thumbs-up strategy; *see* EPR

timbre; *see also* music literacy, elements, 331

time, use of, 126
    flexible and on task, 33
    line, 58

tolerance, teaching, 166, 221, 293

tone and tone color; *see* music literacy, elements

tongue twisters; *see* Seed Strategies Index, energizers

traditional literature; *see* literary genre

transfer of learning; *see also* explicit teaching, 6, 33, 40, 70, 8l, 158, 219, 227, 298, 338, 350

transformation and the arts, 6, 31, 52, 76, 79, 124, 296

Transforming Education through the Arts Challenge, 15

transitions, making; *see also* discipline, 235, 301

trickster stories; *see* literary genre

Trott, L., 368

Trotter, J., 2

truancy, 14

truth(s); *see also* themes, 68, 99, 100, 117

Tuttle, C., 222

Twain, M., 221

understanding; *see* comprehension

unique contributions, arts, 16, 17

units; *see also* LADDM areas; Planning Pages table at front of book
    artist-author study, 65, 114, 160–161, 169–171, 287
    centers, 69, 71–72, 113, 290, 340
    core work, 69, 95, 113, 115, 117
    criteria for, 69, 229

culture unit, 24, 358

event or field based, 69, 114, 229, 293–294

examples, 3, 4, 8, 55, 57, 94, 154, 167, 187, 227–228, 247

genre, 142, 154

planning/development, 9, 12–13, 58–67, 69–71, 73, 114, 227, 278

questions, 59, 67, 71

types or structures of, 8, 56, 59, 66–67, 90, 113, 169

thematic, 68, 71

school-wide, 71, 354

web, 70, 169–170

universal questions/values; *see also* themes and truths; big ideas; moral education; values, 219, 222

unlocking, 81

VAKTH (visual, auditory, kinesthetic, tactile, humor), 85

values; *see also* moral education, 6, 100, 222, 281

Van Allsburg, C., 170

van Gogh, V., 58, 193

Van Valkenburg, R., 31

verbal and nonverbal arts; *see also* drama and dance, 7

Very Special Arts, 37

vignettes; *see* snapshots and spotlights

visual and auditory aids; *see* visuals, 125, 298

visual art(s)
    and creative problem solving (CPS), 152, 157, 159
    and the arts; *see* arts with arts
    and other curricular areas; *see* math, literacy, science, social studies; Seed Strategies Index
    appreciation, creation and response; *see* communication; viewing and doing
Arts Integration Blueprint, visual art, 153–189
    adaptations for diverse needs, 181–185
    aesthetic environment, 172–175
    arts partnerships, 186
    assessment, 159, 185–186
    best teaching practices, 176–179
    collaborative planning, 167–172

instructional design: routines/ structure, 179–181
    literature, visual art-based, 165, 175–176
    philosophy, 155–159
    visual art literacy: elements and concepts, 7, 159–167
as communication, 154, 156, 183, 186

careers, 160

centers and stations, 180–181

DBAE (discipline based art education) defined, 167

design concepts; *see also* visual art literacy, 164

discussion strategies; *see also* discussion; questions, 164, 168, 180, 183–184

elements (color, line, shape, etc.); *see also* Arts Integration Blueprint, arts literacy, 164, 183

integration, meaningful; *see also* integration; Arts Integration Blueprint; Seed Strategies Index, 160

integration, rationale; *see also* Arts Integration Blueprint, philosophy; research, 159

lesson (s) and planning; *see also* lessons; units, 208

making and appreciating; *see* viewing and doing

materials, media, techniques, tools, 162, 196, 200–201
    book making; *see* book making
    collage, 162, 200
    cropping and crosshatching, 198, 200
    diorama, 162
    displays/bulletin boards, 174, 201
    drawing; *see* drawing
    mixed media, 201
    mixing colors, 196–198
    mobiles, 162, 202
    murals, 201
    overlapping, 199
    painting, 199
    photography, 202
    print making, 199–200
    puppets and masks; *see* puppets
    recipes, 203
    rubbing; *see* drawing
    scratchboard, 198
    sculpture/3D, 202
mini-page for parents, 196

multicultural resources; *see also* culture; multicultural, 377

museum trips; *see also* field, 171–172, 404–405

preferences, 184

prints, strategies; *see also* prints, 13

research; *see also* research; Research Updates, 155

resources and professional organizations; *see also* websites, 174, 188–189, 214–215, 406

Seed Strategies; *see* Seed Strategies Index, visual art, 190–215
    and the arts; *see* arts with arts
    and curricular areas; *see also* math; literacy; science; social studies, 205–214
    elements and concepts, teaching, 193–196
    energizers and warm-ups, 192–193

specialists; *see* arts partners; specialists; collaboration; teaching artist

standards; *see* National Standards for Visual Art; INTASC, 167–169

styles, 166
    abstract, 166, 197
    cartooning, 166
    expressionism, 166
    impressionism, 166
    realistic or representational; *see also* drawing, 166
    surrealism, 166

subject matter, types and teaching, 166, 197
    cityscape, landscapes, portraits, seascape, still life, 166, 197

therapy, 156

units; *see also* units; lesson plans, 187

viewing and doing, 158–160, 171, 177, 179, 183

well-known artists, 161

visual literacy; *see* literacy

visualizing and visual imagery; *see also* images, 18, 50, 51, 64, 66, 98

visuals; *see also* images, 66, 156, 201, 297, 351
    five actions, 177, 282

vocabulary, *see also* literacy; arts literacy; words; 66, 78, 84, 171, 219, 247, 278, 282–283, 285, 290, 303, 339

Vygotsky's social development theory; *see also* scaffolding, 46–47

WAD (Word a Day), 84
WAIT (*with, about, in, through*) integration levels; *see also* integration levels, 13, 25, 57–60, 112, 154, 218, 278, 338
wait time; *see also* questioning, 78
Waldorf Schools; *see also* schools, 10
Walker, A., 245
wallpaper book, 58
Ward, W., 223
Warhol, A., 7
Way, B., 223

webbing; *see also* brainstorming; unit development, 366
websites; *see also* resources at chapter ends, 185, 188, 246, 305–306, 335, 406
What do you see? art print strategy, 154, 175
what-if? approach/perspective, 221, 296–297
whole child, 3
wholes and parts, teaching; *see also* details, 30, 31, 80, 83, 124, 160, 351
windows of development; *see* brain
Wolf Trap Institute for Early Learning through the Arts, 27
word(s); *see also* vocabulary
a day (WAD) strategy, 84

decoding; *see* phonics; fix-ups
walls; *see also* literacy, 178, 303
work samples; *see also* evidence-based, 90
workplace skills and the arts, 23–24, 33, 45, 284
Wright, F. L., 162
writing
and the arts, 153, 158, 183, 219, 290
centers, 129
development, 183
forms and patterns; *see also* poem patterns, 141
process or stages; *see also* pre–during–post, 18, 50
writing strategies
journal; *see* journal
pretend and write (drama), 3, 218

public writing, 95
timed, 124
write right away (WRA)/quick write, 95, 129, 218

xenophobia, 99
x-ray drawing, 181

Yenawine, P., 168
young children; *see* early childhood

Zeigler, J., 72
zone of proximal development (ZPD); *see* Vygotsky; scaffolding
zoom in, zoom out; *see also* details; wholes and parts, 31